ISBN 978-0-243-40266-3
PIBN 10795733

1 MONTH OF
FREE
READING

at
www.ForgottenBooks.com

EXPLANATORY CATALOGUE

OF THE

PROOF-IMPRESSIONS

OF

THE ANTIQUE GEMS

POSSESSED BY THE LATE

PRINCE PONIATOWSKI,

AND NOW

IN THE POSSESSION OF JOHN TYRRELL, ESQ.

———

ACCOMPANIED WITH

DESCRIPTIONS AND POETICAL ILLUSTRATIONS OF THE SUBJECTS,

AND PRECEDED BY AN

Essay on Ancient Gems and Gem=engraving.

BY JAMES PRENDEVILLE, A.B.

EDITOR OF "LIVY," "PARADISE LOST," &c

LONDON:
PRINTED BY ROBSON, LEVEY, AND FRANKLYN,
Great New Street, Fetter Lane

TO

HIS ROYAL HIGHNESS PRINCE ALBERT, K.G.

𝕿𝖍𝖎𝖘 𝖂𝖔𝖗𝖐

IS, BY PERMISSION, DEDICATED,

IN TESTIMONY OF THE HIGH RESPECT IN WHICH

HIS ROYAL HIGHNESS'S

PATRONAGE OF THE FINE ARTS IS HELD

BY HIS ROYAL HIGHNESS'S

MOST OBEDIENT AND MOST DEVOTED SERVANT,

JOHN TYRRELL.

PREFACE.

AFTER the revival of civilisation and literature in Europe, there arose among men of learning and rank a rivalry for the preservation of the relics of ancient art. The enlightened family of the Medici acquired early eminence in this noble pursuit. Among the most valued treasures bequeathed from antiquity, Engraved Gems were prominently distinguished; and justly, because the ancient pictures had all perished, except some frescoes, and few of the statues had escaped the wreck of time and barbarism. Engraved Gems, therefore, were held in the highest estimation, not merely for the purity, brilliancy, rarity, and costliness of the stones, but from their constituting the connecting link between the rival and sister arts of Painting and of Sculpture—preserving the excellencies of both. While they present to us the delicacy, the animation, and the various shadows of pictures — (for the artists often adapted, with great taste and judgment, the execution of their subjects to the various shades and colours of the stones) — they possess the boldness and the material palpability of statues; and thus exhibit the most unerring criterion of the artistical talent, grace, and skill of the ancients. As this subject has been treated at some length in the *Introductory Essay*, it is unnecessary here to expatiate. Pliny thus bears testimony to their great value and perfection (lib. xxxvii. c. 1): *Hic in unum coacta rerum naturæ majestas;*

" here we see nature, in all her majesty, developed within a narrow compass."

Among the most ardent admirers and indefatigable collectors of rare Gems were the Kings of Poland. Their collection went on accumulating during successive reigns, until the fall of that dynasty. The Prince Poniatowski, to whom the cabinet descended by inheritance, was unceasing in his endeavours to augment the series. Endowed with a fine perception of the arts, and a correct critical judgment, he succeeded, at great expense, in adding many valuable specimens that had been dispersed through Europe ; and thus formed the most extensive and splendid collection known in modern times. The entire collection of Medallions in this cabinet, amounting to upwards of twelve hundred, having, with very few exceptions, come into my possession, proof impressions, preserving, with the utmost fidelity, all the delineations and expression of the originals, and offering a variety of pleasing and instructive studies to the artist, have been carefully prepared from them under my own immediate inspection, and are now, for the first time, submitted to the public; this being, according to the judgment of many eminent artists who have examined the gems, the only mode of giving a true and perfect fac-simile of their exquisite delineation.

It is unnecessary here to enumerate the testimonies of men of the highest authority as to the consummate purity and splendour of the stones, or the surpassing execution of the sculpture. It may suffice to say, that among other eminent artists who borrowed designs from the Gems in this collection was the celebrated Canova, — his "Mars and Venus," from No. 112, Class I.; and his " Hercules hurling Lichas into the Sea," from No. 463, Class II., &c.

Of the accompanying explanatory volumes to the Impressions and to the Gems, it is sufficient to say, that as the subjects embrace many of the most important and curious particulars of the Grecian and Roman mythology—the achievements and adventures of the celebrated personages recorded in fabulous and heroic history—in the *Iliad*, the *Odyssey*, and the *Æneid*, — explanatory quotations, taken from the English translations of passages from the ancient authors that have treated of these subjects, have (when it was possible) been given, as an unerring, attractive, and instructive mode of elucidation. Thus the work becomes a compilation — of which there is no example in our language — of the most beautiful passages in the best of the ancient authors; and a valuable accession to our literature. Care has been taken to give appropriate quotations, and to avoid the introduction of irrelevant matter. As the proof impressions of the Gems have been divided into five classes — the first class consisting of subjects relating to the Higher Divinities,—the second to the Demigods—the third to Fabulous and Heroic History,—the fourth to the Trojan War — the fifth to the *Odyssey* and the *Æneid*, embracing as well some miscellaneous subjects, — the work has been also divided into five corresponding parts or classes, taking for guide the " Catalogue des Pierres Gravées Antiques de S. A. le Prince Stanislas Poniatowski."

The passages of Homer have, for the most part, been taken from Pope's translation; of Virgil and Ovid, from Dryden's; of Statius, from Lewis's; of Apollonius, from Preston's; of Lycophron, from Lord Royston's; of the Greek tragedians, from Potter's; &c.

It has been deemed expedient, whenever several Gems are referable to one subject, to give a full exposition of all, by uniting and harmonising the series of several passages under one general head.   In some few instances, when an important subject has been differently treated by eminent authors, as in the case of Orestes and Hector, the quotations have been comparatively lengthy; the great object being not merely to explain the original engravings, (for this could be done, for ordinary purposes, by a few lines in prose), but to give collectanea of the passages appropriate to the subjects, from the most approved of the ancient authors.

In the *Introductory Essay on Gems and Gem-engraving*, the substance has been given of whatever the compiler conceived to be instructive and interesting in works of high repute, ancient and modern; not stating facts, nor drawing inferences, without authority.   To the earlier portion of the work, which was compiled by a person whose connexion with it extended only to the commencement of the third class, *Addenda et Corrigenda* have been appended, correcting errors, and supplying omissions.

JOHN TYRRELL.

INTRODUCTORY ESSAY.

SECTION I.

Of all the remaining monuments of the ancient arts, which have been a Value an utility of cient eng gems. source of universal and unmixed delight, admiration, and instruction to succeeding ages, there are none so various in their objects—so pleasing in their contemplation—and so useful in their study, as the *engraved gems* and *seal-rings* of the ancients. They have preserved in palpable, durable, and almost living characters, the images and the attributes of the ancient mythology; and the features, conditions, and adventures, of the most illustrious personages. They exhibit the most curious details of ancient customs and religious ceremonies; often ingenious and moral allegories, displaying a rich and chaste imagination; while they are, at the same time, invaluable models and copies of the most beautiful pieces of ancient sculpture. Thus, according to the unanimous testimony of all writers, ancient as well as modern, on the subject, they preserve for the amateur the finest copies of statues and groups—for the antiquary, the manners and customs of the ancients—for the historian, remarkable events—for the painter, his finest studies—and for the poet, numerous and diversified images.

As these gems were engraven on the most solid substances, and were in general carefully kept, they have not suffered, as statues and pictures have, alteration or injury by time; and are the only specimens of ancient ingenuity and skill that have been transmitted to us in their original freshness, beauty, and perfection. Uniting to the beauty and the value of their materials the merit of the most exquisite execution, they make us admire the wonderful perfection of an art that appears, by the

b

delicacy and correctness of the workmanship, to rival the skill and in-
dustry of Nature in the beautiful formation of the minutest animals—as
the learned Hayley thus well expresses this whole subject :

" As *Nature,* joying in her boundless reign,
Adorns the tiny links of beauty's less'ning chain ;
Her rival—*Art,* whom emulation warms,
Loves to astonish by *diminished forms ;*
And the consummate characters to bring
Within the compass of the costly *ring*—
Delightful talent of the patient hand,
Gaining o'er life such delicate command !

   .   .   .   .   .   .

The heroes of old time were proud to wear
The *seal, engraven* with ingenious care.

   .   .   .   .   .

To this fine branch of *Art* we owe
Treasures that grandeur may be proud to shew—
Features of men, who on fame's list enroll'd,
Gave life and lustre to the world of old—
Worthies, whose STATUES *failed time's flood to stem,*
Yet live effulgent in the *deathless Gem.*"

    Sculpture in its various departments (and gem-engraving was one of
the most prized and important of these departments) had a powerful in-
fluence over the tastes, habits, and emotions of the ancients—especially
of the Greeks. While it was a record of the religion—the military glory
of the people—and the celebrity of individuals, it generated and fostered a
high tone of religious feeling—a martial spirit—and a rivalry for fame.
Their divinities they saw portrayed with their most imposing attributes—
their heroes in their most perilous enterprises—and their good men in
their most trying sufferings. Having seen all this, they were occasionally
warmed into a high sense of religious sensibility and of devotion—roused
into warlike courage—or softened down into humanity and pity. Suetonius
says that, when Julius Cæsar saw in the temple of Hercules, at Cadiz, the
statue of Alexander the Great, he wept at his own comparative inactivity
and obscurity ; and prayed for an opportunity of winning such glory. But

statues were chiefly memorials for public exhibition in the great halls and the temples—seen but comparatively by a few; whereas engraved gems, recording the scenes—the ceremonials—and the achievements portrayed by the statues, were in the possession of every family, and kept alive the emotions of religion, of patriotism, and valour.

Cicero has observed that necessity may be considered as the primitive parent of all those arts which have instructed and charmed mankind; for it produced those inventions that tend to our use, and minister to our wants; and those, when cultivated with diligence and skill, progressively rise to improvement and refinement; and thus are produced those inventions that tend to our edification, and minister to our intellectual luxury and pleasure. " The origin," says Raspe, " of engraving cannot with exactness be traced to any definite period, or to any particular people; for its first mechanical rudiments,—i. e. the art of grinding, polishing, and shaping hard stones,—was certainly taught by necessity to many tribes of savages who never had intercourse with each other. Military weapons, domestic and mechanical vessels and implements, of various forms and for various uses, made of flint, porphyry, jasper, and other hard stones, often curiously cut, polished, and perforated, have been found alike in the sepulchral monuments of the most ancient barbarians of Europe and Asia, and dug out of fields which were the scenes of battles in very remote and uncivilised ages. Hence it is considered right to say of them, what Tacitus (de Morib. Germ. c. vi.) says of the ancient Germans—that they were unacquainted with the use of metals, which would have furnished them with better materials for tools and weapons. In several parts of the kingdom of ancient Mexico stone vessels and implements, worked with great care and elegance, have been also discovered. Weapons, utensils, and even *ornaments* of similar materials and workmanship, have been found among the South-Sea islanders; the execution of some of which (continues Raspe) is really astonishing. Such, in particular, is the excellence of an ornament in the possession of the widow of the late celebrated Captain Cook, who, in his second circumnavigation of the world, brought it from New Zealand, where the chiefs wear such ornaments with as high an air of pride and dignity as our great men wear their stars and ribands.

Rudiment the art kn to many b barous na

It is a singularly beautiful and transparent green stone, of a flinty yet muriatic nature, exceedingly hard, in colour between the emerald and chrysolite; and of a cylindrical form, about ten inches long and half an inch thick, gently bent towards the upper end, where it is perforated to admit the string which fastened it to the ear of the wearer. Its uncommon transparency and polish make it in its kind, and, in the opinion of intelligent naturalists, as inestimably precious as any large diamond can possibly be, though perhaps not so valuable as an article of merchandise in the estimation of the mercenary. So that, considering the great hardness, high polish, and elaboration of the stone, it must have been a work of immense labour; and may, on that account, be looked upon as one of the greatest masterpieces of this first stage of the art of grinding, cutting, and engraving hard stones."

The origin of engraving on precious stones cannot, I repeat, with any accuracy, be traced to any certain period of time; nor can the invention of it be ascribed exclusively to any one nation. But that it is an art of very remote antiquity, we have the most unerring evidence; for it is expressly mentioned in the oldest literary records in existence—the book of Job, and the Pentateuch, or the five books of Moses. There is a high degree of probability that, as Strut intimates, it was known before the deluge; for we find in Genesis (chap. iv.), that Tubal-Cain, the son of Lamech, was "the *instructor of every artificer* in metals;" and it is likely that, as his descendants multiplied, the art was carried to no mean order of excellence. Now the use and artificial application of metal tools was confessedly subsequent to the working of stones; for though one hard stone may be polished, cut, and shaped for use or ornament by another, yet metal tools were necessary in general to give a perfect execution to the engraving. Be this, however, as it may, we find in Genesis, that Judah gave Tamar his *signet*, and his *bracelets;* and that Pharaoh took off his *signet-ring*, and placed it on the finger of Joseph. And (Judges xviii.) in the house of Micah there was a *molten* image and a *graven* image; and in Job we find this passage, "who shall cause my name to be hewn out with a *graving-tool of iron* in the *rock* for ever." Now all signet-rings were engraved, and had some device or inscription. But the most important and decisive passages in the Old Testament in proof of our position are those in Exodus, where Moses mentions *engraved gems* as constituting an essential and prominent part of the habiliments of the Jewish high-priest.

The ephod and pectoral (or breastpiece) were principal parts of the garments of the Jewish high-priest, when officiating. The ephod was a sort of sash, passing over the neck and shoulders, and drawn backwards round the body, and then drawn to the front, acting as a girdle to the tunic. Exod. ch. xxviii.: "And they shall make the ephod of gold, of blue, of purple, of scarlet, and fine twisted linen, with curious work. . . . . And thou shalt take two onyx stones, and *grave* on them the names of the children of Israel: six of their names on the one stone, and six names of the rest on the other stone, according to their birth. With the *work of an engraver in stone*, like the *engravings of a signet*, shalt thou engrave the two stones with the names of the children of Israel : thou shalt make them to be set in ouches (*i. e.* sockets) of gold. And thou shalt put the two stones upon the shoulders of the ephod, for a memorial to the children of Israel."

The pectoral, a piece of many-coloured fine-twisted linen, about ten inches square, was fastened to the ephod, where it crossed the breast. " And thou shalt make the breastplate of judgment with curious work; after the work of the ephod shalt thou make it. . . . And thou shalt set in it settings of stones, even four rows of stones: the first row shall be a sardius, a topaz, and a carbuncle: the second row shall be an emerald, a sapphire, and a diamond: the third row an agate, a ligure, and an amethyst: and the fourth row a beryl, an onyx, and a jasper: and they shall be set in gold in their enclosings : and the stones shall be with the names of the children of Israel, twelve, according to their names, *like the engravings of a signet.*"

Ch. xxxv. Bezaleel and Aholiab were the engravers : " And Moses said unto the children of Israel, See, the Lord hath called by name Bezaleel, the son of Uri ; and hath filled him with the spirit of God, in wisdom, and in understanding, and in knowledge, and in all manner of workmanship ; to devise cunning works, to work in gold, and in silver, and in brass, and in the *cutting of stones, to set them,* and in the carving of wood, to make any manner of curious work. And he hath put in his heart that he may teach, he and Aholiab, the son of Ahisamach. Them hath he filled with wisdom of heart, to work all manner of *work of the engraver,* and of the cunning workman."

Some short-sighted critics take the words, " The Lord filled him with the spirit of God, in wisdom, and all manner of workmanship," and " Them hath he filled with wisdom of heart, to work all manner of work of the engraver," in their strict and literal sense, to mean that God inspired them with a species of knowledge they did not possess before; and to imply that gem-engraving was before this time unknown to the Israelites; and therefore that these passages can determine nothing in favour of the antiquity of the art. Now this interpretation is at variance with the whole scope of the phraseology of the Old Testament, and with the explanations of the best biblical commentators, who say, that, in the language of the Bible, superiority of knowledge in any art or science which was generally in use among the people, is said to be the gift of God; and that the expressions here do not indicate the discovery of a new art, but are only a figurative mode, in the oriental style, of mentioning Bezaleel's and Aholiab's surpassing accomplishment in a known art. Besides, I may add, that we find (as has been already stated) " *engraving a name in stone with a graving-tool of iron*" practised in the time of Job—a time long prior to this; that Moses mentions the signet-ring of Judah, which was presented to Tamar; and the signet-ring of Pharaoh, which was presented to Joseph, long before this time; and that before this time, he mentions Aaron as fashioning *with a graving-tool* the golden calf for the Israelites (Exod. xxxii.). Now, if we suppose with those critics that God inspired (strictly speaking) Bezaleel, who was before ignorant of the art—an art not known to the Jews—to work the ornaments on the ephod and breastplate of the high-priest; we must, by parity of reasoning, suppose that he also inspired the artist that engraved the signet of Judah, before the Israelites ever set foot in Egypt as a people; and Aaron to work and engrave the image for the Israelites, and so encourage them to idolatry, contrary to his own express wish and injunction!

The plain truth is, that Moses,—who, as being reared in the court of Pharaoh, and educated among the priests, the great depositories of the knowledge of the country, " was skilled in all the learning (or arts) of the Egyptians,"—here mentions the use of a highly prized and elegant art (long before this practised in Egypt) for the decoration of the priest's vestments ; and that Bezaleel and Aholiab were called by God's will, as being superior artists (every excellency in knowledge being supposed to be the gift of God), to execute the work. It is not reasonable to suppose, that the Jews, who were so long conversant with the Egyptians, and were originally brought to Egypt under such favourable auspices, introduced there by Joseph, the favourite and chief minister of the king, and were subsequently employed as workmen, should be ignorant of their arts : at all events, Moses evidently was not ; nor did he fail to encourage among his people as much of the arts and institutions of Egypt as might be adapted to their peculiar condition, and subsidiary to their interest. In subsequent stages of the Jewish history, we find engraving practised, not so much for ornament and luxury, as for necessary use. No writing was considered authentic, unless accompanied with a seal. Thus, when Jezebel wrote a letter in the name of Ahab, she impressed it with the prince's seal, to ensure the prompt and certain execution of her orders. The same custom prevailed in Persia ; for we find Ahasuerus presenting his ring to Esther, as a pledge of his confidence.

The Jews were great admirers and collectors of precious stones. It has been asserted, that they were acquainted with all the varieties of them known in the present day. St. John, who is full of the style and imagery of the ancient prophets, says, in the Apocalypse (ch. xxi.), that the foundation of the new or heavenly Jerusalem was decorated with precious stones : " and the foundations of the wall of the city were garnished with all manner of precious stones : the first was jasper ; the second, sapphire ; the third, a chalcedony ; the fourth, an emerald ; the fifth, sardonyx ; the sixth, sardius ; the seventh, chrysolite ; the eighth, beryl ; the ninth, a topaz ; the tenth, a chrysoprasus ; the eleventh, a jacinth ; the twelfth, an amethyst : and the twelve gates were twelve pearls." Though the Bible mentions, in different places, the names of the several precious stones known to us, yet antiquaries and commentators disagree as to the correctness of our translation of the original names; for instance, the translators of our authorised version say, the first row of stones in the breastplate of the high-priest consisted of a *sardius*, a topaz, and a *carbuncle*; while others say, they were a *cornelian*, a topaz, and an *emerald*. But it was not merely for ornament that the Jews used hard, engraved stones : we find that they used cut stones as implements of use. In Exod. iv. we find that they originally used stone knives for the operation of circumcision. In the use of such instruments they were neither original nor singular; for Herodotus (b. ii. c. 2) tells us, that the early Egyptians used such implements to open the bodies of the dead who were to be embalmed; and Pliny (b. xxxiv. c. 12) and Catullus (in his poem on Atys) shew that the priests of Cybele used them in order to emasculate themselves.

edge of among ient)s.   The art was long practised by the Egyptians before it was *generally* known to the Jews; and probably by the Indians before it was known to the Egyptians. The extensive trade and intercourse between Egypt and India, which was called by the old historians the *land of gems and gold*, tended immensely to circulate wealth and a knowledge of the arts (especially of engraving) in Egypt. That India yielded a vast source of riches, luxury, and scientific knowledge to the Egyptians, is a fact established by the concurrent testimony of the most trustworthy writers. " India, from the remotest ages, produced (says Raspe) the best specimens of hard and precious stones which lapidaries and engravers work on, together with every substance and tool they use in their operation : the *real diamond* (which is at once both a material and an instrument), the ruby-sapphire, the emerald, topaz, chrysolite, sardonyx, calcedony, onyx, cornelian, jasper,—nay even, besides the *real diamond*, the stone called the *diamond spar*, which, when pulverised and applied to the engraver's or lapidary's tool, cuts the hardest gems nearly as well as the diamond powder, and much more effectively than the best emery." Raspe confidently asserts (and from the great research he appears to have bestowed on the subject, his opinion is entitled to great respect, if not implicit belief) that neither Egypt, nor any other country of the old world, except India, produced the *real diamond*, or the diamond spar, without which the lapidary's art could not be brought to perfection; and that from India this stone, and a knowledge of its properties, so necessary for gem-engraving, spread to the western nations. Not only did the ancient Indians furnish other nations with precious stones, but they carried the art of engraving on them to a high order of excellence, as many specimens of engraved gems now preserved amply testify.

Without entering into details of the great traffic between India and Egypt in remote ages, and of the advantages accruing to the Egyptians from it, we may mention one surprising fact (as evidence of the wealth of India) which is recorded by the best authority—the Bible (Chron. viii. 18; 1 Kings ix. 26)—*i. e.* that Solomon brought, through the Red Sea, from Ophir (or India) in one voyage, no less than *four hundred and fifty talents* of gold, *i. e.* about 3,240,000*l.* sterling.

Among the principal commodities introduced into Egypt from India, Egyptian and other countries of the East, were *precious stones.* But the Egyptians of the art were not exclusively dependent on foreigners for an imported supply of these articles. Their own mines furnished a vast abundance of emeralds; and these mines were worked so early as the reign of Amunoph III., or 1425 years before Christ. Wilkinson says (vol. i.) :—" That the riches of the country were immense is proved, among other evidences, by the vast quantity of jewels, in gold, silver, *precious stones,* and other objects of luxury in use among them in the earliest times. Their treasures, and cultivation of the arts (especially the art of engraving and working costly stones), became proverbial through the neighbouring states ; and pomp and splendour continued to be their ruling passion till the close of their existence as an independent nation, as is fully demonstrated by the history of the celebrated Cleopatra."

Hieroglyphics may be termed the originals of engraving. Warburton, who has treated the subject of hieroglyphics with his usual ingenuity, has classed them under three heads. He says, the *first* design was to make a part represent the whole : thus, two hands, one holding a bow, the other a shield, represented a battle,—a man casting arrows, a tumult or insurrection,—a scaling-ladder, a siege, &c.

The second and more artificial method was, to put the *instrument*

of a thing, whether real or metaphorical, for the *thing itself:* thus, a pro-
minent *eye* represented God's *omniscience*—an *eye and sceptre,* the duties
and powers of a *monarch*—a *ship and pilot,* the *Governor* of the *universe,* &c.

The third and still more artificial method was, to make *one thing*
stand for *another,* where any resemblance or analogy could be collected
from the form, nature, or qualities of beings and things, or from traditional
superstitions: thus, a *serpent* in a *circle* represented the *universe,* its *spots*
designating the *stars*—the *eyes* of a *crocodile, sunrise,* because the eyes
appear to emerge from the animal's head—a *black pigeon* expressed a
young widow, who would not take a second husband—a *blind beetle,* one
dead from *fever,* or a *sun-stroke*—a *sparrow* and *owl,* a *suppliant* flying for
protection, and not finding it—a *vulture,* an inexorable *tyrant* estranged
from his people—a *grasshopper* (which they imagined had no mouth), one
initiated into the *mysteries.* So, the *sistrum,* or rattle, which was often
placed in the right hand of Isis, was rattled to announce the *swelling of
the Nile;* and the *situla,* or water-ewer, was the symbol of the *retirement*
of the *inundation.* The *persea,* which was often an ornament to the head
of the deities, expressed the *blessings of husbandry;* because the tree,
when growing (according to Galen) in its native country, Persia, produced
a poisonous fruit; but when transplanted to Egypt, and there carefully
cultivated, it yielded a pear-like fruit, which was good for eating. So, a
peach-tree in luxuriant fruit was expressive of *one* who *profited* much by
long travelling; for the peach-tree was said to be more fruitful when
transplanted, than in its native soil. So, a *squatting hare* indicated a
melancholy man; for the hare is a timid and solitary animal. Among
the hieroglyphic inscriptions on gems and in the temples, the *eye* was
a frequent figure, sometimes without eyebrows, sometimes marked only
by two eyelids, without a pupil appearing: sometimes it was adorned
with wings, or other expressive attributes, which shews that the same
symbol represented different ideas and modifications of meaning. It is
the most simple image of vision, and consequently of wisdom and provi-
dence; and it is thus applicable to the *sun,* and to the *Divinity.* Diodorus
and Plutarch expressly state, that it was particularly the symbol of Osiris.
The sphinx was always an emblem of the Divine power, or kingly power

as the earthly representative of the Divine, in different aspects of observation. Though no object so often occurs among the hieroglyphics as the sphinx, yet no decisive or satisfactory explanation of it has been given in its various forms. In general, however, it may be said that, as the Egyptian sphinx presented the head of a *lion* and a *man*, it was typical of power and wisdom: the figure of the lion being indicative of power; and the figure of man indicative of intelligence. There were other combinations of this animal among the Egyptians, such as the ram-headed sphinx, the hawk-headed sphinx, which were only modifications of the same meaning;—the hawk being the symbol of vigilance and swift execution; the ram the sign of power and prosperity: horns were invariably the types of power and strength, and the fleece of the sheep was synonymous with wealth and comfort. The *Grecian* sphinx was a compound of a lion and a *female;* and the Greeks most probably meant to shew by it *power* blended with *elegance, grace,* and the *attraction* of beauty.

Hieroglyphics were not single and detached emblems only; they often formed groups to convey some great moral lesson or religious tenet. Clemens of Alexandria mentions one engraven on one of the gates of the temple at Diospolis. " There appeared a *child* (the symbol of birth), and an *old man* (the symbol of death), a *hawk* (the accepted symbol of the Divinity), a *fish* (the symbol of hatred), and a *frightful crocodile* (the symbol of effrontery and insolence). All these united meant, ' O man, who art born, and who diest; God hateth the shameless and the insolent.'"

But the Egyptians were not the only people who used hieroglyphic symbols. Warburton shews that the Chinese, the Scythians, the Indians, and the Mexicans, used them. All readers of the invasions of America by the Spaniards must recollect how rapidly the intelligence of the first landing of the invaders in Mexico was transmitted to Montezeuma, the emperor, by means of symbols or picture-writing. *The History and Antiquities of Mexico** will shew the perfection to which the Mexicans

---

* The folio work in twelve volumes, compiled chiefly by the labour, and solely at the expense of the late Lord Kingsborough, eldest son of the Earl of Kingston of Michelstown Castle, in the county of Cork (the cost being 31,000*l.*). This noble contributor to the lite-

brought this art; and every classical scholar must recollect the symbolical representation (which is mentioned by Herodotus) sent by the Scythians to Darius, on his invasion of their country : it exhibited a bird, a mouse, and a frog, and five arrows; thus intimating, that if he did not fly away as swiftly as a bird, or hide himself like a mouse or frog, he would perish by their arrows.

The claim to superior antiquity and of prior civilisation set up by the Egyptians, and long acknowledged, has been much shaken by modern discoveries; for the great similarity in customs, manners, and religion between them and the Hindoos and other Eastern nations, has been justly considered evidence of identity of origin. Now, the stream of population, and of civilisation too, has confessedly flowed from the East; and, as many of the oldest religious rites and customs, and specimens of the arts, among the Egyptians, are now proved to have been identical with those ascertained to have existed in Hindostan (some precious stones, for instance, have been discovered with Sanscrit inscriptions and devices coeval with, if not antecedent to, the earliest Egyptian relics),—an inference has been plausibly, if not justly, deduced, that the Egyptians borrowed, and perhaps improved the discovery of others.

But, without entering into a discussion of the relative claims of these nations to the merit of originality, let us concede the merit to the Egyptians. The form of government among the Egyptians had much influence on the cultivation of the fine arts in ancient Egypt. Although there has been much disputation about the most ancient form of settled government in that country, the balance of probabilities appears to incline to the theory, that it was, like that of the Jews, a *hierarchy*, or a priestly government. "From the circumstance," says Wilkinson, " of the earliest names enclosed in *ovals* (or *egg-shaped* engraved stones*) being preceded by the title of priest, instead of king, it is fair to infer that

---

rature of the country, and the author of the most splendid book that ever issued from the press of any nation, died, some two or three years ago, in Dublin.

  * " Among the Egyptian gems," says Dagley, "of which there are more intaglios than cameos, the greater part have the form of the consecrated *scarabæus*, or beetle; and the figures (or subject of the gem) are engraven on its surface. They afterwards ground, or cut

the priestly form of government preceded that of the kingly; and the account of Manetho and other writers, who mention the reign of the gods, would seem to sanction or even *require* such an inference." Yet we must not take this mention of the reign of the gods in its strict and literal acceptation, to imply that there was a time when the Egyptian divinities ruled on earth, any more than we can suppose that Saturn in reality descended from heaven, and governed Latium; but only take it to mean figuratively that the ministers of the gods—the priests—had absolute sway in the land—that the time of their government was a golden age of happiness, piety, and virtue. To this, the character given by Cicero (*de Republ.* iii. 8) of the ancient Egyptians refers: "that *nation uncorrupt* (*gens incorrupta*) which contains literary memorials of countless ages and events."

From Herodotus (lib. ii.), and from Plutarch (*de Is.*), we find that the priests and the inhabitants of the Thebaid did not believe that any Egyptian deity ever ruled on earth. The story, then, of Osiris's rule in this world was purely allegorical, and intimately connected with the most profound and curious mystery of their religion; and so great was the reverence of the priests for the important secret, and for the name of Osiris, that Herodotus scrupled to mention him (the Jews felt a somewhat similar awe to pronounce the name of Jehovah); and Plutarch says, that the priests talked with great reserve even of his well-known character of ruler of the dead. The Egyptians ridiculed the Greeks for pretending to derive their origin from deities. They shewed Hecatæus and Herodotus a series of three hundred and forty-five high-priests, each of whom, they observed, was "a man, the son of man," but in no instance the descendant of a god. "

One great cause of the progress of the Egyptians in civilisation, power, and all their accompanying arts, was the division of the people into castes, or classes (as among the Hindoos): such as the class of priests, who were

---

away, the lower part of the scarabee stone, cut into an oval form, to be more commodiously set into a ring or seal. Such was the origin of the oval engraved stones, which are still called *Scarabees*, although the figure of the insect no longer appears. The early Egyptians conceived the beetle to be the type of the *sun*, or the Divinity, the source of generation, because they thought the beetle had the power of self-production; and of *courage*, because they thought all beetles were males."

exclusively confined to the pursuit of the theories and the practice of the rites of religion, in its various departments; the soldiers; the artificers; the husbandmen, &c. As each class was confined to one pursuit (for instance, among the artificers the particular trade or occupation of the father was followed by the children, down through successive generations), a growing fund of knowledge and improvement was created, that tended to promote abstract science, mechanical dexterity, national wealth, prosperity, and comfort. But however great may have been the success of the Egyptians in many other departments of science and mechanism, especially of architecture, it was, generally speaking, much restrained in *engraving* by the stern and fixed regulations of the priests. These regulations prescribed certain attitudes, a certain position of the limbs, and a certain cast of feature, in the portraiture of the divinities, which gave a character of hardness, stiffness, and immobility to their figures. The figures were mostly in profile; the limbs and lineaments of the features angular, marked by straight lines. This style of engraving and of sculpture pervaded all their copies of the human form. Yet this defect—this deviation from the laws of nature—was compensated for by the vastness of their designs, and their gigantic execution. They surrendered up grace and beauty for the awful and the colossal; and in this department it must be admitted they have excelled. But wherever they were not fettered by the regulations of the priests,—for instance, when free to draw the figures of animals, such as the lion, sphinx, &c.,—they exhibited much ingenuity, taste, and elegance. Engraved gems were not only prized among them for the value of the stone, and the labour and beauty of the engraving, but they were used for many purposes of real or imaginary good. They were worn as amulets, or charms against accident or evil— as medals, and marks of distinction for signal services in peace or war —as proofs of devotion and piety when they had on them the figures of their gods. The priests too wore them on their vestments. Among these gems were frequently the figures of Isis, Osiris, Orus, Anubis, &c.

The Egyptian art of engraving must be divided into two stages: the first, the old and purely Egyptian style; and the second, the Egyptio-Grecian, which took place when Egyptian gems were executed by Grecian artists, who, though engraving Egyptian subjects, and *generally* following the Egyptian rule, yet contrived to infuse into their works a character of motion, ease, and beauty.

" It was not," says Wilkinson (vol. iii. c. 9 and 10), in his learned work on Ancient Egypt, " in architecture alone the Egyptians excelled. The wonderful skill they evinced in sculpturing or *engraving hard stones* is still more surprising; and we wonder at the means they employed for cutting hieroglyphics on stones of the hardest quality. Nor were they deficient in taste—a taste, too, not acquired by imitating approved models, but claiming for itself the praise of originality, and universally allowed to have been the parent of much that was afterwards perfected with such amazing success by the most highly-gifted of nations—the Greeks: and no one can look on the elegant forms of many of the Egyptian vases, and the ornamental designs of their sculptured stones, without conceding to them due praise on this point, and admitting that, however whimsical some of the figures may be in sacred subjects, they often shewed considerable taste where the regulations of the priesthood and religious scruples ceased to interfere. In their temples they were obliged to conform to rules established in the infancy of the art, which custom and prejudice rendered sacred. Plato and Synesius both mention the stern regulations which forbade their artists to introduce innovations in religious subjects; and the more effectually to prevent this, the profession of *artist* or *engraver* was not allowed to be exercised by common or illiterate persons, lest they should attempt any thing contrary to the laws established regarding the figures of the deities. . . . . The same veneration for ancient usage, and the stern regulations of the priesthood, which forbade any innovation in the form of the human figure, fettered the genius of the Egyptian artist. The same formal outline—the same stiff attitude of the body—the same conventional modes of representing the different parts, were adhered to. No improvement resulting from observation in drawing the figure—no attempt to copy nature, and give expression to the features or proper action to the limbs, was resorted to.

" Egyptian bas-relief (in *engraving* as well as statuary) appears to have been, in its origin, a mere copy of painting—its predecessor. The first attempts to represent the figures of the gods, sacred emblems, and other subjects connected with the divine and human form, consisted in painting simple outlines of them on a flat surface, the details being afterwards put in with colour. But, in process of time, these forms were traced on stone with a tool, and the intermediate space between the various figures being afterwards cut away, the once level surface assumed the appearance of a bas-relief. It was, in fact, a pictorial representation on stone; which readily accounts for the imperfect arrangement of their figures. Deficient in conception, and, above all, in a knowledge of grouping, they were unable to form those combinations which give true expression. Every figure was made up of isolated parts, put together according to some general notions, but without harmony, or preconceived effect. The expression of feeling and passion was entirely wanting; and the countenance of the king, whether charging an enemy's phalanx in the heat of battle, or peaceably offering incense in a sombre temple, presented the same outline and the same inanimate look. Nor do they appear to have had any clear conception of the effect required to distinguish the warrior from the priest, beyond the impressions received from characteristic costume, or from the subject of which the figures formed a part. . . . . . Thus, then (as Diodorus, i. 98, observes of Egyptian statues), various portions of the same figure look as if they might be made by several artists in different places, the style and attitude having been previously agreed on, which, when brought together, would form a complete whole.'' Yet this appears never to have been done by the Egyptians, for all their figures on stone were of one piece; though he mentions a Greek statue of Apollo of Samos made in two pieces, by Telecles and Theodorus, at Ephesus and Samos.

" In the reign of the second Rameses, some slight improvement was made in varying the proportions; but still the general form and character of the figures continued the same, which gave rise to the remark of Plato (book ii. *of Laws*), 'that the pictures and statues made by the Egyptians ten thousand years ago are no better or worse than what they now

make.'* .... It must, however, be allowed that, in general, the character
and form of animals (in portraying which they were not restricted to the
same rigid style prescribed by the priests) were executed with great anima-
tion, and an observance of nature. .... The mode of representing men and
animals in profile, as was generally the case in Egyptian sculpture, is cha-
racteristic of a primitive stage of the art, and holds its ground until genius
bursts through the trammels of usage. From its simplicity it is easily
understood: the most inexperienced perceive the object to be repre-
sented; and no effort is required to comprehend it. Hence it is that
few combinations can be made under such restrictions; but those few are
perfectly intelligible, the eye being aware of the perfect resemblance to
the simple exterior: and the modern uninstructed peasant of Egypt, who
is immediately struck with and understands the drawings on the Theban
tombs, is seldom able, if shewn an European drawing, to distinguish men
from animals; and no argument will induce him to tolerate foreshortening,
the omission of those parts of the body concealed from his view by the
perspective of the picture, or the introduction of shadows, particularly on
the human flesh."

Bas-relief may be considered the earliest style of sculpture. It ori-
ginated in those pictorial representations, which were the primeval records
of a people anxious to commemorate their victories, the qualities of a king,
and other events connected with their history. As their skill increased,
the more allegorical representation was extended to that of a descriptive
kind, and some resemblance of the person was attempted; and what was
at first scarcely more than a symbol assumed the more exalted form and
character of a picture. Of a similar nature were all their historical
records; and these pictorial illustrations were a substitute for written
documents. Sculpture, indeed, long preceded letters; and we find that
even in Greece, to describe, draw, engrave, and write, were expressed by
the same word, γραφειν.

---

* However, this remark of Plato must be taken, with considerable qualification, to mean
that no nearer approach to the Grecian excellence—to the *beau idéal* of perfection—was made
then, than before.

The want of letters, and the inability to describe an individual, his occupations, or his achievements, led them, in early ages, to bury with the body some object which might indicate the character and condition of the deceased. Thus warriors were interred with their arms, artisans with the implements they used, and priests with some utensil of their sacred office. In those times we find no inscription mentioned. A simple mound was raised over a chief; sometimes with a στυλος, or rude stone pillar, placed upon it, but no writing: and when, at a later period, any allusion to the occupation of the deceased was attempted, a rude allegorical emblem, of the same nature as the early historical records before alluded to, was engraved on the levelled surface of the stone.

Sculpture dates long before architecture, considered as an art. Architecture is a creation of the mind, having no model in nature; and it requires great imaginative powers to conceive its ideal beauties, and to give a proper combination of parts and a harmony of forms. But the desire in man to imitate and to record what has passed before him,—in fine, to transfer the impression from his own mind to that of another,— is natural in every stage of society.

As the wish to record events gave the *first*, religion gave the *second*, impulse to sculpture. The simple pillar of wood or stone, which was originally chosen to represent the Deity, afterwards assumed the human form, the noblest image of the Power that created it; and the memorial for the primitive substitute for a statue is curiously preserved in the Greek name κιων, implying a column and an idol. Pausanias (b. ii. c. 19) says, that " all statues were in ancient times made of wood, particularly those made in Egypt;" but this must have been at a period so remote as to be far beyond the known history of that country; though it is probable that when the arts were in their infancy the Egyptians were confined to statues of that kind.

Though the *general* character of sculpture continued the same, and a certain conventional mode of representing the human figure was universally adopted throughout the country, which was followed by every artist from the earliest era until the religion of the country and hieroglyphic symbols were abolished by the introduction of Christianity,—yet

several styles were introduced, and the genius of the arts varied consider-
ably during that lengthened period. This was especially so when Greek
artists began to engrave Egyptian subjects.

All the best ancient authors bear united testimony to the fact, that Knowledg
the ancient Phœnicians made great progress in all the arts of civilisation the art a
and of peace. Not only was their commerce and their social intercourse Phœnicia
extensive and varied with the neighbouring nations,—reciprocally com-
municating and receiving wealth, knowledge, and improvement,—but they
carried their discoveries, their trade, and their arts, to the remotest shores
of the then known world. Their invasion of Ireland, and their esta-
blishment there of a colony, introducing and fixing in that country their
institutions religious and civil,—a colony that spread over the country,
disseminating and settling the Asiatic notions, and customs, and arts,—is a
fact that, independently of the old Irish records, is proved by the researches
of the most dispassionate historians and antiquaries. Strabo, Diodorus,
Pliny, and other writers, mention certain islands discovered by the Phœni-
cians, which, from the quantity of tin, or a metal bearing many of its
properties, obtained the name of Cassiterides. This metal was mixed with
other metals, particularly copper, and was employed, according to Homer
(*Iliad*, xviii. 565, 574, 612, 474), for the relief-engraving on the exterior of
shields, as in that of Achilles; for making greaves; binding various parts
of defensive armour; and for household and ornamental purposes. These
islands included Britain, at least the southern and western coasts of it.
Strabo says (b. iii. *ad finem*), " The secret of the discovery was carefully
concealed from all other persons ; and the Phœnician vessels continued to
sail from Gades (Cadiz) in quest of this commodity, without its being
known whence they obtained it; though many endeavours were made by
the Romans, at a subsequent period, to ascertain the secret, and share the
benefits of this discovery. So anxious were the Phœnicians to retain their
monopoly, that on one occasion, when a Roman vessel pursued a Phœni-
cian trader bound to the spot, the latter purposely steered his vessel on a
shoal, preferring to suffer shipwreck (provided he involved his pursuers in
the same fate) to the disclosure of his country's secret. His artifice and
fidelity succeeded. The Roman crew and vessel perished; and the Phœ-

nician, who escaped, was rewarded, on his return home, from the public treasury, for his devotion and his sacrifice."

Two remarkable evidences of the high degree of excellence to which the Phœnicians carried the fine arts (and among them the art of engraving), it will be sufficient to adduce here—these evidences being taken from the most unquestionable and ancient records we possess; the Old Testament and Homer. When Solomon was about to build the temple, one of the noblest monuments ever erected, he obtained his chief artist from Huram, king of Tyre, a Phœnician city (2 Chron. ii. 14). Huram, in his letter complying with the request of Solomon, says, "And now I have sent a cunning man, endued with understanding, skilful to work in gold, in silver, in brass, in iron, in stone, and in timber; also to grave any manner of graving, and to find out every device which shall be put to him, with thy cunning men, and with the cunning men of my lord David thy father."

The prize that Achilles gave to the best runner at the funeral games of Patroclus was a silver cup curiously wrought by the skilful artists of Sidon. (*Iliad*, xxiii. 740 of the original.)

> " And now succeed the gifts, ordained to grace
> The youths contending in the rapid race.
> A silver urn that full six measures held,
> By none in weight or workmanship excell'd :
> *Sidonian artists* taught the frame to shine,
> *Elaborate* with *artifice divine :*
> Whence Tyrian sailors did the prize transport,
> And gave to Thoas at the Lemnian port:
> From him descended good Eunæus heir'd
> The glorious gift ; and, for Lycaon spar'd,
> To brave Patroclus gave the rich reward.
> Now, the same hero's fun'ral rites to grace,
> It stands the prize of swiftness in the race."

Indeed Homer's words are far more expressive than Pope's translation; for he says,

αυταρ καλλει ενικα πᾱσαν επ' αιαν
πολλον, επει Σιδονες πολυδαιδαλοι ευ ησκησαν—

" in beauty it was greatly eminent all over the earth, *because* the variously-accomplished artists of Sidon elaborated it with consummate skill."

This passage in Homer shews that the Phœnicians brought the arts to a high order of excellence at a time when the Greeks were only in the infancy of their civilisation, and many hundred years before the age of Solomon. Homer, who is supposed to have been a contemporary of David and Solomon, lived about 250 years after the Trojan war. Thoas, the king of Lemnos, to whom this highly wrought tankard, or cup, or urn (Homer calls it κρητηρα τετυγμενον: now κρητηρ may mean either, and τετυγμενος in Homer often implies elaborate relief-work), was given by *Phœnician* mariners (Φοινικες ανδρες, not *Tyrian*, as Pope has it), lived in the time of the Argonautic expedition; for his daughter Hypsipale married Jason, the commander of the expedition, when he landed in Lemnos on his way to Colchis, and by him had Eunæus, who inherited this cup from his maternal grandfather, and gave it as the purchase for the captive son of King Priam. Homer does not state whether this vessel, when brought to Thoas, was new or old. He only says, it was famous all over the earth, or the land (for αιαν may signify either). But suppose it was brought to him fresh from the hand of the artist, it shews the advanced state of the arts in Phœnicia, when the Greeks were semibarbarous; for all historians agree that the ship Argo, which bore the Argonauts, was the first large ship ever launched by Greeks from their coasts, and that this expedition was the first distant one they ever undertook. The colonies which the Phœnicians established are sufficient evidence of the early cultivation and prosperity of that people. It is here sufficient to mention one —Carthage, which was so famous for its wealth, power, and knowledge of all the arts and sciences, that Virgil expressly says, at the commencement of the *Æneid*, that the queen of heaven peculiarly cherished and patronised it, as her earthly residence, even in preference to the refined Samos—that there were her own arms and her chariot. The great abundance of precious stones which they possessed, and their acknowleged ingenuity, taste, and wealth, brought the arts to a high state of cultivation.

Though we have undoubted evidence of the great progress made by the Persians at a very remote age in civilisation—indeed, Persian luxury

Knowledg
the art am
the Persia

and pomp were proverbial among the ancient Greeks—yet there are nò proofs of their having made any progress in the art of sculpture : but they did in architecture. The main causes of this were their system of religion, and their aversion to naked images. They did not believe, like the Egyptians, Greeks, and other nations, that the gods had human form : they considered the elements only to be the proper representatives of the divine Power; and so they condemned all statues and images. Hence Xerxes is said to have destroyed, at the instigation of the Magi, or Persian priests or wise men, all the temples of Greece, because it was thought impious to confine within walls the gods, to whom all things were open and free, and whose temple should be the whole world. But there was another cause of their imperfect proficiency in the arts of sculpture and painting—their dislike of naked images, which alone are favourable to the full and elegant development of the human form. All their figures were wrapped up in drapery; and these figures were not so much intended to represent the actual features, attitudes, and emotions of the originals, under the varied circumstances of their condition, as to become general memorials of them.

ledge of
t among
truscans. The first European people who adopted the arts of the Egyptians, especially sculpture in its various departments, were the Etruscans; a people who reached a high degree of prosperity and civilisation, when Greece was in its state of transition from barbarism. Thus Hayley speaks of Etruria (*epistle* iv.) :—

> " Artists defrauded of their deathless due,
> Who once a glory round Etruria threw ;
> When, with her flag of transient fame unfurled,
> She shone the *wonder* of the *western world*—
> *Eclipsing Greece, ere, raised to nobler life,*
> *Greece learned to triumph o'er barbarian strife.*"

The Etruscans had at an early age extensive commerce with the Egyptians, Phœnicians, and other civilised nations of the East, and borrowed from them their arts, which their own native genius and taste enabled them to cultivate and improve with great success. Peace and commerce brought them wealth; this introduced refinement and luxury : and

the art of engraving precious stones, glass, and compound substances, which
were known to the Egyptians, became one of their favourite pursuits. The
curiously wrought vases, and other sculptured relics of that people, which
have been preserved to us, bear ample testimony to their industry, skill, and
elegance. The Etruscans, who had borrowed many of their subjects and
much of their general design of engraving from the Egyptians, adhered, how-
ever, much more to veri-similitude and nature. For instance, their engraved
figures of the *scarabœus* were more in accordance with the natural size of
the animal; whereas the Egyptian figure of it was, in their usual habit
of giving large proportions to every thing, sometimes four inches long.
Etruscan art evidently seems to have been in an intermediate or transition
state between Egyptian and Grecian accomplishment. The Etruscans,
while they adopted many of the outlines of the definitive characteristics of
the angular Egyptian style, yet improved on it considerably, by giving
them a comparative rotundity, smoothness, and a character of elasticity.
Notwithstanding all this, their style of sculpture and engraving still re-
tained much of the Egyptian in elongation of limb and stiffness of attitude.
But it was their evil destiny to be placed in the neighbourhood of Rome,
whose pursuit was mainly war—whose ambition was conquest—and
whose lust was plunder. Their flourishing confederation of twelve states,
each ruled by its *lucumon*, and possessing a representative form of govern-
ment, was lost in the encroachments of those rude and unscrupulous
republicans — the Romans. With their independence sunk their arts;
and never revived. It is true that, when Rome emerged into refine-
ment, the monuments of Etruscan science and taste which escaped were
cherished and admired; but the art irretrievably perished with Etruscan
liberty.

It is allowed that the early Romans adopted from them many of the
ceremonials, and much of the substance, of their religion—the fundamentals
of many of their best civil institutions—their robes of office, and the insignia
of state pageantry; and Ammianus Marcellinus, a historian of much research
and scrupulous accuracy, states that they were acquainted with the tri-
umphal procession, and all its accompanying circumstances, one thousand
years before Rome. At least, it is clear that during the Roman monarchy

they carried some of the arts to perfection, and were rich in curious and costly ornaments, which they carried about them; for Dionysius of Halicarnassus records that the elder Tarquin, having conquered one of the Etruscan states, despoiled the magistrates of the engraved and precious rings they wore.

As it does not come within the scope of this brief essay to descant on the civilisation of Etruria, it may be well to refer the curious reader to Dempster, Gori, Buonarotti, the Latin dissertations of Posseri, and the Saggio di Lingua Etrusca dall' Abate Lanzi. It is here sufficient to remark, that the concurrent testimony of those authors who have sifted the inquiry with judgment, impartiality, and care, proves Etruria to have been the first country on the continent of Europe that rose to civilised prosperity, and cultivated the sciences and all the polite arts of peace with diligence, success, and renown.

un era art.

The Greeks, in the progress of their own civilisation and the diffusion of Egyptian commerce, acquired from the Egyptians a knowledge of their arts, as they borrowed from them much of their philosophy and religion. When once in possession of the art of engraving, they soon brought it, like the other arts of fancy and delineation, to the highest imaginable perfection. Raspe justly observes, that "their improvements were not so much improvements in the *mechanical* parts of the art, *i.e.* the tools or method of engraving (for these, from their simplicity, could undergo but little variation), as in a more extensive and varied use of the tool, and in a better choice and happier treatment of the subject, from their superior knowledge of anatomy and their imitation of nature." One cardinal defect pervaded Egyptian sculpture, *i. e.* rigid immobility : the limbs appear stiff, angular, clumsy, and inactive. The Egyptian style was the colossal and the imposing ; the Grecian, the delicate and the fascinating, breathing, as it were, life into a figure, and touching into motion the group contained within the small precincts of a ring. The commercial intercourse of the Greeks with other nations, especially Egypt, Phœnicia, and Etruria—the constant emulation between the many independent states into which Greece was divided—the encouragement given by ingenious and aspiring artists to the industrious and successful cultivation of mechanism and science—the athletic exercises of the people—the natural symmetry and beauty of their forms—the diversified and charming scenery of their country, together with the genial influence of the climate,—all tended to give an impulse to their genius, and a consummation to their art. To all these causes and qualities a great propelling force was given by the varied enchantments of their mythology, which widely differed from the cold, dry theology of the Asiatics and Africans. It was by the study of Nature and her laws, that the Greeks formed their immortal works—her alone they adored—she alone was their object, standard, and test of art and science—of genius and of taste.

It is impossible to trace with any accuracy the origin, or the gradual stages of the advancement of the art among the Greeks. Pliny, following the traditional accounts of the Greeks, states (*Nat. Hist.* vii. 56), that " Dædalus invented the carpenter's tools, particularly the saw, plumb-line, augur, and glue of isinglass; but that the rule, level, turning-lade, *lock and key,* were invented by Theodore the Samian." But the only Samian artist of the name of Theodorus, whose history is known to us, was the artist who engraved the famous emerald ring of Polycrates king of Samos, and the contemporary of Amasis, king of Egypt. The story of this ring it may be here right to give; for the era of Polycrates and Amasis may be justly considered as the period from which we date an acquired excellence of the pursuit of art, of science, and philosophy, in Greece. Polycrates having enjoyed a long and singular career of uninterrupted prosperity, was advised, by his friend Amasis, to cast away, as a counterpoise to his prosperity, the possession he valued most, and whose loss would most afflict him. Polycrates, acting on the advice, rowed out to sea, and, in presence of the chief men of his court, flung into the water a signet-ring of inestimable value, which he was wont to wear—an emerald, set in gold, beautifully engraved—the work of Theodorus. (Yet Pliny (xxxvii. 2) and Solinus (c. 33) say it was a sardonyx.) So much did he prize this gem, that on his return to the palace he gave way to extreme grief. But in a few days a fisherman sent him, as a present, a large and beautiful fish, which, when opened, was found to contain the identical ring. When Amasis learned this, he renounced all connexion with him, as being a

e

man doomed by Providence to destruction,—a foreboding that, was afterwards realised. The gem of Pyrrhus, king of Epirus, engraved with the figures of Apollo and the nine Muses (in which the spots and various colours of the stone were singularly adapted to the attributes of each character portrayed on it), also obtained much celebrity among the ancients.

It is quite evident that the use of the key was known in Homer's time; for he describes Juno (*Iliad*, xiv.) as opening her cabinet with a *secret key*. That engraving was not only known, but carried to high perfection in his time, is, among many other proofs, attested by the simple fact of his wonderful description of the metal figures on the sculptured shield of Achilles—figures so executed to the life, that he intimates you could imagine you saw them move, and heard them speak. Æschylus says, the shields of the seven chiefs of the Theban war—a war antecedent to the Trojan—had emblematical devices engraved upon them. Nor are we dependent on Homer and Æschylus alone for evidence of the antiquity of the art among the Greeks; for we have the authority of Hesiod as well, in his description of the shield of Hercules.

When the art of engraving in Greece arrived at a high order of execution, the use of signet-rings and engraved stones was not restricted to particular persons or certain ranks; but extended to the people, either as presenting the image of some favourite divinity to the adoring eye of the votary, and so attaching his confidence and fortifying his belief; or perpetuating some signal deed achieved by the possessor of the gem, or by his ancestor, or some hero who had enlisted his sympathies and won his admiration. Thus the perfection of the art gave value and circulation to the engraved stones; while their general estimation and use reciprocally acted in giving encouragement to the art.

In the age of Polycrates there was much intercourse between Greece (which was then rising rapidly to civilisation) and Egypt. It is stated that he was instrumental in introducing Pythagoras to Amasis, and so enabled him to obtain facilities for studying the religious mysteries and occult sciences of the Egyptians,—a privilege that few (if any) strangers before were permitted to enjoy. It is also stated, that Solon visited Egypt in the reign of Amasis; and having got opportunities of learning the laws and religion of the country, transplanted into Greece many of its religious and political institutions. Many other eminent Greeks, Homer, Thales, Plato, &c. at different times visited Egypt, and derived from it much of their philosophy and learning.

From Dædalus to the time immediately preceding Phidias, there intervened a period of about 800 years in attaining a complete delineation of the human form and its various attitudes. It would be tedious and uninteresting to quote here the few fragments of history left to us, to give a shadowy outline of the gradations through which the art slowly but surely crept on to perfection.

About 500 years elapsed between the age of Homer and that of Solon and Pythagoras, who lived about 500 years before the Christian era. That the art of engraving acquired importance we have evidence from one of his laws, which forbade engravers to keep or make copies of seal-rings; lest, no doubt, fraudulent use might be made of them (Diog. Laer. *in vit. Solon*).

, The first great impulse was given to Grecian skill and talent, after the establishment of Grecian independence, by the rout of the Persian invaders. Then they were free to turn their attention to the cultivation of the domestic arts, as well in drawing isolated figures as groups. From this time all the arts advanced with prodigious strides, till the age of Alexander, when they reached their utmost perfection. For many ages they still upheld their excellence; but, in some degree, fell off towards the Roman occupation of Greece. However, Raspe says that " the arts arrived at perfection in the time of Pericles; and so continued through the age of Alexander and his successors, up to the middle of the third century of the Christian era, long after the age of Augustus, *i. e.* about 1250 years of success from the time of Homer."

We have a remarkable instance (told by Lucian in his Συγγραφειν, or *Treatise on History*) of the love of future fame which animated the Grecian artists; and this love tended much to their success. Sostratus, who was employed by Ptolemy to erect the famous lighthouse on the island of Pharos, inscribed on the outside the name of the king; for the king wished that his own name, on a structure so remarkable, " dedicated to

Jove the Saviour, for the good of mariners," should be perpetüated—not the name of the architect. But thus the artist foiled his design. He carved into a solid block of stone, presenting a prominent view to the open sea, his own name: over this he put an incrustation of mortar, on which he inscribed the name of Ptolemy. Time and weather soon swept away the mortar and the imposing superscription, together with all remembrance of the beneficence of Ptolemy; while his own name, as the constructor of that great and useful work, was exhibited in indelible·characters for ages.

The most celebrated engraver of Greece was Pyrgoteles, who lived in the time of Alexander, and alone was privileged to engrave his image, as Apelles was to paint his picture, and Lysippus to make his statue. Next to Pyrgoteles, Pliny (xxxvii. 1) ranks Apollonides and Cromius the elder. He also makes honourable mention of Teucer. Scylax and Admon acquired great eminence before the time of Pericles. Among the eminent engravers of the Periclean age may be mentioned Polygnotus, Mycon, Pamphilus, and Plotarchus; and in the time of Alexander, Pyrgoteles, Aëtion, Apollonides, Solon, Sostratus, and Cromius the younger, were the most celebrated. In general it may be remarked, on the authority of the best authors on this subject, that the ancient sculptors and engravers must have been thoroughly acquainted with the principles of mathematical science—with the laws of proportion and anatomy—to enable them to execute their figures with so much elegance, force, and fidelity to nature. Vitruvius (b. iii.) lays down some rules adopted by the most celebrated Grecian artists, taken from their own writings, for defining the symmetrical proportions of the human figure; as well as the geometrical lines which circumscribe its general form, attitude, and general motion.

oman
he art.   The Romans were for a long time debarred by their religious institution from using engraved stones to perpetuate the symbols, the ceremonials, or the mysteries of their religion; for Numa, the chief founder of their theology, following in many things the precepts of Pythagoras, conceived that a knowledge of the Divinity (as the Supreme Being was not an object of sense, or liable to human infirmity, but invisible and incorruptible) could only be acquired hy the *mind,* and imagined that it

was derogatory to employ material and perishable objects to represent it. (See Plutarch, in his life of Numa.) But this fastidiousness gradually died away with the progress of their polytheism, and with their growing knowledge of the refinements of other nations.

After the Romans had possessed themselves of the spoils of conquered Etruria, and began to acquire a knowledge of Grecian art, a passion, and even a taste, for engraved gems began to spread among them; and as these curious treasures acquired by their arms were inadequate to the public demand, ingenuity was taxed to supply the deficiency. Then their caprice invented all kinds of subjects to be engraved on their seal-rings. Rings were, during the republic, the distinctive mark of the nobility. When a gold ring was bestowed on a plebeian, as the reward of merit, by a dictator or a quæstor, he was admitted into the equestrian order. On the other hand, whenever a Roman knight had dissipated his fortune, or became unworthy of his rank, he was compelled to resign his gold ring; and if any disgraceful act disqualified a citizen from holding a public office, he was deprived of his ring; and even his seal was erased (Pliny, xxxii. 12). But towards the close of the republic, and during the first ages of the empire, a multiplicity of rings, which had been hitherto prohibited, was allowed; and from having been originally used as seals, they became curious and necessary ornaments to every family—at least to every family and person of respectability and station. The Romans frequently covered all their fingers with them, and even carried several on one finger; and often mounted several engraved stones on one ring (Macrob. vii. 3). Pliny says, they loaded their fingers with princely fortunes; and they became so luxuriously fastidious, that some had their summer and their winter rings. Juvenal (sat. i.) describes Crispinus as waving his delicate finger " to cool his light summer ring, being unable to bear the weight of the massy winter *gem*." They not only used their engraved rings to seal their letters and cabinets, but sometimes as keys,—one part of the seal forming the wards of a key. As the head of every family had his own ring, no engraver was permitted to make the same ring for two different persons. These gem-rings they were most careful in preserving. Pompey (the son of Pompey the Great), anticipating his melancholy fate, flung his signet-ring into the sea, to prevent his enemies from converting the application of it to their own purposes after his death (Flor. iv. 2. Paterc. ii. 55).   At the bed of a dying man, his friends and heirs stood anxiously waiting for the disposal of his ring, this being considered an index to his last will.   This custom was not peculiar to the Romans; for we find evidence of it among the Greeks.   When Alexander the Great was on his death-bed, he was asked about his wishes respecting the appointment of his heir, or the partition of his empire.   He made no reply, but gave his ring to Perdiccas.   This has been pronounced, by all historians, a sufficient indication of his will.   Many, from various motives, ordered the signet to be enclosed in their funeral urn.   But if the dying man gave no directions about it, they took it from his finger, sometimes even before he expired,—a practice that Scena laments as one of the reprehensible manners of his age.

   " At Rome chiefly," observes Raspe, " the engravers and their art had encouragement much beyond any thing our times and fashions permit our artists to expect.   Seals were not their only care : such was the magnificence and taste of the ancients, that the art was applied to the working of the richest jewellery, for individual wear and ornament, and for adorning the statues of the gods.   Not only bracelets, earrings, clasps, girdles, &c., were ornamented with gems; but even the robes, gowns, and shoes of the opulent and the elegant were richly set and variegated with engraved stones. The emperor Heliogabalus is stigmatised by Lampridius for wearing such ornaments on his shoes and stockings; ' as if,' says he, ' the works of the celebrated artist could be admired in seal-rings worn on the toes.'   The same taste and profusion sometimes adorned the helmets, breastplates, sword-handles, and even the saddles of their military men.   The large cameos had their place in cabinet-work and furniture; and thousands of gems were set in gold and silver goblets, vases, &c., which glittered on the sideboards of the opulent, or in the temples of the divinities.   We have still left, for our astonishment, beautiful cups and vases of solid onyx, sardonyx, and rock-crystal, exhibiting the finest relievo-work."

   The great estimation in which these treasures, notwithstanding their extensive diffusion among all orders of the wealthy, were held, may be

ijudged of by the fact, that many of the most illustrious characters depo-
sited their own collections, selected with great care and made at great
expense, as precious relics, in public buildings, for the instruction and the
gratification of the community.   Pompey, after his triumph, placed in the
capitol the gems which he found among the treasures of the great king
Mithridates.   Julius Cæsar, who, according to Suetonius (c. 47), was a
great admirer and encourager of the fine arts, and was not prevented
by the excitement and occupations of war, or the glare of his victories,
from turning his attention to the possession of the rarest and most beau-
tiful specimens of engraved stones, consecrated and gave to the temple of
Venus Genetrix, or Venus the Great Mother (it being one of his honours
that his primitive ancestor, Æneas, was the son of Venus), his famous
cabinet of gems, which he collected with vast care and expense.   Mar-
cellus, the son of Octavius, deposited his cabinet in the temple of Apollo;
and others made similar dedications.

It has been already stated that engraved gems were frequently worn
on seals.   The seal of Julius Cæsar had the device of Venus armed with
a dart.   Augustus, when he assumed the sceptre, used the figure of a
sphinx; because, I suppose, the sphinx, which united the human head
and the body of a lion, was a symbol of the Divinity, as incorporating
beauty with intellectual and physical power.   He afterwards changed
this device for the head of Alexander the Great, whom he wished to be
considered as his prototype; and finally adopted his own image, engraved
by Dioscorides.   Pompey's seal had a lion holding a sword; which was
fully indicative of his generous bravery and military prowess.   The seal
of Mecænas had the figure of a frog, which, as being an amphibious
animal, was truly symbolical of the power of this prime minister by sea
and land.   Sylla's seal bore the head of Jugurtha; and the jealousy that
Marius (who was commander-in-chief in that campaign) felt at this was,
according to Plutarch, the original cause of the mortal enmity between
these two leaders, which afterwards drained the best blood of Rome and
Italy.   In the age of Augustus, the genius and the power that acquired and
maintained unchecked and boundless dominion over the vast empire of
Rome were not negligent to encourage those arts that tended to minister

to its luxury, and advance its refinement. But with the Roman power fell
the Greek and Roman arts alike; and though, after the revival of civilisa-
tion and letters in Europe, they have been partially restored, yet they have
not hitherto (especially gem-engraving) been brought to their former state
of excellence.

Dioscorides was a Grecian artist in the time of Augustus. So high
was his reputation, that, as Pyrgoteles alone was allowed to engrave the
effigy of Alexander, so he alone had the privilege of engraving the head of
Augustus. This was used by the successors of Augustus as the imperial
seal. Solon, Evodus, and Scylax, were also celebrated artists of the
Augustan age.

Although a vast number of these precious relics have, in the fall of
those states that practised and encouraged the art, been irretrievably lost,
yet a great number have escaped the ravages of time and barbarism, so as
to enable us to estimate the perfection of the art, and even (though faintly)
the gradations of its improvement. These relics have been better pre-
served than any other. Their smallness exposed them less to the injuries
of *time*. The frequent and different uses to which they were applied,
either as symbols of religion, mementos of eminent men, or rewards of
merit, in seals, rings, or other ornaments, made them useful; and their
exquisite beauty made them valuable: for the natural splendour of the
stone, and the additional perfection of the work, presented at one view
two objects of admiration. The perfection of gem-engraving in intaglio
becomes the more wonderful by contemplating the difficulty of the exé-
cution. The operator, in a measure, pursued his work in the dark : he
must mainly have trusted to the accuracy with which he formed his plan ;
the proper adaptation of his tools ; and the skill and fidelity with which
he guided them. He could not immediately see the effects of his touches,
at the time that these touches gave, as it were, life to the stone. He
could not judge of the progress he made on the stone but by consulting,
almost at every stroke, the impression he made on the wax, or other
plastic substance which he was obliged to apply to the stone, in order
to test the progress he made. These impressions were almost the only
eyes that gave him light to examine his performance. His general con-

ception must have been previously well formed in his mind, and his tools must have been in a suitable condition to obey the guidance of his judg- ment. The engraver in relief executed his work by the eye, and without the aid of wax; but notwithstanding this real (or perhaps imaginary) ad- vantage, it is generally supposed that it required at least as much labour and skill to engrave in relief as in intaglio.

But the singular perfection of these little pieces was not at all dimi- nished by the difficulty of the execution; for they were, for the most part, in the spirit of the age that drew them forth and perfected them; and not merely evidence of the best state to which the science was brought, but of the zeal and rivalry of the artists, and of the general encourage- ment given to their occupation: while the beauty and value of the stones rendered them not simply articles of luxury and wealth, but often objects of commerce.

These gems are equal in every particular to the finest statues, and in many particulars to the finest paintings, of antiquity. They possess all the delineations of proportions, all the development of grace, or dignity, or terror, exhibited by the statues; and with all these much of the light and shadow conveyed by the pictures: for it is one of the singular features in these gems, that the nature, colour, varied shades, and peculiar marks of the stone, were frequently adapted to the particular character of the sub- ject. Gems preserve a more perfect likeness than medals cast to represent the same subjects. They have descended to us with less alteration than those pieces of metal, which are often worn, and disfigured with rust. The concavity of the engraved stone screens the relief from the corrosion that damages the medal; also from attrition, and consequently from wear- ing,—for friction can seldom take place upon a figure that is entrenched and interior. The very incision, too, of the instrument that produces the figure of the stone is susceptible of a more beautiful detail than the mould or balance of the minter.

Besides these advantages, engraved gems possess another merit; inas- much as almost an infinite number of impressions can be taken from them. As in these figured volumes is to be found all that regards the fable or the history, the ceremonies or the exercises, the customs or the habits, of the ancients ; and as they enable us, as it were, to see the features and feel the lineaments of those great personages whose characters and actions, as described by the historians and poets of old, have been a source of instruction and pleasure to all ages, the preservation of the original relics, and the diffusion of their models, must ever be an agreeable acquisition to the curious, and a useful acquisition to the learned.

ADDENDA ET CORRIGENDA

TO PART I.

No. 1.

THE name *Saturn* of the Romans (who is the same in most things with the *Kronos*, or god of time, of the Greeks), Varro says, was derived from *Sator*, the sower, or husbandman. The pruning-hook, or sickle, with which he was represented, may designate him as the personification of husbandry, or of time, which cuts down all things. The circumflexed serpent too, (the serpent being a sign of wisdom), biting its tail, which he was represented as holding in his hand, was symbolical of a revolution, and of the renovation of the crops and seasons. To other gods the Romans sacrificed with their heads veiled, but to Saturn with their heads uncovered, to express the open candour and simplicity of the golden age, when he was supposed to reign, and the fact that time is the great revealer of all things. As much of the ancient mythology is confessedly but a corruption of the true accounts in Holy Writ, many incidents in the life, and many coincidents in the character and condition of Noah and Saturn, have been dwelt on to establish their identity. Martial (b. xii. ep. 63) calls Saturn a denizen of the antique world, under whose reign men led an easy life ; just as Noah was the father of another golden age—

> " Antiqui rex magne poli, mundique prioris,
> Sub quo prima quies, nec labor ullus erat."

God promised Noah that the earth would resume its pristine fecundity, and the righteous enjoy their former happiness. The coins struck in honour of Saturn had on the reverse the figure of a ship. In the time of each there was but one language. Noah was the first planter of vineyards ; Virgil says the same of Saturn—

> " *Vitisator* curvam servans sub imagine falcem."

Noah had three sons (as had Saturn) : Ham (who is generally supposed to be identical with Jupiter Hamon), to whose lot fell Arabia, Egypt, and Africa; Japheth, to whose lot fell Europe, and the isles of the Gentiles, and who was worshipped as Neptune, the god of the sea and the islands; and Shem, to whom Asia fell, among whose posterity a belief of an after state of rewards and punishments was retained, had many points of coincidence with Pluto. The sacrifice of human victims may be explained by the fact, that among the ancients there prevailed a general opinion that there could be no sufficient atonement obtained but by blood ; and human blood (from the superior value of human life) was judged the most acceptable (see the subsequent addenda to No. 116). The Abbé La Pluche, who is followed by many eminent

a

men, supposes that the worship of *Saturn*, a word which he derives from the Egyptian word *seter*, a judge; and of *Kronos*, from *keron*, splendour, was derived from the great annual meeting of the Egyptian judges (who were the priests in the primitive ages). This was notified by an image with a long beard, holding a scythe : in company with this image was always exposed an image of Isis with several breasts, and surrounded with the heads of animals. This they called *Rhea*, from *rahah*, to *feed* (the Greeks supposed the name to be derived from *rheo*, to *flow*, in reference to the all-pervading principle of production) : sometimes he was depicted with eyes before and behind (hence he was occasionally identified with Janus by the Romans); for time, and prudence, and providence, of which he was often the symbol, looks all around —to the future and the past. Thus, too, was he furnished with four wings; and the Mosaic history shews how expressive were these emblems. " The Greeks and Romans," says Bryant, " taking these pictures in a literal sense, turned into fabulous history what was only allegorical."

No. 6.

For " Sardonyx" read " Amethyst."

No. 8.

For " Amethyst" read " Sardonyx."

No. 9.

The explanation of the fable of Cybele's love for Atys is, that he was her zealous priest, who laboured to propagate and extend her worship; and his transformation into a pine-tree was significant of the sacred pine-groves in which this worship was practised. Cybele, who represented the earth, generation, and even all nature, was worshipped under different names, such as the good goddess, the Phrygian mother, the Idæan mother, the mother of the gods, Ops, Rhea, Vesta, Ceres, &c. The derivation of the word is the subject of much doubt and disputation. Bryant says it is " Cu-Bela, the temple of Bela, the feminine of Belus, the chief Chaldaic god." Her worship is said to have originated in Phrygia, and was introduced into Greece by Cadmus : it was not introduced into Rome until the time of the war with Annibal, the Sibylline books having declared that the invader could not be expelled till the Idæan mother were brought to Rome. Her priests were called Curetes, Corybantes, Dactyli, Galli, Semiviri, &c. The animals commonly sacrificed to her were the sow, on account of its fecundity, the bull, and the goat; and her priests sacrificed sitting, touching the earth, and offering the hearts of the victims. She was represented sometimes as drawn by tame lions, because there is nothing so wild, or fierce, or barren, that cannot be subdued and cultivated by care, industry, and tenderness ; sometimes as crowned with towers, for she was a personification of the earth, and all its cities ; sometimes holding a key, to express not only the safe custody of cities, but that in winter the earth locks up those treasures which in summer it unlocks and distributes ; the drum which she held was a symbol of the globe; the vehement gestures, the yells, and the music of her votaries, meant to express the bustle and activity of industry, and the merriment that follows the successful result of labour.

No. 12.

The reader must not suppose that this transformation gave rise to the representation of Cybele being drawn by lions; but that it was (like many other transformations mentioned in mythology) a story that was designed to mark the deserved and suitable punishment of incontinence and profanation.

No. 14.

The radical of the Latin word *Vesta* is *ast*, fire, which the Greeks changed into *Hestia* The worship paid to fire, as being supposed to be the purest and the most active of the elements, and therefore the strongest symbol of the Divinity, was very ancient. Though Zoroaster reduced the worship of fire among the ancient Persians to a regular system, and indeed admitted no visible object of devotion except fire, yet it was held in veneration long before his time. The priestesses of Vesta in Rome were virgins (as best fitted for so pure an element) of the first families, elected by lot, under ten years of age. The fire was kept perpetually burning in her temple, in little earthern vessels called *capeduncula*, and suspended in the air. If the fire went out, it was judged a most unlucky prognostic, which threw the whole city into consternation, and was to be expiated with much pomp and ceremony: it was to be rekindled by rubbing ignitable wood. But among the Greeks it was rekindled by exposing some inflammable matter in the centre of a concave glass, collecting the pure rays of the sun. If a Roman vestal priestess violated her vow of chastity, she was tried by the pontiffs, and sentenced to be buried alive. The palladium was a statue of Minerva, which was said to have fallen from heaven, and was kept in the temple of the goddess in Troy. The Romans believed that Æneas brought it to Italy; and it was kept in the temple of Vesta: hence from the close mythological connexion between divine wisdom and ætherial fire, it is very proper that Vesta should hold the statue of Minerva. Here it may be observed, that the palladium, or statue of Pallas, was said to be the guardian of the cities in which it was kept, because wisdom, and industry and courage, of which Pallas or Minerva was the divinity, are the best security of a people.

No. 15.

Amalthæa was the daughter of Melissus, king of Crete, who fed the infant Jupiter with goat's milk. Hence arose the fable of the goat Amalthæa suckling Jupiter: hence, too, the story of the horn of the goat being the horn of plenty. It is said, that, after the death of the goat, he covered his shield with its skin: hence this shield, which he afterwards gave Minerva, according to some, was called *ægis*, from *aigòs*, a goat. It is quite enough here to state, in general, that Jupiter was the supreme divinity of the Greeks and Romans, and the same as Belus of the Babylonians, Osiris of the Egyptians, and Ammon of the Africans. His first great exploit was the defeat of the Titans. He afterwards routed the giants who attacked Olympus. The Greeks called him *Zeus,* and *Zeus pater,* or God the father: hence the Latin name Jupiter.

No. 18.

Jupiter at first assumed the form of a serpent in order to deceive Proserpine.

No. 23.

For " Cornelian" read " Amethyst."

Nos. 30 and 32.

Transpose these numbers: Ganymede must have been borne to heaven before he received the caresses of Jupiter, or the nectar.

No. 50.

Read as a title, " Danaë receiving the shower of gold."

No. 51.

Read as a title, " Jupiter appearing as a flame of fire to Ægina."

No. 57.

Read as a title, " Io tracing her name on the sand beside the river-god Inachus."

No. 58.

For " Carialos" read " Carilaos."

No. 59.

For " Apollonides. Cornelian" read " Pyrgoteles. Calcedony."

No. 64.

The best authorities affirm that Ammon was the same as Ham, the son of Noah, whose posterity settled in Africa, and that the figure of a ram indicated wealth and power; the fleece of a sheep being the symbol of wealth, and horns being always the symbol of power. The Greeks knowing nothing of the history of Ham, or of the origin of the worship, derived the name from their own word *amma,* sand, and the worship from one of the many imaginary adventures of Bacchus.

No. 71.

It is Minerva, and not Juno, that is here represented. Here the artist adopts another account of the education of the infant Mars. In the background is Pan. This number should immediately precede No. 235.

No. 79.

This number should immediately precede No. 209.

No. 104.

The fable is, that Alectryon was appointed by Mars to watch and warn him and Venus of the approach of Apollo, or the sun's appearance. But Alectryon fell asleep, and they were discovered. Mars, to punish Alectryon for his neglect, changed him into a cock; who, to atone for his fault, has ever since given notice, by his crowing, of the sun's approach.

No. 109.

For " Cornelian" read " Sardonyx."

Nos. 110 and 111.

Transpose these numbers; for she must have arrived at Cyprus before she received attention, or deification.

No. 115.

There are many stories in mythological history detailing the persecutions of the gods from the monster Typhon.

No. 116.

Cyprus was called *Cerastis*, from *keras*, a horn; because it had many promontories protruding like horns. The human victims mentioned here were offered to Venus herself. Here it may be right to state, once for all, that most of the pagan nations offered human victims, as Bryant shews from various authors (volume vi. of his Ancient Mythology, under the article ανθρωποθυσια and τεκνοθυσια) ;—the Egyptians, the Carthaginians, the Phœnicians, the Cretans, the Scythians, the Arabians, the Cyprians, the Rhodians, the Phoceans, the Chians, Lesbians, and other islanders. Every classical reader must recollect the human sacrifices offered to Diana by the inhabitants of the Tauric Chersonese, mentioned by Euripides in his Iphigenia in Tauris ; and the human victims sacrificed by the Druids of Gaul, Germany, and the British isles, and by all the nations of the north. The Persians buried people alive; Amestris, the wife of Xerxes, had twelve men buried alive as a propitiatory offering. The Pelasgi, in a time of scarcity, vowed the tenth of all that should be born to them for a sacrifice, in order to procure plenty. Aristomenes, the Messenian, slew three hundred noble Lacedemonians, among them Theopompus the king, at the altar of Jupiter at Ithome. The Romans often sacrificed their prisoners; but in the year of Rome 657, and in the consulship of Lentulus and Crassus, a law was enacted that there should be *no more* human sacrifices. However, the custom was revived; for Suetonius says, that it was asserted of Augustus that, on the surrender of Perusia, in the second triumvirate, he offered up, on the ides of March, three hundred of the senatorian and equestrian order, at an altar dedicated to the manes of his uncle Julius. Porphyry says, that in his time a man was sacrificed every year at the shrine of Jupiter Latiaris. Heliogabalus offered human victims to the Syrian deity, whose worship he introduced into Rome. It is stated that Aurelian offered captives to Jupiter in the capitol. This custom prevailed in most parts of the Roman empire till the time of Adrian, who took great pains to abolish it. These horrid rites were performed through Gaul and Germany generally in the deep recesses of gloomy forests, and in places especially set apart for this solemnity, which were held in the highest veneration, and only approached at particular seasons. The priests drew omens from the agony and convulsions of the victim, as well as from the effusion of his blood. Among some nations the victims were prisoners of war; among others the victim was selected by lot; and among some northern tribes the importance of the sacrifice was in proportion to the importance of the victim. If the lot fell on a chieftain, or the king, it was received with loud acclamation. The sacrifices were not only offered for occasional purposes, but were offered at regular and stated seasons; and these were times of general feasting and rejoicing. The Egyptians selected the handsomest person, the Albanians the most virtuous, and the Carthaginians the most excellent and at the same time the most dear to them, which induced them to slaughter their own children. Plutarch, περι δεισιδαιμονιας, in reference to this custom, asks, "Would it not have been better for the Galatæ, and for the Scythians, to have had no tradition or conception of any superior beings, than to have formed to themselves notions of gods who delighted in the blood of men—of gods who deemed human victims the most acceptable and perfect sacrifice? Would it not have been better for the Carthaginians to have had the atheist Critias, or Diagoras, their lawgiver at the commencement of their polity, and to have been taught that there was neither god nor demon, than to have sacrificed, in the manner they were wont, to the divinity they adored? Tell me if the monsters of old, the Typhons, or the giants, were to expel the gods and rule the world in their stead, could they require a service more horrid than these infernal rites and sacrifices?"

No. 134.

There are different accounts of the ægis of Minerva. Some say it is so called from being covered with the skin of the goat, *aigos*, that nursed Jupiter. The ægis of Jupiter was a buckler; but Servius, on *Æneid*, viii. 435, says that the ægis of Minerva was a *cuirass*.

Nos. 140 and 141.

Read "Murmex."

No. 142.

Read as a title, " Arachne challenging Minerva."

No. 143.

Read as a title, "Contest between Minerva and Neptune."

No. 146.

The owl, a bird which sees in the dark, was sacred to Minerva; this was a symbol of wisdom, which sees through the gloom of ignorance and error.

No. 149.

Read as a title, "Latona metamorphosing the Lycian peasants into frogs."

No. 150.

Read as a title, " Themis rendering young Apollo immortal." She is represented as coming to him, when dwelling in an island, on a sea-horse, and presenting the cup.

No. 151.

Read " bathed by nymphs." This number should precede the number marked No. 150.

No. 152.

For " Virgil" read " Ovid, *Met.* i." After this number should follow Nos. 161 and 162, in which this monster is represented as slain by Apollo.

No. 153.

For "Virgil" read " Homer, *Odyssey* xi.;" and, as a title, read " Tityus pursuing Latona." In the prose explanation of this subject it is said that Tityus intended to " *destroy* Latona and her children," and yet in the poetic quotation appended, it is stated that his object was to *violate* her person—

" With haughty *love* th' audacious monster strove
To *force* the *goddess*, and to *rival Jove.*"

This is the most prevalent opinion. After this number, the numbers marked 167, 168, and 169, should follow, as describing his death and infernal punishment.

No. 158.

For " Apollo *surprising* Creusa," read " Apollo *caressed* by Creusa;" for this is the plain representation on the gem.

Nos. 161 and 162.

These numbers should immediately follow No. 152.

Nos. 167, 168, and 169.

These should immediately follow No. 153. The liver of Tityus is said to have been selected as the part in which he suffered punishment, as being, according to ancient authors, the seat of lust; and brutal, impious lust was his crime. In No. 168 Tityus is represented by the artist as tortured by a *serpent;* and yet the writer of the explanation in the text says the punishment was inflicted by a *vulture,* and quotes as proof a passage from Virgil. He says, " The artist, taking advantage of the *liberty* accorded by Horace to speak to the imagination, gives the preference to this reptile, as more analogous to the regions of darkness." Setting aside the absurdity of this language, and the weakness of this authority, (for Horace merely says, " painters and poets have the privilege of taking any liberty"), we may observe, that if the writer only consulted ordinary books of reference, he would have found that the artist here did *not* take *any liberty,* but followed a received opinion. There were two traditional or historical accounts of this punishment: *one* was, that he was tortured by a *serpent;* the, *other,* that he was tortured by *vultures;* and the subject is treated here in two different ways, by two different artists, according to the two different accounts. Pharnax engraved the subject on amethyst, adopting the story of the serpent; Apollonides engraved it on cornelian, adopting the story of the vultures. Hyginus (fab. 55) has these words, " Serpens ei appositus est, qui jecur ejus exesset," *i.e.* a *serpent* was set on him, that continually ate away his liver. The Scholiast on Pindar, Olymp. A, says, οφεις τα σπλαγχνα ὑπτιον κειμενου κατεσθιουσιν, *i.e.* serpents eat away his liver while he lies upon his back. In No. 169 he is represented as torn by *two* vultures. This is in accordance with Homer's account (*Odyssey,* b. xi. 587), who further says, that the punishment was inflicted for the outrage to Latona; and yet in place of the quotation from Homer, which would be to the point, the quotation this writer gives is from Virgil, who only mentions *one* vulture, and makes no mention of the *cause* of punishment. Not only is the quotation given from Virgil, but two different versions are given of the same original passage; one of them by Mr. Nathaniel Ogle. To this there is appended a note, announcing that the son of that gentleman is the editor of this work. It therefore becomes necessary to apprise the reader, that, although a Mr. Ogle did prepare for publication several of the commencing numbers, yet his connexion with this work has long since ceased.

No. 170.

For "tortoise" read " coiled serpent;" for this is the representation on the gem, and it agrees with the subject of the next number.

No. 172.

The last line of the prose explanation is incorrect; for the plant was called lotus *before* she plucked the flower, as appears from the quotation given by the writer himself.

No. 183.

Cycnus, who wandered about inconsolable for the loss of Phaeton, was his relation and friend.

No. 199.

Read as a title, " Pyrene weeping over the dead body of Cenchreus."

No. 203.

Ceres, the goddess of husbandry, was generally represented as having her chief residence in Sicily, from the fertility of the soil and the industry of the people. After the abduction of her daughter Proserpine by Pluto, she wandered over the earth to seek her, in a chariot drawn by dragons, bearing at night a torch originally kindled from the flames of Ætna. This event the Sicilians annually commemorated, by running about at night uttering loud cries. When over-exhausted in her wanderings, she received this reviving draught from Bacchus.

No. 206.

This subject should follow No. 208. Read as a title, " Lyncus transformed into a lynx, when about to kill Triptolemus."

No. 208.

Ceres, in gratitude for the hospitality of Celeus, king of Attica, taught his son Triptolemus the science of husbandry ; and sent him over the earth in her chariot to disseminate it. Some say that Triptolemus first introduced the Eleusinia and Thesmophoria, which were the most celebrated and solemn religious festivals and ceremonies in all Greece.

No. 209.

The prose explanation of this subject in the text states that Arion was the offspring of *Zephyrus* and a *harpy*, whereas the quotation given by the writer from Statius mentions him as the offspring of *Neptune*. There were many accounts of the pedigree of Arion. The artist here follows the account of his having been the offspring of Neptune and Ceres transformed into a mare ; and indeed, in No. 79, she is represented as metamorphosed into a mare, in the presence of Neptune. Thus the compiler of the text is palpably wrong, even on his own

b

shewing.   No. 79 ought immediately to precede this number.   Pausanias says (b. viii. c. 25), " Ceres, they say, had by Neptune the famous horse Arion ;" and hence the propriety of the mother presenting the offspring to the sire.   Arion was said to have had a human leg and foot.

No. 213.

For a title, read " Jupiter and Maia."

No. 215.

This number ought immediately to precede No. 229.

No. 216.

Read as a title, " Mercury and Alcmena."

No. 219.

Read as a title, " Mercury transforming Battus."

No. 229.

This subject should immediately follow the subject No. 215; for Lara and Muta were the same being.

No. 239.

Read as a title, " Mars killing Halirrhotius while carrying off Alcippe."

ADDENDA ET CORRIGENDA

TO PART II.

No. 245.

BOCHART says (and his solution of the fable of Æolus having been king of the winds is the most probable of the many solutions given) that the word Æolus is derived from the Phœnician word *aol*, which signifies a tempest; whence the Greeks formed the word *aella*. The Phœnicians observing, in their trading along the Mediterranean, the king of a cluster of islands in the Sicilian seas to be remarkable for his knowledge of navigation and of astronomy, and for his careful observation of the weather, and therefore able to give useful instructions to mariners when to sail, and how to avoid the fury of a storm, called him king *Aolin*, or king of the winds and storms.

No. 250.

Read "Cyclop."

No. 251.

Read as a title, "Galatea, the sea-nymph, escaping from Polyphemus, who has crushed her lover Acis." Acis was metamorphosed into a fountain.

No. 254.

Read as a title, "Jupiter appearing in all his glory to Semele."

No. 255.

The worship of *Bacchus*, called by the Greeks *Dionusos*, was one of the most ancient in Greece. Herodotus says the Greeks themselves could not explain the origin of its introduction from the East. *Bacchus*, or Iachus (says Bryant), is derived from the oriental word *ouc*, king, or great man. It was a custom of the Greeks, when they found a similarity between foreign names, especially of divinities (whose worship was introduced among them), and words in their own language, to devise some fanciful or fabulous explanation of it.

" The history of Dionusos," he adds, " is closely connected with that of Bacchus, though they were in truth two distinct persons: the close similarity between several parts of their history, and of their attributes, has caused them to be identified with each other. It is said of the former, that he was born at Nusa, in Arabia; but the people upon the Indus insisted that he was a native of their country, and that the city Nusa, near Mount Meru, was the true place of his birth. He taught the nations whither he came, to build and plant, and to enter into societies. To effect this, he collected the various rude families, and built towns for them— then gave them laws, and taught them the worship of the gods—taught them to plant the vine, and extract the juice of the grape, besides much other salutary knowledge. This he did through all his travels, till he subdued and civilised every region in the east: his beneficence extended over all the habitable world, subduing nature in its sterility and fierceness. Hence he is represented frequently as drawn by tame panthers, or lions. The account given by the Egyptians is consonant to that of the Indians, except that the Egyptians supposed him to have belonged to their own country, and to have set out by the way of Arabia and the Red Sea, till he arrived at the extremities of the East. He travelled also into Libya, as far as the Atlantic; of which exploit Thymætes is said to have given an account in an ancient Phrygian poem. After his Indian expedition, which occupied three years, he passed over into Thrace, where Lycurgus resisted his efforts, and at last expelled him. He came into Greece; and was then adopted by the people, and represented as their countryman. He also visited many places on the Mediterranean, especially the coasts of Italy, where he was taken prisoner by Etrurian pirates. Some say he conquered all Etruria. The fact is, that Dionusos (or Bacchus) is multiplied into as many personages as Hercules. His history was interesting, and his acts beneficial; and therefore he was a favourite theme with the ancient poets. Diodorus says that he was the same as the Egyptian Osiris."

The fact that the vine (the cultivation of which, among other improvements, he introduced as a source of comfort to mankind) yields the most delicious and exhilarating juice above all the productions of the earth, has given rise to the notion that he was exclusively the god of wine. Now this was not his exclusive attribute; nor did the Greeks (though it may have been his predominant and most attracting attribute) think so. They considered him the primitive father of civilisation, animal enjoyment, and hilarity; and therefore introduced a greater number of festivals in his honour, than to that of any other divinity in the whole range and system of their polytheism. These festivals, by which the Athenians numbered their years, were blended with a great deal of mystery, and celebrated with uncommon pomp. It is not now necessary here to enter into a detailed account of his rites and festivities; but it may be stated that these festivals were called Dionusia and Bacchanalia (from his names), and Orgia, from *orge*, frenzy, in consequence of the licentious and wild behaviour of his votaries.

As there have been various accounts of the birth and exploits of Bacchus, the different artists have given different representations; and even the same artist varies his representations. He is represented sometimes as a full-grown, bearded person; sometimes as a florid-faced boy. A lion or panther is one of his general accompaniments.

Nos. 256, 257, 258, 259.

These numbers are incorrectly arranged and incorrectly described. The subject marked 257 should have come first, and have the following title, "Jupiter commanding Mercury to bear off to Ino the infant Bacchus, transformed into a kid." Then should come the subject marked 258, and be entitled, "Mercury holding Bacchus transformed into a kid." Next the number marked 256, and be entitled, "Mercury wafting young Bacchus through the air;" and next No. 259, "Mercury committing the infant Bacchus to the care of Ino."

No. 262.

There are various accounts of the conduct of Theseus to Ariadne. It is sufficient here to state that the popular statement is, that after she was instrumental in releasing him from the dangers of the labyrinth in which he was confined by her father, he took her and her sister Phædra away with him. When they arrived at the isle of Naxos, he there deserted her, and eloped with her sister to Athens. Bacchus having discovered Ariadne on the island, fell in love with and married her. He gave her a crown set with stars, which Vulcan wrought for Venus. After her death, which was caused by Diana because she had not preserved her virginity, this crown became a constellation.

No. 266.

Read as a title, "Bacchus pointing derisively at Hercules sleeping."

No. 268.

This should follow No. 265.

No. 269.

This subject forms one of the most beautiful representations in the gallery of the Grand Duke of Tuscany. Ampelos means a vine.

> " 'Tis said, that Ampelos of blooming face,
> A nymph and satyr's son, the hills of Thrace
> Adorn'd, whom Bacchus fondly did caress,
> And let him from the grapes the vintage press;
> Once, as a lofty and a spreading vine
> Did through the branches of an elm entwine,
> Th' advent'rous youth climbs up the tree elate,
> And, falling, met with his untimely fate:
> Bacchus, in pity of his mournful case,
> Gave him amongst the starry signs a place."
>
> OVID: *Fasti*, book iii.

No. 274.

The first quotation given is not from Ovid, but from Homer (*Iliad*, book vi.).

No. 286.

Read as a title, " Jupiter, metamorphosed into a swan, visiting Leda."

No. 290.

To prevent confusion in the explanation of this subject, it is necessary to state that the Bebryces migrated from Thrace to Asia.

No. 301.

This number has been inadvertently introduced here.

No. 303.

Read as a title, " Circe poisoning the water in which Scylla bathes."

No. 309.

Read *Myiagrus*, which is the proper compound word. *Myagrius* means *mouse*-catcher.

No. 314.

The huge serpent here is meant to represent the fierce heat of the sun in summer, under which these noxious animals acquire all their strength and activity. The quotation from Ovid properly belongs to the following subject.

No. 320.

The caduceus, or rod entwined by two serpents, was the symbol of peace; hence those ambassadors who went to sue for peace were called *caduceatores*. Camillus first erected a temple to concord in the Capitol, where the magistrates often assembled for public business.

No. 321.

The Greeks worshipped Felicity under the name of Macaria. The children of Hercules having fled from Eurystheus to Athens for protection, the Athenians espoused their cause. But the oracle having declared that the voluntary sacrifice of one of the children was indispensable to the Athenian success, Macaria offered herself; and the Athenians gained a signal victory. The Athenians after this deified her as the representative of Felicity. Lucullus first built a temple to Felicity in Rome, on his return from the war against Mithridates.

No. 322.

This virtue was deified by the Romans on occasion of a discovery made, that a daughter privately sustained with her own milk her aged parent, who had been closely confined, and debarred of all nourishment. This act created such a sensation that the parent was released, and they were both supported at the public expense. A temple was erected to Piety on the spot, by Acilius Glabrio.

No. 323.

For *Meed* read *Medos*. According to Hesiod (*Theog.* 890), Metis was a distinct being from Minerva; being the first wife of Jupiter, whom he devoured in her pregnancy; and he then produced Minerva from his own head. The fable is thus explained by Lord Bacon, in his *Essay on Counsel*. "The ancient times set forth the incorporation of counsel with kings, and the wise and politic use of counsel by kings: the one, in that they say that Jupiter did marry *Metis*, which signifieth *counsel*; the other, in which they say that she conceived by him; but he suffered her not to bring forth, but ate her up; whereby he was himself delivered of Pallas armed out of his head. This fable containeth a secret of empire: how kings are to make use of their council of state—that first they ought to refer matters unto them, which is the begetting or impregnation; but when they are elaborated, and shaped in the womb of their council, and grow ripe, and be ready to be brought forth, that then they suffer not their council to go through with the resolution and direction, as if it depend on them, but take the matter back into their own hands: that the decrees and final directions (which, because they come forth with wisdom and power, are resembled by Pallas armed) proceeded from themselves; and not only from their authority, but the more to add reputation to themselves, from their head and device."

No. 325.

Chastity, Pudicitia, was worshipped by the Romans under the figure of a *matron*, half veiled. There were two temples dedicated to her; one to Pudicitia Patricia, exclusively confined to women of rank; the other to Pudicitia Plebeia. In both temples, no matron was permitted to sacrifice unless her reputation was unsullied, and she had been but once married: matrons, who were admitted, obtained *the crown of chastity*.

No. 326.

The worship of Fidelity, *Fides*, called also *Solafides*, was introduced into Rome by Numa, and maintained at the public cost. No bloody sacrifices were offered in her temple; her priests were dressed in pure white robes, and presented their offerings with the right hand only. So highly was she revered, that, in cases of intricacy, the magistrates often referred the decision of the litigated question to the *faith* of the contending parties.

No. 328.

Men are urged by Hope to become industrious and acquire subsistence, of which ears of corn were the type; are induced by Hope to sleep away and forget their cares, which is indicated by the poppies; and are steered by Hope right onwards to their object, as typified by the rudder.

No. 330.

The representation here is not that she is "seated *in* clouds which *overhang a pyramid*," but that she is seated *on* clouds; and that the *pyramid*, the meet type of her durable deeds and fame, on the summit of which she lays her hand, *out-tops the clouds*. It is more natural to suppose that glory and the lasting monument of her deeds should out-top the clouds, than that the clouds should overhang them, and therefore wrap them in obscurity.

No. 333.

Her attributes here are the horn of plenty and the rudder of a ship, to shew that she distributes riches and abundance, and directs the affairs of the world; or (for there are two explanations of the subject) that she dispenses all the treasures of sea and land. She stands upon a globe.

No. 337.

This was meant to express that sleep subdues, and renders harmless, the strongest and fiercest of all animals; or that the presence of even the greatest danger cannot prevent sleep. In this group sleep holds the soporific poppy-plant; and overhead is the owl, the bird of night.

No. 338.

This should follow No. 428. Charon, according to the *Theogony* of Hesiod, was the son of Erebus and Nox. His office was, in the infernal regions, to ferry across the river Acheron the spirits of the dead for a small fare. Those who could not pay this fare, which was usually put into the mouths of the dying, were, like those who did not receive the rites of burial, obliged to wander on the banks of the river for a hundred years, before they could be admitted to a passage. He was represented as a muscular, ragged, repulsive, grisly-looking person, of a hale and green old age, with rough, matted, and filthy beard and hair. See VIRGIL, *Æneid*, book vi.

No. 339.

Pausanias shews that Latona and Diana interceded to appease the anger of Apollo, and Minerva to appease Hercules. At their intercession he restored the tripod. The priestess usually sat on a tripod.

No. 344.

As Amphitryon was king of Thebes, Hercules was born in that city, and called the Theban Hercules.

No. 345.

Iphicles, or Iphiclus, was the twin brother of Hercules; but while Hercules was the son of Jupiter, Iphicles was the reputed son of Amphitryon.

No. 349.

There is a material error in the explanation here. It was Eurystheus the son of Sthenelus, and not Iphicles the son of Amphitryon, who gave the orders to Hercules. The wife of Sthenelus king of Mycenæ, and Alcmæna, were pregnant at the same time. Jupiter, to appease the jealousy of Juno, declared that the child first born of either should rule the other. Juno delayed the parturition of Alcmæna, and Eurystheus was born first. Eurystheus, actuated partly by jealousy of the rising celebrity of Hercules, but chiefly acting on the divine decree in his favour, imposed his tyrannical commands on Hercules to perform certain feats, which were generally considered impossible. Hence the famous legends of "the labours of Hercules." Here, once for all, it may be sufficient to state that there were many heroes of this name. Varro enumerates forty-three. Indeed almost every nation had one Hercules, or more; hence arises the discordant variety of the accounts about him, which it is not easy to reduce to system or consecutive order. But the achievements and adventures of them all have been condensed by the Greeks in the exploits of the Theban Hercules. Of this hero it is enough here to say, in general, that he was gifted with every accomplishment and power of mind and body that nature, or education through all its range and various departments of instruction, could give him. He was instructed by the most eminent masters in the different branches of philosophy, science, and elegant accomplishment, as well as in the various gymnastic and military exercises. He could touch the lyre as tenderly and skilfully, as he could powerfully and victoriously wield his club. In a word, the Greeks considered him the personification of human power directed for the public good, in destroying monsters and tyrants; and in removing every obstacle to the civilisation and happiness of mankind. From his own reputed intellectuality, and from his instrumentality in advancing civilisation and letters, he was styled *Musagetes*, or *leader of the Muses.* And yet, because physical prowess appears the most prominent engine in the achievement of his greatest victories, there prevails a vulgar opinion that he is the representative of mere manly strength. This is a mistake; for the Greeks represented him as the abstraction of all human power— intellectual as well as physical. He was deified after death, and married to Hebe. He is generally represented with a lion's skin, and a club—sometimes with a bow.

Nos. 357 and 358.

Transpose these numbers.

No. 359.

Read " Pholus."

No. 362.

Read as a title, " Hercules wounding the brazen-footed stag." This stag is generally known as the stag of Mount Mœnalus.

No. 365.

These birds were said to have had beaks, talons, and wings of iron, and to have destroyed and fed on the inhabitants bordering on the lake Stymphalus in Arcadia: the simple explanation of which fable is, that they were a gang of iron-tempered robbers that plundered the country, and evaded pursuit by their fleetness, and defied punishment by their ferocity.

No. 366.

From the entire omission here of any explanation of this subject, it is necessary to state that Minos, king of Crete, who had obtained wide dominion over the circumjacent seas, was so vainglorious as to refuse to offer the rightful sacrifice to Neptune. Neptune, to punish his disobedience and impiety, sent from out the sea a bull-shaped monster to desolate his country. This monster Hercules subdued, and dragged bound to Eurystheus. The plain solution of this fable appears to be, that the usurped supremacy over the free-trading on those seas by Minos raised up a formidable corsair or freebooter that ravaged the coast, but was eventually destroyed by Hercules. It is stated that Eurystheus let loose this bull, which afterwards was known as the famous bull of Marathon, subdued by Theseus. Of this an account is given under the head of Theseus.

No. 367.

Diomedes, a Thracian prince, was not only remarkable for his own ferocity and power, but his fierce horses were trained to attack strangers and devour their flesh: hence the great arduousness of a contest with him. However, Hercules killed him.

No. 368.

There are two versions of this story. One is, that Eurystheus, anxious to obtain for his daughter the belt of Hippolyte, the most famous in the world, ordered Hercules to bring it. Hercules, though attended only by a few followers, encountered the Amazons, the most formidable antagonists in those times—defeated Hippolyte, and gained the girdle, or belt. Another is, that she gave it as the ransom of her sister Menalippe, whom he had taken prisoner.

No. 370.

Here Hercules is represented as driving the butt-end of his club against the cistern (the usual attribute of a river-god), and discharging its contents through the stable, while the river-god is remonstrating against the act. In this stable or shed 3000 oxen were kept; and Hercules was required to perform the labour of cleansing it in one day. The work was considered impossible: but ingenuity and skill effected what physical strength could not. This achievement was of great value as an example, by shewing to the world in general that a slight exercise of skill is of more advantage than a great exercise of physical power; and to the Greek husbandmen in particular, an easy mode of keeping their stalls clean, and their cattle consequently healthy.

Augeas cheated him out of the promised reward—the tenth of the stock. For this treachery Hercules justly sacked his city and slew him; but generously surrendered the kingdom to his son Phyleus, who disapproved of his father's conduct. This story was an example to shew that perfidy and honesty should have, each its adequate reward.

No. 375.

The most probable explanation of the fable of Atlas having sustained the heavens on his shoulders, and of Hercules having for a short time relieved him, is, that he possessed great knowledge of astronomy and of the system of the universe, which Hercules learned and communicated to the Greeks.

Another well-supported opinion is, that on the summit of this lofty mountain, Atlas, there was a famous temple to Cœlus, the religious rites of which contained some sublime mysteries, in which Hercules was initiated.

There are different accounts of this labour of Hercules. Some say that he plucked the apples himself, after he slew the dragon.

No. 378.

Read as a title, " Hercules killing the vulture that fed on the liver of Prometheus." The fables about Prometheus are various. The artist here follows the account that Prometheus, having been chained to a rock over a ravine on Mount Caucasus, while a vulture preyed constantly on his liver, which grew as fast as it was devoured, — a punishment inflicted by Jupiter for his having stolen celestial fire, and with it animated into man a human figure formed of clay, — was released by Hercules, who slew the vulture or eagle. See *Addenda et Corrigenda* to the first number of Class III.

No. 389.

Read as a title, " Hercules enclosing the pigmies in a bag."

No. 391.

Read as a title, " Hercules killing *Sileus* with a spade."

d

No. 402.

There is an error in the explanation of the text here : both mountains are not now known by the name of Calpe. The hill on the African side was called Abyla ; that on the Spanish, Calpe, which the Moors called Tarik. Hence Gibraltar is a contraction of the Moorish words Gebel al Tarik, or the hill of Tarik.

No. 405.

As Adonis was fond of the chase, he is here represented as accompanied by his dog.

Nos. 406, 467, 468.

Achelous had (it is fabled) the power of transforming himself into many shapes. This horn became to Hercules a horn of plenty. The fables of the transformations into a serpent and a bull, and the wrenching off of the horn, are said to mean the serpentine course and roaring of the river, which divided itself into two streams or horns, which flooded the neighbouring country. One of these Hercules cut off, and so drained and fertilised the land.

No. 415.

The arrows of Hercules were exhausted before he prayed to Jupiter for assistance : hence he is here represented as holding up his empty quiver to heaven. The place where these stones fell from the air on the giants was called "the stony field" in Narbonne.

No. 422.

Read as a title, "Hercules dragging Cacus out of his den."

No. 423.

Read as a title, "Hercules griping the throat of Cacus, who discharges volumes of fire and smoke."

No. 424.

Read as a title, "Hercules strangling Cacus." These two numbers ought to be transposed.

No. 426.

This should follow No. 446. Theodamas, with his forces, attacked and wounded Hercules for having slain the ox Dejanira; but was himself slain by Hercules, who took off with him his son Hylas. Hylas afterwards became his constant friend.

· No. 428.

It is generally supposed that Hercules was commanded by Eurystheus to descend to the infernal regions to bring up Cerberus. It is enough to state here that, when he did descend thither, whatever may have been the command or the object, he is represented by different authors to have performed different feats, and to have released several persons.

No. 433.

Read as a title, " Hercules transfixing Pluto with an arrow."

No. 438.

Read as a title, " Hercules meeting Theseus and Pirithous chained to a rock in hell." There are three figures in the group ; and neither of the captives is represented in the act of receiving deliverance. Theseus is holding out his hands in supplication, while Pirithous is bending backward in an agony of despair at being left behind. It is in the following number the delivery of Theseus is represented.

Nos. 445 and 446.

These numbers should immediately precede No. 426.

No. 457.

There is no butterfly, and only one genius, represented. It would be a more appropriate arrangement if Nos. 455, 456, and 457, were immediately to precede No. 467.

No. 471.

" Hyllus cutting off the head of Eurystheus." CHROMIOS; *Cornelian.* This number which has been omitted, ought to precede No. 468.

ADDENDA ET CORRIGENDA

TO PART III.

No. 471.

Æschylus, in his tragedy of *Prometheus Bound*, represents Prometheus as saying that he instructed, from a feeling of benevolence, mankind, and raised them from a state of savage ignorance—having taught them astronomy, letters, agriculture, navigation, medicine, soothsaying, the use of metals, and all the refined arts connected with metals. On the explanation of the fable of Prometheus and Pandora, much learned ingenuity has been expended. Bryant says he was the same as Noah, the second parent of the human race. Another explanation, maintained on high authority, is, that notwithstanding the embellishments of the Grecian poets, the fable is based on the *fall* of Adam. Milton compares Eve to Pandora—

> " More lovely than Pandora, whom the gods
> Endow'd with all their gifts (and oh! too like
> In sad event!), when, to th' unwiser son
> Of Japhet brought by Hermes, she ensnar'd
> Mankind with her fair looks."
>
> *Paradise Lost,* book iv.

But whatever may have been the origin of the fable of Prometheus having stolen celestial fire, and having been, by reason of it, preyed on by a vulture, it is evident that the Greeks, and after them the Romans, deduced a moral lesson from it. It appears that they thought the theft of the fire was symbolical of his introduction of civilisation and luxury; and his punishment by means of a bird of prey was expressive of the cares and passions consequent on luxury. Tityus, as well as Prometheus, were said to have been tortured by eagles or vultures; and the explanation of one punishment may be applied to the other. Lucretius says—

> " But he is *Tityus* here, that lies oppress'd
> With *vexing love,* or whom *fierce cares* molest:
> These are the *eagles* that do *tear* his *breast.*"

Horace (ode iii. book i.) has the following remarkable passage :—

> " Post ignem ætherea domo
> Subductum, macies, et nova febrium
> Terris incubuit cohors,
> Semotique prius tarda necessitas
> Leti corripuit gradum."

Which means, that since the act of Prometheus diseases unknown in simple and primeval ages have brooded on the earth; and that the span of human life has become shortened. In corroboration of this view, there is near the commencement of Hesiod's poem *Works and Days*, the following sentiment :—

> " Posterity the sad effect shall know,
> When, in pursuit of joy, they grasp their woe."

The following passage from a note in Cooke's Hesiod, gives Lord Bacon's explanation of the eagle preying on the liver of Prometheus :—" In the other part of the fable, Prometheus means prudent men who consider for the future, and warily avoid the many evils and misfortunes which human nature is liable to; but this good property is accompanied with many cares, and with the deprivation of pleasures; they defraud their genius of various joys of life—they perplex themselves with intestine fears and troublesome reflections, which are denoted by the eagle gnawing his liver while he is bound to the pillar of necessity: from the night they obtain some relief, but wake in the morning to fresh anxieties. Prometheus having assistance from Hercules means fortitude of mind. The same is the explanation, by the Scholiast, of the eagle. The poet goes farther than what Tzetzes and Lord Bacon have observed; he makes Hercules free Prometheus by the consent of Jupiter: the meaning of which must be, that such miseries are not to be undergone patiently without divine aid to support the spirits."

No. 474.

Read as a title, "Pandora formed by Vulcan." Read first line of explanation, *whom* for *who*.

No. 502.

Read *bow and arrow* for *lance*.

No. 505.

Venus is not here represented: it is his dog that is near him.

No. 514.

Apollo is not represented here. Read as a title, "Metamorphosis of Cyparissus."

No 520.

Read as a title, "Orpheus playing on his lyre before Pluto and Proserpine."

No. 542.

Read *horns* for *tail*.

No. 556.

Read *Simulachrum.*

CATALOGUE.

CATALOGUE.

CLASS I.

GODS AND GODDESSES.

No. 1.

The head of Saturn.

MYRON. *Oriental Sardonyx.*

It would be a vain attempt to try to reconcile the numerous and contradictory traditions of this mythological deity.

The philosophical mythe seems to be, that he was the first cause, or god, of earthly productions, who had existed from unknown time, which his name Kronos signifies; and as time destroys all things brought into existence, he is metaphorically said to devour his own children. He is united to Rhea (ever-flowing), and Ops, the female power of earthly productions. In commemoration of the golden age, over which Saturn reigned, the festival of Saturnalia was celebrated; general festivity and mirth prevailed, the slave and the master were considered on an equality, scholars were released from obedience to their masters, war was not proclaimed, no criminals were executed: the modern carnival is derived from it. Hesiod says that Saturn ruled over the islands of the blest, situated near the "deep eddying ocean" at the confines of the world. His sons were Jupiter, Neptune, and Pluto. Empedocles tells us, that he married also Euronyme, who bore to him Aphrodite, the Fates Clotho (spinster), Lachesis (allotter), and Atropos (unchangeable), whom Plato in his Republic, χ, terms the daughters of necessity. In later ages he had in Egypt the cognomen of Orus, and among the Carthaginians Moloch, so pathetically alluded to in Psalm cvi. Hercules abolished the human sacrifices originally offered to Saturn in Italy, and substituted clay figures, called *oscilla*, which were suspended from trees.

b

" How happy liv'd mankind in Saturn's days,
  Ere tiresome journeys mark'd out tedious ways!
  No ship then ventur'd on the azure main,
  Or spread its sails the speeding winds to gain;
  To coasts unknown then none a voyage made,
  Or stor'd their vessels with a foreign trade.
  No sturdy bull as yet had wore the yoke,
  No horse with bit and bridle yet was broke.

No doors their houses had; and in their grounds
No stone was fix'd to mark each tenant's bounds.
Oaks honey gave; and, of their own accord,
The ewes with swelling dugs their milk afford.
Armies, nor rage, nor wars, as yet were found,
Nor yet the cruel smith had weapons forg'd to
  wound."
            TIDUL. b. i. Eleg. iii. BAKER'S *Trans.*

Juvenal, in his sixth Satire, has some pungent lines on a virtue, in his opinion, only known in Saturn's reign. The islands of the blest are thus described in Pindar's second Olympian Ode, where Seneca (Herc. Æt. act ii.) informs us, dwelt

" A pious offspring and a purer race:
  Such as erewhile in golden ages sprung,
  When Saturn govern'd, and the world was young."
                                        ADDISON'S *Trans.*

" But in the happy fields of light,
    Where Phœbus with an equal ray
  Illuminates the balmy night
    And gilds the cloudless day,
  In peaceful, unmolested joy
  The good their smiling hours employ:

Then no uneasy wants constrain
    To vex the ungrateful soil,
  To tempt the dangers of the billowy main,
    And break their strength with unabating toil,
  A frail disastrous being to maintain.

But in their joyous calm abodes
    The recompense of justice they receive;
  And in the fellowship of gods
    Without a fear eternal ages live.'   WEST'S *Trans.*

No. 2.

Saturn, with the herpè in his hand, devouring one of his children.

APOLLONIDES.   *Oriental Cornelian.*

No. 3.

Saturn and his wife Rhea, with their attributes.

CHROMIOS. *Calcedony, partaking of the Sapphire.*

No. 4.

Saturn receiving from Rhea the stone given him as her child.

APOLLONIDES. *Oriental Cornelian.*

" Then swathing an enormous stone,
She placed it in the hands of heaven's huge son,
The ancient king of gods : that stone he snatch'd,
And in his ravening breast convey'd away :
Wretch ! nor bethought him that the stone sup-
plied
His own son's place, survivor in its room,
Unconquer'd and unharm'd ; the same who soon,
Subduing him with mightiness of arm,
Should drive him from his state, and reign himself
King of immortals.

Swiftly grew the strength
And hardy limbs of that same kingly babe :
And when the great year had fulfill'd its round,
Gigantic Saturn, wily as he was,
Yet foil'd by Earth's considerate craft, and quell'd
By his son's arts and strength, released his race :
The stone he first disgorged, the last devoured ;
This Jove on earth's broad surface firmly fix'd
At Pythos the divine, in the deep cleft
Of high Parnassus ; to succeeding times
A monument and miracle to man." *

HESIOD.

No. 5.

Saturn devouring a horse, and near him Rhea.

PYRGOTELES. *Oriental Cornelian.*

---

* "The stone, which Saturn was supposed to have swallowed instead of a child, stood, according
to Pausanias, at Delphi : it was esteemed very sacred, and used to have libations of wine poured upon
it daily, and upon festivals was otherwise honoured. The purport of the above history I take to
have been this:—It was for a long time the custom to offer children at the altar of Saturn; but in
process of time they removed it, and in its form erected a stone pillar, before which they made their
vows, and offered sacrifices of another nature."—BRYANT.

No. 6.

Saturn, transformed to a horse, caressing Philyra.

CHROMIOS. *Oriental Sardonyx.*

Saturn, surprised by Rhea with Philyra, daughter of Ocean, who became the mother of Chiron, transforms himself into a horse. It is from this circumstance that Chiron is represented partaking equally of the forms of a man and a horse.

> " Such, at the coming of his wife, the swift
> Saturnus' self upon his equine crest
> Pour'd out a mane, and lofty Pelion fill'd
> With his shrill neighings, as away he fled."
>
> *Geor.* book iii. l. 92.

" Soon left Aretias' barren shore behind,
And, swiftly skimming o'er the watery vast,
The Philyræan isle at eve they past;
Where Saturn first fair Philyra survey'd,
When on Olympus he the Titans sway'd
(Nurs'd by the fierce Curetes, yet à child,
Young Jove was hid in Cretan caverns wild).
Unknown to Rhea he the maid compress'd,
But soon to Rhea was the crime confess'd;

Detected Saturn left his bed with speed,
And sprung all vigorous as a mane-crown'd
   steed.
Swift fled fair Philyra, abash'd with shame,
And to the hills of Thessaly she came:
Fam'd Chiron sprung from this embrace so odd,
Ambiguous, half a horse and half a god."
              APOLL. RH.

No. 7.

Philyra nursing her infant child Chiron.

DIOSCORIDES. *Oriental Sardonyx.*

Rhea recognises Saturn, though changed to a horse.

Philyra flies to the mountains of Thessaly, where she gives birth to Chiron. She is here represented nursing her child, who is called by Homer the most upright of the Centaurs; he was celebrated for his skill in surgery. Being accidentally wounded by one of the poisoned arrows of his son Hercules, he suffered great pain, and at his earnest prayer was raised by Zeus to the constellation of the Bowman.—OVID, in the 5th book of the *Fasti*, line 387 *et seq.*

No. 8.

Philyra, in despair at having given birth to a monster, prays the gods to transform her; and, obtaining her wish, is changed to a lime-tree.

APOLLONIDES. *Amethyst.*

No. 9.

Cybele, with her crown of towers, and at her feet a tame lion, caressing Atys, the young and handsome shepherd of mount Ida.

CHROMIOS. *Oriental Cornelian.*

The Lydian legend, that Cybele, the earth, was united to Atys, the personification of the sun, is curious and significant.

> " They tell how Atys, wild with love,
> Roams the mount and haunted grove;
> Cybele's name he howls around —
> The gloomy blast returns the sound."
>
> ANACREON, *by* MOORE.

No. 10.

Cybele in extreme sorrow, and at her feet the lifeless Phrygian shepherd Atys.

CHROMIOS. *Oriental Cornelian.*

The profound grief of Cybele for the death of Atys, whom Saturn in a fit of jealousy slew, was the origin of the worship of Cybele, whose priests were the Curetes and Corybantes.

No. 11.

Atys changed to a pine-tree.

GNAIOS. *Oriental Cornelian.*

There is a statue of Atys in the Altieri Palace at Rome, and another representation of him, at a more advanced age, in the Grand Duke of Tuscany's collection.

> " To Rhea grateful still the pine remains,
> For Atys still some favour she retains;
> He once in human shape her breast had warm'd,
> And now is cherished, to a tree transformed."
>
> OVID, *Met.* b. x. l. 165.

No. 12.

Atalanta and Hippomenes changed into a lion and lioness.

APOLLONIDES. *Oriental Cornelian.*

They having profaned the temple of Cybele, she punishes them by changing Hippomenes to a lion, and Atalanta to a lioness, whom she always keeps attached to her car.

> " A heavier doom such black profaneness draws ;
> Their taper fingers turn to crooked paws ;
> No more their necks the smoothness can retain,
> Now cover'd sudden with a yellow mane.
> Arms change to legs ; each finds the hard'ning breast
> Of rage unknown and wondrous strength possest.
> Their alter'd looks with fury grim appear,
> And on the ground their brushing tails they bear.
> They haunt the woods ; their voices, which before
> Were musically sweet, now hoarsely roar."
>
> OVID, *Met.* book x.

No. 13.

Cybele in her car drawn by lions.

APOLLONIDES. *Oriental Cornelian.*

> " Hence lions, dreadful to the lab'ring swains,
> Are tam'd by Cybele and curb'd with reins,
> And humbly draw her car along the plains."
>
> OVID, *Met.* book x.

> " In humble vales they built their soft abodes :
> Till Cybele, the mother of the gods,
> With tinkling cymbals charm'd th' Idean woods,
> The secret rites and ceremonies taught,
> And to the yoke the savage lions brought."
>
> *Eneid*, iii.

No. 14.

The goddess Vesta, holding in one hand the palladium, in the other the sacred fire.

PYRGOTELES. *Oriental Cornelian.*

The worship of the sacred fire, the domestic hearth, was first established in Phrygia. In the Prytaneion of every Grecian city was placed the hearth on which the sacred fire burnt and offerings were made to Hestia or Vesta. The worship of the goddess was introduced into Italy by Æneas. As the Romans attributed to him the introduction of the palladium also, from that time Vesta was always represented with this emblem.

PART I.—*Strophe* 1.

' Daughter of Rhea! thou whose holy fire
Before the awful seat of Justice flames!
Sister of heaven's almighty sire!
Sister of Juno, who co-equal claims
With Jove to share the empire of the gods!
O virgin Vesta! to thy dread abodes,
Lo! Aristagoras directs his pace.
Receive, and near thy sacred sceptre place
Him and his colleagues, who with honest zeal
O'er Tenedos preside, and guard the public weal.

Antistrophe 1.

And lo! with frequent offerings they adore
Thee, first invok'd in every solemn prayer!
To thee unmix'd libations pour,
And fill with odorous fumes the fragrant air.
Around, in festive songs, the hymning choir
Mix the melodious voice and sounding lyre;
While still, prolong'd with hospitable love,
Are solemnis'd the rites of genial Jove.
Then guard him, Vesta, through his long career,
And let him close in joy his ministerial year."

PINDAR, 11th *Nem. Ode*, WEST'S *Trans.*

No. 15.

The goat Amalthæa nursing the infant Jupiter. An eagle bringing him ambrosia in a cup.

GNAIOS. *Oriental Amethyst.*

" Hail, Saturn's son, dread sov'reign of the skies,
Supreme disposer of all earthly joys:
What man his numbers to thy gifts could raise,—
What man hath sung, or e'er shall sing thy praise?
The bard is yet, and still shall be unborn,
Who can a Jove with worthy strains adorn.

Hail, father! though above all praises, hear;
Grant wealth and virtue to thy servant's prayer;
Wealth without virtue but enhances shame,
And virtue without wealth becomes a name:
Send wealth, send virtue, then; for join'd they prove
The bliss of mortals and the gift of Jove."

CALLIMACHUS, *Hymn to Jupiter.*

> " Jove, her youngest born, vast Earth
> Took to herself, the mighty babe to rear
> With nurturing softness in the spacious isle
> Of Crete. So came she then, transporting him
> With the swift shades of night, to Lyctus first:
> And thence, upbearing in her arms, conceal'd
> Beneath the sacred ground, in sunless cave,
> Where shagg'd with thickening woods th' Egæan mount
> Impends."   Hesiod.

> " To Gnossus brought, the Melian nymphs' abode,
> With joy the Melian nymphs embrac'd the god ;
> His wants Adraste sedulous supplies,
> And in the golden cradle lulls his cries ;
> Milk from the duteous goat the god receives,
> And pleas'd the lab'ring bee her tribute gives:
> Hence Amalthæa 'midst the stars is found ;
> Hence fame the bee and Jove's protection crown'd."
>   Callimachus, *Hymn to Jupiter.*

No. 16.

Jupiter presenting a cup to Saturn containing a liquid which causes him to vomit the children and the swathed stone which he had swallowed.

Chromios.   *Oriental Sardonyx.*

Jupiter, arrived at manhood, and clothed in the skin of the goat Amalthæa, in accordance with the advice of Metis, goddess of prudence, presents himself before Saturn. She offers him a liquid to make him vomit the children he had swallowed, together with the swathed stone which Rhea substituted for Jupiter.

No. 17.

Jupiter in the form of an owl at the feet of Juno.

Gnaios.   *Oriental Cornelian.*

Jupiter having often in vain tried to overcome the coldness of Juno, raises a violent storm on mount Thornax, where Juno was in the habit of walking, and transforming himself to a cuckoo trembling with cold, he seeks shelter in the bosom of the goddess. Immediately resuming his own form, he obtains the favour of Juno, on condition that he will marry her. Such is the subject of this medallion, except that Jupiter is here represented as an owl.

No. 18.

Jupiter resuming his divinity, and manifesting himself to Proserpine.

GNAIOS. *Oriental Cornelian.*

No. 19.

A Titan destroyed by Jupiter with a thunderbolt.

CHROMIOS. *Oriental Cornelian.*

" Titanic gods, and sons
And daughters of old Saturn ; and that band
Of giant brethren, whom, from forth th' abyss
Of darkness under earth, deliverer Jove
Sent up to light: grim forms and strong, with force
Gigantic: arms of hundred-handed gripe
Burst from their shoulders: fifty heads up-sprang,
Cresting their muscular limbs. They thus opposed
In dreadful conflict 'gainst the Titans stood,
In all their sinewy hands wielding aloft
Precipitous rocks. On th' other side, alert
The Titan phalanx closed: then hands of strength
Join'd prowess, and shew'd forth the works of war.
Th' immeasurable sea tremendous dash'd
With roaring; earth re-echoed; the broad heaven
Groan'd shattering: vast Olympus reel'd through-out
Down to its rooted base beneath the rush
Of those immortals: the dark chasm of hell
Was shaken with the trembling, with the tramp
Of hollow footsteps and strong battle-strokes,
And measureless uproar of wild pursuit.
So they against each other through the air
Hurl'd intermix'd their weapons, scattering groans
Where'er they fell. The voice of armies rose
With rallying shout through the starr'd firma-ment,
And with a mighty war-cry both the hosts
Encountering closed. Nor longer then did Jove
Curb down his force ; but sudden in his soul

There grew dilated strength, and it was fill'd
With his omnipotence: his whole of might
Broke from him, and the godhead rush'd abroad.
The vaulted sky, the mount Olympus, flash'd
With his continual presence; for he pass'd
Incessant forth, and lighten'd where he trod.
Thrown from his nervous grasp the lightnings flew
Reiterated swift; the whirling flash
Cast sacred splendour, and the thunderbolt
Fell.

    *   *   *   *   *

                Keen rush'd the light
In quivering splendour from the writhen flash:
Strong though they were, intolerable smote
Their orbs of sight, and with bedimming glare
Scorch'd up their blasted vision.

    *   *   *   *   *

Successive thrice a hundred rocks in air
Hurl'd from their sinewy grasp: with missile storm
The Titan host o'ershadowing, them they drove,
Vain-glorious as they were, with hands of strength
O'ercoming them, beneath th' expanse of earth,
And bound with galling chains: so far beneath
This earth as earth is distant from the sky,
So deep the space to darksome Tartarus.

    *   *   *   *   *

    But now, when Jupiter from all the heaven
Had cast the Titans forth, huge Earth embraced
By Tartarus, through balmy Venus' aid,

c

Her youngest-born Typhœus* bore; whose hands
Of strength are fitted to stupendous deeds,
And indefatigable are the feet
Of the strong god: and from his shoulders rise
A hundred snaky heads of dragon-growth,
Horrible, quivering with their blackening tongues:
In each amazing head, from eyes that roll'd
Within their sockets, fire shone sparkling; fire
Blazed from each head, the whilst he roll'd his
    glance
Glaring around him. In those fearful heads
Were voices of all sound, miraculous:
Now utter'd they distinguishable tones
Meet for the ear of gods, now the deep cry

Of a wild-bellowing bull untamed in strength,
And now the roaring of a lion fierce
In spirit, and anon the yell of whelps
Strange to the ear, and now the monster hiss'd,
That the high mountains echoed back the sound.
Then had a dread event that fatal day
Inevitable fall'n, and he had ruled
O'er mortals and immortals, but the sire
Of gods and men the peril instant knew
Intuitive, and vehement and strong
He thunder'd; instantaneous all around
Earth reel'd with horrible crash: the firmament
Of high heaven roar'd, the streams of Nile, the
    sea,

---

* " Taph, which at times was rendered Tuph, Toph, and Taphos, was a name current among the Ammonians, by which they called their high places. Lower Egypt being a flat, and annually overflowed, the natives were forced to raise the soil on which they built their principal edifices, in order to secure them from the inundation; and many of their sacred towers were erected on conical mounds of earth. There were often hills of the same form constructed for religious purposes, upon which there was no building. These were high altars; on which they used sometimes to offer human sacrifices. Tophet, where the Israelites made their children pass through fire to Moloch, was a mount of this form. Those cities in Egypt which had a high place of this sort, and rites in consequence of it, were styled Typhonian. Many writers say that these rites were performed to Typhon at the tomb of Osiris. Hence he was in later times supposed to have been a person; one of immense size; and he was also esteemed a god. But this arose from the common mistake by which places were substituted for the deities there worshipped. Typhon was the Tuph-on, or altar; and the offerings were made to the Sun, styled On; the same as Osiris and Busiris. What they called his tombs were mounds of earth raised very high; some of these had also lofty towers adorned with pinnacles and battlements. They had also carved on them various symbols, and particularly serpentine hieroglyphics, in memorial of the god to whom they were sacred. In their upper story was a perpetual fire, that was plainly seen in the night. The gigantic stature of Typhon was borrowed from this object; and his character was formed from the hieroglyphical representations in the temples styled Typhonian. This may be inferred from the allegorical description of Typhœus given by Hesiod. Typhon and Typhœus were the same personage; and the poet represents him of a mixed form, being partly a man, and partly a monstrous dragon, whose head consisted of an assemblage of smaller serpents; and as there was a perpetual fire kept up in the upper story, he describes it as shining through the apertures of the building. The tower of Babel was undoubtedly a Tuph-on, or altar of the Sun; though generally represented as a temple. Hesiod certainly alludes to some ancient history concerning the demolition of Babel, when he describes Typhon or Typhœus as overthrown by Jove. He represents him as the youngest son of Earth; as a deity of great strength and immense stature; and adds, what is very remarkable, that had it not been for the interposition of the chief god, this demon would have obtained a universal empire."—BRYANT. See also Völcker on the mythe of the Titans.

And uttermost caverns. While the king in wrath
Uprose, beneath his everlasting feet
The great Olympus trembled, and earth groan'd.
From either god a burning radiance caught
The darkly azured ocean: from the flash
Of lightnings, and that monster's darted flame,
Hot thunderbolts, and blasts of fiery winds.
Earth, air, sea glow'd; the billows, heaved on
     high,
Foam'd round the shores, and dash'd on every side
Beneath the rush of gods. Concussion wild
And unappeasable uprose; aghast
The gloomy monarch of th' infernal dead

Shudder'd; the sub-tartarean Titans heard
E'en where they stood, with Saturn in the midst:
They heard appall'd the unextinguished rage
Of tumult, and the din of dreadful war.
But now when Jove had gather'd all his strength
And grasp'd his weapons, bolts, and bickering
     flames,
He from the mount Olympus' topmost ridge
Leap'd at a bound, and smote him: hiss'd at once
The horrible monster's head enormous, scorch'd
In one conflagrant blaze."
                              HESIOD.

No. 20.

Combat between Jupiter and Typhon the Titan.

CHROMIOS.   *Oriental Cornelian.*

Jupiter, armed with Saturn's scythe, is defending himself, whilst Typhon encircles him with the folds of his tail.

" When with heav'n he strove,
Stood opposite in arms to mighty Jove,
Mov'd all his hundred hands, provok'd the war,
Defied the forky light'ning from afar.
At fifty mouths his flaming breath expires,
And flash for flash returns, and fires for fires:
In his right hand as many swords he wields,
And takes the thunder on as many shields."
                              Eneid, x. DRYDEN.

No. 21.

Typhon, overcoming Jupiter, casts him into the Cave of Corycus, at the foot of Parnassus.

CHROMIOS.   *Oriental Cornelian.*

" Briareus thus (if Phlegra credit claim)
Oppos'd the regents of the starry frame:
The Thund'rer launch'd his flaming bolts in vain,
Nor Phœbus' shafts, nor Pallas' snakes restrain.

The spear of haughty Mars unheeded flies,
And Ætna's forge in vain new bolts supplies.
Unmov'd he stalks along the fields of light,
And with regret beholds th' exhausted fight."

Th. lib. ii. Lewis.

" She sings, from earth's dark womb how Typhon rose,
And struck with mortal fear his heav'nly foes ;
How the gods fled to Egypt's slimy soil,
And hid their heads beneath the banks of Nile ;
How Typhon from the conquer'd skies pursued
Their routed godheads to the seven-mouth'd flood ;
Forc'd ev'ry god, his fury to escape,
Some beastly form to take, or earthly shape :

Jove (so she sung) was chang'd into a ram,
From whence the horns of Libyan Ammon came ;
Bacchus a goat, Apollo was a crow,
Phœbe a cat, the wife of Jove a cow
Whose hue was whiter than the falling snow ;
Venus a fish became, and Mercury
Conceal'd within an ibis-form did lie."

Ovid, *Met.* lib. v. Maynwaring.

No. 22.

Jupiter hurling a thunderbolt at Typhon.

Apollonides.   *Oriental Cornelian.*

Decade 4.

" But they on earth, or the devouring main,
Whom righteous Jove with detestation views,
With envious horror hear the heavenly strain,
Exil'd from praise, from virtue, and the muse.
Such is Typhœus, impious foe of gods,
Whose hundred-headed form Cilicia's cave
Once foster'd in her infamous abodes ;
Till daring with presumptuous arms to brave
The might of thundering Jove, subdued he fell,
Plung'd in the horrid dungeons of profoundest hell.

Decade 5.

" Now under sulphurous Cuma's sea-bound coast,
And vast Sicilia's, lies his shaggy breast,
By snowy Ætna, nurse of endless frost,
The pillar'd prop of heaven, for ever press'd ;
Forth from whose nitrous caverns issuing rise
Pure liquid fountains of tempestuous fire,
And veil in ruddy mists the noon-day skies,
While wrapt in smoke the eddying flames aspire ;
Or gleaming through the night with hideous roar,
Far o'er the reddening main huge rocky fragments pour."

Pindar, *1st Pyth.* West's *Tr.*

No. 23.

Mercury and Pan at the mouth of the Cave Corycus.

Apollonides.   *Oriental Cornelian.*

No. 24.

Mercury and Ægipan sending to sleep the enormous dragon which guards the Cave of Corycus, and delivering Jupiter.

CHROMIOS. *Oriental Cornelian.*

No. 25.

Jasius, a young man of great beauty, being beloved by Ceres, Jupiter becomes jealous of him, and annihilates him with lightning.

PYRGOTELES. *Oriental Cornelian.*

The allegory of the union between Ceres (the Isis of Egypt) the Earth, and Jason, husbandman, is very probably the mythe. Riches, under the figure of their offspring Plutus, are the results of agriculture and industry, exemplified in the " thrice-ploughed field." Proserpine is the personification of corn, part of the year beneath the earth.

> " Jason, a hero through the world renown'd,
> Was with the joyous love of Ceres crown'd ;
> Their joys they acted in a fertile soil
> Of Crete, which thrice had bore the ploughman's toil.
> Of them was Plutus born, who spreads his hand,
> Dispensing wealth o'er all the sea and land :
> Happy the man who in his favour lives,
> Riches to him and all their joys he gives."
>
> HESIOD, *Th.* l. 1832.

> " And when the fair-hair'd Ceres' yielding mind
> In the thrice-labour'd glebe her charms resign'd
> To beautiful Iasion, conscious Jove
> Smote with avenging flames her earthly love.
> Thus, gods, you envy me——"
>
> *Calypso to Mercury, Odyss.* lib. v.

No. 26.

Jupiter, majestically seated on an eagle, with clouds beneath his feet, banishes his daughter Ate (Discord) from heaven.

GNAIOS. *Oriental Cornelian.*

" What could I do? how heaven's decree remove?
How Ate's artful power, stern child of Jove?
She whose soft foot ne'er deigns descend on
     earth,
But passes o'er each head of human birth;
She who distils her venom in the mind,
And weaves the treach'rous net that chains
     mankind;
She who once injur'd Jove, whose sov'reign sway
The gods in heaven and men on earth obey.
Yet him, shrewd Juno, versed in Ate's wile,
The female goddess could the god beguile;
When, in proud Thebes, Alcmena's labour-strife
Toil'd, as the Herculean burden long'd for life.
The Jove exultant spake:—Celestials, hear!
Ye all, each god and goddess, bow the ear!
Hear what my spirit prompts: to me this morn
Shall Ilithya view a hero born,
Who o'er all realms around shall rule the race,
All who their lineage boast from Jove's em-
     brace.
     Then Juno proudful spoke:—We all have
     heard,
But ne'er shall Jove redeem his boastful word.
Yet, by thy oath, the terror on thy brow,
Swear that the realms around to him shall bow;
Him who this day shall, born of woman, trace
His heavenly origin from Jove's embrace.
     Then, reckless of her guile, the Olympian
     swore,
And that tremendous oath but wrong'd him
     more.

Then Juno darting from Olympus' height,
Swift in Achæan Argos stay'd her flight:
She knew that Sthenelus' illustrious bride,
To Jove-born Perseus close in blood allied,
There pregnant dwelt; and there her heavenly
     might
Brought, ere the time, a seven-month'd babe
     to light,
And stay'd Lucina from Alcmena's throes:
Then heralding the birth to heaven uprose.
Sire, lord of thunder, hear: a man this morn,
He who shall rule o'er Argos, now is born;
Eurystheus, son of Sthenelus, thy race
From Perseus sprung: that king shall Argos
     grace.
     She spoke; then deeply grieved, with arms
     outspread,
Jove grasp'd the baleful Ate's bright-hair'd
     head;
And stung with fury, by his terror swore
That ne'er her foot should tread Olympus more;
Ne'er the curs'd fiend who injured all again
Should, back returning, haunt his starr'd do-
     main.
He spoke; and hurl'd her from the star-pav'd
     sky,
To dwell for ever 'mid mortality.
There ever loath'd her, when the Herculean
     birth,
His son, beneath Eurystheus slaved on earth."
          Iliad, lib. xix.: SOTHEBY's *Tr.*

No. 27.

Hebe presenting a cup of nectar to the eagle of Jupiter.

CHROMIOS.   *Oriental Sardonyx.*

No. 28.

Hebe pouring out nectar to Jupiter.

CHROMIOS.   *Oriental Sardonyx.*

No. 29.

Jupiter commanding the eagle to carry off Ganymede, son of Tros, king of Ilium.

CHROMIOS. *Oriental Cornelian.*

" There royal Ganymede . . . .
O'er hills and forests hunts the bounding hart:
From towering Ida shoots the bird of Jove,
And bears him struggling through the clouds above ;
With outstretched hands his hoary guardians cry,
And the loud hounds spring furious at the sky."
VIRGIL'S *Eneid.*

No. 30.

Jupiter caressing Ganymede, who is offering him nectar.

CHROMIOS. *Oriental Cornelian.*

No. 31.

Ganymede presenting a cup of nectar to the eagle of Jupiter.

PYRGOTELES. *Oriental Cornelian.*

No. 32.

Ganymede borne by the eagle of Jupiter.

CHROMIOS. *Cornelian.*

No. 33.

Head of Ganymede, with attributes.

Cornelian.

No. 34.

Jupiter as a satyr surprising Antiope.

DIOSCORIDES. *Oriental Sardonyx.*

The eyes of mortals being unable to sustain the terrible majesty of Jupiter with his celestial attributes, he assumed different forms to appear before them. He is here seen as a satyr surprising Antiope, daughter of Nycteus, king of Thebes, in Bœotia, asleep. After which she became the mother of the twins Zethus and Amphion. Epopeus, king of Sicyon, having carried off Antiope, Nycteus made war against him, and was slain. She was thus thrown into the power of her uncle Lycus and her aunt Dirce, from whom, during several years, she experienced the harshest treatment. At length she escaped to her sons, whose protection she claimed, and they avenged her by killing Lycus, and tying Dirce to the tail of a furious bull. This is the subject of the colossal group known under the name of the *Farnese Bull.* A difference of pursuits led to dissensions between Zethus and Amphion, the former being passionately fond of hunting and war, the latter of music and poetry. Amphion, however, yielded to the counsels of Zethus, and the two brothers together built the walls of Thebes.

> " Antiope, with haughty charms,
> Who blest th' almighty Thunderer in her arms :
> Hence sprung Amphion, hence brave Zethus came,
> Founders of Thebes, and men of mighty name ;
> Though bold in open field, they yet surround
> The town with walls, and mound inject on mound ;
> Here ramparts stood, there towers rose high in air,
> And here through seven wide portals rush'd the war."
>
> HOMER's *Odyssey.*

No. 35.

Jupiter destroying the house of Lycaon, and changing him to a wolf.

CHROMIOS. *Oriental Cornelian.*

Lycaon, son of Titan and the Earth, and king of Arcadia, was celebrated for his cruelties. Jupiter was not ignorant of this; but wishing to ascertain the fact himself, he disguised himself as a pilgrim, and repaired to the dwelling of Lycaon. The king, to discover whether his guests were immortal or not, killed the young Arcas, offspring of his daughter Calisto and Jupiter, and causing him to be cooked, he ordered him to be served at table. Jupiter, seized with horror and indignation, destroyed the house with his thunder, and changed Lycaon to a wolf.

" Disguis'd in human shape, I travell'd round
The world, and more than what I heard I found.
O'er Mænalus I took my steepy way,
By caverns infamous for beasts of prey:
Then cross'd Cyllene, and the piny shade,
More infamous by curst Lycaon made.
Dark night had cover'd heav'n and earth before
I enter'd his unhospitable door.
Just at my entrance I display'd the sign
That somewhat was approaching of divine.
The prostrate people pray, the tyrant grins;
And, adding profanation to his sins,
I'll try, said he, and if a god appear,
To prove his deity shall cost him dear.
'Twas late; the graceless wretch my death pre-
pares,
When I should soundly sleep, opprest with
cares:
This dire experiment he chose, to prove
If I were mortal, or undoubted Jove.
But first he had resolv'd to taste my pow'r:
Not long before, but in a luckless hour,
Some legates, sent from the Molossian state,
Were on a peaceful errand come to treat:

Of these he murders one; he boils the flesh,
And lays the mangled morsels in a dish:
Some part he roasts; then serves it up, so drest,
And bids me welcome to this human feast.
Mov'd with disdain, the table I o'erturn'd,
And with avenging flames the palace buru'd.
The tyrant in a fright, for shelter gains
The neighb'ring fields, and scours along the
plains.
Howling he fled, and fain he would have
spoke;
But human voice his brutal tongue forsook.
About his lips the gather'd foam he churns,
And, breathing slaughters, still with rage he
burns,
But on the bleating flock his fury turns.
His mantle, now his hide, with rugged hairs,
Cleaves to his back; a famished face he bears;
His arms descend, his shoulders sink away
To multiply his legs for chase of prey.
He grows a wolf; his hoariness remains,
And the same rage in other members reigns.
His eyes still sparkle in a narrower space;
His jaws retain the grin and violence of his face."

OVID's *Metam.*

No. 36.

The same subject.

CHROMIOS.   *Oriental Cornelian.*

No. 37.

Jupiter and Calisto.

CHROMIOS.   *Oriental Cornelian.*

Jupiter, enamoured of Calisto, first takes the form of Diana to entice her away, and then resuming his own, possesses himself of her.

d

" Oft passing to and fro, a Nonacrine
The god inflam'd; her beauty, more divine,
'Twas not her art to spin, nor with much care
And fine variety to trick her hair;
But with a zone her looser garments bound,
And her rude tresses in a fillet wound;
Now armed with a dart, now with a bow:
A squire of Phœbe's. Mænalus did know
None more in grace of all her virgin throng;
But favourites in favour last not long.
The parted day in equal balance held,
A wood she enter'd, as yet never fell'd;
There from her shoulder she her quiver takes,
Unbends her bow; and, tir'd with hunting,
    makes
The flow'ry mantled earth her happy bed,
And on her painted quiver lays her head.
When Jove the nymph without a guard did see
In such a positure: This stealth, said he,
My wife shall never know; or, say she did—
Who, ah, who would not for her sake be chid?
Diana's shape and habit then indu'd,
He said: My huntress, where hast thou pursu'd
This morning's chase? She, rising, made reply:
Hail, pow'r more great than Jove (though Jove
    stood by)
In my esteem! He smil'd; and gladly heard
Himself by her before himself preferr'd,
And kiss'd. His kisses too intemperate grow,
Not such as maids on maidens do bestow;
His strict embracements her narration stay'd,
And by his crime his own deceit betray'd.
She did what woman could to force her fate:
(Would Juno saw, it would her spleen abate!)

Although as much as woman could she strove,
What woman, or who, can contend with Jove?
The victor hies him to the ethereal states.
The woods, as guilty of her wrongs, she hates;
Almost forgetting, as from thence she flung,
Her quiver, and the bow by which it hung.
High Mænalus, Dictynna with her train
Now ent'ring, pleased with the quarry slain,
Beheld and call'd her: call'd upon she fled;
And in her semblance Jupiter doth dread.
But when she saw th' attending nymphs ap-
    pear,
She troops amongst them, and diverts her fear.
Ah, how our faults are in our faces read!
With eyes scarce ever rais'd she hangs the head,
Nor perks she now as she was wont to do
By Cynthia's side, nor leads the starry crew.
Though mute she be, her violated shame
Self-guilty blushes silently proclaim;
But that a maid, Diana the ill-hid
Had soon espi'd; they say her sly nymphs did.
    Nine crescents now had made their orbs
        complete,
When, faint with labour and her brother's heat,
She takes the shades; close by the murmuring
And silver current of a fruitful spring.
The place much prais'd, the stream, as cool as
    clear,
Her fair feet glads. No spies, said she, be
    here:
Here will we our disrobed bodies dip.
Calisto blush'd."

                                OVID: SANDYS.

No. 38.

Jupiter confiding Arcas to a Shepherd.

CHROMIOS.   *Oriental Cornelian.*

Jupiter, after punishing Lycaon, collects the scattered limbs of Arcas, restores the child to life, and confides him to a shepherd.

No. 39.

Calisto and Arcas as the Great and Little Bear.

DIOSCORIDES. *Oriental Cornelian.*

Jupiter changes Calisto and Arcas to bears, and placing them in the heavens, they become the constellations of the Great and the Little Bear.

No. 40.

Juno changing Calisto to a bear.

GNAIOS. *Amethyst.*

" This said, her hand within her hair she wound,
Swung her to earth, and dragg'd her on the ground;
The prostrate wretch lifts up her arms in pray'r;
Her arms grow shaggy and deform'd with hair,
Her nails are sharpen'd into pointed claws,
Her hands bear half her weight, and turn to paws;
Her lips, that once could tempt a god, begin
To grow distorted in an ugly grin.
And, lest the supplicating brute might reach
The ears of Jove, she was deprived of speech:
Her surly voice through a hoarse passage came
In savage sounds; her mind was still the same.

The furry monster fix'd her eyes above,
And heav'd her new, unwieldy paws to Jove,
And begg'd his aid with inward groans; and though
She could not call him false, she thought him so.
How did she fear to lodge in woods alone,
And haunt the fields and meadows, once her own !
How often would the deep-mouth'd dogs pursue,
Whilst from her hounds the frighted huntress flew !
How did she fear her fellow-brutes, and shun
The shaggy bear, though now herself was one!
How from the sight of rugged wolves retire,
Although the grim Lycaon was her sire !"

OVID's *Metam.*

No. 41.

Jupiter appearing to Arcas stays his hand at the moment he is about to discharge an arrow at his mother Calisto, whom, transformed to a bear, he does not recognise.

ATHENION. *Oriental Sardonyx.*

" But now her son had fifteen summers told,
Fierce at the chase, and in the forest bold;
When, as he beat the woods in quest of prey,
He chanc'd to rouse his mother where she lay.
She knew her son, and kept him in her sight,
And fondly gaz'd: the boy was in a fright,

And aim'd a pointed arrow at her breast,
And would have slain his mother in the beast;
But Jove forbad, and snatch'd 'em through the air
In whirlwinds up to heav'n and fixed 'em there,
Where the new constellations nightly rise,
And add a lustre to the northern skies."

OVID's *Metam.*

No. 42.

Calisto as a bear discovering herself to her son snatches the arrow
from him.

GNAIOS.   *Oriental Amethyst.*

No. 43.

Europa, daughter of Agenor, king of Phœnicia, caressing the bull to which
Jupiter has metamorphosed himself.

GNAIOS.   *Oriental Cornelian.*

" The dignity of empire laid aside,
(For love but ill agrees with kingly pride,)
The ruler of the skies, the thundering god,
Who shakes the world's foundations with a
    nod,
Among a herd of lowing heifers ran,
Frisk'd in a bull, and bellow'd o'er the plain.
Large rolls of fat about his shoulders clung,
And from his neck the double dewlap hung.
His skin was whiter than the snow that lies
Unsullied by the breath of southern skies;
Small shining horns on his curl'd forehead stand,
As turn'd and polish'd by the workman's hand;
His eye-balls roll'd, not formidably bright,
But gaz'd and languish'd with a gentle light.
His ev'ry look was peaceful, and express'd
The softness of the lover in the beast.

Agenor's royal daughter, as she play'd
Among the fields, the milk-white bull survey'd,
And view'd his spotless body with delight,
And, at a distance, kept him in her sight.
At length she pluck'd the rising flow'rs, and fed
The gentle beast, and fondly strok'd his head.
He stood well pleas'd to touch the charming
    fair,
But hardly could confine his pleasure there.
And now he wantons o'er the neighb'ring
    strand,
Now rolls his body on the yellow sand;
And now, perceiving all her fears decay'd,
Comes tossing forward to the royal maid;
Gives her his breast to stroke, and downward
    turns
His grisly brow, and gently stoops his horns."

OVID's *Metam.*

No. 44.

Jupiter as a bull crossing the sea with Europa on his back, and near him the eagle.*

CHROMIOS. *Oriental Sardonyx.*

" In flow'ry wreaths the royal virgin dress'd
His bending horns, and kindly clapt his
     breast.
Till now grown wanton, and devoid of fear,
Not knowing that she press'd the Thunderer,
She plac'd herself upon his back, and rode
O'er fields and meadows, seated on the god.

The frighted nymph looks backward on the
     shore,
And hears the tumbling billows round her roar ;
But still she holds him fast : one hand is born
Upon his back, the other grasps a horn ;
Her train of ruffling garments flies behind,
Swells in the air, and hovers in the wind."

OVID's *Metam.*

" Methinks the pictur'd bull we see
Is amorous Jove—it must be he !
How fondly blest he seems to bear
That fairest of Phœnician fair !
How proud he breasts the foamy tide,
And spurns the billowy surge aside !
Could any beast of vulgar vein
Undaunted thus defy the main ?
No, he descends from climes above,
He looks the god—he breathes of Jove !"

ANACREON : MOORE's *Trans.*

" Then with a mournful look the damsel said :
' Ah ! whither wilt thou bear a wretched maid ?
Who, and whence art thou, wond'rous crea-
     ture, say ?
How can'st thou fearless tread the wat'ry way ?
On the broad ocean safely sails the ship,
But bulls avoid and dread the stormy
     deep.

Say, can a bull on sea-born viands feed ?
Or, if descended from celestial breed,
Thy acts are inconsistent with a god :
Bulls rove the meads, and dolphins swim the
     flood ;
But earth and ocean are alike to thee,
Thy hoofs are oars that row thee through the
     sea.

* Guido Reni had evidently studied the composition of this gem when painting the same subject ; and his picture was in the Altemira collection, and subsequently sold by Mr. Peacock.

Perhaps, like airy birds, thou soon wilt fly ,
And soar amidst the regions of the sky.
Ah! wretched maid, to leave my native home,
And simply dare with bulls in meads to roam !
And now on seas I ride—ah, wretched maid !
But, O ! I trust, great Neptune, in thy aid ;
Soon let my eyes my great conductor hail,
For not without a deity I sail.'
Thus spoke the nymph, and thus the bull
   replied :
'Courage, fair maid, nor fear the foaming tide:
Though now a bull I seem to mortal eyes,
Thou soon shalt see me ruler of the skies.
What shape I please at will I take and keep,
And now a bull I cross the boundless deep ;
For thy bright charms inspire my breast with
   love.
But soon shall Crete's fair isle, the nurse of Jove,

Receive Europa on its friendly strand,
To join with me in Hymen's blissful band :
From thee shall kings arise in long array,
To rule the world with delegated sway.'
   Thus spoke the god ; and what he spoke
    prov'd true,
For soon Crete's lofty shore appear'd in
   view ;
Jove straight assum'd another form and air,
And loos'd her zone ; the Hours the couch pre-
   pare.
The nymph Europa thus, through powerful
   love,
Became the bride of cloud-compelling Jove ;
From her sprung mighty kings in long array,
Who rul'd the world with delegated sway.

      MOSCHUS, FAWKE's *Trans.*

No. 45.

Jupiter and Europa.

CHROMIOS. *Oriental Cornelian.*

    Jupiter having transported Europa to the island of Crete, and deposited her under a plantain at the mouth of the river Lethe, resuming his own form, and making himself known to her.

  " Through storms and tempests he the virgin bore,
    And lands her safe on the Dictean shore :
    Where now in his divinest form array'd,
    In his true shape he captivates the maid ;
    Who gazes on him, and with wond'ring eyes
    Beholds the new, majestic figure rise,
    His glowing features, and celestial light,
    And all the god discovered to her sight."
      OVID's *Metam.*

No. 46.

Europa reclining under the plantain, and Jupiter as an eagle nestling in the branches.

GNAIOS. *Oriental Cornelian.*

No. 47.

Jupiter in love with Leda, daughter of Thespius, and wife of Tyndarus, king of Sparta, takes the form of a swan to surprise her, and commands Venus to assume that of an eagle and pursue him, in order that Leda may give him shelter.

DIOSCORIDES. *Oriental Cornelian.*

" Now I spied
Leda the fair, the godlike Tyndar's bride ;
Hence Pollux sprung, who wields with furious sway
The deathful gauntlet matchless in the fray ;
And Castor, glorious on th' embattled plain,
Curbs the proud steeds, reluctant to the rein.
By turns they visit this ethereal sky,
And live alternate, and alternate die :
In hell beneath, on earth, in heaven above,
Reign the twin-gods, the favourite sons of Jove.'

VIRGIL's *Eneid.*

No. 48.

Jupiter, enamoured of Elara, daughter of Orchomenus, king of Bœotia, to conceal her from the watchfulness of Juno, secrets her in a deep cave, where she becomes the mother of the giant Tityus.

APOLLONIDES. *Amethyst.*

No. 49.

Jupiter metamorphosed to a horse, to obtain the favours of Dia, daughter of Deioneus.

GNAIOS. *Calcedony, partaking of the Sapphire.*

No. 50.

Jupiter in love with Danaë, daughter of Acrisius, king of Argos, transforming himself to a shower of gold, penetrates the brazen tower in which Danaë is confined by her father, and she becomes the mother of Perseus.

DIOSCORIDES. *Oriental Sardonyx.*

" Thus the beauteous Danaë lay,
  Long doom'd in brass-girt walls to dwell,
Denied the sun's ethereal ray,
  Enclosed in her sepulchral cell.
Yet her rich illustrious blood
From a long line of Argive monarchs flow'd ;
And she unconscious of his secret love,
  Cherish'd the golden gems of Jove.
O fate, resistless is thy pow'r,
Triumphant o'er the heav'n-descended show'r,
The rampired wall, war's furious train,
And the black bark that rides the roaring main !

Antigone, SOPH. : POTTER.

" Of watchful dogs an odious ward
  Might well one hapless virgin guard,
  When in a tower of brass immur'd,
  And by strong gates of oak secur'd—
  Although by gallantry pursued,
  And midnight arts fram'd to delude,—
  Had not great Jove and Venus fair
  Laugh'd at her father's fruitless care ;
For well they knew no fort could hold
Against a god transform'd to gold :
Stronger than thunder's winged force
All-powerful gold can speed its course ;
Through watchful guards its passage make,
And loves through solid walls to break."

HORACE, b. iii. Ode xvi. : FRANCIS.

No. 51.

Jupiter, to obtain the favours of Ægina, daughter of the river Asopus, changed himself to a flame of fire, and made the nymph the mother of Æacus, who was the father of Telamon.

POLYCLETES. *Oriental Cornelian.*

No. 52.

Jupiter captivated by the beauty of Io, daughter of the river Inachus, descended to earth in a thick cloud and surprised the nymph.

AETION. *Oriental Cornelian.*

Probably the history of Io being seized by pirates near Carne, a city of Phœnicia, and carried to Osiris king of Egypt, gave rise to the tale of her being forcibly captured by Jupiter. Lycophron thus makes Cassandra allude to the occurrence:—

" Curs'd be the mariners, the Carnian wolves,
Who bore their prize unto the Memphian king—
The heifer-maid, who cropped the tender flowers
Where humid Lerne spreads her swamps around!
Then Discord waved her torch, and rear'd on high
Flames of immortal hate, strife ne'er to cease,
Rage ne'er to cool; for straight th' Idean boars

In dread reprisal seized upon the maid :
In gallant trim the sculptured vessel flew
Lightly on ocean's wave, the figured bull
High on the prow drove back the dashing surge,
And swift the virgin of Sarapte bore
To Dicte's hills, and on the Cretan lord
Bestowed the lovely maid, the captive bride."

VISCOUNT ROYSTON'S *Trans.*

No. 53.

Jupiter, to conceal his amours with Io from Juno, metamorphoses Io into a heifer; but Juno, suspecting the fraud, begs her of him.

PYRGOTELES. *Amethyst.*

———— " Now
In Io's place appears a lovely cow ;
So sleek her skin, so faultless was her make,
E'en Juno did unwilling pleasure take
To see so fair a rival of her love ;
And what she was and whence, inquired of Jove,
Of what fair herd and from what pedigree ?
The god, half caught, was forced upon a lie,
And said she sprang from earth. She took the word,
And begged the beauteous heifer of her lord."

OVID's *Metam.*

e

No. 54.

Jupiter, yielding to the entreaties of his jealous wife, gives her the heifer Io.

ADMON. *Oriental Amethyst.*

" What should he do? 'twas equal shame to Jove
Or to relinquish or betray his love;
Yet to refuse so slight a gift would be
But more t' increase his consort's jealousy:
Thus fear and love by turns his heart assailed,
And stronger love had sure at length prevailed,
But some faint hope remained his jealous queen
Had not the mistress through the heifer seen.
The cautious goddess, of her gift possessed,
Yet harboured anxious thoughts within her breast."

OVID's Metam.

No. 55.

Juno charging the shepherd Argus to watch the heifer Io.

TEUCER. *Oriental Cornelian.*

" Io now
With horns exalted stands, and seems to low,
(A noble charge) her keeper by her side,
To watch her walks his hundred eyes applied;
And on the brims her sire, the wat'ry god,
Roll'd from a silver urn his crystal flood."

OVID's Metam.

No. 56.

Mercury, by order of Jupiter, having sent Argus to sleep with the sound of his lyre, cut off his head with the herpè, and carried off the heifer Io.

CHROMIOS. *Sardonyx.*

" Now Jove no longer could her suff'rings bear;
But call'd in haste his airy messenger,
The son of Maia, with severe decree,
To kill the keeper, and to set her free.
With all his harness soon the god was sped;
His flying hat was fasten'd on his head,
Wings on his heels were hung, and in his hand
He holds the virtue of the snaky wand.
The liquid air his moving pinions wound,
And in the moment shoot him on the ground.
Before he came in sight, the crafty god
His wings dismiss'd, but still retain'd his rod:
That sleep-procuring wand wise Hermes took,
But made it seem to sight a shepherd's hook.
With this he did a herd of goats control,
Which by the way he met, and slily stole.
Clad like a country swain, he pip'd and sung,
And playing drove his jolly troop along.

. . . . . .

While Hermes pip'd, and sang, and told his
tale,
The keeper's winking eyes began to fail,
And drowsy slumber on the lids to creep,
Till all the watchmen were at length asleep.
Then soon the god his voice and song sup-
press'd,
And with his pow'rful rod confirm'd his rest:
Without delay his crooked falchion drew,
And at one fatal stroke the keeper slew.
Down from the rock fell the dissever'd head,
Opening its eyes in death, and falling bled,
And mark'd the passage with a crimson trail:
Thus Argus lies in pieces, cold and pale;
And all his hundred eyes, with all their light,
Are clos'd at once in one perpetual night.
These Juno takes, that they no more may fail,
And spreads them in her peacock's gaudy tail."

OVID's *Metam.*

No. 57.

Io, tormented by an insect sent by Juno, leads a wandering life. After having traversed Thrace and Scythia, crossed the Ionian Sea and the Bosphorus, she reaches the banks of the river Inachus; and tracing her name on the sand with her hoof, is recognised by her father.

CHROMIOS.   *A fine Calcedony.*

"Io, PROMETHEUS, CHORUS.

Io. Whither, ah, whither am I borne!
To what rude shore, what barb'rous race? O
thou,
Whoe'er thou art, that, chain'd to that black rock,
The seat of desolation, ruest thy crimes,
Say on what shore my wretched footsteps stray.
Again that sting!—Ah me, that form again!—
With all his hundred eyes, the earth-born
Argus!
Cover it, Earth! See, how it glares upon me,
The horrid spectre!—Wilt thou not, O Earth,
Cover the dead, that from thy dark abyss

He comes to haunt me, to pursue my steps,
And drive me foodless o'er the barren strand?
Hoarse sounds the reed-compacted pipe, a note
Sullen and drowsy.   Miserable me!
Whither will these wide-wand'ring errors lead
me?
How, son of Saturn, how have I offended,
That with these stings, these tortures, thou pur-
suest me,
And driv'st to madness my affrighted soul!
Hear me, supreme of gods, O hear the suppliant!
Blast me with lightnings, bury me in the earth,
Or cast me to the monsters of the sea;

But spare these toils, spare these wide-wand'ring errors,
Which drive me round the world, and know no rest.

CHORUS.

Hear'st thou the voice of this lamenting virgin?
For such she is, though in that form disguised.

PROMETHEUS.

I hear her griefs, that whirl her soul to madness,
Daughter of Inachus, whose love inflames
The heart of Jove; hence Juno's jealous rage
Drives the poor wanderer restless through the world.

   .   .   .   .   .

CHORUS. *Strophe.*

Whoe'er thou art, whom young desire
Shall lead to Hymen's holy fire,

Choose from thy equals, choose thy humble love;
Let not the pomp of wealth allure thine eye,
Nor high-trac'd lineage thy ambition move—
Ill suits with low degree t' aspire so high.

Antistrophe.

Never, O never may my fate
See me a splendid victim led
To grace the mighty Jove's imperial bed,
Or share a god's magnific state.
When Io's miseries meet my eyes,
What horrors in my soul arise!
Her virgin bosom, harb'ring high intent,
In man delights not, and his love disdains;
Hence the dire pest by wrathful Juno sent,
Her wide wild wanderings hence, and agonising pains."

POTTER's *Trans.*

No. 58.

Io, terrified at the spectre sent by Juno, throws herself into the sea, which from Io took the name of Ionian.

CARIALOS. *Oriental Cornelian.*

No. 59.

Io on her knees before Jupiter, who recognises her, and restores her to her original form.

APOLLONIDES. *Oriental Cornelian.*

" At length arriving on the banks of Nile,
Wearied with length of ways and worn with toil,
She laid her down; and leaning on her knees
Invoked the cause of all her miseries,
And cast her languishing regards above
For help from heav'n and her ungrateful Jove;
She sigh'd, she wept, she low'd: 'twas all she could,
And with unkindness seem'd to tax the god;

Last with a humble prayer she begg'd repose,
Or death at least to finish all her woes.
Jove heard her vows, and with a flatt'ring look
In her behalf to jealous Juno spoke.

   .   .   .   .   .

The goddess was appeased; and at the word
Was Io to her former shape restored."

OVID's *Metam.*

No. 60.

Jupiter, metamorphosed to an ant, surprising the nymph Clytoris.

DIOSCORIDES. *Amethyst.*

No. 61.

Jupiter surprises Juturna, the daughter of Daunus, and sister of Turnus, king of the Rutuli.

APOLLONIDES. *Oriental Amethyst.*

Jupiter made her immortal, and she became the nymph of rivers and fountains.

" Of goddess Muta if you should demand,
And what by such a name we understand,
Although the story 's not of modern date,
What ancient men have told I'll here relate.
Jove with the nymph Juturna fell in love,
And suffer'd many slights unworthy Jove;
Sometimes in filbert-groves herself she hid,
Sometimes in her kindred waters slid ;
Jove summon'd all the nymphs of Latin race
To meet together in a proper place,
And as he in the shining circle stood,
He thus harangued th' attentive beauteous crowd :

Your sister-nymph much wrongs herself, alas,
By striving to avoid a god's embrace ;
My soft caresses does Juturna flee,
To her the loss is greater than to me;
Then all assist my pleasure to attain,
Which will be vastly to your sister's gain.
If e'er she to the river's bank should run,
When my pursuits she does unkindly shun,
Prevent her plunging in the crystal flood,
And by that favour gratify a god.
This said, the Naiads which in Tiber sport,
Or in the gelid Tev'rone keep their court,
Gave freely their assent."

Fasti, l. ii.: MASSEY'S *Trans.*

No. 62.

Jupiter commanding Vulcan to forge the most formidable arrows that could be made, for Hercules to destroy the monsters which infested the earth.

DAMAS. *Oriental Cornelian.*

This idea seems to have its origin in the very ancient and generally received opinion that Hercules was the representative of the sun, and his arrows the beams of the day-star; which, borrowing their power from the elementary fire, dried the plains which were inundated by the

overflowings of different rivers, especially the Nile, and purged them of the monsters living in
the stagnant waters. The sceptre of Jupiter terminates in a lotus-flower, an aquatic plant of
Egypt, and a symbol of immortality.

Antistrophe 1.

" What fell despoilers of the land,
    The prophet told, what monsters of the main,
Should feel the vengeance of his righteous hand:
    What savage, proud, pernicious tyrant slain,
To Hercules should bow his head,
    Hurl'd from his arbitrary throne,
While glittering pomp his curs'd ambition fed,
    And made indignant nations groan.
Last, when the giant-sons of earth shall dare
To wage against the gods rebellious war,
Pierc'd by his rapid shafts on Phlegra's plain,
With dust their radiant locks the haughty foe shall stain."

PINDAR, *Nem. Ode* 1, WEST'S *Trans.*

No. 63.

Jupiter destroys the Cercopes with his thunderbolts, and then changes
    them to monkeys, for having refused, after promising their assistance
    and received remuneration, to fight against Saturn.

APOLLONIDES.   *Oriental Cornelian.*

" The galleys now by Pythecusa pass;
The name is from the natives of the place.
The father of the gods, detesting lies,
Oft with abhorrence heard their perjuries.
Th' abandon'd race, transform'd to beasts, began
To mimic the impertinence of man.
Flat-nos'd and furrow'd, with grimace they grin,
And look to what they were too near akin;
Merry in make, and busy to no end,
This moment they divert, the next offend;
So much this species of their past retains,
Though lost the language, yet the noise remains."

OVID'S *Metam.*

No. 64.

Origin of the worship of Jupiter Ammon.

GNAIOS. *Oriental Cornelian.*

Bacchus traversing the deserts of Libya, being tormented with thirst, implored the aid of Jupiter. The father of the gods appeared to him in the form of a ram, and brought him to a fountain. Bacchus in gratitude erected on the spot a temple, where he was invoked as *Jupiter Ammon.*

" Now to the sacred temple they draw near,
Whose only altars Libyan lands revere;
There, but unlike the Jove by Rome ador'd,
A form uncouth, stands heaven's almighty lord.
No regal ensigns grace his potent hand,
Nor shakes he there the lightning's flaming brand.
But, ruder to behold, a horned ram
Belies the god, and Ammon is his name.
There, though he reigns unrivall'd and alone
O'er the rich neighbours of the torrid zone;
Though swarthy Æthiops are to him confin'd,
With Araby the blest, and wealthy Inde;

Yet no proud domes are rais'd, no gems are seen,
To blaze upon his shrines with costly sheen;
But plain, and poor, and unprofan'd he stood,
Such as to whom our great forefathers bow'd:
A god of pious times and days of old,
That keeps his temples safe from Roman gold.
Here, and here only, through wide Libya's space,
Tall trees the land and verdant herbage grace;
Here the loose sands by plenteous springs are bound,
Knit to a mass, and moulded into ground;
Here smiling nature wears a fertile dress,
And all things here the present god confess."
APOLL. RHODIUS.

No. 65.

Jupiter, armed with a hatchet, is here called *Labradeus,* or *Labrandeus,* as he is frequently represented on the coins of Caria, where he was worshipped under this invocation.

CHROMIOS. *Oriental Sardonyx.*

No. 66.

A head of Jupiter.

APOLLONIDES. *Amethyst.*

No. 67.

Oceanus and Tethys taking charge of the education of Juno at her birth.

POLYCLETES.   *Oriental Sardonyx.*

" For, lo, I haste to those remote abodes,
Where the great parents (sacred source of gods!)
Ocean and Tethys, their old empire keep,
On the last limits of the land and deep.
In their kind arms my tender years were past,
What time old Saturn, from Olympus cast,
Of upper heaven to Jove resign'd the reign,
Whelm'd under the huge mass of earth and main.

For strife, I hear, has made the union cease,
Which held so long that ancient pair in peace.
What honour and what love shall I obtain,
If I compose those fatal feuds again ;
Once more their minds in mutual ties engage,
And what my youth has ow'd, repay their
    age?"

HOMER'S *Il.*

No. 68.

Flora presenting the secret flower to Juno.

EVODOS.   *Oriental Sardonyx.*

Juno, piqued that Jupiter should have given birth to Minerva without her, undertook a journey towards the eastern ocean, that she might learn the mystery herself. Fatigued with the length of the way, she arrived at a temple dedicated to Flora, and seated herself at the portal. Flora appeared to her; and after having interrogated her on the motives of her journey, gave her secretly a flower, by only touching which women immediately became mothers. It was by this means that Juno gave birth to the god Mars. The moment of action represented on this medallion is that in which Flora is presenting the flower to Juno.

In the *Fasti* of Ovid, book v. line 195 *et seq.*, will be found the history of the origin of this supposed power of Flora.

No. 69.

Juno with the lotus-flower presented to her by Flora.

GNAIOS.   *Calcedony.*

No. 70.

Juno confiding the infant Mars to Priapus to educate.

CHROMIOS.   *Oriental Cornelian.*

No. 71.

Juno confiding the infant Mars to Priapus to educate.

CHROMIOS. *Oriental Cornelian.*

No. 72.

Juno saving the stag with golden horns.

DIOSCORIDES. *Amethyst.*

Diana, whilst hunting in the plains of Thessaly, pursued and killed four stags with golden horns; the fifth saved himself in Juno's arms, whence she was called *Sospita* (*Preserver*).

No. 73.

The figure of Juno Sospita, covered with a goat-skin, and armed with a lance and shield.

APOLLONIDES. *Oriental Cornelian.*

No. 74.

Juno confiding the gardens of the Hesperides to the care of an enormous dragon.

APOLLONIDES. *Oriental Amethyst.*

The Hesperides were, according to Hesiod, islands in the Great Western Ocean—probably the Cape de Verde Isles—other writers place them on the confines of Libya. They are also considered the daughters of Hesperus, the brother of Atlas, and shepherdesses. Hercules carried off their sheep, which, from the fine quality of their fleeces, were called golden, and very likely the oranges were metamorphosed into golden fruit.

The mythe appears to be, that as the light was extinguished in the far west, and re-appeared, so life left man, and he re-appeared in happier regions,—a simile often used by the ancient poets. The stillness of evening, and the repose of death, amid the refulgent clouds of a tropical sunset, was a reflection likely to have an effect on the minds of a people who were perhaps the most imaginative that ever existed. The reader who wishes to see a summary of the opinions of the ancients on the state of the departed souls, will find it in the celebrated Dissertation of Dr. Jortin.

> " And Care, the mother of a doleful train,
> Th' Hesperides she bore, far in the seas,
> Guards of the golden fruit and fertile trees."
>
> HESIOD.

The following is taken from Todd's " Milton," vol. vi. page 413, being a transcript from a MS. at Cambridge of the various readings, or rather intentions for parts, of the *Masque of Comus :* —

> " Amidst th' Hesperian gardens, on whose banks,
> Bedew'd with nectar and celestial songs,
> Eternal roses grow, and hyacinth,
> And fruits of golden rind, on whose fair tree
> The scalie-barnest dragon ever keeps
> His unenchanted eye; around the verge
> And sacred limits of this blissful isle,
> The jealous ocean, that old river, windes
>
> His farre-extended arms, till with steepe fall
> Half his waste flood the wild Atlantique fills,
> And half the slow unfadom'd Stygian pool.
> But soft, I was not sent to court your wonder
> With distant worlds, and strange removed climes.
> Yet thence I come, and oft from thence behold," &c.
>
> MILTON'S *MS.*

No. 75.

The Cyclops presenting the trident to Neptune.

APOLLONIDES.   *Calcedony, partaking of the Sapphire.*

> " The Cyclops brethren, arrogant of heart,
> Undaunted Arges, Brontes, Steropes;
> Who forged the lightning-shaft, and gave to Jove
> His thunder: they were like unto the gods;
> Save that a single ball of sight was fix'd
> In their mid-forehead. Cyclops was their name,
> From that round eyeball in their brow infix'd:
> And strength and force and manual craft were theirs."*
>
> HESIOD.

---

* "Thucydides acquaints us concerning the Cyclopes, that they were the most ancient inhabitants of Sicily, but that he could not find out their race. Strabo places them near Etna and Icontina, and supposes that they once ruled over that part of the island ; and it is certain that a people called Cyclopians did possess that province. It is generally agreed by writers upon the subject, that they were of a size superior to the common race of mankind. Among the many tribes of the Ammonians

No. 76.

Neptune and Cænis seated on a dolphin.

APOLLONIDES.   *Oriental Cornelian.*

Neptune having surprised Cænis, daughter of Elatus Lapithus, she yielded to the wishes of the god, on condition that he would change her sex.   Neptune granted her request, and metamorphosed her to a boy.

> " Cæneus, a woman once, and once a man:
> But ending in the sex she first began."   VIRGIL.

---

who went abroad were to be found people who were styled Anakim, and were descended from the sons of Anak: so that this history, though carried to a great excess, was probably founded in truth. They were particularly famous for architecture; and in all parts whither they came they erected noble structures, which were remarkable for their height and beauty, and were often dedicated to the chief deity, under the name of Elorus and P'Elorus.   People were so struck with their grandeur, that they called every thing great or stupendous Pelorian (πέλωρος, *huge*); and when they described the Cyclopians as a lofty towering race, they came at last to borrow their ideas of this people from the towers to which they alluded.   They supposed them in height to reach the clouds, and in bulk equal to the promontories on which these edifices were founded.   As these buildings were oftentimes light-houses, and had in their upper story one round casement, 'like an Argolic buckler or the moon,' by which they afforded light in the night-season, the Greeks made this a characteristic of the people.   They supposed this aperture to have been an eye, which was fiery and glaring, and placed in the middle of their foreheads.   What confirmed the mistake was the representation of an eye, which was often engraved over the entrance of these temples; the chief deity of Egypt being elegantly represented by the symbol of an eye, which was intended to signify the superintendence of Providence.   The notion of the Cyclopes framing the thunder and lightning for Jupiter, arose chiefly from the Cyclopians engraving hieroglyphics of this sort upon the temples of the deity.   The poets considered them merely in the capacity of blacksmiths, and condemned them to the anvil."—BRYANT.

The proximity of Etna doubtless had its share in this delusion, Virg. Æn. viii. 417:

> " Deep below
> In hollow caves the fires of Etna glow.
> The Cyclops here their heavy hammers deal:
> Loud strokes and hissings of tormented steel
> Are heard around: the boiling waters roar,
> And smoky flames through fuming tunnels soar.
> Hither the father of the fire by night
> Through the brown air precipitates his flight:
> On their eternal anvils here he found
> The brethren beating, and the blows go round."   DRYDEN.

No. 77.

Coronis metamorphosed into a crow.

APOLLONIDES. *Oriental Cornelian.*

Neptune, in love with Coronis, daughter of Coronæus, king of Phocis, leaves the sea to surprise her. Coronis tried to fly, but the sand on the shore retarded her flight, and she implored the aid of Minerva, who changed her to a crow.

" My beauty was the cause of all my harms:
Neptune, as on his shores I wont to rove,
Observ'd me in my walks, and fell in love.
He made his courtship, he confess'd his pain,
And offer'd force when all his arts were vain:
Swift he pursu'd; I ran along the strand,
Till, spent and wearied on the sinking sand,
I shriek'd aloud, with cries I fill'd the air
To gods and men: nor god nor man was there:
A virgin goddess heard a virgin's prayer.
For, as my arms I lifted to the skies,
I saw black feathers from my fingers rise:

I strove to fling my garment on the ground;
My garment turn'd to plumes, and girt me
    round:
My hands to beat my naked bosom try;
Nor naked bosom now nor hands had I:
Lightly I tripp'd, nor weary as before
Sunk in the sand, but skimm'd along the
    shore;
Till, rising on my wings, I was preferr'd
To be the chaste Minerva's virgin bird:
Preferr'd in vain! I now am in disgrace;
Nyctimene, the owl, enjoys my place."

OVID, *Met.*

No. 78.

Neptune restoring the eyesight of Arne.

DIOSCORIDES. *Oriental Sardonyx.*

Neptune, enamoured of Arne, daughter of Eolus, made her the mother of two children, Eolus and Beotas. The outraged father of Arne confined her in a tower, and put out her eyes. Eolus and Beotas, when grown to manhood, released their mother, and Neptune restored her sight.

No. 79.

Ceres escaping from the importunities of Neptune by changing herself into a mare.

APOLLONIDES. *Cornelian.*

No. 80.

Neptune pursuing Tyro.

GNAIOS. *Oriental Cornelian.*

Neptune becoming enamoured of Tyro, daughter of Salmoneus, king of Elis, who, it was believed, was the inventor of a machine which counterfeited the brilliancy of lightning and the noise of thunder, changed himself to the river Enipeus, surprised Tyro, and made her the mother of Pelias, and of Neleus the father of Nestor.

" Tyro began, whom great Salmoneus bred,
The royal partner of famed Cretheus' bed:
For fair Enipeus, as from fruitful urns
He pours his watery store, the virgin burns:
Smooth flows the gentle stream with wanton
    pride,
And in soft mazes rolls a silver tide.
As on his banks the maid enamour'd roves,
The monarch of the deep beholds and loves !
In her Enipeus' form and borrow'd charms,
The amorous god descends into her arms:
Around a spacious arch of waves he throws,
And high in air the liquid mountain rose ;
Thus in surrounding floods conceal'd he proves
The pleasing transport, and completes his
    loves.
Then, softly sighing, he the fair addrest,
And as he spoke her tender hand he prest.
Hail, happy nymph ! no vulgar births are ow'd
To the prolific raptures of a god :

Lo ! when nine times the moon renews her
    horn,
Two brother heroes shall from thee be born ;
Thy early care the future worthies claim,
To point them to the arduous paths of fame ;
But in thy breast th' important truth conceal,
Nor dare the secret of a god reveal :
For know, thou Neptune view'st ! and at my
    nod
Earth trembles, and the waves confess their
    god.
He added not, but mounting spurn'd the
    plain,
Then plung'd into the chambers of the main.
Now in the time's full process forth she brings
Jove's dread vicegerents in two future kings ;
O'er proud Iolcos Pelias stretch'd his reign,
And godlike Neleus ruled the Pylian plain."

HOMER.

No. 81.

Neptune in a dignified attitude. In his right hand he holds the trident, and in the left a dolphin.

PYRGOTELES. *Oriental Cornelian.*

"'Now would that I might cast me in the sea,
And perish not. Great Neptune ! I would be

Advancèd to the freedom of the main,
And stand before your vast creation's plain,

And roam your watery kingdom through and
    through,
And see your branching woods and palace blue,
Spar-built, and domed with crystal; ay, and view
The bedded wonders of the lonely deep,
And see on coral banks the sea-maids sleep—
Children of ancient Nereus—and behold
Their streaming dance about their father old,

Beneath the blue Ægean, where he sate
Wedded to prophecy, and full of fate;
Or rather as Arion harped, indeed,
Would I go floating on my dolphin-steed
Over the billows, and, triumphing there,
Call the white Siren from her cave, to share
My joy, and kiss her willing forehead fair."

               B. CORNWALL.

No. 82.

Ino, with her infant Melicerta, on the back of a dolphin.

CHROMIOS. *Oriental Cornelian.*

Ino, to save herself from the fury of her husband Athamas, threw herself into the sea with her son Melicerta. Neptune took pity on them, and metamorphosed them to sea-gods.

" A rock there stood, whose side the beating
    waves
Had long consum'd, and hollow'd into caves:
The head shot forwards in a bending steep,
And cast a dreadful covert o'er the deep.
The wretched Ino on destruction bent,
Climb'd up the cliff, such strength her fury lent:
Thence with her guiltless boy, who wept in
    vain,
At one bold spring she plung'd into the main.
Her niece's fate touched Cytherea's breast,
And in soft sounds she Neptune thus address'd :
Great god of waters, whose extended sway
Is next to his whom heav'n and earth obey :

Let not the suit of Venus thee displease,
Pity the floaters on th' Ionian seas.
Increase thy subject-gods, nor yet disdain
To add my kindred to that glorious train ;
If from the sea I may such honours claim,
If 'tis desert, that from the sea I came,
As Grecian poets artfully have sung,
And in the name confest from whence I sprung.
    Pleas'd Neptune nodded his assent; and free
Both soon became from frail mortality.
He gave them form and majesty divine,
And bade them glide along the foamy brine.
For Melicerta is Palæmon known,
And Ino once Leucothoë is grown."

               OVID, *Met.*

Antistrophe 2.

" To Ino, goddess of the main,
    The Fates an equal lot decree,
Rank'd with old Ocean's Nereid train,
    Bright daughters of the sea.
Deep in the pearly realms below,
Immortal happiness to know.
    But here our day's appointed end
      To mortals is unknown ;
Whether distress our period shall attend,
And in tumultuous storms our sun go down,
Or to the shades in peaceful calms descend.

For various flows the tide of life,
Obnoxious still to fortune's veering gale;
Now rough with anguish, care, and strife,
O'erwhelming waves the shatter'd bark assail;
Now glide serene and smooth the limpid streams,
And on the surface play Apollo's golden beams."

PINDAR, *Olym.* ii.: WEST'S *Trans.*

No. 83.

Neptune as a sea-horse carrying off Medusa.

GNAIOS. *Oriental Amethyst.*

Neptune, captivated with Medusa, daughter of Phorcus, metamorphosed himself to a horse, carried off Medusa, and crossing the sea, obtained her favour in a temple of Minerva; which so irritated the goddess, that she changed the beautiful hair of Medusa into serpents.

" Yet is it less the horror than the grace
    Which turns the gazer's spirit into stone,
Whereon the lineaments of that dead face
    Are graven, till the characters are grown
Into itself, and thought no more can trace;
    'Tis the melodious hue of beauty thrown
Athwart the darkness and the glare of pain,
Which humanise and harmonise the strain.

And from her head as from one body grow—
    As spired grass out of a watery rock—
Hairs which are vipers, and they curl and flow,
    And their long tangles in each other lock;

And with unending involutions show
    Their mailèd radiance, as it were to mock
The torture and the death within, and saw
The solid air with many a ragged jaw.

.   .   .   .   .   .

'Tis the tempestuous loveliness of terror;
    For from the serpents gleams a brazen glare,
Kindled by that inextricable error,
    Which makes a thrilling vapour of the air
Become a strong and everlasting mirror
    Of all the beauty and the terror there—
A woman's countenance with serpent-locks,
Gazing in death on heaven from those wet rocks."

SHELLEY.

No. 84.

Neptune carrying off Salamina, or Salamis, daughter of Asopus.

APOLLONIDES. *Oriental Cornelian.*

He conveyed her to an island of the Ægean Sea, to which she gave her name.

No. 85.

Neptune causing the Cretan bull to come out of the sea.

GNAIOS.   *Aqua-marine.*

No. 86.

Neptune, in a car drawn by dolphins, calling the Cretan bull from the depths of the ocean.

PYRGOTELES.   *Cornelian.*

No. 87.

Neptune on a sea-horse, with Eumolpus in his arms.

GNAIOS.   *Aqua-marine of rare quality.*

Chione, the daughter of Boreas and Orithya, was beloved by Neptune, by whom she had Eumolpus. To conceal her fault from Boreas, she threw Eumolpus into the sea. Neptune saved the child, and had him educated by Amphitrite.

No. 88.

The dolphin sent by Neptune enticing Amphitrite, daughter of Ocean and Tethys, to follow him.

GNAIOS.   *Oriental Amethyst.*

No. 89.

Neptune and Amphitrite seated on a sea-horse.

CHROMIOS.   *Oriental Jade.*

No. 90.

Pluto carrying off Proserpine.

APOLLONIDES. *Oriental Cornelian.*

" Near Euna's walls a spacious lake is spread,
Famed for the sweetly-singing swans it bred ;
Pergusa is its name : . . . . .
Here, while young Proserpine among the
    maids
Diverts herself in these delicious shades ;
While like a child with busy speed and care
She gathers lilies here, and violets there ;
While first to fill her little lap she strives,
Hell's grizzly monarch at the shade arrives ;
Sees her thus sporting on the flow'ry green,
And loves the blooming maid as soon as
    seen.

His urgent flame impatient of delay,
Swift as his thought he seiz'd the beauteous
    prey,
And bore her in his sooty car away.
The frighted goddess to her mother cries ;
But all in vain, for now far off she flies :
Far she behind her leaves her virgin train ;
To them too cries, and cries to them in vain.
And, while with passion she repeats her call,
The violets from her lap and lilies fall :
She misses 'em, poor heart ! and makes new
    moan ;
Her lilies, ah ! are lost, her violets gone."
                    OVID.

.   .   .   .   .   .

" PROSERPINE.
Hark ! what sound?
Do you see aught?

CHORUS.
Behold, behold, Proserpina !
Dark clouds from out the earth arise,
And wing their way towards the skies,
As they would veil the burning blush of day.
    And look ! upon a rolling car,
    Some fearful being from afar
Comes onward. As he moves along the ground,
    A dull and subterranean sound
Companions him ; and from his face doth shine,
    Proclaiming him divine,
A light that darkens all the vale around.

SEMICHORUS (CYANE).
'Tis he ! 'tis he ! he comes to us
From the depths of Tartarus.
For what of evil doth he roam
From his red and gloomy home

In the centre of the world,
Where the sinful dead are hurl'd ?
Mark him, as he moves along,
Drawn by horses black and strong ;
Such as may belong to Night,
Ere she takes her morning flight.
Now the chariot stops : the god
On our grassy world hath trod.
Like a Titan steppeth he,
Yet full of his divinity.
On his mighty shoulders lie
Raven locks ; and in his eye
A cruel beauty — such as none
Of us may wisely look upon.

PROSERPINE.
He comes indeed. How like a god he looks !
Terribly lovely ! Shall I shun his eye,
Which even here looks brightly beautiful ?
What a wild-leopard glance he has ! I am
Jove's daughter, and shall I then deign to fly ?
I will not ; yet methinks I fear to stay.
Come, let us go, Cyane.

g

(PLUTO *enters.*)

PLUTO.

          Stay! O stay,
Proserpina! Proserpina, I come
From my Tartarian kingdom to behold you.
The brother of Jove am I. I come to say,
Gently beside this blue Sicilian stream,
How much I love you, fair Proserpina.

     .   .   .   .   .

SEMICHORUS (CYANE).

Come with me away, away,
Fair and young Proserpina!
You will die, unless you flee,
Child of crownèd Cybele.
Think of all your mother's love,
Of ev'ry stream and pleasant grove,
That you must for ever leave,
If the dark king you believe.
Think not of his eyes of fire,
Nor his wily heart's desire;
Nor the locks that round his head
Run like wreathed snakes, and fling
A shadow o'er his dark eyes glancing;
Nor the dang'rous whispers hung,
Like honey roofing, o'er his tongue;
But think of all thy mother's glory.

     .   .   .   .   .

Once again I bid thee flee,
Daughter of great Cybele.

PROSERPINE.

You are too harsh, Cyane.

PLUTO.

          O, my love,
Fairer than the white Naiad — fairer far
Than aught on earth, and fair as aught in heav'n;
Hear me, Proserpina!

PROSERPINE.

          Away! away!
I'll not believe you. What a cunning tongue
He has, Cyane! has he not? Away!
Can the gods flatter?

PLUTO.

          By my burning throne,
I love you, sweetest. I will make you queen
Of my great kingdom. One-third of the world
Shall you reign over, my Proserpina;
And you shall rank as high as any she,
Save one, within the starry court of Jove.

PROSERPINE.

Will you be true?

PLUTO.

          I swear it, by myself!
Come, then, my bride!

PROSERPINE.

          Speak thou again, my friend;
Speak, harsh Cyane, in a harsher voice,
And bid me not believe him. Ah! you droop
Your head in silence.

PLUTO.

          Come, my brightest queen!
Come, beautiful Proserpina, and see
The regions over which your husband reigns;
His palaces and radiant treasures, which
Mock and outstrip all fable; his great power,
Which the living own, and wand'ring ghosts
     obey,
And all the elements. Oh! you shall sit
On my illuminated throne, and be
A queen indeed; and round your forehead shall
     run
Circlets of gems, as bright as those which bind
The brows of Juno on heav'n's festal nights,
When all the gods assemble and bend down
In homage before Jove.

PROSERPINE.

          Speak out, Cyane!

PLUTO.

But, above all, in my heart shall you reign
Supreme, a goddess and a queen indeed,
Without a rival. Oh! and you shall share
My subterranean power, and sport upon

The fields Elysian; where, mid softest sounds,
And odours springing from immortal flowers,
And mazy rivers, and eternal groves
Of bloom and beauty, the good spirits walk.
And you shall take your station in the skies
Nearest the queen of heav'n, and with her hold
Celestial talk; and meet Jove's tender smile,
So beautiful——

PROSERPINE.

Away! away! away!
Nothing but force shall ever—Oh, away!
I'll not believe. Fool that I am to smile!
Come round me, virgins. Am I then betray'd?
O fraudful king!

PLUTO.

No; by this kiss, and this,
I am your own, my love; and you are mine,
For ever and for ever. Weep, Cyane.

CHORUS.

They are gone, afar, afar,
Like the shooting of a star.
See! their chariot fades away—
Farewell, lost Proserpina!
[CYANE *is gradually transformed.*
But, ah! what frightful change is here?
Cyane, raise your eyes, and hear!

We call thee vainly—on the ground
She sinks, without a single sound,
And all her garments float around.
Again, again she rises—light,
Her head is like a fountain bright;
And her glossy ringlets fall,
With a murmur musical,
O'er her shoulders, like a river
That rushes and escapes for ever.
Is the fair Cyane gone?
And is this fountain left alone
For a sad remembrance; where
We may in after-times repair,
With heavy heart and weeping eye,
To sing songs to her memory?
O then farewell! and now, with hearts that
   mourn
Deeply, to Dian's temple will we go;
But ever on this day we will return,
   Constant to mark Cyane's fountain flow;
And haply—for among us who can know
   The secrets written on the scroll of fate?—
A day may come when we may cease our
   woe;
And she, redeem'd at last from Pluto's hate,
Rise in her beauty old, pure and regenerate."
B. CORNWALL.

"Cease, cease, fair nymph, to lavish precious
   tears,
And discompose your soul with airy fears.
Look on Sicilia's glitt'ring courts with scorn:
A nobler sceptre shall that hand adorn.
Imperial pomp shall soothe a gen'rous pride;
The bridegroom never will disgrace the bride.
If you above terrestrial thrones aspire,
From heav'n I spring, and Saturn was my sire:
The pow'r of Pluto stretches all around,
Uncircumscrib'd by Nature's utmost bound;
Where matter mould'ring dies, where forms decay,
Through the vast trackless void extends my sway.
Mark not with mournful eyes the fading light,
Nor tremble at this interval of night;

A fairer scene shall open to your view,
An earth more verdant, and a heav'n more
   blue.
Another Phœbus gilds those happy skies,
And other stars with purer flames arise;
Their chaste adorers shall their praises join,
And with the choicest gifts enrich your shrine.
The blissful climes no change of ages knew,
The golden first began, and still is new:
That golden age your world awhile could boast,
But here it flourish'd, and was never lost.
Perpetual zephyrs breathe through fragrant bow'rs,
And painted meads smile with unbidden flow'rs—
Flow'rs of immortal bloom and various hue,
No rival sweets in your own Enna grew.

In the recess of a cool sylvan glade,
A monarch-tree projects no vulgar shade;
Encumber'd with their wealth, the branches bend,
And golden apples to your reach descend.
Spare not the fruit, but pluck the blooming ore,
The yellow harvest will increase the more.
But I too long on trifling themes explain,
Nor speak the unbounded glories of your reign.
Whole Nature owns your pow'r: whate'er have
    birth,
And live and move o'er all the face of earth;
Or in old Ocean's mighty caverns sleep,
Or sportive roll along the foaming deep,
Or on stiff pinions airy journeys take,
Or cut the floating stream or stagnant lake,—
In vain they labour to preserve their breath,
And soon fall victims to your subject, Death.
Unnumber'd triumphs swift to you he brings—
Hail! goddess of all sublunary things!
Empires that sink, above, here rise again,
And worlds unpeopled crowd the Elysian plain:
The rich, the poor, the monarch, and the slave,
Know no superior honours in the grave.

Proud tyrants once, and laurell'd chiefs, shall
    come
And kneel, and trembling wait from thee their
    doom;
The impious, forc'd, shall then their crimes dis-
    close,
And see past pleasures teem with future woes;
Deplore in darkness your impartial sway,
While spotless souls enjoy the fields of day.
When ripe for second birth, the dead shall stand
In shiv'ring throngs on the Lethean strand:
That shade whom you approve shall first be
    brought
To quaff oblivion in the pleasing draught;
Whose thread of life, just spun, you would renew,
But nod, and Clotho shall rewind the clue.
Let no distrust of pow'r your joys abate—
Speak what you wish, and what you speak is fate.
   The ravisher thus sooth'd the weeping fair,
And check'd the fury of his steeds with care:
Possess'd of beauty's charms, he calmly rode,
And love first soften'd the relentless god."
                        CLAUDIAN, *by* EUSDEN, 1764.

" The ravisher o'er hills and valleys speeds,
By name encouraging his foamy steeds;
He rattles o'er their necks the rusty reins,
And ruffles with the stroke their shaggy manes.
O'er lakes he whirls his flying wheels, and comes
To the Palici breathing sulphurous fumes.
And thence to where the Bacchiads of renown
Between unequal havens built their town;
Where Arethusa, round th' imprison'd sea,
Extends her crooked coast to Cyane;
The nymph who gave the neighb'ring lake a
    name,
Of all Sicilian nymphs the first in fame.

She from the waves advanc'd her beauteous head,
The goddess knew, and thus to Pluto said:
   Farther thou shalt not with the virgin run;
Ceres unwilling, canst thou be her son?
The maid should be by sweet persuasion won:
Force suits not with the softness of the fair;
For if great things with small I may compare,
Me Anapis once lov'd; a milder course
He took, and won me by his words, not force.
   Then, stretching out her arms, she stopp'd his
    way;
But he, impatient of the shortest stay,
Throws to his dreadful steeds the slacken'd rein.'

No. 91.

Pluto carrying off Proserpine in a quadriga.

APOLLONIDES. *Cornelian.*

" In Nysia's vale, with nymphs a lovely train,
Sprung from the hoary father of the main,
Fair Proserpine consum'd the fleeting hours
In pleasing sports, and pluck'd the gaudy flowers.
Around them wide the flamy crocus glows,
Through leaves of verdure blooms the opening rose;
The hyacinth declines his fragrant head,
And purple violets deck th' enamell'd mead.
The fair Narcissus far above the rest,
By magic form'd, in beauty rose confest.
So Jove, t' ensnare the virgin's thoughtless mind,
And please the ruler of the shades design'd,
He caus'd it from the opening earth to rise,
Sweet to the scent, alluring to the eyes.
Never did mortal, or celestial power,
Behold such vivid tints adorn a flower:
From the deep root an hundred branches sprung,
And to the winds ambrosial odours flung;
Which lightly wafted on the wings of air,
The gladden'd earth, and heaven's wide circuit
share.
The joy-dispensing fragrance spreads around,
And ocean's briny swell with smiles is crown'd.

Pleas'd at the sight, nor deeming danger
nigh,
The fair beheld it with desiring eye;
Her eager hand she stretch'd to seize the flower,
(Beauteous illusion of th' ethereal power!)
When, dreadful to behold, the rocking ground
Disparted—widely yawn'd a gulf profound!—
Forth rushing from the black abyss, arose
The gloomy monarch of the realm of woes,
Pluto, from Saturn sprung. The trembling maid
He seiz'd, and to his golden car convey'd.
Borne by immortal steeds, the chariot flies;
And thus she pours her supplicating cries:—
Assist, protect me, thou who reign'st above,
Supreme and best of gods, paternal Jove!
But, ah! in vain the hapless virgin rears
Her wild complaint——nor god not mortal
hears!—
Not to the white-arm'd nymphs with beauty
crown'd,
Her lov'd companions, reach'd the mournful
sound."

Homeric Hymn to Ceres.

No. 92.

Pluto, being wounded in the shoulder by Hercules, ascends to Olympus, where he is cured by Pæon, the physician of the gods.

APOLLONIDES. *Amethyst.*

" Ev'n hell's grim king Alcides' power confess'd,
The shaft found entrance in his iron breast;
To Jove's high palace for a cure he fled,
Pierc'd in his own dominions of the dead;
Where Pæon, sprinkling heavenly balm around,
Assuag'd the glowing pangs, and clos'd the wound.
Rash, impious man! to stain the bless'd abodes,
And drench his arrows in the blood of gods!

Iliad, book v.

No. 93.

Pluto and Proserpine seated on a throne. Pluto has the tiara on his head, the bident in his right hand; Proserpine holds a torch turned down and enwreathed with a serpent. At their feet is Cerberus.

CHROMIOS. *Calcedony.*

No. 94.

Head of Pluto.

AULOS. *Sardonyx.*

" Pluto, the grisly god, who never spares,
 Who feels no mercy and who hears no prayers,
 Lives dark and dreadful in deep hell's abodes,
 And mortals hate him as the worst of gods."   *Iliad,* book ix.

" Leaving the cavern of the dead, and gates
 Of darkness, where from all the gods apart
 Dwells Pluto"——   *Hecuba.*

" Foremost th' infernal palaces are seen
 Of Pluto and Persephone his queen :
 A horrid dog, and grim, couch'd on the floor,
 Guards with malicious art the sounding door ;
 On each, who in the entrance first appears,
 He fawning wags his tail and cocks his ears ;
 If any strive to measure back the way,
 Their steps he watches and devours his prey."   HESIOD, *Theog.*

" Go then, sportive Echo, go
 To the sable dome below,
 Proserpine's black dome, repair,
 There to Cleodemus bear
 Tidings of immortal fame :
 Tell, how in the rapid game
 O'er Pisa's vale his son victorious fled ;
 Tell, for thou saw'st him bear away
 The winged honours of the day ;
 And deck with wreaths of fame his youthful head."
          Pindar, 14th Olymp.

No. 95.

Proserpine metamorphosing Ascalaphus into an owl.

KAECAS. *Oriental Sardonyx.*

Pluto having carried off Proserpine, and taken her to the infernal regions, Ceres had recourse to Jupiter, begging to be allowed the power of bringing her daughter back to earth. Jupiter consented, provided Proserpine had taken no nourishment whilst in the infernal regions. Ascalaphus, son of Acheron and the nymph Orphne, having seen Proserpine eat seven pomegranate-seeds, told Pluto of it. Jupiter then decided that she should pass six months of every year with her husband in hell, and six months with her mother on earth. Proserpine, to avenge herself on Ascalaphus, sprinkled some of the waters of the Phlegethon on his head, and metamorphosed him to an owl.

" The goddess now, resolving to succeed,
Down to the gloomy shades descends with speed.
But adverse fate had otherwise decreed:
For, long before, her giddy, thoughtless child
Had broke her fast, and all her projects spoil'd.
As in the garden's shady walks she stray'd,
A fair pomegranate charm'd the simple maid;
Hung in her way, and tempting her to taste,
She pluck'd the fruit, and took a short repast.
Seven times, a seed at once, she ate the food:
The fact Ascalaphus had only viewed,
Whom Acheron begot, in Stygian shades,
On Orphne, fam'd among Avernal maids;
He saw what pass'd, and, by discov'ring all,
Detain'd the ravish'd nymph in cruel thrall.
But now a queen, she with resentment heard,
And chang'd the vile informer to a bird.
In Phlegethon's black stream her hand she dips,
Sprinkles his head, and wets his babbling lips.
Soon on his face, bedropt with magic dew,
A change appear'd, and gaudy feathers grew;

A crooked beak the place of nose supplies,
Rounder his head, and larger are his eyes;
His arms and body waste, but are supplied
With yellow pinions flagging on each side;
His nails grow crooked, and are turn'd to claws,
And lazily along his heavy wings he draws:
Ill-omen'd in his form, th' unlucky fowl,
Abhorr'd by men, and call'd a screeching owl.

Jove some amends for Ceres' loss to make,
Yet willing Pluto should the joy partake,
Gives 'em of Proserpine an equal share,
Who, claim'd by both, with both divides the year.
The goddess now in either empire sways,
Six moons in hell, and six with Ceres stays.
Her peevish temper's chang'd; that sullen mind,
Which made e'en hell uneasy, now is kind.
Her voice refines, her mien more sweet appears,
Her forehead free from frowns, her eyes from
    tears.
As when with golden light the conqu'ring day
Through dusky exhalations clears a way."

OVID, *Met.*

No. 96.

Proserpine, in a car drawn by dragons, having discovered the nymph Minthe holding amorous intercourse with Pluto, metamorphoses her into the plant called *mint*.

GNAIOS.   *Sardonyx.*

" Could Pluto's queen with jealous fury storm,
A Minthe to a fragrant herb transform?"

No 97.

Head of Proserpine.

ALEXANDER.   *Amethyst.*

" Tell me what god, what mortal has convey'd,
Reluctant from these arms my darling maid?
  Daughter of Rhea! he replied, I hear
With grief thy wrongs, and dignity revere.
Blame not th' ethereal race; from heaven's dread king,
Who dwells mid black'ning clouds, thy sorrows spring.
Pluto by his decree the virgin bore
Where, darkly frowning on th' infernal shore,
His lofty palace stands.   No more repine;
No cause for anguish nor for shame is thine.
He, brother to the god who rules on high,
Now hails her empress of the lower sky;
For Saturn's awful race superior reign
O'er heaven, o'er hell, and earth-encircling main."

Homeric Hynn to Ceres.

No. 98.

The infant Vulcan, having fallen from heaven on the island of Lemnos, is saved by Thetis and the nymph Euronyme.

APOLLONIDES.   *Oriental Cornelian.*

" Thetis (replied the god), our powers may claim
An ever-dear, an ever-honour'd name:

When my proud mother hurl'd me from the sky
(My awkward form, it seems, displeas'd her eye),
She and Eurynome my griefs redress'd,
And soft receiv'd me on their silver breast."

HOMER.

No. 99.

The fall of Vulcan.

PYRGOTELES. *Amethyst.*

" Thus Vulcan spoke ; and rising with a bound,
The double bowl with sparkling nectar crown'd,
Which held to Juno in a cheerful way,
Goddess (he cried), be patient and obey.
Dear as you are, if Jove his arm extend,
I can but grieve, unable to defend.
What god so daring in your aid to move,
Or lift his hand against the force of Jove?
Once in your cause I felt his matchless might,
Hurl'd headlong downward from the ethereal
  height ;

Toss'd all the day in rapid circles round,
Nor, till the sun descended, touch'd the ground ;
Breathless I fell, in giddy motions lost ;
The Sinthians rais'd me on the Lemnian coast.
  He said, and to her hands the goblet heav'd,
Which, with a smile, the white-arm'd queen re-
  ceiv'd.
Then to the rest he fill'd ; and in his turn
Each to his lips applied the nectar'd urn.
Vulcan with awkward grace his office plies,
And unextinguish'd laughter shakes the skies."

Iliad, book i.

No. 100.

Bacchus intoxicating Vulcan.

GNAIOS. *Oriental Sardonyx.*

Among the principal works of Vulcan was the throne of gold which he sent to Olympus for Juno. The goddess, not suspecting her son, and delighted with the beauty of the work, did not hesitate to seat herself; but no sooner had she done so, than she found herself unable to move, being kept down by secret springs, and thus exposed to the mockery of the gods. Bacchus, however, had recourse to Vulcan; and having intoxicated him, prevailed on him to go to heaven, and release Juno. Vide Pausanias.

No. 101.

Vulcan unfastening the springs of the seat, and releasing Juno.

DIOSCORIDES. *Sardonyx.*

h

No. 102.

Apollo warning Vulcan of the amours of Venus and Mars.

AMMONIOS.   *Oriental Amethyst.*

" Venus' amour with Mars, the Sun, we're told,
First saw; for all things he does first behold:
Griev'd at the sight, and swift, on mischief bent,
To Venus' husband Juno's son he sent."

OVID, *Met.* book iv.

No. 103.

Vulcan shewing Apollo the net of metal which he had forged to envelope Venus and Mars.

CHROMIOS.   *Oriental Cornelian.*

No. 104.

Vulcan, finding Alectryon asleep, avails himself of the opportunity to surprise Venus and Mars.

APOLLONIDES.   *Calcedony, partaking of the Sapphire.*

No. 105.

Vulcan, having surprised Venus and Mars, encloses them in his brazen net, which united extreme lightness with such solidity, that even the god of war could not break it.

PYRGOTELES.   *Oriental Sardonyx.*

" Meantime the bard, alternate to the strings,
The loves of Mars and Cytherea sings;
How the stern god, enamour'd with her charms,
Clasp'd the gay panting goddess in his arms,
By bribes seduc'd; and how the sun, whose eye
Views the broad heavens, disclos'd the lawless joy.

Stung to the soul, indignant through the skies
To his black forge vindictive Vulcan flies:
Arriv'd, his sinewy arms incessant place
Th' eternal anvil on the massy base.
A wondrous net he labours, to betray
The wanton lovers as entwin'd they lay,

Indissolubly strong. Then instant bears
To his immortal dome the finish'd snares.
Above, below, around, with art dispread,
The sure enclosure folds the genial bed;
Whose texture e'en the search of gods deceives,
Thin as the filmy threads the spider weaves.
Then, as withdrawing from the starry bowers,
He feigns a journey to the Lemnian shores,
His favourite isle. Observant Mars descries
His wish'd recess, and to the goddess flies:
He glows, he burns: the fair-hair'd queen of
    love
Descends smooth gliding from the courts of
    Jove,
Gay blooming in full charms: her hand he
    press'd
With eager joy, and with a sigh address'd:
Come, my belov'd, and taste the soft delights;
Come, to repose the genial bed invites;
Thy absent spouse, neglectful of thy charms,
Prefers his barbarous Sinthians to thy arms.
    Then, nothing loath, th' enamour'd fair he led,
And sunk transported on the conscious bed.
Down rush'd the toils, enwrapping as they
    lay
The careless lovers in their wanton play;
In vain they strive, th' entangling snares deny
(Inextricably firm) the power to fly.

Warn'd by the god who sheds the golden day,
Stern Vulcan homeward treads the starry way;
Arriv'd, he sees, he grieves, with rage he burns;
Full horrible he roars, his voice all heaven re-
    turns.
    O Jove, he cried, O all ye powers above,
See the frail dalliance of the queen of love!
Me, awkward me, she scorns; and yields her
    charms
To that fair hero, the strong god of arms.
If I am lame, that stain my natal hour
By fate imposed; such me my parent bore:
Why was I born? See how the wanton lies!
    .   .   .   .
But yet I trust, this once, e'en Mars would fly
His fair one's arms — he thinks her, once, too
    nigh.
But there remain, ye guilty, in my power,
Till Jove refunds his shameless daughter's dower.
Too dear I priz'd a fair enchanting face;
Beauty unchaste is beauty in disgrace.
    Meanwhile the gods the dome of Vulcan
    throng,
Apollo comes, and Neptune comes along;
With these gay Hermes trod the starry plain;
But modesty withheld the goddess-train.
All heaven beholds, imprison'd as they lie,
And unextinguish'd laughter shakes the sky."
                             Odyss. viii.

No. 106.

Vulcan, armed with an enormous hammer, heated in the furnace, over-
throwing one of the Titans.

AMMONIOS. *Oriental Sardonyx.*

No. 107.

Venus Urania (celestial), who presided over pure and exalted love. She is
resting one hand on a celestial globe, and one foot on a tortoise.

GNAIOS. *Amethyst.*

" Venus, bright goddess of the skies,
  To whom unnumber'd temples rise,
Jove's daughter fair, whose wily arts
Delude fond lovers of their hearts,
O listen gracious to my prayer,
And free my mind from anxious care.

If e'er you heard my ardent vow,
Propitious goddess, hear me now ;
And oft my ardent vow you've heard,
By Cupid's kindly aid preferr'd ;
Oft left the golden courts of Jove,
To listen to my tales of love.

The radiant car your sparrows drew ;
You gave the word, and swift they flew,
Through liquid air they wing'd their way ;
I saw their quivering pinions play ;
To my plain roof they bore their queen,
Of aspect mild, and look serene.

Soon as you came, by your command,
Back flew the wanton feather'd band ;
Then with a sweet enchanting look,
Divinely smiling, thus you spoke:

' Why didst thou call me to thy cell ?
Tell me, my gentle Sappho, tell.

What healing med'cine shall I find
To cure thy love-distemper'd mind ?
Say, shall I lend thee all my charms,
To win young Phaon to thy arms ?
Or does some other swain subdue
Thy heart ? my Sappho, tell me who.

Though now, averse, thy charms he slight,
He soon shall view thee with delight ;
Though now he scorns thy gifts to take,
He soon to thee shall offerings make ;
Though now thy beauties fail to move,
He soon shall melt with equal love.'

Once more, O Venus ! hear my prayer,
And ease my mind of anxious care ;
Again vouchsafe to be my guest,
And calm this tempest in my breast:
To thee, bright queen, my vows aspire ;
O grant me all my heart's desire !"

SAPPHO.

" There too the goddess lives in stone, and fills
  The air around with beauty ; we inhale
The ambrosial aspect which, beheld, instils
Part of its immortality ; the veil
Of heav'n is half withdrawn, within the pale
We stand, and in that form and face behold
What Mind can make when Nature's self
    would fail ;
And to the fond idolators of old
Envy the innate flash which such a soul could
  mould.

We gaze and turn away, we know not where,
Dazzled and drunk with beauty, till the heart
Reels with its fulness ; there—for ever there—
Chain'd to the chariot of triumphal Art,
We stand as captives, and would not depart.

Away ! these need no words nor terms pre-
  cise—
The paltry jargon of the marble mart,
Where Pedantry gulls Folly—we have eyes :
Blood, pulse, and breast confirm the Dardan
  shepherd's prize.

Appear'dst thou not to Paris in this guise ?
Or to more deeply-blest Anchises ? or,
In all thy perfect goddess-ship, when lies
Before thee thy own vanquish'd lord of war,
And, gazing on thy face as toward a star,
Laid on thy lap, his eyes to thee upturn,
Feeding on thy sweet cheek ; while thy lips are
With lava kisses, melting while they burn,
Shower'd on his eyelids, brow, and mouth, as
  from an urn.

Glowing and circumfused in speechless love,
Their full divinity inadequate
That feeling to express, or to improve,
The gods become as mortals; and man's fate
Has moments like their brightest—but the weight
Of earth recoils upon us. Let it go!
We can recall such visions, and create,
From what has been or might be, things which grow
Into thy statue's form, and look like gods below.

I leave to learned fingers and wise hands,
The artist and his ape, to teach and tell
How well his connoisseurship understands
The graceful bend and the voluptuous swell.
Let these describe the indescribable;
I would not their vile breath should crisp the stream
Wherein that image shall for ever dwell—
The unruffl'd mirror of the loveliest dream
That ever left the sky on the deep soul to beam."
BYRON.

No. 108.

Venus (created from the blood of Uranus and the foam of the sea) seated in a shell drawn by dolphins.

GNAIOS. *Sardonyx.*

The ancients differed in opinion on the manner of her arriving at Cyprus. Homer, in his *Hymn in honour of Venus,* says that she was transported thither by Zephyrus. Other mythologians have thought that she repaired to the island herself in the shell in which she was born, carried by dolphins, as represented on this stone.

" Till now swift-circling a white foam arose
From that immortal substance, and a nymph
Was quicken'd in the midst. The wafting waves
First bore her to Cythera's heavenly coast;
Then reach'd she Cyprus, girt with flowing seas,
And forth emerged a goddess, in the charms
Of awful beauty. Where her delicate feet
Had press'd the sands, green herbage flowering sprang.
Her Aphrodite gods and mortals name,
The foam-born goddess; and her name is known
As Cytherea with the blooming wreath,
For that she touch'd Cythera's flowery coast;
And Cypris, for that on the Cyprian shore
She rose amidst the multitude of waves;
And Philomedea, from the source of life.'
HESIOD.

Idyllium 8.

" Sweet Venus, daughter of the main,
Why are you pleas'd with mortals' pain?
What mighty trespass have they done,
That thus you scourge them with your son—
A guileful boy, a cruel foe,
Whose chief delight is human woe?
You gave him wings, alas! and darts,
To range the world and shoot at hearts."
BION.

No. 109.

Venus standing in a shell on the sea.

GNAIOS.   *Oriental Cornelian.*

" And whose immortal hand could shed
Upon this disk the ocean's bed?
And, in a frenzied flight of soul,
Sublime as heaven's eternal pole,
Imagine thus, in semblance warm,
The queen of love's voluptuous form,
Floating along the silv'ry sea
In beauty's naked majesty!
O! he has given the captur'd sight
A witching banquet of delight;
And all those sacred scenes of love,
Where only hallow'd eyes may rove,
Lie faintly glowing, half conceal'd,
Within the lucid billows veil'd.
Light as the leaf, that summer's breeze
Has wafted o'er the glassy seas,
She floats upon the ocean-breast,
Which undulates in sleepy rest,

And stealing on, she gently pillows
Her bosom on the amorous billows.
Her bosom like the humid rose,
Her neck like dewy sparkling snows,
Illume the liquid path she traces,
And burn within the stream's embraces!
In languid luxury soft she glides,
Encircled by the azure tides,
Like some fair lily, faint with weeping,
Upon a bed of violets sleeping!
Beneath their queen's inspiring glance,
The dolphins o'er the green sea dance,
Bearing in triumph young desire,
And baby love with smiles of fire!
While, sparkling on the silver waves,
The tenants of the briny caves
Around the pomp in eddies play
And gleam along the watery way."

ANACREON: MOORE's *Trans.*

No. 110.

Jupiter confiding the education of Venus to the Hours or Seasons.

GNAIOS.   *Oriental Cornelian.*

" Love track'd her steps; and beautiful Desire
Pursued, while soon as born she bent her way
Towards heaven's assembled gods; her honours these
From the beginning; whether gods or men
Her presence bless—to her the portion fell
Of virgin whisperings and alluring smiles,
And smooth deceits, and gentle ecstasy,
And dalliance, and the blandishments of love."

HESIOD.

No. 111.

Venus transported by Zephyrus to the island of Cyprus.*

APOLLONIDES. *Oriental Cornelian.*

" Saturn the parts divided from the wound, ·
Spoils of his parent god, cast from the ground
Into the sea; long through the watery plain
They journey'd on the surface of the main:
Fruitful at length th' immortal substance grows,
Whit'ning it foams, and in a circle flows:
Behold a nymph arise divinely fair,
Whom to Cythera first the surges bear;
Hence is she borne safe o'er the deeps profound
To Cyprus, water'd by the waves around;
And here she walks endow'd with every grace
To charm, the goddess blooming in her face;
Her looks demand respect, and where she goes,
Beneath her tender feet the herbage blows;

And Aphrodite, from the foam, her name,
Among the race of gods and men the same;
And Cytherea from Cythera came;
Whence, beauteous crown'd she safely cross'd the sea,
And call'd, O Cyprus, Cypria from thee;
Nor less by Philomedea known on earth,
A name deriv'd immediate from her birth:
Her first attendants to th' immortal choir
Were Love, the oldest god, and fair Desire;
The virgin whisper and the tempting smile,
The sweet allurements that can hearts beguile,
Soft blandishments which never fail to move,
Friendship, and all the fond deceits in love,
Constant her steps pursue, or she will go
Among the gods above or men below."

HESIOD: *Th.*

" Then gentle zephyrs, with reviving sweets
From gay Eubœa's myrtle-border'd meads,
Perfume the waves, scarce ruffling in their course
The ocean's pearly robe."

Athenaid.

No. 112.

Venus and Mars.

DIOSCORIDES. *Oriental Cornelian.*

" O Love, resistless in thy might,
Triumphant o'er the pow'r of gold,
In youth's soft cheek with beauty bright
Joying thy sweet domain to hold,

Thou rulest o'er th' extended main,
The rural hut, the pastoral plain;
Thy pow'r th' immortal gods obey,
And mortal men confess thy sway:

* Insulam veteribus divitiis abundantem, et ob hoc Veneri sacram, Ptolemæus regebat.—*Annæ Flor.* lib. iii. c. 9.

56 CATALOGUE.

But all who feel thy piercing darts
Feel madness rankling in their hearts.
By thee the virtuous mind beguil'd
Basely to wrong is drawn aside;
By thee contentions fierce and wild
Raise storms in hearts by blood allied;

Desire, in flames now seen to rise,
Caught from the virgin's radiant eyes,
Disdains the curb of laws to own,
But with them shares their potent throne;
While Venus, sovereign of the soul,
Victorious smiles, and scorns control."

SOPHOCLES, *Antigone:* POTTER'S *Trans.*

No. 113.

Venus in the palace of Vulcan caressing Mars to detain him.

DIOSCORIDES. *Oriental Cornelian.*

"This said, with speed the god of battles came
To the grand mansion of the Cyprian dame,
Which crippled Vulcan rais'd, when first he led
The Paphian goddess to his nuptial bed.
The gate they pass, and to the dome retire,
Where Venus oft regales the god of fire:
(He to his forge had gone at early day,
A floating isle contain'd it on the bay,
Here wond'rous works by fire's fierce power he wrought,
And on his anvil to perfection brought).

Fronting the door, all lovely and alone,
Sat Cytherea on a polish'd throne;
Adown the shoulders of the heavenly fair
In easy ringlets flow'd her flaxen hair,
And with a golden comb, in matchless grace,
She taught each lock its most becoming
place.
She saw the deity approach her dome,
And from her hand dismiss'd the golden
comb."

APOLL. RH. book iii.

"Mars entered, clasp'd her hand, and breathed his love:
'Come, fairest, to these arms; we meet alone;
Thy lord, 'mid Sinthians, seeks his Lemnian throne.'
He spake: the goddess by like ardour led,
Retiring, shared with him the nuptial bed."

Odyssey, book viii.

No. 114.

Venus stealing the weapons of Love.

GNAIOS. *Amethyst.*

"His mother's lips while Cupid fondly press'd,
Heedless, he with an arrow raz'd her breast:
The goddess felt it, and with fury stung,
The wanton mischief from her bosom flung;
She thought at first the danger slight, but found
The dart too faithful, and too deep the wound."

OVID'S *Met.* book x.

No. 115.

Typhon chasing Venus.

CHROMIOS. *Calcedony.*

Venus, pursued by the giant Typhon, took flight with her son. Arrived on the shores of the Euphrates, they are each taken on the back of a dolphin to the opposite bank. Jupiter placed the two fish in the heavens, which was the origin of this sign in the Zodiac. (See War of Titans.)

No. 116.

Venus transforming the Cerastes, the inhabitants of the island of Cyprus, to bulls, for immolating human victims.

GNAIOS. *Oriental Cornelian.*

" Venus these barb'rous sacrifices view'd
With just abhorrence, and with wrath pursued:
At first to punish such nefarious crimes
Their towns she meant to leave, her once-lov'd climes;
' But why ?' said she, ' for their offence should I
My dear delightful plains and cities fly ?

No, let the impious people who have sinn'd
A punishment in death or exile find:
If death or exile too severe be thought,
Let them in some vile shape bemoan their fault.
While next her mind a proper form employs,
Admonish'd by their horns she fix'd her choice:
Their former crest remains upon their heads,
And their strong limbs an ox's shape invades."
OVID's *Met.* book x.

No. 117.

Venus in her bath. She is holding a vase of elegant form, filled with perfumed oil.

GNAIOS. *Oriental Cornelian.*

No. 118.

Venus metamorphosing Selimnus and Argyra.

PYRGOTELES. *Oriental Cornelian.*

Argyra, a nymph of Thessaly, was passionately fond of her husband Selimnus, who loved her with equal tenderness. Being near losing her, he was greatly afflicted; and Venus, touched with pity, metamorphosed Selimnus into a river, and Argyra to a fountain; and by underground courses they mingled their waters. (Vide Pausanias, book vii. chap. 23.)

No. 119.

Myrene changing to a myrtle.

GNAIOS.   *Amethyst.*

Myrene was a priestess of Venus, who violated her duty by giving her hand to a young man who had saved her from danger, and who was struck dead by Venus for thus profaning her priesthood.

No. 120.

Venus Victrix.

GNAIOS.   *Amethyst.*

Venus armed, known under that name.   She was worshipped at Lacedæmon to comme-morate the victory gained by the Spartan women over the Messenians.   It is this figure which Julius Cæsar took for his seal.

> " To thee all human passions yield,
> However strong their hold ;
> For thee ambition quits the field,
> And avarice leaves his gold."

> " Great Love ! thy empire o'er the world extends ;
> To thy soft charms the whole creation bends ;
> On hills, in streams, through all the rolling main,
> The leafy forest and the grassy plain,
> Thy kindling warmth the various nations find,
> And rush with joy to generate their kind."
>
> LUCRETIUS, book i.

No. 121.

Cupid stung by a bee shews his wounded finger to Venus.

GNAIOS.   *Amethyst.*

> " Once as Cupid, tir'd with play,
> On a bed of roses lay,
> A rude bee, that slipt unseen
> The sweet-breathing buds between,

> Stung his finger, cruel chance !
> With its little pointed lance.
> Straight he fills the air with cries,
> Weeps, and sobs, and runs, and flies ;

Till the god to Venus came,
Lovely laughter-loving dame;
Then he thus began to plain:
' Oh! undone—I die with pain!
Dear mamma, a serpent small,
Which a bee the ploughmen call,
Imp'd with wings and arm'd with dart,
Oh!—has stung me to the heart.'

Venus thus replied, and smil'd:
' Dry those tears, for shame, my child:
If a bee can wound so deep,
Causing Cupid thus to weep,
Think, O think, what cruel pains
He that's stung by thee sustains.' "

ANACREON: FAWKES'S *Trans.*

No. 122.

Psyche contemplating the murder of Cupid.

PEMALLIO. *Oriental Cornelian.*

Psyche had the imprudence to boast to her sisters that Cupid loved her; and they, being jealous, made her believe that Cupid had deceived her. Indignant at this, she takes a dagger to kill him whilst asleep; but her pity being excited when gazing on him, she changes her purpose.

" Venus has call'd her winged child,
  And with malicious pleasure laugh'd
That boy, who lawless, wicked, wild,
  At random aims the flaming shaft.

Him who all deeds of darkness owns,
  Who breaks so oft the nuptial tie,
And, whilst his luckless victim groans,
  On careless pinions flutters by.

The dangerous power to Psyche's bower
  She with vindictive fury led,
And bade him thus his vengeance shower
  On the detested virgin's head:

  ' By a mother's sacred name,
    By thine arrows tipp'd with flame,
    By thy joys, which often borrow
    Of despair most bitter sorrow,

Make thy parent's rival know
Unimaginable woe!
May her youth's unequall'd bloom
Unrequited love consume,
For some wretch of abject birth,
Wandering outcast of the earth;
Be for him her fond heart torn,
May e'en he her torments scorn;
That all womankind may see
What it is to injure me.
Make thy parent's rival know
Unimaginable woe.'

Then kiss'd her son, and fleet as wind
  She seeks old Ocean's dark green caves;
Her ivory feet, with roses twin'd,
  Brush lightly o'er the trembling waves."

APULEIUS.

" Allow'd to settle on celestial eyes,
Soft sleep exulting now exerts his sway,
From Psyche's anxious pillow gladly flies,
To veil those orbs, whose pure and lambent ray
The powers of heaven submissively obey.

Trembling and breathless, then, she softly rose,
And seiz'd the lamp, where it obscurely lay—
With hand too rashly daring to disclose
The sacred veil which hung mysterious o'er her
woes.

Twice as with agitated step she went,
The lamp expiring shone with doubtful gleam,
As though it waru'd her from her rash intent;
And twice she paus'd, and on its trembling
   beam
Gaz'd with suspended breath, while voices seem,
With murmuring sound, along the roof to sigh;
As one just waking from a troublous dream,
With palpitating heart and straining eye,
Still fix'd with fear remains, still thinks the
   danger nigh.

O daring Muse! wilt thou indeed essay
To paint the wonders which that lamp could
   shew?
And canst thou hope in living words to say
The dazzling glories of that heavenly view?
Ah, well I ween that if with pencil true
That splendid vision could be well exprest,
The fearful awe imprudent Psyche knew
Would seize with rapture every wond'ring
   breast,
When Love's all-potent charms divinely stood
   confest.

All imperceptible to human touch,
His wings display celestial essence light;
The clear effulgence of the blaze is such,
The brilliant plumage shines so heavenly bright,
That mortal eyes turn dazzl'd from the sight:
A youth he seems in manhood's freshest years;
Round his fair neck as clinging with delight
Each golden curl resplendently appears,
Or shades his darker brow, which grace majestic
   wears.

The friendly curtain of indulgent sleep
Disclos'd not yet his eyes' resistless sway;
But from their silky veil there seem'd to peep
Some brilliant glances with a soften'd ray,
Which o'er his features exquisitely play,
And all his polish'd limbs suffuse with light.
Thus through some narrow space the azure day,
Sudden its cheerful rays diffusing bright,
Wide darts its lucid beams to gild the brow of
   night.

His fatal arrows and celestial bow
Beside the couch were negligently thrown;
Nor needs the god his dazzling arms to show
His glorious birth, such beauty round him
   shone
As sure could spring from Beauty's self alone:
The bloom which glowed o'er all of soft desire
Could well proclaim him Beauty's cherish'd
   son;
And Beauty's self will oft these charms admire,
And steal his touching smile, his glance's living
   fire.

Speechless with awe, in transport strangely lost,
Long Psyche stood with fix'd adoring eye,
Her limbs immovable, her senses tost
Between amazement, fear, and ecstacy,
She hangs enamour'd o'er the deity,
Till from her trembling hand extinguish'd falls
The fatal lamp—he starts—and suddenly
Tremendous thunders echo through the halls,
While ruin's hideous crash bursts o'er the af-
   frighted walls."

TIGHE.

No. 123.

Psyche propitiating Ceres.

GNAIOS. *Oriental Cornelian.*

Psyche having lost Cupid, who has been taken from her by Venus, undertakes a long and painful journey to recover him. Arriving at a field consecrated to Ceres, she gathers some ears of corn and offers them to Ceres, praying her to indicate where Cupid might be found.

" Now four long tedious moons are spent,
 She hears no tidings of her lord,
Yet still her wandering steps are bent
 In search of him her soul adored.

She pray'd at Ceres' corn-wreath'd shrine,
 And Juno's altar deck'd with flowers;
But, sternly bound by pact divine,
 No succour lend the pitying powers.

Till, wearied by unnumber'd woes,
 And render'd valiant by despair,
She to the Murtian temple goes—
 Perchance her true love tarries there.

O, turn thee from the perilous way!
 Ah! wherefore work thine own annoy?
Yon priestess, Custom, marks her prey,
 And eyes thee with malignant joy.

Instant she on her victim springs,
 She mocks the unavailing prayer,

Furious her wither'd hand enwrings,
 And drags her by her flowing hair.

Then laughing Venus bids them speed,
 Her handmaids on the pavement throw
Of all the flowering plants the seed
 That in the Hesperian gardens blow.

And she must each assort before
 The dewfall shall the damp grass steep,
While sentry at the chamber-door
 Solicitude and Sorrow keep.

A little ant the mandate heard,
 The oppressive mandate, with disdain;
For e'en the weakest, 'tis averr'd,
 Will on the oppressor turn again.

And insect myriads never ceas'd
 Their labours till the setting sun;
When Venus, rising from the feast,
 With wonder saw the hard task done."
                              APULEIUS.

No. 124.

Psyche and Pan.

GNAIOS. *Amethyst.*

Psyche, in despair at not being able to find Cupid, throws herself into the river, the tutelary god of which conveys her to the bank; Pan finding her there, consoles her, and indicates the means of recovering Cupid.

" In vapoury twilight damp and chill
 The languid star fades pale away,
The high peak of the distant hill
 Is gilded by the gleams of day:

And who is that distracted fair
 Reclined beneath yon spreading yew?
Swoln are her eyes, her dark brown hair
 Is pearly with the morning dew;

Her spring of life now seems to flag,
 In wild delirium now she raves—
O, see! from that o'er-jutting crag,
 She plunges in the foaming waves!

But he who o'er the stream presides
 The frantic girl in pity bore,
Quick darting through his billowy tides,
 In safety to the opposing shore.

There in a bower with wood-moss lin'd,
  With violets blue and cowslips gay,
Old Pan, by Canna's side reclin'd,
  Sung many a rustic roundelay.

While, wandering from his heedless eyes,
  His white goats crop the neighbouring brake,
The god in this unfashion'd guise
  With no ungentle feelings spake:

  'Sweet girl! though rural is the air
  That I the king of shepherds wear,
  As assay'd silver, tried, and sage,
  And prudent are the words of age.

Then list, O list, sweet girl, to me:
  By my divining power I see,
  Both from thy often-reeling pace,
And from thy pale and haggard face,
And from thy deep and frequent sigh,
  While grief hangs heavy on thine eye,
That all the ills thou'rt doom'd to prove
Are judgments of the god of love.
Then list, O list, sweet girl, to me:
  Seek not by death thy soul to free;
But cast thy cares, thy griefs away;
  To Cupid without ceasing pray;
  And soon that soft, luxurious boy
  Will tune anew thy mind to joy.'"

APULEIUS.

No. 125.

Psyche giving the soporific cake to Cerberus.

GNAIOS. *Cornelian.*

Venus commanded Psyche to descend to the kingdom of Pluto to ask Proserpine for a box, in which some of her charms were enclosed.

"'Can beauty no compassion know?
  Sure mercy must her bright beams dart,
And piercing through those hills of snow,
  Melt e'en the adamantine heart.

Ah, no! by Venus' stern command
  Psyche to Proserpine is sped;
Shivering she seeks the dreary land,
  The sunless mansions of the dead.

The unopen'd casket she must bring,
  Whose weak and fragile sides entomb,
From beauty's uncreated spring,
  The essence of eternal bloom.

Fearful and sad she journey'd on,
  While silence rul'd the midnight hour,
To where the unsteady moonbeam shone
  Reflected from a ruin'd tower.

And thence she heard these warning notes,
  Caroll'd as clear as clear might be,
Sweet as the mermaid's lay that floats
  Melodious on the charmed sea:

'Sunk her spirit, whelm'd in woe,
  Does the royal captive go?
  Does her heart, oppress'd with dread,
  Shudder to approach the dead?
Where the cavern yawns around,
Enter there the dark profound;
Soon thy path a crippled ass,
By a cripple led, shall pass,
Fainting they beneath their task,
He assistance oft will ask;
But in these infernal lands
Touch not with unhallow'd hands;
Cautious thou, without delay
Onward, onward, speed thy way.

In old Charon's creaking boat,
O'er the dead stream thou must float;
There the livid corse thou'lt see
Stretch his blue swoln hand to thee;
Frown thou on his suit severe,
Mercy were destruction here!
See those crones that on the left
Weave the many-colour'd weft,
See them, how they this way wend,
Asking thee thy aid to lend;
But in these infernal lands
Touch not with unhallow'd hands;
Cautious thou, without delay
Onward, onward, speed thy way.
Dip the sop in hydromel,
Charm the three-neck'd dog of hell;

Then from her imperial seat
Thee the shadowy queen shall greet,
Shall for thee the feast prepare;
Thou that feast refuse to share;
But upon the pavement spread
Take the black and mouldy bread.
By the queen soon set at large,
Back now bear thy precious charge:
Over all thy curious mind
In the chains of prudence bind,
Nor the strict command infringe,
Move not thou the golden hinge.
Gladsome then, without delay,
Onward, onward, speed thy way.'"

APULEIUS.

No. 126.

The eagle of Jove giving the vase of black water to Psyche.

GNAIOS. *Amethyst.*

" No grace with Venus can she find,
Her stony heart no pity warms,
    Another trial waits behind.

' Down from that cloud-capp'd mountain's
        brow
    A never-ceasing cataract pours,
Whose feathery surges dash below
    In thunder on the Stygian shores.

Thou on the dangerous brink must stand,
    And dip this goblet in the spring;
Descending then with steady hand,
    The black transparent crystal bring.'

Nimbly the mountain-steep she'd climb,
    But thence impervious rocks arise,
Whose awful foreheads frown sublime,
    And lift their bold crags to the skies;

While horrid voices howl around,
    ' Fly!—swiftly fly!'—' Forbear, forbear!'—
Vast stones, with heart-appalling sound,
    Are hurl'd into the groaning air.

And on the right and on the left
    Four ever-watchful dragons fly,
Flame-breathing through each dizzy cleft
    Their long and flexile necks they ply.

Though beauty's queen no pity feels,
    The bold rapacious bird of Jove
His succour to the afflicted deals,
    In reverence to the god of love.

He sees her blasted hopes expire,
    He leaves the liquid fields of light,
And whirling round in many a gyre,
    Majestic wings his rapid flight.

High o'er the dragons see him tower,
  Up-darting through the azure air,
And high above the stony shower
  The bowl his crooked talons bear.

Now to the grateful maid he brings
  The sparkling waters bright and clear;
Then spreads again his ample wings,
  And soaring quits this nether sphere."

APULEIUS.

No. 127.

Psyche receiving the casket of perfumes from Proserpine.

DIOSCORIDES. *Amethyst.*

No. 128.

Psyche with the casket of perfume received from Proserpine.

GNAIOS. *Amethyst.*

At the same time that Psyche obtained the casket from Proserpine, a voice warned her not to open it; but after she had quitted the infernal regions, she could no longer restrain her curiosity.

" She has seen the secrets of the deep,
  And through o'erwhelming horrors past;
How her recovering pulses leap,
  To hail the day-star gleams at last!

' Do I then bear eternal bloom
  Alone to make my tyrant shine?
Say, rather let its tints illume
  These wan and woe-worn cheeks of mine;

Whilst I will revel in the rays
  Of beauty in the casket hid.'
Alas! no beam of beauty plays
  Delightful from the lifted lid;

But from the empty casket sprang
  Of Stygian fogs the baleful breath,
And heavy o'er her blanch'd frame hang
  The damp unwholesome hues of death."

APULEIUS.

No. 129.

Psyche presenting the casket to Venus, which appeases her anger and extinguishes her jealousy.

GNAIOS. *Oriental Cornelian.*

" So have I often seen a purple flow'r,
  Fainting through heat, hang down her drooping head;
But soon refreshed with a welcome show'r,
  Begins again her lively beauties spread,

And with new pride her silken leaves display;
And, while the sun doth now more gentle play,
Lays out her swelling bosom to the day."

PH. FL. P. I.

" ' Psyche, thou hardly hast my favour won,'
With rosy smile, her heavenly parent cried;
' Yet hence thy charms, immortal, deified,
With the young Joys, thy future offspring fair,
Shall bloom for ever at thy lover's side.
All-ruling Jove's high mandate I declare:
Blest denizen of heaven! arise, its joy to share.' "

TIGHE.

No. 130.

Mercury, commanded by Jupiter, bringing Psyche back to Olympus.

GNAIOS. *Cornelian.*

Psyche, according to the idea formed of her by the ancients, combines all that is most perfect in grace, beauty, and youth.

"The fields of nature to deform,
 Not always drives the furious blast;
And shall misfortune's moral storm
 'Gainst meek endurance ever last?

No, though unnumber'd ills assail—
 Though man behold no succour nigh—
Though, with the frailest of the frail,
 Presumption tempt the prying eye—

Yet, if the germ of virtue live,
 Let constant faith her sufferings brave;
Goodness is powerful to forgive,
 And Heaven omnipotent to save.

Cupid, with downcast, humbled mien,
 Has to the Thunderer breath'd his care;
The almighty father smil'd serene,
 And granted his adorer's prayer.

Now flies he joyful to her aid:
 He gently rais'd her falling head,
With his bright arrow touch'd the maid,
 And rous'd her from her cheerless bed.

He animates anew her charms,
 Warm o'er her breathes the light of love,
Then bears her in his circling arms,
 And stands before the throne of Jove.

But on the sovereign of the skies,
 What fleshly optics dare to gaze?
And Psyche, with averted eyes,
 Shrinks trembling from th' excessive blaze.

Till Hebe raising to her lips
 The ambrosial goblet foaming high,
Wrapt in ecstatic trance, she sips
 The fount of immortality.

k

Purpled with roses dance the Hours;
 The Graces, scattering odours, play;
And crown'd with never-fading flowers,
 The Muses hymn the jocund lay.

And onwards up the ethereal arch
 Glad Hymen leads the festive train,
As o'er the rainbow's hues they march,
 And links them in his golden chain.

While soon, to bless the faithful pair,
 With eye of laughter, soul of flame,
Burst into life a daughter fair,
 And Pleasure was the infant's name."

APULEIUS.

No. 131.

Psyche transported by Zephyr to a grove, and placed in the arms of Cupid.

PYRGOTELES.   Oriental Cornelian.

" Two tapers thus, with pure, converging rays,
 In momentary flash their beams unite,
Shedding but one inseparable blaze
Of blended radiance and effulgence bright,
Self-lost in mutual intermingling light.
Thus in her lover's circling arms embrac'd,
The fainting Psyche's soul, by sudden flight,
 With his, its subtlest essence, interlaced :
Oh! bliss too vast for thought, by words how poorly trac'd!"

TIGHE.

" But far above, in spangled sheen,
 Celestial Cupid, her fam'd son, advanc'd,
Holds his dear Psyche sweet entranc'd,
After her wandering labours long,
Till free consent the gods among
Makes her his eternal bride;
And from her fair unspotted side
Two blissful twins are to be born,
Youth and Joy, so Jove hath sworn."

Comus.

No. 132.

Head of Psyche.

ASPASIOS. *Amethyst.*

"Choice nymph! the crown of chaste Diana's
    train,
Thou beauty's lily, set in heav'nly earth,
Thy fairs unpattern'd, all perfection stain:
    Sure heav'n, with curious pencil, at thy birth
In thy rare face her own full picture drew:
It is a strong verse here to write, but true—
Hyperboles in others are but half thy due.

Upon her forehead Love his trophies fits,
    A thousand spoils in silver arch displaying;
And in the midst himself full proudly sits,
    Himself in awful majesty arraying:
Upon her brows lies his bent ebon bow,
And ready shafts; deadly those weapons show,
Yet sweet the death appear'd, lovely that deadly
    blow."

PH. FL. P. I.

"O Love! to vernal sweets, to summer's air,
To bow'rs which temper sultry suns at noon,
Art thou confin'd? to rills in lulling flow,
To flow'rs which scent thy arbours of recess,
To birds who sing of youth and soft desire?
All is thy empire, ev'ry season thine,
Thou universal origin of things,
Sole ruler, oft a tyrant."

Athenaid.

"Monarch Love! resistless boy,
With whom the rosy queen of joy,
And nymphs that glance ethereal blue,
Disporting tread the mountain dew;
Propitious, oh! receive my sighs,
Which, burning with entreaty, rise,
That thou wilt whisper to the breast
Of her I love thy soft behest;
And counsel her to learn from thee
The lesson thou hast taught to me.
Ah! if my heart no flattery tell,
Thou 'lt own I've learn'd that lesson well."

ANACREON, MOORE.

"They sin who tell us love can die :
  With life all other passions fly,
  All others are but vanity.
In heaven ambition cannot dwell,
  Nor avarice in the vault of hell ;
  Earthly, these passions of the earth,
  They perish where they had their birth ;
  But love is indestructible.

Its holy flame for ever burneth,
  From heav'n it came, to heav'n returneth.
Too oft on earth a troubled guest,
  At times deceived, at times distress'd,
It here is tried and purified :
  It hath in heaven its perfect rest.
It soweth here with toil and care,
  But the harvest-time of love is *there*."

              SOUTHEY.

No. 133.

Minerva springing from the head of Jupiter, which Vulcan opens with a blow of his axe.

GNAIOS.   *Oriental Cornelian.*

" That blissful island where a wondrous cloud
  Once rain'd, at Jove's command, a golden
    shower ;
What time, assisted by the Lemnian god,
  The king of heaven brought forth the virgin
    power.

By Vulcan's art the father's teeming head
  Was open'd wide, and forth impetuous
    sprung,
And shouted fierce and loud, the warrior maid :
  Old mother earth and heaven affrighted rung.

Then Hyperion's son, pure fount of day,
  Did to his children the strange tale reveal;
He warn'd them straight the sacrifice to slay,
  And worship the young power with earliest
    zeal.

So would they soothe the mighty father's mind,
  Pleas'd with the honours to his daughter paid ;

And so propitious ever would they find
  Minerva, warlike formidable maid.

On staid precaution, vigilant and wise,
  True virtue and true happiness depend ;
But oft oblivion's darkening clouds arise,
  And from the destin'd scope our purpose
    bend.

The Rhodians, mindful of their sire's behest,
  Straight in the citadel an altar rear'd ;
But with imperfect rites the power address'd,
  And without fire their sacrifice prepar'd.

Yet Jove approving o'er th' assembly spread
  A yellow cloud, that dropp'd with golden
    dews ;
While in their opening hearts the blue-eyed
    maid
Deign'd her celestial science to infuse."

       PINDAR: WEST'S *Trans.*

" And now the king of gods, Jove, Metis led,
  The wisest fair one, to the genial bed ;

Who with the blue-ey'd virgin fruitful proves,
Minerva pledge of their celestial loves.

The sire, from what kind earth and heav'n re-
veal'd,
Artful the matron in himself conceal'd ;
From her it was decreed a race should rise
That would usurp the kingdom of the skies.
And first the virgin, with her azure eyes,
Equal in strength, and as her father wise,

Is born, the offspring of th' almighty's brain.
And Metis by the god conceiv'd again,
A son decreed to reign o'er heav'n and earth,
Had not the sire destroy'd the mighty birth :
He made the goddess in himself reside,
To be in ev'ry act th' eternal guide."

HESIOD, *Theog.*

" Thus she spoke,
And speaking gave the nod : her nod is fate !
Since Jove of all his daughters this high gift
To Pallas only granted, that his pow'r,
Even all her father's glories, she might bear.
No mother bore the goddess, but the head
Of sov'reign Jove. O virgins ! to whate'er
The head of Jove shall give the awful nod,
It stands unalterably sure ; and thus
The nod of Pallas is the stamp of fate."

CALLIMACHUS.

" He from his head disclos'd himself to birth
The blue-eyed maid, Tritonian Pallas ; fierce
Rousing the war-field's tumult ; unsubdued ;
Leader of armies ; awful ; whom delight
The shout of battle and the shock of war.
. . . . Minerva rose, leader of hosts,
Resembling Pallas when she would array
The marshall'd battle. In her grasp the spear,
And on her brows a golden helm : athwart
Her shoulders thrown her ægis."

HESIOD.

No. 134.

Minerva destroying the Gorgon.

APOLLONIDES. *Sardonyx.*

Ægis, a monster born of the Earth, who vomited fire and flame. She desolated Phrygia
and Mount Caucasus, destroying the forests from India and Phœnicia to Egypt and Libya.

Minerva, commanded by Jupiter, fought the monster, killed her, and taking her skin, covered her shield with it, which was thence called *Ægide*. To it she added the head of Medusa.

"Why plagues like these infect the Libyan air;
Why deaths unknown in various shapes appear;
Why, fruitful to destroy, the cursed land
Is temper'd thus by nature's secret hand,—
Dark and obscure the hidden cause remains,
And still deludes the vain inquirer's pains;
Unless a tale for truth may be believ'd,
And the good-natur'd world be willingly deceiv'd.

Where western waves on farthest Libya beat,
Warm'd with the setting sun's descending heat,
Dreadful Medusa fix'd her horrid seat.
No leafy shade with kind protection shields
The rough, the squalid, unfrequented fields;
No mark of shepherds, or the ploughman's toil,
To tend the flocks, or turn the mellow soil;
But rude with rocks, the region all around
Its mistress and her potent visage own'd.
'Twas from this monster, to afflict mankind,
That nature first produc'd the snaky kind;
On her at first their forky tongues appear'd,
From her their dreadful hissings first were heard.
Some wreath'd in folds upon her temples hung;
Some backwards to her waist depended long;
Some with their rising crests her forehead deck;
Some wanton play, and lash her swelling neck:
And while her hands the curling vipers comb,
Poisons distil around, and drops of livid foam.

None who beheld the fury could complain,
So swift their fate, preventing death and pain.
Ere they had time to fear, the change came on,
And motion, sense, and life, were lost in stone.
The soul itself, from sudden flight debarr'd,
Congealing, in the body's fortune shar'd.

The dire Eumenides could rage inspire,
But could no more; the tuneful Thracian lyre
Infernal Cerberus did soon assuage,
Lull'd him to rest, and sooth'd his triple rage;
Hydra's seven heads the bold Alcides view'd,
Safely he saw, and what he saw subdu'd:
Of these in various terrors each excell'd,
But all to this superior fury yield.
Phorcus and Ceto—next to Neptune he,
Immortal both, and rulers of the sea,
This monster's parents—did their offspring dread,
And from her sight her sister gorgons fled.
Old ocean's waters and the liquid air,
The universal world, her power might fear:
All nature's beauteous works she could invade,
Through every part a lazy numbness shed,
And over all a stony surface spread.
Birds in their flight were stopt, and ponderous grown,
Forgot their pinions, and fell senseless down.
Beasts to the rocks were fix'd, and all around
Were tribes of stone and marble nations found.
No living eyes so fell a sight could bear;
Her snakes themselves, all deadly though they were,
Shot backward from her face, and shrunk away for fear.
By her a rock Titanian Atlas grew,
And heav'n by her the giants did subdue.
Hard was the fight, and Jove was half dismay'd,
Till Pallas brought the gorgon to his aid.
The heavenly nation laid aside their fear,
For soon she finish'd the prodigious war;
To mountains turu'd the monster race remains,
The trophies of her power on the Phlegræan plains."

LUCAN: ROWE's *Trans.*

No. 135.

Minerva killing Pallas, the most ferocious of the Titans, who dared to make war against Jupiter.

CHROMIOS. *Oriental Cornelian.*

It is supposed that after this victory Minerva was also known by the name of Pallas.

No. 136.

Minerva and the giant Pallas.

CHROMIOS. *Sardonyx.*

No. 137.

Minerva having shewn Pallas the head of Medusa, he was immediately turned to stone. Demastor, the companion of Pallas, and fierce as he, raised him from the earth, and hurled him at the gods.

CHROMIOS. *Oriental Amethyst.*

No. 138.

Minerva shaking with her lance Mount Etna, under which Enceladus lies crushed.

SOLON. *Oriental Cornelian.*

" Enceladus, they say, transfix'd by Jove,
With blasted limbs came trembling from above ;
And where he fell, th' avenging father drew
This flaming hill, and on his body threw.
As often as he turns his weary sides,
He shakes the solid isle, and smoke the heavens hides."
Æn. iii.

But he, Vulcanian monster, to the clouds
  The fiercest, hottest inundations throws;
While with the burden of incumbent woods
  And Ætna's gloomy cliffs o'erwhelm'd he
    glows.
There on his flinty bed outstretch'd he lies,
  Whose pointed rock his tossing carcase
    wounds;

There with dismay he strikes beholding eyes,
  Or frights the distant ear with horrid
    sounds.
O save us from thy wrath, Sicilian Jove!
Thou that here reign'st, ador'd in Ætna's sacred
    grove!
                    PINDAR, *Pyth.*: WEST'S *Trans.*

" Him too, the dweller of Cilicia's caves,
I saw—with pity saw—Earth's monstrous son,
With all his hundred heads, subdued by Force,
The furious Typhon, who 'gainst all the gods
Made war. His horrid jaws, with serpent-hiss,
Breath'd slaughter; from his eyes the gorgon
    glare
Of baleful lightnings flash'd, as his proud force
Would rend from Jove his empire of the sky.
But him the vengeful bolt, instinct with fire,
Smote sore, and dash'd him from his haughty
    vaunts,
Pierc'd through his soul, and wither'd all his
    strength.

Thus stretch'd out, huge in length, beneath the
    roots
Of Ætna, near Trinacria's narrow sea,
Astonied, blasted, spiritless he lies;
On whose high summit Vulcan holds his seat,
And forms the glowing mass. In times to come,
Hence streams of torrent-fire, with hideous roar,
Shall burst, and with its wasteful mouths devour
All the fair fields of fruitful Sicily.
Such rage shall Typhon, blasted as he is
With Jove's fierce lightning, pour incessant forth
In smoking whirlwinds and tempestuous flame."
                    ÆSCHYLUS, POTTER.

" What oceans shall he (Ulysses) search? what lands explore?
  First shall he see the rocks whose weight oppress
  Stern Typhon's blasted limbs."
                    LYCOPHRON.

No. 139.

Minerva animating the Human Figure formed in clay by Prometheus.

CHROMIOS. *Oriental Cornelian.*

" The nobler creature, with a mind possess'd,
Was wanting yet, that should command the rest.
That maker, the best world's original,
Either him fram'd of seed celestial;
Or earth, which late he did from heav'n divide,
Some sacred seeds retain'd to heaven allied;
Which with the living stream Prometheus mix'd,
And in that artificial structure fix'd

The form of all th' all-ruling deities.
And whereas others see with downcast eyes,
He with a lofty look did man indue,
And bade him heav'n's transcendant glories
    view.
So that rude clay, which had no form before,
Thus chang'd, of man the unknown figure bore.
                    OVID, *Met.*: SANDYS' *Trans.*

" No laws, or human or divine,
Can the presumptuous race of man confine :
Thus from the sun's ethereal beam,
When bold Prometheus stole th' enlivening flame,
Of fevers dire a ghastly brood,
Till then unknown, th' unhappy fraud pursued ;
On earth their horrors baleful spread,
And the pale monarch of the dead,
Till then slow-moving to his prey,
Precipitately rapid swept his way."

HOR. book i. Od. 3 : FRANCIS.

No. 140.

Minerva teaching Murmes, a young girl whom she loved for her chastity, the art of making the plough.

ALLION. *Oriental Amethyst.*

" She first, white Peace, the earth with ploughshares broke,
And bent the oxen to the crooked yoke;
First rear'd the vine, and hoarded first with care
The father's vintage for his drunken heir."

TIBUL. book i. *El.* 10.

No. 141.

Murmes, wanting in gratitude to Minerva, is changed by her to an ant.

GNAIOS. *Oriental Amethyst.*

No. 142.

Arachne metamorphosed by Minerva into a spider.

DIOSCORIDES. *Oriental Cornelian.*

Arachne, the daughter of Idmon, a dyer of Lydia, who was very skilful at embroidery, dared to challenge Minerva to try which could work the best piece of tapestry.

" Whether the shapeless wool in balls she wound,
Or with quick motion turu'd the spindle round,
Or with her pencil drew the neat design,
Pallas, her mistress, shone in every line.

This the proud maid with scornful air denies,
And e'en the goddess at her work defies ;
Disowns her heav'nly mistress ev'ry hour,
Nor asks her aid, nor deprecates her pow'r :—

Let us (she cries) but to a trial come;
And if she conquers, let her fix my doom.

.   .   .   .   .

Straight to their posts appointed both repair,
And fix their threaded looms with equal care:
Around the solid beam the web is tied,
While hollow canes the parting warp divide,
Through which, with nimble flight, the shuttles
    play,
And for the woof prepare a ready way;
The woof and warp unite, press'd by the toothy
    slay.

.   .   .   .   .

This the bright goddess, passionately mov'd,
With envy saw, yet inwardly approv'd.
The scene of heav'nly guilt with haste she tore,
Nor longer the affront with patience bore;
A boxen shuttle in her hand she took,
And more than once Arachne's forehead struck.

Th' unhappy maid, impatient of the wrong,
Down from a beam her injur'd person hung;
When Pallas, pitying her wretched state,
At once prevented and pronounc'd her fate:—
Live, but depend, vile wretch, (the goddess
    cried,)
Doom'd in suspense for ever to be tied;
That all your race, to utmost date of time,
May feel the vengeance, and detest the crime.
    Then, going off, she sprinkled her with juice
Which leaves of baleful aconite produce.
Touch'd with the pois'nous drug, her flowing hair
Fell to the ground, and left her temples bare;
Her usual features vanish'd from their place,
Her body lessen'd all, but most her face;
Her slender fingers, hanging on each side
With many joints, the use of legs supplied;
A spider's bag the rest, from which she gives
A thread, and still by constant weaving lives."
                                        OVID.

No. 143.

The naming of Athens.

PYRGOTELES.   *Oriental Cornelian.*

In the dispute between Pallas and Neptune as to which should give a name to the city built by Cecrops, the gods decided that it should bear the name of whichsoever of the divinities gave it the most useful present. Neptune upon this struck the ground with his trident, and a horse appeared—the emblem of war. Pallas, with her lance, caused an olive-tree in blossom—the symbol of peace—to spring from the earth. The city took the name of *Athens* from Minerva.

' On lofty thrones twice six celestials sate,
  Jove in the midst, and held their warm debate;
  The subject weighty, and well known to fame,
  From whom the city should receive its name.
  Each god by proper features was exprest:
  Jove with majestic mien excell'd the rest;
  His three-fork'd mace the dewy sea-god shook,
  And, looking sternly, smote the ragged rock,
  When from the stone leapt forth a sprightly
      steed,
  And Neptune claims the city for the deed.

Minerva, with a glittering spear,
And crested helm that veil'd her braided hair,
With shield and scaly breastplate, implements
    of war,
Struck with her pointed lance the teeming
    earth,
Seemed to produce a new surprising birth,
When from the glebe the pledge of conquest
    sprung,
A tree pale green with fairest olives hung."

" Twice six celestials sit enthron'd on high,
Replete with awe-infusing gravity;
Jove in the midst: the seated figures took
Their lively forms; Jove had a royal look:
The sea-god stood, and with his trident strake
The cleaving rock, from whence a charger
    brake,
Whereon he grounds his claim. With spear
    and shield

Minerva arms; her head a murrion steel'd,
Her breast her ægis guards; her lance the
    ground
With force doth strike, and from that pregnant
    wound
The hoary olive, charged with fruit, ascends.
The gods admire: with victory she ends."

SANDYS' OVID.

No. 144.

Minerva playing the flute.

GNAIOS. *Amethyst.*

Minerva, the patroness of the arts and sciences, was that of music also. She invented the flute, and played on it so skilfully as to delight both men and gods; but on discovering one day that her features were much distorted while playing on this instrument, she threw it away. Pan found it, and became a very expert player on it. This stone represents Minerva blowing the flute, and Pan, at some distance, listening with attention.

" The maid armipotent, that dreadful pow'r
Who drives th' embattled host and shakes the solid tow'r,
Laid by her spear and all her war-attire,
Now mildly mixes with the softer quire;
The horror of her helm, the warrior's pride,
Wreathes of fair roses innocently hide;
She shines with peaceful decoration dress'd,
And flow'rs nod harmless from her lofty crest."

CLAUDIAN: HUGHES.

No. 145.

Minerva, appearing in a dream to Pericles, indicates a salutary plant to him to cure a workman who had fallen from the edifice of the Areopagus, which was being erected under his inspection.

CHROMIOS. *Oriental Cornelian.*

It is believed that this fact gave rise to the epithet *Medica,* sometimes added to that of Minerva; and to her worship under this title at Athens, and since at Rome.

No. 146.

Minerva with her principal attributes, the olive-branch and owl.

DIOSCORIDES. *Oriental Cornelian.*

" Next day but one Minerva's feast revives,
The which from those five days the name derives.
The first no blood nor sword-play doth admit,
Because Minerva was brought forth in it ;
The four next days the scaffolds all are fill'd —
This warlike queen delights in weapons skill'd.
Come, boys and maids, your gifts to Pallas bring ;
Her favour gives great skill in every thing.
In Pallas' favour let the lasses learn
To empty distaffs and to twist their yarn ;
She also learns to make the shuttle play
About the web, and how to fill the slay.
Fullers and dyers give her honour both —
You that do white, and you that dye the cloth.

No shoemaker a shoe can fashion well
Without her help, though Tychius he excel.
He that Epeus shames in carpentry,
Becomes a dunce if Pallas angry be.
And you physicians that diseases cure,
Salute this lady with some gifts of your.
Dull scholars, curb'd in curst schoolmasters' lore,
Your wits she quickens — honour her, therefore.
Ye that mete heaven, and ye that pencils use,
And he that stones to curious statues hews.
A thousand arts she skills. She verse doth favour :
Inspire my song, if I may ask that favour."

OVID's *Fasti:* GOWER's *Trans.*

No. 147.

Latona and her two children in presence of Neptune descending from his car.

APOLLONIDES. *Oriental Cornelian.*

Latona, daughter of the Titan Cœus and his sister Phœbe, was beloved by Jupiter, who made her the mother of Apollo and Diana. Juno, jealous of her, drove her from Olympus ; and made the earth swear not to grant her an asylum for the birth of her expected offspring. Neptune took pity on Latona ; and from the depths of the sea he caused to spring up the island of Delos, where Apollo and Diana first saw the light.

" Cœus the Titan's vagrant progeny ;
To whom, in travail, the whole spacious earth
No room afforded for her spurious birth.
Not the least part in earth, in heav'n, or seas,
Would grant your outlaw'd goddess any ease ;
Till pitying hers from his own wand'ring case,
Delos, the floating island, gave a place.
There she a mother was, of two at most."

OVID.

No. 148.

Latona seated under a palm-tree, with her infants Apollo and Diana.

PYRGOTELES. *Amethyst.*

" In mingled joy with ægis-wielding Jove,
Latona bore the arrow-shooting Dian,
And Phœbus, loveliest of the heavenly tribe."
HESIOD.

No. 149.

The Lycian peasants turned into frogs.

APOLLONIDES. *Oriental Cornelian.*

Latona, not considering herself secure at Delos, left it with her children; and after a long voyage, landed on the shores of Lycia. Tormented with thirst, she began to drink some water from a marsh, when some malicious peasants, concealing themselves, attempted to disturb the waters.

" Hence, too, she fled the furious step-dame's
    pow'r,
And in her arms a double godhead bore;
And now the borders of fair Lycia gain'd,
Just when the summer solstice parch'd the land.
With thirst the goddess languishing, no more
Her empty'd breast would yield its milky store;
When from below the smiling valley shew'd
A silver lake that in its bottom flow'd:
A sort of clowns were reaping; near the bank,
The bending osier and the bulrush dank,
The cress, and water-lily, fragrant weed,
Whose juicy stalk the liquid fountains feed.
The goddess came, and, kneeling on the brink,
Stoop'd at the fresh repast, prepar'd to drink.
Then thus, being hinder'd by the rabble race,
In accents mild expostulates the case:
    Water I only ask, and sure 'tis hard
From nature's common rights to be debarr'd.
This, as the genial sun and vital air,
Should flow alike to ev'ry creature's share;

Yet still I ask, and as a favour crave,
That which a public bounty nature gave.
Nor do I seek my weary limbs to drench,
Only with one cool draught my thirst I'd
    quench.
Now from my throat the usual moisture dries,
And e'en my voice in broken accents dies;
One draught as dear as life I should esteem,
And water, now I thirst, would nectar seem.
Oh! let my little babes your pity move,
And melt your hearts to charitable love;
They (as by chance they did) extend to you
Their little hands, and my request pursue!
    Whom would these soft persuasions not subdue,
Though the most rustic and unmanner'd crew?
Yet they the goddess's request refuse,
And with rude words reproachfully abuse;
Nay more, with spiteful feet the villains trod
O'er the soft bottom of the marshy flood,
And blacken'd all the lake with clouds of rising
    mud.

Her thirst by indignation was suppress'd ;
Bent on revenge, the goddess stood confess'd.
Her suppliant hands uplifting to the skies,
For a redress to heaven she now applies ;
And may you live, she passionately cried,
Doom'd in that pool for ever to abide !
  The goddess has her wish: for now they choose
To plunge and dive among the wat'ry ooze ;
Sometimes they shew their head above the brim,
And on the glassy surface spread to swim ;
Often upon the bank their station take,
Then spring and leap into the coolly lake.

Still, void of shame, they lead a clam'rous life,
And, croaking, still scold on in endless strife ;
Compell'd to live beneath the liquid stream,
Where still they quarrel and attempt to scream.
Now, from their bloated throat, their voice puts on
Imperfect murmurs in a hoarser tone ;
Their noisy jaws, with bawling now grown wide,
(An ugly sight !) extend on either side ;
Their motley back, streak'd with a list of green,
Join'd to their head, without a neck is seen ;
And with a belly broad and white, they look
Mere frogs, and still frequent the muddy brook."

OVID.

No. 150.

The infant Apollo, after being bathed by the nymphs in the waters of Ocean, was rendered immortal by Themis, who fed him with ambrosia and nectar.

ALLION.   Oriental Amethyst.

" ' O'er the rough waves a well-known island
    roams ;
Yet unconfin'd, like flower of Asphodel,
That yields to every blast, it wanders wide,
As winds and waves direct its doubtful course,
Boreas or Auster, or th' uncertain flood :
Thither thy burden bear; the willing isle
Shall to Latona gladly grant admittance.'
He said ; the isles retiring sought their place,
Obedient to his word. Asteria then,
Of hymns divine regardful, to behold
The sacred choir of Cyclades, came down
In happy hour from fair Euboea's coasts,
Encumber'd in her course with burdening weeds,
From rough Geræstus gather'd. In the midst
She stood ; and with a generous pity touch'd
At fair Latona's sorrows, quick consum'd
The weeds impeding — for indignant flames
Buru'd round her shores — the suffering pangs to
    view
Of female anguish. ' Wreak, dread queen,' she
    cried,

' O Juno, wreak on me what vengeance best
Shall suit thy soul ; thy threats shall not disarm
My honest purpose. Come, Latona, come ;
Asteria waits thee gladly.' Thus her toils
The wish'd-for end obtain'd ; beside the banks
Of deep Inopus (whose proud current wells
Most rapid, where from Ethiopia's rocks
The Nile descending deluges the land,)
Her wearied limbs she laid, the crowded zone
Unloosing ; while against the sacred palm's
Supporting trunk reclin'd, with bitterest pangs
She groan'd distrest, and big cold drops distill'd
Adown her fainting body to the ground.
Breathless amid her throes, ' My son,' she cried,
With intermitted fervency, ah ! why
Thus grieve thy tortur'd mother, when to thee
A kindly isle the wish'd reception grants?
Be born, be born, and ease thy mother's pangs.'
But long the deed from Juno to conceal
'Twere vain to hope : for, trembling with the
    tale,
Her watchful Iris fled ; and whilst her breast

Big pants with conscious fear, ' Oh, queen,' she
cried,
' Majestic, all-ador'd, whose power supreme
Not I alone, but all confess ; of heav'n
Dread empress thou, sister and spouse of Jove ;
Nor fear we ought from other female hand.
Yet for thy rage hear cause : Latona's birth
A little isle presumptuous dares admit :
The rest all fled ; but this, of all least worth,
Asteria, sweeping refuse of the main,
Even this invited, this receiv'd thy foe.
Thou know'st the rest ; but pass not unreveng'd
Their quarrel, who o'er earth thy mandates bear.'
Speaking she sat beneath the golden throne ;
And as a faithful dog, when from the chase
Diana rests, sits watchful at her feet,
While still erect its sharp ears list'ning stand,
And wait each whisper of her voice, so sat
Thaumantian Iris, o'er her weary lids his downy wings,
Spreads o'er her weary lids his downy wings,
Her duty aught foregoing ; by the throne
Her head she leans reclining, and thus laid
Oblique, short slumber and disturb'd she shares ;
Her circling zone not daring to unbrace,
Nor loose the winged sandals from her feet,
Lest sudden Juno's word should claim her speed.
But warm resentment rising in her breast,
Thus Juno vents her ire : ' In sort like this,
Ye vile reproaches of licentious Jove,
May ye in fearful secrecy conceive,
And thus in secret shame produce your births ;
Nor find a shelter to conceal your pangs,
Base as receives the veriest abject wretch
Of human race birth-tortur'd ; but on rocks
And desert cliffs unpitied, unreliev'd,
Thus like the monstrous phocæ yean your brood.
And sure Asteria's favour to my foe
Cannot much rouse my vengeance, since her
shores,
Barren and desolate, can but afford
A wretched hospitality. Yet, prone
To fury though I were, this would disarm
My steadiest purpose, that her virtue scorn'd,
Though courted, to ascend my sacred bed,

And to Jove's arms preferr'd the briny deep.'
She spoke ; when from Pactolus' golden banks
Apollo's tuneful songsters, snowy swans,
Steering their flight, seven times their circling
course
Wheel round the island, carolling meantime
Soft melody, the favourites of the Nine ;
Thus ushering to birth with dulcet sounds
The god of harmony. And hence seven strings
Hereafter to his golden lyre he gave ;
For ere the eighth soft concert was begun,
He sprung to birth. The Delian nymphs aloud,
All grateful to Lucina, tun'd the hymn,
The sacred song rejoicing. Æther hears,
And from his brazen vault returns the sound
Exulting : perfect glory reign'd ; and Jove
Sooth'd even offended Juno, that no ire
Might damp the gen'ral joy when Sol was born.
Then, Delos, thy foundations all became
Of purest gold ; the circling lake, the flood
Of deep Inopus roll'd the splendid ore
Adown their glittering streams, and golden fruit
On golden stems thy favour'd olive bore.
Thou, too, from off the golden soil uprais'd
The new-born god, and fondling in thy breast,
Thus spoke : ' See thou, O earth, so richly
blest,
Thou fertile continent, and ye full isles,
Who boast such num'rous altars, shrines, and
states,
I am that poor uncultivated isle,
Despis'd and barren. Yet observe, from me
Delian Apollo scorns not to receive
An honour'd name ; and hence no other clime
From any god shall equal favour share :
Not Cenchris, by her Neptune so belov'd,
By Hermes nor Cyllene ; nor by Jove
Illustrious Crete ; as Delos, happy isle,
By her Apollo, steadfast in his love :
Here will I fix, and wander hence no more.'
She spoke ; and to the god her snowy breast
Unfolding, gave sweet nurture ; o'er the babe,
Enamour'd, smiling with maternal love."
CALLIMACHUS, *Hymn to Delos.*

" Nor milk to Phœbus, with his golden locks,
  Did fair Latona give ; but Themis brought
  To his immortal hands the heav'nly food
  Of deities, ambrosia and nectar."
                              HOMER's *Hymn to Apollo.*

No. 151.

The infant Apollo nursed by nymphs.

GNAIOS. *Amethyst.*

          " Of the north
  (Chill Boreas' climes, the Arimaspians' seat,)
  The loveliest daughters, Hecaërge blest,
  Bright Upis and fair Loxo, with a choir
  Of chosen youth accompanied, first brought
  The grateful sheaves and hallow'd gifts to Phœbus :
  Thrice-happy throng, ordain'd no more to see
  Their native north, but ever flourish fair
  In fame immortal, servants of their god."
                        CALLIMACHUS, *Hymn to Delos.*

" Iŏ, Carnean, all-ador'd, we bring
  The choicest beauties of the painted spring ;
  Now gentle Zephyr breathes the genial dew,
  That gives each flow'r its variegated hue :
  But on thy altars, when stern winter comes,
  The fragrant saffron breathes its rich perfumes ;
  To thee eternal fires incessant rise,
  And on thy shrine the living coal ne'er dies."
                                    CALLIMACHUS.

" Descend, ye ministers of Phœbus' shrine,
    Unto Castalia's silver wave ;
  Your bodies in its limpid waters lave,
    Then seek the fane divine."
                              Trach. Virg.

No. 152.

Latona flying from the serpent Python, whom Juno had sent in pursuit
of her.

GNAIOS.   *Oriental Cornelian.*

> " From hence the surface of the ground, with mud
> And slime besmear'd (the fæces of the flood),
> Receiv'd the rays of heav'n, and sucking in
> The seeds of heat, new creatures did begin :
> Some were of sev'ral sorts produc'd before,
> But of new monsters earth created more,
> Unwillingly ; but yet she brought to light
> Thee, Python, too, the wond'ring world to fright,
> And the new nations, with so dire a sight :
> So monstrous was his bulk, so large a space
> Did his vast body and long train embrace."
>   VIRGIL.

No. 153.

Tityus attacking Latona.

APOLLONIDES.   *Oriental Cornelian.*

Juno, enraged at Latona and her children, instigates Tityus, the most terrible of the
giants, to destroy them.

> " There Tityus large and long, in fetters bound,
> O'erspreads nine acres of infernal ground ;
> Two ravenous vultures, furious for their food,
> Scream o'er the fiend and riot in his blood,
> Incessant gore the liver in his breast ;
> Th' immortal liver grows, and gives th' immortal feast.
> Far as o'er Panope's enamell'd plains,
> Latona journey'd to the Pythian fanes,
> With haughty love th' audacious monster strove
> To force the goddess, and to rival Jove."
>   VIRGIL.

m

No. 154.

The combat between Idas and Apollo.

DIOSCORIDES.   *Oriental Cornelian.*

Apollo enamoured of Marpessa, daughter of the river Evenus, and wife of Idas, carried her off.   While fighting, they are separated by the bolts of Jupiter.

"Where Calydon on rocky mountains stands,
Once fought th' Ætolian and Curetian bands ;
To guard it those, to conquer these advance,
And mutual deaths were dealt with mutual
    chance.
The silver Cynthia bade Contention rise,
In vengeance of neglected sacrifice ;
On Œneus' field she sent a monstrous boar,
That levell'd harvests, and whole forests tore :
This beast (when many a chief his tusks had
    slain)
Great Meleager stretch'd along the plain.
Then, for his spoils a new debate arose,
The neighbour nations thence commencing foes.

Strong as they were, the bold Curetes fail'd,
While Meleager's thundering arm prevail'd ;
Till rage at length inflam'd his lofty breast
(For rage invades the wisest and the best).
Curs'd by Althæa, to his wrath he yields,
And in his wife's embrace forgets the fields.
She from Marpessa sprung, divinely fair,
And matchless Idas, more than man in war ;
The god of day ador'd the mother's charms ;
Against the god the father bent his arms :
Th' afflicted pair, their sorrows to proclaim,
From Cleopatra chang'd this daughter's name,
And call'd Alcyone ; a name to show
The father's grief, the mourning mother's woe."

Il. ix.

No. 155.

Apollo on the banks of the river Peneus, in pursuit of Daphne, who is saved from being captured by the god by being transformed into a laurel.

GNAIOS.   *Oriental Cornelian.*

"She urg'd by fear, her feet did swiftly move,
But he more swiftly, who was urg'd by love ;
He gathers ground upon her in the chase ;
Now breathes upon her hair, with nearer pace ;
And just is fast'ning on the wish'd embrace.
The nymph grew pale, and in a mortal fright,
Spent with the labour of so long a flight ;
And now despairing, cast a mournful look
Upon the streams of her paternal brook :—
Oh, help, she cried, in this extremest need,
If water-gods are deities indeed !

Gape, earth, and this unhappy wretch intomb,
Or change my form, whence all my sorrows
    come.
Scarce had she finish'd, when her feet she
    found
Benumb'd with cold and fasten'd to the ground ;
A filmy rind about her body grows,
Her hair to leaves, her arms extend to boughs ;
The nymph is all into a laurel gone,
The smoothness of her skin remains alone."

OVID.

No. 156.

Apollo, inconsolable at the loss of Daphne, embracing one of the branches of the laurel to which she has been metamorphosed.

GNAIOS. *Oriental Cornelian.*

" Yet Phœbus loves her still, and casting round
Her bole his arms, some little warmth he found ;
The tree still panted in th' unfinish'd part,
Not wholly vegetive, and heav'd her heart.
He fix'd his lips upon the trembling rind ;
It swerv'd aside, and his embrace declin'd."
OVID.

No. 157.

Apollo, after having gathered the branch of laurel, making garlands for his head and lyre.

GNAIOS. *Oriental Cornelian.*

" To whom the god : Because thou canst not be
My mistress, I espouse thee for my tree :
Be thou the prize of honour and renown,
The deathless poet and the poem crown :
Thou shalt the Roman festivals adorn,
And after poets be by victors worn ;
Thou shalt returning Cæsar's triumph grace,
When pomps shall in a long procession pass,
Wreath'd on the posts before his palace wait,
And be the sacred guardian of the gate.
Secure from thunder, and unharm'd by Jove,
Unfading as th' immortal pow'rs above ;
And as the locks of Phœbus are unshorn,
So shall perpetual green thy boughs adorn."
OVID.

No. 158.

Apollo surprising Creusa, daughter of Erechtheus king of Athens.

APOLLONIDES. *Oriental Cornelian.*

Pausanias (Travels in Attica) says that in his time this grotto was shewn in a temple dedicated to Apollo.

" O, cave of Pan, with rocks o'erhung,
Dark-brow'd recess by poets sung,
Where old Aglauro's daughters led
The festive dance o'er flowery bed,
Before Minerva's fane, to sound
Of hymn and pipe re-echoing round.
Thy pipe, O Pan, whose rustic note
Is wont on ev'ning breeze to float

From that deep cave, where erst a maid,
By Phœbus' treach'rous arts betray'd,
Her infant left, a bloody feast
To mountain bird and rav'nous beast,

That thus her babe might ne'er proclaim
To sneering crowds its mother's shame."

EURIPIDES' *Ion*, HAYGARTH'S *Trans.*

No. 159.

Apollo and Leucothoe.

APOLLONIDES. *Oriental Amethyst.*

Apollo, enamoured of Leucothoe, daughter of Orchamus and Eurynome, first approaches her in the form of Eurynome, and then makes himself known, resuming the majesty of his divine form. Clytie, nymph of Ocean, who loved Apollo, and was jealous of Leucothoe, discovers this interview to Orchamus, who orders his daughter to be buried alive. Apollo, who could not save her, nor change the decrees of fate, sprinkled nectar and ambrosia on her tomb, which, penetrating to the body of Leucothoe, thence sprang the trees from which flows the frankincense.

" Leucothoe has all his soul possest,
  And chas'd each rival passion from his breast.
To this bright nymph Eurynome gave birth
In the blest confines of the spicy earth;
Excelling others, she herself beheld
By her own blooming daughter far excell'd.
The sire was Orchamus, whose vast command,
The seventh from Belus, rul'd the Persian land.

.   .   .   .   .
Confus'd she heard him his soft passion tell,
And on the floor untwirl'd the spindle fell:
Still from the sweet confusion some new
  grace
Blush'd out by stealth and languish'd in her
  face."

OVID.

No. 160.

Orchamus dragging his daughter Leucothoe to the grave, where she is buried alive.

GNAIOS. *Oriental Cornelian.*

" This Clytie knew, and knew she was undone,
Whose soul was fix'd and doated on the Sun.
With envious madness fir'd, she flies in haste,
And tells the king his daughter is unchaste.
The king, incens'd to hear his honour stain'd,
No more the father nor the man retain'd.
In vain she stretch'd her arms and turn'd her
  eyes
To her loved god, the enlight'ner of the skies;

The brutal sire stood deaf to ev'ry pray'r,
And deep in earth entomb'd alive the fair.
What Phœbus could do was by Phœbus done,
Full on her grave with pointed beams he shone:
To pointed beams the gaping earth gave way—
Had the nymph eyes, her eyes had seen the day;
But lifeless now, yet lovely still she lay.
Not more the god wept when the world was fir'd,
And in the wreck his blooming boy expir'd.

The vital flame he strives to light again,
And warm the frozen blood in ev'ry vein;
But since resistless fates denied that pow'r,
On the cold nymph he rain'd a nectar show'r.
Ah! undeserving thus (he said) to die,
Yet still in odours thou shalt reach the sky.

The body soon dissolv'd, and all around
Perfum'd with heav'nly fragrances the ground;
A sacrifice for gods uprose from thence,
A sweet delightful tree of frankincense."

OVID.

No. 161.

Apollo killing the serpent Python.

SOLON. *Oriental Cornelian.*

" Whom Phœbus basking on a bank espied:
Ere now the god his arrows had not tried
But on the trembling deer or mountain goat:
At this new quarry he prepares to shoot.
Though ev'ry shaft took place, he spent the store
Of his full quiver; and 'twas long before
Th' expiring serpent wallow'd in his gore.

Then, to preserve the fame of such a deed,
For Python slain he Pythian games decreed,
Where noble youths for mastership should
    strive
To quoit, to run, and steeds and chariots drive.
The prize was fame: in witness of renown,
An oaken garland did the victor crown."

OVID.—See also *Thebaid* of STATIUS, book i.

" Sing Io Pæan, sing the sacred sound,
The Delphian people to thy honour found;
What time thy golden arrows plenteous flew,
And the fell Python, dreadful serpent, slew:
Swift from thy bow they pierc'd the monster's heart,
While still the people cry'd, ' Elance the dart!'
Each shaft with acclamations they attend,
' Io send forth, another arrow send;
Thee thy blest mother bore, and pleas'd assign'd
The willing saviour of distress'd mankind.' "

CALLIMACHUS, *Hymn to Apollo.*

No. 162.

Apollo trampling on Python.

ADMON. *Oriental Sardonyx.*

Apollo, proud of his victory over Python, meets Cupid and ridicules him, saying, that his arrows had power only on weak minds. Cupid, indignant at his raillery, swears to be revenged.

"Swell'd with the pride that new success attends, | Take up the torch (and lay my weapons
He sees the stripling, while his bow he bends, | by);
And thus insults him: 'Thou lascivious boy, | With that the feeble souls of lovers fry.'
Are arms like these for children to employ? | To whom the son of Venus thus replied:
Know, such achievements are my proper claim, | ' Phœbus, thy shafts are sure on all beside,
Due to my vigour and unerring aim; | But mine on Phœbus; mine the fame shall be
Resistless are my shafts, and Python late | Of all thy conquests, when I conquer thee.' "
In such a feather'd death has found his fate. | OVID.

No. 163.

Apollo and Hercules destroying the Titan.

ALLION.   *Oriental Cornelian.*

Titan seizing an enormous stone to hurl at them: the former has already let fly an arrow,
which has put out his left eye, and Hercules is in the act of shooting another at his right eye.

No. 164.

Midas bathing in the river Pactolus.

CHROMIOS.   *Oriental Cornelian.*

Midas, son of Gordius king of Lydia, received Silenus at his court; and Bacchus, out of
gratitude for the hospitality he had received, promised Midas to grant him whatever he desired.
Midas asked that whatever he touched might become gold; but when he saw that even his food
was changed to that metal, he prayed Bacchus to take back his gift. The god granted his
prayer, and, by his command, he washed himself in the river Pactolus.

"The king through Lydia's fields young Bac- | He had his wish; but yet the god repin'd
    chus sought, | To think the fool no better wish could find.
And to the god his foster-father brought. | .   .   .   .   .
Pleas'd with the welcome sight, he bids him soon | The hungry wretch his folly thus confess'd,
But name his wish, and swears to grant the boon. | Touch'd the kind deity's good-natur'd breast;
A glorious offer! yet but ill bestow'd | The gentle god annull'd his first decree,
On him whose choice so little judgment shew'd. | And from the cruel compact set him free.
Give me, says he (nor thought he ask'd too much), | But then, to cleanse him quite from farther harm,
That with my body wheresoe'er I touch, | And to dilute the relics of the charm,
Chang'd from the nature which it held of old, | He bids him seek the stream that cuts the land
May be converted into yellow gold. | Nigh where the tow'rs of Lydian Sardis stand;

Then trace the river to the fountain-head,
And meet it rising from its rocky bed;
There, as the bubbling tide pours forth amain,
To plunge his body in, and wash away the stain.
The king instructed, to the fount retires,
But with the golden charm the stream inspires;

For while this quality the man forsakes,
An equal pow'r the limpid water takes;
Informs with veins of gold the neighb'ring
   land,
And glides along a bed of golden sand."

OVID.

No. 165.

Apollo killing Caanthus.

GNAIOS. *Oriental Cornelian.*

Apollo carried off Melia, daughter of Ocean. Caanthus, the brother of Melia, angry at this outrage, set fire to a wood consecrated to Apollo; for which the god killed him with his arrows.

No. 166.

Apollo killing Phlegyas, who has set fire to his temple.

APOLLONIDES. *Oriental Cornelian.*

Apollo having seduced Coronis, daughter of Phlegyas, king of the Lapithæ, she became the mother of Esculapius. Phlegyas, to revenge himself, burns the temple of Apollo; and the god kills Phlegyas, and casts him into hell.

No. 167.

Apollo killing Tityus.

CHROMIOS. *Oriental Sardonyx.*

Tityus, one of the giant-children of the earth, of an enormous size, covered with his body nine acres of land. He offered violence to Latona. She had recourse to Apollo, who killed the giant with his arrows.

No. 168.

Tityus in torture.

PHARNAX. *Oriental Amethyst.*

Tityus, after his death, is precipitated by Jupiter into Tartarus, and condemned to have his liver, which always grew again, devoured by a vulture. This stone represents Tityus

chained to a rock; but it is a serpent which feeds on his entrails. The artist, taking advantage
of the liberty accorded by Horace to speak to the imagination, gives the preference to this
reptile, as more analogous to the regions of darkness, as an accompaniment to the Eumenides,
and as best representing the remorse of the wicked.

> " There Tityus' pond'rous length outstretch'd was spread,
>   Titanian-born, o'ershadowing the space
>   Of nine whole acres; and a vulture huge,
>   Plunging his rav'nous and arched beak,
>   Uprooted every fibre, and devour'd
>   His ever-during liver, which again
>   Regenerate and imperishable sprang.
>   No rest the monster found; the winged fiend
>   Still deep entrench'd within his bleeding breast,
>   Pluck'd forth each trembling vital."
>   *Æneid*, book vi. : NATHANIEL OGLE'S *Trans.* *

No. 169.

The same subject.

APOLLONIDES.   *Oriental Cornelian.*

This stone also represents the punishment of Tityus, two vultures being continually gnaw-
ing the always-renewed liver of the giant, as described by Homer in the *Odyssey*, book xi.
verses 606 and 607.

> " There Tityus was to see, who took his birth
>   From heav'n, his nursing from the foodful earth;
>   Here his gigantic limbs, with large embrace,
>   Infold nine acres of infernal space.
>   A rav'nous vulture in his open'd side
>   Her crooked beak and cruel talons tried;
>   Still for the growing liver digg'd his breast,
>   The growing liver still supplied the feast;
>   Still are his entrails fruitful to their pains—
>   Th' immortal hunger lasts, th' immortal food remains."
>   VIRGIL.

---

* The father of the editor, who has left unfinished the finest translation of the *Æneid* extant,
and which will be occasionally quoted in the sequel.

No. 170.

Dryope holding Apollo transformed to a tortoise.

PYRGOTELES. *Oriental Cornelian.*

Apollo, enamoured of Dryope, a young shepherdess of Mount Æta, and daughter of Eurytus, metamorphosed himself to a tortoise. The Hamadryads took it and gave it to Dryope.

No. 171.

Apollo (partly formed as a serpent) pursuing Dryope.

GNAIOS. *Sardonyx.*

Her affrighted companions fled, and Apollo, finding her alone, holds intercourse with her, and makes her the mother of Amphissus.

No. 172.

Dryope changed into a lotus.

GNAIOS. *Amethyst.*

Dryope, with her child at her breast, by the side of a lake, gathers a flower and gives it to her babe; but on seeing drops of blood trickle from the stem, affrighted she shrinks back: Apollo metamorphoses her to the plant from which she had plucked the flower, which was from that time called *Lotus.*

" You, mother, sorrow for no kindred's fate.
But what if I the wond'rous change relate
Of my poor sister? Tears and sorrow seize
My troubled speech. Of all th' Œcalides,
For form few might with Dryope compare;
The only child her dying mother bare:
I born by a second wife. Her virgin-flow'r
Being gather'd by that over-mast'ring pow'r,
Who in Delos and in Delphos doth reside,
Andræmon weds her, happy in his bride.
A lake there is, which shelving borders bound,
Much like a shore, with fragrant myrtles crown'd.
Hither came simple Dryope, and (what more
Afflicts me) to those nymphs she garlands bore;

Her arms her child, a pleasing burden, hold,
Who suck'd her breasts, not yet a twelvemonth old.
Hard by the lake a flow'ry lotus grew,
(Expecting berries) of a crimson hue:
Thence pulling flowers, she gave them to her son
To play withal; so was I like t' have done,
For I was there. I saw the blood descend
From dropping twigs, the boughs with horror bend;
And heard too late, Lotis, a nymph, who fled
From lustful Priapus, to quit her dread,
Assum'd this shape, her name of Lotus kept.
My sister, this not knowing, backward stept,

n

And would depart as soon as she had pray'd;
But roots her feet, for all her struggling, stay'd,
And only above she moves. The bark increas'd,
Ascending from the bottom to her breast.
This seen, she thought t' have tore her hair, but
    tears
Leaves from their twigs; her head green branches
    bears.
The child Amphissus (for his grandfather
Eurytus did that name on him confer)
Now finds his mother's breasts both stiff and
    dry.
I, a spectator of thy tragedy,
Dear sister, had in me no power of aid;
Yet, as I could, thy growing trunk I stay'd,
Clung to thy spreading boughs, and wish'd
    that I,
Entomb'd with thee, might in thy lotus lie.
Behold, Andræmon comes, with him her sire,
(Both wretched) and for Dryope inquire.
When I for Dryope the lotus shew'd,
They kisses on the yet warm wood bestow'd;
And, grovelling on the ground, her roots em-
    brace.
Now all of thee, dear sister, but thy face,
Th' encroaching habit of a tree receives.
With tears she bathes her new created leaves;
And, while she might, while yet a way re-
    main'd
For speaking passion, in this sort complain'd:—
  'If credit to the wretched may be given,
I swear by all the powers above in heaven,
I never this deserv'd. Without a sin
I suffer; innocent my life hath been:
Or if I lie, may my green branches fade,
And, fell'd with axes, on the fire be laid.
This infant from his dying mother bear
To some kind nurse; and often let him here
Be fed with milk; oft in my shadow play.
Let him salute my tree; and sadly say,
When he can speak, This lotus doth contain
My dearest mother. Let him still refrain
All lakes, nor ever dare to touch a flower;
But think that every tree enshrines a power.

Dear husband, sister, father, all, farewell:
If in your gentle hearts compassion dwell,
Suffer no axe to wound my tender boughs,
Nor on my leaves let hungry cattle browse.
And since I cannot unto you decline,
Ascend to me, and join your lips to mine.
My little son, while I can kiss, advance.
But fate cuts off my failing utterance;
For now the softer rind my neck ascends,
And round about my leafy top extends.
Remove your hands; without the help of those
The wrapping bark my dying eyes will close.'
She left to speak, and be. Yet human heat
In her chang'd body long retain'd a seat.
    While Iole this story told, her eyes,
Fill'd with her tears, the kind Alcmena dries,
And weeps herself. Behold, a better change
With joy defers this sorrow, nor less strange:
For Iolaus, twice a youth, came in,
The doubtful down now budding on his chin.
Fair Hebe, at her husband's suit, on thee
This gift bestow'd. About to swear that she
Would never give the like, wise Themis said:
  'Forbear; war raves in Thebes by discord
      sway'd,
And Capaneus but by Jove alone
Can be subdu'd. The brothers then shall groan
With mutual wounds. The sacred prophet, lost
In swallowing earth, alive shall see his ghost;
His son's red hands his mother's life extract,
T' appease his sire — a just, yet wicked fact.
Rapt from his home and senses, with th' affright
Of staring furies and his mother's sprite,
Until his wife the fatal gold demands—
Her husband murder'd by Phegides' hands.
Then Acheloian Callirrhoe
Shall Jove importune, that her infants may
Be turn'd to men, and due revenge require
(As he, for his) of those who slew their sire.
Her pray'rs shall win consent from Jove; who
    then
Will bid thee make Callirrhoe's children men.'
    This Themis with prophetic rapture sung.
Among the gods a grudging murmur sprung,

Why they this gift should not to others give :
Aurora for her husband's age doth grieve ;
Ceres complains of Jasias' hoary hair ;
Vulcan would Erichthonius' youth repair ;

And cares of time to come in Venus' reign,
That her Anchises might wax young again."

SANDYS' *Trans.*

No. 173.

Dryope, at the moment of being changed to a plant, confiding her child to her sister Iole.

GNAIOS. *Oriental Cornelian.*

No. 174.

Clytie transformed to a sunflower.

PYRGOTELES. *Oriental Sardonyx of rare beauty.*

Apollo, being irritated against Clytie, the daughter of Oceanus, for betraying to Orchamus his love for Leucothoe, disdained even to look at her. The afflicted Clytie refused nourishment, and kept her eye always turned to the god of day. Apollo took pity on her, and changed her to the heliotrope (sunflower).

" But angry Phœbus hears unmov'd her sighs,
And scornful from her loath'd embraces flies ;
All day, all night, in trackless wilds, alone
She pin'd, and taught the list'ning rocks her moan.
On the bare earth she lies, her bosom bare,
Loose her attire, dishevell'd is her hair.
Nine times the morn unbarr'd the gates of light,
As oft were spread th' alternate shades of night ;
So long no sustenance the mourner knew,
Unless she drank her tears, or suck'd the dew ;

She turn'd about, but rose not from the ground,
Turu'd to the sun, still as he roll'd his round :
On his bright face hung her desiring eyes,
Till fix'd to earth, she strove in vain to rise.
Her looks their paleness in a flow'r retain'd,
But here and there some purple streaks they gain'd.
Still the lov'd object the fond leaves pursue,
Still move their root, the moving sun to view—
And in the heliotrope the nymph is true."

OVID.

No. 175.

Dædalion metamorphosed to a hawk.

GNAIOS. *Oriental Cornelian.*

Dædalion, son of Lucifer, inconsolable for the loss of Chione his daughter, who was killed

by Diana, throws himself into the sea.   Apollo bears him up while falling, and metamorphoses
him to a sparrow-hawk.

> " O'er the most rugged ways so fast he ran,
> He seem'd a bird already, not a man;
> He left us breathless all behind; and now,
> In quest of death, had gain'd Parnassus' brow;
> But when from thence headlong himself he threw,
> He fell not, but with airy pinions flew.
> Phœbus in pity chang'd him to a fowl,
> Whose crooked beak and claws the birds control,
> Little of bulk, but of a warlike soul.
> A hawk become, the feather'd race's foe,
> He tries to ease his own by others' woe."
>
> OVID.

No. 176.

Apollo tending the flocks of Admetus.

CHROMIOS.   *Oriental Cornelian.*

The care which Apollo took of the flocks of Admetus on the banks of the Amphrysus,
produced extraordinary fecundity in the cows, each of which gave birth to two calves at once.

> " Thee, Nomian, we adoré, for that from heaven
> Descending, thou on fair Amphrysus' banks
> Didst guard Admetus' herds; sithence the cow
> Produc'd an ampler store of milk, and the she-goat
> Not without pain dragg'd her distended udder;
> And ewes that erst brought forth but single lambs,
> Now dropp'd their twofold burdens; blest the cattle
> On which Apollo cast his favouring eye."
>
> CALLIMACHUS, *Hymn to Apollo:* PRIOR's *Trans.*

No. 177.

Apollo guarding the herd of Admetus.

GNAIOS.   *Cornelian.*

" Admetus' herds the fair Apollo drove,
In spite of med'cine's power, a prey to love;
Nor aught avail'd to soothe his amorous care,
His lyre of silver sound, or waving hair.

To quench their thirst, the kine to streams he led,
And drove them from their pasture to the shed;
The milk to curdle, then, the fair he taught,
And from the cheese to strain the dulcet draught.

Oft, oft his virgin sister blush'd for shame,
As bearing lambkins o'er the field he came;
Oft would he sing the listening vales among,
Till lowing oxen broke the plaintive song.
To Delphi trembling anxious chiefs repair,
But got no answer, Phœbus was not there.
Thy curling locks that charm'd a stepdame's eye,
A jealous stepdame, now neglected fly.
To see thee, Phœbus, thus disfigur'd stray,
Who could discover the fair god of day?

Constrain'd by Cupid in a cot to pine,
Where was thy Delos, where thy Pythian shrine?
Thrice-happy days, when love almighty sway'd,
And openly the gods his will obey'd.
Now love's soft power's become a common jest;
Yet those who feel his influence in their breast,
The prude's contempt, the wise man's sneer de-
    spise,
Nor would his chains forego to rule the skies."
                       TIBULLUS.

No. 178.

Apollo exchanging his caduceus for the lyre of Mercury.

DAMAS. *Oriental Cornelian.*

Mercury carried off the flocks which Admetus had confided to the keeping of Apollo. The shepherd Battus gave intelligence of it to the son of Latona, who in searching for his bow and arrow to slay Mercury, discovered that he had stolen them also. They were soon reconciled. Mercury gave his lyre to Apollo, and Apollo presented Mercury with the caduceus, the common attribute of the messenger of the gods.

No. 179.

A sitting figure of Apollo, in the attitude of singing to his lyre.

PYRGOTELES. *Oriental Cornelian.*

" The god his own Parnassian laurel crown'd,
And in a wreath his golden tresses bound,
Graceful his purple mantle swept the ground.
High on the left his iv'ry lute he rais'd;
The lute, emboss'd with glitt'ring jewels, blaz'd.
In his right hand he nicely held the quill;
His easy posture spoke a master's skill:
The strings he touch'd with more than human art."
                       OVID.

No. 180.

Apollo Smintheus.

GNAIOS. *Oriental Amethyst.*

Apollo was known to the Greeks by the epithet of *Smintheus* (*mouse-destroyer*). The following incident gave rise to his worship under this name. Crinis, a priest of Apollo, had omitted in his sacrifices to the god some of the usual ceremonies, and was punished by an innumerable quantity of mice, which destroyed all the produce of his land. Crinis asked pardon of Apollo, and was more exact in the discharge of his ministry. The god himself killed all the mice with his arrows.

" Or view the lord of the unerring bow,
The god of life, and poesy, and light,
The sun in human limbs arrayed, and brow
All radiant from his triumph in the fight.
The shaft hath just been shot — the arrow bright
With an immortal's vengeance; in his eye
And nostril beautiful disdain, and might,
And majesty, flash their full lightnings by,
Developing in that one glance the Deity.

But in his delicate form—a dream of love,
Shaped by some solitary nymph, whose breast
Longed for a deathless lover from above,
And maddened in that vision — are exprest

All that ideal beauty ever blessed
The mind with in its most unearthly mood,
When each conception was a heavenly guest,
A ray of immortality; and stood
Starlike around, until they gathered to a god.

And if it be Prometheus stole from heaven
The fire which we endure, it was repaid
By him to whom the energy was given,
Which this poetic marble hath arrayed
With an eternal glory; which, if made
By human hands, is not of human thought;
And Time himself hath hallowed it, nor laid
One ringlet in the dust; nor hath it caught
A tinge of years, but breathes with which 'twas wrought."

BYRON.

No. 181.

Head of the Sun issuing from the shades of night.

GNAIOS. *Oriental Sardonyx.*

" So toil'd the Greeks; nor yet the morning light
Had pass'd the doubtful confines of the night,
But faintly glimmering on this earthly ball,
Produc'd what mortals morning-twilight call:
To Thynia's neighbouring isle their course they bore,
And safely landed on the desert shore,
When bright Apollo shew'd his radiant face,
From Lycia hastening to the Scythian race.
His golden locks, that flow'd with grace divine,
Hung clustering like the branches of the vine;

In his left hand his bow unbent he bore,
His quiver pendant on his back he wore:
The conscious island trembled as he trod,
And the big rolling waves confess'd the god;
Nor dar'd the heroes, seized with dire dismay,
The splendours of his countenance survey,
But on the ground their downward eyes they cast.
Meanwhile Apollo o'er the watery waste
And through thin æther on his journey flew,
Then thus spoke Orpheus to the martial crew.'
APOL. RHODIUS, *Argonautics*, lib. ii.

" Now the resplendent chariot of the sun
   Shines o'er the earth; from its ethereal fires,
   Beneath the veil of sacred night, the stars
   Conceal themselves. Parnassus' cloven ridge,
   Too steep for human footsteps to ascend,
   Receives the lustre of its orient beams,
   And through the world reflects them."

EURIP. Ion.

" O thou, whom sapphire-spangled night
    (That vanquish'd flies before thy golden ray)
    Calls forth thy orient lustre to display,
   And curtains close thy setting light,
   To thee, O Sun, I call; declare,
   Bright blazing through the lucid air,
   Where dwells the hero through this length of time?
    Where does Alcmena's son reside?
    Rolls he on the ocean's billowy tide?
   Lies he repos'd in some soft eastern clime,
   Or where decline thy west'ring rays?
   O say; for all thy piercing eye surveys."

SOPHOCLES, Trach. Virg.

No. 182.

The fall of Phaeton.

APOLLODOTOS.   *Very fine Oriental Cornelian.*

Phaeton, the son of Phœbus and Clymene, wishing to prove to Epaphus that he was the true offspring of the Sun, begged a favour of his father, without telling him what it was. Phœbus promised with the most solemn oaths to grant whatsoever he should ask. Phaeton then petitioned to be allowed to guide for one day the chariot of the Sun. It was granted; but the celestial coursers perceiving the inexperience of their new driver, departed from the usual track, and approaching the earth too nearly, parched up every thing on it. Jupiter strikes the charioteer with one of his thunderbolts, and hurls him from heaven into the river Eridanus. The Heliades, his sisters, weeping on the banks of the river, were changed into poplars, and their tears into amber; Cycnus, king of Liguria, to a swan; and Phaeton, under the name of Eridanus, was placed among the celestial signs, according to Claudian. In the background of this stone is seen the symbol of the river flowing into the sea.

" Phœbus beheld the youth from off his throne;
And cries aloud, ' What wants my son?—for know
My son thou art, and I must call thee so.'
  ' Light of the world,' the trembling youth re-
    plies,
' Illustrious parent! since you don't despise
The parent's name, some certain token give,
That I may Clymene's proud boast believe,
Nor longer under false reproaches grieve.'
  The tender sire was touch'd with what he said,
And flung the blaze of glories from his head,
And bade the youth advance: ' My son,' said he,
' Come to thy father's arms; for Clymene
Has told thee true; a parent's name I own,
And deem thee worthy to be call'd my son.
As a sure proof, make some request, and I,
Whate'er it be, with that request comply.
By Styx I swear, whose waves are hid in night,
And roll impervious to my piercing sight.'
  The youth, transported, asks, without delay,
To guide the Sun's bright chariot for a day.

    .   .   .   .   .

  He spoke in vain; the youth with active heat
And sprightly vigour vaults into the seat;
And joys to hold the reins, and fondly gives
Those thanks his father with remorse receives.

Half dead with sudden fear, he dropp'd the reins;
The horses felt 'em loose upon their manes,
And, flying out through all the plains above,
Ran uncontroll'd where'er their fury drove;
Rush'd on the stars, and through a pathless way
Of unknown regions hurried on the day.
And now above, and now below they flew,
And near the earth the burning chariot drew.

    .   .   .   .   .

  Jove call'd to witness ev'ry pow'r above,
And ev'n the god whose son the chariot drove,
That what he acts he is compell'd to do,
Or universal ruin must ensue.

Straight he ascends the high ethereal throne,
From whence he us'd to dart his thunder down,
From whence his show'rs and storms he used to
    pour,
But now could meet with neither storm nor
    show'r.
Then, aiming at the youth with lifted hand,
Full at his head he hurl'd the forky brand,
In dreadful thund'rings. Thus th' almighty sire
Suppress'd the raging of the fires with fire.
  At once from life and from the chariot driv'n,
Th' ambitious boy fell thunder-struck from heav'n.

    .   .   .   .   .

          Here the bark increas'd,
Clos'd on their faces, and their words suppress'd.
The new-made trees in tears of amber run,
Which, harden'd into value by the sun,
Distil for ever on the streams below;
The limpid streams their radiant treasure show,
Mixed in the sand; whence the rich drops convey'd,
Shine in the dress of the bright Latian maid.
  Cycnus beheld the nymphs transform'd, allied
To their dead brother on the mortal side:
In friendship and affection nearer bound,
He left the cities, and the realms he own'd,
Through pathless fields and lonely shores to range,
And woods made thicker by the sisters' change.
Whilst here, within the dismal gloom, alone,
The melancholy monarch made his moan,
His voice was lessen'd, as he tried to speak,
And issued through a long-extended neck;
His hair transforms to down, his fingers meet
In skinny films, and shape his oary feet;
From both his sides the wings and feathers break:
And from his mouth proceeds a blunted beak:
All Cycnus now into a swan was turn'd,
Who, still rememb'ring how his kinsman buru'd,
To solitary pools and lakes retires,
And loves the waters as opposed to fires."
                         OVID.

No. 183.

The same subject.

APOLLONIDES. *Amethyst.*

" Be wise, my son,
Th' untrampled zones and stars insidious shun :
With pious caution first the youth proceeds,
But fate at length sets free th' immortal steeds."

STATIUS.

" Yet fire, as stories go, did once prevail,
And once the water too was spread o'er all.
The fire prevail'd when the sun's furious horse,
Disdaining Phaèton's young feeble force,
Ran through the sky in an unusual course;
And, falling near the earth, burnt all below,
Till angry Jove did dreadful thunder throw,
And quench'd the hot-brain'd fiery youth in Po.
But Phœbus gather'd up the scatter'd ray,
And brought to heav'n again the falling day.

The horses, too, that ran through heav'n's wide
    plain,
He caught, and harness'd to the coach again ;
They ever since, in due obedience, drew
The flaming car. This Greece reports as true ;
Yet 'tis absurd : but all may yield to flame,
If great supplies of rapid matter came
From the vast mass; for then those seeds must
    fail,
And sink again, or fire must ruin all."

LUCRETIUS : CREECH'S *Trans.*

No. 184.

Aurora accompanied by the Spirit of Light.

GNAIOS. *Sardonyx.*

" Now through night's shade the early dawning broke,
And changing skies the coming sun bespoke ;
As yet the morn was drest in dusky white,
Nor purpled o'er the east with ruddy light.
At length the Pleiads' fading beams gave way,
And dull Boötes languish'd into day ;
Each larger star withdrew his fainting head,
And Lucifer from stronger Phœbus fled."

LUCAN, book ii.

" I am the god who measure out the years,
The world's vast eye, of light the source serene,
Which all things sees, by which all things are seen."

OVID, *Met.* book iv.

O

" Hither, as to their fountain, other stars
    Repairing, in their golden urns draw light ;
    And hence the morning-planet gilds his horns.

         .   .   .   .

    First in his east the glorious lamp was seen,
    Regent of day ; and all the horizon round,
    Invested with bright rays, jocund to run
    His longitude through heav'n's high road : the gray
    Dawn and the Pleiades before him danc'd,
    Shedding sweet influence."

                 MILTON's *Paradise Lost*, book vii.

" Helios is doom'd to labour every day,
     And rest there never is for him,
   Or for his horses, when rose-finger'd Eos
     Leaves Ocean, and to heaven ascends.
   For through the waves, his loved bed, beneath him
     Hollow, and form'd of precious gold
   By Hephæstus' hand, and wing'd, the water's top
     Along it bears the sleeping god,
   From the Hesperides to the Æthiop's land,
     Where stand his horses and swift car,
   Until the air-born Eos goeth forth :
     Then Helios mounts another car."

                 MIMNERMUS : *Nanno.*

No. 185.

Aurora scattering flowers and dispelling darkness, which is represented by
a bird of night.

GNAIOS.   *Sardonyx.*

" The silver-footed Dawn, her rosy hand
   Glitt'ring with diamond dew, the sable band
   Of Night from off the silent earth withdrew,
   Robing the golden-fretted heaven anew
   With amber blushing into ruby hue,
   As amaranthine flow'rs she gaily threw,
   Bidding the wakeful Hours the horses yoke,
   Whose beamy breaths from Ocean's arms first woke
   Her, th' impatience to begin their heavenly way
   Thus telling to the radiant God of day."

                 N. O.

" The morn had now dispell'd the shades of night,
Restoring toils, as she restor'd the light."

Æn. book xi.: DRYDEN.

No. 186.

Aurora and Orion.

GNAIOS. *Oriental Cornelian.*

Aurora, the daughter of Hyperion and Thea, sister of the Sun and Moon, and the mother of the Winds and of Lucifer, became enamoured of Orion, born of Neptune and Euryale the daughter of Minos, and carried him to the island of Delos.

" This truth shall hundred-handed Gyas prove,
And warm Orion, who with impious love
Tempting the goddess of the sylvan scene,
Was by her virgin darts, gigantic victim,
    slain."

HOR., book iii. ode 4: FRANCIS.

" Gods, when Aurora shared Orion's bed,
Though bless'd yourselves, your souls with envy
    fed,
Till in Ortygia, chaste Diana's dart
In death's soft slumber chill'd the lover's heart."

Odyssey, book v.

No. 187.

The death of Procris.

APOLLONIDES. *Oriental Cornelian.*

Cephalus, beloved by Aurora, was insensible to her charms, and retained his affection for Procris. Aurora, tired of his constancy, sends him back to his wife, telling him that he will repent having loved her so much. Cephalus, doubting the fidelity of his wife, disguises himself to surprise her. Procris, unable to resist his attentions and dazzling promises, listens to him, when he discovers himself. Procris, ashamed of her weakness, conceals herself in the woods ; but her husband, who could not live without her, follows her, and they are reconciled. Procris in her turn becomes jealous of Cephalus, and, suspecting him in love with some nymph, conceals herself in a thicket to watch him. Cephalus, believing it a wild beast, throws the dart which she had presented to him, and kills her. Cephalus was inconsolable, and was carried off by Aurora and transported to heaven.

" When (as upon Hymettus' dewy head,
    For mountain stags my net betimes I spread,)
Aurora spied, and ravish'd me away,—
With rev'rence to the goddess I must say,
Against my will, for Procris had my heart,
Nor would her image from my thoughts de-
    part.

At last, in rage she cried, ' Ungrateful boy,
Go to your Procris, take your fatal joy !'
    .   .   .   .   .
Aurora's envy aided my design,
And lent me features far unlike to mine.
In this disguise to my own house I came ;
But all was chaste, no conscious sign of blame :

With thousand arts I scarce admittance found,
And then beheld her weeping on the ground
For her lost husband; hardly I retain'd
My purpose, scarce the wish'd embrace refrain'd.

.   .   .   .   .   .

How charming was her grief! Then, Phocus, guess
What killing beauties waited on her dress.
Her constant answer, when my suit I press'd,
' Forbear; my lord's dear image guards this breast;
Where'er he is, whatever cause detains,
Whoe'er has his, my heart unmov'd remains.'
    What greater proofs of truth than these could be?
Yet I persist, and urge my destiny.
At length she found, when my own form return'd,
Her jealous lover there, whose loss she mourn'd.
Enrag'd with my suspicion, swift as wind,
She fled at once from me and all mankind;
And so became, her purpose to retain,
A nymph, and huntress in Diana's train.
Forsaken thus, I found my flames increase,
I own'd my folly, and I sued for peace.
It was a fault, but not of guilt to move
Such punishment, a fault of too much love.

Thus I retriev'd her to my longing arms,
And many happy days possess'd her charms.
But with herself she kindly did confer
What gifts the goddess had bestow'd on her;
The fleetest greyhound, with this lovely dart,
And I of both have wonders to impart.

.   .   .   .   .   .

    Next morn I to the woods again repair,
And, weary with the chase, invoke the air:
Approach, dear Aura, and my bosom cheer!—
At which a mournful sound did strike my ear;
Yet I proceeded, till the thicket by,
With rustling noise and motion, drew my eye;
I thought some beast of prey was shelter'd there,
And to the covert threw my certain spear;
From whence a tender sigh my soul did wound;
' Ah me !' it cried, and did like Procris sound.
Procris was there; too well the voice I knew,
And to the place with headlong horror flew;
Where I beheld her gasping on the ground,
In vain attempting from the deadly wound
To draw the dart, her love's dear fatal gift!"

OVID.

No. 188.

Aurora united by Hymen to Tithonus.

DIOSCORIDES.   *Oriental Cornelian.*

Aurora, enamoured of Tithonus, son of Laomedon king of Troy, a young prince celebrated
for his beauty, carried him off and married him.

" The saffron morn, with early blushes spread,
    Now rose refulgent from Tithonus' bed ;
With new-born day to gladden mortal sight,
    And gild the courts of heaven with sacred light."

Odyssey, book v. : POPE.

" Two royal sons were to Tithonus born
  Of thee, Aurora, goddess of the morn;
  Hemathion from whom and Memnon spring,
  Known by his brazen helm was Æthiop's king."
                                        HESIOD.

No. 189.

Tithonus changed to a grasshopper.

GNAIOS.   *Oriental Cornelian.*

Tithonus loved Aurora passionately, and, that he might never be separated from her, besought and obtained immortality of the gods; but he forgot to ask at the same time for perpetual youth. He grew old and decrepit; and as life became insupportable to him, he prayed Aurora to allow him to die. She changed him to a cicada or grasshopper.

" In dew that drops from morning's wings,
  The gay cicada sipping floats;
  And drunk with dew, his matin sings,
  Sweeter than any cygnet's notes."
                    ANTIPATER, *Anthologia.*

" O thou that on the grassy bed
  Which nature's vernal hand has spread,
  Reclinest soft, and tun'st thy song,
  The dewy herbs and leaves among!
  Whether thou liest on springing flowers,
  Drunk with the balmy morning showers,
  Or ——— "
                        PERE RAPIN.

" Happy insect! what can be
  In happiness compar'd to thee?
  Fed with nourishment divine,
  The dewy morning's gentle wine;
  Nature waits upon thee still,
  And thy verdant cup does fill;
  'Tis fill'd wherever thou dost tread,
  Nature's self's thy Ganymede.
  Thou dost drink, and dance, and sing,
  Happier than the happiest king;
  All the fields which thou dost see,
  All the plants belong to thee;
  All that summer hours produce,
  Fertile made with early juice.
  Man for thee does sow and plow;
  Farmer he, and landlord thou;
  Thou dost innocently joy,
  Nor does thy luxury destroy:
  The shepherd gladly heareth thee,
  More harmonious than he;
  Thee country hinds with gladness hear,
  Prophet of the ripen'd year;
  Thee Phœbus loves and does inspire,
  Phœbus is himself thy sire.

To thee, of all things upon earth,
Life is no longer than thy mirth.
Happy insect, happy thou !
Dost neither age nor winter know ;
But when thou'st drunk, and dauc'd, and sung
Thy fill the flowery leaves among,

(Voluptuous and wise withal,
Epicurean animal,)
Sated with thy summer feast,
Thou retir'st to endless rest."

ANACREON : COWLEY.

No. 190.

A bust of Aurora issuing from the clouds, surmounted by the Morning Star.

ILLOS. *Oriental Cornelian.*

" Now Morn, her rosy steps in th' eastern clime
Advancing, sow'd the earth with orient pearl.

.   .   .   .   .

Fairest of stars, last in the train of night,
If better thou belong not to the dawn,
Sure pledge of day, that crown'st the smiling morn
With thy bright circlet."

MILTON.

———————————

" Now the day
Returning, with the morning star arose ;
And from the heav'n Aurora's dawn dispell'd
The dewy shades."

Æn. book iii.: TRAP.

———————————

" Aurora now from Tithon's saffron bed,
With dawning streaks of light the skies o'erspread ;
She shook the sparkling dew-drops from her hair,
And blush'd to find the peeping sun so near.
While, breaking through the clouds, the morning star
Advancing tow'rds her guides his rosy car,
Nor e'er withdraws till Sol's superior ray
Flames in the front of heav'n, and gives the day."

Thebaid, book ii.: LEWIS.

No. 191.

Diana seated, caressing a hind, an animal which was sacred to her.

PYRGOTELES. *Oriental Cornelian.*

" And now equipt to high Parrhasia's mount
The goddess leads; where, wondrous sight!
        behold,
Proud o'er the summit five tall stags advance,
Immense as bulls: their beamy antlers shone
With gold refulgent; rich Anaurus' banks
Ere fed the lordly beasts. Sight so august
With pleasing admiration as she view'd,
Raptur'd, the goddess cried: ' A prey like this
Well merits our acceptance, well deserves

Diana's first gift-offering to be made.'
Light o'er the unbending turf the goddess flies:
Five was the sum, and four she quickly caught
To whirl her flying chariot; but the fifth,
A future labour for Alcmena's son,
By heav'n's dread empress destin'd, fords the
        flood
Of rapid Celadon ; and, breathless half,
Securely pants on Cerynea's brow."

CALLIMACHUS, *Hymn to Diana.*

No. 192.

Diana gazing on Endymion.

APOLLONIDES. *Oriental Sardonyx.*

" Crescented Dian, who,
'Tis said, once wandered from her wastes of blue,
And all for love; filling a shepherd's dreams
With beauty and delight. He slept, he slept,
And on his eyelids white the huntress wept
'Till morning, and look'd through, on nights like this,
His lashes dark, and left his dewy kiss;
But never more upon the Latmos hill
May she descend to kiss that forest-boy,
And give, receive, gentle and innocent joy,
When clouds are distant far, and winds are still :
Her bound is circumscrib'd, and curb'd her will."

BARRY CORNWALL.

" How the pale Phœbe, hunting in a grove,
First saw the boy Endymion, from whose eyes
She took eternal fire that never dies ;
How she convey'd him softly in a sleep,
His temples bound with poppy, to the steep
Head of old Latmos, where she stoops each night,
Gilding the mountains with her brother's light,
To kiss her sweetest."

FLETCHER, *F. S.*

" She, Cynthia, not a huntress, when the chase
Of rugged boars hath flush'd her eager cheek,
But gently stooping from an argent cloud,

Illumining mount Latmos, while she view'd
Her lov'd Endymion, by her magic pow'r
Entranc'd to slumber."

Athenaid.

No. 193.

Diana, accompanied by her dog, in the war with the Titans pierces one of them with an arrow.

DAMAS.   *Oriental Cornelian.*

Euhemerus relates, that in a grove in the island of Panchaia, on a golden pillar in a temple dedicated to Triphylian Zeus, the deeds of Artemis, *i. e.* Diana, in the wars with the Titans, are inscribed.

"Girt with the golden zone, with arms of gold
Richly caparison'd, I see thee mount,
Parthenia, virgin queen (from whose dread arm
Destruction lighten'd on earth's giant sons);
I saw thee mount thy chariot, flashing gold,
While the stags proudly champ the golden bit."

CALLIMACHUS, *Hymn to Diana:* DODD's *Trans.*

No. 194.

Diana, as Hecate, armed with torches, killing a Titan, who is preparing to hurl a large stone at her.

SOLON.   *Oriental Cornelian.*

" Ye gods like gods, with me who dauntless dare
To face the Titans in a dreadful war,
Above the rest in honour shall ye stand,
And ample recompense shall load your hand ;
To Saturn's reign who bow'd, and unpreferr'd,
Void of distinction, and without reward,
Great, and magnificently rich, shall shine,
As right requires, and suits a pow'r divine.
First, as her father counsell'd, Styx ascends,
And her brave offsprings to the god commends;
Great Jove receiv'd her with peculiar grace,
Nor honour'd less the mother than her race.

Enrich'd with gifts, she left the bright abodes,
By Jove ordain'd the solemn oath of gods ;
Her children, as she wish'd, behind remain,
Constant attendants on the thund'rer's train :
Alike the god with all maintain'd his word,
And rules in empire strong of lords the lord.
Phœbe with fondness to her Cœus cleav'd,
And she a goddess by a god conceiv'd ;
Latona, sable veil'd, the produce proves,
Pleasing to all of their connubial loves,
Sweetly engaging from her natal hour,
The most delightful in th' Olympian bow'r.

From them Asterea sprung, a nymph renown'd,
And with the spousal love of Perses crown'd;
To whom she bore Hecate, lov'd by Jove,
And honour'd by th' inhabitants above;
Profusely gifted from th' almighty hand,
With pow'r extensive o'er the sea and land;
And great the honour she, by Jove's high leave,
Does from the starry vault of heav'n receive.
When to the gods the sacred flames aspire
From human off'rings, as the laws require,
To Hecate the vows are first preferr'd:
Happy of men whose pray'rs are kindly heard;
Success attends his every act below,
Honour, wealth, pow'r, to him abundant flow.

The gods, who all from earth and heaven descend,
On her decision for their lots depend;
Nor what the earliest gods, the Titans, claim,
By her ordain'd, of honour or of fame,
Has Jove revok'd by his supreme command,
For her decrees irrevocable stand.
To Hecate they all for safety bow,
And to their god and her prefer the vow.
O'er infants she, so Jove ordain'd, presides,
And the upgrowing youth to merit guides;
Great is the trust the future man to breed,
A trust to her by Saturn's son decreed."

HESIOD.

" The northern Bear was sunk beneath the hills,
And all the air a solemn silence fills;
Jason to lonely haunts pursu'd his way
(All rites adjusted the preceding day):
'Twas Argus' care a lambkin to provide,
And milk,—the rest the ready ship supplied.
A sweet sequester'd spot the hero found,
Where silence reigns, and swelling streams
    abound;
And here, observant of due rites, he laves,
His limbs immerging in the cleansing waves;
Then o'er his shoulders, pledge of favours past,
The gift of fair Hypsipyla he cast,
A sable robe; a deep round foss he made,
And on the kindling wood the victim laid:

The mix'd libation pouring o'er the flame,
Loud he invok'd infernal Brimo's name;
Then back retires: his call her ears invades,
And up she rises from the land of shades:
Snakes, wreath'd in open boughs, curl'd round
    her hair,
And gleaming torches cast a dismal glare.
To guard their queen, the hideous dogs of hell
Rend the dark welkin with incessant yell;
The heaving ground beneath her footsteps shakes;
Loud shriek the naiads of the neighbouring lakes,
And all the fountain-nymphs astonish'd stood
Where amaranthine Phasis rolls his flood.
Fear seiz'd the chief, yet backward he withdrew,
Nor till he join'd his comrades turn'd his view."

Argonautics, book iii.: FAWKES' *Trans.*

No. 195.

The Metamorphosis of Actæon.

APOLLONIDES. *Oriental Cornelian.*

Diana coming out of the water, accompanied by her nymphs, who stand round her to conceal her from the indiscreet gaze of Actæon, on whom the goddess has just sprinkled some water, thus transforming him to a stag.

" Now all undrest the shining goddess stood,
When young Actæon, wilder'd in the wood,

To the cool grot by his hard fate betray'd,
The fountains fill'd with naked nymphs survey'd.

P

The frighted virgins shriek'd at the surprise,
(The forest echo'd with their piercing cries,)
Then in a huddle round their goddess press'd:
She, proudly eminent above the rest,
With blushes glow'd; such blushes as adorn
The ruddy welkin, or the purple morn;
And, though the crowding nymphs her body hide,
Half backward shrunk, and view'd him from aside.

Surpris'd, at first she would have snatch'd her bow,
But sees the circling waters round her flow;
These in the hollow of her hand she took,
And dash'd 'em in his face, while thus she spoke:
' Tell, if thou canst, the wondrous sight disclos'd,
A goddess to thy naked view expos'd.'
　This said, the man began to disappear
By slow degrees, and ended in a deer."

OVID.

No. 196.

Actæon, changed to a stag, torn to pieces by his dogs.

GNAIOS.　*Amethyst.*

" He bounded off with fear, and swiftly ran
O'er craggy mountains and the flow'ry plain;
Through brakes and thickets forc'd his way, and
　flew
Through many a ring where once he did pursue.
From shouting men, and horns, and dogs he flies,
Deafen'd and stunn'd with their promiscuous cries;
When now the fleetest of the pack, that prest
Close at his heels and sprang before the rest,
Had fasten'd on him; straight another pair
Hung on his wounded haunch, and held him
　there,

Till all the pack came up, and ev'ry hound
Tore the sad huntsman grov'lling on the ground.
His servants, ignorant of what had chanc'd,
With eager haste and joyful shouts advanc'd,
And call'd their lord Actæon to the game:
He shook his head in answer to the name:
He heard, but wish'd he had indeed been gone,
Or only to have stood a looker-on:
But, to his grief, he finds himself too near,
And feels his rav'nous dogs with fury tear
Their wretched master, panting in a deer."

OVID.

No. 197.

Actæon expiring in the arms of his mother.

APOLLONIDES.　*Oriental Cornelian.*

No. 198.

Diana discharged an arrow at a stag, and inadvertently killed Cenchreus,
son of the nymph Pyrene.

GNAIOS.　*Amethyst.*

" The goddess paus'd ; and, held in deep amaze,
Now views the victim, now the mother's face.
Different in each, yet equal beauty glows ;
That the full moon, and this the crescent shews.
Thus rais'd beneath its parent tree is seen
The laurel shoot, while in its early green
Thick sprouting leaves and branches are essay'd,
And all the promise of a future shade.

Or blooming thus, in happy Pæstan fields,
One common stock two lovely roses yields :
Mature by vernal dews, this dares display
Its leaves full blown, and boldly meets the day ;
That, folded in its tender nonage, lies
A beauteous bud, nor yet admits the skies."

Ex Epitha. Hon. et Mar.
CLAUDIAN : HUGHES.

No. 199.

This stone represents Cenchreus lifeless, and near him his mother weeping.
She shed so many tears that she was changed to a fountain.

GNAIOS. *Oriental Cornelian.*

" She said, and melting as in tears she lay,
In a soft silver stream dissolved away.
The silver stream her virgin coldness keeps,
For ever murmurs, and for ever weeps ;
Still bears the name the hapless mother bore,
And bathes the forest where she rang'd before."

POPE.

" Some one I o'erheard,
Appearing not to listen, as I came
Where aged men sit near Pyrene's fount
And hurl their dice—say, that from Corinth's land,
Creon, the lord of these domains, will banish
The children with their mother."

EURIPIDES, *Medea.*

No. 200.

Diana Taurica seated on a bull.

GNAIOS. *Amethyst.*

The goddess holds a torch in her hand ; and on her head is the crescent.

" In the extremest bounds
Of Attica, near steep Carysthus' mount,
There is a sacred spot known by the name
Of Halas to my people ; there erect
A temple to receive the statue call'd

Tauric Diana; thus to future times
Transmitting a remembrance of thy toils
And wanderings through all Greece, from realm to realm
Chas'd by the furies.　Hence unnumber'd throngs
Shall join the choral hymn, and by that name
The goddess celebrate."

　　　　　　　EURIPIDES, *Iph. in Tauris:* WOODHULE'S *Trans.*

No. 201.

Diana Ærea (Hecaté) extinguishing the torch of Day.

GNAIOS.　*Oriental Cornelian.*

" Hear me, O queen ! Jove's daughter, various-nam'd,
　Bacchian and Titan, noble huntress queen,
　Shining on all, *torch-bearer,* bright Dictynna."

　　　　　　　　CALLIMACHUS : 35*th Hymn.*

—————

" But whither bore thee first thy rapid wheels?
　To Thracian Hæmus; whence the north wind's blasts
　Through loop'd and window'd ruggedness infest
　The houseless habitants.　But whence the torch
　Light-shedding didst thou hew ?　Whence shot the flame
　That gave the kindling touch?　Olympus' mount
　The first supplied; the unextinguish'd blaze
　Of Jove's blue lightning flashing gave the last."

　　　　　　　　CALLIMACHUS: *Hymn to Diana.*

—————

" And now (the sacred altars plac'd around)
　The priestess enters with her hair unbound,
　And thrice invokes the pow'rs below the ground.
　Night, Erebus, and Chaos she proclaims,
　And threefold Hecate with her hundred names,
　With three Dianas.　Next she sprinkles round,
　With feign'd Auvernian drops, the hallow'd ground ;
　Culls hoary simples found by Phœbe's light,
　With brazen sickles reap'd at noon of night."

　　　　　　　　Æn. iv. ; vide also *Iph. in. Tauris,* passim.

No. 202.

A bust of Diana.

PAMPHILOS. *Cornelian.*

" But mild the beauties of Diana were,
And all her charms serene and sweetly fair;
Her brother's looks adorn her radiant face,
Her cheeks and sparkling eyes express his
    grace.
The same she were, did not her sex alone
A difference cause, and make the virgin known.
Her arms are naked to th' admiring eye,
And in the wind her careless tresses fly;

Her famish'd quivers on her shoulders hung,
And her neglected bow was now unstrung.
Her Cretan vest, short gather'd from the ground,
A double girdle regularly bound.
There floating Delos the rich robes displays,
And round thy wand'ring isle is wrought a
    golden sea."

        CLAUD., *Rapt. Pros.*

" The bright-hair'd Vesper from a golden cloud
Beholds the fainting goddess; he alone
Earth's deity persuades to taste the draught
Refreshing, when through many a clime unknown
She sought her ravish'd daughter. Say, dread pow'rs,
How the long journey could thy tender feet
Support, enfeebled, to the distant west,
The tawny Ethiopians, and the climes
Fam'd for the golden fruit?"

        CALLIMACHUS.

No. 203.

Ceres receiving from Bacchus a restorative cup.

GNAIOS. *Oriental Cornelian.*

The god pours from a cup with one hand, holding at the same time a torch in the other, which are emblematical of heat and moisture being necessary to revive vegetation.

No. 204.

The amours of Ceres with the young Iasius, or Iasion, the son of Jupiter and Electra, one of the Atlantides, in a field of corn.

PYRGOTELES. *Oriental Cornelian.*

" And when the fair-hair'd Ceres' yielding mind
In the thrice-labour'd glebe her charms resign'd
To beautiful Iasion, conscious Jove
Smote with avenging flames her earthly love."
                                        Odyssey, lib. v.: SOTHEBY.

No. 205.

Plemneus confiding his daughter Chrysorte to Ceres.

DIOSCORIDES.   *Oriental Cornelian.*

Plemneus, a king of Sicyon, was the father of several children, who perished soon after their birth. Afflicted at their loss, and fearing a like fate for another child just born, Ceres appears to him and offers to take charge of it : it lived and prospered. When he discovered the nature of the nurse, he built a temple to her (PAUSANIAS, ii. c. 5 and 11).

No. 206.

Ceres changes Lyncus into a lynx.

PYRGOTELES.   *Oriental Sardonyx.*

Lyncus king of Scythia, at the moment when, armed with an axe, he surprises Triptole-mus his guest asleep, to kill him, and carry off the vase of corn received by him from Ceres, is by that goddess changed to a lynx.

" By me the goddess who the fields befriends
These gifts, the greatest of all blessings, sends :
The grain she gives, if in your soil you sow,
Thence wholesome food in golden crops shall
    grow.
Soon as the secret to the king was known,
He grudg'd the glory of the service done,
And wickedly resolved to make it all his own.

To hide his purpose, he invites his guest,
The friend of Ceres, to a royal feast ;
And when sweet sleep his heavy eyes had
    seiz'd,
The tyrant with his steel attempts his breast.
Him straight a lynx's shape the goddess gives,
And home the youth her sacred dragon drives."
                                        OVID, *Met.*

No. 207.

Ceres changes Stellio into an eft.

PYRGOTELES.   *Oriental Cornelian.*

Ceres, while traversing Trinacria, fatigued and without food, knocks at the hut of old Baubo, and craves assistance. Baubo prepares her a refreshing drink composed of corn and honey. Stellio, an inhabitant of the country, dared to laugh at the eagerness of the goddess, who threw over him what remained of the liquid, and metamorphosed him to an eft, a kind of lizard, often seen on the monuments representing Ceres.

" O'er mountains erst with hasty tread
　Did the celestial mother stray,
Nor stop where branching thickets spread,
Where rapid torrents cross'd her way,
Or on the margin of the billowy deep ;
　Her daughter, whom we dread to name,
　She wept while hailing the majestic dame.
Cymbals of Bacchus from the craggy steep
　Sent forth their clear and piercing sound ;

Her car the harness'd dragons drew,
Following the nymph torn from her virgin crew ;
　Amidst her maidens swift of foot were found.
Diana, skill'd the bow to wield ;
　Minerva who in glittering state
Brandish'd the spear, and rais'd her gorgon
　shield :
But Jove look'd down from heaven t' award
　another fate.

" Thirsty at last by long fatigue she grows,
But meets no spring, no riv'let near her flows.
Then looking round, a lowly cottage spies,
Smoking among the trees, and thither hies.
　The goddess knocking at the little door,
'Twas open'd by a woman old and poor,
Who, when she begg'd for water, gave her ale,
Brew'd long, but well preserv'd from being stale.
The goddess drank ; a chuffy lad was by,
Who saw the liquor with a grudging eye,
And grinning cries, ' She's greedy more than
　dry.'
Ceres offended at his foul grimace,
Flung what she had not drank into his face.

The sprinklings speckle where they hit the skin,
And a long tail does from his body spin ;
His arms are turn'd to legs, and, lest his size
Should make him mischievous, and he might
　rise
Against mankind, diminutive 's his frame,
Less than a lizard, but in shape the same.
Amaz'd the dame the wondrous sight beheld,
And weeps, and fain would touch her quondam
　child.
Yet her approach th' affrighted vermin shuns,
And fast into the greatest crevice runs.
A name they gave him which the spots express'd,
That rose like stars, and varied all his breast."
　　　　　　　　　　　　　　　　　OVID.

No. 208.

Ceres presenting Triptolemus with a vase of gold filled with corn to sow the earth with, which was replenished again as soon as it was empty.

GNAIOS.　*Oriental Cornelian.*

" Meantime around this isle, harmonious muse !
　The brightest beams of shining verse diffuse ;
　This fruitful island, with whose flowery pride
Heaven's awful king endow'd great Pluto's beau-
　teous bride.
Sicilia with transcendant plenty crown'd,
　Jove to Proserpina consign'd ;
Then with a nod his solemn promise bound
Still farther to enrich her fertile shores

With peopled cities, stately towers,
And sons in arts and arms refin'd,
Skill'd to the dreadful works of war,
　The thundering steed to train,
Or mounted on the whirling car,
Olympia's all-priz'd olive to obtain.
Abundant is my theme ; nor need I wrong
The fair occasion with a flattering song."
　　　　　　　　　　　　PINDAR : WEST.

" First Ceres taught the lab'ring hind to plough
The pregnant earth, and quick'ning seed to sow.
She first for man did wholesome food provide,
And with just laws the wicked world supplied:
All good from her deriv'd, to her belong
The grateful tributes of the Muse's song.
Her more than worthy of our verse we deem,
Oh! were our verse more worthy of the theme."

" Ceres takes
Her golden car, and yokes her fiery snakes;
With a just rein, along mid-heav'n she flies
O'er earth and seas, and cuts the yielding skies.
She halts at Athens, dropping like a star,
And to Triptolemus resigns her car.
Parent of seed, she gave him fruitful grain,
And bade him teach to till and plough the plain;
The seed to sow as well in fallow fields,
As where the soil manur'd a richer harvest yields."

No. 209.

Ceres presenting the horse Arion to Neptune.

GNAIOS.   *Oriental Cornelian.*

Ceres in her long wanderings employed the horse Arion, born of Zephyrus and a Harpy.

" Mighty god of verse,
Theirs and their princely master's names re-
    hearse;
For ne'er was a more gen'rous race of steeds
Collected for the course on Grecian meads.
As if a numerous flock of birds should try
Their active pow'rs, and wing the midway sky;
Or Æolus to the mad winds propose
The palm of swiftness,—such a tumult rose.
Before them all was fleet Arion led,
Distinguish'd by his mane of fiery red;
From Ocean's god (if ancient fame says true)
The gen'rous horse his honour'd lineage drew. .

'Tis said he rein'd him first with forming hand
And curbing bit upon the dusty strand,
But spar'd the lash; for free he scours the
    plain,
Swift as the surge that skims along the main.
Oft in the car with other steeds, design'd
To swim the Libyan billows, was he join'd,
And train'd to carry his cerulean sire
To any coast.   The tardier clouds admire
His active strength; and each contending wind,
Notus or Eurus, follows far behind."

STATIUS, *Th.* book vi.

" Beneath the gate his fiery coursers stand;
And while the groom divides with artful hand
His flowing mane, reluctant to the car
Arion bounds, and hopes the promised war."

STATIUS, book iv.

" Steeds, erst to Peleus by the sea-god given;
By him to me, th' immortal breed of heaven."

Il. xxiii.

No. 210.

The Nymphs washing the horse Arion in the waters of the sea.

The same man's foot is here observed as in the former medallion.

GNAIOS. *Amethyst.*

No. 211.

Ceres Mallophora (*lanam ferens*), the producer of wool, seated on a sheep.

DIOSCORIDES. *Oriental Cornelian.*

No. 212.

Metanira discovering herself while watching Ceres holding her son over the flames.

APOLLONIDES. *Oriental Cornelian.*

Ceres so ardently loved Deiphon, brother of Triptolemus, and son of Celeus and Metanira, that she wished to render him immortal; and to purify him from any remaining particles of mortality, she placed him every evening on burning coals. Metanira, surprised at the rapid growth of her son, watched the goddess to discover what she did to make him so vigorous; and alarmed at what she saw, screamed and disturbed the mysterious operations of Ceres, who mounted her car drawn by dragons, and left Deiphon to perish in the flames.

" 'Be it thy care to nurse this lovely boy,
Child of my age, an unexpected joy
By favouring gods bestow'd! Should, through thy cares,
My Deiphon arrive at manhood's years,
Others shall at thy happier state repine,
Such high rewards, such treasure shall be thine.'
'O woman! favour'd by the powers of heaven,
To whom the gods this beauteous child have given,'
Ceres replied, 'I take with joy thy heir;
No nurse unskill'd receives him to her care:
Nor magic spell, nor roots of mighty power
From earth's dark bosom torn àt midnight hour,

Shall hurt thy offspring; to defeat each charm,
And herb malignant of its power disarm,
Full well I know.' She said, and to her breast
The infant clasp'd, and tenderly carest.
Thus Ceres nurs'd the child; exulting joy
Reign'd in his parents' hearts. Meanwhile the boy
Grew like an offspring of ethereal race;
Health crown'd his frame, and beauty deck'd his face.
No mortal food he ate: the queen ador'd,
Around him oft ambrosial odours pour'd;
Oft as the child was on her bosom laid,
She heavenly influence to his soul convey'd.

At night, to purge from earthly dross his frame,
She kindled on the earth th' annealing flame;
And like a brand, unmark'd by human view,
Amid the fire wide-blazing frequent threw
Th' unconscious child. His parents woud'ring
    trace
Something divine, a more than mortal grace
Shine in his form; and she design'd the boy,
To chance superior and to time's annoy,
Crown'd with unceasing joys in heaven should
    reign :
Those thoughts a mother's rashness render'd vain.
  One fatal night, neglectful of repose,
Her couch forsaking, Metanira rose;
And from her secret stand beheld the flame
Receive the infant. Terror shakes her frame;
She shrieks in agony; she smites her thighs;
And thus she pours her loud-lamenting cries:—
  ' O Deiphon, my child, this stranger-guest
What causeless rage, what frenzy has possest?
Consuming flames around thy body roll,
And anguish rends thy mother's tortur'd soul.'
  Wrath seiz'd the goddess; her immortal hands
Sudden she plung'd amid the fiery brands;
And full before th' afflicted mother's view,
On the cold floor the blameless infant threw,
And furious thus began :—' O mortals vain,
Whose folly counteracts what gods ordain ;
Who, lost in error's maze, will never know
Approaching blessings from impending woe :
Long, for the rashness that thy soul possest,
Shall keen reflection agonise thy breast.
For, by that oath which binds the powers su-
    preme,
I swear by sable Styx, infernal stream !

Else had thy son in youth's perpetual prime
Shar'd heavenly joys, and mock'd the rage of
    time.
But now 'tis past; from fate he cannot fly ;
Man's common lot is his—he breathes to die.
But since a goddess on her knees carest
Thy child, since oft he slumber'd on her breast,
Fame shall attend his steps, and bright renown
With wreathes unfading shall his temples crown.
In future times, torn by discordant rage,
Eleusis' sons commutual war shall wage ;
(Then Deiphon)——

      .   .   .   .   .
  ' Know, then, that Ceres, from whose bounty flow
Those blessings the revolving years bestow,
Who, both from gods and man's frail race
    demands
Her honours due, before thy presence stands.
Away, and let Eleusis' sons unite,
Where steep Callichorus' projecting height
Frowns o'er the plain, a stately fane to rear;
Her awful rites its goddess shall declare.
There with pure hearts upon the hallow'd shrine
Your victims slay, and soothe a power divine.'
  This said, the front of age so late assum'd
Dissolv'd; her face with charms celestial bloom'd:
The sacred vesture that around her flew,
Through the wide air ambrosial odours threw ;
Her lovely form with sudden radiance glow'd ;
Her golden locks in wreaths of splendour flow'd:
Through the dark palace stream'd a flood of light,
As cloud-engender'd fires illume the night
With dazzling blaze, then swiftly from their view."
                    HOMER'S *Hymn to Ceres:*
                    HOLE'S *Trans.*

<hr>

No. 213.

Maia, the eldest of the daughters of Atlas, was beloved by Jupiter, who
    surprised her in the cave of Cylleneius, and she became the mother of
    Mercury.

GNAIOS. *Oriental Cornelian.*

" Daughter of Atlas, Maia, bore to Jove
The glorious Hermes, herald of the gods,
The sacred couch ascending."

" Maia, of Atlas born, and mighty Jove
Join in the sacred bonds of mutual love;
From whom behold the glorious Hermes rise,
A god renown'd, the herald of the skies."

HESIOD, *Theogony.*

No. 214.

Mercury transforming Aglauros to a stone.

CHROMIOS. *Oriental Cornelian.*

Aglauros, eldest daughter of Cecrops king of Attica, promised Mercury, in case he would remunerate her, to forward his amours with Herse, another daughter of Cecrops. Minerva, indignant at this compact, created in Aglauros so much jealousy with respect to her sister, that she did all in her power to sow discord between Mercury and Herse. Mercury, in consequence, changes Aglauros to a stone.

" His ornaments with nicest art display'd,
He seeks th' apartment of the royal maid.
The roof was all with polish'd iv'ry lin'd,
That richly mix'd in clouds of tortoise shin'd.
Three rooms, contiguous, in a range were plac'd,
The midmost by the beauteous Herse grac'd;
Her virgin sisters lodg'd on either side.
Aglauros first th' approaching god descried,
And, as he cross'd her chamber, ask'd his name,
And what his business was, and whence he came.
' I am the son and messenger of Jove,
My name is Mercury, my bus'ness love:
Do you, kind damsel, take a lover's part,
And gain admittance to your sister's heart.'

She star'd him in the face with looks amaz'd,
As when she on Minerva's secret gaz'd,
And asks a mighty treasure for her hire,
And, till he brings it, makes the god retire.

.   .   .   .   .   .

Giv'n up to envy (for, in ev'ry thought,
The thorns, the venom, and the vision wrought),
Oft did she call on death; as oft decreed,
Rather than see her sister's wish succeed,

To tell her awful father what had past;
At length before the door herself she cast;
And, sitting on the ground, with sullen pride,
A passage to the love-sick god denied.
The god caress'd, and for admission pray'd,
And sooth'd, in softest words, th' envenom'd
        maid.
In vain he sooth'd: ' Begone!' the maid replies,
' Or here I keep my seat, and never rise.'
' Then keep thy seat for ever,' cries the god,
And touch'd the door, wide op'ning to his rod.
Fain would she rise and stop him, but she found
Her trunk too heavy to forsake the ground;
Her joints all benumb'd, her hands are pale,
And marble now appears in ev'ry nail.
As when a cancer in the body feeds,
And gradual death from limb to limb proceeds,
So does the chillness to each vital part
Spread by degrees, and creeps into her heart;
Till, hard'ning ev'ry where, and speechless grown,
She sits unmov'd, and freezes to a stone.
But still her envious hue and sullen mien
Are in the sedentary figure seen."

OVID.

116 CATALOGUE.

No. 215.

Mercury, touched with pity, withdraws Lara from the gates of the infernal
regions.

CHROMIOS. *Oriental Sardonyx.*

Lara, daughter of the river Almon, had the indiscretion to reveal to Juno the gallantries of
Jupiter, who in revenge cut off her tongue, and ordered Mercury to convey her to the infernal
regions. The messenger of the gods, captivated by her beauty, falls in love with her, and she
becomes the mother of twins, which were the gods called Lares.

" The angry god exclaim'd,
' Since, tattling girl, you indiscreetly use
Your tongue, and Jupiter himself abuse,
That tongue I take away. Come, Hermes, here;
To Hades, suited to the silent, bear
This nymph, a naiad of the Stygian wave;
Th' example many naiads' fame may save.'
The mandate of the angry Jove's obey'd,
Through darksome woods the tongueless girl's
    convey'd.

The silent nymph so pleas'd the god of speech,
Vain were the looks with which she did be-
    seech:
Wrapt in resistless Mercury's embrace,
She was in time the mother of a race,
Who from her take the household Lares' name,
And day and night the guard of thresholds
    claim."

Fasti, book ii.: N. O.

No. 216.

Mercury near the lifeless body of Alcmena, which he is commanded by
Jupiter to conduct to the Islands of the Blessed, inhabited by shades,
where she espouses Rhadamanthus, judge of the infernal regions.

APOLLONIDES. *Oriental Cornelian.*

"There with soft step the fair Alcmena trod,
Who bore Alcides to the trembling god."
VIRGIL.

"Thee, where the earth's extremest bounds extend,
The powers immortal to Elysium send;
Where gold-hair'd Rhadamanthus ever dwells,
And blissful life all bliss of man excels.
There hail nor snow earth's beauteous face deform,
Nor winter's bitter blast, nor pelting storm;

But, in sweet murmurs heard, the wintry wind
Breathes o'er the ocean to refresh mankind :
There shalt thou, blissful as the gods above,
'Live."

Odyssey, book iv.

No. 217.

Mercury killing Hippolytus, one of the Giants who made war against Jupiter.

CHROMIOS. *Oriental Sardonyx.*

No. 218.

The Amazon Myrto seated by the side of Mercury, by whom she became the mother of Myrtilus, the celebrated arm-bearer of Œnomaus, father of Hippodamia.

APOLLONIDES. *Amethyst.*

No. 219.

Mercury, after carrying off the kine of Apollo, gave the shepherd Battus one of the finest cows, on condition that he should not reveal the theft. Battus betrayed the secret for a double bribe, and Mercury changed him to a touchstone.

APOLLONIDES. *Oriental Cornelian.*

" As once, attentive to his pipe, he play'd,
The crafty Hermes from the god convey'd
A drove that sep'rate from their fellows stray'd:
The theft an old insidious peasant view'd
(They call him Battus in the neighbourhood),
Hir'd by a wealthy Pylian prince to feed
His fav'rite mares, and watch the gen'rous breed.
The thievish god suspected him, and took
The hind aside, and thus in whispers spoke :
' Discover not the theft, whoe'er thou be,
And take that milk-white heifer for the fee.'
' Go, stranger,' cries the clown, ' securely on,
That stone shall sooner tell;' and shew'd a
        stone.

The god withdrew, but straight return'd again,
In speech and habit like a country swain ;
And cries out, ' Neighbour, hast thou seen a stray
Of bullocks and of heifers pass this way?
In the recov'ry of my cattle join,
A bullock and a heifer shall be thine.'
The peasant quick replies, ' You'll find 'em there
In yon dark vale:' and in the vale they were.
The double bribe had his false heart beguil'd ;
The god, successful in the trial, smil'd ;—
' And dost thou thus betray myself to me ?
Me to myself dost thou betray?' says he.
Then to a touchstone turns the faithless spy,
And in his name records his infamy."

OVID.

No. 220.

Mercury weighing the souls of the dead.

GNAIOS.   *Oriental Cornelian.*

" Cyllenius now to Pluto's dreary reign
  Conveys the dead, a lamentable train."

Odyssey, xxiv.

" Unspotted spirits you consign
  To blissful seats and joys divine ;
  And powerful with your golden wand,
  The light unbodied crowds command.
  Thus grateful does your office prove
  To gods below and gods above."

HOR. book i. Od. 10.

No. 221.

Mercury evoking the spirits of the dead on the banks of Lethe.

GNAIOS.   *Oriental Cornelian.*

It was a received opinion among the ancients, that the souls of the departed, after wandering for a thousand years in the Elysian fields, were recalled to earth by Mercury to animate new bodies.

" And thee,
Hermes, the chief, tremendous king, whose throne
Awes with supreme dominion, I adjure :
Send from your gloomy regions, send his shade
Once more to visit this ethereal light."

ÆSCHYLUS, *Persians.*

" ' What urg'd the busy and impatient throng
To hover near the stream ?' To whom the sire :
' At these slow ling'ring waters all those souls
Destin'd to change their forms here first must
          quaff
A long oblivion of their former cares.
Pleasing forgetfulness ! Thine eyes now ope,
The hour is come when all thy glorious line
Shall pass before thee. So much thou the more
Wilt prize th' Ausonian land.' To whom the
          son :
' Believ'st thou that these pure celestial souls,
Resuming mortal bodies, will return
Spontaneously to sluggish earth again ?
Whence such great love of life ?' The ghost
          replied,
' Thy doubts remain no longer. Hear me now :'
And thus divulg'd these awful truths sublime.

' Know that a great pervading spirit fills
The air, the earth, and all the mighty waste
Of waters ; all the starry vault above
With silver lamp of night ; and scatt'ring wide,
Inspires, actuates, impregns the mass.
Hence is the being of man, and beast, and bird,
Each in its order ; hence beneath the flood
The uncouth monsters roll ; all are alike
Inspirited with energy divine ;
But that this mixture mortal and terrene
Imbrutes the heav'nly vigour, gend'ring
The tumults of the soul, whence joy, and fear,
And grief (perplexing the perturbed mind),
Still drag them downward with their earthy load,
Marring the seed celestial innate :
E'en after death some old degenerate stains
(Inveterate infections) linger still,

Ingrafted deep ; when ev'ry former taint
Is cleans'd by suff'rings various. To the wind
Some parch in air suspended ; others steep
The rank contagion in the whelming tide,
Or dissipate the dross by sulphurous fire—
All pass through torment ere they peaceful rest
In plains of bliss (nor that the lot of all).
When at the destin'd hour, after long space
Of pain, the dregs concreted be exhal'd,
Leaving th' original spirit unconfin'd,
Ethereal, and pure, the spark divine,—
All these, though ling'ring for a thousand years,
At the god's summons drowning all their cares,
Flock to the stream Lethean, and there quaff
Oblivion of the past, that they may long
Unheedful to return to life above.'
Thus spake the prescient sire.''

Æneis, book vi.: NATH. OGLE'S *Trans.*

No. 222.

Mercury changing Chelone to a tortoise.

DIOSCORIDES. *Oriental Cornelian.*

Jupiter, to render his nuptials with Juno more impressive, commanded Mercury to invite not only all the gods, but both man and beast also. The nymph Chelone ridiculed this marriage, and was the only person who refused to assist at it. Mercury was sent in search of her, and finding her, he cast herself and her house into the river on the banks of which she dwelt, changed her to a tortoise, and condemned her to perpetual silence, of which this animal became the emblem.

No. 223.

Mercury alighting on the tortoise to which Chelone is changed.

ANTEROTOS. *Oriental Cornelian.*

No. 224.

Mercury with his caduceus lulling Chione to sleep.

APOLLONIDES. *Oriental Cornelian.*

Chione, the daughter of Dædalion, was beloved at the same time by Apollo and Mercury, and became in one day the mother of Philammon and Autolycus. The first, the son of Apollo, was a skilful player on the lute; the second, the son of Mercury, was an expert and cunning thief.

" Hermes with golden pinions binds
His flying feet, and mounts the western winds ;
And whether o'er the seas or earth he flies,
With rapid force they bear him down the skies.
But first he grasps within his awful hand
The mark of sov'reign pow'r, his magic wand :
With this he draws the ghosts from hollow graves ;
With this he drives them down the Stygian waves ;
With this he seals in sleep the wakeful sight,
And eyes, though clos'd in death, restores to light.

To Mercury Autolycus she brought,
Who turn'd to thefts and tricks his subtle thought;
Possess'd he was of all his father's sleight,
At will made white look black, and black look
    white.
Philammon, born to Phœbus, like his sire,
The Muses lov'd, and finely struck the lyre,
And made his voice and touch in harmony
    conspire."
                                    OVID.

No. 225.

The same subject.

CHROMIOS.   *Oriental Cornelian.*

No. 226.

Mercury near Chione, who is asleep on a bank strewed with flowers.

PYRGOTELES.   *Oriental Cornelian.*

No. 227.

The origin of the Caduceus.

GNAIOS.   *Oriental Cornelian.*

The principal attribute of Mercury is represented on this stone. Mercury threw between two serpents that were fighting on mount Cithæron the rod which Apollo had given him; and the reptiles twining themselves round it, Mercury chose it as an emblem of peace and alliance. He added wings, to indicate the force of eloquence and the power of persuasion over men.

No. 228.

Mercury seated in a car drawn by rams.

GNAIOS.   *Oriental Cornelian.*

Mercury on a car drawn by two rams, and laden with the attributes which, according to the fable, he had stolen from the different gods,—the sceptre of Neptune, the arrows of Apollo, the girdle of Venus. It may here be observed, that the Mercury of the Romans and Hermes of the Greeks was the same as the Thoth or Phtas (Egyptian Vulcan), the celestial elementary fire, *igneus vigor*, that is to say, the Supreme Intelligence, which animates and governs the universe, and to which belongs the qualities that mythology, before changing the principles of primitive philosophy, so beautiful from its simplicity, had attributed to each of the gods.

No. 229.

Mercury and Muta, the goddess of silence, seated at the entrance of the infernal regions.

DIOSCORIDES. *Oriental Cornelian.*

No. 230.

Mercury, holding the caduceus, seated on a ram.

DIOSCORIDES. *Cornelian.*

No. 231.

Head of Mercury.

PYRGOTELES. *Calcedony, partaking of the Sapphire.*

" Offspring of Attas and my nephew dear,
Of hell and heav'n the common messenger ;
Who canst alone appear in either court,
Free of both worlds, which own thy glad resort :
Wing on the rapid winds thy flight above,
And bear my message to the haughty Jove.
Scarce had he spoke when, with despatchful flight,
The sacred envoy gain'd the realms of light."

CLAUDIAN: HUGHES.

No. 232.

Hermaphroditus and Salmacis.

GNAIOS. *Amethyst.*

Hermaphroditus, born of Mercury and Venus, was a young man of rare beauty, in whom were united the manly form of his father and the softness and grace of his mother. The naiad Salmacis became enamoured of him,. and, concealing herself in a thicket, wished to surprise him while bathing in a fountain.

No. 233.

Salmacis metamorphosed.

DAMAS. *Calcedony.*

Salmacis surprises Hermaphroditus at the fountain, but he is indifferent to her; and Salmacis entreats the gods to unite her inseparably with Hermaphroditus, and that she may be allowed to form one being with him. This is granted, and the external appearance of the sexes were manifested in Hermaphroditus.

No. 234.

The metamorphosis of Hermaphroditus.

GNAIOS. *Amethyst.*

Hermaphroditus, astonished at his metamorphosis, is at the same time afflicted at no longer seeing Salmacis, who had at length succeeded in inspiring him with an equal passion. Cupid is shewing him the foliage of a plant growing by the side of the fountain of Salmacis.

No. 235.

Mars put in chains by the Aloides.

PEMALLIO. *Oriental Cornelian.*

In the wars with the Giants, in which all the gods undertook to defend the throne of Jupiter, Mars was wounded, and taken by the Aloides, Otus and Ephialtes, who detained him prisoner during thirteen months.

> " The mighty Mars, in mortal fetters bound,
> And lodg'd in brazen dungeons underground,
> Full thirteen moons imprison'd, roar'd in vain ;
> Otus and Ephialtes held the chain :
> Perhaps had perish'd, had not Hermes' care
> Restor'd the groaning god to upper air."
> *Iliad,* book v.

" For Tartarus descends a double space
Through the dark caverns of the realms of night.
Deeper than to the canopy of heav'n
Is the ascent: here that old earth-born race,
Hurl'd headlong by the angry bolts of Jove,
Lie rolling in the abyss. I there beheld
Th' Allian brethren of gigantic mould,
Neptunian sprung, whose brutal force defied
The Thunderer's arm, and to the vault above
Menac'd annihilation."

Æneis, book vi.: NATH. OGLE'S *Trans.*

No. 236.

Mercury came down from Mount Olympus, burst the chains which bound Mars, and delivered him, unknown to the Giants.

GNAIOS. *Oriental Sardonyx.*

No. 237.

Mars, hastening to defend Olympus from the attack of the Titans, kills two of them with his formidable lance.

APOLLONIDES. *Oriental Cornelian.*

No. 238.

Mars, in the war with the Titans, killed with a thrust of his lance the most formidable of these monstrous children of the earth.

DIOSCORIDES. *Oriental Cornelian.*

No. 239.

Halirrhotius and Alcippe.

APOLLONIDES. *Oriental Sardonyx.*

124

Halirrhotius, the son of Neptune, passionately loved Alcippe, daughter of the god Mars. He ravished her and carried her off. Mars killed the ravisher. Neptune, inconsolable for the loss of his son, summoned the murderer to judgment before the Areopagus, who unanimously declared Mars " not guilty."

> " But, nam'd from Mars, there is a certain hill
> Where the immortal powers in judgment sat
> On murder, when the cruel god of war
> Slew lustful Halirrhotius, fir'd with rage
> Against that impious miscreant, Neptune's son,
> Who had by force defil'd his daughter's bed ;
> There each decision since that time pronounc'd
> Is sacred, and awarded by the gods."
>
> EUR., *Elec.*

> " The sacred judgment-seat
> Is there, at which Jove erst ordain'd that Mars,
> Whose hands had been defil'd with recent gore,
> Should undergo a trial."
>
> EUR., *Iphigenia.*

No. 240.

Mars and Cupid.

CHROMIOS. *Cornelian.*

> " Then Love, most beauteous of immortals, rose ;
> He of each god and mortal man at once
> Unnerves the limbs, dissolves the wiser breast
> By reason steel'd, and quells the very soul."
>
> HESIOD.

" Once to the Lemnian cave of flame
The crested lord of battles came ;
'Twas from the ranks of war he rush'd,
His spear with many a life-drop blush'd :
He saw the mystic darts, and smil'd
Derision on the archer child.
' And dost thou smile ?' said little Love :
' Take this small dart, and thou may'st prove,
That though they pass the breeze's flight,
My bolts are not so feathery light.'

He took the shaft ; and, O thy look,
Sweet Venus ! when the shaft he took :
He sigh'd, and felt the urchin's art—
He sigh'd in agony of heart.
' It is not light ; I die with pain ;
Take—take thy arrow back again.'
' No,' said the child, ' it must not be ;
That little dart was made for thee ' "

ANACREON : MOORE

No. 241.

Mars changing Alectryon to a cock.

DIOSCORIDES. *Amethyst.*

Mars, in his frequent interviews with Venus, charged Alectryon to keep watch for him, and to guard his arms. Alectryon, however, fell asleep, and Phœbus giving intelligence to Vulcan, he surprised Mars with his wife, and exposed them to the railleries of the inhabitants of Olympus. Mars changes Alectryon to a cock, commanding him to announce every day the rising of the sun.

No. 242.

Head of Mars.

CAECAS. *Cornelian.*

" Now Mars showers down a fiery sleet, and winds
His trumpet shell, distilling blood ; and now,
Knit with the furies and the fates in dance,
Leads on the dreadful revelry : the fields
With iron harvests of embattled spears
Gleam ; from the towers I hear a voice of woe
Rise to the stedfast empyrean ; crowds
Of zoneless matrons rend their flowing robes,
And sobs and shrieks cry loud into the night."

LYCOPHRON : VISCOUNT ROYSTON'S *Trans.*

No. 243.

Mars Gradivus.

PYRGOTELES. *Oriental Cornelian.*

" Frantic are ye who seek renown
Amid the horrors of th' embattled field ;
Who masking guilt beneath a laurel-crown,
    With nervous arm the falchion wield :
Not slaughter'd thousands can your fury
    sate,
    If still success the judgment guide ;
If bloody battle right and wrong decide,
Incessant strife must vex each rival state.

Hence from her home departs each Phrygian wife,
    O Helen, when the cruel strife
    Which from thy charms arose
One conference might have clos'd ; now myriads
    dwell
    With Pluto in the shades of hell,
    And flames, as when Jove's vengeance throws
The bolt, have caught her towers, and finish'd
    Ilion's woes."

EURIPIDES, *Helen.:* WOODHULL.

" Lo ! the ministers of Fate
   Hover o'er this guilty land ;
Bloated Anger, livid Hate,
   Guide the desolating band.
Wide the hosts of Rapine spread,
   Battle leads the dusky van ;
Fiery clouds half shroud his head,
   Gales of Death his banners fan ;
Famine crouches at his side ;
   Underneath his ample shield
Pestilence, with nostrils wide,
   Scents the carnage of the field."
               HAYGARTH'S *Cassandra.*

CLASS II.

DEMI-GODS.

No. 244.

Chaos.

CHROMIOS. *Sardonyx.*

" Before the seas, and this terrestrial ball,
And heav'n's high canopy that covers all,
One was the face of nature, if a face—
Rather a rude and indigested mass ;
A lifeless lump, unfashion'd and unfram'd,
Of jarring seeds, and justly Chaos nam'd.
No sun was lighted up the world to view ;
No moon did yet her blunted horns renew ;
Nor yet was earth suspended in the sky,
Nor pois'd did on her own foundations lie ;
Nor seas about the shores their arms had thrown ;
But earth, and air, and water were in one.
Thus air was void of light, and earth unstable,
And water's dark abyss unnavigable.
No certain form on any was imprest ;
All were confus'd, and each disturb'd the rest.
For hot and cold were in one body fix'd ;
And soft with hard, and light with heavy mix'd.

．　　．　　．　　．　　．　　．

From the beginning say who first arose ;
First of all beings Chaos was."

OVID.

" Now I will sing how moving seeds were hurl'd,
How toss'd to order, how they fram'd the world :
How sun and moon began ; what steady force
Mark'd out their walk ; what makes them keep
　　their course.
For sure unthinking seeds did ne'er dispose
Themselves by counsel, nor their order chose ;
Nor any compacts made how each should move,
But from eternal through the vacuum strove,
By their own weight, or by eternal blows,
All motions tried, to find the best of those ;
All unions too, if, by their various play,
They could compose new beings any way :
Thus long they whirl'd, most sorts of motion
　　past,
Most sorts of union too, they join'd at last
In such convenient order, whence began
The sea, the heav'n, and earth, and beasts, and
　　man :
But yet no glitt'ring sun, no twinkling star,
No heav'n, no roaring sea, no earth, no air,
Nor any thing like these did then appear,

But a vast heap; and from this mighty mass
Each part retir'd, and took its proper place:
Agreeing seeds combin'd; each atom ran
And sought his like, and so the frame began.
From disagreeing seeds the world did rise,
Because their various motion, weight, and size,
And figure, would not let them all combine,
And lie together, nor friendly motions join:
Thus skies, and thus the sun first rais'd his head,
Thus stars, thus seas o'er proper places spread."

LUCRETIUS, book iv.

" And now let this as the first rule be laid,
Nothing was by the gods of nothing made.
From hence proceeds all our distrust and fear,
That many things in heaven and earth appear,
Whose causes far remote and hidden lie,
Beyond the ken of vulgar reason's eye,
And therefore men ascribe them to the Deity.
But this once prov'd, it gives an open way
To nature's secrets, and we walk in day."

LUCRETIUS, book i.

——" I saw the rising birth
Of nature from the unapparent deep;
I saw, when, at God's word, this formless mass,
The world's material mould, came to a heap:
Confusion heard his voice, and wild uproar
Stood rul'd, stood vast infinitude confin'd;
Till at his second bidding, darkness fled,
Light shone, and order from disorder sprung.
Swift to their sev'ral quarters hasten'd then
The cumb'rous elements, earth, flood, air, fire;
And the ethereal quintessence of heaven
Flew upward, spirited with various forms,
That roll'd orbicular, and turn'd to stars:
Each had his place appointed, each his course.
Thus God the heav'ns created, thus the earth,
Matter unform'd and void: darkness profound
Cover'd th' abyss: but on the wat'ry calm
His brooding wings the Spirit of God outspread,
And vital virtue infus'd, and vital warmth
Throughout the fluid mass; but downwards purg'd
The black, tartareous, cold, infernal drugs,
Adverse to life: then founded, then conglob'd
Like things to like; the rest to several place
Disparted, and between spun out the air;
And earth, self-balanc'd, on her centre hung."

MILTON.

" He sung the secret seeds of nature's frame:
How seas, and earth, and air, and active flame,
Fell through the mighty void; and in their fall
Were blindly gather'd in this goodly ball!
The tender soil then, stiff'ning by degrees,
Shut from the bounded earth the bounding seas:
Then earth and ocean various forms disclose,
And a new sun to the new world arose;
And mists, condens'd to clouds, obscure the sky;
And clouds, dissolv'd, the thirsty ground supply:
The rising trees the lofty mountains grace;
The lofty mountains feed the savage race,
Yet few, and strangers in the unpeopled place."

VIRGIL, Ec.: DRYDEN.

No. 245.

Head of Æolus.

AULOS. *Cornelian.*

" In a spacious cave of living stone,
The tyrant Æolus, from his airy throne,
With power imperial curbs the struggling winds,
And sounding tempests in dark prisons binds ;
This way and that th' impatient captives tend,
And pressing for release the mountains rend.
High in his hall th' undaunted monarch stands,
And shakes his sceptre, and their rage commands ;
Which did he not, their unresisted sway
Would sweep the world before them in their way ;
Earth, air, and seas, through empty space would roll,
And heaven would fly before the driving soul !
In fear of this, the father of the gods
Confin'd their fury to those dark abodes,
And lock'd them safe within, oppress'd with mountain loads ;
Impos'd a king, with arbitrary sway,
To loose their fetters, or their force allay."

VIRGIL.

" There he commands the changing clouds to stray,
There thund'ring terrors mortal minds dismay ;
And, with the lightning, winds engend'ring snow,
Yet not permitted every way to blow,
Who hardly now to tear the world refrain
(So brothers jar), though they divided reign.
To Persis and Sabæa Eurus flies,
Whose gums perfume the blushing morn's uprise.
Next to the evening, and the coast that glows
With setting Phœbus, flow'ry Zeph'rus blows.
In Scythia horrid Boreas holds his reign,
Beneath Boötes and the frozen wain.
The land to this oppos'd doth Auster steep
With fruitful show'rs, and clouds which ever weep."

OVID'S *Met.:* SANDYS.

" At length we reach'd Æolia's sea-girt shore,
Where great Hippotades the sceptre bore ;
A floating isle ! High rais'd by toil divine,
Strong walls of brass the rocky coast confine.
Six blooming youths, in private grandeur bred,
And six fair daughters grac'd the royal bed :
These sons their sisters wed, and all remain
Their parents' pride, and pleasure of their reign.
All day they feast, all day the bowls flow round,
And joy and music through the isle resound.
At night each pair on splendid carpets lay,
And crown'd with love the pleasures of the day.
This happy port affords our wandering fleet
A month's reception and a safe retreat.
Full oft the monarch urg'd me to relate
The fall of Ilion and the Grecian fate :
Full oft I told ; at length for parting mov'd ;
The king with mighty gifts my suit approv'd.
The adverse winds in leathern bags he brac'd,
Compress'd their force, and lock'd each struggling blast.
For him the mighty sire of gods assign'd
The tempest's lord, the tyrant of the wind ;
His word alone the listening storms obey,
To smooth the deep or swell the foamy sea."

Odyssey.

" Now rising all at once and unconfin'd,
From every quarter roars the rushing wind.
First from the wide Atlantic ocean's bed
Tempestuous Corus rears his dreadful head ;

S

Th' obedient deep his potent breath controls,
And mountain-high the foamy flood he rolls.
Him the north-east encountering fierce defied,
And back rebuffeted the yielding tide.
The curling surges loud conflicting meet,
Dash their proud heads, and bellow as they beat;
While piercing Boreas from the Scythian strand
Ploughs up the waves, and scoops the lowest sand.
Nor Eurus then I ween was left to dwell,
Nor showery Notus in the Æolian cell;

But each from every side, his power to boast,
Rang'd his proud forces to defend his coast.
Equal in might, alike they strive in vain,
While in the midst the seas unmov'd remain.
In lesser wars they yield to stormy heaven,
And captive waves to other deeps are driven;
The Tyrrhene billows dash Ægean shores,
And Adria in the mix'd Ionian roars."

LUCAN'S *Phar.*: ROWE.

No. 246.

Æolus menacing his daughter Canace.

APOLLONIDES.   *Oriental Cornelian.*

She holds in her arms the child born of her illicit marriage with her brother Macareus.

" The babe he seiz'd, the feigned rites unveil'd,
And hapless me with raging voice assail'd;
As ocean quivers to the passing breeze,
As stormy south winds shake the rustling trees,
My pale limbs shiv'ring at his voice and frown,
So shook beneath my frame the bed of down.
A father's tongue proclaim'd his daughter's shame,
And e'en from violence could scarce refrain.

O'erwhelm'd with conscious guilt and fears,
I only answer'd him with sobs and tears.
To vultures and to hungry dogs a prey,
He bids them cast our helpless babe away;
The guiltless child, as conscious of his doom,
With cries implor'd to snatch him from the
     tomb."

OVID'S *Ep. Can. to Mac.*: N. O.

No. 247.

Oceanus borne by a sea-crab.

CHROMIOS.   *Oriental Cornelian.*

Oceanus, son of Cœlus and Vesta, was the father of all the principal rivers, and of three thousand nymphs called Oceanides, whom he had by his wife Tethys. The sea-crab was consecrated to him. He holds a sceptre and a rudder, and majestically traverses the sea.

" Thetis to Ocean brought the rivers forth,
In whirlpool waters roll'd: Eridanus
Deep-eddied, and Alpheus, and the Nile;
Fair-flowing Ister, Strymon, and Meander,
Phasis and Rhesus; Achelous bright

With silver-circled tides; Heptaporus,
And Nessus; Haliacmon and Rhodius;
Granicus and the heavenly Simois;
Æsapus, Hermus, and Sangarius vast;
Peneus, and Caicus smoothly flowing;

And Ladon, and Parthenius, and Evenus;
Ardescus, and Scamander the divine:
Three thousand graceful Oceanides
Long stepping tread the earth; or far and wide
Dispers'd, they haunt the glassy depth of lakes,
A glorious sisterhood of goddess-birth.

As many rivers also, yet untold,
Rushing with hollow-dashing echoes, rose
From awful Tethys: but their every name
Is not for mortal man to memorate,
Arduous, yet known to all the borderers round."
HESIOD.

No. 248.

A head of Ocean.

CHROMIOS. *Amethyst.*

" Ah, me! what draws thee hither? Art thou come,
Spectator of my toils? How hast thou ventur'd
To leave the ocean-waves, from thee so call'd,
Thy rock-roof'd grottoes, arch'd by Nature's hand,
And land upon this iron-teeming earth?
Com'st thou to visit and bewail my ills?"
ÆSCHYLUS, *Prometheus:* POTTER.

No. 249.

Galatea, daughter of Nereus and Doris, accompanied by a Triton, who, playing on a sea-shell, calms the angry waves.

DIOSCORIDES. *Amethyst.*

" Triton, at his call, appears
Above the waves; a Tyrian robe he wears,
And in his hand a crooked trumpet bears.
The sov'reign bids him peaceful sounds inspire,
And give the waves the signal to retire.
His writhen shell he takes, whose narrow vent
Grows by degrees into a large extent;

Then gives it breath: the blast, with doubling sound,
Runs the wide circuit of the world around.
The Sun first heard it in his early east,
And met the rattling echoes in the west;
The waters, list'ning to the trumpets' roar,
Obey the summons, and forsake the shore."
OVID.

No. 250.

Polyphemus the Cyclops, enamoured of Galatea, arranging his hair, and looking at himself in the sea, which serves him as a mirror.

CHROMIOS. *Calcedony.*

" On a steep
Rough-pointed rock, that overlook'd the deep,
And with brown horror high impending hung,
The giant monster sat, and thus he sung :—
 ' Fair nymph, why will you thus my passion
  slight ?
Softer than lambs you seem, than curds more white;
Wanton as calves before the udder'd kine,
Harsh as the unripe fruitage of the vine.
You come when pleasing sleep has clos'd mine eye,
And like a vision with my slumbers fly,
Swift as before the wolf the lambkin bounds,
Panting and trembling, o'er the furrow'd grounds.
Then first I lov'd, and thence I date my flame,
When here to gather hyacinths you came ;
My mother brought you—'twas a fatal day—
And I, alas! unwary led the way.
E'er since my tortur'd mind has known no rest;
Peace is become a stranger to my breast:
Yet you nor pity nor relieve my pain—
Yes, yes, I know the cause of your disdain.
For, stretch'd from ear to ear with shagged grace,
My single brow adds horror to my face ;
My single eye enormous lids enclose,
And o'er my blubber'd lips projects my nose.
Yet homely as I am, large flocks I keep,
And drain the udders of a thousand sheep ;
My pails with milk, my shelves with cheese they
  fill,
In summer scorching, and in winter chill.
The vocal pipe I tune with pleasing glee,
No other Cyclops can compare with me ;
Your charms I sing, sweet apple of delight!
Myself and you I sing the live-long night.

For you ten fawns, with collars deck'd, I feed,
And four young bears for your diversion breed.
Come, live with me ; all these you may command,
And change your azure ocean for the land :
More pleasing slumbers will my cave bestow ;
There spiry cypress and green laurels grow ;
There round my trees the sable ivy twines,
And grapes as sweet as honey load my vines ;
From grove-crown'd Etna, rob'd in purest snow,
Cool springs roll nectar to the swains below.
Say, who would quit such peaceful scenes as these
For blustering billows and tempestuous seas ?
Though my rough form's no object of desire,
My oaks supply me with abundant fire ;
My hearth unceasing blazes : though I swear
By this one eye, to me for ever dear,
Well might that fire to warm my breast suffice,
That kindled at the lightning of your eyes.
Had I, like fish, with fins and gills been made,
Then might I in your element have play'd ;
With ease have div'd beneath your azure tide,
And kiss'd your hand, though you your lips
  deny'd ;
Brought lilies fair, or poppies red that grow
In summer's solstice, or in winter's snow :
These flowers I could not both together bear,
That bloom'd in different seasons of the year.
Well, I'm resolv'd, fair nymph, I'll learn to dive,
If e'er a sailor at this port arrive ;
Then shall I surely by experience know
What pleasures charm you in the depths below.
Emerge, O Galatea ! from the sea,
And here forget your native home like me."
         THEOCRITUS.

 " Forgot his caverns and his woolly care,
  Assum'd the softness of a lover's air,
 And comb'd with teeth of rakes his rugged hair.
 Now with a crooked scythe his beard he sleeks,
 And mows the stubborn stubble of his cheeks,
 Now in the crystal stream he looks to try
 His simagres, and rolls his glaring eye."
         OVID.

No. 251.

Galatea escaping from Polyphemus.

CHROMIOS. *Oriental Cornelian.*

Polyphemus, having surprised Galatea with the young Acis the son of Faunus, hurled a piece of rock at him and crushed him. Galatea, fearing the same fate, saved herself as is represented on this stone.

" Affrighted with his monstrous voice, I fled,
And in the neighb'ring ocean plung'd my
head.
Poor Acis turu'd his back, and, 'Help,' he cried,
' Help, Galatea, help, my parent gods,
And take me dying to your deep abodes.'
The Cyclops follow'd ; but he sent before
A rib which from the living rock he tore :

Though but an angle reach'd him of the stone,
The mighty fragment was enough alone
To crush all Acis ; 'twas too late to save,
But what the fates allow'd to give, I gave :
That Acis to his lineage should return,
And roll, among the river-gods, his urn.
Straight issu'd from the stone a stream of blood ;
Which lost the purple, mingling with the flood."

OVID.

No. 252.

Glaucus addressing Scylla.

APOLLONIDES. *Cornelian.*

Glaucus, the son of Neptune, loved the nymph Scylla, and wished to marry her, but she refused to listen to him, and fled.

" While Scylla, fearful of the wide-spread
main,
Swift to the safer shore returns again.
There o'er the sandy margin unarray'd,
With printless footsteps flies the bounding maid ;
Or in some winding creek's secure retreat
She bathes her weary limbs, and shuns the noon-
day's heat.
Her Glaucus saw as o'er the deep he rode,
New to the seas, and late receiv'd a god.
He saw, and languish'd for the virgin's love ;
With many an artful blandishment he strove
Her flight to hinder, and her fears remove.
The more he sues, the more she wings her
flight,
And nimbly gains a neighb'ring mountain's
height.

Steep shelving to the margin of the flood,
A neighb'ring mountain bare and woodless
stood;
Here, by the place secur'd, her steps she stay'd,
And, trembling still, her lover's form survey'd.
His shape, his hue, her troubled sense appall,
And dropping locks that o'er his shoulders fall :
She sees his face divine and manly brow
End in a fish's wreathy tail below :
She sees, and doubts within her anxious mind
Whether he comes of god or monster kind.
This Glaucus soon perceiv'd ; and, ' O ! forbear,
(His hand supporting on a rock lay near)
' Forbear,' he cried, ' fond maid, this needless
fear ;
Nor fish am I, nor monster of the main,
But equal with the wat'ry gods I reign.'"

OVID.

No. 253.

Nereus and Doris.

GNAIOS. *Oriental Amethyst.*

Children of Ocean and Tethys, of whom were born the fifty Nereids.

No. 254.

The birth of Rhodus, one of the Oceanides, beloved by Apollo, who gave her name to an island called Rhodes.

PYRGOTELES. *Oriental Sardonyx.*

"Some say, that when by lot th' immortal gods
  With Jove these earthly regions did divide,
All undiscover'd lay Phœbean Rhodes,
  Whelm'd deep beneath the salt Carpathian
    tide:

That, absent on his course, the god of day
  By all the heavenly synod was forgot,
Who, his incessant labours to repay,
  Nor land nor sea to Phœbus did allot;

That Jove, reminded, would again renew
  Th' unjust partition, but the god denied;
And said, beneath yon hoary surge I view
  An isle emerging through the briny tide;

A region pregnant with the fertile seed
  Of plants, and herbs, and fruits, and foodful
    grain;
Each verdant hill unnumber'd flocks shall feed;
  Unnumber'd men possess each flow'ry plain.

Then straight to Lachesis he gave command,
  Who binds in golden cauls her jetty hair;
He bade the fatal sister stretch her hand,
  And by the Stygian rivers bade her swear;

Swear to confirm the Thunderer's decree
  Which to his rule that fruitful island gave,

When from the oozy bottom of the sea
  Her head she rear'd above the Lycian wave.

The fatal sister swore, nor swore in vain;
  Nor did the tongue of Delphi's prophet err;
Upsprung the blooming island through the main,
  And Jove on Phœbus did the boon confer.

In this fam'd isle, the radiant fire of light,
  The god whose reins the fiery steeds obey
Fair Rhodos saw, and, kindling at the sight,
  Seiz'd, and by force enjoy'd the beauteous
    prey:

From whose divine embraces sprung a race
  Of mortals, wisest of all human kind;
Seven sons, endow'd with every noble grace—
  The noble graces of a sapient mind.

Of these Ialysus and Lindus came,
  Who with Camirus shar'd the Rhodian lands;
Apart they reign'd, and sacred to his name
  Apart each brother's royal city stands.

Here a secure retreat from all his woes
  Astydameia's hapless offspring found;
Here, like a god in undisturb'd repose,
  And like a god with heav'nly honours crown'd."

PINDAR, *Homeric Stanzas:* WEST.

No. 255.

The birth of Bacchus.

DIOSCORIDES. *Oriental Sardonyx.*

Jupiter appears to Semele, who, instigated by Juno under the form of her nurse Beroë, desired to see him in all his glory. He heard her request with horror; but as he had sworn by the Styx to grant whatsoever she should ask, he acquiesced; and Semele was consumed, but Bacchus was saved from the flames.

" To keep his promise he ascends, and
    shrouds
His awful brow in whirlwinds and in clouds;
Whilst all around, in terrible array,
His thunders rattle and his lightnings play.
Thus dreadfully adorn'd, with horror bright,
Th' illustrious god, descending from his height,
Came rushing on her in a storm of light.

The mortal dame, too feeble to engage
The lightning's flashes and the thunder's rage,
Consum'd amidst the glories she desir'd,
And in the terrible embrace expir'd.
    But, to preserve his offspring from the tomb,
Jove took him, smoking, from the blasted womb;
And, if on ancient tales we may rely,
Enclos'd the half-born infant in his thigh."
                  OVID.

" Thy hapless daughters' various fate
  This moral truth, O Cadmus, shews;
  Who, vested now with godlike state,
  On heavenly thrones repose,
  And yet affliction's thorny road
  In bitter anguish once they trod.
  But bliss superior hath eras'd
    The memory of their woe;
  While Semele, on high Olympus plac'd,

To heavenly zephyrs bids her tresses flow,
Once by devouring lightnings all defac'd.
    There, with immortal charms improv'd,
  Inhabitant of heaven's serene abodes
  She dwells, by virgin Pallas lov'd;
  Lov'd by Saturnius, father of the gods;
  Lov'd by her youthful son, whose brows divine,
  In twisting ivy bound, with joy eternal shine."
         PINDAR, *Olym.* ii.: WEST.

" When sudden throes her entrails tore,
  As wing'd from heav'n the rapid lightnings came,
  The mother an abortive infant bore,
  And died o'ercome by that celestial flame.
  But Jove, in such distressful state,
  Did for his son another womb supply;
  And safe within his fostering thigh
  Conceal him from Saturnia's hate.
  At length the horned god he bore,
  Form'd by the Fates with plastic care,
  Who on his head a wreath of serpents wore,
The Mænades hence twine the spoils around their hair.'
        EURIP. *Bacch.:* WOODHULL.

No. 256.

Mercury conveying Bacchus to the nymph Ino.

GNAIOS. *Sardonyx.*

" By those who wander o'er the briny deep
She's call'd Leucothea, and her son obtains
The sailor's worship by Palæmon's name."

EURIP. Frag.

" Whom first
By stealth his careful aunt, kind Ino, nurst ;
Then given to the Nysseides, and bred
In secret caves, with milk and honey fed."

OVID : SANDYS.

" Thee saw the wild and rocky steep,
  Whose forked summits proudly rise,
  And stretch their rude brows to the skies,
Where the Corycian nymphs their orgies keep.
Thee, the flames blazing on the mount ;
Thee, pure Castalia's sacred fount ;
Thee, the Nysæan mountain's craggy sides,

O'er which the mantling ivy twines,
The swelling hillocks green with vines,
Whose purple fruit their foliage hides ;
And waking harmony's enchanting pow'rs
On thee attends, thy raptur'd train ;
Raises the high immortal strain,
And hails thee guardian of the Theban tow'rs."

SOPH. Antig.: POTTER.

No. 257.

Bacchus changed to a kid.

DIOSCORIDES. *Calcedony.*

Jupiter, to conceal from Juno the fruit of his amours with Semele, changes Bacchus to a kid, and commands Mercury to convey him to the Nysæan nymphs.

No. 258.

Mercury carrying the kid Bacchus.

DIOSCORIDES. *Amethyst.*

No. 259.

Mercury confiding the infant Bacchus to Ino-Leucothoe, the sister of Semele, that he might be educated by her, with the assistance of the Hyads, the Hours, and the Nymphs.

DIOSCORIDES. *Oriental Cornelian.*

" Ino first took him for her foster-child ;
Then the Nyseans, in their dark abode,
Nurs'd secretly with milk the thriving god."

No. 260.

Bacchus, enamoured of Erigone, daughter of Icarius, changes himself to a bunch of grapes to deceive her.

PYRGOTELES. *Oriental Cornelian.*

" There Bacchus, imaged like the clust'ring grape,
Melting, bedrops Erigone's fair lap."
OVID'S *Met.* book vi.

" I bloom'd awhile in happy flower,
Till Love approach'd one fatal hour,
And made my tender branches feel
The wounds of his avenging steel ;
Then, then I fell like some poor willow,
That tosses on the wintry billow."
ANACREON : MOORE.

No. 261.

Bacchus bringing Semele from Hades.

SCYLAX. *Oriental Cornelian.*

Semele, the mother of Bacchus, who was consumed by beholding Jupiter in all his radiance, descended to the infernal regions. The first adventure of Bacchus was to bring her thence.

"With golden horn supremely bright,
 You darted round the bending light,
 Far-beaming through the gloom of hell;
 When Cerberus, with fear amaz'd,
 Forgot his rage, and frowning gaz'd,
 And at thy feet adoring fell."

                    HOR. book ii. Od. 19.

———————————

            "Thy prayers have sped,
 And hell no more withholds the hallow'd dead;
 Elysian landscapes shine expos'd to day,
 And yawning chasms the nether shades display.

    .   .   .   .

 The next in order as they pass along,
 Vary in sex and age, a mingled throng:
 Autonoë, the first, is bath'd in tears,
 And Semele the bolt she merits fears."

                    APOLL. RH. book iv.

No. 262.

Ariadne, daughter of Minos king of Crete, weeping in the Isle of Naxos
    because she was forsaken by Theseus, who had carried off her sister
    Phædra.

           GNAIOS.   *Oriental Amethyst.*

 "When Theseus, aided by the virgin's art,
  Had trac'd the guiding thread through ev'ry part,
  He took the gentle maid that set him free,
  And, bound for Dias, cut the briny sea.
  There quickly cloy'd, ungrateful and unkind,
  Left his fair consort in the isle behind."

———————————

 "You, Ariadne, on a coast unknown,
  The perjur'd Theseus wept, and wept alone;
  But learn'd Catullus in immortal strains
  Has sung his baseness, and has wept your pains."

                    TIBULLUS: GRAINGER.

"Than savage beasts more fierce, more to be fear'd,
Expos'd by thee, by them I yet am spar'd!

These lines from that unhappy shore I write,
Where you forsook me in your faithless flight,

And the most tender lover did betray,
While lock'd in sleep and in your arms she lay.
When morning dew on all the fields did fall,
And birds with early songs for day did call,
Then I, half-sleeping, stretch'd me tow'rds your place,
And sought to press you with a new embrace;
Oft sought to press you close, but still in vain,
My folding arms came empty back again.
Startled, I rose, and found that you were gone,
Then on my widow'd bed fell raging down;
Beat the fond breast where, spite of me, you dwell,
And tore that hair which once you lik'd so well.

By the moon's light I the wide shore did view,
But all was desert, and no sight of you.
Then ev'ry way with love's mad haste I fly,
But ill my feet with my desires comply;
Weary they sink in the deep-yielding sands,
Refusing to obey such wild commands.
To all the shore of Theseus I complain,
The hills and rocks send back that name again;
Oft they repeat aloud the mournful noise,
And kindly aid a hoarse and dying voice."

OVID, *Ep.*

No. 263.

Bacchus discovering Ariadne asleep on a rock.

GNAIOS. *Oriental Cornelian.*

" The royal Minos Ariadne bred,
  She Theseus lov'd, from Crete with Theseus fled:
  Swift to the Dian isle the hero flies,
  And tow'rds his Athens bears the lovely prize;
  There Bacchus with fierce rage Diana fires,
  The goddess aims her shaft, the nymph expires."

No. 264.

Ariadne presenting a cup to Bacchus containing a most exquisite liquid.

DIOSCORIDES. *Oriental Cornelian.*

" What time with large nectareous draughts oppress'd,
  On the soft vesture Bacchus sunk to rest,
  Close by his side the Cretan maid reclin'd,
  At Naxos' isle whom Theseus left behind;
  From that bless'd hour the robe, with odours fill'd,
  Ambrosial fragrance wide around distill'd."

APOLL. RHO.

" Now Bacchus calls me to his jolly rites:
- Who would not follow, when a god invites?
He helps the poet, and his pen inspires,
Kind and indulgent to his former sires.

Fair Ariadne wander'd on the shore,
Forsaken now, and Theseus loves no more.
Loose was her gown, dishevell'd was her hair,
Her bosom naked, and her feet were bare;

Exclaiming, on the water's brink she stood,
Her briny tears augment the briny flood;
She shriek'd and wept, and both became her face,
No posture could that heav'nly form disgrace.
She beat her breast: ' The traitor's gone,' said she;
' What shall become of poor forsaken me?
What shall become—' She had not time for more,
The sounding cymbals rattled on the shore.
She swoons for fear, she falls upon the ground,
No vital heat was in her body found:
The Mimallonian dames about her stood,
And scudding satyrs ran before their god.
And now the god of wine came driving on,
High on his chariot by swift tigers drawn;
Her colour, voice, and sense forsook the fair;
Thrice did her trembling feet for flight prepare,
And thrice affrighted did her flight forbear.

She shook, like leaves of corn when tempests blow,
Or slender reeds that in the marshes grow:
To whom the god,—' Compose thy fearful mind,
In me a truer husband thou shalt find.
With heav'n I will endow thee; and thy star
Shall with propitious light be seen afar,
And guide on seas the doubtful mariner.'
He said; and from his chariot leaping light,
Lest the grim tigers should the nymph affright,
His brawny arms around her waist he threw,
(For gods, whate'er they will, with ease can do,)
And swiftly bore her thence: th' attending throng
Shout at the sight, and sing the nuptial song.
Now in full bowls her sorrow she may steep;
The bridegroom's liquor lays the bride asleep."

Ovid, Ar. Am.

No. 265.

Bacchus placing the crown of stars on the head of Ariadne.

Gnaios.   Sardonyx.

" Fair Ariadne's crown shall rise,
And add new glories to the skies."

Hor. book iii. Od. 19.

" Next night thou Ariadne's crown mayst see,
Install'd divine by Theseus' perjury.
Now she that gave her thankless love the thread
Had chang'd for Bacchus that perjurious bed;
Joy'd in her match, ' Fool that I was to mourn;
'Tis my advantage that he prov'd forsworn.'
The long-lock'd Indians Liber i' th' mean time
Subdu'd, and came enrich'd from th' eastern clime.
Among the captive maids which did excel
In beauty, he the princess lov'd too well.
His wife bewails; and wand'ring on the shore
With scatter'd hairs, her case doth thus deplore:
' Once more, ye waves, hear my old mournful cares;
Once more, ye sands, swim in a flood of tears.

I Theseus once accus'd for perjury—
He's gone; and Bacchus proves as false as he.
Once more I cry, No woman trust a man;
In change of names my act is new begun.
O that my fate had its first course held on!
Now had my essence with my woes been done.
Why didst thou, Liber, me from dying save?
My sorrows then but one release did crave.
Light Bacchus, lighter than thy brow-bound leafs!
O Bacchus, known but to my tears and griefs!
.   .   .   .   .
Ah! where's thy faith? those solemn vows indented?
Ah me, how oft have I these dirges vented!

Thou blamedst Theseus, and him false didst style;
In thine own judgment thou art far more vile.
In secret griefs I burn, and dare not tell,
Lest it be thought I am thus oft serv'd well.
O let not Theseus know't, of all, lest he
Triumph the more in thy society.
Perhaps her white complexion you prefer
Before my tanu'd : that colour be to her.
But what's all this? She's lik'd the better in
Her black defects: take heed she stains thy skin.
O keep thy vow; nor strangers' beds approve
Before thy wife's! A man I e'er did love.
The white bull's horns my mother caught: thine,
me;
But this thy base love wounds me heavily.
Make not my love my bane: thine did not prove
So when to me thyself confess'd thy love.

Thou burn'st me; 'tis not strange : thou wert
conceiv'd
In fire; from fire by father's hand repriev'd.
To me, O Bacchus, thou betrothedst heaven ;
Ah me, for heaven what dowries here are given!'
She ended. Bacchus all the while did mind her
Lamenting, as by chance he came behind her.
He clips her waist, and tears with kisses dries.
' Let's both,' quoth he, ' together mount the skies;
Our beds are one, our names shall be the same,
And Libera shall be thy changèd name;
Thy crown with thee a monument shall be —
What Vulcan gave to Venus, she to thee.'
This said, her pearls to stars, in number nine,
He chang'd, with which she now in gold doth
shine."

OVID, *Fasti*, book iii. : GOWER.

" Whom Bacchus saw,
Resolves the dear engaging dame
Shall shine for ever in the rolls of fame ;
And bids her crown among the stars be plac'd,
With an eternal constellation grac'd.
The golden circlet mounts; and, as it flies,
Its diamonds twinkle in the distant skies ;
There, in their pristine form, the gemmy rays
Between Alcides and the Dragon blaze."

No. 266.

Bacchus laughing at Hercules.

CHROMIOS. *Oriental Sardonyx.*

Hercules is drunk, and seated on the skin of the Nemean lion, on the ground.

" When gay Bacchus fills my breast,
All my cares are lull'd to rest ;
Rich I seem as Lydia's king,
Merry catch or ballad sing ;
Ivy-wreaths my temple shade,
Ivy that will never fade :

Thus I sit in mind elate
Laughing at the farce of state.
Some delight in fighting-fields ;
Nobler transports Bacchus yields.
Fill the bowl; I ever said,
'Tis better to lie drunk than dead."

ANACREON : FAWKES.

" Arm you, arm you, man of might,
Hasten to the sanguine fight;
Let me, O my budding vine,
Spill no other blood than thine !
Yonder brimming goblet see,
That alone shall vanquish me.
Warrior ! shall I tell you true
How we differ, I and you?
You'll be dead, a senseless trunk,
I shall only be—dead drunk !"

MOORE.

No. 267.

Bacchus, in a car drawn by panthers, looking at Hercules drunk under a tree.

PYRGOTELES. *Calcedony.*

" Or that conqueror
Who whirl'd his axle down Nysæan steep,
Bridling fierce tigers, with his purple reins
Wreath'd with vine-tendrils."

Æneis, book vi. : OGLE.

" The god himself with clust'ring grapes was crown'd,
And shook his spear, which curling vines surround :
Tigers and lynxes round him seem'd to lie,
And painted panthers, dreadful to the eye."

OVID, *Met.* book iii.

No. 268.

Head of Ariadne.

ONESAS. *Cornelian.*

" Poor Ariadne! thou must perish here,
Breathe out thy soul in strange and hated air,
Nor see thy pitying mother shed one tear;
Want a kind hand which thy fix'd eyes may close,
And thy stiff limbs may decently compose ;

Thy carcass to the birds must be a prey :
Thus Theseus all thy kindness does repay !
Meanwhile to Athens your swift ship does run,
There tell the wond'ring crowd what you have
    done :

How the mix'd prodigy you did subdue;
The beast and man how with one stroke you slew;
Describe the lab'rinth, and how, taught by me,
You 'scaped from all those perplex'd mazes free.
Tell, in return, what gen'rous things you've done:
Such gratitude will all your triumphs crown!

Sprung sure from rocks, and not of human race,
Thy cruelty does thy great line disgrace.
Yet couldst thou see, as barb'rous as thou art,
These dismal looks, sure they would touch thy heart."

OVID, *Ep.*

No. 269.

Bacchus caressing and looking complaisantly at Ampelus, the son of Silenus.

CHROMIOS. *Oriental Cornelian.*

No. 270.

Bacchus placing the Ram among the signs of the Zodiac.

PYRGOTELES. *Oriental Cornelian.*

Bacchus, wandering over the barren sands of Libya, and worn out with thirst and fatigue, implores the assistance of Jupiter, who appears to him under the form of a ram, and, striking the earth with his foot, indicates a spring of cool and limpid water. Bacchus, in gratitude, placed the ram among the signs of the zodiac.

No. 271.

Bacchus killing Dryas with his thyrsus.

APOLLONIDES. *Oriental Cornelian.*

Bacchus, when he conquered India, where he introduced the culture of the vine, killed Dryas prince of that country with his thyrsus.

" In nought to Mars inferior thee I call,
Great midst the sons of Jove, thou viest with all;
Not Mars with more success his spear does wield,
Than thou thy thyrsus on th' embattled field."

DIONYS. book xviii.

_____

" But in their wrath the peasants,
Harass'd by Bacchus' vot'ries, took up arms.

A wondrous spectacle, O king, ensued ;
For by our brazen spears no blood was drawn,
Hurl'd from their hands ; but where the thyrsus smote,
A grisly wound appear'd."

EURIP. Bacch.: WOODHULL.

" The tardy god arrives at length,
His stedfast promise to fulfil,
Exulting in immortal strength.
Tremble, ye ministers of ill !
With vengeance arm'd he smites the impious head
Of him who dares pollute his shrine,
And madly spurn the powers divine."

· EURIP. Bacch.

No. 272.

Bacchus teaching Œnopion, his son by Ariadne, the art of making wine.

APOLLONIDES. Amethyst.

" Osiris first contriv'd the crooked plough,
And pull'd ripe apples from the novice bough ;
He taught the swains the savage mould to wound,
And scatter'd seed-corn in th' unpractis'd ground ;
He first with poles sustain'd the reptile vine,
And shew'd its infant tendrils how to twine ;
Its wanton shoots instructed man to shear,
Subdue their wildness, and mature the year :
Then too the ripen'd cluster first was trod,
Then in gay streams its cordial soul bestow'd ;
This as swains quaff'd, spontaneous numbers came,
They prais'd the festal cask, and hymn'd thy name.
All ecstacy ! to certain time they bound,
And beat in measur'd awkwardness the ground.
Gay bowls serene the wrinkled front of care,
Gay bowls the toil-oppressed swain repair ;
And let the slave the laughing goblet drain,
He blithsome sings, though manacles enchain."

TIBULLUS : GRAINGER.

" For this the malefactor goat was laid
On Bacchus' altar, and his forfeit paid.
At Athens thus old comedy began,
When round the streets the reeling actors ran ;
In country villages, and crossing ways,
Contending for the prizes of their plays ;
And glad, with Bacchus, on the grassy soil,
Leap'd o'er the skins of goats besmear'd with oil.
Thus Roman youth, deriv'd from ruin'd Troy,
In rude Saturnian rhymes express their joy :
With taunts, and laughter loud, their audience please,
Deform'd with vizards cut from barks of trees ;
In jolly hymns they praise the god of wine,
Whose earthen images adorn the pine,
And there are hung on high, in honour of the vine :
A madness so devout the vineyard fills,
In hollow valleys and on rising hills ;

On whate'er side he turns his honest face,
And dances in the wind, those fields are in his
    grace.
To Bacchus therefore let us tune our lays,
And in our mother tongue resound his praise.
Thin cakes in charges, and a guilty goat,
Dragg'd by the horns, be to his altars brought;
Whose offer'd entrails shall his crime reproach,
And drip their fatness from the hazle broach.
To dress thy vines new labour is requir'd,
Nor must the painful husbandman be tir'd;
For thrice, at least, in compass of a year,
Thy vineyard must employ the sturdy steer
To turn the glebe; besides thy daily pain
To break the clods, and make the surface plain,
T' unload the branches, or the leaves to thin,
That suck the vital moisture of the vine.
Thus in a circle runs the peasant's pain,
And the year rolls within itself again.
E'en in the lowest months, when storms have
    shed
From vines the hairy honours of their head,
Not then the drudging hind his labour ends,
But to the coming year his care extends:
E'en then the naked vine he persecutes;
His pruning-knife at once reforms and cuts.
Be first to dig the ground, be first to burn
The branches lopp'd, and first the props return
Into thy house, that bore the burden'd vines;
But last to reap the vintage of thy wines.

Twice in the year luxuriant leaves o'ershade
Th' encumber'd vine; rough brambles twice in-
    vade;
Hard labour both! commend the large excess
Of spacious vineyards; cultivate the less.
Besides, in woods the shrubs of prickly thorn,
Sallows and reeds on banks of rivers born,
Remain to cut; for vineyards useful found,
To stay thy vines, and fence thy fruitful ground.
Nor when thy tender trees at length are bound,
When peaceful vines from pruning hooks are free,
When husbands have survey'd the last degree
And utmost files of plants, and order'd every
    tree;
E'en when they sing at ease in full content,
Insulting o'er the toils they underwent;
Yet still they find a future task remain,
To turn the soil and break the clods again;
And after all, their joys are insincere,
While falling rains on ripening grapes they fear.
Quite opposite to these are olives found;
No dressing they require, and dread no wound;
No rakes nor harrows need, but fix'd below,
Rejoice in open air, and unconcern'dly grow.
The soil itself due nourishment supplies;
Plough but the furrows, and the fruits arise:
Content with small endeavours till they spring,
Soft peace they figure, and sweet plenty bring:
Then olives plant, and hymns to Pallas sing."
                        Georgics, ii.: DRYDEN.

No. 273.

Bacchus, metamorphosed to a lion, tearing a Titan in pieces.

CHROMIOS.   *Oriental Cornelian.*

" When rising fierce, in impious arms,
    The giant-race with dire alarms
    Assail'd the sacred realms of light,
    With lion-wrath and dreadful paw,
    With blood-besmear'd and foaming jaw,
    You put their horrid chief to flight."
                        HOR. book ii. Od. 19.

u

No. 274.

Bacchus presenting to Thetis the urn containing the ashes of Achilles and Patroclus.

GNAIOS. *Oriental Cornelian.*

Bacchus, to save himself from the sacrilegious fury of Lycurgus king of Thrace, threw himself into the sea, and was saved by Thetis, whose guest he became. Bacchus gratefully offered her in return a golden urn, the beautiful work of Vulcan. It was the same urn that, on the death of Achilles, the goddess took to the Grecian camp, and in which were enclosed the ashes of Patroclus and the son of Peleus.

" Not long Lycurgus view'd the golden light,
That daring man who mix'd with gods in fight.
Bacchus, and Bacchus' votaries, he drove,
With brandish'd steel, from Nyssa's sacred grove:
Their consecrated spears lay scatter'd round,
With curling vines and twisted ivy bound ;
While Bacchus headlong sought the briny flood,
And Thetis' arms receiv'd the trembling god.

Nor fail'd the crime th' immortals' wrath to move
(Th' immortals blest with endless ease above) ;
Depriv'd of sight by their avenging doom,
Cheerless he breath'd, and wander'd in the gloom ;
Then sunk unpitied to the dire abodes,
A wretch accurst, and hated by the gods !"
OVID, *Met.*

" ' Forbear your flight: fair Thetis from the main,
To mourn Achilles, leads her azure train.'
Around thee stand the daughters of the deep,
Robe thee in heav'nly vests, and round thee weep ;
Round thee the Muses, with alternate strain,
In ever-consecrating verse complain.
Each warlike Greek the moving music hears,
And iron-hearted heroes melt in tears ;
Till seventeen nights and seventeen days re-turu'd,
All that was mortal or immortal mourn'd.
To flames we gave thee the succeeding day,
And fatted sheep and sable oxen slay ;
With oils and honey blaze th' augmented fires,
And like a god adorn'd, thy earthly part ex-pires.
Unnumber'd warriors round the burning pile
Urge the fleet coursers o'er the racer's toil ;
Thick clouds of dust o'er all the circle rise,
And the mix'd clamour thunders in the skies.

Soon, as absorb'd in all-embracing flame,
Sunk what was mortal of thy mighty name,
We then collect thy snowy bones, and place
With wines and unguents in a golden vase—
(The vase to Thetis Bacchus gave of old,
And Vulcan's art enrich'd the sculptur'd gold).
There we thy relics, great Achilles, blend
With dear Patroclus, thy departed friend !
In the same urn a separate space contains
Thy next-belov'd, Antilochus' remains.
Now all the sons of warlike Greece surround
Thy destin'd tomb, and cast a mighty mound :
High on the shore the growing hill we raise,
That wide th' extended Hellespont surveys,
Where all, from age to age, who pass the coast,
May point Achilles' tomb, and hail the mighty ghost.
Thetis herself to all our peers proclaims
Heroic prizes and exequial games :
The gods assented, and around thee lay
Rich spoils and gifts that blaz'd against the day.

Oft have I seen with solemn funeral games
Heroes and kings committed to the flames;
But strength of youth, or valour of the brave,
With nobler contest ne'er renown'd a grave.

Such were the games by azure Thetis given,
And such thy honours, O belov'd of heaven!
Dear to mankind thy fame survives, nor fades
Its bloom eternal in the Stygian shades."

Odyssey, book xxiv.

No. 275.

A Head of Bacchus.

APOLLONIDES. *Cornelian.*

" Be warn'd; let none the jolly god offend,
Lest sorer penalties the wretch attend:
Let none behold his rites with eyes impure,
Age is not safe, nor blooming youth secure.
For me, the works of righteousness I love,
And may I grateful to the righteous prove!
For this is pleasing to almighty Jove.
The pious blessings on their sons derive;
But can the children of the impious thrive?

Hail, Bacchus, whom the ruler of the sky,
Great Jove, enclos'd and foster'd in his thigh!
Hail, with thy sisters, Semele renown'd,
Offspring of Cadmus, with bright praises crown'd
In hymns of heroines! Let none defame
This act; from Bacchus the incentive came:
'Tis not for man the deeds of deities to blame."

THEOCRITUS.

" Thee sorrow flies, Osiris, god of wine!
But songs, enchanting love, and dance are thine;
But flowers and ivy thy fair head surround,
And a loose saffron-mantle sweeps the ground.
With purple robes invested, now you glow;
The shrine is shewn, and flutes melodious blow.
Come then, my god, but come bedew'd with wine;
Attend the rites, and in the dance combine;

The rites and dances are to genius due—
Benign Osiris, stand confess'd to view;
Rich unguents drop already from his hair,
His head and neck soft flow'ry garlands share.
O come, so shall my grateful incense rise,
And cates of honey meet thy laughing eyes."

TIBULLUS.

" Great father Bacchus! to my song repair,
For clustering grapes are thy peculiar care;
For thee large bunches load the bending vine,
And the last blessings of the year are thine;
To thee his joys the jolly autumn owes,
When the fermenting juice the vat o'erflows.
Come strip with me, my god, come drench all o'er
Thy limbs in must of wine, and drink at every pore."

VIRG. *Georg.* ii.

" With rosy cheeks plump Bacchus march'd along;
His curling hair with wreathing ivy tied,

And on his back the Parthian tiger's pride;
The gilded claws in equal order meet,
And his crown'd spear assists his erring feet."

CLAUDIAN, *Rapt. Proser.*

" And now his priest proclaims a solemn feast,
That dames and maids from usual labour rest;
That wrapt in skins, their hair-laces unbound,
And dangling tresses with wild ivy crown'd,
They leafy spears assume; who prophesies
Sad haps to such as his command despise.
The matrons and new-married wives obey;
Their webs, their unspun wool aside they lay,
Sweet odours burn, and sing: ' Lyæus, Bacchus,
Nysæus, Bromius, Evan, great Iacchus;
Fire-got, son of two mothers, the twice-born,
Father Eleleus; Thyon, never shorn;
Lenæus, planter of life-cheering vines;
Nyctileus, with all names that Greece assigns

To thee, O Liber;—still dost thou enjoy
Unwasted youth, eternally a boy.
Thou'rt seen in heav'n, whom all perfections
        grace;
And when unhorn'd, thou hast a virgin's face.
Thy conquests through the Orient are renown'd,
Where tawny India is by Ganges bound;
Proud Pentheus and Lycurgus, like profane,
By thee (O greatly to be fear'd) were slain;
The Tuscans drench'd in seas. Thou hold'st in
        awe
The spotted lynxes which thy chariot draw."

OVID, *Met.*

No. 276.

Silenus the nurse, preceptor, and attendant of Bacchus, drunk, and seated
on an ass, supported by fauns.

PAMELLIO.   *Oriental Cornelian.*

" Light Bacchides and skipping satyrs follow,
   Whilst old Silenus reeling still doth halloo,
   Who weakly hangs upon his tardy ass.
   What place soe'er thou ent'rest, sounding brass,
   Loud sackbuts, timbrels, the confused cries
   Of youths and women, pierce the marble skies."

OVID, *Met.* book iv.

—————

" Silenus on his ass did next appear;
   And held upon the mane (the god was clear).
   The drunken sire pursues, the dames retire;
   Sometimes the drunken dames pursue the drunken sire.
   At last he topples over on the plain;
   The satyrs laugh, and bid him rise again."

OVID, *Ar. Am.*

No. 277.

The Giants terrified at the braying of an Ass.

CHROMIOS. *Jade.*

This stone presents one of the most singular subjects of mythology. In the war of the giants against the gods, Silenus' ass, frightened at the sight of the giants, began to bray; and this extraordinary noise, which they thought proceeded from some new monster, so terrified them, that they threw themselves into the infernal regions.

No. 278.

The same subject.

ATHENION. *Oriental Cornelian.*

No. 279.

Ægle, daughter of Sol and Neæra, staining the face of Silenus, who is asleep, with mulberries.

APOLLONIDES. *Oriental Sardonyx.*

"Proceed, my Muse: two satyrs, on the ground,
Stretch'd at his ease, their sire Silenus found;
Dos'd with his fumes, and heavy with his load,
They found him snoring in his dark abode,
And seiz'd with youthful arms the drunken god.
His rosy wreath was dropp'd not long before,
Borne by the tide of wine, and floating on the floor.
His empty can, with ears half worn away,
Was hung on high, to boast the triumph of the day.
Invaded thus, for want of better bands,
His garland they unstring, and bind his hands;
For, by the fraudful god deluded long,
They now resolve to have their promis'd song.
Ægle came in, to make their party good;
The fairest nais of the neighbouring flood,

And while he stares around with stupid eyes,
His brows with berries and his temples dyes.
He finds the fraud, and, with a smile, demands
On what design the boys had bound his hands.
'Loose me,' he cried, ''twas impudence to find
A sleeping god, 'tis sacrilege to bind.
To you the promis'd poem I will pay:
The nymph shall be rewarded in her way.'
He rais'd his voice: and soon a numerous throng
Of tripping satyrs crowded to the song;
And sylvan fauns and savage beasts advanc'd,
And nodding forests to the numbers dauc'd.
Not by Hæmonian hills the Thracian bard,
Nor awful Phœbus was on Pindus heard
With deeper silence or with more regard.
He sung the secret seeds of Nature's frame;
How seas, and earth, and air, and active flame,

Fell through the mighty void, and in their fall
Were blindly gather'd in this goodly ball.
The tender soil then stiffening by degrees,
Shut from the bounded earth the bounding seas;
Then earth and ocean various forms disclose,
And a new sun to the new world arose;
And mists condens'd to clouds obscure the sky,
And clouds dissolv'd the thirsty ground supply.
The rising trees the lofty mountains grace;
The lofty mountains feed the savage race,
Yet few, and strangers in th' unpeopled place.

From thence the birth of man the song pursu'd,
And how the world was lost, and how renew'd.
The reign of Saturn and the golden age;
Prometheus' theft, and Jove's avenging rage;
The cries of Argonauts for Hylas drown'd,
With whose repeated name the shores resound.
Then mourns the madness of the Cretan queen;
Happy for her if herds had never been."

VIRGIL, *Past.* 6.

No. 280.

Perseus holding the head of Medusa, from which drops of blood are falling.

CHROMIOS.   *Oriental Sardonyx.*

On this stone is seen the origin of one of the most beautiful fables of mythology. The horse Pegasus sprang from the blood which flowed from the head of Medusa, when cut off by Perseus. Pegasus accompanied this hero in his exploits, and also Bellerophon in the victory which he gained over the Chimæra. He also struck the earth on Mount Helicon with his foot, and thence sprang the fountain called Hippocrene, where the Muses assembled for the first time.

" The number of the gorgons once was three—
Stheno, Medusa, and Euryale;
Of which two sisters draw immortal breath, .
Free from the fears of age as free from death.
But thou, Medusa, felt a powerful foe,
A mortal thou, and born to mortal woe;
Nothing avail'd of love thy blissful hours
In a soft meadow, on a bed of flow'rs,
Thy tender dalliance with the ocean's king,
And in the beauty of the year, the spring;
You by the conqu'ring hand of Perseus bled,
Perseus, whose sword laid low in dust thy head.

Then started out, when you began to bleed,
The great Chrysaor, and the gallant steed
Call'd Pegasus, a name not giv'n in vain ;
Born near the fountains of the spacious main.
His birth will great Chrysaor's name unfold,
When in his hand glitter'd the sword of gold ;
Mounted on Pegasus he soar'd above,
And sought the palace of almighty Jove:
Loaded with lightning through the skies he
    rode,
And bore it with the thunder to the god."

HESIOD, *Theog.*

" Then shall he mark the towers where Ce-
    pheus ruled,
And fountains springing from the printed steps
Of Laphrian Hermes, and the double rock
'Gainst which the monster of the ocean rushed
Eager, but found far other prize ; and seized
Deep in the spacious cavern of his jaws

The vulture son of gold, who rode the breeze,
Sandal'd with wings, and with his falchion
    smote
Th' enormous orc, wide wallowing on the wave ;
Who rais'd the steed divine, and from the trunk
Sever'd the snaky visage of the fiend
Distilling blood, whence sprung the winged steed

And wondrous rider; who enclosed his foes
In marble robe, and with uncover'd shield
Froze their young blood, and stiffened them to
    stone;

Who stole upon the sisters three, and thence
Joyful returned, but ne'er to them returned
Light, nor the guide of threefold wanderings."
                LYCOPHRON: VIS. ROYSTON.

" Pegasus the steed,* who born beside
Old Nilus' fountains, thence derived a name.
Chrysaor, grasping in his hands a sword
Of gold, flew upward on the winged horse."

"Thus far Minerva was content to rove
With Perseus, offspring of her father Jove:
Now, hid in clouds, Seriphus she forsook,
And to the Theban tow'rs her journey took.
Cythnos and Gyaros, lying to the right,
She pass'd unheeded in her eager flight;
And choosing first on Helicon to rest,
The virgin Muses in these words address'd:
  "Me the strange tidings of a new-found spring,
Ye learned sisters, to this mountain bring.
If all be true that fame's wide rumours tell,
'Twas Pegasus discover'd first your well;
Whose piercing hoof gave the soft earth a blow,
Which broke the surface where the waters flow.
I saw that horse by miracle obtain
Life from the blood of dire Medusa slain:
And now, this equal prodigy to view,
From distant isles to fam'd Bœotia flew.'

The Muse Urania said, 'Whatever cause
So great a goddess to this mansion draws,
Our shades are happy with so bright a guest;
You, queen, are welcome, and we Muses blest.
What fame has publish'd of our spring is
    true;
Thanks for our spring to Pegasus are due.'
  Then with becoming courtesy, she led
The curious stranger to their fountain's head:
Who long survey'd, with wonder and delight,
Their sacred water, charming to the sight;
Their ancient groves, dark grotto, shady bow'rs,
And smiling plains adorn'd with various flow'rs.
' O happy Muses !' she with rapture cried,
' Who, safe from cares, on this fair hill reside;
Blest in your seat, and free yourselves to please
With joys of study and with glorious ease !' "
                OVID, Met.

No. 281.

Terpsichore clipping the wing of one of the Pierides.

APOLLONIDES. *Amethyst.*

---

* "Pegasus received its name from a well-known emblem, the horse of Poseidon; by which we are to understand an ark or ship. 'By horses,' says Artemidorus, ' the poets mean ships;' and hence it is that Poseidon is called Hippius, for there is a strict analogy between the poetical or winged horse on land, and a real ship in the sea. Hence it came that Pegasus was esteemed the horse of Poseidon (Neptune), and often named *scaphius;* a name which relates to a ship, and shews the purport of the emblem. The ark, we know, was preserved by Divine Providence from the sea, which would have overwhelmed it; and as it was often represented under this symbol of a horse, it gave rise to the fable of the two chief deities, Jupiter and Neptune, disputing about horses."—BRYANT.

The Pierides, daughters of Pierus, dared to challenge the Muses to try who could sing best. They were conquered by the Muses, who changed them into magpies.

"The Muse yet spoke, when they began to hear
A noise of wings that flutter'd in the air;
And straight a voice from some high-spreading bough
Seem'd to salute the company below.
The goddess wonder'd, and inquired whence
That tongue was heard that spoke so plainly sense:
It seem'd to her a human voice to be,
But prov'd a bird's; for in a shady tree
Nine magpies perch'd lament their alter'd state,
And what they hear are skilful to repeat.
   The sister to the wond'ring goddess said:
' These, foil'd by us, by us were thus repaid.
These did Evippe of Pæonia bring
With nine hard labour-pangs to Pella's king.
The foolish virgins, of their number proud,
And puff'd with praises of the senseless crowd,
Through all Achaia and th' Æmonian plains
Defied us thus to match their artless strains:
' No more, ye Thespian girls, your notes repeat,
Nor with false harmony the vulgar cheat;
In voice or skill if you with us will vie,
As many we, in voice or skill will try.
Surrender you to us, if we excel,
Famed Aganippe and Medusa's well.
The conquest yours, your prize from us shall be
Th' Æmathian plains to snowy Pæone:

The nymphs our judges.' To dispute the field
We thought a shame, but greater shame to yield;
On seats of living stone the sisters sit,
And by the rivers swear to judge aright.

   .   .   .   .

   The chosen Muse here ends her sacred lays;
The nymphs unanimous decree the bays,
And give the Heliconian goddesses the praise.
Then far from vain that we should thus prevail,
But much provok'd to hear the vanquish'd rail,
Calliope resumes: ' Too long we've borne
Your daring taunts and your insulting scorn;
Your challenge justly merited a curse,
And this unmanner'd railing makes it worse.
Since you refuse us calmly to enjoy
Our patience, next our passions we'll employ;
The dictates of a mind enraged pursue,
And what our just resentment bids us, do.'
The railers laugh, our threats and wrath despise,
And clap their hands, and make a scolding noise.
But in the fact they're seized; beneath their nails
Feathers they feel, and on their faces scales;
Their horny beaks at once each other scare,
Their arms are plum'd, and on their backs they bear
Pied wings, and flutter in the fleeting air.
Chatt'ring, the scandal of the woods they fly,
And there continue still their clam'rous cry;
The same their eloquence, as maids or birds,
Now only noise, and nothing *then* but words."

OVID, Met.

No. 281.

Alpheus pursuing Arethusa.

ADMON. *Oriental Cornelian.*

The nymph Arethusa, the daughter of Nereus and Doris, and the companion of Diana, was, like her, addicted to the chase. One day, fatigued with the exercise, she went to a stream to bathe, when the god Alpheus fell in love with, and, as she fled, endeavoured to overtake her,

Arethusa implored the assistance of Diana, who, surrounding her with a thick cloud, saved her from the pursuit of Alpheus.

"In Elis first I breath'd the living air:
The chase was all my pleasure, all my care ;
None lov'd like me the forest to explore, ⅰ
To pitch the toils, and drive the bristled boar.
Of *fair*, though masculine, I had the name,
But gladly would to that have quitted claim ;
It less my pride than indignation rais'd,
To hear the beauty I neglected prais'd :
Such compliments I loath'd, such charms as these
I scorn'd, and thought it infamy to please.
Once, I remember, in the summer's heat,
Tir'd with the chase, I sought a cool retreat;
And, walking on, a silent current found,
Which gently glidèd o'er the grav'lly ground :
The crystal water was so smooth, so clear,
My eye distinguish'd ev'ry pebble there ;
So soft its motion, that I scarce perceiv'd
The running stream, or what I saw believ'd.
The hoary willow and the poplar made
Along the shelving bank a grateful shade.
In the cool rivulet my feet I dipp'd,
Then waded to the knee, and then I stripp'd ;
My robe I careless on an osier threw,
That near the place commodiously grew ;
Nor long upon the border naked stood,
But plung'd with speed into the silver flood.
My arms a thousand ways I mov'd, and tried
To quicken, if I could, the lazy tide ;
Where, while I play'd my swimming gambols
    o'er,
I heard a murmuring voice, and frighted sprang
    to shore.
'O ! whither, Arethusa, dost thou fly ?'
From the brook's bottom did Alpheus cry.
Again I heard him, in a hollow tone,
'O ! whither, Arethusa, dost thou run ?'

. . . . . .

Alpheus follow'd fast . . .

. . . . . .

As trembling doves from pressing danger fly,
When the fierce hawk comes sousing from the sky,

And as fierce hawks the trembling doves pursue,
From him I fled, and after me he flew.
First by Orchomenus I took my flight,
And soon had Psophis and Cyllene in sight;
Behind me then high Mænalus I lost,
And craggy Erimanthus scal'd with frost ;
Elis was next : thus far the ground I trod
With nimble feet before the distanc'd god.
But here I lagg'd, unable to sustain
The labour longer, and my flight maintain ;
While he, more strong, more patient of the
    toil,
And fir'd with hopes of beauty's speedy spoil,
Gain'd my lost ground, and by redoubled pace
Now left between us but a narrow space.
Unwearied I till now, o'er hills and plains,
O'er rocks and rivers, ran, and felt no pains ;
The sun behind me, and the god I kept :
But when I fastest should have run, I stept.
Before my feet his shadow now appear'd,
As what I saw, or rather what I fear'd.
Yet there I could not be deceiv'd by fear,
Who felt his breath pant on my braided hair,
And heard his sounding tread, and knew him to
    be near.
Tir'd and despairing, 'O celestial maid,
I'm caught,' I cried, 'without thy heav'nly aid.
Help me, Diana, help a nymph forlorn,
Devoted to the woods, who long has worn
Thy livery, and long thy quiver borne.'
The goddess heard ; my pious pray'r prevail'd ;
In muffling clouds my virgin head was veil'd.
The am'rous god, deluded of his hopes,
Searches the gloom, and through the darkness
    gropes ;
Twice, where Diana did her servant hide,
He came, and twice, 'O Arethusa !' cried.
How shaken was my soul, how sunk my heart !
The terror seiz'd on ev'ry trembling part.
Thus when the wolf about the mountain prowls
For prey, the lambkin hears his horrid howls :

X

The tim'rous hare, the pack approaching nigh,
Thus hearkens to the hounds, and trembles at the
    cry;
Nor dares she stir, for fear her scented breath
Direct the dogs, and guide the threaten'd death.
Alpheus in the cloud no traces found
To mark my way, yet stays to guard the ground.
The god so near, a chilly sweat possess'd
My fainting limbs, at ev'ry pore exprest;
My strength distill'd in drops, my hair in dew,
My form was chang'd, and all my substance new,

Each motion was a stream, and my whole frame
Turn'd to a fount, which still preserves my name.
Resolv'd I should not his embrace escape,
Again the god resumes his fluid shape;
To mix his streams with mine he fondly tries,
But still Diana his attempt denies—
She cleaves the ground; through caverns dark I
    run
A diff'rent current, while he keeps his own.
To dear Ortygia she conducts my way,
And here I first review the welcome day."

OVID.

> " Right o'er against Plemmyrium's wat'ry strand
> There lies an isle, once call'd th' Ortygian land :
> Alpheus, as old fame reports, has found
> From Greece a secret passage under ground ;
> By love to beauteous Arethusa led,
> And, mingling here, they roll in the same sacred bed."

> " Alpheus, too, affords his Pisa's aid ;
> By Pisa's wall the stream is first convey'd,
> Then seeks through seas the lov'd Sicilian maid."

LUCAN.

> " Alpheus next affords his Pisa's aid,
> Who seeks through seas the lov'd Sicilian maid."

STATIUS.

No. 283.

Cyrene, daughter of Hypseus king of the Lapithæ, fighting alone with a lion, kills it.

GNAIOS. *Oriental Sardonyx.*

" From Pelion's mount, where winds perpetual
    roar,
Bright-hair'd Apollo fair Cyrene bore,
To those blest realms where flocks in thousands
    stray,
And fullest plenty crowns the smiling
    plain :
In golden car he bore the nymph away,
    And gave her o'er the world's third part to
    reign.

Bright Venus, goddess of the fair,
Who holds her courts and revels there,
    Smiling receiv'd her Delian guest,
And breath'd soft love through each enamour'd
    breast.
While modesty sweet-blushing spread
The happy love-expecting bed,
Where glad Apollo's glowing arms
Might clasp Hypseus' blooming daughter's
    charms.

From Ocean's monarch was Hypseus sprung,
King of the Lapithæ, a warlike throng ;
Peneus the god's, Hypseus Peneus' son,
  Who dalliance fond with fair Creusa held
In Pindus' vale, where he the virgin won,
  And with Cyrene's godlike father fill'd.

  That father, with industrious care,
  Each female virtue taught the fair ;
  But she, a nobler task approving,
    Scorn'd the loom's enervate toys ;
  Far from female trains removing,
  Talking banquets, lazy joys :
  With the bow the quiver arming,
    To the field triumphant flew,
  Where the savage race alarming,
    These her darts unerring slew.
O'er the hills Aurora rising,
    Ere equipp'd the maid beheld ;
Sleep's emollient bliss despising,
    Early hast'ning to the field.
No hostile beasts her father's realms annoy'd,
She purg'd each forest, and each foe destroy'd.

  Once without help of dart or spear,
  Maintaining an unequal war,
  Phœbus on Pelion's top survey'd,
Engag'd with lion fierce, the lovely maid !
Straight Chiron call'd he from his cave :
' Phyllirides, thy bower leave !
Forth, forth, dread centaur, from thy bow'r,
To view the triumphs of a female power.
View with what courage she maintains the fight,
While her great spirit soars beyond her might :
She knows not fear. Relate her happy sire,
  What root its birth to branch so glorious gave ?
What mortal to the honour may aspire,
  Of daughter so undaunted, great, and brave ?

  On the virgin, Chiron, say,
  May we soft compulsion lay,
  Gently force her to our arms,
And crop her virgin flower and full-blown
      charms ?'

  Soften'd to smiles his features grave,
  This answer sober Chiron gave :
  ' Who love's purer flames would share,
By sweet persuasion steal upon the fair ;
And with fond elegance of passion move
The yielding fair one to a virtuous love.
In modest hints first sighing out their flame,
  And delicate alike, though bolder grown ;
For gods and men hate those who know not
      shame,
  But shock the ear with ribald lewdness' tone.

  But thou, of truth great deity,
  Whose proving touch all falsehoods fly ;
  Gentle complaisance inspiring,
    Thus alone to speak hath led :
  Art thou gracious, thou inquiring
    Whence descends the royal maid ?
Thou who all events art knowing,
    Every path that mortals tread ;
Whence their several fates are flowing,
    Where their several actions lead ;
Whose is wisdom past expressing,
    Knowledge past our power to tell —
Sooner count we earth's increasing
    When her pregnant bowels swell ;
Sooner, when waves roll rough and tempests roar,
Number the sands that raging crowd the shore.

  All things are open to thy eyes,
  Both where they flow, and whence they rise ;
  Yet if with one so wise and great,
'Tis granted me, dread king, myself to meet,
  Hear what the centaur hath to tell :
  Destin'd the maid's, you sought this vale ;
  Hither thou cam'st her love to share,
And to Jove's gardens o'er the seas shall bear.
Thither thy people from their isle shall tend,
And to the vale-surrounded hill ascend,
Where rule from thee Cyrene shall receive.
  Now for thy sake glad Libya to the fair
In golden domes reception waits to give,
  And yield her of her spacious empire share.' "
                    PINDAR: DODD.

" Nor was Cyrene second in thy love :
   To her thy favour gave the victor dogs ;
   Wherewith th' Hypsean virgin, at the tomb
   Of fam'd Iolcian Pelias, o'er the plain
   Laid the proud savage prostrate."
              CALLIMACHUS, *Hymn to Diana.*

" The nymph Cyrene, in old times, 'tis said,
Her flocks beside Thessalian Peneus fed ;
Pleas'd with the honours of her virgin name,
Till day's bright god seduc'd the rural dame.
Far from Hæmonia he convey'd the fair,
Brought to the nymphs, and trusted to their care ;
The mountain nymphs that in parch'd Libya keep
Their airy mansions on Myrtosia's steep.
Cyrene there, along the winding shore,
Thee, Aristæus, to Apollo bore ;

To whom rich swains, who in Thessalia live,
The names of Agreus and of Nomius give.
With length of days the god her love repaid,
And fix'd her huntress of the woodland shade ;
But the young boy to Chiron's care he gave,
To reap instruction in his learned cave.
To him, when blooming in the prime of life,
The Muses gave Autonoë to wife ;
And taught their favourite pupil to excel
In arts of healing and divining well."
              APOLL. RHODIUS.

No. 284.

Apollo changing Arge into a doe.

GNAIOS. *Amethyst.*

The nymph Arge, while pursuing a stag, dared to boast, that, were he as rapid as the sun in his course, she would overtake him. Apollo changed the arrogant nymph to a doe.

No. 285.

Aura devouring her children.

CHROMIOS. *Amethyst.*

Aura, one of the nymphs in the train of Diana, was beloved by Bacchus, but refused to listen to him. Venus, to gratify the passion of the god, inspired Aura with a voluptuous delirium, of which Bacchus availed himself, and she became the mother of two children. Aura, growing frantic in consequence, devoured her children, and drowned herself in despair.

No. 286.

Leda.

GNAIOS. *Oriental Cornelian.*

Leda, the daughter of Thespius, and wife of Tyndarus king of Sparta, surprised by Jupiter in the form of a swan.

> " I see the gryphon spread his leathern wings,
> And mount upon the sharp winds of the north,
> To pounce the dove, whom erst the snowy swan
> Engender'd, walking on the wave, what time
> Around the sacred secundines of gold
> Gleamed the pure whiteness of the snowy shell."
>
> LYCOPHRON: VIS. ROYSTON.

" Ne'er may the joys of me and of my race
  Be blasted by such fears
  As shall the pallid face
Of Lydia's wealthy dames o'erspread;
Who, with the Phrygian matrons in accord,
  Shall utter o'er their looms this lay:
  ' From the wretched captive's head,
Who comes to shear my braided locks away,
  While I bewail in plaintive strains
The ruin that o'erwhelms my native plains,

Through her who from that bird did spring,
Graceful with tow'ring neck, if fame
  A true report convey,
  That Jove transform'd, became
A swan, upborne on sounding wing,
When Leda yielded to his flame?
Or haply the fantastic Muse,
From whom these amorous tales begun,
Such shameful legend forg'd, with impious views
To impose on the credulity of man."

EURIPIDES, *Iphigenia:* WOODHULL.

No. 287.

Leda looking with surprise at the two eggs deposited on the ground, from which sprung Castor and Pollux.

GNAIOS. *Amethyst.*

No. 288.

Leda and Jupiter contemplating the births of their children.

DIOSCORIDES. *Oriental Cornelian.*

On this stone is seen the birth of Castor, Pollux, Helen, and Clytemnestra. Jupiter, as a swan, and Leda reclining on a magnificent bed, are contemplating with interest the two eggs from which have already sprung three children.

> "Leda the fair, Ætolia's matchless grace,
> Roused the twin-offspring of celestial race —

From Sparta roused—THIS famed for dauntless force,
THAT skill'd to wheel the steed's unbounded course:
Fruit of her love in Tyndarus' bright abode,
One happy birth released th' heroic load."
                                    APOLLONIUS RHODIUS.

No. 289.

Mercury carrying Castor and Pollux, shortly after their birth, to Pallena, a town of Achaia.

PYRGOTELES.   *Oriental Cornelian.*

No. 290.

Pollux killing Amycus.

APOLLONIDES.   *Oriental Cornelian.*

Amycus, the son of Neptune, was endowed with extraordinary strength. He compelled all the strangers who landed on the shores of Bithynia to a trial of skill at the cestus. He invariably conquered them, and put them to death. Amycus dared to defy the bravest of the Argonauts; and Pollux entering the arena, vanquished and slew him. Amycus was the king of the Bebryces, a people of Thrace, who took their name from Bebryce, one of the daughters of Danaus.

" The twins of Leda, child of Thestius,
   Twice and again we celebrate in song ;
   The Spartan pair, stamped by Ægeochus
   Castor and Pollux, arming with the thong
   His dreadful hands ; both merciful and strong,
   Saviours of men on danger's extreme edge,
   And steeds tossed in the battle's bloody throng,
   And star-defying ships on ruin's ledge,
Swept with their crews by blasts into the cruel
      dredge.

The winds where'er they list the huge wave
      drive,
   Dashing from prow or stern into the hold ;
   Both sides, sail, tackle, yard, and mast, they
      rive,
   Snapping at random: from night's sudden
      fold

Rushes a flood ; hither and thither rolled,
   Broad ocean's heaving volumes roar and hiss,
   Smitten by blasts and the hail-volley cold :
   The lost ship and her crew your task it is,
Bright pair, to rescue from the terrible abyss.

They think to die : but, lo! a sudden lull
   O' the winds; the clouds disperse, and the
      hushed sheen
Of the calmed ocean sparkles beautiful :
   The bears and asses, with the stall between,
   Foreshew a voyage safe and skies serene.
   Blest brothers, who to mortals' safety bring
   Both harpers, minstrels, knights, and warriors
      keen :
   Since both I hymn, with which, immortal king,
Shall I commence my song? Of Pollux first I'll
      sing.

The jutting rocks, the dangerous Euxine's
    mouth
Snow-veiled, when Argo safely passed and ended
Her course at the Bebrycian shore, the youth,
Born of the gods, from both her sides descended,
And on the deep shore, from rude winds de-
    fended,
Their couches spread, and struck the seeds
    of fire
From the pyreian. Forthwith unattended
Did Pollux of the red-brown hue retire
With Castor, whose renown for horsemanship was
    higher.

On a high hill a forest did appear:
The brothers found there a perennial spring,
Under a smooth rock, filled with water clear,
With pebbles paved, which from below did
    fling
A crystal sheen like silver glistening:
The poplar, plane, tall pine, and cypress, grew
Hard by; and odorous flowers did thither bring
Thick swarm of bees their sweet toil to pursue,
As many as in the meads when spring-buds bloom
    to view.

There lay at ease a bulky insolent,
Grim-looked: his ears by gauntlets scored and
    marred;
His vast chest like a ball was prominent;
His back was broad with flesh like iron hard,
Like anvil-wrought Colossus to regard;
And under either shoulder thews were seen
On his strong arms, like round stones which oft
    jarred
In the quick rush, with many a bound between,
A winter-torrent rolls down through the cleft
    ravine.

A lion's hide suspended by the feet
Hung from his neck, and o'er his shoulders fell:
Him the prize-winner Pollux first did greet:
' Hail, stranger! in these parts what people
    dwell?'
' The hail of utter stranger sounds not well,

At least to me.' ' We're not malevolent,
Nor sons of such: take heart.' ' You need not
    tell
Me that—I in myself am confident.'
' You are a savage, quick to wrath and insolent.'

' You see me as I am; upon your land
I do not walk.' ' Come thither, and return
With hospitable gifts.' ' I've none at hand,
Nor want I yours.' ' Pray, let me learn;
Wilt let me drink from out this fountain-urn?'
' You'll know if your thirst-hanging lips are
    dry.'
' How may we coax you from your humour
    stern,
With silver, or what else?' ' The combat try.'
' How, pray? with gauntlets, foot to foot, and eye
    to eye?'

' In pugilistic fight; nor spare your skill.'
' Who is my gauntlet-armed antagonist?'
' At hand! he's here—you see him if you will:
I, Amycus, the famous pugilist.'
' And what the prize of the victorious fist?'
' The vanquish'd shall become the victor's
    thrall.'
' Red-crested cocks so fight, and so desist.'
' Cock-like, or lion-like, the combat call:
This is the prize for which we fight, or none at
    all.'

Then on a conch he blew a mighty blast:
The long-hair'd Bebryces, hearing the sound,
Under the shady planes assembled fast;
And likewise Castor, in the fight renown'd,
Hasten'd, and called his comrades to the
    ground
From the Magnesian ship. With gauntlets
    both
Arm'd their strong hands; their wrists and
    arms they bound
With the long thongs: with one another
    wroth,
Each breathing blood and death, they stood up
    nothing loath.

First each contended which should get the sun
Of his antagonist; but much in sleight
That huge man, Pollux, was by thee undone,
And Amycus was dazzled with the light;
But raging rush'd straight forward to the
    fight,
Aiming fierce blows; but wary Pollux met
    him,
Striking the chin of his vast opposite,
Who fiercer battled, for the blow did fret
    him,
And leaning forward tried unto the ground to
    get him.

Shouted the Bebryces; and for they feared
The man, like Tityus, might their friend
    downweigh
In the sunk places, the heroes Pollux cheer'd;
But shifting here and there, Jove's son made
    play,
And struck out right and left, but kept away
From the fierce rush of Neptune's son un-
    couth,
Who, drunk with blows, reel'd in the hot
    affray
Outspitting purple blood. The princely youth
Shouted when they beheld his batter'd jaws and
    mouth.

His eyes were nearly closed from the contusion
Of his swoln face. The prince amaz'd him
    more
With many feints, and seeing his confusion,
Mid-front he struck a heavy blow and sore,
And to the bone his forehead gashing tore.
Instant he fell, and at his length he lay
On the green leaves; but fiercely as before,
On his up-rising, they renew'd the fray,
Aiming terrific blows, as with intent to slay.

But the Bebrycian champion strove to place
His blows upon the broad breast of his foe,
Who ceaselessly disfigur'd all his face:
His face with sweating shrunk, that he did
    shew
From huge but small; but larger seem'd to
    grow
The limbs of Pollux, and of fresher hue,
The more he toil'd. Muse! for 'tis thine to
    know,
And mine to give interpretation true,
Tell how the son of Zeus that mighty bulk o'er-
    threw.

Aiming at something great, the big Bebrycian
The left of Pollux with his left hand caught,
Obliquely leaning out from his position,
And from his flank his huge right hand he
    brought,
And had he hit him would have surely wrought
Pollux much damage; but escape he found,
Stooping his head, and smote him quick as
    thought
On the left temple; from the gaping wound
A bubbling gush of gore out-spurted on the
    ground.

Right on his mouth his left hand then he
    dash'd,
Rattled his teeth, and with a quicker hail
Of blows he smote him, till his cheeks he
    smash'd.
Outstretch'd he lay, his senses all did fail,
Save that he owned the other did prevail
By holding up his hands. Nor thou didst claim
The forfeit, Pollux, taking of him bail
Of a great oath, in his own father's name,
Strangers to harm no more with word or deed of
    shame."

                      THEOCRITUS.

No. 291.

Apollo transfixing Coronis with a dart.

GNAIOS. *Oriental Amethyst.*

Apollo was enamoured of Coronis, the daughter of Phlegias, and she became the mother of Æsculapius. Coronis loved a young man named Ischys; and Apollo being informed of this attachment by the crow, in the first transport of passion pierced the bosom of the nymph with one of his arrows, and killed her. He repented, however, having revenged himself so cruelly, and withdrew from the side of Coronis the infant Æsculapius; at the same time punishing the crow by changing him from white to black.

" The palm Coronis of Larissa bare
From all the Æmonian dames for matchless
 fair;
Who dearly, Delphian, was beloved by thee,
As long as chaste, or from detection free.
But Phœbus' bird her scopes did soon descry,
Nor could they charm the inexorable spy;
Who forward flew, and told the hurtful truth
Of lost Coronis and the Æmonian youth.
The harp drops from his hand, and from his
 head
The laurel fell; his cheerful colour fled:
Transported with his rage, his bow he took,
And with inevitable arrow struck
That breast which he had hoped true to find.
She shrieks, and from the deadly wound doth
 wind
The biting steel, pursued with streams of blood,
That bathed her pure white in a crimson flood.
She faints; forth life in her blood's torrent
 swims,
And stiff'ning cold benumbs her senseless limbs.
His cruelty to her he loved too late
He now repenteth, and himself doth hate,

Who lent an ear, whom rage could so incense;
He hates his bird, by whom he knew th' of-
 fence;
He hates his art, his quiver, and his bow :
Then takes her up, and all his skill doth shew.
But, ah! too late to vanquish fate he tries,
And surgery without success supplies.
Which when he saw, and saw the funeral pile
Prepared to devour so dear a spoil,
He deeply groans (for no celestial eye
May shed a tear), as when a cow stands by
And lows aloud to see th' advanced mall
Upon the forehead of her suckling fall.
And now uncar'd-for odours pour'd upon her,
And undue death with all due rites doth honour.
But Phœbus not enduring that his seed
(And that by her) the greedy fire should feed,
Snatch'd it forth from her womb, and from the
 flame,
And to the two-shap'd Chiron brought the
 same.
The white-plum'd raven, who reward expects,
He turns to black, and for his truth rejects."
        SANDYS' OVID.

No. 292.

Coronis on her funeral pile.

ADMON. *Oriental Amethyst.*

Apollo holding in his arms the infant Æsculapius, whom he has taken from the side of his mother; and near him is the burning pile, on which the body of Coronis is about to be consumed.

No. 293.

Mercury hovering over the funeral pile of Coronis, having rescued the infant Æsculapius from the flames.

CHROMIOS.   *Oriental Cornelian.*

No. 294.

The infant Æsculapius nursed by a wild goat of Epidaurus.

DIOSCORIDES.   *Oriental Cornelian.*

No. 295.

The infant Æsculapius nursed by the goat, guarded by a dog, and discovered by the shepherd Arestanus.

GNAIOS.   *Oriental Cornelian.*

No. 296.

Apollo confiding the education of Æsculapius to the centaur Chiron, who taught him medicine and botany.

POLYCLETES.   *Oriental Cornelian.*

No. 297.

Ocyroë, the daughter of the centaur Chiron, changed to a mare.

ALPHEUS.   *Oriental Sardonyx.*

The gods, because Ocyroë had dared to penetrate into futurity, and predict the fortunes of the infant Æsculapius, who is seen in the arms of Chiron, changed her to a mare.

" It pleased the half-horse to be so employed,
Who in his honourable trouble joyed.
Behold his daughter of the yellow hair,
Whom formerly the nymph Caricle bare
By the swift river, and Ocyroë named,
Who had her father's healthful art disclaimed,
To sing the depth of fates. Now, when her breast
Was by the prophesying rage possest,

And that th' included god inflamed her mind,
Beholding of the babe she thus divined:
' Health-giver to the world, grow, infant, grow,
To whom mortality so much shall owe ;
Fled souls thou shalt restore to their abodes,
And one against the pleasure of the gods.
To do the like thy grandsire's flames deny,
And thou begotten by a god must die ;
Thou of a bloodless corpse a god shalt be,
And nature twice shall be renewed in thee.
And you, dear father, not a mortal now,
To whom the fates eternity allow,
Shall wish to die ; then, when your wound shall
    smart
With serpent's blood, and slight your helpless art,
Relenting fates will pity you with death,
Against their law, and stop thy groaning breath.'
Not all yet said, her sighs in storms arise,
And ill-aboding tears burst from her eyes ;
Then thus : ' My fates prevent me ; lo ! they tie
My falt'ring tongue, and further speech deny.

Alas, these arts not of that value be,
That they should draw the wrath of heav'n on
    me ;
O, rather would I nothing have foreknown !
My looks seem now not human, nor my own:
I long to feed on grass ; I long to run
About the spacious fields.   Woe's me, undone !
Into a mare (my kindred's shape) I grow :
Yet why throughout — my father but half so ?'
The end of her complaint you scarce could hear
To understand, her words confused were ;
Forthwith nor words nor neighings she exprest,
Her voice yet more inclining to the beast:
Then neighed outright.   Within a little space
Her down-thrust arms upon the meadow pace ;
Her fingers join ; one hoof five nails unite ;
Her neck and head enlarge, not now upright ;
Her voice and shape at once transformed became,
And to itself the monster gives a name."

SANDYS' OVID.

No. 298.

Æsculapius, smitten by the bolts of Jupiter, imploring the aid of his father Apollo.

CHROMIOS. *Oriental Cornelian.*

The opinion which the ancients entertained of the medical knowledge of Æsculapius was so exalted, that they attributed the resurrection of Hippolytus, the son of Theseus, to the remedies administered by him.   They believed that the father of the gods, the depository of the immutable laws of fate, looking upon Æsculapius as impious, because he dared to oppose himself to destiny and break its chain, smote him with thunder.

"Liv'd Æsculapius, Pæan's son,
    On whom his sire bestow'd
The healing art, Alcestes might be won
    From sullen Pluto's loath'd abode—
Those gates of darkness : for he rais'd the dead,
    Banish'd by Jove from yonder starry cope,
Till winged lightning smote the sage's head."

EURIPIDES, *Alcestes.*

No. 299.

Apollo killing the Cyclops, who had forged the bolts by which Æsculapius had been slain.

CHROMIOS.   *Oriental Cornelian.*

" House of Admetus, underneath thy roof
I, though a god, have been reduc'd to share
The servile board : the guilty cause was Jove,
Who my lov'd offspring Æsculapius slew,
Transpiercing with a thunderbolt his breast.
Enrag'd at this atrocious deed, I smote
The Cyclops, curst artificers, who forg'd
The flames which heav'n's vindictive father wields ;
And therefore did the god, in penal wrath,
Make me an abject hireling to a lord
Of human race."

EURIPIDES, *Alcestes :* WOODHULL.

No. 300.

The same subject.

APOLLONIOS.   *Oriental Cornelian.*

No. 301.

Head of Æsculapius.

AULUS.   *Amethyst.*

No. 302.

Circe caressing Glaucus, who repulses her.

DIOSCORIDES.   *Oriental Cornelian.*

Glaucus, a sea-god, loved the nymph Scylla, the daughter of Phorcys and Hecate, but she refused to listen to him ; and Glaucus prayed Circe that, by means of her enchantment, she would inspire Scylla with the affection he desired. Circe herself became enamoured of Glaucus, but he remained faithful to Scylla.

" Now Glaucus, with a lover's haste, bounds o'er
The swelling waves, and seeks the Latian shore.
Messena, Rhegium, and the barren coast
Of flaming Etna, to his sight are lost:
At length he gains the Tyrrhene seas, and views
The hills where baneful filters Circe brews;
Monsters in various forms around her press,
As thus the god salutes the sorceress:
' O Circe, be indulgent to my grief,
And give a love-sick deity relief;
Too well the mighty pow'r of plants I know,
To those my figure and new fate I owe.
Against Messena, on th' Ausonian coast,
I Scylla view'd, and from that hour was lost.

In tend'rest sounds I sued ; but still the fair
Was deaf to vows, and pitiless to pray'r.
If numbers can avail, exert their pow'r;
Or energy of plants, if plants have more.
I ask no cure ; let but the virgin pine
With dying pangs, or agonies like mine.'
No longer Circe could her flame disguise,
But to the suppliant god marine replies:
' When maids are coy, have manlier aims in view ;
Leave those that fly, but those that like pursue.
If love can be by kind compliance won,
See at your feet the daughter of the sun.'
' Sooner (said Glaucus) shall the ash remove
From mountains, and the swelling surges love ;
Or humble sea-weed to the hills repair,
Ere I think any but my Scylla fair."

OVID.

No. 303.

The transformation of Scylla.

PYRGOTELES. *Oriental Cornelian.*

Circe, to revenge herself of the refusal of Glaucus, poured poison into the waters of the fountain where Scylla was accustomed to bathe ; and no sooner had the nymph touched the place, than she found herself transformed, from the waist downwards, into frightful monsters like dogs.

" Straight Circe reddens with a guilty shame,
And vows revenge for her rejected flame.
Fierce liking oft a spite as fierce creates,
For love refus'd without aversion hates.
To hurt her hapless rival she proceeds ;
And by the fall of Scylla Glaucus bleeds.
Some fascinating bev'rage now she brews,
Compos'd of deadly drugs and baneful juice.
At Rhegium she arrives ; the ocean braves,
And treads with unwet feet the boiling waves:
Upon the beach a winding bay there lies,
Sheltered from seas, and shaded from the skies.

This station Scylla chose, a soft retreat
From chilling winds and raging Cancer's heat.
The vengeful sorc'ress visits this recess,
Her charm infuses, and infects the place.
Soon as the nymph wades in, her nether parts
Turn into dogs ; then at herself she starts.
A ghastly horror in her eyes appears,
But yet she knows not who it is she fears ;
In vain she offers from herself to run,
And drags about her what she strives to shun."

OVID

No. 304.

Penelope caressing the goat into which Mercury had changed himself.

DEMOPHILOS.   *Oriental Amethyst.*

The ancients were divided in their opinions respecting the birth of Pan, the god of shepherds and of the country : some thought him the son of Jupiter and Calisto, others of Jupiter and Oueis. Homer makes him the offspring of Mercury by Dryope. Many contend that he was the son of Penelope,* daughter of Icarius, by all the suitors who frequented her palace during the absence of Ulysses ; hence his name Pan, which signifies in Greek *all* or *every thing.* Lucian, Hyginus, &c. maintain that he was the son of this same Penelope and Mercury, who, assuming the form of one of the most beautiful of the goats in the flock of Icarius, surprised Penelope on mount Taygetus.

> · " It is a thing impossible, that they
> Who have committed any foul misdeed
> Should be conceal'd ; for with keen piercing eyes
> Time is endued, and all things can discern."
>
> EURIPIDES, *Frag. Pen.*

No. 305.

Syrinx transformed to reeds.

APOLLONIOS.   *Oriental Sardonyx.*

Pan, enamoured of Syrinx, pursued her; but at the moment of reaching her on the banks of the Ladon, saw her changed into a reed; of which, to console himself, he made the musical instrument which bears her name.

" When Pan, on Ladon's banks deceived,
The fair Syringa clasped, who, snatched from
      shame,
Already had her tuneful form received,
And to the breathing winds in airy music grieved ;

Still in that tuneful form to Dian dear,
She bids it injured innocence befriend ;

Commands her train the sentence to revere,
And in her grove the vocal reed suspend,
Which virtue may from calumny defend.
Self-breathed when virgin purity appears,
What notes melodious they spontaneous send !
While the rash, guilty nymph with horror hears
Deep groans declare her shame to awe-struck
      wond'ring ears.

---

* This scandal against Penelope depends entirely on one short sentence in Herodotus (book ii. c. 145), and is therefore to be discredited.

The spotless virgins shall unhurt approach
The stream's rude ordeal and the sacred fire.
See the pure maid, indignant of reproach,
The dreadful test of innocence require,
Amid the holy priests and virgin choir!

See her leap fearless on the blazing shrine!
The lambent flames bright-circling all aspire
Innoxious wreaths around her form to twine,
And crown with lustrous beams the virgin's brow
divine."
TIGHE.

" Amongst the hamadryade Nonacrines,
(On cold Arcadian hills) for beauty fam'd,
A naïs dwelt, the nymphs her Syrinx nam'd,
Who oft deceived the satyrs that pursued
The rural gods, and those whom woods include.
In exercises and in chaste desire
Diana-like, and such in her attire ;
You either in each other might behold,
Save that her bow was horn, Diana's gold ;
Yet oft mistook.   Pan, crowned with pines, re-
turning
From steep Lycæus, saw her, and love-burning
Thus said : ' Fair virgin, grant a god's request,
And be his wife.' Surcease to tell the rest,

How from his prayers she fled, as from her shame,
Till to smooth Ladon's sandy banks she came.
There stopt, implores the liquid sisters' aid,
To change her shape, and help a helpless maid.
Pan, when he thought he had his Syrinx clasp'd
Between his arms, reeds for her body grasp'd.
He sighs; they stirred therewith ; gave back
again
A mournful sound like one that did complain.
Rapt with the music,—' Yet, O sweet (said he),
Together ever thus converse will we !'
Then of unequal wax-joined reeds he framed
This sevenfold pipe ; from her 'twas Syrinx
nam'd."
SANDYS' OVID.

No. 306.

Pan, under the disguise of a goat, into which he had changed himself,
escaping from the victorious Typhon.

CHROMIOS.   *Oriental Cornelian.*

No. 307.

Pan seated upon a rock, with his pastoral staff (*pedum*) and pipe of reeds :
a goat at his feet.

CHROMIOS.   *Oriental Cornelian.*

HYMN OF PAN.

" From the forests and highlands
We come, we come ;
From the river-girt islands,
Where loud waves are dumb,
Listening to my sweet pipings.

The wind in the reeds and the rushes,
The bees on the bells of thyme,
The birds on the myrtle-bushes,
The cicale above in the lime,
And the lizards below in the grass,
Were as silent as ever old Tmolus was,
Listening to my sweet pipings.

Liquid Peneus was flowing,
　And all dark Tempe lay
In Pelion's shadow, outgrowing
　The light of the dying day,
　　　Speeded by my sweet pipings.
The Sileni, and sylvans, and fauns,
　And the nymphs of the woods and waves,
To the edge of the moist river lawns,
　And the brink of the dewy caves,
And all that did then attend and follow,
Were silent with love, as you now, Apollo,
　　　With envy of my sweet pipings.

I sang of the dancing stars,
　I sang of the dædal earth,
And of heaven and the giants' wars,
　And love, and death, and birth;
　　　And then I changed my pipings,—
Singing, how down the vale of Menelus
I pursued a maiden, and clasped a reed.
Gods and men, we are all deluded thus;
　It breaks in our bosom, and then we bleed!
All wept, as I think both ye now would,
If envy or age had not frozen your blood,
　　　At the sorrow of my sweet pipings."
　　　　　　　　　　　SHELLEY.

No. 308.

The figure of the Nile, with its attributes.

DIOSCORIDES.　*Oriental Cornelian.*

" In summer Nile o'erflows; his waters drown
The fruitful Egypt's fields, and his alone:
Because the mouth of that wide river lies
Oppos'd to north; for when th' Etesias rise
From heavy northern clouds, and fiercely blow
Against the streams, these stop, and rise, and flow.
For northern winds blow full against the streams;
Their spring is south, it boils with mid-day beams,
Then cuts its way through sun-burnt Negro's land,
And hisses passing o'er the fiery sand.

Or else the troubled sea, that rolls to south,
Brings heaps of sand, and chokes the river's mouth;
These stop the headlong floods; they strive in vain
To force a way, but wearied turn again,
And break their banks, and flow o'er all the plain.
　Or else rain makes it swell; th' Etesias bear
The northern vapours through the southern air:
These thicken'd round the hill, the rain compose.
　Or else the sun melts Ethiopian snows,
These swell the river, and the water flows."
　　　　　　　　　LUCRETIUS: CREECH.

" Whence with annual pomp,
Rich king of floods, o'erflows the swelling Nile.
From his two springs in Gojam's sunny realm,
Pure swelling out, he through the lucid lake
Of fair Dambea rolls his infant stream:
There by the Naiads nursed, he sports away
His playful youth amid the fragrant isles
That with unfading verdure smile around.
Ambitious thence the manly river breaks,
And gathering many a flood, and copious fed

With the mellowed treasures of the sky,
Winds in progressive majesty along;
Through splendid kingdoms now devolves his maze,
Now wanders wild o'er solitary tracks
Of life-deserted sand: till glad to quit
The joyless desert, down the Nubian rocks
From thund'ring steep to steep he pours his urn,
And Egypt joys beneath the spreading wave"
　　　　　　　　　　　THOMSON.

No. 309.

The sacrifice to the god Myagrius.

DAMAS. *Oriental Sardonyx.*

On this stone is seen an altar, on which the sacred fire is burning. On one side is the figure of Minerva with an olive-branch; on the other the god called Myagrius, or Myodes (*fly-catcher*), surrounded by those insects. The Arcadians invoked him, that they might not be infested with flies during the sacrifices which at certain periods they offered in honour of Pallas. (PAUSANIAS, *Travels in Arcadia.*)

No. 310.

Iris, a daughter of Thaumas and Electra, and messenger of the gods.

GNAIOS. *Oriental Cornelian.*

" Iris, pois'd on airy wings,
From the bright summit of Olympus springs;
Descends impetuous down the Ægean deeps,
Where in his watery caverns Nereus sleeps.
To Thetis first repairs the winged maid,
Solicits and obtains her potent aid;
Vulcan she next in humble prayer address'd—
The god of fire complied with her request;
His bellows heave their windy sides no more,
Nor his shrill anvils shake the distant shore.
Her wants to Æolus she next disclos'd;
And while her wearied limbs she here repos'd,
Thetis from all her naiad train withdrew,
And from her Nereus to Olympus flew."

APOLL. RHODIUS.

" Swift-footed Iris, nymph of Thaumus born,
Takes with no frequent embassy her way
O'er the broad main's expanse, when haply strife
Be risen, and midst the gods dissension sown.
And if there be among th' Olympian race
Who falsehood utters, Jove sends Iris down
To bring the great oath in a golden ewer;
The far-famed water from steep sky-capt rock,
Distilling in cold stream."

HESIOD.

" Hark, whence that rushing sound?
'Tis like the wondrous strain
That round a lonely ruin swells,
Which, wandering on the echoing shore,
The enthusiast hears at evening;
'Tis softer than the west wind's sigh;
It's wilder than the unmeasur'd notes
Of that strange lyre whose strings
The genii of the breezes sweep.
Those lines of rainbow light
Are like the moonbeams when they fall
Through some cathedral-window; but the tints
Are such as may not find
Comparison on earth."

SHELLEY.

Z

"On the verge,
From side to side, beneath the glittering morn,
An Iris sits amidst the infernal surge,
Like Hope upon a death-bed; and unworn
Its steady dyes, while all around is torn
By the distracted waters, bears serene
Its brilliant hues, with all their beams unshorn;
Resembling, mid the torture of the scene,
Love watching Madness with unalterable mien."

                                              BYRON.

No. 311.

Nature.

PYRGOTELES.   *Amethyst.*

Nature, the daughter of Jupiter, or rather the Supreme Intelligence which creates and preserves all things, is represented under the form of a beautiful woman, from whose breast flows milk, and who is holding a serpent, an emblem of life, as is seen on the coins of Adrian, and on other monuments of antiquity.

"Spirit of Nature! here,
In this interminable wilderness
Of worlds, at whose immensity
Even soaring fancy staggers,
Here is thy fitting temple.
Yet not the lightest leaf
That quivers to the passing breeze
Is less instinct with thee;
Yet not the meanest worm
That lurks in graves, and fattens on the dead,
Less shares thy eternal breath.
Spirit of Nature! thou
Imperishable as this scene,
Here is thy fitting temple!

If solitude hath ever led thy steps
To the wild ocean's echoing shore,
And thou hast linger'd there
Until the sun's broad orb
Seem'd resting on the burnish'd wave,
Thou must have mark'd the lines
Of purple gold that motionless
Hung o'er the sinking sphere;
Thou must have marked the billowy clouds,
Edg'd with intolerable radiancy,
Tow'ring like rocks of jet
Crowned with a diamond-wreath.
And yet there is a moment
When the sun's surest point
Peeps like a star o'er ocean's western edge,
When those far clouds of feathery gold,
Shaded with deepest purple, gleam
Like islands on a dark blue sea,—
Then has thy fancy soar'd above the earth,
And furl'd its wearied wing
Within the fairy's fane."

                                              SHELLEY.

" Dear Nature is the kindest mother still—
  Though ever changing, in her aspect mild ;
  From her bare bosom let me take my fill,
  Her never-wearied, though not her favour'd child.
  Oh, she is fairest in her features wild,
  Where nothing polish'd dares pollute her path :
  To me by day or night she ever smil'd,
  Though I have marked her when none other hath,
And sought her more and more, and loved her best in wrath."

                                                    BYRON.

" But above all, 'tis pleasantest to get
The top of high philosophy, and sit
On the calm, peaceful, flourishing head of it,
Whence we may view, deep, wond'rous deep below,
How poor mistaken mortals wand'ring go,
Seeking the path to happiness : some aim
At learning, wit, nobility, or fame ;
Others with cares and dangers vex each hour,
To reach the top of wealth and sov'reign pow'r.
Blind, wretched man, in what dark paths of strife
We walk this little journey of our life !
While frugal nature seeks for only ease,
A body free from pains, free from disease ;
A mind from cares and jealousies at peace.
  And little too is needful to maintain
The body found in health and free from pain ;
Not delicates, but such as may supply
Contented nature's thrifty luxury.
She asks no more. What though no boys of gold
Adorn the walls, and sprightly tapers hold,
Whose beauteous rays, scattering the gaudy light,
Might grace the feasts and revels of the night ;
What though no gold adorns, no music's sound
With doubled sweetness from the roofs rebound ?
Yet underneath a loving myrtle's shade,
Hard by a purling stream supinely laid,
When spring with fragrant flow'rs the earth has
      spread,
And sweetest roses grow around our head,
Envied by wealth and pow'r, with small expense,
We may enjoy the sweet delights of sense.

Who ever heard a fever tamer grown
In clothes embroider'd o'er, and beds of down,
Than in coarse rags ?
          Since, then, such toys as these
Contribute nothing to the body's ease,
As honour, wealth, and nobleness of blood,
'Tis plain they likewise do the mind no good.
If when thy fierce embattled troops at land
Mock-fights maintain ; or when the navies stand
In graceful ranks, or sweep the yielding seas,—
If then before such martial fights as these
Disperse not all black jealousies and cares,
Vain dread of death, and superstitious fears
Not leave thy mind ;—but if all this be vain ;
If the same cares, and dread, and fears remain ;
If traitor-like they seize thee on the throne,
And dance within the circle of a crown ;
If noise of arms nor darts can make them fly,
Nor the gay sparklings of the purple dye ;
If they on emperors will rudely seize,—
What makes us value all such things as these,
But folly and dark ignorance of happiness ?
For we, as boys at night, by day do fear
Shadows as vain and senseless as those are.
Wherefore that darkness which o'erspreads our
      souls
Day can't disperse ; but those eternal rules,
Which from firm premises true reason draws,
And a deep insight into nature's laws."

                                            LUCRETIUS.

No. 312.

Flora, or Spring.

DIOSCORIDES.	*Oriental Cornelian.*

The nymph Chloris was the wife of Zephyrus, who gave her as her portion the empire of flowers. She was adored under the name of Flora by many of the ancients, especially by the Sabines and the Phocians.

" Fair-handed Spring unbosoms every grace,
Throws out the snow-drop and the crocus first;
The daisy, primrose, violet darkly blue,
And polyanthus of unnumber'd dyes;
The yellow wall-flower, stained with iron brown,
And lavish stock that scents the garden round;
From the soft wing of vernal breezes shed,
Anemonies; auriculas enriched
With shining meal o'er all their velvet leaves,
And full ranunculas of glowing red.
Then comes the tulip race, where beauty plays
Her idle freaks, from family diffused
To family; as flies the father-dust,
The varied colours run; and while they break
On the charmed eye, the exulting florist marks
With secret pride the wonders of his hand:
No gradual bloom is wanting, from the bud
First-born of spring to summer's musky tribes;
Nor hyacinths of purest virgin white,
Low bent and blushing inward; nor jonquils
Of potent fragrance; nor Narcissus fair,
As o'er the fabled fountain hanging still;
Nor broad carnations, nor gay-spotted pinks;
Nor, shower'd from every bush, the damask rose."

" Spring, the year's youth, fair mother of new
flowers,
New leaves, new loves, drawn by the winged
hours,
Thou art returned; but thy felicity
Thou brought'st me last is not return'd with thee.
Thou art returned; but nought returns with thee,
Save my last joys' regretful memory.
Thou art the self-same thing thou wert before,
As fair and jocund; but I am no more
The thing I was, so gracious in her sight,
Who is heav'n's masterpiece and earth's delight.
O bitter sweets of love! far worse it is
To lose than never to have tasted bliss."

Pastor Fido: FANSHAWE.

" Fierce winter melts in vernal gales,
And grateful zephyrs fill the spreading sails;
No more the ploughman loves his fire,
No more the lowing herds their stalls desire;
While earth her richest verdure yields,
Nor hoary frosts now whiten o'er the fields.
Now joyous through the verdant meads,
Beneath the rising moon, fair Venus leads
Her various dance, and with her train
Of nymphs and modest graces shakes the plain;
While Vulcan's glowing breath inspires
The toilsome forge, and blows up all its fires.
Now crown'd with myrtle, or the flowers
Which the glad earth from her free bosom pours,
We'll offer in the shady grove."

HORACE, book i. Od. 4.

No. 313.

A Head of Flora, with its attributes.

PYRGOTELES. *Calcedony.*

" Here stands gay Spring, fair flow'rs her brow surround ;
There Summer, naked, and with wheat-ears crown'd :
With trodden grapes there Autumn stands besmeared ;
And icy Winter with his snowy beard."

OVID, *Met.*

" Or else it, like a ball, half dark, half bright,
Roll'd round its axle, may affect the sight
With diff'rent phases, and shew various light.
Now turn that half, which the full light adorns,
A quarter now, now dwindle into horns.
And this the later Babylonian sect
Asserts, and the Chaldean schemes reject ;
As if it could not either way be done ;
But powerful reasons fix'd our choice on one.

But why the moons a monthly round pursue ?
Why one so long, not every day a new ?
Why are they fram'd, endure, and always cease
At this set time ? The cause is told with ease :
Since other things at certain times appear,
And only then, thus seasons of the year :
First Spring and Venus' kindest pow'rs inspire
Soft wishes, melting thoughts, and gay desire ;
And warm Favonius fans th' amorous fire :
Then mother Flora, to prepare the way,
Makes all the field look glorious, green, and gay ;

And freely scatters with a bounteous hand
Her sweetest, fairest flowers o'er the land.
Next heat and dusty Harvest take the place,
And soft Etesias fans the sun-burnt face.
Then sweaty Autumn treads the noble vine,
And flowing bunches give immortal wine.
Next roars the strong-lung'd southern blast, and
    brings
The infant thunder on his dreadful wings.
Then cold pursues, the north severely blows,
And drives before it chilling frosts and snows.
And next deep Winter creeps, gray, wrinkled,
    old,
His teeth all shatter, limbs all shake with cold.
Therefore no wonder sure the moon should
    rise
At certain times, and that again she dies
At certain times ; since thousand things are shewn
At fix'd and constant times, and then alone."

LUCRETIUS.

No. 314.

Summer.

GNAIOS. *Calcedony.*

Summer, an aërial figure seated on a dragon, holding in her hand a bunch of corn.

" From bright'ning fields of ether fair disclos'd,
Child of the sun, refulgent summer comes ;
In pride of youth, and felt through nature's
    depth,

She comes, attended by the sultry hours
And ever-fanning breezes on her way.
.   .   .   .   .   The sun
Darts on the head direct his forceful rays ;

O'er heaven and earth, far as the ranging eye
Can sweep, a dazzling deluge reigns, and all ·
From pole to pole is undistinguished blaze.
In vain the sight dejected to the ground
Stoops for relief; thence hot ascending steams
And keen reflection pain.   Deep to the root
Of vegetation parched, the cleaving fields
And slippery lawn an arid hue disclose,
Blast fancy's blooms, and withers e'en the soul.

Echo no more returns the cheerful sound
Of sharpening scythe; the mower, sinking, heaps
O'er him the humid hay with flowers perfum'd;
And scarce a chirping grasshopper is heard
Through the dumb mead.   Distressful nature
    pants;
The very streams look languid from afar,
Or through th' unsheltered glade impatient seem
To hurl into the covert of the grove."

                        THOMSON.

" Pomona flourish'd in those times of ease;
Of all the Latian hamadryades,
None fruitful hortyards held in more repute,
Or took more care to propagate their fruit;
Whereof so nam'd: nor streams, nor shady groves,
But trees producing generous burdens loves.
Her hand an hook, and not a javelin bare,
Now prunes luxurious twigs, and boughs that dare
Transcend their bounds; now slits the bark, the
    bud
Inserts, enforc'd to nurse another's brood.
Nor suffers them to suffer thirst, but brings
To moisture-sucking roots soft-sliding springs.
Such her delight, her care.   No thoughts extend
To love's unknown desires; yet to defend
Herself from rapeful rurals, round about
Her hortyard walls t' avoid and keep them out.
What left the skipping satyrs unassay'd—
Rude Pan, whose horns pine-bristled garlands
    shade,
Or he who thieves with hook and members fears,—
To taste her sweetness: but far more than all,
Vertumnus loves; yet were his hopes as small.
How often like a painful reaper came,
Laden with weighty sheaves, and seem'd the same;
Oft wreaths of new-mow'd grass his brows array,
As though then exercis'd in making hay;
A goad now in his harden'd hand he bears,
And newly seems to have unyok'd his steers;
Oft vines and fruit-trees with a pruning hook
Corrects and dresses; oft a ladder took
To gather fruit.   Now with his sword the god
A soldier seems, an angler with his rod;

And various figures daily multiplies
To win access, and please his longing eyes.
Now with a staff an old wife counterfeits,
On hoary hair a painted mitre sets:
The hortyard ent'ring, he admires the fair
And pleasant fruit: ' So much,' said he, 'more
    rare
Than all the nymphs whom Albula enjoy,
Hail, spotless flower of maiden chastity !'
And kiss'd the prais'd.   Nor did the virgin know
(So innocent) that old wives kiss'd not so.
Then sitting on a bank, observeth how
The pregnant boughs with autumn's burdens bow;
Hard by, an elm with purple clusters shin'd;
This praising, with the vine so closely join'd—
' Yet,' saith he, ' if this elm should grow alone,
Except for shade, it would be priz'd by none;
And so this vine, in amorous foldings wound,
If but disjoin'd would creep upon the ground.
Yet art not thou by such examples led,
But shunn'st the pleasures of an happy bed.
I would thou wert: not Helen was so sought,
Nor she for whom the lustful centaurs fought,
As thou shouldst be; no, nor the wife of bold
Or cautelous Ulysses.   Yet, behold,
Though thou averse to all, and all eschew,
A thousand men, gods, demi-gods, pursue
The constant scorn, and every deathless power,
Which Alba's high and shady hills embower.
If thou art wise, and would'st well married be,
Or an old woman trust, who, credit me,
Affects thee more than all the rest, refuse
These common wooers, and Vertumnus choose.

Accept me for his gage; since so well none
Can know him, by himself not better known.
He is no wanderer; this his delight:
Nor loves, like common lovers, at first sight.
Thou art the first, so thou the last shalt be;
His life he only dedicates to thee.
Besides his youth perpetual, excellent
His beauty, and all shapes can represent;
Wish what you will, whatever hath a name:
Such shall you see him — your delights the same.
The first-fruits of your hortyard are his due,
Which joyfully he still accepts from you:

But neither what these pregnant trees produce
He now desires, nor herbs of pleasant juice;
Nor aught, but only you. O pity take!
And what I speak, suppose Vertumnus spake.'
Revengeful gods, Idalia, still severe
To such as slight her, and Rhamnusia, fear;
The more to fright you from so foul a crime,
Receive (since much I know from aged Time)
A story, generally through Cyprus known,
To mollify an heart more hard than stone."

OVID: SANDYS.

No. 315.

Autumn.

DIOSCORIDES. *Oriental Cornelian.*

Vertumnus was, according to the commentators of Ovid, a king of Etruria, who, from the care he bestowed on the culture of fruits and gardens, received on his death the honours of apotheosis; and was considered by the Etruscans as the god who presided over Autumn. His worship found its way to Rome, where a temple was erected to Vertumnus, near the forum, or market-place.

" Crown'd with the sickle and the wheaten sheaf,
While Autumn nodding o'er the yellow plain
Comes jovial on, the Doric reed once more
Well pleased I tune . . . . .
When the bright virgin gives the beauteous days,
And Libra weighs in equal scales the year,
From heav'n's high cope the fierce effulgence shook
Of parting Summer, a serener blue,
With golden light enliven'd, wide invests
The happy world. Attemper'd suns arise,
Sweet-beam'd, and shedding oft through lucid clouds

A pleasing colour; while broad and brown below
Extensive harvests hang the heavy head.
Rich, silent, deep they stand; for not a gale
Rolls its light billows o'er the bending plain.
A calm of plenty! till the ruffled air
Falls from its poise, and gives the breeze to blow.
Rent is the fleecy mantle of the sky,
The clouds fly different, and the sudden sun
By fits effulgent gilds the illumin'd field,
And black by fits the shadows sweep along:
A gaily checkered, heart-expanding view,
Far as the circling eye can shoot around,
Unbounded, tossing in a flood of corn."

THOMSON.

No. 316.

Winter, with objects of the chase analogous to the season.

GNAIOS.   *Calcedony.*

" See, Winter comes, to rule the varied year,
Sullen and sad, with all his rising train,
Vapours, and clouds, and storms.   .   .
The keener tempests rise, and fuming dun
From all the livid east or piercing north.
Thick clouds ascend, in whose capacious womb
A vapoury deluge lies to snow congeal'd.
Heavy they roll their fleecy world along ;
And the sky saddens with the gather'd storm.
Through the hushed air the whitening shower
          descends,
At first thin wavering ; till at last the flakes
Fall broad, and wide, and fast, dimming the day
With a continual flow.   The cherished fields
Put on their winter-robe of purest white ;
'Tis brightness all, save where the new snow
          melts
Along the mazy current.   Low the woods
Bow their hoar head ; and ere the languid sun
Faint from the west emits his evening ray,
Earth's universal face, deep hid and chill,   .
Is one wide dazzling waste, that buries wide
The works of man.
                    Thick around
Thunders the sport of those who with the gun,
And dog impatient bounding at the shot,
Worse than the season desolate the fields ;
And, adding to the ruins of the year,
Distress the footed or the feather'd game.
'Tis done, dread Winter spreads his latest glooms,
And reigns tremendous o'er the conquer'd year.
How dead the vegetable kingdom lies !
How dumb the tuneful !   Horror wide extends
His desolate domain.   Behold, fond man !
See here thy pictur'd life !   Pass some few years :
Thy flowering Spring — thy Summer's ardent
          strength —
Thy sober Autumn fading into age —
And pale concluding Winter comes at last,

And shuts the scene.   Ah, whither now are fled
Those dreams of greatness ? those unsolid hopes ?
Those restless cares ? those busy bustling days ?
Those gay-spent festive nights, whose burning
          thoughts
Lost between good and ill, that shared thy life ?
All now are vanished !   Virtue sole survives,
Immortal, never-failing friend of man,—
His guide to happiness on high.   And see !
'Tis come, the glorious morn !   the second birth
Of heaven and earth !   awakening Nature hears
The new-creating word, and starts to life,
In every brighten'd form, from pain and death
For ever free.   The great eternal scheme
Involving all, and in a perfect whole
Uniting, as the prospect wider spreads,
To reason's eye refined clears up apace.
Ye vainly wise !   ye blind presumptuous !   now,
Confounded in the dust, adore that POWER
And WISDOM oft arraign'd !   see now the cause
Why unassuming worth in secret lived,
And died neglected ; why the good man's share
In life was gall and bitterness of soul ;
Why the lone widow and her orphans pined
In starving solitude, while luxury
In palaces lay straining her low thought
To form unreal wants ; why heaven-born truth
And moderation fair wore the red marks
Of superstition's scourge ; why licensed pain,
That cruel spoiler, that embosom'd foe,
Embitter'd all our bliss.   Ye good distress'd !
Ye noble few !   who here unbending stand
Beneath life's pressure, yet bear up awhile ;
And what your bounded view, which only saw
A little part, deem'd evil, is no more :
The storms of WINTRY TIME will quickly pass,
And one unbounded SPRING encircle all."

                              THOMSON.

" Not so the Scythian shepherd tends his fold ;
Nor he who bears in Thrace the bitter cold ;
Nor he who treads the bleak Meotian strand,
Or where proud Ister rolls his yellow sand.
Early they stall the flocks and herds ; for there
No grass the fields, no leaves the forests wear :
The frozen earth lies buried there below
A hilly heap, seven cubits deep in snow,
And all the West allies of stormy Boreas blow.
　The sun from far peeps with a sickly face,
Too weak the clouds and mighty fogs to chase,
When up the skies he shoots his rosy head,
Or in the ruddy ocean seeks his bed.
Swift rivers are with sudden ice constrain'd,
And studded wheels are on its back sustain'd—
An hostry now for wagons, which before
Tall ships of burden on its bosom bore.
The brazen cauldrons with the frost are flaw'd ;
The garment, stiff with ice, at hearths is thaw'd ;
With axes first they cleave the wine, and thence
By weight the solid portions they dispense.

From locks uncomb'd and from the frozen beard
Long icicles depend, and crackling sounds are
　heard.
Meantime perpetual sleet and driving snow
Obscure the skies, and hang on herds below ;
The starving cattle perish in their stalls,
Huge oxen stand enclos'd in wintry walls
Of snow congeal'd ; whole herds are buried there
Of mighty stags, and scarce their horns appear :
The dext'rous huntsman wounds not these afar,
With shafts or darts, or makes a distant war
With dogs, or pitches toils to stop their flight,
But close engages in unequal fight ;
And while they strive in vain to make their way
Through hills of snow, and pitifully bray,
Assaults with dint of sword or pointed spears,
And homeward on his back the joyful burden
　bears.
The men to subterranean caves retire,
Secure from cold, and crowd the cheerful fire."
　　　　　　　　　　　　VIRGIL, *Georg.* iii.

No. 317.

Time devouring his children.

PYRGOTELES. *Amethyst.*

" Even Time, the conqueror, fled thee in his
　fear,
That hoary giant, who in lonely pride
So long had ruled the world, that nations fell
Beneath his silent footstep. Pyramids,
That for millenniums had withstood the tide
Of human things, his storm-breath drove in sand
Across that desert where their stones survived
The name of him whose pride had heaped them
　there.

Yon monarch, in his solitary pomp,
Was but the mushroom of a summer-day,
That his light-winged footstep press'd to dust.
Time was the king of earth ; all things gave
　way
Before him, but the fix'd and virtuous will,
The sacred sympathies of soul and sense,
That mock'd his fury and prepared his fall."
　　　　　　　　　　　　　　SHELLEY.

" Unfathomable sea, whose waves are years !
　Ocean of time, whose waters of deep woe
Are brackish with the salt of human tears !
　Thou shoreless flood, which in thy ebb and flow
Claspest the limits of mortality,

a a

And sick of prey, yet howling on for more,
Vauntest thy wrecks on its inhospitable shore !
Treach'rous in calm, and terrible in storm,
    Who shall put forth on thee,
    Unfathomable sea ?"

SHELLEY.

" So from our lights, our meaner fires below,
Our lamps, or brighter torches, streams do flow,
And drive away the night ; they still supply
New flames as swiftly as the former die,
New beams still tremble in the lower sky.
No space is free, but a continued ray
Still keeps a constant, though a feeble day ;
So fast, e'en hydra-like, the fruitful fires
Beget a new beam as the old expires.
So sun and moon, with many a num'rous birth,
Bring forth new rays, and send them down to
    earth,
Which die as fast, lest some fond fools believe
That these are free from fate, that these must live.
    E'en strongest towns and rocks, all feel the rage
Of pow'rful time ; e'en temples waste by age.
Nor can the gods themselves prolong their date,
Change nature's laws, or get reprieve from fate ;

E'en tombs grow old and waste, by years o'er-
    thrown,
Men's graves before, but now become their own.
How oft the hardest rock dissolves, nor bears
The strength but of a few though pow'rful years !
Now if that rock for infinite ages past
Stood still secure, if it was free from waste,
Why should it fail, why now dissolve at last ?
    Lastly, look round, view that vast track of sky,
In whose embrace our earth and waters lie ;
Whence all things rise, to which they all return,
As some discourse, the same both womb and urn.
'Tis surely mortal all ; for that which breeds,
That which gives birth to other things, or seeds,
Must lose some parts ; and when these things do
    cease,
It gets some new again, and must increase."

LUCRETIUS, book v.

No. 318.

Time raising the veil of Truth.

GNAIOS.   Oriental Cornelian.

    Truth was the daughter of Saturn, and mother of Virtue ; and by the Greeks was known as an allegorical divinity called *Aletheia.*

      " At length, when like some blooming nymph her charms
      Contemplating, he to our eyes holds up
      His mirror, every guilty wretch displays."

EURIPIDES : Hippolytus.

" From darkness deep a radiant blaze
  Broke forth, dazzling my fear-fraught gaze,
  Vaulting a space in diamond light
  Concentrating, and beaming bright.
  Upon an adamantine throne,
  As still and pure as Parian stone,

A gleaming figure veiled sat.
Calm and majestic was her mien,
Her eye both gentle, clear, and keen ;
A soften'd radiance rob'd her round,
Pervading heav'n above and depths beneath the
    ground.

Then from lips unseen mysterious words made
known,
That veiled Truth sat on her everlasting throne—
I gaz'd in awe, and sank before that beauteous form.

Now passing sounds, like whisp'ring wind,
Recall'd to life my wand'ring mind:
I look'd, and saw a winged man,
Whose shadow seem'd himself again,
As if an emanation grew,
While into boundless space he flew.
The moving blast her veil withdrew,
And tenfold glories met my view:

It seem'd as if her piercing ray
Had swept all human doubts away,
And left the book of nature's laws,
The mind of man, th' exciting cause,
The histories of ages past,
The records that for ever last,
In mental light
Before my sight.
It seem'd to shew, that false and erring man must
find
It vain, the force of everlasting truth to bind."

NON. *Frag. Eleu.*

No. 319.

Justice.

GNAIOS. *Oriental Cornelian.*

A female figure, seated on a square base or pedestal, an emblem of firmness, and of the unalterable intention to award to every man his own:—a definition due to the Roman judicaturists, who were also profound philosophers. Justice is holding in one hand a balance, in the other a sceptre. A star on her head recalls her divine origin; for which reason the ancients raised temples and altars to her under the name of *Astræa.*

" What call ye *justice?* Is there one who ne'er
In secret thought has wished another's ill?
Are ye all pure? Let those stand forth who hear
And tremble not. Shall they insult and kill,
If such they be? Their mild eyes can they fill
With the false anger of the hypocrite?
Alas, such were not pure: the chasten'd will
Of virtue sees that justice is the light
Of love; and not revenge, and terror, and despite."

SHELLEY.

No. 320.

Concord.

DIOSCORIDES. *Amethyst.*

She holds in one hand some rods bound together, to signify union; and in the other the caduceus and two ears of corn, characteristics of plenty.

No. 321.

Happiness.

GNAIOS.   *Calcedony.*

Born of the union of Peace and Plenty, holding in her right hand the caduceus, and leaning with her left arm on two cornucopias.

No. 322.

Piety.

GNAIOS.   *Amethyst.*

Known by the Greeks under the name of *Eusebia.*   One hand is placed on her breast, and in the other she is holding a cornucopia; whilst near her is a stork, the emblem of filial piety.

> " True Piety is cheerful as the day—
> Will weep, indeed, and heave a pitying groan
> For others' woes; but smiles upon her own."

" All joy to the believer! He can speak,
Trembling yet happy, confident yet meek :
' Since the dear hour that brought me to Thy foot,
And cut up all my follies by the root,
I never trusted in an arm but thine,
Nor hoped but in thy righteousness divine.
My alms and prayers, imperfect and defil'd,
Were but the feeble efforts of a child :
Howe'er performed, it was their brightest part,
That they proceeded from a grateful heart,
Cleansed in thine own all-purifying blood,
Forgive their evil, and accept their good :
I cast them at thy feet ;—my only plea
Is what it was, dependence upon thee,
While struggling in the vale of tears below ;
That never failed, nor shall it fail me now.' "

COWPER.

No. 323.

Prudence, characterised by the mirror and serpent.

GNAIOS.   *Oriental Cornelian.*

Metis, or Meed, a name of Minerva, is synonymous with Prudentia.   This goddess is usually represented as a beautiful female, with hair formed of a wreath of serpents.   In the temple of Cephisus in Argolis was a head of Medusa, or Metis, fabulously reported to have been the work of the Cyclops, surrounded by wreaths of snakes.

> " If Prudence be thy sole unerring guide,
> Thou need'st no guardian deity beside."

JUVENAL.

The opinion of Cicero smacks of the quibbling of the lawyer, and the selfishness of the heathen :— " The art of prudence lies in gaining the esteem of the world, and turning it to a man's own advantage."

No. 324.

Temperance.

GNAIOS. *Oriental Cornelian.*

She holds in one hand a curb to restrain the passions, and in the other a palm-branch, an emblem of her victory over them.

" O, if the foolish race of man, who find
A weight of cares still pressing on their mind,
Could find as well the cause of this unrest,
And all this burden lodg'd within their breast,
Sure they would change their course ; not live as
    now,
Uncertain what to wish, or what to vow.
Uneasy both in country and in town,
They search a place to lay their burden down :
One, restless in his palace, walks abroad,
And vainly thinks to leave behind the load —
But straight returns ; for he 's as restless there,
And finds there 's no relief in open air :
Another to his villa would retire,
And spurs as hard as if it were on fire ;
No sooner enter'd at his country door,
But he begins to stretch, and yawn, and snore ;
Or seeks the city, which he left before.

Thus ev'ry man o'erworks his weary will
To shun himself, and to shake off his ill ;
The shaking fit returns, and hangs upon him
    still :
No prospect of repose, nor hope of ease,
The wretch is ignorant of his disease ;
Which known would all his fruitless troubles
    spare,
For he would know the world not worth his
    care.
Then would he search more deeply for the cause,
And study nature well, and nature's laws.
For in this moment lies not the debate,
But on our future, fix'd, eternal state ;
That never-changing state which all must keep
Whom death has doom'd to everlasting sleep."

LUCRETIUS: DRYDEN.

" Then still to treat thy ever-craving mind
With ev'ry blessing and of ev'ry kind,
Yet never fill thy rav'ning appetite,
Though years and seasons vary the delight ;
Yet nothing to be seen of all the store,
But still the wolf within thee barks for more,—
This is the fable's moral, which they tell,
Of fifty foolish virgins damn'd in hell
To leaky vessels which the liquor spill,
To vessels of their sex, which none could ever fill."

LUCRETIUS: DRYDEN.

" O wretched man! in what a mist of life,
Enclos'd with dangers and with noisy strife,
He spends his little span, and overfeeds
His cramm'd desires with more than nature needs!
For nature wisely stints our appetites,
And craves no more than undisturb'd delights,
Which minds unmix'd with cares and fears obtain —
A soul serene, a body void of pain.
So little this corporeal frame requires,
So bounded are our natural desires,
That wanting all, and setting pain aside,
With bare privation sense is satisfied."

LUCRETIUS: DRYDEN.

" See, fresh as Hebe, blooming Temperance stand,
Present the nectar'd fruits, and crown the bowl;
While bright-eyed Honour leads the choral band,
Whose songs divine can animate the soul,
Led willing captive to their high control.
They sing the triumphs of their spotless queen,
And proudly bid immortal Fame enroll
Upon her fairest page such as had been
Champions of her cause, the favourites of her reign."

TIGHE.

" 'Tis yet in vain, Town, to keep a pother
About one vice, and fall into the other;
Between excess and famine lies a mean,
Plain but not sordid, though not splendid clean.
He knows to live who keeps the middle state,
And neither leans on this side nor on that."

HOR. *Sat.:* POPE'S *Trans.*

No. 325.

Modesty, or Chastity.

CHROMIOS. *Calcedony.*

This virtue the Greeks and Romans had placed among the divinities, and raised temples and altars in her honour. She is represented under the form of a young and beautiful woman veiled, contemplating a butterfly, emblem of the soul.

" The chaste queen
Like Dian mid her circling nymphs appeared,
Or as Minerva on Parnassus seen,
When condescendingly with smiles she cheered
The silent Muses, who her presence fear'd.
A starry crown its heavenly radiance threw
O'er her pale cheek; for there the rose revered
The purer lilies of her saint-like hue,
Yet oft the mantling blush its transient visits
 knew.

The hand of Fate, which wove of spotless white
Her wondrous robe, bade it unchangeably
Preserve unsullied its first lustre bright—
Nor e'er might be renewed that sacred spell,
If once destroyed; wherefore, to guard it well,
Two handmaids she entrusts with special care,
Prudence and Purity, who both excel,
The first in matron dignity of air,
The last in blooming youth unalterably fair.

Favourite of heaven! she at her birth receiv'd
With it the brilliant zone that bound her
 waist;
Which, were the earth of sun and stars be-
 reav'd,
By its own light, beneficently cast,
Could cheer the innocent and guide the chaste.
Nor armour ever had the virgin bore,
Though oft in warlike scenes her youth was
 past;
For while her breast this dazzling cestus wore,
The foe who dared to gaze beheld the light no
 more.

But when her placid hours in peace are spent,
Conceal'd she bids its latent terrors lie,
Sheathed in a silken scarf, with kind intent
Wove by the gentle hand of modesty."

TIGHE.

No. 326.

Fidelity.

GNAIOS. *Amethyst.*

Divine honours were rendered to her; and she is represented as a young girl caressing a dog, the emblem of fidelity.

No. 327.

Providence.

DIOSCORIDES. *Oriental Cornelian.*

A divinity to whom Augustus was the first to raise temples and altars. She is represented under the form of a dignified woman, holding a wand over the globe, indicating command: the cornucopia reversed is emblematical of the abundance which she sheds upon the earth. The eagle hovering above shews that Providence derives its origin from the father of gods and men.

" Receive my counsel, and securely move ;
Entrust thy fortune to the powers above.

Leave them to manage for thee, and to grant
What their unerring wisdom sees thee want:
In goodness, as in greatness, they excel—
Ah, that we lov'd ourselves but half so well!"
                                                    JUVENAL.

No. 328.

Hope.

PYRGOTELES. *Amethyst.*

Hope, to whom the ancients also paid divine honours, is here represented leaning against a column, holding in one hand some ears of corn, and in the other some poppies and a rudder.

"Through the wide rent in Time's eternal veil,
Hope was seen beaming through the mists of fear;
    Earth was no longer hell;
    Love, freedom, health, had given
Their ripeness to the manhood of its prime;
    And all its pulses beat
Symphonious to the planetary spheres.
    Then dulcet music swell'd
Concordant with the life-strings of the soul;

It throbbed in sweet and liquid beating there,
Catching new life from transitory death.
Like the vague sighing of a wind at even,
That makes the wavelets of the slumb'ring sea,
And dies on the creation of its breath,
And sinks and rises, fails and swells by fits,
    Was the pure stream of feeling
    That sprung from these sweet notes."
                                                    SHELLEY.

" When from this wicked world the gods withdrew,
Hope stay'd behind, nor hence among them flew.
She cheers the shackled slave that digs the mine,
And cries, Sweet liberty will soon be thine.
Through her, though wreck'd where not a shore he spies,
Amidst the waves his arms the sailor plies.
Physicians often give the patient o'er,
But Hope still stays, though Death be at the door.
Prisoners condemn'd in dungeons hope reprieve,
Nor even on the cross does hope the wretched leave."
                                            Ov. *Pont.* vii.

———————

" Thousands in death would seek an end of woe,
But Hope, deceitful Hope, prevents the blow.
Hope plants the forests, and she sows the plain,
And feeds with future granaries the swain;
Hope snares the winged vagrants of the sky,
Hope cheats in reedy brooks the scaly fry;

By Hope the fetter'd slave, the drudge of fate,
Sings, shakes his irons, and forgets his state;
Hope promis'd you, you haughty still deny—
Yield to the goddess, O my fair, comply."
TIBULLUS: GRAINGER, book ii. el. 7.

No. 329.

Fame.

GNAIOS. *Oriental Sardonyx.*

An allegorical divinity worshipped at Athens. She is here represented under the form of a female figure with wings, hovering over the globe, who by the sound of the trumpet she holds in her hand announces mighty deeds. In the other hand is a torch, a symbol of the enthusiasm which animates heroes, inspiring them with the ardent wish to live in the annals of the most distant ages.

" Now Fame through every Libyan city sped,
Than whom no swifter fiend : as she careers,
Her form expatiates in her rapid course,
Each moment gath'ring strength and vigour new;
Cautious and small at first, but soon on earth
She stalks gigantic, midst the clouds of heav'n
Shrouding her head. This pest (as legends say)
Old parent Earth, in vengeance to the gods,
Last-born engender'd, kin to that huge brood
Of rebel Titans : either swift on foot,
Or on the wing, a monster, wondrous, vast;
And under every plume a watchful eye
Lurks, with as many tongues and whisp'ring mouths,
And ears that ever listen : in mid space,
'Twixt heav'n and earth, at dead of night she roams
On rushing wings ; no sleep her eyelid seals,
But at the day-dawn from some towers she peers,
Ambush'd, dismaying many a city proud
With rumours manifold, or false or true."
Æneis, book iv. : OGLE'S *Trans.*

"Amid the world, between air, earth, and seas,
A place there is, the confines to all these;
Where all that's done, though far remov'd, appear,
And every whisper penetrates the ear,—
The house of Fame, who in the highest tower
Her lodging takes. To this capacious bower
Innumerable ways conduct, no way
Barr'd up, the doors stand open night and day.
All built of ringing brass, throughout resounds
Things heard, reports, and every word rebounds.
No rest within, no silence ; yet the noise,
Not loud, but like the murmuring of a voice,
Such as from far by rolling billows sent;
Or as Jove's fainting thunder almost spent.
Hither the idle vulgar come and go ;
Millions of rumours wander to and fro ;
Lies mixt with truths, in words that vary still.
Of these with news unknowing ears some fill ;
Some carry tales, all in the telling grows,
And every author adds to what he knows.
Here dwells rash Error, light Credulity,
Dejected Fear, and vainly grounded Joy ;
New rais'd sedition, secret whisperings
Of unknown authors, and of doubtful things ;
All done in heaven, earth, ocean, Fame reviews,
And through the ample world inquires for news."
OVID'S *Met.* book xii.

b b

" Where is the fame
Which the vain-glorious mighty of the earth
Seek to eternise ?   O, the faintest sound
From time's light footfall, the remotest wave
That swells the flood of ages, whelms in nothing
The unsubstantial bubble !   Ay, to-day
Stern is the tyrant's mandate ; red the gaze
That flashes desolation ; strong the arm
That scatters multitudes !   To-morrow comes !
That mandate is a thunder-peal that died
In ages past; that gaze a transient flash
On which the midnight closed; and on that arm
The worm has made his meal.   .   .
    .   .   .   The virtuous man,
Who great in his humility as kings
Are little in their grandeur ; he who leads
Invincibly a life of resolute good,

And stands amid the silent dungeon-depths
More free and fearless than the trembling judge,
Who, clothed in venal power, vainly strove
To bind the impassive spirit,—when he falls,
His mild eye beams benevolence no more ;
Withered the hand outstretched but to relieve ;
Sunk reason's simple eloquence, that rolled
But to appal the guilty.   Yes, the grave
Hath quench'd that eye, and death's relentless
    frost
Wither'd that arm : but the unfading fame
Which virtue hangs upon its votary's tomb ;
The deathless memory of that man whom kings
Call to their mind and tremble ; the remembrance
With which the happy spirit contemplates
Its well-spent pilgrimage on earth,—
Shall never pass away."

SHELLEY.

No. 330.

Glory.

DIOSCORIDES. *Oriental Cornelian.*

A young and beautiful woman, her head arrayed with stars, seated with dignity in the clouds which overhang a pyramid—a species of monument which in the remotest times was erected to those who had distinguished themselves by glorious actions.   She holds in her right hand a figure of Victory.

" There Glory sits in all her pomp and state :
    Hence places, dignities, preferments flow,
    And all that men admire and wish below ;
    High honours, offices, in suits success,
    Right to make laws, and bid the world have peace :
    Hence sceptres and supreme command accrue,
    And power to give them where rewards are due."

MANIL. book ii. : CREECH.

" Here glory 's but a dying flame,
    And immortality a name."

No. 331.

Fortune on a globe, with her cornucopia.

PYRGOTELES. *Amethyst.*

No. 332.

Fortune, with her attributes.

GNAIOS. *Amethyst.*

No. 333.

Equestrian Victory.

GNAIOS. *Oriental Cornelian.*

No. 334.

Victory, in a car drawn by two horses.

PYRGOTELES. *Oriental Cornelian.*

No. 335.

Victory, with her emblems.

GNAIOS. *Oriental Cornelian.*

" THE GREATEST OF MISFORTUNES NEXT TO A DEFEAT."*
WELLINGTON.

No. 336.

Victory, depicted on the prow of a ship, with the caduceus, the emblem of commerce, and a palm-branch, the emblem of victory.

GNAIOS. *Oriental Cornelian.*

---

* The saying of a true hero, and worth all I can find on the subject in the classics.

No. 337.

Sleep, reposing on a couched lion.

DIOSCORIDES.   *Oriental Cornelian.*

" O thou best comforter of that sad heart
  Whom fortune's spite assails ! come, gentle sleep,
The weary mourner soothe ! for well the art
  Thou know'st, in soft forgetfulness to steep
The eyes which sorrow taught to watch and weep.
Let blissful visions now her spirit cheer,
  Or lull her cares to peace in slumbers deep ;
Till from fatigue refreshed and anxious fear,
Hope like the morning-star again shall re-appear."
                                   TIGHE.

" How wonderful is Death—
    Death and his brother Sleep !
One pale as yonder roaming moon,
    With lips of lurid blue;
The other rosy as the morn,
    When, thron'd on ocean's wave,
It blushes o'er the world :
    Yet both so passing wonderful.

    Hath then the gloomy power,
Whose reign is in the tainted sepulchres,
    Seiz'd on her sinless soul ?
    Must then that peerless form,
Which love and admiration cannot view
Without a beating heart—those azure veins,
Which steal like streams along a field of snow—
    That lovely outline, which is fair
    As breathing marble—perish ?
    Must putrefaction's breath
Leave nothing of this heav'nly sight
    But loathsomeness and ruin—
Spare nothing but a gloomy theme,
On which the lightest heart might moralise ?

Or is it only a sweet slumber
    Stealing o'er sensation,
Which the breath of roseate morning
    Chaseth into darkness ?
    Will Ianthe wake again,
And give that faithful bosom joy,
Whose sleepless spirit waits to catch
Light, life, and rapture from her smile ?

    Yes, she will wake again,
Although her glowing limbs are motionless,
    And silent those sweet lips,
    Once breathing eloquence
That might have sooth'd a tiger's rage,
Or thaw'd the cold heart of a conqueror.
    Her dewy eyes are clos'd,
    And on their lids, whose texture fine
Scarce hides the dark blue orbs beneath,
    The baby Sleep is pillowed ;
    Her golden tresses shade
    The bosom's stainless pride,
Curling like tendrils of the parasite
    Around a marble column."
                                   SHELLEY.

" Sleep, Death's half-brother, sons of gloomy Night,
  There hold they habitation, Death and Sleep.

Dread deities; nor them the shining sun
E'er with his beam contemplates, when he climbs
The cope of heaven, or when from heaven descends."

HESIOD.

No. 338.

Head of Charon.

LYCOS. *Cornelian.*

No. 339.

Hercules and Apollo contending for the tripod.

APOLLONIDES. *Oriental Cornelian.*

" Favoured by them, Alcides' nervous arm
Repelled the monarch of the briny flood ;
Nor did the silver bow his heart alarm,
But firmly angry Phœbus' rage he stood ;
Nor could stern Pluto's rod his breast dismay,
Which drives the dying to his drear abodes :—
Rash Muse, desist! nor urge the impious lay ;
Hateful's the wisdom that blasphemes the gods.
'Tis madness, strength absurdly thus to boast,
And mortal might compare with heaven's triumphant host."

" Ex eo igitur et Lysito est is Hercules, quem concertasse cum Apolline de tripode accepimus."

CIC. *de Nat. Deor.* lib. iii. c. 16.

No. 340.

Hercules seizing the tripod of the Priestess of Delphi.

APOLLONIDES. *Oriental Sardonyx.*

Hercules, after the death of Iphitus, whom he had killed by precipitating him from the walls of Tirynthus, repaired to Delphi to consult the oracle; but Xenoclea, the priestess of Apollo, refused to answer him until he had expiated the murder of Iphitus. This so enraged Hercules, that he seized on the tripod, and only restored it at the reiterated entreaties of the priestess. The moment chosen is that in which Hercules is carrying off the tripod, and Xenoclea is persuading him to desist from the sacrilegious attempt.

No. 341.

Hercules carrying off the tripod.

DIOSCORIDES.   *Oriental Cornelian.*

No. 342.

Amphitryon killing the Mycenæan fox.

GNAIOS.   *Amethyst.*

Amphitryon, the son of Alcæus and Hipponome, and grandson of Perseus, was enamoured of Alcmena, daughter of Electryon, king of Mycenæ, and demanded her in marriage of her father. Electryon consented, on condition that he would deliver the kingdom from a savage fox which desolated it.

> " Is there on earth a stranger to the man
> Who shared the same auspicious nuptial bed
> With Jove—Amphytrion born at Argos, sprung
> From Perseus' son Alcæus—me, the sire
> Of Hercules ?" . . . . .
>   EURIPIDES, *Her. Dis.*

No. 343.

Alcmena visited by Jupiter, who, to deceive her, assumed the form of Amphitryon.

GNAIOS.   *Oriental Sardonyx.*

> " O ye, the partners of one nuptial bed,
> Happy Amphitryon, sprung from mortal race,
> And Jove, who rush'd to the embrace
> Of bright Alcmena; for of thee aright,
> Though erst, O Jove, I doubted, was it said
>   Thou didst enjoy that beauteous dame ;
>   With the renown his triumphs claim,
> Time through the world displays Alcides' might,
> Emerg'd from grisly Pluto's realms abhorr'd,
> Who quits the darksome caverns of the earth—
>   To me a far more welcome lord
> Than you, vile tyrant of ignoble birth."
>   EURIPIDES, *Her. Dis.*

No. 344.

The birth of Hercules.

DIOSCORIDES. *Oriental Cornelian.*

Alcmena, in labour with Hercules, was an object of Juno's hatred; and to prevent her being brought to bed, she sent Lucina, disguised as an old woman, to her house. Hercules would not have been born, had it not been for Galanthis, one of Alcmena's slaves, who, suspecting something wrong from seeing Lucina seated during seven successive days on an altar with her legs and arms crossed, ran to her suddenly, bidding her to rejoice at the happy termination of her mistress's sorrows. Lucina, taken by surprise, uncrossed her legs and arms, and Alcmena gave birth to Hercules.

" For when Alcmena's nine long months were
    run,
And Jove expected his immortal son,
To gods and goddesses th' unruly joy
He shew'd, and vaunted of his matchless boy:
From us (he said) this day an infant springs,
Fated to rule, and born a king of kings.
Saturnia ask'd an oath, to vouch the truth,
And fix'd dominion on the favour'd youth.
The Thunderer, unsuspicious of the fraud,
Pronounc'd those solemn words that bind a god.
The joyful goddess from Olympus' height
Swift to Achaian Argos bent her flight:
Scarce seven moons gone lay Sthenelus's wife,
She push'd her lingering infant into life;
Her charms Alcmena's coming labours stay,
And stop the babe, just issuing to the day.

Then bids Saturnius bear his oath in mind;
'A youth,' said she, 'of Jove's immortal kind
Is this day born; from Sthenelus he springs,
And claims thy promise to be king of kings.'
Grief seiz'd the Thunderer, by his oath engag'd:
Stung to the soul, he sorrow'd and he rag'd.
From his ambrosial head, where perch'd she sate,
He snatch'd the fury-goddess of debate,
The dread, th' irrevocable oath he swore,
Th' immortal seats should ne'er behold her more;
And whirl'd her headlong down, for ever driven
From bright Olympus and the starry heaven:
Thence on the nether world the fury fell,
Ordain'd with man's contentious race to dwell.
Full oft the god his son's hard toils bemoan'd,
Curs'd the dire fury, and in secret groan'd.
E'en thus, like Jove himself, was I misled."

Il. xix.

" Sev'n days and nights, amidst incessant
    throes,
Fatigued with ills I lay, nor knew repose;
When, lifting high my hands, in shrieks I pray'd,
Implor'd the gods, and call'd Lucina's aid.
She came, but prejudic'd to give my fate
A sacrifice to vengeful Juno's hate.
She hears the groaning anguish of my fits,
And on the altar at my door she sits.

O'er her left knee her crossing leg she cast,
Then knits her fingers close, and wrings them
    fast.
This stay'd the birth: in mutt'ring verse she
    pray'd,
The mutt'ring verse th' unfinish'd birth delay'd.
Now with fierce struggles, raging with my
    pain,
At Jove's ingratitude I rave in vain.

How did I wish for death! such groans I sent,
As might have made the flinty heart relent.
　　Now the Cadmeïan matrons round me press,
Offer their vows, and seek to bring redress;
Among the Theban dames Galanthis stands,
Strong-limb'd, red-hair'd, and just to my com-
　　mands:
She first perceiv'd that all these racking woes
From the persisting hate of Juno rose.
As here and there she pass'd, by chance she sees
The seated goddess; on her close-press'd knees

Her fast-knit hands she leans.　With cheerful
　　voice
Galanthis cries, ' Whoe'er thou àrt, rejoice!
Congratulate the dame, she lies at rest—
At length the gods Alcmena's womb have blest.'
Swift from her seat the startled goddess springs,
No more conceal'd, her hands abroad she flings;
The charm unloos'd, the birth my pangs re-
　　liev'd,
Galanthis' laughter vex'd the pow'r deceiv'd."
　　　　　　　　　　　　　　　　　OVID.

No. 345.

Hercules, in presence of Amphitryon and the infant Iphicles, strangling the
serpents which Juno had sent to destroy him in his cradle.

APOLLONIDES.　*Calcedony, partaking of Sapphire.*

" Wash'd with pure water, and with milk well
　　fed,
To pleasing rest her sons Alcmena led ;
Alcides ten months old, yet arm'd with might,
And twin Iphiclus, younger by a night.
On a broad shield of fine brass metal made,
The careful queen her royal offspring laid
(The shield from Pterilus Amphitryon won
In fight—a noble cradle for his son !)
Fondly the babes she view'd, and on each head
She plac'd her tender hands, and thus she said :
' Sleep, gentle babes, and sweetly take your
　　rest ;
Sleep, dearest twins, with softest slumbers blest:
Securely pass the tedious night away,
And rise refresh'd with the fair rising day.'
She spoke, and gently rock'd the mighty shield ;
Obsequious slumbers soon their eyelids seal'd.
But when at midnight sunk the bright-ey'd Bear,
And broad Orion's shoulder 'gan appear,
Stern Juno, urg'd by unrelenting hate,
Sent two fell serpents to Amphitryon's gate,
Charg'd with severe commission to destroy
The young Alcides, Jove-begotten boy.

Horrid and huge, with many an azure fold,
Fierce through the portal's opening valves they
　　roll'd ;
Then on their bellies prone, high swoln with
　　gore,
They glided smooth along the marble floor ;
Their fiery eye-balls darted sanguine flame,
And from their jaws destructive poison came.
Alcmena's sons, when near the serpents prest,
Darting their forked tongues, awoke from rest ;
All o'er the chamber shone a sudden light,
For all is clear to Jove's discerning sight.
When on the shield his foes Iphiclus saw,
And their dire fangs that arm'd each horrid jaw,
Aghast he rais'd his voice with bitter cry,
Threw off the covering, and prepar'd to fly.
But Hercules stretch'd out his hands to clasp
The scaly monsters in his iron grasp ;
Fast in each hand the venom'd jaws he prest
Of the curst serpents, which e'en gods detest.
Their circling spires, in many a dreadful fold,
Around the slow-begotten babe they roll'd ;
The babe unwean'd, yet ignorant of fear,
Who never utter'd cry, nor shed a tear:

At length their curls they loos'd; for, rack'd with
    pain,
They strove to 'scape the dreadful gripe in vain.
Alcmena first o'erheard the mournful cries,
And to her husband thus : ' Amphitryon, rise !
Distressful fears my boding soul dismay ;
This instant rise, nor for thy sandals stay.
Hark, how for help the young Iphiclus calls !
A sudden splendour, lo! illumes the walls,
Though yet the shades of night obscure the
    skies ;
Some dire disaster threats : Amphitryon, rise !'
She spoke; the prince, obedient to her word,
Rose from the bed, and seiz'd his rich-wrought
    sword,
Which on a glittering nail above his head
Hung by the baldric to the cedar bed ;
Then from the radiant sheath, of lotos made,
With ready hand he drew the shining blade :
Instant the light withdrew, and sudden gloom
Involv'd again the wide-extended room.
Amphitryon call'd his train, that slumbering
    lay,
And slept secure the careless hours away :
' Rise, rise, my servants, from your couches
    straight,
Bring lights this instant, and unbar the gate.'
He spoke; the train, obedient to command,
Appear'd with each a flambeau in his hand :
Rapt with amaze, young Hercules they saw
Grasp two fell serpents close beneath the jaw.
The mighty infant shew'd them to his sire,
And smil'd to see the wreathing snakes expire ;
He leapt for joy that thus his foes he slew,
And at his father's feet the scaly monsters threw.
With tender care Alcmena fondly prest,
Half-dead with fear, Iphiclus to her breast ;
While o'er his mighty son Amphitryon spread
The lamb's soft fleece, and sought again his bed.
    When thrice the cock pronounc'd the morning
      near,
Alcmena call'd the truth-proclaiming seer,
Divine Tiresias; and to him she told
This strange event, and urg'd him to unfold

Whate'er the adverse deities ordain.
' Fear not,' she cried, ' but fate's whole will ex-
    plain,
For well thou know'st, O venerable seer !
Those ills which fate determines, man must bear.'
She spoke; the holy augur thus replied : -
' Hail, mighty queen, to Perseus near allied—
Parent of godlike chiefs ! by these dear eyes,
Which never more shall view the morning rise,
Full many Grecian maids for charms renown'd,
While merrily they twirl the spindle round,
Till day's decline thy praises shall proclaim,
And Grecian matrons celebrate thy fame.
So great, so noble will thy offspring prove,
The most gigantic of the gods above ;
Whose arm, endow'd with more than mortal
    sway,
Shall many men and many monsters slay.
Twelve labours past, he shall to heav'n aspire,
His mortal part first purified by fire ;
And son-in-law be nam'd of that dread power
Who sent these deadly serpents to devour
The slumbering child : then wolves shall rove the
    lawns,
And strike no terror in the pasturing fawns.
But, O great queen ! be this thy instant care,
On the broad hearth dry faggots to prepare ;
Aspalathus or prickly brambles bind,
Or the tall thorn that trembles in the wind ;
And at dark midnight burn (what time they came
To slay thy son) the serpents in the flame.
Next morn, collected by thy faithful maid,
Be all the ashes to the flood convey'd,
And blown on rough rocks by the favouring
    wind :
Thence let her fly, but cast no look behind.
Next with pure sulphur purge the house, and
    bring
The purest water from the freshest spring ;
This mix'd with salt, and with green olive
    crown'd,
Will cleanse the late contaminated ground.
Last, let a boar on Jove's high altar bleed,
That ye in all achievements may succeed.'

c c

Thus spoke Tiresias, bending low with age,
And to his ivory car retir'd the reverend sage.
Alcides grew beneath his mother's care,
Like some young plant, luxuriant, fresh, and fair,
That screen'd from storms defies the baleful blast,
And for Amphitryon's valiant son he past.
Linus, who claim'd Apollo for his sire,
With love of letters did his youth inspire ;
And strove his great ideas to enlarge,
A friendly tutor, faithful to his charge.
From Eurytus his skill in shooting came,
To send the shaft unerring of its aim ;
Eumolpus tun'd his manly voice to sing,
And call sweet music from the speaking string ;
In listed fields to wrestle with his foe,
With iron arm to deal the deathful blow,
And each achievement where fair fame is fought,
Harpalycus, the son of Hermes, taught,
Whose look so grim and terrible in fight,
No man could bear the formidable sight.
But fond Amphitryon, with a father's care,
To drive the chariot taught his godlike heir ;
At the sharp turn with rapid wheels to roll,
Nor break the grazing axle on the goal.
On Argive plains, for generous steeds renown'd,

Oft was the chief with race-won honours crown'd ;
And still unbroke his ancient chariot lay,
Though cankering time had eat the reins away.
To launch the spear, to rush upon the foe,
Beneath the shield to shun the falchion's blow,
To marshal hosts, opposing force to force,
To lay close ambush, and lead on the horse,—
These Castor taught him, of equestrian fame :
What time to Argos exil'd Tydeus came,
Where from Adrastus he high favour gain'd,
And o'er a kingdom rich in vineyards reign'd,
No chief like Castor, till consuming time
Unnerv'd his youth, and cropp'd the golden
    prime.
Thus Hercules, his mother's joy and pride,
Was train'd up like a warrior ; by the side
Of his great father's his rough couch was spread,
A lion's spoils compos'd his grateful bed.
Roast meat he lov'd at supper to partake,
The bread he fancied was the Doric cake,
Enough to satisfy the labouring hind ;
But still at noon full sparingly he din'd.
His dress, contriv'd for use, was neat and plain ;
His skirts were scanty, for he wore no train."

THEOCRITUS : FAWKES.

" They their blood-gorging bellies on the ground
    Uncoiling rolled ; their eyes shot baleful flame,
And evermore they spat their poison round :
But when, quick-brandishing with evil aim
Their forked tongues, they to the children came,
They both awoke — (what can escape Jove's
    eye ?)—
Light in the chamber shone ; and who can
    blame
Or wonder that Iphiclus did outcry,
Screaming when he did their remorseless teeth
    outspy ?

He kicked aside the woollen coverlet,
Struggling to flee ; but Hercules comprest,
Relaxing not the gripe his hand did get,
With a firm grasp the head of either pest,
Where is their poison, which e'en gods detest.

The boy that in the birth was long confin'd,
    Who ne'er was known to cry, though at the
        breast
A suckling yet, they with their coils entwined ;
Infolding him they strained their own release to
    find,

Till, wearied in their spines, they loosed their
    fold.
Alcmena heard the noise, and woke in fear :
' Amphitryon, up ! for me strange fear doth
    hold :
Up—up ! don't wait for sandals ; don't you
    hear
Iphiclus screaming ? See the walls appear
Distinctly shining in the dead of night,
As though 'twere dawn. There is some danger
    near ;

I'm sure there is, dear man !' He then out-
right
Did leap from off the bed, to hush his wife's af-
fright.

And hastily his costly sword he sought
(Suspended near the cedar-bed it hung),
With one hand raised the sheath of lotus
wrought,
While with the other he the belt unswung.
The room was filled with night again; he
sprung,
And for his household, breathing slumber
deep,
He loudly called; his voice loud echoing
rung:

' Ho! from the hearth bring lights! Quick!
do not creep!
Fling wide the doors — awake! This is no time
for sleep.'

They hastened all with lights at his command:
But when they saw (their eyes they well might
doubt)
A serpent clutched in either tender hand
Of suckling Hercules, they gave a shout,
And clapped their hands. He instantly held out
The serpents to Amphitryon; and wild
With child-like exultation leaped about,
And laid them at his father's feet and smiled—
Laid down those monsters grim, in sleep of death
now mild."

THEOCRITUS.

" Thy early virtues, Chromius, deck'd with praise,
And those first-fruits of Fame, inspire
The Muse to promise for thy future days
A large increase of merit and renown.
So when of old Jove's mighty son,
Worthy his great immortal sire,
Forth from Alcmena's teeming bed
With his twin-brother came,
Safe through life's painful entrance led,
To view the dazzling sun's reviving flame,—
Th' imperial cradle Juno quick survey'd,
Where slept the twins in saffron bands array'd.

Then, glowing with immortal rage,
The gold-enthroned empress of the gods,
Her eager thirst of vengeance to assuage,
Straight to her hated rival's curs'd abode
Bade her vindictive serpents haste.
They through the opening valves with speed
On to the chamber's deep recesses past,
To perpetrate their murderous deed.
And now in knotty mazes to enfold
Their destin'd prey, on curling spires they roll'd,
His dauntless brow when young Alcides rear'd,
And for their first attempt his infant arms pre-
par'd.

Fast by the azure necks he held
And grip'd in either hand his scaly foes;
Till from their horrid carcasses expell'd,
At length the poisonous soul unwilling flows.
Meantime intolerable dread
Congeal'd each female's curdling blood;
All who, attendant on the genial bed,
Around the languid mother stood.
She with distracting fear and anguish stung,
Forth from her sickly couch impatient sprung;
Her cumb'rous robe regardless off she threw,
And to protect her child with fondest ardour flew.

But with her shrill, distressful cries alarm'd,
In rush'd each bold Cadmean lord,
In brass refulgent, as to battle arm'd;
With them Amphitryon, whose tumultuous
breast
A crowd of various cares infest;
High brandishing his gleaming sword,
With eager, anxious step he came:
A wound so near his heart
Shook with dismay his inmost frame,
And rous'd the active spirits in every part.
To our own sorrows serious heed we give,
But for another's woe soon cease to grieve.

Amaz'd the trembling father stood,
While doubtful pleasure, mix'd with wild sur-
        prise,
Drove from his troubled heart the vital flood ;
His son's stupendous deed with wond'ring eyes
    He view'd, and how the gracious will
    Of Heav'n to joy had chang'd his fear,
And falsified the messengers of ill.
    Then straight he calls th' unerring seer,
Divine Tiresias, whose prophetic tongue
Jove's sacred mandates from the tripod sung ;
Who then to all th' attentive throng explain'd
What fate th' immortal gods for Hercules or-
        dain'd.

    What fell despoilers of the land,
The prophet told, what monsters of the main,
Should feel the vengeance of his righteous
        hand :
What savage, proud, pernicious tyrant slain,
    To Hercules should bow his head ;
    Hurl'd from his arbitrary throne,

Whose glitt'ring pomp his curs'd ambition fed,
    And made indignant nations groan.
Last, when the giant sons of earth shall dare
To wage against the gods rebellious war,
Pierc'd by his rapid shafts on Phlegra's plain,
With dust their radiant locks the haughty foe
        shall stain.

Then shall his generous toils for ever cease,
    With fame with endless life repaid,
With pure tranquillity, and heavenly peace.
Then led in triumph to his starry dome,
    To grace his spousal bed shall come,
    In beauty's glowing bloom array'd,
Immortal Hebe, ever young.
    In Jove's august abodes
    Then shall he hear the bridal song ;
Then, in the blest society of gods,
The nuptial banquet share ; and, rapt in praise
And wonder, round the glittering mansion
        gaze."
                        PINDAR: WEST'S *Trans.*

No. 346.

The same subject.

CHROMIOS.   *Oriental Cornelian.*

No. 347.

Juno, yielding to the entreaties of Pallas, nourishes with her milk the
infant Hercules in presence of Jupiter.

POLYCLETES.   *Oriental Sardonyx.*

" With thee (*i. e.* Theseus) shall come the lion-whelp, who drew
    Tl e milky globes which swell on Juno's breast."
                        LYCO.: VISCOUNT ROYSTON'S *Trans.*

No. 348.

Hercules sucking the milk too greedily, some drops fell, and thence sprung the *via lactea,* or milky way, so celebrated among the poets.

CHROMIOS. *Oriental Cornelian.*

" Nor with inquiring eyes need we survey
The distant skies to find the milky way.
By all it must be seen ; for ev'ry night
It forcibly intrudes upon the sight,
And will be mark'd : there shining streaks adorn
The skies, as op'ning to let forth the morn ;
Or as a beaten path, that spreads between
A trodden meadow and divides the green ;

Or as when seas are plough'd, behind the ship
White foam rolls o'er the surface of the deep,
In heav'n's dark arch this way distinguish'd lies,
And with its brightness parts the azure skies.
Fame says (nor shall with me the fable die),
That Juno's breast, o'erflowing, stain'd the sky,
And left that whiteness; whence it justly draws
The name of milky from the milky cause."

MANIL. book i.: CREECH.

No. 349.

The herald of Eurystheus delivering the orders to Hercules to perform the twelve great labours.

APOLLONIDES. *Oriental Cornelian.*

Iphicles, the son of Amphytrion and Alcmena, king of Argos and Mycenæ, was born before Hercules, and was jealous of his reputation ; and fearing that he might at some time be dethroned by this hero, he commanded him to execute twelve of the most difficult and danger-ous enterprises he could devise, in the persuasion that he must fall a victim.

No. 350.

Eurystheus imposing on Hercules the twelve labours.

APOLLONIDES. *Oriental Amethyst.*

"Com'st thou, detested wretch ? at length hath
            justice
O'ertaken thee? First, hither turn thy head,
And dare to face thine enemies ; for, dwindled
Into a vassal, thou no longer rul'st.
Art thou the man (for I would know the truth)
Who did'st presume to heap unnumber'd wrongs,
Thou author of all mischief, on my son

While yet he lived, wherever now resides
His dauntless spirit? For in what one instance
Didst thou not injure him ? At thy command,
Alive he travell'd to th' infernal shades ;
Thou sent'st, and did commission him to slay
Hydras and lions. Various other mischiefs
Which were by thee contriv'd, I mention not—
For an attempt to speak of them at large

Would be full tedious. Nor was it enough
For thee to venture on these wrongs alone:
But thou, moreover, from each Grecian state,
Me and these children hast expell'd, though
    seated
As suppliants at the altars of the gods,
Confounding those whose locks are grey through
    age

With tender infants. But thou here hast found
Those who were men indeed, and a free city
Which fear'd thee not. Thou wretchedly shalt
    perish,
And pay this bitter usury to atone
For all thy crimes, whose number is so great,
That it were just thou more than once shouldst
    die."

            EURIPIDES, *Ch. Hen.*: WOODHULL.

No. 351.

The first great exploit of Hercules, the victory over the Nemean lion.

GNAIOS.   *Oriental Sardonyx.*

" 'Son of Augeus, what of me you heard
Is strictly true, nor has the stranger err'd.
But since you wish to know, my tongue shall tell
From whence the monster came, and how he fell.
Though many Greeks have mention'd this affair,
None can the truth with certainty declare.
'Tis thought some god, by vengeful anger sway'd,
Sent this sore plague for sacrifice unpaid,
To punish the Phoronians: like a flood
He deluged the Pisean fields with blood.
The Bembinæans, miserable men,
Felt his chief rage, the neighbours to his den.
The hardy task this hideous beast to kill
Eurystheus first enjoin'd me to fulfil,
But hop'd me slain. On the bold conflict bent,
Arm'd to the field with bow and darts I went;
A solid club, of rude wild-olive made,
Rough in his rugged rind, my right hand sway'd:
On Helicon's fair hill the tree I found,
And with the roots I wrench'd it from the ground.
When the close covert I approach'd, where lay
The lordly lion lurking for his prey,
I bent my bow, firm fix'd the string, and straight
Notch'd on the nerve the messenger of fate;
Then circumspect I pry'd with curious eye,
First, unobserv'd, the ravenous beast to spy.
Now mid-day reign'd; I neither could explore
His paw's broad print, nor hear his hideous roar;

Nor labouring rustic find, nor shepherd swain,
Nor cowherd tending cattle on the plain,
To point the lion's lair. Fear chill'd them all,
And kept the herds and herdsmen in the stall.
I search'd the groves, and saw my foe at length;
Then was the moment to exert my strength.
Long ere dim evening clos'd he sought his den,
Gorg'd with the flesh of cattle and of men:
With slaughter stain'd his squalid mane appear'd,
Stern was his face, his chest with blood be-
    smear'd,
And with his pliant tongue he lick'd his gory
    beard.
Mid shady shrubs I hid myself with care,
Expecting he might issue from his lair.
Full at his flank I sent a shaft — in vain,
The harmless shaft rebounded on the plain.
Stunn'd at the shock, from earth the savage
    rais'd
His tawny head, and all around him gaz'd;
Wondering from whence the feather'd vengeance
    flew,
He gnash'd his horrid teeth, tremendous to the
    view.
Vex'd that the first had unavailing fled,
A second arrow from the nerve I sped;
In his broad chest, the mansion of his heart,
I launch'd the shaft with ineffectual art:

His hair, his hide, the feather'd death repel,
Before his feet it innocently fell.
Enrag'd, once more I tried my bow to draw,
Then first his foe the furious monster saw.
He lash'd his sturdy sides with stern delight,
And rising in his rage, prepar'd for fight.
With instant ire his mane erected grew,
His hair look'd horrid, of a brindled hue;
Circling his back, he seem'd in act to bound,
And like a bow he bent his body round,
As when the fig-tree skilful wheelers take
For rolling chariots rapid wheels to make;
The fellies first, in fires that gently glow,
Gradual they heat, and like a circle bow;
Awhile in curves the pliant timber stands,
Then springs at once elastic from their hands.
On me thus from afar, his foe to wound,
Sprung the fell lion with impetuous bound.
My left hand held my darts direct before,
Around my breast a thick strong garb I wore;
My right, club-guarded, dealt a deadly blow
Full on the temples of the rushing foe.
So hard his skull, that with the sturdy stroke,
My knotted club of rough wild olive broke;
Yet ere I clos'd, his savage fury fled,
With trembling legs he stood and nodding head:
The forceful onset had confus'd his brain,
Dim mists obscur'd his eyes and agonizing pain.

This I perceiv'd; and now, an easy prey,
I threw my arrows and my bow away,
And ere the beast recover'd of his wound,
Seiz'd his thick neck, and pinn'd him to the
        ground;
With all my might on his broad back I press'd,
Lest his fell claws should tear my adverse breast.
Then mounting, close my legs in his I twin'd,
And with my feet secur'd his paws behind.
My thighs I guarded, and with all my strength
Heav'd him from earth, and held him at arm's
        length;
And strangled thus, the fellest of the fell,
His mighty soul descending sunk to hell.
The conquest gain'd, fresh doubts my mind
        divide,
How shall I strip the monster's shaggy hide?
Hard task! for the tough skin repell'd the dint
Of pointed wood, keen steel, or sharpest flint:
Some god inspir'd me, standing still in pause,
To flay the lion with the lion's claws—
This I accomplish'd, and the spoil now yields
A firm security in fighting-fields.
Thus, Phyleus, was the Nemean monster slain,
The terror of the forest and the plain,
That flocks and herds devour'd, and many a
        village swain."
                        THEOCRITUS, *Idyll.* xxv.

" Of Cadmus fatal; from the same dire veins
  Sprung the stern ranger of Nemean plains,
  The lion nourish'd by the wife of Jove,
  Permitted lord of Tretum's mount to rove;
  Nemea he and Apesas commands,
  Alarms the people, and destroys their lands.
  In Hercules at last a foe he found,
  And from his arm receiv'd a mortal wound."
                        HESIOD.

No. 352.

The same subject.

DIOSCORIDES.   *Oriental Cornelian.*

No. 353.

Hercules resting himself on the vanquished lion.

PYRGOTELES.   *Oriental Cornelian.*

No. 354.

Hercules presenting Eurystheus with the lion which he had slain.

APOLLONIDES.   *Oriental Sardonyx.*

No. 355.

Hercules bitten by a crab.

CHROMIOS.   *Oriental Cornelian.*

No. 356.

Hercules killing the hydra.

CHROMIOS.   *Oriental Cornelian.*

The victory of Hercules over the hydra of lake Leona in Argolis, a monstrous amphibious serpent with seven heads, who devoured both men and cattle, was the second of his great feats.

> " Upsprang the hydra pest of Leona's lake,
> Whom Juno, white-arm'd goddess, fostering rear'd,
> With deep resentment fill'd insatiable
> 'Gainst Hercules. But he, the son of Jove,
> Nam'd of Amphitryon, in the dragon's blood
> Bath'd his unpitying steel; by warlike aid
> Of Iolaus, and the counsels high
> Of Pallas the despoiler."
>
>   HESIOD.

> " Art thou proportioned to the hydra's length,
> Who by his wounds received augmented strength ?

She raised a hundred hissing heads in air;
When one I lopt, up sprang a dreadful pair.
By his wounds fertile, and with slaughter strong,
Singly I quell'd him, and stretch'd dead along."

OVID.

" Nor did Alcides, ranging through the world,
Fulfil such rare achievements, though he pierc'd
The brazen stag, and silenc'd all the grove
Of Erimanth, staining his angry shafts
With blood Lernean."

Æneis, book vi.: OGLE'S *Trans.*

" Not hydra stronger, when dismember'd, rose
Against Alcmena's much-enduring son;
Grieving to find from his repeated blows
The foe redoubled, and his toil begun."

HOR. book iv. Od. 4.

" The fires curl high; the Salii dance around
To sacred strains, with shady poplars crown'd;
The quires of old and young in lofty lays
Resound great Hercules' immortal praise.
How first his infant hands the snakes o'erthrew
That Juno sent, and the dire monsters slew.
What mighty cities next his arms destroy,
Th' Œchalian walls, and stately tow'rs of Troy.
The thousand labours of the hero's hands,
Enjoin'd by proud Eurystheus' stern commands,
And Jove's revengeful queen. Thy matchless
    might
O'ercame the cloud-born centaurs in the fight;
Hylæus, Pholus sunk beneath thy feet,
And the grim bull whose rage dispeopled Crete.

Beneath thy arm the Nemean monster fell;
Thy arm with terror fill'd the realms of hell;
E'en hell's grim porter shook with dire dismay,
Shrunk back, and trembled o'er his mangled
    prey.
No shapes of danger could thy soul affright,
Nor huge Typhœus, tow'ring to the fight,
Nor Lerna's fiend thy courage could confound,
With all her hundred heads that hiss'd around.
Hail, mighty chief, advanc'd to heaven's abodes!
Hail, son of Jove; a god among the gods!
Be present to the vows thy suppliants pay,
And with a smile these grateful rites survey."

Æneis, book viii.: PITT'S *Trans.*

" For these deserts, and this high virtue shewn,
Ye warlike youths, your heads with garlands
    crown;
Fill high the goblets with a sparkling flood,
And with deep draughts invoke our common god.
This said, a double wreath Evander twin'd,
And poplars, black and white, his temples bind;
Then brims his ample bowl; with like design
The rest invoke the god with sprinkled wine.

Meantime the sun descended from the skies,
And the bright evening-star began to rise;
And now the priests, Potitius at their head,
In skins of beasts involv'd, the long procession
    led;
Held high the flaming tapers in their hands,
As custom had prescrib'd their holy bands;
Then with a second course the tables load,
And with full chargers offer to the god.

d d

The Salii sing, and cense his altars round
With Saban smoke, their heads with poplar
    bound ;
One choir of old, another of the young,
To dance, and bear the burden of the song.
The lay records the labour, and the praise,
And all th' immortal acts of Hercules.
First, how the mighty babe, when swath'd in
    bands,
The serpents strangled with his infant hands.
Then, as in years and matchless force he grew,
Th' Œchalian walls and Trojan overthrew ;
Besides a thousand hazards they relate,
Procur'd by Juno's and Euristheus' hate.

Thy hands, unconquer'd hero, could subdue
The cloud-born Centaurs and the monster-crew :
Nor thy resistless arm the bull withstood ;
Nor he the roaring terror of the wood.
The triple porter of the Stygian seat,
With lolling tongue, lay fawning at thy feet,
And, seiz'd with fear, forgot thy mangled
    meat.
Th' infernal waters trembled at the sight ;
Thee, god, no face of danger could affright ;
Not huge Typhœus, nor th' unnumber'd snake,
Increas'd with hissing heads, in Lerna's lake."

Æneis.

No. 357.

Hercules, after killing the hydra, steeping his arrows in the poisonous blood of the monster.

DIOSCORIDES.   *Sardonyx.*

" Preserve with care
The clotted blood which issues from my wound ;
The gore of the Lernean hydra tinged
The blacken'd shaft."

SOPHOCLES, *Trach. Virg.*: POTTER.

No. 358.

Iolas assisting Hercules to kill the hydra.

ADMON.   *Oriental Sardonyx.*

Hercules could not have gained a complete victory over the hydra without the assistance of fire. Iolas, the son of Iphiclus and nephew of Hercules, and also the conductor of his car, seeing that the heads of the monster grew again as quickly as Hercules cut them off, set fire to a forest near lake Lerna ; and bringing lighted brands thence, burnt the wound of each as Alcides cut them off, by which means the serpent was exterminated.

" Now on the woody coast the warrior strays,
And soon the fam'd Lernean lake surveys,

Where the fell hydra was by flames subdu'd,
(For blows in vain the toiling chief renew'd).
And Nemea, where e'en now the timid swains,
Rarely, as erst, chant forth their artless strains."

Thebaid: LEWIS.

SEMICHORUS I.

" See there Jove's son, who with his golden falchion
Slays the Lernean hydra; O my friend,
Observe him well.

SEMICHORUS II.

I do.

SEMICHORUS I.

Another stands
Beside him brandishing a kindled torch.

SEMICHORUS II.

He whose exploits I on my woof describ'd?

SEMICHORUS I.

The noble Iolaus, who sustain'd
Alcides' shield, and in those glorious toils
Was the sole partner with the son of Jove.
Him also mark who on a winged steed
Is seated, how with forceful arm he smites
The triple-form'd chimæra breathing fire."

EURIPIDES.

No. 359.

The centaur Phobus pouring out wine for his guest Hercules.

SCYLAX. *Oriental Cornelian.*

Hercules, when he was going against the boar of Erymanthus, stopped at the dwelling of the centaur Phobus, the son of Silenus and Melia, who received him kindly, and offered him the most exquisite of their wines in skins.

" With summer's sweets, and autumn's redolence;
Apples and pears lay strew'd in heaps around,
And the plum's loaded branches kiss'd the ground.
Wine flow'd abundant from capacious tuns,
Matur'd divinely by four summers' suns.
Say, nymphs of Castaly! for ye can tell,
Who on the summit of Parnassus dwell,
Did Chiron e'er to Hercules produce
In Pholus' cave such bowls of generous juice?"

THEOCRITUS.

No. 360.

Hercules dragging the Erymanthean boar by one of its feet.

CHROMIOS. *Oriental Cornelian.*

" Next Hercules, endu'd with dauntless mind,
At Jason's summons staid not long behind:
For warn'd of this adventurous band, when last
The chief to Argos from Arcadia past—
(What time in chains he brought the living boar,
The dread, the bane of Erymanthia's moor;
And at the gates of proud Mycenæ's town,
From his broad shoulders hurl'd the monster down)—
Unask'd the stern Mycenian king's consent."

                          APOLL. RHOD., book i.

No. 361.

Eurystheus concealing himself in a tub, being seized with astonishment and terror at sight of the Erymanthean boar, brought to him by Hercules.

APOLLONIDES.   *Oriental Cornelian.*

No. 362.

Hercules, after having pursued for a whole year the stag of Œnoe with golden horns and brazen feet, wounding it with one of his arrows.

APOLLONIDES.   *Oriental Cornelian.*

" Then traversing the hills, whose jutting base
   Indents Arcadia's meads,
To where the virgin goddess of the chase
   Impels her foaming steeds
To Scythian Ister he directs his way,
   Doom'd by his father to obey
The rigid pleasures of Mycenæ's king,
   And thence the rapid hind to bring,
Whom, sacred present for the Orthian maid,
With horns of branching gold Taygeta array'd.

There as the longsome chase the chief pursu'd,
The spacious Scythian plains he view'd ;
   A land beyond the chilling blast
   And northern caves of Boreas cast.
There too the groves of olive he survey'd,
And gaz'd with rapture on the pleasing shade ;
   Thence by the wond'ring hero borne,
   The goals of Elis to adorn."
        PINDAR, *Olym.* book iii. : WEST.
    See also CALLIMACHUS, *Hymn to Diana.*

         " Nor Hercules more lands or labours knew,
           Not though the brazen-footed hind he slew,
           Freed Erymanthus from the foaming boar,
           And dipp'd his arrows in Lernean gore.

Nor Bacchus, turning from his Indian war,
By tigers drawn triumphant in his car,
From Nisus' top descending on the plains,
With curling vines around his purple reins."

APOLL. RHOD.

No. 363.

Hercules catching the wounded stag.

DEMOPHILOS. *Very fine Sardonyx.*

No. 364.

Hercules bringing the stag alive on his shoulders to Eurystheus, at Mycenæ.

CHROMIOS. *Oriental Amethyst.*

No. 365.

Hercules killing the birds of the Lake Stymphalus.

CHROMIOS. *Oriental Cornelian.*

" What verse can soar on so sublime a wing
As reaches his deserts? What muse can sing
As he requires? What poet now can raise
A stately monument of lasting praise,
Great as his vast deserts, who first did shew
These useful truths; who taught us first to know
Nature's great pow'rs? 'Tis more than man can
    do:
For if we view the mighty things he shew'd,
His useful truths proclaim he was a god!
He was a god who first reform'd our souls,
And led us, by philosophy and rules,
From cares, and fears, and melancholy night,
To joy, to peace, to ease, and shew'd us light.
    For now compare what other gods bestow:
Kind Bacchus first the pleasing vine did shew,
And Ceres corn, and taught us how to plough;
Yet men might still have liv'd without these two,
They might have liv'd as other nations do.
But what content could man, what pleasure find,
What joy in life, while passions vex'd the mind?
Therefore that man is more a god than these,
That man who shew'd us how to live at ease,
That man who taught the world delight and peace.
    His useful benefits are rais'd above
Alcides' acts, the greatest son of Jove;
For tell me how the fierce Nemean roar
Could fright us now? How could th' Arcadian
    boar,
The Cretan bull, the plague of Lerne's lakes,
The pois'nous hydra with her num'rous snakes?
How could Geryon's force, or triple face?
How Diomed's fiery horse, those plagues of
    Thrace?

How could the birds that o'er th' Arcadian
   plains
With crooked talons tore th' affrighted swains,
Offend us here? Whom had the serpent struck,
Mighty in bulk, and terrible in look;
That, arm'd with scales, and in a dreadful fold,
Twin'd round the tree, and watch'd the growing
   gold,
Remov'd as far as the Atlantic shore,
Deserts untrod by us and by the Moor?

Those others, too, that fell and rais'd his fame,
That gave him this diffus'd and lasting name,
And made him rise a god from Œta's flame:
Had they still liv'd, what mischief had they done?
Whom had they torn? whom frighted? Surely
   none.
For now, e'en now, vast troops of monsters fill
Each thick and darksome wood and shady hill;
Yet who complains, yet who their jaws endure?
For men may shun their dens, and live secure."

                        LUCRETIUS, book v.: CREECH.

No. 366.

Hercules leading in bonds the Cretan bull.

CHROMIOS.   *Oriental Cornelian.*

No. 367.

Hercules giving the body of Diomedes to be devoured by his own horses.

APOLLONIDES.   *Oriental Cornelian.*

HERCULES.

" Tribes of Pheræa, strangers, shall I find
Admetus in the palace?

CHORUS.

Pheres' son
Is here within, O Hercules. But say,
What errand brings you to Thessalia's land;
Or why you visit these Pheræan walls?

HERCULES.

I, by Eurystheus, the Tirynthian king,[*]
Enjoin'd, a certain labour must perform.

CHORUS.

But whither would you go, and in what realm
Are you prepar'd to wander?

HERCULES.

        The four steeds
Of Thracian Diomedes I must win.

---

[*] The city of Tirynthia appears to have been not far distant from Argos, with whose troops those it furnished for the Trojan war are united by Homer, who calls it τειχιόεσσαν, or " strongly fortified." It became an independent state under Prætus, who, being driven from Argos by his brother Acrisius, was assisted by the Cyclops in erecting bulwarks and a citadel for its defence. In this account Strabo, Apollodorus, and Pausanias, all accord. The latter of these writers mentions the demolition of Tirynthia by the Argives, and speaks of its ruins as consisting of stones of a most enormous size; but in Pliny's time there seems to have been no traces of its situation remaining, for he represents it as known only by tradition. There is room to infer that Tirynthia stood either

CHORUS.

How can you execute this bold emprise?
Are you a stranger to that tyrant's might?

HERCULES.

I am a stranger; the Bistonian land
These feet have never enter'd.

CHORUS.

You those coursers
Without a combat cannot tame.

HERCULES.

From labours,
Whate'er they are, yet cannot I recoil.

CHORUS.

You either will return when you have slain
Their master, or a breathless corpse there lie.

HERCULES.

Nor am I now to run my first career.

CHORUS.

What will you gain if you their lord subdue?

HERCULES.

Those captive steeds to the Tirynthian king
I mean to drive.

CHORUS.

Within their mouths to fix
The galling bit, were not an easy task.

HERCULES.

Unless they from their nostrils breathe forth
fire.

CHORUS.

But with rapacious jaws on human flesh
They prey.

HERCULES.

Such food as this, to beasts who haunt
The mountains, not to horses, doth belong.

CHORUS.

Sprinkled with gore their mangers will you
view.

HERCULES.

As for the man by whom they have been nou-
rished,
What father doth he boast of?

CHORUS.

Mars; and reigns
O'er Thrace distinguish'd by its golden shields.

HERCULES.

The labour too thou speak'st of have the Fates
Ordain'd; them ever have I found severe,
And to the pinnacle of high renown
Urging my steps. I sure am doom'd to war
With all the valiant progeny of Mars;
Lycaon* first, then Cygnus, and advance
To this my third encounter with those steeds
And with their lord. But none shall ever see
Alcmena's offspring tremble at the might
Of any foe."

EURIPIDES.

---

on the sea-coast, or the banks of the Inachus, which is the only river of any consequence we meet
with in that part of the Peloponnesus, from Stephanus Byzantinus saying it was called 'Αλιεῖς, Halies,
from the multitude of fishermen who inhabited it, till it received the name of Tirynthe from the sister
of Amphitrion.

* The Lycaon killed by Hercules was a son of Neleus, and brother to Nestor. He had Neptune,
and not Mars, for his grandfather.

No. 368.

Hercules holding Hippolyte, queen of the Amazons, by the hair.

APOLLONIDES.   *Oriental Sardonyx of exquisite quality.*

No. 369.

Hippolyte, vanquished, is seated on a rock, and is presenting her girdle to Hercules.

APOLLONIDES.   *Oriental Cornelian.*

" Thence with the rising sun they stoutly row,
Near where Carambis lifts his rocky brow;
All day, all night, with unremitted oar
They coast along Ægialus's shore.
Then to the Syrian clime the heroes sped,
Where Jove, by hasty promises misled,
Sinope plac'd, and, all she wish'd to claim,
Gave her the honours of a virgin's name.
For know, the god, by love's strong power op-
    press'd,
Promis'd to grant whate'er she might request;
And this request th' insidious damsel made,
That her virginity might never fade.
Hence Phœbus foil'd could no one wish obtain ;
Hence winding Alys woo'd the maid in vain :
No mortal force such virtue could o'ercome,
Defeat Jove's promise, and impair her bloom.

Here dwelt Deïmachus's offspring fam'd,
Deileon Autolycus and Phlogius nam'd ;
What time they ceas'd with Hercules to roam,
And at Sinope found a settled home.
They, when they saw the bold Thessalian band,
Met them on shore, and welcom'd them to land ;
And loathing longer in these climes to stay,
Join'd the brave crew, and with them sail'd away.
Bless'd with the zephyr's breeze that briskly blew,
Near Halys' stream and Isis' sail'd the crew ;
Near Syria's coast, and ere night's shades abound,
Near th' Amazonian cape, for many a bay re-
    nown'd,
Where Hercules surpris'd, in days of yore,
Bold Menalippe wandering on the shore;
A belt Hippolyta her sister paid,
And for this ransom he restor'd the maid."
                          APOLL. RRODIUS.

" That day the Grecian band with one consent
To the king's hospitable palace went;
Cheerful they there on choicest dainties din'd,
And there with converse sweet regal'd the mind.
Then Jason to the king recounts the name
And race of all these chosen sons of fame,
Who lent their aid at Pelias' dire command ;
Their strange adventures on the Lemnian land ;
What griefs, what woes at Cyzicus they bore ;
And how they landed on the Mysian shore,

Where Hercules, distress'd his friend to find,
They left at land unwillingly behind.
What Glaucus spoke prophetic from the main,
How with his subjects Amycus was slain,
The prince relates : what Phineus, poor and old,
Worn out with sufferings, to the chiefs foretold;
How through Cyanean rocks they safely steer'd,
And in what isle the god of day appear'd.
The king rejoic'd his guests so well had sped,
But griev'd that Hercules was left, and said :

' Think how, my friends, this hero's aid denied,
Rashly ye tempt a length of seas untried.
Full well I knew that valiant son of fame,
When here on foot through Lydia's coast he came
(For here my hospitable father dwelt),
To fetch Hippolyta's embroider'd belt.
The hero found me then a beardless swain,
Mourning my brother by the Mysians slain—
(The nation dearly lov'd the blooming chief,
And still lament in elegies of grief) :
Then at the funeral games he prov'd his might,
And vanquish'd Titias in the gauntlet-fight;
Though young and stout, and eager for the fray,
From his bruis'd jaws he dash'd the teeth away.

The Mysian country and the Phrygian plains
The conqueror added to my sire's domains ;
And the rude nations that Bithynia till,
To foaming Rhebas and Colona's hill ;
And Paphlagonia to its utmost bounds,
Which sable Billis with his waves surrounds.
But now proud Amycus, and all his host,
Since Hercules has left the neighbouring coast,
Have spoil'd my realms, and spread their hostile
   bands
Wide as where Hipias' streams enrich the lands.
At length their lawless insolence they rue,
And by your hands have suffer'd vengeance due."
APOLL. RHODIUS.

" But, O Demophoron, what beyond the ties
Of family you to these children owe
Will I inform you ; and relate how erst
With Theseus in one bark I sail'd, and bore
Thy father's shield, when we that belt, the cause
Of dreadful slaughter, sought; and from the caves
Of Pluto Hercules led back your sire."
EURIPIDES, *Chil. of Her.* : WOODHULL.

" The lion-whelp
Who seiz'd the girdle, rais'd the double storm
Of war; for far from high Themiscyra
He bore the zone, and what of love the zone
Bounded, Orthosia, joying in the bow
And shafts of missile might : but on shall come
Her kindred virgins, like a cloud of night,
Breathing revenge ; from Telamus shall come

Eris, and Lagmus, and Thermodon's stream ;
Thence rush by Danaw's wave, dark as the storm,
And spur their Scythian steeds, and on the sons
Of fam'd Eristheus and the Grecian host
Pour the loud shout of battailous delight,
Throw down the leaguer'd tow'rs, and roll the
   tide
Of ruddy flame o'er all Mopsopia's field."
LYCOPHRON : VISCOUNT ROYSTON.

No. 370.

Hercules cleansing the Augean stable.

CHROMIOS. *Calcedony, partaking of Sapphire.*

Hercules cleansing the stables of Augeas, king of Elis and one of the Argonauts, who pos-
sessed innumerable flocks, by turning the course of the river Alpheus, and making it pass
through the stables.

e e

" When emulation warms the breast,
    The youth (heav'n aiding) matchless fame shall
        gain ;
But few the envied prize obtain
By slothful luxury and inglorious rest.
Now custom bids my muse proclaim
Jove's festival and solemn game,
With which Alcides honour'd Pelops' shrine,
When Neptune's baffled sons confess'd his power
        divine—

When his triumphant arm had laid,
O blameless Cteatus, thy glory low ;
And bold Eurytas felt the blow,
O'ercome by stratagem in Cleon's glade,
From proud Augeas to obtain
The promised meed of toil and pain ;

And wreak on Molion's sons the fatal day,
    When stretch'd on Elis' plains his slaughter'd
        army lay.

Soon did the faithless king his fraud repay—
He saw his country's fairest hopes expire ;
Saw his exulting cities fall a prey
To vengeful slaughter and consuming fire ;
Saw desolation's iron reign
Extend o'er all his fair domain.
Vain are the endeavours to withstand
The vengeance of a mightier hand ;
Awhile he rashly tried to oppose
The forceful entry of his shouting foes ;
Till seeing fell destruction round him wait,
Amidst the press he sought a voluntary fate."

                                        PINDAR.

No. 371.

Hercules killing Augeas.

CHROMIOS.   *Oriental Cornelian.*

He refused to give him the tenth of his flocks, as he had promised him.

No. 372.

Hercules chaining Nereus to a rock.

APOLLONIDES.   *Oriental Sardonyx.*

Nereus, the son of Ocean, was looked upon in a very remote age as the principal god of the sea before Neptune, according to Hesiod. Nereus married his sister Doris, by whom he had fifty daughters, called Nereides. To Nereus was attributed a knowledge of future events. Hercules wishing to consult him about the situation of the gardens of the Hesperides, of which he was ignorant, he assumed successively different forms to avoid giving Alcides the information he wished ; at length, taking his first disguise of a venerable and peaceable old man, Hercules chains him to a rock.

No. 373.

Hercules interrogating Nereus while chained to the rock.

APOLLONIDES. *Oriental Cornelian.*

No. 374.

Hercules killing the dragon which guarded the gardens of the Hesperides.

CHROMIOS. *Oriental Cornelian.*

The last but one, or according to some mythologians, the last of the twelve great labours of Hercules, was his journey to the country of the Hesperides, to obtain the golden apples from the gardens of Atlas, son of Jupiter and Clymene, and brother of Prometheus. These gardens were surrounded by strong walls, and guarded day and night by a terrible dragon. Hercules penetrated into the enclosure, and killed the dragon.

" Let those who, glowing with their country's love,
Resolve with me these dreadful plains to prove:
These Pallas loves, so tells reporting fame,
Here first from heaven to earth the goddess came
(Heaven's neighbourhood the warmer clime betrays,
And speaks the nearer sun's immediate rays),
Here her first footsteps on the brink she stay'd,
Here in the watery glass her form survey'd,
And call'd herself from hence the chaste Tritonian maid.
Here Lethe's streams, from secret springs below,
Rise to the light; here heavily and slow
The silent, dull, forgetful waters flow.
Here, by the wakeful dragon kept of old,
Hesperian plants grew rich with living gold;

Long since, the fruit was from the branches torn,
And now the gardens their lost honours mourn.
Such was in ancient times the tale receiv'd,
Such by our good forefathers was believ'd;
Nor let inquirers the tradition wrong,
Or dare to question now the poet's sacred song.
Then take it for a truth, the wealthy wood
Here under golded boughs low bending stood;
On some large tree his folds the serpent wound,
The fair Hesperian virgins watch'd around,
And join'd to guard the rich forbidden ground.
But great Alcides came to end their care,
Stripp'd the gay grove, and left the branches bare;
Then back returning sought the Argive shore,
And the bright spoil to proud Eurystheus bore.'
LUCAN, book IX.: ROWE.

"This wond'rous tale the tuneful nine recite,
And as the Muses dictate I must write.
This have I heard, and this as truth proclaim,
That you, O princely peers, of deathless fame,
By the joint efforts of united hands,
Twelve days and nights through Libya's burning sands

High on your shoulders rais'd the vessel's weight,
All that its womb contain'd, a mighty freight.
What woes o'ertook them, and what toils befell,
No verse can celebrate, no tongue can tell.
Such brave exploits proclaim'd their godlike line,
For, as their lineage, were their deeds divine.

But when Tritonis' lake the chiefs attain,
They eas'd their shoulders, and embark'd again.
Doom'd to acuter griefs, they now are curs'd
With all the miseries of burning thirst;
Like dogs they run its fury to assuage,
And at a fountain's head suppress its rage.
Nor wander'd they in vain; but soon explor'd
The sacred spot with golden apples stor'd,
In Atlas' realm : the serpent's wakeful eyes
Watch'd till but yesterday the golden prize.
The fair Hesperides with kind survey
Tended the serpent as they tun'd their lay;
But, lo! the monster by Alcides slain,
Beneath a branching pear-tree press'd the plain.
His tail still vibrates, though his ghastly head
And spine immense lie motionless and dead;
Flies in thick swarms his gory sides surround,
Drink his black blood, and dry the dripping
   wound
Made by the darts, whose poison'd tips detain
The deadly venom of the Hydra slain.
As Ladon's fate the pensive maids deplore,
Their hands they wrung, their golden locks they
   tore;
But sudden as the heroes hasten'd near,
They to the dust descend and disappear.
Struck with the prodigy his eyes survey'd,
Thus to the nymphs observant Orpheus pray'd :
 ' Ye goddesses, with bloom and beauty bless'd,
Look with benevolence on men distress'd.
Whether ye grace the splendid courts of Jove,
Or on this humble earth auspicious move;
Whether to flowery pastures ye repair,
And the lov'd name of shepherdesses bear;
Illustrious nymphs, from ocean sprung, arise,
Bless with a recent view our longing eyes,
Bid from the thirsty soul a torrent burst,
Or open some hard rock to slake our thirst.
Should we again our tatter'd sails expand,
And greet at last the dear Achaian land,

Grateful we then these favours will repay,
And choicest offerings on your altars lay :
No goddess who frequents the court of Jove
Shall greater honour share, or greater love.'
   Thus Orpheus pray'd, with feeble voice and
      low;
The listening nymphs commiserate their woe.
First tender grass they bade the soil disclose;
Then high above it verdant branches rose,
Erect and strong, the spreading boughs display'd
Wide o'er the barren soil an ample shade.
A poplar's trunk fair Hespera receives,
And in a weeping willow Ægle grieves :
But Erytheïs in an elm remains;
Each in her tree her proper shape retains.
Stupendous sight! first Ægle silence broke,
And kindly thus the suppliant band bespoke :
 ' Hither some lawless plunderer came of late,
Who will reverse the colour of your fate.
Yon beast he slew for whom we sorrow now,
And tore the golden apples from their bough.
But yesterday the desperate giant came;
From his black eye-brows flash'd the livid flame :
A lion's shaggy skin, besmear'd with gore,
Wide o'er his shoulders spread, the monster
      wore;
On his stout staff his fearless step rely'd,
And by his deadly dart the serpent died.
He like a sturdy traveller stalk'd along,
Seeking some fount to cool his fiery tongue :
With eager haste he trod the dusty plain,
And still for water look'd, but look'd in vain.
To this tall rock, hard by Titonis' lake,
Some god conducted him, his thirst to slake;
Struck by his heel its deep foundation shook,
And from the yawning clefts a torrent broke.
Prone on the ground the limpid streams he
      swills,
And, grovelling like a beast, his belly fills.' ”
                              APOLL. RHODIUS.

No. 375.

Hercules bearing the globe on his shoulders, whilst Atlas gathers the fruit.

DIOSCORIDES. *Oriental Cornelian.*

Hercules was unable to complete his undertaking without the assistance of Atlas; and for this reason he himself undertook to sustain the celestial globe, whilst Atlas gathered the apples. Hercules being unable to support the weight of the globe, makes a sign to Atlas to take it again.

> " Atlas, enforc'd by stern necessity,
> Drops the broad heav'n on earth's far borders where
> Full opposite th' Hesperian virgins sing
> With shrill sweet voice : he rears his head and hand,
> Aye unfatiguable—heav'n's counsellor
> So doom'd his lot."
>
> HESIOD.

No. 376.

Hercules sustaining the globe, whilst Atlas is gathering a branch from the tree full of apples.

CARPOS. *Oriental Cornelian.*

No. 377.

Hercules carrying away the apples of the Hesperides.

CHROMIOS. *Oriental Cornelian.*

No. 378.

Hercules delivering Prometheus, the son of Iapetus and Clymene, from the Caucasian rock, to which he had been chained by order of Jupiter, and killing with one of his arrows the eagle which fed upon his liver, that grew as quickly as it was devoured.

CHROMIOS. *Oriental Cornelian of a very rich colour.*

" Prometheus for his artifice renown'd,
And Epimetheus of unstedfast mind,
Lur'd to false joys, and to the future blind;
Who, rashly weak, by soft temptations mov'd,
The bane of arts and their inventors prov'd;
Who took the work of Jove, the virgin fair,
Nor saw beneath her charms the latent snare.
Blasted by lightning from the hands of Jove,
Menœtius fell in Erebus to rove;
His dauntless mind that could not brook com-
        mand,
And prone to ill, provok'd th' almighty hand.
Atlas, so hard necessity ordains,
Erect the pond'rous vault of stars sustains;
Not far from the Hesperides he stands,
Nor from the load retracts his head or hands:
Here was he fix'd by Jove in counsel wise,
Who all disposes, and who rules the skies.

To the same god Prometheus ow'd his pains,
Fast bound with hard inexorable chains
To a large column, in the midmost part,
Who bore his suff'rings with a dauntless heart.
From Jove an eagle flew, with wings wide spread,
And on his never-dying liver fed;
What with his rav'nous beak by day he tore,
The night supplied, and furnish'd him with more.
Great Hercules to his assistance came,
Born of Alcmena, lovely-footed dame;
And first he made the bird voracious bleed,
And from his chains the son of Japhet freed.
To this the god consents, th' Olympian sire,
Who for his son's renown suppress'd his ire,
The wrath he bore against the wretch who strove
In counsel with himself, the pow'rful Jove.
Such was the mighty Thund'rer's will, to raise
To greatest height the Theban hero's praise."

APOLL. RHOD.

" From thence they sail by long Macronian
        strands,
And where Bechira's ample coast expands;
Shores where Byzerians wander far and wide,
And fierce Sapirians, stigmatis'd for pride;
And favour'd by the soft-impelling wind,
Leave numerous coasts and lands unnam'd be-
        hind.
And sailing swiftly o'er the waves, survey
Far on the Pontic main an opening bay;
Then, Caucasus, thy hills were seen on high,
That rear their rocky summits in the sky.
Fix'd to these rocks Prometheus still remains,
For ever bound in adamantine chains;

On the rude cliffs a rav'nous eagle breeds,
That on the wretch's entrails ever feeds.
The Grecians saw him, ere th' approach of night,
Soar high in air, loud hissing in his flight;
Around the ship he flew in airy rings,
The sails all shiv'ring as he shook his wings.
Not as a light aerial bird he soars,
But moves his pinions like well-polish'd oars.
The rav'nous bird now rushing from the skies,
Sudden they heard Prometheus' piercing cries;
The heav'ns re-echo'd to the doleful sound,
While the fell eagle gnaw'd the recent wound:
Till gorg'd with flesh, the bird of Jove they spied
Again descending from the mountain's side."

APOLL. RHOD.

No. 379.

Hercules releasing Prometheus.

CHROMIOS. *Oriental Cornelian.*

Hercules, after killing the eagle, which is seen lying on the ground, unfastens the chains of Prometheus.

No. 380.

Echidna, with her offspring, Cerberus and Chimera.

GNAIOS. *Oriental Cornelian.*

Echidna, the daughter of Chrysoar and Callirhoe, had the body of a beautiful woman to the waist, while the lower part terminated in an enormous serpent. Concealed in a cavern in the country of the Hyperborei, she left it only to annoy the passengers. She was the mother of several monsters, amongst which were the dog Cerberus and the Chimera. She is here represented with these two monsters by her side.

"Callirhoe in a cave conceiv'd again,
And for Echidna bore maternal pain;
A monster she of an undaunted mind,
Unlike the gods, nor like the human kind:
One half a nymph of a prodigious size,
Fair her complexion, and asquint her eyes;
The other half a serpent dire to view,
Large and voracious, and of various hue.

Deep in a Syrian rock, her horrid den,
From the immortal gods remote and men,
There, so the council of the gods ordains,
Forlorn and ever young the nymph remains.
In love Echidna with Typhaon join'd,
Outrageous he and blust'ring as the wind."

HESIOD, *Theog.*

"Echidna, the untameable of soul,
Above a nymph with beauty-blooming cheeks,
And eyes of jetty lustre; but below
A speckled serpent horrible and huge,
Gorg'd with blood-banquets monstrous, hid in caves
Of sacred earth. There in the utmost depth

Her cavern is within a vaulted rock;
Alike from mortals and immortals deep,
Remote: the gods have there decreed her place
In mansions known to fame. So pent beneath
The rocks of Arima Echidna dwelt
Hideous; a nymph immortal, and in youth
Unchanged for evermore."

No. 381.

Echidna stealing the horses of Hercules.

SOLON. *Oriental Cornelian.*

Hercules, according to Herodotus, having gone into the country of the Hyperboreans, fell asleep on a rock. Echidna then carried off his horses, and took them to her cave.

No. 382.

Echidna promising Hercules to restore his horses.

DIOSCORIDES.   *Oriental Sardonyx.*

No. 383.

Echidna having restored the horses, receives from Hercules his bow.

SOLON.   *Oriental Sardonyx.*

Hercules reconciling himself with Echidna, he fell in love with her, and she became the mother of three children, Agathyrsus, Gelonus, and Scytha, chiefs of three Hyperborean nations, each of which took the name of its founder. Echidna restored the horses of Hercules, who on taking leave of her, gave her his bow, saying, "Thou wilt keep only him of thy sons who can bend this bow;" and Scytha, chief of the Scythians, was the only one who succeeded.

No. 384.

The death of Echidna, killed while sleeping by the shepherd Argus.

DIOSCORIDES.   *Oriental Sardonyx.*

No. 385.

Hercules wounding with an arrow the monster to which Hesione was exposed.

APOLLONIDES.   *Oriental Sardonyx.*

Neptune, to punish the perfidy of Laomedon king of Ilium, who refused to reward Apollo and himself for assisting him to build the walls of his city, visited Troy with a great pestilence. Laomedon consulted the oracle, and obtained for answer that the plague would not cease unless a virgin were annually offered to a sea-monster. After some years the lot fell upon Hesione, the daughter of Laomedon, to the great grief of her father, who loved her tenderly. Hercules arriving at Troy at the time, went to the king and offered to deliver his daughter, on condition that he should have as his reward some fine horses. Hesione is chained to a rock, and the monster from the sea about to devour her, when Hercules from his bow sends an arrow steeped in the blood of the hydra, which pierces the monster.

" Nor this appeas'd the god's revengeful mind,
For still a greater plague remains behind :
A huge sea-monster lodges on the sands,
And the king's daughter for his prey demands.
To him that sav'd the damsel was decreed
A set of horses of the sun's fine breed ;
But when Alcides from the rock untied
The trembling fair, the ransom was denied.

He in revenge the new-built walls attack'd,
And the twice-perjur'd city bravely sack'd ;
Telamon aided, and in justice shar'd
Part of the plunder as his due reward—
The princess, rescu'd late, with all her charms,
Hesione, was yielded to his arms."

OVID, *Met.*

No. 386.

Hercules rescuing Hesione from the monster.

APOLLONIDES. *Very fine Oriental Sardonyx.*

The monster, whom the poisoned arrow has rendered furious, is here seen redoubling his efforts to seize Hesione, and Hercules is preparing to strike him with his club.

" Ah, luckless muse ! enwrapped in ruddy flame,
Then when the lion, sprung from triple night,
Steer'd his dark pine across th' Ægean wave,
And hid her host within her hollow womb ;
Who fearless leap'd into the cavern'd jaws
Of the sea-monster, through the black abyss
Cleaving his bloody way ; whose shadowy locks,
Sing'd in the flameless furnace, wave no more ;
Who dyed his hands in infant blood, the pest
And fell pollution of my native tow'rs ;
Who 'gainst his stepdame's deathless bosom wing'd
The iron shaft ; and wrestling with his sire—
(Fast by the rocks of Cronus, where the tomb
Of earth-born Ischenus, gigantic birth,
Bears its cold marble, whence the courser starts)—

Twin'd round his limbs the sinewy strength of arm ;
Who slew the fiend, that, frowning in the wave,
Guards all the narrow pass where billows roll
Between Ausonian regions and the shores
Of Trinacris, where from the sea-beat rocks
She feasts upon the scaly shoals, and laughs
At Death, and Hades' impotent domain.
For on the vivifying pile her sire
Heap'd high her limbs, and wav'd the burning torch ;
Kindling the bright resuscitating flame ;
Whom nor with sword, nor shield, nor massive mail,
The dead subdu'd, and gave again to view
The dark pavilions and the glooms of hell."

LYCOPHRON : VISCOUNT ROYSTON.

f f

No. 387.

Hercules giving Hesione to Telamon.

APOLLONIDES. *Oriental Sardonyx.*

After the deliverance of Hesione, Laomedon refused to give Hercules the six horses sent by Jupiter to Troy as an indemnity for Ganymede (whom he had carried off), and which had descended to Laomedon. Hercules revenged himself for this perfidy; and, aided by his companions, carried Troy by assault. Telamon was the first to enter the city, which was sacked, and Laomedon killed by Jupiter, who became the possessor of Hesione. Hercules was jealous of the success of Telamon, and wished to slay him; and Telamon having been warned of this, collected a great quantity of stones, and to calm him declared his intention of erecting a very high altar in honour of Hercules (the conqueror). Alcides then, forgetting all former malice, loads him with praises, and gives him Hesione in marriage.

" In Salamis' profound retreat,
  Fam'd for the luscious treasures of the bee,
High rais'd above th' encircling sea,
Thou, Telamon, didst fix thy regal seat.
Near to those sacred hills, where spread
The olive first its fragrant sprays,
To form a garland for Minerva's head,
And the Athenian splendour raise :
With the fam'd archer, with Alcmena's son,
Thou cam'st exulting with vindictive joy ;
By your confed'rate arms was Ilion won,
When from thy Greece thou cam'st, our city to
    destroy.

  Repining for the promis'd steeds,
From Greece Alcides led a chosen band ;
With hostile prows th' indented strand
He reach'd, and anchor'd near fair Simois'
    meads.
Selected from each ship, he led
Those who with dextrous hand could wing
Th' unerring shaft, till slaughter reach'd thy
    head,
Laomedon, thou perjur'd king.
Those battlements which Phœbus' self did
    rear
The victor wasted with devouring flame ;

Twice o'er Troy's walls hath wav'd the hostile
    spear,
Twice have insulting shouts announc'd Dardania's
    shame.

  Thou bear'st the sparkling wine in vain,
With step effeminate, O Phrygian boy ! •
Erewhile didst thou approach with joy
To fill the goblet of imperial Jove :
For now thy Troy lies levell'd with the plain,
And its thick smoke ascends the realms above.
On th' echoing coast our plaints we vent,
As feather'd songsters o'er their young bewail ;
A child or husband these lament,
And those behold their captive mothers sail.
The founts where thou didst bathe, th' athletic
    sports,
Are now no more. Each blooming grace
Sheds charms unheeded o'er thy placid face,
And thou frequent'st heav'n's splendid courts.
Triumphant Greece hath levell'd in the dust
The throne where Priam rul'd the virtuous and
    the just.

  With happier auspices, O Love,
Erst didst thou hover o'er this fruitful plain,
Hence caught the gods thy thrilling pain ;

By thee embellish'd, Troy's resplendent tow'rs
Rear'd their proud summits blest by thund'ring
    Jove,
For our allies were the celestial pow'rs.
But I no longer will betray
Heav'n's ruler to reproach and biting shame.
The white-wing'd morn, blest source of day,
Who cheers the nations with her kindling flame,

Beheld these walls demolish'd, and th' abode
Of that dear prince who shar'd her bed
In fragments o'er the wasted champaign spread;
While swift along the starry road,
Her golden car his country's guardian bore:
False was each amorous god, and Ilion is no
    more."
        EURIPIDES, *Trojan Captives.*

No. 388.

Hercules in the act of striking Telamon, who, to appease him, points to the altar he is constructing in his honour.

SCYLAX. *Oriental Cornelian.*

No. 389.

Hercules bagging the pigmies in the skin of the Nemean lion.

CHROMIOS. *Oriental Cornelian.*

The ancients believed that there existed in Libya a race of men whose stature did not exceed a cubit. Hercules conquered them, and killed Antheas their chief, after which exploit he fell asleep. The pigmies, resolved on revenging the death of their prince, dared to attack Hercules, and placed themselves on his body. Alcides, awakened by the noise, seized all of them, and enclosing them in the skin of the Nemean lion, as in a bag, carried them to Eurystheus.

No. 390.

Hercules killing Busiris.

APOLLONIDES. *Oriental Cornelian.*

Busiris, the son of Neptune and Libya, reigned in Egypt about 1400 years before our era. The kingdom being afflicted during a long period with famine, Busiris, to find a remedy, consulted Thrasius of Cyprus the soothsayer, who replied that the dearth would cease if all foreigners who came to Egypt were sacrificed to Neptune. The king first sacrificed the soothsayer, and then all the foreigners, or men with red hair, who landed in Egypt. Hercules, after overcoming Antæus, went thither, and was condemned to the same fate. He was bound, and led to the altar as a victim; but having broken his bonds, he put to death Busiris, his son, his herald, and the priests. The moment represents Hercules, after having killed several persons in the train of Busiris, dragging the king to the altar, and about to strike him with his club.

" Have I thus gain'd
For slain Busiris, who Jove's temple stain'd
With strangers' blood? that from the earth earth-
 bred
Antæus held? whom Geryon's triple head,
Nor thine, O Cerberus, could once dismay?
These hands, these made the Cretan bull obey:
Your labours, Elis, smooth Stymphalian floods
Confess with praises, and Parthenian woods.
You got the golden belt of Thermodon,
And apples from the sleepless dragon won.
Nor cloud-born Centaurs, nor th' Arcadian boar,
Could me resist; nor Hydra, with her store

Of frightful heads, which by their loss increas'd.
I, when I saw the Thracian horses feast
With human flesh, their mangers overthrew,
And with his steeds their wicked master slew.
These hands the Nemean lion chok'd; these
 quell'd
Huge Cacus; and these shoulders heav'n upheld.
Jove's cruel wife grew weary to impose;
I never to perform. But, O these woes,
This new-found plague, no virtue can repel,
Nor arms, nor weapons."

      OVID's *Met.:* SANDYS.

No. 391.

Hercules killing Aulis with a spade.

APOLLONIDES. *Oriental Amethyst.*

Sileus, king of Aulis, obliged all strangers who passed through his territory to help till the land. He dared to compel Hercules to do this, and gave him a spade, with which the indignant Hercules kills him.

No. 392.

Polygonus and Telegonus, the sons of Proteus, killed by Hercules, whom they had challenged to wrestle with them.

CHROMIOS. *Oriental Sardonyx.*

No. 393.

Hercules killing Erginus.

CHROMIOS. *Oriental Cornelian.*

Erginus, king of Orchomenos, invaded Bœotia, and threatened the city of Thebes. Hercules put himself at the head of the young Thebans to repulse him; and having no arms, he took those of Minerva, which were hung up in her temple.　He attacked the Orchomenians, subdued them, and killed Erginus.

No. 394.

The same subject.

DIOSCORIDES.　*Oriental Cornelian.*

No. 395.

The bolt of Jove separating Mars and Hercules combating.

CHROMIOS.　*Oriental Sardonyx.*

Hercules vanquished Cycnus in the race, and killed him ; and Mars, to revenge the death of his son, challenged Hercules to fight.　Jupiter hurled a bolt, which falling between them separated them.

"As a lion, who has fall'u
Perchance on some stray beast, with griping claws
Intent strips down the lacerated hide,
Drains instantaneous the sweet life, and gluts
E'en to the fill his gloomy heart with blood ;
Green-eyed he glares in fierceness ; with his tail
Lashes his shoulders and his swelling sides,
And with his feet tears up the ground ; not one
Might dare to look upon him, nor advance
Nigh with desire of conflict ;—such in truth
The war-insatiate Hercules to Mars
Stood in array, and gather'd in his soul
Prompt courage.　But the other near approach'd
Anguish'd at heart ; and both encountering rush'd
With cries of battle.　As when from high ridge
Of some hill-top abrupt, tumbles a crag
Precipitous and sheer a giddy space,
Bounds in a whirl, and rolls impetuous down :
Shrill rings the vehement crash, till some steep clift
Obstructs ; to this the mass is borne along ;
This wedges it immovable ;—e'en so
Destroyer Mars, bowing the chariot, rush'd,
Yelling vociferous with a shout ; e'en so,
As utterance prompt, met Hercules the shock,
And firm sustain'd."

HESIOD, *Shield of Hercules.*

No. 396.

Hercules combating the Centaurs at the marriage of Pirithous and Hippodamia.

APOLLONIDES.　*Oriental Sardonyx.*

No. 397.

Hercules killing the centaur Polenor for attacking the centaur Pholus, his host and friend.

APOLLONIDES.   *Oriental Cornelian.*

No. 398.

Hercules strangling Antæus.

APOLLONIDES.   *Cornelian.*

" From thence he seeks the heights renown'd
  by fame,
And hallow'd by the great Cornelian name ;
The rocks and hills which long, traditions say,
Were held by huge Antæus' horrid sway.
Here, as by chance he lights upon the place,
Curious he tries the reverend tale to trace ;
When thus, in short, the ruder Libyans tell,
What from their sires they heard, and how the
  case befell.
The teeming earth, for ever fresh and young,
Yet after many a giant son was strong,
When labouring here with the prodigious birth,
She brought her youngest-born, Antæus, forth.
Of all the dreadful brood which erst she bore,
In none the fruitful beldame gloried more ;
Happy for those above she brought him not,
Till after Phlegra's doubtful field was fought.
That this her darling might in force excel,
A gift she gave : whene'er to earth he fell,
Recruited strength he from his parent drew,
And every slack'ning nerve was strung anew.
Yon cave his den he made ; where oft for food
He snatch'd the mother lion's horrid brood.
Nor leaves, nor shaggy hides, his couch prepar'd,
Torn from the tiger or the spotted pard ;
But stretch'd along the naked earth he lies,
New vigour still the native earth supplies.
Whate'er he meets his ruthless hands invade,
Strong in himself, without his mother's aid.

The strangers that unknowing seek the shore,
Soon a worse shipwreck on the land deplore.
Dreadful to all, with matchless might he reigns,
Robs, spoils, and massacres the simple swains,
And all unpeopled lie the Libyan plains.
At length, around the trembling nations spread
Fame of the tyrant to Alcides fled.
The godlike hero, born by Jove's decree,
To set the seas and earth from monsters free,
Hither in generous pity bent his course,
And set himself to prove the giant's force.
  Now met, the combatants for fight provide,
And either doffs the lion's yellow hide.
Bright in Olympic oil Alcides shone,
Antæus with his mother's dust is strown,
And seeks her friendly force to aid his own.
Now seizing fierce their grasping hands they
  mix,
And labour on the swelling throat to fix ;
Their sinewy arms are writh'd in many a fold,
And front to front they threaten stern and bold.
Unmatch'd before, each bends a sullen frown,
To find a force thus equal to his own.
At length the godlike victor Greek prevail'd,
Nor yet the foe with all his force assail'd ;
Faint dropping sweats bedew the monster's brows,
And panting thick with heaving sides he blows :
His trembling head the slack'ning nerves con-
  fess'd,
And from the hero shrunk his yielding breast.

The conqueror pursues, his arms entwine,
Infolding gripe, and strain his crashing chine,
While his broad knee bears forceful on his groin:
At once his falt'ring feet from earth he rends,
And on the sands his mighty length extends.
The parent earth her vanquish'd son deplores,
And with a touch his vigour lost restores;
From his faint limbs the clammy dew she drains,
And with fresh streams recruits his ebbing veins;
The muscles swell, the hard'ning sinews rise,
And bursting from th' Herculean grasp he flies.
Astonish'd at the sight Alcides stood;
Nor more he wonder'd when in Lerna's flood
The dreadful snake her falling heads renew'd.
Of all his various labours none was seen
With equal joy by heav'n's unrighteous queen;
Pleas'd she beheld what toil, what pains he prov'd,
He who had borne the weight of heav'n unmov'd.
Sudden again upon the foe he flew,
The falling foe to earth for aid withdrew;

The earth again her fainting son supplies,
And with redoubled forces bids him rise;
Her vital pow'rs to succour him she sends,
And earth herself with Hercules contends.
Conscious at length of such unequal fight,
And that the parent touch renew'd his might:
' No longer shalt thou fall,' Alcides cried,
' Henceforth the combat standing shall be tried;
If thou wilt lean, to me alone incline,
And rest upon no other breast but mine,'
He said; and as he saw the monster stoop,
With mighty arms aloft he rears him up:
No more the distant earth her son supplies,
Lock'd in the hero's strong embrace he lies;
Nor thence dismiss'd, nor trusted to the ground,
Till death in ev'ry frozen limb was found.
    Thus, fond of tales, our ancestors of old
The story to their children's children told;
From thence a title to the land they gave,
And call'd this hollow rock Antæus' cave."
                                LUCAN: ROWE.

No. 399.

Hercules at the river Strymon.

CHROMIOS.   *Oriental Cornelian.*

Hercules arriving on the banks of the river Strymon, between Thrace and Macedonia, and not finding it fordable, throws into its bed some large stones. The river is here represented under the human form, appearing overwhelmed by them, and appealing for pity to Hercules.

No. 400.

Hercules, Eurypylus, and Chalciope.

APOLLONIDES.   *Oriental Cornelian.*

Hercules, on his return from his expedition against Laomedon, king of Ilium, landed in the island of Cos; and the inhabitants mistaking him for a pirate, attacked him with stones. Hercules gained a complete victory over them, ravaged their island, slew their king Eurypylus, and carried off his daughter Chalciope.

No. 401.

Hercules extracting the arrow from the centaur Chiron.

SOLON. *Cornelian.*

The centaur Chiron, born of Saturn under the form of a horse, and Philyra daughter of Ocean, was celebrated for his knowledge of astronomy, music, jurisprudence, and medicine. The cave which he selected for his residence, at the foot of mount Pelion in Thessaly, the reputed country of the centaurs, or hippo-centaurs, became a celebrated school, to which resorted the most distinguished men of the heroic ages: Esculapius, Theseus, Hercules, Palamedes, Machaon, Achilles, &c. When Hercules made war against the centaurs, they were defeated, and fled to Malia, where Chiron then was, trusting that his presence would appease the anger of his pupil. Hercules, however, did not desist from pursuing after and shooting at them; and one of the poisoned arrows, taking a wrong direction, hit Chiron on the knee. Hercules, who was greatly distressed at the accident, flew to his assistance, and poured a balsam, the use of which he had learned from Chiron himself, into the wound: but it proved incurable, and the centaur, racked with intolerable pain, raised his hands to heaven, and implored Jupiter to deprive him of immortality, which, as the son of Saturn, he inherited. Jupiter translated him to the heavens, where he became one of the signs of the Zodiac, under the name of *Sagittarius.*

No. 402.

Hercules separating the mountains Abyla and Calpe.

CHROMIOS. *Oriental Cornelian.*

To Hercules was attributed in olden time the opening of the straits which bore the name of this hero (by separating the mountains Abyla and Calpe), and at a much later period Gibraltar, from the rock Calpe, which was so called, and by which name both are now known.

No. 403.

The same subject in high relief.

CHROMIOS. *Oriental Cornelian.*

No. 404.

Apollo presenting the golden cup to Hercules.

POLYCLETES. *Oriental Amethyst.*

Apollo admiring the intrepidity of Hercules, makes him a present of a golden cup, in which he embarks. The word *scaphis* in Greek signifies both *cup* and *vessel*, or *skiff.*

No. 405.

Hercules caressing Adonis.

DIOSCORIDES. *Oriental Cornelian.*

The ancients believed that Hercules was so taken with the beauty of the young Adonis, that Venus became jealous; and that she in consequence inspired the centaur Nessus with the passion for Dejanira which proved fatal to Hercules.

No. 406.

Hercules seizing Achelous, who is changed to a serpent, presses his throat, and endeavours to strangle him.

CHROMIOS. *Oriental Cornelian.*

" O'ermatched in strength, to wiles and arts I take,
And slip his hold in form of spotted snake;
Who when I wreathed in spires my body round,
Or shew'd my forky tongue with hissing sound,
Smiles at my threats : ' Such foes my cradle knew,'
He cries; ' dire snakes my infant hand o'erthrew.' "
OVID.

No. 407.

Achelous metamorphosed to a bull: Hercules tearing off one of his horns.

GNAIOS. *Oriental Sardonyx.*

" Thus vanquish'd too, another form remains,
Chang'd to a bull my lowing fills the plains:
Straight on the left his nervous arms were thrown
Upon my brindled neck, and tugg'd it down;

g g

Then deep he struck my horn into the sand,
And fell'd my bulk among the dusty land.
Nor yet his fury cool'd ; 'twixt rage and scorn
From my maim'd front he tore the stubborn horn :
This heap'd with flowers and fruits the naïads bear,
Sacred to plenty and the bounteous year."

OVID.

No. 408.

Achelous vanquished by Hercules.

CHROMIOS.   *Oriental Sardonyx.*

This stone represents the complete victory gained by Hercules over Achelous, when he compelled him to throw himself into the river Thoas, which was henceforth called Achelous. The personified river is holding an oar, and near him is the urn whence flows the spring or source.

" Achelous in his oozy bed
Deep hides his brow-deform'd and rustic head ;
No real wound the victor's triumph shew'd,
But his lost honours griev'd the wat'ry god.
Yet e'en that loss the willows' leaves o'erspread,
And verdant reeds in garlands bind his head."

OVID.

" Sov'reign resistless in her sway,
O'er the charm'd heart victorious Venus reigns.
Not her sweet force, which gods obey,
Which Jove's firm soul subdu'd, attunes these strains ;
Which taught the gloomy pow'r to bow,
The monarch of the realms below ;
And him who gives his thund'ring waves to roar,
And furious shake the solid shore.
To other themes these humbler strains belong,
The warring rivals claim the song ;
In arms contending for this bride,
The contest dust, and toil, and wounds decide.

Rising in all his strength the flood,
In form a bull terrific to the sight

Ætolian Achelous stood,
With horns his threat'ning forehead arm'd for fight.
From Thebes the chief of mighty fame
Fierce to the rough encounter came,
The son of Jove ; his massy club he rears,
His bow unbent, his arrows bears.
Inflam'd with jealous love and rival rage,
In horrid combat they engage ;
While Venus with severe delight
Awards the prize, and arbitrates the fight.

Dauntless each the fight provokes,
Loud the thunder of their strokes ;
The clanging bow now aims the wound,
With dreadful clash the bull's strong horns resound.

Now front meets front, the furious blow
With horrid conflict threatens death;
Now in strong grasp each struggling foe
Strains ev'ry nerve, and lab'ring pants for
   breath.
Meanwhile the beaut'ous nymph, whose
   charms
Inflam'd the combatants to arms,

Anxious and doubtful of her fate,
Conspicuous on the river's margin sate—
  (My song records the voice of fame):
  All was suspense and awful dread,
  Till victor now the hero came,
And from her mother's arms the trembling virgin
   led."
              SOPHOCLES, *Trach. Virg.*

No. 409.

Callirhoe supplicating Jupiter.

APOLLONIDES. *Oriental Cornelian.*

Callirhoe, the daughter of Achelous, married Alcmæon, the son of Amphiaraus. Alcmæon having been slain by Temenus and Axion, the brothers of his first wife Alphesibœa, Callirhoe presented her sons, still children, to Jupiter, praying him that they might instantly become men to avenge the death of their father. Her prayer was granted.

"Thebes is embroil'd in war. Capaneus stands
Invincible but by the Thund'rer's hands.
Ambition shall the guilty brothers fire,
But rush to mutual wounds, and both expire;
The reeling earth shall ope her gloomy womb,
Where the yet breathing hard shall find his tomb.
The son shall bathe his hands in parent's blood,
And in one act be both unjust and good:

Of home and sense depriv'd, where'er he flies
The furies and his mother's ghost he spies.
His wife the fatal bracelet shall implore,
And Phegeas stain his sword in kindred gore;
Callirhoe shall then with suppliant pray'r
Prevail on Jupiter's relenting ear;
Jove shall with youth her infant sons inspire,
And bid their bosoms glow with manly fire."
              Met. book ix.

No. 410.

Hercules killing Porphyrion.

POLYCLETES. *Oriental Cornelian.*

Hercules being called on by Jupiter to fight against the giants, killed Porphyrion, one of the most valiant amongst them, whilst in pursuit of Juno.

"Jove, whose equal sway
The pond'rous mass of earth and stormy seas
  obey—
O'er gods and mortals, o'er the dreary plains,
And shadowy ghosts, supremely just he reigns,

But dreadful in his wrath,—to hell pursu'd,
With thunder's headlong rage, the fierce Titanian
  brood;
Whose horrid youth, elate with impious pride,
Unnumber'd on their sinewy force relied:

Mountain on mountain pil'd they rais'd in air,
And shook the throne of Jove, and bade the
   Thund'rer fear.
But what could Minas, of enormous might,
Typhœus, or Porphyrion's threat'ning height;
Or bold Enceladus, fierce darting far
The trunks of trees uptorn, dire archer of the war,

Though with despair and rage inspir'd they rose,
To sage Minerva's sounding shield oppose?
While Vulcan here in flames devour'd his way,
There matron Juno stood, and there the god of
   day."

Hor. lib. iii. Od. 4.

No. 411.
Hercules slaying the giant Eurytus.
ADMON. *Oriental Cornelian.*

Hercules attacking the giant Eurytus, kills him with a large oak.

" By Venus was Œchalia's* maid,
  Of hymeneal bonds afraid,
   Consign'd in days of yore
  Like a wild filly to the yoke,
  Espous'd 'midst horrid slaughter, smoke,
   And rites profan'd with gore:
  Indignant was the virgin led,
  Streaming with dishevell'd hair,
  To the stern Alcides' bed,
While bridal shouts were mingled with despair."

EURIPIDES, *Hippolytus:* WOODHULL.

No. 412.
Alcyoneus, the brother of Porphyrion, hurling a piece of rock at Hercules, who parries the blow with his club.
APOLLONIDES. *Oriental Cornelian.*

No. 413.
Minerva seizing the monster Alcyoneus by the hair, after he had been wounded by Hercules with an arrow.
CHROMIOS. *Cornelian.*

---

* Iöle, daughter of Eurytus, king of Œchalia, after having been promised by her father, as Apollodorus informs us, to be given in marriage to the man who should excel him and his sons in archery, was by them unjustly withheld from Hercules, who had given sufficient proofs of his supe-

No. 414.

Hercules and the sons of Boreas.

ADMON. *Oriental Cornelian.*

Hercules to revenge himself on Calais and Zethes, the sons of Boreas, for inducing the Argonauts not to take him on board their vessel on his return from seeking Ila, kills them. One of the sons of Boreas is here seen dead at the feet of Hercules, the other is wounded.

"Then rose contention keen and pungent grief,
For thus abandoning their bravest chief.
In silence Jason sat, and long suppress'd,
Though griev'd, the labouring anguish of his
   breast.
Brave Telamon, with anger kindling, spoke :
' Mute is thy tongue, and unconcern'd thy look ;
To leave unconquer'd Hercules behind
Was a base project, and by thee design'd ;
Lest, when to Greece we steer the sailing pine,
His brighter glories should out-dazzle thine.
But words avail not ; I renounce the band,
Whose selfish wiles this stratagem have plann'd.'
   Thus spoke Æacides, inflam'd with ire,
His eye-balls sparkling like the burning fire ;
On Tiphys then, by rage impell'd, he flew,
And once more Mysia had receiv'd the crew.

Again the heroes the same course had sail'd,
Though roaring winds and raging waves pre-
   vail'd ;
Had not bold Boreas' sons the chief address'd,
And, nobly daring, his rough rage repress'd.
Ill fated youths ! for that heroic deed
Doom'd by the hands of Hercules to bleed :
For when returning home their course they sped,
From funeral games perform'd for Pelias dead,
In sea-girt Tenos he the brother slew,
And o'er their graves in heapy hillocks threw
The crumbling mould : then with two columns
   crown'd,
Erected high the death-devoted ground.
And one still moves—how marvellous the tale !—
With every motion of the northern gale.
But these are facts reserv'd for future years."
                                   APOLL. RHOD. : FAWKES.

No. 415.

Jupiter hurling aerolites at the Giants.

CHROMIOS. *Sardonyx.*

On the giants Albion and Bergion opposing Hercules in his endeavours to cross the Rhone, they were crushed by stones hurled at them from heaven by Jupiter.

---

riority in the use of the bow, a weapon for which he was particularly renowned ; upon which the enraged hero took the city by assault, and having slain her father and brothers, bore off the princess in triumph. The ancient geographers say there were several towns of the name of Œchalia ; but although this city of Eurytus has had the honour of being twice mentioned, and expressly marked out as such by Homer in his catalogue of the Grecian forces—where he speaks of it with Tricca and Ithome, which were in Thessaly, and receives from Virgil the epithet of *egregia*,—Strabo, and all subsequent writers, seem totally unable to ascertain its situation with any degree of precision.

No. 416.

Hercules killing Eryx.

ALLION. *Oriental Sardonyx.*

Eryx, the son of Butes and Lycasta, who from his rare beauty was called Venus, was descended from Boreas, king of Thrace. Driven from Bithynia by Amycus, king of the Bebryces, whom some mythologians consider his father, Eryx passed into Sicily, where he became the king of a country which took the name of *Erycia*. Vain of his extraordinary strength, he challenged all strangers who landed on the shores of Erycia to fight with him; and when he had subdued he slew them. Eryx dared to try his strength with Hercules, who had just arrived in Sicily with the oxen of Geryon. The conditions were these: that if Hercules fell, the oxen should belong to Eryx; and if the latter were vanquished, that Hercules should be master of the country. Hercules overthrew Eryx, and slew him. He was buried in the temple which he had raised to his mother, under the name of Venus Erycina, on mount Eryx, near *Drepanum* (now *Trapani*), where divine honours were rendered to this king (VIRGIL's *Æneid*, book v.). This stone represents Hercules seizing with one hand the throat of the prostrate Eryx, and about to strike him with the other, armed with the cestus, or gauntlet, of great power.

> " ' What,' said Eutellus, ' had your wonder been,
> Had you the gauntlets of Alcides seen,
> Or viewed the stern debate on this unhappy green?
> These which I bear your brother Eryx bore,
> Still mark'd with batter'd brains and mingled gore :
> With these he long sustained th' Herculean arm.' "
>
> VIRGIL.

No. 417.

Eryx slain at the feet of Hercules, who, proud of his victory, continues his journey, taking with him one of the bulls which he has preserved.

APOLLONIDES. *Oriental Cornelian.*

No. 418.

Hercules striking the rock in the desert.

CHROMIOS. *Oriental Cornelian.*

Hercules while journeying through the deserts of Africa, where he destroys all the monsters, is overcome with thirst and fatigue, and striking a rock with his foot obtains water from it.

No. 419.

Juno protecting Geryon.

APOLLONIDES. *Oriental Cornelian.*

Geryon, son of Chrysaor and Callirhoe the daughter of Ocean, was, according to Hesiod, king of the island of Erythea, between Gades and Spain, and the strongest of men. According to this idea, the poets who took Hesiod for their guide represented Geryon as a giant with three heads. Possessing a species of oxen as beautiful as they were ferocious, he had them fed with human flesh. They were guarded by the shepherd Eurythion, by Orthrus, a dog with two heads, and by a monstrous dragon with seven heads. Hercules landed in the island of Erythea, attacked Geryon, and threatened Juno herself, who had come to the assistance of the giant.

No. 420.

Hercules killing the dog Orthrus and the shepherd Eurythion.

APOLLONIDES. *Oriental Cornelian.*

" Geryon rose,
Three-headed form ; him the strong Hercules
Despoil'd of life among his hoof-cloven herds
On Erythea girdled by the wave,
What time those oxen ample-brow'd he drove
To sacred Tyrinth, the broad ocean frith
Once past ; and Orthrus, the grim herd-dog, stretch'd
Lifeless ; and in their murky den beyond
The billows of the long-resounding deep,
The keeper of those herds, Eurythion, slain."

HESIOD.

No. 421.

Cacus robbing Hercules.

APOLLONIDES. *Calcedony, partaking of Sapphire.*

Hercules sleeping at the foot of mount Aventin, whilst Cacus, the son of Vulcan, a cunning and cruel robber, is dragging by the tail into his cavern one of the bulls that Alcides had taken from Geryon.

No. 422.

Cacus strangled by Hercules.

DAMAS. *Oriental Sardonyx.*

Hercules on discovering that Cacus had concealed his oxen in a cave, which was closed
with a huge stone suspended by iron chains forged by Vulcan, tore up the rocks to which the
door was fastened, removed the stone, and entering the cavern he dragged Cacus thence, in
spite of the fire which issued from his mouth.

No. 423.

Hercules, after overthrowing Cacus, seizes him with such force by the
throat, that he strangles him.   The hands of Cacus are formed like
claws, to indicate his rapacity.

CHROMIOS. *Oriental Cornelian.*

No. 424.

Hercules strangling Cacus, in spite of the flames and smoke which issue
from his mouth.

CHROMIOS. *Oriental Cornelian.*

" But sav'd from danger, with a grateful sense
The labours of a god we recompense.
See from afar yon rock that mates the sky,
About whose feet such heaps of rubbish lie,
Such indigested ruin : bleak and bare,
How desert now it stands, expos'd in air !
'Twas once a robber's den ; enclos'd around
With living stone, and deep beneath the ground,
The monster Cacus, more than half a beast,
This hold, impervious to the sun, possess'd ;
The pavement ever foul with human gore ;
Heads and their mangled members hung the
       door.
Vulcan this plague begot ; and, like his sire,
Black clouds he belch'd, and flakes of livid fire.

Time, long expected, eas'd us of our load,
And brought the needful presence of a god :
Th' avenging force of Hercules, from Spain,
Arriv'd in triumph from Geryon slain ;
Thrice liv'd the giant, and thrice liv'd in vain.
His prize, the lowing herds Alcides drove
Near Tiber's bank to graze the shady grove ;
Allur'd with hope of plunder, and intent
By force to rob, by fraud to circumvent,
The brutal Cacus, as by chance they stray'd,
Four oxen thence and four fair kine convey'd.
And lest the printed footsteps might be seen,
He dragg'd them backwards to his rocky den ;
The tracks averse a lying notice gave,
And led the searcher backward from the cave.

Meantime the herdsman hero shifts his place,
To find fresh pasture and untrodden grass;
The beasts, who miss'd their mates, fill'd all
  around
With bellowings, and the rocks restor'd the sound:
One heifer, who had heard her love complain,
Roar'd from the cave, and made the project vain.
Alcides found the fraud; with rage he shook,
And toss'd about his head his knotted oak;
Swift as the winds, or Scythian arrows' flight,
He climb'd with eager haste th' aërial height.
Then first we saw the monster mend his pace;
Fear in his eye, and paleness in his face,
Confess'd the god's approach: trembling he
  springs,
As terror had increas'd his feet with wings;
Nor stay'd for stairs; but down the depth he
  threw
His body; on his back the door he drew—
The door a rib of living rock; with pains
His father hew'd it out, and bound with iron
  chains.
He broke the heavy links; the mountain clos'd,
And bars and levers to his foe oppos'd.
The wretch had hardly made his dungeon fast,
The fierce avenger came with bounding haste;
Survey'd the mouth of the forbidden hold,
And here and there his raging eyes he roll'd.
He gnash'd his teeth; and thrice he compass'd
  round
With winged speed the circuit of the ground;
Thrice at the cavern's mouth he pull'd in vain,
And, panting, thrice desisted from his pain.
A pointed flinty rock, all bare and black,
Grew gibbous from behind the mountain's back;
Owls, ravens, all ill omens of the night,
Here built their nests, and hither wing'd their
  flight.
The leaning head hung threat'ning o'er the flood,
And nodded to the left; the hero stood
Averse, with planted feet, and from the right
Tugg'd at the solid stone with all his might.
Thus heav'd, the fix'd foundations of the rock
Gave way; heaven echo'd at the rattling shock.

Tumbling it chok'd the flood; on either side
The banks leap backward, and the streams di-
  vide;
The sky shrunk upward with unusual dread;
And trembling Tiber div'd beneath his bed:
The court of Cacus stands reveal'd to sight,
The cavern glares with new admitted light.
So pent the vapours with a rumbling sound
Heave from below and rend the hollow ground.
A sounding flaw succeeds; and from on high
The gods with hate beheld the nether sky:
The ghosts repine at violated night,
And curse th' invading sun, and sicken at the
  sight.
The graceless monster, caught in open day,
Enclos'd, and in despair to fly away,
Howls horrible from underneath, and fills
His hollow palace with unmanly yells.
The hero stands above; and from afar
Plies him with darts, and stones, and distant war:
He from his nostrils and huge mouth expires
Black clouds of smoke amidst his father's fires,
Gathering with each repeated blast the night,
To make uncertain aim and erring fight.
The wrathful god then plunges from above,
And where in thickest waves the sparkles drove,
There lights; and wades through fumes, and
  gropes his way,
Half sing'd, half stifled, till he grasp'd his prey.
The monster spewing fruitless flames he found;
He squeez'd his throat, he writh'd his neck
  around,
And in a knot his crippled members bound;
Then from their sockets tore his burning eyes,—
Roll'd on a heap the breathless robber lies:
The doors unbarr'd receive the rushing day,
And thorough lights disclose the ravish'd prey;
The bulls redeem'd breathe open air again;
Next by the feet they drag him from his den.
The wond'ring neighbourhood, with glad sur-
  prise,
Beheld his shagged breast, his giant size,
His mouth that flames no more, and his extin-
  guish'd eyes.

h h

From that auspicious day, with rites divine,
We worship at the hero's holy shrine.
Potitius first ordain'd these annual vows,
As priests were added the Pinarian house;

Who rais'd this altar in the sacred shade,
Where honours, ever due, for ever shall be
    paid."

Æneis: DRYDEN.

No. 425.

Dejanira mounting the centaur Nessus.

CHROMIOS. *Sardonyx.*

Hercules, accompanied by his wife Dejanira, arriving on the banks of the river Evenus, in Ætolia, the centaur Nessus offered to transport Dejanira on his back to the opposite side. The subject of this stone is Dejanira on the point of placing herself on the back of the centaur, to whom Hercules is indicating the spot where he is to put her down.

" As the strong son of Jove his bride conveys
Where his paternal lands their bulwarks raise,
Where from her slopy urn Evenus pours
Her rapid current, swell'd by wint'ry show'rs,
He came. The frequent eddies whirl'd the tide,
And the deep-rolling waves all pass denied.
As for himself he stood unmov'd by fears—
For now his bridal charge employ'd his cares,—
The strong-limb'd Nessus thus officious cried
(For he the shallows of the stream had tried):
' Swim thou, Alcides, all thy strength prepare;
On yonder bank I'll lodge thy nuptial care.'"

OVID.

No. 426.

Dejanira wounded.

GNAIOS. *Oriental Cornelian.*

Dejanira while fighting by the side of Hercules against the Dryopes, commanded by their king Theodamas, was wounded. Hercules is here seen supporting his wounded wife, at whose feet Theodamas lies slain.

No. 427.

Nessus giving the empoisoned tunic to Dejanira.

Tyrphon. *Oriental Sardonyx.*

Nessus, receiving his death-wound from one of the arrows dipped in the blood of the hydra, whilst expiring resolved on being revenged on Hercules. To this end he gave Dejanira his own tunic stained with blood, assuring her that it was an efficacious remedy against the infidelities of her husband.

" Th' Aönian chief to Nessus trusts his wife,
All pale and trembling for her hero's life;
Cloth'd as he stood in the fierce lion's hide,
The laden quiver o'er his shoulder tied,
(For cross the stream his bow and club were cast,)
Swift he plung'd in : ' These billows shall be pass'd,'
He said; nor sought where smoother waters glide,
But stemm'd the rapid dangers of the tide.
The bank he reach'd; again the bow he bears;
When, hark ! his bride's known voice alarms his ears.
' Nessus, to thee I call,' aloud he cries;
' Vain is thy trust in flight, be timely wise :
Thou monster double-shap'd, my right set free ;
If thou no rev'rence owe my fame and me,

Yet kindred should thy lawless lust deny.
Think not, perfidious wretch, from me to fly—
Though wing'd with horse's speed, wounds shall pursue.'
Swift as his words the fatal arrow flew :
The centaur's back admits the feather'd wood,
And through his breast the barbed weapon stood ;
Which when in anguish through the flesh he tore,
From both the wounds gush'd out the spinning gore
Mix'd with Lernæan venom. This he took,
Nor dire revenge his dying breast forsook :
His garment in the reeking purple dyed,
To rouse love's passion, he presents the bride."

OVID.

No. 428.

Hercules and Charon.

Chromios. *Amethyst.*

Hercules descended to the kingdom of Pluto to bring back to earth Alceste, the wife of Admetus king of Thessaly. Hercules is here seen on the banks of the Styx, menacing Charon, and obliging him to convey him to the opposite shore.

ALCESTIS.

" O sun, O thou resplendent light of day !
And ye, O fleecy clouds, with swift career
Whirl'd through the heavens!

ADMETUS.

Our sufferings they behold,
Although we have committed 'gainst the gods
No sin for which thou mightst deserve to die.

ALCESTIS.

Thou too, O earth! ye roofs of stately domes,
And gay apartments, which in bridal pomp
My native land Iolchos erst array'd.

ADMETUS.

Unhappy woman, from thy couch arise,
Forsake me not; but to the powers supreme
Sue for their pity.

ALCESTIS.

　　　　　I behold the boat,
And him who ferries o'er the dead ; he grasps
The pole; by Charon am I summon'd hence.
He cries : ' What mean these fond delays? rouse,
　　rouse !
Thou stay'st behind when all things else are
　　ready.'
Thus eagerly he hastens my career.

ADMETUS.

The voyage which thou speak'st of is to me
Most bitter. Ah, how grievous are our woes !

ALCESTIS.

He leads me (see'st thou?) to yon hall of death ;
'Tis winged Pluto, who with glaring eyes

Darts horror. What art thou about? release me !
Through what strange paths most wretched am I
　　borne ?

ADMETUS.

By every friend, yet most of all by me,
And these our offspring, partners in my grief,
Lamented.

ALCESTIS.

　　　　Loose me, loose me ! lay me down ;
I have no strength, grim Pluto is at hand,
And thickest night o'erspreads these eyes. My
　　children,
Your mother, O my children, is no more ;
May ye with joy this radiant sun behold !

ADMETUS.

Ah, me ! the words I hear are to my soul
More grievous far than death in any form.
Forsake me not, I by the gods implore,
And by our children, who of thee bereft
Will mourn their orphan state ; but O resume
Thy spirits : I no longer can exist
When thou art dead ; on thee, on thee alone
Depends it, whether I yet live, or quit
This world; for thee I love, and thee I revere."

　　　　　　　EURIPIDES : WOODHULL.

" Daughter of Pelias, doom'd by fate to dwell
　　In Pluto's loath'd abode, that vale
Where the sun darts no cheering beams, all
　　hail !
Inform the swarthy god of hell,
And that old ferryman who plies the oar,
Maintaining ever at the leaky helm
　　His station, and to Orcus' realm
Conveys the dead, on Acheron's bleak shore
He now hath landed her who did her sex excel.

For thee shall oft the votaries of the muse
　　To plaintive sounds attune the lyre ;
Long shall thy praises fill the vocal choir,
　　When Sparta's vernal moon renews,
As in meridian lustre through the skies
It glides, that feast from Carnus which its
　　name
　　Derives, and as a tribute to thy fame."

　　　　　　　　　　EURIPIDES.

" What though the bark to distant lands
　　Unfurl a prosperous sail,
Not Ammon's fane on Afric's parching sands,
　　Not Lycia's oracles avail

To free her spirit from the realms of night;
Stern fate draws near and meditates the blow.
E'en where heaven's altars flame with holier
　　light

Each divine response hath ceas'd :
No longer now to any priest
Desponding can I go.

Liv'd Æsculapius, Pæan's son,
On whom his sire bestow'd
The healing art, Alcestis might be won
From sullen Pluto's loath'd abode,

Those gates of darkness; for he rais'd the dead,
Brandish'd by Jove from yonder starry cope,
Till winged light'ning smote the sage's head.
But 'midst youth's bloom her life must end ;
Its short duration to extend,
How can I form a hope?"

EURIPIDES: WOODHULL.

———

" Now, O my heart, inur'd to many toils,
And thou, my enterprising soul, give proof
How great a son in me Tirynthia's fair
Alcmena, daughter of Electryon, bore
To Jove. For I this woman newly dead
Must save; and by establishing afresh
In these abodes his dearest wife, repay
Admetus' kindness : therefore will I go
In quest of death, king of the shades, who flits
On sable wings; him I expect to find
As at the tomb he quaffs the victim's gore.
If rushing forth from ambush, by surprise
Him with these vigorous arms I can enfold ;
No power shall from captivity redeem,
Till he this woman loose, the struggling god.
But if I fail of seizing on this prey,

And he attend not at the hilloc drench'd
With blood, I to that murky realm beneath,
Which the sun never visits, the abode
Of Proserpine and Pluto, will descend,
And my petition urge, with a firm trust
That to this upper world I shall convey,
And place again Alcestis in the arms
Of that kind host, who opening wide his doors
Receiv'd me for a guest; nor drove away,
Though deeply smitten by such grievous woe,
Which with a noble spirit he conceal'd,
Revering me. By what Thessalian chief
Are hospitable deeds like these surpass'd,
Or by what fam'd inhabitant of Greece?
This generous friend shall therefore never say
He on a worthless man his bounty shower'd."

EURIPIDES.

———

HERCULES.
" Say, do'st thou hold her?

ADMETUS.
Yes, I hold her fast.
HERCULES (taking off the veil).
With care preserve her, and in future times
Thou wilt proclaim, that he who sprung from
Jove
Hath been a noble guest. Observe her face,
If it resemble thy departed wife ;
Bless'd as thou art, no longer grieve.

ADMETUS.
Ye gods,
What shall I say ? a miracle like this
Was most unhop'd for. But do I indeed
Behold my wife? or would some fraudful god
Surprise my senses with ideal joy?

HERCULES.
Not thus; in her thou view'st thy real
wife.'

EURIPIDES.

———

" Thee, O Admetus, hath this goddess caught,
Bound with inevitable chains ;
Yet, O despair not; for tears never wrought
Such wonders as again to earth's domains
Conducting the deceas'd from yon infernal shore.

They whom th' immortal powers by stealth begot,
In the cold grave are doom'd to rot
When life's short day is o'er.
Belov'd while present, and in death still dear,
Thy matchless wife this house for ever shall revere.

Deem not she sleeps like those devoid of fame,
  Unconscious in the lap of earth ;
Such homage as the gods from mortals claim,
    Each traveller shall pay her matchless worth,
Digressing from his road, and these bold thoughts,
      express'd

In no faint language, utter o'er her grave :
  ' She who expir'd her lord to save,
    Resides among the bless'd.
Hail, awful goddess, and this realm befriend !'
To her their pious vows shall thus the skies
      ascend."

                      EURIPIDES.

ADMETUS.

  " But why thus mute.
Yet stands my wife ?

HERCULES.

  Thou must not hear her voice
Till those sepulchral rites have been annull'd
By which she to the gods of hell beneath
Was render'd sacred, and the radiant morn
For the third time arise.   Conduct her steps
Into the royal mansion ; and do thou,
Who art already eminently just,
Hereafter with the same benignant zeal

Treat strangers, O Admetus.   Now farewell,
For I must go to execute those labours
My king the son of Sthenelus ordained.

    .   .   .   .   .   .

CHORUS.

  A thousand shapes our varying fates assume ;
The gods perform what we could least expect,
And oft the things for which we fondly hop'd
Come not to pass ; but heaven still finds a clue
To guide our steps through life's perplexing
      maze,
And thus doth this important business end."

                      EURIPIDES.

  " Down to these worlds I trod the dismal way,
    And dragg'd the three-mouth'd dog to upper day ;
    E'en hell I conquer'd, through the friendly aid
    Of Maia's offspring, and the martial maid."

              Odyssey, book xi.

No. 429.

Hercules restrained by Mercury in Hades.

POLYCLETES.   *Oriental Cornelian.*

    When Hercules entered the infernal regions, all the spirits fled, except Meleager and
Medusa.   Hercules attempted to strike Medusa, but he was prevented by Mercury, who said
to him, " Thy arms, though invincible, are useless against shadows."

No. 430.

Hercules attacking Menœtius, the herdsman of Pluto, whose life is spared at the intercession of Proserpine.

APOLLONIDES.   *Cornelian.*

No. 431.

Hercules securing Cerberus.

APOLLONIDES. *Oriental Cornelian.*

"The stubborn god, inflexible and hard,
Forgets my service and deserv'd reward :
Sav'd I for this his favourite son distress'd,
By stern Eurystheus with long labours press'd ?
He begg'd, with tears he begg'd, in deep dismay :
I shot from heaven, and gave his arm the day.
Oh ! had my wisdom known this dire event,
When to grim Pluto's gloomy gates he went,
The triple dog had never felt his chain,
Nor Styx been cross'd, nor hell explor'd in vain."

Il. viii.

No. 432.

Hercules dragging Cerberus from the infernal mansions.

CHROMIOS. *Oriental Cornelian.*

No. 433.

Hercules and Pluto.

DAMAS. *Oriental Cornelian.*

Amongst the boldest exploits of Hercules is that of having dared to attack Pluto at the entrance to the infernal regions, and wound him: it is apparently an allegory of the Sun, emblemed by Hercules, who, with his rays represented by arrows, made war against Night, and dispelled him from the two hemispheres, which he lights alternately in the twenty-four hours.

No. 434.

The same subject.

CHROMIOS. *Oriental Cornelian.*

No. 435.

Hercules chaining Death.

APOLLONIDES.   *Oriental Cornelian.*

Hercules finding in the infernal regions that Death, armed with a poniard, was carrying away Alceste, chained him, and delivered the faithful wife of Admetus.

> " But from the shades
> How did you bring her to this upper world?
>
> HERCULES.
> By furiously encountering the stern king
> Of disembodied ghosts.
>
> ADMETUS.
>   'Twixt you and Death,
> Where say you was this stubborn battle fought?
>
> HERCULES.
> From ambush at the tomb I sprung, and grasp'd
> The tyrant in my arms."
>   EURIPIDES: WOODHULL.

No. 436.

Hercules, after having chained Death, conducting Alceste from the kingdom of Pluto.

CHROMIOS.   *Oriental Cornelian.*

No. 437.

The Souls of the Guilty drinking the blood of the victim offered by Hercules.

SOLON.   *Oriental Cornelian.*

Hercules, when descending to hell to bring back Theseus, prepared to sacrifice a sterile cow to Proserpine.   The souls of the guilty, thirsting for blood, hastened to drink that of the victim.

No. 438.

Hercules in Hell delivering Theseus.

APOLLONIDES.   *Oriental Cornelian.*

No. 439.

Hercules freeing Theseus from his chains.

CHROMIOS. *Oriental Cornelian.*

No. 440.

Hercules conducting Theseus from the infernal regions.

CHROMIOS. *Oriental Cornelian.*

No. 441.

Telephus suckled by a hind.

CHROMIOS. *Oriental Cornelian.*

Augea, the daughter of Aleus, king of Tegæa, was beloved by Hercules, and she became the mother of a child named Telephus. To conceal from her father Aleus the birth of Telephus, she exposed him in a forest, where he was found by a hind, who nourished him with her milk.

> " Plac'd in the centre of those realms which bear
> The name of Pelops, O my native land,
> All hail; and thou who tread'st the frozen rock
> Of Arcady, from whose illustrious race
> I boast my origin, for me in secret
> Auge, the daughter of Aleus, bore
> To the Tirynthian Hercules, Parthenius
> Can witness, for Lucina there releas'd
> My mother from the burden of her womb."
>
> EURIPIDES, *Frag.*

No. 442.

Hercules passing through the forest finds Telephus nursed by the hind; and, seating himself, he contemplates him.

CHROMIOS. *Oriental Cornelian.*

i i

No. 443.

Augea and Telephus separated by a serpent.

PYRGOTELES. *Oriental Cornelian.*

Telephus, warned by an oracle, repaired to Mysia to find his mother Augea, whom Teuthras, king of that country, had adopted as his daughter. This prince being engaged in a war which threatened his crown, had promised the hand of Augea to whomsoever should deliver him from his enemies. Telephus, at the head of the Mysians, gained a complete victory. At the celebration of his marriage with Augea, his mother, urged by a secret presentiment, repulsed him, and the gods sent a serpent to separate them. Augea, alarmed, solicited the protection of the gods.

No. 444.

Phillo discovered by Hercules.

CHROMIOS. *Oriental Sardonyx.*

Hercules was enamoured of Phillo, the daughter of Alcimedon, and had by her the infant Ecmagoras; which so exasperated her father, that he exposed Phillo and her child on mount Ostracine, that they might be devoured by wild beasts. A magpie in the neighbourhood, who frequently heard Ecmagoras cry, learned to imitate him; and when Hercules was passing he mistook his note for the crying of a child; and being led by it to the place where Phillo was exposed, he saved her and her child. This circumstance gave rise to the name of a neighbouring fountain.

No. 445.

Hercules killing one of the oxen of Thiodamas.

APOLLONIDES. *Oriental Cornelian.*

Hercules, accompanied by his wife Deianira and his son Hyllus, meeting Thiodamas his relation seated on a car drawn by two oxen, begged some provisions of him for Hyllus, who was hungry. On Thiodamas refusing, Hercules killed one of the oxen, the whole of which his son and himself devoured.

No. 446.

Hercules dragging the ox which he has killed by the tail, while Deianira and Hyllus appear to be impatiently awaiting their repast.

APOLLONIDES. *Oriental Cornelian.*

No. 447.

Hercules seated upon a rock.

PYRGOTELES. *Oriental Cornelian.*

Hercules, after leaving the ship Argo, which the enormous weight of his body often exposed to the risk of sinking, retired to a rock in Thessaly.

No. 448.

Hercules sending Hylas to the fountain for water.

DIOSCORIDES. *Oriental Sardonyx.*

Hylas, the son of Thiodamas, king of Mysia, was from an early age a follower of Hercules, whom he tenderly loved. Hylas having followed this hero in the Argonautic expedition to Colchis, he went down into the plains of Troy to fetch some water, when the nymphs or naiads who guarded the fountain were so taken with his beauty, that they carried him off, and he returned no more. Hercules and his companions, inconsolable for his loss, caused the banks of the Hellespont to resound with their cries, as they called on the name of Hylas (VIRG. *Ecl.* vi. 43, 44).

" When Jason sail'd to find the golden fleece,
And in his train the choicest youth of Greece ;
Then with the worthies from the cities round
Came Hercules, for patient toil renown'd,
And Hylas with him ; from Iolchos they
In the good Argo plough'd the watery way ;
Touch'd not the ship the dark Cyanean rocks
That justled evermore with crashing shocks,
But bounded through, and shot the swell o' the flood
Like to an eagle, and in Phasis stood ;

Thence either ridgy rock in station lies.
But at what times the Pleiades arise,
When to the court the borders of the field
(The spring to summer turning) herbage yield,
The flow'r of heroes minded then their sailing ;
And the third day a steady south prevailing,
They reach'd the Hellespont ; and in the bay
Of long Propontis hollow Argo lay.
Their oxen, for Cranaians dwelling there,
The ploughshare in the broad'ning furrow wear.

They land at eve; in pairs their mess they keep,
And many strow a high and rushy heap;
A meadow broad convenient lay thereby,
With various rushes prankt abundantly;
And gold-tress'd Hylas is for water gone,
For Hercules and sturdy Telamon,
Who messmates were; a brazen urn he bore,
And soon perceiv'd a fountain straight before.
It was a gentle slope, round which was seen
A multitude of rushes, parsley green,
And the close couch-grass creeping to entwine
Green maiden hair and pale blue calendine.
Their choir the wakeful nymphs, the rustic's dread,
In the mid sparkle of the fountain led;
Malis and young Nachæa looking spring,
And fresh Euxica.   These the youth did bring,
And o'er the water hold his goodly urn,
Eager at once to dip it and return.
The nymphs all clasp'd his hand; for love seiz'd all,
Love for the Argive boy; and he did fall,
Plumping at once into the water dark:
As when a meteor glides with many a spark,

Plumping from out the heavens into the seas;
And then some sailor cries, ' A jolly breeze !
Up with the sail, boys !' Him upon their knees
The nymphs soft held; him dropping many a tear,
With soft enticing words they strive to cheer.

Anxious Alcides linger'd not to go,
Arm'd like a Scythian with his curved bow;
He grasp'd his club, and thrice he threw around
His deep, deep voice at highest pitch of sound.
Thrice call'd on Hylas, thrice did Hylas hear,
And from the fount a thin voice murmur'd near—
Though very near, it very far appear'd.
As when a lion, awful with its beard,
Hearing afar the whining of a fawn,
Speeds to his banquet from the mountain lawn,
In such wise Hercules, the boy regretting,
Off at full speed through pathless brakes was setting.
Who love much suffer: what fatigue he bore
What thickets pierc'd! what mountains clamber'd o'er!
What then to him was Jason's enterprise?"

THEOCRITUS.

" Far from the train with brazen vase the boy
Explores the silver fount with faithful joy;
The lucid stream, the genial meal, his care,
Plac'd for his lord's return in order fair:
Attention's office great Alcides taught,
First from a father's arms the infant brought.
Pierc'd mid Dryopian plains by matchless might,
A lowly lab'rer urg'd the baleful fight;
For he, while sorrow clouds his low'ring brow,
Guides o'er the stubborn earth the sev'ring plough,
The warrior marks, and rushing to the soil,—
' Resign,' he cries, ' the partner of thy toil !'
Yet vainly cries; 'gainst all the native train
Alcides burns to try th' embattled plain,
Foes as they liv'd to right's eternal laws.
Yet wand'ring from her task the muse withdraws:
And now the fountain smiles to youthful haste,
With Pega's name by circling nations grac'd;
Ev'n at the moment greets th' inquirer's view,
When virgin choirs the festal mirth pursue;

For ev'ry nymph, whose spotless charms the pride
Of meads that heave, or lovely Pega's tide,
Join at the darkling hour the votive throng,
Who wake to Dian's praise the hallow'd song;
The nymphs from mountain brow, from cave advance,
From forest wide to join the mystic dance.
One (all were wont their snowy limbs to lave)
Fair Ephidatia rising from the wave,
Ey'd the fair boy, whose charms with vernal claim
Beam in his face, and triumph in his frame.
The full-orb'd moon her cloudless light resign'd,
Love's charming goddess fascinates her mind
Each thought entranc'd her, wild'ring transports thrill.
He from the stream th' entrusted urn to fill,
Obliquely bends; the gathering waters round
Dash'd gurgling to the vessel's brazen sound:

Fond o'er his neck one wanton arm she throws,
And seeks with his her rosy lips to close;
The other clasps his elbow's polished gleam,
And sinks his beauties in the central stream.
Thy son, great Eilatus, whose footsteps stray
Far from th' associate train their onward way,
Heard the lost Hylas' shriek; his anxious sight
Expectant waits to hail the man of might.
Wing'd to the fount he bursts: the savage flies
Less swift to bleating innocency's cries,
Urg'd by keen hunger, rushing to his food
In vain; for caution mocks his scent of blood,
While fost'ring shepherds guard: with baffled toil
Panting he roars, and tir'd resigns the spoil.
Thus frets the hero, roams the fatal space;
Fruitless the tumults—fruitless is the chase!
Impetuous in return he grasps the blade,
Lest to the beast's devouring jaw betray'd,
His mangled corse may glut their rage of prey,
Or sink the spoil of man's ensnaring sway.
The falchion glitt'ring from his sheath he stalks,
And marks Alcides in his homeward walks;
Knows the bold warrior to the bark his stride,
That form in vain would circling darkness hide.

Fix'd on the melancholy tale of death,
With sighs he slowly heaves his throbbing breath:
'Unhappy master, mine the note of woe!
Hylas shall ne'er from Pega's purer flow
Greet thy fond looks; some fiends, a plund'ring train,
Withhold the captive, or some beast hath slain:
Still, still his clamours pierce me to the soul!'
He ceas'd; the briny sweat's big currents roll
Adown th' herculean face; the black blood round
Each entrail frets; resentful to the ground
He casts the pine's huge load: now here, now there,
Wayward he veers, as swells the blast of care.
Thus wand'ring, frantic with th' envenomed sting,
Forsakes his green domains, the lowing thing.
Heedless of shepherds and their flocks, his course
Wide he pursues: now boundless in his force,
Now stopping, fix'd; now rearing his huge head,
He swells the murmurs as his tortures spread.
The hero thus, while ev'ry fibre bleeds,
With anguish headlong as the tempest speeds.
Stops short faint, panting from his toil, and vents
His waste of woe in wildness of laments."

APOLL. RHODIUS.

No. 449.

Alcides presenting to Licymnius the urn containing the ashes of his son Argeas.

APOLLONIDES. *Oriental Sardonyx.*

Argeas, the son of Licymnius, brother of Alcmena, was also among the followers of Hercules, who promised to bring him back to his father. Argeas died on the journey; and Hercules, to fulfil as far as he was able his engagement with Licymnius, caused the young man's body to be burned, and collecting the ashes, he enclosed them in an urn and took them to his father. This is the first instance on record of burning a corpse.

No. 450.

Hercules and Omphale.

SOLON. *Oriental Cornelian.*

Hercules, captivated with Omphale, queen of Lydia, exchanged his club and lion's skin for her distaff and spindle. He is here seen arranging the extremities of the lion's skin, with which she has clad herself, on the neck of Omphale, who is leaning on the club.

" And where through flow'ry vales Meander glides
With winding waves, and turns with refluent tides,
Has Hercules been seen in shameless guise,
Ill suiting him whose shoulders bore the skies,
With bracelets deck'd, and other female gear
Which wanton damsels at their revels wear.
Bright chains of gold around those arms they view,
Which in Nemæan woods the lion slew,
Whose skin, a glorious robe, he proudly wore,
And on his back the dreadful trophy bore.
See his rude locks with gaudy ribands bound,
And purple vests his manly limbs surround,
Such as the soft Mæonian virgins wear,
To catch in silken folds the flowing hair.
Now horror in your mind his image breeds,
Who fed with human flesh his pamper'd steeds;
His conqu'ror had Busiris thus beheld,
He'd doubt his fall, and still dispute the field:
These toys Anteus from your neck would tear,
Asham'd his victor should such trinkets wear.
'Tis said you with Ionian girls are seen,
In base attendance on their haughty queen;
That baskets in your hands like them you bear,
And the vain menace of your mistress fear.
For shame! were those victorious hands design'd
For women's service; or to free mankind?
How think you to the wond'ring world 'twill sound,
That at command you turn the spindle round?

Your work's set out, your mistress you must please,
And your toils dwindle to such tasks as these!
But your rough fingers break the slender thread,
And from the fair a drubbing oft you dread
Now at her feet, methinks, I see you lie,
While she looks from you with an angry eye.
To plead for pity you your error own,
And brag, in your excuse, what deeds you've done:
How, when a child, two serpents you o'ercame,
And then the Erymanthean boar did tame.
The heads that were on Thracian gates affix'd,
And what to them you did you vaunt of next;
Of Diomedes and his mares you boast,
Of your fam'd conquests on th' Iberian coast;
Of Gerion's herd, and Cerberus, you tell,
And the dread wonders you perform'd in hell—
How thrice they both reviv'd, and thrice they fell;
How the huge giant, by a fierce embrace,
You grip'd to death, and kill'd with a caress;
How the swift horses, that outflew the wind,
By you were left in race, and lagg'd behind;
You put them on Thessalian hills to flight,
Nor you their speed, nor double forms affright.
But ill by you are such high things express'd,
A suppliant, like Sidonian harlots dress'd.
Your tongue might by your figure well be tied,
And you, for shame, the tale you tell her hide.
Nor can all this alone preserve her smiles,
She wears your arms, and triumphs with your spoils.

Go, boast your glorious acts, while all that see
Your differing garbs, will guess you both to be,
Thou the soft harlot, and the hero she.
As greater you than all your conquests are,
The less you to your conqu'ror can compare;
And as you can't your lewd desires subdue,
The mightier she who masters them and you.
To her the glory of your deeds redounds,
And fame her pow'r with your disgrace re-
    sounds :
The victor's praise, the laurel-wreath resign,
Those songs and trophies are no longer thine;
She heirs them all. Eternal shame, to see
That skin on her which suited none but thee!

And the rude robe that thou with pride hast worn,
Her feeble limbs enfold, and sink to scorn.
These spoils, mistaken man, are not her aim,
Thyself's her triumph, and her spoil's thy fame.
By her the merit of thy might's suppress'd ;
Her conquest was thyself; and thine, a beast.
She leaves the laden reel, and learns the use
Of arrows poison'd with Lernæan juice.
She who can scarce the flying wheel command,
And turn the spindle with her trembling hand,
Now teaches it the massy club to wield,
Which tam'd the fiercest monsters of the field.
This with delight she in her mirror views,
Fights o'er thy fights, and all thy foes subdues.'

OVID, *Ep.*: OLDMIXON.

No. 451.

Hercules spinning, while Omphale, dressed in the lion's skin and armed with the club, is looking on.

DIOSCORIDES. *Oriental Cornelian.*

The expression of Omphale, proud of her complete victory over Hercules, is worthy of remark.

No. 452.

Hercules giving Omphale the axe which he had taken from Hippolita, queen of the Amazons.

DIOSCORIDES. *Amethyst.*

The kings of Lydia preserved the remembrance by always making use of this weapon in battle.

No. 453.

Pan detected attempting to surprise Omphale.

CHARILAOS. *Oriental Cornelian.*

248   CATALOGUE.

Hercules and Omphale, fatigued with a long journey, are on the point of entering a cave to repose themselves, and the god Pan, who is enamoured of Omphale, conceals himself behind a tree, and joyfully watches for a favourable opportunity to surprise her.

" Tradition tells a merry jest.
Perchance Tirynthius by his sweetheart's side
Walk'd, whereas Faunus on a bank them spied.
He eyes and fries ; and, ' Country lasses,' cries,
' None for my diet; here my Cupid lies.'
The Lydian's shoulders with perfumed hair,
Her breasts with glitt'ring gold begaudied were.
A golden fan Sol's rival heat repell'd,
Which Hercules' kind hand before her held.
To Bacchus' groves and Tmoles' vineyards now
They came when Hesper in the west did glow.
A cave by which there plays a cheerful brook,
With topazes and pumice arch'd they took.
Now, while the servants had prepar'd the feast,
In her attire her Hercules she dress'd.
She puts on him her purple waistcoat slender,
And girdle, which embrac'd her body tender.
Her zone's too little, and her waistcoat's bands
He stretches out to thrust forth his huge hands ;
Her bracelets break, not made for that intent,
His huge plaice-foot her pretty sandals rent.
His weighty club and lion's spoils she tries,
And quiver-weapons of a lesser size.
Thus supper ended, both themselves apply
To sleep, and on two several couches lie ;
Because next day some rites to Jove's wine-son
They should perform, which must be purely done.

Pan comes (what dares not vent'rous love as-
    sault ?)
In midnight darkness to the silent vault;
He finds the servants clogg'd with wine and sleep,
And hopes the same clogs did the lovers keep.
In comes the lecher bold, roams here and there ;
His groping hands his wary ushers were.
At last he on the lady's bed lays hold,
At first right happy in his venture bold.
Soon as he touch'd the lion's bristly hide,
He plucks his hand back greatly terrified.
Then trembling comes again, again goes back,
Just like a traveller that spies a snake.
Then feels he to the softer-clothed bed,
Which stood at hand, by coz'ning signs misled.
Meanwhile the feet he softly doth uncover ;
His legs with bristly hairs were harsh all over.
. . . . . Alcides from the couch
Throws him quite off: down lumps the lustful
    slouch.
Mæonia at the noise for lights doth cry,
Which brought there make a strange discovery.
He with his fall much bruised, groans and moans,
And much ado heaves up his heavy bones.
Alcides laugh'd, and all, at that night-rover ;
And Omphale laughs at her goodly lover."

                                    OVID, *Fasti.*

No. 454.

Hercules carrying off Iole.

CHROMIOS.   *Oriental Cornelian.*

Hercules having demanded of Eurytus, king of Œchalia, his daughter Iole in marriage, was refused ; and making war against Eurytus, killed him and all his children, but Iole, whom he carried off.

DEIANIRA.

" Who, by the gods, and whence are these?
If right
I judge of misery, wretched is their state.

LICHAS.

These, when the town of Eurytus he raz'd,
He for himself selected, and the gods.

DEIANIRA.

Advanc'd against this town was he engag'd
In tedious war all this vast length of time?

LICHAS.

No; but in Lydia he was long detain'd,
Not free—such his account—but sold a slave.
We should not censure, lady, what appears
Wrought by the hand of Jove. Betray'd, and sold
To the barbaric Omphale, he pass'd
One tedious year a slave ; but the disgrace
So stung his noble soul, that with an oath
He vow'd the author of this wrong, his wife,
And children should be slaves. Nor vow'd in
vain :
But expiation made, with social hosts
Vengeful he march'd against the rampired walls
Of Eurytus; for him of all mankind
Alone he deem'd the cause of his disgrace,
Who to his hearth when he approach'd—a friend
With hospitable rites receiv'd of old—
Insulted him aloud with taunting words,
And all the outrage of an hostile mind :
Reviling him as holding in his hands
Arrows by fate assign'd to reach the mark;
But that his sons excell'd him in the skill
To draw the bow ; that by the nobly born
He as a slave should be trod down and crush'd ;
Nay, more, with wine when heated, from his house
He spurn'd him forth. Indignant at these wrongs,
O'er the Tirynthian hills when Iphitus
Search'd for his steeds that from their pastures
rov'd,
His eye on other objects bent, his mind
On other thoughts engag'd, he hurl'd the youth
From the steep summit of the tow'ring rock.

Offended at the deed, Olympian Jove,
The supreme king and father, sent him thence,
To slavery sold, nor brook'd a treacherous act
Unpractised but against this hapless youth.
With manly fortitude, and front to front,
In arms had he oppos'd him, heav'n's high king
Had pardon'd him, and deem'd his vengeance
just ;
But base insidious wrong the gods abhor.
But all those boasters, whose reviling tongues
Were wanton in their insolence, have now
Their mansions in the gloomy realms beneath,
And their proud city is enslav'd. These dames,
Which here thou seest, from high and happy life
Sunk to this wretched state, attend thy will.
Such are thy lord's commands, which I perform
With faithful zeal. When to his father Jove
The hallow'd victims for his conquest vow'd
Are slain, expect him here. Of my long speech,
Though grateful all, this gives thee highest joy.

CHORUS.

Now, royal lady, certain joy is thine ;
This captive train gives proof of his report.

DEIANIRA.

Yes, my heart feels it ; I have cause, just cause
Of joy ; it bounds to hear my lord returns
Victorious : all within me is alive
To tender sympathy. Yet those who deep
Resolve the change of fortune must have fears,
Lest he, who triumphs now, may sometime know
A sad reverse. E'en now, my friends, my heart
Feels the warm touch of pity, while I see
These wretched females, from their country torn,
Torn from their parents, in a foreign land
To exile doom'd ; yet these, perhaps, are sprung
From generous lineage, but must now sustain
A servile life. O Jove, whose guardian pow'r
Averts misfortune, never may I see
My offspring by thy anger thus assail'd ;
Or if to suff'rings thou hast doom'd them, spare
My anguish, nor inflict them whilst I live !
Such are my fears, these females as I view."
SOPHOCLES.

k k

No. 455.

Hercules seated, leaning on his club, and surrounded by his trophies; while Fame, by the sound of the trumpet, is announcing his deeds to the Universe.

ALLION.   *Oriental Cornelian.*

" The lay records the labours, and the praise,
And all th' immortal acts of Hercules.
First how the mighty babe, when swath'd in bands,
The serpents strangled with his infant's hands;
Then as in years and matchless force he grew,
Th' Œchalian walls and Trojan overthrew.
Besides a thousand hazards they relate,
Procur'd by Juno's and Eurystheus' hate.
Thy hands, unconquer'd hero, could subdue
The cloud-born centaurs, and the monster crew.

Nor thy resistless arm the bull withstood,
Nor he the roaring terror of the wood.
The triple porter of the Stygian seat,
With lolling tongue lay fawning at thy feet,
And seiz'd with fear, forgot thy mangled meat.
Th' infernal waters trembl'd at thy sight;
Thee, god, no face of danger could affright:
Not huge Typhœus, nor th' unnumber'd snake,
Increas'd with hissing heads, in Lerna's lake.
Hail, Jove's undoubted son! an added grace
To heav'n, and the great author of thy race."

VIRGIL.

No. 456.

Hercules Musagete, or Conductor of the Muses.

CHROMIOS.   *Oriental Cornelian.*

No. 457.

Hercules triumphant.

PYRGOTELES.   *Oriental Cornelian.*

Hercules after his different exploits had different appellations: that of *Buphagus* (eater of oxen), *Addephagus* (insatiable), *Bibax* (drinker), *Musagete* (conductor of the Muses), *Muscarius* (the driver away of flies), &c. That of *Thespicus* appears on this stone, from the circumstance of his having slept successively with the fifty daughters of Thespius, the son of Agenor, and made them all mothers, with the consent of their father. Hercules is seated on the skin of the Nemean lion, attended by two genii, one of whom places a chaplet on his club for each victory, surmounted by a butterfly, the emblem of life; while the other is pouring out a restorative liquid for Hercules.

No. 458.

Hercules tying to his club Passalus and Achemon.

APOLLONIDES. *Oriental Cornelian.*

Hercules Melampyges, a statue of whom is seen near Thermopylæ, in memory of his tying to his club Passalus and Achemon, the sons of Sennon daughter of Ocean, who had ventured to insult him while he was sleeping under a tree. They belonged to the nation called Cereopes, whom Jupiter, as a punishment for their want of honour, changed to monkeys.

No. 459.

Hercules carrying Passalus and Achemon on his club, suspended by the feet, who in this posture ridiculed his black back, calling him Melampyges.

ADMON. *Oriental Sardonyx.*

No. 460.

Hercules emerging from the body of the sea-monster.

CHROMIOS. *Calcedony, partaking of Sapphire.*

It was believed that Hercules had been swallowed by a sea-monster, where he remained three nights (a circumstance which gave rise to the name of *Trivesperus*), and that he released himself by tearing the entrails of the animal.

No. 461.

Lichas giving Hercules the poisoned tunic which Deianira, jealous of his love for Iole, had sent him.

TEUCER. *Oriental Sardonyx.*

"Fame (who falsehood clothes in truth's disguise,
And swells her little bulk with growing lies)
Thy tender ear, O Deianira, moved
That Hercules the fair Iole loved.

Her love believes the tale; the truth she fears
Of his new passion, and gives way to tears.
The flowing tears diffused her wretched grief—
'Why seek I thus from streaming eyes relief?'

She cries: 'indulge not thus these fruitless cares,
The harlot will but triumph in thy tears.
Let something be resolv'd while yet there's time:
My bed not conscious of a rival's crime,
In silence shall I mourn, or loud complain—
Shall I seek Calidon, or here remain?
What though allied to Meleager's fame,
I boast the honours of a sister's name?
My wrongs perhaps now urge me to pursue
Some desp'rate deed by which the world shall
    view

How far revenge and woman's rage can rise,
When weltering in her blood the harlot dies.'
Thus various passions rul'd by turns her breast:
She now resolves to send the fatal vest,
Dyed with Lernean gore, whose power might
    move
His soul anew, and rouse declining love;
Nor knew she what her sudden rage bestows,
When she to Lichas trusts her future woes:
With soft endearments, she the boy commands
To bear the garment to her husband's hands."

OVID.

    " But, my friends,
What I possess of pow'r to heal my griefs
I will inform you. In a brazen vase,
A present from the ancient centaur long
Have I preserv'd; while yet in youth's fresh
    bloom,
This from the shaggy Nessus I receiv'd,
When dying from his wound. It was his wont
O'er the deep flood Evenus rolls to bear
For hire, who wish'd to reach the further bank,
In his strong arms; nor dashing oar was his,
Nor barge with swelling sails. Me thus he bore,
When, unattended with my father's train,
I follow'd Hercules; but when he reach'd
The middle of the stream, his wanton hands
'Gainst modesty transgress'd; I cried aloud:
The son of Jove sprung forward, in his hand
His ready bow, from which a feather'd shaft
Wing'd with impetuous fury pierc'd his side.
Me then the dying monster thus address'd:
' Daughter of aged Œneus, I no more
Shall pass this flood; but since my arms have
    borne
Thee their last charge, derive thou thence this
    good,
Observant of my words:—Preserve with care
The clodded blood which issues from my wound;
The gore of the Lernæan hydra ting'd
The blacken'd shaft: this will have pow'r to
    charm
The heart of Hercules to thee assur'd,

That never woman shall his eyes behold
Fair and attractive of his love like thee.'
To memory this recalling (for with care
The dying centaur's gift I have preserv'd),
With it, my friends, this vestment I have ting'd,
Nothing omitted which he gave in charge
While yet he liv'd. These things are now pre-
    par'd.
The boldness of ill arts I would not know,
I would not learn; those women I abhor
Who dare attempt them: yet her youthful bloom
Could I by charms o'ercome, and soothe the heart
Of Hercules to love, I would assay
Their potency; but if you deem th' attempt
Unmeet, or void of force, I will forbear.

CHORUS.

If thou hast aught of confidence in deeds
Like this, we judge that thou hast purpos'd well.

DEIANIRA.

My confidence is only such as gives
Strength to opinion not assured by proof.

CHORUS.

Then put it to the proof; opinion else,
Though built on reason, no assurance yields.

DEIANIRA.

We soon shall know; for Lichas from the gate
I see advance; he quickly will be here.

Only be secret; for e'en shameful things
In dark concealment are secur'd from shame.

LICHAS.

Daughter of Œneus, give me thy commands;
Too long already I have linger'd here.

DEIANIRA.

Lichas, in this my care hath been employ'd,
Whilst converse with the strangers thou hast held,
That thou may'st bear this beaut'ous woven vest,
Wrought by my hands, a present to thy lord.
This give him, with a charge that but himself

No mortal in it proudly be array'd;
Nor ever let the sun's resplendent beam
Behold it, nor the altar's sacred flame,
Nor the bright-blazing hearth, till he shall stand
In public view, and shew it to the gods,
When on some solemn day the victim bleeds:
For such my vow, if e'er I saw or heard
That he return'd in safety, with this robe
To deck his person, that before the gods
Gorgeous in new attire he might appear,
And offer sacrifice. Bear this, in proof
I gave such charge; my signet he will know."

SOPHOCLES: POTTER.

No. 462.

Hercules having put on the fatal tunic, becomes furious, and seizes Lichas.

CHROMIOS. *Oriental Cornelian.*

HYLLUS.

" If thou wouldst know it, I must tell thee all.
The far-fam'd town of Eurytus destroy'd,
The trophies of his conquest, and the spoils
He to Cenæum brought, a rocky point
High-rising on the Eubœan shore, and wash'd
On each side by the sea; his altars there,
And the green foliage of a grove, he rais'd
To Jove his father: there my longing eyes
With joy first saw him. But as he prepar'd
The various victims, hence his servant came,
The herald Lichas, and thy present brought,
The fatal vest. With this, for such thy charge,
He rob'd himself, and slew twelve beaut'ous bulls
Selected from the prey; but to the god
An hundred various victims he had brought.
At first th' unhappy hero, with a mind

Cheerful and joying in his gorgeous robe,
Offer'd his vows; but when the bloody flame
Blaz'd from the hallow'd sacrifice, and heat
Glow'd from the unctuous firs, close to his sides
And to each limb, as by some artist fix'd,
The robe adher'd; and through his bones shot
        fierce
Convulsive pains; then as the poisonous gore
Of the detested hydra rankled deep,
He ask'd th' unhappy Lichas, for thy crime
In nothing blameable, by whose base arts
He brought this robe. Unconscious what he
        brought,
Th' ill-fated herald said, from thee alone
It was a present to his charge assign'd,
And brought as he receiv'd it."

SOPHOCLES.

No. 463.

Hercules throwing Lichas into the sea.

APOLLONIDES. *Oriental Cornelian.*

" Th' unwitting hero takes the gift in haste,
And o'er his shoulders Lerna's poison cast:
As first the fire with frankincense he strows,
And utters to the gods his holy vows,
And on the marble altar's polish'd frame
Pours forth the grapy stream ; the rising flame
Sudden dissolves the pois'nous juice,
Which taints his blood, and all his nerves be-
dews.
With wonted fortitude he bore the smart,
And not a groan confess'd his burning heart.
At length his patience was subdu'd by pain,
He rends the sacred altar from the plain ;
Œte's wide forests echo with his cries ;
Now to rip off the deathful robe he tries.
Where'er he plucks the vest, the skin he tears,
The mangled muscles and huge bones he bares,
(A ghastful sight!) or raging with his pain,
To rend the sticking plague he tugs in vain.
   As the red iron hisses in the flood,
So boils the venom in his curdling blood.
Now with the greedy flame his entrails glow,
And livid sweats down all his body flow ;
The cracking nerves, burnt up, are burst in
twain,
The lurking venom melts his swimming brain.
   Then, lifting both his hands aloft he cries ;
' Glut thy revenge, dread empress of the skies ;
Sate with my death the rancour of thy heart,
Look down with pleasure, and enjoy my smart.
Or, if e'er pity mov'd a hostile breast,
(For here I stand thy enemy profess'd,)
Take hence this hateful life, with tortures torn,
Inur'd to trouble, and to labours born.
Death is the gift most welcome to my woe,
And such a gift a stepdame may bestow.

Was it for this Busiris was subdu'd,
Whose barb'rous temples reek'd with strangers'
blood ?
Press'd in these arms, his fate Antæus found,
Nor gain'd recruited vigour from the ground.
Did I not triple-form'd Geryon fell ?
Or did I fear the triple dog of hell ?
Did not these hands the bull's arm'd forehead
hold ?
Are not our mighty toils in Elis told ?
Do not Stymphalian lakes proclaim my fame ?
And fair Parthenian woods resound my name ?
Who seiz'd the golden belt of Thermodon ?
And who the dragon-guarded apples won ?
Could the fierce Centaur's strength my force
withstand,
Or the fell boar that spoil'd th' Arcadian land?
Did not these arms the hydra's rage subdue,
Who from his wounds to double fury grew ?
What if the Thracian horses, fat with gore,
Who human bodies in their mangers tore,
I saw, and with their barb'rous lord o'erthrew ?
What if these hands Nemæa's lion slew ?
Did not this neck the heav'nly globe sustain ?
The female partner of the Thund'rer's reign
Fatigu'd, at length suspends her harsh com-
mands,
Yet no fatigue hath slack'd these valiant hands.
But now new plagues pursue me, neither force,
Nor arms, nor darts, can stop their raging course.
Devouring flame through my rack'd entrails
strays,
And on my lungs and shrivell'd muscles preys ;
Yet still Eurystheus breathes the vital air.
What mortal now shall seek the gods with
pray'r ?'

The hero said ; and with the torture stung,
Furious o'er Œte's lofty hills he sprung :
Stuck with the shaft, thus scours the tiger round,
And seeks the flying author of his wound.
Now might you see him trembling, now he vents
His anguish'd soul in groans and loud laments ;
He strives to tear the clinging vest in vain,
And with uprooted forests strews the plain.
Now kindling into rage his hands he rears,
And to his kindred gods directs his pray'rs ;
When Lichas, lo ! he spies ; who trembling flew,
And in a hollow rock conceal'd from view,
Had shunn'd his wrath.   Now grief renew'd his
    pain,
His madness chaf'd, and thus he raves again :
' Lichas, to thee alone my fate I owe,
Who bore the gift, the cause of all my woe.'
The youth all pale, with shiv'ring fear was stung,
And vain excuses falter'd on his tongue.

Alcides snatch'd him, as with suppliant face
He strove to clasp his knees, and beg for grace :
He toss'd him o'er his head with airy course,
And hurl'd with more than with an engine's
    force ;
Far o'er th' Eubœan main aloof he flies,
And hardens by degrees amid the skies.
So show'ry drops, when chilly tempests blow,
Thicken at first, then whiten into snow ;
In balls congeal'd the rolling fleeces bound,
In solid hail result upon the ground.
Thus whirl'd with nervous force through distant
    air,
The purple tide forsook his veins with fear ;
All moisture left his limbs. Transform'd to stone,
In ancient days the craggy flint was known :
Still in th' Eubœan waves his front he rears,
Still the small rock in human form appears,
And still the name of hapless Lichas bears."

OVID, *Met.* .

                        " At these words,
Rack'd as he was with agonising pains,
He seiz'd him by the foot above the part
Where the joint bends, and dash'd him 'gainst the
    rock
Projecting o'er the waves that wash its sides ;
A mingled mass of hair, and brains, and blood,
Flow'd from his shatter'd head.   Th' assembled
    crowds
Lament the hero's suff'rings, and the fate
Of Lichas ; but of all the train not one
Had courage to approach him.   To the ground
One while he bent convuls'd ; anon erect
He cried aloud ; the promontories round,
The rocks of Locris, and Eubœa's heights,
Resounded with his cries : but now grown faint,
And oft with anguish writhing on the earth,
With many a groan he curs'd thy nuptial bed,
Inhuman as thou art, to his repose
So fatal ; curs'd thy father's bridal rites,
Whence to his life this pest.   Then through the
    mist
That darken'd o'er him, his distorted eyès

He rais'd, and saw me 'midst the numerous
    crowd
Weeping his fate ; he look'd on me, and cried :
' My son, come to me ; do not fly my ills,
Though with thy dying father thou shouldst
    die ;
But bear me hence, and see thou lay me where
No mortal may behold me : if thy soul
Is sensible of pity, from this land
Remove me ; haste, that here I may not die.'
Thus as he urg'd, we plac'd him in a bark,
And brought him to this shore, no easy task,
Roaring aloud through anguish ; him thou soon
Or living wilt behold, or lately dead.
This 'gainst my father have thy arts devis'd,
This hast thou done, my mother ; and this deed
May rigorous justice on thy head repay,
And the avenging fury, if my pray'rs
Be righteous.   They are righteous ; thou hast
    cast
All that is righteous from thee, and hast slain
The best, the noblest man the earth could boast ;
His equal never more shalt thou behold.

CHORUS.

Without reply why dost thou haste away?
Silence, be thou assur'd, confirms the charge.

HYLLUS.

Nay, let her go; and may a favouring gale
Swell as she goes, and waft her from my sight.
Why should I cherish with a son's fond pride
The name of mother? Nothing hath she done
That shews a mother's part: let her then go,
And take this farewell with her, May she find
Such joys as to my father she hath given!

CHORUS.

See, virgins, see, the doom of old
By the prophetic voice foretold,
Advances with impetuous speed,
    For thus the Fates decreed:
' Twelve times the moon shall bend her silver
    bow,
Then rest from toils the son of Jove shall know.'
    See, th' event with secret force
    Onward holds its destin'd course;
For he who sinks to Pluto's peaceful shore
    Is to toils a slave no more.

ANTISTROPHE I.

For if the centaur o'er his head
Guileful the sanguine cloud has spread;
If from the venom-tinctur'd vest
    He feels the rankling pest

Of death, and of the spotted hydra born;
How shall he see another orient morn?
    Ours the hero to deplore,
    Wasted by the hydra's gore;
As the rough centaur's wiles their pangs impart,
    Burning in his tortur'd heart.

STROPHE II.

    But as fear her love alarms,
    When now the royal dame with dread
Beholds a rival to her nuptial bed;
    Confiding in these fatal charms,
She thoughtless is ensnar'd with hostile wiles,
Whilst hope to win her lord her heart beguiles.
    Now the ruin she deplores,
    Now the tear of anguish pours:
For fate advancing all the treach'ry shews,
    Whence this mighty mischief flows.

ANTISTROPHE II.

    Forth hath burst the fount of tears:
    The pest is spread. From all thy foes
Never on thee, Alcides, fell such woes
    To rouse dejected pity's fears.
Alas, th' illustrious hero's fatal spear,
That flam'd terrific in the front of war!
    From Œchalia's summit hoar,
    This the captive virgin bore.
The deed declares Idalia's sportive queen,
    Acting silent and unseen."

SOPHOCLES.

No. 464.

Hercules frenzied on mount Œta, felling the trees for his funeral pyre,
which Philoctetes is engaged in raising.

APOLLONIDES. *Amethyst.*

HERCULES.

" Ye hallow'd altars, whose firm base is fix'd
On high Cenæum, what a recompense
For all my victims to unhappy me
Have you repaid! O Jove, with what fierce pains

Hast thou afflicted me! This dire disease,
Whose unextinguish'd rage to madness fires
My bursting veins, O that I had not known!
What potent charm, what skill medicinal
Can mitigate, without the pow'r of Jove,
These agonising pangs! O might I see

This miracle, though distant! Let me lie,
Ah, let me lie repos'd. Why dost thou touch,
Why dost thou raise me up? Each touch is death.
Thou hast awaken'd pangs that were at rest:
Again my tortures are inflam'd, again
They rush upon me. Ah, where are you now,
Ye most unjust of all the Grecian race?
With many toils th' infested seas I clear'd,
And all the ruffian-haunted woods; yet now
I miserably perish; not a man
Will bring or fire or sword to put an end
To my afflictions; not a man will come
Willing to rend from me this hated life.

ATTENDANT.

O thou his son, this task requires a strength
Greater than mine,—assist him thou; thine eye
Quicker than mine sees what may give him aid.

HYLLUS.

I touch him, but to mitigate his pains
Exceeds my pow'r; and all the healing art
Avails not: that must be the work of Jove.

HERCULES.

My son, my son, where art thou? In thy arms
Raise me, support me. O my cruel fate!
This fierce, immedicable, wasting pest
Attacks, again attacks me; wretched me!
O Pallas, it consumes me. O my son,
In pity to thy father draw thy sword,
And plunge it deep into my throat; the deed
Will not be impious: heal these torturing pangs,
Inflicted by thy mother's wicked hands.
O might I see her fall'n, thus fall'n, as me
Her arts have sunk! Thou monarch of the dead,
Brother of Jove, give me a speedy death,
And lay, O lay a tortured wretch at rest!

CHORUS.

My friends, chill horror shakes me, as I hear
The miseries which th' illustrious hero bears.

HERCULES.

What fiery and unutterable pains
With rankling venom pierce my hands, my back!

Such not the wife of Jove to me assign'd,
Nor stern Eurystheus, as this treach'rous dame,
Daughter of Œneus, whose entangling net,
The texture of the Furies, burns my limbs,
And works me death: close to my sides it sticks,
Eats through my skin, and rioting beneath,
My vitals drains: already hath it drank
The fresh streams of my blood, and all my flesh
Is wasted, by these gnawing bands consum'd.
This not the spear on the ensanguin'd plain
Uplifted, nor the terrible array
Of earth-born giants, nor the furious force
Of savage beasts roused from their horrid dens,
Nor Grecian, nor Barbarian, nor the rage
Of ruffian bands from which I purg'd the earth,
Effected; but a single woman, form'd
By nature weak—a woman to the ground,
Without a sword, hath brought me. But, my
	son,
Now prove thyself my son, nor more revere
A mother's name; but bring her from the house,
And give her to my hands, that I may know
If more my wretched state afflicts thy heart
Than hers, when thou shalt see her ruin'd form
Defac'd by my just vengeance. Go, my son!
Dare this; have pity on me. Many feel
The touch of pity for me, as I weep
Like a sick girl lamenting; till this hour
No man can say that e'er his eyes beheld
Such weakness in me, but without a groan
Toils and afflictions always I sustain'd:
But now my firmness sinks, and I am found
Amidst my ills a woman. But, my son,
Come to me, nearer stand; come all, observe
From what a malady these torturing pains
I suffer; look, I throw my vests aside—
Behold this wretched body; what a sight
To move your pity! Ah, this burning spasm
Rends me afresh, it pierces through my sides!
No rest this cruel, gnawing pest allows.
Receive me, O thou monarch of the dead!
Strike me, ye bolts of Jove; O king supreme,
Roll thy red thunders, hurl them on this head,
My father! for it riots now again,

11

Gains strength, grows fiercer. O my hands, my
    hands,
My back, my breast, my arms! Are these the
    nerves
In which I gloried once, whose matchless strength
Quell'd the Nemean lion with the blood
Of slaughter'd herds distain'd, whose savage rage
None dar'd approach? Are these the nerves,
    whose might
Crush'd the Lernæan hydra, and subdu'd
The host of monsters to the horse's strength
Joining the human form, a lawless band,
To outrage train'd, exulting in brute force?
The boar of Erymanthus? the grim dog
Of hell, three-headed monster, by no arms
To be attack'd, from dire Echidna sprung?

The dragon, guardian of the golden fruit
On earth's remotest verge? These glorious toils,
These and a thousand more have I achiev'd;
But never mortal o'er my glory raised
A trophy. Nerveless now this hardy frame
Is shatter'd, and beneath this blind disease
I waste away; my mother's virtuous name
Avails me not, nor through the starry skies
That I am call'd the son of thund'ring Jove.
Yet know you this, though I am nothing now,
A weak exhausted nothing, yet e'en thus
I will inflict just vengeance on her head
Who brought me to this state; that she may
    learn,
And publish to the world, that it is mine
In life or death to punish impious deeds."

SOPHOCLES.

No. 465.

Hercules giving Philoctetes his bow and arrow.

ADMON. *Oriental Sardonyx.*

" But now the hero of immortal birth
    Fells Œte's forests; on the groaning earth
    A pile he builds: to Philoctetes' care
    He leaves his deathful instruments of war;
    To him commits those arrows, which again
    Shall see the bulwarks of the Trojan reign."

No. 466.

Hercules extended on the funeral pile, and near him Philoctetes holding a lighted torch.

CHROMIOS. *Oriental Cornelian.*

" The son of Pæan lights the lofty pyre,
    High round the structure climbs the greedy fire:
    Plac'd on the top, thy nervous shoulders spread
    With the Nemean spoils, thy careless head
    Rais'd on the knotty club with look divine,

Here thou, dread hero, of celestial line,
Wert stretch'd at ease ; as when, a cheerful guest,
Wine crown'd thy bowls, and flow'rs thy temples dress'd.
Now on all sides the potent flames aspire,
And crackle round those limbs that mock the fire."

OVID.

No. 467.

Head of Hercules.

Oriental Amethyst.

The jealousy and hatred which Eurystheus bore to Hercules and his family were not extinguished by the death of that hero : he pursued the mother and children of Alcides to Athens, where they had sought refuge under the protection of Theseus. Eurystheus made war against them, and was slain by Hyllus, one of the sons of Hercules.

" For Linus' death, by all the tuneful Nine
  Bewail'd, doth Phœbus' self complain,
  And loudly uttering his auspicious strain,
Smite with a golden quill the lyre : but mine
  Shall be the task, while songs of praise
  I chant, and twine the laureat wreath,
  His matchless fortitude t' emblaze,
Who sought hell's inmost gloom, the dreary
    shades beneath ;
  Whether I call the Hero son of Jove,
  Or of Amphitryon ; for the fame
To which his labours have so just a claim
Must e'en in death attract the public love :
In the Nemæan forest first he slew
  That lion huge, whose tawny hide
  And grinning jaws extended wide
  He o'er his shoulders threw.

The winged arrows whizzing from his bow
  Did on their native hills confound
The Centaurs' race with many a deadly wound :
Alcides' matchless strength doth Peneus know,
  Distinguish'd by his limpid waves,
  The fields laid waste of wide extent,
  With Pelion, and the neighbouring caves
Of Homoles, uprooting from whose steep ascent

Tall pines that cast a venerable shade,
  The monsters arm'd their forceful hands,
  And strode terrific o'er Thessalia's lands :
Then breathless on th' ensanguin'd plain he laid
  That hind distinguish'd by her golden horns,
  And still in Dian's temple seen ;
  His prize, to glad the huntress queen,
    Œnoe's walls adorns.

The chariot with triumphal ensigns grac'd
  Ascending, to his stronger yoke
He Diomedes' furious coursers broke,
Scorning the bit, in hateful stalls who placed
  By their fell lord, the flesh of man
  Raging devour'd, accursed food :
  A stream from their foul mangers ran,
Fill'd with unholy gore, and many a gobbet
    crude.
O'er Hebrus' silver tide, at the command
  Of Argos' unrelenting king
Eurystheus, he these captive steeds did bring,
Close to Anauros' mouth on Pelion's strand.
Inhuman Cycnus, son of Mars, next felt
  The force of his resounding bow,
  Unsocial wretch, the stranger's foe,
    Who in Amphanea dwelt.

Then came he to th' harmonious nymphs, that band
Who in Hesperian gardens hold
Their station, where the vegetative gold
Glows in the fruitage,—with resistless hand
To snatch the apple from its height;
The dragon wreath'd his folds around
The tree's huge trunk, portentous sight,
In vain: that monster fell transfix'd with many a wound.
Into those straits of the unfathom'd main
He enter'd with auspicious gales,
Where fear'd the mariner t' unfurl his sails,
And fixing limits to the wat'ry plain,
His columns rear'd. Then from the heavens' huge load
The wearied Atlas he reliev'd:
His arm the starry realms upheav'd,
And propp'd the gods' abode.

˒ Foe to the Amazons' equestrian race,
He cross'd the boist'rous Euxine tide,
And gave them battle by Mæotis' side.
What friends through Greece collected he to face
Hippolita, th' intrepid maid,
That he the belt of Mars might gain,
And tissu'd robe with golden braid:
Still doth exulting Greece the virgin's spoils retain,

Lodg'd in Mycene's shrine, with gore imbru'd.
The dog of Lerna's marshy plain,
Who unresisting multitudes had slain,
The hundred-headed hydra, he subdued,
Aided by fire and winged shafts combin'd;
These from his well-stor'd quiver flew,
And triple-form'd Geryon slew,
Fierce Erythræa's hind.

But having finish'd each adventurous strife,
At length in evil hour he steers
To Pluto's mansion, to the house of tears,
The jail of labour, there to end his life,
Thence never, never to return:
His friends dismay'd forsake these gates,
In hopeless solitude we mourn.
Hell's stern award is pass'd, the boat of Charon waits
To their eternal home his sons to bear,
Most impious, lawless homicide!
For thee, O Hercules, thee erst his pride,
Thy sire now looks with impotent despair.
Had I the strength which I possess'd of yore,
I with my Theban friends, array'd
In brazen arms, thy sons would aid:
But youth's blest days are o'er."

EURIPIDES: WOODHULL.

No. 468.

Hyllus presenting the head of Eurystheus to Alcmena.

APOLLONIDES. *Oriental Sardonyx.*

MESSENGER.
" Your eyes indeed behold, O royal dame,
Yet shall this tongue declare, that we have brought
Eurystheus hither; unexpected sight,
Reverse of fortune his presumptuous soul
Foresaw not; this oppressor little deem'd

That he should ever fall into your hands,
When from Mycene, by the Cyclops' toil
Erected, he those squadrons led, and hoped
With pride o'erweening to lay Athens waste.
But heaven our situation hath revers'd;
And therefore with exulting Hyllas joins
The valiant Iolaus, in erecting

Trophies to Jove, the author of our conquest.
But they to you commanded me to lead
This captive, wishing to delight your soul :
For 'tis most grateful to behold a foe
Fall'n from the height of gay prosperity.

ALCMENA.

Com'st thou, detested wretch? at length hath
    justice
O'ertaken thee.   First hither turn thy head,
And dare to face thine enemies ; for, dwindled
Into a vassal, thou no longer rul'st.
Art thou the man (for I would know the truth)
Who didst presume to heap unnumber'd wrongs,
Thou author of all mischief, on my son
While yet he liv'd, wherever now resides
His dauntless spirit ?   For in what one instance
Didst thou not injure him ?   At thy command,

Alive he travell'd to th' infernal shades ;
Thou sent'st, and didst commission him to slay
Hydras and lions.   Various other mischiefs,
Which were by thee contriv'd, I mention not ;
For an attempt to speak of them at large
Would be full tedious.   Nor was it enough
For thee to venture on these wrongs alone ;
But thou, moreover, from each Grecian state
Me and these children hast expell'd, though
    seated
As suppliants at the altars of the gods,
Confounding those whose locks are grey through
    age
With tender infants.   But thou here hast found
Those who were men indeed, and a free city
Which fear'd thee not."

EURIPIDES : WOODHULL.

No. 469.

Hebe and Iolas.

DIOSCORIDES.   *Oriental Sardonyx.*

Hercules in Olympus petitioned Jupiter to restore Iolas, the companion of his labours, to youth, and he obtained his request.   On this stone Hebe is seen presenting Iolas with nectar, which, although then at a very advanced age, makes him young again.

" Iolas stands before their eyes,
A youth he stood, and the soft down began
'O'er his smooth chin to spread, and promise man.
Hebe submitted to her husband's prayers,
Instill'd new vigour, and restored his years."

OVID.

No. 470.

Iolas, become young again, looking up at two stars, symbolical of Hercules
and Hebe his wife.

APOLLONIDES.   *Oriental Sardonyx.*

CLASS III.

FABULOUS AND HEROIC HISTORY.

No. 471.

Prometheus stealing the sacred fire.

CHROMIOS. *Fine Sardonyx.*

Prometheus,* to animate the figure of a man which he had formed of clay, ascended to heaven, accompanied by Minerva, and thence stole some of the sacred fire with the stalk of a plant called *ferula.*

> " But Jove
> Benevolent Prometheus did beguile:
> For in a hollow reed he stole from high
> The far-seen splendour of unwearied flame.
> Then deep resentment stung the Thund'rer's soul,
> And his heart chaf'd in anger, when he saw
> The fire far gleaming in the midst of men;
> And, for the flame restor'd, he straight devised
> A mischief to mankind."
>
> HESIOD.

---

* Prometheus, who renewed the race of men, was Noos, or Noah. Prometheus raised the first altar to the gods, constructed the first ship, and transmitted to posterity many useful inventions. He was supposed to have lived at the time of the deluge, and to have been guardian of Egypt at that season. He was the same as Osiris, the great husbandman, the planter of the vine, and inventor of the plough. Prometheus is said to have been exposed on mount Caucasus, near Colchis, with an eagle placed over him, preying on his heart. These strange histories are undoubtedly taken from the symbols and devices which were carved upon the front of the ancient Amonian temples, and especially those of Egypt. The eagle and vulture were the insignia of that country. We are told by Orus Apollo that a heart over burning coals was an emblem of Egypt. The history of Tityus,

No. 472.

Prometheus descending with the sacred fire from heaven.

CHROMIOS. *Oriental Cornelian.*

" At length, then, to the wide earth's. extreme
    bounds,
To Scythea are we come, those pathless wilds,
Where human footstep never mark'd the ground.
Now, Vulcan, to thy task : at Jove's command
Fix to these high projecting rocks this vain
Artificer of man ; each massy link
Draw close, and bind his adamantine chains.

The radiant pride, the fiery flame, that lends
Its aid to ev'ry art, he stole, and bore
The gift to mortals ; for which bold offence
The gods assign him this first punishment :
That he may learn to reverence the pow'r
Of Jove, and moderate his love to man."

             ÆSCHYLUS : POTTER.

No. 473.

The Centaur Chiron healing the wound of Prometheus.

APOLLONIDES. *Oriental Cornelian.*

After Hercules had delivered Prometheus by killing the eagle, and breaking the chains by which he was bound to mount Caucasus, the centaur Chiron hastened to him to heal the wounds in his side, by applying the leaves of a vulnerary plant, probably that called *Promethea* by Plutarch, by Apollonius in *Argonaütica*, and by others of the old authors. This herb, indigenous to the Caucasus, and the same as the *Crocus* of Colchis, was also frequently employed by Medea. No longer known, it is perhaps among the many objects in natural history which have not yet been re-discovered, or which have altogether disappeared from the face of the earth.

No. 474.

Vulcan forming the figure of Pandora.

GNAIOS. *Oriental Cornelian.*

Pandora was the first woman who, according to Hesiod (*Theogony*), Vulcan, by command of Jupiter, formed of clay ; after which he animated her, and placing a veil and crown of gol

---

Prometheus, and many other poetical personages, was certainly taken from hieroglyphics misunderstood and badly explained. Prometheus was worshipped by the Colchians as a deity, and had a temple and high place upon mount Caucasus ; and the device upon the portal was Egyptian, an eagle over a heart.—BRYANT.

on her head, he led her to Jupiter in the council of the gods. All admired her, and each bestowed on her his principal attribute: Venus endowed her with beauty, Mercury with eloquence, and Minerva with wisdom; while Jupiter gave her a sealed box, containing the woes, commanding her to give it to Prometheus, as a punishment for the theft he had committed. Prometheus suspected the intention of Jupiter, and would not open the fatal vase. In this engraving the artist has given only as much expression to the beautiful form of Pandora as is consistent with a recently animated figure of clay.

" Fools, blind to truth! nor knows their erring
    soul
How much the half is better than the whole;
How great the pleasure wholesome herbs afford,
How blest the frugal and an honest board!
Would the immortal gods on men bestow
A mind how few the wants of life to know,
They all the year from labour free might live,
On what the bounty of a day would give;
They soon the rudder o'er the smoke would lay,
And let the mule and ox at leisure stray.
This sense to man the king of gods denies,
In wrath to him who daring robb'd the skies;
Dread ills the god prepar'd, unknown before,
And the stol'n fire back to his heav'n he bore.
But from Prometheus 'twas conceal'd in vain,
Which for the use of man he stole again,
And, artful in his fraud, brought from above
Clos'd in a hollow cane, deceiving Jove.
Again defrauded of celestial fire,
Thus spoke the cloud-compelling god in ire:
' Son of Iapetus, o'er subtle, go
And glory in thy artful theft below;
Now of the fire you boast, by stealth retriev'd,
And triumph in almighty Jove deceiv'd:
But thou, too late, shalt find the triumph vain,
And read thy folly in succeeding pain;
Posterity the sad effect shall know,
When, in pursuit of joy, they grasp their woe.'
He spoke, and told to Mulciber his will,
And smiling bade him his commands fulfil;
To use his greatest art, his nicest care,
To frame a creature exquisitely fair;
To temper well the clay with water, then
To add the vigour and the voice of men;

To let her first in virgin lustre shine,
In form a goddess, with a bloom divine.
And next the sire demands Minerva's aid,
In all her various skill to train the maid;
Bids her the secrets of the loom impart,
To cast a curious thread with happy art.
And golden Venus was to teach the fair
The wiles of love, and to improve her air;
And then, in awful majesty, to shed
A thousand graceful charms around her head.
Next Hermes, artful god, must form her mind,
One day to torture, and the next be kind;
With manners all deceitful, and her tongue
Fraught with abuse, and with detraction hung.
Jove gave the mandate; and the gods obey'd.
First Vulcan form'd of earth the blushing maid;
Minerva next perform'd the task assign'd,
With ev'ry female art adorn'd her mind.
To dress her Suada and the Graces join;
Around her person, lo! the diamonds shine,
To deck her brows the fair tress'd Seasons bring
A garland breathing all the sweets of spring.
Each present Pallas gives it proper place,
And adds to ev'ry ornament a grace.
Next Hermes taught the fair the heart to move
With all the false alluring arts of love;
Her manners all deceitful, and her tongue
With falsehoods fruitful, and detraction hung.
The finish'd maid the gods Pandora call,
Because a tribute she receiv'd from all;
And thus, 'twas Jove's command, the sex began,
A lovely mischief to the soul of man.
When the great sire of gods beheld the fair,
The fatal guile, th' inevitable snare,
Hermes he bids to Epimetheus bear.

m m

Prometheus, mindful of his theft above,
Had warn'd his brother to beware of Jove ;
To take no present that the god should send,
Lest the fair bribe should ill to man portend :
But he, forgetful, takes his evil fate,
Accepts the mischief, and repents too late.
Mortals at first a blissful earth enjoy'd,
With ills untainted, nor with cares annoy'd ;
To them the world was no laborious stage,
Nor fear'd they then the miseries of age.
But soon the sad reversion they behold,
Alas! they grow in their afflictions old ;
For in her hand the nymph a casket bears,
Full of diseases and corroding cares ;
Which open'd, they to taint the world begin,
And hope alone remains entire within.
Such was the fatal present from above,
And such the will of cloud-compelling Jove.
And now unnumber'd woes o'er mortals reign,
Alike infected is the land and main ;
O'er human race distempers silent stray,
And multiply their strength by night and day.
'Twas Jove's decree they should in silence rove ;
For who is able to contend with Jove ?
And now the subject of my verse I change,
To tales of profit and delight I range ;
Whence you may pleasure and advantage gain,
If in your mind you lay the useful strain."

HESIOD : COOKE'S *Trans.*

No. 475.

Pandora, holding the vase containing the woes, conducted by Mercury.

DIOSCORIDES. *Oriental Cornelian.*

No. 476.

Pandora, accompanied by Mercury, presenting the vase to Epimetheus,
the brother of Prometheus.

ASPASIOS. *Oriental Sardonyx.*

No. 477.

Epimetheus, less wise and wary than his brother, and more curious than
Pandora, now his wife, opens the fatal vase.

CHROMIOS. *Oriental Cornelian.*

No. 478.

Deucalion explaining to Pyrrha the oracle of Themis.

APOLLONIDES. *Oriental Cornelian.*

Deucalion, the son of Prometheus and king of Thessaly, with his wife Pyrrha, the daughter of Epimetheus, after the deluge, which had desolated the kingdom and overwhelmed all the inhabitants, had recourse to the oracle of Themis, to learn how best to re-people Thessaly. The oracle told them that they must cover their heads with a veil, collect the bones of their grandmother, and throw them behind them. Deucalion and Pyrrha at first were at a loss to comprehend the meaning of Themis; but at length Deucalion observed that the earth was our common mother, and that her bones must be the stones. The present subject is Deucalion pointing out the stones to Pyrrha.

" The careful couple join their tears,
And then invoke the gods with pious pray'rs.
Thus, in devotion having eas'd their grief,
From sacred oracles they seek relief;
And to Cephysus' brook their way pursue—
The stream was troubled, but the ford they knew:
With living waters, in the fountain bred,
They sprinkle first their garments and their head,
Then took the way which to the temple led:
The roofs were all defil'd with moss and mire,
The desert altars void of solemn fire.
Before the gradual prostrate they ador'd;
The pavement kiss'd, and thus the saint implor'd:
' O righteous Themis, if the pow'rs above
By pray'rs are bent to pity and to love;
If human miseries can move their mind;
If yet they can forgive, and yet be kind,—
Tell how we may restore, by second birth,
Mankind, and people desolated earth.'
Then thus the gracious goddess nodding said:
' Depart, and with your vestments veil your head;

And stooping lowly down, with loosen'd zones,
Throw each behind your backs your mighty mother's bones.'
Amaz'd the pair and mute with wonder stand,
Till Pyrrha first refus'd the dire command.
' Forbid it, heav'n,' said she, ' that I should tear
These holy relics from the sepulchre!'
They ponder'd the mysterious words again
For some new sense; and long they sought in vain:
At length Deucalion clear'd his cloudy brow,
And said: ' The dark enigma will allow
A meaning, which, if well I understand,
From sacrilege will free the god's command.
This earth our mighty mother is; the stones
In her capacious body are her bones,—
These we must cast behind.' With hope and fear
The woman did the new solution hear:
The man diffides in his own augury,
And doubts the gods; yet both resolve to try."

OVID, *Met.*

No. 479.

Deucalion and Pyrrha throwing the stones behind them : those thrown by Deucalion become men, and those by Pyrrha women.

GNAIOS. *Oriental Cornelian.*

" Descending from the mount, they first unbind
Their vests, and veil'd they cast the stones behind.
The stones (a miracle to mortal view,
But long tradition makes it pass for true)

Did first the rigour of their kind expel,
And suppled into softness as they fell;
Then swell'd, and swelling by degrees grew warm,
And took the rudiments of human form,

Imperfect shapes. In marble such are seen,
When the rude chisel does the man begin ;
While yet the roughness of the stone remains,
Without the rising muscles and the veins.
The sappy parts, and next resembling juice,
Were turu'd to moisture for the body's use,
Supplying humours, blood, and nourishment ;
The rest, too solid to receive a bent,

Converts to bones ; and what was once a vein,
Its former name and nature did retain.
By help of pow'r divine, in little space,
What the man threw assum'd a manly face ;
And what the wife, renew'd the female race.
Hence we derive our nature ; born to bear
Laborious life, and harden'd into care."

OVID, *Met.*

No. 480.

The metamorphosis of Atlas.

CHROMIOS. *Oriental Cornelian.*

Atlas, warned by an oracle to beware of a son of Jupiter, refuses hospitality to Perseus, who, enraged at this, carries off the apples from the gardens of the Hesperides, and shewing Atlas the head of Medusa, metamorphoses him to a mountain.

" Here Atlas reign'd, of more than human size,
And in his kingdom the world's limit lies ;
Here Titan bids his wearied coursers sleep,
And cools the burning axle in the deep.
The mighty monarch, uncontroll'd, alone
His sceptre sways ; no neighb'ring states are known.
A thousand flocks on shady mountains fed,
A thousand herds o'er grassy plains were spread ;
Here wond'rous trees their shining stores unfold,
Their shining stores too wond'rous to be told ;
Their leaves, their branches, and their apples, gold.
Then Perseus the gigantic prince address'd,
Humbly implor'd a hospitable rest.
' If bold exploits thy admiration fire,
(He said,) I fancy mine thou wilt admire ;
Or if the glory of a race can move,
Not mean my glory, for I spring from Jove.'
At this confession Atlas ghastly star'd,
Mindful of what an oracle declar'd,
That the dark womb of time conceal'd a day
Which should, disclos'd, the bloomy gold betray :

All should at once be ravished from his eyes,
And Jove's own progeny enjoy the prize.
For this, the fruit he loftily immur'd,
And a fierce dragon the strait pass secur'd ;
For this, all strangers he forbade to land,
And drove them from th' inhospitable strand.
To Perseus then : ' Fly quickly, fly this coast,
Nor falsely dare thy acts and race to boast.'
In vain the hero for one night entreats ;
Threat'ning he storms, and next adds force to threats.
By strength not Perseus could himself defend,
For who in strength with Atlas could contend ?
' But since short rest to me thou wilt not give,
A gift of endless rest from me receive,'
He said, and backward turu'd, no more conceal'd
The present, and Medusa's head reveal'd.
Soon the high Atlas a high mountain stood :
His locks and beard became a leafy wood,
His hands and shoulders into ridges went,
The summit-head still crown'd the steep ascent,
His bones a solid rocky hardness gained :
He thus immensely grown (as fate ordained),
The stars, the heavens, and all the gods sustain'd."

OVID, *Met.*

" Thy brother's fate, th' unhappy Atlas,
Afflicts me; on the western shore he stands,
Supporting on his shoulders the vast pillar
Of heav'n and earth, a weight of cumbrous grasp."

ÆSCHYLUS: POTTER.

No. 481.

Danae supplicating Acrisius.

PYRGOTELES. *Oriental Sardonyx.*

Acrisius, king of Argos, when he discovers that his daughter has given birth to a child, is greatly enraged, and threatens her. Danae, throwing herself at his feet, strives to dissipate his anger by shewing him the infant Perseus.

MERCURY.

" These mansions, and this fortress well begirt
With lofty ramparts, no vain pomp display.
Monarch and priest, Acrisius here commands;
Among the Greeks this city is called Argos.
But eager to obtain a son, the king
Enter'd the Pythian temple, and address'd
This question to Apollo: by what means
With a male offspring he his house might
    strengthen,
Through what propitious god, or human aid ?
But dark was the response which Phœbus ut-
    ter'd:
' In time shall a male progeny be given,
Not sprung from thy own loins. Thou must beget
A daughter first; she, knowing yet not knowing
By stealth a paramour, shall to her sire
A winged lion for his grandchild bear,
Who over these domains shall rule supreme.'
Hearing these oracles, he for a time
The genial couch abandon'd; but unmindful
Of his resolves, and by desire o'ercome,
He afterwards a daughter did beget,

On whom he, from this long delay, bestow'd
The name of Danae. Soon as she was born,
He in those female chambers * he had rear'd
Consign'd her to the care of Argive virgins;
Using precautions lest she should behold
The face of man. But after she was grown
To full maturity, and through all Greece
Distinguish'd for her charms, Jove, mighty sire,
By love's inevitable magic caught,
Attempted to ascend her bed in secret.
But by the open language of persuasion
Failing to win the nymph, he next devis'd
This artifice: transform'd to purest gold
(Aware that gold 's what mortals covet most),
From the steep roof to glide into the hands
Of th' inexperienc'd virgin: the deep fraud
She knew not, and receiv'd the molten god
Into her bosom. But when she at length
Perceiv'd the growing burden of her womb,
She was o'erwhelm'd with wonder, nor could
    guess
How it was possible for her to fall
Into such infamy, when she her honour

---

* The place of Danae's confinement is by Apollodorus said to have been a brazen dungeon, built for that purpose by her father Acrisius, on being informed by the oracle that she was to bear a son who would kill his grandfather, and take possession of his kingdom.

Had still preserv'd. But while in secrecy
She hence would fly, her father, having learn'd
The cause, inflam'd with anger, hath confin'd
And keeps her in a dungeon, that the truth
With his own eyes he may explore; resolving,
Soon as her shame he shall perceive confirm'd
Beyond all doubt, to cast into the sea
His daughter and her child. Me, therefore, Jove
To Danae hath with acceptable tidings
Despatch'd, which I shall instantly convey;
For every prudent messenger with zeal
Ought to perform the mandates of his lord.

CHORUS OF ARGIVE VIRGINS.

What wondrous tidings reach our ears!
With speed augmented by my fears,

I seek the palace of the king.
Whence can these envious rumours spring,
That through each street with loud acclaim
Belie fair Danae's virgin fame?
Curs'd be that slanderer's baleful tongue
Which first her honour dar'd to wrong;
And, " by some paramour defil'd,"
Says, " she is pregnant." But his child
Acrisius tends with anxious guard,
Her chambers closely hath he barr'd;
The real truth I wish to learn.
But from the palace I discern
The sov'reign of this Argive state
Now coming hither; with a weight
Of griefs oppress'd he seems to tread,
Because his daughter would have fled."

EURIPIDES, *Fragments:* WOODHULL.

No. 482.

Mercury fastening wings on the feet of Perseus before he mounts Pegasus.

APOLLONIDES.   *Oriental Cornelian.*

" The rising Phosphor, with a purple light,
·   Did sluggish mortals to new toils invite;
   His feet again the valiant Perseus plumes,
   And his keen sabre in his hand resumes:
   Then nobly spurns the ground, and upward springs,
   And cuts the liquid air with sounding wings."

OVID.

" There was the horseman, fair-hair'd Danae's
      son,
Perseus; nor yet the buckler with his feet
Touch'd, not yet distant hover'd. Strange to
      think;
For no where on the surface of the shield
He rested: so the crippled artist-god
Illustrious framed him, with his hands in gold.
Bound to his feet were sandals wing'd; a sword
Of brass, with hilt of sable ebony,
Hung round him from the shoulders by a thong.
Swift e'en as thought he flew. The visage grim

Of monstrous gorgon all his back o'erspread;
And wrought in silver, wondrous to behold,
A veil was drawn around it, whence in gold
Hung glittering fringes; and the dreadful helm
Of Pluto clasp'd the temples of the prince,
Shedding a night of darkness. Thus outstretch'd
In air, he seem'd like one to trembling flight
Betaken. Close behind the gorgons twain,
Of nameless terror, unapproachable,
Came rushing; eagerly they stretch'd their arms
To seize him: from the pallid adamant,
Audibly as they rush'd, the clattering shield

Clank'd with a sharp shrill sound. Two grisly snakes
Hung from their girdles, and with forking tongues
Lick'd their inflected jaws, and violent gnash'd

Their fangs fell glaring; from around their heads
Those gorgons grim a flickering horror cast
Through the wide air."

HESIOD: *Shield of Hercules.*

PERSEUS.

"To what barbarian land, with winged feet,
Ye gods, have I been borne? for through the midst
Of ether's trackless fields my path dividing,
Here for a while I, Perseus, stay my flight,
Bound on a voyage to the Argive realm,
Thither the gorgon's head ordain'd to bear.
But, ha! what rock do I behold, what nymph,
Fair as a goddess, like some anchor'd ship
Bound fast with cords, stands on the craggy beach?

ANDROMEDA.

On me most wretched damsel, generous stranger,
Take pity; loose, O loose these galling chains.

PERSEUS.

With pity I behold thee bound, O virgin.

ANDROMEDA.

But who art thou that pitiest my distress?

PERSEUS.

Some weakness harbours in each human breast:
But me the love of this fair nymph hath seiz'd.
Tyrant of gods and men, O Love, forbear
To dress up evil in that specious form;
Or to these labours grant a bless'd event,
In which thou prompt'st the lover to engage.
By acting thus, thou from the gods themselves
Shalt gain due honours; but if thou refuse,
E'en they whose breasts thou fill'st with warm desire
Thee of thy wonted homage shall bereave.

Sacred Night,
O what a long career dost thou perform,
Driving thy chariot through the starry space
Of ether, and Olympus' hallow'd fields!

PERSEUS.

O virgin, if I save thee, with what thanks
Wilt thou repay me?

ANDROMEDA.

Take me to thyself,
O stranger, for a servant, if thou list;
Or for thy consort.

But thither the whole band of shepherds came;
One brought a cup of iv'ry fill'd with milk,
The sweet refreshment of his toils; a second
The generous liquor of the vine.

I will not give consent to your begetting
A spurious progeny, for though inferior
In no respect to children born in wedlock,
Yet are they harshly treated by the laws,
A ndof this grievance ought you to beware.

Thou canst not see Jove's power, how great,
Presiding o'er the work of fate;
For some he causes every day
To flourish, others to decay.

I gain'd not fame but with unnumber'd toils.
There's nothing by necessity ordain'd
Which can to man be shameful: but for thee
'Tis sweet to recollect past toils in safety.
To this adventurous deed am I impell'd
By youthful vigour and a daring soul."

EURIPIDES, *Frag.*: WOODHULL.

No. 483.

Perseus cutting off the head of Medusa.

DIOSCORIDES. *Sardonyx.*

No. 484.

Perseus displaying to the Monster the head of Medusa.

APOLLONIDES. *Calcedony.*

Cassiopeia, the wife of Cepheus king of Æthiopia, and mother of Andromeda, presumed to boast that herself and daughter surpassed in beauty Juno herself and the Nereids. These last petitioned Neptune to punish such an insolent vaunt; and he sent a sea-monster to devastate Æthiopia. Cepheus consulted the oracle of Jupiter, who replied that its ravages would cease only when Andromeda should be chained to a rock, and left to be devoured by the monster. Perseus, mounted on Pegasus, arrived in Æthiopia, and presenting himself to Cepheus, offered to deliver Andromeda by killing the monster.

" As well-rigg'd galleys, which slaves sweat-
    ing row,
With their sharp beaks the whiten'd ocean
    plough,
So when the monster mov'd, still at his back
The furrow'd waters left a foamy track.
Now to the rock he was advanc'd so nigh,
Whirl'd from a sling a stone the space would
    fly;
Then bounding upwards the brave Perseus
    sprung,
And in mid air on hov'ring pinions hung.
His shadow quickly floated on the main,
The monster could not his wild rage restrain,
But at the floating shadow leap'd in vain.
As when Jove's bird a speckled serpent spies,
Which in the shine of Phœbus basking lies,
Unseen he souses down, and bears away,
Truss'd from behind, the vainly hissing prey ;
To writhe his neck the labour nought avails,
Too deep th' imperial talons pierce his scales.
Thus the wing'd hero now descends, now soars,
And at his pleasure the vast monster gores :

Full in his back, swift stooping from above,
The crooked sabre to its hilt he drove.
The monster rag'd, impatient of the pain,
First bounded high, and then sunk low again.
Now, like a savage boar, when chaf'd with
    wounds
And bay'd with op'ning mouths of hungry hounds,
He on the foe turns with collected might,
Who still eludes him with an airy flight,
And wheeling round, the scaly armour tries
Of his thick sides; his thinner tail now plies :
Till, from repeated strokes, out-gush'd a flood,
And the waves redden'd with the streaming blood.
At last the dropping wings, befoam'd all o'er,
With flaggy heaviness their master bore :
A rock he spied, whose humble head was low,
Bare at an ebb, but cover'd at a flow.
A ridgy hold he thither flying gain'd,
And with one hand his bending weight sustain'd ;
With the other vig'rous blows he dealt around,
And the home-thrusts th' expiring monster own'd.
In deaf'ning shouts the glad applauses rise,
And peal on peal runs rattling through the skies."

OVID, *Met.*

" Then shall he mark the tow'rs where Cepheus
    rul'd,
And fountains springing from the printed steps
Of Laphrian Hermes, and the double rock

'Gainst which the monster of the ocean rush'd
Eager, but found far other prize ; and seiz'd
Deep in the spacious cavern of his jaws
The vulture son of gold, who rode the breeze

Sandal'd with wings, and with his falchion smote
Th' enormous orc, wide wallowing on the wave:
Who rais'd the steed divine, and from the trunk
Sever'd the snaky visage of the fiend,
Distilling blood whence sprung the winged steed
And wondrous riders; who enclos'd his foes

In marble robe, and with uncover'd shield
Froze their young blood, and stiffen'd them to
stone;
Who stole upon the sisters three, and thence
Joyful return'd; but ne'er to them return'd
Light, nor the guide of threefold wanderings."

LYCOPHRON: VISCOUNT ROYSTON.

No. 485.

Perseus and Andromeda.

ALCEUS.   *Oriental Cornelian.*

The monster becoming petrified, Perseus is supporting Andromeda with his right arm, and with his left is concealing the parazonium (sword) and the head of Medusa.

No. 486.

Phineus resisted by Perseus.

APOLLONIDES.   *Calcedony, partaking of Sapphire.*

Perseus, on obtaining from Cepheus the hand of his daughter in marriage, offered a sacrifice to the gods. Phineus, the uncle of Andromeda, opposed the marriage, and tried to kill Perseus with an arrow; but he avoided it, and seizing a lighted brand from the altar of Jupiter, attacked him with it.

" The beauteous bride moves on, now loos'd
    from chains,
The cause and sweet reward of all the hero's
    pains.
Meantime on shore triumphant Perseus stood,
And purg'd his hands, smear'd with the monster's
    blood;
Then in the windings of a sandy bed
Compos'd Medusa's execrable head.
But to prevent the roughness, leaves he threw,
And young green twigs which soft in waters
    grew;
There soft and full of sap, but here when laid,
Touch'd by the head, that softness soon decay'd;

The wonted flexibility quite gone,
The tender scions harden'd into stone;
Fresh juicy twigs surpris'd the Nereids brought,
Fresh juicy twigs the same contagion caught.
The nymphs the petrifying seeds still keep,
And propagate the wonder through the deep:
The pliant sprays of coral yet declare
Their stiff'ning nature when expos'd to air;
Those sprays which did like bending osiers move,
Snatch'd from their element obdurate prove,
And shrubs beneath the waves grow stones
    above."

OVID.

n n

" The great immortals grateful Perseus prais'd,
And to three pow'rs three turfy altars rais'd :
To Hermes this, and that he did assign
To Pallas ; the hind honours, Jove, were thine.
He hastes for Pallas a white cow to call,
A calf for Hermes, but for Jove a bull ;
Then seiz'd the prize of his victorious fight,
Andromeda, and claim'd the nuptial right—
Andromeda alone he greatly sought,
The dowry kingdom was not worth a thought.
Pleas'd Hymen now his golden torch displays,
With rich oblations fragrant altars blaze ;
Sweet wreathes of choicest flowers are hung on
    high,
And cloudless pleasure smiles in ev'ry eye ;
The melting music melting thoughts inspires,
And warbling songsters aid the warbling lyres.

.   .   .   .   .

Chief in the riot Phineus first appear'd,
The rash ringleader of this boist'rous herd ;
And brandishing his brazen-pointed lance,—
' Behold (he said) an injured man advance,
Stung with resentment for his ravish'd wife.
Nor shall thy wings, O Perseus, save thy life ;
Nor Jove himself, though we've been often told
Who got thee in the form of tempting gold.'
His lance was aim'd, when Cepheus ran, and said :
' Hold, brother, hold ! what brutal rage has made
Your frantic mind so black a crime conceive ?
Are these the thanks that you to Perseus give ?
This the reward that to his worth you pay,
Whose timely valour sav'd Andromeda ?

Nor was it he, if you would reason right,
That forc'd her from you, but the jealous spite
Of envious Nereids, and Jove's high decree ;
And that devouring monster of the sea,
That ready with his jaws wide gaping stood
To eat my child, the fairest of my blood.
You lost her then, when she seem'd past relief,
And wish'd, perhaps, her death, to ease your grief
With my afflictions.   Not content to view
Andromeda in chains, unhelp'd by you,
Her spouse and uncle, will you grieve that he
Expos'd his life the dying maid to free ?
And shall you claim his merit ? Had you thought
Her charms so great, you should have bravely
    sought
That blessing on the rocks where fix'd she lay.
But now let Perseus bear his prize away,
By service gain'd, by promis'd faith possess'd ;
To him I owe it, that my age is bless'd
Still with a child : nor think that I prefer
Perseus to thee, but to the loss of her.'
Phineus on him and Perseus roll'd about
His eyes in silent rage, and seem'd to doubt
Which to destroy ; till, resolute at length,
He threw his spear with the redoubled strength
His fury gave him, and at Perseus struck ;
But missing Perseus, in his seat it stuck :
Who, springing nimbly up, return'd the dart,
And almost plung'd it in his rival's heart—
But he for safety to the altar ran,
Unfit protection for so vile a man."

OVID.

No. 487.

The birth of Orion,

DIOSCORIDES. *Oriental Cornelian.*

Jupiter, Neptune, and Mercury, in the course of a journey which they made on earth, arrived at the dwelling of Hyrieus, a poor man, a widower without children, who, though he had made a vow never to marry again, earnestly desired a son, and besought the gods to grant him one. They, grateful for the hospitable reception they had met with from Hyrieus, caused the skin of an ox which had been sacrificed to their divinity to be brought them; and steeping it in water, they directed Hyrieus to bury it in the ground for nine months, assuring him that from it would proceed a child.

No. 488.

Orion and Merope.

APOLLONIDES. *Oriental Sardonyx.*

Orion was very skilful in the chase, and when in Scio, for the purpose of destroying the wild beasts which infested the island, he became enamoured of Merope, the daughter of Œnopion, king of that country, and asked her in marriage of her father.

No. 489.

Œnopion intoxicating Orion.

CHROMIOS. *Oriental Cornelian.*

Œnopion, to revenge himself on Orion, intoxicates him and puts out his eye.

No. 490.

Orion consulting Vulcan.

APOLLONIDES. *Oriental Sardonyx.*

Orion on finding himself blind, consulted Vulcan about a remedy for his misfortune, who advised him to keep his face always turned towards the sun; and thus Orion recovered his sight.

No. 491.

The death of Orion.

DIOSCORIDES. *Oriental Sardonyx.*

Orion made a vow to exterminate all the wild beasts which he met with. Diana, indignant at this, sent a scorpion, whose sting proved fatal to him, and he died.

" Who that the scorpion's insect-form surveys
  Would think how ready Death his call obeys?
  Threat'ning, he rears his knotty tail on high:
  The vast Orion thus he doom'd to die,
  And fix'd him his proud trophy in the sky."

                          LUCAN, book ix.: ROWE.

No. 492.

Diana killing Orion.

PEMALLIO.   *Oriental Cornelian.*

Some mythologians assert that Diana, jealous of Orion's skill in the chase, killed him
herself.

" Ungracious gods! with spite and envy curst,
  Still to your own ethereal race the worst;
  Ye envy mortal and immortal joy,
  And love, the only sweet of life, destroy.
  Did ever goddess by her charms engage
  A favour'd mortal, and not feel your rage?
  So when Aurora sought Orion's love,
  Her joys disturb'd your blissful hours above,
  Till, in Ortygia, Dian's winged dart
  Had pierc'd the hapless hunter to the heart."

                          HOMER, *Odyssey* v.

_____

" And warm Orion, who, with impious love
  Tempting the goddess of the sylvan scene,
  Was by her virgin darts, gigantic victim! slain."

                          HOR. book iii. Od. 14.

No. 493.

Orion in Hades.

LICINIOS.   *Oriental Cornelian.*

Homer (*Odyssey*, book ii.) has transmitted to us the opinion of the ancients, who believed
that in the kingdom of Pluto the souls of the departed continued to occupy themselves with the
same pursuits which interested them on earth.   Orion is here seen, still gigantic in figure, armed
with two lances, and pursuing a lion, a tiger, and a wolf, in the infernal regions.

" There huge Orion, of portentous size,
Swift through the gloom a giant-hunter flies;
A ponderous mace of brass with direful sway
Aloft he whirls, to crush the savage prey ;
Stern beasts in trains that by his truncheon fell,
Now grisly forms shoot o'er the lawns of hell."

HOMER, Odyssey v.

" Next the bright twins see great Orion rise,
His arms extended stretch o'er half the skies ;
His stride as large; and with a stately pace
He marches on, and measures a vast space.
On each broad shoulder a bright star's display'd,
And three obliquely grace his shining blade ;
In his vast head, immers'd in boundless spheres,
Three stars less bright, but yet as great, he bears ;
Though, farther off remov'd, their splendour 's lost :
Thus grac'd and arm'd, he leads the starry host."

MANILIUS : CREECH.

No. 494.

The same subject.

APOLLONIDES. *Oriental Cornelian.*

No. 495.

Venus animating her statue made by Pygmalion.

ONESAS. *Oriental Cornelian.*

Pygmalion, king of Cyprus and grandfather of Adonis, was so intoxicated with the beauty of a statue he had made, that he begged of Venus to endue it with life. Venus consented, and she became his wife, and the mother of Paphus and Cinyras.

" Pygmalion, frighted with the many crimes
That rule in women, chose a single life,
And long forbore the pleasures of a wife.
Meanwhile in ivory with happy art
A statue carves, so graceful in each part,
As woman never equall'd it ; and stands
Affected to the fabric of his hands.

It seem'd a virgin full of living flame,
That would have mov'd, if not withheld by
    shame.
Such art his art conceal'd ; which he admires,
And from it draws imaginary fires ;
Then often feels it with his hands, to try
If 'twere a body, or cold ivory :

Nor could resolve. Who kissing, thought it kiss'd;
Oft courts, embraces, wrings it by the wrist,
The flesh impressing (his conceit was such),
And fears to hurt it with too rude a touch.
Now flatters her; now sparkling stones presents,
And orient pearl (love's witching instruments);
Soft-singing birds, each several-colour'd flower:
First, lilies, painted balls, and tears that pour
From weeping trees.   Rich robes her person
        deck;
Her fingers, rings; reflecting gems, her neck;
Pendants, her ears; a glitt'ring zone, her breast,—
In all shew'd well; but shew'd when naked best.
Now lays he her upon a gorgeous bed,
With carpets of Sidonian purple spread.
Now calls her wife.   Her head a pillow press'd
Of plumy down, as if with sense possess'd.
Now came the day of Venus' festival,
Through wealthy Cyprus solemnised by all;
White heifers, deck'd with golden horns, by
        strokes
Of axes fall; ascending incense smokes.
He with his gift before the altar stands:
' You gods, if all we crave be in your hands,
Give me the wife I wish; one like,' he said,
But durst not say, ' Give me my ivory maid.'
The golden Venus, present at her feast,
Conceives his wish, and friendly signs express'd :

The fire thrice blazing, thrice in flames aspires.
To his admired image he retires :
Lies down beside her, rais'd her with his arm;
Then kiss'd her tempting lips, and found them
        warm.
That lesson oft repeats; her bosom oft
With amorous touches feels, and felt it soft.
The ivory, dimpled with his fingers, lacks
Accustom'd hardness; as Hymettia wax
Relents with heat, which chafing thumbs reduce
To pliant forms, by handling fram'd for use.
Amaz'd with doubtful joys, and hope that reels,
Again the lover what he wishes feels;
The veins beneath his thumb's impression beat,—
A perfect virgin full of juice and heat.
The Cyprian prince, with joy-expressing words,
The pleasure-giving Venus thanks affords.
His lips to her he joins, which seems to melt—
The blushing virgin now his kisses felt;
And fearfully erecting her fair eyes,
Together with the light her lover spies.
Venus the marriage bless'd which she had made :
And when nine crescents had at full display'd
Their joining horns, replete with borrow'd flame,
She Paphus bore, who gave that isle a name ;
He Cinyras begot, who might be styl'd
Of men most happy, if without a child."

OVID: SANDYS.

No. 496.

Cinyras discovering Myrrha.

PYRGOTELES.   *Calcedony, partaking of Sapphire.*

Cinyras, king of Cyprus, son of Pygmalion and the statue, desirous. to ascertain who was
in his bed, lighted a torch, and discovered his daughter Myrrha. He seized a sword to kill
her, but Myrrha, covering her face, fled.

No. 497.

Cinyras striking with his sword the tree Myrrha.

Chromios. *Calcedony, partaking of Sapphire.*

Myrrha, pursued by her father to the forest, whither she had fled, implores the protection of the gods; and she was metamorphosed to the odorous plant which bears her name.

" Sabæan fields afford her needful rest.
There loathing life, and yet of death afraid,
In anguish of her spirit thus she pray'd:
' Ye pow'rs, if any so propitious are
T' accept my penitence and hear my pray'r;
Your judgments I confess are justly sent,—
Great sins deserve as great a punishment:
Yet since my life the living will profane,
And since my death the happy dead will stain,
A middle state your mercy may bestow,
Betwixt the realms above and those below:
Some other form to wretched Myrrha give,
Nor let her wholly die, nor wholly live.'
The prayers of penitents are never vain;
At least she did her last request obtain:
For while she spoke, the ground began to rise,
And gather'd round her feet, her legs, and thighs;
Her toes in roots descend, and spreading wide,
A firm foundation for the trunk provide;
Her solid bones convert to solid wood,
To pith her marrow, and to sap her blood;
Her arms are boughs, her fingers change their kind,
Her tender skin is harden'd into rind.
And now the rising tree her form invests,
Now shooting upwards still, invades her breasts,
And shades the neck; when, weary with delay,
She sunk her head within, and met it half the way.
And though with outward shape she lost her sense,
With bitter tears she wept her last offence;
And still she weeps, nor sheds her tears in vain
For still the precious drops her name retain."

Ovid.

No. 498.

The birth of Adonis in the midst of the Naiads.

Dioscorides. *Amethyst.*

" The ready nymphs receive the crying child,
And wash him in the tears the parent plant distill'd;
They swath'd him with their scarfs, beneath him spread
The ground with herbs, with roses rais'd his head.
The lovely babe was born with ev'ry grace,
E'en envy must have prais'd so fair a face.
Such was his form as painters when they shew
Their utmost art on naked loves bestow;
And that their arms no diff'rence might betray,
Give him a bow, or his from Cupid take away.
Time glides along with undiscover'd haste,
The future but a length behind the past;
So swift are years."

Ovid.

No. 499.

Venus presenting the infant Adonis in a basket to Proserpine.

APOLLONIDES.   *Oriental Sardonyx.*

No. 500.

Adonis wounded by the thorns of a rose.

GNAIOS.   *Oriental Cornelian.*

No. 501.

Venus foreseeing the misfortune which would befall Adonis, who is about
to depart to hunt the wild boar, seeks to detain him.

DIOSCORIDES.   *Sardonyx.*

" Thee too, Adonis, with a lover's care
She warns, if warn'd thou wouldst avoid the
      snare.
To furious animals advance not nigh,
Fly those that follow, follow those that fly;
'Tis chance alone must the survivors save,
Whene'er brave spirits will attempt the brave.
O, lovely youth ! in harmless sports delight,
Provoke not beasts which armed by nature fight :
For me, if not thyself, vouchsafe to fear,
Let not thy thirst of glory cost me dear.

Boars know not how to spare a blooming age ;
No sparkling eyes can soothe the lion's rage.
Not all thy charms a savage breast can move,
Which have so deeply touch'd the queen of love.
When bristled boars from beaten thickets spring,
In grinded tusks a thunderbolt they bring.
The daring hunters lions roused devour,
Vast is their fury, and as vast their power,—
Curst be their tawny race !"

OVID.

" If Love hath lent you twenty thousand tongues,
   And every tongue more moving than your own,
   Bewitching, like the wanton mermaid's songs,
   Yet from mine ear the tempting tune is blown ;
   For know, my heart stands armed in my ear,
   And will not let a false sound enter there.

   With this he breaketh from the sweet embrace
   Of those fair arms, which bound him to her breast,
   And homewards through the dark lawns runs apace."

SHAKSPEARE.

No. 502.

Adonis, armed with a lance, attacking the wild boar.

POLYCLETES.   *Oriental Cornelian.*

No. 503.

Adonis mortally wounded in the thigh by the wild boar.

APOLLONIDES.   *Oriental Cornelian.*

" Thus cautious Venus school'd her fav'rite boy,
But youthful heat all cautions will destroy ;
His sprightly soul beyond grave counsels flies,
While with yok'd swans the goddess cuts the skies.
His faithful hounds, led by the tainted wind,
Lodg'd in thick coverts chanc'd a boar to find ;
The callow hero shew'd a manly heart,
And pierc'd the savage with a side-long dart.
The flying savage wounded turn'd again,
Wrench'd out the gory dart, and foam'd with pain.
The trembling boy by flight his safety sought,
And now recall'd the lore which Venus taught ;
But now too late to fly the boar he strove,
Who in the groin his tusks impetuous drove :
On the discolour'd grass Adonis lay,
The monster trampling o'er his beauteous prey."

OVID.

No. 504.

Adonis dying in the arms of Venus.

GNAIOS.   *Sardonyx.*

No. 505.

Adonis lifeless, and near him Venus in despair, who is producing the anemone.

CHROMIOS.   *Oriental Cornelian.*

LAMENT FOR ADONIS.

" I and the Loves Adonis dead deplore ;
The beautiful Adonis is indeed
Departed—parted from us. Sleep no more
In purple, Cypris ! but in loathed weed
All wretched beat thy breast, and all aread,
' Adonis is no more !' The Loves and I
Lament him. O, her grief to see him bleed !
Smitten by white tooth on a whiter thigh,
Outbreathing life's faint sight upon the mountain high :
Adown his snowy flesh drops the black gore ;
Stiffen beneath his brow his sightless eyes ;
The rose is off his lip. With him no more
Lives Cytherea's kiss, but with him dies ;
He knows not that her lip his cold lip tries,
But she finds pleasure still in kissing him.
Deep is his thigh-wound ; her's yet deeper lies,
E'en in her heart. The Oreads' eyes are dim ;
His hounds whine piteously, in most disorder'd trim.

Distraught, unkempt, unsandall'd, Cypris
  rushes
Madly along the tangled thicket-steep;
Her sacred blood is drawn, by bramble-bushes
Her skin is torn; with wailings wild and deep
She wanders through the valley's weary sweep,
Calling her boy-spouse her Assyrian fere.
But from his thigh the purple jet doth leap
Up to his snowy navel; on the clear
Whiteness beneath his paps the deep red streaks
  appear.

' Alas for Cypris!' sigh the Loves: ' depriv'd
Of her fair spouse she lost her beauty's pride;
  ypris was lovely whilst Adonis lived,
But with Adonis all her beauty died.'
Mountains, and oaks, and streams that broadly
  glide,
Or wail or weep for her; in fearful rills
For her gush fountains from the mountain-side;
Redden the flow'rs from grief; city and hills
With ditties sadly wild lorn Cytherea fills.

Alas for Cypris! dead is her Adonis!
And echo ' dead Adonis' doth resound.
Who would not grieve for her whose love so
  lone is?
But when she saw his cruel, cruel wound,
The purple gore that ran his wan thigh round,
She spread her arms, and lowly murmur'd —
  ' Stay thee!
That I may find thee as before I found,
My hapless own Adonis! and embay thee,
And mingle lips with lips whilst in my arms I
  lay thee.

' Up for a little! kiss me back again
The latest kiss—brief as itself, that dies
In being breathed—until I fondly drain
The last breath of thy soul, and greedywise
Drink it into my core. I will devise
To guard it as Adonis; since from me
To Acheron my own Adonis flies,
And to the drear, dread king; but I must be
A goddess still and live, nor can I follow thee.

But thou, Persephona! my spouse receive,
Mightier than I, since to thy chamber drear
All bloom of beauty falls; but I must grieve
Unceasingly. I have a jealous fear
Of thee, and weep for him. My dearest dear,
Art dead indeed? Away my love did fly,
E'en as a dream! At home my widow'd cheer
Keeps the Loves idle; with thy latest sigh
My cestus perished too. Thou rash one! why,
  O why

Did'st hunt — so fair contend with monsters
  grim ?'
Thus Cypris wail'd; but dead Adonis lies.
For ev'ry gout of blood that fell from him
She drops a tear: sweet flowers each dew sup-
  plies—
Roses his blood, her tears anemonies.
Cypris no longer in the thickets creep,
The couch is furnished! There in loving guise,
Upon thy proper bed, that odorous heap,
The lovely body lies—how lovely! as in sleep.

Come, in those vestments now array him
In which he slept the livelong night with thee,
And in the golden settle gently lay him—
A sad yet lovely sight! and let him be
High heap'd with flowers, though wither'd all
  when he
Surceas'd. With essences him sprinkle o'er,
And ointments; let them perish utterly,
Since he who was thy sweetest is no more !
He lies in purple ; him the weeping Loves deplore.

Their curls are shorn: one breaks his bow,
  another
His arrows and the quiver; this unstrings
And takes Adonis' sandals off; his brother
In golden urn the fountain-water brings;
This bathes his thighs, that fans him with his
  wings.
The Loves, ' Alas for Cypris!' weeping say :
' Hymen hath quench'd his torches, shreds
  and flings
The marriage-wreath away ; and for the lay
Of love is only heard the doleful ' weal-away !'

Yet more than Hymen for Adonis weep :
The Graces shriller than Dione vent
Their shrieks; for him the Muses wail, and
    keep
Singing the songs he hears not, with intent
To call him back ; and would the nymph relent,

How willingly would he the Muses hear!
Hush, hush, to-day, sad Cypris ! and consent
To spare thyself—no more thy bosom tear ;
For thou must wail again, and weep another
    year."
                                BION.

"Since thou art dead, lo ! here I prophesy,
  Sorrow on love hereafter shall attend ;
It shall be waited on with jealousy,
  Find sweet beginning, but unsavoury end ;
Ne'er settled equally, too high or low,
That all love's pleasures shall not match his woe.

It shall be fickle, false, and full of fraud,
  And shall be blasted in a breathing while ;
The bottom poison, and the top o'erstraw'd
    With sweets that shall the sharpest sight be-
      guile.
The strongest body shall it make most weak,
Strike the wise dumb, and teach the fool to speak.

It shall be sparing, and the fool of riot,
  Teaching decrepit age to tread the measures ;
The staring ruffian shall it keep in quiet,
    Pluck down the rich, enrich the poor with
      treasures :

It shall be raging mad and silly mild,
Make the young old, the old become a child.

It shall suspect, where is no cause of fear ;
  It shall not fear, where it should most mis-
    trust ;
It shall be merciful, and too severe,
  And most deceiving when it seems most just :
Perverse it shall be, when it seems most toward ;
Put fear to valour, courage to the coward.

It shall be cause of war and dire events,
  And set dissension 'twixt the son and sire ;
Subject and servile to all discontents,
  As dry combustious matter is to fire.
Sith in his prime death doth my love destroy,
They that love best their love shall not enjoy."
      SHAKSPEARE, *Lamentation of Venus*
                     on Adonis.

" Alas ! poor world, what treasure hast thou lost !
What face remains alive that's worth the viewing ?
Whose tongue is music now ? What canst thou boast
Of things long since, or any thing ensuing ?
The flowers are sweet, their colours fresh and trim,
But true sweet beauty liv'd and died in him."
                  SHAKSPEARE.

" Fair Cytherea, Cypris scarce in view,
Heard from afar his groans, and own'd them
    true,
And turn'd her snowy swans, and backward flew.
But as she saw him gasp his latest breath,
And quiv'ring agonise in pangs of death,
Down with swift flight she plung'd, nor rage for-
    bore :
At once her garments and her hair she tore ;

With cruel blows she beat her guiltless breast,
The Fates upbraided, and her love confess'd.
' Nor shall they yet (she cried) the whole de-
    vour
With uncontroll'd inexorable pow'r ;
For thee, lost youth, my tears and restless pain
Shall in immortal monuments remain.
With solemn pomp in annual rites return'd,
Be thou for ever, my Adonis, mourn'd.'

Could Pluto's queen with jealous fury storm,
And Menthe to a fragrant herb transform ;
Yet dares not Venus with a change surprise,
And in a flow'r bid her fall'n hero rise ?
Then on the blood sweet nectar she bestows,
The scented blood in little bubbles rose,
Little as rainy drops, which flutt'ring fly
Borne by the winds along a low'ring sky.
Short time ensu'd till where the blood was shed,
A flower began to rear its purple head :

Such as on Punic apples is revealed,
Or in the filmy rind but half concealed ;
Still here the fate of lovely forms we see,
So sudden fades the sweet anemony :
The feeble stems to stormy blasts a prey,
Their sickly beauties droop and pine away ;
The winds forbid the flow'rs to flourish long,
Which owe to winds their names in Grecian
    song."

OVID.

No. 506.

Adonis metamorphosed into a rose.

PYRGOTELES. *Oriental Sardonyx.*

In spite of the general opinion of mythologians, that Adonis was metamorphosed to an anemone, the artist has here represented a rose, the cherished flower of Venus; and to render it well, he has taken advantage of a more transparent portion of the stone.

No. 507.

Liriope (Lily-voice), daughter of Ocean and Tethys, and mother of Narcissus, consulting Tiresias on the fate of her son.

APOLLONIDES. *Oriental Sardonyx.*

" The tender dame, solicitous to know
  Whether her child should reach old age or no,
  Consults the sage Tiresias ; who replies,
  If e'er he knows himself, he surely dies."

OVID.

No. 508.

Narcissus gazing on himself in the waters of a fountain.

GNAIOS. *Oriental Cornelian.*

" There stands a fountain in a darksome wood,
Nor stain'd with falling leaves nor rising mud ;
Untroubled by the breath of winds it rests,
Unsullied by the touch of men or beasts;

High bow'rs of shady trees above it grow,
And rising grass and cheerful greens below.
Pleas'd with the form and coolness of the place,
And over-heated by the morning chase,

Narcissus on the grassy verdure lies;
But whilst within the crystal fount he tries
To quench his heat, he feels new heats arise.
For as his own bright image he survey'd,
He fell in love with the fantastic shade;
And o'er the fair resemblance hung unmov'd,
Nor knew, fond youth, it was himself he lov'd.
The well-turu'd neck and shoulders he descries,
The spacious forehead and the sparkling eyes;
The hands that Bacchus might not scorn to shew,
And hair that round Apollo's head might flow;

With all the purple youthfulness of face,
That gently blushes in the wat'ry glass:
By his own flames consum'd the lover lies,
And gives himself the wound by which he dies.
To the cold water oft he joins his lips,
Oft catching at the beauteous shade he dips
His arms, as often from himself he slips,
Nor knows he who it is his arms pursue
With eager clasps, but loves he knows not who.'

OVID.

No. 509.

Narcissus, even after his death captivated by his own beauty, gazing on himself in the muddy waters of Acheron.

CHROMIOS.   *Oriental Cornelian.*

No. 510.

Echo pursuing Narcissus.

POLYCLETES.   *Oriental Sardonyx.*

The nymph Echo, daughter of Earth and Air, inhabited the banks of the Cephisus. Falling desperately in love with Narcissus, he slighted her, and she retired into the deepest caverns and thickest forests, where, perpetually shedding tears, she at length became a stone with the power of speech.

" And many a maid his beauty set on fire:
Yet in his tender age his pride was such,
That neither youth nor maiden might him touch.
The vocal nymph this lovely boy did spy,
(She could not proffer speech, nor yet reply),
When, busy in pursuit of savage spoils,
He drove the deer into his corded toils.
Echo was then a body, not a voice;
Yet then as now of words she wanted choice,
But only could reiterate the close
Of every speech.   This Juno did impose.

For often when she might have taken Jove
Compressing there the nymphs who weakly strove,
Her long discourses made the goddess stay
Until the nymphs had time to run away.
Which when perceiv'd, she said: ' For this abuse
Thy tongue henceforth shall be of little use.'
Those threats are deeds; she yet ingeminates
The last of sounds, and what she hears relates.
   Narcissus seen, intending thus the chase,
She forthwith glows, and with a noiseless pace

His steps pursues. The more she did pursue,
More hot (as nearer to her fire) she grew;
And might be likened to a sulph'rous match,
Which instantly th' approached flame doth catch.
How oft would she have woo'd him with sweet words !
But nature no such liberty affords.
Begin she could not, yet full readily
To his expected speech she would reply.
The boy, from his companions parted, said :
' Is any nigh ?'—' I !' Echo answer made.
He round about him gazed (much appall'd),
And cried out, ' Come.' She him who called, call'd.
Then looking back, and seeing none appear'd,
' Why shun'st thou me ?' The self-same voice he heard.
Deceived by the image of his words,
' Then let us join,' said he. No sound accords
More to her wish ; her faculties combine
In dear consent, who answer'd, ' Let us join.'
Flattering herself, out of the woods she sprung,
And would about his struggling neck have hung.
Thrust back, he said, ' Life shall this breast forsake,
Ere thou, light nymph, on me thy pleasure take.'
' On me thy pleasure take,' the nymph replies
To that disdainful boy, who from her flies.
Despis'd, the wood her sad retreat receives,
Who covers her asham'd face with leaves,
And skulks in desert caves. Love still possess'd
Her soul, through grief of her repulse increas'd.
Her wretched body pines with sleepless care,
Her skin contracts, her blood converts to air :
Nothing was left her now but voice and bones—
The voice remains, the other turn to stones :
Conceal'd in woods, in mountains never found,
Yet heard in all; and all is but a sound."

OVID.

No. 511.

The death of Hyacinthus.

DIOSCORIDES. *Oriental Cornelian.*

Hyacinthus of Amyclæ, a town of Laconia, was the son of Œbolus, or, as some affirm, of Amyclas and Diomede, and a young man of extraordinary beauty. He was beloved at the same time by Apollo and Boreas; and while playing at quoits with Apollo, who was the first to throw, Boreas from spite turned it aside with his breath, and caused it to fall on the head of Hyacinthus, which killed him. Apollo, inconsolable for his loss, changed him into a hyacinth, that "sanguine flower inscribed with woe," and which is sculptured springing up near the lifeless body.

" The mid-day sun now shone with equal light
Between the past and the succeeding night ;
They strip, then, smooth'd with suppling oil, essay
To pitch the rounded quoit, their wonted play.
A well-pois'd disk first hasty Phœbus threw,
It cleft the air, and whistled as it flew ;
It reach'd the mark, a most surprising length,
Which spoke an equal share of art and strength.
Scarce was it fall'n, when with too eager hand
Young Hyacinth ran to snatch it from the sand ;
But the curst orb, which met a stony soil,
Flew in his face with violent recoil.
Both faint, both pale and breathless now appear,
The boy with pain, the am'rous god with fear;
He ran, and rais'd him bleeding from the ground,
Chafes his cold limbs, and wipes the fatal wound ;

Then herbs of noblest juice in vain applies,
The wound is mortal, and his skill defies.
As in a water'd garden's blooming walk,
When some rude hand has bruis'd its tender
    stalk,
A fading lily droops its languid head,
And bends to earth, its life and beauty fled ;
So Hyacinth with head reclin'd decays,
And sick'ning, now no more his charms displays.
' O, thou art gone, my boy (Apollo cried),
Defrauded of thy youth in all its pride !
Thou, once my joy, art all my sorrow now,
And to my guilty hand my grief I owe ;
Yet from myself I might the fault remove,
Unless to sport and play a fault should prove,
Unless it too were call'd a fault to love.
O, could I for thee, or but with thee die !
But cruel fates to me that pow'r deny.
Yet on my tongue thou shalt for ever dwell,
Thy name my lyre shall sound, my verse shall
    tell :

And to a flow'r transform'd, unheard of yet,
Stamp'd on thy leaves my cries thou shalt repeat.
The time shall come, prophetic I foreknow,
When join'd to thee a mighty chief shall grow,
And with my plaints his name thy leaf shall shew.'
    While Phœbus thus the laws of Fate reveal'd,
Behold the blood which stain'd the verdant field
Is blood no longer ; but a flow'r full blown
Far brighter than the Tyrian scarlet shone.
A lily's form it took ; its purple hue
Was all that made a diff'rence to the view.
Nor stopp'd he here ; the god upon its leaves
The sad expression of his sorrow weaves ;
And to this hour the mournful purple wears
' Ai, Ai,' inscrib'd in funeral characters.
Nor are the Spartans, who so much are fam'd
For virtue, of their hyacinth asham'd ;
But still, with pompous woe and solemn state,
The hyacinthian feasts they yearly celebrate."

OVID.

" Phœbus tried all his means, and thought of new,
    Scarce knowing what he did in his distress ;
With nectar bathed him, with ambrosial dew,
    But Fate made remedies remediless."

BION.

No. 512.

Apollo, touching the body of Hyacinthus with his bow, changes it to a flower.

APOLLONIDES.   *Oriental Cornelian.*

No. 513.

Apollo consoling Cyparissus.

PYRGOTELES.   *Oriental Amethyst.*

Cyparissus, the son of Telaphus, was beloved by Apollo. He had a tame stag, of which he was exceedingly fond, and Cyparissus being one day at the chase, accidentally killed it, which so afflicted him, that he petitioned Apollo to deprive him of life.

" 'Twas when the summer sun at noon of day
Through glowing Cancer shot his burning ray;
'Twas then the fav'rite stag in cool retreat
Had sought a shelter from the scorching heat;
Along the grass his weary limbs he laid,
Inhaling freshness from the breezy shade;
When Cyparissus with his pointed dart,
Unknowing, pierc'd him to the panting heart.
But when the youth, surpris'd, his error found,
And saw him dying of the cruel wound,

Himself he would have slain through desp'rate
    grief.
What said not Phœbus that might yield relief?
To cease his mourning he the boy desir'd,
Or mourn no more than such a loss requir'd.
But he, incessant griev'd, at length address'd
To the superior pow'rs a last request;
Praying, in expiation of his crime,
Thenceforth to mourn to all succeeding time."
                                        OVID.

No. 514.

Apollo changing young Cyparissus to a tree.

CHROMIOS.   *Oriental Cornelian.*

" And now of blood exhausted he appears,
    Drain'd by a torrent of continual tears;
    The fleshy colour in his body fades,
    And a green tincture all his limbs invades;
    From his fair head, where curling locks late hung,
    A horrid bush with bristled branches sprung,
    Which, stiff'ning by degrees, its stem extends
    Till to the starry skies the spire ascends.
    Apollo sad look'd on, and sighing cried,
    'Then be for ever what thy pray'r implied;
    Bemoan'd by me, in others grief excite,
    And still preside at ev'ry fun'ral rite.' "
                                        OVID.

No. 515.

Marsyas teaching Olympus to play on the flute.

DIOSCORIDES.   *Calcedony.*

Marsyas, the Phrygian, in the form of a faun, indicated by his horns and tail, in the act of teaching music to young Olympus, who afterwards became celebrated in the art by his invention of the double flute and the Lydian measure, which is animated, tender, and passionate.

No. 516.

The punishment of Marsyas.

SOLON. *Oriental Sardonyx.*

Marsyas challenging Apollo to a trial of his skill as a musician, was vanquished, and punished by the god for his temerity by being tied to a tree and flayed by a Scythian.

"Thus much I know not by what Theban said,
Another mention of a satyr made,
By Phœbus with Tritonia's reed o'ercome,
Who for presuming felt an heavy doom.
'Me from myself, ah! why do you distract?
O! I repent, he cried: alas! this fact
Deserves not such a vengeance.' Whilst he cried,
Apollo from his body stript his hide:
His body was one wound, blood every way
Streams from all parts; his sinews naked lay,
His bare veins pant; his heart you might behold,
And all the fibres in his breast have told.

For him the fauns that in the forests keep,
For him the nymphs and brother satyrs weep;
His end Olympus (famous then) bewails,
With all the shepherds of those hills and dales.
The pregnant earth conceiveth with their tears,
Which in her penetrated womb she bears,
Till big with water, then discharg'd her fraught.
This purest Phrygian stream a way outsought
By downfalls, till to toiling seas he came,
Now called Marsyas of the satyr's name."

OVID: SANDYS.

"'This I fain would learn,' said I,
'Why this thy day is called Quinquatrie.'
'March hath my feasts too of this name,' said she:
''Twas my invention rais'd this company.
I first the pipe of bored box did frame
With certain holes, and play'd upon the same.
Sweet were the notes; but when as I beheld
My face i' th' spring, I spy'd my cheeks all swell'd:
'I prize thee not so high, my pipe,' said I;
'Farewell,' and cast it on a bank thereby.

A satyr finds it; but the use unfound,
Admires; at last he blows, and hears a sound.
Now could his warbling fingers play their part,
And make the nymphs admire his vaunted art.
He challeng'd Phœbus; Phœbus got the day,
Who hung him up, and took his skin away.
Yet I'm th' inventress of this pipe; therefore
This company these days do me adore.'"

Fasti: GOWER.

No. 517.

Chiron and Orpheus trying their skill on the lyre.

CHROMIOS. *Cornelian.*

Orpheus, the son of Œager, king of Thrace, was among the number of the Argonauts. When the ship Argo touched on the shores of Thessaly, at the foot of mount Pelion, Orpheus and Jason disembarked, and proceeded to the dwelling of the centaur Chiron. Jason prevailed

P P

on the two heroes to play on the lyre, when the superiority of Orpheus in this science was acknowledged even by Chiron himself.

" First in the list, to join the princely bands,
    The tuneful bard, enchanting Orpheus, stands;
    Whom fair Calliope, on Thracia's shore,
    Near Pimpla's mount to bold Œagrus bore.
    Hard rocks he soften'd with persuasive song,
    And sooth'd the rivers as they roll'd along.
    Yon beeches tall, that bloom near Zona, still
    Remain memorials of his vocal skill:
    His lays Pieria's listening trees admire,
    And move in measures to his melting lyre.
    Thus Orpheus charm'd, who o'er the Bistons reign'd,
    By Chiron's art to Jason's interest gain'd."

                        APOL. RHODIUS.

" Ye sisters, smile, sweet harbingers of verse,
    Your Orpheus foremost of the train rehearse;
    Whom, fair Calliope, thy virgin charms
    Gave to the raptures of Œagrus' arms;
    Sprung from soft Pimpla's ever-verdant height
    First wak'd the infant harmonist to light,
    Pierc'd by the magic of whose shell the streams
    To silence sink, the rock with beauty teems;
    The vast beech, conscious of his warbled lore,
    Whose zones of foliage gloom the sullen shore
    E'en to earth's central reign, the dulcet song
    Led from Pieria's vale, a ravish'd throng."

                        APOL. RHODIUS.

" The Thracian bard, surrounded by the rest,
    There stands conspicuous in his flowing vest;
    His flying fingers and harmonious quill
    Strike sev'n distinguish'd notes, and sev'n at once they fill."

                        VIRGIL.

"Twas then, the jarring heroes to compose,
Th' enchanting bard, Œagrian Orpheus rose,
And thus, attuning to the trembling strings
His soothing voice, of harmony he sings:
'How at the first, beneath chaotic sway,
Heaven, earth, and sea, in wild disorder lay;
Till nature parted the conflicting foes,
And beauteous order from confusion rose.

How in yon bright ethereal fields above
The lucid stars in constant orbits move;
How the pale queen of night and golden sun
Through months and years their radiant journeys run;
Whence rose the mountains, clad with waving woods,
The crystal founts, and hoarse-resounding floods,

With all their nymphs: from what celestial seed
Springs the vast species of the serpent breed;
How o'er the new-created world below,
On high Olympus' summits crown'd with snow,
Ophion, and, from ocean sprung of old,
The fair Eurynome reign'd uncontroll'd;
How haughty Saturn, with superior sway,
Exil'd Ophion from the realms of day;
Eurynome before proud Rhea fled,
And how both sunk in ocean's billowy bed.
Long time they rul'd the blest Titanian gods,
While infant Jove possess'd the dark abodes
Of Dictè's cave; yet uninform'd his mind
With heavenly wisdom, and his hand confin'd.

Forg'd by earth's giant sons, with livid rays
Flam'd not as yet the lightning's piercing blaze,
Nor roar'd the thunder through the realms above,
The strength and glory of almighty Jove.'
 Here the sweet bard his tuneful lyre unstrung,
And ceas'd the heavenly music of his tongue;
But, with the sound entranc'd, the listening ear
Still thought him singing, and still seem'd to hear;
In silent rapture every chief remains,
And feels within his heart the thrilling strains.
Forthwith the bowl they crown with rosy wine,
And pay due honours to the powers divine;
Then on the flaming tongues libations pour,
And wait salubrious sleep's composing hour."
                                    APOL. RHO.

" The wood-born race of men whom Orpheus tam'd,
From acorns and from mutual blood reclaim'd:
This priest divine was fabled to assuage
The tiger's fierceness and the lion's rage.
Thus rose the Theban wall; Amphion's lyre
And soothing voice the listening stones inspire.
Poetic wisdom mark'd, with happy mean,
Public and private, sacred and profane;
The wand'ring joys of lawless love suppress'd,
With equal rites the wedded couple bless'd;
Plann'd future towns, and instituted laws:
So verse became divine, and poets gain'd applause."
                                    HOR. *Art. Poet.*

" Lead'st thou the votive choir
To Nyssa's mount, where savage beasts abound;
Qn steep Corycian summits art thou found;
Or dost thou haunt Olympus' shadowy cave,
 Where Orpheus erst, with magic lyre,
Collected trees that listen'd to his strain,
And lur'd the howling lion from the plain?
 O blest Pierian mount!

Revering thee, ere long will Bacchus lead
His shouting followers to the Muses' fount;
 And crossing Axius' rapid spring,
 The Mænades to Lydia bring,
Streaming with joys exhaustless and refin'd,
 Bounteous parent of mankind,
 Whose waters glide through regions fam'd
For coursers which outstrip the wind."
                        EURIPIDES, *Bacch.:* WOODHULL.

No. 518.

Orpheus charming the brutes with the sound of his lyre.

GNAIOS. *Oriental Cornelian.*

No. 519.

Eurydice bitten by a serpent while pursued by Aristæus.

APOLLONIDES. *Sardonyx.*

" To shun thy lawless lust, the dying bride
Unwary took along the river's side,
Nor at her heels perceived the deadly snake,
That keeps the bank in covert of the brake.
But all her fellow-nymphs the mountains tear
With loud laments, and break the yielding air;
The realms of Mars re-murmured all around,
And echoes to the Athenian shores resound."

VIRGIL.

No. 520.

Orpheus redeeming Eurydice.

AGLAOS. *Oriental Cornelian.*

Eurydice, the wife of Orpheus, while pursued by Aristæus, was bitten by a serpent, which caused her death, and left Orpheus inconsolable. Her husband, however, resolved on going to the kingdom of Pluto to endeavour to regain her, and bring her back to earth; which is granted, on condition that he does not look at her till they reach the earth.

" Sad Orpheus doom'd, without a crime, to mourn
His ravish'd bride, that never shall return,
Wild for her loss, calls down th' inflicted woes,
And deadlier threatens, if no fate oppose.
When urged by thee along the marshy bed,
Th' unhappy nymph in frantic terror fled,
She saw not, doom'd to die, across her way,
Where, couch'd beneath the grass, the serpent lay.
But ev'ry dryad, their companion dead,
O'er the high rocks their echo'd clamour spread;
The Rhodopeian mounts with sorrow rung;
Deep wailings burst Pangæa's cliffs among;
Sad Orythyia and the Getæ wept,
And loud lament down plaintive Hebrus swept.

He, lonely, on his harp, mid wilds unknown,
Sooth'd his sad love with melancholy tone.
On thee, sweet bride, still dwelt th' undying lay,
The first at dawn deplor'd, the last at close of day.
For thee he dar'd to pass the jaws of hell,
And gates where death and darkness ever dwell,
Trod with firm foot in horror's gloomy grove,
Approach'd the throne of subterraneous Jove,
Nor fear'd the manes and stern host below,
And hearts that never felt for human woe.
Drawn by his song from Erebus profound,
Shades and unbodied phantoms flock around,
Countless as birds that fill the leafy bow'r
Beneath pale eve, or winter's driving show'r;
Matrons and sires, and unaffianc'd maids,
Forms of bold warriors and heroic shades,

Youths and pale infants laid upon the pyre,
While their fond parents saw th' ascending fire:
All whom the squalid reeds and sable mud
Of slow Cocytus' unrejoicing flood,
All whom the Stygian lake's dark confine bounds,
And with nine circles maze in maze surrounds—
On him, astonish'd, Death and Tartarus gaz'd,
Their viper-hair the wond'ring Furies rais'd ;
Grim Cerberus stood, his triple jaws half clos'd ;
And fix'd in air Ixion's wheel repos'd.
Now ev'ry peril o'er, when Orpheus led
His rescued prize in triumph from the dead,
And the fair bride, so Proserpine enjoin'd,
Press'd on his path and follow'd close behind,
In sweet oblivious trance of amorous thought
The lover err'd, to sudden frenzy wrought.
Oh ! venial fault, if hell had ever known
Mercy, or sense of suff'ring not its own :
He stopp'd, and, ah ! forgetful, weak of mind,
Cast, as she reach'd the light, one look behind,
And scatter'd all his labour to the wind—

That law he broke by hell's stern tyrant bound.
Thrice o'er the Stygian lake a hollow sound
Portentous murmur'd from its depth profound.
Alas ! what fates our hapless love divide !
What frenzy, Orpheus, tears thee from thy bride !
' Again I sink,' a voice resistless calls ;
' Lo ! on my swimming eyes cold slumber falls.
Now, now, farewell ! involv'd in thickest night,
Borne far away, I vanish from thy sight ;
And stretch towards thee, all hope for ever o'er,
These unavailing arms, ah ! thine no more.'
She spoke, and from his gaze for ever fled,
Swift as dissolving smoke through ether spread,
No more beheld him ; while he fondly strove
To catch her shade, and pour the plaints of love.
Deaf to his pray'r, no more stern Charon gave
To cross the Stygian lake's forbidden wave.
What shall he do ? where, dead to hope, reside,
Reft of all joy, and doubly lost his bride ?
What tears shall soothe th' inexorable god ?
Pale swam her spirit to its last abode."

VIRG. *Geo*. iv. : SOTHEBY'S *Trans.*

No. 521.

Eurydice vanishing from Orpheus.

PYRGOTELES. *Oriental Amethyst.*

Orpheus yielding to his desire to see his wife, turns to look at her, and she instantly disappears.

No. 522.

Orpheus repulsed by Charon.

APOLLONIDES. *Oriental Cornelian.*

Orpheus returned to earth, but the loss of Eurydice was so insupportable to him, that he resolved on quitting it a second time for the realms of darkness. Arrived on the banks of the Styx, he is rudely repulsed by Charon.

No. 523.

The death of Orpheus.

APOLLONIDES.   *Oriental Cornelian.*

Orpheus while journeying in Egypt, where he remained some time, adopted the dietetic regimen of the Egyptian priests, which forbade the use of wine and other intoxicating liquids. This circumstance made him so much hated by the followers of Bacchus, that the infuriated Bacchantes tore him to pieces.

> " The Thracian matrons, who the youth accus'd
> Of love disdain'd and marriage-rites refus'd,
> With furies and nocturnal orgies fir'd,
> At length against his sacred life conspir'd :
> Whom e'en the savage beasts had spar'd, they kill'd,
> And strew'd his mangled limbs about the field ;
> Then when his head from his fair shoulders torn,
> Wash'd by the waters, was on Hebrus borne,
> E'en then his trembling tongue invok'd his bride;
> With his last voice, ' Eurydice !' he cried ;
> ' Eurydice !' the rocks and river-banks replied."
>   VIRGIL.

No. 524.

The murderers of Orpheus changed into trees.

APOLLONIDES.   *Oriental Cornelian.*

Bacchus highly reprobated the ferocious fanaticism of the Bacchantes ; and to revenge the death of Orpheus, he assembled them all in one place, and changed them into trees.

> " Bacchus, resolving to revenge the wrong
> Of Orpheus murder'd on the madding throng,
> Decreed that each accomplice-dame should stand
> Fix'd by the roots along the conscious land.
> Their wicked feet, that late so nimbly ran
> To wreak their malice on the guiltless man,
> Sudden with twisted ligatures were bound,
> Like trees deep planted in the turfy ground.
> And as the fowler with his subtle gins
> His feather'd captives by the feet entwines,
> That flutt'ring pant, and struggle to get loose,
> Yet only closer draw the fatal noose ;
> So these were caught, and as they strove in vain
> To quit the place, they but increas'd their pain :
> They flounce and toil, yet found themselves con-
> troll'd,
> The root, though pliant, toughly keeps its hold.
> In vain their toes and feet they look to find,
> For e'en their shapely legs are cloth'd with
> rind.

One smites her thighs with a lamenting
stroke,
And finds the flesh transform'd to solid oak;
Another, with surprise and grief distress'd,
Lays on above, but beats a wooden breast.

A rugged bark their softer neck invades,
Their branching arms shoot up delightful shades;
At once they seem and are in real grove,
With mossy trunk below, and verdant leaves
above."

OVID.

No. 525.

Apollo changing the serpent to stone for attempting to devour the head of Orpheus.

GNAIOS. *Oriental Cornelian.*

The Bacchantes, after tearing the body of Orpheus to pieces, threw his head and lyre into the Hebrus, a river of Thrace, and the tide carried them both to the opposite shore, where a serpent, intent on devouring the head, began by licking the blood with which the hair was saturated. Apollo succeeded in preserving the head of Orpheus, and changed the serpent to a stone.

" His head and harp a better fortune found;
In Hebrus' streams they gently roll'd along,
And sooth'd the waters with a mournful song.
Soft deadly notes the lifeless tongue inspire,
A doleful tune sounds from the floating lyre;
The hollow banks in solemn concert mourn,
And the sad strain in echoing groans return.
Now with the current to the sea they glide,
Borne by the billows of the briny tide;
And driv'n where waves round rocky Lesbos roar,
They strand and lodge upon Methymna's shore:

But here, when landed on the foreign soil,
A venom'd snake, the product of the isle,
Attempts the head, and sacred locks embru'd
With clotted gore and still fresh-dropping blood.
Phœbus at last his kind protection gives,
And from the fact the greedy monster drives;
Whose marbled jaws his impious crime atone,
Still grinning ghastly, though transform'd to
stone."

OVID.

" What could the Muse herself that Orpheus bore,
The Muse herself, for her enchanting son,
Whom universal nature did lament,
When by the rout that made the hideous roar
His gory visage down the stream was sent,
Down the swift Hebrus to the Lesbian shore?"

MILTON.

No. 526.

Head of Medusa.

Cornelian.

No. 527.

Leander, guided by the torch of Hero, swimming across the Hellespont.

GNAIOS. *Oriental Cornelian.*

Hero, a young priestess of Venus at Sestos, a town situated on the European side of the straits of the Hellespont, was beloved by Leander, a young man of Abydos, a city on the opposite shore of Asia, who swam across nightly to visit her.

> " What dares not ardent youth when love inspires,
> Boils in his blood, and pours unsated fires?
> Lonely at midnight, when the tempest raves,
> Fearless he flings his bosom to the waves;
> Above dire thunder rolls, seas boil below,
> Round his pale head portentous lightnings glow:
> Nor heav'n, nor seas, nor roaring winds appal,
> Nor billows breaking on the rocks recall,
> Nor his deserted parents' boding cry,
> Nor on his corse the virgin doom'd to die."
>
> *Geor.* iii.: SOTHEBY's *Trans.*

" Sing, Muse! the conscious torch, whose nightly ray
Led the bold lover through the wat'ry way,
To share those joys which mutual faith hath seal'd,
Joys to divine Aurora unreveal'd.
Abydos, Sestos, ancient towns, proclaim
Where gentlest bosoms glow'd with purest flame.
I hear Leander dash the foaming tide;
Fix'd high in air I see the glimmering guide,
The genial flame, the love-enkindling light,
Signal of joy, that buru'd serenely bright,
Whose beams, in fair effulgency display'd,
Adorn'd the nuptials of the Sestian maid;
Which Jove, its friendly office to repay,
Should plant all-glorious in the realms of day,
To blaze for ever midst the stars above,
And style it gentle harbinger of love;
For sure on earth it shone supremely kind,
To soothe the anguish of the love-sick mind;
Till cloth'd in terrors rose the wint'ry blast,
Impetuous howling o'er the wat'ry waste.

And O, inspire me, goddess, to resound
The torch extinguish'd, and the lover drown'd.
　Against Abydos sea-beat Sestos stood,
Two neighb'ring towns, divided by the flood;
Here Cupid prov'd his bow's unerring art,
And gain'd two conquests with a single dart.
On two fond hearts the sweet infection prey'd,
A youth engaging, and a beauteous maid:
Of Sestos she, fair Hero was her name;
The youth, Leander, from Abydos came:
Their forms divine a bright resemblance bore,
Each was the radiant star of either shore.
　Thou whom the Fates commission here to stray,
A while the turret's eminence survey;
Thence Hero held the blazing torch, to guide
Her lover rolling on the boist'rous tide—
The roaring Hellespont, whose wave-worn strait
Still in loud murmurs mourns Leander's fate.
Say, heav'nly Muse, had Hero charms to move,
And melt the Abydinian into love?
Say, with what wiles the am'rous youth inspir'd,
Obtain'd the virgin whom his soul admir'd?

Fair Hero, priestess to th' Idalian queen,
Of birth illustrious, as of graceful mien,
Dwelt on a high sequester'd tower, that stood
Firm on the ramparts, and o'erlooked the flood.
Chaste, and unconscious of love's pleasing pain,
She seem'd a new-born Venus of the main;
But nice of conduct, prudently withdrew
Far from the follies of the female crew.
Bless'd in retreat, she shunn'd the vain delight
Of daily visits, and the dance at night,
Content in sweet tranquillity to screen
Her blooming beauty from malignant spleen :
For where superior beauty shines confess'd,
It kindles envy in each female breast.
To soften Venus oft with pray'r she strove,
Oft pour'd libations to the god of love ;
Taught by th' example of the heavenly dame,
To dread those arrows that were tipt with flame.
Vain all her caution, fruitless prov'd her pray'r,
Love gains an easy conquest o'er the fair.
For now the sacred festival appear'd,
By pious Sestians annually rever'd,
At Venus' fane to pay the rites divine,
And offer incense at Adonis' shrine.

.   .   .   .   .

As through the temple pass'd the Sestian maid,
Her face a soften'd dignity display'd ;
Thus silver Cynthia's milder glories rise,
To glad the pale dominion of the skies.

.   .   .   .   .

Thus as she shone superior to the rest,
In the sweet bloom of youth and beauty dress'd,
Such softness temper'd with majestic mien,
The earthly priestess match'd the heav'nly queen.
The wond'ring crowds the radiant nymph admire,
And every bosom kindles with desire ;
Eager each longs, transported with her charms,
To clasp the lovely virgin in his arms. •

.   .   .   .   .

Leander saw the blooming fair ;
Love seiz'd his soul instead of dumb despair :
Resolv'd the lucky moments to improve,
He sought occasion to reveal his love ;

The glorious prize determin'd to obtain,
Or perish for those joys he could not gain.
Her sparkling eyes, instilling fond desire,
Entranc'd his soul, and kindled amorous fire.
Such radiant beauty, like the pointed dart,
With piercing anguish stings th' unguarded
        heart :
For on the eye the wound is first impress'd,
Till by degrees it rankles in the breast.
Now hope and confidence invade his soul ;
Then fear and shame alternately control.
Fear through his bosom thrill'd ; a conscious
        shame
Confess'd the passion which it seem'd to blame :
Her beauties fix'd him in a wild amaze,—
Love made him bold, and not afraid to gaze.
With step ambiguous, and affected air,
The youth advancing, fac'd the charming fair :
Each amorous glance he cast, though form'd by
        art,
Yet sometimes spoke the language of his heart ;
With nods and becks he kept the nymph in
        play,
And tried all wiles to steal her soul away.
Soon as she saw the fraudful youth beguil'd,
Fair Hero conscious of her beauty smil'd ;
Oft in her veil conceal'd her glowing face,
Sweetly vermilion'd with the rosy grace :
Yet all in vain to hide her passion tries,
She owns it with her love-consenting eyes.
Joy touch'd the bosom of the gentle swain,
To find his love was not indulg'd in vain.
Then while he chid the tedious lingering day,
Down to the west declin'd the solar ray ;
And dewy Hesper shone serenely bright,
In shadowy silence leading on the night.
Soon as he saw the dark-involving shade,
Th' embolden'd youth approach'd the blooming
        maid,
Her lily hand he seiz'd and gently press'd,
And softly sigh'd the passion of his breast ;
Joy touch'd the damsel, though she seem'd dis-
        pleas'd,
And soon withdrew the lily hand he seiz'd.

The youth perceiv'd, through well-dissembled
  wiles,
A heart just yielding by consenting smiles;
Then to the temple's last recess convey'd
The unreluctant, unresisting maid :
Her lovely feet, that seem'd to lag behind,
But ill conceal'd her voluntary mind.
She feign'd resentment with an angry look,
And sweetly chiding, thus indignant spoke :
' Stranger, what madness has possess'd thy brain,
To drag me thus along the sacred fane?
Go—to your native habitation go——
'Tis quite unkind to pull my garments so.
Rich are my parents; urge not here your fate,
Lest their just vengeance you repent too late.
If not of me, of Venus stand afraid,
In her own fane soliciting a maid;
Hence speed your flight, and Venus' anger dread,
'Tis bold aspiring to a virgin's bed.'
Thus chid the maid, as maids are wont to do,
And shew'd her anger and her fondness too.
The wily youth, as thus the fair complain'd,
Too well perceiv'd the victory was gain'd ;
For nymphs enrag'd the more complying prove,
And chidings are the harbingers of love.
He kiss'd her snowy neck, her fragrant breast,
And thus the transport of his soul express'd :
' O lovely fair, in whom combin'd are seen
The charms of Venus and Minerva's mien !
For sure no virgin of terrestrial race
Can vie with Hero in the blooms of face ;
I deem your lineage from the gods above,
And style you daughter of Saturnian Jove.
Blest is the father from whose loins you sprung,
Blest is the mother at whose breast you hung ;
Blest, doubly blest, the fruitful womb that
  bore
This heavenly form for mortals to adore.
Yet, beauteous Hero, grant a lover's prayer,
And to my wishes prove as kind as fair;
As Venus' priestess just to Venus prove,
Nor shun the gentle offices of love.
O let us, while the happy hour invites
Propitious, celebrate the nuptial rites.

No maid can serve in Cytherea's fane,
Her eyes delight not in the virgin train.
But would fair Hero secret rites explore,
The laws of Venus, and her pleasing lore,
Those rites are practis'd in the bridal bed,
And there must Hero, yet a maid, be led.
Then, as you fear the goddess to offend,
In me behold your husband and your friend ;
Ordain'd by Cupid, greatest god above,
To teach you all the mysteries of love :
As winged Mercury, with golden wand,
Made Hercules, with distaff in his hand,
To every task of Omphale submit,
Thus Love, more powerful than the god of wit,
Sent me to you. 'Tis needless to relate
The chaste Arcadian Atalanta's fate,
Who from th' embraces of Milanion fled,
Her faithful lover, and the nuptial bed ;
But vengeful Venus caus'd the nymph to burn
With equal flame, and languish in her turn.
O let example warn you to revere
The wrathful goddess, and your lover hear!'
Thus spoke the youth ; his magic words control
Her wavering breast, and soften all her soul.
Silent she stood, and wrapt in thought profound,
Her modest eyes were fix'd upon the ground ;
Her cheeks she hid, in rosy blushes drest,
And veil'd her lily shoulders with her vest ;
On the rich floor, with Parian marble laid,
Her nimble foot involuntary play'd.
By secret signs a yielding mind is meant,
And silence speaks the willing maid's consent.
Now had the wily god's envenom'd dart
Diffus'd the pleasing poison to her heart;
Leander's form, instilling soft desire,
Woo'd her pleas'd eyes, and set her soul on fire.

        .   .   .   :   .

                        Modest grace
Conceal'd the new-born beauties of her face ;
For on her cheeks the roseate blush that hung
Seem'd to condemn the language of her tongue.
Meanwhile Leander feeds the hidden fire,
Glows in each vein, and burns with fierce de-
  sire;

But anxious doubt his musing breast alarms,
How shall he gain admittance to her charms.
Nor long he paus'd, for Love in wiles abounds,
Well pleas'd to heal the bosoms which he
    wounds
'Twas he whose arrows men and gods control,
That heal'd Leander's love-afflicted soul ;
Who thus, while sighs upheav'd his anxious
    breast,
The nymph with artful eloquence address'd :
' For thee, dear object of my fond desire,
I'll cross the ocean though it flame with fire ;
Nor would I fear the billows' loud alarms,
While every billow bore me to thy arms;
Uncheck'd, undaunted by the boisterous main,
Tempestuous winds should round me roar in
    vain:
But oft as Night her sable pinions spread,
I through the storm would swim to Hero's bed,—
For rich Abydos is the home I boast,
Not far divided from the Thracian coast.
Let but my fair a kindly torch display,
From the high turret to direct my way ;
Then shall thy daring swain securely glide
The bark of Cupid o'er the yielding tide,
Thyself my haven, and thy torch my guide.
And while I view the genial blaze afar,
I'll swim regardless of Boòtes' car,
Of fell Orion, and the northern wain,
That never bathes his brightness in the main ;
Thy star, more eminently bright than they,
Shall lead the lover to his blissful bay.
But let the torch, O nymph divinely fair !
My only safety, be thy only care :
Guard well its light when wint'ry tempests roar,
And hoarse waves break tumultuous on the shore,
Lest the dire storms that blacken all the sky
The flame extinguish, and the lover die.
More wouldst thou know—Leander is my name,
The happiest husband of the fairest dame.'
    Thus mutual vow'd the lovers to employ
The nights in raptures of mysterious joy ;
Her task secure th' extended torch to keep,
And his to cross the unfathomable deep.

On promis'd bliss their fruitful fancies fed,
Ecstatic pleasures of the nuptial bed ;
Till the fond nymph, when decency requir'd,
Back to her tower unwillingly retir'd.

        His lovely limbs undress'd,
And folded round his head the various vest;
Then dauntless plunging in the foaming tide,
Dash'd with his arms th' intruding waves aside :
Full in his view he kept the shining mark,
Himself the pilot, passenger, and bark.
While faithful Hero, to her promise true,
Watch'd on the turret every wind that blew ;
Oft with her robe she screen'd the torch's blaze
From dangerous blasts that blew a thousand
    ways ;
Till the tir'd youth, on rolling surges toss'd,
Securely landed on the Sestian coast.
Soon as she saw her lover safe on shore,
Eager she ran and led him to her tower ;
Welcom'd with open arms her panting guest,
And sweetly smiling to her bosom press'd.
Then dumb with joy the shivering youth she led,
Still wet and weary, to the genial bed,
Wip'd his fair limbs, and fragrant oils applied
To cleanse his body from the oozy tide ;
Then clasp'd him close, still panting, to her
    breast,
And thus with fond endearing words address'd :
' My life, my lover, thou hast suffer'd more
Than fondest bridegroom e'er endur'd before;
Destin'd, alas ! dread troubles to sustain
On the rough bosom of the briny main :
Now let sweet joy succeed in sorrow's place,
And lull thy labours in my warm embrace.'
She spoke ; he loos'd her virgin zone to prove
The sacred rites and mysteries of love.

Thus wrapp'd in hidden joys, each blissful night
They pass'd in ecstasies of full delight.
But soon, alas ! those dear-bought pleasures fled,
And short the transports of that bridal bed !
For now relentless winter, that deforms
With frost the forest and the sea with storms,

Bade the wild winds o'er all the ocean reign,
And raise the rapid whirlpools of the main.
The hoarse wild winds obey, and with harsh
    sound
Roar o'er the surface of the vast profound ; ·
Rouse from their beds the scatter'd storms that
    sleep
In the dark caverns of the dreary deep :
The trembling sailor hears the dreadful roar,
Nor dares the wint'ry turbulence explore,
But drags his vessel to the safer shore.
But thee, bold youth, no wint'ry storms restrain,
Nor all the deathful dangers of the main.
For when thou saw'st the torch's blaze from
    far,
(Of nuptial bliss the bright prophetic star,)
Thee not the furious tempest could control,
Nor calm the glowing raptures of the soul.
Yet sure fair Hero, when the gloomy sky
With gathering clouds proclaim'd rough winter
    nigh,
Without her lover should have pass'd the night,
Nor from the tower ill-omen'd shewn the light.
But she, ah, hapless ! burns with fond desire,
'Tis love inflames her while the Fates conspire ;
The torch of death now glimmer'd from above,
No more the gentle harbinger of love.
'Twas night, and angry Æolus had hurl'd
The winds tempestuous o'er the wat'ry world ;
The bellowing winds with rage impetuous roar,
And dash the foaming billows on the shore :
E'en then the youth, with pleasing visions fed,
Glows with remembrance of the bridal bed ;
And while fierce tempests howl on every side,
Floats on the bosom of the briny tide.
Waves roll'd on waves, in hideous heaps are
    driven,
Swell'd into mountains, and upheav'd to heaven ;
Bleak blasts, loud roaring, the vex'd ocean sweep,
Foam the dash'd billows, and resounds the deep.

From every part the blustering terrors fly,
Rage o'er the main, and battle in the sky ;
The growling thunder of the vast profound
The rocks rebellow, and the shores rebound.
Amidst the wat'ry war with toils oppress'd,
O'erwhelm'd with billows, and in gulfs distress'd,
Leander oft with suppliant prayer implor'd
The sea-sprung goddess, and old ocean's lord.
Thee, Boreas, too, he summon'd to his aid,
Nor was unmindful of th' Athenian maid ;
But prayers are fruitless, and petitions vain,
Love must submit to what the Fates ordain.
From wave to wave the hapless youth is toss'd,
Now heav'd on high, and now in whirlpools lost ;
His wearied feet no more his will obey,
His arms hang useless, and forget to play :
Borne on the surge supine, and void of breath,
He drinks the briny wave, and draws in death.
Thus while in fatal rage each wind conspires,
Extinct at once the flame and lover's fires,
Fainting he sinks, and with the torch expires.
    While on the turret Hero mourn'd his stay,
And fondly sighing chid his long delay,
Perplexing anguish in her bosom rose,
Nor knew her eyes the blessings of repose.
Now rose the morn, in russet vest array'd,
Still from th' impatient fair the lover stay'd ;
Watchful she stood, and cast her eyes around,
O'er the wide beach, and o'er the depths pro_
    found,
Haply to spy her lover, should he stray,
The light extinguish'd midst the wat'ry way.
But when she saw him breathless on the sand,
Stretch'd ghastly pale by death's relentless hand,
She shriek'd aloud, and from her throbbing breast
Rent the gay honours of her flowery vest.
Then from the tow'r her beauteous body cast,
And on her lover's bosom breath'd her last ;
Nor could the Fates this faithful pair divide—
They liv'd united, and united died."

             Musæus: Fawkes's *Trans.*

No. 528.

Head of Leander.

Cornelian.

No. 529.

Althæa extinguishing the brand on which depended the duration of the life of her infant son Meleager.

PYRGOTELES. *Calcedony.*

Althæa, the daughter of Thestius and Eurythemis, and wife of Æneus, king of Calydon, at the moment of giving birth to Meleager, saw the Parcæ, or Fates, enter her room and place a lighted brand on the hearth, telling her that the life of her infant would last as long as the brand continued unconsumed. The Parcæ then retired, and Althæa extinguished the brand.

> " There lay a log unlighted on the hearth,
> When she was lab'ring in the throes of birth
> For th' unborn chief; the fatal sisters came,
> And rais'd it up, and toss'd it on the flame.
> Then on the rock a scanty measure place
> Of vital flax, and turn'd the wheel apace ;
> And turning, sung : ' To this red brand and thee,
> O new-born babe, we give an equal destiny !'
> So vanish'd out of view. The frighted dame
> Sprang hasty from her bed, and quench'd the flame ;
> The log in secret lock'd she kept with care,
> And that while thus preserv'd, preserv'd her heir."
>
> OVID.

No. 530.

The chase of the Calydonian boar.

AMMONIOS. *Oriental Cornelian.*

Atalanta, daughter of Schœneus king of Scyros, or, according to others, of Jasius, first wounded the monster, which was then killed by Meleager.

> " But Meleager is the name thou bear'st,
> Doom'd to pursue an inauspicious prey."
>
> EURIP. *Frag.*

" There stood a forest on a mountain's brow,
Which overlook'd the shaded plains below;
No sounding axe presum'd those trees to bite,
Coeval with the world, a venerable sight.
The heroes there arriv'd; some spread around
The toils, some search the footsteps on the ground,
Some from the chains the faithful dogs unbound.
Of action eager, and intent in thought,
The chiefs their honourable danger sought.
A valley stood below, the common drain
Of waters from above, and falling rain;
The bottom was a moist and marshy ground,
Whose edges were with bending osiers crown'd:
The knotty bulrush next in order stood,
And all within of reeds a trembling wood.
From hence the boar was rous'd, and sprang
      amain,
Like lightning sudden on the warrior-train;
Beats down the trees before him, shakes the
      ground,
The forest echoes to the crackling sound;
Shout the fierce youth, and clamours ring around.
All stood with their protended spears prepar'd,
With broad steel heads the brandish'd weapons
      glar'd.
The beast impetuous with his tusks aside
Deals glancing wounds; the fearful dogs divide:
All spend their mouths aloof, but none abide.

Meantime the virgin huntress was not slow
T" expel the shaft from her contracted bow;
Beneath his ear the fasten'd arrow stood,
And from the wound appear'd the trickling
      blood.
She blush'd for joy; but Meleagrus rais'd
His voice with loud applause, and the fair archer
      prais'd.
He was the first to see, and first to shew
His friends the marks of the successful blow:
' Nor shall thy valour want the praises due,'
He said.   A virtuous envy seiz'd the crew.

Two spears from Meleager's hand were sent,
With equal force, but various in th' event;
The first was fix'd in earth, the second stood
On the boar's bristled back, and deeply drank
      his blood.
Now while the tortur'd savage turns around,
And flings about his foam, impatient of the
      wound,
The wound's great author close at hand provokes
His rage, and plies him with redoubled strokes;
Wheels as he wheels, and with his pointed dart
Explores the nearest passage to his heart."

                                        OVID.

" A golden eagle deck'd the massive shield
Of Telamon, which dauntless he oppos'd
To the fierce savage; with the clustering vine
His brows he girt: this warrior was the pride
Of happy Salamis his native land.
Hated by Venus, from th' Arcadian fields
Came Atalanta, with her hounds, her bow,
And biting axe, in an embroider'd vest.
The sons of Thestius follow'd her; all bare
Was their left foot, their right in sandals clad,
That they with greater ease might bend the knee;
Such is the usage of Ætolian youths."

                              EURIP., *Frag.*

No. 531.

Meleager.

PYRGOTELES. *Oriental Cornelian.*

Leaning against a pedestal, on which is the head of the boar, Meleager meditates presenting it to Atalanta, as a reward for her courage. Diana *lucifera* on a rock appears to be occupied in exciting discord.

> " But he, the conqu'ring chief, his foot impress'd
> On the strong neck of that destructive beast :
> And gazing on the nymph with ardent eyes,—
> ' Accept,' said he, ' fair Nonacrine, my prize ;
> And though inferior, suffer me to join
> My labours and my part of praise with thine.'
> At this, presents her with the tusky head
> And chine, with rising bristles roughly spread.
> Glad she receiv'd the gift, and seem'd to take
> With double pleasure for the giver's sake."
>
> OVID.

No. 532.

Meleager presenting the head of the wild boar to Atalanta.

LYCOS. *Oriental Sardonyx.*

No. 533.

Meleager, sword in hand, attacking the two brothers of Althæa, who had carried off the boar's head from Atalanta, kills them.

GNAIOS. *Oriental Cornelian.*

" The rest were seiz'd with sullen discontent,
And a deaf murmur through the squadron went.
All envied ; but the Thestian brethren shew'd
The least respect, and thus they vent their spleen
    aloud :
' Lay down these honour'd spoils, nor think to
    share,
Weak woman as thou art, the prize of war ;
Ours is the title, thine a foreign claim,
Since Meleagrus from our lineage came.
Trust not thy beauty : but restore the prize,
Which he, besotted on that face and eyes,
Would rend from us.' At this, inflam'd with
    spite,
From her they snatch'd the gift, from him the
    giver's right.

But soon th' impatient prince his falchion drew,
And cried : ' Ye robbers of another's due,
Now learn the diff'rence at your proper cost
Betwixt true valour and an empty boast.'
At this advanc'd, and sudden as the word
In proud Plexippus' bosom plung'd the sword.

Toxeus amaz'd, and with amazement slow
Or to revenge or ward the coming blow,
Stood doubting ; and while doubting thus he
 stood,
Receiv'd the steel bathed in a brother's blood.''
          OVID.

No. 534.

Cleopatra entreating Meleager to defend the city of Calydon against the Curetes.

GNAIOS. *Oriental Cornelian.*

Meleager, enraged with his mother Althæa, refused to defend the city of Calydon, which was attacked by the Curetes, and which they were preparing to carry by assault. Æneus, the father of Meleager, Althæa herself, and the deputation from Calydon, endeavoured in vain to persuade him. His wife Cleopatra at length succeeded in calming him, and induced him to fight against the Curetes, whom he put to flight.

" Where Calydon on rocky mountains stands,
Once fought the Ætolian and Curetian bands ;
To guard it those, to conquer these advance,
And mutual deaths were dealt with mutual chance.
The silver Cynthia bade contention rise,
In vengeance of neglected sacrifice ;
On Œneus' fields she sent a monstrous boar,
That levell'd harvests, and whole forests tore :
This beast (when many a chief his tusks had
 slain)
Great Meleager stretch'd along the plain.
Then for his spoils a new debate arose,
The neighbour-nations thence commencing foes ;
Strong as they were, the bold Curetes fail'd,
While Meleager's thundering arm prevail'd :
Till rage at length inflam'd his lofty breast,
(For rage inflames the wisest and the best).
Curs'd by Althæa, to his wrath he yields,
And in his wife's embrace forgets the fields.
She, from Marpessa sprung, divinely fair,
And matchless Idas, more than man in war ;
The god of day ador'd the mother's charms,
Against the god the father bent his arms.
Th' afflicted pair, their sorrows to proclaim,
From Cleopatra chang'd this daughter's name,

And call'd Alcyone—a name to shew
The father's grief, the mourning mother's woe.
To her the chief retir'd from stern debate,
But found no peace from fierce Althæa's hate ;
Althæa's hate th' unhappy warrior drew,
Whose luckless hand his royal uncle slew.
She beat the ground, and call'd the powers be-
 neath
On her own son to wreak her brother's death ;
Hell heard her curses from the realms profound,
And the red fiends that walk the nightly round.
In vain Ætolia her deliverer waits,
War shakes her walls, and thunders at her gates.
She sent ambassadors, a chosen band,
Priests of the gods, and elders of the land ;
Besought the chief to save the sinking state,—
Their prayers were urgent, and their proffers
 great
(Full fifty acres of the richest ground,
Half pasture green, and half with vineyards
 crown'd).
His suppliant father, aged Œneus, came ;
His sisters follow'd ; e'en the vengeful dame
Althæa sues ; his friends before him fall :
He stands relentless, and rejects them all.

Meanwhile the victors' shouts ascend the skies,
The walls are scal'd, the rolling flames arise.
At length his wife (a form divine) appears;
With piercing cries and supplicating tears,

She paints the horrors of a conquer'd town—
The heroes slain, the palaces o'erthrown,
The matrons ravish'd, the whole race enslav'd :
The warrior heard, he vanquish'd, and he sav'd."

HOMER, Il. ix.

No. 535.

Althæa destroying the brand on which the life of her son Meleager depended.

AMPHION.   Oriental Cornelian.

Althæa, exasperated at the loss of her brothers, threw the brand on which depended the life of Meleager into the fire, and he perished in extreme agony.

> " For the last time she lifts her hand,
> Averts her eyes, and half unwilling drops the brand.
> The brand amid the flaming fuel thrown,
> Or drew or seem'd to draw a dying groan ;
> The fires themselves but faintly lick'd their prey,
> Then loath'd their impious food, and would have shrunk away.
> Just then the hero cast a doleful cry,
> And in those absent flames began to fry ;
> The blind contagion rag'd within his veins,
> But he with manly patience bore his pains :
> He fear'd not fate, but only griev'd to die
> Without an honest wound, and by a death so dry."

HOMER, Il. ix.

No. 536.

Atalanta discovered nurtured by a bear.

ALLION.   Oriental Amethyst.

The father of Atalanta, desiring only male children, exposed her in a desert place, where she was suckled by a bear. She was discovered by some hunters, who took her home and brought her up ; and she became very skilful at the chase and in running races.

r r

No. 537.

Atalanta killing the centaurs Rhœcus and Hylæus.

SOSTRATOS. *Oriental Cornelian.*

No. 538.

The same subject.

POLYCLETES. *Oriental Cornelian.*

" Iasian Atalanta, fam'd for speed,
Admitted of thy choir, was taught by thee
T' elance the dart unerring : from her arm
Light'ning, behold, it trembles in the heart
Of Calydonia's monster. Nor the deed
Shall the brave hunters envy; while thy realms,
Arcadia, boast the trophies, the sharp tusks
Of the wide-wasting boar. Nor can I deem

The vengeful centaurs with such fury fraught,
Rhœcus and mad Hylæus (by her arm
Though level'd bleeding on Mænalion's top),
As to pursue the huntress with their hate
In Pluto's realms ; yet will their wounds not lie,
But speak the truth and testify their shame."
CALLIMACHUS, *Hymn to Diana :*
DODD'S *Trans.*

No. 539.

The race between Atalanta and Hippomenes.

APOLLONIDES. *Oriental Cornelian.*

Atalanta, on account of her great beauty, was sought in marriage by several suitors; and to rid herself of them, she proposed that whoever arrived first at the goal should be her husband. Hippomenes, who entered the lists with her, received from Venus some golden apples; and when he had started in the course, he artfully threw them down at intervals from each other. Atalanta stooping to pick them up, Hippomenes passes her, wins the race, and claims her hand.

" Amongst the rest fair Atalanta came,
Grace of the woods; a diamond buckle bound
Her vest behind, that else had flow'd upon the
    ground,
And shew'd her buskin'd legs; her head was
    bare,
But for her native ornament of hair,

Which in a simple knot was tied above—
Sweet negligence ! unheeded bait of love !
Her sounding quiver, on her shoulder tied,
One hand a dart, and one a bow supplied.
Such was her face, as in a nymph display'd,
A fair fierce boy, or in a boy betray'd
The blushing beauties of a modest maid.

. . . . .
The signal sounding by the king's command,
Both start at once, and sweep th' unprinted sand.
So swiftly move their feet, they might with ease,
Scarce moisten'd, skim along the glassy seas;
Or with a wond'rous levity be borne
O'er yellow harvests of unbending corn.
Now fav'ring peals resound from ev'ry part,
Spirit the youth, and fire his fainting heart:
' Hippomenes,' they cried, ' thy life preserve,
Intensely labour, and stretch ev'ry nerve:
Base fear alone can baffle thy design,
Shoot boldly onward, and the goal is thine.'
'Tis doubtful whether shouts like these con-
vey'd
More pleasures to the youth, or to the maid.
When a long distance oft she could have gain'd,
She check'd her swiftness, and her feet restrain'd ;
She sigh'd, and dwelt, and languish'd on his face,
Then with unwilling speed pursu'd the race.
O'erspent with heat his breath he faintly drew ;
Parch'd was his mouth, nor yet the goal in
view,
And the first apple on the plain he threw.
The nymph stopp'd sudden at the unusual sight,
Struck with the fruit so beautifully bright ;
Aside she starts the wonder to behold,
And eager stoops to catch the rolling gold.

Th' observant youth pass'd by, and scour'd along,
While peals of joy rung from the applauding
throng.
Unkindly she corrects the short delay,
And to redeem the time fleets swift away,
Swift as the lightning, or the northern wind,
And far she leaves the panting youth behind.
Again he strives the flying nymph to hold
With the temptation of the second gold ;
The bright temptation fruitlessly was toss'd,
So soon, alas! she won the distance lost.
Now but a little interval of space
Remain'd for the decision of the race.
' Fair author of the precious gift (he said),
Be thou, O goddess, author of my aid !'
Then of the shining fruit the last he drew,
And with his full-collected vigour threw ;
The virgin still the longer to detain,
Threw not directly, but across the plain.
She seem'd awhile perplex'd in dubious thought,
If the far-distant apple should be sought;
I lur'd her backward mind to seize the bait,
And to the massy gold gave double weight.
My favour to my votary was shew'd,
Her speed I lessen'd, and increas'd her load.
But lest, though long, the rapid race he run
Before my longer tedious tale is done,
The youth the goal, and so the virgin won."

OVID.

No. 540.

Sisyphus in Hades.

DIOSCORIDES. *Sardonyx.*

The opinions of mythologians respecting Sisyphus, who was the son of Æolus and husband of Merope, daughter of Atlas, and also the founder of Ephysa, since called Corinth, are numerous and varied. That of Homer (*Iliad*, book vi.) appears the most probable. He represents Sisyphus as the wisest and most prudent of men and of kings; and believes that he was only condemned in hell to roll a large stone up hill, which, on reaching the summit, always fell back again, because he chained up Death, or, in other words, avoided war and bloodshed. His character is the more worthy of admiration, because in those times of barbarous heroism all rights were based on violence, and men attributed even to the gods the passions of ferocity, vengeance, thirst for blood, and aversion to peace. Sisyphus, indefatigable in the difficult task imposed on him, appears to be an emblem of those rare and really great men, who, keeping constantly in view the public good, never allow themselves to be discouraged; and who, though they may once fail in a laborious undertaking, resume it with the same feeling, firmness, and patience, as before.

> " A mournful vision! the Sisyphian shade,
> With many a weary step, and many a groan,
> Up the high hill he heaves a huge round stone;
> The huge round stone, resulting with a bound,
> Thunders impetuous down, and smokes along the ground.
> Again the restless orb his toil renews,
> Dust mounts in clouds, and sweat descends in dews."
>
> OVID.

No. 541.

Mercury forcing Sisyphus to return to Hades.

GNAIOS. *Oriental Cornelian.*

Sisyphus, when dying, wished to prove the love of his wife Merope, and therefore ordered her to leave his body unburied in the market-place; but she was too faithful to him to comply with his mandate. Sisyphus begged permission of Pluto to return for a short time to earth, in order to punish the pretended inhumanity of his wife; but having begun to breathe the ethereal air, he refused at the time prescribed to go back to the infernal regions; and Pluto was compelled to send Mercury to take him by force.

No. 542.

The death of Dirce.

GNAIOS. *Oriental Cornelian.*

Zethus and Amphion, born of Jupiter and Antiope, the first wife of Lycus king of Thebes, to punish their mother-in-law Dirce for the cruelties she had inflicted on Antiope, fastened her to the tail of a wild bull, which dragged her about till she died.

> " But an old tradition
> Among the race of Cadmus hath prevail'd,
> That Lycus, Dirce's husband, erst bore rule

Over this city, till Jove's sons, Amphion
And Zethus, who on milk-white coursers rode,
Became its sovereigns. Lycus' son, who bears
His father's name, no Theban, but arriving
From the Eubœan state, slew royal Creon ;
And having slain him, seiz'd the throne, invading
The city with tumultuous broils convuls'd."

EURIPIDES.

" From Achelous' slimy bed,
O lovely Dirce, who deriv'st thy birth ;
When first Jove's son young Bacchus grac'd
    the earth,
Thy streams were sprinkled o'er his head.
Th' abortive infant, his relenting sire
Snatch'd from the lightning's livid fire,
    And shelter'd in his thigh :
Let this male womb contain thee,' cried aloud
The parent god, ' till to Thebes' wondering crowd
Thee I produce, their deity,

By Dithyrambus' name.' Our solemn rite,
    Yet thou, O Dirce, dost confound,
Regardless of our train with garlands crown'd.
Why scorn my pray'r? what means thy
    flight?
Obedient to young Bromius' nod,
Soon shall thy current hail the jocund god,
    Shaded by ripen'd clusters bright,
And vineyards blushing rich delight."

EURIPIDES.

" Wherever came the bull, he whirl'd around,
And with the woman bore away the rock,
The oak, and ever chang'd his wild career."

EURIPIDES, *Frag.*

No. 543.

Bacchus metamorphosing Dirce into a fountain.

APOLLONIDES. *Oriental Cornelian.*

Bacchus had compassion on Dirce, and touching her with his thyrsus, changed her to a fountain of the same name.

No. 544.

Cadmus thrusting his lance with such force through the dragon's neck, as to drive it deep into the trunk of an old oak.

CHROMIOS. *Oriental Sardonyx.*

" When Cadmus from the Tyrian strand
Arriving trod this destin'd land,
Heav'n-taught the heifer led his way,
Till down to willing rest she lay,
    Marking his future seat:
By fate assign'd the furrow'd plain,
Thick waving with the golden grain;
Assign'd the verdure-vested meads,
Through which the beauteous Dirce leads
    Her crystal currents fleet.
The pregnant mother here of yore
To Jove the blooming Bacchus bore;
And instant o'er the boy divine
With wanton wreaths the ivy-twine
    Entrail'd its pale-green shade.
To Bacchus hence through festive groves
The train of Theban matrons roves;
The virgins hence in frolic bands,
Waving their ivy-twisted wands,
    The dance fantastic lead.

A dragon there, in scales of gold,
Around his fiery eyeballs roll'd,
By Mars assign'd that humid shade,
To guard the green extended glade,
    And silver-streaming tide:
Him, as with pious haste he came
To draw the purifying stream,
Dauntless the Tyrian chief repress'd,
Dash'd with a rock his sanguine crest,
    And crush'd his scaly pride.
Then at the martial maid's command,
With his deep ploughshare turns the land,
The dragon's teeth wide scattering round;
When sudden from the furrow'd ground
    Embattled hosts arise.
But slaughter's iron arm again
Consigns them to their native plain,
And their lov'd earth, that to the day
Shew'd them in heav'n's ethereal ray.
                    EURIPIDES: POTTER.

No. 545.

Minerva commanding Cadmus to sow the teeth of the dragon which
he has slain.

CHROMIOS.   *Oriental Sardonyx.*

Vide Illustration No. 544.

No. 546.

The armed host springing from the ground on which Cadmus had scattered
the dragon's teeth.

PYRGOTELES.   *Oriental Cornelian.*

Vide Illustration No. 544.

No. 547.

Cadmus, instigated by the lowing of a heifer, prostrates himself to Apollo, kisses the ground, and founds the city of Thebes.

DIOSCORIDES. *Oriental Chrysolite.*

Vide Illustration No. 544.

" Now to this land, the realms of Thebes, I
    come,
Bacchus, the son of Jove, whom Semele,
Daughter of Cadmus, midst the lightning flames
Brought forth; the god beneath a mortal's form
Concealing, on the brink of Dirce's fount,
And where Ismenus rolls his stream, I tread.
I see my mother's tomb rais'd near the house
In which she perish'd by the thunder; yet
Its ruins smoke, th' ethereal fire yet lives,
The everlasting mark of Juno's hate
Wreck'd on my mother. Cadmus hath my praise,
Who to his daughter rais'd this shrine, the ground
Hallow'd from vulgar tread; the clust'ring vine
I gave to wreath around its verdant boughs.
Leaving the Lydian fields profuse of gold,
The Phrygian and the Persian plains expos'd
To the sun's rays, and from the tow'red forts
Of Bactria passing, from the frozen soil
Of Media, from Arabia the blest,
And all that tract of Asia which along
The salt sea lies, where with barbarians mix'd
The Grecians many a stately-structur'd town
Inhabit,—to this city, first of Greece,
I come; here lead my dance, my mystic rites
Establish here, that mortals may confess
The manifest god. Of all the realms of Greece,
In Thebes I first have rais'd my shouts, thus
    cloth'd
With a fawn's dappled hide, and in my hand
Thy thyrsus hold, this ivy-wreathed spear.
For that the sisters of my mother (least
Becomes it them) declared that not from Jove
I sprung, but pregnant by some mortal's love,
That Semele on Jove had falsely charg'd

Her fault, the poor device of Cadmus; whence
They arrogantly said that Jove enraged
Slew her, because she falsely urg'd his love
As her excuse: for this my mad'ning stings
Impell'd them to forsake the house, and roam
Distracted o'er the mountain, where perforce
They wear the habit of my orgies. All
The females who from Cadmus draw their birth
Have I driv'n frantic from their houses forth;
And with the sons of Cadmus mix'd, beneath
The dark-green firs whose boughs o'er-roof the
    rocks,
They sit. This city must be taught to know,
Howe'er averse, that with my mystic rites
She is not hallow'd; and that I defend
The cause of Semele, to mortal men
Avow'd a god, the son of thund'ring Jove.
Cadmus his honours and imperial state
Resigns to Pentheus, from his daughter sprung;
He with profane contempt against me wars,
Drives me from the libations, in his vows
Deems me not worthy mention: for which cause
To him and all the Thebans will I shew
Myself a god. Things well appointed here,
Hence to some other realm will I remove,
And shew myself; but should the Theban state
In rage attempt with hostile arms to drive
My Bacchæ from their confines, I will head
My Mænades, and lead them to the fight:
For this have I put off my godlike form,
Taking the semblance of a mortal man.
But you, my frolic train, who left the heights
Of Tmolus, Lydian mount, ye female troop,
Whom from barbaric coasts I led with me,
Associates and attendants on my march,

Resume your Phrygian timbrels fram'd by me
And mother Rhea; round the royal house
Of Pentheus let their hoarse notes roar, that
    Thebes

May see you.   To Cithæron's heights I go,
And with my circling Bacchæ join the dance."

              EURIPIDES: POTTER.

" Love lights his torch, and bids thee come
    away;
Thou slothful bridegroom, whence this cold
    delay?
Favour'd of heaven, who midst th' enchanting
    scene,
Where young Adonis woo'd the Cyprian queen,
Dwell'st near the gates of Byblis.   But in thee
I am mistaken; for thou ne'er didst see
Adonis' fount, and Byblis' land, where reign
The Graces, worshipp'd in a stately fane;

Where in the dance Assyrian Venus moves,
And Pallas frowns not on their wedded loves:
Not Dian, but Persuasion, who the bride
Adorns with smiles auspicious, is thy guide;
Cherish'd by her, man's amorous flames increase.
Long hast thou roam'd, thy labours now shall
    cease;
Harmonia's plighted hand with joy receive,
And to the bull's embrace Europa leave."

              NONNUS, lib. iii.

" Cadmus Harmonia lov'd, the fair and young,
    A fruitful dame from golden Venus sprung :
    Ino and Semele, Agave fair,
    And thee, Autonoë, thy lover's care,
    (Young Aristæus with his comely hair,)
    She bore ; and Polydore completes the race
    Born in the walls of Thebes, a stately place."

              HESIOD, *Theog.*

" O thou, who through the starry heavens divid'st
    Thy path, and on a golden chariot sitt'st
    Exalted, radiant sun, beneath the hoofs
    Of whose swift steeds the fiery volumes roll :
    How inauspicious, o'er the Theban race
    Didst thou dart forth thy beams, the day when Cadmus
    Came to this land from the Phœnician coast ;
    He erst obtain'd Harmonia for his bride,
    Daughter of Venus.   Of their loves the fruit
    Was Polydorus, and from him, as fame
    Relates, descended Labdacus the sire."

            EURIP., *Ph.:* WOODHULL.

    " Some where stately flows
    The flood Illyricum expect repose;
    Beside whose bank a lofty tower they rear'd,
    Where Cadmus' and Harmonia's tomb appear'd."

              APOLL. RHOD.

No. 548.

Dijoleon, one of the companions of Cadmus, killed by the serpent at the fountain of Dirce.

CHROMIOS.   *Cornelian.*

No. 549.

Pentheus assailed by his mother Agave.

GNAIOS.   *Oriental Cornelian.*

Pentheus, observing the excesses which this liquor produced in a yet barbarous people, especially among the women, opposed the innovation; and proceeding to Mount Cytheron, he interrupted the orgies that were being celebrated by the Bacchantes. His mother Agave was the first to attack him, and to instigate her infuriated companions to revenge the insult offered to Bacchus. Such is the subject of this stone.

STROPHE.

" Go, ye fleet dogs of madness, go,
   Sweep o'er the mountain's rugged brow,
Where sport the dames of Cadmus' royal race;
   Inflame their frantic fury high,
To hold this female-vested wretch in chase,
Who madly dares their hallow'd haunts espy.
   Him from Cithæron's rocky head,
   Or some enclosure's rising mound,
His mother first shall view in ambush laid;
   Then shouting call the Mænades around—
These heights, these heights, ye Bacchæ, who
Ascends, our mountain-ranging train to view?
   Whence is his lineage trac'd?
   His birth he to no woman owes;
But from some tigress in the howling waste,
   Or Libyan gorgon rose.
Vengeance, in all thy terrors clad, appear,
   High thy thund'ring falchion rear,
Stain it in his unrighteous, impious gore,
And ruin on this earth-born tyrant pour.

ANTISTROPHE.

He with unjust nefarious thought,
   And with unholy madness fraught,
Against thy orgies, Bacchus, dares to fight,
   Against his mother's hallow'd train,
By force to conquer thy unconquer'd might,
Swoln with obdurate pride and malice vain.
   With peace their cloudless days shall shine,
   Who wisdom's temp'rate pow'r obey;
But death on him that spurns at rites divine
   Comes undisguis'd, and rushes on his prey.
With joy I see their greatness rise,
And envy not when glory crowns the wise;
   In honour train'd their lives
   By day, by night the gods adore:
But lawless is his rage who madly strives
   T' insult their slighted pow'r.
Vengeance, in all thy terrors clad, appear,
   High thy thund'ring falchion rear,
Stain it in his unrighteous, impious gore,
And ruin on this earth-born tyrant pour.

S S

His sense, O son of Jove, confound :
A bull to his astonish'd eyes appear ;
   Or as a dragon rear
An hundred threat'ning heads; or to his sight
   A lion breathing flames around,
     His guilty soul affright.
   Go, hunter-god, pursue the chase,
   Whilst the smile brightens on thy face ;
   Go, hunter-god, thy Bacchæ lead :
   Their unabating fatal speed
   Shall seize the savage as he flies,
   And triumph o'er their trembling prize.

    .   .   .   .

MESSENGER.

Soon as we left Therapnæ, to our Thebes
Adjacent, and had pass'd Asopus' stream,
We mount Cithæron's steep, Pentheus, myself,
(I on my lord attended), and our guide,
The stranger; to the forest first we came,
And trod with silent step the grassy ground,
Nor breath'd a whisper, for we went to see,
Not to be seen.   A hollow glen was here,
On each side crags arose, and through the midst,
With pine-trees shaded round, a streamlet flow'd.
There sat the Mænades, their hands employ'd
In grateful tasks : around the thyrsus some,
Deserted of its foliage, wreath'd afresh
The ivy-twine ; some from the various heights
Like hinds descending, with melodious voice
Respondent each to each the sprightly song
To Bacchus rais'd.   Th' unhappy Pentheus here
The female band not seeing, thus bespoke
The stranger : ' Where I stand my searching eye
Descries not their employ ; let me ascend
Some pine that waves his tall top o'er yon mound,
Thence might I view distinct their shameful deeds.'
There with amaze a wond'rous act I saw,
A pine's aërial branch the stranger took,
And downward drew it, drew it to the ground ;
Till as one bends a bow, or curves the line
That marks the rolling wheel's circumference,
The stranger with his hands the mountain-pine

Drew down, and bent it to the earth—a deed
Exceeding mortal strength : amidst the boughs
He seat'd Pentheus, to its upright state
Then let the branch with gentle motion rise,
Lest the too quick and violent recoil
Should toss him from his hold ; and now the tree
Stood firm its upright height, and bore my lord,
Seen by the Bacchæ, more than seeing them,
As more conspicuous in his lofty seat.
And now the stranger was no more beheld ;
But from th' ethereal height a voice was heard,
Of Bacchus, it should seem, calling aloud :
' Ye blooming females, him I bring, who held
Your train and me and my mysterious rites
In proud derision ; pour your vengeance on him !'
He spoke, and to the sky and to the earth
Display'd a steady blaze of sacred light.
The air was hush'd, through all the pastur'd grove
And all its leaves a solemn silence reign'd,
Nor sound of beast was heard : the Theban dames,
The voice not heard distinct, start from their seats,
And roll their eyes around.   Again he gave
The dread command ; but when they clearly
     knew
The bidding of the god, with rapid speed,
Swift as the flight of doves, they forward rush'd,
Agave, and the dames of royal blood,
And all the Bacchæ ; with the god inspir'd,
They bounded o'er the torrent of the grove,
And up the crags.   But when my lord they saw
High-seated on the pine, they mount a cliff
Full opposite, and at his head first hurl
What of the rock their hands could grasp ; and
    some
The broken branches of a pine-tree dart ;
Others aloft at his uneasy seat
The thyrsus cast, but reach'd him not, the height
Beyond their aim, where my unhappy lord
Astonied sat, nor had what to devise.
And now the boughs of oaks, and their tough roots
Rent from the ground, nor wanted they for this
Poles arm'd with iron, in a volley'd storm
They hurl'd ; but when Agave saw their toils
Wasted in vain, she cried,—' Haste, form a ring,

And grasp the stem around, that we may seize
This mounted savage; let him not divulge
The secret orgies of the god.' At once
A thousand hands were to the pine applied,
And instant from the ground uprooted it;
Pentheus high-seated with it from his height
Came headlong to the earth with many a groan,
For mischief now he saw was nigh at hand.
Agave, as the priestess of the rites,
Began the murd'rous work, and rushes on him;
The mitre from his hair he rent, that known
His mother might not kill him; on her cheek
He plac'd his soothing hand, and suppliant said:
' 'Tis Pentheus; O my mother, 'tis thy son,
Thine and Echion's son, who sues to thee;
Have pity on me, mother, do not kill
Thy son for his offence.' She foam'd with rage,
Rolling her eyes askance, nor harbour'd thoughts
She ought to harbour, frantic with the god,
Nor listen'd to his pray'rs; but his left hand
She seiz'd, and pressing on his side tore off
His shoulder with a force not hers, the deed
Made easy by the god. On th' other side
Ino assisted in the dreadful work,
Rending his flesh; Autonoe hung upon him,
And all the Bacchæ; every voice was rais'd
At once; his dying breath was spent in groans.
They shouted wild; one snatch'd an arm, and one
A sandal'd foot; dismember'd by their force
Lay the bare trunk; in their ensanguin'd hands
Each hurl'd the flesh of Pentheus to and fro:
His limbs were scatter'd,—on the craggy rocks
Some, on the close-entwined thickets some,
No easy search; the miserable head

His mother, as she caught it in her hands,
Fix'd on her thyrsus, o'er Cithæron bears
High-lifted, as some mountain lion's spoils.
Leaving her sisters with the Mænades,
And proud of her ill-fated prize, her steps
She this way bends, on Bacchus calling loud,
The partner of the chase and of the prize,
The glorious conqueror, who this conquest gain'd
Of tears to her. This horrid scene I fled,
Ere to this house Agave should return.
A modest awe and reverence of the gods
I deem the most distinguish'd ornament,
And wisdom's noblest height in mortal man.

CHORUS.

To Bacchus raise the choral strain,
And celebrate the god for Pentheus slain.
This tyrant of the dragon race,
Our hallow'd haunts to trace,
Conceal'd a female stole beneath,
The thyrsus shook with impious pride,
The faithful wand of death,
And on his ruin rush'd, a bull his guide.
Ye Theban dames, to Bacchus dear,
Your god hath led the vaunting foe;
His hopes of conquest vanish'd into air,
To groans, to tears, to woe.
A glorious conquest, when her hand,
With her son's gushing blood distain'd,
The mother rais'd.——
No more: I see her; to this royal house
Agave speeds, rolling her furious eyes
Askance. Receive th' associate of the god."

EURIPIDES: POTTER.

No. 550.

Pentheus attacked by Agave and her sisters Ino and Autonoe.

POLYCLETES. *Oriental Cornelian.*

"Three troops three sisters to the mountains led:
Agave, with her cheeks that blossom'd red
The bloom of apple; and, in wildest mood,
Autonoe and Ino. From the wood

They stripp'd oak-leaves, and ivy green as well,
And from the ground the lowly asphodel.
In a pure lawn, with these twelve altars plac'd,
Nine Dionysus, three his mother grac'd;

Then from the chest the sacred symbols mov'd,
And as their god had taught them and approv'd,
Upon the leafy altars reverent laid.
Hid in a native mastic's sheltering shade,
Them from a steep rock Pentheus then survey'd:
Him perched aloft Autonoe first discern'd,
And dreadful shriek'd, and spurning overturn'd
The sacred orgies of the frenzied one,
Which none profane may ever look upon.
She madden'd, madden'd all: scared Pentheus
    fled,
And they with robes drawn up pursued. He said,
' What want ye, dames?' Autonoe then, 'Thou,
    fellow,
Shalt know, not hear;' and mightily did bellow,
Loud as a lioness her brood defending.
His mother clutched his head, whilst Ino rending

Tore off his shoulder, trod and trampled o'er him;
Autonoe likewise: limb from limb they tore him.
Then all returned to Thebes, defiled with gore;
They of their Pentheus only fragments bore.
Their after-grief—this troubles not my mind:
Nor let another, impotent and blind,
Name Dionysus as hereby defiled;
Nor though he harsher used some curious child.
May I my life to holy courses give,
Dear to the holy who reproachless live.
This omen sent from ægis-bearing Jove
Shews what he hates, and what his thoughts ap-
    prove:
Blest are the children of the godly ever;
Blest are the children of the godless never."

                                    THEOCRITUS.

No. 551.

The finding of Œdipus.

GNAIOS. *Amethyst.*

Œdipus, the infant son of Laius king of Thebes, being exposed by order of his father (because the oracle said he would perish by the hand of his son), was found and saved by Phorbus, shepherd to Polybus king of Corinth.

" O thou that, whirling midst the stars of
    heaven
Thy radiant course, and on thy golden car
High-seated, glorying in thy fiery steeds,
Rollest the orient light, resplendent sun,
How inauspicious didst thou dart thy beams
That day on Thebes, when from the sea-wash'd
    coast
Of fair Phœnicia Cadmus on this land
Set his ill-omen'd foot! Yet to his arms
The queen of love consign'd her beauteous
    daughter
Harmonia; and from her, to crown his joys,
Sprung Polydorus; Labdacus from him
Derived his birth; the father he of Laius.
Menœceus was my sire, and from one mother

Creon my brother; me my father nam'd
Jocasta, and to Laius wedded me.
Year after year roll'd on, our nuptial bed
Yet childless, when to Phœbus he his way
Inquiring took, and of the god requests
The sweet society of a son to cheer
His house. The oracle replied: ' O king
Of warlike Thebes, sow not, the gods averse,
For such a fatal harvest: should a son
Spring up, that son shall kill thee, and thine
    house
Shall sink in blood.' Yet one night in his wine
He yielded to his pleasure, and a son
From thence arose; but conscious of his fault,
Offending 'gainst th' oracular voice, that son
He to his herdsmen gave in charge t' expose him

In the rich meads of Juno, where Cithæron
O'ershades the vale, and with sharp-pointed steel
Bor'd through his legs; hence Greece gave him
    the name
Of Œdipus. Him there the wand'ring grooms
That watch'd the grazing steeds of Polybus
Took up, and to their royal mistress bore;
She cherish'd at her breast the child that cost me
A mother's throes, and works upon her lord
To deem it hers."

SOPHOCLES.

No. 552.

Phorbus presenting the infant Œdipus to Polybus.

GNAIOS. *Oriental Cornelian.*

    " When now the blooming down
Spoke manhood in my son, by instinct mov'd,
Or some report, t' Apollo's shrine he went,
Ardent to know his parents. At that time
To the same shrine went Laius, to inquire,
If haply he might learn what fate attended
His exposed child: at Phocis, where the road
Divides itself, they met; the charioteer
of Laius sternly bids him quit the way,
Yielding to kings; he silent moved and slow,
Greatly indignant; but the rushing steeds
Rent with their trampling hoofs his bleeding
    feet.
At this—(but why relate each circumstance
Of bloody action distant far?)—the son
There kills the father, and to Polybus
In triumph sends the chariot."

SOPHOCLES.

No. 553.

Œdipus unconsciously killing his father Laius.

PYRGOTELES. *Oriental Cornelian.*

    Œdipus killed his father without knowing him. He then married his mother Jocasta, and sustained heavy calamities, the lot of all the race of Laius.

    " Now the sphynx
Prey'd with a vulture's talons on the city.
My husband now no more, my brother Creon
Proclaim'd to him whose deep thought should
    unfold
The subtle monster's intricate enigma,
My bed the prize. Chance then brought Œdipus
My son; the sphynx's riddle he explain'd,
And as the monarch of this land assumes
The sceptre, his just meed; and marries me
His mother, hapless he, and knew it not;
Nor did she know that her son shar'd her bed.
I to my child bore children: two brave sons,
Eteocles, and the illustrious worth
Of Polynices; and two daughters, one
Her father call'd Ismene, but the elder
I nam'd Antigone. But when he knew,
Much-suffering Œdipus, that sharing mine
He shar'd his mother's bed, in grief, in rage,
He did a deed of desperate horror—rent
His eyes, and with his golden buckles bor'd
Their bleeding orbs."

SOPHOCLES.

" Thus fate, O Theron, that with bliss divine
And glory once enrich'd thy ancient line,
Again reversing ev'ry gracious deed,
Woe to thy wretched sires and shame decreed,
What time, encountering on the Phocian plain,
By luckless Œdipus was Laius slain.
To parricide by fortune blindly led,
His father's precious life the hero shed ;
Doom'd to fulfil the oracles of heaven,
To Thebes' ill-destin'd king by Pythian Phœbus
        given.

But with a fierce avenging eye
Erinnys the foul murder view'd,
And bade his warring offspring die,
    By mutual rage subdu'd :
Pierc'd by his brother's hateful steel
Thus haughty Polynices fell.
Thersander, born to calmer days,
    Surviv'd his falling sire,
In youthful games to win immortal praise,
Renown in martial combats to acquire."

                                PINDAR : WEST.

" When on the floor the wretched corse was laid,
The golden clasps with which she was adorn'd
He from her vestments snatch'd ; then, dreadful
        deed !
Rais'd high his hand, and plung'd their piercing
        points
Deep in his orbs of sight, exclaiming thus :
That her no more they should behold, his woes,
His horrid deeds no more ; but henceforth dark,
Nor see whom it beseem'd him not to see,
Nor those with whom he should have converse
        know.

Thus oft exclaiming, he his eyelids rais'd,
And rent the orbs of sight ; the bleeding balls
Imbath'd his cheeks, nor ceas'd the gushing
        drops,
But rain'd a show'r of black and streaming gore.
This the unhappy fate of both, the woes
Of wife and husband blended dreadfully.
Their former happiness, with ample right
Of old call'd happiness, is now this day
Misfortune, lamentation, death, disgrace,
And all the names that misery ever knew."

                    SOPHOCLES, Phœn. Virg.

No. 554.

Œdipus explaining the enigma of the Sphynx.

GNAIOS.   *Oriental Sardonyx.*

After having killed Laius, Œdipus proceeded to Thebes, and presenting himself to Creon,
the successor of Laius, offered to subdue the sphynx.

" O winged fiend, who from the earth
And an infernal viper drew'st thy birth,
    Thou cam'st, thou cam'st, to bear away
    Amidst incessant groans thy prey,
        And harass Cadmus' race ;
    Thy frantic pinions did resound,
    Thy fangs impress'd the ghastly wound,
Thou ruthless monster with a virgin's face :

What youths from Dirce's fount were borne
        aloof,
While thou didst utter thy discordant song !
    The Furies haunted ev'ry roof,
And o'er these walls sat Slaughter brooding
        long.
Sure from some god whose breast no mercy knew
    Their source impure these horrors drew.

From house to house the cries
Of matrons did resound,
And wailing maidens rent the skies
With frequent shrieks, loud as the thunder's burst,
Oft as the sphynx accurst
Some youth, whom in the Theban streets she
found,
Bore high in air; all gaz'd in wild affright,
Till she vanished from their sight.

At length the Pythian god's command
Brought Œdipus to this ill-fated land ;
Each heart did then with transport glow,
Though now his name renew their woe :
By angry heav'n beguil'd,
When he th' enigma had explain'd,
His mother for a bride he gain'd ;
With incest hence the city was defil'd.

Fresh murders soon his curses will inspire,
Urging his sons to an unnatural strife.
We that heroic youth admire,
Who in his country's cause resigns his life ;
He, though his father Creon wail his fate,
With triumph in the fell debate
Will crown these sevenfold tow'rs.
Of heav'n I ask no more
Than that such children may be ours.
Thy aid, O Pallas, in th' adventurous deed
Caus'd Cadmus to succeed,
And slay the dragon, whose envenom'd gore
Was sprinkled on these rocks ; by heav'n's com-
mand
Hence some pest still haunts the land."

EURIPIDES : WOODHULL.

" Where hast thou e'er display'd a prophet's skill ?
Why, when the ravening hound of hell her charm
Mysterious chanted, for thy country wise
Didst thou not solve it ? Of no vulgar mind
Was this the task ; the prophet this requir'd.
No knowledge then from birds didst thou receive,
None from the gods t' unfold it ; but I came,
This nothing-knowing Œdipus, and quell'd
The monster, piercing through her dark device
By reason's force, not taught by flight of birds."

SOPHOCLES, Œdipus: POPE.

" Far from the town two shaded hills arise,
And lose their adverse summits in the skies;
One side is bounded by the grove's embrace,
A mountain's brow o'erhangs the middle space.
The nature of the place and gloomy site
Seem'd form'd for ambuscade and deeds of
night :
A path obscure here winds the rocks between,
Beneath are spacious fields, a flow'ring scene
Here posted on a cliff's declining brow,
From whence she might survey the vale below,
The sphynx once dwelt. Her cheeks were pale
to view,
And her fell eyes suffus'd with gory dew.

Oft with expanded wings the monster prest
The mould'ring bones of mortals to her breast,
And hurl'd her eyes along the winding way,
Lest unobserving she should lose her prey :
But if his fate or the avenging gods
Had drawn some wretch to her obscene abodes,
She clapp'd her wings distain'd with human gore,
And fill'd with yellings the retentive shore ;
Then with protended nails his face she struck,
And oft her breaking teeth their hold forsook.
Thus long she reign'd : at last with headlong
flight
Sprung from the rocks, and sought the realms of
night ;

For Œdipus by Phœbus' aid disclos'd
The dark enigma which she'd long propos'd.
Untouch'd the grass, neglected lies the wood,
And hungry beasts at distance seek their food;

The Dryads never haunt these loathsome bow'rs,
Nor swains with incense bribe the rural pow'rs;
To other groves ill-omen'd birds repair,
And from afar abhor the tainted air."

STATIUS, *Thebaid.*

No. 555.

Œdipus killing the Sphynx.

APOLLONIDES. *Oriental Cornelian.*

" The Theban monster that propos'd
Her riddle, and him that solv'd it not devour'd,
That once found out and solv'd, for grief and spite
Cast herself headlong from th' Ismenian steep."

MILTON.

STROPHE.

" It rose, on iron wings it rose:
From the monster-teeming earth,
And the viperous brood of hell,
Drew the hideous fiend its birth;
Nigh affrighted Thebes to dwell,
Big with mischief, big with woes.
Once where sacred Dirce springs,
Clanging fierce thy horrid wings,
Didst thou, darting from the skies,
Seize and bear the youth on high;
There, exulting o'er the prey,
Chant thy unharmonious lay;
And whilst Erinnys nigh thee stood,
Lap thy mangled country's blood:
Blood that vengeful god must please,
Who could prompt to deeds like these.
 The matron's moans,
 The virgin's groans,
Through each sorrowing house resound;
 To dismal cries
 Like cries arise,
And shriek succeeds to shriek th' affright'd city
 round:

Like the mingled din of war,
Like the thunder's deep'ning roar,
Such the groan that rent the air
When high her prey the winged virgin bore.

ANTISTROPHE.

But in heav'n's appoint'd hour,
(Such the answers Phœbus gave,)
Œdipus, with fate his foe,
Came this bleeding land to save.
High the joys, the transports flow,
Victor of her subtile lore,
When he shew'd the monster dead.
But new miseries soon succeed,
From the nuptial bed they spring:
Son and mother!—Wretched king!
Sick'ning at the guilty rite,
Nature starts with pale affright;
And pollution's baleful dews
O'er the town their pest diffuse.
Hence the curse in anguish pour'd,
Ruthless call'd the vengeful sword:
Hence his sons with mutual hate
Hurried rush upon their fate.—
 Be fame his meed,
 Who dares to bleed,

When his suff'ring country calls :
He goes, he goes ;
To Creon woes
He leaves ; but Thebes shall stand, and conquest
grace her walls.

With such sons may we be blest,
Virgin queen, at whose command
Cadmus crush'd the dragon's crest,
Whence rav'nous fiends rang'd through this
groaning land."

EURIPIDES, *Phœn. Virg.* : POTTER.

No. 556.

The Simulacra of Juno imposed upon Ixion.

CHROMIOS. *Oriental Cornelian.*

Ixion, king of the Lapithæ in Thessaly, son of Phlegas, or, as some say, of Antion and Perimela, was admitted to Olympus by Jupiter, and when there became violently enamoured of Juno. She complained of his overtures to Jupiter, who, to deceive Ixion, formed a cloud like Juno, and substituted it for the goddess. Deceived by this phantom, Ixion believed that he had obtained the favours of the real Juno, and had the imprudence to boast of it ; for which Jupiter condemned him to perpetual punishment in hell.

" There he who dar'd to tempt the queen of heav'n
Upon an ever-turning wheel is driv'n."

TIBULLUS, book i. E. 3 : GRAINGER.

" A lover built for Juno's bed."

Met. book xii.

" Though far as hell he (Jason), rash adventurer, go,
To free Ixion, link'd in chains of wo."

APOLL. RHO. book iii.

" Such miseries never did mine eyes behold ;
But fame records from times of old
That when Ixion with ambitious love
Assay'd to stain the bed of Jove,
Seized by the Thunderer, on the whirling wheel
Enchain'd, such tortures he was doom'd to feel."

SOPH.: POTTER.
See DIODORUS SICULUS, book iv.

t t

No. 557.

The punishment of Phlegyas.

SOLON. *Oriental Cornelian.*

Phlegyas, son of Mars and Chryse, and father of Coronis the mother of Æsculapius, was king of that part of Bœotia which took the name of Phlegyæ. Indignant at the insult offered him by Apollo in seducing his daughter, he set fire to the temple at Delphi; and Apollo, in revenge, slew him and cast him into hell, where he was condemned to perpetual alarm by the dread of the huge stone which is suspended over his head falling on him.

> " And Phlegyas (sad example) through the gloom
> Repentant, ever crying, ' By my fate,
> Ye mortals, know how awful justice is,
> Nor scorn the will of heav'n."
>
> Æneis vi. : OGLE.

> " Megæra, fiercest fiend, at thy command
> For e'er incumbent, shakes her vengeful brand
> O'er the devoted head of the rash sire
> Who wrapt the Delphic fane in impious fire;
> He views the proferr'd food, yet dares not taste,
> And dreads the cavern'd rock above him plac'd."
>
> STATIUS, Thebaid, book i.: LEWIS's Trans.

No. 558.

Polynices giving the bracelet to Eriphyle.

APOLLONIDES. *Oriental Cornelian.*

Amphiaraus, son of Oicleus, a descendant of Deucalion, and Hypermnestra, one of the daughters of Thestius, was king of a part of the country of Argos, and celebrated for his knowledge of futurity. When Adrastus declared war against Thebes, Amphiaraus, knowing he should be killed in the expedition, secreted himself that he might not be called on to accompany it. Eriphyle his wife discovered his place of concealment to Polynices, who gave her in return a bracelet of gold and jewels.

ALCMEON.

" Thou art the brother of the dame who slew
Her husband.

ADRASTUS.

The detested murderer thou

Of her who bore thee.

'Twas Œdipus' deceitful son that caus'd
Thy sire and me to perish, when he brought
That golden necklace to the Argive land."
Sophocles.

———————————

" Capaneus stands
Invincible but by the Thund'rer's hands.
Ambition shall the guilty brothers* fire,
Both rush to mutual wounds, and both expire;
The reeling earth shall ope her gloomy womb,
Where the yet-breathing bard † shall find his tomb.
The son ‡ shall bathe his hands in parent's blood,
And in one act be both unjust and good.
Of home and sense depriv'd, where'er he flies
The furies and his mother's ghost he spies:
His wife the fatal bracelet shall implore,
And Phegeus stain his sword in kindred gore.'
Ovid.

" With many a gem 'twas fraught and precious
    stone,
To deck the partner of the Theban throne.
Long did the Cyclops o'er their anvils sweat,
And their swoln sinews echoing blows repeat,
Ere th' artist had attain'd his vast design,
And stamp'd perfection on the work divine.

Of polish'd em'ralds was the curious ground,
And fatal forms of adamant surround;
Sparks of ethereal temper flame above,
Filed remnants of the swift-wing'd bolts of Jove;
A dragon's scaly pride is here impress'd,
And there Medusa rears her snaky crest;
From golden boughs Hesperian apples sprung,
And gay to view the Colchian tree was hung;
Torn from the furies' hair a serpent shines:
To this foul lust and various plagues he joins,

Then dips the whole in foam of lunar rays,
And hides the venom in a sprightly blaze.
Where'er this came th' affrighted Graces fled;
Love pined, and Beauty droop'd her sick'ning
    head;
Sorrow still haunts the mansion where it lies,
And hate-engender'd rage and fears arise.

.   .   .   .   .

Fair Eriphyle the rich gift beheld,
And her sick breast with secret envy swell'd:
Not the late omens and the well-known tale
To cure her vain ambition ought avail.
Oh, had the wretch by self-experience known
The future woes and sorrows not her own!
But fate decrees her wretched spouse must bleed,
And the son's phrenzy clear the mother's deed."
Statius.

———————————

ANTIGONE.
" O thou aged man;
But who is he who on yon chariot, drawn
By milk-white coursers, seated, guides the reins?

ATTENDANT.
The seer Amphiareus, O royal maid;
He bears the victims that with crimson tides
Must drench the ground.

———————————————————————————

* Eteocles and Polynices.   † Amphiaraus.   ‡ Alcmæon.

ANTIGONE.

Encircled with a zone
Of radiance, O thou daughter of the Sun,
Pale Moon, who from his beams thy golden orb

Illum'st, behold with what a steady thong,
And how discreetly, he those coursers guides!
But where is Capaneus, who proudly utters
Against this city the most horrid threats?"

EURIPIDES: WOODHULL.

" Amphiareus the seer
March'd to the gates of Prætus, on his car
Conveying victims. No unseemly pride
In his armorial bearings was express'd;
But on his modest buckler there appear'd
A vacant field."

EURIPIDES, *Phœn.*

_____

" There Eriphyle came, who basely sold
The husband of her youth for barter'd gold."

Odyssey.

_____

" Oicleus gave Amphiareus birth,
By Jove and Phœbus lov'd o'er all the earth;
Yet ere old age in Thebes the prophet died,
Through a brib'd woman's guilt and tempted pride:
From him Amphalocus was foremost bred,
And brave Alcmæon bless'd his nuptial bed."

Odyssey: SOTHEBY'S *Trans.*

No. 559.

Alcmæon, the son of Amphiaraus, by order of his father, taking from
Eriphyle the bracelet, the origin of so much misfortune, and killing
her.

DIOSCORIDES. *Oriental Cornelian.*

No. 560.

The battle between Eteocles and Polynices.

APOLLONIDES. *Oriental Sardonyx.*

Eteocles and Polynices, twin brothers who were born of the incestuous marriage of Œdipus
and Jocasta, were entitled, according to the order of succession established by their father, to
reign alternately at Thebes. Eteocles, who was the first to ascend the throne, did not choose

to relinquish it to his brother when his turn arrived; and his obstinacy and injustice gave rise to the expedition of the seven warriors to the walls of Thebes, so celebrated in the pages of heroic history.

<table>
<tr><td>

STROPHE.

" Woe, woe, woe, woe!
Trembling, shudd'ring with my fears,
    Thrilling horror shakes my frame;
Pity fills mine eyes with tears,
    Pity for th' afflicted dame,
For the griefs her heart that rend,
Whilst her furious sons contend.
Pierc'd through mail and shatter'd shield,
Which shall stain the crimson'd field?
O Jove, O earth, O fatal strife;
Brother seeking brother's life!
Which, ah, which shall I deplore,
Breathless welt'ring in his gore!

</td><td>

ANTISTROPHE.

O earth, earth, earth!
Shaking each his angry lance,
    Each inflam'd with lion-rage;
Breathing slaughter they advance,
    Soon in dreadful fight t' engage:
Soon from many a flowing wound
Shall their blood distain the ground;
Higher raise the notes of woe,
For the slain my tears shall flow.
Ruin nigh and slaughter wait,
And this sun decides their fate;
Dreadful, dreadful is their doom,
Dark the Fury's baleful gloom."

SOPHOCLES.

</td></tr>
</table>

" But when now the youthful sons
Of the old Œdipus in radiant arms
Had sheath'd their limbs, advancing to the space
'Twixt host and host the rival chieftains stood,
Ready to lift their spears in single fight;
His eye tow'rds Argos Polynices roll'd,
And utter'd thus his pray'r: ' Imperial Juno,
Goddess rever'd,—for thine I am, since join'd
In marriage with the daughter of Adrastus,
Thy land receiv'd me an inhabitant,—
Give me to kill my brother, and to stain
With his warm life-blood this victorious hand
In the fierce contest; an inglorious crown
I ask, to kill a brother.' Tears gush'd forth
From many, as their eyes each glanc'd on each,
Pitying their fate. But to the hallow'd dome
Of Pallas, glorious with her golden shield,
His eyes Eteocles turn'd, and thus address'd her:
' Daughter of Jove, give my victorious spear,
Lanc'd by this hand, to pierce my brother's breast,
And kill him, for he came to waste my country.'
But when the torch was hurl'd, which, as the sound
Of the Tyrrhenian trumpet, gives the signal

Of bloody battle, furiously they rush'd
In dreadful opposition; as two boars
Whetting their savage tusks, their jaws be-
    smear'd
With foam, they met impetuous with their spears.
But each beneath his round shield lay at ward,
That the steel glanc'd in vain: if either rais'd
His eye above the verge, the other drove
With eager haste full at his face the lance;
But to the grated openings that adorn
The rim, his eye with caution each applies,
And disappoints the spear. With throbbing
    hearts,
More than the combatants, their friends around
Intent and anxious for their chieftain glow.
It chanc'd against a stone Eteocles
Impress'd his foot, thus turn'd without the verge
Of his broad shield: this Polynices saw,
And where the part was open to the blow
Drove through the plated greave his Argive
    spear;
All the Pelasgian troops shouted aloud.
His shoulder in the effort left exposed
The wounded chief observ'd, and aim'd his lance

With well-directed force against the breast
Of Polynices; to the sons of Thebes
Requiting joy: but, faithless to his hand,
The steel point broke. Now in the headless
        truncheon
No more confiding, quick a backward step
He mov'd, then seiz'd and whirl'd a rugged
        stone;
Full on the spear the pond'rous marble fell,
And crash'd it in the midst: the combat now
Was equal, of the spear each chief depriv'd.
Their falchions then they grasp'd, and furious
        rush'd
To closer conflict; shield to shield advanc'd
Sustain'd the clashing tumult of the fight:
Eteocles, with presage of success,
Call'd to his aid the wily discipline

Learn'd in Thessalia, from the pressing toil
Withdrew his left foot backward, guarding well
His body, with his right advancing wheel'd
Oblique, and plung'd his sword deep in his
        bowels,
Driven to the chine. Th' unhappy Polynices
Stood writhing with his torturing wound awhile,
Then fell, the blood fast welling from the wound.
And now the victor, as secure of conquest,
Threw down his sword to strip him of his arms,
Heedless of him, and on the spoil intent.
A fatal oversight: he breathing yet,
And grasping in his dreadful fall his sword,
Scarce rais'd it as he lay; Eteocles
Stooping receiv'd it in his heart. Thus both
Together fell, together lie in blood,
Biting the ground, the conquest undecided."
                    SOPHOCLES, *Phœn. Virg.*

" But you my sons! Away, you are not mine.
For this cause fortune looks upon thee now
Not as she soon will look, when thou shalt lead
These troops to Thebes: it is not in thy fate
To rend her rampires down, but there to fall
Welt'ring in blood; such too thy brother's fate.
These curses on you I before denounced,
And now as my associates call them down,
That to a parent you may learn to shew
Due reverence, nor disdain a father more
Though blind. My daughters have not been thus
        base;
Therefore thy seat, thy throne shall they possess;
Since Justice long renown'd, by laws of old
Establish'd, shares th' imperial throne of Jove.
But get thee hence, thou hast no father here,
Detested wretch, thou vilest of the vile,

And take these curses with thee on thy head
Which I call down: By arms thy native land
Never may'st thou recover, nor again
Visit the vales of Argos; may'st thou die
Slain by thy brother's hand, and may thy hand
Slay him by whom thou art to exile driv'n.
These curses I call on thee, and invoke
The parent gloom of Erebus abhorr'd
To give thee in his dark Tartarean realms
A mansion; I invoke these awful pow'rs,
And the stern god of war, who 'twixt you rais'd
This horrid hate. Thou hast my answer; go!
Tell all the Thebans, tell thy faithful friends
Confederate in thy cause, that Œdipus
Confers this meed of merit on his sons."
                SOPHOCLES, *Œdipus Col.*: POTTER.

CHORUS.
" O Jove supreme,
And all ye gods that guard this state,
Should I the joyful pæan raise,
And celebrate your praise?

Your guardian care, propitious pow'rs,
Preserv'd our walls, preserv'd our tow'rs!
Or bid the solemn, doleful strain,
Lament the chiefs, the brothers slain—
        A mournful theme;

Through mad ambition's impious pride
Childless, unbless'd, in youth's warm tide
Fall'n, fall'n by too severe a fate !

STROPHE.

Thou gloomy curse, too prompt to ill,
A father's vengeance to fulfil,
I feel, I feel thee in my shiv'ring breast !
Soon as I heard th' unhappy slain
Lay welt'ring on th' ensanguin'd plain,
With inspiration's raging pow'r possess'd,
I form'd the funeral strains to flow,
With all the melody of woe.

ANTISTROPHE.

Thou fell, ill-omen'd, cruel spear,
Couldst thou the father's curses hear,
And wing'd with fury drink the brother's gore?
Now, Laius, boast the frantic deed ;
Thy disobedience has its meed,
The fatal oracle delays no more.
These are your works ; and round them
stand
Horrors, and death's avenging band.

EPOD.

Is this a tale of fair-created woe?
In very deed before our eyes
[*The dead bodies of* ETEOCLES *and* PO-
LYNICES *are here brought on the stage.*
A twofold scene of misery lies,
And from a double slaughter double horrors
flow ;
Whilst grief on grief, and groan on groan
Rush in, and make this house their own.
Come then, ye virgins, from the mournful
bands,
    To wail the mighty slain ;
And ever and anon at each sad ause
    The dying cadence draws,
    Together smite your high-rais'd hands ;
The sullen sound attemper'd to the strain,
    That with many a dismal note
    Accompanies the sable boat,
Slow as it sails on Acheron's dull stream,
    Wafting its joyless numbers o'er
    To that unlovely, dreary shore,
Which Phœbus never views, nor the light's golden
    beam."

ÆSCHYLUS: POTTER.

No. 561.

Capaneus threatened by Jupiter.

DIOSCORIDES. *Oriental Sardonyx.*

No. 562.

Capaneus killed by Jupiter.

DIOSCORIDES. *Oriental Sardonyx.*

"Th' immortals blush to fear ; but when they spy
In midway air an earth-born warrior stand
Oppos'd to Jove, and the mad fight demand,
Th' unwonted scene in silence they admire,
And doubt if he'll employ th' ethereal fire.

Now 'gan the pole just o'er th' Ogygian tow'r
To thunder, prelude of almighty pow'r,
And heav'n was ravish'd from each mortal
eye.
Yet still he grasps the spires he can't descry ;

And oft as gleams shone through the breaking cloud,
' This flash comes opportune,' he cries aloud,
' To wrap proud Thebes in fire; at my demand
'Twas sent to wake anew my smould'ring brand.'
While thus he spake, the lord of all above
Bar'd his right arm, and all his thunder drove:
Dispers'd in ambient air his plumes upflew,
And his shield falls discolour'd to the view;
And now his manly members all lie bare.
Both hosts astounded at the dazzling glare

Recede, lest rushing with his whelming weight
And flaming limbs he hasten on their fate.
His helmet, hair, and torch now hiss within,
And from the touch quick shrinks his shudd'ring skin;
He shoves his mail away, amaz'd to feel
Beneath his breast the cinders of the steel,
And places full against the hated wall
His smoking bosom, lest half-burnt he fall.
At length his earthly part resolv'd away,
The spirit quits its prison-house of clay."

STATIUS, *Thebiad.*

" Forsooth, you deem
That justice was infring'd, when smok'd the body
Of frantic Capaneus, by thunder smitten,
Upon that ladder which he at the gates
Erecting swore he would lay waste our city,
Or with dread Jove's consent, or in despite
Of the vindictive god; nor should th' abyss
Have snatch'd away that augur, swallowing up
His chariot in the caverns of the earth:
Nor was it fitting that those other chiefs
Should at the gates lie breathless, with their limbs

Disjointed by huge stones; boast that your wisdom
Transcends e'en that of Jove himself, or own
The gods may punish sinners. It behoves
Those who are wise to love their children first,
Their aged parents next, and native land,
Whose growing fortunes they are bound t' improve,
And not dismember it. In him who leads
An host, or pilot station'd at the helm,
Rashness is dangerous; he who by discretion
His conduct regulates, desists in time,
And caution I esteem the truest valour."

EURIPIDES.

No. 563.

The same subject.

PYRGOTELES.   *Calcedony, partaking of Sapphire.*

No. 564.

Evadne, the wife of Capaneus, inconsolable for the loss of her husband, throws herself on the pile which consumed him.

CHROMIOS.

CHORUS.

" And now the pyre of Capaneus I see;
And there without the gates the sacred tomb
By Theseus rais'd, sad honour to the dead,
Th' illustrious wife of him, who by the stroke
Of thunder fell transfix'd, Evadne nigh,
Daughter of aged Iphis. Why this way
Advancing, on the rock's aerial height
That overlooks this dome takes she her stand?

STROPHE.—EVADNE.

Where now the golden flood of light,
Roll'd from the glorious-beaming orb of day?
Where the moon's silver-waving ray,
That to her swift train riding through the night
Spreads her pale lustre through the air?
What time, the festive joy to share,
Applauding Argos join'd my nuptial train,
And swell'd the high ecstatic strain,
Hailing in votive verse the bride,
With Capaneus their hero at my side?
Now raving from my house I came,
Bent to partake my lost lord's doom;
To share with him the funeral flame,
With him to sink into the tomb;
With him to Pluto's dark abodes to go,
There end a toilsome life of woe.
Sweetest the death, if ratified on high,
Together with our dying friends to die.

CHORUS.

There from thy rocky station dost thou see
That pyre, the sacred right of Jove, where lies
Thy husband, by the thunder's flame subdu'd?

ANTISTROPHE.—EVADNE.

I see my end; for this I came,
For this the station of this rock I chose;
The tangling fates around me close.
Hence will I throw me, led by honest fame,
And headlong from this cliff's steep brow
Plunge in the flaming pile below.
With my lov'd lord's my body shall be laid;
And as the flames around us spread,

My corse with his dear corse shall join,
Pleas'd thus to tread the courts of Proserpine.
Thee, though the iron hand of death
Hath seiz'd thy livid limbs his prey,
Never shall thy Evadne's breath,
In fondness for this earth, betray.
Bright sun, farewell; farewell my nuptial bed;
Happier in Argos be thou spread.
My generous lord glow'd with love's purest fire,
And with him shall the generous wife expire.

CHORUS.

But see, thy father, aged Iphis, near
Advances; thy last words, if unexpected
They hit his ear, will fill his soul with grief.

IPHIS.

O thou unhappy! I too in mine age
Unhappy; from the gods a double grief
Lies on me: to his country would I bear
My son, who by the Theban spear was slain,
Eteoclus;—my daughter too I seek;
She disappear'd at once, leaving my house
With abrupt flight, the wife of Capaneus,
To die with her dead husband her warm wish.
My care was watchful o'er her, and a while
Prevented this; but through these pressing ills
My vigilance suspended, she escap'd
Most likely hither: if you know, inform me.

EVADNE.

Why ask of them, my father? on this rock,
Like some poor bird, I hover o'er the pyre
Of Capaneus, a wretch, and soon to fall.

.   .   .   .   .

IPHIS.

Some senseless riddle this; what may it mean?

EVADNE.

Hence to the pyre of Capaneus I plunge.

IPHIS.

My daughter, let not many hear such words.

u u

EVADNE.

It is my wish that every Argive heard them.

IPHIS.

To such a deed I never will consent.

EVADNE.

It matters not; thou canst not reach me here.
Now plunge I headlong down: to thee my fall
Not pleasing, but to me and to my husband,
Thus join'd in death, and in one funeral pile."

EURIPIDES: POTTER.

" With what a bound and placid smile
Evadne leap'd upon the fun'ral pile;
And, folding in her arms her husband's corse,
Explor'd the traces of the lightning's force."

STATIUS, *Thebaid.*

No. 565.

Hæmon and Antigone.

DIOSCORIDES.   *Oriental Sardonyx.*

Antigone was put to death by order of Creon king of Thebes, because, contrary to his orders, she had given sepulture to the body of her brother Polynices. Hæmon the son of Creon, by whom she was passionately beloved, killed himself on her body.

CREON.

" If mournful cries and wailings before death
Avail'd, there is not one, be well assured,
That e'er would cease them. Instant take her
      hence,
Enclose her in the rock's sepulchral cave,
As I commanded; leave her there alone,
Either to die, or there to live entomb'd.
We from her death receive no stain; but she
No more shall with the living converse hold.

ANTIGONE.

O thou dark tomb, thou rugged bridal bed !
Deep mansion, which shalt ever close me round !
To thee I go : I go to join my friends,
A numerous train, whom sunk among the dead
Hath Proserpine receiv'd. I go the last
And most unhappy, ere th' allotted space
Of life I reach. Yet glowing at my heart
I feed this hope—that to my father dear,
And dear to thee, my mother—dear to thee,

My brother,—I shall go ; since with these hands
Your bodies I with cleansing lavers wash'd,
Added each ritual ornament, and pour'd
Libations at your tombs. And now thy corse,
Loved Polynices, in the earth I laid,
And for the pious deed have this reward;
Yet those of better judgment will approve
My care, which paid these honours to the dead.
Were I a mother now, were I a wife,
Mouldering in death if child or husband lay,
I would not, if the state opposed the deed,
In such a task engage. Ask you what rules
Direct my conduct ? If an husband dies,
Another might be wedded ; to a child,
One lost, another father might give birth :
But when both parents in the earth are laid
Entomb'd, a brother can no more be born.
Me, by these thoughts impell'd with hallow'd rites
To honour thee, my brother, Creon deem'd
Deep stain'd with guilt, and daring heinous
      deeds;

He seized me with rude hands, he leads me now,
Of nuptial rites, of hymeneal song,
Of bridal bed depriv'd, and the sweet joys
A mother in her children's nurture knows;
But thus oppress'd with wretchedness, by friends
Abandon'd, to the caves of death I go
Alive. What rites, what honours of the gods
Have I transgress'd? But why, unhappy me,
Why to the gods look more? What heav'nly
　　pow'r
Shall I invoke, since for my pious deeds
I bear the vengeance to the impious due?
If this the justice of the gods demands,
And I offend, these sufferings I forgive:
If these offend, no greater ill be theirs
Than they to me unjustly have assign'd.

CHORUS.

The tempest of her passions yet is high;
The same impetuous spirit rules her yet.

CREON.

For this the slaves that lead her shall be taught
With tears their slow obedience to repent.

ANTIGONE.

Death from that menace is not distant far.

CREON.

I will not soothe thee with the flattering hope
That thy fixed doom shall ever be reversed.

ANTIGONE.

Thou city of my fathers, royal Thebes,
And you, who from my country drew your birth,
Ye gods, I hence am forced; I am no more!
And you, who o'er the Theban state preside,
See the last virgin of an honour'd line,
Your kings: see what I suffer, and from whom,
See me condemn'd for pious deeds to die!"
　　　　　　　　SOPHOCLES: POTTER.

No. 566.

Theophane borne by Neptune, transformed into a ram, to the island of Crumissa.

GNAIOS. *Oriental Cornelian.*

Under this transformation he had by her the golden-fleeced ram that bore Phryxus to Colchis.

No. 567.

Phryxus and Helle.

DIOSCORIDES. *Oriental Amethyst.*

Phryxus and his sister Helle, the children of Athamas king of Thebes and Nephele his second wife, whom he repudiated that he might take back Ino his first wife, were the origin of the beautiful allegory of the Golden Fleece. Ino was resolved on the death of these children, and to accomplish her purpose caused sentence of death to be passed on them by means of an oracle, pretending that this sacrifice was necessary to stay the ravages which a famine was then making in the city. The children of Nephele fled on the ram of the golden fleece, and took the route to Colchis; but as they were crossing the arm of the sea which separates Europe and Asia, Helle grew giddy and fell into the strait, which from her took the name of Hellespont. Phryxus continued his flight, and, arriving at Colchis, where Æëtes was king, sacrificed the ram to Jupiter, and suspended the rich fleece on a tree in a wood dedicated to the god of war. He then married Chalciope, the daughter of Æëtes, but was afterwards murdered by order of the king, that he might gain possession of the fleece, which was recovered by Jason in the year 1294 before our era, and the 85th before the taking of Troy.

" Now may you lift your eyes to heaven, and say,
' Sol back'd the Phryxean wether yesterday.'
The seeds all scorch'd by wicked Ino's wile,
No fruits would grow, as they were wont ere while ;
A message is to Delphian Tripos sent,
To beg some help for souls with famine spent.
He with the seeds corrupt brought word : ' Fates stood
To have both Phryxus' and his sister's blood.'
Time, people, Ino, all do urging stand
Th' abhorring king t' obey the sad command.
Phryxus and Helle crown'd with flow'rs stand by
The altars, moaning their joint destiny.

Their mother spies them as in th' air she hung,
And hands against her frighted bosom flung ;
Leaps into Thebes, girt with a troop of clouds,
And snatch'd her children from amid the crowds.
And for their flight the ram with golden fleece
Was given to both, which bears them o'er the seas.
The fainting maid with weak left hand the ram
Held by the horn, when she that sea did name ;
Her brother, whilst he strain'd to help, and gave
His hand stretch'd to her, scarce himself could save.
He for his double-dangers mate miscarried
Laments, not knowing Neptune her had married.
Ashore the ram was to the heavens extoll'd,
And Colchis kept his precious fleece of gold."

Ovid's *Festivals.*

" Phryxus, whose smiles Æëtes' realm behold
Borne on the lordly ram of fleecy gold ;
Proud work of Hermes ! still its honours seen
Suspended from the oak's eternal green ;
Itself to Jove a sacred victim spread,
The god commanding to the wand'rer's dread,
Who smoothed the path of flight ; thy spousal arms,
Divine Chalciope, of matchless charms,
A sire to brave Æëtes' love resigned."

Apoll. Rhodius.

No. 568.

Phryxus hearing with surprise the ram speak.

Pyrgoteles. *Amethyst.*

No. 569.

Helle falling from the ram into the waves of the Hellespont.

Gnaios. *Sardonyx.*

No. 570.

Phryxus slaying a ram before the altar of Jupiter.

GNAIOS. *Amethyst.*

No. 571.

Phryxus burning the ram on the altar, whilst the fleece is suspended on a tree.

APOLLONIDES. *Oriental Cornelian.*

No. 572.

Minerva instructing Argus in building the ship Argo.

DIOSCORIDES. *Oriental Cornelian.*

Argus, a celebrated architect of the heroic ages, constructed the ship which bore his name, and in which the heroes who reconquered the golden fleece embarked for Colchis. This was the first large ship built in Greece. Minerva, or Pallas, gave the architect a beam of wood from the sacred forest of Dodona (some say, for a mast; some say, for a bow), which possessed an oracular power.

"From Pelion Argo's keel loud murmurs broke, / Urgent to sail; the keel of sacred oak, / Endu'd with voice and marvellously wrought, / Itonian Pallas from Dodona brought. / For though wise Argus with ingenious art / Form'd the fair ship compact in every part, / Vigour divine propitious Pallas gave, / And pow'r assign'd her o'er the wind and wave."
APOLL. RHOD.

No. 573.

Jason supplicating Juno to convey him across the river Enipeus.

PYRGOTELES. *Amethyst.*

Jason, the son of Æson and Alcimede, at the age of twenty quitted the abode of Chiron, which had served him as an asylum, and where he had been instructed by the centaur in the arts and sciences, but more particularly in medicine. He resolved on going to Pelias, his maternal uncle, and claiming the sceptre of Iolchos, which he had wrested from his father Æson. Arriving on the banks of the Enipeus, Jason met Juno, the implacable enemy of Pelias, who, under the form of an old woman, offers to transport him to the opposite shore. In crossing, Jason loses one of his sandals.

No. 574.

Jason, after having been conveyed across the river, discovers that he has lost his sandal.

PYRGOTELES.   *Sardonyx.*

No. 575.

Jason in presence of Pelias.

CHROMIOS.   *Sardonyx.*

Jason, presenting himself before Pelias, demands the crown of Iolchos, usurped by him. Pelias promises to restore it to him when he returns victorious with the golden fleece from Colchis.

No. 576.

Jason engaging the great poet Orpheus to accompany him in the expedition to Colchis.

CHROMIOS.   *Sardonyx.*

" Offspring of Æson, thou with wisdom fraught,
By Chiron's precepts and example taught,
Thou lov'st the minstrel partner of thy way,
Who cheer'd Bistonia's earth with lenient sway."

APOLL. RHOD.

No. 577.

Jason taking leave of Chiron, who is carrying the infant Achilles on his back.

CHROMIOS.   *Oriental Cornelian.*

No. 578.

Jason, before his departure for Colchis, offering a sacrifice to Neptune for a prosperous voyage.

CHROMIOS.   *Oriental Cornelian.*

" If Jason, friends, dear object of your choice,
Tow'r to the sacred charge, be ours no more
To woo soft dalliance on th' inglorious shore;
Yet to the pow'r of light our zeal employ
The pious incense and the festal joy ;

Then urge the vassals, to whose skill preferr'd
To cull the richest of the lordly herd ;
Ere at the shrine they shed their sacred blood
The vessel drag we to th' encircling flood ;

Fix'd the well-order'd arms' terrific grace,
Th' allotted oar its seat of labour trace;
Through the wide strand, auspicious god, rever'd,
Now the rich altar to thy name be rear'd

By parting mariners; nor thou in vain,
Guide of our course, our guardian o'er the main,
Deign'st to announce, oracular, thy aid,
The year's first off'rings on thy shrine display'd."

APOLL. RHOD.

No. 579.

Jason conferring with Triton.

APOLLONIDES. *Calcedony, of rare beauty.*

The ship Argo was driven by contrary winds near the shores of Lydia into the lake Tritonis, where it remained some time. At last a Triton appeared, and indicated to Jason the best and least dangerous means of getting the ship out of the lake. He unloosed one of the horses from Neptune's car, and sent it before the Argonauts to guide them on their way.

"In sad suspense, still wishing to forsake,
And cross with favouring gales Tritonis' lake,
They loiter long, and waste the useful day
In idle contest and in vain delay.
A serpent thus, long scorch'd with summer's heat,
Winds to some secret chink, his cool retreat;
Enrag'd he hisses, rears his crest on high,
And furious darts his fire-emitting eye,
Till haply he the wished-for chink pervade,
And in its cool recess secure a shade.
Uncertain thus the ship explor'd in vain
The lake's wide mouth that opened to the main.
With pious care, as Orpheus gives command,
They place Apollo's tripod on the strand,
That those auspicious powers the coast who guard,
Pleas'd with th' oblation, may their toils reward.
Clad like a youth, before them stood confess'd.

.   .   .   .   .

Heartening he spoke : the decks they reascend,
And, rowing brisk, to cross the lake contend.
The proffer'd tripod friendly Triton takes,
And hides his head beneath the dimpling lakes.

Thus with the costly prize the god withdrew,
Instant invisible to mortal view.
Inspir'd with joy, that some superior guest
Had comfort given them, and with counsel
    bless'd,
The choicest sheep they bade their leader slay,
And to the power benign due honours pay.
He to the galley's poop with speed convey'd
The choicest sheep, and, as he offer'd, pray'd :
' Dread deity, who late conspicuous stood
On the clear margin of this rolling flood,
Whether great Triton's name delight thine ear,
Triton whom all the watery gods revere,
Or Ocean's daughters, as they sound thy fame,
Thee mighty Nereus, or thee Phorcus name,
Be bounteous still; bid all our labours cease,
And reinstate us in our native Greece.'
Thus pray'd the chief, as on the poop he stood,
And sunk the slaughter'd victim in the flood.
His head above the billows Triton rear'd,
And in his proper shape the god appear'd."

APOLL. RHOD.

"The son of Neptune, in his awful mood,
Up-heaves a form majestic, and his own;
No borrow'd shape of man !—the courser known
Thus 'mid th' embattled circus speeds his way :
Wild floats his mane; he, practis'd to obey,

Rears his arch'd neck sublime; from side to
    side
Grinds the champ'd bit, his slavery and his pride;
So, firmly grasping Argo's polish'd keel,
He winds her o'er the surge with monarch-zeal !

The back, the head, the loins, the structure prove
His faithful lineage from the gods above;
The tail's strong nerves a monster-fish display,
And lash the surface of the wat'ry way,
Obliquely darting their divided gleam,
Soft as thy crescent swells, thou lunar beam!
Her guide, till roll'd o'er Ocean's central round,
Then dashing plunges in the dark profound.

Each wond'ring warrior murmurs, as he eyes
The form celestial of portentous size.
Ev'n now th' Argöan port, th' attesting signs
Of sacred Argo, and th' exalted shrines
To Ocean's god, to Ocean's child appear;
Shrines on that awful day the warriors rear!
Light's orient dawn allures the zephyr gale;
Earth's deserts they explore with spreading sail."

APOLL. RHOD.

No. 580.

Jason, in gratitude to Triton for his assistance, gives him a golden tripod.

GNAIOS. *Oriental Cornelian.*

No. 581.

Triton with the tripod.

CHROMIOS. *Amethyst.*

No. 582.

Medea conducting Jason to the altar of Diana, or Hecate, that they may bind each other by vows of mutual fidelity.

APOLLONIDES. *Calcedony, partaking of Sapphire.*

Jason having landed at Colchis, Medea, the daughter of Æëtes and priestess of Hecate, became enamoured of him, and conducted him to a grove consecrated to the goddess.

" Meanwhile the maid her secret thoughts enjoy'd,
And one dear object all her soul employ'd;
Her train's gay sports no pleasure can restore;
Vain was the dance, and music charm'd no more.
She hates each object, every face offends;
In every wish her soul to Jason sends:
With sharpen'd eyes the distant lawn explores,
To find the hero whom her soul adores;
At every whisper of the passing air,
She starts, she turns, and hopes her Jason there;
Again she fondly looks, nor looks in vain;
He comes: her Jason shines along the plain.

As when, emerging from the wat'ry way,
Refulgent Sirius lifts his golden ray,
He shines terrific, for his burning breath
Taints the red air with fevers, plagues, and death:
Such to the nymph approaching Jason shews,
Bright author of unutterable woes;
Before her eyes a swimming darkness spread,
Her flush'd cheeks glow'd, her very heart was dead:
No more her knees their wonted office knew,
Fix'd without motion, as to earth, they grew.
Her train recedes—the meeting lovers gaze
In silent wonder and in still amaze:

As two fair cedars on the mountain's brow,
Pride of the groves, with roots adjoining grow;
Erect and motionless the stately trees
Short time remain, while sleeps each fanning
    breeze,
Till from th' Æolian caves a blast unbound
Bends their proud tops, and bids their boughs re-
    sound :
Thus gazing they, till by the breath of love
Strongly at last inspir'd, they speak—they move;
With smiles the love-sick virgin he survey'd,
And fondly thus address'd the blooming maid :
  ' Dismiss, my fair, my love, thy virgin fear;
'Tis Jason speaks, no enemy is here;
Dread not in me a haughty heart to find :
In Greece I bore no proud inhuman mind.
Whom wouldst thou fly? stay, lovely virgin, stay;
Speak every thought; far hence be fears away ;
Speak, and be truth in every accent found ;
Scorn to deceive ; we tread on hallow'd ground.
By the stern power who guards this sacred place,
By the fam'd authors of thy royal race,
By Jove, to whom the stranger's cause belongs,
To whom the suppliant, and who feels their
    wrongs,—
O guard me, save me, in the needful hour;
Without thy aid thy Jason is no more;
To thee a suppliant in distress I bend,
To thee a stranger, one who wants a friend ;

Then when between us seas and mountains rise,
Medea's name shall sound in distant skies;
All Greece to thee shall owe her hero's fates,
And bless Medea through her hundred states.
The mother and the wife, who now in vain
Roll their sad eyes fast streaming o'er the main,
Shall stay their tears ; the mother and the wife
Shall bless thee for a son's or husband's life !
Fair Ariadne, sprung from Minos' bed,
Sav'd valiant Theseus, and with Theseus fled ;
Forsook her father and her native plain,
And stemm'd the tumults of the surging main.
Yet the stern sire relented, and forgave
The maid whose only crime it was to save;
E'en the just gods forgave, and now on high
A star she shines, and beautifies the sky.
What blessings, then, shall righteous heaven de-
    cree
For all our heroes sav'd, and sav'd by thee ?
Heaven gave thee not to kill so soft an air,
And cruelty sure never look'd so fair !'
He ceas'd, but left so charming on her ear
His voice, that listening still she seem'd to hear :
Her eyes to earth she bends with modest grace,
And heaven in smiles is open'd on her face.
A look she steals ; but rosy blushes spread
O'er her fair cheek, and then she hangs her head."

APOLL. RHOD.

No. 583.

Jason and Medea, at the altar of Diana or Hecate, exchanging vows of mutual fidelity.

KARPOS. *Oriental Cornelian.*

No. 584.

Medea presenting the charm to Jason.

GNAIOS. *Amethyst.*

x x

" A thousand words at once to speak she tries
In vain; but speaks a thousand with her eyes:
Trembling the shining casket she expands,
Then gives the magic virtue to his hands;
And had the power been granted to convey
Her heart, had given her very heart away.
For Jason beam'd in beauty's charms so bright,
The maid admiring, languish'd with delight;
Thus when the rising sun appears in view,
On the fair rose dissolves the radiant dew.
Now on the ground both cast their bashful eyes,
Both view each other now with mild surprise.
The rosy smiles now dimpling on their cheeks,
The fair at length in faltering accents speaks:
' Observant thou, to my advice attend,
And hear what succour I propose to lend:
Soon as my sire Æëta shall bestow
The dragon's teeth in Mars's field to sow,
The following night in equal shares divide;
Bathe well thy limbs in some perennial tide:
Then all retir'd, thyself in black array,
Dig the round foss, and there a victim slay,
A female lamb; the carcass place entire
Above the foss, then light the sacred pyre,
And Perseus' daughter, Hecate, appease
With honey, sweetest labour of the bees:
This done retreat, nor while the relics burn
Let howling dogs provoke thee to return,
Nor human footsteps; lest thou render vain
The charm, and with dishonour join thy train.
Next morn, the whole enchantment to fulfil,
This magic unguent on thy limbs distil;

Then thou with ease wilt strong and graceful move,
Not like a mortal, but the gods above.
Forget not with this unguent to besmear
Thy sword, thy buckler, and tremendous spear;
No giant's falchions then can harm thy frame,
Nor the fell rage of bulls' expiring flame.
One day, nor longer, wilt thou keep the field;
Nor thou to perils nor to labour yield.
But mark my words: when thou with ceaseless
     toil
Hast yok'd the bulls, and plough'd the stubborn
'   soil;
And seest up-springing on the teeth-sown land
Of giant foes a formidable band.

.   .   .   .
All bath'd in tears she sits; her hand sustains
     her head:
There sits she pondering in a pensive state,
What dire distresses on her counsels wait.
But Jason, eager to return, withdrew
With his two friends, and join'd his social crew,
Who throng'd impatient round, while he display'd
The secret counsels of the Colchian maid,
And shew'd the potent herbs; Idas apart
Conceal'd the choler rankling in his heart.
Meanwhile the rest, when glimmering daylight
     clos'd,
Wrapp'd in the mantle of the night, repos'd.
Next morn they sent Æthalides, the son
Of Mercury, and valiant Telamon,
(For thus in council had the Greeks decreed,)
Of fierce Æëta to demand the seed."

APOLL. RHOD.

No. 585.

Jason taming the wild bulls.

APOLLONIDES. *Oriental Cornelian.*

The recovery of the golden fleece could only be effected by whosoever should succeed in taming two furious bulls, from whose nostrils issued flames, and plough with them four acres of a field consecrated to Mars. Jason, aided by Medea, succeeded in this enterprise.

" Meanwhile, instructed by the magic maid,
The chief his shield, his spear, and trenchant blade
With unguents smear'd : the Greeks, approaching
    nigh,
In vain their efforts on his armour try ;
But chief the spear such magic charms attend,
No force can break it, and no onset bend.
Idas enrag'd deals many a furious wound :
But as hard hammers from an anvil bound,
So from the spear his sword recoiling sprung ;
The distant vales with loud applauses rung.
Next, with the potent charm the chief anoints
His well-turu'd limbs, and supples all his joints ;
And, lo ! new pow'rs invigorate his hands,
And arm'd with strength intrepidly he stands.
As the proud steed, exulting in his might,
Erects his ears, impatient for the fight,
And pawing snuffs the battle from afar,
So pants the hero for the promis'd war.
Firmly he moves, incapable of fear ;
One hand his shield sustains, and one the spear.
Thus when black clouds obscure the darkening
    day,
And rains descend, the living lightnings play.
And now the fight draws near ; the Grecian train
Sail up the Phasis to the martial plain,
Which from as far the towers of Æa stand,
As when the chieftains, who the games com-
    mand
For some dead king, the bounding barriers place
For steeds or men contending in the race.
Æeta there they found, of mind elate ;
On Phasis' banks his chariot rolls in state ;
On the Caucasian summits that command
The field of Mars, the crowded Colchians stand.
Now Argo moor'd, the prince invades the field,
Arm'd with his magic spear and ample shield ;
With serpents' teeth his brazen helm was stor'd,
And 'cross his shoulder gleam'd his glittering
    sword :
Like Mars the chief enormous power display'd,
Or Phœbus brandishing his golden blade.
O'er the rough tilth he cast his eyes around,
And soon the plough of adamant he found,

And yokes of brass ; his helm (approaching near)
He plac'd on earth, and upright fix'd his spear.
To find the bulls he farther went afield,
And trac'd their steps, arm'd only with his shield.
In a dark cave which smoky mists surround,
Horrid and huge their safe retreat he found ;
With rage impetuous forth the monsters came,
And from their nostrils issued streams of flame.
Fear seiz'd the Greeks, but he their fury braves,
Firm as a rock defies the roaring waves :
Screen'd by his shield, intrepidly he scorns
The bulls' loud bellowing and their butting
    horns ;
Collected firm he wards each threat'ning blow.
As at the forge where melting metals glow,
While now the bellows heave, now sink by turns,
The flame subsides, or with fresh fury burns,
Stirr'd to the bottom roars the raging fire ;
So roar the bulls, and living flame expire,
That fierce as lightning round the hero play'd,
In vain, now shelter'd by the magic maid.
One bull he seiz'd that aim'd a deadly stroke—
Seiz'd by the horns, and dragg'd him to the
    yoke,
Then hurl'd the roaring monster on the ground :
An equal fate his fellow captive found.
Loos'd from his arm he flung his shield aside,
And the two monsters manfully he ply'd ;
Dragg'd on their knees his fiery foes o'ercame,
And shifting artfully escap'd the flame.
Æeta view'd him with astonish'd eyes ;
When, lo ! the sons of Tyndarus arise,
As erst it was decreed, and from the land
Heav'd the strong yokes, and gave them to his
    hand ;
These o'er the bulls' low-bended necks he flung ;
The brazen beams by rings suspended hung.
The youths retreating from the burning field,
The chief resum'd his loaded helm, his shield
Behind him thrown ; then grasp'd his massy spear,
(Thus arm'd the hinds of Thessaly appear,
With long sharp goads to prick their bullocks'
    sides)
And the firm plough of adamant he guides.

The restive bulls, with indignation fir'd,
From their broad nostrils living flames expir'd,
Loud as the blasts when wint'ry winds prevail,
And trembling sailors furl the folding sail.
Urg'd by his spear the bulls their task fulfil,
Prove their own prowess, and the ploughman's
    skill.
As the sharp coulter cleft the clodded ground,
The roughen'd ridges sent a rattling sound.
Firm o'er the field undaunted Jason treads,
And scattering wide the serpents' teeth he
    spreads:
Yet oft looks back, suspecting he should find
A legion rising up in arms behind;
Unwearied still the bulls their toil pursue,
Their brazen hoofs the stubborn soil subdue.
When now three portions of the day were spent,
And weary hinds at evening homeward went,
The chief had till'd four acres of the soil;
He then releas'd the monsters from their toil.
Away they scamper'd wildly o'er the plain;
Himself rejoin'd his delegated train,
Till on the field his earth-born foes appear;
The Greeks their animated hero cheer.
He in his helm, replenish'd at the springs,
To slake his burning thirst fresh water brings;
His limbs renew'd with forceful vigour play,
His heart beats boldly and demands the fray.
Thus the fell boar disdains the hunter-bands—
Foams—whets his tusks—and in defiance stands.
Now rose th' embattled squadron in the field,
In glittering helms array'd, with spear and shield;
Bright o'er the martial train the splendous rise,
And dart in streams of radiance to the skies.
Thus when thick snow the face of nature shrouds,
And nightly winds dispel the wint'ry clouds,
The stars again their splendid beams display:
So shone the warriors in the face of day.
But Jason, mindful of the maid's command,
Seiz'd a vast rock, and rais'd it from the land;
Not four stout youths, for strength of limbs re-
    nown'd,
Could lift a weight so pond'rous from the ground;

This 'midst his foes, embattled on the field,
He hurl'd, and safe retir'd behind his shield.
The Colchians shout, as when the raging main
Roars round tremendous rocks, but roars in vain.
In silence fix'd Æëta stands aghast
To see the fragment with such fury cast.
The host, like dogs contending o'er their prey,
With curs'd ferocity their comrades slay;
Then leave on earth their mangled trunks be-
    hind,
Like pines of oaks uprooted by the wind.
As shoots a star from heaven's ethereal brow,
Portending vengeance to the world below,
Who through dark clouds descry its radiant
    light;
Thus Jason rush'd in glittering armour bright.
His brandish'd falchion fell'd the rising foes:
Succinct in arms, some half their lengths disclose,
Some scarce their shoulders; others feebly stand,
While others, treading firm, the fight demand.
As on the bounds which separate hostile states,
Eternal source of battle and debates,
The cautious hind the cruel spoiler fears,
And reaps his wheat with yet unripen'd ears,
Ere yet the spikes their wonted growth attain,
Ere yet the sunbeams have matur'd the grain:
So Jason's arms the rising squadrons mow'd,
Their blood profusely in the furrows flow'd.
Some sidelong fall on earth, and some supine,
Some prone lie grovelling, and their lives resign,
Like whales incumbent on the buoyant main;
Some wounded perish ere they tread the plain:
As late in air they held their heads on high,
So lowly humbled in the dust they lie.
Thus tender plants, by copious torrents drown'd,
Strew their fresh leaves uprooted from the
    ground;
The tiller views with heart-corroding pain
His fostering care, and all his labours vain.
Æëta thus with wild vexation burn'd,
And with his Colchians to the town return'd,
Some weightier task revolving in his mind.
Thus clos'd the combat, and the day declin'd."
                                    APOLL. RHOD.

No. 586.

Jason sowing the field of Mars with dragon's teeth.

CHARILAOS.

Jason, after having ploughed the field of Mars, sowed in it the teeth of the dragon consecrated to the same god, when he saw an army of men spring from the ground and run towards him. He threw a stone in the midst of them, and they fought amongst each other till all were destroyed. (See the preceding quotation.)

No. 587.

Jason obtains the golden fleece.

PYRGOTELES. *Oriental Cornelian.*

See explanation to No. 585.

" Here, as by Argus taught, the chiefs with-
  drew,
While their lone course the regal pair pursue
Through the thick grove, impatient to behold
The spreading beech that bears the fleecy gold;
Suspended here it darts a beamy blaze,
Like a cloud tipp'd with Phœbus' orient rays.
With high arch'd neck in front the dragon lies,
And tow'rds the strangers turns his sleepless
  eyes;
Aloud he hisses, the wide woods around
And Phasis' banks return the doleful sound.
Colchians far distant from Titanus' shore,
Heard e'en to Lycus' streams the hideous roar—
Lycus who, sever'd from Araxis' tides,
A boisterous flood, with gentle Phasis glides;
One common course their streams united keep,
And roll united to the Caspian deep.
The mother, starting from her bed of rest,
Fears for her babe reclining on her breast;
And closely clasping to her fondling arms,
Protects her trembling infant from alarms.
As from some wood, involv'd in raging fires,
Clouds following clouds ascend in curling spires,

The smoky wreaths in long succession climb,
And from the bottom rise in air sublime;
The dragon thus his scaly volumes roll'd,
Wreath'd his huge length, and gather'd fold in
  fold.
Him, winding slow, beheld the magic dame,
And sleep invok'd, the monster's rage to tame.
With potent song the drowsy god she sway'd
To summon all his succour to her aid;
And Hecate from Pluto's coast she drew,
To lull the dauntless monster, and subdue.
Jason advanc'd with awe—with awe beheld
The dreaded dragon by her magic quell'd:
Lifeless he lay, each languid fold unbound,
And his vast spine extended on the ground:
Thus when the boist'rous wave forbears to
  roar,
It sinks recumbent on the peaceful shore.
Still strove the monster his huge head to heave,
And in his deadly jaws his foe receive.
A branch of juniper the maid applies,
Steep'd in a baneful potion to his eyes;
Its odours strong the branch diffus'd around,
And sunk th' enormous beast in sleep profound.

Supine he sunk; his jaws forgot to move,
And his unnumber'd folds are spread o'er half the
    grove.
Then Jason to the beech his hand applies,
And grasps at her command the golden prize.
Still she persists to ply the potent spell,
And the last vigour of the monster quell,
Till he advis'd her to rejoin the crew :
Then from the grove of Mars the maid withdrew.
As some fair dame, when Cynthia rises bright,
Beholds the beamy splendours with delight,
Which from her vestment strong-reflected rise,
Thus gloried Jason in the glistering prize.
The flaming rays that from its surface flow'd,
Beam'd on his cheeks and on his forehead
    glow'd.
Large as the heifer's hide, or as the hind's,
Which in Achaia's plains the hunter finds,
Shone the thick, pond'rous fleece, whose golden
    rays
Far o'er the land diffus'd a beamy blaze.
He on his shoulders now the spoil suspends,
Low at his feet the flowing train descends.
Collecting now within its pond'rous folds,
His grasping hand the costly capture holds :
Fearful he moves, with circumspect survey,
Lest men or gods should snatch the prize away.
Now as returning morn illumes the land,
The royal pair rejoin the gallant band;
The gallant band beheld with wond'ring eyes,
Fierce as Jove's fiery bolt, the radiant prize;
Their hands extending as they flock around,
All wish to heave the trophy from the ground.

But Jason interdicting singly threw
O'er the broad fleece a covering rich and new;
Then in the ship he plac'd the virgin-guest,
And thus the listening demigods address'd :
' No longer doubt ye, comrades, to regain
Far o'er a length of seas your lov'd domain.
For see, the end of all our glorious toil,
Won by Medea's aid, this precious spoil !
Her, not reluctant, I to Greece will bear,
And with connubial honours crown her there.
Guard your fair patroness, ye gallant crew,
Who sav'd your country when she succour'd
    you.
Soon will Æëta with his Colchian train
Preclude, I ween, our passage to the main.
Some with your oars resume your destin'd seat,
Some with your shields secure your wish'd re-
    treat;
This rampire forming we their darts defy,
Nor home returning unreveng'd will die.
Lo, on our prowess all we love depends—
Our children, parents, country, and our friends !
Greece, as we speed, through future times shall
    boast
Her empire fix'd, or wail her glory lost.'
He said, and arm'd : the heroes shout applause :
Then from its pendent sheath his sword he draws,
Severs the hauser, and, in arms array'd,
His station fixes near the magic maid,
And where Ancæus' hand the pilot's art dis-
    play'd.
Keen emulation fir'd the labouring crew,
As down the stream of Phasis Argo flew."

                                    APOLL. RHOD.

No. 588.

Medea and Jason murdering Absyrtus.

CHROMIOS.   *Oriental Sardonyx.*

Jason and Medea fled from Colchis, taking with them the golden fleece and the treasures
stolen from Æëtes. The king sent his son Absyrtus in pursuit of them, and he overtook them
near the mouth of the Danube. Medea enticed him into the temple of Diana, pretending that

she desired an interview with him, when Jason slew him while she lighted him with a torch: but she averts her head, struck with a natural and sudden impulse of horror.

" Her guileful purposes the magic maid
In order thus before the heralds laid :
That soon as Night her sable shade had spread,
And to the temple was Medea led,
Thither Absyrtus should repair, and hear
A project pleasing to a brother's ear:
How she, the golden fleece in triumph borne,
Would to Æëta speed her wish'd return ;
How Phryxus' treacherous sons prolonged her stay,
And her to cruel foes consign'd a prey :
Then far she flung her potent spells in air,
Which lur'd the distant savage from his lair.
Curse of mankind ! from thee contentions flow,
Disastrous love, and every heartfelt woe:
Thy darts the children of thy foes infest,
As now they rankle in Medea's breast.
How vanquish'd by her wiles, Absyrtus fell,
In seemly order now my muse must tell.
    Medea now secur'd in Dian's fane,
The Colchians hasten to their ships again.

Jason meanwhile lies in close ambush, bent
Absyrtus and his friends to circumvent.
Him, yet unpractis'd in his sister's guile,
His ready ship had wafted to the isle :
Conceal'd in night, they tugg'd their toilsome oars,
Till in the bay secure the vessel moors.
Alone in confidence the stripling came,
And at Diana's porch approach'd the dame,
(She like a torrent look'd when swoln with rain,
Which foaming terrifies the village swain,)
To learn what snare her wily art could lay
To drive these bold adventurers away.
And all was plann'd ; when from his ambuscade
Sprung Æson's son, and shook his lifted blade.
The conscious sister, stung with secret dread,
Lest her own eyes should view Absyrtus dead,
Turn'd from the murderous scene aside distress'd,
And veil'd her guilty face beneath her vest.
As falls an ox beneath the striker's blow,
So was Absyrtus laid by Jason low."

APOLLONIUS.

No. 589.

Medea scatters the limbs of Absyrtus in the way, to retard the pursuit of Æëtes, who would naturally stop to pick up the fragments of his child.

APOLLONIDES.   *Oriental Cornelian.*

No. 590.

Jason and Medea near the ship Argo.

APOLLONIDES.   *Oriental Amethyst.*

" Mild grasping in his own her hand ;
The oars, obedient to her lov'd command,
Sweep to the covert of the grove, in peace
Veil'd by the gloom ; her wish the radiant fleece,

Spite of Æétes' frown : no listless stay—
Quick as the word the vessel scuds away.
Forth they ascend; and heaving from the soil
The host incumbent, o'er the sounding toil
Dash fearless."

APOLL. RHOD.

No. 591.

Circe expiating Jason and Medea.

ALLION.   *Sardonyx.*

To expiate the murder of Absyrtus, Jason and Medea repair to the magician Circe.

" Close in her guileful hand she grasp'd each guest,
And bade them follow where her footsteps press'd:
The crowd aloof at Jason's mandate stay'd,
While he accompanied the Colchian maid.
Together thus they Circe's steps pursue,
Till her enchanting cave arose in view.
  Their visit's cause her troubled mind distress'd:
On downy seats she plac'd each princely guest;
They round her hearth sat motionless and mute;
(With plaintive suppliants such manners suit):

Her folded hands her blushing face conceal;
Deep in the ground he fix'd the murderous steel ;
Nor dare they once, in equal sorrow drown'd,
Lift their dejected eyelids from the ground.
Circe beheld their guilt : she saw they fled
From vengeance hanging o'er the murderer's head.
The holy rites, approv'd of Jove, she pays,
(Jove thus appeas'd his hasty vengeance stays;)
These rites from guilty stains the culprits clear,
Who lowly suppliant at her cell appear."

APOLL. RHOD.

No. 592.

The nuptials of Jason and Medea.

ASPASIOS.   *Oriental Cornelian.*

Jason holds the hand of Medea, while Love is uniting them. From his left arm depends the fleece; and at his feet there is an urn.

No. 593.

Medea preparing the juices of herbs to restore Æson to youth.

PYRGOTELES.   *Oriental Cornelian.*

It was believed that Medea, who was skilled in botany and in the secret properties of plants, performed wonderful cures. She was one of the most famous of the ancient sorceresses.

" She leaps into the wain,
Strokes the snakes' necks, and shakes the golden
rein.
That signal giv'n, they mount her to the skies:
And now beneath her fruitful Tempè lies,
Whose stores she ransacks; then to Crete she flies;
There Ossa, Pelion, Othrys, Pindus, all
To the fair ravisher a booty fall;
The tribute of their verdure she collects:
Not proud Olympus' height his plants protects.

Some by the roots she plucks; the tender tops
Of others with her culling sickle crops.
Nor could the plunder of the hills suffice ;
Down to the humble vales and meads she flies:
Apidanus, Amphrysus, the next rape
Sustain, nor could Enipeus' banks escape:
Through Beebè's marsh, and through the border
rang'd,
Whose pasture Glaucus to a Triton chang'd."

OVID.

No. 594.

Medea restoring Æson to youth.

DIOCLES. *Oriental Cornelian.*

Medea, after having drawn all the blood from the body of Æson, substitutes a decoction of plants that she had collected from different countries, which makes him young again and prolongs his life.

" The foaming juices now the brink o'er-
swell ;
The barren heath, where'er the liquor fell,
Sprang out with vernal grass, and all the pride
Of blooming May. When this Medea spy'd,
She cuts her patient's throat; th' exhausted
blood
Recruiting with her new enchanted flood;
While at his mouth, and through his op'ning
wound,
A double inlet her infusion found ;

His feeble frame resumes a youthful air ;
A glossy brown his hoary beard and hair ;
The meagre paleness from his aspect fled,
And in its room sprang up a florid red ;
Through all his limbs a youthful vigour flies ;
His emptied art'ries swell with fresh supplies :
Gazing spectators scarce believe their eyes.
But Æson is the most surpris'd, to find
A happy change in body and in mind ;
In sense and constitution the same man,
As when his fortieth active year began."

OVID.

No. 595.

Talus expiring through the enchantment of Medea.

APOLLONIDES. *Oriental Sardonyx.*

Jupiter had confided the care of the island of Crete to the giant Talus. Talus thrice a day made the round of the island to prevent strangers from landing, which he did by hurling large stones at them, and killing them. Jason and Medea arrived at Crete, and would have shared the

y y

same fate, had not Medea by her art discovered that all the vital power of the giant lay in the blood of a single vein in his right foot. By means of her enchantment she caused a piece of a rock which Talus held in his hand to fall on the foot and open the vein: streams of blood flowed from the vein, and the giant expired in extreme agony.

" The evening star now lifts, as daylight fades,
His golden circlet in the deep'ning shades:
Stretch'd at his ease the weary labourer shares
A sweet forgetfulness of human cares.
At once in silence sleep the sinking gales;
The mast they drop, and furl the flagging sails;
All night, all day, they ply their bending oars
Tow'rds Carpathus, and reach the rocky shores;
Thence Crete they view, emerging from the main,
The queen of isles; but Crete they view in vain.
There Talus mountains hurls with all their woods,
Whole seas roll back, and tossing swell in floods:
Amaz'd the towering monster they survey,
And trembling view the interdicted bay.
His birth he drew from giants sprung from oak,
Or the hard entrails of the stubborn rock:
Fierce guard of Crete! who thrice each year explores
The trembling isle, and strides from shores to shores,
A form of living brass! one part beneath
Alone he bears, a part to let in death;
Where o'er the ankle swells the turgid vein,
Soft to the stroke, and sensible of pain.
Pining with want, and sunk in deep dismay,
From Crete far distant had they sail'd away;
But the fair sorceress their speed repress'd,
And thus the crew disconsolate address'd:
' Attend: this monster, ribb'd with brass around,
My art, I ween, will level to the ground.
Whate'er his name, his strength however great,
Still, not immortal, must he yield to fate.
But from the far-thrown fragments safe retreat,
Till prostrate fall the giant at my feet.'
She said; retiring at her sage command,
They wait the movement of her magic hand:

Wide o'er her face her purple veil she spread,
And climb'd the lofty decks, by Jason led.
And now her magic arts Medea tries;
Bids the red furies, dogs of Orcus, rise,
That starting dreadful from th' infernal shade,
Ride heaven in storms, and all that breathes invade.
Thrice she applies the power of magic pray'r—
Thrice, hellward bending, mutters charms in air;
Then turning towards the foe bids mischief fly,
And looks destruction as she points her eye:
Then spectres, rising from Tartarean bow'rs,
Howl round in air, or grin along the shores.
Father supreme! what fears my breast annoy,
Since not disease alone can life destroy,
Or wounds inflicted fate's decrees fulfil;
But magic's secret arts have pow'r to kill!
For by Medea's incantations plied,
Enfeebled soon the brazen monster died.
While rending up the earth in wrath he throws
Rock after rock against the aerial foes;
Lo! frantic as he strides, a sudden wound
Bursts the life-vein, and blood o'erspreads the ground.
As from a furnace in a burning flood
Pours melting lead, so pours in streams his blood:
And now he staggers as the spirit flies,
He faints—he sinks—he tumbles—and he dies.
As some huge cedar on a mountain's brow,
Pierc'd by the steel, expects a final blow;
A while it totters with alternate sway,
Till fresh'ning breezes through the branches play,
Then tumbling downward with a thund'ring sound,
Headlong it falls, and spreads a length of ground;
So, as the giant falls, the ocean roars.
Outstretch'd he lies, and covers half the shores."
                              APOLL. RHOD.

No. 596.

Medea, after murdering her children, flies in a car drawn by dragons.

POLYCLETES. *Oriental Sardonyx.*

Jason, whilst residing at Corinth with Medea, by whom he had had two sons, forgot all that he owed to his wife, and became enamoured of Glauce, the daughter of Creon king of that country; and repudiating Medea, he married her. Medea in revenge killed her sons and her rival, set fire to the palace of Creon, which, with the king, was burnt; and mounting a car drawn by dragons, she fled from Corinth.

" Her harness'd dragons now direct she drives
For Corinth, and at Corinth she arrives;
Where, if what old tradition tells be true,
In former ages men from mushrooms grew.
But here Medea finds her place supplied
During her absence by another bride;
And hopeless to recover her lost game,
She sets both bride and palace in a flame.

Nor could a rival's death her wrath assuage,
Nor stopp'd at Creon's family her rage:
She murders her own infants in despite
To faithless Jason, and in Jason's sight;
Yet ere his sword could reach her, up she springs,
Securely mounted on her dragons' wings."

OVID.

STROPHE.

" O earth, and thou who roll'st on high
　　Thy all-illuming flame,
　　Cast from thy radiant car thine eye,
　　And view this raging dame;
To slaughter ere she gives the reins,
Ere in her children's gore her hands she stains:
　　For from thy golden line
　　Their splendid origin they draw;
　　And man with holy awe
Refrains from spilling blood divine;
Check, god of brightness, curb, control
　　This frenzy of her soul;
And far, whilst yet her children live,
Far from the bloody house this fell Erinnys drive!

ANTISTROPHE.

In vain to thee a mother's pain;
　　Thy cares, thy labours lost;
Thine is a mother's name in vain,
　　In vain this dearest boast.
O thou, whose dauntless heart could brave
The pass where howls th' inhospitable wave,

Whose should'ring torrents roll
The dark-brow'd clashing rocks between!
　　Ah, why, unhappy queen,
Why rends this ruthless rage thy soul?
No lavers cleanse the murd'rous hand
　　With kindred blood profan'd:
　　But soon his house in ruins lies,
As desolation marks the vengeance of the skies.

FIRST SON.

What shall I do? how fly my mother's hands?
　　　　　　　　　　[*Within.*

SECOND SON.

I know not; dearest brother, we shall die.

CHORUS.

Heard you the cry? heard you the children's
　　voice?
O thou unhappy, thou ill-fated woman!
Let me go in to them; I deem it right
To snatch the children from her murd'rous hands.

SON.

Nay, by the gods, assist us now, e'en now,
For we are nigh th' inevitable sword.

CHORUS.

Thou wretch, art thou of iron, or of rock,
That thou wilt kill thy sons whom thou brought'st
    forth,
With thine own hands?   The annals of past
    times
Record but one, one only furious dame,
Who plung'd her hands in her dear children's
    blood;

And heav'n-sent madness had o'erturn'd the sense
Of Ino, by the wife of Jove driven forth;
And wand'ring from her house, when she had
    slain
Her sons, as o'er the sea-beat beach she rov'd,
She rush'd into the waves, and perish'd with
    them.
Remains there aught more horrible than this?
Thou female bed, fruitful of various ills,
What woes, what miseries hast thou caus'd to
    man!"

                         EURIPIDES: POTTER.

JASON.

" Instant, ye menial train, unbar the door,
Give me admittance, that I may behold
This aggravated ill, my children slain,
And drag her to deserved punishment.

MEDEA.

Why with this tumult dost thou beat the door,
Seeking the dead, and me who did the deed?
Forbear this uproar.   Wouldst thou aught with
    me?
Speak it; but never shalt thou touch me more:
The Sun, my father, gives me such a car,
A safe protection from each hostile hand.

JASON.

O thou detested woman, most abhorr'd
By the just gods, by me, and all mankind,
In thine own children who couldst plunge the
    sword,
Their mother thou, to 'reave me of my sons;
And having done this deed, dost yet behold
The sun, the earth, this deed of horror done!
Perdition seize thee!   Now I know thee; then
I knew thee not, when from thy home I led thee—
Led thee to Greece from a barbaric shore,
Pernicious monster, to thy father false,
And trait'ress to the land that nurtured thee!
And now the vengeful Furies on my head
Punish thy crimes; for with thy brother's blood

Distain'd, the gallant Argo didst thou mount:
This was a prelude to thy ruthless deeds.
Wedded by me, a mother too by me,
Thy children hast thou murder'd, in revenge
For my new bed; an act no dame of Greece
Would ever dare attempt: yet I preferr'd thee
To all their softer charms, and wedded thee,
Alliance hateful and destructive to me!
A tigress, not a woman; of a soul
More wild, more savage than the Tuscan Scylla!
But millions of reproaches would not gall
That hard unfeeling heart.   Then get thee gone,
Achiever of base mischiefs, blood-stain'd pest,
Stain'd with thy children's blood, begone, and
    perish!
For me remains to wail my hopeless state;
For from my nuptials never shall I taste
The promis'd joy, nor see my sons alive,
Dear objects of my care for ever lost.

MEDEA.

Full answer to thy words could I return,
Recounting each past circumstance; but Jove,
Th' almighty father, knows what grace I shower'd
On thee, and what requital thou hast made.
Thou shalt not pass thy wanton life in joys,
My bed dishonour'd, and make villanous jests
At my disgrace; nor shall thy royal bride,
Nor the proud Creon who betroth'd her, dare
To chase me from this country unchastis'd.

Call me a tigress then, or, if thou wilt,
A Scylla howling 'gainst the Tuscan shore!
I, as is right, have taught thy heart to bleed.

JASON.

Thy heart too bleeds, a sharer in these ills.

MEDEA.

Be thou assured of that: yet in my griefs
I joy thou canst not make a mock at them.

JASON.

My children, a bad mother have you found.

MEDEA.

My sons, you perish'd through your father's folly.

JASON.

Yet my right hand plung'd not the murderous
    sword.

MEDEA.

But thy foul wrongs and thy new nuptials
    plung'd it.

JASON.

And for these nuptials hast thou kill'd thy sons?

MEDEA.

This to a woman deem'st thou a slight pain?

JASON.

To one discreet; but all is ill to thee.

MEDEA.

These are no more; and that shall rend thy heart.

JASON.

Their shades shall pour their vengeance on thy
    head.

MEDEA.

The just gods know which first began these ills.

JASON.

And the gods know thy execrable heart.

MEDEA.

Thou and thy bitter speech are hateful to me.

JASON.

And thine to me: this soon may have an end.

MEDEA.

How? for I wish to free me from thy sight.

JASON.

Give me my sons, to mourn and bury them.

MEDEA.

Never: for on the height, where Juno's shrine
Hallows the ground, this hand shall bury them,
That hostile rage may not insult their ashes,
And rend them from the tomb: a solemn feast
And sacrifice hereafter to this land
Will I appoint to expiate this deed
Of horrid murder. In the friendly land
Where once Erechtheus reign'd, the house of
    Ægeus,
Pandion's son, is open to receive me:
Thither I go. But thou, as thy vile deeds
Deserve, shalt vilely perish; thy base head,
Crush'd with the mouldering relics of thy Argo,
And of my nuptials feel, that wretched end.

JASON.

Thee may th' Erinnys of thy sons destroy,
And Justice, which for blood vindictive calls—
For blood."   EURIPIDES: POTTER.

Note.—The Scholiast observes here, that Medea appears above in a chariot drawn by dragons, bearing with her the bodies of her slaughtered son.]

No. 597.

Medea in her car: also a burning vase of enchanted herbs.

GNAIOS. *Oriental Cornelian.*

See the last speech of Medea in the preceding quotation: see also the quotation from OVID to No. 596.

No. 598.

The Cretan bull rising from the sea, and Minos offering sacrifice.

APOLLONIDES.   *Cornelian.*

Minos, the second king of Crete, was so vain of his naval power, that he refused to recognise Neptune as ruler of the seas, and sacrifice to him a bull which he received from him for that purpose.   Neptune, to punish his insolence, caused a furious bull to arise from the sea, which ravaged the island of Crete.   Minos afterwards offered the sacrifice.

No. 599.

Androgeus, the son of Minos, attacked and killed by the bull of Marathon.

APOLLONIOS.   *Oriental Cornelian.*

Another account is, that he was murdered by order of Ægeus, king of Attica.

No. 600.

Ægeus depositing the sword and sandals beneath a stone.

PYRGOTELES.   *Oriental Cornelian.*

Ægeus king of Athens being at Trœzene, the court of Pittheus, became enamoured of Æthra, daughter of the king, and married her.   Before the birth of Theseus, Ægeus was com-pelled to return to Athens; and previous to his departure he took a sword and a pair of sandals, and in presence of Æthra deposited them under a large stone, commanding his wife, when Theseus should arrive at manhood, to shew him the place where they were concealed, and send him to Athens, where he should be able by these tokens to recognise him as his son.

No. 601.

Theseus, when a youth, attacking the skin of the Nemæan lion.

CHROMIOS.   *Oriental Sardonyx.*

Theseus at a very early age manifested proofs of that intrepidity for which he was after-wards so celebrated in heroic history.   At Trœzene, where Hercules was the guest of king Pittheus, he saw the skin of the Nemæan lion, and supposing it to be the lion itself, he seized an axe to attack it.

No. 602.

Theseus discovering the sword and sandals indicated to him by Æthra.

DIOSCORIDES. *Oriental Cornelian.*

No. 603.

Ægeus preventing Theseus from quaffing the poisoned cup.

GNAIOS. *Oriental Sardonyx.*

Ægeus married Medea, and had a son by her. Medea, to secure the crown to him, attempted to murder Theseus, who was not on his first arrival at Athens recognised by his father. Medea persuaded Ægeus that he was an ill-disposed stranger, whom he should treat as an enemy; and she prepared a poisoned draught for the king to present to his guest to drink. Theseus on taking the cup laid his sword on the table, when he was immediately recognised by his father, who caught the cup just as he had raised it to his lips.

" Meanwhile his son, from actions of renown,
Arrives at court, but to his sire unknown.
Medea, to despatch a dang'rous heir,
(She knew him,) did a pois'nous draught prepare,
Drawn from a drug, was long reserv'd in store
For desp'rate uses, from the Scythian shore,
That from the echydnæan monster's jaws
Deriv'd its origin, and this the cause.
   Through a dark cave a craggy passage lies,
To ours ascending from the nether skies,
Through which, by strength of hand, Alcides drew
Chain'd Cerberus, who lagg'd and restive grew,
With his blear'd eyes our brighter day to view.
Thrice he repeated his enormous yell,
With which he scares the ghosts and startles hell;
At last outrageous (though compell'd to yield),
He sheds his foam in fury on the field;
Which, with its own and rankness of the ground,
Produc'd a weed, by sorcerers renown'd,
The strongest constitution to confound,

Call'd aconite, because it can unlock
All bars, and force its passage through a rock.
   The pious father, by her wheedles won,
Presents this deadly potion to his son,
Who with the same assurance takes the cup,
And to the monarch's health had drunk it up,
But in the very instant he applied
The goblet to his lips, old Ægeus spied
The iv'ry-hilted sword ——
The certain signal of his son he knew,
And snatch'd the bowl away; the sword he drew,
Resolv'd, for such a son's endanger'd life,
To sacrifice the most perfidious wife.
Revenge is swift, but her more active charms
A whirlwind rais'd, that snatch'd her from his
    arms.
While conjur'd clouds their baffled sense surprise,
She vanishes from their deluded eyes,
And through the hurricane triumphant flies.'
               OVID.

No. 604.

Theseus and his father, seized with horror, quit the table.

PYRGOTELES.   *Oriental Cornelian.*

No. 605.

The sacrifice to Venus by Theseus.

APOLLONIDES.   *Oriental Cornelian.*

Before proceeding on the expedition to Crete to destroy the Minotaur, Theseus offered a sacrifice to Venus on the sea-shore.   The victim was a female goat, which, at the moment of immolating, became a male; from which circumstance Theseus bestowed on Venus the epithet of *Epitragia.*

No. 606.

Theseus on a dolphin, bearing the ring of Minos and the crown of Ariadne.

ADMON.   *Veined oriental Cornelian of the rarest quality, which in some points exhibits the colours of the rainbow.*

When Theseus landed in Crete, Minos II., the king, refused to acknowledge him the son of Neptune; and to put him to the proof, he threw his ring into the sea, declaring that Theseus could not get it back.   Theseus plunged into the waves, where he was met by a shoal of dolphins.   He recovered the ring; and received as a present from Amphytrite the crown which Venus had given her on her wedding-day.   Theseus restored the ring to Minos, and gave the crown to Ariadne.

No. 607.

Theseus instructed by Ariadne how to return from the depths of the labyrinth.

POLYCLETES.   *Oriental Cornelian.*

Ariadne, the daughter of Minos II., enamoured of Theseus, tells him how to kill the Minotaur, and gives him a thread by which he may retrace his steps to the mouth of the labyrinth.

" Not far from thence he grav'd the wond'rous maze,
A thousand doors, a thousand winding ways ;
Here dwells the monster, hid from human view,
Not to be found but by the faithful clue :
Till the kind artist, mov'd with pious grief,
Lent to the loving maid this last relief ;
And all those erring paths describ'd so well,
That Theseus conquer'd, and the monster fell."

VIRGIL's *Æneid.*

" Crete I betray'd for you ; and, what's more dear,
Betray'd my father, who that crown does wear.
When to your hands the fatal clue I gave,
Which through the winding lab'rinth led you safe ;
Then how you lov'd, how eagerly embrac'd !
How oft you swore, by all your dangers past,
That with my life your love should ever last !"

OVID, *Ep.*

No. 608.

Theseus receiving from Ariadne the clue of thread to guide him through the labyrinth.

PYRGOTELES. *Amethyst.*

" So Dædalus compil'd
Innumerable by-ways, which beguil'd
The troubled sense, that he who made the same
Could scarce retire, so intricate the frame.
Within this fabric Minos then enclos'd
This double form, of man and beast compos'd :
The monster with Athenian blood twice fed,
The third lot, in the ninth year, vanquished ;
Who by a clue was guided to the door
(A virgin's counsel) never found before."

OVID, *Met.:* SANDYS.

No. 609.

Theseus conquering the Minotaur.

APOLLONIDES. *Oriental Cornelian.*

z z

No. 610.

Theseus slaying the Cretan bull at the altar of Minerva.

CHROMIOS. *Oriental Sardonyx.*

The Cretan bull is known also as the bull of Marathon, from the village of that name in Attica, whither Hercules had carried it alive.

No. 611.

The same subject.

APOLLONIDES. *Oriental Cornelian.*

No. 612.

Theseus carrying off Helen, the daughter of Leda.

APOLLONIDES. *Sardonyx.*

Theseus, while at Lacedæmon, seeing Helen, then very young, in the temple of Diana, exhibiting in a dance called the "dance of innocence," became enamoured of her, and carried her off.

> " For so the Fates,
> Ancient of days, dread daughters of the main,
> Have stamp'd their web, and ratified her doom.
> Two eagles,* stooping from the clouds, shall seize
> The trembling bird,† and swoop upon their prey."
>
> LYCOPHRON : VISC. ROYSTON.

No. 613.

Theseus restoring Helen to her brothers Castor and Pollux.

ANTEROTOS. *Oriental Sardonyx.*

Theseus, after he carried Helen away, confided her education to Æthra. Castor and Pollux, her brothers, went and by force of arms compelled him to restore her.

---

* Theseus and Paris.   † Helen.

No. 614.

Theseus kills Sinis, after he has bound him between two pine-trees.

CHROMIOS. *Amethyst.*

Sinis was a terrible giant and robber in the environs of Corinth, who attacked passengers and tied them to the bent branches of two pine-trees, which giving way by their elasticity, the miserable creatures were torn in pieces. Theseus vanquished Sinis, and made him die by the same cruel means he had invented for others.

> " By him the tort'rer Sinis was destroyed,
> Of strength (but strength to barb'rous use employ'd)
> That tops of tallest pines to earth could bend,
> And thus in pieces wretched captives rend."
> OVID.

No. 615.

Theseus and Perigone.

APOLLONIDES. *Amethyst.*

Perigone, terrified by the death of her father Sinis, and fearing his fate, hid herself. Theseus discovered her, and carried her off. He had by her a son named Menalippus.

No. 616.

Theseus abandoning Ariadne, and eloping with her sister Phædra.

APOLLONIDES. *Oriental Sardonyx.*

Theseus, forgetting all that he owed to Ariadne, abandoned her in the island of Naxos, or Dia, while she was sleeping on a rock, and took with him her sister Phædra.

> " When Theseus, aided by the virgin's art,
> Had trac'd the guiding thread through ev'ry part,
> He took the gentle maid that set him free,
> And, bound for Dia, cut the briny sea.
> There, quickly cloy'd, ungrateful and unkind,
> Left his fair consort in the isle behind.
> Whom Bacchus saw, and straining in his arms
> Her rifled bloom and violated charms,
> Resolves for this the dear engaging dame
> Should shine for ever in the rolls of fame ;
> And bids her crown among the stars be plac'd,
> With an eternal constellation grac'd."
> OVID, *Met.* viii.

No. 617.

Theseus conquering Periphates.

APOLLONIDES. *Oriental Sardonyx.*

Epidaurus, in the province of Argos, is described by Strabo as being situated near the bay of Saron, and opposite to the island Ægina : the distance is not great from thence to Trœzene, the city of Pittheus, under whose care Theseus was educated. Plutarch speaks of that hero's killing Periphates, a famous robber in the neighbourhood of Epidaurus, as his earliest exploit. Theseus, as a mark of his triumph, used to bear the club he took from his vanquished foe, whom Pausanias and Ovid have dignified with the appellation of the son of Vulcan. The ancient poets often put such weapons into the hands of their heroes, in order to convey to the reader an idea of superior strength.

No. 618.

Theseus destroys the centaur Eurytion, who is carrying off Hippodamia.

ADMON. *Amethyst.*

The combat of the Lapithæ and the Centaurs, on the occasion of the nuptials of Pirithous, king of the Lapithæ, and Hippodamia, is one of the most celebrated of the exploits of fabulous history. At the festival Eurytion the Centaur became enamoured of the bride, and attempted to carry her off; but is slain in the attempt by Theseus, who was a guest. (See OVID, *Met.* xii.)

No. 619.

Theseus killing Sciron the brigand, who infested Attica.

CHROMIOS. *Oriental Sardonyx.*

" Inhuman Sciron now has breath'd his last,
And now Alcatho's road's securely past,
By Theseus slain, and thrown into the deep :
But earth nor sea his scatter'd bones would keep ;
Which, after floating long, a rock became,
Still infamous with Sciron's hated name."

OVID.

No. 620.

Theseus slaying the brigand Sisyphus : his hand rests on a rock, the symbol of his punishment in hell.

DIOSCORIDES. *Oriental Cornelian.*

No. 621.

Theseus (on his way from Trœzene to Athens) killing Phæa.

CHROMIOS. *Sardonyx.*

She was a prostitute of Cromyon, near Corinth, who lured strangers to her embraces; then robbed and murdered them.

No. 622.

Phæa, under the representation of a ferocious sow (a proper type of her character), slain by Theseus.

CHROMIOS. *Oriental Cornelian.*

No. 623.

Theseus, his wife Antiope the queen of the Amazons, and Hippolytus their son.

DIOSCORIDES. *Oriental Cornelian.*

No. 624.

The head of Theseus.

GNAIOS. *Amethyst.*

" Theseus, whose name signifies the *Establisher of Social Order*, can only be regarded as an imaginary person. Being the patron-hero of the people among whom literature flourished most, he is presented to us under a more historic aspect than the other heroes. Though his adventures are manifestly founded on those of Hercules, whom he is said to have emulated, we are struck with the absence of the marvellous in them. If we except the descent to Erebos, they are hardly more wonderful than those of Aristomenes. He always appears as the model of a just and moderate ruler, the example of a strict obedience to the dictates of law and equity, the protector of the suppliant, the scourge of the evil-doer, and the author of good and wise regulations. In the spirit of casting splendour on actual political relations by throwing them back to the mythic ages, the dramatists and orators of Athens did not hesitate to make Theseus the founder of the democracy."—KEIGHTLEY.

" Noble, vulgar, all
Together celebrate that festival,
Thus singing, when full bowls their spirits raise:
Great Theseus, Marathon resounds thy praise
For slaughter of the Cretan bull. Secure
They live who Cromyon's wasted field manure,
By thy exploit and bounty. Vulcan's seed
By thee glad Epidaure beheld to bleed.
Savage Procrustes' death Cephisia viewed;
Eleusis Cercyon's. Scinis, ill endued
With strength so much abus'd, who beeches bent,
And tortur'd bodies 'twixt their branches rent,

Thou slewst. The way which to Alcathoë led
Is now secure, inhuman Sciron dead.
The earth his scatter'd bones a grave denied,
Nor would the sea his hated relics hide;
Which, tossed to and fro, in time became
A solid rock : the rock we Sciron name.
If we thy years should number with thy acts,
Thy years would prove a cipher to thy facts.
Great soul, for thee, as for our public wealth,
We pray and quaff Lyæus to thy health.
The palace with the people's praises rings,
And sacred joy in ev'ry bosom springs."

OVID, *Met.:* SANDYS.

No. 625.

Phædra soliciting the love of Hippolytus, who shrinks from her.

GNAIOS.   *Oriental Cornelian.*

Hippolytus, the son of Theseus by Hippolyte, queen of the Amazons, was a man of great chastity ; his whole life being devoted to the worship of Diana, and the pursuit of the chase. Phædra, his step-mother, became rapturously enamoured of him. He virtuously rejected her addresses. She died in despair, having accused him to his father of an attempt on her chastity. The father banished him, imprecating the vengeance of heaven on his head. In his flight along the shore, Neptune, listening to his father's curses, sends a sea-monster to affright his horses: he is flung from his chariot, and dashed to pieces. This story is the subject of a play by Euripides.

" O love, O love, that through the eyes
Instillest softly warm desire,
Pleas'd in the soul with sweet surprise
Entrancing rapture to inspire,
Never with wild ungovern'd sway
Rush on my heart. and force it to obey :
For not the lightning's fire,
Nor stars swift-darting through the sky,
Equal the shafts sent by this son of Jove,
When his hand gives them force to fly,
Kindling the flames of love."

Phædra, in the excess of her love, wishes for the enjoyments of Hippolytus—

" O bear me to the mountain ; to the pines—
The forest would I go, where the fleet hounds
Pursue the dappled hinds ! O, by the gods,

I long to cheer the dogs of chase, to wave
O'er my bright tresses the Thessalian dart,
And grasp the pointed javelin in my hands!"

She afterwards moralises on the folly and guilt of her conduct, and resolves to die—

" Soon as I felt
The wound of love, my thoughts were turn'd
    how best
To bear it.   Hence in silence I conceal'd
My pain; for faithless is the tongue: it knows
T' enforce the passions when discover'd, oft
Working the greatest ills.   My next resolve
Was well to bear the madness, and o'ercome it
With chaste austerity.   When these avail'd not
To vanquish love, I deem'd it noblest for me
To die: these resolutions none will blame.
For be this mine: if virtuous be my deeds,
Let them not lie obscure; nor (be they base)
Let me have many to attest my shame.
I knew how foul this fond desire; I knew
How infamous; and, as a woman, well
I knew in what abhorrence it is held.
O that she perish'd, suff'ring every ill,
Who with adulterate love the nuptial bed
First shamed!   The houses of the great gave
    birth
To this disease, and thence th' infection spread:

For when base deeds from those of highest rank
Receive a sanction, all below esteem them
As objects of their honest imitation.
But her I hate, whose tongue to modest phrase
Is filed, whilst thoughts of lewdness in her heart
She dares to harbour.   Sovereign, sea-born Venus!
How can such look their husbands in the face,
Nor tremble at the darkness that assists them,
And fear the roof, the walls, should find a tongue
To publish their misdeeds?   I will not live,
My friends, to shame my husband and my sons:
No; 'midst the splendour of th' Athenian state
Free let them dwell, and flourish in renown,
Illustrious for their mother; for the mind,
Though form'd for noble daring, sinks enslaved,
When conscious of a mother's foul misdeeds,
Or of a father's; for the honest mind,
Conscious of just and virtuous thought, possesses
A worth excelling life; and time will shew
The bad distinct, as when a virgin holds
Her mirror: ne'er 'mongst such may I be seen!"
                              EURIPIDES: POTTER.

No. 626.

Phædra striving to detain Hippolytus.

APOLLONIDES.   *Amethyst.*

The feelings of Hippolytus can be judged of by the following portion of his speech to the nurse.

"Happier who 'scapes both these, and to his
    house
Leads a plain, gentle-manner'd, simple wife.
I hate the knowing dame; nor in my house
Be one more wise than woman ought to be:
For Venus in these knowing dames with ease
Engenders wiles; from all which folly far

Simplicity removes th' unplotting wit.
But female servant never on the wife
Should be attendant; let them rather dwell
With animals that want the pow'r of speech;
That they may neither have with whom to talk,
Nor hear their conversation in return.
But now the wicked mistress in the house

Contrives her wicked purpose, and abroad
The base attendant bears the lewd design.
So thou, vile wretch, art come to me, to form
Detested commerce with my father's bed,
Too holy to be touch'd : thy impure words
Pollute my ears, and in the living stream
They must be cleans'd : how then should I
     commit
A villany, when but to hear it nam'd
Defiles me ?"

No. 627.

Death of Hippolytus.

GNAIOS.   *Sardonyx.*

No. 628.

The same subject.

DIOSCORIDES.   *Sardonyx.*

Of the many poetical descriptions of this event (see OVID, *Met.* xv.), the following, from the Hippolytus of EURIPIDES, who represents the monster as a bull, is the most circumstantial.

THESEUS.

" O gods! Now, Neptune, thou art proved
     indeed.
My father, rightly hast thou heard my pray'rs.
But say, how perish'd he ? how did the mace
Of justice crush him for his wrongs to me ?

MESSENGER.

We on the margin of the wave-wash'd shore
His coursers held, and comb'd their flowing
     manes,
Weeping ; for one had come with tidings to us
That on this land Hippolytus no more
Must set his foot—by thy severe decree
A wretched exile. He too came, and brought
The same sad sentence to us on the strand ;
Not unattended, for a numerous train
Of youths, his lov'd associates, follow'd him.
After some time, mast'ring his griefs, he spoke :
' What boots it to lament ? My father's bidding
Must be obey'd : my servants, quickly yoke
My coursers to the car, this is a city

For me no more.' Each to his office thence
Hasten'd, and in an instant to our lord
We led his coursers harness'd : from the nave
He snatch'd the reins, and sprung into the seat;
Then to the gods stretch'd forth his hands, and
     said :
' If ever baseness stain'd my heart, O Jove,
May I no longer breathe this vital air ;
And let my father know how much he wrongs
     me,
Whether I die, or view the light of heav'n.'
Then lash'd his steeds ; attendant on our lord,
We follow near the reins the way to Argos
Leading, and Epidaurus. When we reach'd
The tract of desert where our shore swells high
'Gainst the Saronic gulf, a roaring sound
Came o'er the earth, loud as the voice of Jove,
Horrid to hear : the coursers toss'd their heads
High, and tow'rds heav'n erect their ears : our
     train,
Trembling like children, marvell'd whence the
     noise

Proceeded : to the sea-beat shore we cast
Our eyes, and saw a wave so vast—it swell'd
Reaching the skies—that to our view were lost
The cliffs of Sciron ; and the isthmus now
No more appear'd—no more appear'd the rocks
Of Æsculapius : swelling on, and round
Dashing its roaring foam, on the high tide
It reach'd the shore close to the harness'd car:
There from its rolling and tempestuous flood
Cast forth a bull—a monster wild and vast,
Whose horrid bellowings through th' affrighted
    land
Resounded : such an hideous sight the eye
Could not endure : a dreadful terror seiz'd
The starting horses ; and their lord, much train'd
In all equestrian lore, in his strong hand
Held firm the reins ; like one that at the oar
Bends backward—backward so he bent, and drew
The straiten'd reins : champing their iron bits
They rush impetuous on ; nor guiding hand,
Nor straiten'd rein, nor well-compacted car
Regard. If to the level plain his wheels
He guided, there, to force him back, the bull

Appear'd before him, and the madd'ning steeds
Affrighted : on the rough rocks if they rush'd
With wild and frantic fright, approaching nigh
In silence he accompanied the car,
Till dash'd against a crag the clashing wheel
High bounding cast him headlong from his seat.
All then was foul disorder: upward flew
The pierc'd nave and the axle's point infix'd.
Th' unhappy youth, inexplicably bound
Amidst the tangling harness—'guinst the rocks
His dear head dash'd, his flesh all rent—was heard
With lamentable voice t' address his steeds ;
' Stop, O my coursers, mindful that these hands
Have fed you in my stalls, destroy me not :
How dreadful is my father's imprecation !
Is no one nigh—no one to save a man
Of unstain'd innocence ?' Though many wish'd,
We were left far behind, and our best speed
Was slow. He, disengag'd, I know not how,
From the rent harness, falls, a little life
Yet breathing : but the steeds were seen no
    more."

No. 629.

Æsculapius restoring Hippolytus to life, in presence of Diana and her nymphs.

PYRGOTELES.   *Oriental Cornelian.*

Diana, knowing the innocence of Hippolytus, besought Æsculapius to restore him to life ; which he did by pouring on his head the juice of a certain flower. After this, he assumed the name of Virbius, and, conveyed to Italy, devoted his life to the service of Diana and the chase. (OVID, *Met.* xv.; VIRG. *Æn.* vii.)

No. 630.

Pirithous attacking one of the Centaurs.

APOLLONIDES.   *Cornelian.*

No. 631.

Pirithous, while bringing away Proserpine from hell, attacked by the dog Cerberus.

GNAIOS.   *Cornelian.*

Pirithous, after the death of Hippodamia, accompanied by his friend Theseus, went to hell to release Proserpine, and marry her.   Some accounts represent him as attacked and torn to pieces by Cerberus, while Theseus was kept chained to the gates till released by Hercules. (VIRGIL, *Æn.* vi.; HOR. *Od.*, book iii. and iv.)

No. 632.

Pirithous torn to pieces by Cerberus.

CHROMIOS.   *Cornelian.*

No. 633.

Theseus chained, while Cerberus is tearing Pirithous.

PAMPHILOS.   *Cornelian.*

No. 634.

Minerva shewing to Bellerophon the bridle for the winged steed Pegasus.

APOLLONIDES.   *Cornelian.*

Bellerophon (whose original name was Hipponous, because he was supposed to be in-structed by the goddess of wisdom herself in the successful management of the horse,) was famous for his virtue and valour.   Having accidentally slain his brother Beller (whence his name), he fled to the court of Prætus, king of Argos, who gave him hospitable protection. Antæa, the queen, in revenge for his rejection of her amorous solicitations, accused him to the king of an attempt on her virtue.   Prætus, unwilling to violate the laws of hospitality by punishing him, sent him, under the pretence of deputing him as an ambassador, to his father-in-law Jobates, king of Lycia, with a letter detailing the supposed offence.   Jobates felt some scruples about putting him to death, but sent him on many perilous enterprises, all of which he performed triumphantly.   One of these was his victory over the monster Chimæra.   Jobates was so convinced of his virtue, and charmed with his bravery, that he gave him his daughter in marriage. It is said that he became so vain of his exploits, as to attempt to ascend to heaven on his winged steed Pegasus; but was hurled down by Jupiter as a punishment for his presumption; and that he ever after led a melancholy and solitary life in the Aleian territory. (See HOMER, Il. vi.)

ANTISTROPHE III.

"When warred the Greeks on Phrygia's hostile strand,
On either side her sons embattled stood,
Though to bear Helen from the ill-fated land,
Her warriors with the Atridæ crossed the flood;
Yet some, who those with vengeful spears repell'd,
From Corinth's race their honour'd lineage held;
For Lycian Glaucus, to the Achaian host
Trembling before his lance, would often boast
His sires' abode, and wealth, and wide domain,
Where fair Pirene's waves enrich the fertile plain.

EPODE III.

Who by the silver fountain's side
Much labour found and much affliction knew,
While winged Pegasus he tried,
Medusa's offspring, to subdue;
Till, sleeping on his native plains,
Minerva gave the golden reins:
' Awake, Æolian king! awake!
This sacred gift with transport take;
Shew it to Neptune, potent god of steeds,
While at his hallowed shrine the votive bullock bleeds.'

STROPHE IV.

The ægis-bearing maid Minerva spoke,
While midnight slumbers clos'd his heavy eyes;
Straight from the dull embrace of sleep he broke,
And seized with eager hand the glittering prize:

Cæranus' son he sought, the neighbouring seer,
And pour'd the wondrous tidings in his ear;
That, as in awful Pallas' holy fane,
Sleep o'er his temples spread her leaden reign,
Before him stood confess'd the warlike maid,
And by his side at once the golden bridle laid.

ANTISTROPHE IV.

The wondering augur bade him straight obey
Each mystic mandate of the dream divine;
To Neptune first the votive bullock pay,
Then to equestrian Pallas rear a shrine.
Beyond his hopes the gods with favouring will
The object of his wishes soon fulfil;
For brave Bellerophon, with joyful look,
The sacred present of th' immortals took;
Threw it with ease about his aching head,
And peaceful in his hand th' ethereal courser led.

EPODE IV.

Now, shining in refulgent arms,
The winged Pegasus his limbs bestrode;
And seeking war's severe alarms,
To Amazonia's plains he rode;
And, 'midst the chilling reigns of frost,
O'ercame the female archer-host.
His arms Chimæra's flames subdue;
The dauntless Solymi he slew.—
I pass the death his cruel fate decreed,
When Jove's eternal stalls receiv'd th' immortal steed."
PINDAR, Olym. xiii.: PYE.

" Last came forth
Chimæra, breathing fire unquenchable;
A monster grim and huge, and swift and strong.
Her's were three heads; a glaring lion's one,
One of a goat, a mighty snake's the third:
In front the lion threatened, and behind

The serpent, and the goat was in the midst,
Exhaling fierce the strength of burning flame.
But the wing'd Pegasus his rider bore,
The brave Bellerophon, and laid her dead."

HESIOD.

No. 635.

Minerva putting the bridle on Pegasus.

SOLON.   *Amethyst.*

No. 636.

Minerva leading Pegasus to Bellerophon.

APOLLONIDES.   *Sardonyx.*

No. 637.

Bellerophon, mounted on Pegasus, attacking Chimæra.

DIOSCORIDES.   *Calcedony.*

No. 638.

Bellerophon falling from Pegasus.

DIOSCORIDES.   *Sardonyx.*

The explanation of the story of Bellerophon's fall from Pegasus (a steed sacred to the Muses), and his subsequent wandering over the "Aleian field," appears to be that he culti- vated poetry in his later years, became unsuccessful in his poetic flights, and grew melancholy. This Milton prays may not be his case:

" Return me to my native element;
Lest from this flying steed unrein'd (as once
Bellerophon, though from a lower clime),
Dismounted, on the Aleian field I fall,
Erroneous there to wander, and forlorn."

MILTON, *Paradise Lost*, book vii. v. 16.

No. 639.

Boreas carrying off Orithyia.

GNAIOS. *Cornelian.*

Boreas, king of Thrace (who was deified as the personification of the north wind, the most boisterous known to the ancients), carried off Orithyia, daughter of Erechtheus, king of Athens, and had by her Calais and Zethes, the Argonauts, who rescued Phineus from the persecution of the Harpies, and drove them to the islands Strophades. The story of the rape is thus told by Ovid (*Met.* vi.). At first his suit is rejected: then the poet says—

" Blust'ring with ire, he quickly has recourse
To rougher arts and his own native force.
' 'Tis well,' he said ; ' such usage is my due,
When thus disguis'd by foreign ways I sue;
When my stern airs and fierceness I disclaim,
And sigh for love, ridiculously tame ;
When soft addresses foolishly I try,
Nor my own stronger remedies apply.
By force and violence I chiefly live,
By them the low'ring stormy tempests drive ;
In foaming billows raise the hoary deep,
Writhe knotted oaks, and sandy deserts sweep ;
Congeal the falling flakes of fleecy snow,
And bruise with rattling hail the plains below.
I and my brother winds, when, join'd above,
Through the waste campaign of the skies we rove,
With such a boist'rous full career engage,
That heav'n's whole concave thunders at our
    rage ;
While, struck from nitrous clouds, fierce light-
    nings play,
Dart through the storm, and gild the gloomy day;
Or when, in subterraneous caverns pent,
My breath against the hollow earth is bent,
The quaking world above, and ghosts below,
My mighty pow'r, by dear experience, know,
Tremble with fear, and dread the fatal blow.
This is the only cure to be applied ;
Thus to Erechtheus I should be allied ;
And thus the scornful virgin should be woo'd,
Not by entreaty, but by force subdu'd.'
    Boreas, in passion, spoke these huffing things,
And, as he spoke, he shook his dreadful wings;

At which, afar the shiv'ring sea was fanu'd,
And the wide surface of the distant land :
His dusty mantle o'er the hills he drew,
And swept the lowly valleys as he flew :
Then with his yellow wings embrac'd the maid,
And, wrapt in dusky clouds, far off convey'd.
The sparkling blaze of love's prevailing fire
Shone brighter as he flew, and flam'd the higher.
And now the god, possessed of his delight,
To northern Thrace pursues his airy flight,
Where the young ravish'd nymph became his bride,
And soon the luscious sweets of wedlock tried.
    Two lovely twins, th' effect of this embrace,
Crown their soft labours, and their nuptials grace;
Who, like their mother, beautiful and fair,
Their father's strength and feather'd pinions
    share :
Yet these, at first, were wanting, as 'tis said,
And after, as they grew, their shoulders spread.
Zethes and Calais, the pretty twins,
Remain'd unfledg'd while smooth their beardless
    chins ;
But when, in time, the budding silver down
Shaded their face, and on their cheeks were
    grown,
Two sprouting wings upon their shoulders sprung,
Like those in birds, that veil the callow young ;
Then as their age advanc'd, and they began
From greener youth to ripen into man,
With Jason's Argonauts they cross'd the seas,
Embark'd in quest of the fam'd golden fleece :
There, with the rest, the first frail vessel tried,
And boldly ventur'd on the swelling tide."

No. 640.

Boreas and Orithyia on a mountain in Thrace.

GNAIOS. *Cornelian.*

No. 641.

Boreas dashing the nymph Pithys on a rock.

DIOSCORIDES. *Amethyst.*

Boreas and Pan were rivals for the love of the nymph Pithys: she preferred Pan. Boreas in a rage caught her up in a whirlwind, and dashed her against a rock. She became transformed into a pine-tree, which was ever after sacred to the god of shepherds.

No. 642.

Æacus praying to Jupiter to restore his subjects.

ADMON. *Oriental Sardonyx.*

The subjects of Æacus, king of Ægina, having nearly all perished by a pestilence, he prayed for relief to Jupiter, who, in compliance with his prayer, transformed swarms of ants that issued from an old oak into human beings. These new subjects Æacus called Myrmidons, from *murmex,* an ant. Their descendants were, according to some authors, the soldiers of Achilles.

The explanation of the fable appears to be, that Æacus (who was so famous for his justice and wisdom, that he was represented to have become after death one of the judges in the infernal regions,) drew from their caves the rude and scattered population, and taught them to become a civilised and industrious people.

Ovid (*Met.* vii.), after beautifully describing at length the progress of the pestilence, thus describes the restoration :—

"Despairing under grief's oppressive weight,
And sunk by these tempestuous blasts of fate,
'O Jove,' said I, 'if common fame says true,
If e'er Ægina gave those joys to you—
If e'er you lay enclos'd in her embrace,
Fond of her charms, and eager to possess—
O father, if you do not yet disclaim
Paternal care, nor yet disown thy name—
Grant my petitions, and with speed restore
My subjects, num'rous as they were before,
Or make me partner of the fate they bore.'
I spoke, and glorious lightning shone around,
And rattling thunder gave a prosp'rous
    sound ;
'So let it be ; and may these omens prove
A pledge,' said I, ' of your returning love.'

By chance a rev'rend oak was near the place,
Sacred to Jove, and of Dodona's race,
Where frugal ants laid up their winter meat,
Whose little bodies bear a mighty weight:
I saw them march along and hide their store,
And much admir'd their number and their pow'r;
Admir'd at first, but after envy'd more.
Full of amazement, thus to Jove I pray'd,
' O grant, since thus my subjects are decay'd,
As many subjects to supply the dead.'
I pray'd, and strange convulsions mov'd the
    oak,
Which murmur'd, though by ambient winds un-
    shook:
My trembling hands and stiff-erected hair
Express'd all tokens of uncommon fear;
Yet both the earth and sacred oak I kiss'd,
And scarce could hope, yet still I hop'd the
    best;
For wretches, whatsoe'er the fates divine,
Expound all omens to their own design.
    But now 'twas night, when ev'n distraction
    wears
A pleasing look, and dreams beguile our cares.
Lo! the same oak appears before my eyes,
Nor alter'd in his shape nor former size;
As many ants the num'rous branches bear,
The same their labour and their frugal care;
The branches too a like commotion found,
And shook th' industrious creatures on the ground,
Who, by degrees (what's scarce to be believ'd)
A nobler form and larger bulk receiv'd,
And on the earth walk'd an unusual pace,
With manly strides and an erected face;

Their num'rous legs and former colour lost,
The insects could a human figure boast.
    I wake, and waking find my cares again,
And to the unperforming gods complain,
And call their promise and pretences vain.
Yet in my court I heard the murm'ring voice
Of strangers, and a mix'd uncommon noise:
But I suspected all was still a dream,
Till Telamon to my apartment came,
Op'ning the door with an impetuous haste;
' O come,' said he, ' and see your faith and hopes
    surpass'd.'
I follow, and, confused with wonder, view
Those shapes which my presaging slumbers
    drew:
I saw, and own'd, and called them subjects;
    they
Confess'd my pow'r, submissive to my sway.
To Jove, restorer of my race decay'd,
My vows were first with due oblations paid;
I then divide with an impartial hand
My empty city and my ruin'd land,
To give the new-born youth an equal share,
And call them Myrmidons, from what they were.
You saw their persons, and they still retain
The thrift of ants, though now transform'd to
    men;
A frugal people and inur'd to sweat,
Lab'ring to gain, and keeping what they get.
These, equal both in strength and years, shall
    join
Their willing aid, and follow your design,
With the first southern gale that shall present
To fill your sail and favour your intent."

OVID, *Met.* vii.

No. 643.

Thisbe pursued by a lion.

GNAIOS. *Cornelian.*

Pyramus and Thisbe, two young lovers in Babylon, lived in houses adjoining each other.
As their parents interdicted all intercourse between them, they continued to communicate

with one another through a chink in the partition-wall.   At length they made an assignation
to meet by night outside the city.   The subsequent events are thus described by Ovid
(*Met.* iv.):—

" Thus they their vain petition did renew
Till night, and then they softly sigh'd adieu.
But first they strove to kiss, and that was all ;
Their kisses died untasted on the wall.
Soon as the morn had o'er the stars prevail'd,
And, warm'd by Phœbus, flowers their dews
      exhal'd,
The lovers to their well-known place return ;
Alike they suffer, and alike they mourn.
At last their parents they resolve to cheat,
(If to deceive in love be called deceit)
To steal by night from home, and thence un-
      known
To seek the fields, and quit th' unfaithful town.
But, to prevent their wand'ring in the dark,
They both agree to fix upon a mark ;
A mark that could not their designs expose:
The tomb of Ninus was the mark they chose.
There they might rest secure beneath the
      shade,
Which boughs, with snowy fruit encumber'd,
      made :
A wide-spread mulberry its rise had took
Just on the margin of a gurgling brook.
Impatient for the friendly dusk they stay,
And chide the slowness of departing day :
In western seas down sunk at last the light;
From western seas uprose the shades of night.
The loving Thisbe ev'n prevents the hour;
With cautious silence she unlocks the door,
And veils her face, and marching through the
      gloom
Swiftly arrives at th' assignation-tomb :
For still the fearful sex can fearless prove ;
Boldly they act, if spirited by love.
When, lo ! a lioness rush'd o'er the plain,
Grimly besmear'd with blood of oxen slain ;
And, what to the dire sight new horrors brought,
To slake her thirst the neighb'ring spring she
      sought :

Which, by the moon, when trembling Thisbe
      spies,
Wing'd with her fear, swift as the wind she
      flies,
And in a cave recovers from her fright;
But dropp'd her veil, confounded in her flight.
When, sated with repeated draughts, again
The queen of beasts scour'd back along the
      plain,
She found the veil, and mouthing it all o'er,
With bloody jaws the lifeless prey she tore.
      The youth, who could not cheat his guards so
            soon,
Late came, and noted by the glimm'ring moon
Some savage feet new printed on the ground ;
His cheeks turu'd pale, his limbs no vigour found:
But when, advancing on, the veil he spied
Distain'd with blood and ghastly torn, he cried,
' One night shall death to two young lovers give;
But she deserv'd unnumber'd years to live !
'Tis I am guilty, I have thee betray'd,
Who came not early as my charming maid.
Whatever slew thee, I the cause remain ;
I nam'd and fix'd the place where thou wast
      slain.
Ye lions, from your neighb'ring dens repair,
Pity the wretch—this impious body tear !
But cowards thus for death can idly cry ;
The brave still have it in their pow'r to die.'
Then to th' appointed tree he hastes away,
The veil first gather'd, though all rent it lay ;
The veil all rent yet still itself endears,
He kiss'd, and kissing wash'd it with his tears.
' Though rich,' he cried, ' with many a precious
      stain,
Still from my blood a deeper tincture gain.'
Then in his breast his shining sword he drown'd,
And fell supine, extended on the ground.
As out again the blade he, dying, drew,
Out spun the blood, and streaming upwards flew.

So, if a conduit-pipe e'er burst you saw,
Swift spring the gushing waters through the flaw;
Then, spouting in a bow, they rise on high,
And a new fountain plays amid the sky.
The berries, stain'd with blood, began to shew
A dark complexion, and forgot their snow;
While, fatten'd with a flowing gore, the root
Was doom'd for ever to a purple fruit.
   Meantime poor Thisbe fear'd — so long she
     stay'd—
Her lover might suspect a perjur'd maid.
Her fright scarce o'er, she strove the youth to find
With ardent eyes which spoke an ardent mind.
Already in his arms, she hears him sigh
At her destruction, which was once so nigh.
The tomb—the tree, but not the fruit she knew—
The fruit she doubted for its alter'd hue:
Still as she doubts, her eyes a body found
Quiv'ring in death, and gasping on the ground.
She started back—the red her cheeks forsook;
And ev'ry nerve with thrilling horrors shook:
So trembles the smooth surface of the seas,
If brush'd o'er gently with a rising breeze.
But when her view her bleeding love confess'd,
She shriek'd—she tore her hair—she beat her
     breast—
She rais'd the body, and embrac'd it round,
And bath'd with tears unfeign'd the gaping
     wound.
Then her warm lips to the cold face applied;
' And is it thus, ah! thus we meet!' she cried.
' My Pyramus! whence sprung thy cruel fate?
My Pyramus!—ah! speak, ere 'tis too late.
I, thy own Thisbe, but one word implore—
One word thy Thisbe never ask'd before.'

At Thisbe's name awak'd, he open'd wide
His dying eyes; with dying eyes he tried
On her to dwell, but clos'd them slow, and—died!
   The fatal cause was now at last explor'd;
Her veil she knew, and saw his sheathless sword:
' From thy own hand thy ruin thou hast found,'
She said; 'but love first taught that hand to
     wound.
E'en I for thee as bold a hand can shew,
And love which shall as true direct the blow.
I will against the woman's weakness strive,
And never thee, lamented youth, survive.
The world may say I caus'd, alas! thy death,
But saw thee breathless, and resign'd my breath.
Fate, though it conquers, shall no triumph gain;
Fate that divides us, still divides in vain.
   ' Now, both our cruel parents, hear my pray'r;
My pray'r to offer for us both I dare:
Oh! see our ashes in one urn confin'd,
Whom love at first, and fate at last, has join'd.
The bliss you envied is not our request;
Lovers when dead may sure together rest.
Thou, tree, where now one lifeless lump is laid,
Ere long o'er two shalt cast a friendly shade.
Still let our loves from thee be understood,
Still witness in thy purple fruit our blood.'
She spoke, and in her bosom plung'd the sword,
All warm and reeking from its slaughter'd lord.
   The pray'r which dying Thisbe had preferr'd
Both gods and parents with compassion heard.
The whiteness of the mulberry soon fled,
And rip'ning, sadden'd in a dusky red;
Whilst both their parents their lost children
     mourn,
And mix their ashes in one golden urn."

No. 644.

The hunter Epytus, son of Elatus king of Arcadia, killed by a serpent.

DIOSCORIDES.   *Oriental Cornelian.*

See PAUSAN. book viii.

3 B

No. 645.

Lycurgus cutting down the vines.

CHROMIOS.   *Oriental Cornelian.*

Lycurgus, king of the Edoni, near the river Strymon in Thrace, seeing the evil effects of drunkenness, cut down all the vines in his territory, and banished from it the worship of Bacchus and all his votaries.   It is said that Bacchus, as a punishment, struck him with madness; so that, while cutting down the vineyards, he slew his own son, mistaking him for a vine, and maimed himself: he ended his days in misery.

"Not long Lycurgus view'd the golden light—
That daring man who mix'd with gods in fight.
Bacchus, and Bacchus' votaries, he drove
With brandish'd steel from Nyssa's sacred grove:
Their consecrated spears lay scatter'd round,
With curling vines and twisted ivy bound;
While Bacchus headlong sought the briny flood,
And Thetis' arm received the trembling god.

Nor fail'd the crime th' immortals' wrath to move,
(Th' immortals bless'd with endless ease above).
Depriv'd of sight by their avenging doom,
Cheerless he breath'd, and wander'd in the gloom;
Then sunk unpity'd to the dire abodes,
A wretch accurst, and hated by the gods!"
        HOMER, *Il.* book vi.   See OVID, *Trist.* v.,
        El. 3, *Fast.* 3; APOLLOD. iii. c. 5.

No. 646.

Lycurgus killing his own son.

CHROMIOS.   *Sardonyx.*

No. 647.

The same subject.

CHROMIOS.   *Sardonyx.*

No. 648.

Pyrene devoured by wild beasts.

DIOSCORIDES.   *Cornelian.*

Pyrene, daughter of Bebryx, a king in Spain, was violated by Hercules on his way to attack Geryon.   She brought forth a serpent; and was so horror-struck at this, that she fled to the mountains, and was devoured by wild beasts.   (See SIL. ITAL. book iii.)

No. 649.

Erisichthon cutting down the sacred oak of Ceres, while a Dryad seated on its boughs is denouncing vengeance against him.

CHROMIOS. *Cornelian.*

Erisichthon, a prince of Thessaly, impiously disregarding the bounties of Ceres, and profaning her worship, cut down a grove sacred to her. The goddess, to punish this act of sacrilege, sent Famine to torment him with such insatiable hunger, that he at last devoured his own flesh. The story is thus told by Ovid (*Met.* viii.) :—

"This atheist sire the slighted gods defied,
And ritual honours to their shrines denied.
As fame reports, his hand an axe sustain'd,
Which Ceres' consecrated grove profan'd ;
Which durst the venerable gloom invade,
And violate with light the awful shade.
An ancient oak in the dark centre stood,
The covert's glory, and itself a wood ;
Garlands embrac'd its shaft, and from the boughs
Hung tablets, monuments of prosp'rous vows.
In the cool dusk its unpierc'd verdure spread,
The Dryads oft their hallow'd dances led ;
And oft, when round their gaging arms they cast,
Full fifteen ells it measur'd in the waist :
Its height all under standards did surpass,
As they aspir'd above the humbler grass.
　　These motives, which would gentler minds restrain,
Could not make Triope's bold son abstain ;
He sternly charg'd his slaves with strict decree
To fell with gashing steel the sacred tree.
But whilst they, ling'ring, his commands delay'd,
He snatch'd an axe, and thus blaspheming said :
' Was this no oak, nor Ceres' fav'rite care,
But Ceres's self, this arm, unaw'd, should dare
Its leafy honours in the dust to spread,
And level with the earth its airy head.'
He spoke, and as he pois'd a slanting stroke,
Sighs heav'd, and tremblings shook the frighted oak ;
Its leaves look'd sickly, pale its acorns grew,
And its long branches sweat a chilly dew.

But when his impious hand a wound bestow'd,
Blood from the mangled bark in currents flow'd.
When a devoted bull of mighty size,
A sinning nation's grand atonement, dies—
With such a plenty from the spouting veins,
A crimson stream the turfy altars stains.
　　They wonder all amaz'd ; yet one more bold,
The act dissuading, strove his axe to hold.
But the Thessalian, obstinately bent—
Too proud to change, too harden'd to repent—
On his kind monitor his eyes, which burn'd
With rage, and with his eyes his weapon turn'd ;
' Take the reward,' says he, ' of pious dread :'
Then with a blow lopp'd off his parted head.
No longer check'd, the wretch his crime pursu'd,
Doubled his strokes, and sacrilege renew'd ;
When from the groaning trunk a voice was heard :
' A Dryad I, by Ceres' love preferr'd,
Within the circle of this clasping rind
Coeval grew, and now in ruin join'd ;
But instant vengeance shall thy sin pursue,
And death is cheer'd with this prophetic view.'
　　At last the oak with cords enforc'd to bow,
Strain'd from the top, and sapp'd with wounds below,
The humbler wood, partaker of its fate,
Crush'd with its fall, and shiver'd with its weight.
　　The grove destroy'd, the sister Dryads moan,
Griev'd at its loss, and frighted at their own ;
Straight, suppliants for revenge, to Ceres go,
In sable weeds, expressive of their woe.

The beauteous goddess, with a graceful air,
Bow'd in consent, and nodded to their pray'r.
The awful motion shook the fruitful ground,
And wav'd the fields with golden harvests crown'd.
Soon she contriv'd in her projecting mind
A plague severe, and piteous in its kind—
If plagues for crimes of such presumptuous
　　height
Could pity in the softest breast create—
With pinching want and hunger's keenest smart
To tear his vitals and corrode his heart.
But since her near approach by fate's denied
To Famine, and broad climes their pow'rs divide,
A nymph, the mountain's ranger, she address'd,
And, thus resolv'd, her high commands express'd:

DESCRIPTION OF FAMINE.

'Where frozen Scythia's utmost bound is
　　plac'd,
A desert lies, a melancholy waste:
In yellow crops there Nature never smil'd—
No fruitful tree to shade the barren wild.
There sluggish cold its icy station makes—
There paleness frights, and aguish trembling
　　shakes.
Of pining Famine this the fated seat,
To whom my orders in these words repeat:
Bid her this miscreant with her sharpest pains
Chastise, and sheath herself into his veins;
Be unsubdu'd by Plenty's baffled store,
Reject my empire, and defeat my pow'r.
And lest the distance and the tedious way
Should with the toil and long fatigue dismay,
Ascend my chariot, and, convey'd on high,
Guide the rein'd dragons through the parting
　　sky.'
The nymph, accepting of the granted car,
Sprung to the seat, and posted through the air;
Nor stopp'd till she to a bleak mountain came,
Of wondrous height, and Caucasus its name.
There in a stony field the fiend she found,
Herbs gnawing, and roots scratching from the
　　ground.

Her elf-lock hair in matted tresses grew;
Sunk were her eyes, and pale her ghastly hue;
Wan were her lips; and foul with clammy glue
Her throat was furr'd; her guts appear'd within
With snaky crawlings through her parchment
　　skin:
Her jutting hips seem'd starting from their place,
And for a belly was a belly's space:
Her dugs hung dangling from her craggy spine,
Loose to her breast, and fasten'd to her chine:
Her joints protuberant by leanness grown,
Consumption sunk the flesh, and rais'd the bone:
Her knees large orbits bunch'd to monstrous size,
And ancles to undue proportion rise.
This plague the nymph, not daring to draw near,
At distance hail'd, and greeted from afar:
And though she told her charge without delay—
Though her arrival late, and short her stay,
She felt keen famine, or she seem'd to feel,
Invade her blood, and on her vitals steal.
She turn'd, from the infection to remove,
And back to Thessaly the serpents drove.

　　The fiend obey'd the goddess's command
(Though their effects in opposition stand);
She cut her way, supported by the wind,
And reach'd the mansion by the nymph assign'd.
　　'Twas night, when ent'ring Erisichthon's room,
Dissolv'd in sleep, and thoughtless of his doom,
She clasp'd his limbs, by impious labour tir'd,
With battish wings, but her whole self inspir'd;
Breath'd on his throat and chest a tainting blast,
And in his veins infus'd an endless fast.
　　The task despatch'd, away the fury flies
From plenteous regions and from rip'ning skies;
To her old barren north she wings her speed,
And cottages distress'd with pinching need.
　　Still slumbers Erisichthon's senses drown,
And soothe his fancy with their softest down:
He dreams of viands delicate to eat,
And revels on imaginary meat—
Chews with his working mouth, but chews in vain,
And tires his grinding teeth with fruitless pain—
Deludes his throat with visionary fare,
Feasts on the wind, and banquets on the air.

The morning came, the night and slumbers past,
But still the furious pangs of hunger last;
The cank'rous rage still gnaws with griping pains,
Stings in his throat, and in his bowels reigns.
  Straight he requires, impatient in demand,
Provisions from the air, the seas, the land ;
But, though the land, air, seas, provisions grant,
Starves at full tables, and complains of want.
What to a people might in dole be paid,
Or victual cities for a long blockade,
Could not his wolfish appetite assuage ;
For glutting nourishment increas'd its rage.
As rivers pour'd from ev'ry distant shore,
The sea insatiate drinks, and thirsts for more ;
Or as the fire, which all materials burns,
And wasted forests into ashes turns,

Grows more voracious as the more it preys,
Recruits, dilates the flame, and spreads the blaze ;
So impious Erisichthon's hunger raves,
Receives refreshments, and refreshments craves :
Food raises a desire for food, and meat
Is but a new provocative to eat :
He grows more empty, as the more supply'd ;
And endless cramming but extends the void.
  Now riches, hoarded by paternal care,
Were sunk, the glutton swallowing up the heir;
Yet the devouring flame no stores abate,
Nor less his hunger grew with his estate.
  At last all means, as all provisions, fail'd ;
For the disease by remedies prevail'd :
His muscles with a furious bite he tore—
Gorg'd his own tatter'd flesh, and gulp'd his gore :
Wounds were his feast—his life to life a prey—
Supporting nature by its own decay."

No. 650.

Ceres sending her nymph to bring Famine to Erisichthon.

APOLLONIDES. *Cornelian.*

No. 651.

Famine tormenting Erisichthon.

CHROMIOS. *Amethyst.*

No. 652.

Phineus and the Harpies.

CHROMIOS. *Amethyst.*

. The fables respecting Phineus have been very much varied. Some authors represent him as king of Thrace, some as king of Arcadia. Sophocles relates that he was punished with blindness, because he deprived his sons by Cleopatra of sight at the instigation of his wife Dia.

Hesiod attributes it to his having assisted Phryxus; Apollonius to his having revealed the will of Fate to all inquirers. Phineus was made the subject of a drama both by Æschylus and Sophocles. He is represented as one of the great prophets of antiquity. His persecution by the harpies—winged monsters with human faces, and the bodies and talons of vultures—is a celebrated story. He was relieved from them by Otus and Ephialtes, sons of Boreas, two of the Argonauts, to whom he gave very useful information for the prosecution of their voyage. The story is thus told by Apollonius Rhodius (*Argonautics*, book ii.):—

" With the succeeding morn they gain the land,
And moor their ship on the Bithynian strand.
The wretched Phineus dwelt upon that shore,
Who pangs beyond the lot of mortals bore.
From Phœbus' bounty all his suff'rings flow'd;
The power of augury the god bestow'd.
Regardless he of vengeance from above,
To men reveal'd the secret will of Jove.
Th' offended pow'r inflicts a dreadful doom—
Endless decrepitude in cheerless gloom—
No relish left of health or young delight—
No comfort beaming through the Stygian night:
No viands gratify his famish'd taste,
Though daily care supplied the rich repast.
The natives round his far-fam'd prescience led,
And plenteous off'rings on his board they spread;
But rushing from the clouds the harpy brood
Snatch from his hands and mouth th' untasted food,
With crooked talons and with rav'ning jaws:
Their inroads knew nor interval nor pause.
Unwearied plunderers! Sometimes nought remain'd;
And sometimes scarce what loathsome life sustain'd,
Reserv'd for torture. Such a stench imbu'd
Whate'er they touch'd, that none might taste the food
Spar'd by their ravage, or in haunts remain
Stain'd by the visits of that odious train;
Save him by dire necessity confin'd
To bear th' annoyance of their hateful kind.

The wretched sufferer heard th' approaching crowd,
With trampling steps and mingled voices loud;
And well could read, in oracles of Jove,
Those strangers came his famine to remove.
Rais'd from his couch, a lifeless thing—a shade,
Scarce with his staff the phantom-frame he stay'd.
As dark, with tottering limbs, he sought the doors,
His trembling hand the guiding wall explores.
Feeble and old, scarce differing from the dead—
An hideous squalor o'er his body spread.
When to the portal of his house he came,
His knees unnerv'd refus'd to bear his frame.
Distemper'd vision mocks his darkling eyes;
And wheeling earth in giddy circle flies.
Speechless he sinks, absorb'd in trance profound—
Th' astonish'd Greeks the wretched man surround.
Regaining breath, the seer prophetic spoke;
Scarce from his breast the feeble accents broke:
' Hear, flower of Greeks, if ye, indeed, are they,
Who, doom'd by Pelias, plough the wat'ry way—
Whom Argo wafts, a gallant band enroll'd,
And Jason leads, to win the fleece of gold,—
Hail, noble strangers, welcome to this heart!
Hail, glad event, long promis'd by my art!
Son of Latona,* thanks to thee be paid!
O, king of prophets, I have felt thine aid
My sole support in anguish to this hour.
By hospitable Jove†—tremendous pow'r
To him that slights the suppliant's hallow'd claim—
By Phœbus, and by matron Juno's name—

---

* Apollo.   † Jupiter Xenius.

The guardian pow'rs, that guide you through the main,
Oh let not sorrow supplicate in vain !
Despise me not; but, ere ye plough the wave,
A wretch from pangs unutterable save.
'Tis not that furies trample on my head—
That darkling thus I am to pleasure dead—
That slow decrepit age has made my life
A ling'ring death, with nature still at strife.
Curses on curses, plagues on plagues, I bear :
The harpies from my mouth the viands tear.
No prudence, aid, or comfort, can supply;
They stoop impetuous, rushing through the sky.
I may not 'scape them : present as my thought,
Sudden they come, with dire annoyance fraught—
Of food and social intercourse bereave :
Such poisonous scents the parting furies leave,

Men loathe the relicts of their tasted food,
And shun the place polluted by that brood.
An heart of adamant could scarce endure :
Yet I must bear these ills without a cure,
By famine driv'n (though horror chills my breast)
To feed on noxious fragments of their feast.
But late relenting Jove beholds my grief;
Divine predictions promise sure relief.
The sons of Borèas, sprung from kindred race,
Are doom'd by heav'n th' infernal brood to chase.
If I, indeed, am Phineus, known to fame,
For mighty riches and an augur's name—
Our lineage if Agenor has supplied,
Or if in Thrace their sister was my bride—' "

Here Phineus is interrupted by the sons of Boreas, who undertake to grant his request. The narrative then proceeds—

" Meantime, the juniors of the band, with haste,
To cheer the prophet furnish the repast—
A parting spoil to gorge the harpy train.
The sons of Boreas* nigh the board remain,
With falchions to repel th' accursed brood :
And scarcely had the prophet touch'd the food—
They rushing sudden from the darken'd air,
Swift as the whirlwind's blast or lightning's glare,
With sounding pinions and with fearful cry,
Stoop from the clouds, and on the viands fly.
The gallant youths, undaunted at the view,
With threat'ning shouts upon the monsters flew.
With keen despatch the shrieking monsters fed ;
Consum'd the viands, and o'er ocean fled.
As, vanishing from sight, aloft they rose ;
Diffus'd around th' infectious odour flows.
The youths pursued them with incessant flight,
For Jove infus'd unconquerable might :

And close behind their falchions they display'd ;
But vain the chase, had Jove withheld his aid.
For, when they sought the prophet, or withdrew,
More swift than Zephyr's blast the harpies flew.
As when with eager speed sagacious hounds
The wooded valley trace or forest bounds,
And see the mountain-goats, or branching deer,
Fly full in view upon the wings of fear,
Stretch'd at full speed they follow close behind—
They think to seize the prey—they champ the wind ;
The plumy brethren thus pursued the chase,
With hands outstretch'd to grasp that hateful race;
And now, and now they aim'd a mortal blow.
In heaven's despite they had subdued the foe :
On the Plotæan isles, their swords had freed
Abhorrent earth of that detested breed ;
But Iris swift, who made these birds her care,
From heaven observant cut the yielding air.

---

* Calais and Zetes.

She check'd the youths, with monitory words:
' O, sons of Boreas, cease; withhold your swords;
For know, the fates prohibit mortal arm
These huntress dogs of sov'reign Jove to harm.
Their dire approach no more shall Phineus feel;
Most solemn oaths this peaceful compact seal.'
She said, and swore by Styx—a sound of fear—
Tremendous oath that all the gods revere !
' That never more (so destinies ordain)
Should Phineus suffer from the harpy train.'
Confiding in that oath, the youths return:
Hence have those isles their appellation borne
Of Strophades *—a name that still remains,
And memory of the past event maintains.
　　The Grecian leaders pious cares engage.
Lustrations purify the darkling sage,
Whose frame neglected squalid filth o'erspread.
The chosen victims for the gods they led,
With care selected from Bebrycia's spoil ;
Then spread the feast, more welcome after toil.
In Phineus' halls the banquet they prepar'd ;
And with the chiefs the noble sufferer shar'd—
Eager he shar'd ; and these returning gleams
Of ease and comfort seem'd but blissful dreams.
Now, fully satisfied with food and wine,
Sleep fled the band, till morn began to shine.
With anxious heart for Boreas' sons they wait.
Meanwhile the seer unfolds the book of fate.
He sate before the hearth ; around, the youth
Bend forward, and imbibe prophetic truth—
What various incidents their course attend—
What toils await them—what propitious end."

No. 653.

Allirothius mortally wounded by his own axe.

DIOSCORIDES.　　*Amethyst.*

Allirothius, in revenge for the defeat sustained by his father Neptune, in the contest with Minerva, about the right of giving a name to Athens when just built, attempted to cut down the olive produced by her. For this the goddess punished him, by causing him to wound himself mortally in the leg. (See APOLLOD. iii.)

No. 654.

Æsacus in grief at the death of Hesperia.

GNAIOS.　　*Cornelian.*

Æsacus, one of Priam's sons, was enamoured of the nymph Hesperia. While following her through a wood, he found her stung to death by a serpent. Then, in despair at her loss, he flung himself from a cliff into the sea ; but as he fell was transformed into a cormorant by Thetis, standing on a shell drawn by dolphins.

---

* From *strepho*, to turn.

THE STORY OF ÆSACUS.

"These some old man sees wanton in the air,
And praises the unhappy constant pair.
Then to his friend the long-neck'd corm'rant shows,
The former tale reviving others' woes:
'That sable bird,' he cries, 'which cuts the flood
With slender legs, was once of royal blood;
His ancestors from mighty Tros proceed,
The brave Laomedon, and Ganymede
(Whose beauty tempted Jove to steal the boy),
And Priam, hapless prince! who fell with Troy:
Himself was Hector's brother, and (had fate
But giv'n this hopeful youth a longer date)
Perhaps had rivall'd warlike Hector's worth,
Though on the mother's side of meaner birth;
Fair Alyxothe, a country maid,
Bare Æsacus by stealth in Ida's shade.
He fled the noisy town and pompous court,
Lov'd the lone hills and simple rural sport,
And seldom to the city would resort.
Yet he no rustic clownishness profess'd,
Nor was soft love a stranger to his breast:
The youth had long the nymph Hesperie woo'd—
Oft through the thicket or the mead pursued:
Her haply on her father's bank he spied,
While fearless she her silver tresses dried;
Away she fled: not stags with half such speed,
Before the prowling wolf, scud o'er the mead;
Not ducks, when they the safer flood forsake,
Pursued by hawks, so swift regain the lake.

As fast he follow'd in the hot career;
Desire the lover wing'd, the virgin fear.
A snake unseen now pierc'd her heedless foot;
Quick through the veins the venom'd juices shoot:
She fell, and 'scap'd by death his fierce pursuit.
Her lifeless body, frighted, he embrac'd,
And cried, 'Not this I dreaded, but thy haste:
O had my love been less, or less thy fear!
The victory, thus bought, is far too dear.
Accursed snake! yet I more curs'd than he!
He gave the wound; the cause was given by me.
Yet none shall say that unreveng'd you died.'
He spoke; then climb'd a cliff's o'er-hanging side,
And, resolute, leap'd on the foaming tide.
Tethys receiv'd him gently on the wave,
The death he sought denied, and feathers gave.
Debarr'd the surest remedy of grief,
And forc'd to live, he curs'd th' unask'd relief;
Then on his airy pinions upward flies,
And at a second fall successless tries;
The downy plume a quick descent denies.
Enrag'd, he often dives beneath the wave,
And there in vain expects to find a grave.
His ceaseless sorrow for th' unhappy maid
Meager'd his look, and on his spirits prey'd.
Still near the sounding deep he lives; his name
From frequent diving and emerging came."

OVID, *Met.* xi.

No. 655.

Transformation of Æsacus.

GNAIOS. *Calcedony.*

No. 656.

Crinisus in the shape of a dog surprising a nymph.

GNAIOS. *Sardonyx.*

3 c

Crinisus, or Cremissus, was (according to some, for the stories about him vary) a Trojan prince, who exposed his daughter on the sea, sooner than allow her to be consigned to the monster sent to punish the perfidy of Laomedon. Hearing that she was wafted safely to Sicily, he went in quest of her. The gods, to reward his fidelity, granted him the power of assuming various shapes, in order to facilitate her discovery. This privilege he used to win the favour of many nymphs. He gave his name to a river in Sicily, which is here represented as issuing from an open-mouthed vase. (See *Æn.* v.)

No. 657.

Cyanippus dragged by his daughter to the altar.

GNAIOS.   *Sardonyx.*

Cyanippus, king of Syracuse, derided the worship of Bacchus; for this the god so inebriated him that he attempted to offer violence to his own daughter. A plague having raged through his dominions, the oracle declared that it could only cease with his death. On this he was seized, and dragged by his daughter to the altar of Bacchus, to be sacrificed. (PLUTARCH, *Parallel.*)

No. 658.

Tisiphone and Cythæron.

ADMON.   *Cornelian.*

The fury Tisiphone became enamoured of the shepherd Cythæron; but as he declined her suit, she snatched one of the snakes from her hair and flung it at him, which stung him to death. He gave his name to a mountain in Bœotia, where the orgies of Bacchus, which were in a great measure under the influence of the Furies, were celebrated.

No. 659.

Acastus stealing the arrows of Peleus while asleep.

APOLLONIDES.   *Cornelian.*

Peleus, a king in Thessaly, the son of Æacus and Endeis, daughter of the centaur Chiron, having accidentally slain his father-in-law during the chase of the Calydonian boar, fled to the court of Acastus, king of Iolchos, where he was purified, according to the rites observed in those times, of the murder. There the queen Astidamia fell in love with him. He virtuously rejected her overtures. She then, through revenge, accused him to her husband of an attempt to corrupt her. Acastus, believing the charge, took him to hunt on Mount Pelion; and there, as he lay asleep through fatigue, he stole his arrows, and left him to be devoured by wild beasts. Jupiter, knowing his virtue, sent Pluto to release him, and supply him with arms to avenge his wrongs. On his release he drove Acastus from his dominions, and put Astidamia to death. He subsequently married the goddess Thetis, by whom he had Achilles.

No. 660.

Pluto giving Peleus a sword.

Lycos. *Cornelian.*

No. 661.

The same subject.

Chromios. *Cornelian.*

No. 662.

Peleus killing Astidamia.

Gnaios. *Cornelian.*

No. 663.

Peleus wounding the centaur Clanis.

Apollonides. *Cornelian.*

Many of the greatest heroes of historic fable took a part in this engagement between the Centaurs and Lapithæ. The subject was a fertile one to poets, painters, and sculptors. The centaurs were the first who in that region rode on horseback; and the novelty of their appearance when mounted, and their dexterous management of their horses, first suggested the idea, which afterwards became a constant representation, of their being compound animals. The name is said to be derived from κεντεῖν ταύρους (*goading bulls*), because they hunted the wild oxen of the country. (See Ovid, *Met.* xii.)

No. 664.

Peleus piercing the hand and forehead of Dorylas.

CHROMIOS. *Calcedony.*

" For want of other ward,
He lifted up his hand his front to guard :
His hand it pass'd, and fixed it to his brow.

.   .   .   .   .

Him Peleus finish'd with a second wound,
Which through the navel pierced : he reeled around,
And dragg'd his dangling bowels on the ground—
Trod what he dragg'd, and what he trod he crush'd ;
And to his mother earth with empty belly rush'd."

OVID, *Met.* xii.

No. 665.

Peleus slaying Dorylas.

APOLLONIDES. *Sardonyx.*

No. 666.

Eurytus, the centaur, carrying off the bride Hippodamia.

GNAIOS. *Sardonyx.*

This attempt of Eurytus, or Eurytion, was the commencement of the fight.

No. 667.

Amycus hurling a candelabrum at Celadon.

CHROMIOS. *Calcedony.*

" Bold Amycus, from the robb'd vestry brings
The chalices of heav'n, and holy things
Of precious weight: a sconce that hung on high,
With tapers fill'd, to light the sacristy,
Torn from the cord, with his unhallow'd hand
He threw amid the Lapithæan band :
On Celadon the ruin fell ; and left
His face of feature and of form bereft.

So, when some brawny sacrificer knocks,
Before an altar led, an offer'd ox,
His eye-balls rooted out are thrown to ground ;
His nose, dismantled, in his mouth is found ;
His jaws, cheeks, front, one undistinguish'd
    wound.

This Belates, th' avenger, could not brook ;
But by the foot a maple board he took,
And hurl'd at Amycus ; his chin it bent
Against his chest, and down the centaur sent :
Whom, sputt'ring bloody teeth, the second blow
Of his drawn sword despatch'd to shades below."

OVID, *Met.* xii.

No. 668.

Belates attacking Amycus with the leg of a table.

APOLLONIDES. *Cornelian.*

No. 669.

Cyllarus wounded.

GNAIOS. *Cornelian.*

No. 670.

Death of Cyllarus and Hylonome.

APOLLONIDES. *Sardonyx.*

Hylonome, the lover of Cyllarus, threw herself on the point of the arrow that trans-pierced him.

THE STORY OF CYLLARUS AND HYLONOME.

" Nor could thy form, O Cyllarus, foreshew
Thy fate (if form to monsters men allow):
Just bloom'd thy beard—thy beard of golden hue;
Thy locks in golden waves about thy shoulders
    flew ;
Sprightly thy look ; thy shapes in ev'ry part
So clean, as might instruct the sculptor's art,
As far as man extended ; where began
The beast, the beast was equal to the man :
Add but a horse's head and neck, and he,
O Castor, was a courser worthy thee.
So was his back proportion'd for the seat ;
So rose his brawny chest ; so swiftly mov'd his feet.

Coal-black his colour, but like jet it shone ;
His legs and flowing tail were white alone.
Belov'd by many maidens of his kind,
But fair Hylonome possess'd his mind—
Hylonome for features and for face
Excelling all the nymphs of double race.
Nor less her blandishments than beauty move ;
At once both loving and confessing love.
For him she dress'd ; for him with female care
She comb'd and set in curls her auburn hair ;
Of roses, violets, and lilies mix'd,
And sprigs of flowing rosemary betwixt,
She form'd the chaplet that adorn'd her front :
In waters of the Pegasæan fount,

And in the streams that from the fountain play,
She wash'd her face and bath'd her twice a day.
The scarf of furs that hung below her side
Was ermine, or the panther's spotted pride—
Spoils of no common beast. With equal flame
They lov'd : their sylvan pleasures were the same;
All day they hunted, and when day expir'd
Together to some shady cave retir'd.
Invited to the nuptials, both repair ;
And side by side they both engage in war.
Uncertain from what hand, a flying dart
At Cyllarus was sent, which pierc'd his heart.
The jav'lin drawn from out the mortal wound,
He faints with stagg'ring steps, and seeks the
    ground ;

The fair within her arms receiv'd his fall,
And strove his wand'ring spirits to recall ;
And while her hand the streaming blood oppos'd,
Join'd face to face, his lips with hers she clos'd.
Stifled with kisses, a sweet death he dies ;
She fills the fields with undistinguish'd cries :
At least her words were in her clamour drown'd,
For my stunn'd ears receiv'd no vocal sound.
In madness of her grief, she seiz'd the dart
New-drawn and reeking from her lover's heart,
To her bare bosom the sharp point applied,
And wounded fell ; and falling by his side,
Embrac'd him in her arms, and thus embracing—
    died !"

OVID'S *Met.* xii.

No. 671.

Erechtheus killing the serpent that attacked his son Phalerus.

APOLLONIDES.   *Sardonyx.*

No. 672.

A serpent inspiring Melampus while asleep with the power of divination.

PYRGOTELES.   *Cornelian.*

The servant of Melampus, of Pylos in the Peloponnesus, having killed a serpent that
made its nest at the bottom of an oak, Melampus burned it with great respect on a funeral
pile, and very tenderly reared up its brood.   Some time after, as he lay asleep under the oak,
one of these serpents played about him and licked his ear : when he awoke he found himself
inspired with supernatural knowledge.   He understood the chirping of birds ; all the mysteries
of the healing art ; and obtained a knowledge of futurity.   He was one of the most celebrated
soothsayers and physicians of antiquity.   (See HOM. *Odys.* xi. and xv.; PROPERT. ii. el. 2 ;
APOLLOD. ii. c. 2.)

No. 673.

Neptune and Iphimedia.

GNAIOS.   *Sardonyx.*

Iphimedia, wife of the giant Aloëus, had by Neptune twins, Otus and Ephialtes, who were educated by Aloëus as his own children, and called Aloidæ. They joined the giants in their war against the gods, were defeated by Apollo, and consigned to torments in hell.

In this representation Iphimedia is pouring from a shell salt-water on her person ; and all this is meant to exemplify the great producing power of the sea.

" The consort of Aloëus next I view'd, Iphimedia. She to Neptune bore, For him she call'd their father, a short-liv'd But godlike pair of never-dying fame, Otus and Ephialtes. Such for height, And such for beauty, never by the fruits Of Earth were nourish'd since Orion died. Nine cubits were the breadth, nine ells the length, At nine years' growth, of each. The gods themselves They menac'd, and preparing to disturb With all-confounding war the realms above, On the Olympian summit thought to fix Huge Ossa, and on Ossa's tow'ring head Pelion with all his forests ; so to climb, By mountains heap'd on mountains, to the skies. Nor had they fail'd, to full-grown youth matur'd ; But, by the son of fair Latona slain, Both perish'd, ere the cheeks of either yet The fleecy down of blooming manhood wore."

HOMER, *Odyss.* xi. : COWPER's *Trans.*

No. 674.

Otus and Ephialtes shot by Apollo.

CHROMIOS. *Cornelian.*

No. 675.

Otus and Ephialtes entwined by serpents, and further tormented by an owl in hell.

CHROMIOS. *Cornelian.*

No. 676.

Pasiphaë soliciting the assistance of Dædalus.

APOLLONIDES. *Cornelian.*

Pasiphaë, the wife of Minos king of Crete, fell in love with a young prince named Taurus, or Bull ; and was assisted in her assignations with him by Dædalus, a celebrated artist, and a man very fertile in devices, who had built for the king the famous labyrinth. She brought forth male twins, who grew up very strong men ; one of whom resembled Minos, and the other

Taurus. Minos, to conceal this evidence of the queen's guilt and his own shame, had them confined in the labyrinth; and also imprisoned Dædalus and his son Icarus, who at length made their escape from the island in a boat, impelled by means of sails which Dædalus made. Icarus, in his youthful ardour not heeding his father's advice, was drowned : hence that part of the sea was afterwards called the Icarian sea. These circumstances gave rise to the fables of Pasiphaë being inspired, by the anger of the god, with an unnatural passion for a bull; of her being enclosed in a brazen cow made by Dædalus; of her bringing forth a ferocious monster—half man, half bull—called the Minotaur; of the escape of Dædalus and his son by means of wings; and of his son imprudently mounting too near the sun, which melted the cement of the wax of his wings.

> " Meanwhile the monster of a human beast
> His family's reproach and stain increas'd :
> His double kind the rumour swiftly spread,
> And evidenc'd the mother's beastly deed.
> When Minos, willing to conceal the shame
> That sprung from the reports of tattling fame,
> Resolves a dark enclosure to provide,
> And far from sight the two-form'd creature hide."
>
> <div align="right">Ovid's <i>Met.</i> viii.</div>

No. 677.

Dædalus and Icarus.

Gnaios.   *Amethyst.*

STORY OF DÆDALUS AND ICARUS.

" In tedious exile now too long detain'd,
Dædalus languish'd for his native land.
The sea foreclos'd his flight; yet thus he said :
' Though earth and water in subjection laid,
O cruel Minos, thy dominions be,
We'll go through air; for sure the air is free.'
Then to new arts his cunning thought applies,
And to improve the work of nature tries.
A row of quills, in gradual order plac'd,
Rise by degrees in length from first to last;
As on a cliff th' ascending thicket grows,
Or different reeds the rural pipe compose :
Along the middle runs a twine of flax,
The bottom stems are join'd by pliant wax.
Thus, well compact, a hollow bending brings
The fine composure into real wings.

His boy, young Icarus, that near him stood,
Unthinking of his fate, with smiles pursu'd
The floating feathers, which the moving air
Bore loosely from the ground, and wafted here
    and there;
Or with the wax impertinently play'd,
And with his childish tricks the great design de-
    lay'd.
The final master-stroke at last impos'd,
And now the neat machine completely clos'd ;
Fitting his pinions on a flight he tries,
And hung self-balanc'd in the beaten skies.
Then thus instructs his child :—' My boy, take
    care
To wing your course along the middle air;
If low, the surges wet your flagging plumes ;
If high, the sun the melting wax consumes :

Steer between both; nor to the northern skies,
Nor south Orion, turn your giddy eyes;
But follow me: let me before you lay
Rules for the flight, and mark the pathless way.'
Then teaching with a fond concern his son,
He took the untried wings and fix'd them on—
But fix'd with trembling hands; and, as he
    speaks,
The tears roll gently down his aged cheeks;
Then kiss'd, and in his arms embrac'd him fast,
But knew not this embrace must be the last.
And mounting upward, as he wings his flight,
Back on his charge he turns his aching sight—
As parent birds, when first their callow care
Leave the high nest to tempt the liquid air—
Then cheers him on, and oft, with fatal art,
Reminds the stripling to perform his part.
  These, as the angler at the silent brook,
Or mountain-shepherd leaning on his crook,
Or gaping ploughman, from the vale descries,
They stare, and view 'em with religious eyes,
And straight conclude them gods; since none but
    they
Through their own azure skies could find a way.

  Now Delos, Paros, on the left are seen,
And Samos, favour'd by Jove's haughty queen—
Upon the right, the isle Lebynthos nam'd,
And fair Calymne for its honey fam'd.
When now the boy, whose childish thoughts
    aspire
To loftier aims, and make him ramble higher,
Grown wild and wanton, more embolden'd flies
Far from his guide, and soars among the skies;
The soft'ning wax, that felt a nearer sun,
Dissolv'd apace, and soon began to run.
The youth in vain his melting pinions shakes;
His feathers gone, no longer air he takes:
' O, father, father!' as he strove to cry,
Down to the sea he tumbled from on high,
And found his fate; yet still subsists by fame
Among those waters that retain his name.
  The father, now no more a father, cries,
' Ho! Icarus! where are you?' as he flies;
' Where shall I seek my boy?'—he cries again,
And saw his feathers scatter'd on the main:
Then curs'd his art, and fun'ral rites conferr'd—
Naming the country from the youth interr'd."
          OVID'S *Met.* viii.

No. 678.

Phyllius dragging the bull to the altar.

APOLLONIDES. *Sardonyx.*

  Phyllius, a Bœotian youth, was enjoined by Cygnus, as the conditions of returning his friendship and attachment, to perform certain feats; one of which was to bring him a wild bull that ravaged the country, in order to sacrifice it at the altar of Jupiter.

"Then Hyrie's lake, and Tempe's field o'er-
    ran,
Fam'd for the boy who there became a swan;
For there enamour'd Phyllius, like a slave,
Perform'd what tasks the wayward youth would
    crave.
For presents he had mountain-vultures caught;
And from the desert a tame lion brought:

Then a wild bull commanded to subdue,
The conquer'd savage by the horns he drew;
But, mock'd so oft, the treatment he disdains,
And from the craving boy this prize detains.
Then thus in choler the resenting lad:
' Won't you deliver him?—You'll wish you had.'
No sooner said, but, in a peevish mood,
Leap'd from the precipice on which he stood.

3 D

The standers-by were struck with fresh sur-
    prise,
Instead of falling, to behold him rise
A snowy swan, and soaring to the skies.

But dearly the rash prank his mother cost,
Who ignorantly gave her son for lost—
For his misfortune wept; till she became
A lake, and still renown'd with Hyrie's name."

Ovid, Met. vii.

No. 679.

Slaying of the serpent that stung Archemorus or Opheltes.

APOLLONIDES. Cornelian.

Bacchus induced the nymphs to poison all the fountains and streams that lay on the way of the Argive army, when proceeding to the attack of his favourite city Thebes. The allies, half dead with thirst, are met by Hypsipile, the famous Lemnian princess, who spared her father's life (when the other Lemnian women all murdered their male relations), and, afterwards reduced to slavery, became nurse to Archemorus (called also Opheltes from his subsequent fate), son of Lycurgus king of Nemea, by his wife Eurydice. She conducted them to the river Langia, having left the infant playing on the grass. On her return the child was found to have been killed by a serpent. The serpent itself was afterwards killed by one of the Argive leaders. The obsequies of the child were celebrated with great solemnity, and funeral games, called the *Nemean*, instituted in honour of him. These were afterwards revived by Hercules, to commemorate his victory over the Nemean lion. This whole story, which has been used as the subject of many representations, is given in the fourth and fifth books of the *Thebais* of Statius. The following portions of the narrative are enough for the present purpose:—

" When, rising from amidst a circling crowd
Of Naiads, thus the god * exclaims aloud:
'Ye nymphs, that o'er each stream exert your reign,
Partake our honours and adorn our train;
Assist me to repel our common foes;
Nor grudge the toil unwilling I impose.
Withhold your sluices—dry the fertile source,
And clog with dust each stream's impetuous course;
But Nemea's most, from whence the guided foe
Pursues his wasteful path to Thebes below.
Let ev'ry torrent quit its craggy steep,
And disembogue its waters in the deep.'

He spoke; and straight a gath'ring filth o'er-
    spreads,
And binds the streams, suspended on their heads;

No more the spring its wonted influence yields;
Increasing thirst inflames the wither'd fields:
Huge heaps of moisten'd dust condens'd to mud
Charge the discolour'd channel of the flood:
Pale Ceres sickens on the barren soil,
And wither'd ears elude the peasant's toil:
The flocks on the fallacious margin stood,
And mourn th' unwonted absence of the flood.

Langia only, as the god ordain'd,
Preserves his stream with dust and filth un-
    stain'd—
Langia, yet unknown to vulgar fame,
Nor glorying in the slaughter'd infant's name.
Inviolate the grove and spring remain,
And all their wonted properties retain.

---

* Bacchus.

But, O, what honours the fair nymph await,
When Greece, to solemnise her infant's fate,
Shall institute triennial feasts and games,
And ages hence record their sacred names!
No more the plates their swelling chests confine—
No more the bucklers on their shoulders shine:
The fever spreads through each interior part,
And from the mouth invades the beating heart:
With raging pain their with'ring entrails burn,
And fiery breathings from their lungs return;
The shrinking veins contract their purple flood,
Nor feel the circling motion of the blood.
The gaping earth exhales unwholesome steams,
Resolv'd to dust by Sol's increasing beams.
The thirsty steed, impatient of the reins,
In wild disorder scours along the plains;
On the dry bit no floods of moisture flow,
In whiteness equal to the Scythian snow;
But from his mouth depends the lolling tongue,
Or to the parched roof adhesive hung.

At length a ray of hope dispels their grief,
And cheers them with the prospect of relief.
Hypsipile, as through the woods they stray'd,
A beauteous mourner, haply they survey'd.
Opheltes in her soft embraces press'd,
(Another's hope,) hung smiling at her breast.
With graceful negligence her tresses flow;
Her humble weeds were suited to her woe:
Yet all those studied arts could not efface
Her native grandeur and majestic grace;
With decent mixture in her stately mien,
The captive and the princess might be seen.
Th' Inachian monarch first his silence broke;
And, aw'd, the royal exile thus bespoke:
' O thou, whose features and celestial air
A more than mortal origin declare,
Let not an humble suppliant sue in vain.

Here fiery thirst our just designs controls—
Consumes our vigour, and unmans our souls.
Whate'er you grant, with joy we shall partake,
Nor scorn the troubled stream or standing lake.

O give us strength to match our warm desires,
And nerves to second what our soul inspires.
So may this infant thrive beneath the care
Of heav'n, and long inhale the vital air.'

The Lemnian princess fix'd her modest eyes
Prone to the ground, and thus at length replies:
' 'Tis true, O Greeks, from heav'n I claim my
    birth,
And far in woe surpass the race of earth.
Hard is my lot, a nurse's cares to prove,
And tend the produce of another's love;
While mine, perchance, the pangs of hunger know,
And crave what on an alien I bestow:
Yet for the author of my birth I claim
A monarch great in empire as in fame.
But why do I delay to give redress,
And aggravate with converse your distress?
Come, then, if haply yet Langia glides,
And rolls beneath the ground his silent tides.'

She spoke; and to procure the promis'd aid,
In haste her charge on the soft herbage laid:
Then heap'd around the choicest flow'rs, and tries
With lulling sounds to close his streaming eyes.

Meanwhile in childish sports Opheltes pass'd
The fatal day—of all his days the last.
One while the rising blades of grass he spurns,
Then, as his thirst or lust of food returns,
Recalls his absent nurse with feeble cries,
Or seeks in sleep to close his heavy eyes.
To form the speech of man he now essays,
And harmless thoughts in broken sounds con-
    veys;
Erects his list'ning ears at ev'ry sound,
And culls the tender flow'rs that grow around—
Too credulous to the fallacious grove,
Nor conscious of the fate decreed by Jove.

Thus she repeated, as she pass'd along,
Her promises, and cheer'd the drooping throng.
Soon as the rocky murmur greets their ears,
And in full view the grateful vale appears,

' A stream !' the leading chief exclaims aloud,
And waves the standard o'er the joyful crowd—
' A stream !' at once ten thousand voices cry !
' A stream !' the list'ning hills and rocks reply.

.   .   .   .

Eager to drink, the rushing crowds descend,
Unmindful of their sov'reign or their friend—
Horses and charioteers, a mingled throng ;
Steed press'd on steed, and man drove man along.
Here kings themselves in vain precedence claim—
In rank superior, yet their thirst the same :
Some tumble headlong from the slipp'ry rock ;
Others are whelm'd beneath the wat'ry shock.

.   .   .   .

The tender infant whom she left behind
(So the stern gods advis'd and fates design'd)
In fatal slumbers hangs his drooping head—
The skies his canopy—the ground his bed,—
And cloy'd with sport, and weary with his toils,
Grasp'd in his hand the grass and Flora's spoils.
Meanwhile along the fields a serpent roves,
Earth-born, the terror of Achæan groves :
Sublime on radiant spires he glides along,
And brandishes by fits his triple tongue :
An hideous length of tail behind he draws,
And foamy venom issues from his jaws ;
Three rows of teeth his mouth expunded shews,
And from his crest terrific glories rose.

.   .   .   .

One while he rolls his curling volumes round
The sylvan fane, or ploughs the furrow'd ground ;
Then round an oak his scaly length he twines,
And breaks in his embrace the toughest pines.

After violent resistance, he is at length slain—

" Swift through his gaping jaws the weapon
          glides,
And the rough texture of his tongue divides :
The point was seen above his crested head ;
Then stains the ground with gory filth dispread.
The furious monster, unappall'd with pain,
In rapid mazes bounds along the plain.

.   .   .   .

Then to the temple of his patron fled.

From bank to bank extended oft he lies :
Cut by his scales the waves high-bubbling rise.
But now, when earth is furrow'd o'er with chinks,
And ev'ry nymph within her channel sinks,
He twists, impatient of th' autumnal heats,
His spiry length, and wide destruction threats ;
And through exhausted springs and standing
          lakes
In winding folds his noxious progress takes.
One while he bares his lolling tongue in air,
Through impotence of pain and wild despair ;
Then crawls adhesive to the groaning plain,
If haply dew or moisture yet remain.

.   .   .   .

Smit with his tail, the dying babe awoke,
(Nor was the serpent conscious of the stroke) ;
Sleep soon invades his stiff'ning limbs again,
And locks them in an adamantine chain.
His nurse, alarm'd at his half-finish'd screams
(Such as are utter'd in terrific dreams),
Essays to fly ; but destitute of force,
Her falt'ring limbs desert her in the course.

.   .   .   .

Him as the princess unsuspecting view'd,
With sudden shrieks she rends the spacious wood.
Unmov'd the monster keeps his former post :
Her piercing clamours reach th' Argolic host :
Sent by the king, th' Arcadian hero learn'd
The fatal cause, and with the chiefs return'd.
Soon as the glare of arms the monster spies,
And hears the growing thunder of their cries,
He rears his crest, and with a fiery glance
Expects th' assailant's terrible advance."

.   .   .   .

Here long he struggles in the pangs of death ;
And hissing threats, at length resigns his breath.
Him Lerna's lakes in gentle murmurs mourn,
And Nemea, by his frequent windings worn—
Him ev'ry nymph that late was wont to bring
Her early tribute from the rifled spring—
For him the fauns were seen to break their reeds,
And tear the leafy honours from their heads."

          STATIUS, books iv. and v.

No. 680.

Tiresias observing Minerva naked, after she has bathed in the fountain Hippocrene.

CHARITON. *Cornelian.*

Tiresias of Thebes was perhaps the most celebrated augur and seer of antiquity. During his lifetime he was looked on as an infallible oracle all over Greece; and he has been represented as giving answers to several who went to consult him in the infernal regions after his death. The numerous accounts of him in the ancient authors are various, and sometimes contradictory. He is generally represented as having been afflicted with blindness. Many of the greatest sages, and prophets and poets (for poets and prophets meant the same), recorded in ancient history, such as Tiresias, Phineus, Homer, &c., were said to have been blind. The most probable solution of such a story is, that they were physically blind in comparison to the light and keenness of their intellectual vision, or that Providence had thus compensated for a natural defect. To this Milton seems to allude in the opening of the third book of *Paradise Lost*, when, after comparing himself to " Thamyris, and blind Mæonides (Homer), and Tiresias, and Phineus—prophets old," he says,

> " So much the rather thou, celestial light!
> Shine inward, and the mind through all her powers
> Irradiate. There plant eyes—all mist from thence
> Purge and disperse; that I may *see* and *tell*
> Of things invisible to mortal sight!"

See the notes of Prendeville's edition of the *Paradise Lost.* London, 1840.

No. 681.

The same subject.

DIOSCORIDES. *Amethyst.*

No. 682.

Tiresias receiving the wisdom-giving wand from Minerva.

CHROMIOS. *Cornelian.*

No. 683.

Tiresias striking the serpents, and undergoing the process of transformation.

GNAIOS.　*Cornelian.*

Ovid (*Met.* iii.) gives the following account of this subject. Others represent the cause of blindness differently. However, the explanation of the fables adopted here by the artist is, that Tiresias saw all the secrets of wisdom, and knew the mysteries of nature.

" ' The sense of pleasure in the male is far
More dull and dead than what you females share.'
Juno the truth of what Jove said denied :
Tiresias, therefore, must the cause decide,
For he the pleasure of each sex had tried.
　It happen'd once, within a shady wood,
Two twisted snakes he in conjunction view'd ;
When with his staff their slimy folds he broke,
And lost his manhood at the fatal stroke.
But after seven revolving years, he view'd
The self-same serpents in the self-same wood :
' And if,' says he, ' such virtue in you lie,
That he who dares your slimy folds untie
Must change his kind, a second stroke I'll try.'

Again he struck the snakes, and stood again
New sex'd, and straight recover'd into man ;
Him, therefore, both the deities create
The sov'reign umpire in their grand debate ;
And he declar'd for Jove ; when Juno, fir'd
More than so trivial an affair requir'd,
Deprived him in her fury of his sight,
And left him groping round in sudden night.
But Jove (for so it is in heav'n decreed,
That no one god repeal another's deed,)
Irradiates all his soul with inward light,
And with the prophet's art relieves the want of
　　sight."

No. 684.

Minerva, Vulcan, and Ericthonius.

DIOSCORIDES.　*Cornelian.*

While Minerva was escaping from the pursuit of Vulcan, the monster Ericthonius is produced from the ground. He afterwards became king of Athens, and a most celebrated charioteer. At the Panathenæa, or games in honour of Minerva, of which, according to some authors, he was the inventor, he won the prize.

" Once upon a time,
The two-shap'd Ericthonius had his birth
(Without a mother) from the teeming earth ;
Minerva nurs'd him, and the infant laid
Within a chest of twining osiers made.
The daughters of king Cecrops undertook
To guard the chest, commanded not to look

On what was hid within. I stood to see
The charge obey'd, perch'd on a neighb'ring
　　tree.
The sisters Pandrosos and Herse keep
The strict command ; Aglauros needs would peep,
And saw the monstrous infant in a fright,
And call'd her sisters to the hideous sight :

A boy's soft shape did to the waist prevail,
But the boy ended in a dragon's tail.
I told the stern Minerva all that pass'd ;
But, for my pains, discarded and disgrac'd

The frowning goddess drove me from her sight,
And for her fav'rite chose the bird of night.
Be then no tell-tale ; for I think my wrong
Enough to teach a bird to hold her tongue."

OVID, *Met.* iii.

" Bold Ericthonius was the first who join'd
Four horses for the rapid race design'd,
And o'er the dusty wheels presiding sate."

VIRGIL, *Georg.* iii.

No. 685.

Minerva placing Ericthonius in a basket.

ALLION. *Amethyst.*

No. 686.

The daughters of Cecrops looking at Ericthonius.

CHROMIOS. *Cornelian.*

No. 687.

Ceyx and Alcyone.

APOLLONIDES. *Cornelian.*

Ceyx having prepared to go and consult the oracle of Claros, his wife Alcyone followed him to the shore ; and when she could not detain him, or induce him to take her with him, swooned away. On his return he was shipwrecked, and his body was washed ashore. When she saw it, she flung herself through grief into the sea ; and they were both transformed into sea-birds, called Halcyones. It was said that the sea during the incubation of the halcyon bird was calm : hence the phrase " halcyon days," to signify days of tranquillity.

" He purposes to seek the Clarian god,
Avoiding Delphi, his more fam'd abode,
Since Phrygian robbers made unsafe the road.
Yet could he not from her he lov'd so well
The fatal voyage he resolv'd conceal :
But when she saw her lord prepar'd to part,
A deadly cold ran shiv'ring to her heart ;

Her faded cheeks are chang'd to boxen hue,
And in her eyes the tears are ever new.
She thrice essay'd to speak ; her accents hung,
And falt'ring died unfinish'd on her tongue,
Or vanish'd into sighs : with long delay
Her voice return'd, and found the wonted
way.

'Tell me, my lord,' she said, 'what fault un-
    known
Thy once-belov'd Alcyone has done?
Whither, ah, whither, is thy kindness gone?
Can Ceyx, then, sustain to leave his wife,
And unconcern'd forsake the sweets of life?
What can thy mind to this long journey move—
Or need'st thou absence to renew thy love?
Yet if thou go'st by land, though grief possess
My soul ev'n then, my fears will be the less.
But, ah! be waru'd to shun the wat'ry way;
The face is frightful of the stormy sea.

   .   .   .   .

But if not fears or reasons will prevail,
If fate has fix'd thee obstinate to sail,
Go not without thy wife, but let me bear
My part of danger with an equal share,
And, present, what I suffer only fear:
Then o'er the bounding billows shall we fly,
Secure to live together, or to die.'

These reasons mov'd her starlike husband's heart,
But still he held his purpose to depart:
For as he lov'd her equal to his life,
He would not to the seas expose his wife;
Nor could be wrought his voyage to refrain;
But sought by arguments to soothe her pain.
Nor these avail'd; at length he lights on one,
With which so difficult a case he won:
'My love, so short an absence cease to fear,
For by my father's holy flame I swear,
Before two moons their orb with light adorn,
If heav'n allow me life, I will return.'
This promise of so short a stay prevails;
He soon equips the ship, supplies the sails,
And gives the word to launch; she trembling
    views
This pomp of death, and parting tears renews;
Last with a kiss she took a long farewell,
Sigh'd with a sad presage, and swooning fell.'
                    OVID, *Met.* xi.

No. 688.

Althæmenes discovering that he has unwittingly killed his father.

CHROMIOS. *Cornelian.*

The oracle having declared that Althæmenes would be instrumental in causing the death of his father Crateus, king of Crete, was so horror-stricken at the announcement, that he quitted the island and retired to Rhodes, in order to place himself beyond the reach of any collision with his father. His father went in search of him, and, arriving at Rhodes, was taken for an enemy by the people, who accordingly attacked him. Althæmenes was one of the assailants, and slew him. When he recognised the dead body of his father, he became frantic with grief, and implored of the gods to remove him from the earth. The earth then opened under him, and swallowed him up. (See APOLLODORUS, iii. 2.)

No. 689.

Eleathus attacking the winged monster.

APOLLONIDES. *Sardonyx.*

The river-god Liris promised his daughter, the nymph Pholoë, in marriage to whoever would deliver her from a winged monster that persecuted her. Eleathus undertook her deliverance, and slew the monster; but died of his own wounds before he could obtain the hand of his promised spouse.

No. 690.

Pholoë bewailing the death of Eleathus.

GNAIOS. *Cornelian.*

No. 691.

Ancæus killed by the Calydonian boar.

CHROMIOS. *Cornelian.*

There were two heroes named Ancæus: one the son of Lycurgus king of Thrace; the other a Samian, the son of Neptune. Both were in the Argonautic expedition; the son of Neptune being pilot of the ship the greater part of the voyage. The Ancæus alluded to here was the son of Lycurgus, and one of the heroes engaged in the famous attack on the Calydonian boar, described by Ovid and others. The following particulars are extracted from Ovid (*Met.* viii.) :—

" The cause, a boar, who ravag'd far and near,
Of Cynthia's wrath th' avenging minister:
For Œneus, with autumnal plenty bless'd,
By gifts to heav'n his gratitude express'd—
Cull'd sheafs to Ceres—to Lyæus wine—
To Pan and Pales offer'd sheep and kine,
And fat of olives to Minerva's shrine.
Beginning from the rural gods, his hand
Was lib'ral to the pow'rs of high command;
Each deity in ev'ry kind was bless'd,
Till at Diana's fane th' invidious honour ceas'd.
Wrath touches e'en the gods : the queen of night,
Fir'd with disdain, and jealous of her right,—
' Unhonour'd though I am, at least,' said she,
' Not unreveng'd that impious act shall be.'
Swift as the word she sped the boar away,
With charge on those devoted fields to prey.
No larger bulls th' Egyptian pastures feed,
And none so large Sicilian meadows breed :

His eyeballs glare with fire suffus'd with blood;
His neck shoots up a thickset thorny wood;
His bristled back a trench impal'd appears,
And stands erected like a field of spears;
Froth fills his chaps, he sends a grunting sound,
And part he churns, and part befoams the ground;
For tusks with Indian elephants he strove;
And Jove's own thunder from his mouth he drove.
He burns the leaves; the scorching blast invades
The tender corn, and shrivels up the blades,
Or, suff'ring not their yellow beards to rear,
He tramples down the spikes, and intercepts the year.
In vain the barns expect their promis'd load;
Nor barns at home, nor ricks are heap'd abroad;
In vain the hinds the threshing-floor prepare,
And exercise their flails in empty air.

3 E

With olives ever green the ground is strew'd,'
And grapes ungather'd shed their gen'rous
    blood.
Amid the fold he rages, nor the sheep
Their shepherds, nor the grooms their bulls can
    keep.
  From fields to walls the frighted rabble run,
Nor think themselves secure within the town ;
Till Meleagros and his chosen crew
Contemn the danger, and the praise pursue.

    .   .   .   .

There stood a forest on a mountain's brow,
Which overlook'd the shaded plains below :
No sounding axe presum'd those trees to bite—
Coeval with the world—a venerable sight !
The heroes there arriv'd, some spread around
The toils — some search the footsteps on the
    ground—
Some from the chains the faithful dogs un-
    bound.
Of action eager, and intent in thought,
The chiefs their honourable danger sought :
A valley stood below, the common drain
Of waters from above, and falling rain ;
The bottom was a moist and marshy ground,
Whose edges were with bending oziers crown'd ;
The knotty bulrush next in order stood,
And all within of reeds a trembling wood.
  From hence the boar was rous'd, and sprung
    amain,
Like lightning sudden, on the warrior-train ;
Beats down the trees before him—shakes the
    ground ;
The forest echoes to the crackling sound ;
Shout the fierce youth, and clamours ring
    around :

All stood with their protended spears prepar'd,
With broad steel heads the brandish'd weapons
    glar'd.
The beast impetuous with his tusks aside
Deals glancing wounds : the fearful dogs divide ;
All spend their mouths aloof, but none abide.

    .   .   .   .

Meantime the virgin-huntress was not slow
T' expel the shaft from her contracted bow ;
Beneath his ear the fastened arrow stood,
And from the wound appear'd the trickling blood.
She blush'd for joy ; but Meleagros rais'd
His voice with loud applause, and the fair archer
    prais'd.
He was the first to see, and first to shew
His friends the marks of the successful blow :
' Nor shall thy valour want the praises due,'
He said ; a virtuous envy seiz'd the crew.
They shout ; the shouting animates their hearts ;
And all at once employ their thronging darts :
But out of order thrown, in air they join,
And multitude makes frustrate the design.
With both his hands the proud Ancæus takes
And flourishes his double-biting axe ;
Then forward to his fate he took a stride
Before the rest, and to his fellows cried :
' Give place, and mark the difference, if you can,
Between a woman-warrior and a man :
The boar is doom'd ; nor though Diana lend
Her aid, Diana can her beast defend.'
Thus boasted he ; then stretch'd on tiptoe stood,
Secure to make his empty promise good.
But the more wary beast prevents the blow,
And upward rips the groin of his audacious foe.
Ancæus falls ; his bowels from the wound
Rush out, and clotted blood distains the ground.'

    Meleager finally slew the monster, and presented the head and hide to Atalanta, as a
reward for her having inflicted the first wound.

No. 692.

Thetis and Phasis.

APOLLONIDES. *Cornelian.*

Thetis was enamoured of Phasis, a youth of Colchis, who was insensible to her charms; upon which she transformed him into a river of that name, which flows into the Euxine. The entrance of the Argonauts into this river, after a long and dangerous voyage, gave rise to the phrase "sailing to Phasis." It is said that pheasants were first brought from the banks of the Phasis to Europe.

No. 693.

Harpalyce defending her father.

APOLLONIDES. *Cornelian.*

Harpalyce, daughter of Harpalycus king of the Amymneans in Thrace, was trained up by her father to the chase and the use of arms. Neoptolemus, son of Achilles, having once attacked and wounded him, she bravely repelled the assailant. After the death of her father, who was expelled from his throne in a civil war, she was forced to flee to the woods, where she subsisted by plunder. Having for a long time evaded all pursuit, or attempts to capture her, by her surprising swiftness, dexterity, and courage, she was at length ensnared in a net, and put to death. A contest having arisen among her captors for the property she had taken away, many of them were killed: hence a custom arose of offering at stated times sacrifices, and solemnising games, at her tomb, as pacificatory offerings to her manes.

No 694.

Menæceus slaying himself to save his country.

APOLLONIDES. *Cornelian.*

During the Theban war, Tiresias the soothsayer declared to the Thebans, that nothing but the sacrifice of one of the descendants of those who sprung from the dragon's teeth sown by Cadmus could save the city. Menæceus, the son of Creon the former king, accordingly slew himself for the salvation of his country; and the enemy were repulsed. The following extracts are selected from the *Thebais* of Statius, book x.

" The prophet then gave loose to rage, and cried:
' Ye guilty Thebans, hear what fates betide
Your city—the result of sacrifice:
Its safety may be bought, though high the price.

The snake of Mars, as his due rite, demands
A human victim from the Theban bands;
Fall he, whoe'er amidst our num'rous trains
The last of the fell dragon's race remains.
Thrice happy who can thus adorn his death,
And for so great a meed resign his breath!'
   Near the fell altars of the boding chief
Sad Creon stood, and fed his soul on grief;
Yet then he only wept his common fate,
And the near ruin of the Aonian state :
When sudden as the vengeful shaft arrests
Some hapless wretch, deep sinking in his breasts,

Pale horror fix'd him, when he heard the call,
Which summons brave Menæceus to his fall.
A clammy sweat crept cold o'er ev'ry part,
Fear froze his veins and thrill'd through all his
      heart.
Whilst for the victim the stern prophet cries,
Full of th' inspiring god ; in suppliant guise
Around his knees the tender father clung,
And strove in vain to curb his boding tongue.
   Swift fame then makes the sacred answer
      known,
And the dread oracle flies round the town."

Clio, the goddess of glory, descends from heaven to the field of battle, and, disguised as a
venerable Theban, informs Menæceus of the prediction. She says—

      " ' Thee all Thebes demands,
To save the rest of her devoted bands.
Fame sings the sacred answer, and our youth
With shouts of triumph hail the voice of truth.
Embrace the glorious offer, then ; nor waste
The time away ; but to fruition haste.' "

He announces his intention to the troops, and quits the field, while the battle rages outside
the walls, and the Thebans are sorely pressed.

" At length, supported by his menial train,
He goes : the vulgar hail him o'er the plain
With names of ' Patriot!' 'Champion!' ' God!'
     —inspire
An honest pride, and set his soul on fire.
And now to Thebes his course Menæceus bends,
Well pleas'd to have escap'd his wretched friends,
When Creon met him, and would fain accost ;
But his breath fail'd—his utterance was lost !
Awhile both silent and dejected stand ;
At length his sire began with kind demand :
' Say, prithee, what new stroke of fortune calls
My son from fight, when Greece surrounds our
     walls ?
What worse than cruel war dost thou prepare ?
Why do thy eyes with rage unwonted glare ?
Why o'er thy cheeks such savage paleness reigns,
And ill thy face a father's look sustains?
Heard'st thou the forg'd responses ?—It appears
Too well. My son, by our unequal years

I pray thee, and thy wretched mother's breasts,
Trust not—O trust not, what the seer suggests !
     .   .   .
Nor think I check thee through excess of fear:
Go—mix in combat—toss the pointed spear,
And dare the thickest horrors of the plain :
Where chance is equal, I will ne'er restrain.
O let me cleanse with tears the stain of blood,
And with my hairs dry up the surging flood ;
Thus thou may'st fight—o'ercome, and triumph
     still :
This is thy country's choice—thy father's will.'
Thus in embrace his troubled son he holds,
And round his neck his arms encircling folds ;
But neither could the copious stream of grief,
Nor words, unbend the heav'n-devoted chief.
Yet more the gods suggesting, he relieves
His father's fears, and with this tale de-
     ceives.
     .   .   .   .

Meanwhile Menœceus on the walls was seen—
Divine his aspect, more august his mien:
His casque aside the pious hero threw,
And stood awhile confess'd to public view:
From thence he cast an eye of pity down
On either host that fought before the town;
And silence and a truce from war enjoin'd,
Thus spoke the purpose of his gen'rous mind :
' Ye pow'rs of war, and thou, whose partial love
Grants me this honour, Phœbus, son of Jove,
O give to Thebes the joys so dearly sought—
Those mighty joys, by my own life-blood bought:
Return the war—on Lerna's captive coast
Dash the foul remnants of her vanquish'd host;
And let old Inachus with adverse waves
Shun his fam'd offspring, now dishonour'd slaves.
But let the Thebans by my death obtain
Their fanes — lands — houses — children —wives
again.

If aught of merit my submission claim—
If undismay'd I heard the prophet name
Myself the victim, nor with fear withdrew,
Assenting ere my country deem'd it true;
To Thebes, I pray, in lieu of me be kind,
And teach my credulous sire to be resign'd.'
He said; and, pointing to his virtuous breast
The glitt'ring blade, attempts to set at rest
Th' indignant soul, that frets and loathes to stay
Imprison'd in its tenement of clay.
He lustrates with his blood the walls and tow'rs,
And throws himself amidst the banded pow'rs,
And, grasping still the sabre in his hands,
Essays to fall on the stern Grecian bands.
But Piety and Virtue bear away,
And gently on the ground his body lay;
While the free spirit stands before the throne
Of Jove, and challenges the well-earn'd crown."

No. 695.

Phalegus devoured by a lioness.

CHROMIOS. *Cornelian.*

The explanation of the fable of Phalegus, king of Ambracia, having been devoured by a lioness while attempting to take away her young, as a punishment inflicted on him by Diana, the goddess of chastity, is, that for his licentiousness and tyranny he was killed by his subjects.

No. 696.

Circe alluring Picus with the phantom of a boar.

GNAIOS. *Amethyst.*

The full explanation of this and the three following subjects is the annexed fable in Ovid (*Met.* xiv.):—

THE STORY OF PICUS, CIRCE, AND CANENS.
" Picus, who once th' Ausonian sceptre held,
Could rein the steed, and fit him for the field.

So like he was to what you see, that still
We doubt if real, or the sculptor's skill.
The graces in the finish'd piece you find
Are but the copy of his fairer mind.

Four lustres scarce the royal youth could name,
Till ev'ry love-sick nymph confess'd a flame;
Oft for his love the mountain Dryads su'd,
And ev'ry silver sister of the flood :
Those of Numicus, Albula, and those
Where Almo creeps, and hasty Nar o'erflows ;
Where sedgy Anio glides through smiling meads ;
Where shady Farfar rustles in the reeds,
And those that love the lakes, and homage owe
To the chaste goddess of the silver bow.
 In vain each nymph her brightest charms
   puts on ;
His heart no sov'reign would obey but one—
She whom Venilla on mount Palatine
To Janus bore, the fairest of her line.
Nor did her face alone her charms confess ;
Her voice was ravishing, and pleas'd no less ;
Whene'er she sung, so melting were her strains,
The flocks unfed seem'd list'ning on the plains ;
The rivers would stand still—the cedars bend ;
And birds neglect their pinions to attend ;
The savage kind in forest-wilds grow tame :
And *Canens*—from her heavenly voice—her name.
 Hymen had now in some ill-fated hour
Their hands united, as their hearts before.
Whilst their soft moments in delights they waste,
And each new day was dearer than the past,
Picus would sometimes o'er the forests rove,
And mingle sports with intervals of love.
It chanc'd, as once the foaming boar he chas'd,
His jewels sparkling on his Tyrian vest,
Lascivious Circe well the youth survey'd,
As simpling on the flow'ry hills she stray'd.
Her wishing eyes their silent message tell,
And from her lap the verdant mischief fell.
As she attempts at words, his courser springs
O'er hills and lawns, and e'en a wish outwings.
 'Thou shalt not 'scape me so,' pronounc'd the
   dame,
' If plants have pow'r, and spells be not a name.'
She said, and forthwith form'd a boar of air,
That sought the covert with dissembled fear.
Swift to the thicket Picus wings his way
On foot, to chase the visionary prey.

Now she invokes the daughters of the night,
Does noxious juices smear, and charms recite ;
Such as can veil the moon's more feeble fire,
Or shade the golden lustre of her sire.
In filthy fogs she hides the cheerful noon ;
The guard at distance, and the youth alone,
' By those fair eyes,' she cries, ' and ev'ry grace
That finish all the wonders of your face,
Oh ! I conjure thee, hear a queen complain,
Nor let the sun's soft lineage sue in vain.'
 ' Whoe'er thou art,' replied the king, ' forbear,
None can my passion with my *Canens* share.
She first my ev'ry tender wish possess'd,
And found the soft approaches to my breast.
In nuptials bless'd, each loose desire we shun ;
Nor time can end what innocence begun.'
 ' Think not,' she cried, ' to saunter out a life
Of form with that domestic drudge—a wife ;
My just revenge, dull fool, ere long shall shew
What ills we women, if refus'd, can do ;
Think me a woman, and a lover too :
From dear successful spite we hope for ease,
Nor fail to punish, where we fail to please.'
 Now twice to east she turns, as oft to west ;
Thrice waves her wand, as oft a charm express'd.
On the lost youth her magic pow'r she tries ;
Aloft he springs, and wonders how he flies ;
On painted plumes the woods he seeks, and still
The monarch oak he pierces with his bill.
Thus chang'd, no more o'er Latian lands he
   reigns ; ·
Of Picus nothing but the name remains.
 The winds from drizzling damps now purge the
   air,
The mist subsides, the settling skies are fair :
The court their sov'reign seek with arms in hand ;
They threaten Circe, and their lord demand.
Quick she invokes the spirits of the air,
And twilight elves, that on dun wings repair
To charnels and th' unhallow'd sepulchre.
 Now, strange to tell, the plants sweat drops
   of blood,
The trees are toss'd from forests where they
   stood :

Blue serpents o'er the tainted herbage slide;
Pale glaring spectres on the ether ride;
Dogs howl—earth yawns—rent rocks forsake
  their beds,
And from their quarries heave their stubborn
  heads.
The sad spectators stiffen'd with their fears
She sees, and sudden ev'ry limb she smears—
Then each of savage beasts the figure bears.
  The sun did now to western waves retire,
In tides to temper his bright world of fire.
Canens laments her royal husband's stay;
Ill suits fond love with absence or delay.
Where she commands, her ready people run;
She wills—retracts—bids—and forbids anon.

Restless in mind, and dying with despair,
Her breasts she beats, and tears her flowing
  hair.
Six days and nights she wanders on, as chance
Directs, without or sleep or sustenance:
Tiber at last beholds the weeping fair;
Her feeble limbs no more the mourner bear;
Stretch'd on his banks, she to the flood com-
  plains,
And faintly tunes her voice to dying strains.
The sick'ning swan thus hangs her silver wings,
And as she droops her elegy she sings.
Ere long, sad *Canens* wastes to air; whilst fame
The place still honours with her hapless name."

No. 697.

Circe transforming Picus into a woodpecker, or the bird *Picus*.

GNAIOS. *Cornelian.*

No. 698.

The same subject.

GNAIOS. *Cornelian.*

No. 699.

Canens bewailing the loss of Picus.

GNAIOS. *Amethyst.*

No. 700.

The infant Cæculus found in the fire by shepherds.

CHROMIOS. *Cornelian.*

The story of Cæculus has been variously represented. The artist here had in view the account that shepherds, having found an infant enveloped in flames, rescued and reared him up;

and from the weakness of his eyes, which had been affected by the flames, called him *Cæculus*, or (as we may say in English) *Blindy*. He subsequently became the leader of an enterprising band, and founded, as some say, the famous town Præneste. Whether from the accident of his being surrounded in infancy by fire, or his subsequent achievements, or both, he was called the son of Vulcan. This view has been adopted by Virgil (*Æn.* vii. 678), and others.

> " Nor was Præneste's founder wanting there,
> Whom fame reports the son of Mulciber :
> Found in the fire, and fostered in the plains,
> A shepherd and a king at once he reigns."

No. 701.

Athamas excited by the Fury to slay his wife and children.

APOLLONIDES.　*Cornelian.*

Athamas, king of Thebes, married Ino, who reared up young Bacchus, the son of her sister Semele by Jupiter. Bacchus became the favourite of the Thebans. Juno, enraged at this, and at the neglect of the honours due to herself, sent Tisiphone to inspire both with madness. Athamas, in a paroxysm of phrensy, mistaking Ino and their children Learchus and Melecerta for a lioness and her cubs, attempted to kill them. Learchus was slain ; but Ino, bearing Melecerta in her arms, was saved by Bacchus. She afterwards flung herself and the child into the sea ; and both were changed by Neptune, at the intercession of Venus, into sea divinities. The whole story is thus given by Ovid (*Met.* iv.) :—

ATHAMAS AND INO.

" The pow'r of Bacchus now o'er Thebes had flown ;
With awful rev'rence soon the god they own.
Proud Ino all around the wonder tells,
And on her nephew-deity still dwells.
Of num'rous sisters, she alone yet knew
No grief but grief which she from sisters drew.
　Imperial Juno saw her with disdain,
Vain in her offspring—in her consort vain,
Who rul'd the trembling Thebans with a nod ;
But saw her vainest in her foster-god.
' Could then,' she cried, ' a bastard boy have pow'r
To make a mother her own son devour ?

Could he the Tuscan crew to fishes change,
And now three sisters damn to forms so strange ?
Yet shall the wife of Jove find no relief ?
Shall she, still unreveng'd, disclose her grief ?
Have I the mighty freedom to complain ?
Is that my pow'r ? is that to ease my pain ?
A foe has taught me vengeance : and who ought
To scorn that vengeance which a foe has taught ?
What sure destruction frantic rage can throw,
The gaping wounds of slaughter'd Pentheus shew.
Why should not Ino, fir'd with madness, stray,
Like her mad sisters her own kindred slay ?
Why she not follow where they lead the way ?'

DESCRIPTION OF HELL.

Down a steep yawning cave, where yews dis-
    play'd
In arches meet, and lend a baleful shade,
Through silent labyrinths a passage lies
To mournful regions and infernal skies.
Here Styx exhales its noisome clouds, and here,
The fun'ral rites once paid, all souls appear:
Stiff cold, and horror with a ghastly face
And staring eyes, infest the dreary place.
Ghosts, new-arriv'd, and strangers to these plains,
Know not the palace where grim Pluto reigns;
They journey doubtful, nor the road can tell
Which leads to the metropolis of hell.
A thousand avenues those tow'rs command—
A thousand gates for ever open stand.
As all the rivers, disembogu'd, find room
For all their waters in old Ocean's womb;
So this vast city worlds of shades receives,
And space for millions still of worlds she leaves.
Th' unbody'd spectres freely rove, and shew
Whate'er they lov'd on earth they love below.
The lawyers still or right or wrong support:
The courtiers smoothly glide to Pluto's court:
Still airy heroes thoughts of glory fire:
Still the dead poet strings his deathless lyre:
And lovers still with fancied darts expire.

    The queen of heav'n, to gratify her hate
And soothe immortal wrath, forgets her state.
Down from the realms of day, to realms of night,
The goddess swift precipitates her flight.
At hell arriv'd, the noise hell's porter heard;
Th' enormous dog his triple head uprear'd:
Thrice from three grizly throats he howl'd pro-
    found,
Then suppliant couch'd, and stretch'd along the
    ground.
The trembling threshold, which Saturnia press'd,
The weight of such divinity confess'd.
    Before a lofty adamantine gate,
Which clos'd a tow'r of brass, the furies sate—

Misshapen forms, tremendous to the sight—
Th' implacable foul daughters of the night:
A sounding whip each bloody sister shakes,
Or from her tresses combs the curling snakes.
But now great Juno's majesty was known;
Through the thick gloom, all heav'nly bright, she
    shone:
The hideous monsters their obedience shew'd,
And rising from their seats, submissive bow'd.
    This is the place of woe: here groan the dead:
Huge Tityus o'er nine acres here is spread.
Fruitful for pain th' immortal liver breeds—
Still grows, and still th' insatiate vulture feeds.
Poor Tantalus to taste the water tries,
But from his lips the faithless water flies:
Then thinks the bending tree he can command,
The tree starts backwards, and eludes his hand.
The labour, too, of Sisyphus is vain;
Up the steep mount he heaves the stone with pain;
Down from the summit rolls the stone again.
The Belides* their leaky vessels still
Are ever filling, and yet never fill;
Doom'd to this punishment for blood they shed,
For bridegrooms slaughter'd in the bridal bed.
Stretch'd on the rolling wheel Ixion lies;
Himself he follows, and himself he flies.
' Ixion, tortur'd !' Juno sternly eyed,
Then turn'd, and toiling Sisyphus espy'd:
' And why,' she said, ' so wretched is the fate
Of him whose brother proudly reigns in state?
Yet still my altars unador'd have been
By Athamas and his presumptuous queen.'
    What caus'd her hate the goddess thus confess'd;
What caus'd her journey now was more than
    guess'd:
That hate relentless its revenge did want,
And that revenge the furies soon could grant:
They could the glory of proud Thebes efface,
And hide in ruin the Cadmean race.
For this she largely promises—entreats;
And to entreaties adds imperial threats.

---

* Called also Danaides.

Then fell Tisiphone with rage was stung,
And from her mouth th' untwisted serpents flung.
' To gain this trifling boon, there is no need,'
She cried, ' in formal speeches to proceed.
Whatever thou command'st to do, is done ;
Believe it finish'd, though not yet begun ;
But from these melancholy seats repair
To happier mansions and to purer air.'
She spoke : the goddess, darting upwards, flies,
And joyous re-ascends her native skies ;
Nor enter'd there, till round her Iris threw
Ambrosial sweets, and pour'd celestial dew.
    The faithful fury, guiltless of delays,
With cruel haste the dire command obeys.
Girt in a bloody gown, a torch she shakes,
And round her neck twines speckled wreaths of
    snakes.
Fear, and Dismay, and agonising Pain,
With frantic Rage, complete her loveless train.
To Thebes her flight she sped, and hell forsook ;
At her approach the Theban turrets shook :
The sun shrunk back ; thick clouds the day o'er-
    cast ;
And springing greens were wither'd as she pass'd.
    Now, dismal yellings heard, strange spectres
        seen,
Confound as much the monarch as the queen.
In vain to quit the palace they prepar'd ;
Tisiphone was there, and kept the ward.
She wide extended her unfriendly arms,
And all the fury lavish'd all her harms.
Part of her tresses loudly hiss, and part
Spread poison, as their forky tongues they dart ;

Then from her middle locks two snakes she drew,
Whose merit from superior mischief grew :
Th' envenom'd ruin, thrown with spiteful care,
Clung to the bosoms of the hapless pair.

. . . .

Then toss'd her torch in circles still the same,
Improv'd their rage, and added flame to flame.
The grinning fury her own_conquest spied,
And to her rueful shades return'd with pride,
And threw th' exhausted, useless snakes aside.
    Now Athamas cries out, his reason fled :
' Here, fellow-hunters, let the toils be spread.
I saw a lioness, in quest of food,
With her two young, run roaring in this wood.'
Again the fancied savages were seen,
As through his palace still he chas'd his queen.

. . . .

    A rock there stood, whose side the beating
        waves
Had long consum'd, and hollow'd into caves ;
The head shot forwards in a bending steep,
And cast a dreadful covert o'er the deep.
The wretched Ino, on destruction bent,
Climb'd up the cliffs ; such strength her fury lent :
Thence with her guiltless boy, who wept in vain,
At one bold spring she plung'd into the main.

. . . .

Pleased Neptune nodded his assent, and free
Both soon became from frail mortality.
He gave them form and majesty divine,
And bade them glide along the foamy brine.
For Melicerta is Palemon known ;
And Ino, once, Leucothoé is grown."

No. 702.

Athamas attempting to slay Ino.

PYRGOTELES.   *Cornelian.*

No. 703.

Ino saved by Bacchus.

APOLLONIDES. *Cornelian.*

No. 704.

Athamas killing Learchus.

APOLLONIDES. *Cornelian.*

No. 705.

Athamas espying the wolves.

DIOSCORIDES. *Cornelian.*

Athamas, after the perpetration of his crime, was (says APOLLODORUS, book i.) expelled from Bœotia; and, finding no resting-place, was told by the Oracle to locate himself where he would find beasts of prey devouring a sheep. In his wanderings he met wolves devouring a sheep, who fled at his approach. He settled in that place, and built there a city, which he called Athamantia.

No. 706.

Pyrene and Cenchreus.

DIOSCORIDES. *Sardonyx.*

Cenchreus, the son of the nymph Pyrene, having been accidentally killed with an arrow by Diana, Pyrene became so dissolved with grief, that it was said she was transformed by the goddess into a fountain.

No. 707.

Amymone wounding a satyr.

GNAIOS. *Cornelian.*

Amymone, daughter of Danaus, while hunting in the woods and aiming at a stag, shot a satyr, who suddenly presented himself. The wounded satyr pursued her; but she was saved by Neptune, who bore her off, and subsequently had by her Nauplius. In the place where she stood he raised a fountain by striking a rock with his trident. It is said that he transformed her into a fountain.

No. 708.

Amymone protected by Neptune.

GNAIOS.   *Cornelian.*

No. 709.

Amymone and Neptune.

APOLLONIDES.   *Cornelian.*

No. 710.

The same subject.

GNAIOS.   *Amethyst.*

She is here represented as detaching the trident, by Neptune's direction, from the rock whence the water is issuing.

No. 711.

Prospylea and Arcas.

GNAIOS.   *Cornelian.*

Arcas, son of Jupiter, introduced great improvements in agriculture, and gave his name to Arcadia, a country so celebrated in fabulous history.   Prospylea, one of the Hamadryads, or nymphs of the woods, each of whose existence was only coeval with that of the particular tree she inhabited, besought Arcas to drain away the water that was rotting the roots of her favourite tree.

No. 712.

Tydeus gnawing the head of Menalippus.

APOLLONIDES.   *Cornelian.*

Tydeus, the father of Diomedes, so celebrated in the *Iliad,* was one of the bravest and most eminent of the heroes who fought against Thebes.   After performing prodigies of valour, he received his death-wound from Menalippus, a Theban, whom he slew in return.   The head of his enemy having been brought to him, while in the agonies of death, he was impelled with frenzy by Tisiphone to gnaw it. Æschylus in his *Seven Chiefs*, and Statius in his *Thebaid*, have exerted all their power in describing Tydeus, especially at the close of his career. The following extracts are sufficient.

SOLDIER.

" Now I can tell thee, for I know it well,
The disposition of the foe, and how
Each at our gates takes his allotted post.
Already near the Prætian gate in arms
Stands Tydeus, raging; for the prophet's voice
Forbids his foot to pass Ismenus' stream,
The victims not propitious. At the pass
Furious, and eager for the fight, the chief,
Fierce as the dragon when the mid-day sun
Calls forth his glowing terrors, raves aloud—
Reviles the sage, as forming tim'rous league
With war and fate. Frowning he speaks, and
        shakes
The dark crest streaming o'er his shaded helm
In triple wave; whilst dreadful ring around
The brazen bosses of his shield, impress'd
With this proud argument—a sable sky
Burning with stars; and in the midst full-orb'd
A silver moon, the eye of night, o'er all,
Awful in beauty, pours her peerless light.
Clad in these proud habiliments, he stands
Close to the river's margin; and with shouts
Demands the war, like an impatient steed,
That pants upon the foaming curb, and waits
With fiery expectation the known signal,
Swift at the trumpet's sound to burst away.
Before the Prætian gate, its bars remov'd,

What equal chief wilt thou appoint against
        him?

ETEOCLES.

   This military pride!—it moves not me:
The gorgeous blazonry of arms—the crest
High waving o'er the helm—the roaring boss,
Harmless without the spear, imprint no wound.
The sable night, spangled with golden stars,
On his proud shield impress'd, perchance may
        prove
A gloomy presage. Should the shades of night
Fall on his dying eyes, the boastful charge
May to the bearer be deem'd ominous,
And he the prophet of his own destruction.
Against his rage the son of Astacus,
That breathes deliberate valour, at that gate
Will I appoint commander; bent on deeds
Of glory, but a votary at the shrine
Of modesty, he scorns the arrogant vaunt
As base, but bids brave actions speak his worth.
The flow'r of that bold stem, which from the
        ground
Rose arm'd, and fell not in the dreadful fight,
Is Menalippus: him his parent earth
Claims as her own, and in her natural right
Calls him to guard her from the hostile spear:
But the brave deed the die of war decides."
                                   ÆSCHYLUS.

" Meanwhile Bellona* wak'd anew the fray,
And turn'd the doubtful fortune of the day:
She chang'd her torch, and other serpents wore—
Heap'd slain on slain, and swell'd the stream of
        gore;
As if the toil of fight was scarce begun,
Much work of death remaining to be done.

But Tydeus shines the most; though sure to
        wound,
Parthenopæus deals his shafts around.
Though fierce Hippomedon impels his horse
Through the gor'd war, and crushes many a corse;
And Capaneus's javelin wings its flight,
Afar distinguish'd in the ranks of fight,

---

* The goddess of war.

His was the day; before him trembling flies
The Theban herd, as thus aloud he cries:
' Why this retreat, when unreveng'd remain
Your valiant comrades, late in ambush slain?
Behold the man by whom alone they bled —
Behold, and wreak on his devoted head
Your wrath collected. Can ye thus forego
The chance of war, and spare the present foe?
Is there a man whom this wide-wasting steel
Has wrong'd?—for vengeance let him here ap-
peal.'

. . . .

And now the prince, unweary'd yet with toils,
Block'd himself up with carcases and spoils;
With him alone the circling hosts engage—
The single object of their missile rage.
Part glitter on the surface of his skin—
Part frustrate fall; and part are lodg'd within:
Some Pallas plucks away. His targe appears
An iron-grove, thick set with gleamy spears.
No crest is extant; through the bristling hide
His naked back and shoulders are descried:
And Mars, which on his casque depictur'd fate,
Fell off—a joyless omen of his fate!
The shiver'd brass into his body pent,
Wrought him such pain as might have made
relent
The bravest heart; when, lo! a stroke descends,
And from the gums his gnashing grinders rends.
His breast is delug'd with a tide of gore,
With dust embrown'd, while each dilated pore
In copious drops perspires. Pleas'd he sur-
vey'd
His bands applauding, and the martial maid,*
Who o'er her eyes the spreading ægis threw,
As to her sire in his behalf she flew.
But see! an ashen jav'lin cuts the wind,
And leaves, with anger charg'd, the clouds be-
hind.
Long was the author of the deed unknown —
Great Menalippus—for he durst not own:

At length the foe's untimely joy display'd,
The warrior, herding in his troop, betray'd;
For the pierc'd hero, now no longer steel'd
Against the growing anguish, loos'd his shield,
And bent beneath the wound. This seen, the
Greeks
Rush to his aid with groans, not manly shrieks;
The sons of Cadmus, smiling at their grief,
With shouts triumphant intercept relief.
The chief, inspecting close the adverse side,
The marksman, lurking in the crowd, espied—
Collects his whole remains of life and strength,
And throws a weapon of enormous length,
Which neighb'ring Hopleus gave, nor gave in
vain:
Forth spouts the blood, extorted by the strain.
By force his sad companions drag him thence,
(While yet unconscious of his impotence,)
Then bear him to the margin of the field,
His sides supported in a double shield;
And promise he shall quickly re-engage,
When strength shall second his undaunted rage.
But he himself perceives his failing breath,
And shudd'ring at the chilling hand of death,
Reclines on earth, and cries: ' I die in peace;
But pity me, O sons of fertile Greece!
I ask you not these relics to convey
To Argos, or the seat of regal sway,
Regardless of my body's future doom,
Nor anxious for the honours of the tomb.
Curs'd are the brittle limbs, which thus desert
The soul, when most their strength they should
exert!
All I solicit farther, is the head
Of Menalippus; for my jav'lin sped,
And stretch'd, I trust, the dastard on the plains:
Then haste, Hippomedon, if aught remains
Of Argive blood; and thou, Arcadian youth,
In praise of whom Fame e'en detracts from truth—
Go, valiant Capaneus, thy country's boast,
And now the greatest of th' Argolic host.

* Minerva.

All mov'd; but Capaneus arrives the first,
Where breathing yet he lay, deform'd with dust,
And took him on his shoulders: down his back
Flows the warm blood, and leaves a crimson
    track.
Such look'd Alcides, when in times of yore
He enter'd Argos with the captive boar.
O'ercome with joy and anger, Tydeus tries
To raise himself, and meets with eager eyes
The deathful object—pleas'd as he survey'd
His own condition in his foe's portray'd.
The sever'd head impatient he demands,
And grasps with fervour in his trembling hands,
While he remarks the restless balls of sight,
That sought and shun'd alternately the light.
Contented now, his wrath began to cease,
And the fierce warrior had expir'd in peace ;

But the fell fiend a thought of vengeance bred,
Unworthy of himself and of the dead.
Meanwhile, her sire unmov'd, Tritonia came
To crown her hero with immortal fame ;
But when she saw his jaws besprinkled o'er
With spatter'd brains, and ting'd with living
    gore,
Whilst his imploring friends attempt in vain
To calm his fury and his rage restrain ;
Again, recoiling from the loathsome view,
The sculptur'd target o'er her face she threw;
And, her affection chang'd to sudden hate,
Resign'd Œnides to the will of fate :
But, ere she join'd the senate of the skies,
Purg'd in Ilyssos her unhallow'd eyes."

                        STATIUS, book viii.

No. 713.

Theone carried off by a pirate.

DIOSCORIDES. *Cornelian.*

    Theone, daughter of Thestor, and sister of the celebrated Calchas, the augur who accompanied the Grecian expedition to Troy, was carried off by pirates, and sold to Icarus, king of Caria. Thestor pursued them, was wrecked on the coast of Caria, and afterwards imprisoned there. Leucippe, anxious for her father's and her sister's fate, went in search of them, disguised (by advice of the oracle) in the character of a priest of Apollo. In this character she was introduced to Theone (both being unknown to each other), who fell in love with her. Theone, enraged at the rejection of her addresses, resolved to put her to death ; and Thestor was employed as the agent, he then not knowing, and not known by, Theone. Shocked at being compelled to become a murderer, he uttered, while about to give the fatal blow, among other exclamations, the name of his daughters. This led to the discovery ; and he then attempted, in a paroxysm of horror, to kill himself; but was prevented by Leucippe. Theone was afterwards discovered to both. The king, moved by this strange adventure, permitted them to return home, and made them valuable presents. See HYGIN. *Fab.* 190.

No. 714.

Thestor about to kill his daughter Leucippe.

APOLLONIDES. *Sardonyx.*

No. 715.

Thestor prevented by Leucippe from killing himself.

PYRGOTELES. *Cornelian.*

No. 716.

Thyestes and Pelopea.

DIOSCORIDES. *Cornelian.*

The history of Thyestes is full of horrors. The following circumstances are enough to explain this and the two following subjects. Having been banished by his brother Atreus, king of Argos, for an intrigue with the queen, he met during his exile with his own daughter Pelopea in a grove; and had by her a son, who was exposed in the woods, and was subsequently found by shepherds sucking a goat: hence the child was named Ægisthus. Thyestes gave Pelopea a sword, as a token by which they may at some future time recognise one another. She recovered her child, and afterwards went to Argos, where she married her uncle Atreus, who reared up Ægisthus. When Ægisthus arrived at maturity, his mother gave him his father's sword. Thyestes was subsequently brought to Argos, and thrown into prison; and Ægisthus was sent by Atreus to assassinate him. But the sword which he carried led to a discovery, in presence of Pelopea, of the relation existing between all the parties. Pelopea was so horrified, that she snatched up the sword and slew herself; and Ægisthus murdered Atreus.

No. 717.

Ægisthus found by the shepherds.

APOLLONIDES. *Cornelian.*

No. 718.

Pelopea presenting the sword to Ægisthus.

DIOSCORIDES. *Cornelian.*

No. 719.

Pelopea killing herself in presence of Thyestes and Ægisthus.

APOLLONIDES. *Cornelian.*

No. 720.

Hippodamas hurling his daughter Perimele from a rock.

APOLLONIDES. *Amethyst.*

No. 721.

Acheloüs, the river-god, receiving Perimele.

APOLLONIDES. *Sardonyx.*

Hippodamas, enraged at his daughter Perimele for having received the addresses of the river-god Acheloüs, flung her into the Ionian sea, where she was transformed into an island, one of the Echinades, at the mouth of the Acheloüs.

THE STORY OF PERIMELE.

" But yonder far—lo! yonder does appear
An isle—a part to me for ever dear.
I, doating, forc'd by rape a virgin's fame:
From that it sailors Perimele name.
Hippodamas's anger grew so strong—
Gall'd with the abuse, and fretted at the wrong,
He cast his pregnant daughter from a rock:
I spread my waves beneath, and broke the shock;
And as her swimming weight my stream con-
    vey'd,
I su'd for help divine, and thus I pray'd:
' O pow'rful thou, whose trident does command
The realm of waters which surround the land!
We sacred rivers, wheresoe'er begun,
End in thy lot, and to thy empire run.
With favour hear, and help with present aid;
Her whom I bear 'twas guilty I betray'd.

Yet if her father had been just or mild,
He would have been less impious to his child—
In her, have pitied force in the abuse—
In me, admitted love for my excuse.
O let relief for her hard case be found—
Her, whom paternal rage expell'd from ground—
Her, whom paternal rage relentless drown'd.
Grant her some place, or change her to a place,
Which I may ever clasp with my embrace.'
His nodding head the sea's great ruler bent,
And all his waters shook with his assent.
The nymph still swam, though with the fright
    distrest,
I felt her heart leap trembling in her breast;
But hard'ning soon, whilst I her pulse explore,
A crusting earth cas'd her stiff body o'er;
And as accretions of new-cleaving soil
Enlarg'd the mass, the nymph became an isle."

OVID, *Met.* viii.

No. 722.

Mercury presenting Protesilaus to his wife Laodamia.

CHROMIOS. *Calcedony.*

Protesilaus, a prince of Thessaly, was one of the leaders in the Grecian expedition against Troy. He was the first Greek who was slain in the Trojan war; the Oracle having declared that the first Greek who should set foot on the Trojan soil should lose his life. His wife Lao-

3 G

damia, to keep alive his memory, and in some degree console herself for his absence, kept an image of him in her bed. It is said that the gods, yielding to her prayer, when hearing of his death, to be allowed the enjoyment of his society for three hours, despatched Mercury to bring him from the infernal regions; and that she died in his embraces, from the vehemence of her emotions.

" Now I must own I fear'd to let thee go:
My trembling lips had almost told thee so.
When from thy father's house thou didst with-
    draw,
Thy fatal stumble at the door I saw—
I saw it—sigh'd, and pray'd the sign might be
Of thy return a happy prophecy.
I cannot but acquaint thee with my fear ;
Be not too brave—remember, have a care ;
And all my dreads will vanish into air.
    Among the Grecians some one must be found
That first shall set his foot on Trojan ground :
Unhappy she that shall his loss bewail !
Grant, O ye gods, thy courage then may fail !
Of all the ships, be thine the very last—
Thou the last man that lands : there needs no
    haste
To meet a potent and a treach'rous foe :
Thou'lt land, I fear, too soon, though e'er so
    slow.
At thy return ply ev'ry sail and oar,
And nimbly leap on thy deserted shore.
    All the day long, and all the lonely night,
Black thoughts of thee my anxious soul affright :
Darkness, to other women's pleasures kind,
Augments, like hell, the torments of my mind.
I court e'en dreams on my forsaken bed :
False joys must serve, since all my true are fled.
What's that same airy phantom so like thee ?
What wailings do I hear—what paleness see ?
I wake, and hug myself !—'tis but a dream !
The Grecian altars know I feed their flame :
The want of hallow'd wine my tears supply,
Which make the sacred fire burn bright and high.
When shall I clasp thee in these arms of mine—
These longing arms—and lie dissolv'd in thine ?
When shall I have thee by thyself alone,
To learn the wond'rous actions thou hast done ?

Which when in rapt'rous words thou hast begun,
With many and many a kiss—pr'ythee tell on :
Such interruptions graceful pauses are :
A kiss in story's but an halt in war.
    .   .   .   .   .
    Ye Trojans ! with regret methinks I see
Your first encounter with your enemy—
I see fair Helen put on all her charms
To buckle on her lusty bridegroom's arms :
She gives him arms, and kisses she receives—
(I hate the transports each to other gives)—
She leads him forth, and she commands him come
Safely victorious and triumphant home.
And he (no doubt) will make no nice delay,
But diligently do whate'er she say.
Now he returns !—see with what am'rous speed
She takes the pond'rous helmet from his head,
And courts the weary champion to her bed !
We women, too, too credulous, alas !
Think what we fear will surely come to pass.
Yet while before the leaguer thou dost lie,
Thy picture is some pleasure to my eye :
That I caress in words most kind and free,
And lodge it on my breast as I would thee :
There must be something in it more than art—
'Twere very thee, could it thy mind impart.
I kiss the pretty idol, and complain,
As if, like thee, 'twould answer me again.
By thy return—by thy dear self, I swear—
By our loves' vows, which most religious are—
By thy beloved head, and those grey hairs
Which time may on it snow in future years,—
I come where'er thy fate shall bid thee go,
Eternal partner of thy weal and woe !
So thou but live, though all the gods say No !
    Farewell !—but pr'ythee very careful be
Of thy beloved self—I mean, of me !"
            OVID, *Epis.*, *Laodamia to Protesilaus.*

No. 723.

Laodamia and Protesilaus.

PYRGOTELES. *Cornelian.*

No. 724.

The death of Callirhoë.

GNAIOS. *Cornelian.*

This story is thus told by Pausanias (book vii. c. 21):—In this part of the city there is a temple of Bacchus, who is called Calydonius; for the statue of the god was brought from Calydon. While Calydon stood, Coresus was one of the priests of Bacchus, and suffered very unjustly through love : for he was in love with a virgin, Callirhoë; but the hatred of the virgin rose in proportion to the ardour of his love. When he found, therefore, that he was unable, either by prayers or gifts, to move the virgin, he came in a suppliant posture to the statue of Bacchus, who heard the prayer of his priest, and afflicted the Calydonians with a degree of insanity like that produced by intoxication; through which great numbers of them continually perished. In consequence of this, the inhabitants fled to the Oracle in Dodona : the Oracle therefore told them that their calamity was produced by the anger of Bacchus, and that they would not be relieved from their disease till Coresus either sacrificed Callirhoé, or some other person who had the courage to die in her stead. As the virgin, however, found no one willing thus to procure her safety, nothing now remained for her but to die. Every thing being ready for the sacrifice, she was led after the manner of a victim to the altar. Coresus himself presided over the sacrifice ; but giving way to his love, and not to his anger, he slew himself instead of Callirhoë. Callirhoë, as soon as she saw that Coresus had slain himself, found her hatred of the youth vanish, and love succeed in its stead. Hence, through pity of Coresus, and shame for her behaviour towards him, she slew herself by the fountain which is not far from the port in Calydon ; and this fountain afterwards was called Callirhoë, from the name of the virgin.

No. 725.

The Sphinx killing one of her victims.

APOLLONIDES. *Cornelian.*

During the reign of Creon, king of Thebes, the Sphinx, a monster with the head and breasts of a woman, the limbs and tail of a lion, the body of a dog, and the wings of a vulture, was sent as a divine visitation to ravage the country. She made the solution of the following riddle the condition of sparing the lives of those who fell into her power: "What animal is that which goes on four feet in the morning, upon two at noon, and upon three at night?" The

Oracle having been consulted, declared that the destruction of the Sphinx herself would imme-
diately follow the solution. The solution was attempted by several; but they failed, and were
torn to pieces. Among them was Æmon, the son of Creon. Upon this, Creon issued a pro-
clamation that he would resign the throne to any one who would solve the riddle. Œdipus,
who arrived in Thebes, a stranger and an adventurer, solved it, by saying that man in childhood
went on all-fours, in the maturity of life on his legs, and in old age went supported by a staff.
On hearing this, the Sphinx flung herself from a precipice, and perished.

> " In ill hour did thy virgin-wing,
>   Dire Sphinx!—thou mountain-monster! bring
> Woes to this land with thy untuneful lay;
>   When o'er the walls thy circling flight
> Smote its desponding sons with pale affright—
>   When thy fierce talons seiz'd their prey,
> And bore it to the rock's aërial brow:
> Thee hell's relentless king, with dread command,
> Unhallow'd fiend! to waste this groaning land,
> Sent from the gloom of Erebus below."
>
>   EURIPIDES, *Phœnissæ.*

> " Where hast thou e'er display'd a prophet's skill?
> Why, when the ravening hound of hell her charm
> Mysterious chanted, for thy country wise
> Didst thou not solve it? Of no vulgar mind
> Was this the task; the prophet this requir'd.
> No knowledge then from birds didst thou receive—
> None from the gods t' unfold it: but I came—
> This 'nothing-knowing Œdipus!' and quell'd
> The monster, piercing through her dark device
> By reason's force—not taught by flight of birds."
>
>   SOPHOCLES, *Œdipus Tyrannus.*

" Here, posted on a cliff's declining brow,
From whence she may survey the vale below,
The Sphinx once dwelt. Her cheeks were pale
    to view,
And her fell eyes suffused with gory dew.
Oft with expanded wings the monster prest
The mouldering bones of mortals to her breast;
And hurl'd her eyes along the winding way,
Lest, unobserving, she should lose her prey.
But if his fate, or the avenging gods,
Had drawn some wretch to her obscene abodes,
She clapp'd her wings distain'd with human gore,
And fill'd with yellings the retentive shore.
Then with protended nails his face she struck;
And oft her breaking teeth their hold forsook.
Thus long she reign'd. At last with headlong
    flight
Sprung from the rocks, and sought the realms of
    night:
For Œdipus, by Phœbus' aid, disclos'd
The dark enigma, which she'd long propos'd."

                          STATIUS, *Thebais*, book ii.

The explanations of the fable of the Sphinx are numerous. The plainest and most obvious
one is, that (if the story of the Sphinx has exclusive reference to Thebes) a band of savage

marauders, who infested the Theban territory during the feeble reign of Cleon, used profligate women as their ostensible instruments in luring persons to their haunts; that they were singularly dexterous and swift in evading justice; and that Œdipus, a man of great sagacity and courage, broke up the bandit society—a service for which he was rewarded by his elevation to the throne. Some think, as there was an image of the Sphinx in the vestibule of the temple of the Egyptian Isis (who was the same as the Grecian Minerva), and as the Romans adopted the custom of placing the figure in the vestibules, or *pronaoi*, of their temples, that the Sphinx is a religious representation of the human mind, and of its connexion with the divinity.

No. 726.

The same subject.

APOLLONIDES. *Cornelian.*

No. 727.

Tydeus sparing the life of Mæon.

GNAIOS. *Sardonyx.*

This subject relates to one of the incidents connected with the famous Theban war. When Polynices, being refused a participation in the sovereignty of Thebes by his brother Eteocles, fled to Argos and married the daughter of Adrastus the king, it was determined to restore him to his right. Accordingly Tydeus, the father of the great Diomede, who had married another daughter of Adrastus, was despatched as ambassador to negotiate between the brothers. Tydeus, having failed in his mission, was waylaid on his return by fifty hired assassins. He slew them all except one, whom he allowed to return to convey the news to the king. This is one of the bravest achievements recorded in ancient history. The following passages, from Homer (*Iliad*, book iv.) and Statius (*Thebais*, book ii.), fully explain the story. The elaborate description by Statius has been much admired by critics.

" O, son of Tydeus—he whose strength could tame
The bounding steed—in arms a mighty name !
Canst thou, remote, the mingling hosts descry,
With hands unactive and a careless eye ?
Not thus thy sire the fierce encounter fear'd ;
Still first in front the matchless prince appear'd :
What glorious toils, what wonders they recite,
Who view'd him labouring through the ranks of fight !
I saw him once, when, gathering martial powers,
A peaceful guest, he sought Mycenæ's towers ;

Armies he ask'd, and armies had been given—
Not we denied, but Jove forbade from heaven !
While dreadful comets, glaring from afar,
Forewarn'd the horrors of the Theban war.
Next, sent by Greece from where Asopus flows,
A fearless envoy, he approach'd the foes ;
Thebes' hostile walls, unguarded and alone,
Dauntless he enters, and demands the throne.
The tyrant feasting with his chiefs he found,
And dared to combat all those chiefs around—
Dared and subdued, before their haughty lord !
For Pallas strung his arm and edg'd his sword.

Stung with the shame, within the winding way,
To bar his passage fifty warriors lay ;
Two heroes led the secret squadron on,
Mæon the fierce, and hardy Lycophon ;
Those fifty slaughter'd in the gloomy vale,
He spared but one to bear the dreadful tale.

Such Tydeus was, and such his martial fire,
Gods ! how the son degenerates from the sire !
    No words the godlike Diomed return'd,
    But heard respectful, and in secret burn'd."

                                            HOMER.

" Thus anger'd, Tydeus left the guilty town,
And seem'd to make his brother's cause his
        own.
On earth the fruitless branch * in haste he threw,
And o'er the plains with winged ardour flew.
The matrons eye from their balconies' height
The chief, and vent in curses their despite ;
But not on him alone—the tyrant bears
His share of hate, convey'd in secret pray'rs.
Nor does the monarch's turn for treachery fail,
By nature taught too often to prevail :
With bribes and threats he gains a chosen throng
T' assault young Tydeus as he pass'd along,
Whose daring spirit and intrepid mien
Made them fit actors of so vile a scene.
O, fatal madness of th' ambitious soul !
What lengths can bind it, or what heights con-
        trol ?
Which dares attack what each preceding age
Had justly deem'd exempt from hostile rage.†
No arts he'd leave untried, no means forego,
Would fortune yield him up his brother-foe.
Meanwhile th' unfolding gates disclose a train
Of chiefs ne'er destin'd to return again ;
In one firm orb was rang'd the glitt'ring band,
Oppos'd—ye gods ! to Tydeus' single hand ;
As if prepar'd to storm some hostile town,
Or beat the walls with batt'ring engines down ;
For fear had thus the scatter'd troop combin'd,
The sure attendant of a guilty mind.
Through thorny woods, a near and secret way,
They march'd unnotic'd, wedg'd in firm array.

Far from the town two shaded hills arise,
And lose their adverse summits in the skies :
One side is bounded by the grove's embrace ;
A mountain's brow o'erhangs the middle space.
The nature of the place, and gloomy site,
Seem'd form'd for ambuscade and deeds of
        night.
A path obscure here winds the rock between,
Beneath are spacious fields—a flow'ring scene.

      .   .   .   .

Untouch'd the grass—neglected lies the wood—
And hungry beasts at distance seek their food !
The Dryads never haunt these loathsome bow'rs ;
Nor swains with incense bribe the rural pow'rs.
To other groves ill-omen'd birds repair,
And from afar abhor the tainted air.
Meanwhile the Thebans, urg'd by cruel fate,
Th' Ætolian chief in silent pomp await,
Reclining on their spears—the wood surround,
And rest their bucklers on the dewy ground.
The sun recall'd his unavailing light,
And on the shaded ocean rush'd the night :
When Tydeus, from an eminence, survey'd
Their shields and helmets glitt'ring through the
        shade ;
Where through the scanty branches Phœbe
        gleams
On their bright armour with refracted beams.
Amazement seiz'd him ; 'yet he onward hied,
And grasp'd the faithful sabre at his side :
A pointed javelin glitter'd in his hand,
While he accosts them with this stern demand :

---

* The olive-branch, which he bore as the sign of peace.
† The sacred character of ambassador.

'Warriors! whence come ye? and why thus profane
With war's alarms the night's alternate reign?'
Silent they stood; and no return of sound
Convinc'd the chief he treads on hostile ground.
A javelin soon supplies the want of tongue,
By Chthonius hurl'd, the leader of the throng.
The weapon whizzes in its airy course,
Nor miss'd the mark, though destitute of force:
It pierc'd th' Ætolian boar's erected hide,
(The chief's defence, and erst the monster's pride)
And o'er his shoulder flew, unstain'd with blood,
Where the false point deserts the feeble wood.
Then paleness clothed his face, but such as shews
Excess of wrath—his stiff'ning hair arose!
And now he hurls his angry looks around,
And views, amaz'd, the numerous foe surround.
'Whence does,' he said, ' this needless terror grow,
Of meeting on the plain a single foe?
Advance, like sons of Thebes, and bravely wield
Your glitt'ring weapons on this open field.'
Scarce had he spoke, when rushing from their holds,
A num'rous band th' intrepid chief enfolds;
From hill and dale they pour — their bucklers yield
A silver sound, and brighten all the field.
So, when the mingled cry of men and hounds
Invades the forest, or the wood surrounds,
From covert bound the stags—a fearful train—
And scour in num'rous herds the verdant plain.
The hero then ascends a mountain's height—
The best retreat from such unequal fight:
From hence, when posted on th' impending brow,
He might with ease annoy the foes below.
Enrag'd, he tore the fragment of a rock,
(Earth deeply groan'd beneath the mighty shock)
Then swung it round, and poising it on high,
Sought where to let the pond'rous ruin fly:
Two steers beneath th' enormous weight would groan,
But Tydeus hurl'd it from the rock alone.

.   .   .   .   .

The Thebans felt it, ere they saw it fly,
And crush'd in one promiscuous ruin lie.
Four chiefs, entomb'd beneath th' oppressive weight,
Clos'd their dim eyes in one united fate;
The rest to their strongholds again repair,
Unmindful of their charge and promis'd care.

When fiercer now he saw them quit the fray,
He rush'd, a lion, on his helpless prey;
With swift-whirl'd javelins fed their growing fear—
Annoy'd the front, and gall'd them in the rear.
With headlong rage he issues on the plain;
Nor cares of life or safety can detain.
Then seiz'd a glitt'ring target, which before,
While fate permitted, valiant Theron bore:
The spacious orb he moves on ev'ry part,
And stands impervious to each hostile dart.
The flaming sabre waves their heads above,
(The shining earnest of paternal love):
Now these, now those, with fatal blows he plied;
And the red slaughter swells on ev'ry side.
But while the Theban troops prolong the fray,
Involv'd in night—disorder—and dismay!
With heedless rage they deal their blows around,
And on their comrades oft inflict a wound;
O'er breathless heaps alternately they reel,
Darts hiss on darts, and steel descends on steel.
He presses on, o'ercoming those who try
The conflict, and o'ertaking those who fly.
Briareus thus (if Phlegra credit claim)
Oppos'd the regents of the starry frame—
The Thunderer launch'd his flaming bolts in vain,
Nor Phœbus' shafts, nor Pallas' snakes restrain—
The spear of haughty Mars unheeded flies,
And Etna's forge in vain new bolts supplies;
Unmov'd he stalks along the fields of light,
And with regret beholds th' exhausted fight.
Thus Tydeus in the glorious conflict glows,
And pours, like lightning, on his trembling foes;
Then, as if bent on flight, around them wheel'd,
And intercepts their anger with his shield.
Oft from its orb he pluck'd a bristling wood:
The darts, returning, drink their master's blood.

His wounded breast stopp'd many a weapon's
    course;
But Heaven disarm'd them of their fatal force.

   .   .   .   .   .

Thus when the king of brutes has storm'd the
    fold,
By famine press'd—by shepherds uncontroll'd,
He feasts luxurious on the tempting food,
And shakes his mane, erect with clotted blood;
But quickly pamper'd, bids his wrath subside,
And views the ground with slipp'ry slaughter
    dy'd;
Then bites the air, and ere he hies away,
Licks the spare remnants of his mangled prey.
The warrior now to Thebes had bent his course,
And shewn the marks of his superior force;
When rushing from the skies, th' Athenian maid *
His rash attempt and daring ardour stay'd.
' O thou, by whose right arm unerring fate
Decrees destruction to the Theban state !
With moderation use whate'er is giv'n,
Nor dare beyond the bounds prescrib'd by Heav'n.

All you can wish beyond these glorious spoils,
Is public credit to reward your toils.
Hæmon's prophetic offspring only lives,
Nor willing he his slaughter'd friends survives.
He, who in wisdom and experience old,
Could fates foresee, and mystic dreams unfold,
Had warn'd the king ; but by the gods' decree,
He heard and disbeliev'd the prophecy.'
To him, while for delaying death he pines,
The victor-chief this odious task consigns.
' Whoe'er thou art, whom mercy prompts to
    spare,
This message to the Theban monarch bear;
Bid him prevent each nodding turret's fall,
And with deep trenches fortify the wall—
Arm ev'ry son of Cadmus in his cause,
And subject all to military laws :
Ere soon he see me, like a ray of light,
Break through the cloud of hosts oppos'd in
    fight.'
To Pallas then, assistant in his toils,
The hero dedicates the bloody spoils."

No. 728.

Neanthus torn to pieces by dogs.

APOLLONIDES. *Sardonyx.*

Neanthus having obtained the lyre of Orpheus from the priests of Apollo, boasted that he could play on it as well as that god. For this rashness Apollo caused him to be torn to pieces by dogs.

No. 729.

The same subject.

GNAIOS. *Cornelian.*

No. 730.

Glaucus devoured by his mares.

DIOSCORIDES. *Cornelian.*

---

* Minerva.

Glaucus, son of Sisyphus king of Corinth, born at Potnia in Bœotia, in order to preserve the fleetness of his mares, called by Virgil the Potnian, restrained the indulgence of their natural impulses. This so maddened them, that they tore him to pieces on returning from the funeral games celebrated by Adrastus in honour of his father. The following extract from Virgil (*Georg.* iii.) will fully explain this fable :—

" I pass the wars that spotted lynxes make
With their fierce rivals for the female's sake—
The howling wolf's—the mastiff's am'rous rage;
When ev'n the fearful stag dares for his hind
    engage.
But, far above the rest, the furious mare,
Barr'd from the male, is frantic with despair ;
For, when her pouting vent declares her pain,
She tears the harness and she rends the rein.
For this (when Venus gave them rage and pow'r)
Their master's mangled members they devour,
Of love defrauded in their longing hour.

For love they force through thickets of the wood ;
They climb the steepy hills and stem the flood.
When, at the spring's approach, their marrow
    burns
(For with the spring their genial warmth returns),
The mares to cliffs of rugged rocks repair,
And with wide nostrils snuff the western air ;
Then, fir'd with am'rous rage, they take their
    flight
Through plains, and mount the hill's unequal
    height."

No. 731.

The infant Linus attacked by dogs.

GNAIOS. *Cornelian.*

This story is thus related by Statius (*Thebaid*, book i.) :—

" To th' Argive court repair'd the victor-god,[*]
And with his presence honour'd our abode.
The king Crotopus (as the Fates decreed)
Was blest with no male issue to succeed :
A nymph,[†] unmatch'd in manners as in face,
Was the sole product of his first embrace.
Thrice-happy maid ! had Phœbus fail'd to move
Her tender breast, nor kindled mutual love ;
For by the enamour'd god compress'd, she bore
A godlike son[‡] on Nemea's winding shore,
Ere the tenth moon had with her borrow'd light
Supplied the want of day and rul'd the night.
For this constrain'd to quit her native place,
And shun approaching vengeance and disgrace,

Among the rustic swains she seeks a friend,
To whom she might her precious charge com-
    mend.
The wretched babe, beneath an homely shed,
With bleating lambkins shares a common bed ;
While with the pipe his foster-father tries
To soothe his plaints and close his infant eyes.
Hard was his lot ! yet still relentless fate
Forbade him to enjoy this poor retreat :
For while abandon'd to blind Fortune's care,
Beneath the shade he breathes the morning air,
The furious dogs his tender carcass tore,
And fed luxurious on the recent gore."

---

[*] Apollo, after slaying the monster Python.   [†] Psamathe.   [‡] Linus.

No. 732.

Ixion hurling his father-in-law into a furnace.

PYRGOTELES. *Calcedony.*

Ixion, a king of Thessaly, promised Dioneus a large sum for obtaining his consent to his marriage with his daughter Dia. After his marriage, he failed to fulfil his promise ; whereupon his father-in-law forcibly took away some of his cattle. Ixion, under pretence of adjusting all matters of dispute between them, invited his father-in-law to a feast ; and, having got him in his power, he hurled him into a furnace. This atrocious act so exasperated the neighbouring princes, that neither of them would afford him hospitable shelter, or perform the usual ceremonies of purification for homicides in those times.

No. 733.

Dercetis metamorphosed.

GNAIOS. *Cornelian.*

Dercetus, or Dercetis, was the same as Atargatis, the goddess of the Ascalonites in Syria ; the upper part of whose image resembled a woman, the lower that of a fish. The Greek fable is, that having had a child by a Syrian youth, she was so much horrified at the crime, that she slew her lover, exposed her child in a desert place, and threw herself into a lake, where she was metamorphosed into a fish. This is one of those numerous fables that have reference to the ark (which was typified by a fish), and to the state of existence in it. The Greeks, not knowing that their mythology mainly sprung from hieroglyphic representations, made a personal story out of every figure. See LUCIAN, *de Deâ Syriâ.*

> " And knew not whether she should first relate
> The poor Dercetis and her wondrous fate :
> The Palestines believe it to a man,
> And shew the lake in which her scales began."
>
>   OVID, *Met.*

No. 734.

Ismenus, son of Niobe, slain by Apollo, and transformed into a river.

DIOSCORIDES. *Sardonyx.*

Niobe, wife of Amphion, the powerful king of Thebes, intended to prevent the Thebans from offering due worship to Latona and her children, Apollo and Diana, because she thought herself more worthy of adoration, from the power of the king and her more numerous offspring. Latona, incensed at the affront, induced Apollo to slay the male children, and Diana to slay the female. Niobe, dissolved in grief at the death of her children, was turned into a stone.

This story has been a fertile subject for poets and artists. The following portions of Ovid's account (*Met.* vi.) are selected :—

" Meanwhile, surrounded with a courtly guard,
The royal Niobe in state appear'd ;
Attir'd in robes embroider'd o'er with gold,
And mad with rage, yet lovely to behold :
Her comely tresses, trembling as she stood,
Down her fine neck with easy motion flow'd ;
Then, darting round a proud disdainful look,
In haughty tone her hasty passion broke,
And thus began : ' What madness this ! to court
A goddess, founded merely on report ?
Dare ye a poor pretended power invoke,
While yet no altars to my godhead smoke ?
Mine, whose immediate lineage stands confess'd
From Tantalus, the only mortal guest
That e'er the gods admitted to their feast.
A sister of the Pleiads gave me birth ;
And Atlas, mightiest mountain upon earth,
Who bears the globe of all the stars above,
My grandsire was, and Atlas sprung from Jove.
The Theban towns my majesty adore,
And neighb'ring Phrygia trembles at my pow'r :
Rais'd by my husband's lute, with turrets crown'd,
Our lofty city stands secure around.
Within my court, where'er I turn my eyes,
Unbounded treasures to my prospect rise :
With these my face I modestly may name,
As not unworthy of so high a claim :
Sev'n are my daughters, of a form divine,
With sev'n fair sons, an indefective line.
Go, fools ! consider this ; and ask the cause
From which my pride its strong presumption
        draws :
Consider this,—and then prefer to me
Cæus the Titan's vagrant progeny !
To whom, in travail, the whole spacious earth
No room afforded for her spurious birth ;
Not the least part in earth, in heav'n, or seas,
Would grant your outlaw'd goddess any ease ;
Till, pitying hers from his own wand'ring case,
Delos, the floating island, gave a place.
There she a mother was of two at most ;
Only the seventh part of what I boast.
My joys all are beyond suspicion fix'd,
With no pollutions of misfortune mix'd ;

Safe on the basis of my pow'r I stand,
Above the reach of Fortune's fickle hand.
Lessen she may my inexhausted store,
And much destroy, yet still must leave me more.
Suppose it possible that some may die
Of this my num'rous lovely progeny,
Still with Latona I might safely vie ;
Who by her scanty breed, scarce fit to name,
But just escapes the childless woman's shame.
Go then, with speed your laurell'd heads uncrown,
And leave the silly farce you have begun.'
    The tim'rous throng their sacred rites forbore,
And from their heads the verdant laurel tore ;
Their haughty queen they with regret obey'd,
And still in gentle murmurs softly pray'd.
    High on the top of Cynthus' shady mount,
With grief the goddess saw the base affront ;
And, the abuse revolving in her breast,
The mother her twin-offspring thus address'd :
' Lo ! I, my children, who with comfort knew
Your godlike birth, and thence my glory drew—
And thence have claim'd precedency of place
From all but Juno of the heav'nly race,
Must now despair, and languish in disgrace ;
My godhead question'd, and all rites divine,
Unless you succour, banish'd from my shrine.
Nay more, the imp of Tantalus has flung
Reflections with her vile paternal tongue ;
Has dar'd prefer her mortal breed to mine,
And call'd me childless, which, just Fate, may she
        repine !'
    When to urge more the goddess was prepar'd,
Phœbus in haste replies, ' Too much we've heard,
And ev'ry moment's lost while vengeance is de-
        ferr'd.'
Diana spoke the same. Then both enshroud
Their heavenly bodies in a sable cloud,
And to the Theban tow'rs descending light,
Through the soft yielding air direct their flight.
    Without the wall there lies a champaign ground,
With even surface far extending round,
Beaten and levell'd, while it daily feels
The trampling horse and chariot's grinding
        wheels.

Part of proud Niobe's young rival breed
Practising there to ride the manag'd steed,
Their bridles boss'd with gold, were mounted high
On stately furniture of Tyrian dye.
Of these, Ismenus, who by birth had been
The first fair issue of the fruitful queen,

Just as he drew the rein to guide his horse
Around the compass of the circling course,
Sigh'd deeply, and the pangs of smart express'd,
While the shaft stuck, engor'd within his breast;
And, the reins dropping from his dying hand,
He sunk quite down, and tumbled on the sand."

The other sons are killed in succession, the death of each being graphically described.

" Swift to the mother's ears the rumour came,
And doleful sighs the heavy news proclaim;
With anger and surprise inflam'd by turns,
In furious rage her haughty stomach burns.
First she disputes th' effects of heav'nly pow'r,
Then at their daring boldness wonders more:
For poor Amphion, with sore grief distress'd,
Hoping to soothe his cares by endless rest,
Had sheath'd a dagger in his wretched breast.
And she, who toss'd her high, disdainful head,
When through the streets in solemn pomp she
     led
The throng that from Latona's altar fled,
Assuming state beyond the proudest queen,
Was now the miserablest object seen.
Prostrate among the clay-cold dead she fell,
And kiss'd an undistinguish'd last farewell.
Then her pale arms advancing to the skies,
' Cruel Latona! triumph now,' she cries.
' My grieving soul in bitter anguish drench,
And with my woes your thirsty passion quench;
Feast your black malice at a price thus dear,
While the sore pangs of seven such deaths I bear.
Triumph, too cruel rival, and display
Your conq'ring standard, for you've won the
     day.
Yet I'll excel; for yet, though seven are slain,
Superior still in number I remain.'
Scarce had she spoke, the bow-string's twanging
     sound
Was heard, and dealt fresh terrors all around,
Which all, but Niobe alone, confound.
Stunn'd and obdurate by her load of grief,
Insensible she sits, nor hopes relief.
 Before the fun'ral biers, all weeping sad,
Her daughters stood in vests of sable clad.

When one, surpris'd, and stung with sudden
     smart,
In vain attempts to draw the sticking dart;
But to grim death her blooming youth resigns,
And o'er her brother's corpse her dying head re-
     clines.
This, to assuage her mother's anguish tries,
And, silenc'd in the pious action, dies;
Shot by a secret arrow, wing'd with death,
Her falt'ring lips but only gasp'd for breath.
One, on her dying sister breathes her last;
Vainly in flight another's hopes are plac'd.
This hiding, from her fate a shelter seeks;
That trembling stands, and fills the air with
     shrieks:—
And ell in vain; for now all six had found
Their way to death, each by a diff'rent wound.
The last, with eager care, the mother veil'd
Behind her spreading mantle close conceal'd,
And with her body guarded, as a shield.
' Only for this, this youngest, I implore,
Grant me this one request, I ask no more;
O grant me this!' she passionately cries: •
But while she speaks, the destin'd virgin dies!

THE TRANSFORMATION OF NIOBE.

Widow'd and childless, lamentable state!
A doleful sight, among the dead she sate;
Harden'd with woes, a statue of despair—
To ev'ry breath of wind unmov'd her hair—
Her cheek still redd'ning, but its colour dead—
Faded her eyes, and set within her head.
No more her pliant tongue its motion keeps,
But stands congeal'd within her frozen lips.
Stagnate and dull within her purple veins,
Its current stopp'd, the lifeless blood remains.

Her feet their usual offices refuse,	Yet still she weeps, and whirl'd by stormy winds,
Her arms and neck their graceful gestures lose;	Borne through the air, her native country finds;
Action and life from ev'ry part are gone,	There fix'd, she stands upon a bleaky hill—
And ev'n her entrails turn to solid stone.	There yet her marble cheeks eternal tears distil!"

No. 735.

Abaris receiving the arrow from Apollo.

GNAIOS. *Sardonyx.*

Abaris was a famous poet and prophet of antiquity, who visited several countries; hence it was said that Apollo constituted him his priest, and gave him an arrow that conveyed to him the power of divination, and of travelling through the air. It was said that he built the Palladium, on which the safety of Troy depended.

No. 736.

The pretensions of Danaus to the crown of Argos proved by a sign.

CHROMIOS. *Sardonyx.*

The circumstance here represented is thus described by Pausanias (book ii. c. 19):— "When Danaus came to Argos, he contended for the kingdom with Gelanor; and as each of them addressed many arguments to the people both of a just and probable nature, and as those of Gelanor appeared to be not less valid, hence the decision was deferred till the next day. On the next day, a wolf, in the presence of the people, rushed on a herd of oxen that were feeding before the walls, and attacked the bull that was the leader of the herd. This circumstance occasioned the Argives to assimilate Gelanor to the bull, and Danaus to the wolf; because as the wolf is an animal that has no association with men, so Danaus till that time had no correspondence with the Argives. Then, as the wolf vanquished the bull, on this account Danaus obtained the kingdom. Danaus, being of opinion that Apollo sent the wolf to this herd of oxen, built the temple of Lycian Apollo."

No. 737.

The mother of Branchus dreaming.

DIOSCORIDES. *Cornelian.*

The story of Branchus has been variously given. Varro says that the mother of Branchus, when pregnant, dreamed that the sun entered her throat, and passed through her body; hence the child was called Branchus, from βρόγχος, *the throat.* When he grew up, Apollo met him in the woods, kissed him, and gave him a sceptre and crown. Branchus after this became a celebrated prophet. A magnificent temple was erected to him and Apollo at Didyme, called the temple of the Branchidæ, which was one of the most famous of antiquity for its oracular responses. It was plundered and burned by Xerxes; but was afterwards rebuilt by the Milesians, and so magnificently, as to exceed in extent all the temples of Greece.

No. 738.

Apollo and Branchus.

PYRGOTELES. *Cornelian.*

No. 739.

Crinisus, in the shape of a bear, paying court to Egesta.

GNAIOS. *Calcedony.*

Crinisus, who gave his name to a river in Sicily, had the power of transforming himself into various shapes. In the form of a bear, he had by Egesta, a Trojan princess, Acestes, mentioned by Virgil (*Æn.* v.) as giving hospitable reception to Æneas and his companions.

> " Meantime Acestes, from a lofty stand,
> Beheld the fleet descending on the land ;
> And, not unmindful of his ancient race,
> Down from the cliff he ran, with eager pace,
> And held the hero* in a strict embrace.
> Of a rough Libyan bear the spoils he wore ;
> And either hand a pointed jav'lin bore.
> His mother was a dame of Dardan blood ;
> His sire Crinisus, a Sicilian flood.
> He welcomes his returning friends ashore
> With plenteous country cakes and homely store."

No. 740.

Daphnis found by shepherds.

APOLLONIDES. *Amethyst.*

---

* Æneas.

Daphnis was a son of Mercury by a Sicilian nymph. He was found, when an infant exposed in the woods, by shepherds; and educated by the nymphs. He became a famous musician, poet, and sportsman. It was supposed that he was the first who wrote pastoral poetry. After his death he was translated by his father Mercury to heaven. His praises are thus sung in Virgil (*Ecl.* v.):—

MOPSUS.

" No more, but sit and hear the promis'd lay :
The gloomy grotto makes a doubtful day.
The nymphs about the breathless body wait
Of Daphnis, and lament his cruel fate.
The trees and floods were witness to their tears :
At length the rumour reach'd his mother's ears.
The wretched parent, with a pious haste,
Came running, and his lifeless limbs embrac'd.
She sigh'd, she sobb'd, and furious with despair,
She rent her garments and she tore her hair,
Accusing all the gods and every star.
The swains forgot their sheep, nor near the brink
Of running waters brought their herds to drink.
The thirsty cattle of themselves abstain'd
From water, and their grassy fare disdain'd.
The death of Daphnis woods and hills deplore ;
They cast the sound to Libya's desert shore ;
The Libyan lions hear, and hearing roar.
Fierce tigers Daphnis taught the yoke to bear,
And first with curling ivy dress'd the spear.
Daphnis did rites to Bacchus first ordain,
And holy revels of his reeling train.
As vines the trees—as grapes the vines adorn—
As bulls the herds—and fields the yellow corn ;
So bright a splendour, so divine a grace,
The glorious Daphnis cast on his illustrious race.
When envious Fate the godlike Daphnis took,
Our guardian gods the fields and plains forsook ;
Pales no longer swell'd the teeming grain,
Nor Phœbus fed his oxen on the plain ;
No fruitful crop the sickly fields return ;
But oats and darnel choke the rising corn.

And where the vales with violets once were
 crown'd,
Now knotty burrs and thorns disgrace the ground.
Come, shepherds, come, and strew with leaves
 the plain ;
Such fun'ral rites your Daphnis did ordain.
With cypress-boughs the crystal fountains hide,
And softly let the running waters glide.
A lasting monument to Daphnis raise,
With this inscription to record his praise :
' Daphnis, the fields' delight, the shepherd's love,
Renown'd on earth, and deified above ;
Whose flock excell'd the fairest on the plains,
But less than he himself surpass'd the swains.'

MENALCAS.

Daphnis, the guest of heav'n, with wond'ring eyes
Views in the milky way the starry skies ;
And far beneath him, from the shining sphere
Beholds the moving clouds and rolling year.
For this with cheerful cries the woods resound ;
The purple spring arrays the various ground ;
The nymphs and shepherds dance ; and Pan him-
 self is crown'd.
The wolf no longer prowls for nightly spoils,
Nor birds the springes fear, nor stags the toils ;
For Daphnis reigns above, and deals from thence
His milder beams and peaceful influence.
The mountain-tops unshorn—the rocks rejoice ;
The lowly shrubs partake of human voice.
Assenting Nature, with a gracious nod,
Proclaims him, and salutes the new-admitted
 god."

No. 741.

Mercury conveying Daphnis to heaven.

DIOSCORIDES.   *Sardonyx.*

· No. 742.

The children of Melanippe suckled by a cow.

PYRGOTELES.   *Cornelian.*

The story of these children is thus told by Hyginus (*fable* 186) :—" Melanippe, daughter of Desmontes, or (as some poets say) of Æolus, had twins by Neptune ; which, when her father discovered, he blinded his daughter and confined her in a prison ; moreover, he ordered the children to be cast out to wild beasts.   When they had been cast out, a milch cow came and gave the children her teats.   The herdsmen having seen this, took them up and reared them. Meanwhile Metapontus, king of Icaria, demanded of his wife Theano to bring him children, or abdicate.   She, in her fear, sends word to the shepherds to procure for her some infant, that she may present it as her own to the king.   They sent her the two just found ; and she presented them to the king.   But Theano afterwards did herself beget two children by Metapontus.   As Metapontus loved the former children very much, because they were very beautiful, Theano sought an opportunity to make away with them, and preserve the crown for her own children.   There came a time when Metapontus went to offer sacrifice at the temple of Metapontine Diana.   Theano, using this occasion, tells her own children that the others were foundlings ; and, said she, " when they go out to hunt, kill them with your knives."   When they had all gone out to the mountain, they fought ; but, with Neptune's aid, the sons of Neptune conquered : and when the dead bodies of Theano's children were brought back to the palace, she slew herself with a hunter's knife, whereupon the avengers, Bœotus and Æolus, fled to the shepherds among whom they had been reared.   There Neptune discovers to them that they are his children, and that their mother is kept in custody.   They go to Desmontes, and kill him ; and they liberate their mother, to whom Neptune restores her eyesight.   They bring her to Icaria, to Metapontus the king, and explain to him the perfidy of Theano.   After this Metapontus married Melanippe, and adopted them as his own children.   They afterwards founded settlements in Propontis, called after their own names—Bœotus, Bœotia ; and Æolus, Æolia."

No. 743.

Mars holding the infant Æropus to the breast of his dead mother.

GNAIOS. *Amethyst.*

This circumstance is thus mentioned by Pausanias (book viii. c. 44): "There is an ascent from Asea to the mountain Boreum, upon the summit of which there are vestiges of a temple. Ulysses, when he returned from Troy, is said to have raised this temple to Minerva the Saviour. In that place which they call the *causeway*, the boundaries between the Megalopolitans, Tegeatæ, and Pallantienses, are contained. On the right hand of this road there is a mountain of no great magnitude, which is called Cresius, and in which there is a temple of Aphneus: for, according to the Tegeatæ, Mars had connexion with Ærope, the daughter of Cepheus, and granddaughter of Aleus. Now Ærope died in childbed; but the boy of which she was delivered clung to his dead mother, and drew from her breasts milk in abundance. This circumstance happened by the will of Mars; and, on account of it, they called the god Aphneus: but the name of the boy was, they say, Æropus."

No. 744.

Chiron the centaur restoring sight to Phœnix.

APOLLONIDES. *Calcedony.*

Phœnix figures in the *Iliad* as the preceptor of Achilles, whom he accompanied to the Trojan war. The main facts of his history are detailed by himself (*Iliad*, book ix.), in the speech which he makes to induce Achilles to return to the battle, and save the Greeks. Though Homer does not there mention his blindness, as one of the punishments inflicted on him by his father, or of his cure by Chiron, the centaur and famous physician, at the intercession of Peleus; yet the fact is mentioned by Propertius (book ii.), by Apollodorus (book ii.), and by others.

"The son of Peleus ceas'd; the chiefs around,
In silence wrapt—in consternation drown'd,
Attend the stern reply. Then Phœnix rose—
Down his white beard a stream of sorrow flows—
And, while the fate of suff'ring Greece he mourn'd,
With accent weak these tender words return'd:
'Divine Achilles! wilt thou then retire,
And leave our hosts in blood, our fleets on fire?
If wrath so dreadful fill thy ruthless mind,
How shall thy friend—thy Phœnix, stay behind?

The royal Peleus when from Pthia's coast
He sent thee early to th' Achaian host,
Thy youth as then in sage debates unskill'd,
And new to perils of the direful field;
He bade me teach thee all the ways of war,
To shine in councils, and in camps to dare.
Never—ah never, let me leave thy side!
No time shall part us, and no fate divide:
No—though the god that breath'd my life restore
The bloom I boasted, and the part I bore

3 I

When Greece of old beheld my youthful flames—
Delightful Greece, the land of lovely dames!
My father, faithless to my mother's arms,
Old as he was, ador'd a stranger's charms.
I tried what youth could do (at her desire)
To win the damsel, and prevent my sire.
My sire with curses loads my hated head,
And cries, ' Ye furies ! barren be his bed.'
Infernal Jove, the vengeful fiends below,
And ruthless Proserpine, confirm'd his vow.
Despair and grief distract my lab'ring mind!
Gods! what a crime my impious heart design'd!
I thought (but some kind god that thought sup-
        press'd)
To plunge the poniard in my father's breast—
Then meditate my flight ; my friends in vain
With pray'rs entreat me, and with force detain.
On fat of rams, black bulls, and brawny swine,
They daily feast, with draughts of fragrant
        wine:
Strong guards they plac'd, and watch'd nine
        nights entire ;
The roofs and porches flam'd with constant fire.

The tenth, I forc'd the gates, unseen of all ;
And, favour'd by the night, o'erleap'd the wall.
My travels thence through spacious Greece ex-
        tend :
In Pthia's court * at last my labours end.
Your sire receiv'd me—as his son caress'd—
With gifts enrich'd, and with possessions bless'd.
The strong Dolopians thenceforth own'd my reign,
And all the coast that runs along the main.
By love to thee his bounties I repaid,
And early wisdom to thy soul convey'd :
Great as thou art, my lessons made thee brave,
A child I took thee, but a hero gave.
Thy infant breast a like affection shew'd ;
Still in my arms (an ever-pleasing load)
Or at my knee, by Phœnix wouldst thou stand—
No food was grateful but from Phœnix' hand.
I pass my watchings o'er thy helpless years—
The tender labours—the compliant cares.
The gods (I thought) revers'd their hard decree,
And Phœnix felt a father's joys for thee:
Thy growing virtues justified my cares,
And promis'd comfort to my silver hairs.' "

No. 745.

Antigone, daughter of Laomedon, metamorphosed into a stork by Juno.

CHROMIOS.   *Amethyst.*

" In a third part, the rage of heav'n's great queen,
    Display'd on proud Antigone, was seen ;
    Who with presumptuous boldness dar'd to vie,
    For beauty, with the empress of the sky.
    Ah! what avails her ancient princely race,
    Her sire a king, and Troy her native place :
    Now, to a noisy stork transform'd, she flies,
    And with her whiten'd pinions cleaves the skies."
                                OVID, *Met.* vi.

* The court of Peleus, the father of Achilles.

No. 746.

The Hamadryad frightening away Parhelius, who attempted to cut down her oak.

GNAIOS. *Cornelian.*

No. 747.

The bone of Pelops recovered by a fisherman.

APOLLONIDES. *Aqua Marine.*

This circumstance is thus related by Pausanias (book v. c. 13):—"When the war against Troy became so protracted, the prophets told the Greeks that the city could not be taken till they brought away with them the arrows of Hercules and some portion of the bones of Pelops. Hence, they say, Philoctetes was called into the camps; and of the bones of Pelops, they brought the shoulder-blade from Pisa. But as the Greeks were returning home with the bone of Pelops, they were shipwrecked near Euboea, and the ship that carried the bone lost in the storm. Many years after this, and after Troy had been taken, Demarmenus, an Eretriensian fisherman, having thrown his net into the sea, drew up the bone of Pelops; and wondering at its magnitude, concealed it in the sand. At last he came to Delphos, and inquired whose bone it was, and what he should do with it. But then, through the providential interposition of divinity, certain persons were present, whom the Eleans had sent to inquire by what means they might be freed from the pestilence with which they were afflicted. The Pythian deity, therefore, gave them for answer, an injunction to preserve the bones of Pelops; and ordered Demarmenus to give to the Eleans what he had found. Demarmenus, therefore, on complying with the Oracle, received gifts from the Eleans; and the care of the bone was committed to him and his posterity."

CLASS IV.

SUBJECTS PRINCIPALLY FROM THE ILIAD.

No. 748.

Jupiter presenting horses of celestial breed to Tros.

APOLLONIDES. *Sardonyx.*

Jupiter having in the shape of an eagle carried off the beautiful youth Ganymede to heaven, where he became cup-bearer to the gods, presented to his father, Tros king of Troy, horses of celestial breed as a compensation.

No. 749.

Hecuba dreaming.

APOLLONIDES. *Sardonyx.*

Hecuba, wife of Priam king of Troy, dreamed in the first month of her pregnancy that she was to bring forth a firebrand; and announced her dream to the king. The soothsayers being consulted, declared that the child would cause the destruction of his country. To prevent such a calamity, Priam ordered the child, called Paris, to be given to his slave Archelaus, to be destroyed. Archelaus exposed him on mount Ida, where he was found by shepherds, and reared up by them. He became celebrated for his courage, beauty, and address. He made himself known to his mother, and was received at court. The goddess of discord, determined to have revenge for not having been invited with the other divinities to the banquet at the marriage of Peleus and Thetis, flung into the assembly a golden apple, bearing the inscription, " Be it given to the most beautiful." This produced a contest between the goddesses present. At last the competitors resigned their pretensions to Juno, Minerva, and Venus. Paris was appointed the judge; and when the goddesses, conducted by Mercury, appeared

before him on mount Ida, Juno, to induce him to decide in her favour, promised him empire;
Minerva, wisdom and valour; and Venus, the enjoyment of the most beautiful woman. He
decided in favour of Venus. He afterwards went to Greece, was hospitably entertained by
Menelaus, and, in his absence, took off his wife Helen; which led to the Trojan war, and the
destruction of Troy. Before he knew Helen, he was married to Œnone.

" Now in my mother's womb shut up I lay,
Her fatal burden longing for the day;
When she in a mysterious dream was told,
Her teeming womb a burning torch did hold:
Frighted she rises, and her vision she
To Priam tells, and to his prophets he.
They sing that I all Troy should set on fire:
But sure fate meant the flames of my desire.
For fear of this among the swains expos'd,
My native greatness every thing disclos'd:
Beauty, and strength, and courage, join'd in one,
Through all disguise spoke me a monarch's son.
A place there is in Ida's thickest grove
With oaks and fir-trees shaded all above;
The grass here grows untouch'd by bleating flocks,
Or mountain goat, or the laborious ox.
From hence Troy's tow'rs, magnificence and pride,
Leaning against an aged oak, I spied.
When straight methought I heard the trembling
        ground
With the strange noise of trampling feet resound.
In the same instant Jove's great messenger,*
On all his wings borne through the yielding air,
Lighting before my wond'ring eyes did stand—
His golden rod shone in his sacred hand:
With him three charming goddesses there came,
Juno, and Pallas, and the Cyprian dame.
With an unusual fear I stood amaz'd,
'Till thus the god my sinking courage rais'd:
' Fear not—thou art Jove's substitute below,
The prize of heav'nly beauty to bestow:
Contending goddesses appeal to you—
Decide their strife.' He spake, and up he flew.
Then bolder grown, I throw my fears away,
And ev'ry one with curious eyes survey.

Each of them merited the victory,
And I, their doubtful judge, was griev'd to see,
That one must have it, when deserv'd by three.
But yet that one there was which most prevail'd,
And with more powerful charms my heart as-
        sail'd.
Ah! would you know who thus my breast could
        move?
Who could it be but the fair queen of love?
With mighty bribes they all for conquest strive—
Juno will empires—Pallas valour give:
Whilst I stand doubting which I should prefer,
Empire's soft ease, or glorious toils of war;
But Venus gently smil'd, and thus she spake:
' They're dang'rous gifts, O do not—do not take!
I'll make thee Love's immortal pleasures know,
And joys that in full tides for ever flow.
For, if you judge the conquest to be mine,
Fair Leda's fairer daughter shall be thine.'
She spake; and I gave her the conquest due,
Both to her beauty, and her gift of you.
    Meanwhile (my angry stars more gentle grown)
I am acknowledg'd royal Priam's son:
All the glad court—all Troy does celebrate,
With a new festival, my change of fate.
And as I languish now, and die for thee,
So did the beauties of all Troy for me.
You in full pow'r over a heart do reign,
For which a thousand virgins sigh'd in vain:
Nor did queens only fly to my embrace,
But nymphs of form divine and heav'nly race.
I all their loves with cold disdain repress'd,
Since hopes of you first fir'd my longing breast.
Your charming form all day my fancy drew,
And when night came, my dreams were all of you."
            OVID's *Epist., Paris to Helen.*

* Mercury.

No. 750.

Priam commanding Hecuba to have Paris exposed by the slave.

POLYCLETES. *Cornelian.*

No. 751.

The slave, Paris, and a wild beast.

APOLLONIDES. *Amethyst.*

No. 752.

Paris shewing the swaddling-clothes, in which he was exposed, to his mother, by which she recognised him.

DIOSCORIDES. *Sardonyx.*

No. 753.

Paris receiving from Mercury the golden apple, the prize to be awarded to the victorious goddess.

DIOSCORIDES. *Cornelian.*

No. 754.

The judgment of Paris.

PYRGOTELES. *Amethyst.*

At the feet of Juno, who is in the foreground, stands the peacock ; at the feet of Venus, who is in the centre of the group, Cupid; while Minerva is distinguished by her helmet and spear.

No. 755.

Paris, Venus, and Cupid.

DIOSCORIDES.　*Sardonyx.*

Venus holds the apple adjudged to her; while Paris receives the arrow of Cupid.

No. 756.

Paris and Œnone.

GNAIOS.　*Cornelian.*

" Whilst thou a prince, and I a shepherdess,
My raging passion can have no redress.
Would heav'n, when first I saw thee, thou hadst
　　been
This great—this cruel, celebrated thing ;
That without hope I might have gaz'd and bow'd,
And mix'd my adoration with the crowd !
Unwounded then I had escap'd those eyes—
Those lovely authors of my miseries.
Not that less charms their fatal pow'r had dress'd,
But fear and awe my love had then suppress'd ;
My unambitious heart no flame had known,
But what devotion pays to gods alone.
I might have wonder'd, and have wish'd that he,
Whom heav'n should make me love, might look
　　like thee.
More in a silly nymph had been a sin :
This had the height of my presumption been.
But thou a flock didst feed on Ida's plain,
And hadst no title but ' the lovely swain.'
A title ! which more virgin hearts has won,
Than that of being own'd king Priam's son.
Whilst me a harmless neighb'ring cottager
You saw, and did above the rest prefer—
You saw ! and at first sight you lov'd me too,
Nor could I hide the wounds receiv'd from you.
Me all the village herdsmen strove to gain,
For me the shepherds sigh'd and sued in vain :
Thou hadst my heart ; and they my cold dis-
　　dain !

Not all their offerings, garlands, and first-born
Of their lov'd ewes, could bribe my native scorn.
My love, like hidden treasure long conceal'd,
Could only, where 'twas destin'd, be reveal'd.
And yet how long my maiden blushes strove
Not to betray the easy new-born love.
But at thy sight the kindling fire would rise,
And I, unskill'd, declare it by my eyes.
But oh the joy ! the mighty ecstacy
Possess'd thy soul at this discovery !
Speechless and panting at my feet you lay,
And short-breath'd sighs told what you could not
　　say :
A thousand times my hand with kisses press'd,
And look'd such darts as none could e'er resist.
Silent we gaz'd, and as my eyes met thine,
Now joy fill'd theirs, new love and shame fill'd
　　mine !
You saw the fears my kind disorder shows,
And broke your silence with a thousand vows !
Heav'ns, how you swore ! by ev'ry pow'r divine '
You would be ever true !—be ever mine !
Each god a sacred witness you invoke,
And wish'd their curse, whene'er those vows you
　　broke.
Quick to my heart the perjur'd accents ran,
Which I took in—believ'd—and was undone !
　　Vows are Love's poison'd arrows, and the
　　heart
So wounded rarely finds a cure in art :

At least this heart, which Fate has destin'd yours—
This heart unpractis'd in Love's mystic pow'rs;
For I am soft and young as April flow'rs.

Now uncontroll'd we meet—uncheck'd improve
Each happier minute in new joys of love!
Soft were our hours! and lavishly the day
We gave entirely up to love and play.
Oft to the cooling groves our flocks we led,
And, seated on some shady flow'ry bed,
Watch'd the united wantons as they fed.
And all the day my list'ning soul I hung
Upon the charming music of thy tongue,
And never thought the blessed hours too long.
No swain—no god—like thee could ever move,
Or had so soft an art in whispering love:
No wonder that thou art allied to Jove.
And when you pip'd—or sung—or danc'd—or
    spoke,
The god appear'd in ev'ry grace and look—
Pride of the swains, and glory of the shades,
The grief and joy of all the love-sick maids!
Thus whilst all hearts you rul'd without control,
I reign'd the abs'lute monarch of your soul:
Each beach my name yet bears, carv'd out by
    thee—
Paris and his Œnone fill each tree;
And, as they grow, the letters largely spread—
Grow still a witness of my wrongs—when dead!

Close by a silent silver brook there grows
A poplar, under whose dear gloomy boughs
A thousand times we have exchang'd our vows.
Oh mayst thou grow to an endless date of years!
Who on thy bark this fatal record bears,
' When Paris to Œnone proves untrue,
Back Xanthus' streams shall to their fountain
    flow.'
Turn—turn your tide! back to your fountains run!
The perjur'd swain from all his faith is gone!
Curs'd be that day, may fate point out the hour
As ominous in his black calendar!
When Venus, Pallas, and the wife of Jove
Descended to thee in the myrtle grove,
In shining chariots drawn by winged clouds.
Naked they came, no veil their beauty shrouds,

But ev'ry charm and grace expos'd to view—
Left heav'u to be survey'd and judg'd by you.
To bribe thy voice Juno would crowns bestow;
Pallas, more gratefully, would dress thy brow
With wreaths of wit; Venus propos'd the choice
Of all the fairest Greeks, and—had thy voice!
Crowns, and more glorious wreaths, thou didst
    despise,
And promis'd beauty more than empire prize!
This when you told, gods! what a killing fear
Did over all my shivering limbs appear!
And I presag'd some ominous change was near!
The blushes left my cheeks—from ev'ry part
The blood ran swift to guard my fainting heart.
You in my eyes the glimmering light perceiv'd
Of parting life, and on my pale lips breath'd
Such vows as all my terrors undeceiv'd.
But soon the envying gods disturb our joys,
Declare thee great, and all my bliss—destroys!

And now the fleet is anchor'd in the bay
That must to Troy the glorious youth convey.
Heav'ns, how he look'd! and what a godlike grace
At their first homage beautified your face!
Yet this no wonder or amazement brought—
You still a monarch were in soul and thought!
Nor could I tell which most the sight augments,
Your joys of pow'r, or parting discontents.
You kiss'd the tears which down my cheeks did glide,
And mingled yours with the soft-falling tide,
And 'twixt your sighs a thousand times you said,
' Cease, my Œnone!—cease, my charming maid!
If Paris lives his native Troy to see,
My lovely nymph, thou shalt a princess be.'
But my prophetic fear no faith allows;
My breaking heart resisted all thy vows.
' Ah, must we part!' I cried; ' those killing words
No further language to my grief affords.'
Trembling I fell upon thy panting breast,
Which was with equal love and grief oppress'd;
Whilst sighs and looks, all dying, spoke the rest.
About thy neck my feeble arms I cast:
Not vines nor ivy circle elms so fast.
To stay what dear excuses didst thou frame,
And fancied tempests when the seas were calm!

3 K

How oft the winds contrary feign'd to be,
When they, alas! were only so to me!
How oft new vows of lasting faith you swore,
And 'twixt your kisses all the old run o'er.
  But now the wisely grave, who love despise,
(Themselves past hope) do busily advise;
Whisper renown and glory in thy ear,
Language which lovers fright, and swains ne'er
    hear.

'For Troy,' they cry; 'these shepherd's weeds lay
    down!
Change crooks for sceptres, garlands for a crown!'
Be sure that crown does far less easy sit
Than wreaths of flow'rs—less innocent and sweet.
Nor can thy beds of state so grateful be,
As those of moss and new-fall'u leaves with
    me!'"

           OVID's *Epist., Œnone to Paris.*

No. 757.

Paris carrying off Helen.

APOLLONIDES. *Cornelian.*

"What pleasures, then, must you yourself im-
    part,
Whose shadows only so surpris'd my heart?
And oh! how did I burn approaching nigher,
That was so scorch'd by so remote a fire!
  For now no longer could my hopes refrain
From seeking their wish'd object through the main.
I fell the stately pine, and ev'ry tree
That best was fit to cut the yielding sea;
Fetch'd from Gargarian hills, tall firs I cleave,
And Ida naked to the winds I leave;
Stiff oaks I bend, and solid planks I form,
And ev'ry ship with well-knit ribs I arm.
To the tall mast I sails and streamers join;
And the gay poops with painted gods do shine;
But on my ship does only Venus stand,
With little Cupid smiling in her hand;
Guide of the way she did herself command.
My fleet thus rigg'd, and all my thoughts on thee,
I long to plough the vast Ægean sea;
My anxious parents my desires withstand,
And both with pious tears my stay command:
Cassandra too, with loose dishevell'd hair,
Just as our hasty ships to sail prepare,
Full of prophetic fury cries aloud,
'Oh whither steers my brother through the flood?
Little, ah! little dost thou know or heed
To what a raging fire these waters lead.'

True were her fears, and in my breast I feel
The scorching flames her fury did foretel.
Yet out I sail, and favour'd by the wind,
On your bless'd shore my wish'd-for haven find.
Your husband then, so heav'n, kind heav'n or-
    dains,
In his own house his rival entertains;
Shews me whate'er in Sparta does delight
The curious traveller's inquiring sight.
But I, who only long'd to gaze on you,
Could taste no pleasure in the idle show.
But at thy sight—oh! where was then my heart!
Out from my breast it gave a sudden start,
Sprung forth, and met half-way the fatal dart.
Such, or less charming, was the queen of love
When with her rival goddesses she strove:
But, fairest, hadst thou come among the three,
Even she the prize must have resign'd to thee.
Your beauty is the only theme of fame,
And all the world sounds with fair Helen's name;
Nor lives there she whom pride itself can raise
To claim with you an equal share of praise.
Do I speak false? rather report does so,
Detracting from you in a praise too low.
More here I find than that could ever tell;
So much your beauty does your fame excel.
Well then might Theseus, he who all things knew,
Think none was worthy of his theft but you:

I this bold theft admire; but wonder more
He ever would so dear a prize restore:
Ah! would these hands have ever let you go?
Or could I live, and be divorc'd from you?
No; sooner I with life itself could part,
Than e'er see you torn from my bleeding heart.
But could I do as he, and give you back,
Yet sure some taste of love I first would take—
Would first in all your blooming excellence,
And virgin sweets, feast my luxurious sense!
Or if you would not let that treasure go,
Kisses at least you should — you would, bestow,
And let me smell the flow'r as it did grow.
Come then into my longing arms, and try
My lasting — fix'd — eternal constancy!
Which never, till my fun'ral pile, shall waste:
My present fire shall mingle with my last.
Sceptres and crowns for you I did disdain,
With which great Juno tempted me in vain;
And when bright Pallas did her bribes prepare,
One soft embrace from you I did prefer
To courage—strength—and all the pomp of war.
Nor shall I ever think my choice was ill:
My judgment's settled, and approves it still.
Do you but grant my hopes may prove as true
As they were plac'd above all things but you.
I am, as well as you, of heav'nly race;
Nor will my birth your mighty line disgrace:
Pallas and Jove our noble lineage head,
And them a race of godlike kings succeed.
All Asia's sceptres to my father bow,
And half the spacious east his pow'r allow.
There you shall see the houses roof'd with gold,
And temples glorious as the gods they hold.
Troy you shall see, and walls divine admire,
Built to the concert of Apollo's lyre.
What need I the vast flood of people tell,
That over its wide banks does almost swell?
You shall gay troops of Phrygian matrons meet,
And Trojan wives shining in ev'ry street.
How often then will you yourself confess
The emptiness and poverty of Greece!

How often will you say, one palace there
Contains more wealth than do whole cities here!
I speak not this your Sparta to disgrace;
For wheresoe'er your life began its race
Must be to me the happiest, dearest place.
Yet Sparta's poor; and you, that should be dress'd
In all the riches of the shining east,
Should understand how ill that sordid place
Suits with the beauty of your charming face;
That face with costly dress and rich attire
Should shine, and make the gazing world admire!
When you the habit of my Trojans see,
What, think ye, must that of their ladies be!
Oh! then be kind, fair Spartan! nor disdain
A Trojan in your bed to entertain.
He was a Trojan, and of our great line,
That to the gods does mix immortal wine:
Tithonus too, whom to her rosy bed
The goddess of the morning blushing led;
So was Anchises of our Trojan race;
Yet Venus self to his desir'd embrace,
With all her train of little loves, did fly,
And in his arms learn'd for a while to lie.
Nor do I think that Menelaus can,
Compar'd with me, appear the greater man.
I'm sure my father never made the sun
With frighted steeds from his dire banquet run:*
No grandfather of mine is stain'd with blood,
Or with his crime names the Myrtoan flood.
None of our race does in the Stygian lake
Snatch at those apples he wants pow'r to take.
But stay; since you with such a husband join,
Your father Jove is forc'd to grace his line.

.   .   .   .   .

But now I've nothing left to do but pray,
And myself prostrate at your feet to lay.
O thou, thy house's glory, brighter far
Than thy two shining brothers' friendly star!†
O worthy of the bed of heav'n's great king,
If aught so fair but from himself could spring!
Either with thee I back to Troy will fly,
Or here a wretched banish'd lover die.

---

* This refers to the ancestors of Helen's husband.
† Castor and Pollux, translated to heaven as the constellation Gemini.

With no slight wound my tender breast does
    smart,
My bones and marrow feel the piercing dart;
I find my sister true did prophesy,
I with a heav'nly dart should wounded die;
Despise not then a love by heav'n design'd,
So may the gods still to your vows be kind.

.   .   .   .

But you forget your lord's command,* I see,
Nor take you any care of love or me.
And think you such a thing as he does know
The treasure that he holds in holding you?
No: did he understand but half your charms,
He durst not trust them in a stranger's arms.
If neither his nor my request can move,
We're forced by opportunity to love;
We should be fools, e'en greater fools than he,
Should so secure a time unactive be.
Then will I swear by all the pow'rs above,
And in their awful presence seal my love.
Then, if my wishes may aspire so high,
I with our flight shall win you to comply;
But if nice honour little scruples frame,
The force I'll use shall vindicate your fame.
Of Theseus and your brothers I can learn;
No precedents so nearly you concern;
You Theseus, they Leucippus' daughter, stole;
I'll be the fourth in the illustrious roll.
Well mann'd, well arm'd, for you my fleet does
    stay,
And waiting winds murmur at our delay.
Through Troy's throng'd streets you shall in
    triumph go,
Ador'd as some new goddess here below.
Where'er you tread, spices and gums shall smoke,
And victims fall beneath the fatal stroke.
My father—mother—all the joyful court—
All Troy, to you with presents shall resort.
Alas! 'tis nothing what I yet have said;
What there you'll find shall what I write exceed.

Nor fear, lest war pursue our hasty flight,
And angry Greece should all her force unite.
What ravish'd maid did ever wars regain?
Vain the attempt, and fear of it as vain !
The Thracians Orythia stole from far;
Yet Thrace ne'er heard the noise of following
    war.
Jason too stole away the Colchian maid;
Yet Colchos did not Thessaly invade.
He who stole you, stole Ariadne too;
Yet Minos did not with all Crete pursue.
Fear in these cases than the danger's more;
And when the threat'ning tempest once is o'er,
Our shame's then greater than our fear before.
But say, from Greece a threat'ned war pursue;
Know I have strength and wounding weapons too.
In men and horse more numerous than Greece
Our empire is, nor in its compass less.
Nor does your husband Paris aught excel
In generous courage, or in martial skill.
E'en but a boy, from my slain foes I gain'd
My stolen herd, and a new name attain'd;
E'en then o'ercome by me I could produce
Deïphobus and great Ilioneus.
Nor hand to hand more to be fear'd am I,
Than when from far my certain arrows fly.
You for his youth can no such actions feign,
Nor can he e'er my envied skill attain.
But could he, Hector's your security;
And he alone an army is to me.
You know me not, nor the hid prowess find
Of him that heav'n has for your bed design'd.
Either no war from Greece shall follow thee,
Or if it does, shall be repell'd by me.
Nor think I fear to fight for such a wife—
That prize would give the coward's courage life.
All after-ages shall your fame admire,
If you alone set the whole world on fire.
To sea—to sea ! while all the gods are kind,
And, all I promise, you in Troy shall find."

                  OVID's *Epist., Paris to Helen.*

---

* Menelaus, being obliged to go to Crete, directed Helen to be attentive in his absence to their guest, Paris.

No. 758.

Nereus, a sea-god, announcing to Paris, during his voyage, the calamities he is about to bring on his country by carrying off Helen.

GNAIOS. *Cornelian.*

This is the subject of the 15th ode (book i.) of Horace :—

NEREUS' PROPHECY OF THE DESTRUCTION OF TROY.

" When the perfidious shepherd bore
The Spartan dame to Asia's shore,
Nereus the rapid winds oppress'd,
And calm'd them to unwilling rest,
That he might sing the dreadful fate
Which should their guilty loves await.
' Fatal to Priam's ancient sway,
You bear th' ill-omen'd fair away,
For soon shall Greece in arms arise,
Deep-sworn to break thy nuptial ties.
What toils do men and horse sustain!
What carnage loads the Dardan plain!
Pallas prepares the bounding car—
The shield, and helm—and rage of war!
Though proud of Venus' guardian care,
In vain you comb your flowing hair—
In vain you sweep th' unwarlike string,
And tender airs to females sing;
For though the dart may harmless prove
(The dart that frights the bed of love),
Though you escape the noise of fight,
Nor Ajax can o'ertake thy flight,

Yet shalt thou, infamous of lust,
Soil those adulterous hairs in dust!
Look back and see, with furious pace,
That ruin of the Trojan race!
Ulysses drives; and sage in years
Famed Nestor, hoary chief, appears.
Intrepid Teucer sweeps the field,
And Sthenelus, in battle skill'd—
Or skill'd to guide with steady rein,
And pour his chariot o'er the plain.
Undaunted Merion shalt thou feel,
While Diomed, with furious steel,
In arms superior to his sire,
Burns after thee with martial fire.
As when a stag at distance spies
A prowling wolf, aghast he flies,
Of pasture heedless; so shall you,
High-panting, fly when they pursue.
Not such the promises you made,
Which Helen's easy heart betray'd.
Achilles' fleet with short delay,
Vengeful protracts the fatal day:
But when ten rolling years expire,
Thy Troy shall blaze in Grecian fire!' "

Euripides, in his *Iphigenia in Aulis*, thus explains the reason why the chiefs of Greece all united to avenge the rape of Helen. As so great a number of these representations has reference to the incidents of the Trojan war, this preparatory explanation is necessary.

AGAMEMNON.

" To Leda were three beauteous daughters born,
Phœbe—and Clytemnestra now my wife—
And Helena: to her the youths of Greece,
Those of the noblest rank, as wooers came.

Each menac'd high, on deeds of blood resolv'd,
Should he not win the virgin: this was cause
To Tyndarus her father of much doubt,
To give—or not to give her—and how best
To make good fortune his: at length this thought

Occurr'd, that each to each the wooers give
Their oath, and plight their hands, and on the
flames
Pour the libations, and with solemn vows
Bind their firm faith that him, who should obtain
The virgin for his bride, they all would aid;
If any dar'd to seize and bear her off,
And drive by force her husband from her bed —
All would unite in arms, and lay his town,
Greek or barbaric, level with the ground.
Their faith thus pledg'd, the aged Tyndarus
Beneath them well with cautious prudence
wrought:
He gave his daughter of her wooers one

To choose, tow'rds whom the gentle gales of love
Should waft her; and she chose (O had he ne'er
Obtain'd that envied favour!) Menelaus.
To Lacedemon now the Phrygian came —
The judge between the beauties of the sky;
So fame reports him: gorgeous was his dress,
Glitt'ring with gold and vermeil-tinctur'd dyes—
Barbaric elegance: he lov'd — was lov'd,
And bore the beauteous Helena away
To Ida's pastoral groves; for Menelaus
Was absent then: deserted thus through Greece
He rav'd, the oaths attesting giv'n of old
To Tyndarus, conjuring all t' avenge
His wrongs. On this the Grecians rush to war."

No. 759.

Teuthis and Minerva.

ADMON. *Cornelian.*

This subject is thus explained in Pausanias (book viii. c. 28):—" Teuthis, which is now a village, but was formerly a city, is near Thisoa, in Arcadia. In the Trojan war, this place sent a general whose name was Teuthis; but others call him Ornytus. While the Greeks were detained at Aulis by adverse winds, a disagreement arose between Teuthis and Agamemnon; and in consequence of this, Teuthis, they say, was about to lead back his forces; but Minerva, in the form of Melas the son of Ops, opposed his design. Teuthis, in his anger at the time, pierced the thigh of the goddess with his spear; and led back his army from Aulis. But when he returned home, the goddess appeared to him, and shewed him her wounded thigh. From that time Teuthis was seized with a deadly kind of consumption; and the earth was barren in that part of Arcadia alone. Some time after, however, an oracle from Dodona admonished the Arcadians to appease the goddess; in consequence of which they made a statue of Minerva, with a wound in the thigh. This statue I have seen with a purple bandage round its thigh."

No. 760.

Transformation of the daughters of Anius.

GNAIOS. *Cornelian.*

The daughters of Anius, king of Delos and priest of Apollo, were gifted with the power of converting whatever they touched to corn, wine, and oil. Agamemnon, when going to the

Trojan war, determined to carry them with him to supply his army. But they appealed to Bacchus; who transformed them into doves. The story is thus told by Ovid (*Met.* xiii.) :—

" The Delian isle receives the banish'd train,
Driv'n by kind gales, and favour'd by the main.
  Here pious Anius, priest and monarch, reign'd,
And either charge with equal care sustain'd—
His subjects rul'd—to Phœbus homage paid,
His god obeying, and by those obey'd.
  The priest displays his hospitable gate,
And shews the riches of his church and state,
The sacred shrubs which eas'd Latona's pain,
The palm, and olive, and the votive fane.
Here grateful flames with fuming incense fed,
And mingled wine ambrosial odours shed ;
Of slaughter'd steers the crackling entrails burn'd ;
And then the strangers to the court return'd.
  On beds of tap'stry plac'd aloft they dine,
With Ceres' gift and flowing bowls of wine ;
When thus Anchises spoke, amidst the feast,
' Say, mitred monarch, Phœbus' chosen priest,
Or (ere from Troy by cruel fate expell'd)
When first mine eyes these sacred walls beheld,
A son and twice two daughters crown'd thy bliss ?
Or errs my mem'ry, and I judge amiss ?'
  The royal prophet shook his hoary head,
With snowy fillets bound, and sighing, said :
' Thy mem'ry errs not, prince ; thou saw'st me then
The happy father of so large a train.
Behold me now (such turns of chance befal
The race of man !) almost bereft of all.
For, ah ! what comfort can my son bestow—
What help afford, to mitigate my woe !
While far from hence, in Andros' isle, he reigns
(From him so nam'd), and there my place sustains.
Him Delius prescience gave ; the twice-born god
A boon more wond'rous on the maids bestow'd.

Whate'er they touch'd, he gave them to transmute
(A gift past credit, and above their suit)
To Ceres', Bacchus', and Minerva's fruit.
How great their value, and how rich their use,
Whose only touch such treasures could produce !
The dire destroyer of the Trojan reign,
Fierce Agamemnon, such a price to gain
(A proof we also were design'd by fate
To feel the tempest that o'erturn'd your state),
With force superior, and a ruffian crew,
From these weak arms the helpless virgins drew ;
And sternly bade them use the grant divine,
To keep the fleet in corn, and oil, and wine.
Each, as they could, escap'd : two strove to gain
Eubœa's isle, and two their brother's reign.
The soldier follows, and demands the dames ;
If held by force, immediate war proclaims.
Fear conquer'd nature in their brother's mind,
And gave them up to punishment assign'd.
Forgive the deed—nor Hector's arm was there ;
Nor thine, Æneas, to maintain the war !
Whose only force upheld your Ilium's tow'rs,
For ten long years against the Grecian pow'rs.
Prepar'd to bind their captive arms in bands,
To heav'n they rear'd their yet unfetter'd hands :
' Help, Bacchus, author of the gift,' they pray'd :
The gift's great author gave immediate aid ;
If such destruction of their human frame,
By ways so wondrous, may deserve the name.
Nor could I hear, nor can I now relate
Exact the manner of their alter'd state ;
But this in gen'ral of my loss I knew,
Transform'd to doves, on milky plumes they flew,
Such as on Ida's mount thy consort's chariot drew. ' ":

No. 761.

Agamemnon killing the hind sacred to Diana.

APOLLONIDES. *Cornelian.*

No. 762.

Sacrifice of Iphigenia.

POLYCLETES. *Cornelian.*

The story of Iphigenia was a favourite one with the ancient poets. The main facts are these :—The combined fleet of Greece having been detained at port Aulis, on its way to Troy, by contrary winds, the soothsayer Calchas declared that the detention was caused by the anger of Diana against Agamemnon, the commander, who had shot a hind sacred to her; and that nothing but the pacificatory immolation of his favourite daughter Iphigenia to her could rescue the Greeks from their difficulties. Agamemnon's natural affection revolted at this crime; but he was at last prevailed on for the public good to yield. Iphigenia was brought from home under the pretence of being married to Achilles. When at the altar, she was snatched away in a cloud by Diana, who substituted a hind in her place. This, being considered a satisfactory victim to the goddess, was sacrificed; and the fleet sailed safely off. The following extracts from the *Agamemnon* of Æschylus, and the *Iphigenia in Aulis* of Euripides, will be enough to convey a full exposition of the circumstances here represented.

AGAMEMNON.

EPODE.

"The virgin goddess of the chase,
Fair from the spangled dew-drops that adorn
   The breathing flow'rets of the morn—
   Protectress of the infant race
   Of all that haunt the tangled grove,
   Or o'er the rugged mountains rove—
She, beauteous queen, commands me to declare
   What by the royal birds is shewn,
   Signal of conquest—omen fair,
   But darken'd by her awful frown !
   God of the distant-wounding bow,
Thee, Pæan—thee I call ; hear us, and aid.
   Ah ! may not the offended maid
   Give the sullen gales to blow,

Adverse to this eager train,
   And bar th' unnavigable main ;
   Nor other sacrifice demand,
At whose barbaric rites no feast is spread ;
   But discord rears her horrid head,
   And calls around her murd'rous band :
   . Leagued with hate, and fraud, and fear,
   Nor king nor husband they revere ;
   Indignant o'er a daughter weep,
   And burn to stamp their vengeance deep.

.   .   .   .   .

STROPHE.

When now in Aulis' rolling bay
   His course the refluent floods refus'd,

And sick'ning with inaction lay
In dead repose th' exhausted train,
Did the firm chief of chance complain.
  No prophet he accus'd ;
His eyes towards Chalcis bent, he stood,
And silent mark'd the surging flood.
Sullen the winds from Strymon sweep
  (Mischance and famine in the blast),
Ceaseless torment the angry deep—
  The cordage rend—the vessels waste—
With tedious and severe delay
Wear the fresh flow'r of Greece away.

ANTISTROPHE 2.

When in Diana's name the seer*
  Pronounc'd the dreadful remedy,
More than the stormy sea severe ;
Each chieftain stood in grief profound,
And smote his sceptre on the ground :
  Then with a rising sigh
The monarch, while the big tears roll,
Express'd the anguish of his soul ;
' Dreadful the sentence ! not t' obey,
  Vengeance and ruin close us round—
Shall then the sire his daughter slay,
  In youth's fresh bloom with beauty crown'd ?
Shall on these hands her warm blood flow ?
Cruel alternative of woe !

STROPHE 3.

This royal fleet—this martial host—
  The cause of Greece shall I betray ?
The monarch in the father lost !
To calm these winds, to smooth this flood,
Diana's wrath a virgin's† blood
  Demands : 'tis our's t' obey.'
Bound in necessity's iron chain
Reluctant nature strives in vain :
Impure, unholy thoughts succeed,
  And dark'ning o'er his bosom roll ;
Whilst madness prompts the ruthless deed,
Tyrant of the misguided soul :

Stern on the fleet he rolls his eyes,
And dooms the hateful sacrifice.

ANTISTROPHE 3.

Arm'd in a woman's cause, around
  Fierce for the war the princes rose ;
No place affrighted pity found.
In vain the virgin's streaming tear—
Her cries in vain ! Her pleading pray'r—
  Her agonising woes—
Could the fond father hear unmov'd ?
The fates decreed—the king approv'd—
Then to th' attendants gave command
  Decent her flowing robes to bind ;
Prone on the altar with strong hand
  To place her, like a spotless hind ;
And check her sweet voice, that no sound
Unhallow'd might the rites confound.

EPODE.

Rent on the earth her maiden veil she throws,
  That emulates the rose ;
  And on the sad attendants rolling
The trembling lustre of her dewy eyes,
  Their grief-impassion'd souls controlling,
  That ennobled, modest grace,
  Which the mimic pencil tries
  In the imag'd form to trace,
  The breathing picture shews :
And as, amidst his festal pleasures,
  Her father oft rejoic'd to hear
Her voice in soft mellifluous measures
  Warble the sprightly-fancied air ;
So now in act to speak the virgin stands.
But when, the third libation paid,
  She heard her father's dread commands
Enjoining silence, she obey'd !
  And for her country's good,
With patient, meek, submissive mind,
  To her hard fate resign'd !"

ÆSCHYLUS, Agamemnon.

---

* Calchas.   † Iphigenia.

3 L

IPHIGENIA IN AULIS.

ATTENDANT.

"The blazing lamp didst thou display, and write
That letter, which thou holdest in thy hand
E'en now—the writing didst thou blot—then
    seal—
And open it again—then on the floor
Cast it in grief, the warm tear from thine eye
Fast flowing, in thy thoughts distracted near,
As it should seem, to madness. What new care,
My royal lord? say what new care disturbs thee!
Tell me—impart it to me—to a man
Honest and faithful wilt thou speak—a man
By Tyndarus of old sent to thy wife,
A nuptial present, to attend the bride:
One of tried faith, and to his office just.

AGAMEMNON.

Collected and embodied, here we sit
Unactive; and from Aulis wish to sail
In vain. The prophet Calchas, midst the gloom
That darken'd on our minds, at length pronounc'd
That Iphigenia—my virgin daughter—
    to Diana, goddess of this land,
Must sacrifice! This victim giv'n, the winds
Shall swell our sails, and Troy beneath our arms
Be humbled in the dust; but, if denied,
These things are not to be. This when I heard,
I said, that by the herald's voice the troops
Should be discharg'd; for never would I bear
To slay my daughter; till my brother came,
And, urging many a plea, persuaded me
To bear these dreadful things. I wrote—I seal'd
A letter to my wife, that she should send
Her daughter to Achilles, as a bride
Affianc'd: of his worth I spoke in terms
Of amplest honour—said he would not sail
With Greece, unless from us his nuptial bed
Was deck'd in Phthia. With my wife this found
Easy belief—the false tale that announc'd
Her daughter's destin'd marriage. Of the Greeks
None but Ulysses, Calchas, and my brother,
To this are conscious. What I then resolv'd
Imprudently, I prudently retract,
Committed to this letter, which thou saw'st me
This night, old man, unfold and fold again.
Take, then, this letter—haste—to Argos go.
What there is written, in its secret folds
Enclos'd, I will explain to thee; for thou
Art faithful to my wife, and to my house.

ATTENDANT.

Read it—explain its purport—that my words
May aptly with thy writing correspond.

AGAMEMNON.

(*Reads.*) 'Whate'er my former letter gave in
    charge,
Daughter of Leda,* this I write to thee:
That to Euboea's winding way thou send not
Thy daughter, nor to Aulis rising high
Above the waves; for to some other time
The nuptials of the virgin we defer.'

ATTENDANT.

Will not Achilles, frustrate of his bride,
Be fir'd with rage 'gainst thee, and 'gainst thy wife?
This might be dang'rous—is not such thy thought?

AGAMEMNON.

His name indeed we used, but nothing more:
Achilles knows not of the nuptials—knows
Of our transactions naught; nor that I nam'd
My daughter his, as to his bed betroth'd."

Iphigenia and her mother Clytemnestra arrive at the Grecian fleet, expecting the marriage with Achilles. When told of the horrid purpose which Iphigenia was sent for, they both make the most affecting remonstrances. Clytemnestra throws herself and her child on the gallantry and pity of Achilles, to save her. Achilles nobly promises his aid; but is afterwards overruled

---

* His wife, Clytemnestra.

by the mutinous spirit of his forces. The grief of Agamemnon is excessive at the prospect of being obliged to sacrifice his child. Menelaus himself—he whose interest and passions were most concerned in the success of the expedition—becomes melted into compassion, retracts his former remonstrances, and yields to the natural impulses of his brother. But the soothsayer declares that the sacrifice must take place, to ensure success to the expedition and save the people. Then Agamemnon yields: so does Iphigenia. After uttering some natural lamentations, she consents to sacrifice herself, as the promised means of punishing crime, and obtaining safety and glory for Greece.

AGAMEMNON.

" Have I not leave in mine own house to rule ?

MENELAUS.

How wayward is thy mind ! thy present thoughts
At variance with the past, and soon to change !

AGAMEMNON.

Finely thy words are tun'd ; but know thou this,
The wily tongue is a detested ill.

MENELAUS.

The wav'ring mind is a base property,
And darkens to our friends—I will convince thee.
But if through pride thou turn thee from the truth,
Small share of praise shalt thou receive from me.
Thou knowest, when thy aim was to command
The troops of Greece at Troy, thy semblance
    form'd
As if affecting nothing, but thy wish
Most ardent : what humility was thine !
Pressing the hand of each : thy door to all
Was open—to the meanest ; and thy speech
To all address'd in order, e'en to those
Who will'd no converse with thee, seeking thus
By courteous manners thy ambitious wish
To purchase. The supreme command obtain'd,
Soon were thy manners chang'd, and to thy
    friends
Not friendly as before ; nor was access
Easy—oft too denied. Ill it becomes
An honest man, when rais'd to pow'r, to change
His manners ; but then most to be approv'd
Firm to his friends, when through his advanc'd
    state

He most can serve them. This I urge against
    thee
As my first charge, where first I found thee base.
But when thou cam'st to Aulis, with the troops
Of Greece in arms, to nothing didst thou sink—
Astonish'd at thy fortune—by the gods
Denied a gale to swell thy sails. The Greeks
Requir'd thee to dismiss the ships, nor toil
In vain at Aulis : how dejected then
Thy visage—thy confusion then how great,
Not to command the thousand ships, and fill
The fields of Priam with embattled hosts !
Me then didst thou address : ' What shall I do,
Or what expedient find, of this command—
Of this high honour, not to be depriv'd ?'
When Calchas at the hallow'd rites declar'd
That to Diana thou must sacrifice
Thy daughter, and the Grecians then should sail ;
With joy thy thoughts were heighten'd—willingly
The virgin as a victim didst thou promise,
And freely, not by force (urge not that plea),
Dost thou dispatch a message to thy wife
To send thy daughter hither (the pretence,
Her nuptials with Achilles). But thy mind
Was soon averse, and secretly devis'd
Letters of diff'rent import : now, in sooth,
Thou wilt not be the murd'rer of thy daughter !
This air is witness, which hath heard these things
Of thee. To thousands this hath chanc'd in tasks
Of arduous nature : freely they engage ;
Then from the high attempt retreat with shame—
Th' ill judgment of their countrymen in part,
Justice in part, the cause—for in the proof
They feel their want of pow'r to guard the state.
But most I mourn th' unhappy fate of Greece,

Who, prompt her noble vengeance to inflict
On the barbarians, worthless as they are,
Shall let them now go scoffing off, through thee,
And through thy daughter. Never for his wealth
Would I appoint a ruler o'er the state,
Or chief in arms : wisdom should mark the man
Who in his country bears the sov'reign sway—
Every man sage in counsel is a leader.

AGAMEMNON.

For this I will rebuke thee ; but in brief—
Not raising high the eye of insolence,
But with more temperance, because thou art
My brother ! for a good man loves to act
With modesty. But tell me, why with rage
Dost thou thus swell ? — why rolls thy blood-
      streak'd eye ?
Who injures thee ?—of what art thou in want ?—
A rich connubial bed ! is that thy wish ?
This to procure thee is not in my pow'r.
Thou didst possess one, but ill govern'd it.
Shall I, who with no fault have e'er been charg'd,
Suffer for thy ill conduct ? Is thy heart
Rack'd at my honours ? But a beauteous wife
In thy fond arms it is thy wish to hold,
Transgressing decency and reason : base
Of a bad man the pleasures ! But if I,
Before ill-judging, have with sober thought
My purpose chang'd, must I be therefore deem'd
Reft of my sense ? Thou rather, who hast lost
A wife that brings thee shame, yet dost with
      warmth
Wish to regain her, would the fav'ring god
Grant thee that fortune. Of the nuptials eager,
The suitors pledg'd to Tyndarus their oath—
Unwise ! the hope, I ween, of the fair bride
Effected this, more than thy grace or pow'r.
Take these, and march to war ; soon wilt thou
      find
What oaths avail ill plighted, with slight thought,
And by compulsion. But I will not slay

My children ; and thy wishes o'erleap justice,
The punishment of thy flagitious wife.
My nights—my days would pass away in tears,
Should I with outrage and injustice wrong
Those who from me deriv'd their birth.

.   .   .   .   .

IPHIGENIA TO AGAMEMNON.

But I have nothing to present thee now
Save tears, my only eloquence ; and those
I can present thee. On thy knees I hang
A suppliant wreath—this body, which she * bore
To thee. Ah ! kill me not in youth's fresh prime.
Sweet is the light of heav'n : compel me not
What is beneath † to view. I was the first
To call thee father : me thou first didst call
Thy child. I was the first that on thy knees
Fondly caress'd thee, and from thee receiv'd
The fond caress ! This was thy speech to me,
' Shall I, my child, e'er see thee in some house
Of splendour—happy in thy husband—live
And flourish, as becomes my dignity ?'
My speech to thee was, leaning 'gainst thy cheek,
Which with my hand I now caress, ' And what
Shall I then do for thee ? shall I receive
My father when grown old, and in my house
Cheer him with each fond duty, to repay
The careful nurture which he gave my youth ?'
These words are on my mem'ry deep impress'd—
Thou hast forgot them—and wilt kill thy child !
By Pelops I entreat thee !—by thy sire
Atreus !—by this my mother, who before
Suffer'd for me the pangs of childbirth, now
These pangs again to suffer—do not kill me !
If Paris be enamour'd of his bride—
His Helen, what concerns it me ? and how
Comes he to my destruction ? Look upon me—
Give me a smile—give me a kiss, my father !
That, if my words persuade thee not, in death
I may have this memorial of thy love.
My brother ! small assistance canst thou give

---

* Her mother.   † In the regions of the dead.

Thy friends; yet for thy sister with thy tears
Implore thy father that she may not die!—
E'en infants have a sense of ills. And see,
My father, silent though he be, he sues
To thee. Be gentle to me—on my life
Have pity! Thy two children by this beard
Entreat thee—thy dear children! one is yet
An infant—one to riper years arriv'd.

.   '   .   .   .   .

IPHIGENIA.

My mother, hear ye now my words: for thee
Offended with thy husband I behold.
Vain anger! for where force will take its way,
To struggle is not easy. Our warm thanks
Are to this stranger for his prompt good will
Most justly due: yet, it behoves thee, see
Thou art not by the army charg'd with blame:
Nothing the more should we avail—on him
Mischief would fall. Hear then what to my mind
Deliberate thought presents: it is decreed
For me to die. This then I wish—to die
With glory—all reluctance banish'd far!
My mother! weigh this well, that what I speak
Is honour's dictate. All the pow'rs of Greece
Have now their eyes on me—on me depends
The sailing of the fleet—the fall of Troy;
And not to suffer, should a new attempt
Be dar'd, the rude barbarians from blest Greece
To bear in future times her dames by force—
This ruin bursting on them for the loss
Of Helena, whom Paris bore away.
By dying, all these things shall I achieve;
And blest, for that I have deliver'd Greece,
Shall be my fame. To be too fond of life
Becomes not me; nor for thyself alone,
But to all Greece a blessing didst thou bear me.
Shall thousands, when their country's injur'd, lift
Their shields—shall thousands grasp the oar, and
    dare,
Advancing bravely 'gainst the foes, to die
For Greece? And shall my life—my single life,
Obstruct all this? Would this be just? What
    word

Can we reply? Nay, more; it is not right
That he with all the Grecians should contend
In fight, should die, and—for a woman! No:
More than a thousand women is one man
Worthy to see the light of life. If me
The chaste Diana wills t' accept, shall I,
A mortal, dare oppose her heav'nly will?
Vain the attempt! for Greece I give my life.
Slay me—demolish Troy: for these shall be
Long time my monuments—my children these'—
My nuptials and my glory! It is meet
That Greece should o'er barbarians bear the
    sway,
Not that barbarians lord it over Greece:
Nature hath form'd them slaves—the Grecians
    free.

.   .   .   .   .

I suffer not a tear to fall. But you,
Ye virgins, to my fate attune the hymn,
'Diana, daughter of almighty Jove.'
With fav'ring omens sing 'Success to Greece!'
Come, with the basket one begin the rites—
One with the purifying cakes the flames
Enkindle; let my father his right hand
Place on the altar: for I come to give
Safety to Greece, and conquest to her arms..

 Lead me, mine the glorious fate
 To o'erturn the Phrygian state;
 Ilium's tow'rs their head shall bow.
 With the garlands bind my brow:
 Bring them—be these tresses crown'd..
 Round the shrine, the altar round,
 Bear the lavers, which you fill
 From the pure translucent rill.
 High your choral voices raise,
 Tun'd to hymn Diana's praise—
 Blest Diana—royal maid.
 Since the fates demand my aid,
 I fulfil their awful pow'r
 By my slaughter—by my gore.
 Swell the notes, ye virgin train;
 To Diana swell the strain—
 Queen of Chalcis, adverse land—
 Queen of Aulis, on whose strand,,

Winding to a narrow bay,
Fierce to take its angry way
Waits the war, and calls on me
Its retarded force to free.
O my country, where these eyes
Open'd on Pelasgic skies !
O, ye virgins, once my pride,
In Mycenæ who reside !
Me you rear'd a beam of light :
Freely now I sink in night.
Ah, thou beaming lamp of day,
Jove-born—bright—ethereal ray,
Other regions me await—
Other life, and other fate !
Farewell, beauteous lamp of day—
Farewell, bright ethereal ray !

.   .   .   .

MESSENGER.

Of thy daughter have I things
Astonishing and awful to relate.

CLYTEMNESTRA.

Delay not, then, but speak them instantly.

MESSENGER.

Yes, honour'd lady, thou shalt hear them all,
Distinct from first to last, if that my sense
Disorder'd be not faithless to my tongue.
When to Diana's grove and flow'ry meads
We came, where stood th' assembled host of
          Greece,
Leading thy daughter, straight in close array
Was form'd the band of Argives : but the chief,
Imperial Agamemnon, when he saw
His daughter as a victim to the grove
Advancing, groan'd, and bursting into tears,
Turn'd from the sight his head, before his eyes
Holding his robe. The virgin near him stood,
And thus address'd him, ' Father, I to thee
Am present : for my country, and for all
The land of Greece, I freely give myself
A victim : to the altar let them lead me,
Since such the oracle. If aught on me

Depends, be happy ; and attain the prize
Of glorious conquest, and revisit safe
Your country : of the Grecians for this cause
Let no one touch me : with intrepid spirit
Silent will I present my neck.' She spoke,
And all that heard admir'd the noble soul
And virtue of the virgin. In the midst
Talthybius standing—such his charge—proclaim'
Silence to all the host : and Calchas now,
The prophet, in the golden basket plac'd,
Drawn from its sheath, the sharp-edg'd sword,
          and bound
The sacred garlands round the virgin's head.
The son of Peleus, holding in his hands
The basket and the laver, circled round
The altar of the goddess, and thus spoke :
' Daughter of Jove—Diana ! in the chase
Of savage beasts delighting, through the night
Who rollest thy resplendent orb, accept
This victim, which th' associate troops of Greece,
And Agamemnon, our imperial chief,
Present to thee, the unpolluted blood
Now from this beauteous virgin's neck to flow.
Grant that secure our fleets may plough the main ;
And that our arms may lay the rampir'd walls
Of Troy in dust.' The sons of Atreus stood,
And all the host fix'd on the ground their eyes.
The priest then took the sword, preferr'd his
          pray'r,
And with his eye mark'd where to give the blow.
My heart with grief sunk in me, on the earth
Mine eyes were cast ; when sudden to the view
A wonder ! for the stroke each clearly heard,
But where the virgin was none knew ! aloud
The priest exclaims, and all the host with shouts
Rifted the air, beholding from some god
A prodigy, which struck their wond'ring eyes,
Surpassing faith when seen : for on the ground
Panting was laid an hind of largest bulk,
In form excelling ; with its spouting blood
Much was the altar of the goddess dew'd.
Calchas at this—think with what joy—exclaim'd,
' Ye leaders of th' united host of Greece,
See you this victim, by the goddess brought,

And at her altar laid—a mountain hind?
This, rather than the virgin, she accepts,
Not with the rich stream of her noble blood
To stain the altar—this she hath receiv'd
Of her free grace; and gives a fav'ring gale
To swell our sails, and bear th' invading war
To Ilium: therefore rouse, ye naval train,
Your courage—to your ships! for we this day,
Leaving the deep recesses of this shore,

Must pass th' Ægean sea.' Soon as the flames
The victim had consum'd, he pour'd a pray'r,
That o'er the waves the host might plough their
    way.
Me Agamemnon sends, that I should bear
To thee these tidings, and declare what fate
The gods assign him, and through Greece t' obtain
Immortal glory."

        EURIPIDES, *Iphigenia in Aulis.*

No. 763.

Agamemnon and Priam arranging the conditions of the combat between Paris and Menelaus.

DIOSCORIDES. *Cornelian.*

    The Greek and Trojan armies being ready to engage in the first pitched battle mentioned in the *Iliad*, a single combat was agreed on between Paris and Menelaus, for the determination of the war, and the restoration or retention of Helen. Priam was sent for to ratify the covenant. As this event, in its various accompaniments, has been made the subject of many of these representations, the following account of its origin is necessary.

" Now front to front the hostile armies stand,
Eager to fight, and only wait command;
When, to the van, before the sons of fame
Whom Troy sent forth, the beauteous Paris came—
In form a god! the panther's speckled hide
Flow'd o'er his armour with an easy pride;
His bended bow across his shoulders flung;
His sword beside him negligently hung;
Two pointed spears he shook with gallant grace,
And dared the bravest of the Grecian race.

    As thus, with glorious air and proud disdain,
He boldly stalk'd the foremost on the plain,
Him Menelaus, lov'd of Mars, espies,
With heart elated and with joyful eyes:
So joys a lion, if the branching deer,
Or mountain goat, his bulky prize, appear;
Eager he seizes and devours the slain,
Press'd by bold youths, and baying dogs in vain.
Thus fond of vengeance, with a furious bound,
In clanging arms he leaps upon the ground

From his high chariot: him approaching near,
The beauteous champion views with marks of
    fear—
Smit with a conscious sense, retires behind,
And shuns the fate he well deserved to find.
As when some shepherd, from the rustling trees
Shot forth to view, a scaly serpent sees;
Trembling and pale, he starts with wild affright,
And all confus'd precipitates his flight:
So from the king the shining warrior flies,
And plunged amid the thickest Trojans lies.

    As godlike Hector sees the prince retreat,
He thus upbraids him with a generous heat:
' Unhappy Paris! but to women brave!
So fairly formed, and only to deceive!
Oh hadst thou died when first thou saw'st the
    light,
Or died at least before thy nuptial rite—
A better fate than vainly thus to boast,
And fly, the scandal of the Trojan host!

Gods! how the scornful Greeks exult to see
Their fears of danger undeceived in thee!
Thy figure promised with a martial air,
But ill thy soul supplies a form so fair.
In former days, in all thy gallant pride,
When thy tall ships triumphant stemm'd the tide—
When Greece beheld thy painted canvass flow,
And crowds stood wondering at the passing show;
Say, was it thus, with such a baffled mien,
You met th' approaches of the Spartan queen—
Thus from her realm convey'd the beauteous prize,
And both her warlike lords * outshined in Helen's eyes?
This deed—thy foes' delight—thy own disgrace—
Thy father's grief, and ruin of thy race;
This deed recalls thee to thy proffer'd fight;
Or hast thou injured whom thou darest not right?
Soon to thy cost the field would make thee know
Thou keep'st the consort of a braver foe.
Thy graceful form instilling soft desire—
Thy curling tresses, and thy silver lyre—
Beauty and youth! in vain to these you trust,
When youth and beauty shall be laid in dust:
Troy yet may wake, and one avenging blow
Crush the dire author of his country's woe.'
His silence here, with blushes, Paris breaks:
''Tis just, my brother, what your anger speaks:
But who, like thee, can boast a soul sedate,
So firmly proof to all the shocks of fate?
Thy force, like steel, a temper'd hardness shows,
Still edged to wound, and still untired with blows:
Like steel uplifted by some strenuous swain,
With falling woods to strew the wasted plain.
Thy gifts I praise; nor thou despise the charms
With which a lover golden Venus arms—
Soft moving speech, and pleasing outward show:
No wish can gain them, but the gods bestow.
Yet, wouldst thou have the proffer'd combat stand,
The Greeks and Trojans seat on either hand;

Then let a midway space our hosts divide,
And on that stage of war the cause be tried.
By Paris there the Spartan king be fought,
For beauteous Helen and the wealth she brought;
And who his rival can in arms subdue,
His be the fair, and his the treasure too.
Thus with a lasting league your toils may cease,
And Troy possess her fertile fields in peace;
Thus may the Greeks review their native shore,
Much famed for generous steeds—for beauty more.'
He said. The challenge Hector heard with joy,
Then with his spear restrain'd the youth of Troy,
Held by the midst, athwart; and near the foe
Advanced with steps majestically slow:
While round his dauntless head the Grecians pour
Their stones and arrows in a mingled shower.
Then thus the monarch, great Atrides, cried:
'Forbear, ye warriors! lay the darts aside;
A parley Hector asks—a message bears—
We know him by the various plume he wears.'
Awed by his high command, the Greeks attend,
The tumult silence, and the fight suspend.
While from the centre Hector rolls his eyes
On either host, and thus to both applies.
'Hear, all ye Trojans—all ye Grecian bands!
What Paris, author of the war, demands.
Your shining swords within the sheath restrain,
And pitch your lances in the yielding plain.
Here in the midst, in either army's sight,
He dares the Spartan king to single fight;
And wills that Helen and the ravish'd spoil
That caused the contest shall reward the toil.
Let these the brave triumphant victor grace,
And differing nations part in leagues of peace.'
He spoke: in still suspense on either side
Each army stood, the Spartan chief replied:
'Me too, ye warriors, hear, whose fatal right
A world engages in the toils of fight.
To me the labour of the field resign—
Me Paris injured—all the war be mine.

* Theseus and Menelaus.

Fall he that must, beneath his rival's arms,
And live the rest secure of future harms.
Two lambs, devoted by your country's rite—
To earth a sable, to the sun a white—
Prepare, ye Trojans! while a third we bring,
Select to Jove,* th' inviolable king.
Let reverend Priam in the truce engage,
And add the sanction of considerate age:
Cool age advances venerably wise,
Turns on all hands its deep-discerning eyes:
Sees what befell, and what may yet befall,
Concludes from both, and best provides for all.'

    The nations hear, with rising hopes possess'd,
And peaceful prospects dawn in every breast:
Within the lines they drew their steeds around,
And from their chariots issued on the ground;
Next, all unbuckling the rich mail they wore,
Laid their bright arms along the sable shore.
On either side the meeting hosts are seen
With lances fix'd, and close the space between.
Two heralds now, dispatch'd to Troy, invite
The Phrygian monarch to the peaceful rite;
Talthybius hastens to the fleet, to bring
The lamb for Jove, th' inviolable king."

  "Next from the car descending on the plain,
Amid the Grecian host and Trojan train,
Slow they proceed. The sage Ulysses then
Arose, and with him rose the king of men.†
On either side a sacred herald stands;
The wine they mix, and on each monarch's hands
Pour the full urn: then draws the Grecian's
    lord
His cutlass, sheath'd beside his ponderous sword—
From the sign'd victims crops the curling hair—
The heralds part it, and the princes share;
Then loudly thus, before th' attentive bands,
He calls the gods, and spreads his lifted hands:
  ' O first and greatest power! whom all obey—
Who high on Ida's holy mountain sway—
Eternal Jove! and you bright orb that roll
From east to west, and view from pole to pole!
Thou mother earth! and all ye living Floods!
Infernal Furies, and Tartarian Gods,
Who rule the dead, and horrid woes prepare
For perjured kings, and all who falsely swear!
Hear, and be witness! If, by Paris slain,
Great Menelaus press the fatal plain,
The dame and treasures let the Trojan keep,
And Greece returning plough the watery deep.
If by my brother's lance the Trojan bleed,
Be his the wealth and beauteous dame decreed:

Th' appointed fine let Ilion justly pay,
And every age record the signal day.
Thus, if the Phrygians shall refuse to yield,
Arms must revenge, and Mars decide the field.'
  With that the chief the tender victims slew,
And in the dust their bleeding bodies threw:
The vital spirit issued at the wound,
And left the members quivering on the ground.
From the same urn they drink the mingled
    wine,
And add libations to the powers divine,
While thus their prayers united mount the sky:
  ' Hear, mighty Jove! and hear, ye gods, on
    high!
And may their blood, who first the league con-
    found,
Shed like this wine, distain the thirsty ground—
May all their consorts serve promiscuous lust,
And all their race be scatter'd as the dust!'
Thus either host their imprecations join'd—
Which Jove refused, and mingled with the
    wind!
  The rites now finish'd, reverend Priam rose,
And thus express'd a heart o'ercharged with
    woes:
  ' Ye Greeks and Trojans, let the chiefs engage,
But spare the weakness of my feeble age;

---

* Jupiter Xenius, the avenger of violated hospitality.
† Agamemnon, the commander-in-chief.

3 M

In yonder walls that object let me shun,
Nor view the danger of so dear a son.
Whôse arms shall conquer, and what prince shall
    fall,
Heaven only knows, for heaven disposes all.'

This said, the hoary king no longer stayed,
But on his car the slaughter'd victims laid ;
Then seized the reins his gentle steeds to guide,
And drove to Troy, Antenor at his side."

No. 764.

Iris, disguised as Laodicea, inviting Helen to witness the combat.

POLYCLETES.   *Cornelian.*

" Meantime, to beauteous Helen, from the skies
The various goddess of the rainbow flies
(Like fair Laodicè in form and face,
The loveliest nymph of Priam's royal race).
Her in the palace at her loom she found ;
The golden web her own sad story crown'd.
The Trojan wars she weav'd (herself the prize)
And the dire triumphs of her fatal eyes.
To whom the goddess of the painted bow :
' Approach, and view the wondrous scene below !
Each hardy Greek and valiant Trojan knight,
So dreadful late, and furious for the fight,
Now rest their spears, or lean upon their shields :
Ceased is the war, and silent all the fields.

Paris alone and Sparta's king advance,
In single fight to toss the beamy lance ;
Each met in arms, the fate of combat tries,
Thy love the motive, and thy charms the prize.'
    This said, the many-colour'd maid inspires
Her husband's love, and wakes her former
    fires :
Her country—parents—all that once were dear,
Rush to her thought, and force a tender tear.
O'er her fair face a snowy veil she threw,
And, softly sighing, from the loom withdrew :
Her handmaids, Clymenè and Æthra, wait
Her silent footsteps to the Scæan gate."

No. 765.

Hector and Ulysses casting the lots for Paris and Menelaus.

DIOSCORIDES.   *Cornelian.*

" Bold Hector and Ulysses now dispose
The lists of combat, and the ground enclose ;
Next to decide by sacred lots prepare,
Who first shall launch his pointed spear in air.

.   .   .   .

With eyes averted, Hector hastes to turn
The lots of fight, and shakes the brazen urn :
Then, Paris, thine leaped forth—by fatal chance
Ordain'd the first to whirl the weighty lance."

No. 766.

The combat of Paris and Menelaus.

DIOSCORIDES. *Cornelian.*

" Both armies sat the combat to survey;
Beside each chief his azure armour lay ;
And round the lists the generous coursers neigh.
The beauteous warrior now arrays for fight,
In gilded arms magnificently bright:
The purple cuishes clasp his thighs around,
With flowers adorn'd, with silver buckles bound ;
Lycaon's corslet his fair body dress'd,
Braced in, and fitted to his softer breast ;
A radiant baldric, o'er his shoulder tied,
Sustain'd the sword that glitter'd at his side ;
His youthful face a polish'd helm o'erspread ;
The waving horse-hair nodded on his head ;
His figured shield, a shining orb, he takes,
And in his hand a pointed javelin shakes.
With equal speed, and fired by equal charms,
The Spartan hero sheaths his limbs in arms.
   Now round the lists th' admiring armies stand,
With javelins fix'd, the Greek and Trojan band.
Amidst the dreadful vale the chiefs advance,
All pale with rage, and shake the threat'ning
      lance.
The Trojan first his shining javelin threw ;
Full on Atrides' ringing shield it flew ;
Nor pierced the brazen orb, but with a bound
Leap'd from the buckler blunted on the ground.
Atrides then his massy lance prepares,
In act to throw, but first prefers his prayers:
' Give me, great Jove ! to punish lawless lust,
And lay the Trojan gasping in the dust ;
Destroy th' aggressor—aid my righteous cause—
Avenge the breach of hospitable laws !
Let this example future times reclaim,
And guard from wrong fair friendship's holy
      name.'

He said, and poised in air the javelin sent—
Through Paris' shield the forceful weapon went—
His corslet pierces, and his garment rends,
And glancing downward, near his flank descends.
The wary Trojan, bending from the blow,
Eludes the death, and disappoints his foe ;
But fierce Atrides waved his sword, and strook
Full on his casque ; the crested helmet shook ;
The brittle steel, unfaithful to his hand,
Broke short—the fragments glitter'd on the sand.
The raging warrior to the spacious skies
Raised his upbraiding voice, and angry eyes :
' Then is it vain in Jove himself to trust ?
And is it thus the gods assist the just ?
When crimes provoke us, heaven success denies ;
The dart falls harmless, and the falchion flies !'
Furious he said, and tow'rd the Grecian crew
(Seized by the crest) th' unhappy warrior drew ;
Struggling he follow'd, while the embroider'd
      thong
That tied his helmet dragg'd the chief along.
Then had his ruin crown'd Atrides' joy,
But Venus trembled for the prince of Troy :
Unseen she came, and burst the golden band,
And left an empty helmet in his hand !
The casque, enraged, amidst the Greeks he threw :
The Greeks with smiles the polish'd trophy view.
Then as once more he lifts the deadly dart,
In thirst of vengeance, at his rival's heart,
The queen of love her favour'd champion shrouds
(For gods can all things) in a veil of clouds.
Raised from the field, the panting youth she led,
And gently laid him on the bridal bed ;
With pleasing sweets his fainting sense renews,
And all the dome perfumes with heavenly dews. "

No. 767.

The same subject.

APOLLONIDES.   *Cornelian.*

See preceding quotation.

No. 768.

Menelaus dragging Paris.

CHROMIOS.   *Cornelian.*

See preceding quotation.

No. 769.

Venus conducting Helen to Paris.

GNAIOS.   *Cornelian.*

Helen had witnessed the combat from the walls of Troy, and knew that Paris was worsted, and escaped.   The following extract will sufficiently explain this and the next subject.

" Meantime the brightest of the female kind—
The matchless Helen—o'er the walls reclined ;
To her, beset with Trojan beauties, came,
In borrow'd form, the laughter-loving dame *
(She seem'd an ancient maid, well skill'd to cull
The snowy fleece, and wind the twisted wool).
The goddess softly shook her silken vest,
That shed perfumes, and, whispering, thus ad-
      dress'd :
' Haste, happy nymph ! for thee thy Paris calls,
Safe from the fight, in yonder lofty walls.
Fair as a god ! with odours round him spread,
He lies, and waits thee on the well-known bed—
Not like a warrior parted from the foe,
But some gay dancer in the public show.'

She spoke, and Helen's secret soul was moved :
She scorn'd the champion, but the man she loved.
Fair Venus' neck, her eyes that sparkled fire,
And breast, reveal'd the queen of soft desire.
Struck with her presence, straight the lively red
Forsook her cheek ; and, trembling, thus she
      said :
' Then is it still thy pleasure to deceive ?
And woman's frailty always to believe ?
Say, to new nations must I cross the main,
Or carry wars to some soft Asian plain ?
For whom must Helen break her second vow ?
What other Paris is thy darling now ?
Left to Atrides (victor in the strife)
An odious conquest, and a captive wife,

* Venus.

Hence let me sail; and if thy Paris bear
My absence ill, let Venus ease his care—
A handmaid goddess at his side to wait—
Renounce the glories of thy heavenly state—
Be fix'd for ever to the Trojan shore—
His spouse, or slave—and mount the skies no more.
For me, to lawless love no longer led,
I scorn the coward, and detest his bed:
Else should I merit everlasting shame,
And keen reproach from every Phrygian dame.
Ill suits it now the joys of love to know,
Too deep my anguish, and too wild my woe.'

Then, thus incensed, the Paphian queen replies:
'Obey the power from whom thy glories rise:
Should Venus leave thee, every charm must fly—
Fade from thy cheek, and languish in thy eye.
Cease to provoke me, lest I make thee more
The world's aversion, than their love before—
Now the bright prize for which mankind engage,
Then the sad victim of the public rage.'

At this, the fairest of her sex obey'd,
And veil'd her blushes in a silken shade:
Unseen and silent from the train she moves,
Led by the goddess of the smiles and loves..

Arrived, and enter'd at the palace-gate,
The maids officious round their mistress wait;
Then all dispersing, various tasks attend;
The queen and goddess to the prince ascend.
Full in her Paris' sight, the queen of love
Had placed the beauteous progeny of Jove;

Where, as he view'd her charms, she turn'd away
Her glowing eyes, and thus began to say:
'Is this the chief, who, lost to sense of shame,
Late fled the field, and yet survives his fame?
Oh, hadst thou died beneath the righteous sword
Of that brave man whom once I call'd my lord!
The boaster Paris oft desired the day
With Sparta's king to meet in single fray:
Go now—once more thy rival's rage excite—
Provoke Atrides, and renew the fight:
Yet Helen bids thee stay, lest thou, unskill'd,
Shouldst fall an easy conquest on the field:'

The prince replies: 'Ah, cease, divinely fair!
Nor add reproaches to the wounds I bear;
This day the foe prevail'd by Pallas' power;
I yet may vanquish in a happier hour.
There want not gods to favour me above:
But let the business of our life be love;
These softer moments let delights employ,
And kind embraces snatch the hasty joy.
Not thus I loved thee, when from Sparta's shore
My forced, my willing, heavenly prize I bore—
When first entranced in Cranae's isle I lay,
Mix'd with thy soul, and all dissolved away!'

Thus having spoke, th' enamour'd Phrygian
boy
Rush'd to the bed, impatient for the joy.
Him Helen follow'd slow, with bashful charms,
And clasp'd the blooming lover in her arms."

No. 770.

Paris replying to the reproaches of Helen.

APOLLONIDES. *Cornelian.*

See preceding quotations.

No. 771.

The Council of the Gods—Jupiter sending down Minerva.

PYRGOTELES. *Cornelian.*

The gods deliberated in council concerning the Trojan war, and they agreed upon the continuation of it. Jupiter, yielding to the advice of Juno, sent down Minerva to break the truce. She persuaded Pandarus to wound Menelaus with an arrow. The following extracts, from the fourth book of the *Iliad*, explain this and the next two subjects.

"And now Olympus' shining gates unfold;
The gods, with Jove, assume their thrones of
    gold:
Immortal Hebe, fresh with bloom divine,
The golden goblet crowns with purple wine.
While the full bowls flow round, the powers em-
    ploy
Their careful eyes on long-contended Troy.

.   .   .   .   .

The sire of men, and monarch of the sky,
Th' advice approved, and bade Minerva fly—
Dissolve the league, and all her arts employ
To make the breach the faithless act of Troy.
   Fired with the charge, she headlong urged her
    flight,
And shot like lightning from Olympus' height.
As the red comet, from Saturnius sent
To fright the nations with a dire portent
(A fatal sign to armies on the plain,
Or trembling sailors on the wintry main),
With sweeping glories glides along in air,
And shakes the sparkles from its blazing hair:
Between both armies thus, in open sight,
Shot the bright goddess in a trail of light.
With eyes erect, the gazing hosts admire
The power descending, and the heavens on fire!
'The gods,' they cried, 'the gods this signal sent,
And fate now labours with some vast event:
Jove seals the league, or bloodier scenes prepares—
Jove, the great arbiter of peace and wars!'
   They said, while Pallas through the Trojan
    throng
(In shape a mortal) pass'd disguised along;

Like bold Laödócus, her course she bent,
Who from Antenor traced his high descent.
Amidst the ranks Lycaön's son she found,
The warlike Pandarus, for strength renown'd;
Whose squadrons, led from black Æsepus' flood,
With flaming shields in martial circle stood.
   To him the goddess: 'Phrygian! canst thou
    hear
A well-timed counsel with a willing ear?
What praise were thine, couldst thou direct thy
    dart,
Amidst his triumph, to the Spartan's heart!
What gifts from Troy, from Paris wouldst thou
    gain,
Thy country's foe, the Grecian glory slain!
Then seize th' occasion, dare the mighty deed,
Aim at his breast, and may that aim succeed!
But first, to speed the shaft, address thy vow
To Lycian Phœbus with the silver bow;
And swear the firstlings of thy flock to pay
On Zelia's altars to the god of day.'
   He heard, and madly at the motion pleased,
His polish'd bow with hasty rashness seized:
'Twas form'd of horn, and smooth'd with artful
    toil—
A mountain-goat resign'd the shining spoil,
Who pierced long since beneath his arrows bled;
The stately quarry on the cliffs lay dead,
And sixteen palms his brow's large honours
    spread:
The workman join'd, and shaped the bended
    horns,
And beaten gold each taper point adorns.

This, by the Greeks unseen, the warrior bends,
Screen'd by the shields of his surrounding friends.
There meditates the mark, and couching low,
Fits the sharp arrow to the well-strung bow.
One from a hundred feather'd deaths he chose,
Fated to wound, and cause of future woes.
Then offers vows, with hecatombs to crown
Apollo's altars in his native town.
   Now with full force the yielding horn he bends,
Drawn to an arch, and joins the doubling ends;
Close to his breast he strains the nerve below,
Till the barb'd point approach the circling bow :
Th' impatient weapon whizzes on the wing,
Sounds the tough horn, and twangs the quivering
   string.
   But thee, Atrides ! in that dangerous hour
The gods forget not, nor thy guardian power.
Pallas assists, and (weaken'd in its force)
Diverts the weapon from its destined course :

So from her babe, when slumber seals his eye,
The watchful mother wafts th' envenom'd fly.
Just where his belt with golden buckles join'd,
Where linen folds the double corslet lined,
She turn'd the shaft, which, hissing from above,
Pass'd the broad belt, and through the corslet
   drove ;
The folds it pierced, the plaited linen tore,
And razed the skin, and drew the purple gore.
As when some stately trappings are decreed
To grace a monarch on his bounding steed,
A nymph, in Caria or Mæonia bred,
Stains the pure ivory with a lively red :
With equal lustre various colours vie,
The shining whiteness and the Tyrian dye :
So, great Atrides ! shew'd thy sacred blood,
As down thy snowy thigh distill'd the streaming
   flood."

No. 772.

Pandarus preparing his bow and arrow.

ALLION. *Amethyst.*

See preceding illustration.

No. 773.

Pandarus screened by the shields of his friends, while he wounds
Menelaus.

APOLLONIDES. *Sardonyx.*

No. 774.

Agamemnon declaring the vengeance of the Gods against the Trojans.

POLYCLETES. *Amethyst.*

" With horror seized, the king of men descried
The shaft infix'd, and saw the gushing tide :
Nor less the Spartan fear'd, before he found
The shining barb appear above the wound.
Then with a sigh that heaved his manly breast,
The royal brother thus his grief express'd,
And grasp'd his hand ; while all the Greeks around
With answering sighs return'd the plaintive sound.
' Oh, dear as life ! did I for this agree
The solemn truce—a fatal truce to thee !
Wert thou exposed to all the hostile train,
To fight for Greece, and conquer to be slain !
The race of Trojans in thy ruin join,
And faith is scorn'd by all the perjured line.

Not thus our vows, confirm'd with wine and gore,
Those hands we plighted, and those oaths we swore,
Shall all be vain : when heaven's revenge is slow,
Jove but prepares to strike the fiercer blow.
The day shall come—that great avenging day—
Which Troy's proud glories in the dust shall lay,
When Priam's powers and Priam's self shall fall,
And one prodigious ruin swallow all.
I see the god already from the pole
Bare his red arm, and bid the thunder roll ;
I see th' Eternal all his fury shed,
And shake his ægis o'er their guilty head.
Such mighty woes on perjured princes wait :
But thou, alas ! deservest a happier fate.' "

Iliad, book iv.

No. 775.

Paris and Hector returning through the Scæan gate to the battle.

GNAIOS.   *Cornelian.*

After Menelaus was wounded, the Trojans attacked the Greeks ; and the battle raged furiously.   The Greeks having repulsed the Trojans, Hector went, by advice of the augur Helenus, to the city to appoint a solemn procession of the queen and matrons to the temple of Minerva, in order to implore the favour of the goddess.   When in the city, he induced Paris to return with him to the field.

" Near Priam's court and Hector's palace stands
The pompous structure,* and the town commands.
A spear the hero bore of wondrous strength—
Of full ten cubits was the lance's length ;
The steely point with golden ringlets join'd,
Before him brandish'd, at each motion shined.
Thus entering, in the glittering rooms he found
His brother-chief, whose useless arms lay round,
His eyes delighting with their splendid show,
Brightening the shield, and polishing the bow.

Beside him Helen with her virgins stands—
Guides their rich labours, and instructs their hands.
   Him thus unactive, with an ardent look
The prince beheld, and high resenting spoke :
' Thy hate to Troy is this the time to shew ?
(O wretch ill-fated, and thy country's foe !)
Paris and Greece against us both conspire—
Thy close resentment, and their vengeful ire.
For thee great Ilion's guardian heroes fall,
Till heaps of dead alone defend her wall ;

---

* The house of Paris.

For thee the soldier bleeds, the matron mourns,
And wasteful war in all its fury burns.
Ungrateful man! deserves not this thy care,
Our troops to hearten, and our toils to share?
Rise, or behold the conquering flames ascend,
And all the Phrygian glories at an end.'
  ' Brother, 'tis just,' replied the beauteous youth;
' Thy free remonstrance proves thy worth and
    truth;
Yet charge my absence less, O generous chief!
On hate to Troy, than conscious shame and grief.
Here, hid from human eyes, thy brother sat,
And mourn'd in secret his and Ilion's fate.
'Tis now enough: now glory spreads her charms,
And beauteous Helen calls her chief to arms.
Conquest to-day my happier sword may bless:
'Tis man's to fight, but heaven's to give success.
But while I arm, contain thy ardent mind;
Or go, and Paris shall not lag behind.'

.   .   .   .   .

   But now, no longer deaf to honour's call,
Forth issues Paris from the palace wall.
In brazen arms that cast a gleamy ray,
Swift through the town the warrior bends his
    way.
The wanton courser thus, with reins unbound,
Breaks from his stall, and beats the trembling
    ground;

Pamper'd and proud, he seeks the wonted tides,
And laves, in height of blood, his shining sides;
His head now freed, he tosses to the skies;
His mane dishevell'd o'er his shoulders flies ;
He snuffs the females in the distant plain,
And springs, exulting, to his fields again.
With equal triumph, sprightly, bold, and gay,
In arms refulgent as the god of day,
The son of Priam, glorying in his might,
Rush'd forth with Hector to the fields of fight.
 · And now the warriors passing on the way,
The graceful Paris first excused his stay.
To whom the noble Hector thus replied:
' O chief! in blood, and now in arms, allied!
Thy power in war with justice none contest;
Known is thy courage, and thy strength confess'd.
What pity sloth should seize a soul so brave,
Or godlike Paris live a woman's slave!
My heart weeps blood at what the Trojans say,
And hopes thy deeds shall wipe the stain away.
Haste, then, in all their glorious labours share;
For much they suffer, for thy sake, in war.
These ills shall cease whene'er, by Jove's decree,
We crown the bowl to Heaven and Liberty:
While the proud foe his frustrate triumphs
    mourns,
And Greece indignant through her seas re-
    turns.' "

                           Iliad, book vi.

No. 776.

Paris slaying Menestheus.

GNAIOS. *Cornelian.*

    When Hector and Paris returned to the field, Paris was the first to charge the enemy. He then behaved with great bravery, and performed great feats all through the remainder of the campaign.

" So spoke the guardian of the Trojan state,
Then rush'd impetuous through the Scæan gate.
Him Paris follow'd to the dire alarms—
Both breathing slaughter—both resolved in arms!

As when to sailors labouring through the main,
That long had heaved the weary oar in vain,
Jove bids at length th' expected gales arise;
The gales blow grateful, and the vessel flies ;

3 N

So welcome these to Troy's desiring train—
The bands are cheer'd, the war awakes again.
  Bold Paris first the work of death begun
On great Menestheus, Areithous' son:

Sprung from the fair Philomeda's embrace;
The pleasing Arnè was his native place."

Iliad, book vii.

No. 777.

Apollo directing Paris to slay Achilles.

APOLLONIDES.   *Cornelian.*

" The sire of Cygnus, monarch of the main,
Meantime laments his son in battle slain,
And vows the victor's death; nor vows in vain.
For nine long years the smother'd pain he bore—
Achilles was not ripe for fate before—
Then when he saw the promis'd hour was near,
He thus bespoke the god that guides the year:
' Immortal offspring of my brother Jove,
My brightest nephew, and whom best I love—
Whose hands were join'd with mine to raise the wall
Of tott'ring Troy, now nodding to her fall,
Dost thou not mourn our pow'r employ'd in vain,
And the defenders of our city slain?
To pass the rest, could noble Hector lie
Unpity'd—dragg'd around his native Troy?
And yet the murderer lives—himself by far
A greater plague than all the wasteful war!
He lives—the proud Pelides lives—to boast
Our town destroy'd—our common labour lost.
Oh, could I meet him! But I wish too late;
To prove my trident is not in his fate!
But let him try (for that's allow'd) thy dart:
Then pierce his only penetrable part.'

Apollo bows to the superior throne;
And to his uncle's anger adds his own.
Then, in a cloud involv'd, he takes his flight,
Where Greeks and Trojans mix'd in mortal
        fight;
And found out Paris, slaying where he stood,
And stain'd his arrows with plebeian blood:
Phœbus to him alone the god confess'd,
Then to the valiant knight he thus address'd:
' Dost thou not blush to spend thy shafts in vain,
On a degenerate and ignoble train?
If fame or better vengeance be thy care,
There aim; and, with one arrow, end the war.'
  He said; and shew'd from far the blazing shield
And sword, which but Achilles none could wield;
And how he mov'd a god, and mow'd the stand-
        ing field.
The deity himself directs aright
The envenom'd shaft, and wings the fatal flight.
  Thus fell the foremost of the Grecian name;
And he, the base adult'rer! boasts the fame—
A spectacle to glad the Trojan train;
And please old Priam, after Hector slain."*

OVID, *Met.*; book xii.

No. 778.

Chryses praying to Apollo.

CHROMIOS.   *Cornelian.*

---

* This account of Achilles having been slain in battle agrees with Homer's. It appears from several passages in the *Iliad*, and from the beginning of the twenty-fourth book of the *Odyssey*, that he was slain on the field of battle, and that a fight for the possession of his arms and body lasted the whole day. Another account is, that he was treacherously slain by Paris in the temple, while about to be married to his sister Polyxena.

In the Trojan war, the Greeks having sacked some Phrygian towns, took away certain female captives. One of these, Chryseis the daughter of Chryses, priest of Apollo, was allotted to Agamemnon; another, Briseis, was allotted to Achilles. Chryses came to the Grecian camp to ransom his daughter; but Agamemnon refused to release her. Then Chryses prayed to Apollo to punish the Greeks; and Apollo, listening to his suit, inflicted on them a pestilence. Achilles summoned the people to a general council. Calchas, the augur, declared the cause of the public affliction. Upon this, Agamemnon, yielding to the public interest, consented to restore Chryseis; but said he should have some other chief's captive in lieu of her. This Achilles denounces as an act of great injustice. An angry debate ensues. At last Agamemnon, as commander-in-chief, seizes on Briseis; and Achilles, in rage, secedes, together with his forces. This anger of Achilles, and its consequences, form the subject of the *Iliad*.

"Declare, O Muse! in what ill-fated hour
Sprung the fierce strife — from what offended
    power?
Latona's son* a dire contagion spread,
And heap'd the camp with mountains of the dead:
The king of men his reverend priest defied;
And for the king's offence the people died.
  For Chryses sought with costly gifts to gain
His captive daughter from the victor's chain.
Suppliant the venerable father stands:
Apollo's awful ensigns grace his hands:
By these he begs; and lowly bending down,
Extends the sceptre and the laurel crown.
He sued to all; but chief implored for grace
The brother-kings of Atreus' royal race.
  'Ye kings and warriors! may your vows be
    crown'd,
And Troy's proud walls lie level with the ground!
May Jove restore you, when your toils are o'er,
Safe to the pleasures of your native shore!
But, oh! relieve a wretched parent's pain,
And give Chryseis to these arms again.
If mercy fail, yet let my presents move,
And dread avenging Phœbus, son of Jove!'
  The Greeks in shouts their joint assent declare,
The priest to reverence, and release the fair.
Not so Atrides: he, with kingly pride,
Repulsed the sacred sire, and thus replied:

'Hence, on thy life, and fly these hostile plains;
Nor ask, presumptuous, what the king detains—
Hence, with thy laurel crown and golden rod;
Nor trust too far those ensigns of thy god.
Mine is thy daughter, priest, and shall remain;
And prayers, and tears, and bribes, shall plead in
    vain,
Till time shall rifle every youthful grace,
And age dismiss her from my cold embrace,
In daily labours of the loom employ'd;
Or doom'd to deck the bed she once enjoy'd.
Hence, then, to Argos shall the maid retire—
Far from her native soil and weeping sire.'
  The trembling priest along the shore return'd,
And in the anguish of a father mourn'd.
Disconsolate, not daring to complain,
Silent he wander'd by the sounding main:
Till, safe at distance, to his god he prays—
The god who darts around the world his rays.
  'O Smintheus! sprung from fair Latona's line,
Thou guardian power of Cilla the divine—
Thou source of light whom Tenedos adores,
And whose bright presence gilds thy Chrysa's
    shores;
If e'er with wreaths I hung thy sacred fane,
Or fed the flames with fat of oxen slain—
God of the silver bow! thy shafts employ—
Avenge thy servant, and the Greeks destroy.'"
                          Iliad, book i.

---

* Apollo.

No. 779.

Apollo discharging his vengeful arrows in view of the Grecian fleet.

PYRGOTELES.   *Amethyst.*

> " Thus Chryses pray'd : the favouring power attends,
> And from Olympus' lofty tops descends.
> Bent was his bow, the Grecian hearts to wound :
> Fierce as he moved, his silver shafts resound.
> Breathing revenge, a sudden night he spread,
> And gloomy darkness roll'd about his head.
> The fleet in view, he twang'd his deadly bow,
> And hissing fly the feather'd fates below.
> On mules and dogs the infection first began ;
> And last—the vengeful arrows fix'd in man !
> For nine long nights through all the dusky air
> The pyres, thick-flaming, shot a dismal glare."

No. 780.

Agamemnon charging the heralds Talthybius and Eurybates to bring him Briseis.

APOLLONIDES.   *Amethyst.*

Agamemnon says to Achilles—

> " Then thus the king : ' Shall I my prize resign
> With tame content, and thou possess'd of thine ?
> Great as thou art, and like a god in fight,
> Think not to rob me of a soldier's right.
> At thy demand shall I restore the maid ?
> First let the just equivalent be paid—
> Such as a king might ask ; and let it be
> A treasure worthy her, and worthy me.
> Or grant me this, or, with a monarch's claim,
> This hand shall seize some other captive dame—
> The mighty Ajax shall his prize resign,
> Ulysses' spoils, or e'en thine own be mine.
> The man who suffers loudly may complain ;
> And rage he may, but he shall rage in vain.' "

Achilles threatens to return home.   Then Agamemnon says—

> " ' Haste—launch thy vessels—fly with speed away—
> Rule thy own realms with arbitrary sway ;
> I heed thee not, but prize at equal rate
> Thy short-lived friendship, and thy groundless hate.

Go, threat thy earth-born myrmidons; but here
'Tis mine to threaten, prince, and thine to fear!
Know, if the god the beauteous dame demand,
My bark shall waft her to her native land;
But then prepare, imperious prince!—prepare,
Fierce as thou art, to yield thy captive fair:

E'en in thy tent I'll seize the blooming prize—
Thy lov'd Briseis with the radiant eyes.
Hence shalt thou prove my might, and curse the hour
Thou stood'st a rival of imperial power;
And hence to all our host it shall be known,
That kings are subject to the gods alone.' "

After Achilles retired to his tent, Agamemnon despatched the heralds.

"Atrides still with deep resentment raged:
To wait his will two sacred heralds stood,
Talthybius, and Eurybates the good.
'Haste to the fierce Achilles' tent,' he cries,
'Thence bear Briseis as our royal prize.
Submit he must; or if they will not part,
Ourself in arms shall tear her from his heart.'

Th' unwilling heralds act their lord's commands;
Pensive they walk along the barren sands:
Arrived, the hero in his tent they find,
With gloomy aspect, on his arm reclined.
At awful distance long they silent stand,
Loath to advance, or speak their hard command;
Decent confusion! this the godlike man
Perceived, and thus with accent mild began.'

Iliad, book i.

No. 781.

Jupiter, Juno, and Vulcan.

SOLON. *Cornelian.*

Achilles having resigned Briseis, complained to his mother Thetis. She supplicated Jupiter to avenge the wrong done him; and Jupiter promised to grant her suit. This produced an angry debate between Jupiter and Juno. Vulcan appeased Juno. The following passages are necessary, in order to give the unlearned reader a full conception not merely of the present, but of many of the succeeding subjects.

"Patroclus now th' unwilling beauty brought.
She, in soft sorrows, and in pensive thought,
Pass'd silent, as the heralds held her hand,
And oft look'd back, slow moving o'er the strand.
Not so his loss the fierce Achilles bore;
But sad retiring to the sounding shore,
O'er the wild margin of the deep he hung—
That kindred deep from whence his mother sprung—
There, bathed in tears of anger and disdain,
Thus loud lamented to the stormy main:

'O parent goddess! since in early bloom
Thy son must fall by too severe a doom;
Sure, to so short a race of glory born,
Great Jove in justice should this span adorn:
Honour and fame at least the Thund'rer ow'd,
And ill he pays the promise of a god,
If yon proud monarch thus thy son defies—
Obscures my glories, and resumes my prize.'
Far from the deep recesses of the main,
Where aged Ocean holds his wat'ry reign,
The goddess-mother heard. The waves divide;
And like a mist she rose above the tide."

Thetis supplicates Jupiter—

> " Suppliant the goddess stood ; one hand she placed
>   Beneath his beard, and one his knees embraced.
> ' If e'er, O father of the gods !' she said,
> ' My words could please thee, or my actions aid ;
>   Some marks of honour on my son bestow,
>   And pay in glory what in life you owe.
>   Fame is at least by heavenly promise due
>   To life so short, and now dishonour'd too.
>   Avenge this wrong, O ever just and wise !
>   Let Greece be humbled, and the Trojans rise ;
>   Till the proud king, and all th' Achaian race,
>   Shall heap with honours him they now disgrace.' "

Jupiter promises to grant her suit—

> " ' But part in peace, secure thy prayer is sped :
>   Witness the sacred honours of our head—
>   The nod that ratifies the will divine—
>   The faithful—fix'd—irrevocable sign !
>   This seals thy suit, and this fulfils thy vows.'
>   He spoke, and awful bends his sable brows,
>   Shakes his ambrosial curls, and gives the nod—
>   The stamp of fate, and sanction of the god !
>   High heaven with trembling the dread signal took,
>   And all Olympus to the centre shook."

Vulcan appeases Juno—

> " Then thus the god : ' Oh, restless fate of pride !
> That strives to learn what heaven resolves to hide ;
> Vain is the search—presumptuous, and abhorr'd—
> Anxious to thee, and odious to thy lord !
> Let this suffice ; the immutable decree
> No force can shake : what is, that ought to be.
> Goddess, submit, nor dare our will withstand ;
> But dread the power of this avenging hand :
> Th' united strength of all the gods above
> In vain resists th' omnipotence of Jove.'
>   The Thunderer spoke, nor durst the queen reply :
> A reverend horror silenced all the sky.
> The feast disturb'd, with sorrow Vulcan saw
> His mother menaced, and the gods in awe ;
> Peace at his heart, and pleasure his design,
> Thus interposed the architect divine :
>
> ' The wretched quarrels of the mortal state
> Are far unworthy, gods ! of your debate.
> Let men their days in senseless strife employ—
> We, in eternal peace and constant joy !
> Thou, goddess-mother, with our sire comply,
> Nor break the sacred union of the sky ;
> Lest, roused to rage, he shake the blest abodes,
> Launch the red lightning, and dethrone the gods.
> If you submit, the Thunderer stands appeased :
> The gracious power is willing to be pleased.'
> Thus Vulcan spoke ; and rising with a bound,
> The double bowl with sparkling nectar crown'd,
> Which held to Juno in a cheerful way,
> ' Goddess,' he cried, ' be patient and obey :
> Dear as you are, if Jove his arm extend,
> I can but grieve, unable to defend.
> What god so daring in your aid to move,
> Or lift his hand against the force of Jove ?

Once in your cause I felt his matchless might,
Hurl'd headlong downward from th' ethereal
    height;
Toss'd all the day in rapid circles round;
Nor, till the sun descended, touch'd the ground:
Breathless I fell, in giddy motion lost;
The Sinthians raised me on the Lemnian coast.'

He said, and to her hands the goblet heaved,
Which, with a smile, the white-arm'd queen re-
    ceived.
Then to the rest he fill'd; and in his turn,
Each to his lips applied the nectar'd urn.
Vulcan with awkward grace his office plies,
And unextinguish'd laughter shakes the skies."

Iliad, book i.

No. 782.

Agamemnon in the tent of Nestor.

CHROMIOS. *Amethyst.*

Night having put an end to the battle, and the Greeks having been driven to their forti-
fications before the ships, the Trojans continued on the field, and kept watch-fires all night.
Agamemnon, unable from distress of mind to sleep, rose, and went to the tent of Nestor, to
consult with him in this crisis of affairs. This subject is thus described in the beginning of the
tenth book of the *Iliad.*

" All night the chiefs before their vessels lay,
And lost in sleep the labours of the day—
All but the king! With various thoughts op-
    press'd,
His country's cares lay rolling in his breast.
As when by lightnings Jove's ethereal power
Foretells the rattling hail or weighty shower;
Or sends soft snows to whiten all the shore;
Or bids the brazen throat of war to roar;
By fits one flash succeeds as one expires,
And heaven flames thick with momentary fires,—
So, bursting frequent from Atrides' breast,
Sighs following sighs his inward fears confess'd.
Now o'er the fields, dejected, he surveys
From thousand Trojan fires the mounting blaze;
Hears in the passing wind their music blow,
And marks distinct the voices of the foe.
Now looking backwards to the fleet and coast,
Anxious he sorrows for th' endanger'd host.
He rends his hairs in sacrifice to Jove,
And sues to him that ever lives above:
Inly he groans, while glory and despair
Divide his heart, and wage a doubtful war.

A thousand cares his labouring breast revolves:
To seek sage Nestor now the chief resolves—
With him in wholesome counsels to debate
What yet remains to save th' afflicted state.
He rose, and first he cast his mantle round;
Next on his feet the shining sandals bound;
A lion's yellow spoils his back conceal'd;
His warlike hand a pointed javelin held.
Meanwhile his brother, press'd with equal
    woes,
Alike denied the gifts of soft repose,
Laments for Greece—that in his cause before
So much had suffer'd, and must suffer more.
A leopard's spotted hide his shoulders spread;
A brazen helmet glitter'd on his head:
Thus (with a javelin in his hand) he went
To wake Atrides in the royal tent.
Already waked, Atrides he descried,
His armour buckling at his vessel's side.
Joyful they met: the Spartan thus begun
' Why puts my brother his bright armour on?
Sends he some spy amidst these silent hours,
To try yon camp, and watch the Trojan powers?

But say, what hero shall sustain that task—
Such bold exploits uncommon courage ask;
Guideless, alone, through night's dark shade to go,
And midst a hostile camp explore the foe?'
  To whom the king: 'In such distress we stand,
No vulgar counsels our affairs demand;
Greece to preserve is now no easy part,
But asks high wisdom, deep design, and art.
For Jove averse our humble prayer denies,
And bows his head to Hector's sacrifice.
What eye has witness'd, or what ear believed,
In one great day, by one great arm achieved,
Such wondrous deeds as Hector's hand has done,
And we beheld, the last revolving sun?
What honours the beloved of Jove adorn!
Sprung from no god, and of no goddess born,
Yet such his acts, as Greeks unborn shall tell,
And curse the battle where their fathers fell.
Now speed thy hasty course along the fleet,
There call great Ajax, and the prince of Crete;
Ourself to hoary Nestor will repair;
To keep the guards on duty be his care
(For Nestor's influence best that quarter guides,
Whose son with Merion o'er the watch presides).'

  .   .   .   .   .

  This said, each parted to his several cares;
The king to Nestor's sable ship repairs.
The sage protector of the Greeks he found
Stretch'd in his bed with all his arms around;
The various-colour'd scarf, the shield he rears,
The shining helmet, and the pointed spears:
The dreadful weapons of the warrior's rage,
That, old in arms, disdain'd the peace of age.
Then, leaning on his hand his watchful head,
The hoary monarch raised his eyes, and said:
  'What art thou—speak—that on designs unknown,
While others sleep, thus range the camp alone?
Seek'st thou some friend, or nightly sentinel?
Stand off—approach not—but thy purpose tell.'
  'O son of Neleus,' thus the king rejoin'd,
'Pride of the Greeks, and glory of thy kind!
Lo, here the wretched Agamemnon stands,
Th' unhappy general of the Grecian bands;

Whom Jove decrees with daily cares to bend,
And woes, that only with his life shall end!
Scarce can my knees these trembling limbs sustain,
And scarce my heart support its load of pain.
No taste of sleep these heavy eyes have known;
Confus'd, and sad, I wander thus alone,
With fears distracted, with no fix'd design;
And all my people's miseries are mine.
If aught of use thy waking thoughts suggest
(Since cares, like mine, deprive thy soul of rest),
Impart thy counsel, and assist thy friend.
Now let us jointly to the trench descend,
At every gate the fainting guard excite,
Tired with the toils of day and watch of night;
Else may the sudden foe our works invade,
So near, and favour'd by the gloomy shade.'
  To him thus Nestor: 'Trust the powers above,
Nor think proud Hector's hopes confirmed by Jove.
How ill agree the views of vain mankind,
And the wise counsels of th' eternal mind!
Audacious Hector, if the gods ordain
That great Achilles rise and rage again,
What toils attend thee, and what woes remain!
Lo, faithful Nestor thy command obeys;
Thy care is next our other chiefs to raise:
Ulysses, Diomed, we chiefly need;
Meges for strength, Oïleus famed for speed.
Some other be dispatch'd of nimbler feet,
To those tall ships, remotest of the fleet,
Where lie great Ajax and the king of Crete.
To rouse the Spartan I myself decree;
Dear as he is to us, and dear to thee,
Yet must I tax his sloth, that claims no share
With his great brother in this martial care:
Him it behoved to every chief to sue,
Preventing every part perform'd by you;
For strong necessity our toils demands—
Claims all our hearts, and urges all our hands.'
  To whom the king: 'With reverence we allow
Thy just rebukes, yet learn to spare them now.
My generous brother is of gentle kind,
He seems remiss, but bears a valiant mind;

Through too much deference to our sovereign
    sway,
Content to follow when we lead the way.
But now, our ills industrious to prevent,
Long ere the rest he rose, and sought my tent.
The chiefs you named, already at his call,
Prepare to meet us near the navy wall;
Assembling there between the trench and gates,
Near the night-guards, our chosen council waits.'
   ' Then none,' said Nestor, ' shall his rule with-
    stand,
For great examples justify command.'

With that the venerable warrior rose;
The shining greaves his manly legs enclose;
His purple mantle golden buckles join'd,
Warm with the softest wool, and doubly lined.
Then, rushing from his tent, he snatch'd in
    haste
His steely lance, that lighten'd as he pass'd:
The camp he traversed through the sleeping
    crowd,
Stopp'd at Ulysses' tent, and call'd aloud.
Ulysses, sudden as the voice was sent,
Awakes, starts up, and issues from his tent."

Iliad, book x.

No. 783.

Agamemnon wounded by Coön.

DIOSCORIDES. *Cornelian.*

Agamemnon, after performing prodigies of valour, had slain the brother of Coön.

"Coön, Antenor's eldest hope, was nigh:
Tears, at the sight, came starting from his eye,
While pierced with grief the much-loved youth
    he view'd,
And the pale features now deform'd with blood.
Then with his spear, unseen, his time he took,
Aim'd at the king, and near his elbow strook.
The thrilling steel transpierced the brawny part,
And through his arm stood forth the barbed dart.
Surprised the monarch feels, yet void of fear
On Coon rushes with his lifted spear:

His brother's corpse the pious Trojan draws,
And calls his country to assert his cause,
Defends him breathless on the sanguine field,
And o'er the body spreads his ample shield.
Atrides, marking an unguarded part,
Transfix'd the warrior with the brazen dart;
Prone on his brother's bleeding breast he lay,
The monarch's falchion lopp'd his head away:
The social shades the same dark journey go,
And join each other in the realms below."

Iliad, book xi.

No. 784.

Agamemnon killing Coön.

POLYCLETES. *Amethyst.*

See preceding quotation.

3 o

No. 785.

Head of Agamemnon.

#### AGEDES.	*Cornelian.*

Agamemnon was one of the bravest of all the Grecian chiefs.	After his return home he was assassinated by his wife Clytemnestra, and her paramour Ægysthus.

No. 786.

Menelaus killing Scamandrius.

#### APOLLONIDES.	*Sardonyx.*

" Then died Scamandrius, expert in the chase,
In woods and wilds to wound the savage race:
Diana taught him all her sylvan arts—
To bend the bow, and aim unerring darts.
But vainly here Diana's arts he tries,
The fatal lance arrests him as he flies;
From Menelaus' arm the weapon sent,
Through his broad back and heaving bosom went:
Down sinks the warrior with a thundering sound—
His brazen armour rings against the ground!"

Iliad, book v.

No. 787.

Menelaus defending the dead body of Patroclus.

#### SOLON.	*Cornelian.*

" On the cold earth divine Patroclus spread,
Lies pierced with wounds among the vulgar dead.
Great Menelaus, touch'd with generous woe,
Springs to the front and guards him from the foe:
Thus round her new-fallen young the heifer moves,
Fruit of her throes, and firstborn of her loves;
And anxious (helpless as he lies, and bare)
Turns, and returns her, with a mother's care.
Opposed to each that near the carcass came,
His broad shield glimmers, and his lances flame.
The son of Panthus, skill'd the dart to send,
Eyes the dead hero, and insults the friend:

' This hand, Atrides, laid Patroclus low—
Warrior, desist, nor tempt an equal blow!
To me the spoils my prowess won resign;
Depart with life, and leave the glory mine.'
The Trojan thus: the Spartan monarch buru'd
With generous anguish, and in scorn return'd:
' Laugh'st thou not, Jove! from thy superior throne,
When mortals boast of prowess not their own?
Not thus the lion glories in his might—
Nor panther braves his spotted foe in fight—
Nor thus the boar (those terrors of the plain)—
Man only vaunts his force, and vaunts in vain.

But far the vainest of the boastful kind,
These sons of Panthus vent their haughty mind :
Yet, 'twas but late beneath my conquering steel
This boaster's brother, Hyperenor, fell ;
Against our arm, which rashly he defied,
Vain was his vigour, and as vain his pride.
These eyes beheld him on the dust expire,
No more to cheer his spouse, or glad his sire.
Presumptuous youth ! like his shall be thy doom ;
Go, wait thy brother to the Stygian gloom !
Or, while thou mayst, avoid the threaten'd fate;
Fools stay to feel it, and are wise too late.'
  Unmov'd, Euphorbus thus : 'That action known,
Come—for my brother's blood repay thy own.
His weeping father claims thy destined head,
And spouse, a widow in her bridal bed ;
On these thy conquer'd spoils I shall bestow,
To soothe a consort's and a parent's woe.
No longer then defer the glorious strife,
Let heaven decide our fortune, fame, and life.'
  Swift as the word the missile lance he flings,
The well-aim'd weapon on the buckler rings,
But blunted by the brass innoxious falls.
On Jove the father great Atrides calls,
Nor flies the javelin from his arm in vain—
It pierced his throat, and bent him to the plain :

Wide through the neck appears the grisly wound,
Prone sinks the warrior, and his arms resound.
The shining circlets of his golden hair,
Which e'en the graces might be proud to wear,
Instarr'd with gems and gold, bestrew the shore,
With dust dishonour'd, and deform'd with gore.
As the young olive, in some sylvan scene,
Crown'd by fresh fountains with eternal green,
Lifts the gay head, in snowy flow'rets fair,
And plays and dances to the gentle air—
When, lo ! a whirlwind from high heav'n invades
The tender plant, and withers all its shades—
It lies uprooted from its genial bed,
A lovely ruin now defac'd and dead.
Thus young, thus beautiful, Euphorbus lay,
While the fierce Spartan tore his arms away.
Proud of his deed, and glorious in the prize,
Affrighted Troy the tow'ring victor flies—
Flies as before some mountain lion's ire
The village curs and trembling swains retire;
When o'er the slaughter'd bull they hear him
            roar,
And see his jaws distil with smoking gore ;
All pale with fear, at distance scatter'd round,
They shout incessant, and the vales resound."
                              Iliad, book xvii.

No. 788.

Menelaus exhorting the Greeks to rally for the protection of the dead body of Patroclus.

Gnaios. *Amethyst.*

Menelaus for a time defended the body of Patroclus ; but on the approach of Hector was forced to retire. He then shouted to the Greeks to come to the rescue. The following extracts, from the seventeenth book of the *Iliad*, sufficiently explain this subject.

" Atrides from the voice the storm divined,
And thus explored his own unconquer'd mind :
  ' Then shall I quit Patroclus on the plain—
Slain in my cause, and for my honour slain—
Desert the arms, the relics of my friend ?
Or, singly, Hector and his troops attend ?

Sure where such partial favour heav'n bestow'd,
To brave the hero were to brave the god.
Forgive me, Greece, if once I quit the field—
'Tis not to Hector, but to heaven I yield.
Yet, not the god, nor heaven, should give me fear,
Did but the voice of Ajax reach my ear:

Still would we turn, still battle on the plains,
And give Achilles all that yet remains
Of his and our Patroclus.' This, no more,
The time allow'd : Troy thicken'd on the shore,
A sable scene! the terrors Hector led.
Slow he recedes, and sighing quits the dead.
　So from the fold th' unwilling lion parts,
Forced by loud clamours, and a storm of darts :
He flies indeed, but threatens as he flies,
With heart indignant and retorted eyes.
Now enter'd in the Spartan ranks, he turn'd
His manly breast, and with new fury buru'd—
O'er all the black battalions sent his view,
And through the cloud the godlike Ajax knew ;
Where labouring on the left the warrior stood,
All grim in arms, and cover'd o'er with blood.

　The warrior raised his voice, and wide around
The field re-echoed the distressful sound :
' O chiefs ! O princes ! to whose hand is given
The rule of men ! whose glory is from heaven !

Whom with due honours both Atrides grace—
Ye guides and guardians of our Argive race !
All, whom this well-known voice shall reach from
　　far—
All whom I see not through this cloud of war—
Come all ! let generous rage your arms employ,
And save Patroclus from the dogs of Troy.'
　Oïlean Ajax first the voice obey'd,
Swift was his pace, and ready was his aid ;
Next him Idomeneus, more slow with age,
And Merion, burning with a hero's rage.
The long succeeding numbers who can name ?
But all were Greeks, and eager all for fame.
Fierce to the charge great Hector led the throng ;
Whole Troy embodied rush'd with shouts along.
Thus, when a mountain billow foams and raves,
Where some swoll'n river disembogues his waves,
Full in the mouth is stopp'd the rushing tide,
The boiling ocean works from side to side,
The river trembles to his utmost shore,
And distant rocks rebellow to the roar."

Iliad, book xvii.

No. 789.

Menelaus killing Pisander.

CHROMIOS. *Calcedony.*

" Behold ! Pisander, urged by Fate's decree,
Springs through the ranks to fall—and fall by thee,
Great Menelaus ! to enhance thy fame :
High-towering in the front the warrior came.
First, the sharp lance was by Atrides thrown :
The lance far distant by the winds was blown.
Nor pierced Pisander through Atrides' shield :
Pisander's spear fell shiver'd on the field.
Not so discouraged, to the future blind,
Vain dreams of conquest swell his haughty mind !
Dauntless he rushes where the Spartan lord
Like lightning brandish'd his far-beaming sword.
His left arm high opposed the shining shield :
His right, beneath, the cover'd poleaxe held
(An olive's cloudy grain the handle made,
Distinct with studs ; and brazen was the blade) ;

This on the helm discharged a noble blow ;
The plume dropp'd nodding to the plain below,
Shorn from the crest.　Atrides waved his steel :
Deep through his front the weighty falchion fell :
The crashing bones before its force gave way ;
In dust and blood the groaning hero lay ;
Forc'd from their ghastly orbs, and spouting
　　gore,
The clotted eyeballs tumble on the shore.
The fierce Atrides spurn'd him as he bled,
Tore off his arms, and, loud exulting, said :
" Thus, Trojans—thus, at length be taught to
　　fear ;
O race perfidious, who delight in war !
Already noble deeds ye have perform'd,
A princess raped transcends a navy storm'd :

In such bold feats your impious might approve,
Without the assistance or the fear of Jove.
The violated rites, the ravish'd dame,
Our heroes slaughter'd, and our ships on flame,
Crimes heap'd on crimes shall bend your glory
    down,
And whelm in ruins yon flagitious town.
O thou, great Father! lord of earth and skies,
Above the thought of man supremely wise!
If from thy hand the fates of mortals flow,
From whence this favour to an impious foe—
A godless crew—abandon'd and unjust—
Still breathing rapine, violence, and lust?

The best of things beyond their measure cloy—
Sleep's balmy blessing—love's endearing joy—
The feast—the dance : whate'er mankind de-
    sire—
E'en the sweet charms of sacred numbers tire.
But Troy for ever reaps a dire delight
In thirst of slaughter, and in lust of fight.'
    This said, he seized (while yet the carcass
        heaved)
The bloody armour, which his train received :
Then sudden mix'd among the warring crew."

Iliad, book xiii.

No. 790.

Menelaus stamping on the dead body of Pisander.

CHROMIOS. *Cornelian.*

No. 791.

Menelaus despoiling the body of Pisander.

CHROMIOS. *Cornelian.*

See preceding quotation.

No. 792.

Head of Menelaus.

HYDROS. *Cornelian.*

Homer, in the *Odyssey*, states that Menelaus, on his return home from the Trojan war, lived happily with Helen.

No. 793.

Minerva and Mars retired from the field of battle.

GNAIOS. *Cornelian.*

Minerva, after inspiring Diomedes with supernatural valour, induced Mars, who was favourable to the Trojans, to retire from the battle; so that Diomedes might remain uuquestioned possessor of the glories of the day.

"Struck with amaze and shame, the Trojan crew,
The sons, or slain, or fled, of Dares view,
When the blood-stain'd hand Minerva press'd
The god of battles, and this speech address'd:
' Stern power of war! by whom the mighty fall,
Who bathe in blood, and shake the lofty wall!
Let the brave chiefs their glorious toils divide;
And whose the conquest mighty Jove decide:

While we from interdicted fields retire,
Nor tempt the wrath of heaven's avenging sire.'
Her words allay'd the impetuous warrior's heat;
The god of arms and martial maid retreat:
Removed from fight, on Xanthus' flowery bounds
They sat, and listen'd to the dying sounds."

Iliad, book v.

No. 794.

Nestor, in his youth, escaping from a wild boar.

GNAIOS. *Cornelian.*

No. 795.

Head of Nestor.

PERGAMOS. *Cornelian.*

Nestor, son of Neleus and king of Pylos, is famous in ancient history for his bravery, for his longevity, and for his wisdom. He brought in his old age a large fleet and army to the aid of the Greeks in the Trojan war; and was one of the most eminent of the combined chiefs. After the Trojan war he returned safely home, and died in happiness and glory. The word Nestor is now become synonymous with venerable sage. It is said he saw three generations of men. The following extracts from Homer will be sufficient to convey a fair estimate of his character and great sagacity; and an outline of the most distinguished events in which he was engaged.

He endeavours to prevent dissension between Achilles and Agamemnon—

" To calm their passions with the words of age,
Slow from his seat arose the Pylian sage—
Experienced Nestor, in persuasion skill'd:
Words sweet as honey from his lips distill'd.
Two generations now had pass'd away,
Wise by his rules, and happy by his sway:
Two ages o'er his native realm he reign'd,
And now the example of the third remain'd.

All view'd with awe the venerable man;
Who thus with mild benevolence began:
' What shame, what woe is this to Greece! what joy
To Troy's proud monarch, and the friends of Troy!
That adverse gods commit to stern debate
The best, the bravest of the Grecian state.

Young as ye are, this youthful heat restrain,
Nor think your Nestor's years and wisdom vain.
A godlike race of heroes once I knew,
Such as no more these aged eyes shall view!
Lives there a chief to match Pirithous' fame,
Dryas the bold, or Ceneus' deathless name;
Theseus, endued with more than mortal might,
Or Polyphemus, like the gods in fight!
With these of old to toils of battle bred,
In early youth my hardy days I led—

Fired with the thirst which virtuous envy breeds,
And smit with love of honourable deeds.
Strongest of men, they pierced the mountain boar,
Ranged the wild deserts red with monsters' gore,
And from their hills the shaggy centaurs tore.
Yet these with soft, persuasive arts I sway'd:
When Nestor spoke, they listen'd and obey'd.
If in my youth e'en these esteem'd me wise—
Do you, young warriors, hear my age advise.' "
Iliad, book i.

The high estimation in which he was held may be judged of from the following extract from the speech of Agamemnon—

" To him the king: ' How much thy years excel
In arts of council, and in speaking well!
O would the gods, in love to Greece, decree
But ten such sages as they grant in thee!
Such wisdom soon should Priam's force destroy,
And soon should fall the haughty towers of Troy.' "
Iliad, book ii.

His good generalship may be judged of from the following passages—

" Among those counsels let not mine be vain—
In tribes and nations to divide thy train;
His separate troops let every leader call—
Each strengthen each—and all encourage all.
What chief, or soldier, of the numerous band,
Or bravely fights, or ill obeys command,
When thus distinct they war, shall soon be known,
And what the cause of Ilion not o'erthrown—
If fate resists, or if our arms are slow—
If gods above prevent, or man below."
Iliad, book ii.

" Old Nestor saw, and roused the warrior's rage:
' Thus, heroes!—thus, the vigorous combat wage!
No son of Mars descend, for servile gains,
To touch the booty while a foe remains.
Behold yon glittering host—your future spoil!
First gain the conquest—then reward the toil.' "
Iliad, book vi.

Agamemnon having proposed to the Greeks to return home, Diomede opposes this; and thus Nestor seconds him—

" Wise Nestor then his reverend figure rear'd ;
He spoke : the host in still attention heard.
' O truly great ! in whom the gods have join'd
Such strength of body with such force of mind ;
In conduct, as in courage, you excel—
Still first to act what you advise so well.
Those wholesome counsels which thy wisdom
   moves,
Applauding Greece with common voice approves.
Kings thou canst blame ; a bold but prudent
   youth ;
And blame e'en kings with praise, because with
   truth.
And yet those years that since thy birth have run,
Would hardly style thee Nestor's youngest son.
Then let me add what yet remains behind,
A thought unfinish'd in that generous mind :
Age bids me speak ; nor shall the advice I bring
Distaste the people, or offend the king :
Cursed is the man, and void of law and right—
Unworthy property—unworthy light—
Unfit for public rule, or private care—
That wretch—that monster, who delights in war!

Whose lust is murder, and whose horrid joy,
To tear his country, and his kind destroy !
This night refresh and fortify thy train ;
Between the trench and wall let guards remain.
Be that the duty of the young and bold ;
But thou, O king, to council call the old—
Great is thy sway, and weighty are thy cares ;
Thy high commands must spirit all our wars.
With Thracian wines recruit thy honour'd guests,
For happy councils flow from sober feasts.
Wise, weighty councils aid a state distress'd,
And such a monarch as can choose the best.
See ! what a blaze from hostile tents aspires—
How near our fleet approach the Trojan fires !
Who can, unmoved, behold the dreadful light,
What eye beholds them, and can close to-night ?
This dreadful interval determines all—
To-morrow Troy must flame, or Greece must
   fall !'
   Thus spoke the hoary sage : the rest obey—
Swift through the gates the guards direct their
   way."
                    Iliad, book ix.

In the council of the chiefs he proposes to send spies to the enemy's camp : a proposal
that proved of vital benefit to the Greeks.

" There sat the mournful kings ; when Neleus'
   son,
The council opening, in these words begun :
' Is there,' said he, ' a chief so greatly brave,
His life to hazard, and his country save ?
Lives there a man who, singly, dares to go
To yonder camp, or seize some straggling foe ?
Or, favour'd by the night, approach so near,
Their speech — their counsels — and designs to
   hear ?

If to besiege our navies they prepare,
Or Troy once more must be the seat of war ?
This could he learn, and to our peers recite,
And pass unharm'd the dangers of the night ;
What fame were his through all succeeding days,
While Phœbus shines, or men have tongues to
   praise ?
What gifts his grateful country would bestow ?
What must not Greece to her deliverer owe ?' "
                    Iliad, book ix.

He relates to Patroclus, when sent to learn certain events of the battle, some portions of
his former history.

" ' Can then the sons of Greece,' the sage rejoin'd,
' Excite compassion in Achilles' mind ?
Seeks he the sorrows of our host to know ?
This is not half the story of our woe.

Tell him not great Machaon bleeds alone,
Our bravest heroes in the navy groan ;
Ulysses, Agamemnon, Diomed,
And stern Eurypylus, already bleed.

But, ah! what flattering hopes I entertain!
Achilles heeds not, but derides our pain:
E'en till the flames consume our fleet he stays,
And waits the rising of the fatal blaze.
Chief after chief the raging foe destroys;
Calm he looks on, and every death enjoys.
Now the slow course of all-impairing time
Unstrings my nerves, and ends my manly prime.
Oh! had I still that strength my youth pos-
    sess'd,
When this bold arm th' Epeian powers op-
    press'd—
The bulls of Elis in glad triumph led,
And stretch'd the great Itymonæus dead!
Then from my fury fled the trembling swains,
And ours was all the plunder of the plains:
Fifty white flocks, full fifty herds of swine,
As many goats, as many lowing kine;
And thrice the number of unrivall'd steeds—
All teeming females, and of generous breeds.
These, as my first essay of arms, I won;
Old Neleus gloried in his conquering son.
Thus Elis forced, her long arrears restored,
And shares were parted to each Pylian lord.
The state of Pyle was sunk to last despair,
When the proud Elians first commenced the war;
For Neleus' sons Alcides' rage had slain;
Of twelve bold brothers I alone remain;
Oppress'd we arm'd; and now this conquest
    gain'd,
My sire three hundred chosen sheep obtain'd
(That large reprisal he might justly claim,
For prize defrauded, and insulted fame,
When Elis' monarch at the public course
Detain'd his chariot and victorious horse).
The rest the people shared; myself survey'd
The just partition, and due victims paid.
Three days were past, when Elis rose to war,
With many a courser and with many a car;
The sons of Actor at their army's head
(Young as they were) the vengeful squadrons
    led.
High on a rock fair Thryoëssa stands,
Our utmost frontier on the Pylian lands;

Not far the streams of famed Alphæus flow;
The stream they pass'd, and pitch'd their tents
    below.
Pallas, descending in the shades of night,
Alarms the Pylians, and commands the fight.
Each burns for fame, and swells with martial
    pride—
Myself the foremost; but my sire denied—
Fear'd for my youth, exposed to stern alarms—
And stopp'd my chariot, and detain'd my arms.
My sire denied in vain: on foot I fled
Amidst our chariots: for the goddess led.
Along fair Arene's delightful plain
Soft Minyas rolls his waters to the main.
There, horse and foot, the Pylian troops unite,
And, sheathed in arms, expect the dawning light.
Thence, ere the sun advanced his noonday flame,
To great Alphæus' sacred source we came.
There first to Jove our solemn rites were paid:
An untamed heifer pleased the blue-eyed maid;
A bull Alphæus; and a bull was slain
To the blue monarch of the watery main.
In arms we slept, beside the winding flood,
While round the town the fierce Epeians stood.
Soon as the sun, with all-revealing ray,
Flamed in the front of heaven, and gave the
    day,
Bright scenes of arms and works of war ap-
    pear;
The nations meet; there Pylos, Elis here.
The first who fell, beneath my javelin bled;
King Augias' son, and spouse of Agamede
(She that all simples' healing virtues knew,
And every herb that drinks the morning dew).
I seized his car—the van of battle led;
The Epeians saw—they trembled—and they fled.
The foe dispersed, their bravest warrior kill'd,
Fierce as a whirlwind now I swept the field:
Full fifty captive chariots graced my train;
Two chiefs from each fell breathless to the plain.
Then Actor's sons had died, but Neptune shrouds
The youthful heroes in a veil of clouds.
O'er heapy shields, and o'er the prostrate throng,
Collecting spoils, and slaughtering all along,

3 P

Through wide Buprasian fields we forced the foes,
Where o'er the vales the Olenian rocks arose;
Till Pallas stopp'd us where Alisium flows.
E'en there the hindmost of their rear I slay,
And the same arm that led concludes the day,
Then back to Pyle triumphant take my way.

There to high Jove were public thanks as-
     sign'd,
As first of gods; to Nestor, of mankind.
Such then I was, impell'd by youthful blood;
So proved my valour for my country's good.' "
                                        Iliad, book xi.

No. 796.

Machaon, wounded by Paris, borne off in the car of Nestor to the fleet.

POLYCLETES. *Sardonyx.*

" But Hector, from this scene of slaughter
     far,
Raged on the left, and ruled the tide of war :
Loud groans proclaim his progress through the
     plain,
And deep Scamander swells with heaps of slain.
There Nestor and Idomeneus oppose
The warrior's fury—there the battle glows—
There fierce on foot, or from the chariot's height,
His sword deforms the beauteous ranks of fight.
The spouse of Helen,* dealing darts around,
Had pierced Machaon with a distant wound :

In his right shoulder the broad shaft appear'd,
And trembling Greece for her physician fear'd.
To Nestor then Idomeneus begun :
  ' Glory of Greece, old Neleus' valiant son !
Ascend thy chariot, haste with speed away,
And great Machaon to the ships convey.
A wise physician, skill'd our wounds to heal,
Is more than armies to the public weal.'
Old Nestor mounts the seat : beside him rode
The wounded offspring of the healing god.
He lends the lash ; the steeds with sounding feet
Shake the dry field, and thunder toward the fleet."
                                        Iliad, book xi.

No. 797.

Interview of Ulysses and Helen in Troy.

APOLLONIDES. *Cornelian.*

According to Homer, Helen lived with Menelaus after the destruction of Troy. Tele-
machus, the son of Ulysses, in his wanderings in quest of his father, went to the court of
Menelaus, and was hospitably entertained. There Helen related this singular adventure.

" Meantime with genial joy to warm the soul,
Bright Helen mix'd a mirth-inspiring bowl ;
The bev'rage now prepar'd t' inspire the feast,
The circle thus the beauteous queen address'd :—

  ' Thron'd in omnipotence, supremest Jove
Tempers the fates of human race above ;
By the firm sanction of his sov'reign will,
Alternate are decreed our good and ill.

---

* Paris.

To feastful mirth be this white hour assigned,
And sweet discourse, the banquet of the mind.
Myself assisting in the social joy,
Will tell Ulysses' bold exploit in Troy:
Sole witness of the deed I now declare;
Speak you (who saw) his wonders in the war.'
  Seam'd o'er with wounds, which his own sabre
    gave,
In the vile habit of a village-slave,
The foe deceiv'd, he pass'd the tented plain,
In Troy to mingle with the hostile train.
In this attire secure from searching eyes,
Till haply piercing through the dark disguise,
The chief I challeng'd : he, whose practis'd wit
Knew all the serpent-mazes of deceit,
Eludes my search; but when his form I view'd
Fresh from the bath, with fragrant oils renew'd,
His limbs in military purple dress'd,
Each brightning grace the genuine Greek con-
  fess'd.

A previous pledge of sacred faith obtain'd,
Till he the lines and Argave fleet regain'd,
To keep his stay conceal'd ; the chief declar'd
The plans of war against the town prepar'd.
Exploring then the secrets of the state,
He learn'd what best might urge the Dardan
  fate :
And safe returning to the Grecian host,
Sent many a shade to Pluto's dreary coast.
Loud grief resounded through the tow'rs of Troy,
But my pleas'd bosom glow'd with secret joy :
For then with dire remorse, and conscious shame,
I view'd th' effects of that disastrous flame,
Which, kindled by th' imperious queen of love,
Constrain'd me from my native realm to rove :
And oft in bitterness of soul deplor'd
My absent daughter, and my dearer lord—
Admir'd among the first of human race,
For every gift of mind and manly grace.' "
                      Odyssey, book iv.

No. 798.

Minerva urging Ulysses to detain the Greeks.

PYRGOTELES. *Amethyst.*

Agamemnon, after the secession of Achilles, proposed to the Greeks (in order to sound their dispositions) to return home. They approved of the proposal; but are detained by the arts of Ulysses, who was urged to the measure by Minerva.

" His deep design unknown, the hosts ap-
  prove
Atrides' speech. The mighty numbers move.
So roll the billows to th' Icarian shore,
From east and south when winds begin to roar—
Burst their dark mansions in the clouds, and
  sweep
The whitening surface of the ruffled deep.
And as on corn when western gusts descend,
Before the blast the lofty harvests bend :
Thus o'er the field the moving host appears,
With nodding plumes and groves of waving
  spears.

The gathering murmur spreads, their trampling
  feet
Beat the loose sands, and thicken to the fleet.
With long-resounding cries they urge the train
To fit the ships, and launch into the main.
They toil—they sweat—thick clouds of dust arise—
The doubling clamours echo to the skies.
E'en then the Greeks had left the hostile plain,
And fate decreed the fall of Troy in vain.
  But Jove's imperial queen their flight survey'd,
And sighing thus bespoke the blue-eyed maid :
' Shall then the Grecians fly ! oh, dire disgrace !
And leave unpunish'd this perfidious race?

Shall Troy, shall Priam, and the adulterous
   spouse,
In peace enjoy the fruits of broken vows?
And bravest chiefs, in Helen's quarrel slain,
Lie unrevenged on yon detested plain?
No; let my Greeks, unmoved by vain alarms,
Once more refulgent shine in brazen arms.
Haste, goddess—haste! the flying host detain,
Nor let one sail be hoisted on the main.'
   Pallas obeys, and from Olympus' height
Swift to the ships precipitates her flight:
Ulysses, first in public cares, she found,
For prudent counsel like the gods renown'd;
Oppress'd with generous grief the hero stood,
Nor drew his sable vessels to the flood.
   ' And is it thus, divine Laertes' son!
Thus fly the Greeks!' the martial maid begun—
' Thus to their country bear their own disgrace,
And fame eternal leave to Priam's race?
Shall beauteous Helen still remain unfreed—
Still unrevenged a thousand heroes bleed?
Haste, generous Ithacus! prevent the shame—
Recall your armies, and your chiefs reclaim.
Your own resistless eloquence employ,
And to th' immortals trust the fall of Troy.'
   The voice divine confess'd the warlike maid;
Ulysses heard, nor uninspir'd obey'd.
Then meeting first Atrides, from his hand
Received th' imperial sceptre of command.
Thus grac'd, attention and respect to gain,
He runs—he flies through all the Grecian train:
Each prince of name, or chief in arms approved,
He fired with praise, or with persuasion moved.

' Warriors like you, with strength and wisdom
   bless'd,
By brave examples should confirm the rest.
The monarch's will not yet reveal'd appears;
He tries our courage, but resents our fears.
Th' unwary Greeks his fury may provoke;
Not thus the king in secret council spoke.
Jove loves our chief, from Jove his honour
   springs:
Beware! for dreadful is the wrath of kings.'
   But if a clamorous vile plebeian rose,
Him with reproof he check'd, or tamed with
   blows.
' Be still, thou slave, and to thy betters yield:
Unknown alike in council and in field!
Ye gods! what dastards would our hosts com-
   mand!
Swept to the war, the lumber of a land.
Be silent, wretch, and think not here allow'd
That worst of tyrants, an usurping crowd.
To one sole monarch Jove commits the sway;
His are the laws, and him let all obey.'
   With words like these the troops Ulysses ruled,
The loudest silenced and the fiercest cool'd.
Back to th' assembly roll the thronging train,
Desert the ships, and pour upon the plain.
Murmuring they move, as when old Ocean roars,
And heaves huge surges to the trembling shores:
The groaning banks are burst with bellowing
   sound,
The rocks remurmur, and the deeps rebound.
At length the tumult sinks, the noises cease,
And a still silence lulls the camp to peace."
                 Iliad, book ii.

No. 799.

Ulysses receiving the sceptre from Agamemnon.

APOLLONIDES.   *Cornelian.*

See preceding quotation.

No. 800.

Ulysses proceeding through the camp.

PYRGOTELES. *Amethyst.*

See preceding quotation.

No. 801.

Ulysses killing Socus, who had wounded him.

TEUCER. *Cornelian.*

" Now on the field Ulysses stands alone,
The Greeks all fled, the Trojans pouring on ;
But stands collected in himself and whole,
And questions thus his own unconquer'd soul :
' What farther subterfuge, what hopes remain ?
What shame inglorious, if I quit the plain !
What danger, singly if I stand the ground,
My friends all scatter'd, all the foes around !
Yet wherefore doubtful ? let this truth suffice—
The brave meets danger, and the coward flies :
To die or conquer proves a hero's heart ;
And knowing this, I know a soldier's part.'
    Such thoughts revolving in his careful breast,
Near, and more near, the shady cohorts press'd ;
These in the warrior their own fate enclose ;
And round him deep the steely circle grows.
So fares a boar whom all the troop surrounds
Of shouting huntsmen, and of clamorous hounds ;
He grinds his ivory tusks ; he foams with ire ;
His sanguine eyeballs glare with living fire ;
By these, by those, on every part is plied ;
And the red slaughter spreads on every side.
Pierced through the shoulder, first Deiopis fell ;
Next Ennomus and Thoön sunk to hell ;
Chersidamas, beneath the navel thrust,
Falls prone to earth, and grasps the bloody dust.
Charops, the son of Hippasus, was near ;
Ulysses reach'd him with the fatal spear ;
But to his aid his brother Socus flies—
Socus, the brave—the gen'rous—and the wise !

Near as he drew the warrior thus began :
    ' O great Ulysses, much-enduring man !
Not deeper skill'd in every martial sleight,
Than worn to toils, and active in the fight !
This day two brothers shall thy conquest grace,
And end at once the great Hippasian race,
Or thou beneath this lance must press the field.'
He said, and forceful pierced his spacious shield :
Through the strong brass the ringing javelin
        thrown,
Plough'd half his side, and bared it to the bone.
By Pallas' care, the spear, though deep infix'd,
Stopp'd short of life, nor with his entrails mix'd.
    The wound not mortal, wise Ulysses knew,
Then furious thus (but first some steps with-
        drew):
' Unhappy man ! whose death our hands shall
        grace !
Fate calls thee hence, and finish'd is thy race.
No longer check my conquests on the foe ;
But, pierced by this, to endless darkness go,
And add one spectre to the realms below !'
    He spoke ; while Socus, seized with sudden
        fright,
Trembling gave way, and turn'd his back to
        flight ;
Between his shoulders pierced the following dart,
And held its passage through the panting heart.
Wide in his breast appear'd the grisly wound ;
He falls ; his armour rings against the ground.

Then thus Ulysses, gazing on the slain:
' Famed son of Hippasus! there press the plain;
There ends thy narrow span assign'd by Fate—
Heaven owes Ulysses yet a longer date.
Ah, wretch! no father shall thy corpse compose,
Thy dying eyes no tender mother close;
But hungry birds shall tear those balls away,
And hovering vultures scream around their prey.
Me Greece shall honour, when I meet my doom,
With solemn funerals and a lasting tomb.'
Then raging with intolerable smart,
He writhes his body, and extracts the dart.
The dart a tide of spouting gore pursued,
And gladden'd Troy with sight of hostile blood.
Now troops on troops the fainting chief invade,
Forced he recedes, and loudly calls for aid.
Thrice to its pitch his lofty voice he rears;
The well-known voice thrice Menelaus hears:
Alarm'd, to Ajax Telamon he cried,
Who shares his labours, and defends his side:
' O friend! Ulysses' shouts invade my ear;
Distress'd he seems, and no assistance near.
Strong as he is, yet, one opposed to all,
Oppress'd by multitudes, the best may fall.

Greece, robb'd of him, must bid her host despair,
And feel a loss not ages can repair.'
Then, where the cry directs, his course he bends;
Great Ajax, like the god of war, attends.
The prudent chief in sore distress they found,
With bands of furious Trojans compass'd round.
As when some huntsman, with a flying spear,
From the blind thicket wounds a stately deer;
Down his cleft side while fresh the blood distils,
He bounds aloft, and scuds from hills to hills;
Till life's warm vapour issuing through the wound,
Wild mountain wolves the fainting beast surround;
Just as their jaws his prostrate limbs invade,
The lion rushes through the woodland shade—
The wolves, though hungry, scour dispersed away—
The lordly savage vindicates his prey.
Ulysses thus, unconquer'd by his pains,
A single warrior, half a host sustains;
But soon as Ajax heaves his tower-like shield,
The scatter'd crowds fly frighted o'er the field;
Atrides' arm the sinking hero stays,
And, sav'd from numbers, to his car conveys."

Iliad, book xi.

No. 802.

Ulysses led off wounded from the field by Menelaus, while Ajax protects him with his shield.

APOLLONIDES. *Cornelian.*

See preceding quotation.

No. 803.

Neptune encouraging Agamemnon.

CHROMIOS. *Cornelian.*

" The god of ocean (to inflame their rage)
Appears a warrior furrow'd o'er with age ;
Press'd in his own the general's hand he took,
And thus the venerable hero spoke :
' Atrides, lo ! with what disdainful eye
Achilles sees his country's forces fly ;
Blind, impious man ! whose anger is his guide,
Who glories in unutterable pride.
So may he perish, so may Jove disclaim
The wretch 'relentless, and o'erwhelm with shame!
But heaven forsakes not thee : o'er yonder sands
Soon shalt thou view the scatter'd Trojan bands

Fly diverse ; while proud kings and chiefs re-nown'd,
Driven heaps on heaps, with clouds involved around
Of rolling dust, their winged wheels employ
To hide their ignominious heads in Troy.'
He spoke, then rush'd amid the warrior-crew,
And sent his voice before him as he flew,
Loud as the shout encountering armies yield,
When twice ten thousand shake the labouring field :
Such was the voice, and such the thundering sound
Of him whose trident rends the solid ground.
Each Argive bosom beats to meet the fight,
And grisly war appears a pleasing sight."

Iliad, book xiv.

No. 804.

Neptune exciting the two Ajaces.

APOLLONIDES.   *Cornelian.*

" But Neptune rising from the seas profound—
The god whose earthquakes rock the solid ground,
Now wears a mortal form ; like Calchas seen—
Such his loud voice, and such his manly mien :
His shouts incessant every Greek inspire,
But most th' Ajaces, adding fire to fire.
' 'Tis yours, O warriors, all our hopes to raise :
Oh, recollect your ancient worth and praise !
'Tis yours to save us, if you cease to fear :
Flight, more than shameful, is destructive here.
On other works though Troy with fury fall,
And pour her armies o'er our batter'd wall ;
There Greece has strength : but this—this part o'erthrown,
Her strength were vain : I dread for you alone.
Here Hector rages like the force of fire,
Vaunts of his gods, and calls high Jove his sire.
If yet some heavenly power your breast excite,
Breathe in your hearts, and string your arms to fight,
Greece yet may live, her threaten'd fleet remain ;
And Hector's force, and Jove's own aid, be vain.'

Then with his sceptre, that the deep controls,
He touch'd the chiefs, and steel'd their manly souls :
Strength not their own the touch divine imparts—
Prompts their light limbs, and swells their daring hearts.
Then, as a falcon from the rocky height,
Her quarry seen, impetuous at the sight
Forth-springing, instant darts herself from high—
Shoots on the wing, and skims along the sky :
Such, and so swift, the power of Ocean flew—
The wide horizon shut him from their view.
Th' inspiring god, Oïleus' active son
Perceived the first, and thus to Telamon :
' Some god, my friend, some god in human form
Favouring descends, and wills to stand the storm.
Not Calchas this, the venerable seer ;
Short as he turn'd, I saw the power appear :
I mark'd his parting, and the steps he trod ;
His own bright evidence reveals a god.
E'en now some energy divine I share,
And seem to walk on wings, and tread in air !'

‘ With equal ardour,’ Telamon returns,
‘ My soul is kindled, and my bosom burns :
New rising spirits all my force alarm—
Lift each impatient limb, and brace my arm.

This ready arm, unthinking, shakes the dart ;
The blood pours back, and fortifies my heart ;
Singly, methinks, yon towering chief I meet,
And stretch the dreadful Hector at my feet.’ ”

No. 805.

Iris sent by Juno to the Genius of Sleep, to announce to Alcyone the death of her shipwrecked husband, Ceyx.

GNAIOS.　*Cornelian.*

“ Then Iris thus bespoke : ‘ Thou faithful maid,
By whom thy queen's commands are well con-
　vey'd,
Haste to the house of sleep, and bid the god
Who rules the night by visions with a nod,
Prepare a dream, in figure and in form
Resembling him who perish'd in the storm ;
This form before Alcyone present,
To make her certain of the sad event.'
Indu'd with robes of various hue she flies,
And, flying, draws an arch (a segment of the
　skies) ;
Then leaves her bending bow, and from the steep
Descends, to search the silent house of sleep.”

THE HOUSE OF SLEEP.

“ Near the Cymmerians, in his dark abode,
Deep in a cavern dwells the drowsy god ;
Whose gloomy mansion nor the rising sun,
Nor setting, visits ; nor the lightsome noon ;
But lazy vapours round the region fly—
Perpetual twilight and a doubtful sky :
No crowing cock does there his wings display,
Nor with his horny bill provoke the day—
Nor watchful dogs, nor the more wakeful geese,
Disturb with nightly noise the sacred peace—
Nor beast of nature, nor the tame are nigh—
Nor trees with tempests rock'd, nor human cry ;
But safe repose, without an air of breath,
Dwells here, and a dumb quiet next to death !

An arm of Lethe, with a gentle flow
Arising upwards from the rock below,
The palace moats, and o'er the pebbles creeps,
And with soft murmurs calls the coming sleeps.
Around its entry nodding poppies grow,
And all cool simples that sweet rest bestow :
Night from the plants their sleepy virtue drains,
And, passing, sheds it on the silent plains :
No door there was th' unguarded house to keep,
On creaking hinges turu'd to break his sleep.
　But in the gloomy court was rais'd a bed,
Stuff'd with black plumes, and on an ebon-sted :
Black was the cov'ring too, where lay the god,
And slept supine, his limbs displayed abroad :
About his head fantastic visions fly,
Which various images of things supply,
And mock their forms ; the leaves on trees not
　more,
Nor bearded ears in fields, nor sands upon the
　shore.
　The virgin ent'ring bright, indulg'd the day
To the brown cave, and brush'd the dreams away :
The god, disturb'd with this new glare of light
Cast sudden on his face, unseal'd his sight,
And rais'd his tardy head, which sunk again,
And, sinking, on his bosom knock'd his chin ;
At length shook off himself, and ask'd the dame,
(And, asking, yawu'd) for what intent she came.
　To whom the goddess thus : ‘ O sacred rest,
Sweet pleasing sleep, of all the pow'rs the best !

,O peace of mind—repairer of decay—
Whose balms renew the limbs to labours of the day,
Care shuns thy soft approach, and sullen flies
    away!
Adorn a dream, expressing human form,
The shape of him who suffer'd in the storm,
And send it flitting to the Trachin court,
The wreck of wretched Ceyx to report:
Before his queen bid the pale spectre stand,
Who begs a vain relief at Juno's hand.'
She said, and scarce awake her eyes could keep,
Unable to support the fumes of sleep;
But fled, returning by the way she went,
And swerv'd along her bow with swift ascent.

    The god, uneasy till he slept again,
Resolv'd at once to rid himself of pain;
And, though against his custom, call'd aloud,
Exciting Morpheus from the sleepy crowd:
Morpheus, of all his num'rous train, express'd
The shape of man and imitated best;
The walk—the words—the gesture could supply—
The habit mimic, and the mien belie—
Plays well; but all his action is confin'd,
Extending not beyond our human kind.
Another, birds and beasts and dragons apes,
And dreadful images, and monster-shapes:
This demon, Icelos, in heaven's high hall,
The gods have nam'd; but men Phobetor call.

A third is Phantasus, whose actions roll
On meaner thoughts, and things devoid of soul;
Earth, fruits, and flow'rs he represents in dreams,
And solid rocks unmov'd, and running streams.
These three to kings and chiefs their scenes dis-
    play,
The rest before th' ignoble commons play.
Of these the chosen Morpheus is dispatch'd;
Which done, the lazy monarch, over-watch'd,
Down from his propping elbow drops his head,
Dissolv'd in sleep, and shrinks within his bed.
Darkling the demon glides, for flight prepar'd,
So soft, that scarce his fanning wings are heard.
To Trachin, swift as thought, the flitting shade
Through air his momentary journey made:
Then lays aside the steerage of his wings,
Forsakes his proper form—assumes the king's;
And pale as death, despoil'd of his array,
Into the queen's apartment takes his way,
And stands before the bed at dawn of day:
Unmov'd his eyes, and wet his beard appears;
And shedding vain, but seeming real, tears;
The briny waters dropping from his hairs.
Then staring on her with a ghastly look
And hollow voice, he thus the queen bespoke:—
'Know'st thou not me? Not yet, unhappy wife!
Or are my features perish'd with my life?'"

                    OVID, *Met*. xi.

No. 806.

Juno persuading the Genius of Sleep to shed his influence over Jupiter.

ADMON. *Sardonyx.*

" Meantime Saturnia from Olympus' brow,
High-throned in gold, beheld the fields below;
With joy the glorious conflict she survey'd,
Where her great brother gave the Grecians aid.
But placed aloft, on Ida's shady height
She sees her Jove, and trembles at the sight.
Jove to deceive, what method shall she try,
What arts to blind his all-beholding eye?

At length she trusts her power; resolved to prove
The old, yet still successful, cheat of love—
Against his wisdom to oppose her charms,
And lull the lord of thunders in her arms.
    Swift to her bright apartment she repairs,
Sacred to dress and beauty's pleasing cares:
With skill divine had Vulcan form'd the bower,
Safe from access of each intruding power.

3 Q

Touch'd with her secret key, the doors unfold ;
Self-closed, behind her shut the valves of gold.
Here first she bathes, and round her body pours
Soft oils of fragrance, and ambrosial showers.

  .   .   .   .   .

Forth from the dome th' imperial goddess moves,
And calls the mother of the Smiles and Loves.
  ' How long,' to Venus thus apart she cried,
' Shall human strife celestial minds divide ?
Ah ! yet will Venus aid Saturnia's joy,
And set aside the cause of Greece and Troy ?'
  ' Let heaven's dread empress,' Cytheræa said,
' Speak her request, and deem her will obey'd.'
    ' Then grant me,' said the queen, ' those con-
      quering charms—
That power which mortals and immortals warms—
That love which melts mankind in fierce desires,
And burns the sons of heaven with sacred fires !'

  .   .   .   .   .

She said. With awe divine the queen of love
Obey'd the sister and the wife of Jove ;
And from her fragrant breast the zone unbraced,
With various skill and high embroidery graced.
In this was every art and every charm,
To win the wisest and the coldest warm :
Fond love—the gentle vow—the gay desire—
The kind deceit—the still-reviving fire—
Persuasive speech—and more persuasive sighs—
Silence that spoke, and eloquence of eyes.
This on her hand the Cyprian goddess laid :
' Take this, and with it all thy wish,' she said.
With smiles she took the charm, and, smiling,
  press'd
The powerful cestus to her snowy breast.
  Then Venus to the courts of Jove withdrew ;
Whilst from Olympus pleased Saturnia flew.
O'er high Pieria thence her course she bore—
O'er fair Emathia's ever-pleasing shore—
O'er Hæmus' hills with snows eternal crown'd ;
Nor once her flying foot approach'd the ground.
Then taking wing from Athos' lofty steep,
She speeds to Lemnos o'er the rolling deep,
And seeks the cave of Death's half-brother, Sleep.

  ' Sweet, pleasing Sleep !' Saturnia thus began,
' Who spread'st thy empire o'er each god and man :
If e'er obsequious to thy Juno's will,
O Power of Slumbers ! hear, and favour still ;
Shed thy soft dews on Jove's immortal eyes,
While sunk in love's entrancing joys he lies.
A splendid footstool, and a throne, that shine
With gold unfading, Somnus, shall be thine—
The work of Vulcan—to indulge thy ease,
When wine and feasts thy golden humours please.'

  .   .   .   .

Then, swift as wind, o'er Lemnos' smoky isle
They wing their way, and Imbrus' seabeat soil ;
Through air unseen, involved in darkness, glide,
And light on Lectos, on the point of Ide
(Mother of savages, whose echoing hills
Are heard resounding with a hundred rills) ;
Fair Ida trembles underneath the god ;
Hush'd are her mountains, and her forests nod.

  .   .   .   .

To Ida's top successful Juno flies ;
Great Jove surveys her with desiring eyes :
The god whose lightning sets the heavens on fire,
Through all his bosom feels the fierce desire ;
Fierce as when first by stealth he seized her
  charms,
Mix'd with her soul, and melted in her arms ;
Fix'd on her eyes he fed his eager look,
Then press'd her hand, and thus with transport
  spoke.

  .   .   .   .

Gazing he spoke, and kindling at the view,
His eager arms around the goddess threw.
Glad earth perceives, and from her bosom pours
Unbidden herbs and voluntary flowers :
Thick new-born violets a soft carpet spread,
And clustering lotos swell'd the rising bed,
And sudden hyacinths the turf bestrow,
And flamy crocus made the mountain glow.
There golden clouds conceal'd the heavenly pair,
Steep'd in soft joys, and circumfused with air—
Celestial dews, descending o'er the ground,
Perfume the mount, and breathe ambrosia round."
                Iliad, book xiv.

No. 807.

Jupiter, Juno, and the Genius of Sleep.

CHROMIOS. *Cornelian.*

See last quotation.

No. 808.

The Genius of Sleep conveying Juno's message to Neptune.

GNAIOS. *Cornelian.*

" Now to the navy borne on silent wings,
To Neptune's ear soft Sleep his message brings;
Beside him, sudden, unperceived he stood,
And thus with gentle words address'd the god :
' Now, Neptune ! now the important hour employ,
To check awhile the haughty hopes of Troy :
While Jove yet rests, while yet my vapours shed
The golden vision round his sacred head ;
For Juno's love, and Somnus' pleasing ties,
Have closed those awful and eternal eyes.' "

Iliad, book xiv.

No. 809.

Neptune, in compliance with the advice of Juno, urging the Grecian chiefs to renew the battle.

APOLLONIDES. *Chrysolite.*

" Neptune, with zeal increased, renews his care,
And towering in the foremost rank of war,
Indignant thus : ' O once of martial fame !
O Greeks ! if yet ye can deserve the name !
This half-recover'd day shall Troy obtain ?
Shall Hector thunder at your ships again ?
Lo, still he vaunts, and threats the fleet with fires,
While stern Achilles in his wrath retires.
One hero's loss too tamely you deplore :
Be still yourselves, and we shall need no more.
Oh, yet, if glory any bosom warms,
Brace on your firmest helms, and stand to arms— His strongest spear each valiant Grecian wield—
Each valiant Grecian seize his broadest shield ;
Let to the weak the lighter arms belong,
The pond'rous targe be wielded by the strong.
Thus arm'd, not Hector shall our presence stay—
Myself, ye Greeks ! myself will lead the way.'
The troops assent ; their martial arms they change,
The busy chiefs their banded legions range.
The kings, though wounded, and oppress'd with pain,
With helpful hands themselves assist the train.

The strong and cumb'rous arms the valiant wield,
The weaker warrior takes a lighter shield.
Thus sheath'd in shining brass, in bright array
The legions march, and Neptune leads the way:

His brandish'd falchion flames before their eyes,
Like lightning flashing through the frighted skies.
Clad in his might, the earth-shaking pow'r appears—
Pale mortals tremble, and confess their fears."

Iliad, book xiv.

No. 810.

Iris delivering to Neptune the commands of Jupiter, to desist from aiding the Greeks.

PYRGOTELES.   *Cornelian.*

When Jupiter awoke, he was incensed that Neptune was aiding the Greeks; and despatched Iris to prevent him.   The following extract from the *Iliad* (book xv.) fully explains this and the two subsequent representations.

" The Almighty spoke; the goddess wing'd her flight
To sacred Ilion from th' Idean height,
Swift as the rattling hail or fleecy snows
Drive through the skies when Boreas fiercely blows;
So from the clouds descending Iris falls,
And to blue Neptune thus the goddess calls:
' Attend the mandate of the sire above;
In me behold the messenger of Jove.
He bids thee from forbidden wars repair
To thy own deeps, or to the fields of air.
This if refused, he bids thee timely weigh
His elder birthright, and superior sway.
How shall thy rashness stand the dire alarms,
If heaven's omnipotence descend in arms?
Striv'st thou with him by whom all power is given?
And art thou equal to the lord of heaven?'
' What means the haughty sovereign of the skies?'
The king of ocean, thus incensed, replies—
' Rule as he will his portion'd realms on high,
No vassal god, nor of his train, am I.
Three brother-deities from Saturn came,
And ancient Rhea, earth's immortal dame:

Assign'd by lot, our triple rule we know:
Infernal Pluto sways the shades below;
O'er the wide clouds, and o'er the starry plain,
Ethereal Jove extends his high domain;
My court beneath the hoary waves I keep,
And hush the roarings of the sacred deep.
Olympus and this earth in common lie—
What claim has here the tyrant of the sky?
Far in the distant clouds let him control,
And awe the younger brothers of the pole;
There to his children his commands be given—
The trembling—servile—second race of heaven.'
' And must I then,' said she, ' O sire of floods!
Bear this fierce answer to the king of gods?
Correct it yet, and change thy rash intent;
A noble mind disdains not to repent.
To elder brothers guardian-fiends are given,
To scourge the wretch insulting them and heaven.'
' Great is the profit,' thus the god rejoin'd,
' When ministers are bless'd with prudent mind:
Warn'd by thy words, to powerful Jove I yield,
And quit, though angry, the contended field.
Not but his threats with justice I disclaim,
The same our honours, and our birth the same.

If yet—forgetful of his promise given
To Hermes, Pallas, and the queen of heaven—
To favour Ilion, that perfidious place,
He breaks his faith with half th' ethereal race;
Give him to know, unless the Grecian train
Lay yon proud structures level with the plain,
Howe'er th' offence by other gods be past,
The wrath of Neptune shall for ever last.'
 Thus speaking, furious from the field he
  strode,
And plunged into the bosom of the flood.
The lord of thunders from his lofty height
Beheld, and thus bespoke the Source of Light:

' Behold ! the god whose liquid arms are hurl'd
Around the globe, whose earthquakes rock the
 world ;
Desists at length his rebel war to wage,
Seeks his own seas, and trembles at our rage ;
Else had my wrath, heaven's thrones all shaking
 round,
Burn'd to the bottom of the seas profound ;
And all the gods that round old Saturn dwell,
Had heard the thunders to the deeps of hell,
Well was the crime and well the vengeance
 spared :
E'en power immense had found such battle hard.' "

No. 811.

Neptune, complying with the orders of Jupiter given by Iris, retires
from the battle into the sea.

PYRGOTELES. *Amethyst.*

No. 812.

The same subject.

CHROMIOS. *Sardonyx.*

See the concluding part of the last quotation.

No. 813.

Jupiter giving Apollo his ægis, and commanding him to assist Hector
and the Trojans.

POLYCLETES. *Sardonyx.*

Jupiter gave this commission to Apollo at the time when he sent the command to Neptune.
The following quotation from the *Iliad* (book xv.) fully explains this and the two subsequent
representations.

" ' Go thou, my son! the trembling Greeks alarm,
Shake my broad ægis on thy active arm ;
Be god-like Hector thy peculiar care,
Swell his bold heart, and urge his strength to war :
Let Ilion conquer till th' Achaian train
Fly to their ships and Hellespont again :
Then Greece shall breathe from toils.' The godhead said :
His will divine the son of Jove obey'd.
Not half so swift the sailing falcon flies,
That drives a turtle through the liquid skies,
As Phœbus, shooting from th' Idæan brow,
Glides down the mountain to the plain below.
There Hector seated by the stream he sees,
His sense returning with the coming breeze;
Again his pulses beat—his spirits rise ;
Again his lov'd companions meet his eyes ;
Jove thinking of his pains, they pass'd away :
To whom the god who gives the golden day—
' Why sits great Hector from the field so far,
What grief, what wound, withholds him from the war?'
  The fainting hero, as the vision bright
Stood shining o'er him, half unseal'd his sight :
' What blest immortal, with commanding breath,
Thus wakens Hector from the sleep of death?
Has fame not told how, while my trusty sword
Bath'd Greece in slaughter, and her battle gor'd,
The mighty Ajax with a deadly blow
Had almost sunk me to the shades below?—
E'en yet, methinks, the gliding ghosts I spy,
And hell's black horrors swim before my eye.'
  To him Apollo : ' Be no more dismay'd ;
See, and be strong ! the Thund'rer sends thee aid.
Behold ! thy Phœbus shall his arms employ—
Phœbus, propitious still to thee and Troy.
Inspire thy warriors, then, with manly force,
And to the ships impel thy num'rous horse :
E'en I will make thy fiery coursers' way,
And drive the Grecians headlong to the sea.'
  Thus to bold Hector spoke the son of Jove,
And breath'd immortal ardour from above.

As when the pamper'd steed, the reins unbound,
Breaks from his stall, and pours along the ground;
With ample strokes he rushes to the flood,
To bathe his sides, and cool his fiery blood.
His head, now freed, he tosses to the skies;
His mane dishevell'd o'er his shoulders flies ;
He snuffs the females in the well-known plain,
And springs, exulting, to his fields again.
Urged by the voice divine, thus Hector flew,
Full of the god, and all his hosts pursue.
As when the force of men and dogs combin'd,
Invade the mountain-goat, or branching hind;
Far from the hunter's rage secure they lie
Close in the rock, not fated yet to die ;
When, lo ! a lion shoots across the way !
They fly—at once the chasers and the prey.
So Greece, that late in conqu'ring troops pursu'd,
And mark'd their progress through the ranks in blood,
Soon as they see the furious chief appear,
Forget to vanquish, and consent to fear.
  Thoas with grief observ'd his dreadful course—
Thoas, the bravest of th' Ætolian force :
Skill'd to direct the jav'lin's distant flight,
And bold to combat in the standing fight ;
Nor more in councils fam'd for solid sense,
Than winning words and heav'nly eloquence.
' Gods ! what portent,' he cried, ' these eyes invades ?
Lo ! Hector rises from the Stygian shades !
We saw him late by thund'ring Ajax kill'd—
What god restores him to the frighted field,
And, not content that half of Greece lie slain,
Pours new destruction on her sons again ?
He comes not, Jove ! without thy pow'rful will :
Lo ! still he lives, pursues, and conquers still !
Yet hear my counsel, and his worst withstand ;
The Greeks' main body to the fleet command ;
But let the few whom brisker spirits warm,
Stand the first onset, and provoke the storm.
Thus point your arms, and when such foes appear,
Fierce as he is, let Hector learn to fear.'
  The warrior spoke, the list'ning Greeks obey,
Thick'ning their ranks, and form a deep array ;

Each Ajax, Teucer, Merion, gave command,
The valiant leader of the Cretan band,
And Mars-like Meges : these the chiefs excite,
Approach the foe, and meet the coming fight.
Behind unnumber'd multitudes attend,
To flank the navy, and the shores defend.
Full on the front the pressing Trojans bear,
And Hector first came towering to the war.
Phœbus himself the rushing battle led—
A veil of clouds involved his radiant head—
High held before him, Jove's enormous shield
Portentous shone, and shaded all the field ;
Vulcan to Jove th' immortal gift consign'd,
To scatter hosts and terrify mankind.
The Greeks expect the shock, the clamours rise
From different parts, and mingle in the skies.

Dire was the hiss of darts by heroes flung,
And arrows leaping from the bowstring sung ;
These drink the life of generous warriors slain,
Those guiltless fall, and thirst for blood in vain.
As long as Phœbus bore unmoved the shield,
Sat doubtful Conquest hovering o'er the field ;
But when aloft he shakes it in the skies—
Shouts in their ears, and lightens in their eyes,
Deep horror seizes every Grecian breast—
Their force is humbled, and their fear confess'd.
So flies a herd of oxen, scatter'd wide,
No swain to guard them, and no day to guide,
When two fell lions from the mountain come,
And spread the carnage through the shady gloom.
Impending Phœbus pours around them fear,
And Troy and Hector thunder in the rear."

No. 814.

Apollo rousing Hector to return to the battle.

DIOSCORIDES. *Cornelian.*

See last quotation.

No. 815.

Apollo and Hector rushing to the battle.

DIOSCORIDES. *Cornelian.*

See last quotation.

No. 816.

Apollo and Hector dashing through the Grecian rampart.

APOLLONIDES. *Cornelian.*

" The Greeks, dismay'd, confus'd, disperse or
    fall ;
Some seek the trench—some skulk behind the
    wall ;

While these fly trembling, others pant for breath,
And o'er the slaughter stalks gigantic death.
On rush'd bold Hector, gloomy as the night—
Forbids to plunder—animates the fight—

Points to the fleet : ' For, by the gods, who flies—
Who dares but linger, by this hand he dies ;
No weeping sister his cold eye shall close,
No friendly hand his fun'ral pyre compose.
Who stops to plunder, in this signal hour,
The birds shall tear him, and the dogs devour.'

　　.　　　　.　　　　.　　　　.　　　　.

Apollo, planted at the trench's bound,
Push'd at the bank : down sunk th' enormous
　　mound :
Roll'd in the ditch the heapy ruin lay ;
A sudden road ! a long and ample way !
O'er the dread fosse (a late-impervious space)
Now steeds, and men, and cars, tumultuous pass.
The wond'ring crowds the downward level trod :
Before them flam'd the shield, and march'd the god.

Then with his hand he shook the mighty wall :
And, lo ! the turrets nod, the bulwarks fall !
Easy, as when ashore an infant stands,
And draws imagin'd houses in the sands ;
The sportive wanton, pleas'd with some new
　　play,
Sweeps the slight works and fashion'd domes
　　away :
Thus vanish'd at thy touch the tow'rs and walls ;
The toil of thousands in a moment falls !
The Grecians gaze around with wild despair,
Confus'd, and weary all the pow'rs with pray'r ;
Exhort their men with praises—threats—com-
　　mands ;
And urge the gods with voices—eyes—and
　　hands."

Iliad, book xv.

No. 817.

Minerva restraining Mars from disobeying the prohibitory command of Jupiter.

APOLLONIDES.　*Cornelian.*

　　Jupiter, after awaking, and finding that his command, that none of the deities should interfere in the battle, was disregarded, was incensed against Juno, whom he commands to return to heaven. Juno, at the assembly of the gods, while professing great submission to the high authority of Jupiter, artfully inflames the party among the gods favourable to the Greeks, especially Mars.

" Thus she proceeds : ' Attend, ye powers
　　above !
But know, 'tis madness to contest with Jove—
Supreme he sits ; and sees in pride of sway
Your vassal godheads grudgingly obey—
Fierce in the majesty of power controls—
Shakes all the thrones of heaven, and bends the
　　poles.
Submit, immortals ! all he wills obey ;
And thou, great Mars, begin and shew the way.
Behold Ascalaphus ! behold him die ;
But dare not murmur—dare not vent a sigh ;

Thy own loved boasted offspring lies o'erthrown,
If that loved boasted offspring be thy own.'
　　Stern Mars, with anguish for his slaughter'd
　　son,
Smote his rebelling breast, and fierce begun :
' Thus then, immortals ! thus shall Mars obey—
Forgive me, gods, and yield my vengeance way—
Descending first to yon forbidden plain,
The god of battles dares avenge the slain—
Dares, though the thunder bursting o'er my
　　head
Should hurl me blazing on those heaps of dead !'

With that he gives command to Fear and
    Flight,
To join his rapid coursers for the fight:
Then, grim in arms, with hasty vengeance flies—
Arms that reflect a radiance through the skies.
And now had Jove, by bold rebellion driven,
Discharg'd his wrath on half the host of heaven:
But Pallas, springing through the bright abode,
Starts from her azure throne to calm the god.
Struck for th' immortal race with timely fear,
From frantic Mars she snatch'd the shield and
    spear;
Then the huge helmet lifting from his head,
Thus to th' impetuous homicide she said:
  ' By what wild passion, furious! art thou
    toss'd?
Striv'st thou with Jove?—thou art already lost.

Shall not the Thunderer's dread command re-
    strain?
And was imperial Juno heard in vain?
Back to the skies wouldst thou with shame be
    driven,
And in thy guilt involve the host of heaven?
Ilion and Greece no more should Jove engage;
The skies would yield an ampler scene of rage,
Guilty and guiltless find an equal fate,
And one vast ruin whelm th' Olympian state.
Cease then thy offspring's death unjust to call;
Heroes as great have died, and yet shall fall.
Why should heav'n's law with foolish man
    comply,
Exempted from the race ordain'd to die?'
  This menace fix'd the warrior to his throne;
Sullen he sat, and curb'd the rising groan."

No. 818.

Thetis transforming herself into a tigress, to avoid Peleus.

DIOSCORIDES. *Cornelian.*

Thetis was a sea-nymph of surpassing beauty. Jupiter resolved to possess her; but the
Fates having declared that her child would surpass his father, he resigned her to Peleus.
She at first rejected the suit of Peleus, and endeavoured to elude him by assuming various
forms; such as that of a bird—a tigress—a tree—a serpent—a flame of fire. The simple ex-
planation of all which is, that she, at different times, exhibited the swiftness of a bird—the fury
of a tigress—the insensibility of a tree—the cunning of a serpent—the violence of fire. Peleus
at last succeeded, and had by her Achilles. The story is thus related by Ovid (*Met.* xi.):—

THE STORY OF THETIS AND PELEUS, &c.

" For Proteus thus to virgin Thetis said:
' Fair goddess of the waves, consent to wed,
And take some sprightly lover to your bed.
A son you'll have, the terror of the field,
To whom in fame and pow'r his sire shall yield.'
  Jove, who ador'd the nymph with boundless
    love,
Did from his breast the dang'rous flame remove:
He knew the fates, nor cared to raise up one
Whose fame and greatness should eclipse his own.

On happy Peleus he bestow'd her charms,
And bless'd his grandson in the goddess' arms.
  A silent creek Thessalia's coast can shew;
Two arms project, and shape it like a bow;
'Twould make a bay, but the transparent tide
Does scarce the yellow-gravell'd bottom hide;
For the quick eye may through the liquid wave
A firm unweedy level beach perceive.
A grove of fragrant myrtle near it grows,
Whose boughs, though thick, a beauteous grot
    disclose;

3 R

The well-wrought fabric, to discerning eyes,
Rather by art than nature seems to rise.
A bridled dolphin oft fair Thetis bore
To this her lov'd retreat, her fav'rite shore.
Here Peleus seiz'd her, slumb'ring while she lay,
And urg'd his suit with all that love could say :
But when he found her obstinately coy,
Resolv'd to force her, and command the joy.
The nymph o'erpowered, to art for succour flies,
And various shapes the eager youth surprise :
A bird she seems, but plies her wings in vain ;
His hands the fleeting substance still detain :
A branchy tree high in the air she grew ;
About its bark his nimble arms he threw :
A tigress next, she glares with flaming eyes ;
The frighten'd lover quits his hold, and flies.
The sea-gods he with sacred rites adores,
Then a libation on the ocean pours ;
While the fat entrails crackle in the fire,
And sheets of smoke in sweet perfume aspire :
Till Proteus, rising from his oozy bed,
Thus to the poor desponding lover said :

' No more in anxious thoughts your mind employ,
For yet you shall possess the dear expected joy.
You must once more th' unweary nymph surprise,
As in her cooly grot she slumb'ring lies ;
Then bind her fast with unrelenting hands,
And strain her tender limbs with knotted bands.
Still hold her under ev'ry different shape,
Till, tir'd, she tries no longer to escape.'
Thus he : then sunk beneath the glassy flood,
And broken accents flutter'd where he stood.
   Bright Sol had almost now his journey done,
And down the steepy western convex run ;
When the fair Nereid left the briny wave,
And, as she us'd, retreated to her cave.
He scarce had bound her fast, when she arose,
And into various shapes her body throws :
She went to move her arms, and found them tied ;
Then with a sigh, ' Some god assists ye,' cried,
And in a proper shape stood blushing by his side.
About her waist his longing arms he flung,
From which embrace the great Achilles sprung."

No. 819.

Thetis transformed to a tree.

PYRGOTELES.   *Cornelian.*

See preceding explanation.

No. 820.

The same subject.

PYRGOTELES.   *Amethyst.*

See preceding quotation.

No. 821.

Thetis transformed into a serpent.

APOLLONIDES.   *Sardonyx.*

See preceding quotation.

No. 822.

Thetis transformed into a flame.

APOLLONIDES.   *Cornelian.*

See preceding explanation.

No. 823.

The same subject.

GNAIOS.   *Cornelian.*

No. 824.

Peleus making an offering to Proteus, to obtain the hand of Thetis.

CHROMIOS.   *Cornelian.*

See preceding quotation.

No. 825.

Thetis, Peleus, and the centaur Chiron.

GNAIOS.   *Cornelian.*

Chiron the centaur, so famous for his skill in medicine, music, and archery, was the maternal grandfather of Peleus, and aided him in securing Thetis. Catullus, in his description of the marriage-feast of Peleus and Thetis, represents him as bringing the first offerings:

" Chiron the first, when all the dome was still,
His rural offering bore from Pelion's hill.

Whatever flowers the meads produce, whate'er
Thessalia's broad and fertile mountains bear,
Whatever blossom some pure streamlet near
The tepid breezes of Favonius rear,
He brought in chaplets of promiscuous bloom ;
And all the palace breathed their glad perfume."

And Valerius Flaccus represents him as seated by Peleus, celebrating the nuptials with his lyre.

No. 826.

Peleus conducted by Cupid and Hymen to Thetis, in her grotto.

CHROMIOS. *Cornelian.*

No. 827.

Thetis immersing Achilles in the Styx.

APOLLONIDES. *Cornelian.*

Thetis adopted various expedients to render Achilles invulnerable: one was by immersing him in the infernal river Styx. The heel by which she held him was the only part of him that was vulnerable.

No. 828.

Thetis exposing Achilles to the flames.

PYRGOTELES. *Sardonyx.*

This story is thus mentioned by Apollonius (*Argonautics*, book iv.)—

" O'er flaming lamps, amid the nightly gloom,
Her infant's mortal flesh she would consume ;
Immortal being to the babe to give,
And bid him free from age and sickness live.
She pour'd upon his little limbs, by day,
Ambrosial streams preventive of decay.
As, starting from his couch, th' indignant sire
Beheld his darling panting in the fire,
Untaught to read the dictates of the sky,
Forward he rush'd, with a tremendous cry.
The goddess heard, with rage and grief profound,
And cast her infant screaming to the ground.
Like fading airy visions forth she pass'd,
With motion swifter than the northern blast ;
And wrathful plung'd beneath the briny foam,
Divorc'd from Peleus, and estrang'd from home."

No. 829.

Peleus committing young Achilles to the care of the centaur Chiron.

CHROMIOS. *Sardonyx.*

Chiron taught Achilles medicine, music, and archery—

> " But thou, Patroclus! act a friendly part,
> Lead to my ships, and draw this deadly dart—
> With lukewarm water wash the gore away—
> With healing balms the raging smart allay,
> Such as sage Chiron, sire of pharmacy,
> Once taught Achilles, and Achilles thee."
>
> *Iliad*, book xi.

When the ambassadors from Agamemnon went to Achilles, they found him playing on the harp—

> " Amus'd, at ease, the godlike man they found,
> Pleas'd with the solemn harp's harmonious sound—
> The well-wrought harp from conquer'd Thebæ came,
> Of polish'd silver was its costly frame:
> With this he soothes his angry soul, and sings
> Th' immortal deeds of heroes and of kings."
>
> *Iliad*, book ix.

No. 830.

Chiron giving Peleus an ash-tree, from which to make the spear of Achilles.

APOLLONIDES. *Cornelian.*

> " And now he shakes his great paternal spear,
> Ponderous and huge! which not a Greek could rear.
> From Pelion's cloudy top an ash entire
> Old Chiron fell'd, and shaped it for his sire:
> A spear which stern Achilles only wields—
> The death of heroes, and the dread of fields."
>
> *Iliad*, book xix.

No. 831.

Chiron teaching Achilles the use of the bow.

APOLLONIDES.   *Cornelian.*

No. 832.

Achilles discovered by Ulysses.

APOLLONIDES.   *Cornelian.*

Thetis, knowing that Achilles would be slain if he went to the Trojan war, sent him, disguised as a young lady, to the court of Lycomedes, king of Scyros. But Calchas having declared that Troy could not be taken without him, Ulysses discovered him by the following stratagem. Having in the habit of a merchant gone to the court, he exposed for sale female ornaments and military weapons. The ladies admired the ornaments; but Achilles confined his examination to the weapons. Ulysses relates the circumstance (OVID, book xiii.) in his contest with Ajax for the arms of Achilles.

"Thetis, who knew the fates, applied her care
To keep Achilles in disguise from war;
And till the threat'ning influence was past,
A woman's habit on the hero cast:
All eyes were cozen'd by the borrow'd vest,
And Ajax (never wiser than the rest)
Found no Pelides there: at length I came
With proffer'd wares to this pretended dame;
She, not discover'd by her mien or voice,
Betray'd her manhood by her manly choice;

And while on female toys her fellows look,
Grasp'd in her warlike hand a javelin shook;
Whom, by this act reveal'd, I thus bespoke:
  'O goddess-born! resist not heav'n's de-
        cree—
The fall of Ilium is reserv'd for thee;'
Then seiz'd him, and produc'd in open light,
Sent blushing to the field the fatal knight.
Mine then are all his actions of the war."

He had by Deïdamia, one of the daughters of Lycomedes, a son called Neoptolemus, and also Pyrrhus, who signalised himself in the Trojan war. Achilles thus speaks of him in his lamentation for Patroclus (*Iliad,* book xix.)—

"What greater sorrow could afflict my breast,
What more, if hoary Peleus were deceased?
Who now, perhaps, in Phthia dreads to hear
His son's sad fate, and drops a tender tear.
What more, should Neoptolemus the brave
(My only offspring) sink into the grave?
If yet that offspring lives (I distant far,
Of all neglectful, wage a hateful war).

I could not this, this cruel stroke attend;
Fate claim'd Achilles, but might spare his friend.
I hoped Patroclus might survive, to rear
My tender orphan with a parent's care.
From Scyros' isle conduct him o'er the main,
And glad his eyes with his paternal reign,
The lofty palace, and the large domain."

No. 833.

Achilles and Ulysses.

PYRGOTELES. *Cornelian.*

No. 834.

Peleus consecrating the hair of Achilles to the river-god Spercheius.

APOLLONIDES. *Cornelian.*

It was a custom of the ancients to consecrate not only their own hair, but also that of their children, to the river-gods of their country. Pausanias mentions this act of Peleus (book i. c. 37). " Before you pass the river Cephissus, you will see the tomb of Theodorus, who was the most excellent tragic actor of his time. Near the river there are two statues; one of Mnesimachus, the other of his son cutting off his hair as an offering to the river: for, that it was an ancient custom with the Greeks to cut off locks of their hair to rivers, may be inferred from Homer's poetry, in which he relates that Peleus vowed to consecrate to the river-god Spercheius the hair of his son Achilles, for his safe return from Troy." The reason why he consecrated the hair to Spercheius, rather than to any other river of Thessaly, seems to be that the river-god Spercheius was allied to the family of Peleus; for Menesthius, one of the generals under Achilles in the Trojan war, was the son of Spercheius, by Polydora, daughter of Peleus.

> " Five chosen leaders the fierce bands obey,
> Himself supreme in valour, as in sway.
> First march'd Menesthius, of celestial birth,
> Derived from thee, whose waters wash the earth,
> Divine Spercheius! Jove-descended flood!
> Great Peleus' daughter mixing with a god."
>
> *Iliad,* book xvi. 175.

No. 835.

Combat of Achilles and Cygnus.

DIOSCORIDES. *Cornelian.*

Achilles finding that Cygnus, the son of Neptune, was invulnerable, threw him on the ground and strangled him. When he attempted to despoil him of his armour, he found he was transformed into a swan.

" From these first onsets, the Sigæan shore
Was strew'd with carcasses, and stain'd with gore:
Neptunian Cygnus troops of Greeks had slain:
Achilles in his car had scour'd the plain,
And clear'd the Trojan ranks: where'er he fought,
Cygnus, or Hector, through the fields he sought:
Cygnus he found; on him his force essay'd:
For Hector was to the tenth year delay'd.
His white-maned steeds, that bow'd beneath the
       yoke,
He cheer'd to courage with a gentle stroke;
Then urg'd his fiery chariot on the foe;
And, rising, shook his lance, in act to throw.
But first he cried, ' O youth be proud to bear
Thy death, ennobled by Pelides' spear.'
The lance pursu'd the voice without delay,
Nor did the whizzing weapon miss the way,
But pierc'd his cuirass, with such fury sent,
And sign'd his bosom with a purple dint.
At this the seed of Neptune: ' Goddess-born,
For ornament, not use, these arms are worn:
This helm and heavy buckler I can spare,
As only decorations of the war:
So Mars is arm'd for glory, not for need.
'Tis somewhat more from Neptune to proceed,
Than from a daughter of the sea to spring:
Thy sire is mortal—mine is ocean's king.
Secure of death, I should contemn thy dart,
Though naked, and impassable depart.'
    He said, and threw; the trembling weapon
       pass'd
Through nine bull-hides, each under other plac'd
On his broad shield, and stuck within the last.
Achilles wrench'd it out; and sent again
The hostile gift—the hostile gift was vain.
He tried a third, a tough well-chosen spear;
Th' inviolable body stood sincere,
Though Cygnus then did no defence provide,
But scornful offer'd his unshielded side.
    Not otherwise th' impatient hero far'd
Than as a bull, encompass'd with a guard,
Amid the circus roars, provok'd from far
By sight of scarlet and a sanguine war:

They quit their ground, his bended horns elude;
In vain pursuing, and in vain pursued.
    Before to farther fight he would advance,
He stood considering, and survey'd his lance;
Doubts if he wielded not a wooden spear
Without a point: he look'd, the point was there.
' This is my hand, and this my lance,' he said,
' By which so many thousand foes are dead:
O whither is their usual virtue fled?
I had it once; and the Lyrnessian wall,
And Tenedos, confess'd it in their fall.
Thy streams, Caicus, roll'd a crimson flood;
And Thebes ran red with her own natives' blood.
Twice Telephus employ'd their piercing steel,
To wound him first, and afterward to heal.
The vigour of this arm was never vain:
And that my wonted prowess I retain,
Witness these heaps of slaughter on the plain.'
    He said; and, doubtful of his former deeds,
To some new trial of his force proceeds.
He chose Menœtes from among the rest;
At him he launch'd his spear, and pierc'd his
       breast:
On the hard earth the Lycian knock'd his head,
And lay supine; and forth the spirit fled.
    Then thus the hero: ' Neither can I blame
The hand or jav'lin; both are still the same.
The same I will employ against this foe,
And wish but with the same success to throw.'
So spoke the chief; and while he spoke he threw.
The weapon with unerring fury flew,
At his left shoulder aim'd: nor entrance found,
But back, as from a rock, with swift rebound
Harmless return'd—a bloody mark appear'd,
Which with false joy the flatter'd hero cheer'd.
Wound there was none: the blood that was in
       view,
The lance before from slain Menœtes drew.
    Headlong he leaps from off his lofty car,
And in close fight on foot renews the war.
Raging with high disdain, repeats his blows;
Nor shield, nor armour, can their force oppose.
Huge cantlets of his buckler strew the ground,
And no defence in his bor'd arms is found,

But on his flesh no wound or blood is seen ;
The sword itself is blunted on the skin.
  This vain attempt the chief no longer bears ;
But round his hollow temples and his ears
His buckler beats : the son of Neptune, stunn'd
With these repeated buffets, quits his ground ;
A sickly sweat succeeds, and shades of night—
Inverted nature swims before his sight.
Th' insulting victor presses on the more,
And treads the steps the vanquish'd trod before,
Nor rest, nor respite gives.   A stone there lay
Behind his trembling foe, and stopp'd his way :

Achilles took th' advantage which he found,
O'erturn'd and push'd him backward on the
  ground.
His buckler held him under, while he press'd
With both his knees above his panting breast ;
Unlac'd his helm : about his chin the twist
He tied, and soon the strangled soul dismiss'd.
  With eager haste he went to strip the dead—
The vanish'd body from his arms was fled.
His sea-god sire, t' immortalise his frame,
Had turn'd it to a bird that bears his name."
                                   OVID, *Met.* xii.

No. 836.

Achilles, stained with the blood of his enemies, washing himself at the fountain Achillea, near Miletus.

CHROMIOS. *Cornelian.*

This refers to one of the adventures of Achilles in destroying, at the commencement of the war, the tributary towns.

No. 837.

Achilles and Agamemnon.

APOLLONIDES. *Cornelian.*

Achilles, in his quarrel about Briseis—which was the cause of his secession from the allied forces, and is the subject of the *Iliad*—thus addresses Agamemnon (*Iliad*, book i.) :—

  " ' O monster ! mix'd of insolence and fear—
Thou dog in forehead, but in heart a deer !
When wert thou known in ambush'd fights to
    dare,
Or nobly face the horrid front of war ?
'Tis ours the chance of fighting-fields to try—
Thine to look on, and bid the valiant die !
So much 'tis safer through the camp to go,
And rob a subject, than despoil a foe.
Scourge of thy people—violent and base—
Sent in Jove's anger on a slavish race !—

Who, lost to sense of gen'rous freedom pass'd,
Are tam'd to wrongs—or this had been thy last.
Now by this sacred sceptre—hear me swear !
Which never more shall leaves or blossoms bear,
Which sever'd from the trunk (as I from thee)
On the bare mountains left its parent tree—
This sceptre, form'd by temper'd steel to prove
An ensign of the delegates of Jove,
From whom the power of laws and justice
    springs—
Tremendous oath ! inviolate to kings !—

3 s

By this I swear, when bleeding Greece again
Shall call Achilles, she shall call in vain :
When, flush'd with slaughter, Hector comes to
  spread
The purpled shore with mountains of the dead,
Then shalt thou mourn th' affront thy madness
  gave—
Forced to deplore, when impotent to save :

Then rage in bitterness of soul, to know
This act has made the bravest Greek thy foe.'
  He spoke ; and furious hurl'd against the
  ground
His sceptre, starr'd with golden studs around.
Then sternly silent sat. With like disdain,
The raging king return'd his frowns again."
                                Iliad, book i.

No. 838.

Achilles, in grief for the loss of Briseis, addressing his mother Thetis.

GNAIOS.   *Cornelian.*

" Not so his loss the fierce Achilles bore ;
But sad retiring to the sounding shore,
O'er the wild margin of the deep he hung—
That kindred deep from whence his mother sprung.
There, bath'd in tears of anger and disdain,
Thus loud lamented to the stormy main :
  ' O parent goddess ! since in early bloom
Thy son must fall by too severe a doom ;

Sure, to so short a race of glory born,
Great Jove in justice should this span adorn :
Honour and fame at least the Thund'rer ow'd ;
And ill he pays the promise of a god,
If yon proud monarch thus thy son defies—
Obscures my glories, and resumes my prize.' "
                                Iliad, book i.

No. 839.

Thetis inquiring of Achilles the cause of his affliction.

SCYLAX.   *Cornelian.*

" Far in the deep recesses of the main,
  Where aged Ocean holds his wat'ry reign,
The goddess-mother heard. The waves divide ;
And like a mist she rose above the tide—
Beheld him mourning on the naked shores,
And thus the sorrows of his soul explores :
' Why grieves my son ? Thy anguish let me share ;
Reveal the cause, and trust a parent's care.' "
                                Iliad, book i.

No. 840.

Thetis consoling Achilles.

ADMON. *Sardonyx.*

" 'Unhappy son !' fair Thetis thus replies,
While tears celestial trickle from her eyes ;
' Why have I borne thee with a mother's throes,
To fates averse, and nursed for future woes ?
So short a space the light of heaven to view !—
So short a space ! and fill'd with sorrow too !
O might a parent's careful wish prevail,
Far, far from Ilion should thy vessels sail !
And thou, from camps remote, the danger shun,
Which now, alas ! too nearly threats my son.
Yet (what I can) to move thy suit I'll go
To great Olympus crown'd with fleecy snow.

Meantime, secure within thy ships, from far
Behold the field, nor mingle in the war.
The sire of gods and all th' ethereal train,
On the warm limits of the farthest main,
Now mix with mortals, nor disdain to grace
The feast of Æthiopia's blameless race ;
Twelve days the powers indulge the genial
rite,
Returning with the twelfth revolving light.
Then will I mount the brazen dome, and move
The high tribunal of immortal Jove.' "

Iliad, book i.

No. 841.

Interview of Thetis with Jupiter.

CHROMIOS. *Amethyst.*

" Twelve days were past, and now the dawn-
ing light
The gods had summon'd to th' Olympian height :
Jove first ascending from the wat'ry bow'rs
Leads the long order of ethereal pow'rs.
When, like the morning mist in early day,
Rose from the flood the daughter of the sea,
And to the seats divine her flight address'd.
There, far apart, and high above the rest,
The Thund'rer sat ; where old Olympus shrouds
His hundred heads in heav'n, and props the
clouds.
Suppliant the goddess stood : one hand she
plac'd
Beneath his beard, and one his knee embrac'd.
' If e'er, O father of the gods !' she said,
' My words could please thee, or my actions
aid,

Some marks of honour on my son bestow,
And pay in glory what in life you owe.
Fame is at least by heav'nly promise due
To life so short, and now dishonour'd too.
Avenge this wrong, O ever just and wise !
Let Greece be humbled, and the Trojans rise,
Till the proud king and all the Achaian race
Shall heap with honours him they now dis-
grace.'
Thus Thetis spoke ; but Jove in silence held
The sacred councils of his breast conceal'd.
Not so repuls'd, the goddess closer press'd,
Still grasp'd his knees, and urg'd the dear re-
quest :
' O sire of gods and men ! thy suppliant hear ;
Refuse or grant—for what has Jove to fear ?
Or, oh ! declare, of all the pow'rs above,
Is wretched Thetis least the care of Jove ?'

She said; and, sighing, thus the god replies,
Who rolls the thunder o'er the vaulted skies:
' What hast thou ask'd ? Ah! why should Jove
    engage
In foreign contests and domestic rage—
The gods' complaints, and Juno's fierce alarms,
While I, too partial, aid the Trojan arms ?

Go, lest the haughty partner of my sway
With jealous eyes thy close access survey ;
But part in peace, secure thy pray'r is sped—
Witness the sacred honours of our head,
The nod that ratifies the will divine—
The faithful, fix'd, irrevocable sign.' "

Iliad, book i.

No. 842.

Achilles receiving Ulysses, who was at the head of the ambassadors from Agamemnon, sent to deprecate his wrath.

ALCEOS. *Cornelian.*

" The rite perform'd, the chiefs their thirst
    allay,
Then from the royal tent they take their way :
Wise Nestor turns on each his careful eye—
Forbids t' offend—instructs them to apply :
Much he advised them all, Ulysses most,
To deprecate the chief, and save the host.
Through the still night they march, and hear the
    roar
Of murmuring billows on the sounding shore.
To Neptune, ruler of the seas profound,
Whose liquid arms the mighty globe surround,
They pour forth vows their embassy to bless,
And calm the rage of stern Æacides.
And now, arrived where on the sandy bay
The Myrmidonian tents and vessels lay,
Amused at ease the godlike man they found,
Pleased with the solemn harp's harmonious sound

(The well-wrought harp from conquer'd Thebæ
    came,
Of polish'd silver was its costly frame).
With this he soothes his angry soul, and sings
Th' immortal deeds of heroes and of kings.
Patroclus only of the royal train,
Placed in his tent, attends the lofty strain ;
Full opposite he sat, and listen'd long,
In silence waiting till he ceased the song.
Unseen the Grecian embassy proceeds
To his high tent ; the great Ulysses leads.
Achilles starting, as the chiefs he spied,
Leap'd from his seat and laid the harp aside.
With like surprise arose Menœtius' son:
Pelides grasp'd their hands, and thus begun—
' Princes, all hail! whatever brought you
    here.' "

Iliad, book ix.

No. 843.

Antilochus announcing to Achilles the death of Patroclus.

GNAIOS. *Cornelian.*

" Thus, like the rage of fire, the combat burns;
And now it rises—now it sinks, by turns.
Meanwhile, where Hellespont's broad waters flow,
Stood Nestor's son—the messenger of woe !

There sat Achilles, shaded by his sails,
On hoisted yards extended to the gales :
Pensive he sat ; for all that fate design'd
Rose in sad prospect to his boding mind.

Thus to his soul he said: 'Ah! what constrains
The Greeks, late victors, now to quit the plains?
Is this the day which heaven so long ago
Ordain'd, to sink me with the weight of woe?
(So Thetis waru'd) when by a Trojan hand
The bravest of the Myrmidonian band
Should lose the light? Fulfill'd is that decree!
Fallen is the warrior, and Patroclus he!
In vain I charged him soon to quit the plain,
And waru'd to shun Hectorian force—in vain!'
  Thus while he thinks, Antilochus appears,
And tells the melancholy tale with tears.

' Sad tidings, son of Peleus! thou must hear;
And wretched I, th' unwilling messenger!
Dead is Patroclus!—for his corse they fight—
His naked corse—his arms are Hector's right!'
  A sudden horror shot through all the chief,
And wrapt his senses in the cloud of grief:
Cast on the ground, with furious hands he spread
The scorching ashes o'er his graceful head;
His purple garments, and his golden hairs—
Those he deforms with dust, and these he tears:
On the hard soil his groaning breast he threw,
And roll'd and grovell'd, as to earth he grew."

Iliad, book xviii.

No. 844.

Iris delivering the order of Juno to Achilles.

POLYCLETES.   *Sardonyx.*

" The various goddess of the showery bow,
Shot in a whirlwind to the shore below;
To great Achilles at his ships she came,
And thus began the many-colour'd dame:
  ' Rise, son of Peleus! rise, divinely brave!—
Assist the combat, and Patroclus save;
For him the slaughter to the fleet they spread,
And fall by mutual wounds around the dead.
To drag him back to Troy the foe contends,
Nor with his death the rage of Hector ends—
A prey to dogs he dooms the corse to lie,
And marks the place to fix his head on high.
Rise, and prevent (if yet you think of fame)
Thy friend's disgrace—thy own eternal shame!'
  ' Who sends thee, goddess, from th' ethereal
    skies?'
Achilles thus. And Iris thus replies:
' I come, Pelides, from the queen of Jove,
Th' immortal empress of the realms above,
Unknown to him who sits remote on high—
Unknown to all the synod of the sky.'
  ' Thou comest in vain,' he cries, with fury
    warm'd;
Arms I have none, and can I fight unarm'd?

Unwilling as I am, of force I stay,
Till Thetis bring me, at the dawn of day,
Vulcanian arms: what other can I wield,
Except the mighty Telamonian shield?
That, in my friend's defence, has Ajax spread,
While his strong lance around him heaps the dead.
The gallant chief defends Menœtius' son,
And does what his Achilles should have done.'
  ' Thy want of arms,' said Iris, ' well we know,
But though unarm'd, yet clad in terrors, go!
Let but Achilles o'er yon trench appear,
Proud Troy shall tremble, and consent to fear:
Greece from one glance of that tremendous eye
Shall take new courage, and disdain to fly.'
  She spoke, and pass'd in air. The hero rose—
Her ægis Pallas o'er his shoulder throws:
Around his brow a golden cloud she spread—
A stream of glory flamed above his head.
As when from some beleaguer'd town arise
The smokes high curling to the shaded skies
(Seen from some island o'er the main afar,
When men distress'd hang out the sign of war);
Soon as the sun in ocean hides his rays,
Thick on the hills the flaming beacons blaze;

With long-projected beams the seas are bright,
And heaven's high arch reflects the ruddy light:
So from Achilles' head the splendours rise,
Reflecting blaze on blaze against the skies.
Forth march'd the chief, and distant from the
        crowd,
High on the rampart raised his voice aloud;
With her own shout Minerva swells the sound.
Troy starts astonish'd, and the shores rebound.
As the loud trumpet's brazen mouth from far
With shrilling clangour sounds th' alarm of
        war,

Struck from the walls, the echoes float on high,
And the round bulwarks and thick towers reply;
So high his brazen voice the hero rear'd,
Hosts drop their arms, and trembled as they
        heard;
And back the chariots roll, and coursers bound,
And steeds and men lie mingled on the ground.
Aghast they see the livid lightnings play,
And turn their eyeballs from the flashing ray.
Thrice from the trench his dreadful voice he
        raised;
And thrice they fled—confounded—and amazed!"

Iliad, book xviii.

No. 845.

Minerva throwing her ægis over Achilles.

APOLLONIDES.   *Cornelian.*

See last paragraph of the preceding quotation.

No. 846.

Achilles striking terror into the Trojans.

CHROMIOS.   *Cornelian.*

See last paragraph of the preceding quotation.

No. 847.

Achilles over the dead body of Patroclus vowing to avenge his death.

PEMALLIO.   *Sardonyx.*

"While the long night extends her sable reign,
Around Patroclus mourn'd the Grecian train.
Stern in superior grief Pelides stood:
Those slaughtering arms so used to bathe in blood
Now clasp'd his clay-cold limbs; then gushing
        start
The tears, and sighs burst from his swelling heart.

The lion thus, with dreadful anguish stung,
Roars through the desert and demands his young,
When the grim savage, to his rifled den
Too late returning, snuffs the track of men,
And o'er the vales and o'er the forest bounds;
His clamorous grief the bellowing wood re-
        sounds.

So grieves Achilles; and impetuous vents
To all his Myrmidons his loud laments:
' In what vain promise, gods! did I engage,
When, to console Menœtius' feeble age,
I vow'd his much-loved offspring to restore,
Charged with rich spoils, to fair Opuntia's shore?
But mighty Jove cuts short, with just disdain,
The long—long views of poor designing man!
One fate the warrior and the friend shall strike,
And Troy's black sands must drink our blood
    alike:
Me, too, a wretched mother shall deplore—
And aged father never see me more!
Yet, my Patroclus! yet, a space I stay;
Then swift pursue thee on the darksome way.

Ere thy dear relics in the grave are laid,
Shall Hector's head be offer'd to thy shade!
That, with his arms, shall hang before thy shrine;
And twelve the noblest of the Trojan line,
Sacred to vengeance, by this hand expire—
Their lives effused around thy flaming pyre.
Thus let me lie till then! thus, closely press'd,
Bathe thy cold face, and sob upon thy breast!
While Trojan captives here thy mourners stay—
Weep all the night, and murmur all the day—
Spoils of my arms and thine! when, wasting wide,
Our swords kept time, and conquer'd side by side.'
    He spoke, and bid the sad attendants round
Cleanse the pale corse, and wash each honour'd
    wound."

Iliad, book xviii.

No. 848.

Thetis received by Charis, the spouse of Vulcan.

DIOSCORIDES. *Cornelian.*

    Thetis having dissuaded Achilles from entering the battle, until she had procured him a new suit of impenetrable armour of celestial workmanship (his former suit having been stripped by Hector from the body of Patroclus), repaired for that purpose to Vulcan; who granted her prayer, in gratitude for her former services to him.

" Meanwhile the silver-footed dame
Reach'd the Vulcanian dome—eternal frame!
High eminent amid the work divine,
Where heaven's far-beaming brazen mansions
    shine.
There the lame architect the goddess found,
Obscure in smoke, his forges flaming round,
While bathed in sweat from fire to fire he flew;
And, puffing loud, the roaring bellows blew.
That day no common task his labour claim'd:
Full twenty tripods for his hall he framed,
That placed on living wheels of massy gold
(Wondrous to tell) instinct with spirit roll'd
From place to place around the bless'd abodes,
Self-moved, obedient to the beck of gods:

For their fair handles now, o'erwrought with
    flowers,
In moulds prepared the glowing ore he pours.
Just as responsive to his thought the frame
Stood prompt to move, the azure goddess came:
Charis, his spouse, a Grace divinely fair
(With purple fillets round her braided hair),
Observed her entering! her soft hand she press'd,
And, smiling, thus the watery queen address'd:
' What, goddess! this unusual favour draws?
All hail, and welcome! whatsoe'er the cause:
Till now a stranger, in a happy hour
Approach, and taste the dainties of the bower.'
    High on a throne, with stars of silver graced,
And various artifice, the queen she placed;

A footstool at her feet; then, calling, said,
' Vulcan, draw near; 'tis Thetis asks your aid.'
  ' Thetis,' replied the god, ' our powers may
    claim—
An ever dear—an ever honour'd name!
When my proud mother* hurl'd me from the sky
(My awkward form, it seems, displeased her eye),
She and Eurynome my griefs redress'd,
And soft received me on their silver breast.
E'en then, these arts employ'd my infant thought,
Chains, bracelets, pendants—all their toys I
    wrought.
Nine years kept secret in the dark abode,
Secure I lay conceal'd from man and god.
Deep in a cavern'd rock my days were led;
The rushing ocean murmur'd o'er my head.
Now since her presence glads our mansion, say,
For such desert what service can I pay?
Vouchsafe, O Thetis! at our board to share
The genial rites and hospitable fare;
While I the labours of the forge forego,
And bid the roaring bellows cease to blow.'

Then from his anvil the lame artist rose;
Wide with distorted legs oblique he goes,
And stills the bellows, and (in order laid)
Locks in their chests his instruments of trade.
Then with a sponge the sooty workman dress'd
His brawny arms imbrown'd, and hairy breast.
With his huge sceptre graced, and red attire,
Came halting forth the sovereign of the fire:
The monarch's steps two female forms uphold,
That moved, and breathed, in animated gold;
To whom was voice, and sense, and science given
Of works divine (such wonders are in heaven!):
On these supported, with unequal gait,
He reach'd the throne where pensive Thetis sate;
There placed beside her on the shining frame,
He thus address'd the silver-footed dame:
  ' Thee, welcome goddess! what occasion calls
(So long a stranger) to these honour'd walls?
'Tis thine, fair Thetis, the command to lay,
And Vulcan's joy and duty to obey.'
  To whom the mournful mother thus replies—
The crystal drops stood trembling in her eyes."

Iliad, book xviii.

No. 849.

Vulcan shewing Thetis the arms of Achilles.

DIOSCORIDES. *Cornelian.*

" To her the artist-god: ' Thy griefs resign;
Secure, what Vulcan can, is ever thine.
O could I hide him from the Fates as well,
Or with these hands the cruel stroke repel,
As I shall forge most envied arms, the gaze
Of wondering ages, and the world's amaze!'
  Thus having said, the father of the fires
To the black labours of his forge retires.
Soon as he made them blow, the bellows turn'd
Their iron mouths; and, where the furnace burn'd,
Resounding breathed: at once the blast expires,
And twenty forges catch at once the fires:

Just as the god directs, now loud, now low,
They raise a tempest, or they gently blow.
In hissing flames huge silver bars are roll'd,
And stubborn brass, and tin, and solid gold,
Before, deep fix'd, th' eternal anvils stand;
The ponderous hammer loads his better hand,
His left with tongs turns the vex'd metal round,
And thick, strong strokes the doubling vaults re-
    bound.
  Then first he form'd th' immense and solid
    shield;
Rich various artifice emblazed the field;

---

* Juno.

Its utmost verge a threefold circle bound ;
A silver chain suspends the massy round ;
Five ample plates the broad expanse compose,
And godlike labours on the surface rose.
There shone the image of the master-mind :
There earth—there heaven—there ocean, he de-
   sign'd—
Th' unwearied sun—the moon completely round—
The starry lights that heaven's high convex
   crown'd.
       .   .   .   .   .

Thus the broad shield complete the artist
   crown'd
With his last hand, and pour'd the ocean round :
In living silver seem'd the waves to roll,
And beat the buckler's verge, and bound the
   whole.
This done, whate'er a warrior's use requires,
He forged—the cuirass that outshines the fires—
The greaves of ductile tin—the helm impress'd
With various sculpture—and the golden crest.
At Thetis' feet the finish'd labour lay."

As the shield of Achilles contained such a number of devices, the artist, who was confined to the narrow compass of a gem, judiciously abstained here from attempting a portraiture of them, and contented himself with giving only an outline of the shield itself; and therefore it is unnecessary to quote here Homer's minute description of it. But as it was so celebrated a piece of mechanism and specimen of engraving, and as the poet fully displays in it his genius for description, a brief sketch may be useful and interesting to the unlearned reader.

Homer says that the figures were executed so naturally, that you could imagine you saw their motions, and heard their voices. The shield is supposed to have been quite round, capable of covering the whole body of Achilles (who is represented as a man of gigantic size), and four feet in diameter ; the convex surface being divided into four concentric circles, and into twelve compartments, for the twelve different subjects. The centre of the shield, round the boss, contained a representation of earth, sea, heaven, the sun, moon, and all the celestial signs.

The *first* compartment represented a town in peace, with a nuptial procession through the town, and festival—dancing in a circle, singing, and playing on the flute and lyre ; while the women stood in the porches, looking on with delight and wonder. The *second* compartment contained a representation of a public assembly, and two men pleading about a fine for murder : the murderer contending that he had paid the fine, the relative of the murdered man affirming that he himself had not received it ; the multitude expressing approbation or disapprobation, according to their opinions of the force of argument on either side. The *third* compartment represented the decision on the case ; the people ranged in order by the heralds ; the judges standing up and pronouncing, each with sceptre in hand, his verdict in succession ; while two talents of gold are lying before them, as a reward to him who should, in the opinion of the people, pronounce the ablest and most righteous sentence. The *fourth* compartment represented a beleaguered city : the besieged issue forth for an ambuscade, Mars and Minerva majestically glittering at their head ; while the old men, the women, and children, are posted to defend the walls. The *fifth* compartment represented them as arrived at the banks of a river ; to which two herdsmen, playing on their flutes, are conducting oxen and sheep to drink. The *sixth* compartment represented a sanguinary encounter between the besiegers and the besieged for the possession of the cattle. The *seventh* compartment represented a ploughed field : some are ploughing, while others are regaling themselves after arriving at the furrow's end. The *eighth* compart-

3 T

ment represented a corn-field, with reapers: the boys are gathering up the swarths after the reapers, and binding them into sheaves; while the lord of the field is superintending the entire work, with his staff in his hand.   Under the shade of an oak his servants are preparing to slay an ox, while the women are making bread, for the feast.   The *ninth* compartment represented a vineyard: young men and maids are carrying off the fruit in baskets through a pathway; among them a youth is playing on a lyre and singing, while the rest keep time to his music with step and voice.   The *tenth* compartment represented a herd of oxen issuing from their stalls to drink at a river, with their keepers, followed by large dogs attending them.   Two lions rush on the herd, and fasten on a bull; while the herdsmen are struck with terror, and the dogs stand barking at a distance.   The *eleventh* compartment represented a flock of sheep grazing in a rich valley, with shepherds, folds, and cottages.   The *twelfth* compartment represented the various evolutions of the Cretan dance, invented by Dædalus for Ariadne.   The young men and maidens danced hand in hand; the maidens dressed in linen garments, with flowery crowns upon their heads; the men in rich and shining stuffs, with swords of gold hanging from their sides in belts of silver.   Now they whirled in a circle—then they moved in many figures: sometimes they met; and sometimes wound from one another.   The spectators stood around in wonder and delight.   In the midst two nimble tumblers played their feats, while the whole circle united in the song.

Then, last of all, he represented the vast and mighty ocean rolling round the outer border of the shield.

No. 850.

Vulcan giving Thetis the arms.

GNAIOS.   *Cornelian.*

No. 851.

Thetis carrying the arms to Achilles.

GNAIOS.   *Cornelian.*

Here the artist, by representing Thetis as proceeding through the sea mounted on a sea-horse, deviates a little from Homer, who places Vulcan's forge in heaven; but seems to adopt Virgil's account, which places it in a cavern at the bottom of Hiera, one of the Lipari islands; and thus the representation becomes correct and characteristic.

No. 852.

Thetis presenting the arms to Achilles.

APOLLONIDES.   *Calcedony.*

"A ray divine her heavenly presence shed,
And thus, his hand soft-touching, Thetis said:
'Suppress, my son, this rage of grief, and know
It was not man, but heaven that gave the blow;
Behold what arms by Vulcan are bestow'd—
Arms worthy thee, or fit to grace a god.'
Then drops the radiant burden on the ground:
Clang the strong arms, and ring the shores around:

Back shrink the myrmidons with dread surprise,
And from the broad effulgence turn their eyes.
Unmoved, the hero kindles at the show,
And feels with rage divine his bosom glow:
From his fierce eyeballs living flames expire,
And flash incessant like a stream of fire:
He turns the radiant gift, and feeds his mind
On all th' immortal artist had design'd."

Iliad, book xix.

No. 853.

Achilles lamenting over the dead body of Patroclus.

CHARILAOS.   *Cornelian.*

"His rage they calm not, nor his grief control;
He groans—he raves—he sorrows from his soul.
'Thou too, Patroclus!' thus his heart he vents,
'Once spread th' inviting banquet in our tents:
Thy sweet society—thy winning care,
Once stay'd Achilles rushing to the war.

But now, alas! to death's cold arms resign'd,
What banquet but revenge can glad my mind?
What greater sorrow could afflict my breast—
What more, if hoary Peleus were deceased?
What more, should Neoptolemus the brave,
My only offspring, sink into the grave?'"

Iliad, book xix.

No. 854.

The reconciliation of Achilles and Agamemnon.

ÆTION.   *Cornelian.*

"'That unavailing care be laid aside,'
The azure goddess to her son replied:
'Whole years untouch'd, uninjur'd shall remain
Fresh as in life, the carcass of the slain.
But go, Achilles (as affairs require);
Before the Grecian peers renounce thine ire:
Then uncontroll'd in boundless war engage,
And heaven with strength supply the mighty rage!'
Then in the nostrils of the slain she pour'd
Nectareous drops, and rich ambrosia shower'd
O'er all the corse. The flies forbid their prey;
Untouch'd it rests, and sacred from decay.
Achilles to the strand obedient went:
The shores resounded with the voice he sent.

The heroes heard, and all the naval train
That tend the ships, or guide them o'er the main,
Alarm'd—transported, at the well-known sound—
Frequent and full, the great assembly crown'd;
Studious to see that terror of the plain,
Long lost to battle, shine in arms again.
Tydides and Ulysses first appear,
Lame with their wounds, and leaning on the spear;
These on the sacred seats of council placed,
The king of men, Atrides, came the last—
He, too, sore wounded by Agenor's son.
Achilles, rising in the midst, begun
'O monarch! better far had been the fate
Of thee—of me—of all the Grecian state,

If (ere the day when, by mad passion sway'd,
Rash we contended for the black-eyed maid)
Preventing Dian had dispatch'd her dart,
And shot the shining mischief to the heart:
Then many a hero had not press'd the shore,
Nor Troy's glad fields been fatten'd with our gore:
Long — long shall Greece the woes we caused be-
    wail,
And sad posterity repeat the tale!
But this no more ; the subject of debate
Is past—forgotten, and resign'd to fate.
Why should, alas! a mortal man, as I,
Burn with a fury that can never die?
Here, then, my anger ends: let war succeed,
And e'en as Greece has bled, let Ilion bleed.
Now call the hosts, and try, if in our sight,
Troy yet shall dare to camp a second night?

I deem their mightiest, when this arm he knows,
Shall 'scape with transport, and with joy repose.'
    He said: his finish'd wrath with loud acclaim
The Greeks accept, and shout Pelides' name.
When thus, not rising from his lofty throne,
In state unmov'd, the king of men begun:
    ' Hear me, ye sons of Greece! with silence
        hear!
And grant your monarch an impartial ear—
Awhile your loud, untimely joy suspend,
And let your rash, injurious clamours end:
Unruly murmurs, or ill-timed applause,
Wrong the best speaker and the justest cause.
Nor charge on me, ye Greeks, the dire debate—
Know, angry Jove, and all-compelling Fate,
With fell Erinnys, urged my wrath that day
When from Achilles' arms I forced the prey.' "

No. 855.

Briseis lamenting the death of Patroclus.

Lycos.   *Cornelian.*

Agamemnon restored Briseis, accompanied with valuable presents, to Achilles.

" Briseis, radiant as the queen of love,
Slow as she pass'd, beheld with sad survey
Where, gash'd with cruel wounds, Patroclus
    lay.
Prone on the body fell the heav'nly fair,
Beat her sad breast, and tore her golden hair ;
All beautiful in grief, her humid eyes,
Shining with tears, she lifts, and thus she cries:
    ' Ah, youth for ever dear, for ever kind—
Once tender friend of my distracted mind!
I left thee fresh in life, in beauty gay ;
Now find thee cold, inanimated clay !
What woes my wretched race of life attend?
Sorrows on sorrows, never doom'd to end !

The first-lov'd consort of my virgin-bed
Before these eyes in fatal battle bled :
My three brave brothers in one mournful day
All trod the dark, irremeable way :
Thy friendly hand uprear'd me from the plain,
And dried my sorrows for a husband slain.
Achilles' care you promis'd I should prove—
The first, the dearest partner of his love ;
That rites divine should ratify the band,
And make me empress in his native land.
Accept these grateful tears ! for thee they flow —
For thee, that ever felt another's woe !'
    Her sister-captives echo'd groan for groan,
Nor mourn'd Patroclus' fortunes, but their own."

Iliad, book xix.

No. 856.

Achilles arming.

APOLLONIDES.   *Sardonyx.*

" Full in the midst, high towering o'er the rest,
His limbs in arms divine Achilles dress'd—
Arms which the father of the fire bestow'd,
Forged on th' eternal anvils of the god.
Grief and revenge his furious heart inspire—
His glowing eyeballs roll with living fire—
He grinds his teeth, and furious with delay,
O'erlooks th' embattled host, and hopes the
    bloody day.
The silver cuishes first his thighs infold ;
Then o'er his breast was braced the hollow gold ;
The brazen sword a various baldric tied,
That, starr'd with gems, hung glittering at his
    side ;
And, like the moon, the broad refulgent shield
Blaz'd with long rays, and gleam'd athwart the
    field.
So to night-wandering sailors, pale with fears,
Wide o'er the watery waste a light appears,

Which, on the far-seen mountain blazing high,
Streams from some lonely watch-tower to the sky :
With mournful eyes they gaze, and gaze again :
Loud howls the storm, and drives them o'er the
    main.
Next his high head the helmet graced ; behind
The sweeping crest hung floating in the wind :
Like the red star, that from his flaming hair
Shakes down diseases, pestilence, and war ;
So stream'd the golden honours from his head,
Trembled the sparkling plumes, and the loose
    glories shed.
The chief beholds himself with wondering eyes ;
His arms he poises, and his motions tries ;
Buoy'd by some inward force, he seems to swim,
And feels a pinion lifting every limb.
And now he shakes his great paternal spear,
Ponderous and huge, which not a Greek could
    rear."

Iliad, book xix.

No. 857.

Achilles, in his chariot, addressing his horses.

POLYCLETES.   *Cornelian.*

" Automedon and Alcimus prepare
Th' immortal coursers and the radiant car,
(The silver traces sweeping at their side),
Their fiery mouths resplendent bridles tied ;
The ivory-studded reins, return'd behind,
Wav'd o'er their backs, and to the chariot
    join'd.
The charioteer then whirl'd the lash around,
And swift ascended at one active bound.
All bright in heavenly arms, above his squire,
Achilles mounts, and sets the field on fire ;
Not brighter Phœbus, in th' ethereal way,
Flames from his chariot, and restores the day.

High o'er the host all terrible he stands,
And thunders to his steeds these dread commands :
' Xanthus and Balius ! of Podarges' strain
(Unless ye boast that heavenly race in vain),
Be swift—be mindful of the load ye bear,
And learn to make your master more your care :
Through falling squadrons bear my slaughtering
    sword,
Nor, as ye left Patroclus, leave your lord.'
    The generous Xanthus, as the words he said,
Seem'd sensible of woe, and droop'd his head ;
Trembling he stood before the golden wain,
And bow'd to dust the honours of his mane."

Iliad, book xix.

No. 858.

Combat of Achilles and Æneas.

APOLLONIDES. *Cornelian.*

" He spoke. With all his force the javelin flung,
Fix'd deep, and loudly in the buckler rung.
Far on his outstretch'd arm Pelides held
(To meet the thundering lance) his dreadful shield,
That trembled as it stuck ; nor void of fear
Saw, ere it fell, th' immeasurable spear.
His fears were vain ; impenetrable charms
Secured the temper of the ethereal arms.
Through two strong plates the point its passage held,
But stopp'd, and rested, by the third repell'd.
Five plates of various metal, various mould,
Composed the shield ; of brass each outward fold ;
Of tin each inward; and the middle gold :
There stuck the lance. Then, rising ere he threw,
The forceful spear of great Achilles flew,
And pierced the Dardan shield's extremest bound,
Where the shrill brass return'd a sharper sound :
Through the thin verge the Pelion weapon glides,
And the slight covering of expanded hides ;
Æneas his contracted body bends,
And o'er him high the riven targe extends,
Sees through its parting plates the upper air,
And at his back perceives the quivering spear :
A fate so near him chills his soul with fright ;
And swims before his eyes the many-colour'd light.
Achilles, rushing in with dreadful cries,
Draws his broad blade, and at Æneas flies.
Æneas, rousing as the foe came on,
With force collected, heaves a mighty stone :
A mass enormous ! which in modern days
No two of earth's degenerate sons could raise.
But ocean's god, whose earthquakes rock the ground,
Saw the distress, and moved the powers around."
Iliad, book xx.

No. 859.

Neptune rescuing Æneas.

CHROMIOS. *Cornelian.*

" The king of ocean to the fight descends ;
Through all the whistling darts his course he bends ;
Swift interpos'd between the warriors flies,
And casts thick darkness o'er Achilles' eyes.
From great Æneas' shield the spear he drew,
And at its master's feet the weapon threw.
That done, with force divine he snatch'd on high
The Dardan prince, and bore him through the sky,
Smooth gliding without step above the heads
Of warring heroes and of bounding steeds.
Till at the battle's utmost verge they light,
Where the slow Caucans close the rear of fight."

No. 860.

The combat of Achilles and Hector interrupted by a cloud.

ADMON. *Cornelian.*

" Full in Achilles' dreadful front he came,
And shook his javelin like a waving flame.
The son of Peleus sees, with joy possess'd,
His heart high-bounding in his rising breast:
And, ' Lo! the man on whom black fates attend—
The man that slew Achilles in his friend!
No more shall Hector's and Pelides' spear
Turn from each other in the walks of war.'
Then with revengeful eyes he scann'd him o'er:
' Come, and receive thy fate!' He spake no more.
Hector, undaunted, thus: ' Such words employ
To one that dreads thee—some unwarlike boy:
Such we could give, defying and defied,
Mean intercourse of obloquy and pride!

I know thy force to mine superior far;
But heaven alone confers success in war:
Mean as I am, the gods may guide my dart,
And give it entrance in a braver heart.'
Then parts the lance: but Pallas' heavenly breath
Far from Achilles wafts the winged death;
The bidden dart again to Hector flies,
And at the feet of its great master lies.
Achilles closes with his hated foe,
His heart and eyes with flaming fury glow:
But present to his aid, Apollo shrouds
The favour'd hero in a veil of clouds.
Thrice struck Pelides with indignant heart;
Thrice in impassive air he plunged the dart:
The spear a fourth time buried in the cloud,
He foams with fury, and exclaims aloud."

Iliad, book xx.

No. 861.

Lycaon supplicating Achilles.

POLYCLETES. *Cornelian.*

" The next, that god whom men in vain withstand
Gives the same youth to the same conquering hand;
Now never to return! and doom'd to go
A sadder journey to the shades below.
His well-known face when great Achilles eyed
(The helm and vizor he had cast aside
With wild affright, and dropp'd upon the field
His useless lance and unavailing shield),
As trembling, panting, from the stream he fled,
And knock'd his faltering knees, the hero said:

' Ye mighty gods! what wonders strike my view!
Is it in vain our conquering arms subdue?
Sure I shall see yon heaps of Trojans kill'd,
Rise from the shades, and brave me on the field;
As now the captive, whom so late I bound
And sold to Lemnos, stalks on Trojan ground!
Not him the sea's unmeasured deeps detain,
That bar such numbers from their native plain:
Lo! he returns. Try, then, my flying spear!—
Try, if the grave can hold the wanderer;
If earth at length this active prince can seize—
Earth, whose strong grasp has held down Hercules.'

Thus while he spake, the Trojan, pale with fears,
Approach'd, and sought his knees with suppliant
tears ;
Loath as he was to yield his youthful breath,
And his soul shivering at th' approach of death.
Achilles raised the spear, prepared to wound ;
He kiss'd his feet extended on the ground :
And while above the spear suspended stood,
Longing to dip its thirsty point in blood,
One hand embraced them close, one stopp'd the
dart,
While thus these melting words attempt his heart:
  ' Thy well-known captive, great Achilles ! see,
Once more Lycaon trembles at thy knee.
Some pity to a suppliant's name afford,
Who shared the gifts of Ceres at thy board ;
Whom late thy conquering arm to Lemnos bore,
Far from his father, friends, and native shore.'

.   .   .   .   .

These words, attended with a shower of tears,
The youth address'd to unrelenting ears:
' Talk not of life or ransom,' he replies,
' Patroclus dead, whoever meets me, dies.
In vain a single Trojan sues for grace ;
But least, the sons of Priam's hateful race.
Die then, my friend ! what boots it to deplore ?—
The great, the good Patroclus is no more !
He, far thy better, was foredoom'd to die,
And thou—dost thou bewail mortality ?
Seest thou not me, whom Nature's gifts adorn,
Sprung from a hero, from a goddess born ;
The day shall come (which nothing can avert)
When by the spear, the arrow, or the dart,
By night or day, by force or by design,
Impending death and certain fate are mine."
                                  Iliad, book xxi.

No. 862.

Achilles slaying Lycaon.

ALPHEOS. *Cornelian.*

" Sudden, Achilles his broad sword display'd,
  And buried in his neck the reeking blade.
  Prone fell the youth ; and panting on the land,
  The gushing purple dyed the thirsty sand :
  The victor to the stream the carcass gave,
  And thus insults him, floating on the wave."
                                  Iliad, book xxi.

No. 863.

Achilles binding one of the twelve Trojan captives.

APOLLONIDES. *Amethyst.*

Achilles having plunged into the river Scamander (called, according to Homer, Xanthus
by the gods) after the fugitive Trojans, drew out twelve captives ; whom he bound, and after-
wards sacrificed at the funeral pile of Patroclus.

" So plunged in Xanthus by Achilles' force,
Roars the resounding surge with men and horse.
His bloody lance the hero cast aside
(Which spreading tamarisks on the margin hide);
Then, like a god, the rapid billows braves,
Arm'd with his sword high brandish'd o'er the
    waves:
Now down he plunges, now he whirls it round;
Deep groan'd the waters with the dying sound:
Repeated wounds the reddening river dyed,
And the warm purple circled on the tide.
Swift through the foamy flood the Trojans fly,
And close in rocks or winding caverns lie:

So the huge dolphin tempesting the main,
In shoals before him fly the scaly train;
Confus'dly heap'd, they seek their inmost caves,
Or pant and heave beneath the floating waves.
Now tired with slaughter, from the Trojan band
Twelve chosen youths he drags alive to land;
With their rich belts their captive arms con-
    strains
(Late their proud ornaments, but now their
    chains):
These his attendants to the ships convey'd,
Sad victims! destined to Patroclus' shade."
Iliad, book xxi.

No. 864.

Achilles in the river Scamander.

AËTION. *Sardonyx.*

Achilles having made great slaughter of the Trojans in the Scamander, was requested by the river-god to desist. But he replied,

" No!—not till Troy the destin'd vengeance pay !"

Scamander then attacked him with all his waves; but Neptune and Pallas, when he was nearly exhausted, assured him that he was not destined to perish so ignobly, and urged him to proceed. After this, Scamander solicited the assistance of the river-god Simoïs, and they both assailed Achilles. But Juno sent to his aid Vulcan, who dried up the waters.

" Then, rising in his rage above the shores,
From all his deep the bellowing river roars—
Huge heaps of slain disgorges on the coast,
And round the banks the ghastly dead are toss'd.
While all before, the billows ranged on high
(A watery bulwark) screen the bands who fly.
Now bursting on his head with thundering sound,
The falling deluge whelms the hero round;
His loaded shield bends to the rushing tide;
His feet, upborne, scarce the strong flood di-
    vide—
Sliddering—and staggering ! On the border stood
A spreading elm, that overhung the flood;
He seized a bending bough his steps to stay;
The plant uprooted to his weight gave way,

Heaving the bank, and undermining all;
Loud flash the waters to the rushing fall
Of the thick foliage. The large trunk display'd
Bridged the rough flood across: the hero staid
On this his weight, and, raised upon his hand,
Leap'd from the channel, and regain'd the land.
Then blacken'd the wild waves; the murmur
    rose—
The god pursues—a huger billow throws,
And bursts the bank—ambitious to destroy
The man whose fury is the fate of Troy.
He, like the warlike eagle, speeds his pace
(Swiftest and strongest of th' aërial race):
Far as a spear can fly, Achilles springs
At every bound : his clanging armour rings—

3 u

Now here—now there, he turns on every side,
And winds his course before the following tide:
The waves flow after wheresoe'r he wheels,
And gather fast, and murmur at his heels.

.   .   .   .   .

Still flies Achilles, but before his eyes
Still swift Scamander rolls where'er he flies:
Not all his speed escapes the rapid floods—
The first of men, but not a match for gods.
Oft as he turn'd the torrent to oppose,
And bravely try if all the powers were foes;
So oft the surge, in watery mountains spread,
Beats on his back, or bursts upon his head.
Yet dauntless still the adverse flood he braves,
And still indignant bounds above the waves.
Tired by the tides, his knees relax with toil;
Wash'd from beneath him slides the slimy soil:
When thus (his eyes on heaven's expansion
        thrown)
Forth bursts the hero with an angry groan:
' Is there no god Achilles to befriend—
No power t' avert his miserable end?
Prevent, O Jove! this ignominious date,
And make my future life the sport of Fate.
Of all heaven's oracles believed in vain,
But most of Thetis, must her son complain;
By Phœbus' darts she prophesied my fall
In glorious arms before the Trojan wall.

O! had I died in fields of battle warm—
Stretch'd like a hero—by a hero's arm!
Might Hector's spear this dauntless bosom rend,
And my swift soul o'ertake my slaughter'd friend!
Ah, no! Achilles meets a shameful fate!
Oh how unworthy of the brave and great!
Like some vile swain, whom on a rainy day,
Crossing a ford, the torrent sweeps away,
An unregarded carcass, to the sea.'
    Neptune and Pallas haste to his relief,
And thus, in human form, address the chief—
The power of ocean first: ' Forbear thy fear,
O son of Peleus! Lo, thy gods appear!
Behold! from Jove descending to thy aid,
Propitious Neptune and the blue-eyed maid.
Stay, and the furious flood shall cease to rave;
'Tis not thy fate to glut his angry wave.
But thou the counsel heaven suggests attend;
Nor breathe from combat—nor thy sword sus-
        pend,
Till Troy receive her flying sons—till all
Her routed squadrons pant beneath their wall:
Hector alone shall stand his fatal chance;
And Hector's blood shall smoke upon thy lance.
Thine is the glory doom'd.' Thus spake the gods:
Then swift ascended to the bright abodes."
                    Iliad, book xxi.

No. 865.

Neptune and Pallas encouraging Achilles.

DIOSCORIDES. *Cornelian.*

See preceding explanation.

No. 866.

Achilles attacked by the rivers Scamander and Simoïs conjointly.

CHROMIOS. *Cornelian.*

See preceding explanation.

" Stung with new ardour, thus by heav'n im-
    pell'd,
He springs impetuous, and invades the field:
O'er all th' expanded plain the waters spread;
Heav'd on the bounding billows danc'd the dead,
Floating 'midst scatter'd arms; while casques of
    gold
And turn'd-up bucklers glitter'd as they roll'd.
High o'er the surging tide, by leaps and bounds,
He wades and mounts: the parted wave resounds.
Not a whole river stops the hero's course,
While Pallas fills him with immortal force.
With equal rage indignant Xanthus roars,
And lifts his billows and o'erwhelms his shores.
    Then thus to Simois: ' Haste, my brother
        flood !
And check this mortal that controls a god.
Our bravest heroes else shall quit the fight,
And Ilion tumble from her tow'ry height.
Call, then, thy subject-streams and bid them
    roar:
From all thy fountains swell thy watery store:

With broken rocks, and with a load of dead
Charge the black surge, and pour it on his head.
Mark how resistless through the floods he goes,
And boldly bids the warring gods be foes !
But nor that force, nor form divine to fight,
Shall aught avail him, if our rage unite:
Whelm'd under our dark gulfs those arms shall
    lie,
That blaze so dreadful in each Trojan eye ;
And deep beneath a sandy mountain hurl'd,
Immers'd remain this terror of the world.
Such pond'rous ruin shall confound the place,
No Greek shall e'er his perish'd relics grace ;
No hand his bones shall gather, or inhume—
These his cold rites, and this his watery tomb.'
    He said ; and on the chief descends amain,
Increas'd with gore, and swelling with the slain :
Then, murm'ring from his beds, he boils, he raves,
And a foam whitens on the purple waves :
At ev'ry step, before Achilles stood
The crimson surge, and delug'd him with blood."
                            Iliad, book xxi.

No. 867.

Vulcan attacking Scamander.

Anterotos. *Cornelian.*

See preceding explanation.

" Fear touch'd the queen of heaven: she saw
    dismay'd—
She call'd aloud, and summon'd Vulcan's aid.
    ' Rise to the war ! th' insulting flood re-
        quires
Thy wasteful arm—assemble all thy fires !
While to their aid, by our command enjoin'd,
Rush the swift eastern and the western wind:
These from old ocean at my word shall blow,
Pour the red torrent on the watery foe,
Corses and arms to one bright ruin turn,
And hissing rivers to their bottoms burn.

Go, mighty in thy rage !—display thy power—
Drink the whole flood—the crackling trees de-
    vour—
Scorch all the banks : and (till our voice reclaim)
Exert th' unwearied furies of the flame !'
    The power ignipotent her word obeys :
Wide o'er the plain he pours the boundless
    blaze—
At once consumes the dead, and dries the soil;
And the shrunk waters in their channel boil.
As when autumnal Boreas sweeps the sky,
And instant blows the water'd gardens dry :

So look'd the field—so whiten'd was the ground,
While Vulcan breath'd the fiery blast around.
Swift on the sedgy reeds the ruin preys ;
Along the margin winds the running blaze :
The trees in flaming rows to ashes turn—
The flowery lotos and the tamarisk burn—
Broad elm, and cypress rising in a spire :
The watery billows hiss before the fire.
Now glow the waves—the fishes pant for breath—
The eels lie twisting in the pangs of death :

Now flounce aloft—now dive the scaly fry,
Or, gasping, turn their bellies to the sky.
At length the river rear'd his languid head,
And thus, short panting, to the god he said :
  ' Oh, Vulcan—oh ! what power resists thy
        might ?
I faint—I sink, unequal to the fight—
I yield—let Ilion fall—if fate decree—
Ah—bend no more thy fiery arms on me !' "
                              Iliad, book xxi.

No. 868.

Combat between Mars and Minerva.

APOLLONIDES.   *Cornelian.*

The annexed quotation fully explains this and the three following subjects.

" While these* by Juno's will the strife resign,
The warring gods in fierce contention join :
Rekindling rage each heavenly breast alarms :
With horrid clangour shock'd th' ethereal arms :
Heaven with loud thunder bids the trumpet
        sound ;
And wide beneath them groans the rending
        ground.
Jove, as his sport, the dreadful scene descries,
And views contending gods with careless eyes.
The Power of battles lifts his brazen spear,
And first assaults the radiant queen of war :
  ' What moved thy madness, thus to disunite
Ethereal minds, and mix all heaven in fight ?
What wonder this, when in thy frantic mood
Thou drov'st a mortal to insult a god ?
Thy impious hand Tydides' javelin bore,
And madly bathed it in celestial gore.'
  He spoke, and smote the loud-resounding
        shield,
Which bears Jove's thunder on its dreadful field—
The adamantine ægis of her sire,
That turns the glancing bolt and forked fire.

Then heav'd the goddess in her mighty hand
A stone, the limit of the neighbouring land,
There fix'd from eldest times—black, craggy,
        vast—
This at the heavenly homicide she cast.
Thundering he falls, a mass of monstrous size ;
And seven broad acres covers as he lies.
The stunning stroke his stubborn nerves un-
        bound :
Loud o'er the fields his ringing arms resound :
The scornful dame her conquest views with
        smiles,
And glorying thus the prostrate god reviles :
  ' Hast thou not yet, insatiate fury, known
How far Minerva's force transcends thy own ?
Juno, whom thou rebellious dar'st withstand,
Corrects thy folly thus by Pallas' hand—
Thus meets thy broken faith with just disgrace,
And partial aid to Troy's perfidious race.'
  The goddess spoke, and turn'd her eyes away,
That, beaming round, diffused celestial day.
Jove's Cyprian daughter, stooping on the land,
Lent to the wounded god her tender hand :

---

* Scamander and Simoïs. .

Slowly he rises—scarcely breathed with pain,
And, propp'd on her fair arm, forsakes the plain.
This the bright empress of the heavens survey'd,
And, scoffing, thus to War's victorious maid :
　' Lo! what an aid on Mars's side is seen—
The Smiles' and Love's unconquerable queen !
Mark with what insolence, in open view,
She moves : let Pallas, if she dares, pursue.'
　Minerva smiling heard, the pair o'ertook,
And slightly on her breast the wanton strook :

She, unresisting, fell (her spirits fled) ;
On earth together lay the lovers spread.
' And like these heroes be the fate of all,'
Minerva cries, ' who guard the Trojan wall !
To Grecian gods such let the Phrygians be—
So dread, so fierce, as Venus is to me—
Then from the lowest stone shall Troy be moved.'
Thus she ; and Juno, with a smile, approved."
　　　　　　　Iliad, book xxi.

No. 869.

The same subject.

GNAIOS. *Sardonyx.*

See foregoing quotation. As boundary or landmark-stones were deified by the ancients (being, as it were, the sacred guardians of private property amongst a rural people), they were generally represented as posts with the figure of a head on the top of them.

No. 870.

Venus coming to the aid of Mars.

CHROMIOS. *Sardonyx.*

See preceding quotation.

No. 871.

Venus struck down by Minerva.

APOLLONIDES. *Sardonyx.*

See preceding quotation.

No. 872.

Apollo reproaching Achilles.

APOLLONIDES. *Cornelian.*

The Trojans, having been defeated, fled to the city, pursued by Achilles. Agenor (the son of Antenor) stood to meet him. During the combat, Apollo wrapped Agenor in a cloud, and dismissed him from the field; then assumed his form and fled, pursued by Achilles—thus deluding Achilles until the Trojans were safely lodged within the walls.

" Meanwhile the god, to cover their escape,
Assumes Agenor's habit, voice, and shape—
Flies from the furious chief in this disguise:
The furious chief still follows where he flies.
Now o'er the fields they stretch with lengthen'd
 strides—
Now urge the course where swift Scamander
 glides:
The god now, distant scarce a stride before,
Tempts his pursuit, and wheels about the shore;
While all the flying troops their speed employ,
And pour on heaps into the walls of Troy:
No stop, no stay—no thought to ask, or tell,
Who 'scaped by flight—or who by battle fell.
'Twas tumult all—and violence of flight—
And sudden joy confused—and mix'd affright!
Pale Troy against Achilles shuts her gate;
And nations breathe, deliver'd from their fate.

Apollo now to tired Achilles turns
(The power confess'd in all his glory burns).
' And what,' he cries, 'has Peleus' son in view,
With mortal speed a godhead to pursue?
For not to thee to know the gods is given—
Unskill'd to trace the latent marks of heaven.
What boots thee now, that Troy forsook the plain?
Vain thy past labour, and thy present vain:
Safe in their walls are now her troops bestow'd,
While here thy frantic rage attacks a god.'
 The chief incensed : ' Too partial god of day!
To check my conquests in the middle way—
How few in Ilion else had refuge found!
What gasping numbers now had bit the ground!
Thou robb'st me of a glory justly mine,
Powerful of godhead, and of fraud divine—
Mean fame, alas! for one of heavenly strain,
To cheat a mortal who repines in vain.' "
     Iliad, book xxi. and xxii.

No. 873.

Achilles fastening the dead body of Hector to his chariot.

Sosocles.   *Cornelian.*

" High o'er the slain the great Achilles stands,
Begirt with heroes and surrounding bands;
And thus aloud, while all the host attends:
' Princes and leaders! countrymen and friends!
Since now at length the powerful will of heaven
The dire destroyer to our arm has given,
Is not Troy fallen already? Haste, ye powers!
See, if already their deserted towers
Are left unmann'd; or if they yet retain
The souls of heroes, their great Hector slain?
But what is Troy, or glory what to me?
Or why reflects my mind on aught but thee,
Divine Patroclus? Death has seal'd his eyes!
Unwept—unhonour'd—uninterr'd he lies!
Can his dear image from my soul depart,
Long as the vital spirit moves my heart?

If, in the melancholy shades below,
The flames of friends and lovers cease to glow,
Yet mine shall sacred last—mine undecay'd
Burn on through death, and animate my shade!
Meanwhile, ye sons of Greece, in triumph bring
The corse of Hector, and your pæans sing.
Be this the song, slow moving toward the shore,
' Hector is dead, and Ilion is no more!'
 Then his fell soul a thought of vengeance bred
(Unworthy of himself and of the dead),
The nervous ancles bored, his feet he bound
With thongs inserted through the double wound;
These fix'd up high behind the rolling wain,
His graceful head was trail'd along the plain.
Proud on his car th' insulting victor stood,
And bore aloft his arms distilling blood.

He smites the steeds—the rapid chariot flies—
The sudden clouds of circling dust arise.
Now lost is all that formidable air !
The face divine and long-descending hair

Purple the ground, and streak the sable sand—
Deform'd—dishonour'd—in his native land !
Given to the rage of an insulting throng ;
And in his parents' sight now dragg'd along !"

Iliad, book xxii.

No. 874.

The spirit of Patroclus appearing to Achilles.

DIOSCORIDES. *Cornelian.*

Achilles having dragged the body of Hector to the sea-shore, and driven three times round the bier of Patroclus at the head of his armed myrmidons, left the body on the ground, and ordered a funeral feast for his troops. Then, determined not to cleanse himself from the bloody stains until he paid all the due honours to the remains of his friend, he threw himself on the ground and fell asleep ; when the spirit of Patroclus appeared to him.

" But great Pelides stretched along the shore,
Where dash'd on rocks the broken billows roar,
Lies inly groaning ; while on either hand
The martial myrmidons confus'dly stand.
Along the grass his languid members fall,
Tired with his chase around the Trojan wall :
Hush'd by the murmurs of the rolling deep,
At length he sinks in the soft arms of sleep.
When lo ! the shade, before his closing eyes,
Of sad Patroclus rose, or seem'd to rise ;
In the same robe he living wore he came—
In stature, voice, and pleasing look, the same.
The form familiar hover'd o'er his head :
' And sleeps Achilles,' (thus the phantom said)—
' Sleeps my Achilles, his Patroclus dead ?
Living, I seem'd his dearest, tend'rest care ;
But now forgot, I wander in the air.
Let my pale corse the rites of burial know,
And give me entrance in the realms below :
Till then the spirit finds no resting-place,
But here and there th' unbodied spectres chase
The vagrant dead around the dark abode,
Forbid to cross th' irremeable flood.
Now give thy hand : for to the farther shore
When once we pass, the soul returns no more—
When once the last funereal flames ascend,
No more shall meet Achilles and his friend ;

No more our thoughts to those we loved make
    known ;
Or quit the dearest, to converse alone.
Me fate has sever'd from the sons of earth—
The fate foredoom'd that waited from my birth :
Thee, too, it waits ; before the Trojan wall
E'en great and godlike thou art doom'd to fall.
Hear, then ; and as in fate and love we join,
Ah, suffer that my bones may rest with thine !
Together have we lived—together bred—
One house received us—and one table fed ;
That golden urn thy goddess-mother gave,
May mix our ashes in one common grave.'
    ' And is it thou ?' he answers ; ' to my sight
Once more return'st thou from the realms of night?
Oh, more than brother ! Think each office paid,
Whate'er can rest a discontented shade ;
But grant one last embrace, unhappy boy !—
Afford at least that melancholy joy.'
    He said ; and with his longing arms essay'd
In vain to grasp the visionary shade ;
Like a thin smoke he sees the spirit fly,
And hears a feeble lamentable cry.
Confused he wakes ; amazement breaks the bands
Of golden sleep, and, starting from the sands,
Pensive he muses with uplifted hands."

Iliad, book xxiii.

No. 875.

Achilles offering his hair to the body of Patroclus.

APOLLONIDES. *Cornelian.*

The soldiers having returned from the forests of Ida, with wood for the funeral pile of Patroclus, Achilles ordered a military procession round his body; and, according to the custom of the ancient Greeks and eastern nations, cut off a portion of his hair in honour of the dead.

" There, on the spot which great Achilles shew'd,
They eased their shoulders and disposed the load,
Circling around the place, where times to come
Shall view Patroclus' and Achilles' tomb.
The hero bids his martial troops appear
High on their cars in all the pomp of war:
Each in refulgent arms his limbs attires;
All mount their chariots—combatants and squires.
The chariots first proceed, a shining train;
Then clouds of foot that smoke along the plain.
Next these a melancholy band appear;
Amidst lay dead Patroclus on the bier:
O'er all the corse their scatter'd locks they throw:
Achilles next, oppress'd with mighty woe,
Supporting with his hands the hero's head,
Bends o'er th' extended body of the dead.
Patroclus decent on th' appointed ground
They place, and heap the sylvan pile around.
But great Achilles stands apart in prayer,
And from his head divides the yellow hair—
Those curling locks which from his youth he vow'd,
And sacred grew, to Sperchius' honour'd flood—
Then sighing, to the deep his looks he cast,
And roll'd his eyes around the watery waste:
' Sperchius! whose waves, in mazy errors lost,
Delightful roll along my native coast!
To whom we vainly vow'd, at our return,
These locks to fall and hecatombs to burn—
Full fifty rams to bleed in sacrifice,
Where to the day the silver fountains rise,
And where in shade of consecrated bowers
Thy altars stand, perfumed with native flowers!
So vow'd my father, but he vow'd in vain:
No more Achilles sees his native plain:
In that vain hope these hairs no longer grow,
Patroclus bears them to the shades below.'
    Thus o'er Patroclus while the hero pray'd,
On his cold hand the sacred lock he laid."

Iliad, book xxiii.

No. 876.

The same subject.

GNAIOS. *Cornelian.*

No. 877.

Patroclus setting out for the battle: Achilles offering libation and
prayers to Jove for his success.

POLYCLETES. *Sardonyx.*

The Greeks having been beaten back with great slaughter, and the most distinguished
leaders wounded, Patroclus, by the advice of Nestor (*Iliad*, book xi.), requested of Achilles
to allow him to wear his armour, and lead out the myrmidons, as the only means of saving the
Greeks. Achilles consented; counselling him, however, to return after he had saved the fleet,
and not to encounter Hector.

" Far o'er the rest, in glittering pomp appear,
There bold Automedon, Patroclus here—
Brothers in arms, with equal fury fired—
Two friends—two bodies, with one soul inspired.
But mindful of the gods, Achilles went
To the rich coffer in his shady tent:
There lay on heaps his various garments roll'd,
And costly furs, and carpets stiff with gold,
(The presents of the silver-footed dame).
From thence he took a bowl, of antique frame,
Which never man had stain'd with ruddy wine,
Nor raised in offerings to the powers divine,
But Peleus' son; and Peleus' son to none
Had raised in offerings, but to Jove alone.
This tinged with sulphur, sacred first to flame,
He purged, and wash'd it in the running stream.
Then cleansed his hands; and fixing for a space
His eyes on heaven, his feet upon the place
Of sacrifice, the purple draught he pour'd
Forth in the midst; and thus the god implored:
' O thou Supreme! high throned all height
     above!
O great Pelasgic, Dodonæan Jove!

Who 'midst surrounding frosts and vapours chill,
Presid'st on bleak Dodona's vocal hill:
(Whose groves the Selii, race austere! surround,
Their feet unwash'd, their slumbers on the ground;
Who hear from rustling oaks thy dark decrees,
And catch the fates low-whisper'd in the breeze.)
Hear, as of old! thou gavest, at Thetis' prayer,
Glory to me, and to the Greeks despair.
Lo, to the dangers of the fighting-field
The best—the dearest of my friends I yield;
Though still determined to my ships confined.
Patroclus gone, I stay but half behind.
Oh! be his guard thy providential care—
Confirm his heart, and string his arm to war—
Press'd by his single force, let Hector see
His fame in arms not owing all to me.
But when the fleets are saved from foes and fire,
Let him with conquest and renown retire;
Preserve his arms—preserve his social train,
And safe return him to these eyes again!'
     Great Jove consents to half the chief's request,
But heaven's eternal doom denies the rest."

Iliad, book xvi.

No. 878.

Patroclus routing the Trojans.

APOLLONIDES. *Cornelian.*

3 x

" Thus from the tents the fervent legion swarms,
So loud their clamour, and so keen their arms.
Their rising rage Patroclus' breath inspires,
Who thus inflames them with heroic fires:
' O warriors! partners of Achilles' praise!
Be mindful of your deeds in ancient days:
Your godlike master let your acts proclaim,
And add new glories to his mighty name.
Think your Achilles sees you fight: be brave,
And humble the proud monarch whom you save.'
Joyful they heard, and kindling as he spoke,
Flew to the fleet involved in fire and smoke.
From shore to shore the doubling shouts resound,
The hollow ships return a deeper sound.

The war stood still, and all around them gazed,
When great Achilles' shining armour blazed:
Troy saw, and thought the dread Achilles nigh,
At once they see—they tremble—and they fly!

.   .   .   .   .

And now the chief (the foremost troops repell'd)
Back to the ships his destined progress held—
Bore down half Troy in his resistless way,
And forced the routed ranks to stand the day.
Between the space where silver Simois flows,
Where lay the fleets, and where the rampires rose,
All grim in dust and blood, Patroclus stands,
And turns the slaughter on the conquering bands."

Iliad, book xvi.

No. 879.

Sarpedon slain by Patroclus.

DIOSCORIDES. *Amethyst.*

Sarpedon is represented as addressing Glaucus, while Patroclus is about to pluck the spear from his body.

" When now Sarpedon his brave friends beheld
Grov'lling in dust, and gasping on the field,
With this reproach his flying host he warms,
' Oh, stain to honour! oh, disgrace to arms!
Forsake, inglorious, the contended plain;
This hand, unaided, shall the war sustain:
The task be mine this hero's strength to try,
Who mows whole troops, and makes an army fly.'
He spake; and speaking, leap'd from off the car:
Patroclus lights, and sternly waits the war.
As when two vultures on the mountain's height
Stoop with resounding pinions to the fight;
They cuff—they tear—they raise a screaming cry;
The desert echoes, and the rocks reply:

The warriors, thus opposed in arms, engage
With equal clamours and with equal rage.

.   .   .   .   .

Now met in arms, the combatants appear;
Each heaved the shield and poised the lifted spear:
From strong Patroclus' hand the javelin fled,
And pass'd the groin of valiant Thrasymed;
The nerves unbraced, no more his bulk sustain;
He falls, and falling bites the bloody plain.
Two sounding darts the Lycian leader threw;
The first aloof with erring fury flew,
The next transpierced Achilles' mortal steed,
The generous Pedasus of Theban breed,*
Fix'd in the shoulder's joint he reel'd around,
Roll'd in the bloody dust, and paw'd the slippery ground.

---

* The other horses, Xanthus and Balius, were of immortal breed.

His sudden fall th' entangled harness broke;
Each axle crackled, and the chariot shook:
When bold Automedon, to disengage
The starting coursers, and restrain their rage,
Divides the traces with his sword, and freed
Th' encumber'd chariot from the dying steed:
The rest move on obedient to the rein;
The car rolls slowly o'er the dusty plain.

The towering chiefs to fiercer fight advance;
And first Sarpedon whirl'd his weighty lance,
Which o'er the warrior's shoulder took its course,
And spent in empty air its dying force.
Not so Patroclus' never-erring dart;
Aim'd at his breast, it pierced the mortal part,
Where the strong fibres bind the solid heart.
Then, as the mountain oak, or poplar tall,
Or pine (fit mast for some great admiral),
Nods to the axe, till with a groaning sound
It sinks, and spreads its honours on the ground:
Thus fell the king; and laid on earth supine,
Before his chariot stretch'd his form divine:
He grasp'd the dust distain'd with streaming
          gore,
And, pale in death, lay groaning on the shore.
So lies a bull beneath the lion's paws,
While the grim savage grinds with foamy jaws

The trembling limbs, and sucks the smoking blood;
Deep groans and hollow roars rebellow through
          the wood.

Then to the leader of the Lycian band
The dying chief address'd his last command:
' Glaucus, be bold; thy task be first to dare
The glorious dangers of destructive war—
To lead my troops—to combat at their head—
Incite the living—and supply the dead.
Tell them, I charged them with my latest breath
Not unrevenged to bear Sarpedon's death.
What grief—what shame—must Glaucus undergo,
If these spoil'd arms adorn a Grecian foe!
Then as a friend, and as a warrior, fight—
Defend my body—conquer in my right;
That, taught by great examples, all may try
Like thee to vanquish, or like me to die.'

He ceased; the Fates suppress'd his labouring
          breath,
And his eyes darken'd with the shades of death.
Th' insulting victor with disdain bestrode
The prostrate prince, and on his bosom trod;
Then drew the weapon from his panting heart,
The reeking fibres clinging to the dart;
From the wide wound gush'd out a stream of blood,
And the soul issued in the purple flood."

Pope remarks, " If we conceive this said by the expiring hero—his dying looks fixed on
his wounded, disconsolate friend—the spear remaining in his body—and the victor standing
over him in a kind of ecstacy, surveying his conquest—these circumstances will form a very
moving picture."

Pope further justly remarks, " This hero is by birth superior to all the chiefs of either
side, being the only son of Jupiter engaged in this war: and his qualities are in no way un-
worthy of his high descent. He is the most faultless character in the *Iliad*. The poet, by his
death, even before that of Hector, prepares us to expect the destruction of Troy, when its two
great defenders are no more; and in order to make it the more signal, it is the only death in
the *Iliad* attended with prodigies. Even his funeral is performed by divine assistance; he
being the only hero whose body is carried back to be interred in his native country, and
honoured with monuments erected to his fame." Heaven wept at his fate—

" The cloud-compeller, overcome,
Assents to fate, and ratifies the doom.
Then, touch'd with grief, the weeping heav'ns distill'd
A show'r of blood o'er all the fatal field;

The god, his eyes averting from the plain,
Laments his son, predestin'd to be slain
Far from the Lycian shores, his happy native reign."

After a furious struggle for the possession of his arms, the Greeks prevailed—

" Here Troy and Lycia charge with loud alarms;
Thessalia there and Greece oppose their arms.
With horrid shouts they circle round the slain;
The clash of armour rings o'er all the plain.
Great Jove, to swell the horrors of the fight,
O'er the fierce armies pours pernicious night;
And round his son confounds the warring hosts.
His fate ennobling with a crowd of ghosts."

Iliad, book xvi.

No. 880.

Apollo pouring fragrant waters over the body of Sarpedon.

DIOSCORIDES. *Cornelian.*

" The radiant arms are by Patroclus borne—
Patroclus' ships the glorious spoils adorn.
  Then thus to Phœbus, in the realms above,
Spoke from his throne the cloud-compelling Jove:
' Descend, my Phœbus! on the Phrygian plain,
And from the fight convey Sarpedon slain;
Then bathe his body in the crystal flood—
With dust dishonour'd, and deform'd with blood:
O'er all his limbs ambrosial odours shed,
And with celestial robes adorn the dead.
Those rites discharged, his sacred corse bequeath
To the soft arms of silent Sleep and Death.
They to his friends the mournful charge shall bear,
His friends a tomb and pyramid shall rear;
What honours mortals after death receive,
Those unavailing honours we may give!'

Apollo bows, and from mount Ida's height
Swift to the field precipitates his flight;
Thence from the war the breathless hero bore,
Veil'd in a cloud, to silver Simoïs' shore;
There bath'd his honourable wounds, and dress'd
His manly members in th' immortal vest;
And with perfumes of sweet ambrosial dews
Restores his freshness, and his form renews.
Then Sleep and Death, two twins of winged race,
Of matchless swiftness, but of silent pace,
Received Sarpedon at the god's command,
And in a moment reach'd the Lycian land;
The corse amidst his weeping friends they laid,
Where endless honours wait the sacred shade."

Iliad, book xvi.

No. 881.

Sleep and Death, by command of Apollo, conveying the body of
Sarpedon to Lycia.

POLYCLETES. *Cornelian.*

See preceding explanation.

No. 882.

Apollo repulsing Patroclus from the Trojan wall.

POLYCLETES. *Sardonyx.*

" Now Troy had stoop'd beneath his matchless power;
But flaming Phœbus kept the sacred tower.
Thrice at the battlements Patroclus strook :
His blazing ægis thrice Apollo shook :
He tried the fourth ; when, bursting from the cloud,
A more than mortal voice was heard aloud :
' Patroclus ! cease ; this heaven-defended wall
Defies thy lance—not fated yet to fall ;
Thy friend, thy greater far, it shall withstand—
Troy shall not stoop e'en to Achilles' hand.'
So spoke the god who darts celestial fires :
The Greek obeys him, and with awe retires."

Iliad, book xvi.

No. 883.

Apollo disabling Patroclus.

ANTEROTOS. *Cornelian.*

See the following explanation.

No. 884.

The death of Patroclus.

SCHIMMIOS. *Sardonyx.*

As the death of Patroclus was the immediate cause of the return of Achilles to the battle, and of the consequent death of Hector and the fall of Troy, Homer is minute and forcible in his description of it. This description it is necessary to give.

" Then Hector, checking at the Scæan gates
His panting coursers, in his breast debates—
Or in the field his forces to employ—
Or draw the troops within the walls of Troy.
Thus while he thought, beside him Phœbus stood
In Asius' shape, who reign'd by Sangar's flood
(Thy brother, Hecuba! from Dymas sprung,
A valiant warrior, haughty—bold—and young);
Thus he accosts him: ' What a shameful sight!
Gods! is it Hector that forbears the fight?
Were thine my vigour, this successful spear
Should soon convince thee of so false a fear.
Turn, then—ah! turn thee to the field of fame,
And in Patroclus' blood efface thy shame!
Perhaps Apollo shall thy arm succeed,
And heaven ordain him by thy lance to bleed.'
    So spoke th' inspiring god; then took his flight,
And plunged amidst the tumult of the fight.
He bids Cebrion drive the rapid car—
The lash resounds—the coursers rush to war.
The god the Grecians' sinking souls depress'd,
And pour'd swift spirits through each Trojan
        breast.
Patroclus lights, impatient for the fight;
A spear his left, a stone employs his right:
With all his nerves he drives it at the foe—
Pointed above, and rough and gross below;
The falling ruin crush'd Cebrion's head
(The lawless offspring of king Priam's bed),
His front, brows, eyes, one undistinguish'd wound;
The bursting balls drop sightless to the ground.
The charioteer, while yet he held the rein,
Struck from the car, falls headlong on the plain.
To the dark shades the soul unwilling glides,
While the proud victor thus his fall derides:
' Good heav'ns! what active feats yon artist
        shews—
What skilful divers are our Phrygian foes!
Mark with what ease they sink into the sand—
Pity that all their practice is by land!'

Then rushing sudden on his prostrate prize,
To spoil the carcass fierce Patroclus flies;
Swift as a lion, terrible and bold,
That sweeps the fields—depopulates the fold—
Pierc'd through the dauntless heart, then tumbles
        slain,
And from his fatal courage finds his bane.
At once bold Hector, leaping from his car,
Defends the body, and provokes the war.
Thus for some slaughter'd hind, with equal rage,
Two lordly rulers of the wood engage;
Stung with fierce hunger, each the prey in-
        vades,
And echoing roars rebellow through the shades.
Stern Hector fastens on the warrior's head,
And by the foot Patroclus drags the dead;
While all around, confusion, rage, and fright,
Mix the contending host in mortal fight.
So, pent by hills, the wild winds roar aloud
In the deep bosom of some gloomy wood:
Leaves—arms—and trees, aloft in air are blown—
The broad oaks crackle, and the sylvans groan;
This way and that the rattling thicket bends,
And the whole forest in one crash descends.
Not with less noise, nor less tumultuous rage,
In dreadful shock the mingled hosts engage.
Darts, shower'd on darts, now round the carcass
        ring;
Now flights of arrows bounding from the string:
Stones follow stones; some clatter on the fields,
Some hard and heavy shake the sounding shields.
But where the rising whirlwind clouds the plains,
Sunk in soft dust the mighty chief remains,
And, stretch'd in death, forgets the guiding reins!
    Now flaming from the zenith, Sol had driven
His fervid orb through half the vault of heaven;
While on each host with equal tempest fell
The showering darts, and numbers sunk to hell.
But when his evening wheels o'erhung the main,
Glad conquest rested on the Grecian train.

Then from amidst the tumult and alarms
They draw the conquer'd corse and radiant arms:
Then rash Patroclus with new fury glows,
And, breathing slaughter, pours amid the foes.
Thrice on the press like Mars himself he flew,
And thrice three heroes at each onset slew.
There ends thy glory! there the Fates untwine
The last—black remnant of so bright a line!
Apollo dreadful stops thy middle way;
Death calls, and heaven allows no longer day!

For, lo! the god, in dusky clouds enshrined
Approaching, dealt a staggering blow behind.
The weighty shock his neck and shoulders feel;
His eyes flash sparkles; his stunn'd senses reel
In giddy darkness: far to distance flung,
His bounding helmet on the champain rung.
Achilles' plume is stain'd with dust and gore,
That plume which never stoop'd to earth before;
Long used, untouch'd, in fighting-fields to shine,
And shade the temples of the man divine.
Jove dooms it now on Hector's helm to nod;
Not long—for fate pursues him—and the god!

His spear in shivers falls; his ample shield
Drops from his arm; his baldric strews the field:
The corselet his astonish'd breast forsakes;
Loose is each joint; each nerve with horror shakes;
Stupid he stares, and all assistless stands—
Such is the force of more than mortal hands!

A Dardan youth there was, well known to fame,
From Panthus sprung, Euphorbus was his name;
Famed for the manage of the foaming horse,
Skill'd in the dart, and matchless in the course:
Full twenty knights he tumbled from the car,
While yet he learn'd his rudiments of war.
His venturous spear first drew the hero's gore—
He struck, he wounded, but he durst no more;
Nor, though disarm'd, Patroclus' fury stood,
But swift withdrew the long-protended wood,
And turned him short, and herded in the crowd.
Thus, by an arm divine, and mortal spear,
Wounded at once, Patroclus yields to fear;
Retires for succour to his social train,
And flies the fate which heaven decreed in
    vain.

Stern Hector, as the bleeding chief he views,
Breaks through the ranks, and his retreat pur-
    sues:
The lance arrests him with a mortal wound;
He falls—earth thunders—and his arms resound!
With him all Greece was sunk; that moment all
Her yet-surviving heroes seem'd to fall.

So, scorch'd with heat, along the desert shore,
The roaming lion meets a bristly boar,
Fast by the spring; they both dispute the flood
With flaming eyes and jaws besmear'd with
    blood;
At length the sovereign savage wins the strife,
And the torn boar resigns his thirst and life.
Patroclus thus, so many chiefs o'erthrown—
So many lives effused, expires his own!

As dying now at Hector's feet he lies,
He sternly views him, and triumphing cries:
' Lie there, Patroclus! and with thee the joy
Thy pride once promised of subverting Troy—
The fancied scenes of Ilion wrapt in flames,
And thy soft pleasures served with captive dames!
Unthinking man! I fought those towers to free,
And guard that beauteous race from lords like
    thee:
But thou a prey to vultures shalt be made;
Thy own Achilles cannot lend thee aid;
Though much at parting that great chief might
    say,
And much enjoin thee, this important day:
' Return not, my brave friend,' perhaps he said,
' Without the bloody arms of Hector dead.'
He spoke—Patroclus march'd—and thus he sped!'

    Supine, and wildly gazing on the skies,
With faint, expiring breath the chief replies:
' Vain boaster! cease, and know the pow'rs
    divine:
Jove's and Apollo's is this deed, not thine;
To heaven is owed whate'er your own you call,
And heaven itself disarm'd me ere my fall.
Had twenty mortals, each thy match in might,
Opposed me fairly, they had sunk in fight:
By fate and Phœbus was I first o'erthrown,
Euphorbus next; the third mean part thy own.

But thou, imperious! hear my latest breath;
The gods inspire it, and it sounds thy death.
Insulting man, thou shalt be soon as I;
Black fate hangs o'er thee, and thy hour draws
    nigh;
E'en now on life's last verge I see thee stand,
I see thee fall—and by Achilles' hand!'
    He faints; the soul unwilling wings her way
(The beauteous body left a load of clay),
Flits to the lone, uncomfortable coast—
A naked—wandering—melancholy ghost!

    Then Hector, pausing as his eyes he fed
On the pale carcass, thus address'd the dead:
    'From whence this boding speech, this stern
        decree
Of death denounced, or why denounced to me?
Why not as well Achilles' fate be given
To Hector's lance?—who knows the will of
        heaven?'
    Pensive he said; then treading as he lay
His breathless bosom, tore the lance away."
                            Iliad, book xvi.

No. 885.

Menelaus and Merion carrying the body of Patroclus.

Pyrgoteles.   *Cornelian.*

" ''Tis well,' said Ajax, 'be it then thy care,
With Merion's aid, the weighty corse to rear;
Myself and my bold brother will sustain
The shock of Hector and his charging train:
Nor fear we armies, fighting side by side;
What Troy can dare we have already tried—
Have tried it—and have stood.' The hero said.
High from the ground the warriors heave the
        dead.
A general clamour rises at the sight:
Loud shout the Trojans, and renew the fight.

Not fiercer rush along the gloomy wood,
With rage insatiate and with thirst of blood,
Voracious hounds, that many a length before
Their furious hunters drive the wounded boar;
But if the savage turns his glaring eye,
They howl aloof, and round the forest fly.
Thus on retreating Greece the Trojans pour,
Wave their thick falchions, and their javelins
        show'r;
But Ajax turning, to their fears they yield,
All pale they tremble, and forsake the field."
                            Iliad, book xvi.

No. 886.

Thetis preserving the body of Patroclus from putrefaction.

Teucer.   *Sardonyx.*

" 'Goddess,' he cried, 'these glorious arms that
        shine
With matchless art, confess the hand divine.
Now to the bloody battle let me bend:
But, ah! the relics of my slaughter'd friend!

In those wide wounds through which his spirit
        fled,
Shall flies, and worms obscene, pollute the dead?'
    'That unavailing care be laid aside,'
The azure goddess to her son replied:

' Whole years untouch'd, uninjur'd shall remain
Fresh as in life, the carcass of the slain.
But go, Achilles (as affairs require);
Before the Grecian peers renounce thine ire :
Then uncontroll'd in boundless war engage,
And heaven with strength supply the mighty rage !'

Then in the nostrils of the slain she pour'd
Nectareous drops, and rich ambrosia shower'd
O'er all the corse. The flies forbid their prey,
Untouch'd it rests, and sacred from decay."

Iliad, book ix.

No. 887.

Iris instigating Boreas and Zephyrus to light up the pile of Patroclus.

GNAIOS. *Cornelian.*

" Nor yet the pile, where dead Patroclus lies,
Smokes, nor as yet the sullen flames arise :
But fast beside Achilles stood in prayer—
Invoked the gods whose spirit moves the air ;
And victims promised, and libations cast,
To gentle Zephyr and the Boreal blast :
He called the aërial powers along the skies
To breathe and whisper to the fires to rise.
The winged Iris heard the hero's call,
And instant hasten'd to their airy hall,
Where, in old Zephyr's open courts on high,
Sat all the blustering brethren of the sky.
She shone amidst them on her painted bow ;
The rocky pavement glitter'd with the show.
All from the banquet rise, and each invites
The various goddess to partake the rites.
' Not so,' the dame replied ; ' I haste to go
To sacred Ocean, and the floods below :
E'en now our solemn hecatombs attend,
And heaven is feasting on the world's green end

With righteous Æthiops—uncorrupted train !—
Far on th' extremest limits of the main.
But Peleus' son entreats, with sacrifice,
The western spirit, and the north, to rise ;
Let on Patroclus' pile your blast be driven,
And bear the blazing honours high to heaven.'
  Swift as the word she vanish'd from their
    view—
Swift as the word the winds tumultuous flew :
Forth burst the stormy band with thundering
    roar,
And heaps on heaps the clouds are toss'd before.
To the wide main then stooping from the skies,
The heaving deeps in watery mountains rise :
Troy feels the blast along her shaking walls,
Till on the pile the gather'd tempest falls.
The structure crackles in the roaring fires,
And all the night the plenteous flame aspires."

Iliad, book xxiii.

No. 888.

Achilles pouring libations at the pile of Patroclus.

CHROMIOS. *Amethyst.*

" All night Achilles hails Patroclus' soul
  With large libations from the golden bowl.
  As a poor father, helpless and undone,
  Mourns o'er the ashes of an only son—

3 Y

Takes a sad pleasure the last bones to burn,
And pours in tears, ere yet they close the urn ;
So stay'd Achilles, circling round the shore—
So watch'd the flames, till now they flame no more."

Iliad, book xiii.

No. 889.

Achilles presenting the prize-cup to Nestor.

CHROMIOS. *Cornelian.*

Achilles instituted funeral games ; a chariot-race ; a fight with the gauntlet ; wrestling ;
a foot-race ; single combat ; pitching the *discus,* or quoit ; shooting with arrows ; and darting
the javelin.   Antilochus, the son of Nestor, though driving inferior horses, yet, by observing
the skilful instructions of his father, obtained the second prize.   Then Achilles gave Nestor
himself a prize, as a reward for his wisdom.

" The fifth reward, the double bowl, remain'd.
Achilles this to reverend Nestor bears,
And thus the purpose of his gift declares :
 ' Accept thou this, O sacred sire !' he said,
' In dear memorial of Patroclus dead—
Dead, and for ever lost, Patroclus lies—
For ever snatch'd from our desiring eyes !

Take thou this token of a grateful heart,
Though 'tis not thine to hurl the distant dart,
The quoit to toss, the ponderous mace to wield,
Or urge the race, or wrestle on the field.
Thy pristine vigour age has overthrown,
But left the glory of the past thy own.' "

Iliad, book xxiii.

No. 890.

Achilles seated near the urn which contained the ashes of Patroclus.

DIOSCORIDES. *Cornelian.*

No. 891.

Achilles commanding his handmaids to wash and anoint the dead body of Hector.

DIOSCORIDES. *Cornelian.*

Jupiter having determined, at a council of the gods, to rescue the body of Hector (who
when alive was distinguished for his virtues and his piety) from the shocking indignities of

Achilles, despatched Thetis to induce Achilles to accept a ransom; and Mercury to urge Priam to offer it. Mercury conducted Priam unseen to the tent of Achilles at night. Achilles, melted into pity by the address and appearance of Priam, restored to him the body of Hector; and, unsolicited, granted him a truce of eleven days, that he might perform the usual obsequies, and raise a tomb for Hector. The following quotation is directly descriptive of this and the following subject.

" Achilles, like a lion, rush'd abroad;
Automedon and Alcimus attend,
Whom most he honour'd since he lost his friend:
These to unyoke the mules and horses went,
And led the hoary herald to the tent;
Next heap'd on high the numerous presents bear
(Great Hector's ransom) from the polish'd car.
Two splendid mantles and a carpet spread,
They leave to cover and enwrap the dead.
He called the handmaids, with assistant toil
To wash the body and anoint with oil,
Apart from Priam; lest th' unhappy sire,
Provoked to passion, once more rouse to ire
The stern Pelides; and nor sacred age,
Nor Jove's command, should check the rising
    rage.
This done, the garments o'er the corse they
    spread;
Achilles lifts it to the funeral bed!
Then, while the body on the car they laid,
He groans, and calls on loved Patroclus' shade."
                                    Iliad, book xxiv.

No. 892.

Achilles placing the body of Hector on the funeral bed.

GNAIOS.   *Calcedony.*

See preceding quotation.

No. 893.

Hercules, in presence of Telamon, imploring Jupiter to render young Ajax invulnerable.

ANTEROTOS.   *Cornelian.*

No. 894.

The same subject.

CHROMIOS.   *Cornelian.*

No. 895.

Telamon Ajax killing Simoïsius.

ALLION.   *Sardonyx.*

" In blooming youth fair Simoïsius fell,
Sent by great Ajax to the shades of hell—
Fair Simoïsius, whom his mother bore
Amid the flocks on silver Simoïs' shore :
The nymph descending from the hills of Ide,
To seek her parents on his flowery side,
Brought forth the babe, their common care and
    joy,
And thence from Simoïs named the lovely boy.
Short was his date ! by dreadful Ajax slain
He falls, and renders all their cares in vain !

So falls a poplar, that in watery ground
Raised high the head, with stately branches
    crown'd
(Fell'd by some artist with his shining steel,
To shape the circle of the bending wheel),
Cut down it lies, tall, smooth, and largely spread,
With all its beauteous honours on its head ;
There, left a subject to the wind and rain,
And scorch'd by suns, it withers on the plain.
Thus pierced by Ajax, Simoïsius lies
Stretch'd on the shore—and thus neglected dies !"
                                Iliad, book iv.

No. 896.

Telamon Ajax and Eurypylus.

APOLLONIDES.   *Amethyst.*

" As the slow beast, with heavy strength endued,
In some wide field by troops of boys pursued,
Though round his sides a wooden tempest rain,
Crops the tall harvest, and lays waste the plain ;
Thick on his hide the hollow blows resound,
The patient animal maintains his ground,
Scarce from the field with all their efforts chased,
And stirs but slowly when he stirs at last.
On Ajax thus a weight of Trojans hung ;
The strokes redoubled on his buckler rung ;
Confiding now in bulky strength he stands,
Now turns, and backward bears the yielding bands ;
Now stiff recedes, yet hardly seems to fly,
And threats his followers with retorted eye.
Fix'd as the bar between two warring powers,
While hissing darts descend in iron showers :
In his broad buckler many a weapon stood—
Its surface bristled with a quivering wood ;
And many a javelin, guiltless, on the plain
Marks the dry dust, and thirsts for blood in vain.

But bold Eurypylus his aid imparts,
And dauntless springs beneath a cloud of darts ;
Whose eager javelin launch'd against the foe,
Great Apisaon felt the fatal blow ;
From his torn liver the red current flowed,
And his slack knees desert their dying load.
The victor rushing to despoil the dead,
From Paris' bow a vengeful arrow fled :
Fix'd in his nervous thigh the weapon stood,
Fix'd was the point, but broken was the wood.
Back to the lines the wounded Greek retired,
Yet thus, retreating, his associates fired :
    ' What god, O Grecians ! has your heart dis-
        may'd ?
Oh, turn to arms ; 'tis Ajax claims your aid.
This hour he stands the mark of hostile rage,
And this the last brave battle he shall wage ;
Haste, join your forces ; from the gloomy grave
The warrior rescue, and your country save."
                                Iliad, book xi.

No. 897.

Paris wounding Eurypylus.

APOLLONIDES. *Cornelian.*

See preceding quotation.

No. 898.

Telamon Ajax defending the ships.

CHROMIOS. *Cornelian.*

The Trojans having broken through the Grecian rampart, and boarded the ships, attempted to set them on fire; but are driven back, mainly by the bravery and prowess of Ajax.

" First of the field great Ajax strikes their eyes,
His port majestic, and his ample size :
A ponderous mace with studs of iron crown'd,
Full twenty cubits long, he swings around ;
Nor fights like others fixed to certain stands,
But looks a moving tower above the bands ;
High on the decks with vast gigantic stride,
The godlike hero stalks from side to side.
So when a horseman from the watery mead
(Skill'd in the manage of the bounding steed)
Drives four fair coursers, practised to obey,
To some great city through the public way ;
Safe in his art, as side by side they run,
He shifts his seat, and vaults from one to one ;
And now to this, and now to that he flies ;
Admiring numbers follow with their eyes.
  From ship to ship thus Ajax swiftly flew,
No less the wonder of the warring crew.
As furious Hector thunder'd threats aloud,
And rush'd enraged before the Trojan crowd ;
Then swift invades the ships, whose beaky prores
Lay rank'd contiguous on the bending shores :
So the strong eagle from his airy height,
Who marks the swans' or cranes' embodied flight,
Stoops down impetuous, while they light for food,
And, stooping, darkens with his wings the flood.

Jove leads him on with his almighty hand,
And breathes fierce spirits in his following band.
The warring nations meet—the battle roars—
Thick beats the combat on the sounding prores.
Thou wouldst have thought, so furious was their
    fire,
No force could tame them, and no toil could
    tire ;
As if new vigour from new fights they won,
And the long battle was but then begun.
Greece, yet unconquer'd, kept alive the war,
Secure of death, confiding in despair ;
Troy in proud hopes already view'd the main,
Bright with the blaze, and red with heroes slain !
Like strength is felt from hope and from de-
    spair,
And each contends as his were all the war.
  'Twas thou, bold Hector ! whose resistless hand
First seized a ship on that contested strand ;
The same which dead Protesilaus bore,
The first that touch'd th' unhappy Trojan shore :
For this in arms the warring nations stood,
And bathed their generous breasts with mutual
    blood.
No room to poise the lance or bend the bow ;
But hand to hand, and man to man they grow :

Wounded they wound; and seek each other's
  hearts
With falchions — axes — swords — and shorten'd
  darts.
The falchions ring—shields rattle—axes sound—
Swords flash in air, or glitter on the ground:
With streaming blood the slippery shores are
  dyed,
And slaughter'd heroes swell the dreadful tide.
  Still raging Hector with his ample hand
Grasps the high stern, and gives this loud com-
  mand:
' Haste, bring the flames! the toil of ten long
  years
Is finish'd! and the day desired appears!—
This happy day with acclamations greet—
Bright with destruction of yon hostile fleet!
The coward counsels of a timorous throng
Of reverend dotards check'd our glory long:
Too long Jove lull'd us with lethargic charms,
But now in peals of thunder calls to arms:
In this great day he crowns our full desires,
Wakes all our force, and seconds all our fires.'
  He spoke. The warriors, at his fierce command,
Pour a new deluge on the Grecian band.
E'en Ajax paused (so thick the javelins fly),
Stepp'd back, and doubted or to live or die.
Yet where the oars are placed he stands to wait
What chief approaching dares attempt his fate:

E'en to the last his naval charge defends,
Now shakes his spear, now lifts, and now pro-
  tends;
E'en yet the Greeks with piercing shouts inspires,
Amidst attacks—and deaths—and darts—and
  fires!
  ' O friends! O heroes! names for ever dear,
Once sons of Mars, and thunderbolts of war!
Ah! yet be mindful of your old renown—
Your great forefathers' virtues and your own!
What aids expect you in this utmost strait?
What bulwarks rising between you and fate?
No aids—no bulwarks, your retreat attend—
No friends to help—no city to defend.
This spot is all you have to lose or keep;
There stand the Trojans, and here rolls the deep:
'Tis hostile ground you tread; your native lands
Far, far from hence—your fates are in your
  hands.'
  Raging he spoke; nor farther wastes his breath,
But turns his javelin to the work of death.
Whate'er bold Trojan arm'd his daring hands,
Against the sable ships with flaming brands,
So well the chief his naval weapons sped,
The luckless warrior at his stern lay dead:
Full twelve, the boldest, in a moment fell,
Sent by great Ajax to the shades of hell.''

                                    Iliad, book xv.

No. 899.

Telamon Ajax in his madness attacking the sheep.

Chromios.   *Sardonyx.*

    After the death of Achilles, his armour was set up as a prize for the most meritorious of
the Grecian chiefs.   All others having resigned their claims to Ajax and Ulysses, the armour
was, after a full examination of the relative merits of each, adjudged to Ulysses.   Upon this,
Ajax ran mad; and in his phrensy slaughtered a flock of sheep, which he took for the judges;
and subsequently slew himself.   Some authors, however, represent his death differently; among
them, Dictys Cretensis,—*i. e.* that being infuriated at the decision, he vowed vengeance against
Agamemnon, and in consequence was assassinated in his tent.

No. 900.

Death of Ajax.

DIOSCORIDES. *Cornelian.*

" He who could often and alone withstand
The foe—the fire—and Jove's own partial hand,
Now cannot his unmaster'd grief sustain,
But yields to rage—to madness—and disdain!
Then snatching out his falchion, 'Thou,' said he,
' Art mine: Ulysses lays no claim to thee.
O often tried, and ever-trusty sword,
Now do thy last kind office to thy lord:
'Tis Ajax who requests thy aid, to shew
None but himself himself could overthrow.'
He said, and with so good a will to die,
Did to his breast the fatal point apply;

It found his heart, a way till then unknown,
Where never weapon enter'd but his own.
No hands could force it thence, so fix'd it stood,
Till out it rush'd, expell'd by streams of spouting
    blood.
The fruitful blood produc'd a flow'r, which grew
On a green stem, and of a purple hue,*
Like his whom unaware Apollo slew:
Inscrib'd in both the letters are the same,
But those express the grief, and these the name."
              OVID, *Met.* x.

Ovid (*Met.* x.) says that Apollo, having at a game of quoits inadvertently slain his favourite Hyacinthus, transformed him into a hyacinth.

" ' Yet on my tongue thou shalt for ever
    dwell;
Thy name my lyre shall sound, my verse shall
    tell;
And to a flow'r transform'd, unheard of yet,
Stamp'd on thy leaves my cries thou shalt repeat.
The time shall come, prophetic I foreknow,
When join'd to thee, a mighty chief shall grow,
And with my plaints his name thy leaf shall
    shew.'

While Phœbus thus the laws of fate reveal'd,
Behold, the blood which stain'd the verdant field
Is blood no longer; but a flower full-blown,
Far brighter than the Tyrian scarlet shone.
A lily's form it took; its purple hue
Was all that made a diff'rence to the view.
Nor stopp'd he here; the god upon its leaves
The sad expression of his sorrow weaves;
And to this hour the mournful purple wears
Ai, Ai, inscrib'd in fun'ral characters."

No. 901.

Metamorphosis of Ajax.

CHROMIOS. *Cornelian.*

The fable is, that the gods having allowed Ajax the privilege of returning (after death) to earth in any shape he pleased, he chose that of a lion.

---

* The hyacinth.

No. 902.

Death of Gorgythion.

POLYCLETES. *Cornelian.*

Teucer, the famous Grecian archer, having shot at Hector, slew Gorgythion.

" To this chief: ' With praise the rest in-
        spire,
Nor urge a soul already fill'd with fire ;
What strength I have be now in battle tried,
Till every shaft in Phrygian blood be dyed.
Since rallying from our wall we forced the
        foe,
Still aim'd at Hector have I bent my bow :
Eight forky arrows from this hand have fled,
And eight bold heroes by their points lie dead :
But sure some god denies me to destroy
This fury of the field—this dog of Troy.'

He said, and twang'd the string. The weapon
        flies
At Hector's breast, and sings along the skies :
He miss'd the mark ; but pierced Gorgythio's
        heart,
And drench'd in royal blood the thirsty dart.
Fair Castianira, nymph of form divine,
This offspring added to king Priam's line.
As full-blown poppies overcharged with rain,
Decline the head, and drooping kiss the plain ;
So sinks the youth : his beauteous head, depress'd
Beneath his helmet, drops upon his breast."

Iliad, book viii.

No. 903.

Ajax Oïleus hurling the head of Imbrius at Hector.

APOLLONIDES. *Cornelian.*

" Meanwhile with rising rage the battle glows,
The tumult thickens, and the clamour grows.
By Teucer's arm the warlike Imbrius bleeds,
The son of Mentor, rich in generous steeds.
Ere yet to Troy the sons of Greece were led,
In fair Pedæus' verdant pastures bred,
The youth had dwelt ; remote from war's alarms,
And bless'd in bright Medesicaste's arms :
(This nymph, the fruit of Priam's ravish'd joy,
Allied the warrior to the house of Troy).
To Troy, when glory call'd his arms, he came,
And match'd the bravest of her chiefs in fame :
With Priam's sons, a guardian of the throne,
He lived beloved and honour'd as his own :
Him Teucer pierced between the throat and ear ;
He groans beneath the Telamonian spear.

As from some far-seen mountain's airy crown,
Subdued by steel, a tall ash tumbles down,
And soils its verdant tresses on the ground :
So falls the youth ; his arms the fall resound.
Then Teucer rushing to despoil the dead,
From Hector's hand a shining javelin fled :
He saw, and shunn'd the death ; the forceful dart
Sung on, and pierced Amphimachus's heart,
Cteatus' son, of Neptune's forceful line ;
Vain was his courage, and his race divine !
Prostrate he falls ; his clanging arms resound,
And his broad buckler thunders on the ground.
To seize his beamy helm the victor flies,
And just had fasten'd on the dazzling prize,
When Ajax' manly arm a javelin flung ;
Full on the shield's round boss the weapon rung ;

He felt the shock, nor more was doom'd to feel,
Secure in mail, and sheath'd in shining steel.
Repulsed he yields; the victor Greeks obtain
The spoils contested, and bear off the slain.
Between the leaders of th' Athenian line,
(Stichius the brave, Menestheus the divine),
Deplored Amphimachus—sad object! lies;
Imbrius remains the fierce Ajaces' prize.

As two grim lions bear across the lawn,
Snatch'd from devouring hounds, a slaughter'd fawn,
In their fell jaws high-lifting through the wood,
And sprinkling all the shrubs with drops of blood;
So these the chief: great Ajax from the dead
Strips his bright arms; Oïleus lops his head:
Toss'd like a ball, and whirl'd in air away,
At Hector's feet the gory visage lay."

Iliad, book xiii.

No. 904.

Ajax Oïleus dragging Cassandra from the temple of Minerva.

GNAIOS. *Cornelian.*

Some authors say that he violated her in the temple. But Virgil describes her (book ii. line 403 of the original) as dragged bound, with her hair dishevelled, out of the temple to which she had fled as an asylum—

" To heaven she strain'd her burning eyes—in vain—
Her eyes; for bonds restrain'd her tender hands."

No. 905.

Ajax Oïleus impiously ascribing to himself his safety from shipwreck.

CHROMIOS. *Calcedony.*

Minerva, as a punishment for the outrage offered by Ajax to Cassandra in her temple at the sacking of Troy, caused his vessel to be wrecked on his return. Virgil (book i.) describes him as blasted, after landing on a rock, with lightning hurled by Minerva—

" Illum expirantem transfixo pectore flammas
Turbine corripuit, scopuloque infixit acuto."

But it appears that the artist here has adopted the representation of Homer.

" By Neptune rescu'd from Minerva's hate,
On Gyræ safe Oïlean Ajax sat,
His ship o'erwhelm'd; but frowning on the floods,
Impious he roar'd defiance to the gods;
To his own prowess all the glory gave,
The pow'r defrauding who vouchsaf'd to save.
This heard the raging ruler of the main;
His spear, indignant for such high disdain,

3 z

He launch'd; dividing with his forky mace
Th' aërial summit from the marble base:
The rock rush'd seaward with impetuous roar
Ingulf'd, and to th' abyss the boaster bore."

Odyssey, book iv.

No. 906.

Diomede, wounded, imploring the aid of Minerva; while Sthenelus is plucking the arrow from his shoulder.

GNAIOS.　*Sardonyx.*

" With grief the leader of the Lycian band *
Saw the wide waste of his destructive hand:
His bended bow against the chief he drew;
Swift to the mark the thirsty arrow flew,
Whose forky point the hollow breastplate tore,
Deep in his shoulder pierced, and drank the gore:
The rushing stream his brazen armour dyed,
While the proud archer thus exulting cried:
' Hither, ye Trojans, hither drive your steeds!
Lo! by our hand the bravest Grecian bleeds.
Not long the dreadful dart he can sustain;
Or Phœbus urg'd me to those fields in vain.'
So spoke he, boastful; but the winged dart
Stopp'd short of life, and mock'd the shooter's art.
The wounded chief behind his car retired,
The helping hand of Sthenelus required;
Swift from his seat he leap'd upon the ground,
And tugg'd the weapon from the gushing wound;
When thus the king his guardian power address'd,
The purple current wandering o'er his vest:
' O progeny of Jove! unconquer'd maid!
If e'er my godlike sire deserv'd thy aid—
If e'er I felt thee in the fighting-field—
Now, goddess, now thy sacred succour yield.

O give my lance to reach the Trojan knight,
Whose arrow wounds the chief thou guard'st in
　　fight;
And lay the boaster grovelling on the shore,
That vaunts these eyes shall view the light no
　　more.'
　　Thus pray'd Tydides, and Minerva heard;
His nerves confirm'd—his languid spirits cheer'd.
He feels each limb with wonted vigour light;
His beating bosom claims the promised fight.
' Be bold,' she cried, ' in every combat shine,
War be thy province, thy protection mine;
Rush to the fight, and every foe control;
Wake each paternal virtue in thy soul:
Strength swells thy boiling breast, infused by me,
And all thy godlike father breathes in thee!
Yet more, from mortal mists I purge thy eyes,
And set to view the warring deities.
These see thou shun through all th' embattled
　　plain,
Nor rashly strive where human force is vain.
If Venus mingle in the martial band,
Her shalt thou wound: so Pallas gives com-
　　mand.' "

Iliad, book v.

No. 907.

Diomede killing Pandarus.

CHROMIOS.　*Cornelian.*

---

* Pandarus.

" With deep concern divine Æneas view'd
The foe prevailing, and his friends pursued;
Through the thick storm of singing spears he flies,
Exploring Pandarus with careful eyes;
At length he found Lycaon's mighty son,
To whom the chief of Venus' race begun :

.   .   .   .   .

'Against yon hero let us bend our course,
And, hand to hand, encounter force with force.
Now mount my seat, and from the chariot's
    height
Observe my father's steeds, renown'd in fight.
Practised alike to turn, to stop, to chase,
To dare the shock, or urge the rapid race:
Secure with these, through fighting-fields we go ;
Or safe to Troy, if Jove assist the foe.
Haste, seize the whip, and snatch the guiding
    rein ;
The warrior's fury let this arm sustain ;
Or, if to combat thy bold heart incline,
Take thou the spear, the chariot's care be mine.'
' O prince !' Lycaon's valiant son replied,
As thine the steeds, be thine the task to guide.
The horses, practised to their lord's command,
Shall bear the rein, and answer to thy hand.
Thine be the guidance then : with spear and shield
Myself will charge this terror of the field.'

Thus while they spoke, the foe came furious on,
And stern Lycaon's warlike race begun :
' Prince, thou art met. Though late in vain
    assail'd,
The spear may enter where the arrow fail'd.'
He said, then shook the pond'rous lance and flung ;
On his broad shield the sounding weapon rung,
Pierc'd the tough orb, and in his cuirass hung.
' He bleeds ! the pride of Greece !' the boaster
    cries ;
' Our triumph now, the mighty warrior lies !'
' Mistaken vaunter !' Diomed replied ;
' Thy dart has err'd ; and now my spear be tried.
Ye 'scape not both ; one, headlong from his car,
With hostile blood shall glut the god of war.'
He spoke ; and, rising, hurl'd his forceful dart,
Which, driven by Pallas, pierc'd a vital part ;
Full in his face it enter'd, and betwixt
The nose and eyeball the proud Lycian fix'd ;
Crash'd all his jaws, and cleft the tongue within,
Till the bright point look'd out beneath the chin.
Headlong he falls, his helmet knocks the ground;
Earth groans beneath him, and his arms resound ;
The starting coursers tremble with affright;
The soul indignant seeks the realms of night."

Iliad, book v.

No. 908.

Combat of Diomede and Æneas.

Evodos. *Cornelian.*

" To guard his slaughter'd friend Æneas flies,
His spear extending where the carcass lies ;
Watchful he wheels—protects it every way,
As the grim lion stalks around his prey.
O'er the fallen trunk his ample shield display'd,
He hides the hero with his mighty shade,
And threats aloud : the Greeks with longing eyes
Behold at distance, but forbear the prize.

Then fierce Tydides stoops ; and from the fields,
Heaved with vast force, a rocky fragment wields :
Not two strong men th' enormous weight could
    raise,
Such men as live in these degenerate days.
He swung it round ; and gathering strength to
    throw,
Discharged the ponderous ruin at the foe.

Where to the hip th' inserted thigh unites,
Full on the bone the pointed marble lights:
Through both the tendons broke the rugged stone,
And stripp'd the skin, and crack'd the solid bone.
Sunk on his knees, and staggering with his pains,
His falling bulk his bended arm sustains;
Lost in a dizzy mist the warrior lies;
A sudden cloud comes swimming o'er his eyes.

There the brave chief who mighty numbers
sway'd,
Oppress'd had sunk to death's eternal shade;
But heavenly Venus, mindful of the love
She bore Anchises in the Idæan grove,
His danger views with anguish and despair,
And guards her offspring with a mother's care."

Iliad, book v.

No. 909.

Venus, who is wounded by Diomede, led away by Iris.

DIOSCORIDES. *Cornelian.*

Minerva instigated Diomede to assail Venus.   See the quotation No. 906.

" Through breaking ranks his furious course
he bends,
And at the goddess his broad lance extends;
Through her bright veil the daring weapon drove—
The ambrosial veil, which all the Graces wove;
Her snowy hand the razing steel profaned,
And the transparent skin with crimson stain'd.
From the clear vein a stream immortal flow'd,
Such stream as issues from a wounded god—
Pure emanation! uncorrupted flood!
Unlike our gross, diseased, terrestrial blood
(For not the bread of man their life sustains,
Nor wine's inflaming juice supplies their veins).
With tender shrieks the goddess filled the place,
And dropp'd her offspring from her weak em-
brace.
Him Phœbus took: he casts a cloud around
The fainting chief, and wards the mortal wound.
Then, with a voice that shook the vaulted
skies,
The king insults the goddess as she flies:
' Ill with Jove's daughter bloody fights agree,
The field of combat is no scene for thee:
Go, let thy own soft sex employ thy care—
Go, lull the coward, or delude the fair.

Taught by this stroke, renounce the war's alarms,
And learn to tremble at the name of arms.'
Tydides thus. The goddess, seized with dread,
Confused, distracted, from the conflict fled.
To aid her, swift the winged Iris flew,
Wrapp'd in a mist above the warring crew.
The queen of love with faded charms she found,
Pale was her cheek, and livid look'd the wound.
To Mars, who sat remote, they bent their way,
Far on the left with clouds involved he lay;
Beside him stood his lance, distain'd with gore,
And, rein'd with gold, his foaming steeds before.
Low at his knee she begg'd, with streaming eyes,
Her brother's car to mount the distant skies;
And shew'd the wound by fierce Tydides given—
A mortal man, who dares encounter heaven.
Stern Mars attentive hears the queen complain,
And to her hand commits the golden rein;
She mounts the seat, oppress'd with silent woe,
Driven by the goddess of the painted bow.
The lash resounds, the rapid chariot flies,
And in a moment scales the lofty skies:
There stopp'd the car, and there the coursers
stood,
Fed by fair Iris with ambrosial food."

Iliad, book v.

No. 910.

Venus, accompanied by Iris, praying Mars to lend her his chariot.

POLYCLETES. *Cornelian.*

See preceding quotation.

No. 911.

Venus and Iris returning to heaven.

DIOSCORIDES. *Cornelian.*

See preceding quotation.

No. 912.

Apollo repulsing Diomede.

ALLION. *Amethyst.*

" Thus they in heaven : while on the plain
    below
The fierce Tydides charged his Dardan foe ;
Flush'd with celestial blood, pursued his way,
And fearless dared the threatening god of day :
Already in his hopes he saw him kill'd,
Though screen'd behind Apollo's mighty shield.
Thrice rushing furious, at the chief he strook ;
His blazing buckler thrice Apollo shook :
He tried the fourth ; when, breaking from the cloud,
A more than mortal voice was heard aloud :

' O son of Tydeus, cease ! be wise, and see
How vast the difference of the gods and thee—
Distance immense ! between the powers that
    shine
Above, eternal, deathless, and divine,
And mortal man !—a wretch of humble birth—
A short-lived reptile in the dust of earth !'
    So spoke the god who darts celestial fires ;
He dreads his fury, and some steps retires."

Iliad, book v.

No. 913.

Hebe cleansing and refreshing Mars.

PYRGOTELES. *Sardonyx.*

Mars was wounded by Diomede. He fled, wrapped in a cloud, to heaven ; and was consigned by Jupiter, who reproached him for his turbulent disposition, to the care of Pæon and Hebe.

" She snatch'd the reins, she lash'd with all
       her force,
And full on Mars impell'd the foaming horse:
But first, to hide her heavenly visage, spread
Black Orcus' helmet o'er her radiant head.
   Just then gigantic Periphas lay slain,
The strongest warrior of th' Ætolian train;
The god who slew him leaves his prostrate prize
Stretch'd where he fell, and at Tydides flies.
Now rushing fierce, in equal arms appear
The daring Greek, the dreadful god of war!
Full at the chief, above his courser's head,
From Mars's arm th' enormous weapon fled:
Pallas opposed her hand, and caused to glance
Far from the car the strong, immortal lance.
Then threw the force of Tydeus' warlike son—
The javelin hiss'd—the goddess urged it on:
Where the broad cincture girt his armour round,
It pierced the god; his groin received the wound.
From the rent skin the warrior tugs again
The smoking steel. Mars bellows with the pain:

Loud as the roar encountering armies yield,
When shouting millions shake the thundering field.
Both armies start, and trembling gaze around;
And earth and heaven rebellow to the sound.

  .   .   .   .   .

   Thus he who shakes Olympus with his nod ;
Then gave to Pæon's care the bleeding god.
With gentle hand the balm he pour'd around,
And heal'd th' immortal flesh, and closed the
       wound.
As when the fig's press'd juice, infused in cream,
To curds coagulates the liquid stream,
Sudden the fluids fix, the parts combined ;
Such, and so soon, th' ethereal texture join'd.
Cleansed from the dust and gore, fair Hebe
       dress'd
His mighty limbs in an immortal vest.
Glorious he sat, in majesty restored,
Fast by the throne of heaven's superior lord."

                                   Iliad, book v.

No. 914.

Diomede and Glaucus.

CHROMIOS.   *Sardonyx.*

   The Greeks having prevailed, chiefly through the prowess of Diomede, Hector quitted the
field to appoint a supplicatory procession of Hecuba and the Trojan matrons to the temple of
Minerva.

" Now paused the battle (godlike Hector gone)
When daring Glaucus and great Tydeus' son
Between both armies met: the chiefs from far
Observed each other, and had mark'd for war.
Near as they drew, Tydides thus began :
  ' What art thou, boldest of the race of man ?
Our eyes, till now, that aspect ne'er beheld,
Where fame is reap'd amid th' embattled field ;
Yet far before the troops thou dar'st appear,
And meet a lance the fiercest heroes fear.

Unhappy they, and born of luckless sires,
Who tempt our fury when Minerva fires !
But if from heaven celestial thou descend;
Know, with immortals we no more contend.'

   .   .   .   .   .

  ' I brave not heaven : but if the fruits of earth
Sustain thy life, and human be thy birth;
Bold as thou art, too prodigal of breath,
Approach and enter the dark gates of death.'

   Glaucus says he is the grandson of the famous Bellerophon, the Greek, whose history he gives. Diomede is transported with joy at finding that their ancestors were bound together by ties of hospitality, and made each other presents as pledges of lasting friendship, and then proceeds—

" ' Mindful of this, in friendship let us join ;
If heaven our steps to foreign lands incline,
My guest in Argos thou, and I in Lycia thine.
Enough of Trojans to this lance shall yield,
In the full harvest of yon ample field ;
Enough of Greeks shall dye thy spear with gore ;
But thou and Diomed be foes no more.
Now change we arms, and prove to either host
We guard the friendship of the line we boast.'

Thus having said, the gallant chiefs alight,
Their hands they join, their mutual faith they plight;
Brave Glaucus then each narrow thought resign'd
(Jove warm'd his bosom and enlarged his mind) :
For Diomed's brass arms, of mean device,
For which nine oxen paid (a vulgar price),
He gave his own, of gold divinely wrought,
A hundred beeves the shining purchase bought."
Iliad, book vi.

No. 915.

Diomede and Ulysses proceeding as spies at night to the Trojan camp.

CHROMIOS. *Cornelian.*

After the defeat of the Greeks, and refusal of Achilles to re-engage in the war, the Grecian chiefs held a council; and Nestor proposed to send some one as a spy to the Trojan camp, to learn, if possible, something about the position and intentions of the enemy. Diomede volunteered to go on the dangerous enterprise, and selected Ulysses as his companion.

" Thus sheath'd in arms, the council they forsake,
And dark through paths oblique their progress take.
Just then, in sign she favour'd their intent,
A long-wing'd heron great Minerva sent ;
This, though surrounding shades obscured their view,
By the shrill clang and whistling winds they knew.
As from the right she soar'd, Ulysses pray'd,
Hail'd the glad omen, and address'd the maid.

The heroes pray'd, and Pallas from the skies
Accords their vow—succeeds their enterprise.
Now, like two lions panting for the prey,
With deathful thoughts they trace the dreary way,
Through the black horrors of th' ensanguin'd plain—
Through dust—through blood—o'er arms—and hills of slain !"
Iliad, book x.

No. 916.

Hector engaging to reward the spy, Dolon.

SOLON. *Cornelian.*

The Trojans likewise held a council, and determined to send Dolon as a spy to the Grecian camp.

" Nor less bold Hector, and the sons of Troy,
On high designs the wakeful hours employ;
Th' assembled peers their lofty chief enclosed;
Who thus the counsels of his breast proposed :
  ' What glorious man, for high attempts pre-
      pared,
Dares greatly venture for a rich reward ?
Of yonder fleet a bold discovery make,
What watch they keep, and what resolves they
    take?
If now subdued they meditate their flight,
And spent with toil neglect the watch of night ?
His be the chariot that shall please him most,
Of all the plunder of the vanquish'd host ;
His the fair steeds that all the rest excel,
And his the glory to have served so well.'
  A youth there was among the tribes of Troy,
Dolon his name, Eumedes' only boy
(Five girls beside the reverend herald told).
Rich was the son in brass, and rich in gold ;
Not bless'd by nature with the charms of face,
But swift of foot, and matchless in the race.
' Hector !' he said, ' my courage bids me meet
This high achievement, and explore the fleet :
But first exalt thy sceptre to the skies,
And swear to grant me the demanded prize ;
Th' immortal coursers, and the glittering car,
That bear Pelides through the ranks of war.
Encouraged thus, no idle scout I go,
Fulfil thy wish, their whole intention know,
E'en to the royal tent pursue my way,
And all their counsels, all their aims betray.'
  The chief then heav'd the golden sceptre high,
Attesting thus the monarch of the sky :
  ' Be witness thou ! immortal Lord of all !
Whose thunder shakes the dark aërial hall :
By none but Dolon shall this prize be borne,
And him alone th' immortal steeds adorn.'
  Thus Hector swore : the gods were call'd in vain,
But the rash youth prepares to scour the plain :
Across his back the bended bow he flung,
A wolf's gray hide around his shoulders hung,
A ferret's downy fur his helmet lined,
And in his hand a pointed javelin shined.

Then (never to return) he sought the shore,
And trod the path his feet must tread no more.
Scarce had he pass'd the steeds and Trojan throng
(Still bending forward as he coursed along),
When, on the hollow way, th' approaching tread
Ulysses mark'd, and thus to Diomed :
  ' O friend ! I hear some step of hostile feet,
Moving this way, or hastening to the fleet ;
Some spy, perhaps, to lurk beside the main ;
Or nightly pillager that strips the slain.
Yet let him pass, and win a little space ;
Then rush behind him, and prevent his pace.
But if too swift of foot he flies before,
Confine his course along the fleet and shore ;
Betwixt the camp and him our spears employ,
And intercept his hoped return to Troy.'
  With that they stepp'd aside, and stoop'd their
    head
(As Dolon pass'd) behind a heap of dead :
Along the path the spy unwary flew ;
Soft, at just distance, both the chiefs pursue.

.   .   .   .   .

Now Dolon, listening, heard them as they pass'd ;
Hector (he thought) had sent, and check'd his
    haste,
Till, scarce at distance of a javelin's throw,
No voice succeeding, he perceived the foe.
As when two skilful hounds the leveret wind,
Or chase through woods obscure the trembling
    hind ;
Now lost, now seen, they intercept his way,
And from the herd still turn the flying prey ;
So fast, and with such fears, the Trojan flew ;
So close, so constant, the bold Greeks pursue.
Now almost on the fleet the dastard falls,
And mingles with the guards that watch the walls ;
When brave Tydides stopp'd ; a generous thought
(Inspired by Pallas) in his bosom wrought,
Lest on the foe some forward Greek advance,
And snatch the glory from his lifted lance.
Then thus aloud : ' Whoe'er thou art, remain ;
This javelin else shall fix thee to the plain.
He said, and high in air the weapon cast,
Which wilful err'd, and o'er his shoulder pass'd ;

Then fix'd in earth. Against the trembling wood
The wretch stood propp'd, and quiver'd as he stood;

A sudden palsy seized his turning head;
His loose teeth chatter'd, and his colour fled;
The panting warriors seize him as he stands,
And with unmanly tears his life demands."

Iliad, book x.

No. 917.

Ulysses and Diomede hanging on a tree the arms of Dolon.

CHROMIOS. *Cornelian.*

Ulysses, in reply to the supplications of Dolon, tells him to take courage; and, without directly promising to spare his life, obtains from him information respecting the state of the Trojan camp, and the position of the auxiliary forces, especially that of Rhesus, who had recently arrived with his celebrated horses, on which the safety of Troy depended; the oracle having declared that the city could not be taken if they once drank of the waters of the Xanthus, or fed on the pasture of Troy.

" To this Tydides, with a gloomy frown:
' Think not to live, though all the truth be shewn.
Shall we dismiss thee, in some future strife
To risk more bravely thy now forfeit life?
Or that again our camps thou may'st explore?
No—once a traitor, thou betray'st no more.'
Sternly he spoke, and as the wretch prepar'd
With humble blandishment to stroke his beard,
Like lightning swift the wrathful falchion flew,
Divides the neck, and cuts the nerves in two;
One instant snatch'd his trembling soul to hell,
The head, yet speaking, mutter'd as it fell.

The furry helmet from his brow they tear,
The wolf's grey hide, th' unbended bow and spear;
These great Ulysses lifting to the skies,
To fav'ring Pallas dedicates the prize:
' Great queen of arms! receive this hostile spoil,
And let the Thracian steeds reward our toil:
Thee first of all the heav'nly host we praise—
Oh, speed our labours, and direct our ways!'
This said, the spoils, with dropping gore defac'd,
High on a spreading tamarisk he plac'd;
Then heap'd with reeds and gather'd boughs the plain,
To guide their footsteps to the place again."

Iliad, book x.

No. 918.

Minerva commanding Diomede to return to the Grecian camp.

GNAIOS. *Cornelian.*

" Through the still night they cross the devious fields,
Slippery with blood, o'er arms and heaps of shields,

Arriving where the Thracian squadrons lay
And eased in sleep the labours of the day.
Ranged in three lines they view the prostrate band:
The horses yoked beside each warrior stand;

4 A

Their arms in order on the ground reclined,
Through the brown shade the fulgid weapons
    shined;
Amidst lay Rhesus, stretch'd in sleep profound,
And the white steeds behind his chariot bound.
The welcome sight Ulysses first descries,
And points to Diomede the tempting prize:
' The man, the coursers, and the car behold!
Described by Dolon, with the arms of gold.
Now, brave Tydides! now thy courage try,
Approach the chariot, and the steeds untie;
Or if thy soul inspire to fiercer deeds,
Urge thou the slaughter, while I seize the steeds.'
   Pallas (this said) her hero's bosom warms,
Breathed in his heart, and strung his nervous
    arms:
Where'er he pass'd, a purple stream pursued;
His thirsty falchion, fat with hostile blood,
Bath'd all his footsteps—dyed the fields with gore,
And a low groan remurmur'd through the shore.
So the grim lion, from his nightly den,
O'erleaps the fences and invades the pen;
On sheep or goats, resistless in his way,
He falls, and foaming rends the guardless prey:
Nor stopp'd the fury of his vengeful hand,
Till twelve lay breathless of the Thracian band.
Ulysses following, as his partner slew,
Back by the foot each slaughter'd warrior drew;
The milk-white coursers studious to convey
Safe to the ships, he wisely clear'd the way;

Lest the fierce steeds, not yet to battles bred,
Should start, and tremble at the heaps of dead.
Now twelve despatch'd, the monarch last they
    found;
Tydides' falchion fix'd him to the ground.
Just then a deathful dream Minerva sent;
A warlike form appear'd before his tent,
Whose visionary steel his bosom tore:
So dream'd the monarch, and awaked no more.
   Ulysses now the snowy steeds detains,
And leads them, fasten'd by the silver reins;
These, with his bow unbent, he lash'd along
(The scourge forgot, on Rhesus' chariot hung),
Then gave his friend the signal to retire;
But him new dangers, new achievements fire.
Doubtful he stood, or with his reeking blade
To send more heroes to th' infernal shade—
Drag off the car where Rhesus' armour lay,
Or heave with manly force, and lift away.
While unresolved the son of Tydeus stands,
Pallas appears, and thus her chief commands:
' Enough, my son; from farther slaughter cease—
Regard thy safety—and depart in peace;
Haste to the ships—the gotten spoils enjoy,
Nor tempt too far the hostile gods of Troy.'
   The voice divine confess'd the martial maid,
In haste he mounted, and her word obey'd;
The coursers fly before Ulysses' bow,
Swift as the wind, and white as winter snow."
                    Iliad, book x.

No. 919.

Ulysses with the horses of Rhesus, and Diomede taking down the arms
of Dolon.

Chromios. *Cornelian.*

" Meanwhile the chiefs, arriving at the shade
   Where late the spoils of Hector's spy were laid,
   Ulysses stopp'd; to him Tydides bore
   The trophy, dropping yet with Dolon's gore:

Then mounts again; again their nimble feet
The coursers ply, and thunder tow'rd the fleet."

Iliad, book x.

No. 920.

Return of Ulysses and Diomede to the camp.

APOLLONIDES. *Amethyst.*

" Then o'er the trench the bounding coursers flew;
The joyful Greeks with loud acclaim pursue.
Straight to Tydides' high pavilion borne,
The matchless steeds his ample stall adorn:
The neighing coursers their new fellows greet,
And the full racks are heap'd with generous wheat;
But Dolon's armour, to his ships convey'd,
High on the painted stern Ulysses laid,
A trophy destined to the blue-eyed maid."

Iliad, book x.

No. 921.

Diomede wounded by Paris.

PYRGOTELES. *Sardonyx.*

" By Tydeus' lance Agastrophus was slain,
The far-famed hero of Pæonian strain;
Wing'd with his fears, on foot he strove to fly—
His steeds too distant, and the foe too nigh—
Through broken orders, swifter than the wind,
He fled; but, flying, left his life behind."

Hector ran to the rescue, but was driven back by Diomede.

" Him, while he triumph'd, Paris eyed from far
(The spouse of Helen, the fair cause of war);
Around the fields his feather'd shafts he sent,
From ancient Ilus' ruin'd monument.
Behind the column plac'd, he bent his bow,
And wing'd an arrow at th' unwary foe;
Just as he stoop'd, Agastrophus's crest
To seize, and drew the corslet from his breast.
The bow-string twang'd; nor flew the shaft in
vain—
But pierc'd his foot, and nail'd it to the plain.
The laughing Trojan, with a joyful spring,
Leaps from his ambush, and insults the king:
' He bleeds!' he cries, ' some god has sped my dart;
Would the same god had fix'd it in his heart!
So Troy, reliev'd from that wide-wasting hand,
Should breathe from slaughter, and in combat
stand;
Whose sons now tremble at his darted spear,
As scatter'd lambs the rushing lion fear.' "

Iliad, book xi.

No. 922.

Ulysses extracting the arrow from the foot of Diomede.

SOLON. *Sardonyx.*

" Ulysses hastens, with a trembling heart —
  Before him steps, and bending draws the dart —
  Forth flows the blood—an eager pang succeeds—
  Tydides mounts—and to the navy speeds."

Iliad, book xi.

No. 923.

Merion attacking Deïphobus, while bearing off the helmet of Ascalaphus.

GNAIOS. *Cornelian.*

" Deïphobus beheld him as he pass'd,
And, fired with hate, a parting javelin cast :
The javelin err'd, but held its course along,
And pierced Ascalaphus, the brave and young.
The son of Mars fell gasping on the ground,
And gnash'd the dust all bloody with his
            wound.

.   .   .   .   .

Now, where in dust the breathless hero lay—
For slain Ascalaphus commenced the fray—

Deïphobus to seize his helmet flies,
And from his temples rends the glittering prize.
Valiant as Mars, Meriones drew near,
And on his loaded arm discharged his spear :
He drops the weight, disabled with the pain ;
The hollow helmet rings against the plain.
Swift as a vulture leaping on his prey,
From his torn arm the Grecian rent away
The reeking javelin, and rejoin'd his friends."

Iliad, book xiii.

No. 924.

Merion attacking Acamas, king of Thrace.

POLYCLETES. *Cornelian.*

" O'ertaken Acamas by Merion bleeds,
  Pierc'd through the shoulder as he mounts his steeds ;
  Back from the car he tumbles to the ground :
  His swimming eyes eternal shades surround."

Iliad, book xiii.

No. 925.

Hector, Paris, and Helen.

DIOSCORIDES. *Cornelian.*

Hector, having left the field of battle, and gone to Troy to appoint a supplicatory procession of the queen and matrons to the temple of Minerva, took the opportunity of inducing Paris to return to the battle.

> " Thus ent'ring, in the glitt'ring rooms he found
> His brother chief, whose useless arms lay round,
> His eyes delighting with the splendid show,
> Bright'ning the shield, and polishing the bow.
> Beside him Helen with her virgins stands—
> Guides their rich labours, and instructs their hands.
> Him thus unactive, with an ardent look
> The prince beheld, and high resenting spoke."
>
> *Iliad,* book vi.

Hector tells Paris of the defeat of the Trojans, and of the necessity of his returning to the battle. Paris promises to go. Helen bewails her own sad destiny in being the cause of so much calamity and carnage; and recommends Hector to take a little rest after his fatigue.

> " The chief replied : ' This time forbids to rest—
> The Trojan bands by hostile fury prest,
> Demand their Hector, and his arm require—
> The combat urges, and my soul's on fire.
> Urge thou thy knight to march where glory calls,
> And timely join me, ere I leave the walls ;
> Ere yet I mingle in the direful fray,
> My wife, my infant, claim a moment's stay ;
> This day (perhaps the last that sees me here)
> Demands a parting word, a tender tear—
> This day, some god who hates our Trojan land
> May vanquish Hector by a Grecian hand."
>
> *Iliad,* book vi.

No. 926.

The interview between Hector and Andromache.

GNAIOS. *Cornelian.*

" He said ; and pass'd with sad presaging heart
To seek his spouse, his soul's far dearer part ;
At home he sought her, but he sought in vain—
She, with one maid of all her menial train,
Had thence retired ; and with her second joy,
The young Astyanax—the hope of Troy.
Pensive she stood on Ilion's towery height—
Beheld the war, and sicken'd at the sight !
There her sad eyes in vain her lord explore,
Or weep the wounds her bleeding country bore.
  But he who found not whom his soul desired,
Whose virtue charm'd him, as her beauty fired,
Stood in the gates, and ask'd what way she bent
Her parting step ? If to the fane she went,
Where late the mourning matrons made resort ;
Or sought her sisters in the Trojan court?
' Not to the court,' replied the attendant train,
' Nor mix'd with matrons to Minerva's fane :
To Ilion's steepy tower she bent her way,
To mark the fortunes of the doubtful day.
Troy fled, she heard, before the Grecian sword :
She heard, and trembled for her absent lord.
Distracted with surprise, she seem'd to fly,
Fear on her cheek, and sorrow in her eye.
The nurse attended with her infant boy,
The young Astyanax, the hope of Troy."

Hector finds Andromache—

" Silent the warrior smiled, and, pleas'd, resign'd
To tender passion all his mighty mind.
His beauteous princess cast a mournful look—
Hung on his hand—and then dejected spoke.
Her bosom labour'd with a boding sigh ;
And the big tear stood trembling in her eye.
' Too daring prince ! ah, whither dost thou run ?—
Ah, too forgetful of thy wife and son !
And think'st thou not how wretched we shall be,
A widow I, a helpless orphan he !
For sure such courage length of life denies ;
And thou must fall—thy virtue's sacrifice !
Greece in her single heroes strove in vain ;
Now hosts oppose thee, and thou must be slain !
Oh, grant me, gods ! ere Hector meets his doom,
All I can ask of heaven—an early tomb !
So shall my days in one sad tenour run,
And end with sorrows, as they first begun.
No parent now remains my griefs to share—
No father's aid—no mother's tender care.
The fierce Achilles wrapp'd our walls in fire,
Laid Thebè waste, and slew my warlike sire !

.   .   .   .

By the same arm my seven bravê brothers fell—
In one sad day beheld the gates of hell.

.   .   .   .

My mother lived to bear the victor's bonds.

.   .   .   .

Yet, while my Hector still survives, I see
My father—mother—brethren—all—in thee !
Alas ! my parents—brothers—kindred—all—
Once more will perish, if my Hector fall !
Thy wife—thy infant in thy danger share :
Oh, prove a husband's, and a father's care !

That quarter most the skilful Greeks annoy,
Where yon wild fig-trees join the walls of Troy:
Thou from this tower defend th' important
    post;
There Agamemnon points his dreadful host,
That pass Tydides—Ajax strive to gain ;
And there the vengeful Spartan fires his train.
Thrice our bold foes the fierce attack have given,
Or led by hopes, or dictated from heaven.
Let others in the field their arms employ,
But stay my Hector here, and guard his Troy.'
  ' The chief replied: ' That post shall be my care,
Not that alone, but all the works of war.
How would the sons of Troy, in arms renown'd,
And Troy's proud dames, whose garments sweep
    the ground,
Attaint the lustre of my former name,
Should Hector basely quit the field of fame?
My early youth was bred to martial pains—
My soul impels me to th' embattled plains:
Let me be foremost to defend the throne,
And guard my father's glories, and my own.
Yet come it will—the day decreed by fates
(How my heart trembles while my tongue re-
    lates)—
The day when thou, imperial Troy ! must bend,
And see thy warriors fall—thy glories end.
And yet no dire presage so wounds my mind—
My mother's death—the ruin of my kind—
Not Priam's hoary hairs defiled with gore—
Not all my brothers gasping on the shore—
As thine, Andromache ! thy griefs I dread:
I see thee trembling—weeping—captive—led !
In Argive looms our battles to design,
And woes, of which so large a part was thine !
To bear the victor's hard commands, or bring
The weight of waters from Hyperia's spring :
There, while you groan beneath the load of life,
They cry, ' Behold the mighty Hector's wife !'

Some haughty Greek, who lives thy tears to see,
Embitters all thy woes by naming me.
The thoughts of glory past, and present shame—
A thousand griefs shall waken at the name !
May I lie cold before that dreadful day,
Press'd with a load of monumental clay !
Thy Hector, wrapp'd in everlasting sleep,
Shall neither hear thee sigh, nor see thee weep.'
  Thus having spoke, the illustrious chief of Troy
Stretch'd his fond arms to clasp the lovely boy.
The babe clung crying to his nurse's breast,
Scared at the dazzling helm and nodding crest.
With secret pleasure each fond parent smiled,
And Hector hasted to relieve his child—
The glittering terrors from his brows unbound,
And placed the beaming helmet on the ground.
Then kiss'd the child, and lifting high in air,
Thus to the gods preferr'd a father's prayer :
  ' O thou ! whose glory fills th' ethereal throne,
And all ye deathless powers ! protect my son !
Grant him, like me, to purchase just renown—
To guard the Trojans—to defend the crown—
Against his country's foes the war to wage—
And rise the Hector of the future age !
So when, triumphant from successful toils
Of heroes slain, he bears the reeking spoils,
Whole hosts may hail him with deserv'd acclaim,
And say, "This chief transcends his father's fame:"
While pleas'd amidst the gen'ral shouts of Troy,
His mother's conscious heart o'erflows with joy.'
  He spoke; and, fondly gazing on her charms,
Restor'd the pleasing burden to her arms;
Soft on her fragrant breast the babe she laid,
Hush'd to repose, and with a smile survey'd.
The troubled pleasure soon chastis'd by fear,
She mingled with the smile a tender tear.
The soften'd chief with kind compassion view'd,
And dried the falling drops, and thus pursu'd."
                          Iliad, book vi.

No. 927.

The same subject.

AËTION. *Cornelian.*

No. 928.

Hector and Ajax exchanging presents after their combat.

DIOSCORIDES. *Cornelian.*

The Trojans having rallied after the return of Hector and Paris to the battle, Minerva and Apollo agreed to produce a suspension of the general engagement for that day; and for this purpose induced Hector, through the instrumentality of his brother Helenus, a seer, or prophet, to challenge the bravest of the Greeks to a single combat. Hector, acting on the suggestion, advanced in front of the ranks, and checked the Trojans. Agamemnon seeing this, and knowing it intimated some proposal, checked the Grecians also.

" Thus in thick orders settling wide around,
At length composed they sit, and shade the ground.
Great Hector first amidst both armies broke
The solemn silence, and their powers bespoke :
' Hear, all ye Trojan—all ye Grecian bands,
What my soul prompts, and what some god commands.
Great Jove, averse our warfare to compose,
O'erwhelms the nations with new toils and woes;
War with a fiercer tide once more returns,
Till Ilion falls, or till yon navy burns.
You, then, O princes of the Greeks ! appear;
'Tis Hector speaks, and calls the gods to hear;
From all your troops select the boldest knight;
And him, the boldest, Hector dares to fight.
Here, if I fall, by chance of battle slain,
Be his my spoil, and his these arms remain ;

But let my body, to my friends return'd,
By Trojan hands and Trojan flames be burn'd.
And if Apollo, in whose aid I trust,
Shall stretch your daring champion in the dust—
If mine the glory to despoil the foe,
On Phœbus' temple I'll his arms bestow :
The breathless carcass to your navy sent,
Greece on the shore shall raise a monument ;
Which when some future mariner surveys,
Wash'd by broad Hellespont's resounding seas,
Thus shall he say, ' A valiant Greek lies there,
By Hector slain, the mighty man of war.'
The stone shall tell your vanquish'd hero's name,
And distant ages learn the victor's fame.'
    This fierce defiance Greece astonish'd heard—
Blush'd to refuse—and to accept it fear'd."

Menelaus was the first to step forward, and propose to accept the challenge; but Agamemnon restrained him. Nestor then addressed the chiefs, and dwelt on the gallantry and glory of their fathers, who would promptly answer such defiance.

" His warm reproofs the listening kings inflame,
And nine, the noblest of the Grecian name,
Up started fierce :"

i. e. Agamemnon, Diomede, the two Ajaces, Idomeneus, Meriones, Eurypilus, Thoas, and Ulysses. The election, however, was determined by lot, which fell on Telamon Ajax.

" Now Ajax braced his dazzling armour on :
Sheath'd in bright steel the giant warrior shone.
He moves to combat with majestic pace ;
So stalks in arms the grisly god of Thrace,*
When Jove to punish faithless men prepares,
And gives whole nations to the waste of wars.
Thus march'd the chief, tremendous as a god ;
Grimly he smiled ; earth trembled as he strode :
His massy javelin quivering in his hand,
He stood, the bulwark of the Grecian band.
Through every Argive heart new transport ran ;
All Troy stood trembling at the mighty man.
E'en Hector paused ; and with new doubt oppress'd,
Felt his great heart suspended in his breast.
'Twas vain to seek retreat, and vain to fear ;
Himself had challenged, and the foe drew near.
Stern Telamon, behind his ample shield,
As from a brazen tower, o'erlook'd the field.
Huge was its orb, with seven thick folds o'ercast
Of tough bull-hides ; of solid brass the last
(The work of Tychius, who in Hylè dwell'd,
And all in arts of armory excell'd).
This Ajax bore before his manly breast,
And threatening, thus his adverse chief address'd :
' Hector ! approach my arm, and singly know
What strength thou hast, and what the Grecian foe.
Achilles shuns the fight ; yet some there are
Not void of soul, and not unskill'd in war :
Let him, unactive on the sea-beat shore,
Indulge his wrath, and aid our arms no more ;
Whole troops of heroes Greece has yet to boast,
And sends thee one, a sample of her host.
Such as I am, I come to prove thy might :
No more—be sudden, and begin the fight.'
' O son of Telamon, thy country's pride !'
To Ajax thus the Trojan prince replied ;
' Me, as a boy or woman, wouldst thou fright,
New to the field, and trembling at the fight ?

Thou meet'st a chief deserving of thy arms,
To combat born, and bred amidst alarms :
I know to shift my ground, remount the car,
Turn, charge, and answer every call of war ;
To right, to left, the dexterous lance I wield,
And bear thick battle on my sounding shield.
But open be our fight, and bold each blow ;
I steal no conquest from a noble foe.'
He said ; and, rising, high above the field
Whirl'd the long lance against the sevenfold
shield.
Full on the brass descending from above
Through six bull-hides the furious weapon drove,
Till in the seventh it fix'd. Then Ajax threw ;
Through Hector's shield the forceful javelin flew,
His corslet enters, and his garment rends,
And glancing downwards near his flank descends.
The wary Trojan shrinks, and, bending low,
Beneath his buckler, disappoints the blow.
From their bored shields the chiefs their javelins
drew,
Then close impetuous, and the charge renew :
Fierce as the mountain lions bathed in blood,
Or foaming boars, the terror of the wood.
At Ajax, Hector his long lance extends ;
The blunted point against the buckler bends :
But Ajax, watchful as his foe drew near,
Drove through the Trojan targe the knotty spear ;
It reach'd his neck, with matchless strength impell'd ;
Spouts the black gore, and dims his shining shield.
Yet ceased not Hector thus ; but, stooping down,
In his strong hand upheaved a flinty stone,
Black—craggy—vast : to this his force he bends ;
Full on the brazen boss the stone descends ;
The hollow brass resounded with the shock.
Then Ajax seized the fragment of a rock,
Applied each nerve, and swinging round on high,
With force tempestuous let the ruin fly :

---

* Mars.

The huge stone thundering through his buckler broke:
His slacken'd knees received the numbing stroke;
Great Hector falls extended on the field,
His bulk supporting on the shatter'd shield;
Nor wanted heavenly aid: Apollo's might
Confirm'd his sinews, and restored to fight.
And now both heroes their broad falchions drew,
In flaming circles round their heads they flew;
But then by heralds' voice the word was given,
The sacred ministers of earth and heaven:
Divine Talthybius, whom the Greeks employ,
And sage Idæus on the part of Troy,
Between the swords their peaceful sceptres rear'd;
And first Idæus' awful voice was heard:

' Forbear, my sons! your farther force to prove,
Both dear to men, and both beloved of Jove.
To either host your matchless worth is known,
Each sounds your praise, and war is all your own.
But now the night extends her awful shade,
The goddess parts you: be the night obey'd.'

To whom great Ajax his high soul express'd:
' O sage! to Hector be these words address'd.
Let him who first provoked our chiefs to fight,
Let him demand the sanction of the night;
If first he ask it, I content obey,
And cease the strife when Hector shews the way.'

' O first of Greeks!' his noble foe rejoin'd,
' Whom heaven adorns, superior to thy kind,
With strength of body and with worth of mind!

Now martial law commands us to forbear;
Hereafter we shall meet in glorious war;
Some future day shall lengthen out the strife,
And let the gods decide of death or life!
Since then the night extends her gloomy shade,
And heaven enjoins it, be the night obey'd.
Return, brave Ajax, to thy Grecian friends,
And joy the nations whom thy arm defends;
As I shall glad each chief, and Trojan wife,
Who wearies heaven with vows for Hector's life.
But let us, on this memorable day,
Exchange some gift; that Greece and Troy may say,
Not hate, but glory, made these chiefs contend;
And each brave foe was in his soul a friend.'

With that, a sword with stars of silver graced,
The baldrick studded, and the sheath enchased,
He gave the Greek. The generous Greek bestow'd
A radiant belt that rich with purple glow'd.
Then with majestic grace they quit the plain;
This seeks the Grecian, that the Phrygian train.

The Trojan bands returning Hector wait,
And hail with joy the champion of their state:
Escaped great Ajax, they survey'd him round,
Alive, unharm'd, and vigorous from his wound.
To Troy's high gates the godlike man they bear,
Their present triumph, as their late despair.
But Ajax, glorying in his hardy deed,
The well-arm'd Greeks to Agamemnon lead."

Iliad, book vii.

No. 929.

Iris delivering the commands of Jupiter to Hector.

TEUCER. *Cornelian.*

" He spoke; and Iris at his word obey'd:
On wings of winds descends the various maid.
The chief she found amidst the ranks of war,
Close to the bulwarks on his glittering car.
The goddess then: ' O son of Priam, hear!
From Jove I come, and his high mandate bear.

While Agamemnon wastes the ranks around,
Fights in the front, and bathes with blood the ground,
Abstain from fight, yet issue forth commands,
And trust the war to less important hands;
But when, or wounded by the spear or dart,
The chief shall mount his chariot, and depart,

Then Jove shall string thy arm, and fire thy
    breast—
Then to her ships shall flying Greece be press'd,
Till to the main the burning sun descend,
And sacred night her awful shade extend.'

    She said, and vanish'd : Hector, with a bound,
Springs from his chariot on the trembling ground,
In clanging arm : he grasps in either hand
A pointed lance, and speeds from band to band—

Revives their ardour—turns their steps from flight,
And wakes anew the dying flames of fight.
They stand to arms : the Greeks their onset dare,
Condense their powers, and wait the coming war.
New force, new spirit, to each breast returns :
The fight renew'd, with fiercer fury burns :
The king leads on ; all fix on him their eye,
And learn from him to conquer or to die."

Iliad, book xi.

No. 930.

Hector breaking open the gate of the Grecian fortifications.

Dioscorides. *Calcedony.*

    The Trojans having attacked the Grecian fortifications, an eagle appeared in the air bearing in his talons a serpent, which stings him. This Polydamas interprets as a bad omen, and urges Hector to withdraw his forces. Hector refuses, and continues the attack. After a long and furious struggle on both sides, Hector at last dashes open one of the gates.

" Meantime, the bravest of the Trojan crew,
Bold Hector and Polydamas, pursue ;
Fierce with impatience on the works to fall,
And wrap in rolling flames the fleet and wall.
These on the further bank now stood and gazed,
By heaven alarm'd—by prodigies amazed :
A signal omen stopp'd the passing host,
Their martial fury in their wonder lost.
Jove's bird on sounding pinions beat the skies ;
A bleeding serpent of enormous size
His talons truss'd ; alive, and curling round,
He stung the bird, whose throat received the
    wound :
Mad with the smart, he drops the fatal prey—
In airy circles wings his painful way—
Floats on the winds, and rends the heavens with
    cries:
Amidst the host the fallen serpent lies.
They, pale with terror, mark its spires enroll'd,
And Jove's portent with beating hearts behold.

.   .   .   .   .

So stood the war, till Hector's matchless might
With Fates prevailing, turns the scale of fight.

Fierce as a whirlwind up the wall he flies,
And fires his host with loud-repeated cries :
' Advance, ye Trojans ! lend your valiant
    hands,
Haste to the fleet, and toss the blazing brands !'
They hear—they run ; and gathering at his
    call,
Raise scaling engines, and ascend the wall :
Around the works a wood of glittering spears
Shoots up, and all the rising host appears.
A ponderous stone bold Hector heaved to throw,
Pointed above, and rough and gross below ;
Not two strong men th' enormous weight could
    raise,
Such men as live in these degenerate days.
Yet this, as easy as a swain could bear
The snowy fleece, he toss'd, and shook in air :
For Jove upheld, and lighten'd of its load
Th' unwieldy rock, the labour of a god.
Thus arm'd, before the folded gates he came,
Of massy substance and stupendous frame ;
With iron bars and brazen hinges strong,
On lofty beams of solid timber hung :

Then, thundering through the planks with force-
ful sway,
Drives the sharp rock ; the solid beams give way—
The folds are shatter'd ; from the crackling door
Leap the resounding bars, the flying hinges roar.
Now rushing in, the furious chief appears
Gloomy as night! and shakes two shining spears :
A dreadful gleam from his bright armour came,
And from his eyeballs flash'd the living flame.

He moves a god, resistless in his course,
And seems a match for more than mortal force.
Then pouring after, through the gaping space,
A tide of Trojans flows, and fills the place ;
The Greeks behold—they tremble—and they fly ;
The shore is heap'd with death, and tumult rends
the sky."

Iliad, book xii.

No. 931.

Æneas pouring water on fainting Hector.

CHROMIOS. *Amethyst.*

Hector was struck in the throat and chest by Ajax with a huge stone, which felled him to the ground.

" Loud shouts of triumph fill the crowded plain ;
Greece sees, in hope, Troy's great defender slain :
All spring to seize him : storms of arrows fly ;
And thicker javelins intercept the sky.
In vain an iron tempest hisses round ;
He lies protected, and without a wound.
Polydamas, Agenor the divine,
The pious warrior of Anchises' line,
And each bold leader of the Lycian band,
With covering shields (a friendly circle) stand.
His mournful followers, with assistant care,
The groaning hero to his chariot bear.

His foaming coursers, swifter than the wind,
Speed to the town, and leave the war behind.
When now they touch'd the mead's enamell'd
side,
Where gentle Xanthus rolls his easy tide,
With watery drops the chief they sprinkle round,
Placed on the margin of the flowery ground :
Raised on his knees, he now ejects the gore ;
Now faints anew, low sinking on the shore ;
By fits he breathes, half views the fleeting skies,
And seals again, by fits, his swimming eyes."

Iliad, book xiv.

No. 932.

Hector putting on the armour of Achilles, after the death of Patroclus.

CHROMIOS. *Cornelian.*

"Then turning to the martial hosts, he cries :
' Ye Trojans, Dardans, Lycians, and allies !
Be men, my friends, in action as in name,
And yet be mindful of your ancient fame.

Hector in proud Achilles' arms shall shine,
Torn from his friend, by right of conquest mine.'
He strode along the field, as thus he said
(The sable plumage nodded o'er his head):

Swift through the spacious plain he sent a look;
One instant saw, one instant overtook
The distant band, that on the sandy shore
The radiant spoils to sacred Ilion bore.
There his own mail unbraced the field be-
    strew'd;
His train to Troy convey'd the massy load.

Now blazing in th' immortal arms he stands,
The work and present of celestial hands;
By aged Peleus to Achilles given,
As first to Peleus by the court of heaven:
His father's arms not long Achilles wears,
Forbid by fate to reach his father's years."
                Iliad, book xvii.

No. 933.

Hector attempting to seize the chariot and horses of Achilles.

APOLLONIDES. *Cornelian.*

" From their high manes they shake the dust, and bear
  The kindling chariot through the parted war:
  So flies a vulture through the clamorous train
  Of geese, that scream, and scatter round the plain.
  From danger now with swiftest speed they flew,
  And now to conquest with like speed pursue;
  Sole in the seat the charioteer remains,
  Now plies the javelin, now directs the reins."
                Iliad, book xvii.

No. 934.

The combat of Hector and Achilles.

SOSTRATOS. *Sardonyx.*

The Trojans having fled into the city, Hector alone remained outside to give Achilles battle.

"Close to the walls advancing o'er the fields,
Beneath one roof of well-compacted shields,
March, bending on, the Greeks' embodied pow'rs,
Far stretching in the shade of Trojan tow'rs.
Great Hector singly stay'd; chain'd down by
    fate,
There fix'd he stood before the Scæan gate;
Still his bold arms determin'd to employ,
The guardian still of long-defended Troy.

Then to the city, terrible and strong,
With high and haughty steps he* tower'd along.
So the proud courser, victor of the prize,
To the near goal with double ardour flies.
Him, as he blazing shot across the field,
The careful eyes of Priam first beheld.
Not half so dreadful rises to the sight,
Through the thick gloom of some tempestuous
    night,

---

* Achilles.

Orion's dog (the year when autumn weighs),
And o'er the feebler stars exerts his rays;
Terrific glory! for his burning breath
Taints the red air with fevers, plagues, and
    death.

So flamed his fiery mail.   Then wept the sage—
He strikes his reverend head, now white with
    age—
He lifts his wither'd arms—obtests the skies—
He calls his much-loved son with feeble cries."

Priam earnestly implored him to retire within the walls. Hecuba joined in the solicitation.
But he is resolute. He ponders on the peril of his situation, exposed not alone to Achilles,
but to the combined host of Greece.

"Thus pond'ring, like a god the Greek drew
    nigh,
His dreadful plumage nodded from on high;
The Pelian javelin in his better hand
Shot trembling rays that glitter'd o'er the land;
And on his breast the beamy splendours shone,
Like Jove's own lightning, or the rising sun.
As Hector sees, unusual terrors rise,
Struck by some god, he fears—recedes—and
    flies!

He leaves the gates, he leaves the walls behind;
Achilles follows like the winged wind.
Thus at the panting dove a falcon flies
(The swiftest racer of the liquid skies),
Just when he holds, or thinks he holds his prey,
Obliquely wheeling through the aërial way;
With open beak and shrilling cries he springs,
And aims his claws, and shoots upon his wings,—
No less fore-right the rapid chase they held,
One urged by fury, one by fear impell'd.

They ran three times round the city walls—

" By these they pass'd, one chasing, one in flight,
(The mighty fled, pursu'd by stronger might);
Swift was the course; no vulgar prize they play,
No vulgar victim must reward the day
(Such as in races crown the speedy strife).
The prize contended was great Hector's life."

The gods having debated in council about the fate of Hector, Jupiter weighs the destinies
of both in a balance; and Hector is doomed to die. Minerva comes down—assures Achilles
of victory—and, in the guise of Deïphobus, the brother of Hector, persuades him to stand the
combat.

"Fraudful she said: then swiftly march'd be-
    fore;
The Dardan hero shuns his foe no more.
Sternly they met. The silence Hector broke;
His dreadful plumage nodded as he spoke:
' Enough, O son of Peleus! Troy has view'd
Her walls thrice circled, and her chief pursu'd.
But now some god within me bids me try
Thine, or my fate: I kill thee, or I die.

Yet on the verge of battle let us stay,
And for a moment's space suspend the day;
Let heav'n's high pow'rs be call'd to arbitrate
The just conditions of this stern debate
(Eternal witnesses of all below,
And faithful guardians of the treasur'd vow!).
To them I swear, if, victor in the strife,
Jove by these hands shall shed thy noble
    life,

No vile dishonòur shall thy corpse pursue;
Stripp'd of its arms alone (the conqueror's due),
The rest to Greece uninjur'd I'll restore:
Now plight thy mutual oath; I ask no more.'
  ' Talk not of oaths,' the dreadful chief replies,
While anger flash'd from his disdainful eyes;
' Detested as thou art, and ought to be,
Nor oath nor pact Achilles plights with thee:
Such pacts as lambs and rabid wolves combine—
Such leagues as men and furious lions join—
To such I call the gods! one constant state
Of lasting rancour and eternal hate;
No thought but rage and never-ceasing strife,
Till death extinguish rage, and thought, and
    life.
Rouse, then, thy forces this important hour,
Collect thy soul, and call forth all thy pow'r.
No farther subterfuge, no farther chance—
'Tis Pallas—Pallas gives thee to my lance.
Each Grecian ghost by thee depriv'd of breath,
Now hovers round, and calls thee to thy death.'
  He spoke, and launch'd his javelin at the foe;
But Hector shunn'd the meditated blow:
He stoop'd, while o'er his head the flying spear
Sung innocent, and spent its force in air.
Minerva watch'd it falling on the land,
Then drew, and gave to great Achilles' hand,
Unseen of Hector; who, elate with joy,
Now shakes his lance, and braves the dread of
    Troy.
  ' The life you boasted to that jav'lin giv'n,
Prince! you have miss'd. My fate depends on
    heav'n;
To thee, presumptuous as thou art, unknown
Or what must prove my fortune, or thy own.
Boasting is but an art our fears to blind,
And with false terrors sink another's mind.
But know, whatever fate I am to try,
By no dishonest wound shall Hector die;
I shall not fall a fugitive at least,
My soul shall bravely issue from my breast.
But first, try thou my arm; and may this dart
End all my country's woes, deep buried in thy
    heart!'

The weapon flew, its course unerring held—
Unerring—but the heavenly shield repell'd
The mortal dart; resulting with a bound
From off the ringing orb, it struck the ground.
Hector beheld his javelin fall in vain;
Nor other lance nor other hope remain;
He calls Deïphobus—demands a spear—
In vain, for no Deiphobus was there!
All comfortless he stands: then, with a sigh,
  ' 'Tis so—heaven wills it, and my hour is nigh!
I deem'd Deïphobus had heard my call,
But he secure lies guarded in the wall.
A god deceived me—Pallas, 'twas thy deed—
Death and black Fate approach!—'tis I must
    bleed.
No refuge now, no succour from above—
Great Jove deserts me, and the son of Jove,
Propitious once, and kind! — then welcome,
    Fate!
'Tis true I perish, yet I perish great—
Yet in a mighty deed I shall expire—
Let future ages hear it, and admire!'
  Fierce, at the word, his weighty sword he drew,
And, all collected, on Achilles flew.
So Jove's bold bird, high balanc'd in the air,
Stoops from the clouds to truss the quiv'ring
    hare:
Nor less Achilles his fierce soul prepares;
Before his breast the flaming shield he bears,
Refulgent orb! above his fourfold cone
The gilded horsehair sparkled in the sun,
Nodding at every step—Vulcanian frame!—
And, as he mov'd, his figure seem'd on flame.
As radiant Hesper shines with keener light,
Far-beaming o'er the silver host of night,
When all the starry train emblaze the sphere;
So shone the point of great Achilles' spear.
In his right hand he waves the weapon round,
Eyes the whole man, and meditates the wound:
But the rich mail Patroclus lately wore
Securely cased the warrior's body o'er.
One place at length he spies to let in Fate,
Where, 'twixt the neck and throat, the jointed
    plate

Gave entrance: through that penetrable part
Furious he drove the well-directed dart:
Nor pierced the windpipe yet, nor took the power
Of speech, unhappy, from thy dying hour!
Prone on the field the bleeding warrior lies,
While thus, triumphing, stern Achilles cries:
  ' At last is Hector stretch'd upon the plain,
Who fear'd no vengeance for Patroclus slain:
Then, prince! you should have fear'd what now
      you feel—
Achilles absent was Achilles still.
Yet a short space the great avenger stay'd:
Then low in dust thy strength and glory laid.
Peaceful he sleeps, with all our rites adorn'd,
For ever honour'd, and for ever mourn'd;
While, cast to all the rage of hostile pow'r,
Thee birds shall mangle, and the dogs devour.'
  Then Hector, fainting at the approach of death:
' By thy own soul! by those who gave thee breath!
By all the sacred prevalence of pray'r!
Ah, leave me not for Grecian dogs to tear!
The common rites of sepulture bestow,
To soothe a father's and a mother's woe;
Let their large gifts procure an urn at least,
And Hector's ashes in his country rest.'
  ' No, wretch accurs'd!' relentless he replies
(Flames, as he spoke, shot flashing from his eyes);
' Not those who gave me breath should bid me
      spare,
Nor all the sacred prevalence of pray'r.
Could I myself the bloody banquet join!
No—to the dogs that carcass I resign.
Should Troy, to bribe me, bring forth all her
      store,
And, giving thousands, offer thousands more;
Should Dardan Priam, and his weeping dame,
Drain their whole realm to buy one fun'ral
      flame;
Their Hector on the pile they should not see,
Nor rob the vultures of one limb of thee.'
  Then thus the chief his dying accents drew:
' Thy rage, implacable! too well I knew:
The Furies that relentless breast have steel'd,
And curs'd thee with a heart that cannot yield.

Yet think, a day will come, when Fate's decree,
And angry gods, shall wreak this wrong on thee;
Phœbus and Paris shall avenge my fate,
And stretch thee here, before this Scæan gate.'
  He ceas'd. The Fates suppress'd his lab'ring
      breath,
And his eyes stiffen'd at the hand of death;
To the dark realm the spirit wings its way
(The manly body left a load of clay),
And plaintive glides along the dreary coast—
A naked—wand'ring—melancholy ghost!
  Achilles, musing as he roll'd his eyes
O'er the dead hero, thus (unheard) replies:
' Die thou the first! When Jove and heaven
      ordain,
I follow thee.' He said, and stripp'd the slain;
Then, forcing backward from the gaping wound
The reeking javelin, cast it on the ground.
The thronging Greeks behold with wondering
      eyes
His manly beauty and superior size:
While some, ignobler, the great dead deface
With wounds ungenerous, or with taunts dis-
      grace:
' How changed that Hector! who like Jove of
      late,
Sent lightning on our fleets and scatter'd fate!'
  High o'er the slain the great Achilles stands,
Begirt with heroes and surrounding bands;
And thus aloud, while all the host attends:
' Princes and leaders! countrymen and friends!
Since now at length the pow'rful will of
      heav'n
The dire destroyer to our arm has giv'n,
Is not Troy fall'n already? Haste, ye pow'rs!
See, if already their deserted tow'rs
Are left unmann'd; or if they yet retain
The souls of heroes, their great Hector slain?
But what is Troy, or glory what to me?
Or why reflects my mind on aught but thee,
Divine Patroclus! death has seal'd his eyes—
Unwept, unhonour'd, uninterr'd he lies!
Can his dear image from my soul depart,
Long as the vital spirit moves my heart?

If in the melancholy shades below,
The flames of friends and lovers cease to glow,
Yet mine shall sacred last; mine, undecay'd,
Burn on through death, and animate my shade.

Meanwhile, ye sons of Greece, in triumph bring
The corpse of Hector, and your pæans sing.
Be this the song, slow-moving tow'rd the shore,
' Hector is dead, and Ilion is no more.' "
Iliad, book xxii.

No. 935.

The same subject.

APOLLONIDES. *Sardonyx.*

See preceding quotation.

No. 936.

Death of Hector.

CHROMIOS. *Cornelian.*

See preceding quotation.

No. 937.

Andromache at her loom, when alarmed by the loud lamentations on the death of Hector.

POLYCLETES. *Cornelian.*

" But not as yet the fatal news has spread
To fair Andromache, of Hector dead;
As yet no messenger had told his fate,
Nor e'en his stay without the Scæan gate.
Far in the close recesses of the dome,
Pensive she plied the melancholy loom;
A growing work employ'd her secret hours,
Confus'dly gay with intermingled flowers.
Her fair-hair'd handmaids heat the brazen urn,
The bath preparing for her lord's return:
In vain, alas! her lord returns no more!
Unbathed he lies, and bleeds along the shore!

Now from the walls the clamours reach her ear,
And all her members shake with sudden fear;
Forth from her ivory hand the shuttle falls,
As thus, astonish'd, to her maids she calls:
' Ah, follow me!' she cried; ' what plaintive noise
Invades my ear? 'Tis sure my mother's voice.
My faltering knees their trembling frame desert,
A pulse unusual flutters at my heart:
Some strange disaster, some reverse of fate
(Ye gods avert it!) threats the Trojan state.

4 c

Far be the omen which my thoughts suggest !
But much I fear my Hector's dauntless breast
Confronts Achilles ; chased along the plain,
Shut from our walls ! I fear—I fear him slain !

Safe in the crowd he ever scorn'd to wait,
And sought for glory in the jaws of fate.
Perhaps that noble heat has cost his breath,
Now quench'd for ever in the arms of death.' "

Iliad, book xxii.

No. 938.

Venus and Apollo preserving the body of Hector from decay.

ANTEROTOS. *Cornelian.*

" So spake he threat'ning ; but the gods made vain
His threat, and guard inviolate the slain :
Celestial Venus hover'd o'er his head,
And roseate unguents, heav'nly fragrance ! shed :
She watch'd him all the night, and all the day,
And drove the bloodhounds from their destin'd prey.
Nor sacred Phœbus less employ'd his care ;
He pour'd around a veil of gather'd air,
And kept the nerves undried, the flesh entire,
Against the solar beam and Sirian fire."

Iliad, book xxiii.

No. 939.

Lamentation of Andromache over the body of Hector.

CHROMIOS. *Cornelian.*

" First to the corse the weeping consort flew ;
Around his neck her milk-white arms she threw.
And, ' O my Hector ! O my lord !' she cries ;
' Snatch'd in thy bloom from these desiring eyes !
Thou to the dismal realms for ever gone !
And I abandon'd—desolate—alone !
An only son, once comfort of our pains,
Sad product now of hapless love, remains !
Never to manly age that son shall rise,
Or with increasing graces glad my eyes ;
For Ilion now (her great defender slain)
Shall sink a smoking ruin on the plain.

Who now protects her wives with guardian care ?
Who saves her infants from the rage of war ?
Now hostile fleets must waft those infants o'er
(Those wives must wait them) to a foreign shore !
Thou too, my son ! to barbarous climes shalt go,
The sad companion of thy mother's woe ;
Driven hence a slave before the victor's sword ;
Condemn'd to toil for some inhuman lord :
Or else some Greek, whose father press'd the plain,
Or son, or brother, by great Hector slain,
In Hector's blood his vengeance shall enjoy,
And hurl thee headlong from the towers of Troy.

Thence many evils his sad parents bore,
His parents many, but his consort more.
Why gav'st thou not to me thy dying hand?
And why received not I thy last command?

Some word thou wouldst have spoke, which sadly dear,
My soul might keep, or utter with a tear;
Which never, never could be lost in air,
Fix'd in my heart, and oft repeated there!' "

Iliad, book xxiv.

No. 940.

Head of Hector.

KOINOS. *Cornelian.*

There is not a character in the *Iliad* that appears in a more noble, amiable, and virtuous point of view than Hector. He was religious, just, humane, and moral. We find him, in order to save bloodshed, proposing to the Greeks to decide the whole issue of the war by a single combat between Paris and Menelaus—the principals concerned: he himself having suggested this course to Paris. After the flight of Paris, and the defeat of the Trojans, we find him resorting to the aid of religion, and going to the city to appoint a supplicatory procession of the queen and matrons to the temple of their tutelar divinity. Although the fortunes of the field depended on his speedy return to the battle, yet the force of natural affection and duty impelled him to pay a hasty visit to his wife and child. Polygamy was allowed, and generally practised among the Trojans of his time; yet he had but one wife, to whom he was devotedly attached. He says that he loves her more than he does all the Trojans—than his mother—or his father—or all his brothers; and utters a wish that the earth may cover him before he should hear her groans, or witness her captivity; and in his supplication to heaven for the prosperity of his child, he again reverts to his wife, and concludes with a prayer that the child may in after-times gladden the heart of his mother. Of his piety there is sufficient proof in the speech of Jupiter, when he foresaw his evil fate in his combat with Achilles—

> " To whom, while eager on the chase they look,
> The sire of mortals and immortals spoke:
> ' Unworthy sight! the *man beloved of heaven,*
> Behold inglorious round yon city driven!
> My *heart* partakes the *generous* Hector's pain—
> Hector, whose *zeal whole hecatombs* has slain—
> Whose grateful fumes the gods received with joy,
> From Ida's summits and the towers of Troy:
> Now see him flying! to his fears resign'd,
> And Fate and fierce Achilles close behind.' "

He was all through the campaign the very soul of his party. His judgment ruled them, as his spirit fired. Before his last mortal combat with Achilles, he proposes to him the generous conditions, to be attested by the gods—that the victor should not treat the body of his fallen foeman with savage indignity : and when his corpse was brought back to Troy, Helen, one of the chief mourners, says, that though she often heard reproaches from others cast on her, as the cause of all the calamities of the country, yet she never heard an unkind or ungenerous word from Hector.

But there is one circumstance in his history—his flight from Achilles—which has been generally considered a stain on his gallantry.   Now, though almost all readers of Homer lament this circumstance, and consider it some indication of cowardice in his character ; yet, I think, a plain exposition of the circumstances of the case will shew that this opinion is unfounded.   First, be it remembered, the Trojans had all fled within their strong walls ; and the Greeks, flushed with victory, were advancing in close phalanx towards the city.   Secondly, Hector alone remained outside the chief gate, gallantly resolved to meet all perils.   Thirdly, he resisted the most affecting and earnest appeals made to him by his father and mother, standing on the city walls, to retire within the fortresses of the town.   Fourthly, when seeing the multitudinous dangers that encompassed him, he yet did not, as he might easily have done, consult his own safety by withdrawing into the city.   Fifthly, he is represented as debating within himself about the propriety of retiring within the walls, or standing out, single-handed and unaided, for his own fame and the safety of Troy.   He is first restrained by a feeling of shame from retiring inside—then he thinks of proposing a compromise to Achilles—then he checks himself, and reflects that even if he did, he was not likely, under present circumstances, to obtain quarter.   His meditations were interrupted by the terrific voice of Achilles, accompanied by the whole Grecian army, thirsting for vengeance.   Then, indeed, he fled, when he *reflected* on his *position*, encircled in a whirlwind of inveterate adversaries.   Be it observed, that the whole Grecian army is represented as advancing *before* Achilles appears—that Hector resolutely determines, after much consideration, to meet the whole force of the enemy.   But when he saw Achilles dashing along, all blazing and terrific, in the centre of the whole Grecian army, a prudential consideration for his own and his country's safety induced him to escape from the imminent and unerring danger.   In a word, he considered, that if he remained his death was inevitable.   What Homer says is this—Ἑκτορα δ᾽ ὡσ ενοησεν ἑλε τρομος, *i. e.* " When Hector *thought,* a terror seized him."   Now, though Pope, and almost all the commentators, translate the word ενοησεν by *saw*, and so represent Hector as flying at the bare appearance of Achilles, yet the whole scope of the passages in Homer will shew to any dispassionate examiner, that it was not personal fear of Achilles that actuated him, at least that it was not the sight of him that terrified him.   Achilles, in his pursuit of him, is represented as checking the Greeks from attacking him (some evidence of the justice of Hector's suspicions that they were not much inclined to spare him) ; and when his body is brought to the Grecian camp, each Greek (to mark his animosity) gave the carcass a stab.

No. 941.

Priam praying to Jupiter for the success of his mission to Achilles.

POLYCLETES. *Cornelian.*

Jupiter having sent Thetis to dispose Achilles to accept ransom for the body of Hector, despatches Iris to Priam, to go and offer it. Priam before setting out offers prayers and libations to Jupiter. The handmaid behind him holds the ewer; Hecuba stands before him; the herald, Idæus, holds the heads of the horses yoked to the chariot that contains the valuable ransom; while overhead appears, as an auspicious sign, Jove's bird, the eagle.

" High on the seat the cabinet they bind:
The new-made car with solid beauty shined:
Box was the yoke, emboss'd with costly pains,
And hung with ringlets to receive the reins:
Nine cubits long, the traces swept the ground;
These to the chariot's polish'd pole they bound,
Then fix'd a ring the running reins to guide,
And close beneath the gather'd ends were tied.
Next with the gifts (the price of Hector slain)
The sad attendants load the groaning wain:
Last to the yoke the well-match'd mules they
          bring
(The gift of Mysia to the Trojan king).
But the fair horses, long his darling care,
Himself received, and harness'd to his car:
Grieved as he was, he not this task denied:
The hoary herald help'd him at his side.
While careful these the gentle coursers join'd,
Sad Hecuba approach'd with anxious mind;
A golden bowl that foam'd with fragrant wine
(Libation destined to the power divine)
Held in her right; before the steeds she stands,
And thus consigns it to the monarch's hands:
  'Take this, and pour to Jove; that, safe from
          harms,
His grace restore thee to our roof and arms.
Since victor of thy fears, and slighting mine,
Heaven, or thy soul, inspire this bold design;
Pray to that god, who high on Ida's brow
Surveys thy desolated realms below,
His winged messenger to send from high,
And lead thy way with heavenly augury:

Let the strong sovereign of the plumy race
Tower on the right of yon ethereal space.
That sign beheld, and strengthen'd from above,
Boldly pursue the journey mark'd by Jove;
But if the god his augury denies,
Suppress thy impulse, nor reject advice.'
  ' 'Tis just (said Priam) to the sire above
To raise our hands; for who so good as Jove?'
He spoke, and bade the attendant handmaid
          bring
The purest water of the living spring
(Her ready hands the ewer and basin held);
Then took the golden cup his queen had fill'd—
On the mid pavement pours the rosy wine—
Uplifts his eyes, and calls the power divine.
  ' O first and greatest! heaven's imperial lord!
On lofty Ida's holy hill adored!
To stern Achilles now direct my ways,
And teach him mercy when a father prays.
If such thy will, despatch from yonder sky
Thy sacred bird, celestial augury!
Let the strong sovereign of the plumy race
Tower on the right of yon ethereal space:
So shall thy suppliant, strengthen'd from above,
Fearless pursue the journey mark'd by Jove.'
  Jove heard his prayer, and from the throne on
          high
Despatch'd his bird, celestial augury!
The swift-wing'd chaser of the feather'd game,
And known to gods by Percnos' lofty name.
Wide as appears some palace-gate display'd,
So broad his pinions stretch'd their ample shade,

As stooping dexter with resounding wings
Th' imperial bird descends in airy rings.
A dawn of joy in every face appears;
The mourning matron dries her timorous tears:
Swift on his car the impatient monarch sprung,
The brazen portal in his passage rung.
The mules preceding draw the loaded wain,
Charged with the gifts: Idæus holds the rein:

The king himself his gentle steeds controls,
And through surrounding friends the chariot rolls.
On his slow wheels the following people wait,
Mourn at each step, and give him up to fate;
With hands uplifted, eye him as he pass'd,
And gazed upon him as they gazed their last.
Now forward fares the father on his way,
Through the lone fields, and back to Ilion they."

Iliad, book xxiv.

No. 942.

Interview between Priam and Mercury.

PHILOLAOS. *Cornelian.*

Jupiter despatched Mercury to conduct him safe. Mercury, disguised as a noble youth, meets and accosts him near the tomb of Ilus as he is refreshing his horses.

" Great Jove beheld him as he cross'd the plain,
And felt the woes of miserable man:
Then thus to Hermes. ' Thou whose constant cares
Still succour mortals, and attend their prayers,
Behold an object to thy charge consign'd,
If ever pity touch'd thee for mankind.
Go, guard the sire; th' observing foe prevent,
And safe conduct him to Achilles' tent.'

The god obeys, his golden pinions binds,
And mounts incumbent on the wings of winds,
That high through fields of air his flight sustain,
O'er the wide earth, and o'er the boundless main:
Then grasps the wand that causes sleep to fly,
Or in soft slumbers seals the wakeful eye;
Thus arm'd, swift Hermes steers his airy way,
And stoops on Hellespont's resounding sea.
A beauteous youth, majestic and divine,
He seem'd; fair offspring of some princely line!
Now twilight veiled the glaring face of day,
And clad the dusky fields in sober gray;
What time the herald and the hoary king
(Their chariots stopping at the silver spring,
That circling Ilus' ancient marble flows)
Allow'd their mules and steeds a short repose.

Through the dim shade the herald first espies
A man's approach, and thus to Priam cries:
' I mark some foe's advance: O king, beware;
This hard adventure claims thy utmost care:
For, much I fear, destruction hovers nigh:
Our state asks counsel. Is it best to fly?
Or, old and helpless, at his feet to fall
(Two wretched suppliants), and for mercy call?'

Th' afflicted monarch shiver'd with despair;
Pale grew his face, and upright stood his hair;
Sunk was his heart; his colour went and came;
A sudden trembling shook his aged frame:
When Hermes, greeting, touch'd his royal hand,
And gently thus accosts with kind demand:
' Say whither, father! when each mortal sight
Is seal'd in sleep, thou wander'st through the night?
Why roam thy mules and steeds the plains along,
Through Grecian foes, so numerous and so strong?
What couldst thou hope, should these thy treasures view—
These, who with endless hate thy race pursue?
For what defence, alas! couldst thou provide;
Thyself not young, a weak old man thy guide?

Yet suffer not thy soul to sink with dread:
From me no harm shall touch thy reverend head;
From Greece I'll guard thee too; for in those
  lines
The living image of my father shines.'
  'Thy words, that speak benevolence of mind,
Are true, my son! (the godlike sire rejoin'd).
Great are my hazards; but the gods survey
My steps, and send thee guardian of my way.
Hail, and be bless'd! For scarce of mortal kind
Appear thy form—thy feature—and thy mind.'
  'Nor true are all thy words, nor erring wide
(The sacred messenger of heaven replied);
But say, convey'st thou through the lonely plains
What yet most precious of thy store remains,
To lodge in safety with some friendly hand:
Prepared, perchance, to leave thy native land?
Or fly'st thou now?—What hopes can Troy retain,
Thy matchless son, her guard and glory, slain?'
  The king, alarm'd: 'Say, what, and whence
  thou art,
Who search the sorrows of a parent's heart,
And know so well how godlike Hector died?'
Thus Priam spoke, and Hermes thus replied:
  'You tempt me, father, and with pity touch
On this sad subject you inquire too much.
Oft have these eyes that godlike Hector view'd
In glorious fight with Grecian blood imbrued:
I saw him when, like Jove, his flames he toss'd
On thousand ships, and wither'd half an host:
I saw, but help'd not: stern Achilles' ire
Forbade assistance, and enjoy'd the fire.
For him I serve, of myrmidonian race;
One ship convey'd us from our native place;
Polyctor is my sire, an honour'd name,
Old like thyself, and not unknown to fame:
Of seven his sons, by whom the lot was cast
To serve our prince, it fell on me, the last.
To watch this quarter my adventure falls:
For with the morn the Greeks attack your walls;
Sleepless they sit, impatient to engage,
And scarce their rulers check their martial rage.'
  'If then thou art of stern Pelides' train
(The mournful monarch thus rejoin'd again),

A h, tell me truly, where, oh! where are laid
My son's dear relics? what befalls him dead?
Have dogs dismember'd (on the naked plains),
Or yet unmangled rest his cold remains?'
  'O favour'd of the skies! (thus answer'd then
The power that mediates 'tween gods and men)
Nor dogs nor vultures have thy Hector rent,
But whole he lies, neglected in the tent:
This the twelfth evening since he rested there,
Untouch'd by worms, untainted by the air.
Still as Aurora's ruddy beam is spread,
Round his friend's tomb Achilles drags the
  dead;
Yet undisfigured, or in limb or face,
All fresh he lies, with every living grace,
Majestical in death! no stains are found
O'er all the corse, and closed is every wound;
Though many a wound they gave. Some hea-
  venly care,
Some hand divine, preserves him ever fair;
Or all the host of heaven, to whom he led
A life so grateful, still regard him dead.'
  Thus spoke to Priam the celestial guide,
And joyful thus the royal sire replied:
  'Bless'd is the man who pays the gods above
The constant tribute of respect and love;
Those who inhabit the Olympian bower
My son forgot not, in exalted power;
And heaven, that every virtue bears in mind,
E'en to the ashes of the just is kind.
But thou, O generous youth! this goblet take,
A pledge of gratitude, for Hector's sake;
And while the favouring gods our steps survey,
Safe to Pelides' tent conduct my way.'
  To whom the latent god: 'O king, forbear
To tempt my youth, for apt is youth to err:
But can I, absent from my prince's sight,
Take gifts in secret, that must shun the light?
What from our master's interest thus we draw,
Is but a licensed theft that 'scapes the law.
Respecting him, my soul abjures th' offence;
And as the crime, I dread the consequence.
Thee, far as Argos, pleased I could convey;
Guard of thy life and partner of thy way—

On thee attend, thy safety to maintain,
O'er pathless forests, or the roaring main.'
  He said, then took the chariot at a bound,
And snatched the reins, and whirled the lash
    around.
Before th' inspiring god that urged them on,
The coursers fly, with spirit not their own.
And now they reach'd their naval walls, and found
The guards repasting, while the bowls go round:
On these the virtue of his wand he tries,
And pours deep slumber on their watchful eyes:
Then heaved the massy gates, removed the bars,
And o'er the trenches led the rolling cars.
Unseen, through all the hostile camp they went,
And now approach'd Pelides' lofty tent.
Of fir the roof was raised, and covered o'er
With reeds collected from the marshy shore;
And, fenced with palisades, a hall of state
(The work of soldiers), where the hero sate.
Large was the door, whose well-compacted strength
A solid pine-tree barr'd, of wondrous length;

Scarce three strong Greeks could lift its mighty
    weight,
But great Achilles singly closed the gate.
This Hermes (such the power of gods) set wide;
Then swift alighted the celestial guide,
And thus reveal'd : ' Hear, prince! and under-
    stand
Thou ow'st thy guidance to no mortal hand :
Hermes I am, descended from above,
The king of arts, the messenger of Jove.
Farewell : to shun Achilles' sight I fly :
Uncommon are such favours of the sky,
Nor stand confess'd to frail mortality.
Now fearless enter, and prefer thy prayers ;
Adjure him by his father's silver hairs,
His son, his mother ! urge him to bestow
Whatever pity that stern heart can know.'
  Thus having said, he vanish'd from his eyes,
And in a moment shot into the skies."
                                Iliad, book xxiv.

No. 943.

Priam conducted into the Grecian camp by Mercury, who lulls the sentinels to sleep.

APOLLONIDES.   *Cornelian.*

See preceding quotation.

No. 944.

Priam left by Mercury at the door of Achilles' tent.

APOLLONIDES.   *Amethyst.*

See conclusion of preceding quotation.

No. 945.

Priam supplicating Achilles.

PHILEMON. *Cornelian.*

"The king, confirm'd from heav'n, alighted there,
And left his aged herald on the car.
With solemn pace through various rooms he went,
And found Achilles in his inner tent.
There sat the hero; Alcimus the brave,
And great Automedon, attendance gave:
These serv'd his person at the royal feast:
Around, at awful distance, stood the rest.

Unseen by these, the king his entry made,
And prostrate now before Achilles laid—
Sudden (a venerable sight!) appears—
Embrac'd his knees, and bath'd his hands in tears:
Those direful hands his kisses press'd, embru'd
Ev'n with the best, the dearest of his blood!

As when a wretch (who, conscious of his crime,
Pursu'd for murder, flies his native clime),
Just gains some frontier—breathless—pale—
amaz'd!

All gaze—all wonder! thus Achilles gaz'd—
Thus stood th' attendants, stupid with surprise—
All mute!—yet seem'd to question with their eyes:
Each look'd on other—none the silence broke,
Till thus, at last, the kingly suppliant spoke:
'Ah, think, thou favour'd of the pow'rs divine!
Think of thy father's age, and pity mine!
In me that father's rev'rend image trace,
Those silver hairs, that venerable face;
His trembling limbs, his helpless person, see!
In all my equal but in misery!
Yet now, perhaps, some turn of human fate
Expels him helpless from his peaceful state:
Think from some pow'rful foe thou seest him fly,
And beg protection with a feeble cry;
Yet still one comfort in his soul may rise—
He hears his son still lives to glad his eyes;

And hearing still may hope a better day
May send him thee, to chase that foe away.
No comfort to my griefs, no hopes remain:
The best, the bravest of my sons are slain!
Yet what a race! ere Greece to Ilion came,
The pledge of many a lov'd and loving dame;
Nineteen one mother bore: dead!—all are dead!
How oft, alas! has wretched Priam bled!
Still one was left, their loss to recompense—
His father's hope, his country's last defence.
Him too thy rage has slain! beneath thy steel,
Unhappy, in his country's cause he fell!

For him through hostile camps I bent my way,
For him thus prostrate at thy feet I lay;
Large gifts proportion'd to thy wrath I bear—
O hear the wretched, and the gods revere!

Think of thy father, and this face behold!
See him in me, as helpless and as old—
Though not so wretched! there he yields to me,
The first of men in sov'reign misery—
Thus forc'd to kneel, thus grov'lling to embrace
The scourge and ruin of my realm and race;
Suppliant my children's murd'rer to implore,
And kiss those hands yet reeking with their
gore!'
These words soft pity in the chief inspire,
Touch'd with the dear remembrance of his sire.
Then with his hand (as prostrate still he lay)
The old man's cheek he gently turn'd away.
Now each by turns indulg'd the gush of woe;
And now the mingled tides together flow:
This low on earth, that gently bending o'er—
A father one, and one a son deplore;
But great Achilles different passions rend,
And now his sire he mourns, and now his friend.
The infectious softness through the heroes ran;

One universal solemn show'r began :
They bore as heroes, but they felt as man.
  Satiate at length with unavailing woes,
From the high throne divine Achilles rose ;
The rev'rend monarch by the hand he rais'd—
On his white beard and form majestic gaz'd,
Not unrelenting ; then serene began
With words to soothe the miserable man :
  ' Alas, what weight of anguish hast thou known !
Unhappy prince ! thus guardless and alone
To pass through foes, and thus undaunted face
The man whose fury has destroy'd thy race ?
Heav'n sure has arm'd thee with a heart of steel,
A strength proportion'd to the woes you feel.
Rise, then ; let reason mitigate our care :
To mourn avails not ; man is born to bear.
Such is, alas ! the gods' severe decree ;
They—only they are bless'd, and only free.
Two urns by Jove's high throne have ever stood,
The source of evil one, and one of good ;
From thence the cup of mortal man he fills,
Blessings to these, to those distributes ills ;
To most he mingles both.   The wretch decreed
To taste the bad unmix'd, is curs'd indeed ;
Pursu'd by wrongs, by meagre famine driv'n,
He wanders, outcast both of earth and heav'n.
The happiest taste not happiness sincere,
But find the cordial draught is dash'd with care.
Who more than Peleus shone in wealth and pow'r ?
What stars concurring bless'd his natal hour !
A realm, a goddess, to his wishes giv'n,
Grac'd by the gods with all the gifts of heav'n !
One evil yet o'ertakes his latest day,
No race succeeding to imperial sway :
An only son ! and he, alas ! ordain'd
To fall untimely in a foreign land !
See him, in Troy, the pious care decline
Of his weak age, to live the curse of thine !
Thou too, old man, hast happier days beheld ;
In riches once, in children once excell'd :
Extended Phrygia own'd thy ample reign,
And all fair Lesbos' blissful seats contain,
And all wide Hellespont's unmeasur'd main.

But since the god his hand has pleas'd to turn,
And fill thy measure from his bitter urn,
What sees the sun but hapless heroes' falls ?
War, and the blood of men, surround thy walls !
What must be must be.   Bear thy lot, nor shed
These unavailing sorrows o'er the dead ;
Thou canst not call him from the Stygian shore,
But thou, alas ! may'st live to suffer more !'
  To whom the king :—' O favour'd of the skies !
Here let me grow to earth ; since Hector lies
On the bare beach, depriv'd of obsequies.
O give me Hector ! to my eyes restore
His corse, and take the gifts : I ask no more.
Thou, as thou may'st, these boundless stores enjoy ;
Safe may'st thou sail, and turn thy wrath from
      Troy :
So shall thy pity and forbearance give
A weak old man to see the light and live.'
  ' Move me no more,' Achilles thus replies,
While kindling anger sparkled in his eyes,
' Nor seek by tears my steady soul to bend ;
To yield thy Hector I myself intend.
For know, from Jove my goddess-mother came,
(Old Ocean's daughter, silver-footed dame,)
Nor com'st thou but by heav'n ; nor com'st alone ;
Some god impels with courage not thy own :
No human hand the weighty gates unbarr'd,
Nor could the boldest of our youth have dar'd
To pass our out-works, or elude the guard.
Cease, lest, neglectful of high Jove's command,
I shew thee, king ! thou tread'st on hostile land.
Release my knees, thy suppliant arts give o'er,
And shake the purpose of my soul no more.'
  The sire obey'd him, trembling and o'eraw'd.
Achilles, like a lion, rush'd abroad ;
Automedon and Alcimus attend
(Whom most he honour'd since he lost his friend) :
These to unyoke the mules and horses went,
And led the hoary herald to the tent ;
Next heap'd on high the num'rous presents bear
(Great Hector's ransom) from the polish'd car."
               Iliad, book xxiv.

No. 946.

Priam warned by Mercury to return.

GNAIOS. *Cornelian.*

Achilles persuaded Priam to sup with him, and sleep that night in the tent.

" Now gods and men the gift of sleep par-
    take ;
Industrious Hermes only was awake,
The king's return revolving in his mind,
To pass the ramparts, and the watch to blind.
The power descending hover'd o'er his head !
' And sleep'st thou, father !' thus the vision said :
' Now dost thou sleep, when Hector is restor'd ?
Nor fear the Grecian foes, or Grecian lord ?
Thy presence here should stern Atrides see,
Thy still surviving sons may sue for thee—

May offer all thy treasures yet contain,
To spare thy age, and offer all in vain.'
    Wak'd with the word, the trembling sire arose,
And raised his friend ; the god before him goes :
He joins the mules, directs them with his hand,
And moves in silence through the hostile land.
When now to Xanthus' yellow stream they drove
(Xanthus, immortal progeny of Jove),
The winged deity forsook their view,
And in a moment to Olympus flew."

Iliad, book xxiv.

No. 947.

Mercury conducting Priam's chariot back.

POLYCLETES. *Sardonyx.*

See preceding quotation.

No. 948.

Priam having brought back the body of Hector, Hecuba and Andromache lament over it.

CHROMIOS. *Cornelian.*

" In thronging crowds they issue to the plains,
Nor man nor woman in the walls remains ;
In ev'ry face the self-same grief is shewn,
And Troy sends forth one universal groan.
At Scæa's gates they meet the mourning wain,
Hang on the wheels, and grovel round the slain.
The wife and mother, frantic with despair,
Kiss his pale cheek, and rend their scatter'd hair.

Thus wildly wailing, at the gates they lay,
And there had sigh'd and sorrow'd out the day ;
But godlike Priam from the chariot rose :
' Forbear,' he cried, ' this violence of woes ;
First to the palace let the car proceed,
Then pour your boundless sorrows o'er the dead.'
    The waves of people at his word divide ;
Slow rolls the chariot through the following tide ;

Ev'n to the palace the sad pomp they wait—
They weep, and place him on the bed of state.
A melancholy choir attend around,
With plaintive sighs, and music's solemn sound:
Alternately they sing; alternate flow
Th' obedient tears, melodious in their woe;
While deeper sorrows groan from each full heart,
And nature speaks at ev'ry pause of art.

 First to the corse the weeping consort flew,
Around his neck her milk-white arms she threw;
And, ' Oh, my Hector! oh, my lord !' she cries—
' Snatch'd in thy bloom from these desiring eyes !
Thou to the dismal realms for ever gone !
And I abandon'd, desolate, alone !
An only son, once comfort of our pains,
Sad product now of hapless love remains !
Never to manly age that son shall rise,
Or with increasing graces glad my eyes;
For Ilion now (her great defender slain)
Shall sink a smoking ruin on the plain.
Who now protects her wives with guardian
  care?
Who saves her infants from the rage of war?
Now hostile fleets must waft those infants o'er
(Those wives must wait 'em) to a foreign shore !
Thou too, my son ! to barb'rous climes shalt go,
The sad companion of thy mother's woe;
Driv'n hence a slave before the victor's sword,
Condemn'd to toil for some inhuman lord.
Or else some Greek, whose father press'd the
  plain,
Or son, or brother, by great Hector slain,

In Hector's blood his vengeance shall enjoy,
And hurl thee headlong from the tow'rs of Troy.
For thy stern father never spar'd a foe :
Thence all these tears, and all this scene of woe !
Thence many evils his sad parents bore,
His parents many, but his consort more.
Why gav'st thou not to me thy dying hand ?
And why receiv'd not I thy last command ?
Some word thou would'st have spoke, which sadly
  dear
My soul might keep, or utter with a tear ;
Which never, never, could be lost in air,
Fix'd in my heart, and oft repeated there !'
 Thus to her weeping maids she makes her
  moan ;
Her weeping handmaids echo groan for groan.
 The mournful mother next sustains her part.
' O thou, the best, the dearest to my heart !
Of all my race thou most by heav'n approv'd,
And by th' immortals ev'n in death belov'd !
While all my other sons in barb'rous bands
Achilles bound, and sold to foreign lands,
This felt no chains, but went a glorious ghost
Free, and a hero to the Stygian coast ;—
Sentenc'd, 'tis true, by his inhuman doom,
Thy noble corse was dragg'd around the tomb—
(The tomb of him thy warlike arm had slain)—
Ungen'rous insult, impotent and vain !
Yet glow'st thou fresh with ev'ry living grace,
No mark of pain, or violence of face ;
Rosy and fair, as Phœbus' silver bow
Dismiss'd thee gently to the shades below.' "
         Iliad, book xxiv.

No. 949.

Hecuba imploring Minerva to spare the Trojans.

Gnaios.   *Cornelian.*

"This heard, she gave command; and sum-
  mon'd came
Each noble matron and illustrious dame.
The Phrygian queen to her rich wardrobe went,
Where treasur'd odours breath'd a costly scent.

There lay the vestures, of no vulgar art ;
Sidonian maids embroider'd ev'ry part,
Whom from soft Sidon youthful Paris bore,
With Helen touching on the Tyrian shore.

Here as the queen revolv'd with careful eyes
The various textures and the various dyes,
She chose a veil that shone superior far,
And glow'd refulgent as the morning star.
Herself with this the long procession leads;
The train majestically slow proceeds.
Soon as to Ilion's topmost tow'r they come,
And awful reach the high Palladian dome :
Antenor's consort, fair Theano, waits
As Pallas' priestess, and unbars the gates.
With hands uplifted and imploring eyes,
They fill the dome with supplicating cries.

The priestess then the shining veil displays,
Plac'd on Minerva's knees, and thus she prays :
  ' Oh, awful goddess ! ever-dreadful maid,
Troy's strong defence, unconquer'd Pallas, aid !
Break thou Tydides' spear, and let him fall
Prone on the dust before the Trojan wall.
So twelve young heifers, guiltless of the yoke,
Shall fill thy temple with a grateful smoke.
But thou, aton'd by penitence and pray'r,
Ourselves, our infants, and our city spare !'
So pray'd the priestess in her holy fane—
So vow'd the matrons ; but they vow'd in vain.''
Iliad, book v.

No. 950.

Hecuba blinding Polymestor.

DIOSCORIDES. *Cornelian.*

The Greeks, on their return from Troy, having put in at the Thracian Chersonese, Hecuba, one of the captives, discovers that her youngest and only surviving son, Polydore, was murdered by Polymestor the king (to whose charge he was entrusted), in order that he might possess his property. In revenge, she, aided by the other Trojan captives, killed his children and blinded himself.

The ghost of Polydore speaks—

" The mansions of the dead, the gates of darkness,
Where Pluto dwells from the blest gods apart,
I leave, the son of Hecuba and Priam.
When danger threaten'd that the Phrygian state
Would sink beneath the conqu'ring spear of Greece,
He, fearing for his much-lov'd Polydore,
In secret sent me from the Trojan land,
To Polymestor's court, his Thracian friend,
Bound to him by each hospitable tie—
Who cultivates this fertile Chersonese,
And with his spear a warlike people rules.
With me he sent in secret stores of gold,
That, if the walls of Troy should fall, his sons,
Whoe'er surviv'd, might find a rich support.

I was the youngest of the sons of Priam,
And therefore sent, because my youthful arm
Could not sustain the shield, or hurl the spear.
Whilst Troy's strong bulwarks stood, and her high tow'rs
Unshaken, and whilst Hector's spear prevail'd,
The Thracian rear'd me with a father's care,
And I, like some fair plant, grew up and flourish'd.
But when Troy sunk, her Hector now no more,
And Priam's palace smok'd upon the ground,
Himself upon the hallow'd altar fall'n
Slain by Achilles' blood-polluted son,
This hospitable friend, to seize my gold,
Kill'd me, and rudely toss'd my lifeless corse
Into the billows of the surging sea ;
There yet it lies, now dash'd upon the strand,

Now whelm'd beneath the tide's returning wave,
Unwept—unburied! For my mother's sake
I wander, having left my breathless body:
Three days I hover here, for now three days
Hath the unhappy Hecuba from Troy
Continued on th' abhorred Chersonese:
Here all the Grecians hold their anchor'd ships,
And sit inactive on the Thracian shore.

· · · · · · · ·

SEMICHORUS.

Hast thou surpris'd, hast thou o'erpower'd the
Thracian?
Say, lady, hast thou done th' appointed deed?

HECUBA.

Soon shalt thou see him here before the tent;
Blind, with blind steps wheeling his oblique path.
His sons are slain, both slain, the Trojan dames
Assisting my revenge, which now he feels.
See, he advances: distant I withdraw,
Shunning the violence of his boist'rous rage.

POLYMESTOR, *coming forth.*

O horrible!
Where shall I go? where stand? where steer my
way?
Prone like a mountain beast, shall my hands learn
The task of feet? Is this my course, or this,
That I may seize these murderous dames of Troy,
Who thus have ruin'd me? Pernicious fiends,
Ye Phrygians, curses on you! in what hole
Hide ye your trembling heads! O sun, couldst
thou
Heal these dark, bleeding orbs, relume their light!
Hist, hist! I hear the soft tread of these women:
How then direct my steps to rush on them,
To tear the savages, to rend them piecemeal,
And glut my vengeance for the wrongs they've
done me?
Ah, whither am I borne, leaving my sons
By these infernal furies to be torn,
And piecemeal on the mountains cast, to dogs,
To rav'nous dogs, a mangled, bleeding prey?

Where shall I stand? where turn? where point
my steps?
For as a ship with all its cables loose,
Its sails all streaming to the wind, I drive,
To guard my sons, to that destructive place
Where murder'd on th' ensanguin'd ground they
lie.

CHORUS.

Wretch, what a load of misery on thee lies,
Thy deeds of baseness by th' avenging gods
With deeds of horror on thy head repaid!

POLYMESTOR.

What, ho! my Thracians, ho! To arms, my
friends,
Bestride your fiery steeds, couch your strong
spears,
Haste to my aid, ye valiant sons of Mars!
Ye Grecians, ho! Ye sons of Atreus, ho!
Holo! holo! Again I call, holo!
Quick, I conjure you by the gods—haste—come.
Hear ye my voice? Comes no man to my aid?
Why are you slow? These women have destroy'd
me,
These captive women. Oh, 'tis horrible,
Horrible what I suffer! Ruin, ruin!
Ah, which way shall I turn me? whither go?
Shall I take wing, and with a lofty flight
Soar through th' ethereal sky to the high man-
sions
Where Sirius and Orion from their eyes
Flash the far-beaming blaze of fiery light?
Or plunging through the darksome depths of hell,
Seek a sad refuge, a sad harbour there?

· · · · · · ·

When her son's death was known to Hecuba,
With treacherous device she lured me hither,
Feigning I know not what of buried gold,
Treasures conceal'd in Troy, the wealth of Priam:
Then with a specious face of secrecy
Within the tent me only and my sons
Admits: I careless in the midst reclin'd;
Around me, as a friend, familiar sat
Bevies of Trojan dames, and to the light

Held the rich texture of th' Edonian loom,
Praising the curious tissue of my robes;
Others admiring view'd my Thracian spear,
So stripp'd me of my double ornament.
Such as were mothers seem'd with fond regard
T' admire my sons, caress'd them, in their arms
Alternately receiv'd them, till from me
They held them distant; 'midst their blandish-
     ments
Suddenly from beneath their robes drew daggers,
And with them stab my sons: me others seize
With hostile violence, my hands, my feet
Lock'd in close grasp; if to protect my sons
I rais'd my head, they held me by the hair;
If I would move my hands, numbers hung on them,
And kept me with their cumbrous weight confin'd.
But their last mischief was a deed of horror
Surpassing savage; for they seize my eyes—
Pierce these poor bleeding orbs, and quench their
     light,
Then vanish through the tent: I started fierce,
Like a chaf'd tiger, and these murderous hounds
Pursue, along the walls searching my way,
Batt'ring and rending."

EURIPIDES, Hecuba.

No. 951.

Hecuba with an urn which contains the ashes of Polyxena and Polydore.

DAMAS. *Cornelian.*

The spirit of Achilles appeared, and demanded the immolation of his affianced bride,
Polyxena, daughter of Priam and Hecuba.

" Awhile, O king, the mournful rites forbear
For my Polyxena, my late slain daughter;
That on one pile the brother and the sister,
To me a double grief, may blaze together,
And mix their ashes in one common urn."

EURIPIDES, Hecuba.

No. 952.

Death of Hecuba.

PYRGOTELES. *Cornelian.*

" The Thracians, fir'd at this inhuman scene,
With darts and stones assail the frantic queen.
She snarls and growls, nor in a human tone;
Then bites impatient at the bounding stone;
Extends her jaws, as she her voice would raise
To keen invectives in her wonted phrase;
But barks, and thence the yelping brute betrays.

Still a sad monument the place remains,
And from this monstrous change its name obtains:
Where she, in long remembrance of her ills,
With plaintive howling the wide desert fills."

OVID'S *Met.* book xiii.

No. 953.

Metamorphosis of Hecuba.

GNAIOS. *Cornelian.*

See preceding quotation.

No. 954.

Peneleus displaying the head of Ilioneus.

GNAIOS. *Cornelian.*

" Heart-piercing anguish struck the Grecian host,
But touch'd the breast of bold Peneleus most;
At the proud boaster he directs his course;
The boaster flies, and shuns superior force:
But young Ilioneus received the spear—
Ilioneus, his father's only care
(Phorbas the rich, of all the Trojan train
Whom Hermes loved, and taught the arts of gain):
Full in his eye the weapon chanced to fall,
And from the fibres scoop'd the rooted ball—
Drove through the neck, and hurl'd him to the plain:
He lifts his miserable arms—in vain!
Swift his broad falchion fierce Peneleus spread,
And from the spouting shoulders struck his head;
To earth at once the head and helmet fly;
The lance, yet striking through the bleeding eye,
The victor seized; and as aloft he shook
The gory visage, thus insulting spoke:
' Trojans! your great Ilioneus behold!
Haste—to his father let the tale be told:
Let his high roof resound with frantic woe,
Such as the house of Promachus must know—
Let doleful tidings greet his mother's ear,
Such as to Promachus' sad spouse we bear';
When we victorious shall to Greece return,
And the pale matron in our triumphs mourn.'
Dreadful he spoke, then toss'd the head on high
The Trojans hear—they tremble—and they fly—
Aghast they gaze around the fleet and wall—
And dread the ruin that impends on all."

Iliad, book xiv.

No. 955.

Wounded Æneas guarded by Venus.

GNAIOS. *Cornelian.*

"To guard his slaughter'd friend Æneas flies,
His spear extending where the carcass lies;
Watchful he wheels, protects it ev'ry way,
As the grim lion stalks around his prey.
O'er the fall'n trunk his ample shield display'd,
He hides the hero with his mighty shade,
And threats aloud: the Greeks with longing eyes
Behold at distance, but forbear the prize.
Then fierce Tydides stoops, and from the fields
Heav'd with vast force, a rocky fragment wields:
Not two strong men th' enormous weight could raise,
Such men as live in these degen'rate days:
He swung it round; and gath'ring strength to throw,
Discharg'd the pond'rous ruin at the foe.
Where to the hip th' inserted thigh unites,
Full on the bone the pointed marble lights;

Through both the tendons broke the rugged stone,
And stripped the skin, and cracked the solid bone:
Sunk on his knees, and stagg'ring with his pains,
His falling bulk his bended arm sustains:
Lost in a dizzy mist the warrior lies,
A sudden cloud comes swimming o'er his eyes.
There the brave chief, who mighty numbers sway'd,
Oppress'd had sunk to death's eternal shade:
But heav'nly Venus, mindful of the love
She bore Anchises in th' Idæan grove,
His danger views with anguish and despair,
And guards her offspring with a mother's care.
About her much-lov'd son her arms she throws—
Her arms whose whiteness match the falling snows—
Screen'd from the foe behind her shining veil,
The swords wave harmless, and the jav'lins fail."

Iliad, book v.

No. 956.

Æneas conveyed to Troy by Apollo, and there attended by Latona and Diana.

PYRGOTELES. *Sardonyx.*

" Then Phœbus bore the chief of Venus' race
To Troy's high fane and to his holy place;
Latona there and Phœbe heal'd the wound,
With vigour arm'd him, and with glory crown'd."

Iliad, book v.

No. 957.

Pandarus killing a wild goat, from whose horns he made his bow.

CHROMIOS. *Cornelian.*

" He heard, and madly at the motion pleas'd,
His polish'd bow with hasty rashness seiz'd:
'Twas form'd of horn, and smooth'd with artful toil;
A mountain-goat resign'd the shining spoil,

4 E

Who pierc'd long since beneath his arrows bled ;
The stately quarry on the cliffs lay dead,
And sixteen palms his brows' large honours spread :
The workman join'd and shap'd the bended horns,
And beaten gold each taper point adorns."

Iliad, book iv.

No. 958.

Polyxena sacrificed by Pyrrhus at the tomb of Achilles.

Dioscorides.　*Cornelian.*

See No. 951.

"Thou know'st that he, appearing o'er his tomb
In all his golden arms, stopp'd their fleet ships,
Their sails unfurl'd and waving in the wind,
Calling aloud, ' And is it thus, ye Greeks,
You speed your course, my tomb unhonour'd left?'

.　　　.　　　.　　　.　　　.

Th' assembled host of Greece before the tomb
Stood in full ranks at this sad sacrifice ;
Achilles' son, holding the virgin's hand,
On the mound's extreme summit ; near him I ;
An honourable train of chosen youths,
In readiness her strugglings to restrain,
Follow'd : the golden goblet crown'd with wine
The hero's son then took, and with his hand
Pour'd the libation to his father's shade.
At his high bidding I aloud proclaim'd
Silence through all the host ; and all were silent.
Then he : ' O son of Peleus, O my father,
Accept my offerings, which evoke—which soothe
The dead : O come, drink the pure purple stream
Which from this virgin we present to thee.
Loose all our cables, wing our flying sails,
Propitious give us to return from Troy,
And safe revisit our paternal Greece.'
He spoke, and with him all the people pray'd.
Then taking by the hilt his golden sword,
He drew it from the scabbard : at his nod
The noble youths advanc'd to hold the virgin ;

Which she perceiving, with these words address'd them :
' Ye Greeks, beneath whose arms my country fell,
Willing I die ; let no hand touch me ; boldly
To the uplifted sword I hold my neck :
You give me to the gods ; then give me free ;
Free let me die ; nor let a royal maid
Blush 'mongst the dead to hear the name of slave.'
Loud was th' applause : the royal Agamemnon
Commands that none should touch her : at the voice
Of their great chief th' obedient youths retire.
Soon as she heard th' imperial word, she took
Her robe, and from her shoulder rent it down,
And bared her bosom—bared her polish'd breast,
Beauteous beyond the sculptor's nicest art !
Then bending to the earth her knee, she spoke
Words the most mournful sure that ear e'er heard :
' If 'tis thy will, young man, to strike this bosom,
Strike : or my throat dost thou require ? behold
Stretch'd to thy sword my throat.' Awhile he paus'd,
In pity of the virgin, then reluctant
Deep in her bosom plung'd the fatal steel ;
Her life-blood gush'd in streams ; yet e'en in death
Studious of modesty, compos'd she fell,

And cover'd with her robe her decent limbs.
Soon as the vital spirit through the wound
Expir'd, in various toils the Greeks engag'd ;
Some on the breathless body scatter'd boughs ;
Some, bringing unctuous pines, the solemn pyre
Funereal rais'd : was one remiss, the active
Rebuk'd him thus, ' Dost thou stand idle here,

Thou drone ? hast thou no robe, no ornament,
Nothing to grace this high heroic spirit,
This glorious excellence ?' Thus they their zeal
With generous ardour to the dead express'd.
But thee, blest parent of the noblest offspring,
Happiest of women, now I see most wretched."
EURIPIDES, *Hecuba.*

No. 959.

Anchises struck with lightning.

APOLLONIDES.   *Sardonyx.*

Anchises was the father of Æneas by Venus. She warned him, that if he boasted of her favours, he would be blasted by the thunderbolt of Jupiter. He did, however, divulge the secret, and was consequently struck with a thunderbolt ; but Venus, seized with sudden compassion, prevented the bolt from taking mortal effect. Some say he was deprived of sight ; Virgil (*Æn.* ii.) only says that he was disabled :—

" Inutilis anuos
Demoror, ex quo me divum pater atque hominum rex
Fulminis afflavit ventis, et contigit igni."

No. 960.

Idomeneus slaying Othryoneus.

SCHIMMIOS.   *Cornelian.*

" Dreadful in arms, and grown in combats gray,
The bold Idomeneus controls the day.
First by his hand Othryoneus was slain,
Swell'd with false hopes—with mad ambition vain !
Call'd by the voice of war to martial fame,
From high Cabesus' distant walls he came ;
Cassandra's love he sought, with boasts of power,
And promised conquest was the proffer'd dower.
The king consented, by his vaunts abused—
The king consented, but the Fates refused !
Proud of himself and of th' imagined bride,
The field he measured with a larger stride.
Him as he stalk'd, the Cretan javelin found.
Vain was his breastplate to repel the wound :

His dream of glory lost, he plunged to hell :
His arms resounded as the boaster fell.
The great Idomeneus bestrides the dead :
' And thus (he cries) behold thy promise sped !
Such is the help thy arms to Ilion bring,
And such the contract of the Phrygian king !
Our offers now, illustrious prince ! receive ;
For such an aid what will not Argos give ?
To conquer Troy, with ours thy forces join,
And count Atrides' fairest daughter thine.
Meantime, on farther methods to advise,
Come, follow to the fleet thy new allies ;
There hear what Greece has on her part to say.'
He spoke, and dragg'd the gory corse away."
Iliad, book xiii.

No. 961.

Eurypilus with the casket which enclosed the image of Bacchus.

PYRGOTELES.   *Calcedony.*

This subject is thus explained by Pausanias (*Achaics*, book vii. c. 19) :—" There is a sepulchre of Eurypilus between the temple of Laphria and the altar. Troy being taken, and the spoils divided, Eurypilus, the son of Euæmon, received a chest, which contained a statue of Bacchus; the work, they say, of Vulcan, and the gift of Jupiter to Dardanus. Of this chest there are two reports. According to some, it was left by Æneas when he quitted Troy; but according to others, it was thrown away by Cassandra, knowing that it would prove unfortunate to any Greek who received it. Eurypilus opened the chest, and was seized with instant madness; though he sometimes recovered the use of his reason, yet he was the greater part of his time insane. He subsequently proceeded to Delphos, to consult the oracle by what means he could be liberated from his calamity. The oracle told him to dedicate the chest, and take up his abode, where he should meet with men sacrificing after a foreign manner. The wind having impelled his ship to the shore near Aroe, he landed, and found men leading along a boy and virgin to be sacrificed on the altar of Triclaria Diana. He then easily perceived that this sacrifice was that to which the oracle referred, and dedicated the chest. The natives too, recollecting that the oracle declared, that the yearly sacrifice (which was required of them as the condition of their release from pestilence and famine—a punishment inflicted by Diana for a violation of her priestess in her temple) would cease when a foreign king should arrive in this country bringing with him a foreign demon,—believed that Eurypilus was the king, and that the chest contained the statue of this divinity. Thus was Eurypilus freed from the visitation, and the country from human sacrifices; and the river was called *Meilichos*, or ' mild.' "

No. 962.

Mercury warning Ægisthus not to attempt the life of Agamemnon.

GNAIOS.   *Sardonyx.*

No. 963.

Death of Agamemnon.

APOLLONIDES.   *Cornelian.*

On the return of Agamemnon from Troy, bringing with him as a captive the prophetess Cassandra, daughter of Priam, he was slain, together with Cassandra, by his queen Clytemnestra, encouraged to the deed by her paramour Ægisthus, Agamemnon's relation, whom he left guardian of the kingdom in his absence. In return, Orestes, the son of Agamemnon and

Clytemnestra, slew his own mother and Ægisthus. The following passages from the *Agamemnon* of Æschylus will fully explain this celebrated event in heroic history. The prominent part which Agamemnon took in the Trojan war, the large space which this subject fills in ancient poetry, and its connexion with other subjects in this collection, are sufficient reasons for the length of the quotations. Clytemnestra rushes outside the palace to meet Agamemnon on his arrival, and thus hypocritically expresses her joy—

" At thy return
The gushing fountains of my tears are dried,
Save that my eyes are weak with midnight
    watchings,
Straining through tears if haply they might see
Thy signal-fires, that claim'd my fix'd attention.
If they were clos'd in sleep, a silly fly
Would with its slightest murm'rings make me
    start,
And wake me to more fears. For thy dear sake
All this I suffer'd : but my jocund heart
Forgets it all, whilst I behold my lord—
My guardian—the strong anchor of my hope—
The stately column that supports my house—
Dear as an only child to a fond parent—
Welcome as land, which the toss'd mariner
Beyond his hope descries—welcome as day
After a night of storms, with fairer beams
Returning—welcome as the liquid lapse
Of fountain to the thirsty traveller :
So pleasant is it to escape the chain
Of hard constraint ! Such greeting I esteem
Due to thy honour : let it not offend ;
For I have suffer'd much. But, my lov'd lord,
Leave now that car, nor on the bare ground set
That royal foot, beneath whose mighty tread
Troy trembled. Haste, ye virgins, to whose care
This pleasing office is entrusted—spread
The streets with tapestry — let the ground be
    cover'd

With richest purple, leading to the palace ;
That honour with just state may grace his entry,
Though unexpected. My attentive care,
Shall, if the gods permit, dispose the rest
To welcome his high glories as I ought.

AGAMEMNON.

Daughter of Leda, guardian of my house,[*]
Thy words are correspondent to my absence,
Of no small length. With better grace my praise
Would come from others : soothe me not with
    strains
Of adulation, as a girl ; nor raise,
As to some proud barbaric king, that loves
Loud acclamations echoed from the mouths
Of prostrate worshippers, a clamorous welcome ;
Nor spread the streets with tapestry — 'tis in-
    vidious :
These are the honours we should pay the gods.
For mortal man to tread on ornaments   ·
Of rich embroid'ry—No : I dare not do it.
Respect me as a man, not as a god.
Why should my foot pollute these vests, that glow
With various-tinctur'd radiance ? My full fame
Swells high without it ; and the temperate rule
Of cool discretion is the choicest gift
Of fav'ring heav'n. Happy the man, whose life
Is spent in friendship's calm security.
These sober joys be mine, I ask no more.

.   .   .   .   .

---

* Agamemnon appears here in the most amiable light. He knows his dignity, and is not insensible to the fame which attends him as the conqueror of Asia : but, by reproving the excessive adulation of Clytemnestra, he shews that manly firmness of mind, that becoming moderation, which distinguishes the sober state of the king of Argos from the barbaric pride of an Asiatic monarch. The part which he has to act is short ; but it gives us a picture of the highest military glory, and of true regal virtue ; and shews us that as a man he was modest, gentle, and humane.

CASSANDRA.

Apollo, O Apollo, fatal leader!
Ah, whither hast thou led me?—to what house?

CHORUS.

Is that unknown?   Let me declare it then—
This is the royal mansion of th' Atridæ.

CASSANDRA.

It is a mansion hated by the gods,
Conscious to many a foul and horrid deed—
A slaughter-house, that reeks with human gore.

.   .   .   .   .

Ye pow'rs of heav'n, what does she now design?
What new and dreadful deed of woe is this?
What dreadful ill designs she in the house—
Intolerable, irreparable mischief,
Whilst far she sends the succouring pow'r away?*

.   .   .   .   .

CHORUS.

These prophecies surpass my apprehension.

CASSANDRA.

Ah, daring wretch! dost thou achieve this deed—
Thus in the bath the partner of thy bed
Refreshing?   How shall I relate th' event?
Yet speedy shall it be.   E'en now advanc'd,
Hand above hand extended threatens high.

CHORUS.

I comprehend her not: her words are dark—
Perplexing me like abstruse oracles.

CASSANDRA.

Ha!   What is this, that I see here before me?
Is it the net of hell?—or rather hers,
Who shares the bed, and plans the murderous
    deed?
Let discord, whose insatiable rage
Pursues this race, howl through the royal rooms

Against the victim destin'd to destruction.

See, see there! from the heifer keep the bull!—
O'er his black brows she throws the entangling
    vest,
And smites him with her huge two-handed engine.
He falls—amidst the cleansing laver falls:
I tell thee of the bath—the treacherous bath.

.   .   .   .   .

Ah me unhappy!   Wretched, wretched fate!
For my own sufferings join'd call forth these
    wailings.
Why hast thou brought me hither?   Wretched
    me!
Is it for this—that I may die with him?

.   .   .   .   .

Ah me!   the fortune of the nightingale
Is to be envied; on her light-pois'd plumes
She wings at will her easy way, nor knows
The anguish of a tear—whilst o'er my head
Th' impending sword threatens the fatal wound.

.   .   .   .   .

For this the sluggard savage, that at ease
Rolls on his bed, nor rouses from his lair,
'Gainst my returning lord—for I must wear
The yoke of slavery—plans the dark design
Of death.   Ah me!   the chieftain of the fleet—
The vanquisher of Troy—but little knows
What the smooth tongue of mischief, filed to
    words
Of glozing courtesy, with Fate her friend,
Like Ate ranging in the dark, can do
Calmly: such deeds a woman dares—she dares
Murder a man!   What shall I call this mis-
    chief?
An Amphisbæna? or a Scylla rather,
That in the vex'd rocks holds her residence,
And meditates the mariner's destruction?
Mother of hell, midst friends enkindling discord
And hate implacable!   With dreadful daring
How did she shout, as if the battle swerv'd!
Yet with feigned joy she welcomes his return!

---

* Orestes.

These words may want persuasion.* What of that?
What must come will come; and e'er long with grief
Thou shalt confess my prophecies are true.

.   .   .   .   .

CHORUS.

The gift of Phœbus this; no trivial grace.

CASSANDRA.

Ah, what a sudden flame comes rushing on me!
I burn—I burn! Apollo, O Apollo!
This lioness, that in a sensual sty
Roll'd with the wolf, the generous lion absent,
Will kill me! And the sorceress, as she brews
Her filt'red cup, will drug it with my blood.
She glories, as against her husband's life
She whets the axe, her vengeance falls on him
For that he came accompanied by me.†
Why do I longer wear these useless honours,
This laurel-wand, and these prophetic wreaths?
Away; before I die I cast you from me—
Lie there, and perish—I am rid of you;
Or deck the splendid ruin of some other.
Apollo rends from me these sacred vestments,
Who saw me in his rich habiliments
Mock'd midst my friends, doubtless without a cause.
When in opprobrious terms they jeer'd my skill,
And treated me as a poor vagrant wretch,
That told events from door to door for bread,
I bore it all: but now the prophet-god,
That with his own arts grac'd me, sinks me down
To this low ruin. As my father fell
Butcher'd e'en at the altar, like the victim's
My warm blood at the altar shall be shed:

Nor shall we die unhonour'd by the gods.
He comes, dreadful in punishment, the son
Of this bad mother, by her death t' avenge
His murder'd father. Distant though he roams,
An outcast and an exile, by his friends
Fenc'd from these deeds of violence,‡ he comes
In solemn vengeance for his father laid
Thus low. But why for foreign miseries
Does the tear darken in my eye, that saw
The fall of Ilium, and its haughty conq'rors
In righteous judgment thus receive their meed?
But forward now; I go to close the scene,
Nor shrink from death. I have a vow in heav'n:
And further I adjure these gates of hell,
Well may the blow be aim'd, that whilst my blood
Flows in a copious stream, I may not feel
The fierce, convulsive agonies of death;
But gently sink, and close my eyes in peace.

.   .   .   .   .

CHORUS.

Thy fate, poor sufferer, fills my eyes with tears.

CASSANDRA.

Yet once more let me raise my mournful voice.
Thou Sun, whose rising beams shall bless no more
These closing eyes! You, whose vindictive rage
Hangs o'er my hated murderers, O avenge me,
Though a poor slave; I fall an easy prey!
This is the state of man: in prosperous fortune
A shadow, passing light, throws to the ground
Joy's baseless fabric: in adversity
Comes malice with a sponge moisten'd in gall,
And wipes each beauteous character away:
More than the first this melts my soul to pity."

---

* Cassandra promised to requite the love of Apollo, on condition of receiving from him the gift of prophecy. When she received it, she broke her word; and for this he caused her to be considered insane, and her predictions to be disbelieved.

† This was one of the excuses of Clytemnestra.

‡ He was sent away from danger, through the agency of his sister Electra, to his uncle Strophius, king of Phocis.

Clytemnestra next boldly avows the act as justifiable—

CLYTEMNESTRA.

" To many a fair speech suited to the times
If my words now be found at variance,
I shall not blush.   For when the heart conceives
Thoughts of deep vengeance on a foe, what means
T' achieve the deed more certain, than to wear
The form of friendship, and with circling wiles
Inclose him in th' insuperable net?
This was no hasty, rash-conceiv'd design;
But form'd with deep, premeditated thought,
Incens'd with wrongs; and often have I stood,
T' assay the execution, where he fell;
And plann'd it so—for I with pride avow it—
He had no pow'r t' escape, or to resist,
Entangled in the gorgeous robe, that shone
Fatally rich.   I struck him twice; and twice
He groan'd—then died!   A third time, as he lay,
I gor'd him with a wound—a grateful present
To the stern god, that in the realms below
Reigns o'er the dead! there let him take his
     seat.
He lay; and spouting from his wounds a stream
Of blood, bedew'd me with these crimson drops.
I glory in them, like the genial earth,
When the warm show'rs of heav'n descend, and
     wake
The flow'rets to unfold their vermeil leaves.
Come, then, ye reverend senators of Argos,
Joy with me, if your hearts be tun'd to joy;
And such I wish them.   Were it decent now
To pour libations* o'er the dead, with justice
It might be done; for his injurious pride
Fill'd for this house the cup of desolation,
Fated himself to drain it to the dregs.

CHORUS.

We are astonish'd at thy daring words,
Thus vaunting o'er the ruins of thy husband.

CLYTEMNESTRA.

Me, like a witless woman, wouldst thou fright?
I tell thee, my firm soul disdains to fear.
Be thou dispos'd t' applaud, or censure me,
I reck it not: there Agamemnon lies,
My husband, slaughter'd by this hand: I dare
Avow his death, and justify the deed.

CHORUS.

What poison hath the baleful-teeming earth,
Or the chaf'd billows of the foamy sea,
Giv'n thee for food, or mingled in thy cup,
To work thee to this frenzy?   Thy curs'd hand
Hath struck—hath slain!   For this thy country's
     wrath
Shall in just vengeance burst upon thy head,
And with abhorrence drive thee from the city.

CLYTEMNESTRA.

And dost thou now denounce upon my head
Vengeance, and hate, and exile?—'gainst this man
Urging no charge!   Yet he, without remorse,
As if a lamb that wanton'd in his pastures
Were doom'd to bleed, could sacrifice his daugh-
     ter,†
For whose dear sake I felt a mother's pains,
T' appease the winds of Thrace.

.   .   .   .   .

Hear then this solemn oath: By that revenge,
Which for my daughter I have greatly taken;
By the dread pow'rs of Ate and Erinnys,
To whom my hand devoted him a victim—
Without a thought of fear I range these rooms,
Whilst present to my aid Ægisthus stands,
As he hath stood, guarding my social hearth:
He is my shield—my strength—my confidence.
Here lies my base betrayer, who at Troy
Could revel in the arms of each Chryseis;
He, and his captive minion—she that mark'd

---

* It was a custom among the ancients, after the defeat of their enemies, to pour libations to the gods their deliverers, in gratitude for their victory and freedom.
     † See No. 762.

Portents and prodigies, and with ominous tongue
Presag'd the fates; a wanton harlotry,
True to the rower's benches: their just meed
Have they receiv'd. See where he lies; and she,
That like the swan warbled her dying notes,
His paranymph, lies with him, to my bed
Leaving the darling object of my wishes.

. . . . . .

CHORUS.

Shalt thou reign king in Argos? Thou, whose
  soul
Plotted this murder; whilst thy coward hand
Shrunk back, nor dar'd to execute the deed?

ÆGISTHUS.

Wiles and deceit are female qualities:

The memory of my ancient enmity
Had wak'd suspicion. Master of his treasures,
Be it my next attempt to gain the people:
Whome'er I find unwilling to submit,
Him, like a high-fed and unruly horse,
Reluctant to the harness, rigour soon
Shall tame: confinement, and her meagre comrade
Keen hunger, will abate his fiery mettle.

CHORUS.

Did not the baseness of thy coward soul
Unman thee to this murder, that a woman,
Shame to her country and her country's gods,
Must dare the horrid deed? But when Orestes,
Where'er he breathes the vital air, returns—
Good fortune be his guide—shall not his hand
Take a bold vengeance in the death of both?"

No. 964.

Electra shewing Orestes and Pylades the bloody robe of Agamemnon.

POLYCLETES. *Cornelian.*

After the murder of Agamemnon, Ægisthus married Clytemnestra, and usurped the throne. Orestes, the son of Agamemnon, who had been under the protection of his uncle Strophius, came in disguise to Argos, accompanied by his cousin and devoted friend Pylades, and slew the assassins; his sister Electra encouraging him to the act, and Apollo sanctioning it. After this he became frantic, and was persecuted by the Furies until he was purified by Apollo, who advised him to take his trial before the court of Areopagus, in Athens. This assembly acquitted him; Minerva presiding on the occasion, and giving the casting vote in his favour. It is said that he also attempted to kill Erigone, the daughter of Ægisthus and Clytemnestra. After his acquittal and cure, he ascended the throne, and carried off and married Hermione (the daughter of Menelaus and Helen, and wife of Pyrrhus, son of Achilles), who had been betrothed to him in his youth. The adventures of Orestes are the subjects of several of the Grecian tragedies that have been preserved to us.

No. 965.

Orestes killing his mother.

POLYCLETES. *Sardonyx.*

4 F

Ægisthus is represented as lying dead at his feet. The length of the annexed quotations, which are taken from the *Choephoræ* of Æschylus, is unavoidable, from the importance attached to the subject by the ancient poets and modern scholars, and from its connexion with other subjects in this collection.

ELECTRA *at the tomb of her Father.*

" O thou, that to the realms beneath the earth
Guidest the dead, be present, Mercury,
And tell me that the pow'rs, whose solemn sway
Extends o'er those dark regions, hear my vows:
Tell me that o'er my father's house they roll
Their awful eyes, and o'er this earth, that bears
And fosters all, rich in their various fruits.
And thee, my father, pouring from this vase
Libations to thy shade, on thee I call—
O pity me—pity my dear Orestes,
That in this seat of kings our hands may hold
The golden reins of pow'r: for now oppress'd,
And harass'd by a mother's cruel hand,
Who for Ægisthus, that contriv'd thy death,
Exchang'd her royal lord, he wanders far,
And I am treated as a slave. Orestes

Orestes discovers himself to his sister—

ELECTRA.

" Am I indeed conversing with Orestes?

ORESTES.

Thou seest me present, yet art slow to know me.
When offer'd on the tomb thou saw'st these locks,
When with thy own th' impression of my feet
Were measur'd, joy gave wings to expectation,
And imag'd me before thee. Mark these locks,
Shorn from my brother's head; observe them well,
Compare them with thy own. This tissue, view
    it;
The texture is thy own, the rich embroidery,
Thine are these figures, by thy curious hand
Imag'd in gold.—Let not thy joy transport thee:
Our nearest friends are now our deadliest foes.

ELECTRA.

Thou dearest pledge of this imperial house,

From his possessions exil'd, they with pride
Wantonly revel in the wealth thy toils
Procur'd. O grant Orestes may return,
And fortune be his guide! Hear me, my father,
And grant me—more than e'er my mother knew—
The grace and blush of unstain'd modesty,
And a more holy hand! For us these vows;
But on our foes may thy avenger rise,
Demanding blood for blood. These vows I breathe
In dreadful imprecations on their heads.
Be thou to us, my father, with the gods—
This earth, and pow'rful justice, be to us,
That breathe this vital air, a guide to good!
With these libations such the vows I offer.
Now let your sorrows flow; attune the pæan,
And soothe his shade with solemn harmony.''

From thee my hopes, water'd with tears, arose:
Thy valour shall support our righteous cause,
And vindicate the glories of thy father.
Pride of my soul, for my fond tongue must speak,
The love my father shar'd, my mother shar'd—
Once shar'd, but justly now my soul abhors her—
And that poor victim my unhappy sister,*
Is centred all in thee: thou art my father—
My mother—sister—my support—my glory—
My only aid! and heav'n's great king shall
    prosper
Thy courage, and the justice of thy cause.

ORESTES.

Look down, great king of heav'n, look down,
    behold
These deeds of baseness! see an orphan race,
Reft of the parent eagle, that, enwreath'd
In the dire serpent's spiry volumes, perish'd.

---

* Iphigenia.

They, unprotected, feel th' oppressive pangs
Of famine, yet too weak to wing their flight,
And, like their parent, fill their nest with prey.
We are the eagle's offspring, of our father
Depriv'd, and driv'n in exile from his house.
Before thy altars, loaded by his hand,
He bow'd with pious reverence : should thy will
Permit his young to perish, who shall pay thee
Like costly honours? Should the eagle's offspring
Be doom'd to perish, who shall bear thy thunders,
Dread sign of wrath awak'd on mortal man?
Nor will this empire, wither'd from its roots,
Adorn thy altars on the solemn day
With hallow'd victims. Save us then—protect us—
To all its former glories raise this house,
Whose ruin'd tow'rs seem bending to their fall.

CHORUS.

Ye generous offspring of this royal house,
And guardians of its honour, check your tran-
    sports;
Lest they are heard, and some incontinent tongue
Bear them to our bad rulers: may these eyes
First see the dark wreaths of the funeral piles.

ORESTES.

The voice of Phœbus never shall deceive :
In dreadful accents, utter'd from his shrine,
Aloud he charg'd me to defy the danger,
Threat'ning to rack my soul with keenest tortures,
Should I forbear t' avenge my father's death
With equal retribution on his murderer,
That proudly riots in my wasted wealth.
This honour'd shade he charg'd me to avenge,
Though round enclos'd with evils; to the dead
This triumph o'er their foes the voice declar'd
A lenient joy; to us denouncing ills,
Corrosive leprosies with rankling tooth
To gnaw our flesh, and taint our healthful bodies

With ulcerous foulness, changing these fresh
    locks
T' untimely white; with trains of heavier woes
Rais'd by the furies from my father's blood,
Who in the realms of night sees this, and bends
His gloomy brows. For the dark shafts, that fly
From those beneath slain by the kindred hand
Of villain baseness,—frenzy, and vain fear
That trembles at the shadows of the night,
Rouse, sting, and drive the vice-polluted wretch
With brazen scourges tortur'd through the city.
He from the friendly bowl, the hallow'd goblet,*
The social intercourse, the incens'd altar,
Is chas'd, condemn'd to bear the secret pangs
Of inly-gnawing guilt : meanwhile the fiends,
Hatred and Infamy, pursue his steps,
And drag him to an execrable death.
Such was the voice of Phœbus, and demands
My prompt obedience. Could my soul refuse
T' obey the awful mandate, yet the deed
Must be accomplish'd : many urgencies
Conspire; the charges of the gods—the grief
That wounds me for my father—the fierce pangs
Of penury compel me; and the shame
That burns the gen'rous soul, to leave my country,
And all those heroes glorious through the world,
Whose conqu'ring arms laid Troy's proud tow'rs
    in dust,
Slaves to two women; for his soul is woman:
If not, th' occasion soon will prove his spirit.

.   .   .   .   .

O thou much-injur'd shade, my suff'ring father,
In thy dear cause what shall I say—what do,
Guided by fortune thither? Where, O where
Is thy couch spread? Our light is shaded o'er
With darkness deep as thine; our youthful graces,
That in this royal house once bloom'd with hope
Fair op'ning, shrink at the rough blast of sorrow.

.   .   .   .   .

---

* " Æschylus here in brief describes the miserable state of the unexpiated murderer, his inter-
diction from every altar, every table, and every house ; no one holding converse or intercourse with
him, as polluted and abominable."—*Stanley*. This, indeed, was usually the punishment inflicted by
the state ; but the poet here finely ascribes it to the vengeance of the Furies.

ELECTRA.

Yet, O my father, hadst thou greatly fallen
Beneath the walls of Troy, pierc'd by the spear
Of some bold Lycian, leaving to thy house
Thy glory, gracing with illustrious splendour
Thy children's steps; on that barbaric coast
The high-rais'd tomb had dignified thy dust,
And sooth'd our sorrows. In the realms beneath
Thy friendly shade, amongst the friendly shades
That fell with honour there, had held its state
Majestic and rever'd—a king, next those
Whose awful pow'r those darksome realms obey.
For to thy last of life thou wast a king;
The golden reins of empire grac'd thy hands,
And thy strong sceptre rul'd a willing people.

.   .   .   .   .

CHORUS.

Supreme of gods, send from the realms of night
The slow-avenging Ate; bid her rise
To blast the fraudful and audacious hands
Of impious mortals: for a father's wrongs
She stamps her vengeance deep. When on this man
The vengeful sword shall fall, and bleeding nigh
Lies this bad woman, be it mine to hear
Their shrieks of death, and answer to their cries
In notes as dismal. Why should I conceal
My honest hopes? Fate spreads her sable wings,
And hovers o'er their heads; before their eyes
Stands Indignation arm'd, and Hate enrag'd,
Ready to rend their hearts, when Jove shall stretch
His puissant hands. O thou, whose pow'r subdues
The mighty, to this country seal thy faith,
And ratify their doom! On th' impious heads
I ask for vengeance. You, whose dreaded pow'r
Th' infernal realms revere, ye Furies, hear me!
There is a law that, for each drop of blood
Shed on the earth, demands that blood be shed;
For from the slain Erinnys calls for slaughter,
On ruin heaping ruin. Ye dread pow'rs

Of hell's dark realms, where are you now? Behold,
Ye potent curses of the slain—behold
The poor remains of this imperial house
Sunk in distress, and all its glories vanish'd!
Where, king of heav'n, where may we seek for
    refuge?

ELECTRA.

Again my throbbing heart sinks at the sound
Of thy laments; and dark'ning o'er my soul
At thy sad voice, comes anguish and despair.
But when thy words breathe courage, my sick griefs
Are fled, and fairer fortune seems to smile.
But with what words to woo her? Speak aloud
The miseries which we suffer from our parents?
Or smooth our tongues to glozing courtesy?
That softens not our miseries; and our spirits,
Rous'd by the wrongs of our ungentle mother,
Contract a wolfish fierceness. With bold hand
She struck the stroke, bold as the Cissian dame
Train'd to the warrior's arms. She struck him
    once;
Again she struck him; her uplifted hands
Redoubled blow on blow; swift on his head
The distant-sounding strokes with steep force fell.
Bold, unrelenting woman, that could bear
Without one pitying sigh t' entomb the king
Unhonour'd with his people's grief, the husband
Without a tear to grace his obsequies.

ORESTES.

All thou hast mentioned are indignities
That swell my grief to rage. But vengeance arms
This hand, assisted by the gods, to punish
The ignominious wrongs done to my father.
May this revenge be mine—then let me die!

ELECTRA.

When she had kill'd, with barbarous hands she
    mangled *

---

* The design of Electra here is to excite her brother to avenge the murder of their father; and we
shall perceive that this is finely carried on. Upon the accidental mention of "fairer fortune," she
says, How shall we obtain it? by speaking our griefs aloud, or by flattering our mother? but they

His manly figure, and with this abuse
Entomb'd him here, studious to make his murder
A deed of horror, that through all thy life
Might shock thy soul. Such was thy father's
   death,
Such were thy father's ignominious wrongs.
But me, a poor, deserted, worthless thing,
Spurn'd like a mischievous cur from my apart-
   ments,
They bid be gone: there I could heave the
   sigh

In secret—there indulge the mournful pleasure
To pour the tear unnotic'd and uncheck'd;
Hear this, and on thy mind imprint it deep—
Engrave it on the tablet of thy heart.
Be resolute and calm. These things are thus:
Know this, and let thine indignation rise:
The time demands a firm, determin'd spirit.
And thou, my father, hear—on thee I call,
And with a friendly voice, though chok'd with
   tears—
Hear us, and aid!"

Orestes, feeling compunction to follow Electra's advice, pauses to inquire why his mother sent offerings to the tomb of his father. Electra replies, that she was terrified by a dream, in which she fancied she gave birth to a dragon, which, when put to her breast, drew blood from her.

ORESTES.

" But to this earth, and to my father's tomb
I make my supplications, that in me
Her dream may be accomplish'd: and I judge
It aptly corresponds; for as this serpent,
Leaving the place that once was mine, and laid
Swath'd like an infant, seiz'd that breast which
   nurs'd
My tender age, and mingled with the milk
Drew clotted blood; and as with the affright
She call'd out in her sleep,—it cannot be
But, as she nurs'd this monster, she must die
A violent death; and with a dragon's rage
This hand shall kill her, as her dream declares.
Or how wilt thou expound these prodigies?

CHORUS.

Thus may it be. But now instruct thy friends
What each must singly do, and each not do.

  .   .   .   .   .

ORESTES.

Few words suffice: then mark me. Let her
   enter;
And keep, I charge thee, keep my purpose secret—
That they who slew an honourable man
By curs'd deceit, may by deceit be caught
In the same snare, and perish; so the god,
Pow'rful Apollo, from whose sacred voice
Nothing but truth can flow, admonish'd me.
I, like a stranger, harness'd in this coarse
And way-worn garb, with Pylades my friend,
Will as a guest and friend knock at the gate:
Our tongues shall imitate the rustic accent
Familiar to the mountain-race of Phocis.*
Nor will the servants ('tis a villanous house)
Receive us cheerfully; but as we are,
There shall we stand; while each that passes by
With shrewd remarks shall shake his head, and
   say,

admit no softening, nor can we ever think of her with any degree of tenderness: she struck the bloody stroke, she repeated it on his unhappy head with all the fierceness of a Cissian virago; then she buried him without his honours. Orestes answers precisely to this, that vengeance, by the assistance of the gods, and by his hand, would inflict punishment for this wrong done to his father; but as he shews himself affected at the revenge to be executed, Electra proceeds to give him an account of the indignities offered to the dead body, and to herself.

   * Clytemnestra had told Agamemnon that Strophius, king of Phocæa, had taken Orestes under his protection from any dangers or disturbances that might arise in the state: the young prince had

'Why are these strangers thus inhospitably
Excluded from the gates, if their arrival
Ægisthus knows midst his domestic train?'
But if I pass the threshold of the gates,
And find him seated on my father's throne,
Or should he come t' accost me, be assur'd,
Quick as the eye can glance, ere he can say
Whence is this stranger? my impatient sword
Shall strike him dead. So shall the fell Erinnys,
That with an horrid joy riots in slaughter,
Quaff this third bowl of blood. Go then, Electra,
Be watchful; see that all things in the house
Be well dispos'd. And you, I charge you, guard
Your tongues; be silent where you ought, and
      where
Your voice can aid me, speak. The rest my
      friend,
That guides my sword to vengeance, will o'ersee.

·   ·   ·   ·   ·

[*Scene changes to the palace.*

CLYTEMNESTRA.

Speak, strangers, what your wants; here shall
      you find
All that becomes an house like this; warm baths,
Refreshment of your toils, the well-spread couch
Inviting soft repose, and over all
An eye regarding justice. If your business
Be of more serious import, asking counsel,
The province this of men; we will inform them.

ORESTES (*as a peasant*).

A Phocian am I, from the town of Daulis.
Occasions of my own call'd me to Argos,
Nor ask'd a better dress than this coarse garb,
Familiar to me: onward as I travell'd
I met a man unknown, myself to him
Unknown; he courteous question'd me how far
I journey'd, and inform'd me of my way—

Strophius of Phocis; so I chanc'd to learn:
'Stranger,' says he, 'since business of thy own
Leads thee to Argos, let me charge thy honour
To tell his parents that the young Orestes
Is dead. Forget it not. Whether his friends
With solemn obsequies will fetch him hence,
Or in eternal rest our friendly earth
Shall lay him in her hospitable bosom,
Bring back their pleasure; for the brazen urn
Now holds the ashes of the honour'd youth
Whom we lament.' This, faithful to my
      charge,
Have I deliver'd; if to kindred ears,
And those whose pow'r is sovereign here, I know
      not:
But it is meet his parent knew the event.

·   ·   ·   ·   ·

CLYTEMNESTRA.

Not less for this shalt thou receive such usage
As thy worth challenges: not less for this
Respected here—another would have come
Charg'd with the same sad message. But the
      hour
Demands refreshment for the stranger, spent
With the long travel of the weary day.
Lead him to those apartments where the men
Are well receiv'd; let his attendant follow,
His fellow-traveller; let thy diligent care,
I charge thee, minister to all his wants.
We to the rulers of this house will bear
These tidings, and amongst our friends consult
What measures in this sad event to form.

ORESTES.

It were my wish to have borne other tidings,
More welcome to the lords of this fair mansion,
And meriting their hospitable favours.

·   ·   ·   ·   ·

---

indeed the good fortune to escape from his mother, and was hospitably received at Phocis, from
whence he now returned in disguise, attended by Pylades, the son of Strophius, whose friendship was
so faithful to Orestes in all his distresses, that it became proverbial.

CHORUS.

What should I say, eternal king,
Or how begin the strain?
These passions how contain,
That in my throbbing breast tumultuous spring?
Oh, that in aid my daring deed
Might all the force of words exceed!
For now, distain'd with blood, the bick'ring sword
The contest ends; if all
This royal race shall fall;
Or the just laws their ancient state resuming,
And liberty her light reluming,
Hail to his father's rights the son restor'd.
'Gainst two fierce wolves the youth contesting
stands
Alone: may heaven-sent conquest grace his hands!

ÆGISTHUS (within).

Oh! I am slain!

CHORUS.

That groan! Again that groan!
Whence? What is done? Who rules the storm
within?
The deed is finish'd. Let us keep aloof,
And seem unconscious of these ills; best stand
At distance, whilst destruction ends her work.

SERVANT.

Woe, woe to me! Woe to my slaughter'd lord!
Woe on my wretched head, and woe again!
Ægisthus is no more. But open here,
Ye females, instantly unbar these doors;
Th' occasion calls for vigour, not t' assist
The slain. Ho, here! What, call I to the
deaf?
Or sleep you? Where is Clytemnestra? How
Employed? Her life stands at the sword's bare
point,
And ready vengeance seems to prompt the blow.

CLYTEMNESTRA.

What means thy clamour? Whence these shrieks
of woe?

SERVANT.

They that were rumour'd dead have slain the
living.

CLYTEMNESTRA.

Ah me! I understand thee, though thy words
Are dark. Now we shall perish in the toils,
E'en as we spread them! Give me instantly
The slaught'ring axe; it shall be seen if yet
We know the way to conquer, or are conquer'd:
These daring measures have my wrongs enforc'd.

ORESTES.

Thee too I seek. He has his righteous meed.

CLYTEMNESTRA.

Ah me! my dear Ægisthus, thou art dead!

ORESTES.

And dost thou love the man? In the same
tomb
Shalt thou be laid, nor e'en in death forsake him.

CLYTEMNESTRA.

Ah, stay thy hand, my son—my child—my
child!
Revere this breast on which thou oft hast slept,
And oft thy infant lips have press'd its milk.

ORESTES.

What shall I do, my Pylades? Restrain'd
By filial reverence, dread to kill my mother?

PYLADES.

Where then the other oracles of Phœbus,
Giv'n from the Pythian shrine? The faithful
vows,
The solemn adjurations, whither vanish'd?
Deem all the world thy foes, save the just gods.

ORESTES.

Thou hast convinc'd me; thy reproofs are just—
Follow him: on his body will I slay thee.
Alive thou held'st him dearer than my father;

Then sleep with him in death, since thou couldst
    love him,
And hate the man who most deserv'd thy love.

   .   .   .   .   .

ORESTES.

Behold the proud oppressors of my country—
The murderers of my father—the destroyers
Of his imperial house : commanding awe
When seated on their thrones, retaining yet
Their loves, of their affection, if with truth
Hence we conjecture ought, and their oath stands
Inviolate ; for to my father's death
They form'd th' unhallow'd compact, and to die
Together : these events confirm their oath.
Behold again, you that attentive mark
These ills ; behold this artifice, the toils
That tangled hand and foot my suff'ring father.
This was his vestment ; form a ring around it,
Spread it, display it to th' all-seeing sun,
That with his awful eye he may behold
My mother's impious deeds, and in the hour
Of judgment be my witness, that with justice
My vengeance fell on her. As for Ægisthus,
I reck not of his death : a sacred law
He dar'd pollute ; and justly has he paid
The dreadful penalty. She 'gainst her husband,
Once the dear object of her love, to which
Her swelling zone bore many a precious pledge,
Now flam'd with ranc'rous hate, and murd'rous
    malice.
What noxious monster, what envenom'd viper,
That poisons with a touch th' unwounded body,
E'er breath'd such pestilent and baleful rage ?
You view that vestment : tell me now, were all
The pow'rs of language mine, what should I call
    it ?
Toils planted for a savage ? Or the bands
That for the tomb enwrap the dead ? A curse
Well may you call it, and the gyves of hell.
Such may the pilferer wear, the thievish slave
That pillages his guests, and trains his life
To plunder ; such the ruffian, whose rude hand
Prompted to murd'rous deeds is stain'd with blood.

Never, ye gods, may such a woman share
My bed : no, rather childless let me perish !

CHORUS.

O horror, horror ! Dreadful were your deeds,
And dreadful is your death ; the ling'ring ven-
    geance
Burst with redoubled force. This was her deed,
Her cursed deed : this vestment is my witness,
Ting'd by Ægisthus' sword ; the gushing blood,
Now stiffen'd, stains its Tyrian-tinctur'd radiance.
Now I applaud his just revenge ; now weep,
Viewing this bloody robe, and mourn these deeds,
The suff'rings of this house, and e'en this con-
    quest—
Dreadful atonement !

   .   .   .   .   .

ORESTES.

Yet let me plead, whilst reason holds its seat,
Plead to my friends, that in the cause of justice
I slew my mother ; for her impious hands,
Stain'd with my father's blood, call'd down re-
    venge
From th' offended gods. And here I plead,
To mitigate the deed, the Pythian prophet,
Phœbus, whose voice pronounc'd me from the
    shrine,
If I achiev'd the vengeance, free from guilt :
To my refusal dreadful was his threat
Of punishments, beyond the reach of thought.
Grac'd with this branch of olive, and this wreath,
I will approach his shrine, his sacred throne,
And his eternal fires, there to be cleans'd
From the pollution of this kindred blood :
No other roof receives me ; so the god
Enjoin'd. Meanwhile let Argos be inform'd,
And all this people witness, what a weight
Of miseries oppress'd me : dead or living,
A vagrant, and an exile from my country,
I leave these words behind me ; having done
What honour gave in charge, I shall not blush
Hearing my name revil'd, nor bear in absence
The tongue of obloquy, the state of Argos

Freed by this hand, that boldly crush'd these
 dragons.—
Ha! look, ye female captives, what are these,
Vested in sable stoles, of Gorgon aspect,
Their starting locks tangled with knots of vipers!
I fly, I fly; I cannot bear the sight!

CHORUS.

What phantoms, what unreal shadows thus
Distract thee? Victor in thy father's cause,
To him most dear, start not at fancied terrors.

ORESTES.

These are no phantoms, no unreal shadows;
I know them now—my mother's angry furies.

CHORUS.

The blood as yet is fresh upon thy hands,
And thence these terrors sink into thy soul.

ORESTES.

Royal Apollo, how their numbers swell!
And the foul gore drops from their hideous eyes.

CHORUS.

Within are lavers: soon as thou shalt reach
His shrine, Phœbus will free thee from these ills.

ORESTES.

And see you nothing there? Look, look! I see
 them:
Distraction 's in the sight; I fly, I fly!

CHORUS.

Blest may'st thou be: and may the god, whose
 eye
Looks on thee, guard thee in these dreadful
 dangers!"

ÆSCHYLUS, Choephoræ.

Euripides and Sophocles agree with Æschylus in the main facts of the story; yet Euripides represents Ægisthus as slain while offering sacrifice.

No. 966.

Diana protecting Erigone from the fury of Orestes.

PYRGOTELES. *Sardonyx.*

Erigone was the daughter of Ægisthus and Clytemnestra. Orestes had by Erigone a son named Penthilus, who shared the regal power with Tisamenus, the legitimate son of Orestes by Hermione, until he was expelled by the Heraclidæ; after which he planted a colony in Lesbos.

No. 967.

Apollo preventing Orestes from slaying himself.

GNAIOS. *Sardonyx.*

4 G

No. 968.

Orestes persecuted by the Furies.

POLYCLETES. *Sardonyx.*

It appears, from the concluding passages of the *Choephoræ*, already quoted, that Orestes was struck with frenzy immediately after assassinating his mother. Æschylus, in his *Furies*, and Euripides in his *Orestes*, have exerted, each in his own characteristic manner, all their powers in describing his sufferings. Those who compose the Chorus in the *Orestes* are friendly to the wretched victim, and to his attached and afflicted sister. It is not necessary to apologise for the length of these quotations. The reader will, no doubt, be pleased to see the different modes in which these celebrated tragedians have treated this celebrated subject.

ELECTRA.

" Not disobedient to the god, he slew her.
I had my share, such as a woman might;
And Pylades assisted in the act.
Since then the poor Orestes pines away,
Impair'd with cruel sickness; on his bed
He lies; his mother's blood to frenzy whirls
His tortur'd sense: th' avenging pow'rs, that haunt
His soul with terrors thus, I dare not name.
The sixth day this, since on the hallow'd pile
My slaughter'd mother purg'd her stains away.
No food hath pass'd his lips, no bath refresh'd
His limbs; but in his garments cover'd close,
When his severe disease abates a little,
He melts in tears; and sometimes from his couch
Starts furious, like a colt burst from his yoke.

.   .   .   .   .

CHORUS.

Again compos'd, he sleeps again.

ELECTRA.

'Tis well.

CHORUS.

Awful queen, whose gentle pow'r
Brings sweet oblivion of our woes,
And in the calm and silent hour
Distils the blessings of repose,

Come—awful Night!
Come from the gloom of Erebus profound,
And spread thy sable-tinctur'd wings around!
    Speed to this royal house thy flight:
    For pale-ey'd Grief, and wild Affright,
And all the horrors of Despair,
Here pour their rage, and threaten ruin here!

ELECTRA.

Softly let your warblings flow;
Further, a further distance keep:
The far-off cadence, sweet and low,
Charms his repose, and aids his sleep.

CHORUS.

Tell us, what end
Awaits his mis'ries?

ELECTRA.

            Death: that end I fear.
He tastes no food.

CHORUS.

            Death then indeed, and near.

.   .   .   .   .

ORESTES.

O gentle Sleep, whose lenient pow'r thus soothes
Disease and pain, how sweet thy visit to me,

Who wanted thy soft aid! Blessing divine,
That to the wretched givest wish'd repose,
Steeping their senses in forgetfulness!—
Where have I been? Where am I? How
    brought thither?
My late distraction blots remembrance out.

ELECTRA.

My most dear brother, O what heartfelt joy
To see thee lie compos'd in gentle sleep!
Wilt thou I touch thee? Shall I raise thee up?

ORESTES.

Assist me, then, assist me! from my mouth
Wipe off this clotted foam; wipe my moist eyes.

ELECTRA.

Delightful office, for a sister's hand
To minister relief to a sick brother.

ORESTES.

Lie by my side, and from my face remove
These squalid locks; they blind my darken'd eyes.

ELECTRA.

How tangled are the ringlets of thy hair,
Wild and disorder'd through this long neglect!

ORESTES.

Pray lay me down again: when this ill frenzy
Leaves me, I am very feeble, very faint.

ELECTRA.

There, there: the bed is grateful to the sick,
A mournful, but a necessary tenure.

ORESTES.

Raise me again—more upright; bend me forward.

CHORUS.

The sick are wayward through their restlessness.
   .   .   .   .   .

ELECTRA.

Alas, my brother, wildly rolls thine eye!
So quickly chang'd! The frantic fit returns!

ORESTES.

Ah, mother! do not set thy furies on me!
See, how their fiery eye-balls glare in blood,
And wreathing snakes hiss in their horrid hair!
There—there they stand! ready to leap upon me!

ELECTRA.

Rest thee, poor brother, rest thee on thy bed:
Thou see'st them not: 'tis fancy's coinage all.

ORESTES.

O Phœbus, they will kill me—these dire forms,
These gorgon-visag'd ministers of hell!

ELECTRA.

Thus will I hold thee—round thee throw mine
    arms,
And check th' unhappy force of thy wild starts.

ORESTES.

Off—let me go! I know thee, who thou art—
One of the furies! and thou grapplest with me,
To whirl me into Tartarus. Avaunt!

ELECTRA.

What shall I do? Ah me, where shall I seek
Assistance, since th' unfriendly god frowns on us!

ORESTES.

Bring me the bow of horn which Phœbus gave
    me,
And with it bade me drive these fiends away,
Should they affright me with their madd'ning
    terrors.

ELECTRA.

Shall any god by mortal hands be wounded?

ORESTES.

Should she not instant vanish from my sight?
Heard you the clang? Saw you the winged shaft
Bound from the distant-wounding bow? Ha, ha—
Here yet! On swift wings mount th' ethereal air,
And there impeach the oracle of Phœbus.—
Whence this disquiet? Why thus pants my breath?

Ah, whither am I wander'd from my bed?
For from the storm the high-swoll'n waves sub-
    side.
Why dost thou weep, my sister? Why decline
Thy drooping head, and hide it in thy vest?
I blush to give thee part in my disease,
And wound with grief thy virgin tenderness.
Let not my ills be thus infectious to thee:
Thou barely didst assent; I did the deed—
I shed her blood. But Phœbus I must blame,
Who urg'd me to this most unholy act;
Then, save with soothing words, assist me not.
Had these eyes seen my father, had I ask'd him
In duty if I ought to slay my mother,
I think he would have pray'd me not to plunge
My murdering sword in her that gave me
    birth;
Since he could not revisit heav'n's sweet light,
And I must suffer all these miseries.
But now unveil thy face and dry thy tears,
My sister! though afflictions press us sore.
And when thou seest me in these fitful moods,
Soothe my disorder'd sense, and let thy voice
Speak peace to my distraction: when the sigh
Swells in thy bosom, 'tis a brother's part
With tender sympathy to calm thy griefs:
These are the pleasing offices of friends.
But to thy chamber go, afflicted maid—
There seek repose—close thy long-sleepless eyes—
With food refresh thee, and th' enlivening bath.
Shouldst thou forsake me, or with too close ten-
    dence
Impair thy delicate and tender health,
Then were I lost indeed! for thou alone,
Abandon'd as I am, art all my comfort.

ELECTRA.

Should I forsake thee! No: my choice is
    fix'd;
And I will die with thee, or with thee live,
Indifferent for myself; for shouldst thou die,
What refuge shall a lonely virgin find,
Her brother lost—her father lost—her friends
All melted from her?—Yet, if such thy wish,

I ought t' obey. Recline thee on thy couch,
Nor let these visionary terrors fright thee;
There rest: though all be fancy's coinage wild,
Yet nature sinks beneath the violent toil.

STROPHE.

  Awful pow'rs, whose rapid flight
  Bears you from the realms of night
  To hearts that groan, and eyes that weep,
  Where you joyless orgies keep;
Ye gloomy pow'rs, that shake the affrighted air,
  And arm'd with your tremendous rod,
    Dealing terror, woe, despair,
    Punish murder, punish blood,—
  For Agamemnon's race this strain,
  This supplicating strain, I pour:
  No more afflict his soul with pain,
  Nor torture him with madness more;
    Breathe oblivion o'er his woes,
    Leave him, leave him to repose.
  Unhappy youth, what toils are thine,
  Since Phœbus from his central shrine
  Bade thee unsheath th' avenging sword,
And Fate confirm'd th' irrevocable word!

ANTISTROPHE.

  Hear us, king of gods, O hear;
  Where is soft-ey'd Pity, where?
  Whence, to plunge thee thus in woes,
  Discord stain'd with gore arose?
What vengeful demon thus, with footstep dread
  Trampling the blood-polluted ground,
    Sternly cruel joys to spread,
    Horror, rage, and madness round?
  Woe, woe is me! in man's frail state
  Nor height nor greatness firm abides:
  On the calm sea, secure of fate,
  Her sails all spread, the vessel rides:
    Now th' impetuous whirlwinds sweep,
    Roars the storm, and swells the deep,
  Till, with the furious tempest tost,
  She sinks in surging billows lost.
  Yet firm their fate will I embrace."
        EURIPIDES, *Orestes.*

In Æschylus the avenging Furies are the Chorus. This foul sisterhood on the Athenian stage amounted at first to fifty; but the consternation arising from their hideous figures and gestures, and terrific denunciations and yellings, had such fatal effects on the children and pregnant women, that the number of the Chorus was reduced, by an express law, to twelve.

Orestes having gone to the shrine of Apollo at Delphos, supplicates the god, who advises him to fly to Athens while the Furies are asleep, and appeal to Minerva.

The PRIESTESS *enters the temple, and returns affrighted.*

" Things horrible to tell, and horrible
To sight, have forc'd me from the fane again :
Trembling with fear, my lax limbs ill support
My frame, save that my hands with eager grasp
Uphold my sinking weakness as I pass.
As to the shrine, with many a garland crown'd,
I bend my age-enfeebled steps, beneath
The central dome I see a man abhorr'd
By the just gods, a suppliant it should seem,
For such his posture ; but his hands are stain'd
With blood : in one he holds a new-drawn
    sword ;
High in the other, crown'd with ample wreaths,
An olive branch, with wreaths of snowy wool
Handsomely wrought : thus far I speak assur'd.
Before him lies a troop of hideous women
Stretch'd on their seats, and sleeping ; yet not
    women,
But Gorgons rather, nor the Gorgon form
Exactly representing, as I have seen them
Drawn by the painter's imitative pencil,
Snatching the viands from the board of Phineus.
These have not wings : but cloth'd in sable
    stoles,
Abhorr'd and execrable. As they sleep,
Hoarse in their hollow throats their harsh breath
    rattles,
And their gall'd eyes a rheumy gore distil.
Ill suit such loathsome weeds the hallow'd fane
Grac'd with the forms of sculptur'd gods, ill suit
The roofs of men : so foul a sisterhood

Till now I never saw. No land can boast   .
To have produc'd a breed so horrible,
But toils, and groans, and mischiefs must ensue.

[The temple opens. APOLLO *is seen;* ORES-
    TES *as a suppliant ; the* FURIES *in a deep
    sleep.]*

APOLLO.

No : I will not forsake thee ; to the end
My guardian care shall favour and assist thee,
Present, or distant far : but to thy foes
I know not mercy. See this grisly troop ;
Sleep has oppress'd them, and their baffl'd rage
Shall fail, grim-visaged hags, grown old
In loath'd virginity : nor god, nor man
Approach'd their bed, nor savage of the wilds ;
For they were born for mischiefs, and their
    haunts
In dreary darkness 'midst the yawning gulfs
Of Tartarus beneath, by men abhorr'd,
And by th' Olympian gods. Fly then, nor yield
To weak distrust : they, be thou sure, will follow
With unremitting chase thy flying steps,
Wide wand'ring o'er the firm terrene, and o'er
The humid sea, and wave-surrounded towns.
But faint thou not, sink not beneath thy toils :
Fly to the city of Minerva ; take
Thy suppliant seat, with reverence in thy arms
Grasp her time-honour'd image. Holding there
Concordant counsels, lenient of these ills,
We shall not want the means to heal thy pains,
And ratify thy peace : for at my bidding
Thy sword is purple with thy mother's blood.''

The spirit of Clytemnestra, retaining still all her ferocity and vengeance, appears—shouts to the Furies—reminds them of the many rich oblations she made, when alive, to them—and rouses them to pursue Orestes, who had escaped.

CHORUS (*asleep*).

" Seize him there, seize him, seize him !—take
   good heed.

CLYTEMNESTRA.

In dreams dost thou pursue him, like the hound
That opens in his sleep, on th' eager chase
E'en then intent.   And is this all ?   Awake—
Arise ! let not thy toil subdue thee ; know
What loss ensues if sleep enfeebles thee ;
And let these just reproaches sting thy mind,
Incentives to the wise.   With fiery breath,
That snuffs the scent of blood, pursue this son—
Follow him, blast him in the prosp'rous chase.

CHORUS (*awaking*).

Awake—arise ! rouse her as I rouse thee.
Yet dost thou sleep ?   Leave thy repose ; arise !
Look we if this firm guard hath been in vain.
   Ha, sisters, ha ! 'tis base, 'tis foul ;
   Vain is our labour, vain our care :
This insult stings my tortur'd soul
   Untaught contempt and wrong to bear.
Whilst overpower'd with sleep I lay,
Burst from the net escapes the prey.

Great triumph, treach'rous son of Jove,
   In youth's fresh prime to mock my age !
Thee could this impious suppliant move
   (And thou a god), whose cruel rage
Plung'd in his mother's breast his sword ?
Yet thou hast screen'd the wretch abhorr'd.
Clashing her scourge with hideous sound,
   Reproach upon my slumbers stole ;
Deep in my heart impress'd the wound—
   E'en yet chill horror shakes my soul.
These are the deeds in misrule's hour,
When youthful gods usurp the pow'r.

See all defil'd with gore thy throne,
   There sate the murd'rer dropping blood.
Yet these pollutions are thy own ;
   From thee the call—th' impulse, flow'd :
Such grace, despis'd th' age-honour'd Fates,
Your new unhallow'd shrines awaits.

And shall this wretch in safety breathe,
   Screen'd by thy pow'r severe to me ?
No : let him fly the earth beneath,
   Never, he never shall be free :
No : as he dar'd this murd'rous deed,
   Murder shall fall upon his head.

APOLLO.

Hence, I command you, from my hallow'd seat
Begone with speed : quit this oracular shrine :
This is no place to snatch your winged serpents,
And hurl them from your golden-twisted string,
To wring the black blood from the human heart
With torture, then disgorge your horrid feast
Of clotted gore : such guests my house abhors.
Begone where vengeance, with terrific rage,
Digs out the eyes, or from the mangled trunk
Remorseless rends the head ; to slaughters go,
Abortions, lurking ambush, rampir'd force,
To suff'rings, to impalements, where the wretch
Writhes on the stake in tortures, yelling loud
With many a shriek.   In feasts like these, ye
      hags
Abhorr'd, is your delight ; sufficient proof
That execrable form.   The desert wild,
Where the blood-rav'ning lion makes his den,
Such should inhabit ; nor with impure tread
Pollute these golden shrines : begone, and graze
Without a keeper ; for of such a herd
Th' indignant gods disdain to take the charge.

        .   .   .   .   .   .

CHORUS.

That moves not me.—These are his marks ; ob-
      serve them—
Unerring guides, though tongueless ; follow, fol-
   low,
And like the hound, that by the drops of blood
Traces the wounded hind, let us pursue him.
      [*The scene changes to the temple of* MINERVA
         at Athens.]

ORESTES.

Hither, divine Minerva, by the mandate
Of Phœbus am I come.   Propitious pow'r !

Receive me, by the Furies' tort'ring rage
Pursu'd, no vile unhallow'd wretch, nor stain'd
With guilty blood, but worn with toil, and spent
With many a painful step to other shrines,
And in the paths of men.   By land, by sea
Wearied alike, obedient to the voice,
The oracles of Phœbus, I approach
Thy shrine—thy statue, goddess ; here to fix
My stand, till judgment shall decide my cause.

[*Here the* FURIES *enter.*

CHORUS.

These toils oppress me, as with breathless haste
I urge the keen pursuit : o'er the long tract
Of continent, and o'er th' extended ocean,
Swift as the flying ship I hold my course,
Though on no pennons borne.   There—there he
    stands !
His speed outstripping mine.   Have I then found
    thee ?
With joy I snuff the scent of human blood !
Take heed, take heed ! keep careful watch ! nor
    let
This murderer of his mother once more 'scape,
By secret flight, your vengeance: trembling, weak,
He hangs upon the image of the goddess,
And wishes to be clear'd of his base deeds.
It may not be—no : when the fluent moisture
Is sunk into the ground, 'tis lost for ever ;
Can then a mother's blood, spilt on the earth,
Be from the earth recover'd ?   No.   Thy hour
Of suff'ring is arriv'd—the hour that gives
The purple stream, that warms thy heart, to
    quench
My thirst, which burns to quaff thy blood, and
    bend
To the dark realms below thy wasted limbs ;
There, for thy mother's murder, shalt thou learn
To taste of pain ; there see whatever mortal
Dar'd an injurious deed—profan'd the gods—
Attack'd with ruffian violence the stranger,
Or rais'd his impious hand against a parent,
Each with vindictive pains condemn'd to groan,
His crimes requiting ; for beneath the earth,

The awful judge of mortals, Pluto, sits,
And with relentless justice marks their deeds.

.   .   .   .   .

No : not Apollo, nor Minerva's pow'r
Shall set thee free, but that an abject outcast
Thou drag thy steps, seeking in vain to find
Rest to thy joyless soul, exhausted—worn—
A lifeless shadow !   Yet thy pride replies not,
Me and my threats despising, though to me
Devoted, my rich victim, and alive
To feed my rage, not offer'd on the altar :
Hear now the potent strain that charms thee
    mine :—

PROSERPINE.

Quickly, sisters, stand around,
Raise your choral warblings high ;
Since the guilty soul to wound
Swells the horrid harmony !
Since to mortal man we shew
How we give his fate to flow ;
Since our will his doom ordains,
Shew that justice 'mongst us reigns.
He whose hands from guilt are pure,
Stands in innocence secure ;
And from youth to honour'd age
Fears not our vindictive rage.
To the wretch, that strives to hide
Ruffian hands with murder dy'd,
Cloth'd in terrors we appear,
Unrelentingly severe ;
And, faithful to th' injur'd dead,
Pour our vengeance on his head.

STROPHE I.

Hear me, dread parent, sable-vested Night—
O hear th' avenger of each impious deed !
    Whether we lie in shades conceal'd,
    Or to the eye of day reveal'd.
Seest thou how Phœbus robs me of my right,
From my just rage the trembling victim freed,
    Destin'd his mother's death t' atone,
    And for her blood to shed his own !

O'er my victim raise the strain,
And let the dismal sound
His tortur'd bosom wound,
And to frenzy fire his brain.
Silent be the silver shell,
Whilst we chant the potent spell;
Then yelling bid th' infernal descant roll,
  To harrow up his soul.

ANTISTROPHE I.

Avenging Fate, as bending o'er the loom
She wove the web, to us this part assign'd,
 'Whoe'er the laws shall dare disdain,
 And his rude hand with murder stain,
Pursue him, Furies—urge his rigorous doom,
Till refuge in the realms below he find.'
  E'en there not free; my chast'ning pow'r
  Pursues him to that dreary shore.
  O'er my victim raise the strain,
  And let the dismal sound
  His tortur'd bosom wound,
  And to frenzy fire his brain.
  Silent be the silver shell,
  Whilst we chant the potent spell;
Then yelling bid th' infernal descant roll,
  To harrow up his soul.

STROPHE II.

This task assign'd us at our natal hour,
Far from th' immortal gods our steps we bend:
  Nor welcome at the social feast,
  Nor honour'd with a splendent vest;
For mine I proudly claim the dreadful pow'r
From its firm base the ruin'd house to rend,
  When in calm peace its ruthless lord
  Distains with a friend's blood his sword.
  Him, though strong, we rush to seize;
  And for the new-pour'd blood
  Demand his purple flood,
  Glorying in the sacrifice;

Duteous hast'ning to remove
Cares like these from angry Jove;
And spare, whilst fierce for blood my vengeance
  flies,
  The terrors of the skies.

ANTISTROPHE II.

His wrathful eye heav'n's mighty monarch rolls,
Awfully silent, on this blood-stain'd race.
  But all the gorgeous blaze of pow'r,
  Which trembling mortals here adore,
When, mantled in these sable-shaded stoles,
With blood-besprinkled feet we urge the chase,
  Sinks darkling to th' infernal shades,
  And all its boasted glory fades.
  Near him, as he flies, I bound,*
  And when, with guilt opprest,
  His weary steps would rest,
  Spurn him headlong to the ground.
  Senseless he, perchance, and blind,
  Such the frenzy of his mind,
Such the deep gloom guilt spreads around his
  walls,
  He knows not that he falls.

EPODE.

But shall shelt'ring wall or gloom
That from dark'ning guilt is spread,
Hide him from his rigorous doom,
Or protect his destin'd head?
Mine the vengeance to design,
And to stamp it deep is mine.
Sternly mindful of the crime,
Nor by man appeas'd, nor time,
When the wretch, whose deed unblest
Dares profane high heav'n's behest,
Though conceal'd from mortal eyes
Through the sunless darkness flies,
We pursue the rugged chase,
And his dubious footsteps trace.

---

* As the Chorus generally danced whilst they sung these odes, and the Athenians were excellent actors, we may be assured that the gestures and the boundings of the Furies at this part were violent, and really horrible.

Hear, then, guilty mortals, hear,
And the righteous god revere;
Hear the task to me assign'd,
Fate the firm decree shall bind;

Mine the prize of old ordain'd,
Never with dishonour stain'd,
Though my drear abode profound
Night and darkness cover round."

ÆSCHYLUS, *Furies.*

No. 969.

Minerva and the court of Areopagus trying the cause of Orestes.

GNAIOS. *Cornelian.*

The Furies impeached Orestes, and Apollo defended him. Minerva is represented addressing the assembly, while the judicial urn containing the little shells, which were the lots, appears in the centre.

MINERVA.

"This is a cause of moment, and exceeds
The reach of mortal man: nor is it mine
To judge, when blood with eager rage excites
To vengeance. Thou with preparation meet
Hast to my shrine approach'd a suppliant pure,
Without offence; and to my favour'd city,
Uncharg'd with blame, I readily receive thee.

. . . . .
But since to me
Th' appeal is made, it shall be mine t' elect
Judges of blood, their faith confirm'd by oath,
And ratify the everlasting law.
Prepare you for the trial—call your proofs—
Arrange your evidence—bring all that tends
To aid your cause: I from the holiest men
That grace my city will select to judge
This cause with justice—men, whose sanctity
Abhors injustice, and reveres an oath.

. . . . .
Ye citizens of Athens, now attend,
Whilst this great council in a cause of blood

First give their judgment. But through future
    ages
This awful court shall to the hosts of Ægeus
With uncorrupted sanctity remain.
Here on this mount of Mars the Amazons
Of old encamp'd, when their embattled troops
March'd against Theseus, and in glitt'ring arms
Breath'd vengeance; here their new-aspiring
    towers
Rais'd high their rampir'd heads to storm his
    towers;
And here their hallow'd altars rose to Mars:
Hence its illustrious name the cliff retains—
The mount of Mars. In this the solemn state
Of this majestic city, and the awe *
That rises thence shall be an holy guard
Against injustice, shall protect the laws
Pure and unsullied from th' oppressive pow'r
Of innovation, and th' adulterate stain
Of foreign mixture: should thy hand pollute
The liquid fount with mud, where wilt thou find
The grateful draught? Let not my citizens

---

* "This whole charge of Minerva is worthy of the goddess of wisdom. By celebrating the high antiquity of the temple, its honourable foundation, the dignity of the court, the authority and impartiality of its sentence, the purity and superior excellence of the laws, she inspires that reverence for the laws, and the administration of them, which constitutes the firmest security of obedience and good manners."—*Potter.*

4 H

Riot in lawless anarchy, nor wear
The chain of tyrant pow'r, nor from their state
Loose all the curb of rigour: this remov'd,
What mortal man, uncheck'd with sense of fear,
Would reverence justice? Let the majesty
That here resides impress your souls with awe;
Your country has a fence, your town a guard,
Such as no nation knows—not those that dwell
In Scythia,* or the cultur'd realms of Pelops:
This court, superior to the alluring glare
Of pestilent gold—this court, that claims your awe
Severely just, I constitute your guard,
Watchful to shield your country and its peace.
These my commands to ev'ry future age
Have I extended. Now behoves you, judges,
Give test of your integrity; bring forth
The shells; with strictest justice give your suffrage,
And reverence your high oath. This is my charge.

. . . .

Last to give suffrage in this cause is mine:
In favour of Orestes shall I add
My vote; for as no mother gave me birth,
My grace in all things, save the nuptial rites,
Attends the male, as from my sire I drew
The vigour of my soul. No woman's fate,
Stain'd with her husband's blood, whom nature
  form'd
Lord of his house, finds partial preference here.
Orestes, if the number of the votes
Be equal, is absolv'd. Now from the urn
Let those among the judges to whose honour
This office is assign'd, draw forth the lots.

. . . .

APOLLO.

Now, strangers, count the lots with righteous heed,
And with impartial justice sever them.

One shell misplac'd haply brings ruin—one
May raise again a desolated house.

MINERVA.

He is absolv'd, free from the doom of blood,
For equal are the numbers of the shells.

ORESTES.

O thou, whose tutelary pow'r preserv'd
The honours of my house—thou, goddess—thou
Hast to his country and his native rites
Restor'd this exile; and each Greek shall say,
'This Argive to his father's throne returns;
So Pallas wills, and Phœbus, and the god
All-powerful to protect:' my father's death
He mark'd severe, and looks indignant down
On those that patronise my mother's cause.
First to this country, and to this thy people,
Through time's eternal course I pledge my faith,
And bind it with an oath. Now to my house
I bend my steps: never may chieftain thence
Advance against this land with ported spear!
If any shall hereafter violate
My oath now made, though then these mould'ring
  bones
Rest in the silent tomb, my shade shall raise
Invincible distress—disasters—toils,
To thwart them, and obstruct their lawless march,
Till in dismay repentant they abhor
Their enterprise. But to the social pow'rs,
That reverence this thy state, and lift the lance
In its defence, benevolent shall be
My gentler influence. Hail, goddess! hail
Ye guardians of the city! be your walls
Impregnable, and in the shock of war
May conquest grace the spear that aids your
  cause!"

       ÆSCHYLUS, Furies.

---

* By this mention of Scythia the poet alludes to Anacharsis, the celebrated lawgiver of that country, contemporary with Solon.

No. 970.

Orestes carrying off Iphigenia, with the statue of Diana, from Tauris.

APOLLONIOS. *Cornelian.*

It has been already stated (No. 762), that the Grecian expedition, on its way to Troy, having been detained at Aulis in Bœotia by adverse winds, the soothsayer declared that this was a punishment inflicted on Agamemnon the commander, for having killed a hind sacred to Diana, and that nothing but the sacrifice of his daughter Iphigenia could appease the goddess. Iphigenia, when at the altar, was snatched away by Diana (who substituted a hind in her place, which was deemed a sufficient sacrifice), and conveyed to Tauris (now called the Crimea), where she was appointed the priestess of her temple, at which all strangers arriving in the country were sacrificed. Though Æschylus has represented Orestes as purified by Apollo at Delphos, yet Euripides, in his *Iphigenia in Tauris*, whose account the artist in this instance follows (for there have been various accounts), says that Apollo declared he could not be released from the persecution of the Furies, until he had brought the statue of the Tauric Diana to Greece. For this he, accompanied by Pylades, went to Tauris—was seized—brought as a victim to the temple—there became known to his sister—and finally escaped with her and the statue of the goddess. The following passages are necessary to be given, to convey a full idea of this subject.

IPHIGENIA.
" My unhappy fate
To Aulis brought me; on the altar there
High was I placed, and o'er me gleam'd the sword,
Aiming the fatal wound: but from the stroke
Diana snatch'd me, in exchange an hind
Giving the Grecians; through the lucid air
Me she convey'd to Tauris, here to dwell,
Where o'er barbarians a barbaric king
Holds his rude sway, named Thoas, whose swift foot
Equals the rapid wing: me he appoints
The priestess of this temple, where such rites
Are pleasing to Diana, that the name
Alone claims honour; for I sacrifice
(Such, ere I came, the custom of the state)
Whatever Grecian to this savage shore
Is driv'n. The previous rites are mine; the deed
Of blood, too horrid to be told, devolves
On others in the temple: but the rest,
In reverence to the goddess, I forbear.
But the strange visions, which the night now past

Brought with it to the air, if that may soothe
My troubled thought, I will relate. I seem'd,
As I lay sleeping, from this land remov'd
To dwell at Argos, resting on my couch
Midst the apartments of the virgin train:
Sudden the firm earth shook; I fled, and stood
Without; the battlements I saw, and all
The rocking roof fall from its lofty height
In ruins to the ground: of all the house—
My father's house—one pillar, as I thought,
Alone was left, which from its cornice wav'd
A length of auburn locks, and human voice
Assum'd: the bloody office, which is mine
To strangers here, respecting, I to death,
Sprinkling the lustral drops, devoted it
With many tears. My dream I thus expound:
Orestes, whom I hallow'd by my rites,
Is dead: for sons are pillars of the house,
They whom my lustral lavers sprinkle die.
I cannot to my friends apply my dream,
For Strophius, when I perish'd, had no son."

Orestes and Pylades, having been brought bound to the temple, are interrogated, before their intended immolation, by Iphigenia, at great length. She learns that they are Greeks, and hears much of the result of the Trojan war, and of the calamities of her family. She also ascertains that her dear brother Orestes is alive. She then avows that she is herself a Greek; and promises to spare the life of Orestes, if he will convey a letter to her friends at Argos. Orestes declines to save his own life by the sacrifice of his friend's; and undertakes to remain the victim while his friend, whom he engaged to accompany him, is to convey the letter. Pylades asks, is he to deliver a verbal message, and to whom, in case he should be shipwrecked and lose the letter? She says, that he is to announce to Orestes her existence and horrid office, and convey to him her prayers to be rescued. This leads to a recognition—to her knowledge of the crime of Orestes—to the object of his arrival—and to the plan and mode of their escape. When Thoas arrives at the temple and inquires whether the strangers were sacrificed, Iphigenia replies that they are stained with their mother's blood, and had polluted the statue of the goddess, and therefore it is necessary for her to purify the statue and the victims privately in the waters of the sea. The escape of Iphigenia and Orestes is thus announced —

MESSENGER.

" When to the shore we came, where station'd
    rode
The galley of Orestes, by the rocks
Conceal'd from us, whom thou hadst sent with her
To hold the strangers' chains, the royal maid
Made signs that we retire, and stand aloof,
As if with secret rites she would perform
The purpos'd expiation. On she went,
In her own hands holding the strangers' chains
Behind them : not without suspicion this,
Yet by thy servants, king, allow'd. At length,
That we might deem her in some purpose high
Employ'd, she rais'd her voice, and chanted loud
Barbaric strains, as if with mystic rites
She cleans'd the stain of blood. When we had sate
A tedious while, it came into our thought
That, from their chains unloos'd, the stranger youths
Might kill her, and escape by flight : yet fear
Of seeing what we ought not kept us still
In silence ; but at length we all resolv'd
To go, though not permitted, where they were.
There we behold the Grecian bark, with oars
Well furnish'd, wing'd for flight ; and at their
    seats,
Grasping their oars, were fifty rowers : free
From chains, beside the stern the two youths stood.

Some from the prow reliev'd the keel with poles ;
Some weigh'd the anchors up ; the climbing ropes
Some hasten'd—through their hands the cables
    drew—
Launch'd the light bark, and gave her to the main.
But when we saw their treach'rous wiles, we rush'd
Heedless of danger—seiz'd the priestess—seiz'd
The halsers—hung upon the helm, and strove
To rend the rudder-bands away. Debate
Now rose : ' what mean you, sailing o'er the seas,
The statue and the priestess from the land
By stealth conveying ? Whence art thou, and who,
That bear'st her, like a purchas'd slave, away ?'
He said, ' I am her brother, be of this
Inform'd—Orestes, son of Agamemnon ;
My sister, so long lost, I bear away,
Recover'd here.' But nought the less for that
Held we the priestess, and by force would lead
Again to thee : hence dreadful on our cheeks
The blows ; for in their hands no sword they held,
Nor we ; but many a rattling stroke the youths
Dealt with their fists ; against our sides and breasts
Their arms fierce darting, till our batter'd limbs
Were all disabled. Now, with dreadful marks
Disfigur'd, up the precipice we fly,
Some bearing on their heads, some in their eyes,
The bloody bruises : standing on the heights

Our fight was safer, and we hurl'd at them
Fragments of rocks ; but, standing on the stern,
The archers with their arrows drove us thence.
And now a swelling wave roll'd in, which drove
The galley tow'rds the land ; the sailors fear'd
The sudden swell. On his left arm sustain'd,
Orestes bore his sister through the tide—
Mounted the bark's tall side, and on the deck
Safe plac'd her, and Diana's holy image
Which fell from heav'n : from the mid ship his voice
He sent aloud : ' Ye youths, that in this bark
From Argos plough'd the deep, now ply your oars,
And dash the billows till they foam : those things
Are ours, for which we swept the Euxine sea,
And steer'd our course within its clashing rocks.'*
They gave a cheerful shout, and with their oars
Dash'd the salt wave. The galley, whilst it rode
Within the harbour, work'd its easy way ;
But having pass'd its mouth, the swelling flood
Roll'd on it, and with sudden force the wind
Impetuous rising drove it back : their oars
They slack'd not, stoutly struggling 'gainst the
    wave ;
But tow'rds the land the refluent flood impell'd

The galley. Then the royal virgin stood,
And pray'd, ' O daughter of Latona, save me—
Thy priestess save—from this barbaric land
To Greece restore me, and forgive my thefts :
For thou, O goddess, dost thy brother love,
Deem then that I love those allied to me.'
The mariners, responsive to her prayer,
Shouted loud pæans, and their naked arms,
Each cheering each, to their stout oars apply.
But nearer, and yet nearer to the rock
The galley drove : some rush'd into the sea,
Some strain'd the ropes that bind the loosen'd sails.
Straight was I hither sent to thee, O king,
T' inform thee of these accidents. But haste,
Take chains and gyves with thee ; for if the flood
Subside not to a calm, there is no hope
Of safety to the strangers. Be assur'd
That Neptune, awful monarch of the main,
Remembers Troy, and, hostile to the race
Of Pelops, will deliver to thy hands,
And to thy people, as is meet, the son
Of Agamemnon ; and bring back to thee
His sister, who the goddess hath betray'd,
Unmindful of the blood at Aulis shed."

No. 971.

Orestes leading away Hermione.

GNAIOS. *Cornelian.*

Hermione, the daughter of Menelaus and Helen, who had been betrothed to Orestes in her youth, was given in marriage by her father, on his return from Troy, to Pyrrhus (or Neoptolemus), the son of Achilles ; but in the absence of her husband at Delphos, where he was slain, was carried off and married by Orestes. The following explanation of the subject is given from the *Andromache* of Euripides.

HERMIONE.
Well dost thou judge ; for me he will destroy,
And justly : what behoves me else to say ?
But I conjure thee, and invoke high Jove,

From whom we draw our race, convey me far—
Far from this land, or to my father's house :
For e'en these walls, had they a voice, I think,
Would drive me hence, and all the realm of Phthia

* The Symplegades, two rocky islands, close to each other, at the entrance of the Euxine, so called because at a distance they appear to mariners, rocking on that agitated sea, to separate and join alternately.

Detests me. Leaving the oracular shrine
Of Phœbus, should my husband first return
Home, he will kill me for my shameful deeds;*
Or to the spurious bed, o'er which my pow'r
Was sovereign once, I shall be made a slave.

ORESTES.

What led thee, then, forgive the word, t' offend?

HERMIONE.

The converse of bad women ruin'd me;
Who oft address'd me with this unsound speech,
' Wilt thou permit a captive—a base slave,
To dwell beneath thy roof, and share thy bed?
By heav'n's dread empress, in my house the light
Of yon bright sun a rival should not see.'
I to these sirens lent my easy ears,
These specious, versatile, insidious pests,
And rais'd to folly's gale my swelling thoughts:
For why behov'd it me with awe to view
My husband? All things, which became my state,
Were mine—abundant wealth was mine—my
      house
I, as it pleas'd me, rul'd; I might have borne
Legitimate offspring, whilst her sons to mine
Had been half-slaves. But never, more than once
Let me repeat it, never let the wise
Give females license to frequent his house,
And hold free converse with his wife; for these
To ill are shrewd instructors: through the hope
Of sordid lucre, one corrupts his wife—
One, who hath fall'n from virtue, like herself
Wishes to make her vile; and many urge,
Through wanton forwardness, their pleas to ill:
Hence the pure fountain of domestic bliss
The husband finds polluted: these against
Let him guard well his gates with locks and bolts;
For nothing good these female visitants
Work by their converse, but abundant ill.

CHORUS.

'Gainst thine own sex too freely hath thy tongue

Inveigh'd; yet this may be forgiv'n thee now:
But woman woman's nature should commend.

ORESTES.

Wisdom was his, who first instructed man
In person of affairs to be inform'd.
I, knowing the confusion of this house,
And all the variance 'twixt thee and the wife
Of Hector, waited not, with cold regard
Attending, to be told thy will, if here
T' abide, or, dreading with well-grounded fear
A captive woman, to withdraw thee hence;
But came, not waiting thy commands, if such
Thy cause of grief as I have heard from thee,
To bear thee from this house; for thou wast mine
Before, though by thy father's falseness now
Thou dwellest with this man: for ere he march'd
Against the Trojan state, to me he pledg'd
Thy hand in marriage; afterwards to him,
Who calls thee now his wife, he promis'd thee,
If he would lay the tow'rs of Troy in dust.
To Phthia when the victor-chief return'd,
Him, for thy father patient I forgave,
Thy nuptials to relinquish I implor'd,
Urging my fortunes, and the vengeful pow'rs
Who then afflicted me; that I perchance
Among my friends, by blood allied, might wed,
A grace from strangers to an outcast wretch,
Outcast like me, not easily indulg'd:
My suit his fiery insolence rejects,
Upbraids me with the murder of my mother,
And the grim-visag'd furies. In despair,
For then the fortunes of my house were low,
I griev'd indeed, but silent bore my grief
With my afflictions sunk, and went away,
Of thee, against my soul's warm wish, depriv'd.
But now, since thou hast found a wayward change
Of fortune, and thy heart desponding sinks,
I from this house will lead thee—guard thee well,
And give thee to thy father's hand; for strong
The bond of kindred, and in ills no zeal
Is warmer than a friend's by blood allied.

---

* Her attempt to kill Andromache, whom Pyrrhus brought from Troy.

HERMIONE.

To what concerns my marriage, with due care
My father will attend: it is not mine
That to determine. But with quickest speed
Convey me hence; lest, should he first return,
My lord prevent me; or should Peleus learn
From his son's house that I have made escape,
He with his fleetest horse pursue my flight.

ORESTES.

Let not the old man's pow'r alarm thy fears;
Nor dread Achilles' son, whose fiery pride

Insulted me: th' entangling toils of fate,
Through which he cannot burst, are by this hand
Fix'd against him: these I explain not now,
But their effect the Delian rock shall know.*
This murderer of his mother, if the oaths
Of my brave friends hold in the Pythian land
Their faith, shall shew him he did wrong to wed
One first to me betroth'd; and he shall rue
His call for vengeance for his father's death
On royal Phœbus; nor avails him now
His thought to reverence chang'd."

No. 972.

Paris and Œnone on Mount Ida.

GNAIOS. *Calcedony.*

Œnone was the wife of Paris.

No. 973.

Death of Paris.

DIOSCORIDES. *Cornelian.*

Philoctetes slew Paris with one of the arrows of Hercules, which had been previously employed in killing the giants. Ovid (*epistle* xvi.) makes Paris say that there was a prophecy that he should be slain by a celestial arrow. Lycophron thus mentions the prophecy—

" But looking, loving, when she † sees her lord
Groan with no med'cinable wound, and lie
Pierced by those shafts, which to the plume were dyed
In giants' blood, down from the battlements—
Down shall she leap, and, frantic with remorse,
Breathe out her soul upon his heaving limbs."

No. 974.

Telephus wounded by Achilles.

GNAIOS. *Sardonyx.*

* He was assassinated at Delphos.　　　　† Œnone.

Telephus, a son of Hercules, king of Mysia, and son-in-law of Priam, made a furious attack on the Greeks, and would have been victorious, had not Bacchus suddenly raised a vine from the ground, which entangled his foot and felled him. He was then wounded by Achilles.

> " Well pleased shall hear
> Enorches,* where the high-hung taper's light
> Gleams on his dread carousals, and when forth
> The savage rushes on the corny field†
> Mad to destroy, shall bid his vines entwist
> His sinewy strength, and hurl him to the ground."

LYCOPHRON. See DICTYS' Cret., book ii.

No. 975.

Telephus cured by Achilles.

APOLLONIDES.   *Sardonyx.*

The oracle having declared that the wound could be healed only by the person who inflicted it, and Ulysses knowing that the presence of a son of Hercules in the Trojan war was indispensable to the success of the Greeks, prevailed on Achilles to cure him, which he did, by applying some of the filings of his spear-head to the wound.

No. 976.

Achilles supporting the wounded Pentheselea.

DIOCLES.   *Sardonyx.*

Pentheselea, the brave queen of the Amazons, who were auxiliaries to the Trojans, was slain by Achilles. He was so transported by her beauty when he stripped off her armour, and so grieved at her death, that he slew Thersites, who had previously wounded her in the eye.

> " Bow down their heads to the brave Amazon,
> Who, borne on foreign waves round foreign shores,
> Shall seek her queen ; what time in fields of war,
> Brass binds her helmed head, brass round her limbs
> Gleams dreadful to the sun. Th' Ætolian Ape‡
> Shall wound the martial glories of those eyes,
> As closed in night they slumber ; but the spear
> Shall nail the dark deformity to earth."

LYCOPHRON.

---

* Bacchus.   † Grecian army.
‡ Thersites is here called "ape" and "deformity" on account of his ugliness.

No. 977.

Achilles killing Thersites.

PAMILLIOS. *Cornelian.*

See preceding quotation.

No. 978.

The body of Pentheselea dragged by Diomede.

PYRGOTELES. *Cornelian.*

The death of Pentheselea is variously described. One account is, that Diomede, enraged at the conduct of Achilles, dragged away her body, and threw it into the river Scamander.

No. 979.

Diomede throwing the body of Pentheselea into the river Scamander.

DIOSCORIDES. *Cornelian.*

No. 980.

Achilles plucking the arrow out of his heel.

CHROMIOS. *Cornelian.*

It has been already stated that Achilles was slain by Paris, who shot him in the only vulnerable part—his heel. Though Homer states that he was slain in the field of battle, Dares of Phrygia, Dictys of Crete, and others, say that he was slain in the temple, when about to be married to Polyxena, daughter of Priam, with whom he fell in love.

No. 981.

Ulysses bearing the dead body of Achilles.

DIOSCORIDES. *Cornelian.*

" Why am I forc'd to name that fatal day
That snatch'd the prop and pride of Greece away?
I saw Pelides sink, with pious grief,
And ran in vain, alas! to his relief;

4 I

For the brave soul was fled.   Full of my friend,
I rush'd amid the war, his relics to defend;
Nor ceas'd my toil till I redeem'd the prey,
And, loaded with Achilles, march'd away:
Those arms which on these shoulders then I bore,
'Tis just you to these shoulders should restore.
You see I want not nerves, who could sustain
The pond'rous ruins of so great a man."

OVID, *Met.* xiii.

No. 982.

The Myrmidons with the dead body of Achilles.

DIOSCORIDES.   *Cornelian.*

The Myrmidons were his soldiers.

No. 983.

Ulysses and Diomede bearing off the Palladium.

APOLLONIDES.   *Calcedony.*

The Palladium was the statue of Pallas Minerva, on the preservation of which the safety of Troy depended.

" Nor doubt the same success, as when before
The Phrygian prophet to these tents I bore,
Surpris'd by night, and forc'd him to declare
In what was plac'd the fortune of the war,
Heav'n's dark decrees and answers to display,
And how to take the town, and where the secret
    lay:
Yet this I compass'd, and from Troy convey'd
The fatal image of their guardian maid.
That work was mine: for Pallas, though our friend,
Yet while she was in Troy did Troy defend.
Now what has Ajax done, or what design'd?
A noisy nothing, and an empty wind.
If he be what he promises in show,
Why was I sent, and why fear'd he to go?

Our boasting champion thought the task not light
To pass the guards—commit himself to night;
Not only through a hostile town to pass,
But scale, with steep ascent, the sacred place—
With wand'ring steps to search the citadel,
And from the priests their patroness to steal:
Then through surrounding foes to force my way,
And bear in triumph home the heav'nly prey;
Which had I not, Ajax in vain had held,
Before that monstrous bulk, his sev'nfold shield.
That night to conquer Troy I might be said,
When Troy was liable to conquest made.
Why point'st thou to my partner of the war?
Tydides had indeed a worthy share
In all my toil and praise."

OVID, *Met.* xiii.

No. 984.

Same subject.

APOLLONIDES. *Cornelian.*

No. 985.

Ulysses holding the Palladium.

APOLLONIDES. *Cornelian.*

No. 986.

Idomeneus and his Son.

GNAIOS. *Sardonyx.*

Idomeneus king of Crete, and one of the most powerful of the Grecian chiefs, having been overtaken on his return from Troy by a violent storm, vowed to Neptune that he would sacrifice to him, if he escaped, the first living being he should meet on his safe arrival in Crete. But, to his horror, he discovered that this was his own son. Some say he fulfilled his vow; others assert that the son was rescued by his subjects, who expelled him, and that he retired to Calabria in Italy, and founded Salentum.

No. 987.

Philoctetes agonised by his wound.

PYRGOTELES. *Cornelian.*

Philoctetes, to whom Hercules at his death bequeathed his poisoned arrows dipped in the blood of the hydra, joined the Grecian expedition against Troy. But having at Aulis received a wound in his foot—(whether from the bite of a serpent, or from one of the arrows which fell upon it, authors disagree)—which disabled him, and emitted an intolerable stench, he was conveyed to a desolate island, and there abandoned. Here he remained for ten years, dwelling in a cave, and subsisting on the animals he shot. But the prophet having declared that Troy could never be taken until the Greeks were aided by Philoctetes and the arrows of Hercules. Ulysses, and Neoptolemus (or Pyrrhus) the son of Achilles, conveyed him to Troy, where he was cured. While at Troy, among other signal feats, he slew Paris. The following passages are given from the *Philoctetes* of Sophocles.

ULYSSES.

" This is the shore of Lemnos' sea-girt isle ;
No human footstep marks the ground ; no hut,
Which man inhabits, rises to the eye :
Here, Neoptolemus, thou noble son
Of the most valiant of the Grecian chiefs,
The Melian Philoctetes I expos'd
In times long past, commanded by the kings
To do this deed ; for from his wounded foot
A rankling ulcer ooz'd, and undisturb'd
Nor victim nor libation could our hands
Present ; through all the camp his dismal groans
And horrid cries resounded.

$\cdot \quad \cdot \quad \cdot \quad \cdot \quad \cdot$

NEOPTOLEMUS.

Thou seest his habitation in this cave,
Where the cleft rock a double entrance yields.

CHORUS.

Where absent is the wretched dweller now ?

NEOPTOLEMUS.

The want of food hath doubtless drawn him forth
To toil with painful step, not distant far :
For he sustains his miserable life
By miserably piercing with his shafts
The beasts that haunt these wilds ; nor for his
    wound
Finds he a cure, or to his pains relief.

CHORUS.

I pity him, no mortal's lenient aid
Tending around him, and no social friend
Near him to soothe his solitary hours.
Alone, and with the anguish of his wound
For ever tortur'd, while each cheerless want
Daily scowls round him, how supports he life ?
Alas, to what hard toils are mortal men
Reduc'd, whose lives, unhappy suff'rers, want
What to sustain them ! So this man, perchance
In noble blood and high-trac'd ancestry
Rank'd with the greatest—destitute of all
That life requires—alone midst shaggy beasts

And birds of various wing his lodging finds,
And, pierc'd with pain and hunger, here endures
Immedicable anguish ; whilst around,
The rock's rude echo, with unceasing voice,
In sullen notes returns his dismal groans !

$\cdot \quad \cdot \quad \cdot$

PHILOCTETES.

As, wearied with the tossing of the waves,
They saw me sleeping on the shore, beneath
This rock's rude cov'ring, with malignant joy
They left me, and sail'd hence ; a few mean rags,
Meet for a wretch like me, beside me laid,
And food, a scanty pittance :—such be theirs !
Think from that sleep, my son, how I awoke
When they were gone ; think on my tears, my
    groans,
Such ills lamenting, when I saw my ships,
With which I hither sail'd, all out at sea,
And steering hence ! no mortal in the place—
Not one to succour me—not one to lend
His lenient hand to mitigate my wound !
On ev'ry side I roll'd my eyes, and saw
Nothing but wretchedness—of that enough.
Time after time roll'd on ; this narrow cave
I made my mansion, and these hands alone
Supplied my wants ; my bow procur'd me food,
Piercing the doves on wing ; beneath my shafts
Whene'er they fell, I trail'd my foot along
In anguish : so when thirst compell'd me forth,
Or the inclement winter's piercing frost,
To break a few dry sticks, out crawl'd this wretch,
Devising shifts ! fire was not here ! I struck
Flint against flint, and rais'd the latent sparks
With pain : thus cherish'd life hath been preserv'd.
This sheltering mansion, with such cheering fire,
Hath furnish'd me with all things, but a cure
To my disease. Now learn from me the state
Of this rude isle : no mariner through choice
Adventures on this coast ; for no safe port
Receives his bark—no mart is open here
For traffic ; and no hospitable door
To give him welcome ; to these shores his course
No wise man steers : some in a length of time,

Which rolls along events surpassing thought,
Have been driv'n hither ; these, my son, when
    here,
In words have pitied me ; nay, they have giv'n,
Touch'd with compassion, some small share of
    food—
Some raiment! but entreaties all were vain,
Not one, though oft I urg'd the fond request,
Would bear me to my household gods, and save
This life ! the tenth sad year now rolls its course,
Since here, with wretchedness and famine pierc'd,
I waste away, and feed my rankling wound.

    .   .   .   .   .

NEOPTOLEMUS.

From this fierce disease no pause,
Be thou assur'd, is thine, whilst in the east
Yon sun shall rise, and rolling its bright course

Sink in the west, till it beholds thee tread
With willing steps the plains of Ilium : there
The sons of Æsculapius shalt thou find,
And of thy wound be heal'd : then shall thy bow,
Join'd by my arms, lay waste the Phrygian state.
How I know this, attend, and thou shalt hear :
Amidst the Grecian camp there is a man
From Troy, a captive, Helenus—a seer
Of high renown : the fates he thus declar'd ;
Adding, that ere the present summer yields
To autumn its dominion, Troy must fall :
That this is true, he sets his life at gage.
Assur'd of this, let thy reluctance cease ;
Embark with us. What honour to be rank'd
First 'mongst the Grecian heroes, by the sons
Of Pæan to be heal'd—to storm the tow'rs
Of Troy, lamenting with deep groans her fall,
And grasp the highest meed that glory gives !"

The ghost of Hercules appears—

HERCULES.

"Not yet, O son of Pœas: to my words
First be attentive. Know thou hear'st the voice
Of Hercules—thine eyes behold his form.
Leaving the heav'nly mansions for thy sake,
I come, announcing the decrees of Jove :
Do thou with fix'd attention mark my words.
My fortunes to thy memory I recal,
What dangers I subdued—what toils achiev'd—
By virtue made immortal, as thine eyes
Behold. And know, thou too must suffer thus ;

And by such toils a life of glory gain.
Go with this leader to the walls of Troy ;
There first thy fell disease shall be reliev'd—
There, midst the host of Greece in valour rank'd
The noblest of her heroes, with thy bow,
Paris, the guilty cause of all these ills,
Thou shalt deprive of life—lay waste the state
Of Troy, and send triumphant to thy house,
To Œta, to thy father, the rich spoils,
Selected by the host, thy glorious prize."

No. 988.

Philoctetes and a Shepherd.

DIOSCORIDES. *Sardonyx.*

See preceding quotation.

No. 989.

Philoctetes pointing out the place where the arrows were deposited.

CHROMIOS.   *Cornelian.*

See preceding quotation.

No. 990.

Philoctetes wounding Paris.

APOLLONIDES.   *Cornelian.*

See the concluding part of the quotation to Nos. 987 and 973.

CLASS V.

SUBJECTS FROM THE ODYSSEY.

ULYSSES, king of the island of Ithaca, stands pre-eminent among the heroes of antiquity for wisdom and valour united. From his attachment to his wife Penelope, he was anxious to avoid joining the Grecian expedition against Troy. He accordingly feigned insanity, and ploughed the sea-shore, in which he sowed salt, saying it would yield a fruitful crop. Palamedes, however, detected and defeated the artifice, by placing before the ploughshare his young child Telemachus, from whom the father turned aside the plough. When at Troy, he performed the most signal services to the Grecian cause as a hero and a counsellor. He was mainly instrumental in preventing the Grecian army, after the secession of Achilles, from returning home, and abandoning the conquest of the country. The soothsayers having declared, at different times, that Troy could not be taken unless the Greeks possessed the Palladium, or image of Pallas (kept in the Trojan citadel); the horses of Rhesus, king of Thrace, a Trojan auxiliary; the arrows of Hercules, kept by Philoctetes, then an exile in the isle of Lemnos; and, after the death of Achilles, the services of his son Neoptolemus,—Ulysses, by his perseverance, courage, and sagacity, procured for them all these benefits. So persuaded were the Grecian chiefs, in full council assembled, of his transcendent services, that they adjudged to him the arms of Achilles, as the great prize to be given to the most meritorious. The *Odyssey* of Homer is mainly a narrative of his adventures after the Trojan war. He was absent from home about twenty years. As he had not returned within a reasonable time after the close of the war, it was reported he was shipwrecked and lost: the chiefs of the neighbouring islands, and some of the chiefs of Ithaca, flocked to the palace, and there lived in riot and luxury, importuning Penelope to select either of them as a husband. She promised to make her selection after she had finished a piece of tapestry on which she was employed; but by unravelling at night what she worked by day, she protracted her labour, until at last Ulysses arrived, and slew them.

No. 991.

Ulysses attacked by a wild Boar.

APOLLONIDES. *Cornelian.*

The following quotation will fully elucidate this and the two subsequent subjects, which refer to one of the adventures of Ulysses in his youth.

" Soon as the morn, new-rob'd in purple light,
Pierc'd with her golden shafts the rear of night,
Ulysses, and his brave maternal race,
The young Autolyci, essay the chase.
Parnassus, thick perplex'd with horrid shades,
With deep-mouth'd hounds the hunter-troop in-
    vades,
What time the sun, from ocean's peaceful stream,
Darts o'er the lawn his horizontal beam.
The pack impatient snuff the tainted gale ;
The thorny wilds the wood-men fierce assail ;
And foremost of the train, his cornel-spear
Ulysses wav'd, to rouse the savage war.
Deep in the rough recesses of the wood,
A lofty copse, the growth of ages, stood :
Nor winter's boreal blast, nor thund'rous show'r,
Nor solar ray, could pierce the shady bow'r,
With wither'd foliage strew'd, a heapy store ;
The warm pavilion of a dreadful boar.
Rous'd by the hounds and hunters' mingling cries,
The savage from his leafy founder flies :
With fiery glare his sanguine eye-balls shine,
And bristles high impale his horrid chine.

Young Ithacus, advanc'd, defies the foe,
Poising his lifted lance in act to throw :
The savage renders vain the wound decreed,
And springs impetuous with opponent speed !
His tusks oblique he aim'd the knee to gore ;
Aslope they glanc'd, the sinewy fibres tore,
And bar'd the bone. Ulysses, undismay'd,
Soon with redoubled force the wound repaid ;
To the right shoulder-joint the spear applied,
His further flank with streaming purple dyed :
On earth he rush'd, with agonising pain ;
With joy, and vast surprise, the applauding train
View'd his enormous bulk extended on the plain.
With bandage firm Ulysses' knee they bound ;
Then chanting mystic lays, the closing wound
Of sacred melody confess'd the force ;
The tides of life regain'd their azure course.
Then back they led the youth with loud acclaim.
Autolycus, enamour'd with his fame,
Confirm'd the cure ; and from the Delphic dome
With added gifts return'd him glorious home.
He safe at Ithaca with joy receiv'd
Relates the chase, and early praise achiev'd."

Odys. b. **xix.**

No. 992.

Ulysses killing the wild Boar.

Pyrgoteles.   *Cornelian.*

See preceding quotation.

No. 993.

Ulysses cured by Autolycus.

Chromios.   *Cornelian.*

See preceding quotation.

No. 994.

Minerva descending to Ithaca, to direct young Telemachus.

GNAIOS. *Cornelian.*

Ulysses having been shipwrecked at the island of Ogygia was detained there for seven years by the queen Calypso, who was enamoured of him. At last Minerva intercedes for his release with Jupiter, who, yielding to her entreaty, despatches Mercury to Calypso; while she herself descends to Ithaca to counsel young Telemachus, the son of Ulysses.

"Now at their native realms the Greeks arriv'd,
All who the wars of ten long years surviv'd,
And 'scap'd the perils of the gulfy main.
Ulysses, sole of all the victor-train,
An exile from his dear paternal coast,
Deplor'd his absent queen, and empire lost.
Calypso in her cave constrain'd his stay,
With sweet, reluctant, amorous delay:
In vain—for now the circling years disclose
The day predestin'd to reward his woes.
At length his Ithaca is giv'n by fate,
Where yet new labours his arrival wait.

.   .   .   .   .

' Father and king ador'd!' Minerva cried,
' Since all who in the Olympian bower reside
Now make the wand'ring Greek their public care,
Let Hermes to the Atlantic isle* repair;
Bid him, arriv'd in bright Calypso's court,
The sanction of the assembl'd powers report—
That wise Ulysses to his native land
Must speed, obedient to their high command.
Meantime Telemachus, the blooming heir
Of sea-girt Ithaca, demands my care:
'Tis mine to form his green, unpractis'd years
In sage debates, surrounded with his peers,

To save the state; and timely to restrain
The bold intrusion of the suitor-train,
Who crowd his palace, and with lawless power
His herds and flocks in feastful rites devour.
To distant Sparta, and the spacious waste
Of sandy Pyle, the royal youth shall haste.
There, warm with filial love, the cause inquire
That from his realm retards his god-like sire;
Deliv'ring early to the voice of fame
The promise of a great, immortal name.'
    She said : the sandals of celestial mould,
Fledg'd with ambrosial plumes, and rich with
        gold,
Surround her feet; with these sublime she sails
Th' aerial space, and mounts the winged gales :
O'er earth and ocean wide prepar'd to soar,
Her dreaded arm a beamy jav'lin bore,
Pond'rous and vast, which, when her fury burns,
Proud tyrants humbles, and whole hosts o'erturns.
From high Olympus prone her flight she bends,
And in the realm of Ithaca descends :
Her lineaments divine the grave disguise
Of Mentes' form conceal'd from human eyes,
(Mentes, the monarch of the Taphian land);
A glitt'ring spear wav'd awful in her hand."
                        Odys. b. i.

No. 995.

Interview of Minerva disguised as Mentes, and Telemachus.

KEPHOS. *Sardonyx.*

See preceding quotation.

---

* Ogygia.

4 K

Henceforward Telemachus appears endued with wisdom and courage far beyond his years. The following description of the riotous conduct of the suitors, and of the embarrassing situation of Penelope and Telemachus, is necessary, in order to give the reader a view of the real object of Minerva's mission, and prepare him for a full comprehension of many of the following subjects.

"There in the portal plac'd, the heav'n-born maid
Enormous riot and misrule survey'd.
On hides of beeves before the palace-gate
(Sad spoils of luxury), the suitors sate:
With rival art, and ardour in their mien,
At chess they vie, to captivate the queen,
Divining of their loves.   Attending nigh,
A menial train the flowing bowl supply:
Others apart the spacious hall prepare,
And form the costly feast with busy care.
There young Telemachus, his bloomy face
Glowing celestial sweet with god-like grace,
Amid the circle shines: but hope and fear
(Painful vicissitude!) his bosom tear.
Now imag'd in his mind, he sees restor'd,
In peace and joy, the people's rightful lord;
The proud oppressors fly the vengeful sword.
While his fond soul these fancied triumphs swell'd,
The stranger-guest the royal youth beheld.
Griev'd that a visitant so long should wait
Unmark'd, unhonour'd, at a monarch's gate,
Instant he flew, with hospitable haste,
And the new friend with courteous air embrac'd:
'Stranger! whoe'er thou art, securely rest
Affianc'd in my faith, a friendly guest:
Approach the dome, the social banquet share,
And then the purpose of thy soul declare.'
   Thus affable and mild, the prince proceeds,
And to the dome th' unknown celestial leads.
The spear receiving from her hand, he plac'd
Against a column, fair with sculpture grac'd;
Where seemly rang'd, in peaceful order, stood
Ulysses' arms, now long disus'd to blood.
He led the goddess to the sov'reign seat,
Her feet supported with a stool of state
(A purple carpet spread the pavement wide);
Then drew his seat, familiar, to her side;
Far from the suitor-train, a brutal crowd,
With insolence and wine elate and loud;

Where the free guest, unnoted, might relate,
If haply conscious of his father's fate.
The golden ewer a maid obsequious brings,
Replenish'd from the cool, translucent springs;
With copious water the bright vase supplies
A silver laver of capacious size:
They wash.   The tables in fair order spread,
They heap the glitt'ring cannisters with bread:
Viands of various kinds allure the taste,
Of choicest sort and savour—rich repast!
Delicious wines th' attending herald brought;
The gold gave lustre to the purple draught.
Lur'd with the vapour of the fragrant feast,
In rush'd the suitors with voracious haste:
Marshall'd in order due, to each a sewer
Presents, to bathe his hands, a radiant ewer.
Luxurious then they feast.   Observant round,
Gay, stripling youths the brimming goblets
      crown'd.
The rage of hunger quell'd, they all advance,
And form to measur'd airs the mazy dance:
To Phemius was consign'd the corded lyre,
Whose hand reluctant touch'd the warbling wire;
Phemius, whose voice divine could sweetest sing
High strains responsive to the vocal string.
   Meanwhile, in whispers to his heav'nly guest,
His indignation thus the prince exprest:—
'Indulge my rising grief, whilst these (my friend)
With song and dance the pompous revel end.
Light is the dance, and doubly sweet the lays,
When for the dear delight another pays.
His treasur'd stores these cormorants consume,
Whose bones, defrauded of a regal tomb
And common turf, lie naked on the plain,
Or doom'd to welter in the whelming main.
Should he return, that troop so blythe and bold,
With purple robes inwrought and stiff with gold,
Precipitant in fear, would wing their flight,
And curse their cumbrous pride's unwieldy weight.

But ah, I dream !—the appointed hour is fled,
And hope, too long with vain delusion fed,
Deaf to the rumour of fallacious fame,
Gives to the roll of death his glorious name !
With venial freedom let me now demand
Thy name, thy lineage, and paternal land :

Sincere, from whence began thy course, recite,
And to what ship I owe the friendly freight :
Now first to me this visit dost thou deign,
Or number'd in my father's social train ?
All who deserv'd his choice he made his own,
And, curious much to know, he far was known.'"

Odyssey, book i.

Mentes says that he was king of the Taphians, and an old friend of Ulysses. Telemachus then details his own and his mother's afflictions.

" With tender pity touch'd, the goddess cried :
' Soon may kind heav'n a sure relief provide !
Soon may your sire discharge the vengeance due,
And all your wrongs the proud oppressors rue !
Oh ! in that portal should the chief appear,
Each hand tremendous with a brazen spear,
In radiant panoply his limbs incas'd,

. . . . . .

Soon should yon boasters cease their haughty
strife,
Or each atone his guilty love with life !
But of his wish'd return the care resign ;
Be future vengeance to the powers divine.
My sentence hear : with stern distaste avow'd,
To their own districts drive the suitor-crowd.
When next the morning warms the purple east,
Convoke the peerage, and the gods attest ;
The sorrows of your inmost soul relate ;
And form sure plans to save the sinking state.
Should second love a pleasing flame inspire,
And the chaste queen connubial rites require,
Dismiss'd with honour let her hence repair
To great Icarius,* whose paternal care
Will guide her passion, and reward the choice
With wealthy dower and bridal gifts of price.
Then let this dictate of my love prevail :
Instant to foreign realms prepare to sail,
To learn your father's fortunes : fame may prove,
Or omen'd voice (the messenger of Jove),
Propitious to the search. Direct your toil
Through the wide ocean, first to sandy Pyle ;
Of Nestor, hoary sage, his doom demand ;
Thence speed your voyage to the Spartan strand,

For young Atrides to the Achaian coast
Arriv'd the last of all the victor-host.
If yet.Ulysses views the light, forbear,
Till the fleet hours restore the circling year ;
But if his soul hath wing'd the destin'd flight,
Inhabitant of deep disast'rous night,
Homeward, with pious speed, repass the main,
To the pale shade funereal rites ordain,
Plant the fair column o'er the vacant grave ;
A hero's honours let the hero have.
With decent grief the royal dead deplor'd,
For the chaste queen select an equal lord.
Then let revenge your daring mind employ ;
By fraud or force the suitor-train destroy,
And, starting into manhood, scorn the boy.
Hast thou not heard how young Orestes, fir'd
With great revenge, immortal praise acquir'd ?
His virgin-sword Ægisthus' veins imbrued ;
The murd'rer fell, and blood aton'd for blood.
O, greatly bless'd with ev'ry blooming grace !
With equal steps the paths of glory trace ;
Join to that royal youth's your rival name,
And shine eternal in the sphere of fame.—
But my associates now my stay deplore,
Impatient on the hoarse-resounding shore.
Thou, heedful of advice, secure proceed ;
My praise the precept is, be thine the deed.'
' The counsel of my friend,' the youth rejoin'd,
' Imprints conviction on my grateful mind.
So fathers speak (persuasive speech and mild !)
Their sage experience to the fav'rite child.
But since to part, for sweet refection due
The genial viands let my train renew :

---

* Her father.

And the rich pledge of plighted faith receive,
Worthy the heir of Ithaca to give.'
' Defer the promis'd boon (the goddess cries,
Celestial azure bright'ning in her eyes),
And let me now regain the Reithrian port:
From Temese return'd, your royal court
I shall revisit ; and that pledge receive,
And gifts, memorial of our friendship, leave.'

Abrupt, with eagle-speed she cut the sky,
Instant invisible to mortal eye.
Then first he recognis'd the ethereal guest ;
Wonder and joy alternate fire his breast :
Heroic thoughts infus'd his heart dilate,
Revolving much his father's doubtful fate :
At length compos'd, he join'd the suitor-throng,
Hush'd in attention to the warbled song."

Odyssey, book i.

No. 996.

Penelope at her loom addressing the suitors.

Polycletes. *Sardonyx.*

" Did not the sun, through heav'n's wide azure
    roll'd,
For three long years the royal fraud behold ?
While she, laborious in delusion, spread
The spacious loom, and mix'd the various thread ;
Where as to life the wond'rous figures rise,
Thus spoke the inventive queen, with artful sighs :
  ' Though, cold in death, Ulysses breathes no
    more,
Cease yet awhile to urge the bridal hour ;
Cease, till to great Laertes I bequeath
A task of grief, his ornaments of death :
Lest when the fates his royal ashes claim,
The Grecian matrons taint my spotless fame ;

When he, whom living mighty realms obey'd,
Shall want in death a shroud to grace his shade.'
  Thus she : at once the gen'rous train complies,
Nor fraud mistrusts in virtue's fair disguise.
The work she plied ; but, studious of delay,
By night revers'd the labours of the day.
While thrice the sun his annual journey made,
The conscious lamp the midnight fraud survey'd ;
Unheard, unseen, three years her arts prevail ;
The fourth, *her maid unfolds the amazing tale.*
We saw, as unperceiv'd we took our stand,
The backward labours of her faithless hand.
Then urg'd, she perfects her illustrious toils ;
A wond'rous monument of female wiles !"

Odyssey, book ii.

No. 997.

Telemachus and Nestor.

Chromios. *Cornelian.*

The owl, the bird of Minerva, is here seen overhead. Telemachus having, under the advice
and guidance of Minerva, sailed from Ithaca unknown to the suitors in quest of his father, and
arrived at Pylos, is received by the old friend of his father, the venerable sage Nestor. Tele-
machus is accompanied by Minerva disguised as Mentor, a faithful friend of Ulysses. They
find Nestor and his Pylian subjects solemnising a festival in honour of Neptune. Having
joined in the festival, and partaken of the king's hospitality, Telemachus, in answer to his re-

quest, announces who he is, and what the object of his voyage. Then Nestor, in reply, gives the following curious and much-prized epitome (according to Homer) of many events, and adventures of the Grecian chiefs, after the war.

"To him experienc'd Nestor thus rejoin'd :
' O friend, what sorrows dost thou bring to mind !
Shall I the long, laborious scene review,
And open all the wounds of Greece anew ?
What toils by sea ! where dark in quest of prey
Dauntless we rov'd : Achilles led the way.
What toils by land ! where, mix'd in fatal fight,
Such numbers fell—such heroes sunk to night :
There Ajax great, Achilles there the brave,
There wise Patroclus, fill an early grave :
There too my son—ah ! once my best delight,
Once swift of foot and terrible in fight ;
In whom stern courage with soft virtue join'd,
A faultless body and a blameless mind :
Antilochus—what more can I relate ?
How trace the tedious series of our fate ?

.   .   .   .   .

But when, by wisdom won, proud Ilion buru'd,
And in their ships the conqu'ring Greeks re-
   turn'd,
'Twas God's high will the victors to divide,
And turn the event, confounding human pride :
Some he destroy'd, some scatter'd as the dust,
(Not all were prudent, and not all were just) ;
Then Discord, sent by Pallas from above,
Stern daughter of the great avenger, Jove,
The brother-kings inspir'd with fell debate ;
Who call'd to council all the Achaian state,
But call'd untimely (nor the sacred rite
Observ'd, nor heedful of the setting light,
Nor herald sworn, the session to proclaim).
Sour with debauch, a reeling tribe, they came :
To these the cause of meeting they explain,
And Menelaus moves to cross the main.
Not so the king of men ; he will'd to stay,
The sacred rites and hecatombs to pay,
And calm Minerva's wrath. O blind to fate !
The gods not lightly change their love or hate.
With ireful taunts each other they oppose,
Till in loud tumult all the Greeks arose.

Now diff'rent counsels ev'ry breast divide ;
Each burns with rancour to the adverse side ;
The unquiet night strange projects entertain'd,
(So Jove, that urg'd us to our fate, ordain'd).
We with the rising morn our ships unmoor'd,
And brought our captives and our stores aboard ;
But half the people with respect obey'd
The king of men, and at his bidding stay'd.
Now on the wings of winds our course we keep,
(For God had smooth'd the waters of the deep) ;
For Tenedos we spread our eager oars,
There land, and pay due victims to the pow'rs ;
To bless our safe return we join in prayer,
But angry Jove dispers'd our vows in air,
And rais'd new discord. Then (so heav'n de-
   creed)
Ulysses first and Nestor disagreed.
Wise as he was, by various counsels sway'd,
He there, though late, to please the monarch,
   stay'd :
But I, determin'd, stem the foamy floods,
Warn'd of the coming fury of the gods.
With us Tydides fear'd, and urg'd his haste ;
And Menelaus came, but came the last :
He join'd our vessels in the Lesbian bay,
While yet we doubted of our wat'ry way ;
If to the right to urge the pilot's toil
(The safer road), beside the Psyrian isle ;
Or the strait course to rocky Chios plough,
And anchor under Mimas' shaggy brow.
We sought direction of the power divine :
The god propitious gave the guiding sign ;
Through the mid seas he bids our navy steer,
And in Euboea shun the woes we fear.
The whistling winds already wak'd the sky ;
Before the whistling winds the vessels fly—
With rapid swiftness cut the liquid way,
And reach Gerestus at the point of day.
There hecatombs of bulls to Neptune slain
High-flaming please the monarch of the main.

The fourth day shone, when, all their labours o'er,
Tydides' vessels touch'd the wish'd-for shore;
But I to Pylos scud before the gales,
The god still breathing on my swelling sails.
Sep'rate from all, I safely landed here;
Their fates or fortunes never reach'd my ear.
Yet what I learn'd, attend; as here I sat,
And ask each voyager each hero's fate;
Curious to know, and willing to relate.

Safe reach'd the Myrmidons their native land,
Beneath Achilles' warlike son's command.
Those whom the heir of great Apollo's art,
Brave Philoctetes, taught to wing the dart;
And those whom Idomen from Ilion's plain
Had led, securely cross'd the dreadful main.
How Agamemnon touch'd his Argive coast,
And how his life by fraud and force he lost,
And how the murd'rer paid his forfeit breath;
What land so distant from that scene of death
But trembling heard the same; and heard, admire
How well the son appeas'd his slaughter'd sire!
E'en to th' unhappy, that unjustly bleed,
Heav'n gives posterity t' avenge the deed.
So fell Ægisthus; and may'st thou, my friend,
(On whom the virtues of thy sire descend),
Make future times thy equal act adore,
And be what brave Orestes was before!

. . . . .

Meantime from flaming Troy we cut the way,
With Menelaus, through the curling sea.
But when to Sunium's sacred point we came,
Crown'd with the temple of th' Athenian dame,

Atrides' pilot, Phrontes, there expir'd—
Phrontes, of all the sons of men admir'd
To steer the bounding bark with steady toil,
When the storm thickens and the billows boil—
While yet he exercis'd the steersman's art,
Apollo touch'd him with his gentle dart:
E'en with the rudder in his hand, he fell.
To pay whose honours to the shades of hell,
We check'd our haste, by pious office bound,
And laid our old companion in the ground.
And now the rites discharg'd, our course we keep
Far on the gloomy bosom of the deep:
Soon as Mallæa's misty tops arise,
Sudden the Thund'rer blackens all the skies,
And the winds whistle, and the surges roll
Mountains on mountains, and obscure the pole.
The tempest scatters and divides our fleet;
Part the storm urges on the coast of Crete,
Where winding round the rich Cydonian plain,
The streams of Jardan issue to the main.
There stands a rock, high, eminent, and steep,
Whose shaggy brow o'erhangs the shady deep,
And views Gortyna on the western side;
On this rough Auster drove th' impetuous tide:
With broken force the billows roll'd away,
And heav'd the fleet into the neighb'ring bay.
Thus sav'd from death, they gain'd the Phæstan shores
With shatter'd vessels and disabled oars:
But five tall barks the winds and waters toss'd
Far from their fellows, on the Ægyptian coast.
There wander'd Menelaus through foreign shores,
Amassing gold, and gathering naval stores.' "
Odyssey, book iii.

No. 998.

The same subject.

CHROMIOS. *Cornelian.*

No. 999.

Polycasta placing the garment on Telemachus.

GNAIOS. *Amethyst.*

" While these officious tend the rites divine,
The last fair branch of the Nestorian line,
Sweet Polycaste, took the pleasing toil
To bathe the prince, and pour the fragrant oil.
When o'er his limbs a flow'ry vest she threw,
He issued, like a god, to mortal view.
His former seat beside the king he found
(His people's father with his peers around);
All plac'd at ease, the holy banquet join,
And in the dazzling goblet laughs the wine."

Odyssey, book iii.

Nestor, after having entertained him and given him all the information in his power, sent him, accompanied by his son Pisistratus, to make inquiries of Menelaus, king of Sparta, because

" He, wand'ring long, a wider circle made,
And many-languag'd nations has survey'd;
And measur'd tracts unknown to other ships,
Amid the monstrous wonders of the deeps;
A length of ocean and unbounded sky,
Which scarce the sea-fowl in a year o'erfly."

No. 1000.

Medon acquainting Penelope with the conspiracy of the suitors.

GNAIOS. *Amethyst.*

The suitors having learned that Telemachus had sailed for Pylos, imagined that he went for reinforcements in order to expel or destroy them: they accordingly conspired to kill him on his return. Penelope was also ignorant of the departure of Telemachus, and was therefore greatly afflicted at these double tidings.

" Swift to the queen the herald Medon ran,
Who heard the consult of the dire divan:
Before her dome the royal matron stands,
And thus the message of his haste demands:

'What will the suitors! must my servant-train
Th' allotted labours of the day refrain,
For them to form some exquisite repast?
Heav'n grant this festival may prove their last!

Or if they still must live, from me remove
The double plague of luxury and love!
Forbear, ye sons of insolence! forbear,
In riot to consume a wretched heir.
In the young soul illustrious thought to raise,
Were ye not tutor'd with Ulysses' praise?
Have not your fathers oft my lord defin'd,
Gentle of speech, beneficent of mind?
Some kings with arbitrary rage devour,
Or in their tyrant-minions vest the power:
Ulysses let no partial favours fall:
The people's parent, he protected all:
But absent now, perfidious and ingrate!
His stores ye ravage, and usurp his state.'
  He thus: 'O, were the woes you speak the worst!
They form a deed more odious and accurs'd;
More dreadful than your boding soul divines :
But pitying Jove avert the dire designs!
The darling object of your royal care
Is mark'd to perish in a deathful snare :
Before he anchors in his native port,
From Pyle resailing and the Spartan court,
Horrid to speak! in ambush is decreed
The hope and heir of Ithaca to bleed!'
  Sudden she sunk beneath the weighty woes,
The vital streams a chilling horror froze :
The big round tear stands trembling in her eye,
And on her tongue imperfect accents die.
At length, in tender language, interwove
With sighs, she thus express'd her anxious love :
'Why rashly would my son his fate explore,
Ride the wild waves, and quit the safer shore?

Did he, with all the greatly wretched, crave
A blank oblivion and untimely grave!'
  ''Tis not,' replied the sage, 'to Medon giv'n
To know if some inhabitant of heav'n
In his young breast the daring thought in-
    spir'd;
Or if, alone with filial duty fir'd,
The winds and waves he tempts in early bloom,
Studious to learn his absent father's doom.'
  The sage retir'd. Unable to control
The mighty griefs that swell her lab'ring soul,
Rolling convulsive on the floor is seen
The piteous object of a prostrate queen.
Words to her dumb complaint a pause supplies,
And breath, to waste in unavailing cries.
Around their sov'reign wept the menial fair,
To whom she thus address'd her deep despair :
  'Behold a wretch, whom all the gods consign
To woe! did ever sorrows equal mine?
Long to my joys my dearest lord is lost—
His country's buckler, and the Grecian boast :
Now from my fond embrace, by tempests torn,
Our other column of the state is borne :
Nor took a kind adieu, nor sought consent!—
Unkind confed'rates in his dire intent!
Ill suits it with your shews of duteous zeal
From me the purpos'd voyage to conceal :
Though at the solemn midnight hour he rose,
Why did you fear to trouble my repose?
He either had obey'd my fond desire,
Or seen his mother, pierc'd with grief, expire.' "
                    Odyssey, book iv.

No. 1001.

The phantom of Iphthime consoling Penelope in her sleep.

GNAIOS.   *Cornelian.*

" Meantime the queen without refection due,
Heart-wounded, to the bed of state withdrew:
In her sad breast the prince's fortunes roll,
And hope and doubt alternate seize her soul.

So when the woodman's toil her cave surrounds,
And with the hunter's cry the grove resounds;
With grief and rage the mother-lion stung,
Fearless herself, yet trembles for her young.

While pensive in the silent, slumb'rous shade,
Sleep's gentle pow'rs her drooping eyes invade;
Minerva, life-like on embodied air,
Impress'd the form of Iphthima the fair*—
(Icarius' daughter she, whose blooming charms
Allur'd Eumelus to her virgin-arms;
A sceptred lord, who o'er the fruitful plain
Of Thessaly wide stretch'd his ample reign).
As Pallas will'd, along the sable skies
To calm the queen the phantom-sister flies.
Swift on the regal dome descending right,
The bolted valves are pervious to her flight.
Close to her head the pleasing vision stands,
And thus performs Minerva's high commands:
  'O why, Penelope, this causeless fear,
To render sleep's soft blessing insincere?
Alike devote to sorrow's dire extreme
The day reflection and the midnight dream!
Thy son the gods propitious will restore,
And bid thee cease his absence to deplore.'
  To whom the queen (whilst yet her pensive
      mind
Was in the silent gates of sleep confin'd):
'O sister, to my soul for ever dear!
Why this first visit to reprove my fear?
How in a realm so distant should you know
From what deep source my ceaseless sorrows
      flow?

To all my hopes my royal lord is lost,
His country's buckler, and the Grecian boast:
And with consummate woe to weigh me down,
The heir of all his honours and his crown,
My darling son, is fled! an easy prey
To the fierce storms, or men more fierce than they;
Who in a league of blood-associates sworn,
Will intercept th' unwary youth's return.'
  'Courage resume,' the shadowy form replied,
'In the protecting care of heav'n confide:
On him attends the blue-ey'd martial maid—
What earthly can implore a surer aid?
Me now the guardian-goddess deigns to send,
To bid thee patient his return attend.'
  The queen replies: 'If in the blest abodes,
A goddess thou hast commerce with the gods,
Say, breathes my lord the blissful realm of light,
Or lies he wrapp'd in ever-during night?'
  'Inquire not of his doom,' the phantom cries;
'I speak not all the counsel of the skies:
Nor must indulge with vain discourse, or long,
The windy satisfaction of the tongue.'
  Swift through the valves the visionary fair
Repass'd, and viewless mix'd with common air.
The queen awakes, deliver'd of her woes;
With florid joy her heart dilating glows:
The vision, manifest of future fate,
Makes her with hope her son's arrival wait."

Odyssey, book iv.

No. 1002.

Calypso giving Ulysses an axe to build his boat.

APOLLONIDES. *Amethyst.*

Jupiter despatched Mercury to Calypso, to command her to allow the departure of Ulysses. The description of her famous grotto, and a portion of her dialogue with Ulysses, it is here necessary to introduce.

"Thus o'er the world of waters Hermes flew,
Till now the distant island rose in view;
Then swift ascending from the azure wave,
He took the path that winded to the cave.

Large was the grot, in which the nymph he found—
The fair-hair'd nymph with ev'ry beauty crown'd;
She sat and sung; the rocks resound her lays;
The cave was brighten'd with a rising blaze—

---

* Penelope's sister.

626

Cedar and frankincense, an od'rous pile,
Flam'd on the hearth, and wide perfum'd the isle;
While she with work and song the time divides,
And through the loom the golden shuttle guides:
Without the grot a various sylvan scene
Appear'd around, and groves of living green;
Poplars and alders ever quiv'ring play'd,
And nodding cypress form'd a fragrant shade;
On whose high branches, waving with the storm,
The birds of broadest wings their mansion form—
The chough, the sea-mew, the loquacious crow—
And scream aloft, and skim the deeps below.
Depending vines the shelving cavern screen,
With purple clusters blushing through the green.
Four limpid fountains from the clefts distil;
And every fountain pours a several rill,
In mazy windings wand'ring down the hill;
Where bloomy meads with vivid greens were
          crown'd,
And glowing violets threw odours round—
A scene, where if a god should cast his sight,
A god might gaze, and wander with delight!
Joy touch'd the messenger of heav'n: he stay'd
Entranc'd, and all the blissful haunt survey'd.
Him, ent'ring in the cave, Calypso knew,
For pow'rs celestial to each other's view
Stand still confess'd, though distant far they lie,
Or habitants of earth, or sea, or sky.

    .   .   .   .

The nymph, obedient to divine command,
To seek Ulysses paced along the sand.
Him pensive on the lonely beach she found,
With streaming eyes in briny torrents drown'd,
And inly pining for his native shore;
For now the soft enchantress pleas'd no more;
For now, reluctant, and constrain'd by charms,
Absent he lay in her desiring arms—
In slumber wore the heavy night away—
On rocks and shores consum'd the tedious day;
There sate all desolate, and sigh'd alone,
With echoing sorrows made the mountains
          groan,
And roll'd his eyes o'er all the restless main,
Till dimm'd with rising grief they stream'd again.

Here on his musing mood the goddess press'd,
Approaching soft; and thus the chief address'd:
'Unhappy man! to wasting woes a prey,
No more in sorrows languish life away:
Free as the winds I give thee now to rove—
Go, fell the timber of yon lofty grove,
And form a raft, and build the rising ship,
Sublime to bear thee o'er the gloomy deep.
To store the vessel let the care be mine,
With water from the rock and rosy wine,
And life-sustaining bread, and fair array,
And prosp'rous gales to waft thee on thy way.
These, if the gods with my desires comply
(The gods, alas! more mighty far than I,
And better skill'd in dark events to come),
In peace shall land thee at thy native home.'
  Thus having said, the goddess march'd be-
          fore:
He trode her footsteps in the sandy shore.
At the cool cave arriv'd, they took their state;
He fill'd the throne where Mercury had sate.
For him the nymph a rich repast ordains,
Such as the mortal life of man sustains;
Before herself were plac'd the cates divine,
Ambrosial banquet, and celestial wine.
Their hunger satiate, and their thirst represt,
Thus spoke Calypso to her godlike guest:
  'Ulysses,' with a sigh she thus began,
'O, sprung from gods! in wisdom more than
          man!
Is, then, thy home the passion of thy heart?
Thus wilt thou leave me? are we thus to part?
Farewell! and ever joyful mayst thou be,
Nor break the transport with one thought of
          me.
But, ah, Ulysses! wert thou giv'n to know
What fate has doom'd thee yet to undergo,
Thy heart might settle in this scene of ease,
And e'en these slighted charms might learn to
          please.
A willing goddess, and immortal life,
Might banish from thy mind an absent wife.
Am I inferior to a mortal dame?
Less soft my feature, less august my frame?

Or shall the daughters of mankind compare
Their earth-born beauties with the heav'nly
    fair?'*
' Alas! for this,' the prudent man replies,
' Against Ulysses shall thy anger rise?
Lov'd and ador'd, O goddess, as thou art,
Forgive the weakness of a human heart!
Though well I see thy graces far above
The dear, though mortal, object of my love—
Of youth eternal well the diff'rence know,
And the short date of fading charms below;
Yet ev'ry day, while absent thus I roam,
I languish to return and die at home.
Whate'er the gods shall destine me to bear,
In the black ocean, or the wat'ry war,
'Tis mine to master with a constant mind—
Enur'd to perils—to the worst resign'd.
By seas, by wars, so many dangers run,
Still I can suffer: their high will be done!'
    Thus while he spoke, the beamy sun de-
        scends,
And rising night her friendly shade extends;

To the close grot the lonely pair remove,
And slept delighted with the gifts of love.
When rosy morning call'd them from their rest,
Ulysses rob'd him in the cloak and vest.
The nymph's fair head a veil transparent grac'd,
Her swelling loins a radiant zone embrac'd,
With flowers of gold: an under-robe, unbound,
In snowy waves flow'd glitt'ring on the ground.
Forth issuing thus, she gave him first to wield
A weighty axe, with truest temper steel'd,
And double-edg'd, the handle smooth and plain,
Wrought of the clouded olive's easy grain;
And next, a wedge, to drive with sweepy sway:
Then to the neighb'ring forest led the way.
On the lone island's utmost verge there stood
Of poplars, pines, and firs, a lofty wood,
Whose leafless summits to the skies aspire,
Scorch'd by the sun, or sear'd by heav'nly fire,
Already dried.† These pointing out to view,
The nymph just shew'd him, and with tears with-
    drew."
                                Odyssey, book v.

No. 1003.
Departure of Ulysses from the Island of Calypso.
CARPOS. *Cornelian.*

Calypso is represented as striving to persuade him to remain, while Mercury is urging him to go. See preceding quotation.

"The nymph dismiss'd him, od'rous garments
    giv'n,
And bath'd in fragrant oils that breath'd of heav'n:
Then fill'd two goat-skins with her hands divine,
With water one, and one with sable wine:
Of ev'ry kind provisions heav'd aboard;
And the full decks with copious viands stor'd.

The goddess, last, a gentle breeze supplies,
To curl old Ocean, and to warm the skies.
    And now, rejoicing in the prosp'rous gales,
With beating heart Ulysses spreads his sails;
Plac'd at the helm he sat, and mark'd the skies;
Nor clos'd in sleep his ever-watchful eyes."
                                Odyssey, book v.

* The reader must consider, that though there may appear a contradiction between her proposal to him, immediately before, to depart, and her indirect solicitations to him, here, to remain, yet there is in reality none. She promised, in obedience to the absolute commands of Jupiter, to let him go, if he pleased; but if he consented to remain, she was absolved from her promise. Jupiter only required that she should not coerce his free agency.

† Green, moist wood, would have been unfit for the purpose.

No. 1004.

Neptune wrecking the boat of Ulysses.

APOLLONIDES.　*Sardonyx.*

Neptune was incensed against Ulysses because he blinded his son Polyphemus.

" But him, thus voyaging the deeps below,
From far, on Solime's aërial brow,
The king of ocean saw, and seeing buru'd
(From Æthiopia's happy climes return'd);*
The raging monarch shook his azure head,
And thus in secret to his soul he said:
  ' Heav'ns! how uncertain are the pow'rs on high!
Is then revers'd the sentence of the sky
In one man's favour, while, a distant guest,
I shar'd secure the Æthiopian feast?
Behold now near Phæacia's land he draws!
The land affix'd by fate's eternal laws
To end his toils. Is, then, our anger vain?
No, if this sceptre yet commands the main.'
  He spoke, and high the forky trident hurl'd—
Rolls clouds on clouds, and stirs the wat'ry world,
At once the face of earth and sea deforms—
Swells all the winds, and rouses all the storms.
Down rush'd the night. East, west, together roar,
And south, and north, roll mountains to the shore.
Then shook the hero, to despair resign'd,
And question'd thus his yet unconquer'd mind:
  ' Wretch that I am! what farther fates attend
This life of toils? and what my destin'd end?
Too well, alas! the island-goddess knew,
On the black sea what perils should ensue.
New horrors now this destin'd head enclose;
Unfill'd is yet the measure of my woes.
With what a cloud the brows of heav'n are
    crown'd!
What raging winds! what roaring waters round!
'Tis Jove himself the swelling tempest rears;
Death—present death, on ev'ry side appears.

Happy! thrice happy! who, in battle slain,
Press'd in Atrides' cause the Trojan plain:
Oh! had I died before that well-fought wall—
Had some distinguish'd day renown'd my fall
(Such as was that when show'rs of jav'lins fled
From conqu'ring Troy around Achilles dead),
All Greece had paid my solemn fun'rals then,
And spread my glory with the sons of men!
A shameful fate now hides my hapless head,
Unwept, unnoted, and for ever dead!'
  A mighty wave rush'd o'er him as he spoke,
The raft it cover'd, and the mast it broke;
Swept from the deck, and from the rudder torn,
Far on the swelling surge the chief was borne;
While, by the howling tempest rent in twain,
Flew sail and sail-yards rattling o'er the main.
Long press'd, he heav'd beneath the weighty wave,
Clogg'd by the cumb'rous vest Calypso gave;
At length emerging, from his nostrils wide,
And gushing mouth, effus'd the briny tide:
E'en then, not mindless of his last retreat,
He seiz'd the raft, and leapt into his seat,
Strong with the fear of death. The rolling flood
Now here, now there, impell'd the floating wood.
As when a heap of gather'd thorns is cast,
Now to, now fro, before the autumnal blast—
Together clung, it rolls around the field;
So roll'd the float, and so its texture held:
And now the south, and now the north, bear sway,
And now the east the foamy floods obey,
And now the west wind whirls it o'er the sea.
  The wand'ring chief, with toils on toils opprest,
Leucothea saw, and pity touch'd her breast

---

* *i. e.* from the annual feast, which, it was fabled, was given to the gods in Æthiopia. The fable arose from the circumstance, that during twelve days in every year the statues of the gods were carried about in solemn procession, and the vòtaries indulged in feasting and amusement.

(Herself a mortal once, of Cadmus' train,
But now an azure sister of the main):
Swift as a sea-mew springing from the flood,
All radiant on the raft the goddess stood;
Then thus address'd him: 'Thou, whom heav'n decrees
To Neptune's wrath, stern tyrant of the seas
(Unequal contest!), not his rage and power,
Great as he is, such virtue shall devour.
What I suggest thy wisdom will perform:
Forsake thy float, and leave it to the storm;
Strip off thy garments; Neptune's fury brave
With naked strength, and plunge into the wave:
To reach Phæacia all thy nerves extend,
There fate decrees thy miseries shall end.
This heav'nly scarf beneath thy bosom bind,
And live; give all thy terrors to the wind.
Soon as thy arms the happy shore shall gain,
Return the gift, and cast it in the main:
Observe my orders, and with heed obey,
Cast it far off; and turn thy eyes away.'
    With that, her hand the sacred veil bestows,
Then down the deeps she div'd, from whence she rose:
A moment snatch'd the shining form away,
And all was cover'd with the curling sea.
    Struck with amaze, yet still to doubt inclin'd,
He stands suspended, and explores his mind:

'What shall I do? Unhappy me! Who knows
But other gods intend me other woes?
Whoe'er thou art, I shall not blindly join
Thy pleaded reason, but consult with mine:
For scarce in ken appears that distant isle
Thy voice foretells me shall conclude my toil.
Thus then I judge: while yet the planks sustain
The wild waves' fury, here I fix'd remain;
But when their texture to the tempest yields,
I launch advent'rous on the liquid fields,
Join to the help of gods the strength of man,
And take this method, since the best I can.'
    While thus his thoughts an anxious council hold,
The raging god a wat'ry mountain roll'd;
Like a black sheet the whelming billow spread,
Burst o'er the float, and thunder'd on his head.
Planks, beams, disparted fly; the scatter'd wood
Rolls diverse, and in fragments strews the flood.
So the rude Boreas, o'er the field new shorn,
Tosses and drives the scatter'd heaps of corn.
And now a single beam the chief bestrides;
There, pois'd awhile above the bounding tides,
His limbs discumbers of the clinging vest,
And binds the sacred cincture round his breast:
Then prone on ocean in a moment flung,
Stretch'd wide his eager arms, and shot the seas
    along."
                            Odyssey, book v.

No. 1005.

Ulysses floating on a fragment of the wreck.

Illos. *Sardonyx.*

Ulysses, Neptune, and the gods of the winds, form the group here. See preceding quotation.

No. 1006.

Ulysses floating, while Minerva lulls the winds.

Admon. *Cornelian.*

" Now, scarce withdrawn the fierce earth-shaking pow'r,
Jove's daughter Pallas watch'd the fav'ring hour;

Back to their caves she bade the winds to fly,
And hush'd the blust'ring brethren of the sky.
The drier blasts alone of Boreas sway,
And bear him soft on broken waves away;
With gentle force impelling to that shore,
Where fate has destin'd he shall toil no more.
And now two nights, and now two days were past,
Since wide he wander'd on the wat'ry waste;
Heav'd on the surge with intermitting breath,
And hourly panting in the arms of death."   *Odyssey*, book v.

No. 1007.

Ulysses aided by Minerva and a river-god.

POLYCLETES. *Cornelian.*

" The third fair morn now blaz'd upon the main;
Then glassy smooth lay all the liquid plain,
The winds were hush'd, the billows scarcely curl'd,
And a dead silence still'd the wat'ry world.
When, lifted on a ridgy wave, he spies
The land at distance, and with sharpen'd eyes.
As pious children joy with vast delight
When a lov'd sire revives before their sight,
(Who ling'ring long has call'd on death in vain,
Fix'd by some demon to his bed of pain,
Till heav'n by miracle his life restore),
So joys Ulysses at th' appearing shore;
And sees, and labours onward, as he sees
The rising forests, and the tufted trees.
And now, as near approaching as the sound
Of human voice the list'ning ear may wound,
Amidst the rocks he hears a hollow roar
Of murm'ring surges breaking on the shore:
Nor peaceful port was there, nor winding bay,
To shield the vessel from the rolling sea;
But cliffs, and shaggy shores, a dreadful sight!
All rough with rocks, with foamy billows white.
Fear seiz'd his slacken'd limbs and beating heart,
As thus he commun'd with his soul apart:
‘Ah me! when o'er a length of waters tost,
These eyes at last behold th' unhop'd-for coast,

No port receives me from the angry main,
But the loud deeps demand me back again.
Above, sharp rocks forbid access; around,
Roar the wild waves; beneath, is sea profound!
No footing sure affords the faithless sand,
To stem too rapid, and too deep to stand.
If here I enter, my efforts are vain,
Dash'd on the cliffs, or heav'd into the main;
Or round the island if my course I bend,
Where the ports open, or the shores descend,
Back to the seas the rolling surge may sweep,
And bury all my hopes beneath the deep;
Or some enormous whale the god may send
(For many such on Amphitrite attend):
Too well the turns of mortal chance I know,
And hate relentless of my heav'nly foe.’
   While thus he thought, a monstrous wave up-
      bore
The chief, and dash'd him on the craggy shore:
Torn was his skin, nor had the ribs been whole,
But instant Pallas enter'd in his soul.
Close to the cliff with both his hands he clung,
And stuck adherent, and suspended hung,
Till the huge surge roll'd off: then backward sweep
The refluent tides, and plunge him in the deep.
As when the polypus, from forth his cave
Torn, with full force reluctant beats the wave,

His ragged claws are stuck with stones and sands:
So the rough rock had shagg'd Ulysses' hands.
And now had perish'd, whelm'd beneath the main,
The unhappy man ; e'en fate had been in vain :
But all-subduing Pallas lent her pow'r,
And prudence sav'd him in the needful hour ;
Beyond the beating surge his course he bore
(A wider circle, but in sight of shore),
With longing eyes, observing, to survey
Some smooth ascent, or safe-sequester'd bay.
Between the parting rocks at length he spied
A falling stream in gentler waters glide,
Where to the seas the shelving shore declin'd,
And form'd a bay impervious to the wind :
To this calm port the glad Ulysses press'd,
And hail'd the river, and its god address'd :
  ' Whoe'er thou art, before whose stream un-
        known
I bend, a suppliant at thy wat'ry throne,
Hear, azure king ! nor let me fly in vain
To thee from Neptune and the raging main.
Heav'n hears and pities helpless men like me,
For sacred e'en to gods is misery :

Let then thy waters give the weary rest,
And save a suppliant, and a man distrest.'
  He pray'd, and strait the gentle stream sub-
        sides—
Detains the rushing current of his tides—
Before the wand'rer smooths the wat'ry way,
And soft receives him from the rolling sea.
That moment, fainting as he touch'd the shore,
He dropt his sinewy arms : his knees no more
Perform'd their office, or his weight upheld :
His swoll'n heart heav'd ; .his bloated body
        swell'd :
From mouth and nose the briny torrent ran ;
And lost in lassitude lay all the man,
Depriv'd of voice, of motion, and of breath,
The soul scarce waking, in the arms of death.
Soon as warm life its wonted office found,
The mindful chief Leucothea's scarf unbound :
Observant of her word, he turn'd aside
His head, and cast it on the rolling tide.
Behind him far, upon the purple waves,
The waters waft it, and the nymph receives."
                              Odyssey, book v.

No. 1008.

Nausicaa presenting garments to Ulysses after his shipwreck.

ILLOS. *Cornelian.*

Ulysses, exhausted by his late struggles in the sea, when he arrived on shore in Phæacia, threw himself under the shade of some trees on the bank of the river, and fell asleep. Nausicaa, daughter of Alcinous the king, came to the river, attended by her maids, to wash the robes of state, preparatory to her own marriage. While the clothes were drying, she and her attendants amused themselves with play. Their noisy mirth awoke Ulysses. Having wrapped some leaves about his person, he appealed to the princess for assistance. She gave him food and raiment, and advised him to go to the palace, and throw himself on the compassion of the sovereign : he did so. Alcinous entertained him hospitably, and, after hearing his adventures, enabled him to reach home. It is stated that his benefactress Nausicaa was afterwards married to his son Telemachus. Ulysses addresses Nausicaa :—

           " If thy race
Be mortal, and this earth thy native place,

Blest is the father from whose loins you sprung—
Blest is the mother at whose breast you hung—

Blest are the brethren who thy blood divide,
To such a miracle of charms allied;
Joyful they see applauding princes gaze,
When stately in the dance you swim th' harmo-
    nious maze:
But blest o'er all the youth, with heav'nly
    charms,
Who clasps thy bright perfection in his arms!
Never, I never view'd till this blest hour
Such finish'd grace! I gaze and I adore!
Thus seems the palm, with stately honours crown'd,
By Phœbus' altars; thus o'erlooks the ground,
The pride of Delos. By the Delian coast
I voyag'd, leader of a warrior host,
But ah how chang'd! from thence my sorrow
    flows;
O fatal voyage, source of all my woes!
Raptur'd I stood, and as this hour amaz'd,
With rev'rence at the lofty wonder gaz'd:
Raptur'd I stand! for earth ne'er knew to bear
A plant so stately, or a nymph so fair.
Aw'd from access, I lift my suppliant hands;
For misery, O queen, before thee stands!
Twice ten tempestuous nights I roll'd, resign'd
To roaring billows and the warring wind;
Heav'n bade the deep to spare! but heav'n, my
    foe,
Spares only to inflict some mightier woe!
Inur'd to cares—to death in all its forms—
Outcast I rove, familiar with the storms!

Once more I view the face of human kind:
Oh, let soft pity touch thy gen'rous mind!
Unconscious of what air I breathe, I stand
Naked, defenceless, on a foreign land.
Propitious to my wants, a vest supply,
To guard the wretch from the inclement sky:
So may the gods, who heav'n and earth control,
Crown the chaste wishes of thy virtuous soul—
On thy soft hours their choicest blessings shed—
Blest with a husband be thy bridal bed—
Blest be thy husband with a blooming race,
And lasting union crown your blissful days.
The gods, when they supremely bless, bestow
Firm union on their favourites below:
Then envy grieves, with inly-pining hate;
The good exult, and heav'n is in our state.'
    To whom the nymph: 'O stranger, cease thy
        care:
Wise is thy soul, but man is born to bear:
Jove weighs affairs of earth in dubious scales,
And the good suffers while the bad prevails.
Bear with a soul resign'd the will of Jove:
Who breathes must mourn: thy woes are from
    above.
But since thou treadst our hospitable shore,
'Tis mine to bid the wretched grieve no more—
To clothe the naked, and thy way to guide:
Know the Phæacian tribes this land divide:
From great Alcinous' royal loins I spring—
A happy nation, and a happy king.' "

Nausicaa directs her maids to attend Ulysses.

    " ' By Jove the stranger and the poor are sent,
        And what to those we give to Jove is lent.
        Then food supply, and bathe his fainting limbs,
        Where waving shades obscure the mazy streams.'
            Obedient to the call, the chief they guide
        To the calm current of the secret tide;
        Close by the stream a royal dress they lay,
        A vest and robe, with rich embroid'ry gay;
        Then unguents in a vase of gold supply,
        That breath'd a fragrance through the balmy sky."
                            Odyssey, book vi.

No. 1009.

Ulysses a suppliant before Alcinous, and his queen Arete.

ASPASIOS. *Cornelian.*

Ulysses was enabled, by the aid of Minerva, to escape notice, until he threw himself at the feet of the king and queen.

" Night now approaching, in the palace stand,
With goblets crown'd, the rulers of the land;
Prepar'd for rest, and off'ring to the god*
Who bears the virtue of the sleepy rod.
Unseen he glided through the joyous crowd,
With darkness circled, and an ambient cloud.
Direct to great Alcinous' throne he came,
And prostrate fell before th' imperial dame.
Then from around him dropp'd the veil of night;
Sudden he shines, and manifest to sight.
The nobles gaze, with awful fear oppress'd,
Silent they gaze, and eye the god-like guest.
' Daughter of great Rhexenor!' thus began,
Low at her knees, the much-enduring man,
' To thee—thy consort, and this royal train—
To all that share the blessings of your reign,
A suppliant bends: oh, pity human woe!
'Tis what the happy to th' unhappy owe.
A wretched exile to his country send,
Long worn with griefs, and long without a friend.
So may the gods your better days increase,
And all your joys descend on all your race—
So reign for ever on your country's breast,
Your people blessing, by your people blest!'
Then to the genial hearth he bow'd his face,
And humbled in the ashes took his place.
Silence ensued. The eldest first began,
Echeneus sage, a venerable man;
Whose well-taught mind the present age surpass'd,
And join'd to that th' experience of the last.

Fit words attended on his weighty sense,
And mild persuasion flow'd in eloquence.
' Oh sight,' he cried, ' dishonest and unjust!
A guest—a stranger, seated in the dust!
To raise the lowly suppliant from the ground
Befits a monarch. Lo! the peers around
But wait thy word, the gentle guest to grace,
And seat him fair in some distinguish'd place.
Let first the herald due libation pay
To Jove, who guides the wand'rer on his way!†
Then set the genial banquet in his view,
And give the stranger-guest a stranger's due.'
His sage advice the list'ning king obeys,
He stretch'd his hand the prudent chief to raise,
And from his seat Laodamas remov'd
(The monarch's offspring, and his best belov'd),
There next his side the god-like hero sat;
With stars of silver shone the bed of state.
The golden ewer a beauteous handmaid brings,
Replenish'd from the cool translucent springs,
Whose polish'd vase with copious streams supplies
A silver laver of capacious size.
The table next in regal order spread,
The glitt'ring canisters are heap'd with bread:
Viands of various kinds invite the taste,
Of choicest sort and favour—rich repast!
Thus feasting high, Alcinous gave the sign,
And bade the herald pour the rosy wine.
Let all around the due libation pay
To Jove, who guides the wand'rer on his way."
Odyssey, book vii.

* Mercury.

† Jupiter Xenius, or Jove the tutelar god of hospitality, under whose protection every suppliant was believed to be the moment he seated himself at the hearthside of a stranger's house.

No. 1010.

Demodocus playing and reciting the story of the Trojan horse to Alcinous and Ulysses.

DIOSCORIDES.   *Hyacinth,* called *Guarnaccino.*

On the following day Alcinous appointed public games, at which Ulysses greatly signalised himself. In the evening, at the public banquet, Demodocus, the bard and minstrel, who had before entertained the company with a recital of the amours of Mars and Venus, was requested by Ulysses to sing and play the introduction of the wooden horse into Troy. Ulysses having wept at the recital, Alcinous is led to inquire his name and fortunes. Then Ulysses relates his adventures.

" Now each partakes the feast, the wine pre-
        pares—
Portions the food, and each his portion shares.
The bard an herald guides : the gazing throng
' Pay low obeisance as he moves along :
Beneath a sculptur'd arch he sits enthron'd—
The peers encircling form an awful round.
Then from the chine Ulysses carves with art
Delicious food, an honorary part:
' This let the master of the lyre receive,
A pledge of love ! 'tis all a wretch can give.
Lives there a man beneath the spacious skies,
Who sacred honours to the bard denies ?
The muse the bard inspires—exalts his mind—
The muse indulgent loves th' harmonious kind.'
    The herald to his hand the charge conveys,
Not fond of flattery, nor unpleas'd with praise.
    When now the rage of hunger is allay'd,
Thus to the lyrist wise Ulysses said :
' O more than man ! thy soul the muse inspires,
Or Phœbus animates with all his fires:
For who by Phœbus uninformed could know
The woe of Greece, and sing so well the woe ?
Just to the tale as present at the fray,
Or taught the labours of the dreadful day,
The song recals past horrors to my eyes,
And bids proud Ilion from her ashes rise.
Once more harmonious strike the sounding string,
Th' Epæan fabric, fram'd by Pallas, sing :

How stern Ulysses, furious to destroy,
With latent heroes sack'd imperial Troy.
If faithful thou record the tale of fame,
The god himself inspires thy breast with flame :
And mine shall be the task henceforth to raise
In ev'ry land thy monument of praise.'
    Full of the god he rais'd his lofty strain,
How the Greeks rush'd tumultuous to the main :—
How blazing tents illumin'd half the skies,
While from the shores the winged navy flies—
How even in Ilion's walls, in deathful bands,
Came the stern Greeks by Troy's assisting hands—
All Troy upheav'd the steed—of diff'ring mind,
Various the Trojans counsell'd—part consign'd
The monster to the sword, part sentence gave
To plunge it headlong in the whelming wave—
The unwise award to lodge it in the towers,
An off'ring sacred to the immortal powers—
The unwise prevail, they lodge it in the walls,
And by the gods' decree proud Ilion falls—
Destruction enters in the treach'rous wood,
And vengeful slaughter, fierce for human blood.
    He sung the Greeks stern issuing from the
        steed,
How Ilion burns—how all her fathers bleed—
How to thy dome, Deiphobus ! ascends
The Spartan king—how Ithacus attends
(Horrid as Mars), and how with dire alarms
He fights—subdues : for Pallas strings his arms !

Thus while he sung, Ulysses' griefs renew,
Tears bathe his cheeks, and tears the ground be-
dew.
As some fond matron views in mortal fight
Her husband falling in his country's right;
Frantic through clashing swords she runs—she
flies,
As ghastly pale he groans—and faints—and dies!
Close to his breast she grovels on the ground,
And bathes with floods of tears the gaping
wound;
She cries—she shrieks! the fierce insulting foe
Relentless mocks her violence of woe,
To chains condemn'd as wildly she deplores,
A widow, and a slave, on foreign shores!
So from the sluices of Ulysses' eyes
Fast fell the tears, and sighs succeeded sighs:
Conceal'd he griev'd. The king observ'd alone
The silent tear, and heard the secret groan:

Then to the bard aloud; ' O cease to sing,
Dumb be thy voice, and mute the tuneful string:
To ev'ry note his tears responsive flow,
And his great heart heaves with tumultuous woe:
Thy lay too deeply moves. Then cease the lay,
And o'er the banquet ev'ry heart be gay.
This social right demands: for him the sails,
Floating in air, invite the impelling gales;
His are the gifts of love: the wise and good
Receive the stranger as a brother's blood.
  But, friend, discover faithful what I crave,
Artful concealment ill becomes the brave:
Say what thy birth, and what the name you bore,
Impos'd by parents in the natal hour?
(For from the natal hour distinctive names,
One common right, the great and lowly claims):
Say from what city—from what regions tost;
And what inhabitants those regions boast?'"
                              Odyssey, book viii.

No. 1011.

Polyphemus closing the door of his cavern on Ulysses and his companions.

CHROMIOS. *Cornelian.*

The Cyclops (i.e. the *round-eyed*) were described as a race of cannibals, of gigantic stature, residing near Mount Ætna, having each but one eye, and this circular, in the forehead. On comparing several explanations of this fable, the best appears to me to be, that they were people of large dimensions—of unsocial and ferocious disposition—worshippers of the sun, of which they wore a bright metal representation on their foreheads; and that they sacrificed all strangers to their divinity, which was a custom among many ancient nations, as I have shewn in this work (*Addenda et Corrigenda*, No. 116, class I.). Ulysses, with a few companions, having landed on the island on an exploring excursion, entered the cave of one of them—Polyphemus. Soon after the savage enters, bringing his sheep with him, and closes the cavern with an enormous rock. He then discovers the visitors, and devours some of them. Next morning he goes out, shutting the survivors in: on his return he makes a similar meal. Then Ulysses, in order to pacificate him, presents to him a cask of very strong wine (which he had previously brought), in order to help his digestion. This giant quaffs off, telling Ulysses that for his kindness he will devour him the last, and drops asleep. Ulysses then sharpens the end of a huge pole, which he hardens in the fire, and bores out the eye of Polyphemus.

Polyphemus starting up, sober and awake, throws open the cavern-door, and there remains groping, in the hope of catching his torturers as they escape. However, they do escape—by hanging under the bellies of the large thick-fleeced sheep as they go out—and carry off the sheep. When they are rowing off, Ulysses raises a shout of triumph: then Polyphemus hurls after the boat a huge rock, that creates such a swell that the boat is well nigh swamped.

The subjoined quotations, which it is better to give as a consecutive whole, will explain this and the five following subjects.

" When to the nearest verge of land we drew,
Fast by the sea a lonely cave we view—
High, and with dark'ning laurels cover'd o'er,
Where sheep and goats lay slumb'ring round the
    shore—
Near this a fence of marble from the rock,
Brown with o'er-arching pine and spreading oak.
A giant-shepherd here his flock maintains
Far from the rest, and solitary reigns,
In shelter thick of horrid shade reclin'd ;
And gloomy mischiefs labour in his mind.
A form enormous ! far unlike the race
Of human birth, in stature, or in face :
As some lone mountain's monstrous growth he
    stood,
Crown'd with rough thickets, and a nodding
    wood.
I left my vessel at the point of land,
And close to guard it gave our crew command :
With only twelve, the boldest and the best,
I seek the adventure, and forsake the rest :
Then took a goatskin fill'd with precious wine,
The gift of Maron, of Evanthus' line.

.   .   .   .

Such was the wine, to quench whose fervent
    steam,
Scarce twenty measures from the living stream
To cool one cup suffic'd : the goblet crown'd
Breath'd aromatic fragrances around.
Of this an ample vase we heav'd aboard,
And brought another with provisions stor'd.
My soul foreboded I should find the bower
Of some fell monster, fierce with barb'rous power—
Some rustic wretch, who liv'd in heav'n's de-
    spite,
Contemning laws, and trampling on the right.

The cave we found, but vacant all within
(His flock the giant tended on the green).
But round the grot we gaze, and all we view,
In order rang'd, our admiration drew :
The bending shelves with loads of cheeses press'd,
The folded flocks each sep'rate from the rest,
(The larger here, and there the lesser lambs,
The new-fall'n young here bleating for their dams ;
The kid distinguish'd from the lambkin lies) ;
The cavern echoes with responsive cries.
Capacious chargers all around were laid,
Full pails, and vessels of the milking trade.
With fresh provision hence our fleet to store
My friends advise me, and to quit the shore ;
Or drive a flock of sheep and goats away—
Consult our safety, and put off to sea.
Their wholesome counsel rashly I declin'd,
Curious to view the man of monstrous kind,
And try what social rites a savage lends—
Dire rites, alas ! and fatal to my friends !
   Then first a fire we kindle, and prepare
For his return with sacrifice and prayer.
The loaden shelves afford us full repast.
We sit expecting. Lo, he comes at last !
Near half a forest on his back he bore,
And cast the pond'rous burden at the door :
It thunder'd as it fell. We trembled then,
And sought the deep recesses of the den.
Now driv'n before him, through the arching rock,
Came tumbling, heaps on heaps, the unnumber'd
    flock :
Big-udder'd ewes, and goats of female kind
(The males were penn'd in outward courts be-
    hind).
Then, heav'd on high, a rock's enormous weight
To the cave's mouth he roll'd, and clos'd the gate

(Scarce twenty four-wheel'd cars, compact and
   strong,
The massy load could bear, or roll along).
He next betakes him to his evening cares,
And, sitting down, to milk his flocks prepares;
Of half their udders eases first the dams,
Then to the mothers' teat submits the lambs.
Half the white stream to hard'ning cheese he
   press'd,
And high in wicker baskets heap'd; the rest,
Reserv'd in bowls, supplied his nightly feast.
His labour done, he fired the pile, that gave
A sudden blaze, and lighted all the cave.

We stand discover'd by the rising fires;
Askance the giant glares, and thus inquires:
   'What are ye, guests? on what adventure,
     say,
Thus far ye wander through the wat'ry way?
Pirates perhaps, who seek, through seas unknown,
The lives of others, and expose your own.'
  His voice like thunder through the cavern
   sounds:
My bold companions thrilling fear confounds,
Appall'd at sight of more than mortal man.
At length, with heart recover'd, I began."

Ulysses tells him they are Greeks returning from the Trojan war, and endeavours to enlist
his sympathy.

" He answer'd with his deed: his bloody hand
Snatch'd two, unhappy! of my martial band,
And dash'd like dogs against the stony floor:
The pavement swims with brains and mingled gore.
Torn limb from limb, he spreads his horrid feast,
And fierce devours it like a mountain beast:
He sucks the marrow, and the blood he drains;
Nor entrails, flesh, nor solid bone remains.
We see the death from which we cannot move,
And humbled groan beneath the hand of Jove.
His ample maw with human carnage fill'd,
A milky deluge next the giant swill'd;
Then, stretch'd in length o'er half the cavern'd
   rock,
Lay senseless and supine amidst the flock.
To seize the time, and with a sudden wound
To fix the slumb'ring monster to the ground,
My soul impels me; and in act I stand
To draw the sword; but wisdom held my hand.
A deed so rash had finish'd all our fate;
No mortal forces from the lofty gate
Could roll the rock. In hopeless grief we lay,
And sigh, expecting the return of day.
Now did the rosy-finger'd morn arise,
And shed her sacred light along the skies.
He wakes—he lights the fire—he milks the dams,
And to the mothers' teat submits the lambs.

The task thus finish'd of his morning hours,
Two more he snatches—murders, and devours!
Then pleas'd and whistling, drives his flock be-
   fore;
Removes the rocky mountain from the door,
And shuts again; with equal ease dispos'd,
As a light quiver's lid is op'd and clos'd.
His giant voice the echoing region fills;
His flocks, obedient, spread o'er all the hills.
  Thus left behind, e'en in the last despair
I thought—devis'd—and Pallas heard my prayer!
Revenge, and doubt, and caution work'd my
   breast;
But this of many counsels seem'd the best:
The monster's club within the cave I spied,
A tree of stateliest growth, and yet undried,
Green from the wood; of height and bulk so vast
The largest ship might claim it for a mast.
This shorten'd of its top, I gave my train
A fathom's length, to shape it and to plane;
The narrower end I sharpen'd to a spire,
Whose point we harden'd with the force of fire,
And hid it in the dust that strew'd the cave.
Then to my few companions, bold and brave,
Propos'd, who first the vent'rous deed should
   try:
In the broad orbit of his monstrous eye

To plunge the brand, and twirl the pointed wood,
When slumber next should tame the man of
 blood.
Just as I wish'd, the lots were cast on four—
Myself the fifth. We stand and wait the hour.
He comes with evening: all his fleecy flock
Before him march, and pour into the rock;
Not one, or male or female, stay'd behind
(So fortune chanc'd, or so some god design'd).
Then heaving high the stone's unwieldy weight,
He roll'd it on the cave, and clos'd the gate.
First down he sits to milk the woolly dams,
And then permits their udder to the lambs.
Next seiz'd two wretches more, and headlong cast,
Brain'd on the rock; his second dire repast.
I then approach'd him reeking with their gore,
And held the brimming goblet foaming o'er:
'Cyclop! since human flesh has been thy feast,
Now drain this goblet, potent to digest:
Know hence what treasures in our ship we lost,
And what rich liquors other climates boast.
We to thy shore the precious freight shall bear,
If home thou send us, and vouchsafe to spare.
But oh! thus furious, thirsting thus for gore,
The sons of men shall ne'er approach thy shore,
And never shalt thou taste this nectar more.'
  He heard, he took, and pouring down his throat
Delighted swill'd the large luxurious draught.
'More! give me more!' he cried: 'the boon be
 thine,
Whoe'er thou art, that bear'st celestial wine!
Declare thy name; not mortal is this juice,
Such as the unblest Cyclopean climes produce
(Though sure our vine the largest cluster yields,
And Jove's scorn'd thunder serves to drench our
 fields);
But this descended from the blest abodes,
A rill of nectar streaming from the gods.'
  He said, and greedy grasp'd the heady bowl,
Thrice drain'd, and pour'd the deluge on his soul.
His sense lay cover'd with the dozy fume:
While thus my fraudful speech I re-assume.
'Thy promis'd boon, O Cyclop! now I claim,
And plead my title: No-man is my name.

By that distinguish'd from my tender years,
'Tis what my parents call me, and my peers.'
  The giant then: 'Our promis'd grace receive,
The hospitable boon we mean to give:
When all thy wretched crew have felt my power,
No-man shall be the last I shall devour.'
  He said: then, nodding with the fumes of wine,
Dropt his huge head, and snoring lay supine.
His neck obliquely o'er his shoulder hung,
Press'd with the weight of sleep, that tames the
 strong;
There belch'd the mingled steams of wine and
 blood,
And human flesh, his undigested food.
Sudden I stir the embers, and inspire
With animating breath the seeds of fire;
Each drooping spirit with bold words repair,
And urge my train the dreadful deed to dare.
The stake now glow'd beneath the burning bed
(Green as it was), and sparkl'd fiery red.
Then forth the vengeful instrument I bring;
With beating hearts my fellows form a ring.
Urg'd by some present god, they swift let fall
The pointed torment on his visual ball.
Myself above them, from a rising ground,
Guide the sharp stake, and twirl it round and
 round.
As when a shipwright stands his workmen o'er,
Who ply the wimble, some huge beam to bore;
Urg'd on all hands it nimbly spins about,
The grain deep-piercing till it scoops it out:
In his broad eye so whirls the fiery wood;
From the pierc'd pupil spouts the boiling blood:
Sing'd are his brows; the scorching lids grow
 black;
The jelly bubbles, and the fibres crack.
And as when arm'rers temper in the ford
The keen-edg'd pole-axe, or the shining sword,
The red-hot metal hisses in the lake;
Thus in his eyeball hiss'd the plunging stake.
He sends a dreadful groan: the rocks around
Through all their inmost winding-caves resound.
Scar'd we receded. Forth, with frantic hand
He tore, and dash'd on earth the gory brand:

Then calls the Cyclops, all that round him dwell,
With voice like thunder, and a direful yell!
From all their dens the one-eyed race repair—
From rifted rocks, and mountains bleak in air.
All haste assembl'd, at his well-known roar—
Inquire the cause, and crowd the cavern-door.
  ' What hurts thee, Polypheme? what strange
    affright
Thus breaks our slumbers, and disturbs the night?
Does any mortal in th' unguarded hour
Of sleep oppress thee, or by fraud or power?
Or thieves insidious the fair flocks surprise?'
Thus they. The Cyclops from his den replies:
  ' Friends, *No-man* kills me: *No-man*, in the
    hour
Of sleep, oppresses me with fraudful power.'
' If no man hurt thee, but the hand divine
Inflict disease, it fits thee to resign:
To Jove, or to thy father Neptune pray,'
The brethren cried, and instant strode away.
  Joy touch'd my secret soul and conscious heart,
Pleas'd with the effect of conduct and of art.
Meantime the Cyclop, raging with his wound,
Spreads his wide arms, and searches round and
    round:
At last, the stone removing from the gate,
With hands extended in the midst he sate;
And search'd each passing sheep, and felt it o'er,
Secure to seize us ere we reach'd the door;
(Such as his shallow wit he deem'd was mine).
But secret I revolv'd the deep design:
'Twas for our lives my lab'ring bosom wrought;
Each scheme I turn'd, and sharpen'd every
    thought:
This way and that I cast to save my friends,
Till one resolve my varying counsel ends.
  Strong were the rams, with native purple fair,
Well fed, and largest of the fleecy care.
These, three and three, with osier bands we tied
(The twining bands the Cyclop's bed supplied);
The midmost bore a man; the outward two
Secur'd each side: so bound we all the crew.
One ram remain'd, the leader of the flock;
In his deep fleece my grasping hands I lock,

And fast beneath, in woolly curls inwove,
There cling implicit, and confide in Jove.
When rosy morning glimmer'd o'er the dales,
He drove to pasture all the lusty males:
The ewes still folded, with distended thighs
Unmilk'd, lay bleating in distressful cries.
But heedless of those cares, with anguish stung,
He felt their fleeces as they pass'd along
(Fool that he was), and let them safely go,
All unsuspecting of their freight below.
  The master-ram at last approach'd the gate,
Charg'd with his wool and with Ulysses' fate.
Him while he past, the monster blind bespoke:
' What makes my lamb the lag of all the flock?
First thou wert wont to crop the flowery mead,
First to the field and river's bank to lead,
And first, with stately step, at ev'ning hour
Thy fleecy fellows usher to their bower.
Now far the last, with pensive pace and slow
Thou mov'st, as conscious of thy master's woe!
Seest thou these lids that now unfold in vain?
(The deed of *No-man* and his wicked train.)
Oh! didst thou feel for thy afflicted lord,
And would but fate the power of speech afford,
Soon mightst thou tell me, where in secret here
The dastard lurks, all trembling with his fear.
Swung round and round, and dash'd from rock to
    rock,
His batter'd brains should on the pavement
    smoke.
No ease, no pleasure, my sad heart receives,
While such a monster as vile *No-man* lives.'
  The giant spoke, and through the hollow rock
Dismiss'd the ram, the father of the flock.
No sooner freed, and through the enclosure past,
First I release myself, my fellows last.
Fat sheep and goats in throngs we drive before,
And reach our vessel on the winding shore.
With joy the sailors view their friends return'd,
And hail us living whom as dead they mourn'd.
Big tears of transport stand in ev'ry eye:
I check their fondness, and command to fly.
Aboard in haste they heave the wealthy sheep,
And snatch their oars, and rush into the deep.

Now off at sea, and from the shallows clear,
As far as human voice could reach the ear,
With taunts the distant giant I accost:
' Hear me, O Cyclop! hear, ungracious host!
'Twas on no coward, no ignoble slave,
Thou meditat'st thy meal in yonder cave ;
But one, the vengeance fated from above
Doom'd to inflict ; the instrument of Jove.
Thy barb'rous breach of hospitable bands,
The god—the god revenges by my hands.'
    These words the Cyclop's burning rage pro-
      voke:
From the tall hill he rends a pointed rock ;
High o'er the billows flew the massy load,
And near the ship came thund'ring on the flood.
It almost brush'd the helm, and fell before:
The whole sea shook, and refluent beat the
      shore.
The strong concussion on the heaving tide
Roll'd back the vessel to the island's side.

Again-I shov'd her off: our fate to fly
Each nerve we stretch, and ev'ry oar we ply.
Just 'scap'd impending death, when now again
We twice as far had furrow'd back the main,
Once more I raise my voice ; my friends, afraid,
With mild entreaties my design dissuade.
' What boots the godless giant to provoke,
Whose arm may sink us at a single stroke?
Already, when the dreadful rock he threw,
Old Ocean shook, and back his surges flew.
The sounding voice directs his aim again ;
The rock o'erwhelms us, and we 'scap'd in vain.'
    But I, of mind elate, and scorning fear,
Thus with new taunts insult the monster's ear.
' Cyclop ! if any, pitying thy disgrace,
Ask who disfigur'd thus that eyeless face ;
Say 'twas Ulysses ; 'twas his deed declare,
Laertes' son, of Ithaca the fair—
Ulysses, far in fighting fields renown'd,
Before whose arm Troy tumbled to the ground.' "

No. 1012.

Polyphemus devouring one of the companions of Ulysses.

APOLLONIDES.   *Sardonyx.*

See preceding quotation.

No. 1013.

Ulysses pouring out the wine for Polyphemus.

CHROMIOS.   *Calcedony.*

See preceding quotation.

No. 1014.

Ulysses and his companions boring out the eye of Polyphemus.

DAMPHILOS.   *Cornelian.*

See preceding quotation.

No. 1015.

Ulysses and his companions escaping from the cave of Polyphemus.

ATHENION. *Cornelian.*

See preceding quotation.

No. 1016.

Polyphemus hurling a rock at the ship of Ulysses.

APOLLONIDES. *Sardonyx.*

See preceding quotation.

No. 1017.

Ulysses receiving from Æolus a bag that encloses the Winds.

POLYCLETES. *Cornelian.*

Ulysses having arrived at the island of Æolus, king of the winds, Æolus gave him prosperous winds at his departure, and enclosed the adverse winds in a bag which he gave him, telling him to keep it carefully closed. But his companions having opened the bag from curiosity, the winds flew out and drove back the ships. Ulysses again supplicated the aid of Æolus, but Æolus refused his prayer. The following quotation will be sufficient for this and the three succeeding subjects.

" This happy port affords our wand'ring fleet
A month's reception and a safe retreat.
Full oft the monarch urg'd me to relate
The fall of Ilion, and the Grecian fate;
Full oft I told: at length for parting mov'd;
The king with mighty gifts my suit approv'd.
The adverse winds in leathern bags he brac'd—
Compress'd their force, and lock'd each struggling blast:
For him the mighty sire of gods assign'd
The tempest's lord, the tyrant of the wind;
His word alone the list'ning storms obey,
To smooth the deep, or swell the foamy sea.

These in my hollow ship the monarch hung,
Securely fetter'd by a silver thong;
But Zephyrus exempt, with friendly gales
He charg'd to fill and guide the swelling sails.
Rare gift! but oh, what gift to fools avails!
    Nine prosp'rous days we plied the lab'ring oar,
The tenth presents our welcome native shore:
The hills display the beacon's friendly light,
And rising mountains gain upon our sight.
Then first my eyes, by watchful toils oppress'd,
Complied to take the balmy gifts of rest;
Then first my hands did from the rudder part
(So much the love of home possess'd my heart),

4 N

When lo! on board a fond debate arose,
What rare device those vessels might enclose?
What sum—what prize from Æolus I brought?
Whilst to his neighbour each express'd his
      thought:
'Say whence, ye gods, contending nations strive
Who most shall please, who most our hero give?
Long have his coffers groan'd with Trojan spoils;
While we, the wretched partners of his toils,
Reproach'd by want, our fruitless labours mourn,
And only rich in barren fame return.
Now Æolus, ye see, augments his store:
But come, my friends, these mystic gifts ex-
      plore.'
They said: and (oh, curs'd fate!) the thongs un-
      bound—
The gushing tempest sweeps the ocean round!
Snatch'd in the whirl, the hurried navy flew,
The ocean widen'd, and the shores withdrew.
Rous'd from my fatal sleep, I long debate
If still to live, or desperate plunge to fate:
Thus doubting, prostrate on the deck I lay,
Till all the coward thoughts of death gave way.
    Meanwhile our vessels plough the liquid plain,
And soon the known Æolian coast regain;
Our groans the rocks remurmur'd to the main;
We leap'd on shore, and with a scanty feast
Our thirst and hunger hastily repress'd:
That done, two chosen heralds straight attend
Our second progress to my royal friend;

And him amidst his jovial sons we found,
The banquet streaming, and the goblets crown'd:
There humbly stopp'd, with conscious shame and
      awe,
Nor nearer than the gate presum'd to draw.
But soon his sons their well-known guest de-
      scried,
And, starting from their couches, loudly cried,
'Ulysses here! what demon couldst thou meet
To thwart thy passage and repel thy fleet?
Wast thou not furnish'd by our choicest care
For Greece, for home, and all thy soul held dear?'
Thus they: in silence long my fate I mourn'd,
At length these words with accent low return'd:
'Me, lock'd in sleep, my faithless crew bereft
Of all the blessings of your god-like gift!
But grant, O grant our loss we may retrieve;
A favour you, and you alone, can give.'
    Thus I with art to move their pity tried,
And touch'd the youths, but their stern sire re-
      plied:
'Vile wretch, begone! this instant I command
Thy fleet accurs'd to leave our hallowed land.
His baneful suit pollutes these bless'd abodes,
Whose fate proclaims him hateful to the gods.'
    Thus fierce he said: we sighing went our way,
And with desponding hearts put off to sea.
The sailors, spent with toils, their folly mourn,
But mourn in vain—no prospect of return!"
                          Odyssey, book x.

No. 1018.

Ulysses carrying the bag which contains the Winds.

GNAIOS.   *Amethyst.*

No. 1019.

The companions of Ulysses opening the bag which contains the Winds.

CHROMIOS.   *Sardonyx.*

See preceding quotation.

No. 1020·

Æolus rejecting the prayer of Ulysses.

DIOSCORIDES.· *Sardonyx.*

See concluding part of preceding quotation.*

No. 1021.

The Læstrygonian giants hurling rocks at the fleet of Ulysses.

CHROMIOS. *Sardonyx.*

Ulysses lost the chief part of his fleet and crew among these giant cannibals, to whose coast in Sicily he was driven after leaving the Æolides.

" Balk'd of his prey, the yelling monster
flies,
And fills the city with his hideous cries:
A ghastly band of giants hear the roar,
And pouring down the mountains, crowd the
shore.
Fragments they rend from off the craggy brow,
And dash the ruins on the ships below :
The crackling vessels burst ; hoarse groans arise,
And mingled horrors echo to the skies ;
The men, like fish, they stuck upon the flood,
And cramm'd their filthy throats with human
food.

Whilst thus their fury rages at the bay,
My sword our cables cut—I call'd to weigh ;
And charg'd my men, as they from fate would
fly,
Each nerve to strain, each bending oar to ply.
The sailors catch the word their oars to seize,
And sweep with equal strokes the smoky seas ;
Clear of the rocks th' impatient vessel flies,
Whilst in the port each wretch encumber'd dies.
With earnest haste my frighted sailors press,
While kindling transports glow'd at our success ;
But the sad fate that did our friends destroy
Cool'd ev'ry breast, and damp'd the rising joy.''

Odyssey, book x.

* The most probable solution of these fables is, that the king of seven islands in the Sicilian Sea (now known as the Lipari islands), from his knowledge of astronomy, his long and acute observation of the winds, became what is termed *weather-wise;* and from his dexterous management of sails, could, as it were, " govern the storm." So the Phœnicians, who traded in those seas, called him king *Aolin,* from *aol,* a *tempest;* whence the Greek word *aella,* and his name Æolos. He gave Ulysses such correct instructions how to shape his course, and avail himself of the shifting currents of wind, that he may be said to have kept the adverse winds confined. But when Ulysses fell asleep through exhaustion, his crew disobeyed the instructions, and were driven back.

No. 1022.

Ulysses in the island of Circe killing a stag.

POLYCLETES. *Cornelian.*

Ulysses was next cast on Æëa, an island (or rather a promontory resembling an island) on the coast of Italy, the residence of Circe, the famous enchantress.

" Two days and nights roll'd on,
And now the third succeeding morning shone :
I climb'd a cliff, with spear and sword in hand,
Whose ridge o'erlook'd a shady length of land ;
To learn if aught of mortal works appear,
Or cheerful voice of mortal strike the ear.
From the high point I mark'd, in distant view,
A stream of curling smoke ascending blue,
And spiry tops, the tufted trees above,
Of Circe's palace bosom'd in the grove.
   Thither to haste, the region to explore,
Was first my thought : but speeding back to shore,
I deem'd it best to visit first my crew,
And send our spies the dubious coast to view.
As down the hill I solitary go,
Some pow'r divine, who pities human woe,
Sent a tall stag, descending from the wood,
To cool his fervour in the crystal flood ;
Luxuriant on the wave-worn bank he lay,
Stretch'd forth, and panting in the sunny ray.
I launch'd my spear, and with a sudden wound,
Transpierc'd his back, and fix'd him to the ground.

He falls, and mourns his fate with human cries :
Through the wide wound the vital spirit flies.
I drew, and casting on the river-side
The bloody spear, his gather'd feet I tied
With twining osiers, which the bank supplied.
An ell in length the pliant whisp I weav'd,
And the huge body on my shoulders heav'd :
Then leaning on the spear with both my hands,
Upbore my load, and press'd the sinking sands
With weighty steps, till at the ship I threw
The welcome burden, and bespoke my crew :
' Cheer up, my friends ! it is not yet our fate
To glide with ghosts through Pluto's gloomy gate.
Food in the desert land, behold ! is giv'n :
Live, and enjoy the providence of heav'n.'
   The joyful crew survey his mighty size,
And on the future banquet feast their eyes,
As huge in length extended lay the beast ;
Then wash their hands, and hasten to the feast.
There, till the setting sun roll'd down the light,
They sat indulging in the genial rite."

Odyssey, book x.

No. 1023.

Ulysses dragging the stag to the ship.

DIOSCORIDES. *Amethyst.*

See preceding quotation.

No. 1024.

Circe, Eurylochus, and the metamorphosed companions of Ulysses.

APOLLONIDES. *Amethyst.*

The explanation and the moral of this transformation into swine are, that these sailors became brutalised by gross indulgence in this place, where there was every incentive to laziness and sensuality. As Circe was the daughter of the sun, she wears here on her head a representation of that luminary.

" In equal parts I straight divide my band,
And name a chief each party to command ;
I led the one ; and of the other side
Appointed brave Eurylochus the guide.
Then in the brazen helm the lots we throw,
And fortune casts Eurylochus to go.
He march'd, with twice eleven in his train :
Pensive they march, and pensive we remain.

The palace in a woody vale they found,
High rais'd of stone ; a shaded space around :
Where mountain wolves and brindled lions roam
(By magic tam'd), familiar to the dome.
With gentle blandishment our men they meet,
And wag their tails, and fawning lick their feet.
As from some feast a man returning late,
His faithful dogs all meet him at the gate,
Rejoicing round, some morsel to receive
(Such as the good man ever us'd to give) :
Domestic thus the grisly beasts drew near ;
They gaze with wonder, not unmix'd with fear.
Now on the threshold of the dome they stood,
And heard a voice resounding through the wood :
Plac'd at her loom within, the goddess sung ;
The vaulted roofs and solid pavement rung.
O'er the fair web the rising figures shine,
Immortal labour ! worthy hands divine.
Polites to the rest the question mov'd
(A gallant leader, and a man I lov'd) :
' What voice celestial, chanting to the loom
(Or nymph or goddess), echoes from the room ?

Say, shall we seek access ?' With that they call ;
And wide unfold the portals of the hall.

The goddess rising, asks her guests to stay,
Who blindly follow where she leads the way :
Eurylochus, alone of all the band
Suspecting fraud, more prudently remain'd.
On thrones around, with downy coverings grac'd,
With semblance fair th' unhappy men she plac'd.
Milk newly press'd, the sacred flow'r of wheat,
And honey fresh, and Pramnian wines the treat :
But venom'd was the bread, and mix'd the bowl
With drugs of force to darken all the soul.
Soon in the luscious feast themselves they lost,
And drank oblivion of their native coast :
Instant her circling wand the goddess waves,
To hogs transforms them, and the sty receives.
No more was seen the human form divine ;
Head, face, and members bristle into swine :
Still curst with sense, their minds remain alone,
And their own voice affrights them when they
        groan.
Meanwhile the goddess in disdain bestows
The mast and acorn, brutal food ! and strows
The fruits of cornel, as the feast, around ;
Now prone and grov'lling on unsav'ry ground.

Eurylochus, with pensive steps and slow,
Aghast returns, the messenger of woe,
And bitter fate. To speak he made essay ;
In vain essay'd, nor would his tongue obey ;
His swelling heart denied the words their way.'

Odyssey, book x.

No. 1025.

Ulysses receiving the plant *moly* from Mercury, as a charm.

MYRON.   *Amethyst.*

When Ulysses heard of the fate of his companions from Eurylochus, he armed himself, and proceeded to the residence of Circe.   On his way he was accosted by Mercury.

" A form divine forth issued from the wood
(Immortal Hermes with the golden rod),
In human semblance : on his bloomy face
Youth smil'd celestial, with each op'ning grace.
He seiz'd my hand, and gracious thus began :
' Ah, whither roam'st thou ? much - enduring
    man !
O blind to fate ! what led thy steps to rove
The horrid mazes of this magic grove ?
Each friend you seek in yon enclosure lies,
All lost their form, and habitants of sties.
Think'st thou by wit to model their escape ?
Sooner shalt thou, a stranger to thy shape,
Fall prone their equal.   First thy danger know,
Then take the antidote the gods bestow.
The plant I give through all the direful bow'r
Shall guard thee, and avert the evil hour.
Now hear her wicked arts.   Before thy eyes
The bowl shall sparkle, and the banquet rise :
Take this, nor from the faithless feast abstain,
For temper'd drugs and poisons shall be vain.

Soon as she strikes her wand, and gives the
    word,
Draw forth and brandish thy refulgent sword,
And menace death : those menaces shall move.
Her alter'd mind to blandishment and love.
Nor shun the blessing proffer'd to thy arms,
Ascend her bed, and taste celestial charms :
So shall thy tedious toils a respite find,
And thy lost friends return to human kind.
But swear her first by those dread oaths that tie
The pow'rs below, the blessed in the sky ;
Lest to the naked secret fraud be meant,
Or magic bind thee, cold and impotent.'
    Thus while he spoke, the sov'reign plant he
    drew,
Where on th' all-bearing earth unmark'd it grew,
And shew'd its nature and its wond'rous pow'r :
Black was the root, but milky white the flow'r ;
Moly the name, to mortals hard to find ;
But all is easy to th' ethereal kind."
                Odyssey, book x.

No. 1026.

Ulysses quaffing off Circe's cup.

CHROMIOS.   *Cornelian.*

" This Hermes gave, then, gliding off the glade,
Shot to Olympus from the woodland shade.
While full of thought, revolving fates to come,
I speed my passage to th' enchanted dome :
Arriv'd before the lofty gates, I stay'd ;
The lofty gates the goddess wide display'd.

She leads before, and to the feast invites ;
I follow sadly to the magic rites.
Radiant with starry studs, a silver seat
Receiv'd her limbs ; a footstool eas'd her feet :
She mix'd the potion, fraudulent of soul ;
The poison mantled in the golden bowl.

I took and quaff'd it, confident in heav'n.
Then wav'd the wand, and then the word was
    giv'n ;
' Hence, to thy fellows ! (dreadful she began)
Go, be a beast !'—I heard, and yet was—man !
  Then sudden whirling, like a waving flame,
My beamy faulchion, I assault the dame.
Struck with unusual fear, she trembling cries,
She faints—she falls—she lifts her weeping eyes.
  ' What art thou, say ? from whence — from
    whom you came ?
O more than human ! tell thy race—thy name.
Amazing strength, these poisons to sustain !
Not mortal thou, nor mortal is thy brain.
Or art thou he, the man to come (foretold
By Hermes, pow'rful with the wand of gold),
The man from Troy, who wander'd ocean
    round—
The man for wisdom's various arts renown'd—

Ulysses ! oh ! thy threat'ning fury cease—
Sheathe thy bright sword, and join our hands in
    peace ;
Let mutual joys our mutual trust combine,
And love and love-born confidence be thine.'
  ' And how, dread Circe ! (furious I rejoin)
Can love and love-born confidence be mine
Beneath thy charms when my companions groan,
Transform'd to beasts, with accents not their own?
O thou of fraudful heart ! shall I be led
To share thy feast-rites, or ascend thy bed,
That, all unarm'd, thy vengeance may have vent,
And magic bind me, cold and impotent?
Celestial as thou art, yet stand denied ;
Or swear that oath by which the gods are tied —
Swear, in thy soul no latent frauds remain—
Swear, by the vow which never can be vain !'
  The goddess swore: then seiz'd my hand, and led
To the sweet transports of the genial bed."

Odyssey, book x.

No. 1027.

Circe supplicating Ulysses.

APOLLONIDES. *Cornelian.*

See preceding quotation.

No. 1028.

Circe soliciting Ulysses to feast.

APOLLONIDES. *Amethyst.*

" The table in fair order spread,
They heap the glitt'ring cannisters with bread ;
Viands of various kinds allure the taste,
Of choicest sort and savour—rich repast !
Circe in vain invites the feast to share ;
Absent I ponder, and absorb'd in care.
While scenes of woe rose anxious in my breast,
The queen beheld me, and these words address'd :

' Why stands Ulysses silent and apart,
Some hoard of grief close-harbour'd at his heart?
Untouch'd before thee stand the cates divine,
And unregarded laughs the rosy wine.
Can yet a doubt or any dread remain,
When sworn that oath which never can be vain ?'
  I answer'd : ' Goddess, humane is thy breast,
By justice sway'd, by tender pity prest :

Ill fits it me, whose friends are sunk to beasts,
To quaff thy bowls, or riot in thy feasts.
Me wouldst thou please? for them thy cares employ,
And them to me restore, and me to joy.'
  With that she parted: in her potent hand
She bore the virtue of the magic wand;
Then hast'ning to the sties, set wide the door,
Urg'd forth, and drove the bristly herd before.
Unwieldy out they rush'd, with gen'ral cry,
Enormous beasts! dishonest to the eye.
Now touch'd by counter-charms, they change again,
And stand majestic, and recall'd to men.

Those hairs of late that bristl'd ev'ry part,
Fall off—miraculous effect of art!
Till all the form in full proportion rise,
More young, more large, more graceful to my eyes.
They saw, they knew me, and with eager pace
Clung to their master in a long embrace:
Sad, pleasing sight! with tears each eye ran o'er,
And sobs of joy re-echo'd through the bow'r:
E'en Circe wept; her adamantine heart
Felt pity enter; and sustain'd her part."
Odyssey, book x.

No. 1029.

Circe restoring the companions of Ulysses to their original form.

ATHENION. *Cornelian.*

See preceding quotation.

No. 1030.

Ulysses soliciting Circe for permission to return home.

CHROMIOS. *Cornelian.*

" But when the shades came on at ev'ning hour,
And all lay slumb'ring in the dusky bow'r,
I came a suppliant to fair Circe's bed,
The tender moment seiz'd, and thus I said:
' Be mindful, goddess, of thy promise made;
Must sad Ulysses ever be delay'd?
Around their lords my sad companions mourn,
Each breast beats homeward, anxious to return:
If but a moment parted from thy eyes,
Their tears flow round me, and my heart complies.'
' Go, then!' she cried; ' ah, go! yet think, not I,
Not Circe, but the fates your wish deny.

Ah, hope not yet to breathe thy native air!
Far other journey first demands thy care;
To tread th' uncomfortable paths beneath,
And view the realms of darkness and of death.
There seek the Theban bard depriv'd of sight,
Within irradiate with prophetic light;
To whom Persephone entire and whole
Gave to retain th' unseparated soul:
The rest are forms of empty ether made,
Impassive semblance, and a flitting shade.' "*
Odyssey, book x.

* Ulysses had by Circe a son named Telegonus. Eustathius ingeniously observes, that the reason why Circe declares to Ulysses the necessity of consulting the great prophet Tiresias in the infernal regions, was, that as he would learn from him that his death was to come from the sea, he might be induced, on his return, to avoid the dangers of the voyage home, and remain with her.

No. 1031.

Circe pointing out to Ulysses one of his companions who chose to remain in his brutalised state.

DIOSCORIDES. *Cornelian.*

Although Homer does not say that any of the companions of Ulysses preferred to remain, yet this is the account given by some authors, to which Horace (ep. vi. b. 1) refers.

No. 1032.

Ulysses listening to the Sirens.

CHROMIOS. *Aquamarine.*

When Ulysses refused to remain any longer with Circe, she, among other instructions for his safe voyage, directed him how to avoid the Sirens. The Sirens were reported to be beautiful females, inhabiting a part of the rocky coast of Sicily, and possessing a superhuman and irresistible power of melody, by which they attracted mariners to their coast, and caused their destruction. Of the many explanations of this fable, the best attested and most simple is, that they were seductive and profligate women, in league with robbers and murderers, who were in the habit of luring sailors to their ruin. Ulysses avoided the danger by stuffing the ears of his crew with wax, and ordering that he himself should be bound to the mast, and his commands to land disobeyed.

" ' Next, where the Sirens dwell you plough the seas ;
Their song is death, and makes destruction please.
Unblest the man whom music wins to stay
Nigh the curs'd shore, and listen to the lay ;
No more that wretch shall view the joys of life,
His blooming offspring or his beauteous wife !
In verdant meads they sport, and wide around
Lie human bones, that whiten all the ground ;

The ground polluted floats with human gore,
And human carnage taints the dreadful shore.
Fly swift the dang'rous coast ; let ev'ry ear
Be stopp'd against the song : 'tis death to hear !
Firm to the mast with chains thyself be bound,
Nor trust thy virtue to th' enchanting sound.
If, mad with transport, freedom thou demand,
Be ev'ry fetter strain'd, and added band to band.' "

Ulysses addresses his crew—

" ' O friends ! oh, ever partners of my woes !
Attend while I what heav'n foredooms disclose ;
Hear all ! fate hangs o'er all ! on you it lies
To live or perish : to be safe be wise !
In flow'ry meads the sportive Sirens play,
Touch the soft lyre, and tune the vocal lay.

Me, me alone, with fetters firmly bound,
The gods allow to hear the dang'rous sound.
Hear, and obey : if freedom I demand,
Be ev'ry fetter strain'd, be added band to band.'
While yet I speak, the winged galley flies,
And, lo ! the Siren shores like mists arise.

4 o

Sunk were at once the winds; the air above,
And waves below, at once forgot to move:
Some demon calm'd the air, and smooth'd the
   deep—
Hush'd the loud winds, and charm'd the waves to
   sleep.
Now ev'ry sail we furl—each oar we ply;
Lash'd by the stroke the frothy waters fly.
The ductile wax with busy hands I mould,
And cleft in fragments; and the fragments roll'd:
Th' aerial region now grew warm with day,
The wax dissolv'd beneath the burning ray;
Then ev'ry ear I barr'd against the strain,
And from access of frenzy lock'd the brain.
Now round the mast my mates the fetters roll'd,
And bound me limb by limb, with fold on fold.
Then bending to the stroke, the active train
Plunge all at once their oars, and cleave the main.
  While to the shore the rapid vessel flies,
Our swift approach the Siren quire descries;

Celestial music warbles from their tongue,
And thus the sweet deluders tune the song:
  'O stay, O pride of Greece! Ulysses, stay!
O cease thy course, and listen to our lay!
Blest is the man ordain'd our voice to hear;
The song instructs the soul, and charms the ear.
Approach! thy soul shall into raptures rise!
Approach! and learn new wisdom from the wise!
We know whate'er the kings of mighty name
Achiev'd at Ilion in the field of fame—
Whate'er beneath the sun's bright journey lies.
O stay, and learn new wisdom from the wise!'
  Thus the sweet charmers warbled o'er the main;
My soul takes wing to meet the heav'nly strain;
I give the sign, and struggle to be free:
Swift row my mates, and shoot along the sea;
New chains they add, and rapid urge the way,
Till, dying off, the distant sounds decay:
Then scudding swiftly from the dang'rous ground,
The deafen'd ear unlock'd, the chains unbound."
                      Odyssey, book xii.

No. 1033.

Lampetia announcing to her father Apollo the slaughter of his sacred oxen.

PYRGOTELES. *Cornelian.*

   Circe warned Ulysses to avoid, on his arrival in Sicily, killing any of a herd of oxen which were consecrated to Apollo; but while Ulysses slept, his companions, impelled by hunger, killed some of them. The consequence was, that after their departure they were shipwrecked, and all perished, except Ulysses, who floated, on the mast tied to the helm, to the island of Calypso, who, at the suggestion of Mercury, afforded him a hospitable reception.

"Meantime Lampetia mounts th' aërial way,
And kindles into rage the god of day.
'Vengeance, ye pow'rs!' he cries; 'and thou
  whose hand
Aims the red bolt, and hurls the writhen brand!
Slain are those herds which I with pride survey,
When through the ports of heav'n I pour the day,
Or deep in ocean plunge the burning ray:
Vengeance, ye gods! or I the skies forego,
And bear the lamp of heav'n to shades below!'

To whom the thund'ring pow'r: 'O source of
  day!
Whose radiant lamp adorns the azure way,
Still may thy beams through heav'n's bright por-
  tals rise,
The joy of earth and glory of the skies:
Lo! my red arm I bare, my thunders guide,
To dash th' offenders in the whelming tide!'"
                    Odyssey, book xii.

No. 1034.

Calypso saving the shipwrecked Ulysses.

CHROMIOS. *Amethyst.*

The following account of the shipwreck and escape of Ulysses is cited by the critics as an evidence that the *Odyssey* occasionally displays much of the boldness, vigour, and fire of the *Iliad.*

" Past sight of shore, along the surge we bound;
And all above is sky, and ocean all around:
When, lo! a murky cloud the thund'rer forms
Full o'er our heads, and blackens heav'n with
    storms.
Night dwells o'er all the deep : and now out flies
The gloomy west, and whistles in the skies.
The mountain billows roar! the furious blast
Howls o'er the shroud, and rends it from the mast :
The mast gives way, and, crackling as it bends,
Tears up the deck ; then all at once descends :
The pilot, by the tumbling ruin slain,
Dash'd from the helm, falls headlong to the main.
Then Jove in anger bids the thunders roll,
And forky lightnings flash from pole to pole ;
Fierce at our heads his deadly bolt he aims,
Red with uncommon wrath, and wrapt in flames :
Full on the bark it fell ; now high, now low,
Toss'd and retoss'd, it reel'd beneath the blow ;
At once into the main the crew it shook,
Sulphureous odours rose, and smould'ring smoke.
Like fowl that haunt the floods, they sink—they
    rise,
Now lost—now seen, with shrieks and dreadful
    cries,
And strive to gain the bark ; but Jove denies.
Firm at the helm I stand, when fierce the main
Rush'd with dire noise, and dash'd the sides in
    twain ;
Again impetuous drove the furious blast—
Snapt the strong helm, and bore to sea the mast.
Firm to the mast with cords the helm I bind,
And ride aloft, to providence resign'd,
Through tumbling billows and a war of wind.

Now sunk the west, and now a southern breeze,
More dreadful than the tempest, lash'd the seas ;
For on the rocks it bore where Scylla raves,
And dire Charybdis rolls her thund'ring waves.
All night I drove ; and at the dawn of day,
Fast by the rocks beheld the desp'rate way :
Just when the sea within her gulfs subsides,
And in the roaring whirlpools rush the tides.
Swift from the float I vaulted with a bound,
The lofty fig-tree seiz'd, and clung around :
So to the beam the bat tenacious clings,
And pendant round it clasps his leathern wings.
High in the air the tree its boughs display'd,
And o'er the dungeon cast the dreadful shade ;
All unsustain'd between the waves and sky,
Beneath my feet the whirling billows fly.
What time the judge forsakes the noisy bar
To take repast, and stills the wordy war ;
Charybdis, rumbling from her inmost caves,
The mast refunded on her refluent waves.
Swift from the tree, the floating mast to gain,
Sudden I dropp'd amidst the flashing main ;
Once more undaunted on the ruin rode,
And oar'd with lab'ring arms along the flood.
Unseen I pass'd by Scylla's dire abodes ;
So Jove decreed (dread sire of men and gods) :
Then nine long days I plough'd the calmer
    seas,
Heav'd by the surge and wafted by the breeze.
Weary and wet th' Ogygian shores I gain,
When the tenth sun descended to the main.*
There, in Calypso's ever-fragrant bow'rs
Refresh'd I lay, and joy beguil'd the hours."
             Odyssey, book xii.

* Ulysses continued in the tree, and the mast remained in the whirlpool, from dawn till noon,

When Mercury (book v.) delivered to Calypso the command of Jupiter to allow Ulysses to depart, she says:—

> " A man, an outcast to the storm and wave,
>   It was my crime to pity, and to save;
>   When he who thunders rent his bark in twain,
>   And sunk his brave companions in the main.
>   Alone—abandon'd—in mid-ocean tost—
>   The sport of winds, and driv'n from ev'ry coast,
>   Hither this man of miseries I led—
>   Receiv'd the friendless, and the hungry fed."

No. 1035.

The Phæacian sailors laying Ulysses asleep under the shelter of a tree.

Nisos. *Cornelian.*

Ulysses, after remaining a few days at the court of Alcinous, was sent to Ithaca by that monarch. Having fallen asleep on board, he was conveyed on shore, and laid under a tree. M. Dacier says: " It was necessary for Ulysses to land alone, in order to his concealment. If he had been discovered, the suitors would have destroyed him—if not as the real Ulysses, at least under the pretext of his being an impostor: they would then have seized on Penelope and his dominions. Even if he had been awake, the Phæacians could not have afforded him sufficient assistance." Ulysses only required to be landed on the coast. This the Phæacians did; and, to avoid discovery, they made the voyage to the island at night, and sailed off again without delay.

> " Thus with spread sails the winged galley flies;
> Less swift an eagle cuts the liquid skies:
> Divine Ulysses was her sacred load,
> A man—in wisdom equal to a god !
> Much danger, long and mighty toils he bore,
> In storms by sea, and combats on the shore;
> All which soft sleep now banish'd from his breast,
> Wrapp'd in a pleasing, deep, and death-like rest.
>
> But when the morning-star, with early ray,
> Flam'd in the front of heav'n, and promis'd day,
> Like distant clouds the mariner descries
> Fair Ithaca's emerging hills arise.
> Far from the town a spacious port appears,
> Sacred to Phorcy's pow'r, whose name it bears:
> Two craggy rocks, projecting to the main,
> The roaring winds' tempestuous rage restrain ;

the time when judges retire to dinner. Before the use of dials or clocks, the ancients distinguished the periods of the day by some remarkable offices or stated occupations. We must here suppose, that as Ulysses was not doomed to perish, he was enabled, by divine assistance, to cling for ten days to the mast without sustenance.

Within, the waves in softer murmurs glide,
And ships secure without their halsers ride.
High at the head a branching olive grows,
And crowns the pointed cliffs with shady boughs.
Beneath, a gloomy grotto's cool recess
Delights the Nereids of the neighb'ring seas;
Where bowls and urns were form'd of living
   stone,
And massy beams in native marble shone;
On which the labours of the nymphs were roll'd,
Their webs divine of purple mix'd with gold.
Within the cave the clust'ring bees attend
Their waxen works, or from the roof depend:

Perpetual waters o'er the pavement glide;
Two marble doors unfold on either side:
Sacred the south, by which the gods descend,
But mortals enter at the northern end.
Thither they bent, and haul'd their ship to land
(The crooked keel divides the yellow sand):
Ulysses sleeping on his couch they bore,
And gently plac'd him on the rocky shore.
His treasures next, Alcinous' gifts, they laid
In the wild olive's unfrequented shade,
Secure from theft: then launch'd the bark again,
Resum'd their oars, and measur'd back the main."
Odyssey, book xiii.

No. 1036.

Ulysses shewing his goods to Minerva who is disguised as a shepherd.

APOLLONIDES. *Cornelian.*

When Ulysses awoke, there was such a mist around him, caused by Minerva to secure his concealment, that he was unable to distinguish the features of the country, or know where he was.

"Then on the sands he rang'd his wealthy
   store—
The gold, the vests, the tripods number'd
   o'er:
All these he found, but still, in error lost,
Disconsolate he wanders on the coast—
Sighs for his country, and laments again
To the deaf rocks, and hoarse resounding main.
When, lo! the guardian-goddess of the wise,
Celestial Pallas, stood before his eyes;
In show a youthful swain of form divine,
Who seem'd descended from some princely
   line.

A graceful robe her slender body dress'd;
Around her shoulders flew the waving vest;
Her decent hand a shining jav'lin bore;
And painted sandals on her feet she wore.
To whom the king: ' Whoe'er of human race
Thou art, that wander'st in this desert place,
With joy to thee, as to some god, I bend—
To thee my treasures and myself commend.
O tell a wretch, in exile doom'd to stray,
What air I breathe, what country I survey?
The fruitful continent's extremest bound,
Or some fair isle which Neptune's arms sur-
   round?'"
. *Odyssey*, book xiii.

The shepherd informs him that he is in Ithaca. Ulysses then tells the shepherd that he is a stranger from Crete—

" But tempests tost,
And raging billows drove us on your coast.
In dead of night an unknown port we gain'd,
Spent with fatigue, and slept secure on land.

But ere the rosy morn renew'd the day,
While in th' embrace of pleasing sleep I lay,
Sudden, invited by auspicious gales,
They land my goods, and hoist their flying sails.
Abandon'd here, my fortune I deplore,
A hapless exile on a foreign shore."

Odyssey, book xiii.

No. 1037.

Ulysses and Minerva concealing the goods of Ulysses.

CHROMIOS.   *Cornelian.*

" Thus while he spoke, the blue-eyed maid
     began
With pleasing smiles to view the god-like man:
Then chang'd her form ; and now, divinely
     bright,
Jove's heav'nly daughter stood confess'd to sight ;
Like a fair virgin in her beauty's bloom,
Skill'd in th' illustrious labours of the loom.
    ' O still the same Ulysses !' she rejoin'd,
' In useful craft successfully refin'd ;
Artful in speech, in action, and in mind !
Suffic'd it not, that, thy long labours past,
Secure thou seest thy native shore at last ?

But this to me ? who, like thyself, excel
In arts of counsel, and dissembling well—
To me, whose wit exceeds the pow'rs divine :
No less than mortals are surpass'd by thine.
Know'st thou not me? who made thy life my care,
Through ten years' wand'ring, and through ten
     years' war—
Who taught thee arts, Alcinous to persuade—
To raise his wonder, and engage his aid ;
And now appear thy treasures to protect—
Conceal thy person—thy designs direct,
And tell what more thou must from fate ex-
     pect.'"

Odyssey, book xiii.

The mist is dispelled, and Ulysses expresses joyful gratitude.

" Then thus Minerva : ' From that anxious breast
     Dismiss those cares, and leave to heav'n the rest.
     Our task be now thy treasur'd stores to save,
     Deep in the close recesses of the cave :
     Then future means consult.' She spoke, and trod
     The shady grot, that brighten'd with the god.
     The closest caverns of the grot she sought ;
     The gold, the brass, the robes Ulysses brought,
     These in the secret gloom the chief dispos'd :
     The entrance with a rock the goddess clos'd."

Odyssey, book xiii.

No. 1038.

Same subject.

Dioscorides. *Cornelian.*

No. 1039.

Minerva transforming Ulysses into the appearance of an old man.

Apollonides. *Cornelian.*

Minerva apprises Ulysses of the wretched state of Penelope and his affairs, and of the departure of Telemachus to the court of Menelaus; and tells him it is necessary for his purpose that he assume the appearance of a ragged old man, and first go to the cottage of his faithful servant Eumæus.

"Now seated in the olive's sacred shade,
Confer the hero and the martial maid :
The goddess of the azure eyes began.

.   .   .   .   .

She spake: then touch'd him with her pow'rful
  wand—
The skin shrunk up, and wither'd at her hand :
A swift old age o'er all his members spread ;
A sudden frost was sprinkled on his head ;
Nor longer in the heavy eye-ball shin'd
The glance divine, forth-beaming from the mind.

His robe, which spots indelible besmear,
In rags dishonest flutters with the air :
A stag's torn hide is lapt around his reins ;
A rugged staff his trembling hand sustains ;
And at his side a wretched scrip was hung,
Wide patch'd, and knotted to a twisted thong.
So look'd the chief—so mov'd ! to mortal eyes
Object uncouth ! a man of miseries !
While Pallas, cleaving the wide fields of air,
To Sparta flies—Telemachus her care."
Odyssey, book xiii.

No. 1040.

Ulysses attacked by the dogs of Eumæus.

Gnaios. *Calcedony.*

Eumæus entertains Ulysses, who retains his disguise, and represents himself as a Cretan who had gone through many adventures.

"But he, deep-musing, o'er the mountains stray'd,
Through mazy thickets of the woodland shade,
And cavern'd ways, the shaggy coast along,
With cliffs and nodding forests overhung.
Eumæus at his sylvan lodge he sought,
A faithful servant, and without a fault.

Ulysses found him, busied as he sate
Before the threshold of his rustic gate.
Around the mansion in a circle shone
A rural portico of rugged stone
(In absence of his lord, with honest toil
His own industrious hands had rais'd the pile):

The wall was stone, from neighb'ring quarries
   borne,
Encircled with a fence of native thorn,
And strong with pales, by many a weary stroke
Of stubborn labour hewn from heart of oak—
Frequent and thick. Within the space were
   rear'd
Twelve ample cells, the lodgment of his herd.
Full fifty pregnant females each contain'd;
The males without (a smaller race) remain'd;
Doom'd to supply the suitors' wasteful feast—
A stock by daily luxury decreas'd;
Now scarce four hundred left. These to defend,
Four savage dogs, a watchful guard, attend.
Here sat Eumæus, and his cares applied
To form strong buskins of well-season'd hide.
Of four assistants who his labour share,
Three now were absent on the rural care;

The fourth drove victims to the suitor-train.
But he, of ancient faith, a simple swain,
Sigh'd while he furnish'd the luxurious board,
And wearied heav'n with wishes for his lord.
  Soon as Ulysses near th' enclosure drew,
With open mouths the furious mastiffs flew :
Down sat the sage ; and, cautious to withstand,
Let fall th' offensive truncheon from his hand.*
Sudden the master runs ; aloud he calls ;
And from his hasty hand the leather falls ;
With show'rs of stones he drives them far away ;
The scatt'ring dogs around at distance bay.
  ' Unhappy stranger ! (thus the faithful swain
Began, with accent gracious and humane)
What sorrow had been mine, if at my gate
Thy rev'rend age had met a shameful fate !
Enough of woes already have I known ;
Enough my master's sorrows and my own.'"

                       Odyssey, book xiv.

No. 1041.

Minerva warning Telemachus to return to Ithaca.

APOLLONIDES. `Sardonyx.`

" Now had Minerva reach'd those ample plains,
Fam'd for the dance, where Menelaus reigns ;
Anxious she flies to great Ulysses' heir—
His instant voyage challeng'd all her care.
Beneath the royal portico display'd,
With Nestor's son, Telemachus was laid.
In sleep profound the son of Nestor lies ;
Not thine, Ulysses ! care unseal'd his eyes :
Restless he griev'd, with various fears oppress'd,
And all thy fortunes roll'd within his breast.
When, ' O Telemachus !' the goddess said,
' Too long in vain, too widely hast thou stray'd ;
Thus leaving careless thy paternal right
The robber's prize, the prey to lawless might.
On fond pursuits neglectful while you roam,
E'en now the hand of rapine sacks the dome.

Hence to Atrides, and his leave implore
To launch thy vessel for thy natal shore :
Fly, whilst thy mother virtuous yet withstands
Her kindred's wishes and her sire's commands ;
Through both, Eurymachus pursues the dame,
And with the noblest gifts asserts his claim.
Hence therefore, while thy stores thy own remain ;
Thou know'st the practice of their female train :
Lost in the children of the present spouse,
They slight the pledges of the former vows ;
Their love is always with the lover past ;
Still the succeeding flame expels the last.
Let o'er thy house some chosen maid preside,
Till heav'n decrees to bless thee in a bride.
But now thy more attentive ears incline,
Observe the warnings of a power divine :

---

* It is, says Eustathius, a natural defence to avert the fury of a dog, to cast away our weapons,
to shew that we intend to offer him no violence. Pliny has a similar remark in the eighth book of
his Natural History.

For thee their snares the suitor-lords shall lay
In Samos' sands, or straits of Ithaca;
To seize thy life shall lurk the murd'rous band,
Ere yet thy footsteps press thy native land.
No!—sooner far their riot and their lust
All-cov'ring earth shall bury deep in dust!
Then distant from the scatter'd islands steer,
Nor let the night retard thy full career;
Thy heav'nly guardian shall instruct the gales
To smooth thy passage, and supply thy sails:
And when at Ithaca thy labour ends,
Send to the town thy vessel with thy friends;

But seek thou first the master of the swine
(For still to thee his loyal thoughts incline):
There pass the night; while he his course pursues,
To bring Penelope the wished-for news,
That thou, safe sailing from the Pylian strand,
Art come to bless her in thy native land.'
  Thus spoke the goddess, and resum'd her flight
To the pure regions of eternal light.
Meanwhile Pisistratus he gently shakes,
And with these words the slumb'ring youth awakes:
' Rise, son of Nestor! for the road prepare,
And join the harness'd coursers to the car.' "

Odyssey, book xv.

No. 1042.

Theoclymenus, the augur, interpreting the omen of the hawk and dove to Telemachus.

CHROMIOS. *Sardonyx.*

Theoclymenus was an augur, who fled from Argos to Pylos in consequence of an accidental homicide. Having arrived when Telemachus was about to sail, and having ascertained who he was, he implored him to receive him on board: with this request Telemachus complied. When they arrived in Ithaca, Telemachus directs him to proceed to the palace, while he himself proposes to visit Eumæus. It was then they witnessed this omen.

"Thus speaking, on the right up-soar'd in air
The hawk, Apollo's swift-wing'd messenger:
His deathful pounces tore a trembling dove;
The clotted feathers, scatter'd from above,
Between the hero and the vessel pour
Thick plumage, mingled with a sanguine show'r.
  Th' observing augur took the prince aside,
Seiz'd by the hand, and thus prophetic cried:

' Yon bird, that dexter cuts th' aërial road,
Rose ominous, nor flies without a god:
No race but thine shall Ithaca obey—
To thine, for ages, heav'n decrees the sway.'
' Succeed the omen, gods!' the youth rejoin'd;
' Soon shall my bounties speak a grateful mind,
And soon each envied happiness attend
The man who calls Telemachus his friend.' "

Odyssey, book xv.

No. 1043.

Ulysses restored by Minerva to his original appearance and vigour.

PHILEMON. *Cornelian.*

Telemachus having arrived at the cottage of Eumæus, enters into a long conversation with the mendicant stranger, whose condition he pities; and despatches Eumæus to announce his safe arrival to Penelope. Meantime Ulysses, who had previously urged Telemachus to take vengeance on the suitors, is restored to his original appearance by Minerva, and makes himself known to Telemachus.

4 P

"Then from the heav'ns the martial goddess
    flies
Through the wide fields of air, and cleaves the
    skies ;
In form a virgin in soft beauty's bloom,
Skill'd in th' illustrious labours of the loom.
Alone to Ithacus she stood display'd,
But unapparent as a viewless shade
Escap'd Telemachus (the pow'rs above,
Seen or unseen, o'er earth at pleasure move).
The dogs intelligent confess'd the tread
Of pow'r divine, and, howling, trembling fled.*
The goddess beck'ning waves her deathless hands;
Dauntless the king before the goddess stands.
' Then why,' she said, ' O favour'd of the skies !
Why to thy godlike son this long disguise ?
Stand forth reveal'd : with him thy cares em-
    ploy
Against thy foes : be valiant, and destroy !
Lo, I descend in that avenging hour,
To combat by thy side—thy guardian pow'r !'
    She said, and o'er him waves her wand of gold :
Imperial robes his manly limbs enfold ;
At once with grace divine his frame improves ;
At once with majesty enlarg'd he moves :
Youth flush'd his redd'ning cheek, and from his
    brows
A length of hair in sable ringlets flows ;
The black'ning chin receives a deeper shade :
Then from his eyes up-sprung the warrior-maid.
    The hero re-ascends : the prince, o'eraw'd,
Scarce lifts his eyes, and bows as to a god.

Then with surprise (surprise chastis'd by fears),
' How art thou chang'd !' he cried ; ' a god
    appears !
Far other vests thy limbs majestic grace !
Far other glories lighten from thy face !
If heav'n be thy abode, with pious care,
Lo ! I the ready sacrifice prepare ;
Lo ! gifts of labour'd gold adorn thy shrine,
To win thy grace : O save us, pow'r divine !'
    ' Few are my days,' Ulysses made reply ;
' Nor I, alas ! descendant of the sky.
I am thy father ! O my son ! my son !—
That father for whose sake thy days have run
One scene of woe ; to endless cares consign'd,
And outrag'd by the wrongs of base mankind.'
Then, rushing to his arms, he kiss'd his boy,
With the strong raptures of a parent's joy.
Tears bathe his cheek, and tears the ground bedew :
He strain'd him close as to his breast he grew.
' Ah me !' exclaims the prince, with fond desire,
' Thou art not—no—thou canst not be my sire !
Heav'n such illusion only can impose,
By the false joy to aggravate my woes.
Who but a god can change the gen'ral doom,
And give to wither'd age a youthful bloom ?
Late, worn with years, in weeds obscene you trod ;
Now, cloth'd in majesty, you move a god !'
    ' Forbear !' he cried ; ' for heav'n reserve that
    name—
Give to thy father but a father's claim :
Other Ulysses shalt thou never see ;
I am Ulysses ; I, my son, am he !' "

Odyssey, book xvi.

No. 1044.

Ulysses and his dog Argus.

CHROMIOS.   *Sardonyx.*

* This was an ancient belief, that the brute creation were sensible of the appearance of a super-
natural spirit, when it was often invisible to mortals. It was the design of the goddess to be invisible
to Telemachus only.

Measures having been concerted privately between the father and son for the destruction of the suitors, Telemachus proceeds to the palace, and is soon followed by Ulysses in the guise of a ragged mendicant, accompanied by Eumæus, who is still ignorant of the identity of Ulysses.

" Thus near the gates, conferring, as they drew,
Argus, the dog, his ancient master knew;
He, not unconscious of the voice and tread,
Lifts to the sound his ear, and rears his head.
Bred by Ulysses, nourish'd at his board,
But ah! not fated long to please his lord!
To him his swiftness and his strength were vain;
The voice of glory call'd him o'er the main.
Till then, in ev'ry sylvan chase renown'd,
With ' Argus! Argus!' rung the woods around:
With him the youth pursu'd the goat or fawn,
Or trac'd the mazy lev'ret o'er the lawn.
Now left to man's ingratitude, he lay
Unhous'd—neglected, in the public way!
And where on heaps the rich manure was spread,
Obscene with reptiles took his sordid bed!
    He knew his lord—he knew, and strove to meet—
In vain he strove to crawl, and kiss his feet!
Yet (all he could) his tail—his ears—his eyes
Salute his master, and confess his joys!
Soft pity touch'd the mighty master's soul;
Adown his cheek a tear unbidden stole—
Stole unperceiv'd: he turn'd his head, and dried
The drop humane; then thus impassion'd cried:
' What noble beast, in this abandon'd state,
Lies here all helpless at Ulysses' gate?
His bulk and beauty speak no vulgar praise;
If, as he seems, he was in better days,

Some care his age deserves: or was he priz'd
For worthless beauty? therefore now despis'd?
Such dogs and men there are, mere things of state,
And always cherish'd by their friends the great.'
    ' Not Argus so,' Eumæus thus rejoin'd,
' But serv'd a master of a nobler kind,
Who never—never shall behold him more!
Long—long since perish'd on a distant shore!
O had you seen him, vig'rous, bold, and young,
Swift as a stag, and as a lion strong:
Him no fell savage on the plain withstood,
None 'scap'd him, bosom'd in the gloomy wood;
His eye how piercing! and his scent how true,
To wind the vapour in the tainted dew!
Such, when Ulysses left his natal coast;
Now years unnerve him, and his lord is lost.
The women keep the gen'rous creature bare—
A sleek and idle race is all their care:
The master gone, the servants what restrains?
Or dwells humanity where riot reigns?
Jove fix'd it certain, that whatever day
Makes man a slave, takes half his worth away.'
    This said, the honest herdsman strode before:
The musing monarch pauses at the door.
The dog, whom fate had granted to behold
His lord, when twenty tedious years had roll'd,
Takes a last look, and having seen him—dies!
So clos'd for ever faithful Argus' eyes!"

Odyssey, book xvii.

No. 1045.

Ulysses overthrowing the sturdy mendicant Irus.

APOLLONIDES.   *Cornelian.*

When Ulysses arrived at the palace, Telemachus ordered Eumæus to give him some food. Ulysses then went round to solicit the assembled guests for charity, giving a fictitious account of his many sufferings and adventures.

"With speaking eyes, and voice of plaintive sound,
Humble he moves, imploring all around.
The proud feel pity, and relief bestow,
With such an image touch'd of human woe;
Inquiring all, their wonder they confess,
And eye the man, majestic in distress!"

But Antinous, provoked by a remark of his, hurled a tripod at him.

"His shoulder-blade receiv'd th' ungentle shock;
He stood, and mov'd not, like a marble rock;
But shook his thoughtful head, nor more complain'd;
Sedate of soul, his character sustain'd,
And inly form'd revenge: then back withdrew;
Before his feet the well-fill'd scrip he threw,
And thus, with semblance mild, address'd the crew."

Odyssey, book xvii.

Penelope having heard that the poor wanderer had lately met Ulysses, makes an appointment to question him, after the retirement of the guests. Meantime Irus, a sturdy beggar, attempts to expel him as an intruder.

"While fix'd in thought the pensive hero sate,
A mendicant approach'd the royal gate;
A surly vagrant of the giant kind—
The stain of manhood, of a coward mind!
From feast to feast, insatiate to devour,
He flew, attendant on the genial hour.
When on his mother's knees a babe he lay,
She nam'd Arnæus on his natal day;
But Irus his associates call'd the boy,
Practis'd the common messenger to fly—
Irus, a name expressive of th' employ.
From his own roof, with meditated blows,
He strove to drive the man of mighty woes.
  'Hence, dotard!—hence! and timely speed
      thy way,
Lest, dragg'd in vengeance, thou repent thy
      stay!
See how with nods assent yon princely train!
But, honouring age, in mercy I refrain:
In peace away! lest if persuasions fail,
This arm with blows more eloquent prevail.'

To whom with stern regards: 'O insolence,
Indecently to rail without offence!
What bounty gives, without a rival share;
I ask—what harms not thee—to breathe this air:
Alike on alms we both precarious live;
And canst thou envy when the great relieve?
Know from the bounteous heav'ns all riches flow,
And what man gives, the gods by man bestow.
Proud as thou art, henceforth no more be proud,
Lest I imprint my vengeance in thy blood;
Old as I am, should once my fury burn,
How wouldst thou fly, nor even in thought re-
      turn!'
  'Mere woman-glutton!' thus the churl replied,
'A tongue so flippant, with a throat so wide!
Why cease I, gods! to dash those teeth away,
Like some vile boar's, that, greedy of his prey,
Uproots the bearded corn? Rise—try the fight—
Gird well thy loins—approach, and feel my might!
Sure of defeat, before the peers engage;
Unequal fight! when youth contends with age.'"

The guests are delighted at the pleasant prospect of the battle; but Telemachus exacts a pledge from them that they will allow it to be a fair fight.

" Now front to front each frowning champion stands,
And poises high in air his adverse hands.
The chief yet doubts, or to the shades below
To fell the giant at one vengeful blow,
Or save his life ; and soon his life to save
The king resolves, for mercy sways the brave.
That instant Irus his huge arms extends,
Full on his shoulder the rude weight descends :
The sage Ulysses, fearful to disclose
The hero latent in the man of woes,
Check'd half his might ; yet rising to the stroke,
His jawbone dash'd ; the crashing jawbone broke :
Down dropp'd he stupid from the stunning wound—
His feet extended quiv'ring beat the ground—
His mouth and nostrils spout a purple flood—
His teeth all shatter'd rush immix'd with blood.
The peers transported, as outstretch'd he lies,
With bursts of laughter rend the vaulted skies.

Then dragg'd along, all bleeding from the wound,
His length of carcass trailing prints the ground ;
Rais'd on his feet, again he reels, he falls,
Till propp'd reclining on the palace-walls :
Then to his hand a staff the victor gave,
And thus with just reproach address'd the slave :
' There ! terrible, affright the dogs, and reign
A dreaded tyrant o'er the bestial train !
But mercy to the poor and stranger shew,
Lest heav'n in vengeance send some mightier woe.'
    Scornful he spoke, and o'er his shoulder flung
The broad-patch'd scrip ; the scrip in tatters hung
Ill join'd, and knotted to a twisted thong.
Then turning short, disdain'd a further stay,
But to the palace measur'd back the way.
There as he rested, gath'ring in a ring,
The peers with smiles address'd their unknown king."

Odyssey, book xviii.

No. 1046.

Minerva pouring on Penelope a cosmetic, which gives her additional beauty.

APOLLONIDES. *Sardonyx.*

Penelope, indignant that outrage should have been offered to a poor stranger within her palace, sends word that she means to appear before the guests.

" Then while Eurynome the mandate bears,
From heav'n Minerva shoots with guardian cares :
O'er all her senses, as the couch she press'd,
She pours a pleasing, deep, and death-like rest—
With ev'ry beauty ev'ry feature arms—
Bids her cheeks glow, and lights up all her charms—
In her love-darting eyes awakes the fires—
(Immortal gifts ! to kindle soft desires)
From limb to limb an air majestic sheds—
And the pure iv'ry o'er her bosom spreads.

Such Venus shines, when with a measur'd bound
She smoothly gliding swims th' harmonious round,
When with the Graces in the dance she moves,
And fires the gazing gods with ardent loves.
    Then to the skies her flight Minerva bends,
And to the queen the damsel-train descends :
Wak'd at their steps, her flowing eyes unclose ;
The tear she wipes, and thus renews her woes."

Odyssey, book xviii.

No. 1047.

The suitors giving presents to Penelope.

DIOSCORIDES. *Cornelian.*

Penelope having appeared before the suitors, is urged by them in flattering speeches to make her election. She dwells on her love for Ulysses, yet holds out to them some faint hopes; but delays her decision—of all which Ulysses is a witness. The suitors then make her presents.

"The peers despatch their heralds to convey
The gifts of love; with speed they take the way.
A robe Antinous gives of shining dyes;
The varying hues in gay confusion rise,
Rich from the artist's hand! twelve clasps of gold
Close to the less'ning waist the vest infold:
Down from the swelling loins the vest unbound
Floats in bright waves, redundant o'er the ground.

A bracelet rich with gold, with amber gay,
That shot effulgence like the solar ray,
Eurymachus presents; and ear-rings bright,
With triple stars, that cast a trembling light.
Pisander bears a necklace, wrought with art
And ev'ry peer, expressive of his heart,
A gift bestows: this done, the queen ascends,
And, slow behind, her damsel-train attends."

Odyssey, book xviii.

No. 1048.

Ulysses and Melantho.

GNAIOS. *Cornelian.*

"Then to the dance they form the vocal strain,
Till Hesperus leads forth the starry train;
And now he raises, as the day-light fades,
His golden circlet in the deep'ning shades:
Three vases heap'd with copious fires display
O'er all the palace a fictitious day;
From space to space the torch wide-beaming burns,
And sprightly damsels trim the rays by turns.
  To whom the king: 'Ill suits your sex to stay
Alone with men: ye modest maids, away!
Go, with the queen the spindle guide, or cull
(The partners of her cares) the silver wool;
Be it my task the torches to supply,
E'en till the morning lamp adorns the sky—
E'en till the morning, with unwearied care,
Sleepless I watch; for I have learn'd to bear.'

Scornful they heard : Melantho, fair and young
(Melantho, from the loins of Dolius sprung,
Who with the queen her years an infant led,
With the soft fondness of a daughter bred),
Chiefly derides : regardless of the cares
Her queen endures, polluted joys she shares
Nocturnal with Eurymachus : with eyes
That speak disdain, the wanton thus replies:
  ' Oh ! whither wanders thy distemper'd brain,
Thou bold intruder on a princely train?
Hence to the vagrant's rendezvous repair,
Or shun in some black forge the midnight air.
Proceeds this boldness from a turn of soul,
Or flows licentious from the copious bowl?
Is it that vanquish'd Irus swells thy mind?
A foe may meet thee of a braver kind,
Who, short'ning with a storm of blows thy stay,
Shall send thee howling all in blood away.'

To whom with frowns : ' O impudent in wrong !
Thy lord shall curb that insolence of tongue ;
Know, to Telemachus I tell th' offence :
The scourge—the scourge shall lash thee into sense.'

With conscious shame they hear the stern re-
buke,
Nor longer durst sustain the sov'reign look."
Odyssey, book xviii.

No. 1049.

Ulysses and Telemachus carrying away the arms, while Minerva holds a torch to them.*

CHROMIOS. *Sardonyx.*

After the suitors retired, Ulysses advised Telemachus to have his arms, which had remained hung up in the banqueting-hall, removed; and as most of the female attendants were in the interest of the suitors, Euryclea, the faithful nurse, was directed to lock them up in their chambers.

"Consulting secret with the blue-ey'd maid,
Still in the dome divine Ulysses stay'd :
Revenge mature for act inflam'd his breast ;
And thus the son the fervent sire address'd :
'Instant convey those steely stores of war
To distant rooms, dispos'd with secret care :
The cause demanded by the suitor-train,
To soothe their fears a specious reason feign.
Say, since Ulysses left his natal coast,
Obscene with smoke, their beamy lustre lost,
His arms deform'd the roof they wont adorn :
From the glad walls inglorious lumber torn.
Suggest that Jove the peaceful thought in-
spir'd,
Lest they by sight of swords to fury fir'd,
Dishonest wounds, or violence of soul,
Defame the bridal feast and friendly bowl.

. . . . . .

Auxiliar to his son, Ulysses bears
The plumy-crested helms and pointed spears,
With shields indented deep in glorious wars.

Minerva viewless on her charge attends,
And with her golden lamp his toil befriends :
Not such the sickly beams which, insincere,
Gild the gross vapour of this nether sphere !
A present deity the prince confess'd,
And wrapt with ecstacy the sire address'd :
' What miracle thus dazzles with surprise ?
Distinct in rows the radiant columns rise :
The walls, where'er my wond'ring sight I turn,
And roofs, amidst a blaze of glory burn !
Some visitant of pure ethereal race,
With his bright presence deigns the dome to grace.'
' Be calm,' replies the sire ; ' to none impart,
But oft revolve the vision in thy heart :
Celestials, mantled in excess of light,
Can visit unapproach'd by mortal sight.
Seek thou repose ; whilst here I sole remain,
T' explore the conduct of the female train :
The pensive queen perchance desires to know
The series of my toils to soothe her woe.' "
Odyssey, book xix.

* Callimachus, the Athenian statuary, worked a figure of Minerva according to this picture in Homer.

No. 1050.

Euryclea, the nurse, recognising Ulysses by the scar on his knee.

DIOSCORIDES. *Cornelian.*

The stranger, having been invited to an interview with Penelope, gives her the consolatory assurance that her husband, whom he had lately met, is safe in Phæacia, and will soon return loaded with riches. She orders refreshment and a bath for him. But, apprehensive that if any of the young female domestics, who were in the interest of the suitors, were (according to the custom of those times) to attend him, she may discover the scar of a wound which had been inflicted in his youth by a boar, and mention it, and thus lead to his premature discovery, he artfully contrives that the office should be assigned to Euryclea, who, from age and infirmity may not notice it—from indifference may not mention it, or if she noticed it, and by it recognised him, would, from her tried fidelity, keep it a secret. The whole of this affecting incident it is necessary here to give.

" 'The delicacy of your courtly train
To wash a wretched wand'rer would disdain ;
But if, in tract of long experience tried,
And sad similitude of woes allied,
Some wretch reluctant views aërial light,
To her mean hand assign the friendly rite.'
    Pleas'd with his wise reply, the queen re-
join'd :
' Such gentle manners and so sage a mind
In all who grac'd this hospitable bow'r
I ne'er discern'd before this social hour.
Such servant as your humble choice requires,
To light receiv'd the lord of my desires
New from the birth ; and with a mother's hand
His tender bloom to manly growth sustain'd :
Of matchless prudence and a duteous mind ;
Though now to life's extremest verge declin'd,
Of strength superior to the toil assign'd.—
Rise, Euryclea ! with officious care
For the poor friend the cleansing bath prepare :
This debt his correspondent fortunes claim,
Too like Ulysses, and perhaps the same !
Thus old with woes my fancy paints him now !
For age untimely marks the careful brow.'
    Instant obsequious to the mild command,
Sad Euryclea rose : with trembling hand

She veils the torrent of her tearful eyes ;
And thus impassion'd to herself replies :
    ' Son of my love, and monarch of my cares !
What pangs for thee this wretched bosom bears !
Are thus by Jove, who constant beg his aid
With pious deed and pure devotion, paid ?
He never dar'd defraud the sacred fane
Of perfect hecatombs in order slain :
There oft implor'd his tutelary power,
Long to protract the sad sepulchral hour ;
That form'd for empire with paternal care,
His realm might recognise an equal heir.
O destin'd head ! the pious vows are lost ;
His god forgets him on a foreign coast !—
Perhaps, like thee, poor guest ! in wanton pride
The rich insult him, and the young deride !
Conscious of worth revil'd, thy gen'rous mind
The friendly rite of purity declin'd :
My will concurring with my queen's command,
Accept the bath from this obsequious hand.
A strong emotion shakes my anguish'd breast ;
In thy whole form Ulysses seems express'd :
Of all the wretched harbour'd on our coast,
None imag'd e'er like thee my master lost.'
    Thus half discover'd through the dark disguise,
With cool composure feign'd, the chief replies :

'You join your suffrage to the public vote;
The same you think have all beholders thought.'
    He said : replenish'd from the purest springs,
The laver straight with busy care she brings ;
In the deep vase, that shone like burnish'd gold,
The boiling fluid temperates the cold.
Meantime revolving in his thoughtful mind
The scar, with which his manly knee was sign'd ;
His face averting from the crackling blaze,
His shoulders intercept th' unfriendly rays.
Thus cautious, in th' obscure he hop'd to fly
The curious search of Euryclea's eye.
Cautious in vain! nor ceas'd the dame to find
The scar, with which his manly knee was sign'd.
This on Parnassus (combating the boar).
With glancing rage the tusky savage tore.

.   .   .   .   .   .

Deep o'er his knee inseam'd remain'd the scar :
Which noted token of the woodland war
When Euryclea found, the ablution ceas'd—
Down dropp'd the leg, from her slack hand re-
    leas'd—
The mingled fluids from the vase redound—
The vase reclining floats the floor around—
Smiles dew'd with tears the pleasing strife ex-
    press'd
Of grief and joy alternate in her breast—
Her flutt'ring words in melted murmurs died ;
At length abrupt : ' My son!—my king!' she
    cried,
His neck with fond embrace enfolding fast.
Full on the queen her raptur'd eye she cast,
Ardent to speak the monarch safe restor'd :
But, studious to conceal her royal lord,
Minerva fix'd her mind on views remote,
And from the present bliss abstracts her thought.

His hand to Euryclea's mouth applied,
' Art thou foredoom'd my pest ?' the hero cried ;
' Thy milky founts my infant-lips have drain'd :
And have the fates thy babbling age ordain'd
To violate the life thy youth sustain'd ?
An exile have I told, with weeping eyes,
Full twenty annual suns in distant skies :
At length return'd, some god inspires thy breast
To know thy king, and here I stand confess'd.
This heav'n-discovered truth to thee consign'd,
Reserve the treasure of thy inmost mind :
Else if the gods my vengeful arm sustain,
And prostrate to my sword the suitor-train ;
With their lewd mates, thy undistinguish'd age
Shall bleed a victim to vindictive rage.'
When thus rejoin'd the dame, devoid of fear :
' What words, my son, have pass'd thy lips
    severe?
Deep in my soul the trust shall lodge secur'd,
With ribs of steel and marble heart immur'd.
When heav'n, auspicious to thy right avow'd,
Shall prostrate to thy sword the suitor-crowd,
The deeds I'll blazon of the menial fair;
The lewd to death devote, the virtuous spare.'
    ' Thy aid avails me not,' the chief replied ;
' My own experience shall their doom decide;
A witness-judge precludes a long appeal :
Suffice it thee thy monarch to conceal.'
    He said : obsequious with redoubled pace,
She to the fount conveys th' exhausted vase :
The bath renew'd, she ends the pleasing toil
With plenteous unction of ambrosial oil.
Adjusting to his limbs the tatter'd vest,
His former seat receiv'd the stranger-guest,
Whom thus with pensive air the queen address'd."
                                Odyssey, book xix.

No. 1051.

Eurynome spreading a mantle over Ulysses.

DAMAS. *Cornelian.*

4 Q

After Ulysses had been bathed and refreshed, Penelope renews her conversation with him—dwells on her dismal situation, and says that, as a last resort, she will propose to wed the suitor who can draw the strong bow of Ulysses, and shoot the mark he used to hit. The stranger urges her to adopt this plan, assuring her that before the game is over, her freedom will be secured. He then retires to rest. The following quotation will suffice for this and the two subsequent subjects.

" An ample hide divine Ulysses spread,
And form'd of fleecy skins his humble bed
(The remnants of the spoil the suitor-crowd
In festival devour'd, and victims vow'd) ;
Then o'er the chief Eurynome the chaste,
With duteous care, a downy carpet cast:
With dire revenge his thoughtful bosom glows ;
And ruminating wrath, he scorns repose.

As thus pavilion'd in the porch he lay,
Scenes of lewd loves his wakeful eyes survey ;
Whilst to nocturnal joys impure repair,
With wanton glee, the prostituted fair.
His heart with rage this new dishonour stung :
Wav'ring his thoughts in dubious balance hung ;
Or, instant should he quench the guilty flame
With their own blood, and intercept the shame ;
Or to their lust indulge a last embrace,
And let the peers consummate the disgrace?
Round his swoll'n heart the murm'rous fury rolls,
As o'er her young the mother-mastiff growls,
And bays the stranger-groom ; so wrath compress'd,
Recoiling, mutter'd thunder in his breast.
' Poor suff'ring heart !' he cried, 'support the pain
Of wounded honour, and thy rage restrain.
Not fiercer woes thy fortitude could foil,
When the brave partners of thy ten years' toil
Dire Polypheme devour'd : I then was freed
By patient prudence from the death decreed.'

Thus anchor'd safe on reason's peaceful coast,
Tempests of wrath his soul no longer toss'd :
Restless his body rolls, to rage resign'd :
As one who long with pale-ey'd famine pin'd,

The sav'ry cates on glowing embers cast
Incessant turns, impatient for repast :
Ulysses so, from side to side devolv'd,
In self-debate the suitors' doom resolv'd.
When in the form of mortal nymph array'd,
From heav'n descends the Jove-born martial maid ;
And hov'ring o'er his head in view confess'd,
The goddess thus her fav'rite care address'd :
' Oh thou, of mortals most inur'd to woes !
Why roll those eyes unfriended of repose ?
Beneath thy palace-roof forget thy care ;
Bless'd in thy queen ! bless'd in thy blooming heir !
Whom, to the gods when suppliant fathers bow,
They name the standard of their dearest vow.'
' Just is thy kind reproach,' the chief rejoin'd ;
Deeds full of fate distract my various mind,
In contemplation wrapt. This hostile crew
What single arm hath prowess to subdue ?
Or if by Jove's and thy auxiliar aid
They're doom'd to bleed ; O say, celestial maid !
Where shall Ulysses shun, or how sustain
Nations embattled to revenge the slain ?"*
' Oh impotence of faith !' Minerva cries,
' If man on frail, unknowing man relies,
Doubt you the gods ? Lo, Pallas' self descends—
Inspires thy counsels, and thy toils attends !
In me affianc'd fortify thy breast,
Though myriads leagu'd thy rightful claim contest ;

* Because among the suitors were many of the princes of the neighbouring islands.

My sure divinity shall bear the shield,
And edge thy sword to reap the glorious field.
Now pay the debt to craving nature due—
Her faded pow'rs with balmy rest renew.'

She ceas'd : ambrosial slumbers seal his eyes ;
His care dissolves in visionary joys :
The goddess, pleas'd, regains her natal skies."

Odyssey, book xx.

No. 1052.

Minerva appearing to Ulysses while on his bed.

PYRGOTELES. *Cornelian.*

See preceding quotation.

No. 1053.

Minerva lulling Ulysses asleep with poppy.

DIOSCORIDES. *Cornelian.*

See conclusion of preceding quotation. .

No. 1054.

Ctesippus casting the foot of an ox at Ulysses.

DIOSCORIDES. *Cornelian.*

On the following morning there is an unusually magnificent feast, as it is the lunar festival in honour of Apollo, the father of light. Among the dependents who brought animals for the occasion was Philætius, the royal herdsman in Cephalonia (then subject to the crown of Ithaca), a trusty old servant of Ulysses, who enters into conversation with the stranger—declares his devotion to his old master, and imprecates destruction on the suitors. The stranger assures him that his prayers will be speedily accomplished. After this Ctesippus commits the outrage on Ulysses.

" By heralds rank'd, in marshall'd order move
The city-tribes to pleas'd Apollo's grove ;
Beneath the verdure of which awful shade
The lunar hecatomb they grateful laid ;
Partook the sacred feast, and ritual honours paid.
But the rich banquet in the dome prepar'd,
(An humble side-board set) Ulysses shar'd.
Observant of the prince's high behest,
His menial train attend the stranger-guest ;

Whom Pallas with unpardoning fury fired,
By lordly pride and keen reproach inspir'd.
A Samian peer, more studious than the rest
Of vice, who teem'd with many a dead-born jest,
And urg'd, for title to a consort queen,
Unnumber'd acres, arable and green,
(Ctesippus nam'd) ; this lord Ulysses ey'd,
And thus burst out, imposthumate with pride :

'The sentence I propose, ye peers, attend ;
Since due regard must wait the prince's friend,
Let each a token of esteem bestow :
This gift acquits the dear respect I owe ;
With which he nobly may discharge his seat,
And pay the menials for the master's treat.'
  He said : and of the steer before him plac'd,
That sinewy fragment at Ulysses cast,

Where to the pastern-bone by nerves com-
    bin'd,
The well-horn'd foot indissolubly join'd ;
Which whizzing high, the wall unseemly sign'd.
The chief, indignant, grins a ghastly smile ;
Revenge and scorn within his bosom boil."

Odyssey, book xx.

No. 1055.

Penelope with the bow and quiver of Ulysses.

Dioscorides.   *Cornelian.*

Penelope, to put an end to the solicitation of the suitors, proposes to marry the person who should first bend the bow of Ulysses, and shoot through twelve rings placed at intervals. Much learned nonsense has been written about this proposal. The simple reason why she made it was, that she knew they were enervated by their dissipation, and could not (either of them) perform such a feat : she therefore would be released from her engagement by their inability to fulfil the proposed conditions.

" And Pallas now, to raise the rival fires,
With her own art Penelope inspires :
Who now can bend Ulysses' bow, and wing
The well-aim'd arrow through the distant ring,
Shall end the strife, and win th' imperial dame :
But discord and black death await the game !
  The prudent queen the lofty stair ascends,
At distance due a virgin-train attends ;
A brazen key she held, the handle turn'd,
With steel and polish'd elephant adorn'd :
Swift to the inmost room she bent her way,
Where safe repos'd the royal treasures lay ;
There shone high-heap'd the labour'd brass and ore,
And there the bow which great Ulysses bore,
And there the quiver, where now guiltless slept
Those winged deaths that many a matron wept.
    .   .   .   .   .
There from the column where aloft it hung,
Reach'd, in its splendid case, the bow unstrung :
Across her knees she laid the well-known bow,
And pensive sate, and tears began to flow.
To full satiety of grief she mourns ;
Then, silent, to the joyous hall returns,

To the proud suitors bears in pensive state
Th' unbended bow, and arrows wing'd with fate.
  Behind, her train the polish'd coffer brings,
Which held th' alternate brass and silver rings.
Full in the portal the chaste queen appears,
And with her veil conceals the coming tears :
On either side awaits a virgin fair ;
While thus the matron, with majestic air :
  ' Say you, whom these forbidden walls enclose,
For whom my victims bleed, my vintage flows,
If these neglected, faded charms can move ?
Or is it but a vain pretence you love ?
If I the prize, if me you seek to wife,
Hear the conditions, and commence the strife.
Who first Ulysses' wond'rous bow shall bend,
And through twelve ringlets the fleet arrow send,
Him will I follow, and forsake my home—
For him forsake this lov'd, this wealthy dome—
Long, long the scene of all my past delight,
And still to last the vision of my night !'
  Graceful she said, and bade Eumæus shew
The rival peers the ringlets and the bow."

Odyssey, book xxi.

No. 1056.

Penelope bearing the bow and arrows to the suitors.

GNAIOS. *Cornelian.*

See preceding quotation.

No. 1057.

Ulysses discovering himself to Eumæus and Philætius.

PYRGOTELES. *Cornelian.*

These faithful old servants retire while the suitors are in vain endeavouring to bend the bow, although they oil it at the fire.

" Then from the hall, and from the noisy crew,
The masters of the herd and flock withdrew.
The king observes them: he the hall forsakes,
And, past the limits of the court, o'ertakes.
Then thus with accent mild Ulysses spoke:
' Ye faithful guardians of the herd and flock!
Shall I the secret of my breast conceal,
Or, as my soul now dictates, shall I tell?
Say, should some fav'ring god restore again
The lost Ulysses to his native reign;
How beat your hearts? what aid would you afford?
To the proud suitors—or your ancient lord?'
    Philætius thus: ' O, were thy word not vain!
Would mighty Jove restore that man again!
These aged sinews, with new vigour strung,
In his blest cause should emulate the young.'
With equal vows Eumæus too implor'd
Each pow'r above with wishes for his lord.
    He saw their secret souls, and thus began:
' Those vows the gods accord—behold the man!
Your own Ulysses! twice ten years detain'd
By woes and wand'rings from this hapless land:
At length he comes; but comes despis'd, un-
        known,
And finding faithful you, and you alone.
All else have cast him from their very thought—
E'en in their wishes and their pray'rs forgot!

Hear, then, my friends! if Jove this arm succeed,
And give yon impious revellers to bleed,
My care shall be to bless your future lives
With large possessions and with faithful wives;
Fast by my palace shall your domes ascend,
And each on young Telemachus attend,
And each be call'd his brother and my friend.
To give you firmer faith, now trust your eye:
Lo! the broad scar indented on my thigh,
When, with Autolycus's sons, of yore,
On Parnass' top I chas'd the tusky boar.'
    His ragged vest then drawn aside disclos'd
The sign conspicuous, and the scar expos'd:
Eager they view'd; with joy they stood amaz'd;
With tearful eyes o'er all their master gaz'd:
Around his neck their longing arms they cast—
His head, his shoulders, and his knees embrac'd.
Tears follow'd tears; no word was in their pow'r;
In solemn silence fell the kindly show'r.
The king, too, weeps—the king, too, grasps their
        hands,
And moveless as a marble fountain stands.
    Thus had their joy wept down the setting
        sun;
But first the wise man ceas'd, and thus begun:
' Enough—on other cares your thought employ,
For danger waits on all untimely joy.

Full many foes, and fierce, observe us near :
Some may betray, and yonder walls may hear.
Re-enter, then, not all at once, but stay
Some moments you ; and let me lead the way.
To me, neglected as I am, I know
The haughty suitors will deny the bow ;
But thou, Eumæus, as 'tis borne away,
Thy master's weapon to his hand convey.
At ev'ry portal let some matron wait,
And each lock fast the well-compacted gate :

Close let them keep, whate'er invades their ear ;
Though arms, or shouts, or dying groans they hear.
To thy strict charge, Philætius, we consign
The court's main gate : to guard that pass be
    thine.'
    This said, he first return'd : the faithful swains
At distance follow, as their king ordains.
Before the flame Eurymachus now stands,
And turns the bow, and chafes it with his hands ;
Still the tough bow unmov'd."

Odyssey, book xxi.

No. 1058.

Ulysses drawing his bow.

ANTEROTOS. *Cornelian.*

As this subject commences the catastrophe of the poem, it is necessary to describe it at
length. When the chiefs failed to draw the bow, and it is proposed to defer the trial till the
next day, the old mendicant solicits permission to make the experiment. He is instantly re-
buked for his presumption. Penelope (who does not know him) kindly interposes to save the
poor old stranger from ill-usage ; but Telemachus (who does know him) insists that he shall
be allowed to make a trial.

"That right complete, up-rose the thoughtful
    man,
And thus his meditated scheme began :
  ' If what I ask your noble minds approve,
Ye peers and rivals in the royal love !
Chief, if it hurt not great Antinous' ear
(Whose sage decision I with wonder hear),
And if Eurymachus the motion please ;
Give heav'n this day, and rest the bow in peace :
To-morrow let your arms dispute the prize,
And take it he, the favour'd of the skies !
But since till then this trial you delay,
Trust it one moment to my hands to-day :
Fain would I prove, before your judging eyes,
What once I was, whom wretched you despise ;
If yet this arm its ancient force retain ;
Or if my woes (a long-continued train),
And wants and insults, make me less than man.'
  Rage flash'd in lightning from the suitors' eyes,
Yet mix'd with terror at the bold emprise.

Antinous then : ' O miserable guest !
Is common sense quite banish'd from thy breast ?
Suffic'd it not within the palace plac'd
To sit distinguish'd, with our presence grac'd—
Admitted here with princes to confer—
A man unknown—a needy wanderer ?
To copious wine this insolence we owe ;
And much thy betters wine can overthrow :
The great Eurytion when this frenzy stung,
Pirithous' roofs with frantic riot rung :
Boundless the Centaur rag'd, till, one and all,
The heroes rose, and dragg'd him from the hall ;
His nose they shorten'd, and his ears they slit,
And sent him sober'd home, with better wit.
Hence with long war the double race was curst,
Fatal to all, but to th' aggressor first.
Such fate I prophesy our guest attends,
If here this interdicted bow he bends ;
Nor shall these walls such insolence contain ;
The first fair wind transports him o'er the main ;

Where Echetus to death the guilty brings
(The worst of mortals, e'en the worst of kings).
Better than that, if thou approve our cheer,
Cease the mad strife, and share our bounty here.'
　To this the queen her just dislike express'd :
' 'Tis impious, prince ! to harm the stranger-guest,
Base to insult who bears a suppliant's name,
And some respect Telemachus may claim.
What if th' immortals on the man bestow
Sufficient strength to draw the mighty bow ?
Shall I, a queen, by rival chiefs ador'd,
Accept a wand'ring stranger for my lord ?
A hope so idle never touch'd his brain :
Then ease your bosoms of a fear so vain.
Far be he banish'd from this stately scene
Who wrongs his princess with a thought so mean.'
　' O fair ! and wisest of so fair a kind !'
Respectful thus Eurymachus rejoin'd ;
' Mov'd by no weak surmise, but sense of shame,
We dread the all-arraigning voice of fame ;
We dread the censure of the meanest slave—
The weakest woman : all can wrong the brave.
' Behold what wretches to the bed pretend
Of that brave chief whose bow they could not bend !

In came a beggar of the strolling crew,
And did what all those princes could not do :'
Thus will the common voice our deed defame ;
And thus posterity upbraid our name.'
　' To whom the queen : ' If fame engage your views,
Forbear those acts which infamy pursues ;
Wrong and oppression no renown can raise :
Know, friend ! that virtue is the path to praise.
The stature of our guest—his port—his face,
Speak him descended from no vulgar race.
To him the bow, as he desires, convey ;
And to his hand, if Phœbus give the day,
Hence, to reward his merit, he shall bear
A two-edg'd faulchion and a shining spear,
Embroider'd sandals, a rich cloak and vest,
And safe conveyance to his port of rest.'
　' O royal mother ! ever-honour'd name !
Permit me,' cries Telemachus, ' to claim
A son's just right.　No Grecian prince but I
Has pow'r this bow to grant, or to deny.
Of all that Ithaca's rough hills contain,
And all wide Elis' courser-breeding plain,
To me alone my father's arms descend ;
And mine alone they are to give or lend.' "

　　Telemachus after this requests his mother to retire.　She complies ; and consequently does
not witness the feats of Ulysses.

" Now through the press the bow Eumæus bore,
And all was riot, noise, and wild uproar.
' Hold, lawless rustic ! whither wilt thou go ?
To whom, insensate, dost thou bear the bow ?
Exil'd for this to some sequester'd den,
Far from the sweet society of men,
To thy own dogs a prey thou shalt be made,
If heav'n and Phœbus lend the suitors aid.'
　Thus they.　Aghast he laid the weapon down,
But bold Telemachus thus urg'd him on :
' Proceed, false slave, and slight their empty
　　words ;
What ! hopes the fool to please so many lords ?
Young as I am, thy prince's vengeful hand,
Stretch'd forth in wrath, shall drive thee from the
　　land.

Oh ! could the vigour of this arm as well
Th' oppressive suitors from my walls expel !
Then what a shoal of lawless men should go
To fill with tumult the dark courts below !'
　The suitors with a scornful smile survey
The youth, indulging in the genial day.
Eumæus, thus encourag'd, hastes to bring
The strifeful bow, and gives it to the king :
Old Euryclea calling then aside,
' Hear what Telemachus enjoins,' he cried ;
' At ev'ry portal let some matron wait,
And each lock fast the well-compacted gate ;
And if unusual sounds invade their ear,
If arms, or shouts, or dying groans they hear,
Let none to call or issue forth presume,
But close attend the labours of the loom.'

Her prompt obedience on his order waits;
Clos'd in an instant were the palace-gates.
In the same moment forth Philætius flies,
Secures the court, and with a cable ties
The utmost gate (the cable strongly wrought
Of Byblos' reed, a ship from Egypt brought);
Then, unperceiv'd and silent, at the board
His seat he takes; his eyes upon his lord.

   And now his well-known bow the master bore—
Turn'd on all sides, and view'd it o'er and o'er;
Lest time or worms had done the weapon wrong,
Its owner absent, and untried so long.
While some deriding: ' How he turns the bow !
Some other like it sure the man must know,
Or else would copy ; or in bows he deals ;
Perhaps he makes them, or perhaps he steals !'
' Heav'n to this wretch,' another cried, ' be
      kind !
And bless, in all to which he stands inclin'd,
With such good fortune as he now shall find.'

   Heedless he heard them, but disdain'd reply ;
The bow perusing with exactest eye.
Then, as some heav'nly minstrel, taught to sing
High notes responsive to the trembling string,
To some new strain when he adapts the lyre,
Or the dumb lute refits with vocal wire,
Relaxes—strains—and draws them to and fro ;
So the great master drew the mighty bow—
And drew with ease ! One hand aloft display'd
The bending horns, and one the string essay'd.

From his essaying hand the string let fly
Twang'd short and sharp, like the shrill swal-
      low's cry.
A gen'ral horror ran through all the race,
Sunk was each heart, and pale was ev'ry face !
Signs from above ensu'd : th' unfolding sky
In light'ning burst : Jove thunder'd from on high.
Fir'd at the call of heav'n's almighty lord,
He snatch'd the shaft that glitter'd on th' board
(Fast by, the rest lay sleeping in the sheath,
But soon to fly the messengers of death).

   Now sitting as he was, the cord he drew,
Through ev'ry ringlet levelling his view ;
Then notch'd the shaft—releas'd, and gave it
      wing ;
The whizzing arrow vanish'd from the string—
Sung on direct, and thredded ev'ry ring !
The solid gate its fury scarcely bounds ;
Pierc'd through and through, the solid gate re-
      sounds.

   Then to the prince : ' Nor have I wrought thee
      shame ;
Nor err'd this hand unfaithful to its aim ;
Nor prov'd the toil too hard ; nor have I lost
That ancient vigour, once my pride and boast.
Ill I deserv'd these haughty peers' disdain ;
Now let them comfort their dejected train,
In sweet repast the present hour employ,
Nor wait till ev'ning for the genial joy.' "

Odyssey, book xxi.

No. 1059.

Ulysses slaying Antinous.

APOLLONIDES. *Cornelian.*

   This act was the commencement of the general slaughter. The following quotation will
suffice for this and the three subsequent subjects.

" He said, then gave a nod ; and at the word
Telemachus girds on his shining sword.
Fast by his father's side he takes his stand ;
The beamy jav'lin lightens in his hand.

Then fierce the hero o'er the threshold strode ;
Stripp'd of his rags, he blaz'd out like a god.
Full in their face the lifted bow he bore,
And quiver'd deaths, a formidable store !

Before his feet the rattling show'r he threw,
And thus terrific to the suitor-crew:
 'One vent'rous game this hand has won to-day;
Another, princes! yet remains to play—
Another mark our arrow must attain.
Phœbus, assist! nor be the labour vain.'
 Swift as the word the parting arrow sings,
And bears thy fate, Antinous, on its wings:
Wretch that he was, of unprophetic soul!
High in his hands he rear'd the golden bowl;
E'en then to drain it lengthen'd out his breath—
Chang'd to the deep—the bitter draught of death!
For fate who fear'd amidst a feastful band—
And fate to numbers by a single hand?
Full through his throat Ulysses' weapon past,
And pierc'd the neck. He falls, and breathes his last.
The tumbling goblet the wide floor o'erflows;
A stream of gore burst spouting from his nose;
Grim in convulsive agonies he sprawls:
Before him spurn'd, the loaded table falls,
And spreads the pavement with a mingled flood
Of floating meats, and wine, and human blood.
Amaz'd, confounded, as they saw him fall,
Uprose the throngs tumultuous round the hall,
O'er all the dome they cast a haggard eye;
Each look'd for arms in vain—no arms were nigh.
 'Aim'st thou at princes?' all amaz'd they said;
'Thy last of games unhappy hast thou play'd;
Thy erring shaft has made our bravest bleed;
And death, unlucky guest, attends thy deed.
Vultures shall tear thee.' Thus incensed they spoke,
While each to chance ascrib'd the wondrous stroke,
Blind as they were! for death e'en now invades
His destin'd prey, and wraps them all in shades.
Then, grimly frowning, with a dreadful look
That wither'd all their hearts, Ulysses spoke:
 'Dogs! ye have had your day: ye fear'd no more
Ulysses vengeful from the Trojan shore;
While to your lust and spoil a guardless prey,
Our house—our wealth—our helpless handmaids lay:

Not so content, with bolder frenzy fir'd,
E'en to our bed presumptuous you aspir'd:
Laws or divine or human fail'd to move,
Or shame of men, or dread of gods above; .
Heedless alike of infamy or praise,
Or fame's eternal voice in future days:
The hour of vengeance, wretches, now is come,
Impending fate is yours, and instant doom.'
 Thus dreadful he. Confus'd the suitors stood,
From their pale cheeks recedes the flying blood;
Trembling they sought their guilty heads to hide,
Alone the bold Eurymachus replied.
 'If, as thy words import,' he thus began,
'Ulysses lives, and thou the mighty man,
Great are thy wrongs; and much hast thou sustain'd
In thy spoil'd palace and exhausted land!
The cause and author of those guilty deeds,
Lo! at thy feet unjust Antinous bleeds.
Not love, but wild ambition was his guide,
To slay thy son—thy kingdoms to divide—
These were his aims, but juster Jove denied.
Since cold in death th' offender lies, oh spare
Thy suppliant people, and receive their pray'r!
Brass, gold, and treasures, shall the spoil defray,
Two hundred oxen ev'ry prince shall pay:
The waste of years refunded in a day.
Till then thy wrath is just.' Ulysses burn'd
With high disdain, and sternly thus return'd:
 'All—all the treasures that enrich'd our throne
Before your rapines, join'd with all your own,
If offer'd, vainly should for mercy call;
'Tis you that offer, and I scorn them all!
Your blood is my demand—your lives the prize,
Till pale as yonder wretch each suitor lies.
Hence with those coward-terms! or fight or fly:
This choice is left ye, to resist or die;
And die I trust ye shall.' He sternly spoke:
With guilty fears the pale assembly shook.
Alone Eurymachus exhorts the train:
 'Yon archer, comrades, will not shoot in vain;
But from the threshold shall his darts be sped
(Whoe'er he be) till every prince lie dead.

Be mindful of yourselves, draw forth your swords,
And to his shafts obtend these ample boards—
So need compels.   Then all united strive
The bold invader from his post to drive;
The city rous'd shall to our rescue haste,
And this mad archer soon have shot his last.'
  Swift as he spoke, he drew his traitor-sword,
And like a lion rush'd against his lord:
The wary chief the rushing foe repress'd,
He launched his shaft, and shot it through his
    breast:
His failing hand deserts the lifted sword,
And prone he falls extended o'er the board!
Before him wide, in mix'd effusion roll
The untasted viands, and the jovial bowl.
Full through his liver pass'd the mortal wound;
With dying rage his forehead beats the ground;
He spurn'd the seat with fury as he fell,
And the fierce soul to darkness div'd, and—hell!
  Next bold Amphinomus his arm extends
To force the pass the godlike man defends.
Thy spear, Telemachus! prevents th' attack;
The brazen weapon driving through his back,
Thence through his breast its bloody passage
    tore;
Flat falls he thund'ring on the marble floor,
And his crush'd forehead marks the stone with
    gore.
He left his jav'lin in the dead, for fear
The long incumb'rance of the weighty spear
To the fierce foe advantage might afford,
To rush between, and use the shorten'd sword.
With speedy ardour to his sire he flies:
And, 'Arm, great father! arm!' in haste he cries;
'Lo, hence I run for other arms to wield,
For missile jav'lins, and for helm and shield;
Fast by our side let either faithful swain
In arms attend us, and their part sustain.'
  'Haste and return,' Ulysses made reply,
'While yet th' auxiliar shafts this hand supply;
Lest thus alone, encounter'd by an host,
Driv'n from the gate, th' important pass be lost.'
  With speed Telemachus obeys, and flies
Where pil'd on heaps the royal armour lies;

Four brazen helmets, eight refulgent spears,
And four broad bucklers, to his sire he bears:
At once in brazen panoply they shone,
At once each servant brac'd his armour on;
Around their king a faithful guard they stand,
While yet each shaft flew deathful from his hand.
Chief after chief expir'd at ev'ry wound,
And swell'd the bleeding mountain on the ground.
Soon as his store of flying fates was spent,
Against the wall he set the bow unbent:
And now his shoulders bear the massy shield,
And now his hands two beamy jav'lins wield;
He frowns beneath his nodding plume, that play'd
O'er the high crest, and cast a dreadful shade.
  There stood a window near, whence looking
    down
From o'er the porch appear'd the subject-town;
A double strength of valves secur'd the place—
A high and narrow, but the only pass:
The cautious king, with all-preventing care,
To guard that outlet, plac'd Eumæus there.
When Agelaus thus: 'Has none the sense
To mount yon window, and alarm from thence
The neighbour-town? the town shall force the
    door,
And this bold archer soon shall shoot no more.'
  Melanthius then: 'That outlet to the gate
So near adjoins, that one may guard the strait.
But other methods of defence remain,
Myself with arms can furnish all the train;
Stores from the royal magazine I bring,
And their own darts shall pierce the prince and
    king.'
  He said; and mounting up the lofty stairs,
Twelve shields, twelve lances, and twelve hel-
    mets bears:
All arm, and sudden round the hall appears
A blaze of bucklers, and a wood of spears.
  The hero stands oppress'd with mighty woe,
On ev'ry side he sees the labour grow:
'Oh curs'd event! and oh unlook'd for aid!
Melanthius, or the women, have betray'd—
Oh my dear son!'—the father, with a sigh;
Then ceas'd.   The filial virtue made reply:

'Falsehood is folly, and 'tis just to own
The fault committed: this was mine alone;—
My haste neglected yonder door to bar,
And hence the villain has supplied their war.
Run, good Eumæus, then, and (what before
I thoughtless err'd in) well secure that door:
Learn if by female fraud this deed were done,
Or (as my thought misgives) by Dolius' son.'
   While yet they spoke, in quest of arms again
To the high chamber stole the faithless swain;
Not unobserv'd.   Eumæus watchful ey'd,
And thus address'd Ulysses near his side:
'The miscreant we suspected takes that way;
Him, if this arm be pow'rful, shall I slay?
Or drive him hither, to receive the meed,
From thy own hand, of this detested deed?'
   'Not so,' replied Ulysses; 'leave him there;
For us sufficient is another care,—
Within the stricture of this palace-wall
To keep enclos'd his masters till they fall.
Go you, and seize the felon; backward bind
His arms and legs, and fix a plank behind;
On this his body by strong cords extend,
And on a column near the roof suspend;
So studied tortures his vile days shall end.'

The ready swains obey'd with joyful haste;
Behind the felon unperceiv'd they pass'd,
As round the room in quest of arms he goes
(The half-shut door conceal'd his lurking foes):
One hand sustain'd a helm, and one the shield
Which old Laertes wont in youth to wield,
Cover'd with dust, with dryness chapp'd and
   worn,
The brass corroded, and the leather torn:
Thus laden, o'er the threshold as he stepp'd,
Fierce on the villain from each side they leapt;
Back by the hair the trembling dastard drew,
And down reluctant on the pavement threw.
Active and pleas'd, the zealous swains fulfil
At ev'ry point their master's rigid will:
First, fast behind his hands and feet they bound,
Then straiten'd cords involv'd his body round;
So drawn aloft, athwart the column tied,
The howling felon swung from side to side.
   Eumæus scoffing, then with keen disdain:
'There pass thy pleasing night, O gentle swain!
On that soft pillow, from that envied height
First may'st thou see the springing dawn of
   light!'"*
                              Odyssey, book xxi.

No. 1060.

Ulysses killing Eurymachus.

DIOSCORIDES.   *Cornelian.*

See preceding quotation.

---

* Let the reader observe, that the chief reason why Ulysses is able to maintain this unequal contest successfully against such superior numbers, is, that he stands on the threshold in a narrow pass, and is well armed; and that the chief cause of his revenge is, that they not only conspired to rob him of his wife and property, but to assassinate his son. He prays to Apollo, as being the god of archery; and he throws the arrows at his feet, that he may the more expeditiously use them. Eurymachus advises the suitors to defend themselves against the arrows with the tables, because each guest had a small separate table; and to alarm the town, because they had a strong party among the citizens, who were impressed with the persuasion that Ulysses was dead. Ulysses sets the bow against the wall, lest the survivors, plucking the arrows out of the bodies of the slain, may use it against him.

No. 1061.

Telemachus killing Amphinomus.

APOLLONIDES. *Cornelian.*

See preceding quotation.

No. 1062.

Melanthius, while bearing the arms to the suitors, arrested by Eumæus and Philætius.

GNAIOS. *Cornelian.*

See preceding quotation.

No. 1063.

Philætius killing Ctesippus.

APOLLONIDES. *Cornelian.*

" Pierc'd through the breast the rude Ctesippus bled;
And thus Philætius gloried o'er the dead :
' There end thy pompous vaunts and high disdain,
O sharp in scandal, voluble and vain!
How weak is mortal pride ! To heav'n alone
Th' event of actions, and our fates are known.
Scoffer, behold what gratitude we bear;
The victim's heel is answer'd with this spear.' " *

No. 1064.

Ulysses slaying the Suitors.

CHROMIOS. *Amethyst.*

---

* Ctesippus flung the shankbone of an ox at Ulysses during the sacrificial feast (see book xx.);
an outrage for which Philætius here says he requites him. This phrase became a proverb, to express
a return of evil for evil.

"Then all at once their mingled lances threw,
And thirsty all of one man's blood they flew:
In vain! Minerva turu'd them in her breath,
And scatter'd short, or wide, the points of death;
With deaden'd sound, one on the threshold falls—
One strikes the gate—one rings against the walls;
The storm past innocent. The godlike man
Now loftier trod, and dreadful thus began:
''Tis now, brave friends! our turn, at once to throw
(So speed them heav'n!) our jav'lins at the foe.
That impious race to all their past misdeeds
Would add our blood. Injustice still proceeds.'
He spoke: at once their fiery lances flew:
Great Demoptolymus Ulysses slew;
Euryades receiv'd the prince's dart;
The goatherd's quiver'd in Pisander's heart;
Fierce Elatus by thine, Eumæus, falls;
Their fall in thunder echoes round the walls.
The rest retreat. The victors now advance,
Each from the dead resumes his bloody lance.
Again the foe discharge the steelly show'r;
Again made frustrate by the virgin pow'r:

Some, turn'd by Pallas, on the threshold fall—
Some wound the gate—some ring against the wall;
Some weak, or pond'rous with the brazen head,
Drop harmless, on the pavement sounding dead.

Now Pallas shines confess'd; aloft she spreads
The arm of vengeance o'er their guilty heads;
The dreadful ægis blazes in their eye;
Amaz'd they see—they tremble, and they fly!
Confus'd—distracted, through the rooms they fling,
Like oxen madden'd by the breeze's * sting,
When sultry days, and long, succeed the gentle spring.
Not half so keen, fierce vultures of the chase
Stoop from the mountains on the feather'd race,
When the wide field extended snares beset, †
With conscious dread they shun the quiv'ring net:
No help—no flight! but, wounded ev'ry way,
Headlong they drop: the fowlers seize the prey.
On all sides thus they double wound on wound;
In prostrate heaps the wretches beat the ground;
Unmanly shrieks precede each dying groan,
And a red deluge floats the reeking stone."

Odyssey, book xxii.

No. 1065.

Minerva striking terror into the Suitors with her shield.

CHROMIOS. *Sardonyx.*

See preceding quotation.

No. 1066.

Leiodes supplicating Ulysses.

APOLLONIDES. *Amethyst.*

* The gadfly.
† This passage shews that the flying of birds of prey, in the nature of hawking, was practised by the ancients. The timorous birds, flying from the falcons, were caught in nets spread on the plains. Arrian (book ii. cap. 1) shews that deer used to be caught in the same way.

" Leiodes first before the victor falls ;
The wretched augur thus for mercy calls :
' O gracious hear, nor let thy suppliant bleed :
Still undishonour'd or by word or deed,
Thy house, for me, remains ; by me repress'd
Full oft was check'd the unjustice of the rest : ꞈ
Averse they heard me when I counsell'd well ;
Their hearts were harden'd, and they justly fell.
Oh spare an augur's consecrated head,
Nor add the blameless to the guilty dead.'
    ' Priest as thou art ! for that detested band
Thy lying prophecies deceiv'd the land :

Against Ulysses have thy vows been made ;
For them thy daily orisons were paid :
Yet more, e'en to our bed thy pride aspires :
One common crime one common fate requires.'
Thus speaking, from the ground the sword he
    took
Which Agelaus' dying hands forsook :
Full through his neck the weighty falchion
    sped :
Along the pavement roll'd the mutt'ring head."
                        Odyssey, book xxii.

No. 1067.

Telemachus interceding for Phemius.

APOLLONIDES. *Sardonyx.*

The following passages illustrate this and the two subsequent subjects.

" Phemius alone the hand of vengeance spar'd—
Phemius the sweet—the heav'n-instructed bard.
Beside the gate the rev'rend minstrel stands ;
The lyre, now silent, trembling in his hands ;
Dubious to supplicate the chief, or fly
To Jove's inviolable altar nigh,
Where oft Laertes holy vows had paid,
And oft Ulysses smoking victims laid.
His honour'd harp with care he first set down,
Between the laver and the silver throne :
Then prostrate stretch'd before the dreadful man,
Persuasive, thus with accent soft began :
    ' Oh king ! to mercy be thy soul inclin'd,
And spare the poet's ever-gentle kind.
A deed like this thy future fame would wrong,
For dear to gods and men is sacred song.
Self-taught I sing : by heav'n and heav'n alone
The genuine seeds of poesy are sown ;
And (what the gods bestow) the lofty lay
To gods alone, and godlike worth, we pay.
Save then the poet, and thyself reward ;
'Tis thine to merit, mine is to record.

That here I sung, was force and not desire ;
This hand reluctant touch'd the warbling wire :
And let thy son attest, nor sordid pay
Nor servile flatt'ry stain'd the moral lay.'
    The moving words Telemachus attends—
His sire approaches, and the bard defends :
' O mix not, father, with those impious dead
The man divine ! forbear that sacred head.
Medon the herald too our arms may spare,
Medon, who made my infancy his care ;
If yet he breathes, permit thy son to give
Thus much to gratitude, and bid him live.'
    Beneath a table, trembling with dismay,
Crouch'd close to earth, unhappy Medon lay,
Wrapp'd in a new-slain ox's ample hide :
Swift at the word he cast his screen aside,
Sprung to the prince, embrac'd his knee with
    tears,
And thus with grateful voice address'd his ears :
    ' Oh prince ! oh friend ! lo, here thy Medon
    stands ;
Ah stop the hero's unresisted hands !

Incens'd too justly by that impious brood,
Whose guilty glories now are set in blood.'
  To whom Ulysses, with a pleasing eye:
' Be bold, on friendship and my son rely ;
Live, an example for the world to read,
How much more safe the good than evil deed :

Thou, with the heav'n-taught bard, in peace resort
From blood and carnage to yon open court :
Me other work requires.' With tim'rous awe
From the dire scene th' exempted two withdraw,
Scarce sure of life, look round, and trembling move
To the bright altars of protector Jove."

Odyssey, book xxii.

No. 1068.

Medon supplicating Telemachus to intercede for him.

CHROMIOS. *Amethyst.*

See preceding quotation.

No. 1069.

Medon supplicating Ulysses to spare him, in presence of Phemius, and of Telemachus who intercedes for him.

APOLLONIDES. *Cornelian.*

See preceding quotation.

No. 1070.

Euryclea announcing to Penelope the return of Ulysses.

GNAIOS. *Amethyst.*

Ulysses, after the slaughter, orders Telemachus to bring Euryclea.

" On heaps of death the stern Ulysses stood,
All black with dust, and cover'd thick with blood.
So the grim lion from the slaughter comes ;
Dreadful he glares, and terrible he foams ;
His breast with marks of carnage painted o'er,
His jaws all dropping with the bull's black gore.
Soon as her eyes the welcome object met—
The guilty fall'n—the mighty deed complete !
A scream of joy her feeble voice essay'd :
The hero check'd her, and compos'dly said :

' Woman, experienc'd as thou art, control
Indecent joy, and feast thy secret soul.
T' insult the dead is cruel and unjust ;
Fate and their crime have sunk them to the dust.
Nor heeded these the censure of mankind,
The good and bad were equal in their mind.
Justly the price of worthlessness they paid,
And each now wails, an unlamented shade.
But thou sincere ! Oh Euryclea, say
What maids dishonour us, and what obey ?"

She informs him that twelve of the female attendants had lent themselves criminally to the suitors. These he orders to remove the dead bodies, and to cleanse and fumigate the hall. This done, he orders them all to be hanged; and then despatches Euryclea to Penelope, to announce his return, and the massacre of the suitors. Penelope, who had been almost in despair of his return, is for a long time incredulous, and delicately cautious: and as she had been lulled into a profound sleep by Minerva in the upper floor of the palace—the place usually appropriated for the women—she did not hear the tumult below. As the conduct of Penelope on this announcement, and the discovery of Ulysses, are events so important in the *Odyssey*, it is necessary to explain them at length.

" Then to the queen, as in repose she lay,
The nurse, with eager rapture, speeds her way;
The transports of her faithful heart supply
A sudden youth, and give her wings to fly.
' And sleeps my child ?' the rev'rend matron
        cries :
' Ulysses lives ! arise, my child—arise !
At length appears the long-expected hour !
Ulysses comes ! The suitors are no more !
No more they view the golden light of day—
Arise, and bless thee with the glad survey !'
    Touch'd at her words, the mournful queen re-
        join'd,
' Ah ! whither wanders thy distemper'd mind ?
The righteous pow'rs who tread the starry skies,
The weak enlighten, and confound the wise,
And human thought, with unresisted sway,
Depress or raise—enlarge or take away :
Truth, by their high decree, thy voice forsakes,
And folly with the tongue of wisdom speaks.
Unkind, the fond illusion to impose !
Was it to flatter, or deride my woes ?
Never did I a sleep so sweet enjoy,
Since my dear lord left Ithaca for Troy :
Why must I wake to grieve, and curse thy shore,
O Troy ?—may never tongue pronounce thee more !
Begone : another might have felt our rage,
But age is sacred, and we spare thy age.'
    To whom with warmth : ' My soul a lie dis-
        dains ;
Ulysses lives—thy own Ulysses reigns !
That stranger, patient of the suitors' wrongs,
And the rude license of ungovern'd tongues—

He—he is thine ! Thy son his latent guest
Long knew, but lock'd the secret in his breast ;
With well-concerted art to end his woes,
And burst at once in vengeance of the foes.'
    While yet she spoke, the queen in transport
        sprung
Swift from the couch, and round the matron
        hung ;
Fast from her eye descends the rolling tear :
' Say, once more say, is my Ulysses here ?
How could that num'rous and outrageous band
By one be slain, though by a hero's hand ?'
    ' I saw it not !' she cries ; ' but heard alone,
When death was busy, a loud dying groan ;
The damsel-train turn'd pale at ev'ry wound ;
Immur'd we sat, and catch'd each passing sound.
When death had seiz'd her prey, thy son at-
        tends,
And at his nod the damsel-train descends ;
There terrible in arms Ulysses stood,
And the dead suitors almost swam in blood ;
Thy heart had leap'd the hero to survey,
Stern as the surly lion o'er his prey,
Glorious in gore !—now with sulphureous fires
The dome he purges, now the flame aspires ;
Heap'd lie the dead without the palace-walls—
Haste, daughter—haste—thy own Ulysses calls !
Thy ev'ry wish the bounteous gods bestow,
Enjoy the present good, and former woe.
Ulysses lives, his vanquish'd foes to see—
He lives to thy Telemachus and thee !'
    ' Ah no !' with sighs Penelope rejoin'd ;
' Excess of joy disturbs thy wand'ring mind ;

How blest this happy hour, should he appear—
Dear to us all—to me supremely dear!
Ah no! some god the suitors' deaths decreed—
Some god descends, and by his hand they bleed,
Blind to contemn the stranger's righteous cause,
And violate all hospitable laws!
The good they hated, and the pow'rs defied;
But heav'n is just, and by a god they died.
For never must Ulysses view this shore—
Never! the lov'd Ulysses is no more!'
　'What words,' the matron cries, ' have reach'd
　　my ears?
Doubt we his presence when he now appears?
Then hear conviction: ere the fatal day
That forc'd Ulysses o'er the wat'ry way,
A boar fierce-rushing in the sylvan war
Plow'd half his thigh; I saw—I saw the scar,
And wild with transport had reveal'd the wound;
But ere I spoke, he rose, and check'd the sound.
Then, daughter, haste away! and if a lie
Flow from this tongue, then let thy servant die!'

To whom with dubious joy the queen replies:
' Wise is thy soul, but errors seize the wise;
The works of gods what mortal can survey?
Who knows their motives? who shall trace their
　way?
But learn we instant how the suitors trod
The paths of death, by man or by a god.'
　Thus speaks the queen, and no reply attends,
But with alternate joy and fear descends;
At ev'ry step debates, her lord to prove;
Or rushing to his arms, confess her love.
Then gliding through the marble valves in state,
Oppos'd, before the shining fire she sat:
The monarch, by a column high enthron'd,
His eye withdrew, and fix'd it on the ground;
Curious to hear his queen the silence break:
Amaz'd she sat, and impotent to speak;
O'er all the man her eyes she rolls in vain,
Now hopes—now fears—now knows—then doubts
　again!"*

Odyssey, book xxiii.

No. 1071.

Penelope recognising Ulysses.

ALLION. *Cornelian.*

Ulysses finding Penelope still incredulous in consequence of his dress and appearance, cleanses himself, and changes his attire.

" Meanwhile the wearied king the bath ascends;
With faithful cares Eurynome attends,
O'er ev'ry limb a show'r of fragrance sheds :
Then dress'd in pomp, magnificent he treads ;

The warrior-goddess gives his frame to shine
With majesty enlarg'd, and grace divine;
Back from his brows in wavy ringlets fly
His thick large locks, of hyacinthine dye.

---

* Euryclea makes no reply to the last remarks of Penelope, because she thought it possible (according to the prevalent belief of those times) that a divinity might have appeared in the shape of a human being. Ulysses takes his seat near the column, because that was the seat of distinction ; and he observes a thoughtful silence, as well from the importance of the events that had just occurred, and from the apprehension he entertained, that, before his return was publicly announced, the friends of the suitors might raise a sudden insurrection, as from a delicate reluctance to offer violence to the modesty of Penelope by his caresses, while she is in this state of uncertainty and agitation.

4 s

As by some artist to whom Vulcan gives
His heav'nly skill, a breathing image lives;
By Pallas taught, he frames the wond'rous
    mould,
And the pale silver glows with fusile gold:
So Pallas his heroic form improves
With bloom divine, and like a god he moves;
More high he treads, and issuing forth in
    state,
Radiant before his gazing consort sate.
And 'Oh, my queen!' he cries, 'what pow'r
    above
Has steel'd that heart, averse to spousal love!
Canst thou, Penelope, when heav'n restores
Thy lost Ulysses to his native shores—
Canst thou, oh cruel! unconcern'd survey
Thy lost Ulysses, on this signal day?
Haste, Euryclea, and despatchful spread
For me, and me alone, th' imperial bed;
My weary nature craves the balm of rest:
But heav'n with adamant has arm'd her breast.'
    'Ah no!' she cries; 'a tender heart I bear,
A foe to pride; no adamant is there:
And now, e'en now it melts! for sure I see
Once more Ulysses, my belov'd, in thee!
Fix'd in my soul, as when he sail'd to Troy,
His image dwells: then haste the bed of joy!
Haste, from the bridal bow'r the bed translate,*
Fram'd by his hand, and be it dress'd in state!'
    Thus speaks the queen, still dubious with dis-
    guise.
Touch'd at her word, the king with warmth re-
    plies:
'Alas for this! what mortal strength can move
Th' enormous burden; who but heav'n above!
It mocks the weak attempts of human hands.

. . . . .

'Tis thine, O queen, to say: and now impart,
If fears remain, or doubts distract thy heart?'

While yet he speaks, her pow'rs of life decay,
She sickens—trembles—falls—and faints away!
At length recov'ring, to his arms she flew,
And strain'd him close, as to his breast she
    grew;
The tears pour'd down amain: and, 'Oh!' she
    cries,
'Let not against thy spouse thine anger rise!
O vers'd in ev'ry turn of human art,
Forgive the weakness of a woman's heart!
The righteous pow'rs that mortal lots dispose,
Decree us to sustain a length of woes;
And from the flow'r of life, the bliss deny
To bloom together—fade away, and—die!
O let me—let me not thine anger move,
That I forbore, thus—thus to speak my love!
Thus in fond kisses, while the transport warms—
Pour out my soul, and die within thy arms!
I dreaded fraud; men—faithless men, betray
Our easy faith, and make the sex their prey:
Against the fondness of my heart I strove;
'Twas caution, oh my lord! not want of love.
Like me had Helen fear'd, with wanton charms
Ere the fair mischief set two worlds in arms,
Ere Greece rose dreadful in th' avenging day,
Thus had she fear'd, she had not gone astray.
But heav'n, averse to Greece, in wrath decreed
That she should wander, and that Greece should
    bleed:
Blind to the ills that from injustice flow,
She colour'd all our wretched lives with woe.
But why these sorrows, when my lord arrives?
I yield—I yield! my own Ulysses lives!
The secrets of the bridal bed are known
To thee, to me, to Actoris alone
(My father's present in the spousal hour,
The sole attendant on our genial bow'r).
Since what no eye has seen, thy tongue reveal'd,
Hard and distrustful as I am, I yield.'

---

* When Penelope ordered the bridal bed to be brought out of its place and prepared for the stranger, she knew it could not be done, and artfully meant, by giving the order, to sound him, as the fixture of the bed was a secret. But when Ulysses remarks that it could not be removed, then there is conclusive proof of his identity.

Touch'd to the soul, the king with rapture
    hears—
Hangs round her neck, and speaks his joy in tears.
As to the shipwreck'd mariner the shores
Delightful rise when angry Neptune roars,
Then, when the surge in thunder mounts the
    sky,
And gulf'd in crowds at once the sailors die,—

If one more happy, while the tempest raves,
Outlives the tumult of conflicting waves,
All pale, with ooze deform'd, he views the strand,
And plunging forth with transport grasps the
    land ;—
The ravish'd queen with equal rapture glows—
Clasps her lov'd lord, and to his bosom grows."
          Odyssey, book xxiii.

No. 1072.

Mercury conducting the souls of the Suitors to the infernal regions.

CHROMIOS. *Sardonyx.*

" Cyllenius now to Pluto's dreary reign
Conveys the dead—a lamentable train !
The golden wand, that causes sleep to fly,
Or in soft slumber seals the wakeful eye,
That drives the ghosts to realms of night or day,
Points out the long, uncomfortable way.
Trembling the spectres glide, and plaintive vent
Thin, hollow screams, along the deep descent.
As in a cavern of some rifted den,
Where flock nocturnal bats and birds obscene,
Cluster'd they hang, till at some sudden shock
They move, and murmurs run through all the rock ;

So cow'ring fled the sable heaps of ghosts,
And such a scream fill'd all the dismal coasts.
And now they reach'd the earth's remotest ends,
And now the gates where ev'ning Sol descends,
And Leuca's rock, and Ocean's utmost streams,
And now pervade the dusky land of dreams ;
And rest at last, where souls unbodied dwell
In ever-flow'ring meads of asphodel.
The empty forms of men inhabit there,
Impassive semblance—images of air !"
          Odyssey, book xxiv.

No. 1073.

Ulysses discovering himself to his father Laertes.

ALLION. *Sardonyx.*

Laertes, afflicted at the long absence of his son, and at the sad condition of the state, withdrew from court, and lived in a retired cottage. Ulysses, on the morning after the destruction of the suitors, went to see him. As this subject is an important one in the *Odyssey*, it is necessary to treat it here at length.

" Thus in the regions of eternal shade
Conferr'd the mournful phantoms of the dead ;

While from the town Ulysses, and his band,
Pass'd to Laertes' cultivated land.

The ground himself had purchas'd with his
    pain,
And labour made the rugged soil a plain:
There stood his mansion of the rural sort,
With useful buildings round the lowly court:
Where the few servants that divide his care
Took their laborious rest and homely fare;
And one Sicilian matron, old and sage,
With constant duty tends his drooping age.
  Here now arriving, to his rustic band
And martial son Ulysses gave command:
' Enter the house, and of the bristly swine
Select the largest to the pow'rs divine.
Alone, and unattended, let me try
If yet I share the old man's memory;
If those dim eyes can yet Ulysses know
(Their light and dearest object long ago),
Now chang'd with time, with absence, and with
    woe !'
  Then to his train he gives his spear and
    shield;
The house they enter, and he seeks the field;
Through rows of shade with various fruitage
    crown'd,
And labour'd scenes of richest verdure round.
Nor aged Dolius, nor his sons were there,
Nor servants, absent on another care—
To search the woods for sets of flow'ry thorn,
Their orchard-bounds to strengthen and adorn.
  But all alone the hoary king he found;
His habit coarse, but warmly wrapp'd around;
His head, that bow'd with many a pensive
    care,
Fenc'd with a double cap of goat-skin hair:
His buskins old, in former service torn,
But well repair'd; and gloves against the thorn.
In this array the kingly gard'ner stood,
And clear'd a plant, encumber'd with its wood.
  Beneath a neighb'ring tree, the chief divine
Gaz'd o'er his sire, retracing ev'ry line—
The ruins of himself! now worn away
With age, yet still majestic in decay!
Sudden his eyes releas'd their wat'ry store;
The much-enduring man could bear no more:

Doubtful he stood, if instant to embrace
His aged limbs—to kiss his rev'rend face—
With eager transport to disclose the whole,
And pour at once the torrent of his soul.
Not so: his judgment takes the winding way
Of question distant, and of soft essay—
More gentle methods on weak age employs,
And moves the sorrows to enhance the joys.
Then to his sire with beating heart he moves,
And with a tender pleasantry reproves;
Who digging round the plant still hangs his
    head,
Nor aught remits the work, while thus he said:
  ' Great is thy skill, O father! great thy
    toil;
Thy careful hand is stamp'd on all the soil;
Thy squadron'd vineyards well thy art declare,
The olive green, blue fig, and pendent pear,
And not one empty spot escapes thy care.
On ev'ry plant and tree thy cares are shewn,
Nothing neglected, but thyself alone.
Forgive me, father, if this fault I blame;
Age so advanc'd may some indulgence claim.
Not for thy sloth I deem thy lord unkind,
Nor speaks thy form a mean or servile mind;
I read a monarch in that princely air,
The same thy aspect, if the same thy care;
Soft sleep, fair garments, and the joys of wine—
These are the rights of age, and should be thine.
Who then thy master, say? and whose the land
So dress'd and manag'd by thy skilful hand?
But chief, O tell me! (what I question most)
Is this the far-fam'd Ithacensian coast?
For so reported the first man I view'd
(Some surly islander, of manners rude),
Nor farther conference vouchsaf'd to stay;
Heedless he whistled, and pursued his way.
But thou, whom years have taught to under-
    stand,
Humanely hear, and answer my demand:
A friend I seek, a wise one and a brave,
Say, lives he yet, or moulders in the grave?
Time was (my fortunes then were at the best) ··
When at my house I lodg'd this foreign guest;

He said, from Ithaca's fair isle he came,
And old Laertes was his father's name.
To him whatever to a guest is ow'd
I paid, and hospitable gifts bestow'd ;
To him seven talents of pure ore I told,
Twelve cloaks, twelve vests, twelve tunics stiff
  with gold,
A bowl that rich with polish'd silver flames,
And, skill'd in female works, four lovely
  dames.'
  At this the father, with a father's fears
(His venerable eyes bedimm'd with tears):
' This is the land ; but, ah ! thy gifts are lost ;
For godless men, and rude, possess the coast :
Sunk is the glory of this once-fam'd shore ;
Thy ancient friend, oh stranger, is no more !
Full recompense thy bounty else had borne ;
For ev'ry good man yields a just return :
So civil rights demand ; and who begins
The track of friendship, not pursuing, sins.

But tell me, stranger, be the truth confess'd,
What years have circled since thou saw'st that
  guest ?
That hapless guest, alas, for ever gone !
Wretch that he was ! and that I am ! my son !
If ever man to misery was born,
'Twas his to suffer, and 'tis mine to mourn !
Far from his friends, and from his native reign,
He lies a prey to monsters of the main,
Or savage beasts his mangled relics tear,
Or screaming vultures scatter through the air :
Nor could his mother fun'ral unguents shed ;
Nor wail'd his father o'er th' untimely dead ;
Nor his sad consort, on the mournful bier
Seal'd his cold eyes, or dropp'd a tender tear !
But tell me who thou art ? and what thy race—
Thy town—thy parents—and thy native place ?
Or if a merchant in pursuit of gain,
What port receiv'd thy vessel from the main ?
Or com'st thou single ? or attend thy train ?' "

Ulysses says that he came from Abylas—was thrown on the Ithacan coast by adverse winds—and had seen Ulysses five years before.

" Quick through the father's heart these accents
  ran ;
Grief seiz'd at once, and wrapp'd up all the man ;
Deep from his soul he sigh'd, and sorrowing
  spread
A cloud of ashes on his hoary head.
Trembling with agonies of strong delight
Stood the great son, heart-wounded with the
  sight :
He ran—he seiz'd him with a strict embrace—
With thousand kisses wander'd o'er his face :
' I—I am he—oh, father ! rise—behold
Thy son, with twenty winters now grown old—
Thy son—so long desir'd—so long detain'd—
Restor'd, and breathing in his native land :
These floods of sorrow, oh, my sire ! restrain :
The vengeance is complete—the suitor-train,
Stretch'd in our palace, by these hands lie slain.'
  Amaz'd, Laertes : ' Give some certain sign,
If such thou art, to manifest thee mine.'

' Lo here the wound,' he cries, ' receiv'd of yore,
The scar indented by the tusky boar,
When by thyself and by Anticlea sent,
To old Autolycus's realms I went.
Yet by another sign thy offspring know ;
The sev'ral trees you gave me long ago,
While yet a child these fields I lov'd to trace,
And trod thy footsteps with unequal pace ;
To ev'ry plant in order as we came,
Well-pleas'd you told its nature and its name—
Whate'er my childish fancy ask'd, bestow'd ;
Twelve pear-trees bowing with their pendent load,
And ten that red with blushing apples glow'd ;
Full fifty purple figs ; and many a row
Of various vines that then began to blow,
A future vintage, when the hours produce
Their latent buds, and Sol exalts the juice.'
  Smit with the signs which all his doubts ex-
  plain,
His heart within him melts ; his knees sustain

Their feeble weight no more; his arms alone
Support him, round the lov'd Ulysses thrown;
He faints—he sinks, with mighty joys opprest!
Ulysses clasps him to his eager breast.

Soon as returning life regains its seat,
And his breath lengthens, and his pulses beat;
'Yes, I believe,' he cries, 'almighty Jove!
Heav'n rules us yet, and gods there are above.' "

Odyssey, book xxiv.

No. 1074.

The servant perfuming Laertes.

CHROMIOS.   *Amethyst.*

The third figure is that of Minerva.

"To this Ulysses: ' As the gods shall please
Be all the rest; and set thy soul at ease.
Haste to the cottage by this orchard side,
And take the banquet which our cares provide;
There wait thy faithful band of rural friends;
And there the young Telemachus attends.'
    Thus having said, they trac'd the garden o'er,
And stooping enter'd at the lowly door.
The swains and young Telemachus they found,
The victim portion'd, and the goblet crown'd.

The hoary king, his old Sicilian maid
Perfum'd and wash'd, and gorgeously array'd.
Pallas attending gives his frame to shine
With awful port, and majesty divine;
His gazing son admires the godlike grace,
And air celestial dawning o'er his face.
' What god,' he cried, ' my father's form im-
        proves?
How high he treads, and how enlarg'd he
        moves!' "

Odyssey, book xxiv.

No. 1075.

Minerva, Ulysses, and Telemachus.

CHROMIOS.   *Sardonyx.*

The friends of the suitors, headed by Eupithes the father of Antinous, raised an insurrec-
tion, but are routed by Ulysses and a few followers, aided by Minerva.

"The op'ning gates at once their war display;
Fierce they rush forth: Ulysses leads the way.
That moment joins them with celestial aid,
In Mentor's form, the Jove-descended maid;
The suff'ring hero felt his patient breast
Swell with new joy, and thus his son address'd:
' Behold, Telemachus! (nor fear the sight)
The brave embattled; the grim front of fight!
The valiant with the valiant must contend:
Shame not the line whence glorious you descend,

Wide o'er the world their martial fame was
        spread;
Regard thyself, the living, and the dead.'
    ' Thy eyes, great father! on this battle cast,
Shall learn from me Penelope was chaste.'
    So spoke Telemachus: the gallant boy
Good old Laertes heard with panting joy;
And, ' Blest! thrice blest this happy day!' he
        cries;
' The day that shews me, ere I close my eyes,

A son and grandson of th' Arcesian name
Strive for fair virtue, and contest for fame !'
  Then thus Minerva in Laertes' ear:
' Son of Arcesius, rev'rend warrior, hear !
Jove and Jove's daughter first implore in pray'r,
Then whirling high, discharge thy lance in air.'
  She said, infusing courage with the word.
Jove and Jove's daughter then the chief implor'd,
And whirling high, dismiss'd the lance in air :
Full at Eupithes drove the deathful spear ;
The brass-cheek'd helmet opens to the wound ;
He falls—earth thunders, and his arms resound.
  Before the father and the conqu'ring son
Heaps rush on heaps ; they fight—they drop—
    they run.
Now by the sword, and now the jav'lin fall
The rebel race, and death had swallow'd all :
But from on high the blue-ey'd virgin cried ;
Her awful voice detain'd the headlong tide :

' Forbear, ye nations ! your mad hands forbear
From mutual slaughter : Peace descends to
    spare.'
  Fear shook the nations. At the voice divine
They drop their jav'lins, and their rage resign.
All scatter'd round their glitt'ring weapons lie ;
Some fall to earth, and some confus'dly fly.
With dreadful shouts Ulysses pour'd along,
Swift as an eagle—as an eagle strong.
But Jove's red arm the burning thunder aims ;
Before Minerva shot the livid flames ;
Blazing they fell, and at her feet expir'd :
Then stopp'd the goddess—trembled—and retir'd.
  ' Descended from the gods ! Ulysses, cease ;
Offend not Jove : obey, and give the peace.'
  So Pallas spoke. The mandate from above
The king obey'd. The virgin-seed of Jove,
In Mentor's form, confirm'd the full accord,
And willing nations knew their lawful lord."

Odyssey, book xxiv.

No. 1076.

Head of Ulysses.

CHROMIOS. *Sardonyx.*

SUBJECTS FROM THE ÆNEID.

No. 1077.

Æolus, at the solicitation of Juno, letting loose the winds, to destroy the fleet of Æneas.

SOLON. *Cornelian.*

Æneas the Trojan, the most distinguished chief next to Hector, having collected those who survived the ruin of the city, set sail for Italy; the oracles having declared that it was fated he should settle there, and there found a great empire. When he was on his voyage, Juno, who was, for many reasons, the implacable enemy of the Trojans—for the judgment of Paris —the honours conferred by Jupiter on Ganymede—but, above all, apprehensive that if Æneas were to reach Italy, his posterity would found Rome, which was destined to destroy her favourite city, Carthage,—persuaded Æolus, king of the winds, to raise a storm, and disperse the fleet.

"Thus rag'd the goddess; and with fury fraught,
The restless regions of the storms she sought,
Where in a spacious cave of living stone,
The tyrant Æolus, from his airy throne,
With pow'r imperial curbs the struggling winds,
And sounding tempests in dark prisons binds.
This way, and that, th' impatient captives tend,
And, pressing for release, the mountains rend.
High in his hall th' undaunted monarch stands,
And shakes his sceptre, and their rage commands;
Which, did he not, their unresisted sway
Would sweep the world before them in their way—
Earth, air, and seas, through empty space would
        roll,
And heav'n would fly before the driving soul.
In fear of this, the father of the gods
Confin'd their fury to those dark abodes,
And lock'd them safe within, oppress'd with
        mountain loads;
Impos'd a king with arbitrary sway,
To loose their fetters, or their force allay;

To whom the suppliant queen her pray'rs ad-
        dress'd,
And thus the tenour of her suit express'd:
'O Æolus! (for to thee the king of heav'n
The pow'r of tempests and of winds has giv'n;
Thy force alone their fury can restrain,
And smooth the waves, or swell the troubled
        main;)
A race of wand'ring slaves, abhorr'd by me,
With prosp'rous passage cut the Tuscan sea;
To fruitful Italy their course they steer,
And for their vanquish'd gods design new tem-
        ples there.
Raise all thy winds—with night involve the
        skies—
Sink or disperse my fatal enemies.
Twice seven, the charming daughters of the main
Around my person wait, and bear my train:
Succeed my wish and second my design,
The fairest, Deiopeia, shall be thine,
And make thee father of a happy line.'

To this the god : ' 'Tis yours, O queen, to will
The work, which duty binds me to fulfil.
These airy kingdoms, and this wide command,
Are all the presents of your bounteous hand ;
Yours is my sovereign's grace ; and, as your guest,
I sit with gods at their celestial feast—
Raise tempests at your pleasure, or subdue—
Dispose of empire which I hold from you.'
He said, and hurl'd against the mountain-side
His quiv'ring spear, and all the god applied.
The raging winds rush through the hollow wound,
And dance aloft in air, and skim along the ground;
Then, settling on the sea, the surges sweep—
Raise liquid mountains, and disclose the deep.
South, east, and west, with mix'd confusion roar,
And roll the foaming billows to the shore.
The cables crack ; the sailors' fearful cries
Ascend ; and sable night involves the skies ;
And heav'n itself is ravish'd from their eyes.
Loud peals of thunder from the poles ensue,
Then flashing fires the transient light renew :
The face of things a frightful image bears ;
And present death in various forms appears."
Æneid, book i.

No. 1078.

Neptune quelling the storm.

ADMON. *Cornelian.*

" Meantime imperial Neptune heard the sound
Of raging billows breaking on the ground.
Displeas'd, and fearing for his wat'ry reign,
He rear'd his awful head above the main—
Serene in majesty, then roll'd his eyes
Around the space of earth, and seas, and skies.
He saw the Trojan fleet dispers'd—distress'd—
By stormy winds and wint'ry heav'n oppress'd.
Full well the god his sister's envy knew,
And what her aims and what her arts pursue.
He summon'd Eurus and the Western blast,
And first an angry glance on both he cast ;
Then thus rebuk'd : ' Audacious winds ! from
  whence
This bold attempt—this rebel insolence ?
Is it for you to ravage seas and land,
Unauthoris'd by my supreme command ?
To raise such mountains on the troubled main ?
Whom I—but first 'tis fit the billows to restrain ;
And then you shall be taught obedience to my
  reign.
Hence ! to your lord my royal mandate bear—
' The realms of ocean and the fields of air
Are mine, not his. By fatal lot to me
The liquid empire fell, and trident of the sea.
His pow'r to hollow caverns is confin'd ;
There let him reign the jailor of the wind,
With hoarse commands his breathing subjects call,
And boast and bluster in his empty hall.'
He spoke; and while he spoke he smooth'd the sea,
Dispell'd the darkness, and restor'd the day.
Cymothoë, Triton, and the sea-green train
Of beauteous nymphs, the daughters of the main,
Clear from the rocks the vessels with their hands:
The god himself with ready trident stands,
·And opes the deep, and spreads the moving sands;
Then heaves them off the shoals. Where'er he
  guides
His finny coursers, and in triumph rides,
The waves unruffle, and the sea subsides.
As when in tumults rise th' ignoble crowd,
Mad are their motions, and their tongues are loud;
And stones and brands in rattling volleys fly,
And all the rustic arms that fury can supply ;
If then some grave and pious man appear,
They hush their noise, and lend a list'ning ear :
He soothes with sober words their angry mood,
And quenches their innate desire of blood :
So when the father of the flood appears,
And o'er the seas his sov'reign trident rears,

Their fury falls—he skims the liquid plains,
High on his chariot, and, with loosen'd reins,
Majestic moves along, and awful peace maintains.

The weary Trojans ply their shatter'd oars
To nearest land, and make the Libyan shores."
Æneid, book i.

No. 1079.

Æneas killing the stags on the African coast.

POLYCLETES.   *Cornelian.*

Æneas, with some of his followers, having been cast on the coast of Libya, kill some
stags for food.

" No vessels were in view; but on the plain
Three beamy stags command a lordly train
Of branching heads; the more ignoble throng
Attend their stately steps, and slowly graze along.
He stood; and while secure they graze below,
He took the quiver and the trusty bow
Achates us'd to bear; the leaders first
He laid along, and then the vulgar pierc'd:
Nor ceas'd his arrows till the shady plain
Sev'n mighty bodies with their blood distain.

For the sev'n ships he made an equal share,
And to the port return'd triumphant from the
    war.
The jars of gen'rous wine (Acestes' gift,
When his Trinacrian shores the navy left)
He set abroach, and for the feast prepar'd,
In equal portions with the ven'son shar'd.
Thus while he dealt it round, the pious chief
With cheerful words allay'd the common grief."
Æneid, book i.

No. 1080.

Venus imploring Jupiter to protect Æneas.

ALLION.   *Sardonyx.*

The following quotation will suffice for this and the two subsequent subjects.

" When, from aloft, almighty Jove surveys
Earth, air, and shores, and navigable seas;
At length on Libyan realms he fix'd his
    eyes;
Whom, pond'ring thus on human miseries,
When Venus saw, she with a lowly look,
Not free from tears, her heav'nly sire bespoke:
' O king of gods and men! whose awful hand
Disperses thunder on the seas and land—
Disposes all with absolute command;
How could my pious son thy pow'rs incense?
Or what, alas! is vanquish'd Troy's offence?

Our hope of Italy not only lost,
On various seas by various tempest toss'd,
But shut from ev'ry shore, and barr'd from ev'ry
    coast.
You promis'd once a progeny divine
Of Romans, rising from the Trojan line,
In after-times should hold the world in awe,
And to the land and ocean give the law.
How is your doom revers'd, which eas'd my care,
When Troy was ruin'd in that cruel war?
Then fates to fates I could oppose: but now,
When Fortune still pursues her former blow,

What can I hope? what worse can still succeed?
What end of labours has your will decreed?
Antenor,* from the midst of Grecian hosts,
Could pass secure, and pierce the Illyrian coasts,
Where, rolling down the steep, Timavus raves,
And through nine channels disembogues his waves.
At length he founded Padua's happy seat,
And gave his Trojans a secure retreat;
There fix'd their arms, and there renew'd their
    name,
And there in quiet rules, and crown'd with fame.
But we, descended from your sacred line,
Entitled to your heav'n and rites divine,
Are banish'd earth, and, for the wrath of one,
Remov'd from Latium, and the promis'd throne.
Are these our sceptres—these our due rewards?
And is it thus that Jove his plighted faith regards?'
  To whom the father of the immortal race,
Smiling with that serene, indulgent face,
With which he drives the clouds and clears the
    skies,
First gave a holy kiss; then thus replies:
' Daughter, dismiss thy fears: to thy desire
The fates of thine are fix'd, and stand entire.
Thou shalt behold thy wish'd Lavinian walls;
And, ripe for heav'n, when fate Æneas calls,
Then shalt thou bear him up sublime to me:
No counsels have revers'd my firm decree.
And lest new fears disturb thy happy state,
Know, I have search'd the mystic rolls of fate:
Thy son (nor is the appointed season far)
In Italy shall wage successful war—
Shall tame fierce nations in the bloody field,
And sov'reign laws impose, and cities build;
Till after ev'ry foe subdued, the sun
Thrice through the signs his annual race shall run:
This is his time prefix'd. Ascanius then,
Now call'd Iulus, shall begin his reign.
He thirty rolling years the crown shall wear;
Then from Lavinium shall the seat transfer;

And with hard labour Alba-longa build.
The throne with his succession shall be fill'd
Three hundred circuits more: then shall be seen
Ilia the fair, a priestess and a queen,
Who, full of Mars, in time, with kindly throes,
Shall at a birth two goodly boys disclose.
The royal babes a tawny wolf shall drain:
Then Romulus his grandsire's throne shall gain,
Of martial tow'rs the founder shall become—
The people Romans call, the city Rome.
To them no bounds of empire I assign,
Nor term of years to their immortal line.
E'en haughty Juno, who with endless broils,
Earth, seas, and heav'n, and Jove himself, tur-
    moils,
At length aton'd, her friendly pow'r shall join,
To cherish and advance the Trojan line.
The subject world shall Rome's dominion own,
And, prostrate, shall adore the nation of the
    gown.
An age is ripening in revolving fate,
When Troy shall overturn the Grecian state,
And sweet revenge her conq'ring sons shall call
To crush the people that conspir'd her fall.
Then Cæsar from the Julian stock shall rise,
Whose empire ocean, and whose fame the skies,
Alone shall bound; whom fraught with eastern
    spoils,
Our heav'n, the just reward of human toils,
Securely shall repay, with rights divine.
And incense shall ascend before his sacred shrine.
Then dire debate, and impious war, shall cease,
And the stern age be soften'd into peace;
Then banish'd Faith shall once again return,
And vestal fires in hallow'd temples burn:
And Remus, with Quirinus, shall sustain
The righteous laws, and fraud and force re-
    strain.
Janus himself before his fane shall wait,
And keep the dreadful issues of his gate

---

  * Antenor, another Trojan prince, migrated with his followers to Italy, and founded Padua on the shores of the Adriatic.

With bolts and iron bars: within remains
Imprison'd Fury, bound in brazen chains:
High on a trophy rais'd, of useless arms,
He sits, and threats the world with vain alarms.'
  He said, and sent Cyllenius with command
To free the ports, and ope the Punic land
To Trojan guests; lest, ignorant of fate,
The queen might force them from her town and
    state.

Down from the steep of heav'n Cyllenius flies,
And cleaves with all his wings the yielding skies.
Soon on the Libyan shore descends the god—
Performs his message, and displays his rod.
The surly murmurs of the people cease,
And, as the fates requir'd, they give the peace.
The queen herself suspends the rigid laws,
The Trojan pities, and protects their cause."
                            Æneid, book i.

No. 1081.

Jupiter declaring to Venus the prosperous destinies of Æneas.

DIOSCORIDES.   *Cornelian.*

See preceding quotation.

No. 1082.

Mercury, in obedience to the orders of Jupiter, inducing Dido to protect Æneas.

CHROMIOS.   *Cornelian.*

See preceding quotation.

No. 1083.

Æneas addressing Venus as she ascends to heaven, after her interview with him in the Libyan wood.

MYRON.   *Cornelian.*

" Beneath a ledge of rocks his fleet he hides:
Tall trees surround the mountain's shady sides;
The bending brow above a safe retreat provides.
Arm'd with two pointed darts, he leaves his
    friends;
And true Achates on his steps attends.
Lo! in the deep recesses of the woods
Before his eyes his goddess-mother stood—

A huntress in her habit and her mien:
Her dress a maid, her air confess'd a queen.
Bare were her knees, and knots her garments
    bind;
Loose was her hair, and wanton'd in the
    wind;
Her hand sustain'd a bow; her quiver hung be-
    hind.

She seem'd a virgin of the Spartan blood :
With such array Harpalyce bestrode
Her Thracian courser, and outstripp'd the rapid
    flood.
  ' Ho, strangers ! have you seen,' she said,
' One of my sisters, like myself array'd,
Who cross'd the lawn, or in the forest stray'd ?
A painted quiver at her back she bore ;
Varied with spots a lynx's hide she wore,
And at full cry pursued the tusky boar.'
  Thus Venus : thus her son replied again—
' None of your sisters have we heard or seen,
O virgin ! or what other name you bear
Above that style : O more than mortal fair !
Your voice and mien celestial birth betray.
If, as you seem, the sister of the day,
Or one at least of chaste Diana's train,
Let not an humble suppliant sue in vain :
But tell a stranger, long in tempests toss'd,
What earth we tread, and who commands the
    coast.
Then on your name shall wretched mortals call,
And offer'd victims at your altars fall.'
  ' I dare not,' she replied, ' assume the name
Of goddess, or celestial honours claim ;
For Tyrian virgins bows and quivers bear,
And purple buskins o'er their ancles wear.
Know, gentle youth, in Libyan lands you are—
A people rude in peace and rough in war.
The rising city, which from far you see,
Is Carthage, and a Tyrian colony.
Phœnician Dido rules the growing state,
Who fled from Tyre, to shun her brother's hate :
Great were her wrongs, her story full of fate ;
Which I will sum in short. Sichæas, known
For wealth, and brother to the Punic throne,
Possess'd fair Dido's bed ; and either heart
At once was wounded with an equal dart.
Her father gave her, yet a spotless maid ;
Pygmalion then the Tyrian sceptre sway'd—
One who contemn'd divine and human laws :
Then strife ensued, and cursed gold the cause.
The monarch, blinded with desire of wealth,
With steel invades his brother's life by stealth ;

Before the sacred altar made him bleed ;
And long from her conceal'd the cruel deed.
Some tale, some new pretence, he daily coin'd,
To soothe his sister, and delude her mind.
At length, in dead of night, the ghost appears
Of her unhappy lord : the spectre stares,
And, with erected eyes, his bloody bosom bares.
The cruel altars, and his fate, he tells,
And the dire secret of his house reveals ;
Then warns the widow, and her household-gods,
To seek a refuge in remote abodes.
Last, to support her in so long a way,
He shews her where his hidden treasure lay.
Admonish'd thus, and seiz'd with mortal fright,
The queen provides companions of her flight :
They meet, and all combine to leave the state,
Who hate the tyrant, or who fear his hate.
They seize a fleet, which ready rigg'd they find :
Nor is Pygmalion's treasure left behind.
The vessels, heavy laden, put to sea
With prosp'rous winds : a woman leads the way.
I know not if by stress of weather driv'n,
Or was their fatal course dispos'd by heav'n ;
At last they landed, where from far your eyes
May view the turrets of new Carthage rise ;
There bought a space of ground, which (*byrsa*
    call'd,)
From the bull's hide,) they first enclos'd and
    wall'd.
But whence are you ? what country claims your
    birth ?
What seek you, strangers, on our Libyan earth ?'
  To whom, with sorrow streaming from his eyes,
And deeply sighing, thus her son replies :
' Could you with patience hear, or I relate,
O nymph ! the tedious annals of our fate ;
Through such a train of woes if I should run,
The day would sooner than the tale be done.
From ancient Troy, by force expell'd, we came—
If you by chance have heard the Trojan name.
On various seas by various tempests toss'd,
At length we landed on your Libyan coast.
The good Æneas am I call'd—a name,
While Fortune favour'd, not unknown to fame :

My household-gods, companions of my woes,
With pious care I rescued from our foes.
To fruitful Italy my course was bent;
And from the king of heav'n is my descent.
With twice ten sail I cross'd the Phrygian sea;
Fate and my mother-goddess led my way.
Scarce sev'n the thin remainders of my fleet,
From storms preserv'd, within your harbour
    meet.
Myself distress'd, an exile, and unknown,
Debarr'd from Europe, and from Asia thrown,
In Libyan deserts wander thus alone.'
  His tender parent could no longer bear;
But, interposing, sought to soothe his care.
  ' Whoe'er you are—not unbelov'd by heav'n,
Since on our friendly shore your ships are driv'n—
Have courage—to the gods permit the rest,
And to the queen expose your just request.
Now take this earnest of success for more:
Your scatter'd fleet is join'd upon the shore;
The winds are chang'd, your friends from danger
    free,
Or I renounce my skill in augury.
Twelve swans behold in beauteous order move,
And stoop with closing pinions from above,
Whom late the bird of Jove had driv'n along,
And through the clouds pursued the scatt'ring
    throng;
Now, all united in a goodly team,
They skim the ground, and seek the quiet stream.

As they, with joy returning, clap their wings,
And ride the circuit of the skies in rings;
Not otherwise your ships, and ev'ry friend,
Already hold the port, or with swift sails descend.
No more advice is needful; but pursue
The path before you, and the town in view.'
  Thus having said, she turn'd, and made appear
Her neck refulgent, and dishevell'd hair,
Which, flowing from her shoulders, reach'd the
    ground,
And widely spread ambrosial scents around.
In length of train descends her sweeping gown;
And by her graceful walk the queen of love is
    known.
The prince pursued the parting deity
With words like these: 'Ah! whither do you fly?
Unkind and cruel! to deceive your son
In borrow'd shapes, and his embrace to shun;
Never to bless my sight but thus unknown;
And still to speak in accents not your own.'
Against the goddess these complaints he made,
But took the path, and her commands obey'd.
They march obscure: for Venus kindly shrouds
With mists their persons, and involv'd in clouds,
That, thus unseen, their passage none might stay,
Or force to tell the causes of their way.
This part perform'd, the goddess flies sublime,
To visit Paphos and her native clime,
Where garlands, ever green and ever fair,
With vows are offer'd, and with solemn prayer."

Æneid, book i.

No. 1084.

Troïlus, the young son of Priam, trailed along the ground by his horses.

PYRGOTELES. *Calcedony.*

Æneas having been rendered invisible by Venus, goes to Carthage, and there sees, in the temple of Juno, the chief events of the Trojan war painted on the wall.

" Elsewhere he saw where Troïlus defied
    Achilles, and unequal combat tried;

Then, where the boy disarm'd, with loosen'd reins,
Was by his horses hurried o'er the plains,
Hung by the neck and hair; and, dragg'd around,
The hostile spear yet sticking in his wound,
With tracts of blood inscrib'd the dusty ground."

Æneid, book i.

No. 1085.

Venus changing Cupid into the appearance of Ascanius.

POLYCLETES. *Calcedony.*

Æneas, while invisible, finds, to his joy, a party of his followers, who, he thought, were lost, supplicating the queen for protection. She willingly grants it when she hears their history, and expresses great concern for the fate of Æneas. Then Æneas suddenly discovers himself. Dido entertains them all at a great banquet. Venus having conveyed Ascanius to Cyprus, substitutes Cupid, who assumes his appearance, makes Dido presents, and inspires her with love for Æneas. The following quotation explains this and the four subsequent subjects.

"The good Æneas, whose paternal care
Iülus' absence could no longer bear,
Despatch'd Achates to the ships in haste,
To give a glad relation of the past,
And, fraught with precious gifts, to bring the boy,
Snatch'd from the ruins of unhappy Troy:
A robe of tissue, stiff with golden wire;
An upper vest, once Helen's rich attire,
From Argos by the fam'd adult'ress brought,
With golden flow'rs and winding foliage wrought—
Her mother Leda's present, when she came
To ruin Troy, and set the world on flame:
The sceptre Priam's eldest daughter bore,
Her orient necklace, and the crown she wore
Of double texture, glorious to behold;
One order set with gems, and one with gold.
Instructed thus, the wise Achates goes,
And in his diligence his duty shews.
But Venus, anxious for her son's affairs,
New counsels tries, and new designs prepares:
That Cupid should assume the shape and face
Of sweet Ascanius, and the sprightly grace;

Should bring the presents, in her nephew's stead,
And in Eliza's veins the gentle poison shed:
For much she fear'd the Tyrians double-tongued,
And knew the town to Juno's care belong'd.
These thoughts by night her golden slumbers broke;
And thus, alarm'd, to winged Love she spoke:
'My son, my strength, whose mighty pow'r alone
Controls the thund'rer on his awful throne,
To thee thy much-afflicted mother flies,
And on thy succour and thy faith relies:
Thou know'st, my son, how Jove's revengeful wife,
By force and fraud, attempts thy brother's life;
And often hast thou mourn'd with me his pains.
Him Dido now with blandishment detains;
But I suspect the town where Juno reigns.
For this, 'tis needful to prevent her art,
And fire with love the proud Phœnician's heart—
A love so violent, so strong, so sure,
That neither age can change, nor heart can cure.

How this may be perform'd, now take my
    mind :
Ascanius by his father is design'd
To come with presents laden, from the port,
To gratify the queen, and gain the court.
I mean to plunge the boy in pleasing sleep ;
And, ravish'd, in Idalian bow'rs to keep,
Or high Cythera, that the sweet deceit
May pass unseen, and none prevent the cheat.
Take thou his form and shape : I beg the grace
But only for a night's revolving space.
Thyself a boy, assume a boy's dissembled face ;
That when, amidst the fervour of the feast,
The Tyrian hugs and fonds thee on her breast,
And with sweet kisses in her arms constrains,
Thou may'st infuse thy venom in her veins.'
The god of love obeys, and sets aside
His bow and quiver, and his plumy pride :
He walks Iülus in his mother's sight,
And in the sweet resemblance takes delight.
    The goddess then to young Ascanius flies,
And in a pleasing slumber seals his eyes ;
Lull'd in her lap, amidst a train of loves,
She gently bears him to her blissful groves ;
Then with a wreath of myrtle crowns his head,
And softly lays him on a flowery bed.
Cupid meantime assum'd his form and face,
Following Achates with a shorter pace,
And brought the gifts. The queen already sate
Amidst the Trojan lords, in shining state,
High on a golden bed : her princely guest
Was next her side ; in order sate the rest.
Then canisters with bread are heap'd on high :
Th' attendants water for their hands supply,

And, having wash'd, with silken towels dry.
Next fifty handmaids in long order bore
The censers, and with fumes the gods adore ;
Then youths and virgins, twice as many, join
To place the dishes, and to serve the wine.
The Tyrian train, admitted to the feast,
Approach, and on the painted couches rest.
All on the Trojan gifts with wonder gaze,
But view the beauteous boy with more amaze,
His rosy-colour'd cheeks, his radiant eyes,
His motions, voice, and shape, and all the god's
    disguise ;
Nor pass unprais'd the vest and veil divine,
Which wand'ring foliage and rich flowers en-
    twine.
But, far above the rest, the royal dame
(Already doom'd to love's disastrous flame),
With eyes insatiate, and tumultuous joy,
Beholds the presents, and admires the boy.
The guileful god about the hero long,
With children's play, and false embraces, hung ;
Then sought the queen : she took him to her
    arms
With greedy pleasure, and devour'd his charms.
Unhappy Dido little thought what guest,
How dire a god, she drew so near her breast.
But he, not mindless of his mother's pray'r,
Works in the pliant bosom of the fair,
And moulds her heart anew, and blots her former
    care.
The dead is to the living love resign'd ;
And all Æneas enters in her mind."
                 Æneid, book i.

No. 1086.

Venus, Cupid, and Ascanius.

DIOSCORIDES. *Sardonyx.*

See preceding quotation.

No. 1087.

Venus conveying Ascanius to Cyprus.

GNAIOS. *Cornelian.*

See preceding quotation.

No. 1088.

Venus laying down Ascanius when asleep.

SOLON. *Cornelian.*

See preceding quotation.

No. 1089.

Cupid, disguised as Ascanius, presenting the gifts to Dido.

NICOMOS. *Cornelian.*

See preceding quotation.

No. 1090.

Laocoon hurling a spear at the wooden horse of Troy.

SOLON. *Cornelian.*

Æneas, at the request of Dido, relates the chief events of the sacking of Troy, and of his own wanderings. He begins by saying that the Greeks had quitted the Trojan territory, and had left behind them a huge wooden structure resembling a horse, secretly filled with armed men. The Trojans are divided in opinion as to the object of this structure. Some advise that it should be drawn into the city; but Laocoon declares it to be some perfidious stratagem of the Greeks, and hurls a spear at it. Meantime a wretched-looking Greek (Sinon) is brought a captive by some shepherds to the city. He is interrogated, and, on the assurance of pardon, concocts a plausible story. The following passages explain this and the three subsequent subjects.

" By destiny compell'd, and in despair,
The Greeks grew weary of the tedious war,
And, by Minerva's aid, a fabric rear'd,
Which like a steed of monstrous height appear'd.
The sides were plank'd with pine: they feign'd it made
For their return, and this the vow they paid..

Thus they pretend; but in the hollow side
Selected numbers of their soldiers hide;
With inward arms the dire machine they load,
And iron bowels stuff the dark abode.
In sight of Troy lies Tenedos, an isle,
While Fortune did on Priam's empire smile,

4 U

Renown'd for wealth; but since, a faithless bay,
Where ships expos'd to wind and weather lay;
There was their fleet conceal'd. We thought for Greece
Their sails were hoisted, and our fears release.
The Trojans, coop'd within their walls so long,
Unbar their gates, and issue in a throng,
Like swarming bees, and with delight survey
The camp deserted, where the Grecians lay:
The quarters of the several chiefs they shew'd—
Here Phœnix, here Achilles, made abode—
Here join'd the battles, there the navy rode.
Part on the pile their wond'ring eyes employ—
The pile by Pallas raised to ruin Troy.
Thymœtes first ('tis doubtful whether hir'd,
Or so the Trojan destiny requir'd)
Mov'd that the ramparts might be broken down,
To lodge the monster-fabric in the town.
But Capys and the rest, of sounder mind,
The fatal present to the flames design'd,
Or to the wat'ry deep; at least to bore
The hollow sides, and hidden frauds explore.
The giddy vulgar, as their fancies guide,
With noise say nothing, and in parts divide.
Laocoon, follow'd by a num'rous crowd,
Ran from the fort, and cried from far aloud:
' O wretched countrymen! what fury reigns?
What more than madness has possess'd your brains?
Think you the Grecians from your coasts are gone?
And are Ulysses' arts no better known?
This hollow fabric either must enclose
Within its blind recess our secret foes,
Or 'tis an engine rais'd above the town,
T' o'erlook the walls, and then to batter down.
Somewhat is sure design'd by fraud or force:
Trust not their presents, nor admit the horse.'
Thus having said, against the steed he threw
His forceful spear, which, hissing as it flew,

Pierc'd through the yielding planks of jointed wood,
And trembling in the hollow belly stood.
The sides, transpierc'd, return a rattling sound,
And groans of Greeks enclos'd come issuing through the wound;
And, had not heav'n the fall of Troy design'd,
Or had not men been fated to be blind,
Enough was said and done t' inspire a better mind:
Then had our lances pierc'd the treach'rous wood,
And Ilian tow'rs and Priam's empire stood.
    Meantime, with shouts, the Trojan shepherds bring
A captive Greek in bands before the king:
Taken, to take—who made himself their prey
T' impose on their belief, and Troy betray;
Fix'd on his aim, and obstinately bent
To die undaunted, or to circumvent.
About the captive tides of Trojans flow;
All press to see, and some insult the foe.
Now hear how well the Greeks their wiles disguis'd;
Behold a nation in a man compris'd.
Trembling the miscreant stood, unarm'd and bound;
He star'd, and roll'd his haggard eyes around,
Then said: ' Alas! what earth remains, what sea
Is open to receive unhappy me?
What fate a wretched fugitive attends,
Scorn'd by my foes, abandon'd by my friends?'
He said, and sigh'd, and cast a rueful eye:
Our pity kindles, and our passions die.
We cheer the youth to make his own defence,
And freely tell us what he was and whence:
What news he could impart we long to know,
And what to credit from a captive foe.
    His fear at length dismiss'd, he said: 'Whate'er
My fate ordains, my words shall be sincere.'"

Sinon says, that the Greeks, having often in vain endeavoured to sail away from Troy, the soothsayer declared that they were not to expect favourable winds until, as at Aulis, on their way to Troy, they offered a human sacrifice; that he himself was selected, through the instrumentality of his enemy Ulysses, as the victim; but that, when decked for the altar, he burst his bonds, escaped, and hid himself in a reedy marsh. He then says that the horse was a pacificatory offering to offended Minerva — that the Greeks will soon return — and had constructed the horse so large that it could not be drawn into the city; for if it were, Troy could not be taken. After he has concluded his address, two huge serpents swim ashore and strangle Laocoon. This the Trojans consider a divine visitation for assailing the horse, and draw the machine into the city. On that night Sinon opens the horse, and lets out the Greeks.

" False tears true pity move: the king com-
    mands
To loose his fetters and unbind his hands;
Then adds these friendly words: ' Dismiss thy
    fears:
Forget the Greeks; be mine as thou wert theirs.
But truly tell, was it for force or guile,
Or some religious end, you rais'd the pile?'
Thus said the king. He, full of fraudful arts,
This well-invented tale for truth imparts:
' Ye lamps of heav'n!' he said, and lifted high
His hands now free; ' thou venerable sky!
Inviolable pow'rs, ador'd with dread!
Ye fatal fillets, that once bound this head!
Ye sacred altars, from whose flames I fled!
Be all of you adjur'd; and grant I may,
Without a crime, the ungrateful Greeks betray—
Reveal the secrets of the guilty state,
And justly punish whom I justly hate!
But you, O king, preserve the faith you gave,
If I, to save myself, your empire save.
The Grecian hopes, and all the attempts they
    made,
Were only founded on Minerva's aid;
But from the time when impious Diomede,
And false Ulysses—that inventive head,
Her fatal image from the temple drew—
The sleeping guardians of the castle slew—
Her virgin statue with their bloody hands
Polluted, and profan'd her holy bands—
From thence the tide of fortune left their shore,
And ebb'd much faster than it flow'd before:
Their courage languish'd, as their hopes decay'd;
And Pallas, now averse, refus'd her aid.
Nor did the goddess doubtfully declare
Her alter'd mind, and alienated care.

When first her fatal image touch'd the ground,
She sternly cast her glaring eyes around,
That sparkled as they roll'd, and seem'd to
    threat:
Her heav'nly limbs distill'd a briny sweat.
Thrice from the ground she leap'd; was seen to
    wield
Her brandish'd lance and shake her horrid
    shield.
Then Calchas bade our host for flight prepare,
And hope no conquest from the tedious war,
Till first they sail'd for Greece—with pray'rs be-
    sought
Her injur'd pow'r, and better omens brought.
And now their navy ploughs the watery main;
Yet soon expect it on your shores again,
With Pallas pleas'd; as Calchas did ordain.
But first, to reconcile the blue-eyed maid,
From her stolen statue and her tow'r betray'd,
Warn'd by the seer, to her offended name
We rais'd and dedicate this wond'rous frame,
So lofty, lest through your forbidden gates
It pass, and intercept our better fates:
For, once admitted there, our hopes are lost;
And Troy may then a new palladium boast.
For so religion and the gods ordain,
That, if you violate with hands profane
Minerva's gift, your town in flames shall burn;
(Which omen, O ye gods, on Græcia turn!)
But if it climb, with your assisting hands,
The Trojan walls, and in the city stands;
Then Troy shall Argos and Mycenæ burn,
And the reverse of fate on us return.'
    With such deceits he gain'd their easy
    hearts,
Too prone to credit his perfidious arts.

What Diomedes, nor Thetis' greater son,
A thousand ships, nor ten years' siege, had done—
False tears and fawning words the city won.
   A greater omen, and of worse portent,
Did our unweary minds with fear torment,
Concurring to produce the dire event.
Laocoon, Neptune's priest by lot that year,
With solemn pomp then sacrific'd a steer;
When (dreadful to behold !) from sea we spied
Two serpents, rank'd abreast, the seas divide,
And smoothly sweep along the swelling tide ;
Their flaming crests above the waves they shew;
Their bellies seem to burn the seas below;
Their speckled tails advance to steer their course,
And on the sounding shore the flying billows
   force :
And now the strand, and now the plain they held.
Their ardent eyes with bloody streaks were fill'd ;
Their nimble tongues they brandish'd as they
   came,
And lick'd their hissing jaws, that sputter'd flame.
We fled amaz'd ; their destin'd way they take,
And to Laocoon and his children make :
And first around the tender boys they wind,
Then with their sharpen'd fangs their limbs and
   bodies grind.
The wretched father, running to their aid
With pious haste, but vain, they next invade ;
Twice round his waist their winding volumes
   roll'd,
And twice about his gasping throat they fold.
The priest thus doubly chok'd, their crests divide,
And, tow'ring o'er his head, in triumph ride :
With both his hands he labours at the knots;
His holy fillets the blue venom blots :
His roaring fills the flitting air around :
Thus when an ox receives a glancing wound,
He breaks his bands, the fatal altar flies,
And with loud bellowing breaks the yielding
   skies.
Their tasks perform'd, the serpents quit their prey,
And to the tow'r of Pallas make their way ;
Couch'd at her feet, they lie protected there
By her large buckler and protended spear.

   Amazement seizes all : the gen'ral cry
Proclaims Laocoon justly doom'd to die,
Whose hand the will of Pallas had withstood,
And dar'd to violate the sacred wood.
All vote t' admit the steed, that vows be paid,
And incense offer'd to th' offended maid.
A spacious breach is made ; the town lies bare :
Some hoisting-levers, some the wheels prepare,
And fasten to the horse's feet ; the rest
With cables haul along the unwieldy beast.
Each on his fellow for assistance calls :
At length the fatal fabric mounts the walls,
Big with destruction. Boys with chaplets
   crown'd,
And choirs of virgins, sing and dance around.
Thus rais'd aloft, and then descending down,
It enters o'er our heads, and threats the town :
O sacred city, built by hands divine !
O valiant heroes of the Trojan line !
Four times he struck : as oft the clashing sound
Of arms was heard, and inward groans rebound.
Yet, mad with zeal, and blinded with our fate,
We haul along the horse in solemn state ;
Then place the dire portent within the tow'r.
Cassandra cried, and curs'd th' unhappy hour ;
Foretold our fate ; and, by the gods' decree,
All heard, but none believ'd, the prophecy.
With branches we the fanes adorn, and waste
In jollity the day ordain'd to be the last.
Meantime the rapid heav'ns roll'd down the
   light,
And on the shaded ocean rush'd the night :
Our men secure, nor guards nor sentries held ;
But easy sleep their weary limbs compell'd.
The Grecians had embark'd their naval pow'rs
From Tenedos, and sought our well-known shores,
Safe under covert of the silent night,
And guided by the imperial galley's light ;
When Sinon, favour'd by the partial gods,
Unlock'd the horse, and op'd his dark abodes ;
Restor'd to vital air our hidden foes,
Who joyful from their long confinement rose."
                    Æneid, book ii.

No. 1091.

Death of Laocoon.

ATHENION. *Cornelian.*

See preceding quotation.

No. 1092.

The Trojans drawing the wooden horse.

APOLLONIDES. *Cornelian.*

See preceding quotation.

No. 1093.

Sinon lighting the Greeks out of the Trojan horse.

PYRGOTELES. *Amethyst.*

See preceding quotation.

No. 1094.

The shade of Hector appearing to Æneas in his sleep.

DIOCLES. *Sardonyx.*

" 'Twas in the dead of night, when sleep repairs
Our bodies worn with toils, our minds with cares,
When Hector's ghost before my sight appears:
A bloody shroud he seem'd, and bath'd in tears;
Such as he was, when, by Pelides slain,
Thessalian coursers dragg'd him o'er the plain.
Swoln were his feet, as when the thongs were thrust
Through the bor'd holes: his body black with dust;
Unlike that Hector who return'd, from toils
Of war, triumphant in Æacian spoils—
Or him who made the fainting Greeks retire,
And launch'd against their navy Phrygian fire.
His hair and beard stood stiffen'd with his gore;
And all the wounds he for his country bore
Now stream'd afresh, and with new purple ran.
I wept to see the visionary man;
And, while my trance continued, thus began:

' O light of Trojans, and support of Troy—
Thy father's champion, and thy country's joy!
O long expected by thy friends! from whence
Art thou so late return'd for our defence?
Do we behold thee wearied as we are
With length of labours and with toils of war?
After so many fun'rals of thy own,
Art thou restor'd to thy declining town?
But say, what wounds are these? what new dis-
    grace
Deforms the manly features of thy face?'
    To this the spectre no reply did frame,
But answer'd to the cause for which he came;
And, groaning from the bottom of his breast,
This warning in these mournful words express'd:
' O goddess-born! escape by timely flight
The flame and horrors of this fatal night:

The foes already have possess'd the wall;
Troy nods from high, and totters to her fall.
Enough is paid to Priam's royal name—
More than enough to duty and to fame:
If by a mortal hand my father's throne
Could be defended, 'twas by mine alone.
Now Troy to thee commends her future state,
And gives her gods companions of thy fate;
From their assistance happier walls expect,
Which, wand'ring long, at last thou shalt erect.'
He said, and brought me from their blest abodes
The venerable statues of the gods,
With ancient Vesta from the sacred choir,
The wreaths, and relics of th' immortal fire.
  Now peals of shouts came thund'ring from afar—
Cries—threats—and loud laments—and mingled
        war!
The noise approaches, though our palace stood
Aloof from streets, encompass'd with a wood.
Louder and yet more loud, I hear th' alarms
Of human cries distinct, and clashing arms.

Fear broke my slumbers: I no longer stay,
But mount the terrace, thence the town survey,
And hearken what the frightful sounds convey.
Thus when a flood of fire by wind is borne,
Crackling it rolls, and mows the standing corn:
Or deluges, descending o'er the plains,
Sweep o'er the yellow year—destroy the pains
Of lab'ring oxen, and the peasant's gains—
Unroot the forest-oaks, and bear away
Flocks, folds, and trees, an undistinguish'd prey,—
The shepherd climbs the cliff, and sees from far
The wasteful ravage of a watery war.
Then Hector's faith was manifestly clear'd;
And Grecian frauds in open light appear'd.

  .   .   .   .   .   .

The fire consumes the town, the foe commands;
And armed hosts, an unexpected force,
Break from the bowels of the fatal horse.
Within the gates, proud Sinon throws about
The flames; and foes for entrance press without."
                              Æneid, book ii.

No. 1095.

Venus dissuading Æneas from killing Helen.

DAMAS.   *Sardonyx.*

After several bloody encounters between the Greeks and Trojans during the night, Æneas,
finding resistance hopeless, and retiring home to save his family, if possible, meets Helen in the
temple of Vesta. The artist represents her as clasping the knees (the seat of mercy) of the statue.

" Thus wand'ring in my way, without a guide,
The graceless Helen in the porch I spied
Of Vesta's temple; there she lurk'd alone;
Muffled she sate, and, as she could, unknown:
But by the flames that cast their blaze around,
That common bane of Greece and Troy I found.
For Ilium burnt she dreads the Trojan sword—
More dreads the vengeance of her injur'd lord—
E'en by those gods who refug'd her abhorr'd.
Trembling with rage the strumpet I regard,
Resolv'd to give her guilt the due reward.
' Shall she triumphant sail before the wind, .
And leave in flames unhappy Troy behind?

Shall she her kingdom and her friends review,
In state attended with a captive crew,
While unreveng'd the good old Priam falls,
And Grecian fires consume the Trojan walls?
For this the Phrygian fields and Xanthian flood
Were swell'd with bodies, and were drunk with
                                      blood.
'Tis true, a soldier can small honour gain,
And boast no conquest, from a woman slain:
Yet shall the fact not pass without applause,
Of vengeance taken in so just a cause.
The punish'd crime shall set my soul at ease,
And murm'ring manes of my friends appease.'

Thus while I rave, a gleam of pleasing light
Spread o'er the place; and, shining heav'nly bright,
My mother stood reveal'd before my sight
(Never so radiant did her eyes appear—
Not her own star confess'd a light so clear);
Great in her charms, as when on gods above
She looks, and breathes herself into their love.
She held my hand, the destin'd blow to break ;
Then from her rosy lips began to speak :
' My son! from whence this madness, this neglect
Of my commands, and those whom I protect?
Why this unmanly rage? Recall to mind
Whom you forsake, what pledges leave behind.

Look if your helpless father yet survive,
Or if Ascanius or Creüsa live :
Around your house the greedy Grecians err ;
And these had perish'd in the nightly war
But for my presence and protecting care.
Not Helen's face nor Paris was in fault;
But by the gods was this destruction brought.
Now cast your eyes around, while I dissolve
The mists and films that mortal eyes involve ;
Purge from your sight the dross, and make you see
The shape of each avenging deity.' "

Æneid, book ii.

No. 1096.

Scene between Æneas, Anchises, and Creüsa.

APOLLONIDES. *Calcedony.*

Æneas returns home, and urges Anchises to quit the city ; he refuses ; Creüsa and young Ascanius (called also Iülus) join in imploring him to consent. The following passages will sufficiently explain this and the three subsequent subjects.

" The good Anchises, whom by timely flight
I purpos'd to secure on Ida's height,
Refus'd the journey, resolute to die,
And add his fun'rals to the fate of Troy,
Rather than exile and old age sustain.
' Go you, whose blood runs warm in ev'ry vein :
Had heav'n decreed that I should life enjoy,
Heav'n had decreed to save unhappy Troy.
'Tis sure enough, if not too much, for one
Twice to have seen our Ilium overthrown.
Make haste to save the poor remaining crew ;
And give this useless corpse a long adieu.
These weak old hands suffice to stop my breath ;
At least the pitying foes will aid my death,
To take my spoils and leave my body bare :
As for my sepulchre, let heav'n take care.
'Tis long since I, for my celestial wife
Loath'd by the gods, have dragg'd a ling'ring life ;

Since ev'ry hour and moment I expire,
Blasted from heav'n by Jove's avenging fire.' *
This oft repeated, he stood fix'd to die.
Myself, my wife, my son, my family,
Intreat, pray, beg, and raise a doleful cry :
' What! will he still persist, on death resolve,
And in his ruin all his house involve ?'
He still persists his reasons to maintain ;
Our pray'rs, our tears, our loud laments are vain
   Urg'd by despair, again I go to try
The fate of arms, resolv'd in fight to die :
What hope remains but what my death must give ?
' Can I without so dear a father live ?
You term it prudence, what I baseness call :
Could such a word from such a parent fall ?
If fortune please, and so the gods ordain,
That nothing should of ruin'd Troy remain,
And you conspire with Fortune to be slain ;

---

* Venus warned Anchises not to boast of her favours. However, he imprudently disobeyed ; and he was accordingly blasted by lightning.

The way to death is wide, th' approaches near;
For soon relentless Pyrrhus will appear,
Reeking with Priam's blood—the wretch who slew
The son (inhuman!) in the father's view,
And then the sire himself to the dire altar drew.
O goddess-mother! give me back to Fate;
Your gift was undesir'd, and came too late.
Did you for this unhappy me convey
Through foes and fires, to see my house a prey?
Shall I my father, wife, and son, behold
Welt'ring in blood each other's arms enfold?
Haste! gird my sword, though spent and over-
    come:
'Tis the last summons to receive our doom.
I hear thee, Fate! and I obey thy call!
Not unreveng'd the foe shall see my fall.
Restore me to the yet unfinish'd fight:
My death is wanting to conclude the night.'
Arm'd once again, my glitt'ring sword I wield,
While th' other hand sustains my weighty shield;
And forth I rush to seek th' abandon'd field.

  I went; but sad Creüsa stopp'd my way,
And 'cross the threshold in my passage lay,
Embrac'd my knees, and, when I would have
    gone,
Shew'd me my feeble sire and tender son.
' If death be your design—at least,' said she,
' Take us along, to share your destiny.
If any farther hopes in arms remain,
This place, these pledges of your love, maintain.
To whom do you expose your father's life,
Your son's, and mine, your now forgotten wife?'
  While thus she fills the house with clam'rous
    cries,
Our hearing is diverted by our eyes:
For while I held my son, in the short space
Betwixt our kisses and our last embrace,
(Strange to relate!) from young Iülus' head
A lambent flame arose, which gently spread
Around his brows, and on his temple fed.
Amaz'd, with running water we prepare
To quench the sacred fire, and slake his hair;
But old Anchises, vers'd in omens, rear'd
His hands to heav'n, and this request preferr'd:

' If any vows, almighty Jove, can bend
Thy will—if piety can pray'rs commend,—
Confirm the glad presage which thou art pleas'd
    to send.'
Scarce had he said, when on our left we hear
A peal of rattling thunder roll in air:
There shot a streaming lamp along the sky,
Which on the winged lightning seem'd to fly:
From o'er the roof the blaze began to move,
And, trailing, vanish'd in th' Idæan grove.
It swept a path in heav'n, and shone a guide,
Then in a streaming stench of sulphur died.
  The good old man with suppliant hands im-
    plor'd
The gods' protection, and their star ador'd.
' No, now,' said he, ' my son, no more delay!
I yield—I follow where heav'n shews the way.
Keep (O my country-gods!) our dwelling-place,
And guard this relic of the Trojan race—
This tender child! These omens are your own;
And you can yet restore the ruin'd town:
At least accomplish what your signs foreshew.
I stand resign'd, and am prepar'd to go.'
He said: the crackling flames appear on high;
And driving sparkles dance along the sky;
With Vulcan's rage the rising winds conspire,
And near our palace roll the flood of fire.
' Haste, my dear father! ('tis no time to wait)
And load my shoulders with a willing freight:
Whate'er befals, your life shall be my care;
One death, or one deliv'rance, we will share.
My hand shall lead our little son; and you,
My faithful consort, shall our steps pursue.
Next you, my servants, heed my strict com-
    mands:
Without the walls a ruin'd temple stands,
To Ceres hallow'd once: a cypress nigh
Shoots up her venerable head on high,
By long religion kept; there bend your feet,
And in divided parties let us meet.
Our country-gods, the relics, and the bands,
Hold you, my father, in your guiltless hands:
In me 'tis impious holy things to bear,
Red as I am with slaughter, new from war,

Till in some living stream I cleanse the guilt
Of dire debate, and blood in battle spilt.'
  Thus, ord'ring all that prudence could provide,
I clothe my shoulders with a lion's hide
And yellow spoils; then, on my bending back,
The welcome load of my dear father take;
While on my better hand Ascanius hung,
And with unequal paces tripp'd along :
Creüsa kept behind. By choice we stray
Through ev'ry dark and ev'ry devious way.
I, who so bold and dauntless just before —
The Grecian darts and shocks of lances bore,
At ev'ry shadow now am seiz'd with fear,
Not for myself, but for the charge I bear;
Till, near the ruin'd gate arriv'd at last,
Secure, and deeming all the danger past,
A frightful noise of trampling feet we hear.
My father, looking through the shades with
    fear,

Cried out, ' Haste, haste, my son! the foes are
  nigh;
Their swords and shining armour I descry.'
  Some hostile god, for some unknown offence,
Had sure bereft my mind of better sense;
For while through winding ways I took my flight,
And sought the shelter of the gloomy night,
Alas! I lost Creüsa : hard to tell
If by her fatal destiny she fell,
Or weary sate, or wander'd with affright;
But she was lost for ever to my sight.
I knew not, or reflected, till I meet
My friends at Ceres' now-deserted seat.
We met : not one was wanting; only she
Deceiv'd her friends—her son, and wretched me!
What mad expressions did my tongue refuse!
Whom did I not of gods or men accuse!
This was the fatal blow, that pain'd me more
Than all I felt from ruin'd Troy before."

Æneid, book ii.

No. 1097.

Creüsa and Ascanius imploring Æneas not to return to the battle.

Chromios. *Cornelian.*

See preceding quotation.

No. 1098.

Anchises, Æneas, and Creüsa in amazement at the miraculous flame that played round the head of Ascanius.

Dioscorides. *Cornelian.*

See preceding quotation.

No. 1099.

The family of Æneas quitting Troy.

Evodos. *Sardonyx.*

See preceding quotation.

4 x

No. 1100.

The ghost of Creüsa disappearing from Æneas.

Sosocles.   *Cornelian.*

Æneas misses Creüsa, and returns back in quest of her: her ghost appears, and announces to him that she is detained by Cybele to become her attendant on Mount Ida.

" Stung with my loss, and raving with despair —
Abandoning my now-forgotten care—
Of counsel, comfort, and of hope bereft—
My sire, my son, my country-gods I left.
In shining armour once again I sheath
My limbs, not feeling wounds, nor fearing death :
Then headlong to the burning walls I run,
And seek the danger I was forc'd to shun.
I tread my former tracks—through night explore
Each passage—ev'ry street I cross'd before.
All things were full of horror and affright,
And dreadful e'en the silence of the night.
Then to my father's house I make repair,
With some small glimpse of hope to find her there.
Instead of her, the cruel Greeks I met ;
The house was fill'd with foes, with flames beset ;
Driv'n on the wings of winds, whole sheets of fire,
Through air transported, to the roofs aspire.
From thence to Priam's palace I resort,
And search the citadel and desert court.
Then, unobserv'd, I pass by Juno's church :
A guard of Grecians had possess'd the porch ;
There Phœnix and Ulysses watch the prey,
And thither all the wealth of Troy convey—
The spoils which they from ransack'd houses
          brought,
And golden bowls from burning altars caught—
The tables of the gods—the purple vests—
The people's treasure, and the pomp of priests :
A rank of wretched youths, with pinion'd hands,
And captive matrons, in long order stands.
    Then, with ungovern'd madness, I proclaim
Through all the silent streets Creüsa's name :
Creüsa still I call : at length she hears,
And sudden through the shades of night appears—

Appears no more Creüsa, nor my wife,
But a pale spectre larger than the life.
Aghast—astonish'd, and struck dumb with fear,
I stood : like bristles rose my stiffen'd hair.
Then thus the ghost began to soothe my grief :
' Nor tears, nor cries, can give the dead relief.
Desist, my much-lov'd lord, t' indulge your pain ;
You bear no more than what the gods ordain :
My fates permit me not from hence to fly,
Nor he, the great Controller of the sky.
Long wand'ring ways for you the pow'rs decree—
On land hard labours, and a length of sea :
Then, after many painful years are past,
On Latium's happy shore you shall be cast,
Where gentle Tiber from his bed beholds
The flow'ry meadows and the feeding folds.
There end your toils ; and there your fates pro-
          vide
A quiet kingdom and a royal bride :
There Fortune shall the Trojan line restore ;
And you for lost Creüsa weep no more.
Fear not that I shall watch, with servile shame,
Th' imperious looks of some proud Grecian dame ;
Or, stooping to the victor's lust, disgrace
My goddess-mother, or my royal race.
And now, farewell ! the parent of the gods
Restrains my fleeting soul in her abodes.
I trust our common issue to your care.'
She said, and gliding pass'd unseen in air.
I strove to speak, but horror tied my tongue ;
And thrice about her neck my arms I flung,
And, thrice deceiv'd, on vain embraces hung :
Light as an empty dream at break of day,
Or as a blast of wind, she rush'd away."
                              Æneid, book ii.

No. 1101.

Æneas at the tomb of Polydorus.

CHROMIOS. *Cornelian.*

After the destruction of Troy and the departure of the Greeks, the Trojans who survived built a fleet, and sailed first for Thrace. There, when Æneas plucks up some shrubs to deck an altar, blood distils from the roots, and a voice announces that it is the blood of young Polydore (buried there), son of Priam, murdered for the sake of his treasures by Polymestor the king, under whose protection he was placed.

" When heav'n had overturn'd the Trojan state,
And Priam's throne, by too severe a fate ;
When ruin'd Troy became the Grecian's prey,
And Ilium's lofty tow'rs in ashes lay,
Warn'd by celestial omens we retreat,
To seek in foreign lands a happier seat.
Near old Antandros, and at Ida's foot,
The timber of the sacred groves we cut,
And build our fleet—uncertain yet to find
What place the gods for our repose assign'd.
Friends daily flock ; and scarce the kindly spring
Began to clothe the ground, and birds to sing,
When old Anchises summon'd all to sea :
The crew my father and the Fates obey.
With sighs and tears I leave my native shore,
And empty fields, where Ilium stood before.
My sire, my son, our less and greater gods,
All sail at once, and cleave the briny floods.
    Against our coast appears a spacious land,
Which once the fierce Lycurgus did command
(Thracia the name—the people bold in war—
Vast are their fields, and tillage is their care):
A hospitable realm, while Fate was kind,
With Troy in friendship and religion join'd.
I land, with luckless omens ; then adore
Their gods, and draw a line along the shore :
I lay the deep foundations of a wall,
And Ænos—nam'd from me—the city call.
To Dionæan Venus vows are paid,
And all the pow'rs that rising labours aid ;
A bull on Jove's imperial altar laid.
Not far a rising hillock stood in view ;
Sharp myrtles on the sides, and cornels grew :

There, while I went to crop the sylvan scenes,
And shade our altar with their leafy greens,
I pull'd a plant—with horror I relate
A prodigy so strange, and full of fate—
The rooted fibres rose, and from the wound
Black bloody drops distill'd upon the ground.
Mute and amaz'd, my hair with terror stood ;
Fear shrunk my sinews, and congeal'd my blood.
Mann'd once again, another plant I try ;
That other gush'd with the same sanguine dye.
Then fearing guilt for some offence unknown,
With pray'rs and vows the Dryads I atone,
With all the sisters of the woods, and most
The god of arms, who rules the Thracian coast ;
That they, or he, these omens would avert—
Release our fears, and better signs impart.
Clear'd as I thought, and fully fix'd at length
To learn the cause, I tugg'd with all my strength ;
I bent my knees against the ground : once more
The violated myrtle ran with gore.
Scarce can I tell the sequel : from the womb
Of wounded earth, and caverns of the tomb,
A groan, as of a troubled ghost, renew'd
My fright, and then these dreadful words en-
        sued :
' Why dost thou thus my buried body rend ?
Oh ! spare the corpse of thy unhappy friend !
Spare to pollute thy pious hands with blood :
The tears distil not from the wounded wood ;
But ev'ry drop this living tree contains
Is kindred blood, and ran in Trojan veins.
Oh ! fly from this inhospitable shore,
Warn'd by my fate ; for I am Polydore !

Here loads of lances, in my blood imbrued,
Again shoot upward, by my blood renew'd.'
  My falt'ring tongue and shiv'ring limbs declare
My horror; and in bristles rose my hair.
When Troy with Grecian arms was closely pent,
Old Priam, fearful of the war's event,
This hapless Polydore to Thracia sent;
Loaded with gold he sent his darling, far
From noise and tumults, and destructive war,
Committed to the faithless tyrant's care;
Who, when he saw the pow'r of Troy decline,
Forsook the weaker, with the strong to join—
Broke ev'ry bond of nature and of truth,
And murder'd, for his wealth, the royal youth.
O sacred hunger of pernicious gold!
What bands of faith can impious lucre hold?
Now, when my soul had shaken off her fears,
I call my father, and the Trojan peers—

Relate the prodigies of heav'n—require
What he commands—and their advice desire.
All vote to leave that execrable shore,
Polluted with the blood of Polydore;
But, ere we sail, his fun'ral rites prepare,
Then to his ghost a tomb and altars rear.
In mournful pomp the matrons walk the round,
With baleful cypress and blue fillets crown'd,
With eyes dejected, and with hair unbound.
Then bowls of tepid milk and blood we pour,
And thrice invoke the soul of Polydore.
  Now, when the raging storms no longer
      reign,
But southern gales invite us to the main,
We launch our vessels with a prosp'rous wind,
And leave the cities and the shores behind."
                      Æneid, book iii.

No. 1102.

Æneas meeting Andromache at the cenotaph of Hector.

SOLON.   *Cornelian.*

  Æneas lands in Epirus, and there meets Andromache the widow of Hector, who, after the death of Pyrrhus son of Achilles (to whom she was assigned as a captive on the sacking of Troy), wedded Helenus, a celebrated soothsayer, and son of Priam.

"The sight of high Phæacia soon we lost,
And skimm'd along Epirus' rocky coast.
Then to Chaonia's port our course we bend,
And, landed, to Buthrotus' heights ascend.
Here wondrous things were loudly blaz'd by
      Fame—
How Helenus reviv'd the Trojan name,
And reign'd in Greece—that Priam's captive son
Succeeded Pyrrhus in his bed and throne—
And fair Andromache, restor'd by Fate,
Once more was happy in a Trojan mate.
I leave my galleys riding in the port,
And long to see the new Dardanian court.
By chance the mournful queen, before the gate,
Then solemnis'd her former husband's fate:

Green altars, rais'd of turf, with gifts she crown'd;
And sacred priests in order stand around,
And thrice the name of hapless Hector sound.
The grove itself resembles Ida's wood:
And Simoïs seem'd the well-dissembled flood.
But when, at nearer distance, she beheld
My shining armour and my Trojan shield,
Astonish'd at the sight, the vital heat
Forsakes her limbs, her veins no longer beat;
She faints — she falls! and scarce recovering
      strength,
Thus, with a falt'ring tongue, she speaks at length:
'Are you alive, O goddess-born?' she said;
'Or if a ghost, then where is Hector's shade?'
At this she cast a loud and frightful cry."
                      Æneid, book iii.

No. 1103.

Parting of Æneas, Ascanius, and Andromache.

ADMON. *Sardonyx.*

Helenus entertained Æneas with much hospitality--traced for him the outlines of his future fortunes—and gave him useful instructions for the prosecution of his voyage.

"Nor less the queen our parting thence deplor'd,
Nor was less bounteous than her Trojan lord.
A noble present to my son she brought,
A robe with flow'rs on golden tissue wrought;
A Phrygian vest; and loads with gifts beside
Of precious texture, and of Asian pride.
' Accept,' she said, ' these monuments of love,
Which in my youth with happier hands I wove :
Regard these trifles for the giver's sake—
'Tis the last present Hector's wife can make.
Thou call'st my lost Astyanax to mind—
In thee his features and his form I find—
His eyes so sparkled with a lively flame—
Such were his motions—such was all his frame ;
And, ah ! had heav'n so pleas'd, his years had
been the same.'
With tears I took my last adieu, and said :
' Your fortune, happy pair, already made,
Leaves you no farther wish. My diff'rent state,
Avoiding one, incurs another fate.

To you a quiet seat the gods allow :
You have no shores to search, no seas to plough,
Nor fields of flying Italy to chase—
Deluding visions and a vain embrace !
You see another Simoïs, and enjoy
The labour of your hands—another Troy,
With better auspice than her ancient tow'rs,
And less obnoxious to the Grecian pow'rs.
If e'er the gods, whom I with vows adore,
Conduct my steps to Tiber's happy shore—
If ever I ascend the Latian throne,
And build a city I may call my own,—
As both of us our birth from Troy derive,
So let our kindred lines in concord live,
And both in equal acts of friendship strive.
Our fortunes, good or bad, shall be the same ;
The double Troy* shall differ but in name :
That what we now begin may never end,
But long to late posterity descend.' "

Æneid, book iii.

No. 1104.

Æneas receiving into his ship Achæmenides, who escaped from the Cyclops.

GNAIOS. *Cornelian.*

Anchises, having arrived at the country of the Cyclops, in Sicily, saves one of the companions of Ulysses, who had been inadvertently left on the coast.†

" ' Scarce had the rising sun the day reveal'd—
Scarce had his heat the pearly dews dispell'd—
When from the woods there bolts, before our sight,
Somewhat betwixt a mortal and a sprite—

So thin—so ghastly meagre—and so wan—
So bare of flesh, he scarce resembled man !
This thing all tatter'd, seem'd from far t' implore
Our pious aid, and pointed to the shore.

---

* Helenus called his city Troy.
† Anchises died after this at Drepanum, on the western coast of Sicily.

We look'd amazed; then view his shaggy beard;
His clothes were tagg'd with thorns, and filth his
    limbs besmear'd:
The rest, in mien, in habit, and in face,
Appear'd a Greek; and such indeed he was.
He cast on us, from far, a frightful view,
Whom soon for Trojans and for foes he knew—
Stood still, and paus'd; then all at once began
To stretch his limbs, and trembled as he ran.
Soon as approach'd, upon his knees he falls,
And thus with tears and sighs for pity calls:
' Now by the pow'rs above, and what we share
From Nature's common gift, this vital air,
O Trojans, take me hence! I beg no more;
But bear me far from this unhappy shore.
'Tis true, I am a Greek, and farther own,
Among your foes besieg'd th' imperial town.
For such demerits if my death be due,
No more for this abandon'd life I sue:
This only favour let my tears obtain,
To throw me headlong in the rapid main:
Since nothing more than death my crime de-
    mands,
I die content to die by human hands.'
He said, and on his knees my knees embrac'd:
I bade him boldly tell his fortune past—
His present state—his lineage, and his name—
Th' occasion of his fears, and whence he came.
The good Anchises rais'd him with his hand:
Who, thus encourag'd, answer'd our demand.
' From Ithaca, my native soil, I came
To Troy; and Achæmenides my name.
Me my poor father with Ulysses sent
(O! had I stay'd, with poverty content!);
But, fearful for themselves, my countrymen
Left me forsaken in the Cyclops' den.
The cave, though large, is dark; the dismal floor
Is pav'd with mangled limbs and putrid gore.
Our monstrous host, of more than human size,
Erects his head, and stares within the skies.
Bellowing his voice, and horrid is his hue—
Ye gods, remove this plague from mortal view!
The joints of slaughter'd wretches are his food;
And for his wine he quaffs the streaming blood.

These eyes beheld, when with his spacious hand
He seiz'd two captives of our Grecian band;
Stretch'd on his back, he dash'd against the stones
Their broken bodies, and their crackling bones:
With spouting blood the purple pavement swims,
While the dire glutton grinds the trembling limbs.
Not unreveng'd Ulysses bore their fate,
Nor thoughtless of his own unhappy state;
For gorg'd with flesh, and drunk with potent
    wine,
While fast asleep the giant lay supine,
Snoring aloud, and belching from his maw
His undigested foam, and morsels raw,—
We pray—we cast the lots—and then surround
The monstrous body, stretch'd along the ground:
Each, as he could approach him, lends a hand
To bore his eye-ball with a flaming brand.
Beneath his frowning forehead lay his eye—
For only one did the vast frame supply—
But that a globe so large, his front it fill'd,
Like the sun's disk, or like a Grecian shield;
The stroke succeeds, and down the pupil bends:
This vengeance follow'd for our slaughter'd friends.
But haste, unhappy wretches! haste to fly!
Your cables cut, and on your oars rely!
Such, and so vast as Polypheme appears,
A hundred more this hated island bears:
Like him in caves they shut their woolly sheep—
Like him, their herds to tops of mountains keep—
Like him, with mighty strides, they stalk from
    steep to steep.
And now three moons their sharpen'd horns re-
    new,
Since thus in woods and wilds, obscure from view,
I drag my loathsome days with mortal fright,
And in deserted caverns lodge by night.
Oft from the rocks a dreadful prospect see
Of the huge Cyclops like a warlike tree:
From far I hear his thund'ring voice resound,
And trampling feet that shake the solid ground.
Cornels and savage berries of the wood,
And roots and herbs, have been my meagre food.
While all around my longing eyes I cast,
I saw your happy ships appear at last.

On those I fix'd my hopes—to these I run—
'Tis all I ask, this cruel race to shun :
What other death you please, yourselves bestow.'
    Scarce had he said, when on the mountain's brow
We saw the giant-shepherd stalk before
His following flock, and leading to the shore—
A monstrous bulk—deform'd—depriv'd of sight—
His staff a trunk of pine, to guide his steps aright.
His pond'rous whistle from his neck descends ;
His woolly care their pensive lord attends :
This only solace his hard fortune sends,
Soon as he reach'd the shore, and touch'd the
    waves,
From his bor'd eye the glutt'ring blood he laves.
He gnash'd his teeth and groan'd ; through seas
    he strides ;
And scarce the topmost billows touch'd his sides.
    Seiz'd with a sudden fear, we ran to sea,
The cables cut, and silent haste away ;
The well-deserving stranger entertain ;
Then buckling to the work, our oars divide the
    main.

The giant hearken'd to the dashing sound :
But when our vessels out of reach he found,
He strided onward, and in vain essay'd
Th' Ionian deep, and durst no farther wade.
With that he roar'd aloud : the dreadful cry
Shakes earth, and air, and seas ; the billows fly
Before the bellowing noise to distant Italy.
The neighb'ring Ætna trembling all around,
The winding caverns echo to the sound.
His brother Cyclops hear the yelling roar,
And rushing down the mountains, crowd the
    shore.
We saw their stern distorted looks from far,
And one-ey'd glance, that vainly threaten'd war—
A dreadful council ! with their heads on high
(The misty clouds about their foreheads fly),
Not yielding to the tow'ring tree of Jove,
Or tallest cypress of Diana's grove.
New pangs of mortal fear our minds assail ;
We tug at ev'ry oar, and hoist up ev'ry sail,
And take th' advantage of the friendly gale."
                                Æneid, book iii.

No. 1105.

Æneas and Dido in the cave.

APOLLONIDES. *Cornelian.*

Æneas and Dido having gone out on a hunting-party, a storm comes on, and they take shelter in a cave. There Juno and Hymen attend, and perform the marriage-ceremony.

"Now had they reach'd the hills, and storm'd
    the seat
Of savage beasts, in dens, their last retreat.
The cry pursues the mountain-goats : they bound
From rock to rock, and keep the craggy ground :
Quite otherwise the stags, a trembling train,
In herds unsingled, scour the dusty plain,
And a long chase in open view maintain.
The glad Ascanius, as his courser guides,
Spurs through the vale, and these and those out-
    rides.

His horse's flanks and sides are forc'd to feel
The clanking lash and goring of the steel.
Impatiently he views the feeble prey,
Wishing some nobler beast to cross his way ;
And rather would the tusky boar attend,
Or see the tawny lion downward bend.
    Meantime the gath'ring clouds obscure the
    skies,
From pole to pole the forky lightning flies ;
The rattling thunders roll ; and Juno pours
A wintry deluge down, and sounding show'rs.

The company, dispers'd, to coverts ride,
And seek the homely cots, or mountain's hollow
    side.
The rapid rains, descending from the hills,
To rolling torrents raise the creeping rills.
The queen and prince, as love or fortune guides,
One common cavern in her bosom hides.
Then first the trembling earth the signal gave ;
And flashing fires enlighten all the cave :

Hell from below, and Juno from above,
And howling nymphs, were conscious to their love.
From this ill-omen'd hour, in time, arose
Debate and death, and all succeeding woes.
The queen, whom sense of honour could not move,
No longer made a secret of her love,
But call'd it marriage, by that specious name
To veil the crime, and sanctify the shame."
                                    Æneid, book iv.

No. 1106.

Jupiter despatching Mercury to command Æneas to quit Carthage.

DIOSCORIDES. *Cornelian.*

The following quotation will suffice for this and the subsequent subject.

" He calls Cyllenius; and the god attends ;
By whom this menacing command he sends :
' Go, mount the western winds, and cleave the
    sky ;
Then, with a swift descent, to Carthage fly :
There find the Trojan chief, who wastes his days
In slothful riot and inglorious ease ;
Nor minds the future city giv'n by Fate.
To him this message from my mouth relate :
' Not so fair Venus hoped, when twice she won
Thy life with pray'rs; nor promis'd such a son.
Her's was a hero, destin'd to command
A martial race, and rule the Latian land ;
Who should his ancient line from Teucer draw,
And on the conquer'd world impose the law.
If glory cannot move a mind so mean,
Nor future praise from fading pleasure wean ;
Yet why should he defraud his son of fame,
And grudge the Romans their immortal name ?
What are his vain designs ? what hopes he more
From his long lingering on a hostile shore,
Regardless to redeem his honour lost,
And for his race to gain th' Ausonian coast ?
Bid him with speed the Tyrian court forsake—
With this command the slumb'ring warrior
    wake.'

Hermes obeys ; with golden pinions binds
His flying feet, and mounts the western winds ;
And whether o'er the seas or earth he flies,
With rapid force they bear him down the skies.
But first he grasps within his awful hand
The mark of sovereign pow'r, his magic wand :
With this he draws the ghosts from hollow graves ;
With this he drives them down the Stygian waves ;
With this he seals in sleep the wakeful sight ;
And eyes, though closed in death, restores to light.
Thus arm'd, the god begins his airy race,
And drives the racking clouds along the liquid
    space ;
Now sees the top of Atlas as he flies,
Whose brawny back supports the starry skies—
Atlas, whose head with piny forests crown'd,
Is beaten with the winds—with foggy vapours
    bound ;
Snows hide his shoulders ; from beneath his chin
The founts of rolling streams their race begin ;
A beard of ice on his large breast depends :
Here, pois'd upon his wings, the god descends :
Then, resting thus, he from the tow'ring height
Plung'd downward with precipitated flight—
Lights on the seas, and skims along the flood.
As water-fowl, who seek their fishy food,

Less, and yet less, to distant prospect shew;
By turns they dance aloft, and dive below—
Like these, the steerage of his wings he plies,
And near the surface of the water flies,
Till, having pass'd the seas, and cross'd the sands,
He clos'd his wings, and stoop'd on Libyan lands;
Where shepherds once were hous'd in homely
    sheds,
Now tow'rs within the clouds advance their heads.
Arriving there, he found the Trojan prince
New ramparts raising for the town's defence:
A purple scarf, with gold embroider'd o'er
(Queen Dido's gift), about his waist he wore;
A sword, with glitt'ring gems diversified,
For ornament, not use, hung idly by his side.
Then thus, with winged words, the god began,
Resuming his own shape, ' Degenerate man!

Thou woman's property! what mak'st thou here,
These foreign walls and Tyrian tow'rs to rear,
Forgetful of thy own? All-pow'rful Jove,
Who sways the world below and heav'n above,
Has sent me down with this severe command:
What means thy ling'ring in the Libyan land?
If glory cannot move a mind so mean,
Nor future praise from flitting pleasure wean;
Regard the fortunes of thy rising heir:
The promis'd crown let young Ascanius wear,
To whom th' Ausonian sceptre and the state
Of Rome's imperial name is owed by Fate.'
So spoke the god; and, speaking, took his
    flight,
Involv'd in clouds; and vanish'd out of sight."
                     Æneid, book iv.

No. 1107.

Mercury delivering the commands of Jupiter to Æneas.

DIOSCORIDES. *Cornelian.*

See preceding quotation.

No. 1108.

Interview between Æneas and Dido.

CHROMIOS. *Sardonyx.*

Dido is represented here as imploring Æneas to remain; and he, about to embark, is signifying that he must obey the divine injunction.

" ' Base and ungrateful! could you hope to fly,
And undiscover'd 'scape a lover's eye?
Nor could my kindness your compassion move,
Nor plighted vows, nor dearer bands of love?
Or is the death of a despairing queen
Not worth preventing, though too well foreseen?
E'en when the wint'ry winds command your stay,
You dare the tempests, and defy the sea.
False as you are, suppose you were not bound
To lands unknown, and foreign coasts to sound;

Were Troy restor'd, and Priam's happy reign,
Now durst you tempt, for Troy, the raging main?
See whom you fly! am I the foe you shun?
Now by those holy vows, so late begun,
By thy right hand (since I have nothing more
To challenge, but the faith you gave before),
I beg you by these tears too truly shed—
By the new pleasures of our nuptial bed;
If ever Dido, when you most were kind,
Were pleasing in your eyes, or touch'd your mind—

4 Y

By these my pray'rs, if prayers may yet have place,
Pity the fortunes of a falling race!
For you I have provok'd a tyrant's hate,
Incens'd the Libyan and the Tyrian state—
For you alone I suffer in my fame,
Bereft of honour, and expos'd to shame!
Whom have I now to trust, ungrateful guest?
(That only name remains of all the rest!)
What have I left? or whither can I fly?
Must I attend Pygmalion's cruelty,
Or till Iarbus shall in triumph lead
A queen that proudly scorn'd his proffer'd bed?
Had you deferr'd, at least, your hasty flight,
And left behind some pledge of our delight—
Some babe to bless the mother's mournful sight—
Some young Æneas to supply your place,
Whose features might express his father's face,
I should not then complain to live bereft
Of all my husband, or be wholly left.'
    Here paus'd the queen.   Unmov'd he holds his eyes,
By Jove's command; nor suffer'd love to rise,
Though heaving in his heart; and thus at length replies:
' Fair queen, you never can enough repeat
Your boundless favours, or I own my debt;
Nor can my mind forget Eliza's name,
While vital breath inspires this mortal frame.
This only let me speak in my defence;
I never hop'd a secret flight from hence,

Much less pretended to the lawful claim
Of sacred nuptials, or a husband's name.
For, if indulgent heav'n would leave me free,
And not submit my life to Fate's decree,
My choice would lead me to the Trojan shore,
Those relics to review, their dust adore,
And Priam's ruin'd palace to restore.
But now the Delphian oracle commands,
And fate invites me to the Latian lands:
That is the promis'd place to which I steer;
And all my vows are terminated there.
If you, a Tyrian and a stranger born,
With walls and tow'rs a Libyan town adorn,
Why may not we—like you, a foreign race—
Like you seek shelter in a foreign place?
As often as the night obscures the skies
With humid shades, or twinkling stars arise,
Anchises' angry ghost in dreams appears,
Chides my delay, and fills my soul with fears;
And young Ascanius justly may complain,
Defrauded of his fate and destin'd reign.
E'en now the herald of the gods appear'd—
Waking I saw him, and his message heard—
From Jove he came commission'd, heav'nly bright
With radiant beams, and manifest to sight
(The sender and the sent I both attest):
These walls he enter'd, and these words express'd.
Fair queen, oppose not what the gods command;
Forc'd by my fate, I leave your happy land.' "
                                        Æneid, book iv.

No. 1109.

Mercury warning Æneas in his sleep to expedite his departure.

CARILAOS.   *Cornelian.*

" These thoughts she brooded in her anxious breast—
On board, the Trojan found more easy rest.
Resolv'd to sail, in sleep he pass'd the night;
And order'd all things for his early flight.

To whom once more the winged god appears:
His former youthful mien and shape he wears,
And with this new alarm invades his ears:
' Sleep'st thou, O goddess-born? and canst thou drown
Thy needful cares so near a hostile town

Beset with foes; nor hear'st the western gales
Invite thy passage and inspire thy sails?
She harbours in her heart a furious hate
(And thou shalt find the dire effects too late),
Fix'd on revenge, and obstinate to die.
Haste swiftly hence, while thou hast power to fly!
The sea with ships will soon be cover'd o'er,
And blazing firebrands kindle all the shore.
Prevent her rage, while night obscures the skies,
And sail before the purple morn arise.
Who knows what hazards thy delay may bring?
Woman's a various and a changeful thing.'
Thus Hermes in the dream; then took his flight
Aloft in air unseen, and mix'd with night.
    Twice warn'd by the celestial messenger,
The pious prince arose with hasty fear;

Then rous'd his drowsy train without delay:
'Haste to your banks! your crooked anchors weigh,
And spread your flying sails, and stand to sea.
A god commands: he stood before my sight,
And urg'd us once again to speedy flight.
O sacred pow'r! what pow'r soe'er thou art,
To thy bless'd orders I resign my heart:
Lead thou the way; protect thy Trojan bands;
And prosper the design thy will commands.'
He said; and drawing forth his flaming sword,
His thund'ring arm divides the many-twisted
    cord.*
An emulating zeal inspires his train—
They run—they snatch—they rush into the main.
With headlong haste they leave the desert shores,
And brush the liquid seas with lab'ring oars."

Æneid, book iv.

No. 1110.

Death of Dido.

GNAIOS. *Cornelian.*

When Dido finds Æneas determined on departing, she resolves not to survive his absence; and under the pretence of performing certain magical rites, in order either to regain the lost love of Æneas, or get rid of her own, orders a funeral pile to be erected, on which were to be placed the clothes and sword of Æneas. On this pile she kills herself with his sword.

"Then swiftly to the fatal place she pass'd,
And mounts the funeral pile with furious haste;
Unsheaths the sword the Trojan left behind
(Not for so dire an enterprise design'd).
But when she view'd the garments loosely spread,
Which once he wore, and saw the conscious bed,
She paus'd, and with a sigh the robes embrac'd;
Then on the couch her trembling body cast,
Repress'd the ready tears, and spoke her last:
'Dear pledges of my love, while heav'n so pleas'd,
Receive a soul, of mortal anguish eas'd.

My fatal course is finish'd; and I go,
A glorious name, among the ghosts below.
A lofty city by my hands is rais'd—
Pygmalion† punish'd, and my lord appeas'd.
What could my fortune have afforded more,
Had the false Trojan never touch'd my shore?'
Then kiss'd the couch: and, 'Must I die?' she
    said,
'And unreveng'd? 'tis doubly to be dead!
Yet e'en this death with pleasure I receive:
On any terms, 'tis better than to live.

---

* The cable.

† Pygmalion, the avaricious and tyrannical king of Tyre, and brother of Dido, slew her husband Sichæus in the temple of which he was priest, in order to get possession of his wealth. But Dido had her revenge by carrying off the treasures, and inducing a great number of the wealthy citizens to accompany her to the coast of Africa, where she founded Carthage.

716 CATALOGUE.

These flames from far may the false Trojan view,
These boding omens his base flight pursue!'
She said, and struck—deep enter'd in her side
The piercing steel, with reeking purple dyed:
Clogg'd in the wound the cruel weapon stands,
The spouting blood comes streaming on her hands.
Her sad attendants saw the deadly stroke,
And with loud cries the sounding palace shook:
Distracted from the fatal sight they fled,
And through the town the dismal rumour spread.
First from the frighted court the yell began;
Redoubled, thence from house to house it ran:
The groans of men, with shrieks, laments, and cries
Of mixing women mount the vaulted skies.
Not less the clamour than if, ancient Tyre,
Or the new Carthage, set by foes on fire,
The rolling ruin, with their lov'd abodes,
Involv'd the blazing temples of their gods.
Her sister hears; and furious with despair,
She beats her breast, and rends her yellow hair;
And calling on Eliza's* name aloud,
Runs breathless to the place, and breaks the crowd:
' Was all that pomp of woe for this prepar'd—
These fires—this funeral pile—these altars rear'd?

Was all this train of plots contriv'd,' said she,
' All only to deceive unhappy me?
Which is the worst? Didst thou in death pretend
To scorn thy sister, or delude thy friend?
Thy summon'd sister and thy friend had come:
One sword had serv'd us both—one common
    tomb!
Was I to raise the pile—the pow'rs invoke,
Not to be present at the fatal stroke?
At once thou hast destroy'd thyself and me—
Thy town—thy senate—and thy colony!
Bring water—bathe the wound; while I in death
Lay close my lips to hers, and catch the flying
    breath.'
This said, she mounts the pile with eager haste,
And in her arms the gasping queen embrac'd;
Her temples chaf'd, and her own garments tore
To stanch the streaming blood, and cleanse the
    gore.
Thrice Dido tried to raise her drooping head,
And, fainting, thrice fell grov'lling on the bed;
Thrice op'd her heavy eyes, and saw the light;
But, having found it, sicken'd at the sight,
And clos'd her lids at last in endless night."
                            Æneid, book iv.

No. 1111.

Combat of Dares and Entellus.

CHROMIOS. *Cornelian.*

Æneas, after quitting Carthage, where he resided nearly a year, was forced by stress of weather to put in at Sicily. Here he is hospitably entertained by Acestes, a prince of Trojan lineage. He institutes games to commemorate his father's death. Among the contests—such as sailing, racing, archery—a combat with the gauntlet holds a prominent rank.

" The race thus ended, and rewards bestow'd,
Once more the prince bespeaks th' assembl'd crowd:
' If there be here whose dauntless courage dare
In gauntlet-fight, with limbs and body bare,
His opposite sustain in open view,
Stand forth the champion, and the games renew!

Two prizes I propose, and thus divide—
A bull with gilded horns, and fillets tied,
Shall be the portion of the conqu'ring chief:
A sword and helm shall cheer the loser's grief.'
    Then haughty Dares in the lists appears;
Stalking he strides—his head erected bears;

* Dido.

His nervous arms the weighty gauntlet wield;
And loud applauses echo through the field.
Dares, alone in combat used to stand,
The match of mighty Paris hand to hand;
The same at Hector's fun'ral undertook
Gigantic Butes, of th' Amycian stock,
And, by the stroke of his resistless hand,
Stretch'd the vast bulk upon the yellow sand.
Such Dares was, and such he strode along,
And drew the wonder of the gazing throng:
His brawny back and ample breast he shews;
His lifted arms around his head he throws,
And deals in whistling air his empty blows.
His match is sought; but through the trembling
    band
Not one dares answer to the proud demand.
Presuming of his force, with sparkling eyes
Already he devours the promis'd prize.
He claims the bull with awless insolence,
And, having seiz'd his horns, accosts the prince:
'If none my matchless valour dares oppose,
How long shall Dares wait his dastard foes?
Permit me, chief—permit, without delay,
To lead this uncontended gift away.'
The crowd assents, and, with redoubled cries,
For the proud challenger demands the prize.
  Acestes, fir'd with just disdain to see
The plain usurp'd without a victory,
Reproach'd Entellus thus, who sat beside,
And heard and saw unmov'd the Trojan's pride:
'Once, but in vain, a champion of renown,
So tamely can you bear the ravish'd crown!
A prize in triumph borne before your sight,
And shun for fear the danger of the fight?
Where is our Eryx now, the boasted name—
The god who taught your thund'ring arm the game?
Where now your baffled honour? where the spoil
That fill'd your house, and fame that fill'd our isle!'
Entellus thus: 'My soul is still the same,
Unmov'd with fear, and mov'd with martial fame:
But my chill blood is curdled in my veins;
And scarce the shadow of a man remains.

Oh! could I turn to that fair prime again—
That prime of which this boaster is so vain—
The brave, who this decrepit age defies,
Should feel my force without the promis'd prize.'
He said; and, rising at the word, he threw
Two pond'rous gauntlets down in open view—
Gauntlets which Eryx wont in fight to wield,
And sheath his hands with, in the listed field.
With fear and wonder seiz'd, the crowd beholds
The gloves of death, with sev'n distinguish'd folds
Of tough bull-hides; the space within is spread
With iron, or with loads of heavy lead.
Dares himself was daunted at the sight—
Renounc'd his challenge, and refus'd to fight.
Astonish'd at their weight, the hero stands,
And pois'd the pond'rous engines in his hands.
  'What had your wonder,' said Entellus, 'been,
Had you the gauntlets of Alcides seen,
And view'd the stern debate on this unhappy
    green?
These which I bear your brother Eryx* bore,
Still mark'd with batter'd brains and mingled gore.
With these he long sustain'd th' Herculean arm;
And these I wielded while my blood was warm—
This languish'd frame while better spirits fed,
Ere age unstrung my nerves, or time o'ersnow'd
    my head.
But if the challenger these arms refuse,
And cannot wield their weight, or dare not use;
If great Æneas and Acestes join
In his request—these gauntlets I resign:
Let us with equal arms perform the fight;
Let him resign his fear, since I resign my right.'
  This said, Entellus for the strife prepares;
Stripp'd of his quilted coat, his body bares;
Compos'd of mighty bones and brawn, he stands
A goodly tow'ring object, on the sands.
Then just Æneas equal arms supplied,
Which round their shoulders to their wrists they
    tied.
Both on the tiptoe stand, at full extent,
Their arms aloft, their bodies inly bent;

* Eryx was the son of Venus, and half-brother of Æneas.

Their heads from aiming blows they bear afar;
With clashing gauntlets then provoke the war.
One on his youth and pliant limbs relies—
One on his sinews and his giant size.
The last is stiff with age—his motion slow—
He heaves for breath—he staggers to and fro,
And clouds of steaming breath his nostrils loudly
    blow.
Yet equal in success, they ward—they strike:
Their ways are diff'rent, but their art alike.
Before—behind—the blows are dealt—around
Their hollow sides the rattling thumps resound.
A storm of strokes, well meant, with fury flies
And errs about their temples, ears, and eyes—
Nor always errs; for oft the gauntlet draws
A sweeping stroke along the crackling jaws.
Heavy with age, Entellus stands his ground,
But with his warping body wards the wound.
His hand and watchful eye keep even pace;
Whiles Dares traverses, and shifts his place,
And like a captain who beleaguers round
Some strong-built castle on a rising ground,
Views all th' approaches with observing eyes;
This and that other part in vain he tries,
And more on industry than force relies.
With hands on high, Entellus threats the foe,
But Dares watch'd the motion from below,
And slipp'd aside, and shunn'd the long-descend-
    ing blow.
Entellus wastes his forces on the wind,
And, thus deluded of the stroke design'd,
Headlong and heavy fell: his ample breast
And weighty limbs his ancient mother press'd.
So falls a hollow pine, that long had stood
On Ida's height, or Erymanthus' wood,
Torn from the roots. The diff'ring nations rise,
And shouts and mingled murmurs rend the skies.
Acestes runs with eager haste to raise
The fall'n companion of his youthful days.
Dauntless he rose, and to the fight return'd;
With shame his glowing cheek, his eyes with fury
    burn'd.

Disdain and conscious virtue fir'd his breast,
And with redoubled force his foe he press'd.
He lays on blows with either hand amain,
And headlong drives the Trojan o'er the plain;
Nor stops, nor stays—nor rest, nor breath allows;
But storms of strokes descend about his brows—
A rattling tempest and a hail of blows.
But now the prince, who saw the wild increase
Of wounds, commands the combatants to cease,
And bounds Entellus' wrath, and bids the peace.
First to the Trojan, spent with toil he came,
And sooth'd his sorrow for the suffer'd shame.
'What fury seiz'd my friend! The gods,' said he,
' To him propitious, and averse to thee,
Have giv'n his arm superior force to thine:
'Tis madness to contend with strength divine.'
The gauntlet-fight thus ended, from the shore
His faithful friends unhappy Dares bore:
His mouth and nostrils pour'd a purple flood;
And pounded teeth came rushing with his blood.
Faintly he stagger'd through the hissing throng,
And hung his head, and trail'd his legs along.
The sword and casque are carried by his train;
But with his foe the palm and ox remain.
    The champion then before Æneas came,
Proud of his prize, but prouder of his fame:
' O goddess-born, and you, Dardanian host,
Mark with attention, and forgive my boast;
Learn what I was by what remains; and know
From what impending fate you sav'd my foe.'
Sternly he spoke, and then confronts the bull;
And on his ample forehead aiming full,
The deadly stroke descending pierc'd the skull.
Down drops the beast, nor needs a second wound,
But sprawls in pangs of death, and spurns the
    ground.
Then thus: ' In Dares' stead I offer this—
Eryx! accept a nobler sacrifice;
Take the last gift my wither'd arms can yield;
Thy gauntlets I resign, and here renounce the
    field.' "

                        Æneid, book v.

No. 1112.

The Trojan women burning the fleet of Æneas.

POLYCLETES.   *Sardonyx.*

Juno, wishing to prevent Æneas from reaching Italy, sends Iris to instigate the Trojan women to fire the fleet, while the men are engaged at the games.

" Swiftly fair Iris down her arch descends,
And, undiscern'd, her fatal voyage ends.
She saw the gath'ring crowd, and gliding thence
The desert shore, and fleet without defence.
The Trojan matrons, on the sands alone,
With sighs and tears Anchises' death bemoan :
Then, turning to the sea their weeping eyes,
Their pity to themselves renews their cries.
' Alas !' said one, ' what oceans yet remain
For us to sail ! what labours to sustain !'
All take the word, and, with a gen'ral groan,
Implore the gods for peace, and places of their
    own.
The goddess great in mischief views their pains,
And in a woman's form her heav'nly limbs re-
    strains.
In face and shape old Beroe she became,
Doryclus' wife, a venerable dame,
Once bless'd with riches and a mother's name.
Thus chang'd, amidst the crying crowd she ran,
Mix'd with the matrons, and these words began :
' O wretched we! whom not the Grecian pow'r
Nor flames destroy'd, in Troy's unhappy hour !
O wretched we ! reserv'd by cruel Fate
Beyond the ruins of the sinking state !
Now sev'n revolving years are wholly run,
Since this unprosp'rous voyage we begun—
Since, toss'd from shores to shores, from lands to
    lands,
Inhospitable rocks and barren sands—
Wand'ring in exile through the stormy sea,
We search in vain for flying Italy.

Now cast by fortune on this kindred land,*
What should our rest and rising walls withstand,
Or hinder here to fix our banish'd band ?
O country lost, and gods redeem'd in vain,
If still in endless exile we remain !
Shall we no more the Trojan walls renew,
Or streams of some dissembled Simois view?
Haste ! join with me ! th' unhappy fleet consume :
Cassandra bids, and I declare her doom.
In sleep I saw her ; she supplied my hands
(For this I more than dreamt) with flaming
    brands :
' With these,' said she, ' these wand'ring ships de-
    stroy—
These are your fated seats, and this your Troy.'
Time calls you now, the precious hour employ ;
Slack not the good presage, while heav'n in-
    spires
Our minds to dare, and gives the ready fires.
See ! Neptune's altars minister their brands :
The god is pleas'd ; the god supplies our hands.'
Then from the pile a flaming fire she drew,
And, toss'd in air, amidst the galleys threw.
Rapt in amaze, the matrons wildly stare :
Then Pyrgo, rev'renc'd for her hoary hair—
Pyrgo, the nurse of Priam's num'rous race :
' No Beroe this, though she belies her face !
What terrors from her frowning front arise !
Behold a goddess in her ardent eyes !
What rays around her heav'nly face are seen !
Mark her majestic voice, and more than mortal
    mien !

* For it was under the dominion of Alcestes, a Trojan.

Beroe but now I left, whom, pin'd with pain,
Her age and anguish from these rites detain.'
She said. The matrons, seiz'd with new amaze,
Roll their malignant eyes, and on the navy gaze.
They fear, and hope, and neither part obey :
They hope the fated land, but fear the fatal way.
The goddess, having done her task below,
Mounts upon equal wings, and bends her painted
    bow.
Struck with the sight, and seiz'd with rage divine,
The matrons prosecute their mad design :

They shriek aloud; they snatch, with impious
    hands,
The food of altars : firs and flaming brands,
Green boughs and saplings, mingled in their haste,
And smoking torches, on the ships they cast.
The flame, unstopp'd at first, more fury gains;
And Vulcan rides at large with loosen'd reins :
Triumphant on the painted stern he soars,
And seizes, in his way, the banks and crackling
    oars."

Æneid, book v.

No. 1113.

Venus entreating Neptune to favour the voyage of Æneas after leaving Sicily.

SOLON. *Sardonyx.*

Æneas left the offenders behind him, and set sail for Italy. The following quotation will suffice for this and the three subsequent subjects.

" Meantime the mother-goddess, full of fears,
To Neptune thus address'd, with tender tears :
' The pride of Jove's imperious queen—the rage—
The malice—which no sufferings can assuage,
Compel me to these pray'rs ; since neither fate—
Nor time—nor pity—can remove her hate.
E'en Jove is thwarted by his haughty wife :
Still vanquish'd, yet she still renews the strife.
As if 'twere little to consume the town
Which aw'd the world, and wore the imperial
    crown,
She prosecutes the ghost of Troy with pains,
And gnaws, e'en to the bones, the last remains.
Let her the causes of her hatred tell ;
But you can witness its effects too well.
You saw the storm she rais'd on Libyan floods,
That mix'd the mounting billows with the clouds,
When, bribing Æolus, she took the main,
And mov'd rebellion in your wat'ry reign.
With fury she possess'd the Dardan dames
To burn their fleet with execrable flames,

And forc'd Æneas, when his ships were lost,
To leave his followers on a foreign coast.
For what remains, your godhead I implore,
And trust my son to your protecting pow'r ;
If neither Jove's nor Fate's decree withstand,
Secure his passage to the Latian land.'
    Then thus the mighty ruler of the main :
' What may not Venus hope from Neptune's reign?
My kingdom claims your birth ; my late defence
Of your endanger'd fleet may claim your confi-
    dence.
Nor less by land than sea my deeds declare,
How much your lov'd Æneas is my care.
Thee, Xanthus ! and thee, Simoïs ! I attest—
Your Trojan troops when proud Achilles press'd,
And drove before him headlong on the plain,
And dash'd against the walls the trembling train,
When floods were fill'd with bodies of the slain ;
When crimson Xanthus, doubtful of his way,
Stood up on ridges to behold the sea
(New heaps came tumbling in and chok'd his way);

When your Æneas fought, but fought with odds
Of force unequal, and unequal gods,
I spread a cloud before the victor's sight,
Sustain'd the vanquish'd, and secur'd his flight—
E'en then secur'd him, when I sought with joy
The vow'd destruction of ungrateful Troy.
My will's the same: fair goddess! fear no more,
Your fleet shall safely gain the Latian shore.
Their lives are giv'n: one destin'd head alone
Shall perish, and for multitudes atone.'
Thus having arm'd with hopes her anxious mind,
His finny team Saturnian Neptune join'd,
Then adds the foamy bridle to their jaws,
And to the loosen'd reins permits the laws.
High on the waves his azure car he guides;
Its axles thunder, and the sea subsides;
And the smooth ocean rolls her silent tides.
The tempests fly before their father's face;
Trains of inferior gods his triumph grace;
And monster whales before their master play,
And choirs of Tritons crowd the watery way.
The marshall'd pow'rs in equal troops divide
To right and left; the gods his better side
Enclose; and, on the worse, the Nymphs and
　　　Nereids ride.
Now smiling hope, with sweet vicissitude,
Within the hero's mind his joys renew'd.
He calls to raise the masts, the sheets display;
The cheerful crew with diligence obey;
They scud before the wind, and sail in open sea.
A-head of all the master-pilot steers;
And, as he leads, the following navy veers.
The steeds of night had travell'd half the sky;
The drowsy rowers on their benches lie;
When the soft god of sleep, with easy flight,
Descends, and draws behind a trail of light.

Thou, Palinurus, art his destined prey;
To thee alone he takes his fatal way.
Dire dreams to thee, and iron sleep he bears;
And, lighting on thy prow, the form of Phorbas
　　　wears.
Then thus the traitor god began his tale:
' The winds, my friend, inspire a pleasing gale;
The ships, without thy care, securely sail:
Now steal an hour of sweet repose, and I
Will take the rudder, and thy room supply.'
To whom the yawning pilot, half asleep:
' Me dost thou bid to trust the treach'rous deep,
The harlot-smiles of her dissembling face,
And to her faith commit the Trojan race?
Shall I believe the siren South again,
And, oft betray'd, not know the monster-main?'
He said: his fasten'd hands the rudder keep;
And, fix'd on heav'n, his eyes repel invading
　　　sleep.
The god was wroth, and at his temples threw
A branch in Lethe dipp'd, and drunk with Stygian
　　　dew;
The pilot, vanquish'd by the pow'r divine,
Soon clos'd his swimming eyes, and lay supine.
Scarce were his limbs extended at their length,
The god, insulting with superior strength,
Fell heavy on him, plung'd him in the sea,
And, with the stern, the rudder tore away.
Headlong he fell, and, struggling in the main,
Cried out for helping hands, but cried in vain.
The victor demon mounts obscure in air,
While the ship sails without the pilot's care;
On Neptune's faith the floating fleet relies:
But what the man forsook, the god supplies; .
And o'er the dang'rous deep secure the navy flies."
　　　　　　　　　　　Æneid, book v.

No. 1114.

The same subject.

Gnaios. *Cornelian.*

See preceding quotation.

No. 1115.

The Genius of Sleep with poppy overpowering Palinurus.

PYRGOTELES.   *Cornelian.*

See last paragraph of preceding quotation.

No. 1116.

Palinurus in the sea, holding the rudder of his ship, while the God of Sleep flies away.

ALLION.   *Sardonyx.*

See last paragraph of preceding quotation.

No. 1117.

The sea-god Triton seizing Misenus.

CHROMIOS.   *Sardonyx.*

Æneas having arrived at Cumæ in Italy, went, accompanied by Achates, to consult the Sibyl. In his absence, Misenus, the famous trumpeter, was killed by Triton, whom he challenged to a trial of skill.

"But soon they found an object to deplore:
Misenus lay extended on the shore—
Son of the god of winds:—none so renown'd
The warrior-trumpet in the field to sound,
With breathing brass to kindle fierce alarms,
And rouse to dare their fate in honourable arms.
He serv'd great Hector, and was ever near,
Not with his trumpet only, but his spear.
But, by Pelides' arm when Hector fell,
He chose Æneas; and he chose as well.
Swoln with applause, and aiming still at more,
He now provokes the sea-gods from the shore.
With envy Triton heard the martial sound,
And the bold champion, for his challenge, drown'd,
Snatch'd from the rock on which he took his stand;
Then cast his mangled carcass on the strand:
The gazing crowd around the body stand.
All weep; but most Æneas mourns his fate,
And hastens to perform the fun'ral state."*

Æneid, book vi.

---

* It is the general opinion of the critics, that, as Homer does not mention the trumpet as having been used during the Trojan war, the instrument was not then known: but this passage shews that Virgil had a different opinion.

No. 1118.

Triton hurling Misenus into the sea.

CHROMIOS. *Sardonyx.*

See preceding quotation.

No. 1119.

Æneas plucking the golden branch.

CHROMIOS. *Cornelian.*

Æneas having, in compliance with the instructions of Helenus, and the advice of his father's shade that appeared to him, consulted the Sibyl of Cumæ about his meditated descent to the infernal regions in order to consult the spirit of his father, she told him that he should first pluck, from a certain tree in a wood sacred to Proserpine, a branch that had golden bark and leaves, which would be a kind of passport.

" Thus while he wrought, revolving in his mind
The ways to compass what his wish design'd,
He cast his eyes upon the gloomy grove ;
And then in vows implor'd the queen of love :
' O! may thy power, propitious still to me,
Conduct my steps to find the fatal tree
In this deep forest ; since the Sibyl's breath
Foretold, alas! too true, Misenus' death.'
Scarce had he said, when, full before his sight,
Two doves descending from their airy flight,
Secure upon the grassy plain alight.
He knew his mother's birds ; and thus he pray'd :
' Be you my guides—lend your auspicious aid,
And lead my footsteps, till the branch be found,
Whose glitt'ring shadow gilds the sacred ground.
And thou, great parent! with celestial care,
In this distress be present to my pray'r.'
Thus having said, he stopp'd, with watchful sight
Observing still the motions of their flight,
What course they took, what happy signs they shew.
They fed, and flutt'ring, by degrees withdrew
Still farther from the place, but still in view ;
Hopping and flying thus they led him on
To the slow lake, whose baleful stench to shun,*
They wing'd their flight aloft; then, stooping low,
Perch'd on the double tree that bears the golden bough.
Through the green leaves the glitt'ring shadows glow ;
As, on the sacred oak, the wint'ry misletoe,
Where the proud mother views her precious brood,
And happier branches which she never sow'd.
Such was the glitt'ring, such the ruddy rind,
And dancing leaves, that wanton'd in the wind.
He seiz'd the shining bough with griping hold,
And rent away with ease the ling'ring gold ;
Then to the Sibyl's palace bore the prize."

Æneid, book vi.

---

* Avernus.

No. 1120.

Æneas, the Sibyl, Charon, and Cerberus, in the infernal regions.

POLYCLETES. *Sardonyx.*

Æneas and the Sibyl, after the performance of many propitiatory rites, descend to the infernal regions.

" Hence to deep Acheron they take their way,
Whose troubled eddies, thick with ooze and clay,
Are whirl'd aloft, and in Cocytus lost.
There Charon stands, who rules the dreary coast—
A sordid god : down from his hoary chin
A length of beard descends—uncomb'd—unclean!
His eyes, like hollow furnaces on fire!
A girdle, foul with grease, binds his obscene attire!
He spreads his canvass ; with his pole he steers ;
The freights of flitting ghosts in his thin bottom
    bears.
He look'd in years ; yet in his years were seen
A youthful vigour and autumnal green.
An airy crowd came rushing where he stood,
Which fill'd the margin of the fatal flood—
Husbands and wives, boys and unmarried maids,
And mighty heroes' more majestic shades,
And youths, entomb'd before their father's eyes,
With hollow groans, and shrieks, and feeble
    cries:
Thick as the leaves in autumn strew the woods,
Or fowls, by winter forc'd, forsake the floods,
And wing their hasty flight to happier lands,—
Such, and so thick, the shiv'ring army stands,
And press for passage with extended hands.
    Now these, now those, the surly boatman bore :
The rest he drove to distance from the shore.
The hero, who beheld, with wond'ring eyes,
The tumult mix'd with shrieks, laments, and cries,
Ask'd of his guide what the rude concourse meant?
Why to the shore the thronging people bent?
What forms of law among the ghosts were us'd ?
Why some were ferried o'er, and some refus'd ?
' Son of Anchises ! offspring of the gods !'
The Sibyl said ; ' you see the Stygian floods,

The sacred streams which heav'n's imperial state
Attests in oaths, and fears to violate.
The ghosts rejected are th' unhappy crew
Depriv'd of sepulchres and fun'ral due.
The boatman, Charon : those—the buried host,
He ferries over to the farther coast.
Nor dares his transport-vessel cross the waves
With such whose bones are not compos'd in
    graves :
A hundred years they wander on the shore ;
At length, their penance done, are wafted o'er.'

.   .   .   .   .

    Now nearer to the Stygian lake they draw :
Whom from the shore the surly boatman saw ;
Observ'd their passage through the shady wood,
And mark'd their near approaches to the flood.
Then thus he call'd aloud, inflam'd with wrath :
' Mortal, whate'er, who this forbidden path
In arms presum'st to tread ! I charge thee, stand
And tell thy name, and bus'ness in this land.
Know this the realm of night—the Stygian shore :
My boat conveys no living bodies o'er.
Nor was I pleas'd great Theseus once to bear,
Who forc'd a passage with his pointed spear ;
Nor strong Alcides—men of mighty fame,
And from th' immortal gods their lineage came.
In fetters one the barking porter tied,
And took him trembling from his sov'reign's
    side :
Two sought by force to seize his beauteous bride.'
To whom the Sibyl thus : ' Compose thy mind ;
Nor frauds are here contriv'd, nor force design'd :
Still may the dog the wand'ring troops constrain
Of airy ghosts, and vex the guilty train ;
And with her grisly lord his lovely queen remain.

The Trojan chief, whose lineage is from Jove,
Much fam'd for arms, and more for filial love,
Is sent to seek his sire in your Elysian grove.
If neither piety, nor heav'n's command,
Can gain his passage to the Stygian strand,
This fatal present shall prevail at least'—
Then shew'd the shining bough, conceal'd within
    her vest.
Nor more was needful; for the gloomy god
Stood mute with awe to see the golden rod;
Admir'd the destin'd off'ring to his queen—
A venerable gift, so rarely seen.
His fury thus appeas'd, he puts to land:
The ghosts forsake their seats at his command:
He clears the deck, receives the mighty freight;
The leaky vessel groans beneath the weight.
Slowly she sails, and scarcely stems the tides:
The pressing water pours within her sides.

His passengers at length are wafted o'er,
Expos'd, in muddy weeds, upon the miry shore.
No sooner landed, in his den they found
The triple porter of the Stygian sound—
Grim Cerberus, who soon began to rear
His crested snakes, and arm'd his bristling hair.
The prudent Sibyl had before prepar'd
A sop, in honey steep'd, to charm the guard,
Which, mix'd with pow'rful drugs, she cast before
His greedy grinning jaws, just op'd to roar:
With three enormous mouths he gapes; and
    straight,
With hunger press'd, devours the pleasing bait.
Long draughts of sleep his monstrous limbs en-
    slave;
He reels, and, falling, fills the spacious cave."
Æneid, book vi.

No. 1121.

Interview of Æneas and Dido in the infernal regions.

ANTEROTOS. *Sardonyx.*

Æneas meets the ghosts of several eminent persons whom he knew in life; among them
Dido and Deïphobus.

"Not far from these Phœnician Dido stood,
Fresh from her wound, her bosom bath'd in blood;
Whom when the Trojan hero hardly knew,
Obscure in shades, and with a doubtful view
(Doubtful as he who sees, through dusky night,
Or thinks he sees, the moon's uncertain light),
With tears he first approach'd the sullen shade,
And, as his love inspir'd him, thus he said:
'Unhappy queen! then is the common breath
Of rumour true, in your reported death,
And I, alas! the cause?—By heav'n I vow,
And all the pow'rs that rule the realms below,
Unwilling I forsook your friendly state,
Commanded by the gods, and forc'd by fate—
Those gods—that fate, whose unresisted might
Have sent me to these regions void of light,
Through the vast empire of eternal night.

Nor dar'd I to presume, that, press'd with grief,
My flight should urge you to this dire relief.
Stay, stay your steps, and listen to my vows!
'Tis the last interview that fate allows!'
In vain he thus attempts her mind to move
With tears and pray'rs and late-repenting love.
Disdainfully she look'd; then turning round,
She fix'd her eyes unmov'd upon the ground,
And what he says and swears regards no more
Than the deaf rocks when the loud billows roar;
But whirl'd away, to shun his hateful sight,
Hid in the forest, and the shades of night;
Then sought Sichæus through the shady grove,
Who answer'd all her cares, and equall'd all her love.
Some pious tears the pitying hero paid,
And followed with his eyes the flitting shade."
Æneid, book vi.

No. 1122.

Helen stealing the arms of Deïphobus.

GNAIOS.   *Cornelian.*

After the death of Paris, his brother Deïphobus married Helen.   On the night when Troy was sacked, she stole his arms as he slept, and admitted Menelaus, who slew him.

" Here Priam's son, Deïphobus, he found,
Whose face and limbs were one continued wound :
Dishonest, with lopp'd arms, the youth appears,
Spoil'd of his nose, and shorten'd of his ears.
He scarcely knew him, striving to disown
His blotted form, and blushing to be known ;
And therefore first began : ' O Teucer's race !
Who durst thy faultless figure thus deface ?
What heart could wish, what hand inflict, this
        dire disgrace ?
'Twas fam'd that, in our last and fatal night,
Your single prowess long sustain'd the fight,
Till, tir'd, not forc'd, a glorious fate you chose,
And fell upon a heap of slaughter'd foes.
But, in remembrance of so brave a deed,
A tomb and fun'ral honours I decreed ;
Thrice call'd your manes on the Trojan plains :
The place your armour and your name retains.
Your body too I sought, and, had I found,
Design'd for burial in your native ground.'
    The ghost replied : ' Your piety has paid
All needful rites to rest my wand'ring shade :
But cruel fate, and my more cruel wife,
To Grecian swords betray'd my sleeping life.

These are the monuments of Helen's love—
The shame I bear below, the marks I bore
        above.
You know in what deluding joys we pass'd
The night that was by heav'n decreed our last :
For when the fatal horse, descending down,
Pregnant with arms, o'erwhelm'd th' unhappy
        town,
She feign'd nocturnal orgies ; left my bed,
And, mix'd with Trojan dames, the dances led ;
Then, waving high her torch, the signal made,
Which rous'd the Grecians from their ambuscade.
With watching overworn, with cares oppress'd,
Unhappy I had laid me down to rest ;
And heavy sleep my weary limbs possess'd.
Meantime my worthy wife our arms mislaid,
And from beneath my head my sword convey'd ;
The door unlatch'd, and, with repeated calls,
Invites her former lord within my walls.
Thus in her crime her confidence she plac'd,
And with new treasons would redeem the past.
What need I more ?   Into the room they ran,
And meanly murder'd a defenceless man.' "

Æneid, book vi.

No. 1123.

Murder of Deïphobus.

DIOSCORIDES.   *Sardonyx.*

See preceding quotation.

No. 1124.

Æneas and Anchises in the Elysian plains.

Dioscorides.   *Sardonyx.*

" To these the Sibyl thus her speech address'd,
And first to him surrounded by the rest
(Tow'ring his height, and ample was his breast) :
' Say, happy souls ! divine Musæus, say
Where lives Anchises, and where lies our way
To find the hero for whose only sake
We sought the dark abodes, and cross'd the bitter
      lake ?'
To this the sacred poet thus replied :
' In no fix'd place the happy souls reside :
In groves we live, and lie on mossy beds,
By crystal streams that murmur through the
      meads.
But pass yon easy hill, and thence descend ;
The path conducts you to your journey's end.'
This said, he led them up the mountain's
      brow,
And shews them all the shining fields below :
They wind the hill, and through the blissful mea-
      dows go.
But old Anchises, in a flow'ry vale,
Review'd his muster'd race, and took the tale—
Those happy spirits which, ordain'd by Fate,
For future being and new bodies wait—
With studious thought observ'd th' illustrious
      throng,
In nature's order as they pass'd along ;
Their names, their fates, their conduct, and their
      care,
In peaceful senates, and successful war.
He, when Æneas on the plain appears,
Meets him with open arms and falling tears.
' Welcome,' he said, ' the gods' undoubted race !
O long-expected to my dear embrace !
Once more 'tis giv'n me to behold your face !

The love and pious duty which you pay
Have pass'd the perils of so hard a way.
'Tis true, computing times, I now believ'd
The happy day approach'd ; nor are my hopes
      deceiv'd.
What length of lands—what oceans have you
      pass'd—
What storms sustain'd—and on what shores been
      cast !
How have I fear'd your fate ! but fear'd it most
When Love assail'd you on the Libyan coast.'
To this the filial duty thus replies :
' Your sacred ghost before my sleeping eyes
Appear'd, and often urg'd this painful enter-
      prise.
After long tossing on the Tyrrhene sea,
My navy rides at anchor in the bay.
But reach your hand, O parent shade ! nor shun
The dear embraces of your longing son.'
He said ; and falling tears his face bedew ;
Then thrice around his neck his arms he threw,
And thrice the flitting shadow slipp'd away,
Like winds, or empty dreams that fly the day.
Now, in a secret vale, the Trojan sees
A sep'rate grove, through which a gentle breeze
Plays with a passing breath, and whispers through
      the trees ;
And just before the confines of the wood,
The gliding Lethe leads her silent flood.
About the boughs an airy nation flew,
Thick as the humming bees, that hunt the golden
      dew
In summer's heat ; on tops of lilies feed,
And creep within their bells to suck the balmy
      seed :

The winged army roams the field around;
The rivers and the rocks remurmur to the sound.
Æneas wond'ring stood, then ask'd the cause
Which to the stream the crowding people draws.

Then thus the sire: 'The souls that throng the
    flood
Are those to whom by Fate are other bodies
    owed.'"

Æneid, book vi.

Anchises explains to Æneas the Pythagorean philosophy of the transmigration of souls; and points out the glorious race of heroes that is to descend from him and his posterity.

No. 1125.

Juno urging the fury Alecto to incite Queen Amata and the Latins against the Trojans.

APOLLONIOS.   *Cornelian.*

Æneas, on his return from the infernal regions, sails for Latium, of which Latinus, a descendant from Saturn, is king. Æneas despatches an embassy to the king, and the king receives it kindly, and, warned by many signs and predictions, promises to give Æneas his only daughter Lavinia in marriage. But Amata the queen is favourable to the suit of Turnus, king of the Rutulians. Juno, the enemy of the Trojans, is instrumental in breaking the treaty which was made, and a war ensues, which terminates in the death of Turnus, the marriage of Æneas, and his succession to the crown.

"Thus having said, she sinks beneath the
    ground
With furious haste, and shoots the Stygian sound,
To rouse Alecto from th' infernal seat
Of her dire sisters, and their dark retreat.
This fury, fit for her intent, she chose—
One who delights in wars and human woes!
E'en Pluto hates his own misshapen race;
Her sister-furies fly her hideous face:
So frightful are the forms the monster takes—
So fierce the hissings of her speckled snakes!
Her Juno finds, and thus inflames her spite:
' O virgin-daughter of eternal night,
Give me this once thy labour, to sustain
My right, and execute my just disdain.
Let not the Trojans, with a feign'd pretence
Of proffer'd peace, delude the Latian prince;
Expel from Italy that odious name,
And let not Juno suffer in her fame.

'Tis thine to ruin realms—o'erturn a state—
Betwixt the dearest friends to raise debate,
And kindle kindred blood to mutual hate—
Thy hand o'er towns the fun'ral torch displays,
And forms a thousand ills ten thousand ways.
Now shake from out thy fruitful breast the seeds
Of envy, discord, and of cruel deeds;
Confound the peace establish'd, and prepare
Their souls to hatred and their hands to war.'
Smear'd as she was with black Gorgonean blood,
The fury sprang above the Stygian flood;
And on her iron wings, sublime through night,
She to the Latian palace took her flight;
There sought the queen's apartment—stood be-
    fore
The peaceful threshold, and besieg'd the door.
Restless Amata lay, her swelling breast
Fir'd with disdain for Turnus dispossess'd,
And the new nuptials of the Trojan guest.

From her black bloody locks the fury shakes
Her darling plague, the fav'rite of her snakes:
With her full force she threw the pois'nous dart,
And fix'd it deep within Amata's heart,
That, thus envenom'd, she might kindle rage,
And sacrifice to strife her house and husband's age.
Unseen, unfelt, the fiery serpent skims
Betwixt her linen and her naked limbs,
His baneful breath inspiring as he glides.
Now like a chain around her neck he rides—
Now like a fillet to her head repairs,
And with his circling volumes folds her hairs.
At first the silent venom slid with ease,
And seiz'd her cooler senses by degrees;
Then, ere th' infected mass was fir'd too far,
In plaintive accents she began the war,
And thus bespoke her husband: 'Shall,' she said,
'A wand'ring prince enjoy Lavinia's bed?
If nature plead not in a parent's heart,
Pity my tears and pity her desert.
I know, my dearest lord, the time will come,
You would, in vain, reverse your cruel doom:
The faithless pirate soon will set to sea,
And bear the royal virgin far away!
A guest like him—a Trojan guest—before,
In shew of friendship, sought the Spartan shore,
And ravish'd Helen from her husband bore.
Think on a king's inviolable word;
And think on Turnus, her once plighted lord.

To this false foreigner you give your throne,
And wrong a friend, a kinsman, and a son!
Resume your ancient care; and if the god,
Your sire, and you, resolve on foreign blood,*
Know all are foreign, in a larger sense,
Not born your subjects, or deriv'd from hence.
Then if the line of Turnus you retrace,
He springs from Inachus of Argive race.'
But when she saw her reasons idly spent,
And could not move him from his fix'd intent,
She flew to rage; for now the snake possess'd
Her vital parts, and poison'd all her breast.
She raves, she runs with a distracted pace,
And fills with horrid howls the public place.
And as young striplings whip the top for sport
On the smooth pavement of an empty court;
The wooden engine flies and whirls about,
Admir'd with clamours by the beardless rout:
They lash aloud; each other they provoke,
And lend their little souls at ev'ry stroke;—
Thus fares the queen; and thus her fury blows
Amidst the crowd, and kindles as she goes.
Not yet content, she strains her malice more,
And adds new ills to those contriv'd before:
She flies the town, and, mixing with the throng
Of madding matrons, bears the bride along,
Wand'ring through woods and wilds, and devious
ways,
And with these arts the Trojan match delays."

Æneid, book vii.

No. 1126.

Alecto rousing Turnus from his sleep to attack the Trojans.

GNAIOS. *Sardonyx.*

"Here in his lofty palace Turnus lay,
Betwixt the confines of the night and day,
Secure in sleep. The fury laid aside
Her looks and limbs, and with new methods tried
The foulness of th' infernal form to hide.

Propp'd on a staff, she takes a trembling
mien,
Her face is furrow'd, and her front obscene;
Deep-dinted wrinkles on her cheek she draws;
Sunk are her eyes, and toothless are her jaws;

---

* He consulted the oracle of his prophetic father Faunus, and, in reply, was advised to wed his daughter to Æneas.

5 A

Her hoary hair with holy fillets bound ;
Her temples with an olive-wreath are crown'd.
Old Chalybe, who kept the sacred fane
Of Juno, now she seem'd, and thus began,
Appearing in a dream, to rouse the careless man :
' Shall Turnus then such endless toil sustain
In fighting-fields, and conquer towns in vain—
Win, for a Trojan head to wear the prize—
Usurp thy crown—enjoy thy victories ?
The bride and sceptre, which thy blood has bought,
The king transfers ; and foreign heirs are sought !
Go now, deluded man, and seek again
New toils, new dangers, on the dusty plain !
Repel the Tuscan foes—their cities seize—
Protect the Latians in luxurious ease !
This dream all-pow'rful Juno sends : I bear
Her mighty mandates, and her words you hear.
Haste ! arm your Ardeans, issue to the plain ;
With faith to friend, assault the Trojan train ;
Their thoughtless chiefs, their painted ships that lie
In Tiber's mouth, with fire and sword destroy.
The Latian king, unless he shall submit,
Own his old promise, and his new forget—
Let him in arms the pow'r of Turnus prove,
And learn to fear whom he disdains to love.
For such is heav'n's command.'　The youthful
　　prince
With scorn replied, and made his bold defence :
' You tell me, mother, what I knew before,
The Phrygian fleet is landed on the shore.

I neither fear nor will provoke the war :
My fate is Juno's most peculiar care.
But time has made you dote, and vainly tell
Of arms imagin'd in your lonely cell.
Go ! be the temple and the gods your care :
Permit to men the thought of peace and war.'
　　These haughty words Alecto's rage provoke ;
And frighted Turnus trembled as she spoke.
Her eyes grow stiffen'd, and with sulphur burn ;
Her hideous looks and hellish form return :
Her curling snakes with hissings fill the place,
And open all the furies of her face ;
Then, darting fire from her malignant eyes,
She cast him backward as he strove to rise,
And ling'ring sought to frame some new replies.
High on her head she rears two twisted snakes :
Her chains she rattles, and her whip she shakes ;
And, churning bloody foam, thus loudly speaks :
' Behold whom time has made to dote, and tell
Of arms imagin'd in her lonely cell !
Behold the fates' infernal minister !
War, death, destruction, in my hand I bear.'
　　Thus having said, her smould'ring torch, im-
　　　press'd
With her full force, she plung'd into his breast.
Aghast he wak'd, and starting from his bed,
Cold sweat, in clammy drops, his limbs o'erspread,
' Arms ! arms !' he cries, ' my sword and shield
　　prepare !'
He breathes defiance, blood, and mortal war."
　　　　　　　　　　　　　　　Æneid, book vii.

No. 1127.

Alecto instigating Ascanius to kill the favourite stag of Silvia.

APOLLONIDES.　*Cornelian.*

　　Silvia, daughter of Tyrrheus, the king's ranger, had a favourite stag : this was killed by
Ascanius.　The cries of Silvia alarmed her brothers and the country people, who collect and
attack the Trojans.　Thus the war is kindled.　The following quotation will suffice for this and
the three subsequent subjects.

　　" While Turnus urges this his enterprise,
The Stygian fury to the Trojans flies :
New frauds invents, and takes a steepy stand
Which overlooks the vale with wide command ;

Where fair Ascanius and his youthful train
With horns and hounds a hunting-match or-
　　dain,
And pitch their toils around the shady plain.

The fury fires the pack; they snuff, they vent,
And feed their hungry nostrils with the scent:
'Twas of a well-grown stag, whose antlers rise
High o'er his front, his beams invade the skies.
From this light cause th' infernal maid prepares
The country churls to mischief, hate, and wars.

The stately beast the two Tyrrhidæ bred,
Snatch'd from his dam, and the tame youngling
    fed;
Their father Tyrrheus did his fodder bring,
Tyrrheus, chief ranger to the Latian king;
Their sister Silvia cherish'd with her care
The little wanton, and did wreaths prepare
To hang his budding horns—with ribands tied
His tender neck, and comb'd his silken hide,
And bath'd his body. Patient of command
In time he grew, and growing, us'd to hand,
He waited at his master's board for food;
Then sought his savage kindred in the wood,
Where grazing all the day, at night he came
To his known lodgings, and his country dame.
This household-beast, that us'd the woodland
    grounds,
Was view'd at first by the young hero's hounds,
As down the stream he swam to seek retreat
In the cool waters, and to quench his heat.
Ascanius, young, and eager of his game,
Soon bent his bow, uncertain in his aim;
But the dire fiend the fatal arrow guides,
Which pierc'd his bowels through his panting
    sides.
The bleeding creature issues from the floods,
Possess'd with fear, and seeks his known abodes,
His old familiar hearth, and household-gods.
He falls; he fills the house with heavy groans,
Implores their pity, and his pain bemoans!
Young Silvia beats her breast, and cries aloud
For succour from the clownish neighbourhood:
The churls assemble; for the fiend, who lay
In the close woody covert, urg'd their way.
One with a brand yet burning from the flame,
Arm'd with a knotty club another came;
Whate'er they catch, or find without their care,
Their fury makes an instrument of war.

Tyrrheus, the foster-father of the beast,
Then clench'd a hatchet in his horny fist,
But held his hand from the descending stroke,
And left his wedge within the cloven oak,
To whet their courage and their rage provoke.

And now the goddess, exercis'd in ill,
Who watch'd an hour to work her impious will,
Ascends the roof, and to her crooked horn,
Such as was then by Latian shepherds borne,
Adds all her breath. The rocks and woods
    around
And mountains tremble at th' infernal sound.
The sacred lake of Trivia from afar,
The Veline fountains, and sulphureous Nar,
Shake at the baleful blast, the signal of the war;
Young mothers wildly stare, with fear possess'd,
And strain their helpless infants to their breast.

The clowns, a boist'rous, rude, ungovern'd crew,
With furious haste to the loud summons flew.
The pow'rs of Troy, then issuing on the plain,
With fresh recruits their youthful chief sustain:
Not theirs a raw and unexperienc'd train,
But a firm body of embattled men.
At first, while fortune favour'd neither side,
The fight with clubs and burning brands was tried;
But now, both parties reinforc'd, the fields
Are bright with flaming swords and brazen shields.
A shining harvest either host displays,
And shoots against the sun with equal rays.

Thus, when a black-brow'd gust begins to rise,
White foam at first on the curl'd ocean fries;
Then roars the main, the billows mount the skies;
Till, by the fury of the storm full blown,
The muddy bottom to the clouds is thrown.

First Almon falls, old Tyrrheus' eldest care,
Pierc'd with an arrow from the distant war;
Fix'd in his throat the flying weapon stood,
And stopp'd his breath, and drank his vital blood.
Huge heaps of slain around the body rise:
Among the rest the rich Galesu lies;
A good old man, while peace he preach'd in vain,
Amidst the madness of the unruly train:
Five herds, five bleating flocks, his pastures fill'd;
His lands a hundred yoke of oxen till'd.

Thus, while in equal scales their fortune stood, | To Juno thus she speaks : ' Behold ! 'tis done,
The fury bath'd them in each other's blood ; | The blood already drawn, the war begun ;
Then, having fix'd the fight, exulting flies, | The discord is complete ; nor can they cease
And bears fulfill'd her promise to the skies. | The dire debate, nor you command the peace.' "

Æneid, book vii.

No. 1128.

Silvia bewailing the loss of her stag.

TEUCER.   *Cornelian.*

See second paragraph of preceding quotation.

No. 1129.

Alecto blowing the trumpet of war.

CHROMIOS.   *Cornelian.*

See third paragraph of preceding quotation. The artist here uses a liberty in representing Alecto as standing on a stag, and in representing the stag as pierced through the throat; whereas Virgil says that she blew her horn from the house-top, and that the stag was wounded in the belly. No doubt these liberties were taken in order to give better effect to the picture.

No. 1130.

The death of Almon and Galesus—Alecto ascending to Heaven.

POLYCLETES.   *Cornelian.*

See last paragraph of preceding quotation.

No. 1131.

Juno opening the gates of the temple of Janus.

SOLON.   *Cornelian.*

In Rome, the temple of Janus was kept open during war, but shut in time of peace.

" A solemn custom was observ'd of old, | Or from the boasting Parthians would regain
Which Latium held, and now the Romans hold : | Their eagles, lost in Carræ's bloody plain,—
Their standard when in fighting-fields they rear | Two gates of steel (the name of Mars they
Against the fierce Hyrcanians, or declare | bear,
The Scythian, Indian, or Arabian war— | And still are worshipp'd with religious fear)

Before his temple stand ; the dire abode,
And the fear'd issues of the furious god,
Are feuc'd with brazen bolts ; without the gates,
The wary guardian Janus doubly waits.
Then, when the sacred senate votes the wars,
The Roman consul their decree declares,
And in his robes the sounding gates unbars.
The youth in military shouts arise,
And the loud trumpets break the yielding
skies.
These rites, of old by sov'reign princes us'd,
Were the king's office ; but the king refus'd,
Deaf to their cries, nor would the gates unbar
Of sacred peace, or loose th' imprison'd war;

But hid his head, and safe from loud alarms,
Abhorr'd the wicked ministry of arms.
Then heav'n's imperious queen shot down from
high ;
At her approach the brazen hinges fly ;
The gates are forc'd, and every falling bar ;
And, like a tempest, issues out the war.
The peaceful cities of the Ausonian shore,
Lull'd in their ease, and undisturb'd before,
Are all on fire ; and some, with studious care,
Their restive steeds in sandy plains prepare ;
Some their soft limbs in painful marches try;
And war is all their wish, and *arms* their gen'ral
cry."

Æneid, book vii.

No. 1132.

The river-god Tiber comforting and counselling Æneas.

ALPHEOS. *Cornelian.*

"While Turnus and th' allies thus urge the
war,
The Trojan, floating in a flood of care,
Beholds the tempest which his foes prepare.
This way and that he turns his anxious mind ;
Thinks and rejects the counsels he design'd ;
Explores himself in vain in ev'ry part,
And gives no rest to his distracted heart.
So when the sun by day, or moon by night,
Strikes on the polish'd brass its trembling light,
The glitt'ring species here and there divide,
And cast their dubious beams from side to side ;
Now on the walls, now on the pavement play,
And to the ceiling flash the glaring day.
    'Twas night ; and weary nature lull'd asleep
The birds of air, and fishes of the deep,
And beasts and mortal men. The Trojan chief
Was laid on Tiber's bank, oppress'd with grief,
And found in silent slumber late relief.
Then, through the shadows of the poplar-wood,
Arose the father of the Roman flood ;

An azure robe was o'er his body spread,
A wreath of shady reeds adorn'd his head :
Thus, manifest to sight, the god appear'd,
And with these pleasing words his sorrow cheer'd :
' Undoubted offspring of ethereal race,
O long expected in this promis'd place !
Who, through the foes, hast borne thy banish'd
    ˙ gods—
Restor'd them to their hearths and old abodes;
This is thy happy home, the clime where fate
Ordains thee to restore the Trojan state ;
Fear not ! The war shall end in lasting peace,
And all the rage of haughty Juno cease.
And that this nightly vision may not seem
Th' effect of fancy, or an idle dream ;
A sow beneath an oak shall lie along,
All white herself, and white her thirty young.
When thirty rolling years have run their race,
Thy son Ascanius, on this empty space,
Shall build a royal town of lasting fame,
Which from this omen shall receive the name.*

---

* Alba.

Time shall approve the truth. For what remains,
And how with sure success to crown thy pains,
With patience next attend. A banish'd band,
Driv'n with Evander from th' Arcadian land,
Have planted here, and plac'd on high their walls:
Their town the founder Pallanteum calls—
Deriv'd from Pallas, his great grandsire's name ;
But the fierce Latians old possession claim,
With war infesting the new colony :
These make thy friends ; and on their aid
To thy free passage I submit my streams.
Wake, son of Venus, from thy pleasing dreams ;
And when the setting stars are lost in day,
To Juno's pow'r thy just devotion pay ;
With sacrifice the wrathful queen appease :
Her pride at length shall fail, her fury cease.

When thou return'st victorious from the war,
Perform thy vows to me with grateful care :
The god am I whose yellow water flows
Around these fields, and fattens as it goes ;
Tiber my name—among the rolling floods,
Renown'd on earth, esteem'd among the gods.
This is my certain seat. In times to come,
My waves shall wash the walls of mighty Rome.'
He said, and plung'd below : while yet he spoke,
His dream Æneas and his sleep forsook.
He rose, and, looking up, beheld the skies
With purple blushing, and the day arise.
Then water in his hollow palm he took
From Tiber's flood, and thus the pow'rs bespoke."

Æneid, book viii.

No. 1133.

Venus soliciting Vulcan to forge armour for Æneas.

DIOSCORIDES. *Amethyst.*

" Now Night had shed her silver dews around,
And with her sable wings embrac'd the ground,
When love's fair goddess, anxious for her son
(New tumults rising, and new wars begun),
Couch'd with her husband in his golden bed,
With these alluring words invokes his aid ;
And that her pleasing speech his mind may move,
Inspires each accent with the charms of love :
' While cruel fate conspir'd with Grecian pow'rs,
To level with the ground the Trojan tow'rs,
I ask'd not aid th' unhappy to restore,
Nor did the succour of thy skill implore ;
Nor urg'd the labours of my lord in vain
A sinking empire longer to sustain,
Though much I ow'd to Priam's house, and more
The danger of Æneas did deplore ;
But now, by Jove's command and fate's decree,
His race is doom'd to reign in Italy—
With humble suit I beg thy needful art,
O still propitious pow'r, that rul'st my heart !

A mother kneels a suppliant for her son.
By Thetis and Aurora thou wert won
To forge impenetrable shields, and grace
With fated arms a less illustrious race.
Behold, what haughty nations are combin'd
Against the relics of the Phrygian kind,
With fire and sword my people to destroy,
And conquer Venus twice in conqu'ring Troy.'
She said ; and straight her arms, of snowy
        hue,
About her unresolving husband threw.
Her soft embraces soon infuse desire—
His bones and marrow sudden warmth inspire !
And all the godhead feels the wonted fire ;
Not half so swift the rattling thunder flies,
Or forky lightnings flash along the skies.
The goddess, proud of her successful wiles,
And conscious of her form, in secret smiles ;
Then thus the pow'r, obedient to her charms,
Panting and half dissolving in her arms :

' Why seek you reasons for a cause so just,
Or your own beauties or my love distrust?
Long since, had you requir'd my helpful hand,
Th' artificer and art you might command,
To labour arms for Troy : nor Jove, nor fate,
Confirm'd their empire to so short a date.
And if you now desire new wars to wage,
My skill I promise, and my pains engage.
Whatever melting metals can conspire,
Or breathing bellows, of the foaming fire,
Is freely yours : your anxious fears remove,
And think no task is difficult to love.'

. . . .

Sacred to Vulcan's name, an isle there lay
Betwixt Sicilia's coasts and Liparè,
Rais'd high on smoky rocks; and deep below,
In hollow caves the fires of Ætna glow.
The Cyclops here their heavy hammers deal ;
Loud strokes, and hissing of tormented steel,

Are heard around ; the boiling waters roar,
And smoky flames through fuming tunnels soar.
Hither the father of the fire, by night,
Through the brown air precipitates his flight.
On their eternal anvils here he found
The brethren beating, and the blows go round.

. . . . .

'My sons!' said Vulcan, 'set your tasks aside ;
Your strength and master-skill must now be tried.
Arms for a hero forge—arms that require
Your force, your speed, and all your forming fire.'
He said. They set their former work aside,
And their new toil with eager haste divide ;
A flood of molten silver, brass, and gold,
And deadly steel, in the large furnace roll'd ;
Of this their artful hands a shield prepare,
Alone sufficient to sustain the war."

Æneid, book viii.

No. 1134.

Venus, attended by Cupid, bringing the arms to Æneas.

GNAIOS. *Amethyst.*

The devices on the shield represented the chief events in Roman history.

" Meantime the mother-goddess, crown'd with charms,
Breaks through the clouds, and brings the fated arms.
Within a winding vale she finds her son,
On the cool river's bank retir'd alone :
She shews her heav'nly form without disguise,
And gives herself to his desiring eyes.
' Behold,' she said, ' perform'd in ev'ry part,
My promise made, and Vulcan's labour'd art :
Now seek secure the Latian enemy,
And haughty Turnus to the field defy.'
She said : and, having first her son embrac'd,
The radiant arms beneath an oak she plac'd.
Proud of the gift, he roll'd his greedy sight
Around the work, and gaz'd with vast delight.

He lifts, he turns, he poises, and admires
The crested helm, that vomits radiant fires :
His hands the fatal sword and corselet hold,
One keen with temper'd steel, one stiff with gold;
Both ample, flaming both, and beamy bright—
So shines a cloud when edg'd with adverse light.
He shakes the pointed spear, and longs to try
The plaited cuishes on his manly thigh ;
But most admires the shield's mysterious mould,
And Roman triumphs rising on the gold ;
For there emboss'd the heav'nly smith had wrought
(Not in the rolls of future fate untaught)
The wars in order, and the race divine
Of warriors issuing from the Julian line."

Æneid, book viii.

No. 1135.

The ships of Æneas, when fired by Turnus, changed into nymphs; while the Rutulians are terror-struck at the sight.

Chromios.   *Cornelian.*

Æneas having gone to solicit assistance from Evander, a neighbouring prince, Turnus—aided by Messapus and others—attacks his camp; and sets fire to his ships, which are changed into nymphs.

" Thus ranges eager Turnus o'er the plain,
Sharp with desire, and furious with disdain;
Surveys each passage with a piercing sight,
To force his foes in equal field to fight.
Thus while he gazes round, at length he spies
Where, fenc'd with strong redoubts, their navy lies,
Close underneath the walls: the washing tide
Secures from all approach this weaker side.
He takes the wish'd occasion, fills his hand
With ready fires, and shakes a flaming brand.
Urg'd by his presence, ev'ry soul is warm'd,
And ev'ry hand with kindled fires is arm'd.
From the fir'd pines the scatt'ring sparkles fly:
Fat vapours, mix'd with flames, involve the sky.
What pow'r, O Muses, could avert the flame,
Which threaten'd, in the fleet, the Trojan name?
Tell: for the fact, through length of time obscure,
Is hard to faith; yet shall the fame endure.
'Tis said, that when the chief prepar'd his flight,
And fell'd his timber from mount Ida's height,
The grandame-goddess then approach'd her son,
And with a mother's majesty begun :*
' Grant me,' she said, ' the sole request I bring,
Since conquer'd heav'n has own'd you for its king.
On Ida's brows for ages past there stood,
With firs and maples fill'd, a shady wood;
And on the summit rose a sacred grove,
Where I was worshipp'd with religious love.
These woods, that holy grove, my long delight,
I gave the Trojan prince, to speed his flight.

Now, fill'd with fear, on their behalf I come:
Let neither winds o'erset, nor waves entomb,
The floating forests of the sacred pine;
But let it be their safety t' have been mine.'
Then thus replied her awful son, who rolls
The radiant stars, and heav'n and earth controls:
' How dare you, mother, endless date demand
For vessels moulded by a mortal hand?
What then is fate?   Shall bold Æneas ride
Of safety certain on th' uncertain tide?
Yet what I can I grant: when, wafted o'er,
The chief is landed on the Latian shore,
Whatever ships escape the raging storms
At my command shall change their fading forms
To nymphs divine, and plough the wat'ry way,
Like Doto and the daughters of the sea.'
To seal his sacred vow, by Styx he swore,
The lake of liquid pitch, the dreary shore,
And Phlegethon's innavigable flood,
And the black regions of his brother-god.
He said; and shook the skies with his imperial nod.
And now at length the number'd hours were come,
Prefix'd by fate's irrevocable doom,
When the great mother of the gods was free
To save her ships, and finish Jove's decree.
First, from the quarter of the morn, there sprung
A light that sign'd the heav'ns, and shot along;
Then from a cloud, fring'd round with golden fires,
Were timbrels heard, and Berecynthian choirs;

---

* Cybele addressing Jupiter.

And last a voice, with more than mortal sounds,
Both hosts, in arms oppos'd, with equal horror
    wounds:
' O Trojan race! your needless aid forbear;
And know my ships are my peculiar care.
With greater ease the bold Rutulian may
With hissing brands attempt to burn the sea,
Than singe my sacred pines. But you, my
    charge,
Loos'd from your crooked anchors, launch at
    large,
Exalted each a nymph: forsake the sand,
And swim the seas at Cybele's command.'

No sooner had the goddess ceas'd to speak,
Than, lo! th' obedient ships their halsers break,
And, strange to tell, like dolphins, in the main
They plunge their prows, and dive, and spring
    again:
As many beauteous maids the billows sweep
As rode before tall vessels on the deep.
The foes surpris'd with wonder stood aghast:
Messapus curb'd his fiery courser's haste:
Old Tiber roar'd, and, rising up his head,
Call'd back his waters to their oozy bed."

                  Æneid, book ix.

No. 1136.

Ascanius killing Numanus.

PLOTARCHOS. *Cornelian.*

" Then young Ascanius, who before this day
Was wont in woods to shoot the savage prey,
First bent in martial strife the twanging bow,
And exercis'd against a human foe—
With this bereft Numanus of his life,
Who Turnus' younger sister took to wife.
Proud of his realm and of his royal bride,
Vaunting before his troops, and with a lengthen'd
    stride,
In these insulting terms the Trojans he defied:
' Twice-conquer'd cowards! now your shame is
    shewn—
Coop'd up a second time within your town!
Who dare not issue forth in open field,
But hold the walls before you for a shield.
Thus threat you war? thus our alliance force?
What gods—what madness, hither steer'd your
    course?
You shall not find the sons of Atreus here;
Nor need the frauds of sly Ulysses fear.
Strong from the cradle, of a sturdy brood,
We bear our new-born infants to the flood;
There bath'd amid the stream our boys we hold,
With winter harden'd, and inur'd to cold.

They wake before the day to range the wood—
Kill ere they eat, nor taste unconquer'd food.
No sports but what belong to war they know—
To break the stubborn colt—to bend the bow.
Our youth, of labour patient, earn their bread:
Hardly they work, with frugal diet fed.
From ploughs and harrows sent to seek renown,
They fight in fields, and storm the shaken town.
No part of life from toils of war is free,
No change in age, or diff'rence in degree.
We plough and till in arms; our oxen feel,
Instead of goads, the spur and pointed steel:
Th' inverted lance makes furrows in the plain.
E'en time, that changes all, yet changes us in
    vain—
The body, not the mind—nor can control
Th' immortal vigour, or abate the soul.
Our helms defend the young—disguise the grey;
We live by plunder and delight in prey.
Your vests embroider'd with rich purple shine;
In sloth you glory, and in dances join.
Your vests have sweeping sleeves: with female
    pride,
Your turbans underneath your chins are tied.

5 B

Go, Phrygians, to your Dindymus again !
Go, less than women in the shapes of men !
Go ! mix'd with eunuchs in the mother's rites
(Where with unequal sound the flute invites),
Sing, dance, and howl, by turns, in Ida's shade :*
Resign the war to men, who know the martial trade.'
  This foul reproach Ascanius could not hear
With patience, or a vow'd revenge forbear.
At the full stretch of both his hands he drew,
And almost join'd the horns of the tough yew.
But first before the throne of Jove he stood,
And thus with lifted hands invok'd the god :
' My first attempt, great Jupiter, succeed !
An annual off'ring in thy grove shall bleed—
A snow-white steer, before thy altar led,
Who, like his mother, bears aloft his head—

Butts with his threat'ning brows, and bellowing
    stands,
And dares the fight, and spurns the yellow sands.'
  Jove bow'd the heav'ns, and lent a gracious
    ear,
And thunder'd on the left, amidst the clear.
Sounded at once the bow ; and swiftly flies
The feather'd death, and hisses through the skies.
The steel through both his temples forc'd the way :
Extended on the ground Numanus lay.
' Go now, vain boaster ! and true valour scorn :
The Phrygians, twice subdued, yet make this
    third return.'
Ascanius said no more.   The Trojans shake
The heav'ns with shouting, and new vigour take."
                                   Æneid, book ix.

No. 1137.

Mezentius killing Orodes.

Pyrgoteles.   *Calcedony.*

Æneas arrives with a considerable body of auxiliaries from Evander, who also sends his son Pallas ; from Etruria, and other places ; and finding the Trojans closely besieged and sorely pressed, gives the enemy battle. Among the most formidable of his enemies is Mezentius, an impious and tyrannical prince of Etruria, who had been expelled by his subjects for his tyranny. Turnus, after killing Pallas, is withdrawn by an artifice of Juno from the battle.

" Meantime, by Jove's impulse, Mezentius
    arm'd,
Succeeding Turnus, with his ardour warm'd
His fainting friends—reproach'd their shameful
    flight—
Repell'd the victors, and renew'd the fight.
Against their king the Tuscan troops conspire :
Such is their hate, and such their fierce desire
Of wish'd revenge ; on him—on him alone,
All hands employ'd, and all their darts are thrown.
He, like a solid rock by seas enclos'd,
To raging winds and roaring waves oppos'd,
From his proud summit looking down, disdains
Their empty menace, and unmov'd remains.

Or as a savage boar on mountains bred,
With forest-mast and fatt'ning marshes fed,
When once he sees himself in toils enclos'd,
By huntsmen and their eager hounds oppos'd,
He whets his tusks, and turns, and dares to war—
Th' invaders dart their jav'lins from afar :
All keep aloof, and safely shout around ;
But none presume to give a nearer wound :
He frets and froths—erects his bristled hide,
And shakes a grove of lances from his side :
Not otherwise the troops, with hate inspir'd,
And just revenge against the tyrant fir'd,
Their darts with clamour at a distance drive,
And only keep the languid war alive.

---

* This refers to the rites observed in the worship of Cybele, called *the Great Mother.*

Then with disdain the haughty victor view'd
Orodes flying, nor the wretch pursued,
Nor thought the dastard's back deserv'd a wound,
But, running, gain'd the advantage of the ground;
Then turning short, he met him face to face,
To give his victory the better grace.
Orodes falls, in equal fight oppress'd:
Mezentius fix'd his foot upon his breast,
And rested lance; and thus aloud he cries:
' Lo ! here the champion of my rebels lies !'
The fields around with ' Iö Pæan !' ring,
And peals of shouts applaud the conq'ring king.

At this the vanquish'd, with his dying breath,
Thus faintly spoke, and prophesied in death :
' Nor thou, proud man, unpunish'd shalt remain :
Like death attends thee on this fatal plain.'
Then sourly smiling, thus the king replied :
' For what belongs to me, let Jove provide ;
But die thou first, whatever chance ensue.'
He said, and from the wound the weapon drew.
A hov'ring mist came swimming o'er his sight,
And seal'd his eyes in everlasting night."

Æneid, book x.

No. 1138.

Lausus interposing in defence of his father Mezentius.

APOLLONIDES. *Cornelian.*

The following quotation will suffice for this and the four subsequent subjects.

"Once more the proud Mezentius, with disdain,
Brandish'd his spear, and rush'd into the plain ;
Where tow'ring in the midmost ranks he stood,
Like tall Orion stalking o'er the flood
(When with his brawny breast he cuts the waves,
His shoulders scarce the topmost billow laves) ;
Or like a mountain-ash, whose roots are spread
Deep fix'd in earth—in clouds it hides its head.
    The Trojan prince beheld him from afar,
And dauntless undertook the doubtful war.
Collected in his strength, and like a rock
Pois'd on his base, Mezentius stood the shock.
He stood, and, measuring first with careful eyes
The space his spear could reach, aloud he cries :
' My strong right hand, and sword, assist my stroke!
(Those only gods Mezentius will invoke.)
His armour from the Trojan pirate torn,
By my triumphant Lausus shall be worn.'
He said ; and with his utmost force he threw
The massy spear, which, hissing as it flew,
Reach'd the celestial shield : that stopp'd the course ;
But glancing thence, the yet unbroken force

Took a new bent obliquely, and betwixt
The side and bowels fam'd Antores fix'd.
Antores had from Argos travell'd far,
Alcides' friend, and brother of the war ;
Till, tir'd with toils, fair Italy he chose,
And in Evander's palace sought repose.
Now falling by another's wound, his eyes
He casts to heav'n—on Argos thinks, and—dies !
    The pious Trojan then his jav'lin sent :
The shield gave way ; through triple plates it went
Of solid brass, of linen triply roll'd,
And three bull-hides which round the buckler
    roll'd.
All these it pass'd, resistless in the course—
Transpierc'd his thigh, and spent its dying force :
The gaping wound gush'd out a crimson flood.
The Trojan, glad with sight of hostile blood,
His falchion drew, to closer fight address'd,
And with new force his fainting foe oppress'd.
    His father's peril Lausus view'd with grief :
He sigh'd—he wept—he ran to his relief.
And here, heroic youth, 'tis here I must
To thy immortal memory be just,

And sing an act so noble and so new,
Posterity will scarce believe 'tis true.
Pain'd with his wound, and useless for the fight,
The father sought to save himself by flight:
Encumber'd, slow he dragg'd the spear along,
Which pierc'd his thigh, and in his buckler hung.
The pious youth, resolv'd on death, below
The lifted sword springs forth to face the foe—
Protects his parent, and prevents the blow.
Shouts of applause ran ringing through the field,
To see the son the vanquish'd father shield:
All, fir'd with gen'rous indignation, strive,
And with a storm of darts to distance drive
The Trojan chief, who, held at bay from far,
On his Vulcanian orb sustain'd the war.

As when thick hail comes rattling in the wind—
The ploughman, passenger, and lab'ring hind,
For shelter to the neighb'ring covert fly,
Or bous'd, or safe in hollow caverns lie;
But that o'erblown, when heav'n above them
    smiles,
Return to travail, and renew their toils:
Æneas thus, o'erwhelm'd on ev'ry side,
The storm of darts undaunted did abide;
And thus to Lausus loud with friendly threat'ning
    cried:
' Why wilt thou rush to certain death, and rage
In rash attempts beyond thy tender age,
Betray'd by pious love?' Nor thus forborne,
The youth desists, but with insulting scorn
Provokes the ling'ring prince, whose patience
    tir'd
Gave place, and all his breast with fury fir'd.
For now the fates prepar'd their sharpen'd
    shears;
And lifted high the flaming sword appears,
Which, full descending with a frightful sway,
Through shield and corslet forc'd th' impetuous
    way,
And buried deep in his fair bosom lay.
The purple streams through the thin armour
    strove,
And drench'd th' embroider'd coat his mother
    wove!

And life at length forsook his heaving heart,
Loath from so sweet a mansion to depart.
    But when, with blood and paleness all o'er-
        spread,
The pious prince beheld young Lausus dead;
He griev'd—he wept (the sight an image brought
Of his own filial love—a sadly-pleasing thought);
Then stretch'd his hand to hold him up, and said:
' Poor hapless youth! what praises can be paid
To love so great—to such transcendant store
Of early worth, and sure presage of more?
Accept whate'er Æneas can afford:
Untouch'd thy arms—untaken be thy sword;
And all that pleas'd thee living still remain
Inviolate, and sacred to the slain.
Thy body on thy parents I bestow,
To rest thy soul—at least if shadows know,
Or have a sense of human things below:
There to thy fellow-ghosts with glory tell,
'Twas by the great Æneas' hand I fell.'
With this, his distant friends he beckons near;
Provokes their duty, and prevents their fear:
Himself assists to lift him from the ground,
With clotted locks, and blood that well'd from
    out the wound.
    Meantime his father—now no father—stood
And wash'd his wounds by Tiber's yellow flood:
Oppress'd with anguish, panting, and o'erspent,
His fainting limbs against an oak he leant.
A bough his brazen helmet did sustain;
His heavier arms lay scatter'd on the plain:
A chosen train of youth around him stand;
His drooping head was rested on his hand;
His grisly beard his pensive bosom sought;
And all on Lausus ran his restless thought.
Careful, concern'd his danger to prevent,
He much inquir'd, and many a message sent
To warn him from the field—alas! in vain!
Behold his mournful followers bear him slain:
O'er his broad shield still gush'd the yawning
    wound,
And drew a bloody trail along the ground."
                    Æneid, book x.

No. 1139.

Æneas and Lausus.

DIOSCORIDES. *Cornelian.*

See preceding quotation.

No. 1140.

Æneas supporting the body of Lausus.

ADMON. *Cornelian.*

See preceding quotation.

No. 1141.

Mezentius bathing his wound in the river Tiber.

SOLON. *Cornelian.*

See preceding quotation. The second person here represented is the river-god Tiber.

No. 1142.

Same subject.

GNAIOS. *Cornelian.*

See preceding quotation.

No. 1143.

Mezentius weeping over the dead body of Lausus.

CHROMIOS. *Amethyst.*

The following quotation explains this and the four subsequent subjects.

"Far off he heard their cries—far off divin'd
The dire event with a foreboding mind.
With dust he sprinkled first his hoary head;
Then both his lifted hands to heav'n he spread;
Last, the dear corpse embracing, thus he said:

'What joys, alas! could this frail being give,
That I have been so covetous to live?
To see my son—and such a son! resign
His life a ransom for preserving mine?

And am I then preserv'd, and art thou lost?
How much too dear has that redemption cost!
'Tis now my bitter banishment I feel:
This is a wound too deep for time to heal.
My guilt thy growing virtues did defame:
My blackness blotted thy unblemish'd name.
Chas'd from a throne, abandon'd, and exil'd
For foul misdeeds, were punishments too mild:
I owed my people these, and from their hate
With less resentment could have borne my fate.
And yet I live, and yet sustain the sight
Of hated men, and of more hated light—
But will not long.' With that he rais'd from
        ground
His fainting limbs, that stagger'd with his wound;
Yet with a mind resolv'd, and unappall'd
With pains or perils, for his courser call'd—
Well-mouth'd, well-manag'd, whom himself did
        dress
With daily care, and mounted with success—
His aid in arms—his ornament in peace!
  Soothing his courage with a gentle stroke,
The steed seem'd sensible while thus he spoke:
' O Rhœbus! we have liv'd too long for me!
If life and long were terms that could agree:
This day thou either shalt bring back the head,
And bloody trophies of the Trojan dead—
This day thou either shalt revenge my woe
For murder'd Lausus, on his cruel foe—
Or, if inexorable Fate deny
Our conquest, with thy conquer'd master die:
For after such a lord, I rest secure
Thou wilt no foreign reins or Trojan load endure.'
He said: and straight th' officious courser kneels
To take his wonted weight. His hand he fills
With pointed jav'lins; on his head he lac'd
His glitt'ring helm, which terribly was grac'd
With waving horse-hair, nodding from afar;
Then spurr'd his thund'ring steed amidst the war.
Love, anguish, wrath, and grief to madness
        wrought—
Despair, and secret shame, and conscious thought
Of inborn worth, his lab'ring soul oppress'd—
Roll'd in his eyes, and rag'd within his breast.

Then loud he call'd Æneas thrice by name;
The loud-repeated voice to glad Æneas came.
' Great Jove,' he said, ' and the far-shooting god,
Inspire thy mind to make thy challenge good!'
He spoke no more, but hasten'd, void of fear,
And threaten'd with his long-protended spear.
  To whom Mezentius thus: ' Thy vaunts are vain:
My Lausus lies extended on the plain:
He's lost! thy conquest is already won;
The wretched sire is murder'd in the son!
Nor fate I fear, but all the gods defy;
Forbear thy threats: my bus'ness is to die;
But first receive this parting legacy.'
He said; and straight a whirling dart he sent:
Another after, and another went.
Round in a spacious ring he rides the field,
And vainly plies th' impenetrable shield.
Thrice rode he round; and thrice Æneas wheel'd—
Turu'd as he turn'd: the golden orb withstood
The strokes, and bore about an iron wood.
Impatient of delay, and weary grown
Still to defend, and to defend alone,
To wrench the darts which in his buckler light,
Urg'd, and o'erlabour'd in unequal fight,
At length resolv'd, he throws, with all his force,
Full at the temples of the warrior-horse.
Just where the stroke was aim'd, th' unerring
        spear
Made way, and stood transfix'd through either ear.
Seiz'd with unwonted pain, surpris'd with fright,
The wounded steed curvets, and, rais'd upright,
Lights on his feet before: his hoofs behind
Spring up in air aloft, and lash the wind.
Down comes the rider headlong from his height;
His horse came after with unwieldy weight,
And flound'ring forward, pitching on his head,
His lord's encumber'd shoulder overlaid.
  From either host, the mingled shouts and cries
Of Trojans and Rutulians rend the skies.
Æneas, hast'ning, wav'd his fatal sword
High o'er his head, with this reproachful word:
' Now! where are now thy vaunts—the fierce
        disdain
Of proud Mezentius, and the lofty strain?'

Struggling, and wildly staring on the skies
With scarce-recover'd sight, he thus replies:
' Why these insulting words—this waste of breath,
To souls undaunted and secure of death?
'Tis no dishonour for the brave to die:
Nor came I here with hopes of victory—
Nor ask I life—nor fought with that design:
As I had us'd my fortune, use thou thine.
My dying son contracted no such band:
The gift is hateful from his murd'rer's hand.
For this, this only favour, let me sue;
If pity can to conquer'd foes be due,

Refuse it not: but let my body have
The last retreat of human kind—a grave.
Too well I know th' insulting people's hate:
Protect me from their vengeance after fate:
This refuge for my poor remains provide:
And lay my much-lov'd Lausus by my side.'
He said; and to the sword his throat applied:
The crimson stream distain'd his arms around,
And the disdainful soul came rushing through the
    wound."

Æneid, book x.

No. 1144.

Mezentius vowing to avenge the death of Lausus.

DIOSCORIDES.   *Cornelian.*

See preceding quotation.

No. 1145.

Mezentius addressing his horse Rhœbus.

ATHENION.   *Cornelian.*

See preceding quotation.

No. 1146.

Æneas wounding the horse of Mezentius.

PYRGOTELES.   *Cornelian.*

See preceding quotation.

No. 1147.

Æneas killing Mezentius.

ADMON.   *Cornelian.*

See preceding quotation.

No. 1148.

Æneas bearing in triumph the arms of Mezentius.

DIOSCORIDES. *Cornelian.*

See following quotation.

No. 1149.

Æneas addressing his companions, after suspending from an oak the arms of Mezentius as a trophy.

DAMAS. *Calcedony.*

" Scarce had the rosy morning raised her head
Above the waves, and left her wat'ry bed,
The pious chief, whom double cares attend
For his unburied soldiers and his friend,*
Yet first to heaven perform'd a victor's vows;
He bared an ancient oak of all its boughs,
Then on a rising ground the trunk he plac'd,
Which with the spoils of his dead foe he grac'd.
The coat of arms by proud Mezentius worn,
Now on a naked snag in triumph borne,
Was hung on high, and glitter'd from afar,
A trophy sacred to the god of war.
Above his arms, fix'd on the leafless wood,
Appear'd his plumy crest besmear'd with blood.
His brazen buckler on the left was seen:
Truncheons of shiver'd lances hung between;
And on the right was plac'd his corslet, bor'd;
And to the neck was tied his unavailing sword.
A crowd of chiefs enclose the godlike man,
Who thus conspicuous in the midst began:
' Our toils, my friends, are crown'd with sure
       success;
The greater part perform'd, achieve the less.

Now follow cheerful to the trembling town.
Press but an entrance, and presume it won.
Fear is no more; for fierce Mezentius lies,
As the first-fruits of war, a sacrifice.
Turnus shall fall, extended on the plain,
And in this omen is already slain.
Prepar'd in arms, pursue your happy chance;
That none unwarn'd may plead his ignorance,
And I, at heav'n's appointed hour may find
Your warlike ensigns waving in the wind.
Meantime the rites and fun'ral pomps prepare,
Due to your dead companions of the war—
The last respect the living can bestow,
To shield their shadows from contempt below.
That conquer'd earth be theirs for which they
       fought,
And which for us with their own blood they
       bought,
But first the corpse of our unhappy friend
To the sad city of Evander send,
Who, not inglorious, in his age's bloom
Was hurried hence by too severe a doom.' "

Æneid, book xi.

---

* Pallas, son of Evander, slain by Turnus.

No. 1150.

Metabus dedicating his infant daughter, Camilla, to Diana.

Lycos. *Cornelian.*

After the expiration of a truce granted by victorious Æneas to the Latins, in order to bury their dead, he advances towards Laurentum, the capital; while the king and leaders are debating about proposing terms of peace to him. Turnus sallies out to intercept his journey. He divides his forces into two bodies; giving Camilla, queen of the Volscians, and one of the most valiant and powerful of his auxiliaries, command of the cavalry. In the catalogue of the Latin allies (book vii.), her character and qualities are thus sketched.

" Last from the Volscians fair Camilla came,
And led her warlike troops—a warrior-dame;
Unbred to spinning, in the loom unskill'd,
She chose the nobler Pallas of the field.*
Mix'd with the first, the fierce virago fought—
Sustain'd the toils of arms—the danger sought—
Outstripp'd the winds in speed upon the plain—
Flew o'er the field, nor hurt the bearded grain;
She swept the seas, and, as she skimm'd along,
Her flying feet unbath'd on billows hung.

Men, boys, and women, stupid with surprise,
Where'er she passes, fix their wond'ring eyes;
Longing they look, and, gaping at the sight,
Devour her o'er and o'er with vast delight;
Her purple habit sits with such a grace
On her smooth shoulders, and so suits her face!
Her head with ringlets of her hair is crown'd,
And in a golden caul the curls are bound.
She shakes her myrtle jav'lin; and, behind,
Her Lycian quiver dances in the wind."

The following is the account of her infancy and education. Diana, foreseeing her death in this encounter, sends Opis, one of her train, to avenge it.

" Meantime Latonian Phœbe from the skies
Beheld th' approaching war with hateful eyes,
And call'd the light-foot Opis to her aid—
Her most belov'd and ever-trusty maid;
Then with a sigh began: ' Camilla goes
To meet her death amidst her fatal foes—
The nymph I lov'd of all my mortal train,
Invested with Diana's arms in vain.
Nor is my kindness for the virgin new:
'Twas born with her, and with her years it grew.
Her father Metabus, when forc'd away
From old Privernum for tyrannic sway,
Snatch'd up, and sav'd from his prevailing foes,
This tender babe, companion of his woes,
Casmilla was her mother; but he drown'd
One hissing letter in a softer sound,

And call'd Camilla. Through the woods he flies;
Wrapp'd in his robe the royal infant lies.
His foes in sight, he mends his weary pace;
With shouts and clamours they pursue the
  chase.
The banks of Amasene at length he gains,
The raging flood his farther flight restrains,
Rais'd o'er its borders with unusual rains.
Prepar'd to plunge into the stream, he fears
Not for himself, but for the charge he bears.
Anxious, he stops a while, and thinks in haste;
Then, desp'rate in distress, resolves at last.
A knotty lance of well-boil'd oak he bore;
The middle part with cork he cover'd o'er;
He clos'd the child within the hollow space;
With twigs of bending osier bound the case;

* Pallas, or Minerva, had two characters: she was the tutelar divinity of all female domestic industry, and was also a military deity.

5 c

Then pois'd the spear heavy with human weight,
And thus invok'd my favour for the freight:
"Accept, great goddess of the woods," he said,
"Sent by her sire, this dedicated maid!
Through air she flies a suppliant to thy shrine;
And the first weapon that she knows is thine."
He said; and with full force the spear he threw:
Above the sounding wave Camilla flew.
Then, press'd by foes, he stemm'd the stormy
    tide,
And gain'd, by stress of arms, the farther side.
His fasten'd spear he pull'd from out the ground;
And, victor of his vows, his infant nymph un-
    bound.
  ' Nor after that in towns which walls enclose
Would trust his hunted life amidst his foes;
But rough, in open air, he chose to lie;
Earth was his couch; his cov'ring was the sky.
On hills unshorn, or in a desert den,
He shunn'd the dire society of men.
A shepherd's solitary life he led;
His daughter with the milk of mares he fed:
The dugs of bears and ev'ry savage beast
He drew, and through her lips the liquor press'd.
The little Amazon could scarcely go—
He loads her with a quiver and a bow;
And, that she might her stagg'ring steps com-
    mand,
He with a slender jav'lin fills her hand.
Her flowing hair no golden fillet bound;
Nor swept her trailing robe the dusty ground.
Instead of these, a tiger's hide o'erspread
Her back and shoulder, fasten'd to her head.

The flying dart she first attempts to fling,
And round her tender temples toss'd the sling;
Then, as her strength with years increas'd, began
To pierce aloft in air the soaring swan,
And from the clouds to fetch the heron and the
    crane.
The Tuscan matrons with each other vied
To bless their rival sons with such a bride:
But she disdains their love, to share with me
The sylvan shades, and vow'd virginity.
And, oh! I wish, contented with my cares
Of savage spoils, she had not sought the wars:
Then had she been of my celestial train,
And shunn'd the fate that doom'd her to be slain.
But since, opposing heav'n's decree, she goes
To find her death among forbidden foes,
Haste with these arms, and take thy steepy flight
Where, with the gods averse, the Latians fight:
This bow to thee, this quiver, I bequeath,
This chosen arrow, to revenge her death;
By whate'er hand Camilla shall be slain,
Or of the Trojan or Italian train,
Let him not pass unpunish'd from the plain.
Then in a hollow cloud myself will aid
To bear the breathless body of my maid;
Unspoil'd shall be her arms, and unprofan'd
Her holy limbs with any human hand,
And in a marble tomb laid in her native land.'
  She said. The faithful nymph descends from
    high
With rapid flight, and cuts the sounding sky:
Black clouds and stormy winds around her body
    fly."

                                    Æneid, book xi.

No. 1151.

Metabus hurling his infant, Camilla, tied to a spear, across the river
Amasenus.

CHROMIOS. *Sardonyx.*

See first paragraph of preceding quotation. The river-god is represented as reclining.

No. 1152.

Metabus, while swimming over the river, assailed by his enemies.

ADMON. *Cornelian.*

The river-god is represented as receiving the child on the opposite bank. See first paragraph of preceding quotation.

No. 1153.

The nursing of Camilla.

APOLLONIDES. *Amethyst.*

See second paragraph of preceding quotation.

No. 1154.

Camilla killing Liris.

CHROMIOS. *Sardonyx.*

Camilla charges the Trojans, while Turnus is guarding the passes through the hills.

"Resistless through the war Camilla rode,
In danger unappall'd, and pleas'd with blood.
One side was bare for her exerted* breast;
One shoulder with her painted quiver press'd.
Now from afar her fatal jav'lins play;
Now with her axe's edge she hews her way;
Diana's arms upon her shoulders sound,
And when, too closely press'd, she quits the
        ground,
From her bent bow she sends a backward wound.
Her maids in martial pomp, on either side,
Larina, Tulla, fierce Tarpeia, ride—
Italians all—in peace their queen's delight—
In war the bold companions of the fight.
So march'd the Thracian Amazons of old,
When Thermodon with bloody billows roll'd,
Such troops as these in shining arms were seen,
When Theseus met in fight their maiden queen:
Such to the field Penthesilea led,
From the fierce virgin when the Grecian fled;

With such return'd triumphant from the war,
Her maids with cries attend the lofty car;
They clash with manly force their moony shields,
With female shouts resound the Phrygian fields.
    Who foremost, and who last, heroic maid,
On the cold earth were by thy courage laid?
Thy spear of mountain-ash, Eunæus first,
With fury driv'n, from side to side transpierc'd:
A purple stream came spouting from the wound;
Bath'd in his blood he lies, and bites the ground.
Liris and Pegasus at once she slew;
The former, as the slacken'd reins he drew
Of his faint steed—the latter as he stretch'd
His arm to prop his friend—the jav'lin reach'd:
By the same weapon, sent from the same hand,
Both fall together, and both spurn the sand.
Amastrus next is added to the slain;
The rest in rout she follows o'er the plain:
Tereus, Harpalycus, Demophoon,
And Chromis, at full speed her fury shun:

---

* Exerted, *exerta*, i. e. exposed, bared.

Of all her deadly darts not one she lost;
Each was attended with a Trojan ghost.

.   .   .   .   .

Orsilochus and she their coursers ply;
He seems to follow, and she seems to fly.
But in a narrow ring she makes the race;
And then he flies, and she pursues the chase.
Gath'ring at length on her deluded foe,
She swings her axe, and rises to the blow:
Full on the helm behind, with such a sway
The weapon falls, the riven steel gives way;
He groans—he roars—he sues in vain for grace,
Brains mingled with his blood besmear his face.
Astonish'd Aunus just arrives, by chance,
To see his fall, nor farther dares advance;
But fixing on the horrid maid his eye,
He stares—he shakes—and finds it vain to fly;
Yet, like a true Ligurian, born to cheat
(At least while Fortune favour'd his deceit),
Cries out aloud, 'What courage have you shewn,
Who trust your courser's strength, and not your
        own?
Forego the 'vantage of your horse; alight;
And then on equal terms begin the fight:
It shall be seen, weak woman, what you can,
When foot to foot you combat with a man.'

He said. She glows with anger and disdain—
Dismounts with speed to dare him on the plain,
And leaves her horse at large among her train:
With her drawn sword defies him to the field,
And, marching, lifts aloft her maiden shield.
The youth, who thought his cunning did succeed,
Reins round his horse, and urges all his speed;
Adds the remembrance of the spur, and hides
The goring rowels in his bleeding sides.
'Vain fool, and coward!' said the lofty maid;
'Caught in the train which thou thyself hast laid!
On others practise thy Ligurian arts;
Thin stratagems, and tricks of little hearts,
Are lost on me: nor shalt thou safe retire,
With vaunting lies, to thy fallacious sire.'
    At this, so fast her flying feet she sped,
That soon she strain'd beyond his horse's head;
Then turning short, at once she seiz'd the rein,
And laid the boaster grov'lling on the plain.
Not with more ease the falcon from above
Trusses, in middle air, the trembling dove,
Then plumes the prey, in her strong pounces
        bound;
The feathers, foul with blood, come tumbling to
        the ground."

                                    Æneid, book xi.

No. 1155.

Camilla killing the son of Aunus.

APOLLONIDES.   *Cornelian.*

See preceding quotation.

No. 1156.

Camilla receiving her mortal wound.

APOLLONIDES.   *Cornelian.*

" Then Aruns, doom'd to death, his arts essay'd
To murder, unespied, the Volscian maid;
This way and that his winding course he bends,
And, wheresoe'er she turns, her steps attends.

When she retires victorious from the chase,
He wheels about with care, and shifts his place;
When, rushing on, she seeks her foes in fight,
He keeps aloof, but keeps her still in sight:

He threats, and trembles, trying ev'ry way
Unseen to kill, and safely to betray.
   Chloreus, the priest of Cybele, from far,
Glitt'ring in Phrygian arms amidst the war,
Was by the virgin view'd.   The steed he press'd
Was proud with trappings; and his brawny chest
With scales of gilded brass was cover'd o'er:
A robe of Tyrian dye the rider wore.
With deadly wounds he gall'd the distant foe;
Gnossian his shafts, and Lycian was his bow;
A golden helm his front and head surrounds;
A gilded quiver from his shoulder sounds.
Gold, weav'd with linen, on his thighs he wore,
With flow'rs of needlework distinguish'd o'er,
With golden buckles bound, and gather'd up
   before.
Him the fierce maid beheld with ardent eyes,
Fond and ambitious of so rich a prize;
Or that the temple might his trophies hold,
Or else to shine herself in Trojan gold.
Blind in her haste, she chases him alone,
And seeks his life, regardless of her own.
This lucky moment the sly traitor chose;
Then, starting from his ambush, up he rose,
And threw, but first to heav'n address'd his vows:
'O patron of Soracte's high abodes!
Phœbus, the ruling pow'r among the gods,
Whom first we serve; whole woods of unctuous
   pine
Are fell'd for thee, and to thy glory shine;
By thee protected, with our naked soles
Through flames unsinged we march, and tread the
   kindled coals.
Give me, propitious pow'r, to wash away
The stains of this dishonourable day:
Nor spoils, nor triumph, from the fact I claim;
But with my future actions trust my fame:
Let me by stealth this female plague o'ercome,
And from the field return inglorious home.'
   Apollo heard, and granting half his prayer,
Shuffled in winds the rest, and toss'd in empty
   air;
He gives the death desir'd: his safe return
By southern tempests to the sea is borne.

   Now, when the jav'lin whizz'd along the skies,
Both armies on Camilla turu'd their eyes,
Directed by the sound.   Of either host
Th' unhappy virgin, though concern'd the most,
Was only deaf; so greedy was she bent
On golden spoils, and on her prey intent:
Till in her pap the winged weapon stood
Infix'd, and deeply drunk the purple blood.
Her sad attendants hasten to sustain
The dying lady drooping on the plain.
Far from their sight the trembling Aruns flies,
With beating heart, and fear confus'd with joys;
Nor dares he farther to pursue his blow,
Or e'en to bear the sight of his expiring foe.
   As when the wolf has torn a bullock's hide
At unawares, or ranch'd a shepherd's side,
Conscious of his audacious deed he flies,
And claps his quiv'ring tail between his thighs:
So, speeding once, the wretch no more attends,
But, spurring forward, herds among his friends.
She wrench'd the jav'lin with her dying hands,
But wedg'd within her breast the weapon stands:
The wood she draws, the steely point remains;
She staggers in her seat with agonising pains—
(A gathering mist o'erclouds her cheerful eyes,
And from her cheeks the rosy colour flies)
Then turns to her, whom of her female train
She trusted most, and thus she speaks with pain:
'Acca, 'tis past! he swims before my sight,
Inexorable Death, and claims his right.
Bear my last words to Turnus, fly with speed,
And bid him timely to my charge succeed—
Repel the Trojans, and the town relieve:
Farewell! and in this kiss my parting breath re-
   ceive.'
She said, and sliding, sunk upon the plain;
Dying, her open'd hand forsakes the rein;
Short and more short she pants; by slow degrees
Her mind the passage from her body frees.
She drops her sword—she nods her plumy crest—
Her drooping head declining on her breast—
In the last sigh her struggling soul expires,
And, murm'ring with disdain, to Stygian sounds
   retires.

A shout that struck the golden stars ensued;
Despair and rage, and languish'd fight renew'd.
The Trojan troops, and Tuscan, in a line,
Advance to charge; the mix'd Arcadians join.
   But Cynthia's maid, high seated, from afar
Surveys the field, and fortune of the war,
Unmov'd a while, till prostrate on the plain,
Welt'ring in blood, she sees Camilla slain,
And round her corpse of friends and foes a fight-
      ing-train.
Then from the bottom of her breast she drew
A mournful sigh, and these sad words ensue:
'Too dear a fine, ah, much-lamented maid!
For warring with the Trojans thou hast paid;
Nor aught avail'd, in this unhappy strife,
Diana's sacred arms to save thy life.
Yet unreveng'd thy goddess will not leave
Her vot'ry's death, nor with vain sorrow grieve.
Branded the wretch, and be his name abhorr'd;
But after-ages shall thy praise record.
Th' inglorious coward soon shall press the plain:
Thus vows thy queen, and thus the Fates ordain.'
   High o'er the field there stood a hilly mound—
Sacred the place, and spread with oaks around—
Where in a marble tomb Dercennus lay,
A king that once in Latium bore the sway.

The beauteous Opis thither bent her flight,
To mark the traitor Aruns from the height.
Him in refulgent arms she soon espied,
Swoln with success; and loudly thus she cried:
'Thy backward steps, vain boaster, are too late;
Turn, like a man, at length, and meet thy fate.
Charg'd with my message, to Camilla go,
And say I sent thee to the shades below—
An honour undeserv'd from Cynthia's bow.'
   She said, and from her quiver chose with speed
The winged shaft predestin'd for the deed;
Then to the stubborn yew her strength applied,
Till the far-distant horns approach'd on either
      side.
The bow-string touch'd her breast, so strong she
      drew;
Whizzing in air the fatal arrow flew.
At once the twanging bow and sounding dart
The traitor heard, and felt the point within his
      heart.
Him, beating with his heels in pangs of death,
His flying friends to foreign fields bequeath.
The conqu'ring damsel, with expanded wings,
The welcome message to her mistress brings."
                                 Æneid, book xi.

No. 1157.

The body of Camilla lying beside her horse.

APOLLONIDES.   *Amethyst.*

See preceding quotation.

No. 1158.

Diana charging Opis to avenge the death of Camilla.

GNAIOS.   *Cornelian.*

See preceding quotation.   See also quotation to No. 1150.

No. 1159.

Opis killing Aruns.

POLYCLETES. *Cornelian.*

See preceding quotation.

No. 1160.

Opis returning to Olympus.

GNAIOS. *Cornelian.*

See conclusion of preceding quotation.

No. 1161.

Juno and Juturna.

DEMIPHILOS. *Sardonyx.*

After the recent victory gained over the forces of Turnus, he is reproached by the Latins as the cause of all their calamities; he therefore resolves to accept the challenge previously given him by Æneas, to determine the issue of the war by single combat. But Juno instigates the nymph Juturna, the sister of Turnus, to defeat the object.

"Meantime the queen of heav'n beheld the sight,
With eyes unpleas'd, from mount Albano's height;
(Since call'd Albano by succeeding fame,
But then an empty hill without a name.)
She thence survey'd the field—the Trojan pow'rs—
The Latian squadrons, and Laurentine tow'rs.
Then thus the goddess of the skies bespake,
With sighs and tears, the goddess of the lake,
King Turnus' sister, once a lovely maid,
Ere to the lust of lawless Jove betray'd—
Compress'd by force, but by the grateful god
Now made the Naïs of the neighb'ring flood :
' O nymph, the pride of living lakes !' said she;
' O most renown'd, and most belov'd by me !
Long hast thou known, nor need I to record,
The wanton sallies of my wand'ring lord.

Of ev'ry Latian fair whom Jove misled
To mount by stealth my violated bed,
To thee alone I grudg'd not his embrace,
But gave a part of heav'n, and an unenvied place.
Now learn from me thy near-approaching grief,
Nor think my wishes want to thy relief.
While Fortune favour'd, nor heav'n's king denied
To lend my succour to the Latian side,
I sav'd thy brother and the sinking state ;
But now he struggles with unequal fate,
And goes, with gods averse, o'ermatch'd in might,
To meet inevitable death in fight ;
Nor must I break the truce, nor can sustain the sight.
Thou, if thou dar'st, thy present aid supply—
It well becomes a sister's care to try.'

At this the lovely nymph, with grief op-
    press'd,
Thrice tore her hair and beat her comely breast.
To whom Saturnia thus: 'Thy tears are late;
Haste—snatch him—if he can be snatch'd—from
    fate.

New tumults kindle—violate the truce:
Who knows what changeful Fortune may produce?
'Tis not a crime t' attempt what I decree;
Or if it were, discharge the crime on me.'
She said, and sailing on the winged wind,
Left the sad nymph suspended in her mind."

All the preliminary ceremonies are gone through, and the lists measured; while the altars
for the sacrifices are still burning, and the victims yet unconsumed.

" Already the Rutulians deemed their man
O'ermatch'd in arms, before the fight began:
First rising fears are whisper'd through the crowd,
Then, gath'ring sound, they murmur more aloud.
Now side to side they measure with their eyes
The champions' bulk, their sinews, and their size;
The nearer they approach, the more is known
Th' apparent disadvantage of their own.
Turnus himself appears in public sight
Conscious of fate, desponding of the fight.
Slowly he moves, and at his altar stands
With eyes dejected, and with trembling hands;
And while he mutters undistinguish'd pray'rs,
A livid deadness in his cheeks appears.
    With anxious pleasure when Juturna view'd
Th' increasing fright of the mad multitude—
When their short sighs and thick'ning sobs she
    heard,
And found their ready minds for change pre-
    par'd,—
Dissembling her immortal form, she took
Camertes' mien, his habit, and his look:
A chief of ancient blood: in arms well known
Was his great sire, and he his greater son.
His shape assum'd, amid the ranks she ran,
And, humouring their first notions, thus began:
' For shame, Rutulians! can you bear the sight
Of one expos'd for all in single fight?
Can we, before the face of heav'n, confess
Our courage colder, or our numbers less?
View all the Trojan host—th' Arcadian band,
And Tuscan army; count them as they stand:
Undaunted to the battle if we go,
Scarce ev'ry second man will share a foe.

Turnus, 'tis true, in this unequal strife,
Shall lose with honour his devoted life,
Or change it rather for immortal fame,
Succeeding to the gods, from whence he came:
But you, a servile and inglorious band,
For foreign lords shall sow your native land—
Those fruitful fields your fighting-fathers gain'd,
Which have so long their lazy sons sustain'd.'
    With words like these, she carried her design:
A rising murmur runs along the line.
Then e'en the city-troops, and Latians, tir'd
With tedious war, seem with new souls in-
    spir'd:
Their champion's fate with pity they lament,
And of the league so lately sworn repent.
    Nor fails the goddess to foment the rage
With lying wonders, and a false presage;
But adds a sign which, present to their eyes,
Inspires new courage and a glad surprise.
For sudden, in the fiery tracts above,
Appears in pomp th' imperial bird of Jove:
A flock of fowl he spies, that swim the lakes,
And o'er their heads his sounding pinions shakes;
Then stooping on the fairest of the train,
In his strong talons truss'd a silver swan.
Th' Italians wonder at th' unusual sight:
But while he lags, and labours in his flight,
Behold the dastard fowl return anew,
And with united force the foe pursue:
Clam'rous around the royal hawk they fly,
And, thick'ning in a cloud, o'ershade the sky.
They cuff—they scratch—they cross his airy
    course:
Nor can th' encumber'd bird sustain their force;

But vex'd, not vanquish'd, drops the pond'rous prey,
And, lighten'd of his burden, wings his way.
Th' Ausonian bands with shouts salute the sight,
Eager of action, and demand the fight.
Then king Tolumnius, vers'd in augurs' arts,
Cries out, and thus his boasted skill imparts:
'At length 'tis granted what I long desir'd!
This, this is what my frequent vows requir'd.

Ye gods! I take your omen, and obey.
Advance, my friends, and charge! I lead the way.
These are the foreign foes, whose impious band,
Like that rapacious bird, infest our land:
But soon, like him, they shall be forc'd to sea
By strength united, and forego the prey.
Your timely succour to your country bring;
Haste to the rescue, and redeem your king.'"

Æneid, book xii.

No. 1162.

Corynæus thrusting a firebrand against the bearded face of Ebusus.

APOLLONIDES. *Amethyst.*

The battle is now renewed:—

" Priest Corynæus arm'd his better hand,
From his own altar, with a blazing brand;
And as Ebusus with a thund'ring pace
Advanc'd to battle, dash'd it on his face:
His bristly beard shines out with sudden fires;
The crackling crop a noisome scent expires.
Following the blow, he seiz'd his curling crown
With his left hand; his other cast him down.
The prostrate body with his knees he press'd,
And plung'd his holy poinard in his breast."

Æneid, book xii.

No. 1163.

Combat between Podalirius and Alsus.

GNAIOS. *Cornelian.*

"While Podalirius with his sword pursued
The shepherd Alsus through the flying crowd,
Swiftly he turns, and aims a deadly blow
Full on the front of his unwary foe.
The broad axe enters with a crashing sound,
And cleaves the chin with one continued wound;
Warm blood and mingled brains besmear his arms around;
An iron sleep his stupid eyes oppress'd,
And seal'd their heavy lids in endless rest."

Æneid, book xii.

5 D

No. 1164.

Iäpis extracting the arrow from wounded Æneas.

APOLLODOTUS.   *Sardonyx.*

" But good Æneas rush'd amid the bands :
Bare was his head and naked were his hands,
In sign of truce ; then thus he cries aloud :
' What sudden rage—what new desire of blood
Inflames your alter'd minds ? O Trojans ! cease
From impious arms, nor violate the peace.
By human sanctions, and by laws divine,
The terms are all agreed : the war is mine.
Dismiss your fears, and let the fight ensue ;
This hand alone shall right the gods and you :
Our injur'd altars, and their broken vow,
To this avenging sword the faithless Turnus owe.'
　Thus while he spoke, unmindful of defence,
A winged arrow struck the pious prince.
But whether from some human hand it came,
Or hostile god, is left unknown by fame :
No human hand or hostile god was found
To boast the triumph of so base a wound.
　When Turnus saw the Trojan quit the plain—
His chiefs dismay'd—his troops a fainting train,
Th' unhop'd event his heighten'd soul inspires ;
At once his arms and coursers he requires ;
Then with a leap his lofty chariot gains,
And with a ready hand assumes the reins.
He drives impetuous, and where'er he goes
He leaves behind a lane of slaughter'd foes.

.　　.　　.　　.　　.

While he triumphs, and while the Trojans yield,
The wounded prince is forc'd to leave the field :
Strong Mnestheus, and Achates often tried,
And young Ascanius, weeping by his side,
Conduct him to his tent.   Scarce can he rear
His limbs from earth, supported on his spear.
Resolv'd in mind—regardless of his smart,
He tugs with both his hands, and breaks the dart :
The steel remains.   No readier way he found
To draw the weapon, than t' enlarge the wound.

Eager of fight, impatient of delay,
He begs ; and his unwilling friends obey.
　Iapis was at hand to prove his art ;
Whose blooming youth so fir'd Apollo's heart,
That for his love he proffer'd to bestow
His tuneful harp and his unerring bow.
The pious youth, more studious how to save
His aged sire, now sinking to the grave,
Preferr'd the pow'r of plants, and silent praise
Of healing arts, before Phœbean bays.
　Propp'd on his lance the pensive hero stood,
And heard and saw unmov'd the mourning crowd.
The fam'd physician tucks his robes around
With ready hands, and hastens to the wound.
With gentle touches he performs his part,
This way and that soliciting the dart,
And exercises all his heav'nly art.
All soft'ning simples, known of sov'reign use,
He presses out, and pours their noble juice.
These first infus'd, to lenify the pain,
He tugs with pincers, but he tugs in vain.
Then to the patron of his art he pray'd :
The patron of his art refus'd his aid.
　Meantime the war approaches to the tents ;
The alarm grows hotter, and the noise augments :
The driving dust proclaims the danger near ;
And first their friends, and then their foes appear :
Their friends retreat ; their foes pursue the rear.
The camp is fill'd with terror and affright ;
The hissing shafts within the trench alight ;
An undistinguish'd noise ascends the sky—
The shouts of those who kill, and groans of those
　　who die.
　But now the goddess-mother, mov'd with grief,
And pierc'd with pity, hastens for relief.
A branch of healing dittany she brought,
Which in the Cretan fields with care she sought—

(Rough is the stem, which woolly leaves surround,
The leaves with flow'rs, the flow'rs with purple
    crown'd)—
Well known to wounded goats—a sure relief
To draw the pointed steel and ease the grief.
This Venus brings, in clouds involv'd, and brews
Th' extracted liquor with ambrosian dews
And od'rous panaceæ. Unseen she stands,
Temp'ring the mixture with her heav'nly hands,
And pours it in a bowl, already crown'd
With juice of med'cinal herbs prepar'd to bathe
    the wound.
    The leech, unknowing of superior art
Which aids the cure, with this foments the part;
And in a moment ceas'd the raging smart.

Stanch'd is the blood, and in the bottom stands:
The steel, but scarcely touch'd with tender hands,
Moves up, and follows of its own accord;
And health and vigour are at once restor'd.
Iapis first perceiv'd the closing wound,
And first the favour of the goddess found:
' Arms! arms!' he cries; ' the sword and shield
    prepare,   ,—
And send the willing chief renew'd to war.
This is no mortal work—no cure of mine—
Nor art's effect, but done by hands divine:
Some god our gen'ral to the battle sends—
Some god preserves his life for greater ends.' "

                              Æneid, book xii.

No. 1165.

Venus preparing the juice of dittany for the cure of Æneas.

GNAIOS. *Cornelian.*

See second-last paragraph of preceding quotation.

No. 1166.

Combat of Æneas and Turnus; and conference of Jupiter and Juno.

Jupiter, who is holding the scales of fate, consoles Juno with the assurance that the death of
    Turnus will lead to the foundation of a mighty empire, in which she will be worshipped
    with peculiar honours.

CHROMIOS. *Sardonyx.*

Æneas returns to the field healed, and with renovated vigour: then follows great slaughter
on both sides. Æneas eventually dashes on towards the city, which he attacks. The queen,
seeing the desperate state of affairs, hangs herself through grief. Turnus at last determines
to decide the whole issue of the war by a single combat with Æneas. The following
description of this famous combat, which it is better to give as a whole, will suffice for
this and the two subsequent subjects.

" As when a fragment, from a mountain torn
By raging tempests, or by torrents borne,

Or sapp'd by time, or loosen'd from the roots—
Prone through the void the rocky ruin shoots,

Rolling from crag to crag, from steep to steep—
Down sink at once the shepherds and their sheep;
Involv'd alike, they rush to nether ground;
Stunn'd with the shock, they fall, and stunn'd,
    from earth rebound;—
So Turnus, hasting headlong to the town,
Should'ring and shoving, bore the squadrons
    down.
Still pressing onward, to the walls he drew,
Where shafts, and spears, and darts, promiscuous
    flew,
And sanguine streams the slipp'ry ground imbrue.
First stretching out his arm in sign of peace,
He cries aloud to make the combat cease:
' Rutulians, hold! and Latin troops, retire!
The fight is mine; and me the gods require.
'Tis just that I should vindicate alone
The broken truce, or for the breach atone.
This day shall free from wars th' Ausonian state,
Or finish my misfortunes in my fate.'
  Both armies from their bloody work desist,
And, bearing backward, form a spacious list.
The Trojan hero, who receiv'd from fame
The welcome sound, and heard the champion's
    name,
Soon leaves the taken works and mounted walls:
Greedy of war where greater glory calls,
He springs to fight, exulting in his force;
His jointed armour rattles in the course.
Like Eryx, or like Athos, great he shews;
Or father Appenine, when, white with snows,
His head divine obscure in clouds he hides,
And shakes the sounding forest on his sides.
The nations, overaw'd, surcease the fight;
Immovable their bodies—fix'd their sight—
E'en death stands still! nor from above they throw
Their darts, nor drive their batt'ring rams below.
In silent order either army stands,
And drop their swords now useless from their
    hands.
Th' Ausonian king beholds, with woud'ring sight,
Two mighty champions match'd in single fight,
Born under climes remote, and brought by Fate
With swords to try their titles to the state.

  Now, in clos'd field, each other from afar
They view: and, rushing on, begin the war.
They launch their spears; then hand to hand they
    meet:
The trembling soil resounds beneath their feet.
Their bucklers clash; thick blows descend from
    high,
And flakes of fire from their hard helmets fly.
Courage conspires with chance; and both engage
With equal fortune yet, and mutual rage.
  As when two bulls for their fair female fight
In Sila's shades, or on Tiburnus' height;
With horns adverse they meet; the keeper flies;
Mute stands the herd; the heifers roll their eyes,
And wait th' event—which victor they shall bear,
And who shall be the lord to rule the lusty year:
With rage of love the jealous rivals burn,
And push for push, and wound for wound return:
Their dewlaps gor'd, their sides are lav'd in blood;
Loud cries and roaring sounds rebellow through
    the wood;—
Such was the combat in the listed ground;
So clash their swords, and so their shields re-
    sound.
  Jove sets the beam: on either scale he lays
The champion's fate, and each exactly weighs.
On this side life and lucky chance ascends;
Loaded with death that other scale descends.
Rais'd on the stretch, young Turnus aims a blow
Full on the helm of his unguarded foe:
Shrill shouts and clamours ring on either side,
As hopes and fears their panting hearts divide:
But all in pieces flies the traitor-sword, ·
And in the middle stroke deserts his lord.
Now 'tis but death or flight: disarm'd he flies,
When in his hand an unknown hilt he spies.
Fame says that Turnus, when his steeds he join'd,
Hurrying to war—disorder'd in his mind,
Snatch'd the first weapon which his haste could
    find:
'Twas not the fated sword his father bore,
But that his charioteer Metiscus wore.
This, while the Trojans fled, its toughness held;
But vain against the great Vulcanian shield:

The mortal-temper'd steel deceiv'd his hand;
The shiver'd fragments shone amid the sand.

Surpris'd with fear, he fled along the field,
And now forthright, and now in orbits wheel'd;
For here the Trojan troops the list surround,
And there the pass is clos'd with pools and marshy
ground.

Æneas hastens, though with heavier pace—
His wound, so newly knit, retards the chase,
And oft his trembling knees their aid refuse;
Yet, pressing foot by foot, his foe pursues.

Thus when a fearful stag is clos'd around
With crimson* toils, or in a river found:
High on the bank the deep-mouth'd hound ap-
pears—
Still op'ning—following still—where'er he steers:
The persecuted creature, to and fro,
Turns here and there, t' escape his Umbrian foe:†
Steep is th' ascent, and if he gains the land,
The purple death is pitch'd along the strand:
His eager foe, determin'd to the chase,
Stretch'd at his length, gains ground at ev'ry
pace;
Now to his beamy head he makes his way,
And now he holds, or thinks he holds, his prey:
Just at the pinch, the stag springs out with fear;
He bites the wind, and fills his sounding jaws
with air:
The rocks—the lakes—the meadows ring with
cries;
The mortal tumult mounts and thunders in the
skies.

Thus flies the Daunian prince, and flying blames
His tardy troops, and, calling by their names,
Demands his trusty sword. The Trojan threats
The realm with ruin, and their ancient seats
To lay in ashes, if they dare supply
With arms or aid his vanquish'd enemy:
Thus menacing, he still pursues the course
With vigour, though diminish'd of his force.
Ten times already round the listed place
One chief had fled, and th' other giv'n the chase.
No trivial prize is play'd; for on the life
Or death of Turnus now depends the strife.

Within the space an olive-tree had stood,
A sacred shade—a venerable wood,
For vows to Faunus paid—the Latins' guardian
god:
Here hung the vests, and tablets were engrav'd,
Of sinking mariners from shipwreck sav'd.‡
With heedless hands the Trojans fell'd the tree,
To make the ground inclos'd for combat free.
Deep in the root, whether by fate, or chance,
Or erring haste, the Trojan drove his lance;
Then stoop'd, and tugg'd with force immense, to
free
Th' encumber'd spear from the tenacious tree;
That whom his fainting limbs pursued in vain,
His flying lance might from afar attain.
Confus'd with fear, bereft of human aid,
Then Turnus to the gods, and first to Faunus,
pray'd:
' O Faunus, pity! and thou, mother Earth,
Where I, thy foster-son, receiv'd my birth,

---

* The hunting-toils or nets were decorated with red feathers, in order to frighten and bewilder
the animals.

† The hound from Umbria, a district in the north of Italy, near the Apennines, famous for stag
and boar-hounds.

‡ It was customary among the Romans, for those who had been saved from shipwreck to hang
up in the temple, as a thanksgiving, the garments they had worn when saved, together with a picture
of the incidents of their escape. But in that rural district, and that rude age, this olive-tree served
the purpose of a temple. Though Virgil does not expressly state the reason why the spear stuck
fast in the root of this sacred tree, yet the best commentators say that the act was a punishment for
the profanation of the Trojans in cutting it down; and Virgil himself gives probability to this opinion
by the subsequent prayer of Turnus.

Hold fast the steel! If my religious hand
Your plant has honour'd, which your foes profan'd,
Propitious hear my pious pray'r!' He said,
Nor with successless vows invok'd their aid.
Th' incumbent hero wrench'd, and pull'd, and
    strain'd;
But still the stubborn earth the steel detain'd.
Juturna took her time; and, while in vain
He strove, assum'd Metiscus' form again,

And in that imitated shape restor'd
To the despairing prince his Daunian sword.
The queen of love (who with disdain and grief
Saw the bold nymph afford this prompt relief)
T' assert her offspring with a greater deed,
From the tough root the ling'ring weapon freed.
    Once more erect, the rival chiefs advance:
One trusts the sword, and one the pointed lance;
And both resolv'd alike to try their fatal chance."

Jupiter sends one of the furies to discomfit Turnus, and drive off Juturna, who assisted him.

"The pest comes whirling down: by far more
    slow
Springs the swift arrow from the Parthian bow,
Or Cydon yew, when, traversing the skies,
And drench'd in pois'nous juice, the sure destruc-
    tion flies.
With such a sudden and unseen a flight
Shot through the clouds the daughter of the
    Night.
Soon as the field enclos'd she had in view,
And from afar her destin'd quarry knew,
Contracted, to the boding bird she turns
Which haunts the ruin'd piles and hallow'd urns,
And beats about the tombs with nightly wings,
Where songs obscene on sepulchres she sings.
Thus lessen'd in her form, with frightful cries
The fury round unhappy Turnus flies—
Flaps on his shield, and flutters o'er his eyes.
A lazy chillness crept along his blood—
Chok'd was his voice—his hair with horror stood.
Juturna from afar beheld her fly,
And knew th' ill omen by her screaming cry,
And stridor of her wing. Amaz'd with fear,
Her beauteous breast she beat, and rent her flow-
    ing hair:
'Ah me!' she cries, 'in this unequal strife
What can thy sister more to save thy life?
Weak as I am, can I, alas! contend
In arms with that inexorable fiend?
Now, now I quit the field! forbear to fright
My tender soul, ye baleful birds of night!

The lashing of your wings I know too well—
The sounding flight, and fun'ral screams of hell!
These are the gifts you bring from haughty Jove—
The worthy recompense of ravish'd love!
Did he for this exempt my life from fate?
O hard conditions of immortal state!
Though born to death—not privileg'd to die,
But forc'd to bear impos'd eternity!
Take back your envious bribes, and let me go
Companion to my brother's ghost below!
The joys are vanish'd: nothing now remains
Of life immortal, but immortal pains.
What earth will open her devouring womb,
To rest a weary goddess in the tomb?'
She drew a length of sighs; nor more she said,
But in her azure mantle wrapp'd her head;
Then plung'd into her stream, with deep de-
    spair,
And her last sobs came bubbling up in air.
    Now stern Æneas waves his weighty spear
Against his foe, and thus upbraids his fear:
'What farther subterfuge can Turnus find?
What empty hopes are harbour'd in his mind?
'Tis not thy swiftness can secure thy flight:
Not with their feet, but hands, the valiant fight.
Vary thy shape in thousand forms, and dare
What skill and courage can attempt in war:
Wish for the wings of wind to mount the sky;
Or hid within the hollow earth to lie!'
The champion shook his head, and made this short
    reply:

'No threats of thine my manly mind can move:
'Tis hostile heav'n I dread and partial Jove.'
He said no more, but, with a sigh, repress'd
The mighty sorrow in his swelling breast.
Then, as he roll'd his troubled eyes around,
An antique stone he saw—the common bound
Of neighb'ring fields, and barrier of the ground—
So vast, that twelve strong men of modern days
Th' enormous weight from earth could hardly
    raise.
He heav'd it at a lift, and, pois'd on high,
Ran stagg'ring on against his enemy;
But so disorder'd, that he scarcely knew
His way, or what unwieldy weight he threw.
His knocking knees are bent beneath the load;
And shiv'ring cold congeals his vital blood.
The stone drops from his arms, and, falling short
For want of vigour, mocks his vain effort.
And as, when heavy sleep has clos'd the sight,
The sickly fancy labours in the night;
We seem to run, and, destitute of force,
Our sinking limbs forsake us in the course:
In vain we heave for breath—in vain we cry;
The nerves, unbrac'd, their usual strength deny;
And on the tongue the falt'ring accents die;—
So Turnus far'd: whatever means he tried—
All force of arms—and points of art employ'd,
The fury flew athwart, and made th' endeavour
    void.
A thousand various thoughts his soul con-
    found;
He star'd about, nor aid nor issue found:
His own men stop the pass; and his own walls
    surround.
Once more he pauses, and looks out again,
And seeks the goddess-charioteer in vain.
Trembling he views the thund'ring chief ad-
    vance,
And brandishing aloft the deadly lance;
Amaz'd he cow'rs beneath his conq'ring foe—
Forgets to ward, and waits the coming blow;

Astonish'd while he stands, and fix'd with fear,
Aim'd at his shield he sees th' impending spear.
    The hero measur'd first, with narrow view,
The destin'd mark; and rising as he threw,
With its full swing the fatal weapon flew.
Not with less rage the rattling thunder falls,
Or stones from batt'ring engines break the
    walls:
Swift as a whirlwind, from an arm so strong,
The lance drove on, and bore the death along.
Nought could his sev'nfold shield the prince
    avail,
Nor aught beneath his arms the coat of mail;
It pierc'd through all, and with a grisly wound
Transfix'd his thigh and doubled him to ground.
With groans the Latians rend the vaulted sky:
Woods, hills, and valleys, to the voice reply.
    Now low on earth the lofty chief is laid,
With eyes cast upward, and with arms dis-
    play'd;
And, recreant, thus to the proud victor pray'd:
'I know my death deserv'd, nor hope to live:
Use what the gods and thy good fortune give.
Yet think—oh, think! if mercy may be
    shewn—
(Thou hadst a father once, and hast a son)—
Pity my sire, now sinking to the grave;
And, for Anchises' sake, old Daunus save!
Or, if thy vow'd revenge pursue my death,
Give to my friends my body void of breath.
The Latin chiefs have seen me beg my life:
Thine is the conquest—thine the royal wife:
Against a yielded man 'tis mean ignoble strife.'
    In deep suspense the Trojan seem'd to stand,
And, just prepar'd to strike, repress'd his hand.
He roll'd his eyes, and ev'ry moment felt
His manly soul with more compassion melt;
When, casting down a casual glance, he spied
The golden belt that glitter'd on his side—
The fatal spoil which haughty Turnus tore
From dying Pallas,* and in triumph wore.

---

* The son of his ally, king Evander.

Then rous'd anew to wrath, he loudly cries
(Flames while he spoke came flashing from his
 eyes),
'Traitor! dost thou—dost thou to grace pretend,
Clad as thou art in trophies of my friend!
To his sad soul a grateful off'ring go:
'Tis Pallas—Pallas gives this deadly blow!

He rais'd his arm aloft, and as he said,
Deep in his bosom fiercely plung'd the blade:
His limbs by death's cold hand relax'd, he fell;
And his indignant soul fled groaning down to
 hell."*

         Æneid, book xii.

No. 1167.

Juturna in despair at the sight of the ill-omened bird that quelled the
vigour of Turnus.

DEMIPHOLOS. *Cornelian.*

See twelfth paragraph of preceding quotation.

---

* Though I have, in my quotations from Virgil, adopted Dryden's translation, as I have adopted
Pope's in my quotations from Homer, because these are the translations that have been generally
stamped with the sanction of public approbation as *the* translations that best convey the poetic fire,
force, and majesty of the originals; yet I have found it occasionally necessary to alter a word or a
phrase, in order the more accurately to express the meaning of the original, and to shew that the
views of the original poet and of the artist coincided. But here I am forced to alter these last three
lines altogether. Virgil says:

  " Hoc dicens, ferrum adverso sub pectore condit
   Fervidus: ast illi solvuntur frigore membra;
   Vitaque cum gemitu fugit indignata sub umbras."

Which literally means: " so saying, fired with fury, he buries the steel deep under his breast in front:
ay, then his limbs are relaxed with cold (the cold of death); and his soul, with a groan, flees indig-
nant to the shades." Now, Dryden's translation is:

  " And at the word
  Deep in his bosom drove the *shining sword:*
  The *streaming blood distain'd his arms around,*
  And the disdainful soul came rushing through the *wound.*"

It will be seen that he omits all notice of some of the most striking expressions in the original, and
introduces images for which there is no authority. The second-last line is wrong in every particular:
Virgil speaks generally by using the word *ferrum*, steel or iron; and *blade* is the most appropriate
general translation. All through the combat Æneas appears armed with a spear: whether he killed
Turnus with the iron, or steel, of his sword or spear, Virgil does not tell us.—J. P.

No. 1168.

Æneas wounding Turnus.

PAMILLIOS. *Sardonyx.*

See preceding quotation.

No. 1169.

Head of Æneas.

DIOSCORIDES. *Cornelian.*

MISCELLANEOUS SUBJECTS.

No. 1170.

Ulysses and Telegonus.

POLYCLETES. *Cornelian.*

Although Homer intimates that Ulysses ended his life peacefully and prosperously in Ithaca, yet there is another account of the close of his life, *i. e.* that Telegonus, his son by Circe, having sailed for Ithaca in order to make himself known to his father, was wrecked on the coast, and was involved in a quarrel with some of the inhabitants, in which Ulysses interfered; and that upon this Telegonus unwittingly slew him: after which he returned to Italy and founded Tusculum, which Horace (book iii. *Od.* 29) calls "Telegoni juga paricidæ."

No. 1171.

Othryades slaying himself.

PYRGOTELES. *Cornelian.*

The Spartans and Argives had been long contending for the possession of Thyre: at length it was agreed that the dispute should be determined by three hundred warriors on each side. Three alone survived the sanguinary conflict—two Argives, and one Spartan—Othryades. The two Argives went home to announce their victory. But Othryades, who remained disabled in the field, recovered, and collecting the spoils of the enemy, bore them to the Spartan camp; there having erected a trophy, and written on it with his still-flowing blood, " I have conquered !" slew himself, unwilling to survive his comrades in arms.

No. 1172.

Same subject.

APOLLONIDES. *Cornelian.*

See preceding explanation.

No. 1173.

Pausanias killing Cleonice.

APOLLONIDES. *Cornelian.*

" They report of Pausanias, king of Sparta, that when he was in Byzantium (now Constantinople) he solicited a young lady of a noble family in the city, whose name was Cleonice. Her parents, dreading his cruelty, were forced to consent, and abandoned their daughter to his embraces. Cleonice had commanded the servants to put out all the lights; so that, approaching silently and in the dark towards his bed, she stumbled upon the lamp that was extinguished, which she overturned and spilled. Pausanias, who had fallen asleep, awoke, and, startled with the noise, thought an assassin was come to murder him; then hastily snatching up his poniard, wounded his supposed enemy to death. After this his mind was never at ease; for her spectre continually haunted his bed, and interrupted his repose with these angry words :

'Go, meet thy doom, the just reward of guilt;
Know, vengeance never sleeps when blood is spilt.'

All the allies looked on this action with the greatest indignation; and joining their forces with Cimon's (the Athenian general), besieged Pausanias in Byzantium. But he escaped out of their hands; and being still terrified by the vision, went to Heraclea. In this place there was a temple, where the spirits of the dead were raised in order to discover future events. Having solemnly invoked Cleonice, and entreated her to be reconciled, she appeared to him and answered : 'As soon as thou goest to Sparta, thou shalt be freed from thy misfortunes;' hereby obscurely foretelling (in my opinion) the death which there awaited him."*—PLUTARCH, *Life of Cimon.*

No. 1174.

The ghost of Cleonice appearing to Pausanias.

CHROMIOS. *Cornelian.*

See preceding explanation.

No. 1175.

Aristodemus killing his daughter.

POLYCLETES. *Sardonyx.*

---

* Having been detected in a negotiation to betray Greece to the Persian king, he fled from the vengeance of the magistrates to the temple of Minerva, as a sanctuary. But the people blocked up the place with stones (his own mother having placed the first), and starved him to death.

Aristodemus was a celebrated chief of Messenia, in the Peloponnesus, who gallantly conducted a war against Sparta. The Messenians, having sustained a signal defeat, consulted the oracle at Delphos : the oracle announced, that, to save Messenia, a virgin of the ancient blood-royal must be sacrificed. Aristodemus, a descendant of the Æpytidæ, offered his daughter as a voluntary sacrifice. But a noble citizen, who was in love with her, claimed her as his own, asserting that she was betrothed to him. This plea proving ineffectual, he then declared that she was pregnant. Aristodemus, enraged at this, slew his daughter; and having cut her open, discovered that the lover's story was a fiction. However, the murder was deemed a sufficient sacrifice. The mother slew herself in grief for her daughter; and Aristodemus, seeing, after many subsequent encounters with the enemy, that he had slain his daughter without producing any advantage to his country, slew himself on her tomb.

This is the substance of what Pausanias states, book iv. caps. 9 and 13.

No. 1176.

The wife of Aristodemus preparing to kill herself beside the dead body of her daughter.

APOLLONIDES. *Cornelian.*

See preceding explanation.

No. 1177.

Aristodemus killing himself at the tomb of his daughter.

PYRGOTELES. *Amethyst.*

See preceding explanation.

No. 1178.

Lysimachus strangling a lion.

APOLLONIDES. *Cornelian.*

Lysimachus, one of Alexander's most distinguished generals, having offended Alexander by avowing his friendship for Callisthenes, was thrown into a lion's den. When the animal sprang at him, he thrust his hand, wrapped in his mantle, into his throat—seized his tongue, and killed him. Alexander was so pleased at this feat that he restored Lysimachus to favour. See JUSTIN, book xv.

No. 1179.

Diogenes in his tub.

GNAIOS. *Cornelian.*

No. 1180.

Alexander and Diogenes.

CHROMIOS. *Sardonyx.*

After Alexander had been appointed generalissimo of the Grecian forces against Persia, he visited the philosopher Diogenes, who at the time was lying in a tub which he used as his house, and basking in the sun. Alexander asked him whether he wanted any thing; but Diogenes replied—" Only stand from between me and the sun." Alexander (says Plutarch) was so struck by this answer, and so surprised at the greatness of the man's soul who had taken so little notice of him, that, as he went away, he said to his followers, who were laughing at the moroseness of the philosopher—" If I were not Alexander, I would wish to be Diogenes."

No. 1181.

Head of Diogenes.

PYRGOTELES. *Amethyst.*

No. 1182.

Alexander cutting the Gordian knot.

DIOSCORIDES. *Cornelian.*

After Alexander subdued Phrygia, he saw in Gordium, the capital city (which is said to have been the seat of Midas), the famous chariot, fastened with cords made of the bark of the cornel-tree; and was informed that the inhabitants had a tradition, that the empire of the world was reserved for the man who should untie the knot. Alexander finding that he could not untie it, because the ends were secretly folded up within it, cut it asunder with his sword, so that several ends appeared. See PLUTARCH, in his *Life of Alexander.*

No. 1183.

Alexander and his physician Philip.

CHROMIOS. *Amethyst.*

This scene is thus described by Plutarch:—" Alexander was detained in Cilicia by sickness, which some say he contracted by fatiguing himself too much; others, by bathing in the river Cydnus, the waters of which are exceedingly cold. However, it so happened that none of his physicians would venture to give him any remedies, thinking his case desperate, and fearing the censure, and even vengeance of the Macedonians, should they fail in the cure; till Philip, the Acarnanian, considering his extreme danger, and confiding in his friendship, resolved to try the utmost efforts of his art, and rather hazard his credit and his life, than suffer him to perish for want of medicine. This medicine he confidently did administer to him, encouraging him to take it boldly, if he desired a speedy recovery in order to prosecute the war. At this very time Parmenio wrote to Alexander, telling him to beware of Philip, as he had been bribed by Darius to kill him—having offered him large sums of money, and his daughter in marriage. Having perused the letter, he put it under his pillow, without shewing it to any of his friends. When Philip came in with the potion, he took it with great cheerfulness and assurance, at the same time giving him the letter to read. This was an encounter well worth being present at—to see Alexander take the draught, and Philip read the letter at the same time, looking earnestly upon one another, but with different sentiments; for Alexander's looks were cheerful and open, a demonstration of his kindness to, and confidence in, his physician; while the other's were full of surprise at the accusation, appealing to the gods to witness his innocence—sometimes lifting up his hands to heaven, and then throwing himself down by the bedside, and beseeching Alexander to lay aside all fear, and rely on his fidelity. The medicine at first wrought so strongly with him, that it overcame his spirits, and brought him so low that he lost his speech, and, falling into a swoon, had scarce any sense or pulse left; but soon after, by Philip's means, his health and strength returned, and he shewed himself in public to the Macedonians, who were in continual fear and dejection till they saw him abroad again." .

No. 1184.

Alexander killing a lion.

PYRGOTELES. *Cornelian.*

" When he perceived that his generals rather more used precious ointments than plain oil when they went to bathe, and that they had servants every where with them, to rub them and wait upon them in their chambers, he reproved them with great mildness and discretion, telling them he wondered that they who had been engaged in so many signal battles, should not know

by experience that labour and industry made people sleep more sweetly and soundly than lazi-
ness; and that if they compared the Persians' manner of living with their own, they would be
convinced it was the most abject, slavish condition in the world to be effeminate and voluptuous;
but the most generous and becoming a great man to take pains. Besides, he reasoned with
them how it was possible for any one who pretended to be a soldier, either to look well after
his horse, or to keep his armour bright and in good order, who thought much to let his hands
be serviceable to what was nearest to him—his own body. ' Are ye still to learn,' said he,
' that the end and perfection of our victories is to avoid the vices and infirmities of those whom
we subdue?' And to strengthen his precepts by example, he applied himself now more
vigorously than ever to hunting and warlike expeditions, readily embracing all opportunities
of hardship and danger; insomuch that old Lacon, who chanced to be by when he encountered
with and mastered a huge lion, told him, ' He had put his empire in competition, and had
fought gallantly with the beast, which of the two should be king.' Craterus caused a representa-
tion of this adventure, consisting of the lion and the dogs—of the king engaged with the lion,
and himself coming in to his assistance—all expressed in figures of brass (some of which were
made by Lysippus, and the rest by Leochares),—to be dedicated to the temple of Apollo at
Delphos. In this manner did Alexander expose his person to danger, whilst he both inured
himself and incited others to the performance of brave and virtuous actions."—PLUTARCH.

No. 1185.

Socrates saving Alcibiades.

ATHENION. *Cornelian.*

" Whilst Alcibiades was very young, he was a soldier in the expedition against Potidæa,
where Socrates lodged in the same tent with him, and seconded him in all encounters. Once
there happened a sharp skirmish, wherein they both behaved themselves with much bravery;
but Alcibiades receiving a wound there, Socrates threw himself before him to defend him, and
most manifestly saved him and his arms from the enemy; and therefore, in all justice, might
have challenged the prize of valour. But the generals appearing earnest to adjudge the honour
to Alcibiades, because of his quality, Socrates, who desired to increase his thirst after glory,
was the first who gave evidence for him, and pressed them to crown him, and to decree to him
the complete suit of armour. Afterwards, in the battle of Delium, when the Athenians were
routed, and Socrates, with a few others, was retreating on foot, Alcibiades, who was on horse-
back, observing it, would not pass on, but stayed to shelter him from the danger, and brought
him safe off, though the enemy pressed hard upon them, and cut off many of the party."—
PLUTARCH.

No. 1186.

Socrates and his disciples.

APOLLONIDES. *Cornelian.*

Socrates, the greatest of the Grecian philosophers, unsparingly attacked the superstition of the Athenians, and propounded the doctrine of an all-disposing Providence. He was impeached by Melitus and Anytus for impiety, and for an endeavour to corrupt the people by bringing their gods into ridicule. He defended himself with great resolution, and maintained the purity of his doctrines. But he was condemned, and ordered to take a dose of poisonous hemlock. The interval between his condemnation and his death he spent in calmly lecturing his pupils, among whom were Plato, Xenophon, Phædon, Crito, Apollodorus. The history of Socrates, who is sometimes designated, from the approximation of his doctrines to the morality of the Bible, the Christian-pagan, is so generally known, that it is unnecessary to dwell on it here.

No. 1187.

Head of Socrates.

ADMON. *Cornelian.*

No. 1188.

Plato meditating on the immortality of the soul.

APOLLONIDES. *Cornelian.*

Plato was the most celebrated of the disciples of Socrates. Quintilian says, that when he read Plato, he seemed to hear, not a man, but a divinity speaking. His writings were so celebrated, and his philosophy so much esteemed, that he was called "the divine Plato." Addison, in his tragedy of *Cato*, gives in Cato's soliloquy the substance of his philosophy on the immortality of the soul.

No. 1189.

Head of Plato.

APOLLONIDES. *Cornelian.*

No. 1190.

Arion upon a dolphin.

DIOSCORIDES. *Calcedony.*

Arion was a famous poet and musician of Methymna, in the island of Lesbos. The dolphin who saved him, when he plunged into the sea to escape from the sailors who conspired to murder him for his riches, was, it is fabled, made a constellation.

This story is thus told by Ovid:—

" The dolphin, whom you lately saw so bright,
Will wholly be obscur'd the following night:
Whether as for a happy spy* to love
He gain'd a place among the stars above;
Or whether for Arion, whom he bore
Upon his back, and carried safe to shore.
Who has not heard of sweet Arion's fame?
What country is a stranger to his name?
He that, with music's all-enchanting force,
Could stop a running river in its course;
Whose voice with magic virtue was endued
To stop a wolf, though he his prey pursued:
The dog and hare their fleeting course have stay'd
To listen when upon his lyre he play'd;
A furious bull his music could assuage,
And mollify the fiercest lion's rage;
The crow and owl,† the hawk and dove, were friends,
To sit and hear his soft melodious strains;
And Cynthia‡ in her orb reluctant hung,
As if she heard her brother's tuneful song.
Long had he ravish'd the Sicilian plains,
And charm'd Ausonia with his lyric strains:
From thence returning home, he went aboard,
And in the ship his late-got riches stor'd.

Perhaps, Arion, thou the sea might'st fear:
Trust not the ship; there is no safety there.
The master and the crew, with sword in hand,
Seize on the lyrist, and his wealth demand:
' But why these hostile arms?' Arion cried;
' Stick to your tackling, and the vessel guide:
Free from all guilt, I'm not afraid to die;
But let me first sing my own elegy."
They grant him leave, but laugh at his request:
Then with a chaplet crown'd, and richly drest
In a wrought mantle, which they all admire,
He with his fingers touch'd the sounding lyre;
And, like the dying swan, he sweetly sung,
The sounding lyre according with his tongue.
This done, and thus adorn'd, without delay
Springing he jump'd into the foamy sea;
Where, wond'rous to relate, a dolphin heav'd
His bending back, and kind the man receiv'd;
On whom he sat, and play'd with tuneful hand,
Till that the dolphin brought him safe to land.
To gracious heav'n let innocency trust;
The gods reward the pious and the just:
It was for this Jove made the dolphin shine
A constellation; and his stars are nine."
OVID. *Fasti*, book ii.

---

* " According to the fabulous tradition, when Neptune had a mind to marry Amphitrite, the coy lady hid herself; but the dolphin found her out, and persuaded her to accept the match; and for that piece of service Neptune gave him a place among the stars."

† " Aristotle says, that the great enmity between the crow and the owl is occasioned by the crow's breaking the owl's eggs by day, and the owl's breaking the crow's eggs by night."

‡ " Diana, or the moon, is called *Cynthia*, from Cynthus, a mountain in the island of Delos."

No. 1191.

Venus presenting a vase of fragrant oil to Phaon.

PYRGOTELES.   *Cornelian.*

Phaon was a mariner of Mitylene, who, after anointing himself with the contents of this vase, became the most beautiful youth of his age. Among his other lovers was the famous poetess Sappho. After returning her love for some time, he abandoned her; upon which she flung herself in despair from Mount Leucate into the sea. See OVID's *Epistles,* " Sappho to Phaon."

No. 1192.

Same subject.

APOLLONIDES.   *Cornelian.*

No. 1193.

Phrynis, the musician of Mitylene, leaning against the altar of Apollo.

GNAIOS.   *Cornelian.*

It is said he was the first who obtained a musical prize at the Panathenæa games in Athens. He added two strings to the lyre, which had been always used with seven by his predecessors.

No. 1194.

Polydamas holding an ox.

APOLLONIDES.   *Sardonyx.*

The exploits of Polydamas are thus related by Pausanias, book vi. cap. 5:—" But the statue, which stands on a lofty basis, is the work of Lysippus. This statue is the image of a man, who, excepting those that are called heroes, or the race of mortals prior to the heroes (if there was any such race), must have been the largest of all men. Scotussa, the native country of this Polydamas, the son of Nicias, is not now inhabited, for it was depopulated by Alexander of Pheræ. . . . . . The mountainous part of Thrace was infested with lions: here Polydamas once, though quite unarmed, slew a large, strong lion, being incited to this daring deed by a desire to emulate the achievements of Hercules. Coming once to a herd of oxen, he seized the largest and fiercest by one of the hind feet. This he so strenuously held, that notwithstanding the animal's violent struggling to get free, it was scarcely able at length to escape with the loss of its hoof. They add, that at this time he was able to stop a chariot at full speed. Darius Nothus having heard of his exploits, sent for him to Susa. When arrived there, he slew three of those called the immortal band, who fought him collectively. These exploits are partly represented on the base of the statue in Olympia, and partly evinced by the inscription. But he fell at last, through too much self-confidence in his own strength. Having once retired, with some companions, to a rocky cavern for shelter, the roof gave way ; and while his companions fled, he remained, and endeavoured to uphold the vast mass of falling rock, which, however, eventually crushed him."

No. 1195.

Polydamas stopping a chariot when driven at full speed.

AGATHEMEROS. *Cornelian.*

See preceding explanation.

No. 1196.

Polydamas killing the guards of Darius.

CHROMIOS. *Amethyst.*

See preceding explanation.

No. 1197.

Polydamas supporting the falling roof of a rocky cave.

APOLLONIDES. *Cornelian.*

No. 1198.

Œbotas victorious in the chariot-race.

APOLLONIDES. *Cornelian.*

" This Œbotas was a Dymæan, who conquered in the seventh Olympiad. But the statue was dedicated in Olympia, in consequence of an oracle given at Delphos in the eightieth Olympiad. Upon this statue there is the following epigram—

' Œbotas, in the stadium victor, raised
His country Palea, in Achaia's realms, to fame.'

That the epigram calls the city Palea, and not Dyme, ought not to disturb the reader; for the more ancient names are employed by the Greeks in poetical composition, instead of the more modern."—PAUSANIAS, book vii. c. 17.

No. 1199.

Arrachion crushing the foot of his adversary.

DIOSCORIDES. *Sardonyx.*

" In the forum of the Phigalenses there is a statue of the pancratist* Arrachion, which is in other respects ancient, and particularly as to its figure. The feet are at no great distance from each other; and the hands adhere to the sides and the hips. This statue is made of stone; and they say that there was an inscription on it, which has become obliterated by time. Arrachion was twice victorious in the Olympic games prior to the fifty-fourth Olympiad; and these victories were obtained as well by the just decision of the judges of the games, as by the merits of Arrachion: for as he was contending for the olive crown with the only antagonist that was left, his antagonist endeavoured to prevent him from gaining the victory by entangling him with his feet, and grasping his neck. But Arrachion crushed one of his toes; and at the moment that he expired, being strangled to death, his adversary through pain of his mangled toe fell to the ground. The Eleans therefore crowned and proclaimed the dead body of Arrachion victorious."—PAUSANIAS, book viii. c. 40.

No. 1200.

Dromeus victor in the foot-race.

PYRGOTELES. *Cornelian.*

" Near this is the statue of the Stymphalian Dromeus, whose name (the *racer*) corresponds with his exercise; for in the longer chariot-race he was twice victorious in the Olympic— twice in the Pythian—thrice in the Isthmian—and five times in the Nemean games. It is said that he was the first who ate animal food; for the Athletæ before him used to eat nothing but fig-cheese. His statue was made by Pythagoras."—PAUSANIAS, book vi. c. 7. He is here represented as holding a garland before the statue of Minerva.

---

* *Pancratium*—from *pan* and *cratos, every* exercise of *strength*—was a sort of contest in which the combatants used every effort to gain the victory, such as by boxing, wrestling, kicking, biting, &c.

No. 1201.

Milo killing the bull.

DIOSCORIDES. *Cornelian.*

Milo of Crotona was celebrated for his prodigious size and strength. He was seven times victor at the Pythian, and six times victor at the Olympian games. He used to bind his forehead tightly with a strong cord, and, by holding in his breath, and swelling out the veins of his head, burst the cord. Setting full against his side the part of the arm between the shoulder and the elbow, he would extend the other part, with his thumb turned upwards and his fingers placed close together; then, his hand being in this position, no one could separate his little finger from the rest. It is said that he carried on his shoulders for forty yards a full-grown bullock, and killed it at a blow. Seeing a large oak, into the trunk of which wedges were driven in order to cleave it, he endeavoured by his own strength to tear it asunder; but the wedges giving way, he was caught by the rebounding parts, and held fast till he was torn to pieces by wild beasts. See PAUSANIAS, book vi. c. 14.

No. 1202.

Death of Milo.

CHROMIOS. *Cornelian.*

See preceding explanation.

No. 1203.

Romulus observing the flight of vultures.

PYRGOTELES. *Cornelian.*

As the history of Romulus, the founder of Rome, is so generally known, it is unnecessary here to enter into any particulars, except, in explanation of the present subject, to say that he and his twin brother Remus agreed to decide by the flight of birds who should give his name to, and have the chief power in, the new city. The augur having gone through the usual ceremonies, Remus took his stand on Mount Aventine, and Romulus on Mount Palatine. Remus first saw a flock of six vultures flying, and soon after Romulus saw twelve. Though Remus had the advantage as to priority of time, yet it was determined that the superiority of numbers rendered the omen of Romulus the more favourable one

No. 1204.

Metamorphosis of Periphas.

APOLLONIDES. *Sardonyx.*

Periphas was one of the first kings of Attica. It is related that his subjects paid him divine honours, for which Jupiter determined to destroy him with his thunderbolt; but, at the prayer of Apollo, only changed him into an eagle.

No. 1205.

Mithras stabbing a bull.

APOLLONIDES. *Cornelian.*

Mithras, or Mithra, is the name of the sun, which alone the Persians worshipped. His worship was introduced into Rome, where he usually was represented as a young man wearing a Persian bonnet, resting his knee on the back of a bull, with one hand holding the animal's head, while with the other he plunges a dagger into its shoulder. The secret rites of Mithras were of a very mysterious character. His mysteries were observed in caverns. In these gloomy recesses the person to be initiated underwent a long process of solitary confinement, then had to endure many kinds of torture (some say eighty), and if he survived these sufferings he was initiated. Most of the candidates lost, in the probation, their reason or life.

No. 1206.

Filial piety.

GNAIOS. *Sardonyx.*

This virtue was worshipped in Rome as a goddess, in consequence of the following circumstance. A man was sentenced to solitary imprisonment, and strict injunctions given that no one should be allowed to bring him food. But his daughter, who was then a nurse, and allowed to visit him, contrived, unknown to the jailor, to nourish him with her milk. This act excited the admiration of the magistrates. The father was released, and he and his daughter were afterwards supported at the public expense; and, according to Pliny, a chapel consecrated to the goddess was erected in the place.

No. 1207.

Homer playing on the lyre, attended by Fame and a Genius.

ALLION. *Cornelian.*

No. 1208.

Apotheosis of Homer.

ARGELAOS. *Cornelian.*

THE END.

LONDON:
PRINTED BY ROBSON, LEVEY, AND FRANKLYN,
Great New Street, Fetter Lane

CPSIA information can be obtained
at www.ICGtesting.com
Printed in the USA
BVHW05s1252020818
523383BV00017B/243/P